BOWDITCH'S

# USEFUL TABLES.

FOURTH EDITION

*NEW YORK:*

PUBLISHED BY E. & G. W. BLUNT, PROPRIETORS,

No. 179 Water Street, corner of Burling Slip.

1863.

C. S. Westcott & Co., Printers,
*No. 79 John Street.*

# PREFACE.

---

The Tables found in the following pages are taken from the Practical Navigator. They have been printed at the suggestion of my friend, Professor Pierce, whose remarks on the same are annexed.

I trust that they will be acceptable to those who require the aid of Logarithms in making their calculations, and may induce others to become acquainted with the power they may acquire from their use.

Tables I. and II. were calculated by the natural sines taken from the fourth edition of Sherwin's Logarithms, which were previously examined, by differences; when the proof-sheets of the first edition were examined, the numbers were again calculated by the natural sines in the second edition of Hutton's Logarithms; and if any difference was found, the numbers were calculated a third time by Taylor's Logarithms.

Table III. contains the meridional parts for every degree and minute of the quadrant, calculated by the following rule, viz.:

$$M = T \times 0.0007915704468,$$

in which T is the log. tangent less radius of half the latitude, increased by 45°, taken to seven places of figures, reckoned as integers; and M is the meridional parts of that latitude in miles.

Table X. contains the distances at which any object is visible, at sea, calculated by the rule given in § 195 of Vince's Astronomy, in which the terrestrial refraction is noticed. This circumstance was neglected by Robertson, Moore, and others, and of course, their tables are erroneous. The rule given by Mr. Vince, expressed in logarithms, is this :

$$0.\bar{1}2155 + \text{half log. of height in feet} = \text{log. of distance in statute miles.}$$

In reducing the rule to logarithms, the radius of the earth was called 20911790 feet, which agrees nearly with the mean value given in De la Lande's Astronomy.

Table X. A. contains the parallax in altitude of a planet.

Table XII. contains the refraction of the heavenly bodies, calculated by Dr. Bradley's rule, supposing the refraction to be as the tangent of the apparent zenith distance of the object, decreased by three times the refraction, the horizontal refraction being supposed equal to 33′. The rule, expressed in logarithms, is this :

$$\text{Log. tang. (app. zen. dist.—3. refraction)—8.2438534} = \text{log. of ref. in sec.}$$

The numbers calculated by this rule agree nearly with those published in Table I. of Maskelyne's Requisite Tables.

Table XIII. contains the dip of the horizon for various heights, calculated by the rule in § 197 of Vince's Astronomy, in which the terrestrial refraction is allowed for. All numbers of this table differ a little from those published by Dr. Maskelyne, who had made a different allowance for that refraction. The rule given by Mr. Vince, expressed in logarithms, is,

$$1.7712711 + \text{half the log. of the height in feet} = \text{log. dip in seconds.}$$

Table XIV. contains the sun's parallax in altitude, calculated by multiplying the natural sine of the apparent zenith distance by the sun's horizontal parallax $8\frac{3}{4}''$. The numbers in this table agree with those published by Dr. Maskelyne.

Table XV. contains the

$$\text{Augmentation of the moon's semi-diameter} = 15''.626 \times \text{sine ☽'s altitude.}$$

This table agrees nearly with that published by Maskelyne.

Table XVI. contains the dip for various distances and heights, calculated by this rule :

$$D = \frac{3}{17} d + 0.56514 \times \frac{h}{d},$$

in which D represents the dip in miles or minutes, *d* the distance of the land in sea-miles, and *h* the height of the eye of the observer in feet.

Table XXI., for turning time into degrees, is the same as in other works of this kind.

Table XXII. contains the proportional logarithms for three hours. The numbers of this table may be found by subtracting the logarithm of the time in seconds from the log. of 10800″, or, which is the same thing, by the following rule :

Prop. log. T=4.0334738—log. of T in seconds,

neglecting the three right-hand figures of the remainder.

Table XXIV. was compared with Sherwin's and Hutton's tables, and a few errors corrected.

Table XXV. contains the log. sines, log. tangents, etc., corresponding to points and quarter points of the compass. This was compared with Sherwin's, Hutton's, and Taylor's logarithms.

Plate XXVI., containing the common logarithms of numbers, was compared with Sherwin's, Hutton's, and Taylor's logarithms.

Table XXVII. contains the common log. sines, tangents, secants, etc. This was compared with Sherwin's, Hutton's, and Taylor's tables. Two additional columns are given in this table, which are very convenient in finding the time from an altitude of the sun ; also, three columns of proportional parts for seconds of space ; and a small table at the bottom of each page, for finding the proportional parts for seconds of time. The degrees are marked to 180°, which saves the trouble of subtracting the given angle from 180° when it exceeds 90°.

Table LI. To change mean solar time into sidereal time.

Table LII. To change sidereal time into mean solar time.

Table on page 76 of the text, contains the corrections in minutes, to be added to the Middle Latitude to obtain the correct Middle Latitude.

J. Ingersoll Bowditch.

*Boston*, 1849.

# REMARKS OF PROFESSOR PIERCE.

By the admirable contrivance of logarithms, the name of their inventor was raised high in the list of the benefactors of his race and the promoters of science. All the numerical calculations in the higher departments of theoretical and practical mathematics are performed by their aid, and the success of the computer principally depends upon the skill and precision with which he uses his logarithmic tables. It is worthy of inquiry, then, whether instruction in their use should not be more common in the schools; they ought to be studied both as the most remarkable instrument for facilitating calculations, and as a useful means of forming the mind to habits of accuracy. Discretion should be exercised in the choice of the tables, for, if ill-constructed and inaccurate, they will certainly lead to awkward and slovenly forms of calculation. They should be well proportioned in their parts; and, if of small extent, they should not be carried beyond five places of decimals. It is a great mistake to carry the small tables to six or seven places of decimals; without any valuable increase of accuracy, they are thus rendered clumsy and inconvenient. Tables of seven places should be proportionally extensive, as the large ones of Taylor; while those of six places are of little value—for they are not delicate enough for the higher orders of calculation, and are not needed for inferior operations; but, on the contrary, the disproportionate labor of using them destroys that brevity of computation, which is the sole recommendation of logarithms. None of the smaller tables can be compared in accuracy with those of Dr. Bowditch; for, besides the repeated and rigid examinations to which they have been subjected by the author and his sons, they have been so long in common use that no important error can have escaped detection. Dr. Bowditch's singular practical tact is also exhibited in their skilful arrangement, of which they are models deserving careful study. Feeling the want of such a set of tables for popular use, I have urged upon their proprietors the expediency of publishing the following selection from them, which will, I hope, be regarded as judiciously made.

This may not be thought an improper occasion to press upon teachers the inexpediency of forcing the youthful intellect to a premature comprehension of abstruse mathematical reasoning, at the expense of failing to impart familiarity with the forms of calculation, and readiness and accuracy in the use of figures, at the flexible age when the seeds of habit most readily germinate. Teach the lad how to obtain results, and you inspire him with the surest stimulus to investigate and apprehend the nature of the process. Imbue him with the spirit of accuracy, and you give him a taste for definite and precise thought, which is the solid foundation of true science, and one of the best antidotes to the laxity of reasoning and vagueness of research with which the atmosphere of the times is infected.

BENJAMIN PIERCE,
*Perkins Professor of Astronomy aud Mathematics,*
HARVARD UNIVERSITY.

*Cambridge*, 1849.

# TABLE I.

## Difference of Latitude and Departure for ¼ Point.

| N. ¼ E. | | | N. ¼ W. | | | S. ¼ E. | | | S. ¼ W. | | | | | |
|---|---|---|---|---|---|---|---|---|---|---|---|---|---|---|
| Dist. | Lat. | Dep. | Dist. | Lat. | Dep. | Dist. | Lat. | Dep. | Dist. | Lat. | Dep. | Dist. | Lat. | Dep. |
| 1 | 01.0 | 00.0 | 61 | 60.9 | 03.0 | 121 | 120.9 | 05.9 | 181 | 180.8 | 08.9 | 241 | 240.7 | 11.8 |
| 2 | 02.0 | 00.1 | 62 | 61.9 | 03.0 | 22 | 121.9 | 06.0 | 82 | 181.8 | 08.9 | 42 | 241.7 | 11.9 |
| 3 | 03.0 | 00.1 | 63 | 62.9 | 03.1 | 23 | 122.9 | 06.0 | 83 | 182.8 | 09.0 | 43 | 242.7 | 11.9 |
| 4 | 04.0 | 00.2 | 64 | 63.9 | 03.1 | 24 | 123.9 | 06.1 | 84 | 183.8 | 09.0 | 44 | 243.7 | 12.0 |
| 5 | 05.0 | 00.2 | 65 | 64.9 | 03.2 | 25 | 124.8 | 06.1 | 85 | 184.8 | 09.1 | 45 | 244.7 | 12.0 |
| 6 | 06.0 | 00.3 | 66 | 65.9 | 03.2 | 26 | 125.8 | 06.2 | 86 | 185.8 | 09.1 | 46 | 245.7 | 12.1 |
| 7 | 07.0 | 00.3 | 67 | 66.9 | 03.3 | 27 | 126.8 | 06.2 | 87 | 186.8 | 09.2 | 47 | 246.7 | 12.1 |
| 8 | 08.0 | 00.4 | 68 | 67.9 | 03.3 | 28 | 127.8 | 06.3 | 88 | 187.8 | 09.2 | 48 | 247.7 | 12.2 |
| 9 | 09.0 | 00.4 | 69 | 68.9 | 03.4 | 29 | 128.8 | 06.3 | 89 | 188.8 | 09.3 | 49 | 248.7 | 12.2 |
| 10 | 10.0 | 00.5 | 70 | 69.9 | 03.4 | 30 | 129.8 | 06.4 | 90 | 189.8 | 09.3 | 50 | 249.7 | 12.3 |
| 11 | 11.0 | 00.5 | 71 | 70.9 | 03.5 | 131 | 130.8 | 06.4 | 191 | 190.8 | 09.4 | 251 | 250.7 | 12.3 |
| 12 | 12.0 | 00.6 | 72 | 71.9 | 03.5 | 32 | 131.8 | 06.5 | 92 | 191.8 | 09.4 | 52 | 251.7 | 12.4 |
| 13 | 13.0 | 00.6 | 73 | 72.9 | 03.6 | 33 | 132.8 | 06.5 | 93 | 192.8 | 09.5 | 53 | 252.7 | 12.4 |
| 14 | 14.0 | 00.7 | 74 | 73.9 | 03.6 | 34 | 133.8 | 06.6 | 94 | 193.8 | 09.5 | 54 | 253.7 | 12.5 |
| 15 | 15.0 | 00.7 | 75 | 74.9 | 03.7 | 35 | 134.8 | 06.6 | 95 | 194.8 | 09.6 | 55 | 254.7 | 12.5 |
| 16 | 16.0 | 00.8 | 76 | 75.9 | 03.7 | 36 | 135.8 | 06.7 | 96 | 195.8 | 09.6 | 56 | 255.7 | 12.6 |
| 17 | 17.0 | 00.8 | 77 | 76.9 | 03.8 | 37 | 136.8 | 06.7 | 97 | 196.8 | 09.7 | 57 | 256.7 | 12.6 |
| 18 | 18.0 | 00.9 | 78 | 77.9 | 03.8 | 38 | 137.8 | 06.8 | 98 | 197.8 | 09.7 | 58 | 257.7 | 12.7 |
| 19 | 19.0 | 00.9 | 79 | 78.9 | 03.9 | 39 | 138.8 | 06.8 | 99 | 198.8 | 09.8 | 59 | 258.7 | 12.7 |
| 20 | 20.0 | 01.0 | 80 | 79.9 | 03.9 | 40 | 139.8 | 06.9 | 200 | 199.8 | 09.8 | 60 | 259.7 | 12.8 |
| 21 | 21.0 | 01.0 | 81 | 80.9 | 04.0 | 141 | 140.8 | 06.9 | 201 | 200.8 | 09.9 | 261 | 260.7 | 12.8 |
| 22 | 22.0 | 01.1 | 82 | 81.9 | 04.0 | 42 | 141.8 | 07.0 | 02 | 201.8 | 09.9 | 62 | 261.7 | 12.9 |
| 23 | 23.0 | 01.1 | 83 | 82.9 | 04.1 | 43 | 142.8 | 07.0 | 03 | 202.8 | 10.0 | 63 | 262.7 | 12.9 |
| 24 | 24.0 | 01.2 | 84 | 83.9 | 04.1 | 44 | 143.8 | 07.1 | 04 | 203.8 | 10.0 | 64 | 263.7 | 13.0 |
| 25 | 25.0 | 01.2 | 85 | 84.9 | 04.2 | 45 | 144.8 | 07.1 | 05 | 204.8 | 10.1 | 65 | 264.7 | 13.0 |
| 26 | 26.0 | 01.3 | 86 | 85.9 | 04.2 | 46 | 145.8 | 07.2 | 06 | 205.8 | 10.1 | 66 | 265.7 | 13.1 |
| 27 | 27.0 | 01.3 | 87 | 86.9 | 04.3 | 47 | 146.8 | 07.2 | 07 | 206.8 | 10.2 | 67 | 266.7 | 13.1 |
| 28 | 28.0 | 01.4 | 88 | 87.9 | 04.3 | 48 | 147.8 | 07.3 | 08 | 207.7 | 10.2 | 68 | 267.7 | 13.2 |
| 29 | 29.0 | 01.4 | 89 | 88.9 | 04.4 | 49 | 148.8 | 07.3 | 09 | 208.7 | 10.3 | 69 | 268.7 | 13.2 |
| 30 | 30.0 | 01.5 | 90 | 89.9 | 04.4 | 50 | 149.8 | 07.4 | 10 | 209.7 | 10.3 | 70 | 269.7 | 13.2 |
| 31 | 31.0 | 01.5 | 91 | 90.9 | 04.5 | 151 | 150.8 | 07.4 | 211 | 210.7 | 10.4 | 271 | 270.7 | 13.3 |
| 32 | 32.0 | 01.6 | 92 | 91.9 | 04.5 | 52 | 151.8 | 07.5 | 12 | 211.7 | 10.4 | 72 | 271.7 | 13.3 |
| 33 | 33.0 | 01.6 | 93 | 92.9 | 04.6 | 53 | 152.8 | 07.5 | 13 | 212.7 | 10.5 | 73 | 272.7 | 13.4 |
| 34 | 34.0 | 01.7 | 94 | 93.9 | 04.6 | 54 | 153.8 | 07.6 | 14 | 213.7 | 10.5 | 74 | 273.7 | 13.4 |
| 35 | 35.0 | 01.7 | 95 | 94.9 | 04.7 | 55 | 154.8 | 07.6 | 15 | 214.7 | 10.5 | 75 | 274.7 | 13.5 |
| 36 | 36.0 | 01.8 | 96 | 95.9 | 04.7 | 56 | 155.8 | 07.7 | 16 | 215.7 | 10.6 | 76 | 275.7 | 13.5 |
| 37 | 37.0 | 01.8 | 97 | 96.9 | 04.8 | 57 | 156.8 | 07.7 | 17 | 216.7 | 10.6 | 77 | 276.7 | 13.6 |
| 38 | 38.0 | 01.9 | 98 | 97.9 | 04.8 | 58 | 157.8 | 07.8 | 18 | 217.7 | 10.7 | 78 | 277.7 | 13.6 |
| 39 | 39.0 | 01.9 | 99 | 98.9 | 04.9 | 59 | 158.8 | 07.8 | 19 | 218.7 | 10.7 | 79 | 278.7 | 13.7 |
| 40 | 40.0 | 02.0 | 100 | 99.9 | 04.9 | 60 | 159.8 | 07.9 | 20 | 219.7 | 10.8 | 80 | 279.7 | 13.7 |
| 41 | 41.0 | 02.0 | 101 | 100.9 | 05.0 | 161 | 160.8 | 07.9 | 221 | 220.7 | 10.8 | 281 | 280.7 | 13.8 |
| 42 | 41.9 | 02.1 | 02 | 101.9 | 05.0 | 62 | 161.8 | 07.9 | 22 | 221.7 | 10.9 | 82 | 281.7 | 13.8 |
| 43 | 42.9 | 02.1 | 03 | 102.9 | 05.1 | 63 | 162.8 | 08.0 | 23 | 222.7 | 10.9 | 83 | 282.7 | 13.9 |
| 44 | 43.9 | 02.2 | 04 | 103.9 | 05.1 | 64 | 163.8 | 08.0 | 24 | 223.7 | 11.0 | 84 | 283.7 | 13.9 |
| 45 | 44.9 | 02.2 | 05 | 104.9 | 05.2 | 65 | 164.8 | 08.1 | 25 | 224.7 | 11.0 | 85 | 284.7 | 14.0 |
| 46 | 45.9 | 02.3 | 06 | 105.9 | 05.2 | 66 | 165.8 | 08.1 | 26 | 225.7 | 11.1 | 86 | 285.7 | 14.0 |
| 47 | 46.9 | 02.3 | 07 | 106.9 | 05.3 | 67 | 166.8 | 08.2 | 27 | 226.7 | 11.1 | 87 | 286.7 | 14.1 |
| 48 | 47.9 | 02.4 | 08 | 107.9 | 05.3 | 68 | 167.8 | 08.2 | 28 | 227.7 | 11.2 | 88 | 287.7 | 14.1 |
| 49 | 48.9 | 02.4 | 09 | 108.9 | 05.3 | 69 | 168.8 | 08.3 | 29 | 228.7 | 11.2 | 89 | 288.7 | 14.2 |
| 50 | 49.9 | 02.5 | 10 | 109.9 | 05.4 | 70 | 169.8 | 08.3 | 30 | 229.7 | 11.3 | 90 | 289.7 | 14.2 |
| 51 | 50.9 | 02.5 | 111 | 110.9 | 05.4 | 171 | 170.8 | 08.4 | 231 | 230.7 | 11.3 | 291 | 290.6 | 14.3 |
| 52 | 51.9 | 02.6 | 12 | 111.9 | 05.5 | 72 | 171.8 | 08.4 | 32 | 231.7 | 11.4 | 92 | 291.6 | 14.3 |
| 53 | 52.9 | 02.6 | 13 | 112.9 | 05.5 | 73 | 172.8 | 08.5 | 33 | 232.7 | 11.4 | 93 | 292.6 | 14.4 |
| 54 | 53.9 | 02.6 | 14 | 113.9 | 05.6 | 74 | 173.8 | 08.5 | 34 | 233.7 | 11.5 | 94 | 293.6 | 14.4 |
| 55 | 54.9 | 02.7 | 15 | 114.9 | 05.6 | 75 | 174.8 | 08.6 | 35 | 234.7 | 11.5 | 95 | 294.6 | 14.5 |
| 56 | 55.9 | 02.7 | 16 | 115.9 | 05.7 | 76 | 175.8 | 08.6 | 36 | 235.7 | 11.6 | 96 | 295.6 | 14.5 |
| 57 | 56.9 | 02.8 | 17 | 116.9 | 05.7 | 77 | 176.8 | 08.7 | 37 | 236.7 | 11.6 | 97 | 296.6 | 14.6 |
| 58 | 57.9 | 02.8 | 18 | 117.9 | 05.8 | 78 | 177.8 | 08.7 | 38 | 237.7 | 11.7 | 98 | 297.6 | 14.6 |
| 59 | 58.9 | 02.9 | 19 | 118.9 | 05.8 | 79 | 178.8 | 08.8 | 39 | 238.7 | 11.7 | 99 | 298.6 | 14.7 |
| 60 | 59.9 | 02.9 | 20 | 119.9 | 05.9 | 80 | 179.8 | 08.8 | 40 | 239.7 | 11.8 | 300 | 299.6 | 14.7 |
| Dist. | Dep. | Lat. | Dist. | Dep. | Lat. | Dist. | Dep. | Lat. | Dist. | Dep. | Lat. | Dist. | Dep. | Lat. |
| E. ¼ N. | | | E. ¼ S. | | | W. ¼ N. | | | W. ¼ S. | | | [For 7¾ Points. | | |

# TABLE I.

## Difference of Latitude and Departure for ½ Point.

| | N.½ E. | | | N.½ W. | | | S.½ E. | | | S.½ W. | | | | |
|---|---|---|---|---|---|---|---|---|---|---|---|---|---|---|
| Dist. | Lat. | Dep. | Dist. | Lat. | Dep. | Dist. | Lat. | Dep. | Dist. | Lat. | Dep. | Dist. | Lat. | Dep. |
| 1 | 01.0 | 00.1 | 61 | 60.7 | 06.0 | 121 | 120.4 | 11.9 | 181 | 180.1 | 17.7 | 241 | 239.8 | 23.6 |
| 2 | 02.0 | 00.2 | 62 | 61.7 | 06.1 | 22 | 121.4 | 12.0 | 82 | 181.1 | 17.8 | 42 | 240.8 | 23.7 |
| 3 | 03.0 | 00.3 | 63 | 62.7 | 06.2 | 23 | 122.4 | 12.1 | 83 | 182.1 | 17.9 | 43 | 241.8 | 23.8 |
| 4 | 04.0 | 00.4 | 64 | 63.7 | 06.3 | 24 | 123.4 | 12.2 | 84 | 183.1 | 18.0 | 44 | 242.8 | 23.9 |
| 5 | 05.0 | 00.5 | 65 | 64.7 | 06.4 | 25 | 124.4 | 12.3 | 85 | 184.1 | 18.1 | 45 | 243.8 | 24.0 |
| 6 | 06.0 | 00.6 | 66 | 65.7 | 06.5 | 26 | 125.4 | 12.4 | 86 | 185.1 | 18.2 | 46 | 244.8 | 24.1 |
| 7 | 07.0 | 00.7 | 67 | 66.7 | 06.6 | 27 | 126.4 | 12.4 | 87 | 186.1 | 18.3 | 47 | 245.8 | 24.2 |
| 8 | 08.0 | 00.8 | 68 | 67.7 | 06.7 | 28 | 127.4 | 12.5 | 88 | 187.1 | 18.4 | 48 | 246.8 | 24.3 |
| 9 | 09.0 | 00.9 | 69 | 68.7 | 06.8 | 29 | 128.4 | 12.6 | 89 | 188.1 | 18.5 | 49 | 247.8 | 24.4 |
| 10 | 10.0 | 01.0 | 70 | 69.7 | 06.9 | 30 | 129.4 | 12.7 | 90 | 189.1 | 18.6 | 50 | 248.8 | 24.5 |
| 11 | 10.9 | 01.1 | 71 | 70.7 | 07.0 | 131 | 130.4 | 12.8 | 191 | 190.1 | 18.7 | 251 | 249.8 | 24.6 |
| 12 | 11.9 | 01.2 | 72 | 71.7 | 07.1 | 32 | 131.4 | 12.9 | 92 | 191.1 | 18.8 | 52 | 250.8 | 24.7 |
| 13 | 12.9 | 01.3 | 73 | 72.6 | 07.2 | 33 | 132.4 | 13.0 | 93 | 192.1 | 18.9 | 53 | 251.8 | 24.8 |
| 14 | 13.9 | 01.4 | 74 | 73.6 | 07.3 | 34 | 133.4 | 13.1 | 94 | 193.1 | 19.0 | 54 | 252.8 | 24.9 |
| 15 | 14.9 | 01.5 | 75 | 74.6 | 07.4 | 35 | 134.3 | 13.2 | 95 | 194.1 | 19.1 | 55 | 253.8 | 25.0 |
| 16 | 15.9 | 01.6 | 76 | 75.6 | 07.4 | 36 | 135.3 | 13.3 | 96 | 195.1 | 19.2 | 56 | 254.8 | 25.1 |
| 17 | 16.9 | 01.7 | 77 | 76.6 | 07.5 | 37 | 136.3 | 13.4 | 97 | 196.1 | 19.3 | 57 | 255.8 | 25.2 |
| 18 | 17.9 | 01.8 | 78 | 77.6 | 07.6 | 38 | 137.3 | 13.5 | 98 | 197.0 | 19.4 | 58 | 256.8 | 25.3 |
| 19 | 18.9 | 01.9 | 79 | 78.6 | 07.7 | 39 | 138.3 | 13.6 | 99 | 198.0 | 19.5 | 59 | 257.8 | 25.4 |
| 20 | 19.9 | 02.0 | 80 | 79.6 | 07.8 | 40 | 139.3 | 13.7 | 200 | 199.0 | 19.6 | 60 | 258.7 | 25.5 |
| 21 | 20.9 | 02.1 | 81 | 80.6 | 07.9 | 141 | 140.3 | 13.8 | 201 | 200.0 | 19.7 | 261 | 259.7 | 25.6 |
| 22 | 21.9 | 02.2 | 82 | 81.6 | 08.0 | 42 | 141.3 | 13.9 | 02 | 201.0 | 19.8 | 62 | 260.7 | 25.7 |
| 23 | 22.9 | 02.3 | 83 | 82.6 | 08.1 | 43 | 142.3 | 14.0 | 03 | 202.0 | 19.9 | 63 | 261.7 | 25.8 |
| 24 | 23.9 | 02.4 | 84 | 83.6 | 08.2 | 44 | 143.3 | 14.1 | 04 | 203.0 | 20.0 | 64 | 262.7 | 25.9 |
| 25 | 24.9 | 02.5 | 85 | 84.6 | 08.3 | 45 | 144.3 | 14.2 | 05 | 204.0 | 20.1 | 65 | 263.7 | 26.0 |
| 26 | 25.9 | 02.5 | 86 | 85.6 | 08.4 | 46 | 145.3 | 14.3 | 06 | 205.0 | 20.2 | 66 | 264.7 | 26.1 |
| 27 | 26.9 | 02.6 | 87 | 86.6 | 08.5 | 47 | 146.3 | 14.4 | 07 | 206.0 | 20.3 | 67 | 265.7 | 26.2 |
| 28 | 27.9 | 02.7 | 88 | 87.6 | 08.6 | 48 | 147.3 | 14.5 | 08 | 207.0 | 20.4 | 68 | 266.7 | 26.3 |
| 29 | 28.9 | 02.8 | 89 | 88.6 | 08.7 | 49 | 148.3 | 14.6 | 09 | 208.0 | 20.5 | 69 | 267.7 | 26.4 |
| 30 | 29.9 | 02.9 | 90 | 89.6 | 08.8 | 50 | 149.3 | 14.7 | 10 | 209.0 | 20.6 | 70 | 268.7 | 26.5 |
| 31 | 30.9 | 03.0 | 91 | 90.6 | 08.9 | 151 | 150.3 | 14.8 | 211 | 210.0 | 20.7 | 271 | 269.7 | 26.6 |
| 32 | 31.8 | 03.1 | 92 | 91.6 | 09.0 | 52 | 151.3 | 14.9 | 12 | 211.0 | 20.8 | 72 | 270.7 | 26.7 |
| 33 | 32.8 | 03.2 | 93 | 92.6 | 09.1 | 53 | 152.3 | 15.0 | 13 | 212.0 | 20.9 | 73 | 271.7 | 26.8 |
| 34 | 33.8 | 03.3 | 94 | 93.5 | 09.2 | 54 | 153.3 | 15.1 | 14 | 213.0 | 21.0 | 74 | 272.7 | 26.9 |
| 35 | 34.8 | 03.4 | 95 | 94.5 | 09.3 | 55 | 154.3 | 15.2 | 15 | 214.0 | 21.1 | 75 | 273.7 | 27.0 |
| 36 | 35.8 | 03.5 | 96 | 95.5 | 09.4 | 56 | 155.2 | 15.3 | 16 | 215.0 | 21.2 | 76 | 274.7 | 27.1 |
| 37 | 36.8 | 03.6 | 97 | 96.5 | 09.5 | 57 | 156.2 | 15.4 | 17 | 216.0 | 21.3 | 77 | 275.7 | 27.2 |
| 38 | 37.8 | 03.7 | 98 | 97.5 | 09.6 | 58 | 157.2 | 15.5 | 18 | 217.0 | 21.4 | 78 | 276.7 | 27.2 |
| 39 | 38.8 | 03.8 | 99 | 98.5 | 09.7 | 59 | 158.2 | 15.6 | 19 | 217.9 | 21.5 | 79 | 277.7 | 27.3 |
| 40 | 39.8 | 03.9 | 100 | 99.5 | 09.8 | 60 | 159.2 | 15.7 | 20 | 218.9 | 21.6 | 80 | 278.7 | 27.4 |
| 41 | 40.8 | 04.0 | 101 | 100.5 | 09.9 | 161 | 160.2 | 15.8 | 221 | 219.9 | 21.7 | 281 | 279.6 | 27.5 |
| 42 | 41.8 | 04.1 | 02 | 101.5 | 10.0 | 62 | 161.2 | 15.9 | 22 | 220.9 | 21.8 | 82 | 280.6 | 27.6 |
| 43 | 42.8 | 04.2 | 03 | 102.5 | 10.1 | 63 | 162.2 | 16.0 | 23 | 221.9 | 21.9 | 83 | 281.6 | 27.7 |
| 44 | 43.8 | 04.3 | 04 | 103.5 | 10.2 | 64 | 163.2 | 16.1 | 24 | 222.9 | 22.0 | 84 | 282.6 | 27.8 |
| 45 | 44.8 | 04.4 | 05 | 104.5 | 10.3 | 65 | 164.2 | 16.2 | 25 | 223.9 | 22.1 | 85 | 283.6 | 27.9 |
| 46 | 45.8 | 04.5 | 06 | 105.5 | 10.4 | 66 | 165.2 | 16.3 | 26 | 224.9 | 22.2 | 86 | 284.6 | 28.0 |
| 47 | 46.8 | 04.6 | 07 | 106.5 | 10.5 | 67 | 166.2 | 16.4 | 27 | 225.9 | 22.2 | 87 | 285.6 | 28.1 |
| 48 | 47.8 | 04.7 | 08 | 107.5 | 10.6 | 68 | 167.2 | 16.5 | 28 | 226.9 | 22.3 | 88 | 286.6 | 28.2 |
| 49 | 48.8 | 04.8 | 09 | 108.5 | 10.7 | 69 | 168.2 | 16.6 | 29 | 227.9 | 22.4 | 89 | 287.6 | 28.3 |
| 50 | 49.8 | 04.9 | 10 | 109.5 | 10.8 | 70 | 169.2 | 16.7 | 30 | 228.9 | 22.5 | 90 | 288.6 | 28.4 |
| 51 | 50.8 | 05.0 | 111 | 110.5 | 10.9 | 171 | 170.2 | 16.8 | 231 | 229.9 | 22.6 | 291 | 289.6 | 28.5 |
| 52 | 51.7 | 05.1 | 12 | 111.5 | 11.0 | 72 | 171.2 | 16.9 | 32 | 230.9 | 22.7 | 92 | 290.6 | 28.6 |
| 53 | 52.7 | 05.2 | 13 | 112.5 | 11.1 | 73 | 172.2 | 17.0 | 33 | 231.9 | 22.8 | 93 | 291.6 | 28.7 |
| 54 | 53.7 | 05.3 | 14 | 113.5 | 11.2 | 74 | 173.2 | 17.1 | 34 | 232.9 | 22.9 | 94 | 292.6 | 28.8 |
| 55 | 54.7 | 05.4 | 15 | 114.4 | 11.3 | 75 | 174.2 | 17.2 | 35 | 233.9 | 23.0 | 95 | 293.6 | 28.9 |
| 56 | 55.7 | 05.5 | 16 | 115.4 | 11.4 | 76 | 175.2 | 17.3 | 36 | 234.9 | 23.1 | 96 | 294.6 | 29.0 |
| 57 | 56.7 | 05.6 | 17 | 116.4 | 11.5 | 77 | 176.1 | 17.3 | 37 | 235.9 | 23.2 | 97 | 295.6 | 29.1 |
| 58 | 57.7 | 05.7 | 18 | 117.4 | 11.6 | 78 | 177.1 | 17.4 | 38 | 236.9 | 23.3 | 98 | 296.6 | 29.2 |
| 59 | 58.7 | 05.8 | 19 | 118.4 | 11.7 | 79 | 178.1 | 17.5 | 39 | 237.8 | 23.4 | 99 | 297.6 | 29.3 |
| 60 | 59.7 | 05.9 | 20 | 119.4 | 11.8 | 80 | 179.1 | 17.6 | 40 | 238.8 | 23.5 | 300 | 298.6 | 29.4 |
| Dist. | Dep. | Lat. | Dist. | Dep. | Lat. | Dist. | Dep | Lat. | Dist. | Dep. | Lat. | Dist. | Dep. | Lat. |
| | E.½ N. | | | E.½ S. | | | W.½ N. | | | W.½ S. | | | [For 7½ Points. | |

# TABLE I.

## Difference of Latitude and Departure for ¾ Point.

N.¾ E. N.¾ W. S.¾ E. S.¾ W.

| Dist. | Lat. | Dep. | Dist. | Lat. | Dep. | Dist. | Lat. | Dep. | Dist. | Lat. | Dep. | Dist. | Lat. | Dep. |
|---|---|---|---|---|---|---|---|---|---|---|---|---|---|---|
| 1 | 01.0 | 00.1 | 61 | 60.3 | 09.0 | 121 | 119.7 | 17.8 | 181 | 179.0 | 26.6 | 241 | 238.4 | 35.4 |
| 2 | 02.0 | 00.3 | 62 | 61.3 | 09.1 | 22 | 120.7 | 17.9 | 82 | 180.0 | 26.7 | 42 | 239.4 | 35.5 |
| 3 | 03.0 | 00.4 | 63 | 62.3 | 09.2 | 23 | 121.7 | 18.0 | 83 | 181.0 | 26.9 | 43 | 240.4 | 35.7 |
| 4 | 04.0 | 00.6 | 64 | 63.3 | 09.4 | 24 | 122.7 | 18.2 | 84 | 182.0 | 27.0 | 44 | 241.4 | 35.8 |
| 5 | 04.9 | 00.7 | 65 | 64.3 | 09.5 | 25 | 123.6 | 18.3 | 85 | 183.0 | 27.1 | 45 | 242.3 | 35.9 |
| 6 | 05.9 | 00.9 | 66 | 65.3 | 09.7 | 26 | 124.6 | 18.5 | 86 | 184.0 | 27.3 | 46 | 243.3 | 36.1 |
| 7 | 06.9 | 01.0 | 67 | 66.3 | 09.8 | 27 | 125.6 | 18.6 | 87 | 185.0 | 27.4 | 47 | 244.3 | 36.2 |
| 8 | 07.9 | 01.2 | 68 | 67.3 | 10.0 | 28 | 126.6 | 18.8 | 88 | 186.0 | 27.6 | 48 | 245.3 | 36.4 |
| 9 | 08.9 | 01.3 | 69 | 68.3 | 10.1 | 29 | 127.6 | 18.9 | 89 | 187.0 | 27.7 | 49 | 246.3 | 36.5 |
| 10 | 09.9 | 01.5 | 70 | 69.2 | 10.3 | 30 | 128.6 | 19.1 | 90 | 187.9 | 27.9 | 50 | 247.3 | 36.7 |
| 11 | 10.9 | 01.6 | 71 | 70.2 | 10.4 | 131 | 129.6 | 19.2 | 191 | 188.9 | 28.0 | 251 | 248.3 | 36.8 |
| 12 | 11.9 | 01.8 | 72 | 71.2 | 10.6 | 32 | 130.6 | 19.4 | 92 | 189.9 | 28.2 | 52 | 249.3 | 37.0 |
| 13 | 12.9 | 01.9 | 73 | 72.2 | 10.7 | 33 | 131.6 | 19.5 | 93 | 190.9 | 28.3 | 53 | 250.3 | 37.1 |
| 14 | 13.8 | 02.1 | 74 | 73.2 | 10.9 | 34 | 132.5 | 19.7 | 94 | 191.9 | 28.5 | 54 | 251.3 | 37.3 |
| 15 | 14.8 | 02.2 | 75 | 74.2 | 11.0 | 35 | 133.5 | 19.8 | 95 | 192.9 | 28.6 | 55 | 252.2 | 37.4 |
| 16 | 15.8 | 02.3 | 76 | 75.2 | 11.2 | 36 | 134.5 | 20.0 | 96 | 193.9 | 28.8 | 56 | 253.2 | 37.6 |
| 17 | 16.8 | 02.5 | 77 | 76.2 | 11.3 | 37 | 135.5 | 20.1 | 97 | 194.9 | 28.9 | 57 | 254.2 | 37.7 |
| 18 | 17.8 | 02.6 | 78 | 77.2 | 11.4 | 38 | 136.5 | 20.2 | 98 | 195.9 | 29.1 | 58 | 255.2 | 37.9 |
| 19 | 18.8 | 02.8 | 79 | 78.1 | 11.6 | 39 | 137.5 | 20.4 | 99 | 196.8 | 29.2 | 59 | 256.2 | 38.0 |
| 20 | 19.8 | 02.9 | 80 | 79.1 | 11.7 | 40 | 138.5 | 20.5 | 200 | 197.8 | 29.3 | 60 | 257.2 | 38.1 |
| 21 | 20.8 | 03.1 | 81 | 80.1 | 11.9 | 141 | 139.5 | 20.7 | 201 | 198.8 | 29.5 | 261 | 258.2 | 38.3 |
| 22 | 21.8 | 03.2 | 82 | 81.1 | 12.0 | 42 | 140.5 | 20.8 | 02 | 199.8 | 29.6 | 62 | 259.2 | 38.4 |
| 23 | 22.8 | 03.4 | 83 | 82.1 | 12.2 | 43 | 141.5 | 21.0 | 03 | 200.8 | 29.8 | 63 | 260.2 | 38.6 |
| 24 | 23.7 | 03.5 | 84 | 83.1 | 12.3 | 44 | 142.4 | 21.1 | 04 | 201.8 | 29.9 | 64 | 261.1 | 38.7 |
| 25 | 24.7 | 03.7 | 85 | 84.1 | 12.5 | 45 | 143.4 | 21.3 | 05 | 202.8 | 30.1 | 65 | 262.1 | 38.9 |
| 26 | 25.7 | 03.8 | 86 | 85.1 | 12.6 | 46 | 144.4 | 21.4 | 06 | 203.8 | 30.2 | 66 | 263.1 | 39.0 |
| 27 | 26.7 | 04.0 | 87 | 86.1 | 12.8 | 47 | 145.4 | 21.6 | 07 | 204.8 | 30.4 | 67 | 264.1 | 39.2 |
| 28 | 27.7 | 04.1 | 88 | 87.0 | 12.9 | 48 | 146.4 | 21.7 | 08 | 205.7 | 30.5 | 68 | 265.1 | 39.3 |
| 29 | 28.7 | 04.3 | 89 | 88.0 | 13.1 | 49 | 147.4 | 21.9 | 09 | 206.7 | 30.7 | 69 | 266.1 | 39.5 |
| 30 | 29.7 | 04.4 | 90 | 89.0 | 13.2 | 50 | 148.4 | 22.0 | 10 | 207.7 | 30.8 | 70 | 267.1 | 39.6 |
| 31 | 30.7 | 04.5 | 91 | 90.0 | 13.4 | 151 | 149.4 | 22.2 | 211 | 208.7 | 31.0 | 271 | 268.1 | 39.8 |
| 32 | 31.7 | 04.7 | 92 | 91.0 | 13.5 | 52 | 150.4 | 22.3 | 12 | 209.7 | 31.1 | 72 | 269.1 | 39.9 |
| 33 | 32.6 | 04.8 | 93 | 92.0 | 13.6 | 53 | 151.3 | 22.4 | 13 | 210.7 | 31.3 | 73 | 270.0 | 40.1 |
| 34 | 33.6 | 05.0 | 94 | 93.0 | 13.8 | 54 | 152.3 | 22.6 | 14 | 211.7 | 31.4 | 74 | 271.0 | 40.2 |
| 35 | 34.6 | 05.1 | 95 | 94.0 | 13.9 | 55 | 153.3 | 22.7 | 15 | 212.7 | 31.5 | 75 | 272.0 | 40.4 |
| 36 | 35.6 | 05.3 | 96 | 95.0 | 14.1 | 56 | 154.3 | 22.9 | 16 | 213.7 | 31.7 | 76 | 273.0 | 40.5 |
| 37 | 36.6 | 05.4 | 97 | 96.0 | 14.2 | 57 | 155.3 | 23.0 | 17 | 214.7 | 31.8 | 77 | 274.0 | 40.6 |
| 38 | 37.6 | 05.6 | 98 | 96.9 | 14.4 | 58 | 156.3 | 23.2 | 18 | 215.6 | 32.0 | 78 | 275.0 | 40.8 |
| 39 | 38.6 | 05.7 | 99 | 97.9 | 14.5 | 59 | 157.3 | 23.3 | 19 | 216.6 | 32.1 | 79 | 276.0 | 40.9 |
| 40 | 39.6 | 05.9 | 100 | 98.9 | 14.7 | 60 | 158.3 | 23.5 | 20 | 217.6 | 32.3 | 80 | 277.0 | 41.1 |
| 41 | 40.6 | 06.0 | 101 | 99.9 | 14.8 | 161 | 159.3 | 23.6 | 221 | 218.6 | 32.4 | 281 | 278.0 | 41.2 |
| 42 | 41.5 | 06.2 | 02 | 100.9 | 15.0 | 62 | 160.2 | 23.8 | 22 | 219.6 | 32.6 | 82 | 278.9 | 41.4 |
| 43 | 42.5 | 06.3 | 03 | 101.9 | 15.1 | 63 | 161.2 | 23.9 | 23 | 220.6 | 32.7 | 83 | 279.9 | 41.5 |
| 44 | 43.5 | 06.5 | 04 | 102.9 | 15.3 | 64 | 162.2 | 24.1 | 24 | 221.6 | 32.9 | 84 | 280.9 | 41.7 |
| 45 | 44.5 | 06.6 | 05 | 103.9 | 15.4 | 65 | 163.2 | 24.2 | 25 | 222.6 | 33.0 | 85 | 281.9 | 41.8 |
| 46 | 45.5 | 06.7 | 06 | 104.9 | 15.6 | 66 | 164.2 | 24.4 | 26 | 223.6 | 33.2 | 86 | 282.9 | 42.0 |
| 47 | 46.5 | 06.9 | 07 | 105.8 | 15.7 | 67 | 165.2 | 24.5 | 27 | 224.5 | 33.3 | 87 | 283.9 | 42.1 |
| 48 | 47.5 | 07.0 | 08 | 106.8 | 15.8 | 68 | 166.2 | 24.7 | 28 | 225.5 | 33.5 | 88 | 284.9 | 42.3 |
| 49 | 48.5 | 07.2 | 09 | 107.8 | 16.0 | 69 | 167.2 | 24.8 | 29 | 226.5 | 33.6 | 89 | 285.9 | 42.4 |
| 50 | 49.5 | 07.3 | 10 | 108.8 | 16.1 | 70 | 168.2 | 24.9 | 30 | 227.5 | 33.7 | 90 | 286.9 | 42.6 |
| 51 | 50.4 | 07.5 | 111 | 109.8 | 16.3 | 171 | 169.1 | 25.1 | 231 | 228.5 | 33.9 | 291 | 287.9 | 42.7 |
| 52 | 51.4 | 07.6 | 12 | 110.8 | 16.4 | 72 | 170.1 | 25.2 | 32 | 229.5 | 34.0 | 92 | 288.8 | 42.8 |
| 53 | 52.4 | 07.8 | 13 | 111.8 | 16.6 | 73 | 171.1 | 25.4 | 33 | 230.5 | 34.2 | 93 | 289.8 | 43.0 |
| 54 | 53.4 | 07.9 | 14 | 112.8 | 16.7 | 74 | 172.1 | 25.5 | 34 | 231.5 | 34.3 | 94 | 290.8 | 43.1 |
| 55 | 54.4 | 08.1 | 15 | 113.8 | 16.9 | 75 | 173.1 | 25.7 | 35 | 232.5 | 34.5 | 95 | 291.8 | 43.3 |
| 56 | 55.4 | 08.2 | 16 | 114.7 | 17.0 | 76 | 174.1 | 25.8 | 36 | 233.4 | 34.6 | 96 | 292.8 | 43.4 |
| 57 | 56.4 | 08.4 | 17 | 115.7 | 17.2 | 77 | 175.1 | 26.0 | 37 | 234.4 | 34.8 | 97 | 293.8 | 43.6 |
| 58 | 57.4 | 08.5 | 18 | 116.7 | 17.3 | 78 | 176.1 | 26.1 | 38 | 235.4 | 34.9 | 98 | 294.8 | 43.7 |
| 59 | 58.4 | 08.7 | 19 | 117.7 | 17.5 | 79 | 177.1 | 26.3 | 39 | 236.4 | 35.1 | 99 | 295.8 | 43.9 |
| 60 | 59.4 | 08.8 | 20 | 118.7 | 17.6 | 80 | 178.1 | 26.4 | 40 | 237.4 | 35.2 | 300 | 296.8 | 44.0 |
| Dist. | Dep. | Lat. | Dist. | Dep. | Lat. | Dist. | Dep. | Lat. | Dist. | Dep. | Lat. | Dist. | Dep. | Lat. |

E.¾ N. E.¾ S. W.¾ N. W.¾ S. [For 7¼ Points.

# TABLE I.

## Difference of Latitude and Departure for 1 Point.

N byE. | N.byW. | S.byE. | S.byW.

| Dist. | Lat. | Dep. | Dist. | Lat. | Dep. | Dist. | Lat. | Dep. | Dist. | Lat. | Dep. | Dist. | Lat. | Dep. |
|---|---|---|---|---|---|---|---|---|---|---|---|---|---|---|
| 1 | 01.0 | 00.2 | 61 | 59.8 | 11.9 | 121 | 118.7 | 23.6 | 181 | 177.5 | 35.3 | 241 | 236.4 | 47.0 |
| 2 | 02.0 | 00.4 | 62 | 60.8 | 12.1 | 22 | 119.7 | 23.8 | 82 | 178.5 | 35.5 | 42 | 237.4 | 47.2 |
| 3 | 02.9 | 00.6 | 63 | 61.8 | 12.3 | 23 | 120.6 | 24.0 | 83 | 179.5 | 35.7 | 43 | 238.3 | 47.4 |
| 4 | 03.9 | 00.8 | 64 | 62.8 | 12.5 | 24 | 121.6 | 24.2 | 84 | 180.5 | 35.9 | 44 | 239.3 | 47.6 |
| 5 | 04.9 | 01.0 | 65 | 63.8 | 12.7 | 25 | 122.6 | 24.4 | 85 | 181.4 | 36.1 | 45 | 240.3 | 47.8 |
| 6 | 05.9 | 01.2 | 66 | 64.7 | 12.9 | 26 | 123.6 | 24.6 | 86 | 182.4 | 36.3 | 46 | 241.3 | 48.0 |
| 7 | 06.9 | 01.4 | 67 | 65.7 | 13.1 | 27 | 124.6 | 24.8 | 87 | 183.4 | 36.5 | 47 | 242.3 | 48.2 |
| 8 | 07.8 | 01.6 | 68 | 66.7 | 13.3 | 28 | 125.5 | 25.0 | 88 | 184.4 | 36.7 | 48 | 243.2 | 48.4 |
| 9 | 08.8 | 01.8 | 69 | 67.7 | 13.5 | 29 | 126.5 | 25.2 | 89 | 185.4 | 36.9 | 49 | 244.2 | 48.6 |
| 10 | 09.8 | 02.0 | 70 | 68.7 | 13.7 | 30 | 127.5 | 25.4 | 90 | 186.3 | 37.1 | 50 | 245.2 | 48.8 |
| 11 | 10.8 | 02.1 | 71 | 69.6 | 13.9 | 131 | 128.5 | 25.6 | 191 | 187.3 | 37.3 | 251 | 246.2 | 49.0 |
| 12 | 11.8 | 02.3 | 72 | 70.6 | 14.0 | 32 | 129.5 | 25.8 | 92 | 188.3 | 37.5 | 52 | 247.2 | 49.2 |
| 13 | 12.8 | 02.5 | 73 | 71.6 | 14.2 | 33 | 130.4 | 25.9 | 93 | 189.3 | 37.7 | 53 | 248.1 | 49.4 |
| 14 | 13.7 | 02.7 | 74 | 72.6 | 14.4 | 34 | 131.4 | 26.1 | 94 | 190.3 | 37.8 | 54 | 249.1 | 49.6 |
| 15 | 14.7 | 02.9 | 75 | 73.6 | 14.6 | 35 | 132.4 | 26.3 | 95 | 191.3 | 38.0 | 55 | 250.1 | 49.7 |
| 16 | 15.7 | 03.1 | 76 | 74.5 | 14.8 | 36 | 133.4 | 26.5 | 96 | 192.2 | 38.2 | 56 | 251.1 | 49.9 |
| 17 | 16.7 | 03.3 | 77 | 75.5 | 15.0 | 37 | 134.4 | 26.7 | 97 | 193.2 | 38.4 | 57 | 252.1 | 50.1 |
| 18 | 17.7 | 03.5 | 78 | 76.5 | 15.2 | 38 | 135.3 | 26.9 | 98 | 194.2 | 38.6 | 58 | 253.0 | 50.3 |
| 19 | 18.6 | 03.7 | 79 | 77.5 | 15.4 | 39 | 136.3 | 27.1 | 99 | 195.2 | 38.8 | 59 | 254.0 | 50.5 |
| 20 | 19.6 | 03.9 | 80 | 78.5 | 15.6 | 40 | 137.3 | 27.3 | 200 | 196.2 | 39.0 | 60 | 255.0 | 50.7 |
| 21 | 20.6 | 04.1 | 81 | 79.4 | 15.8 | 141 | 138.3 | 27.5 | 201 | 197.1 | 39.2 | 261 | 256.0 | 50.9 |
| 22 | 21.6 | 04.3 | 82 | 80.4 | 16.0 | 42 | 139.3 | 27.7 | 02 | 198.1 | 39.4 | 62 | 257.0 | 51.1 |
| 23 | 22.6 | 04.5 | 83 | 81.4 | 16.2 | 43 | 140.3 | 27.9 | 03 | 199.1 | 39.6 | 63 | 257.9 | 51.3 |
| 24 | 23.5 | 04.7 | 84 | 82.4 | 16.4 | 44 | 141.2 | 28.1 | 04 | 200.1 | 39.8 | 64 | 258.9 | 51.5 |
| 25 | 24.5 | 04.9 | 85 | 83.4 | 16.6 | 45 | 142.2 | 28.3 | 05 | 201.1 | 40.0 | 65 | 259.9 | 51.7 |
| 26 | 25.5 | 05.1 | 86 | 84.3 | 16.8 | 46 | 143.2 | 28.5 | 06 | 202.0 | 40.2 | 66 | 260.9 | 51.9 |
| 27 | 26.5 | 05.3 | 87 | 85.3 | 17.0 | 47 | 144.2 | 28.7 | 07 | 203.0 | 40.4 | 67 | 261.9 | 52.1 |
| 28 | 27.5 | 05.5 | 88 | 86.3 | 17.2 | 48 | 145.2 | 28.9 | 08 | 204.0 | 40.6 | 68 | 262.9 | 52.3 |
| 29 | 28.4 | 05.7 | 89 | 87.3 | 17.4 | 49 | 146.1 | 29.1 | 09 | 205.0 | 40.8 | 69 | 263.8 | 52.5 |
| 30 | 29.4 | 05.9 | 90 | 88.3 | 17.6 | 50 | 147.1 | 29.3 | 10 | 206.0 | 41.0 | 70 | 264.8 | 52.7 |
| 31 | 30.4 | 06.0 | 91 | 89.3 | 17.8 | 151 | 148.1 | 29.5 | 211 | 206.9 | 41.2 | 271 | 265.8 | 52.9 |
| 32 | 31.4 | 06.2 | 92 | 90.2 | 17.9 | 52 | 149.1 | 29.7 | 12 | 207.9 | 41.4 | 72 | 266.8 | 53.1 |
| 33 | 32.4 | 06.4 | 93 | 91.2 | 18.1 | 53 | 150.1 | 29.8 | 13 | 208.9 | 41.6 | 73 | 267.8 | 53.3 |
| 34 | 33.3 | 06.6 | 94 | 92.2 | 18.3 | 54 | 151.0 | 30.0 | 14 | 209.9 | 41.7 | 74 | 268.7 | 53.5 |
| 35 | 34.3 | 06.8 | 95 | 93.2 | 18.5 | 55 | 152.0 | 30.2 | 15 | 210.9 | 41.9 | 75 | 269.7 | 53.6 |
| 36 | 35.3 | 07.0 | 96 | 94.2 | 18.7 | 56 | 153.0 | 30.4 | 16 | 211.8 | 42.1 | 76 | 270.7 | 53.8 |
| 37 | 36.3 | 07.2 | 97 | 95.1 | 18.9 | 57 | 154.0 | 30.6 | 17 | 212.8 | 42.3 | 77 | 271.7 | 54.0 |
| 38 | 37.3 | 07.4 | 98 | 96.1 | 19.1 | 58 | 155.0 | 30.8 | 18 | 213.8 | 42.5 | 78 | 272.7 | 54.2 |
| 39 | 38.3 | 07.6 | 99 | 97.1 | 19.3 | 59 | 155.9 | 31.0 | 19 | 214.8 | 42.7 | 79 | 273.6 | 54.4 |
| 40 | 39.2 | 07.8 | 100 | 98.1 | 19.5 | 60 | 156.9 | 31.2 | 20 | 215.8 | 42.9 | 80 | 274.6 | 54.6 |
| 41 | 40.2 | 08.0 | 101 | 99.1 | 19.7 | 161 | 157.9 | 31.4 | 221 | 216.8 | 43.1 | 281 | 275.6 | 54.8 |
| 42 | 41.2 | 08.2 | 02 | 100.0 | 19.9 | 62 | 158.9 | 31.6 | 22 | 217.7 | 43.3 | 82 | 276.6 | 55.0 |
| 43 | 42.2 | 08.4 | 03 | 101.0 | 20.1 | 63 | 159.9 | 31.8 | 23 | 218.7 | 43.5 | 83 | 277.6 | 55.2 |
| 44 | 43.2 | 08.6 | 04 | 102.0 | 20.3 | 64 | 160.8 | 32.0 | 24 | 219.7 | 43.7 | 84 | 278.5 | 55.4 |
| 45 | 44.1 | 08.8 | 05 | 103.0 | 20.5 | 65 | 161.8 | 32.2 | 25 | 220.7 | 43.9 | 85 | 279.5 | 55.6 |
| 46 | 45.1 | 09.0 | 06 | 104.0 | 20.7 | 66 | 162.8 | 32.4 | 26 | 221.7 | 44.1 | 86 | 280.5 | 55.8 |
| 47 | 46.1 | 09.2 | 07 | 104.9 | 20.9 | 67 | 163.8 | 32.6 | 27 | 222.6 | 44.3 | 87 | 281.5 | 56.0 |
| 48 | 47.1 | 09.4 | 08 | 105.9 | 21.1 | 68 | 164.8 | 32.8 | 28 | 223.6 | 44.5 | 88 | 282.5 | 56.2 |
| 49 | 48.1 | 09.6 | 09 | 106.9 | 21.3 | 69 | 165.8 | 33.0 | 29 | 224.6 | 44.7 | 89 | 283.4 | 56.4 |
| 50 | 49.0 | 09.8 | 10 | 107.9 | 21.5 | 70 | 166.7 | 33.2 | 30 | 225.6 | 44.9 | 90 | 284.4 | 56.6 |
| 51 | 50.0 | 09.9 | 111 | 108.9 | 21.7 | 171 | 167.7 | 33.4 | 231 | 226.6 | 45.1 | 291 | 285.4 | 56.8 |
| 52 | 51.0 | 10.1 | 12 | 109.8 | 21.9 | 72 | 168.7 | 33.6 | 32 | 227.5 | 45.3 | 92 | 286.4 | 57.0 |
| 53 | 52.0 | 10.3 | 13 | 110.8 | 22.0 | 73 | 169.7 | 33.8 | 33 | 228.5 | 45.5 | 93 | 287.4 | 57.2 |
| 54 | 53.0 | 10.5 | 14 | 111.8 | 22.2 | 74 | 170.7 | 33.9 | 34 | 229.5 | 45.7 | 94 | 288.4 | 57.4 |
| 55 | 53.9 | 10.7 | 15 | 112.8 | 22.4 | 75 | 171.6 | 34.1 | 35 | 230.5 | 45.8 | 95 | 289.3 | 57.6 |
| 56 | 54.9 | 10.9 | 16 | 113.8 | 22.6 | 76 | 172.6 | 34.3 | 36 | 231.5 | 46.0 | 96 | 290.3 | 57.7 |
| 57 | 55.9 | 11.1 | 17 | 114.8 | 22.8 | 77 | 173.6 | 34.5 | 37 | 232.4 | 46.2 | 97 | 291.3 | 57.9 |
| 58 | 56.9 | 11.3 | 18 | 115.7 | 23.0 | 78 | 174.6 | 34.7 | 38 | 233.4 | 46.4 | 98 | 292.3 | 58.1 |
| 59 | 57.9 | 11.5 | 19 | 116.7 | 23.2 | 79 | 175.6 | 34.9 | 39 | 234.4 | 46.6 | 99 | 293.3 | 58.3 |
| 60 | 58.8 | 11.7 | 20 | 117.7 | 23.4 | 80 | 176.5 | 35.1 | 40 | 235.4 | 46.8 | 300 | 294.2 | 58.5 |
| Dist. | Dep. | Lat. | Dist. | Dep. | Lat. | Dist. | Dep. | Lat. | Dist. | Dep. | Lat. | Dist. | Dep. | Lat. |

E.byN. | E.byS. | W.byN. | W.byS. | [For 7 Points.

# TABLE I.

## Difference of Latitude and Departure for 1¼ Points.

| N.byE.¼E. | | | N.byW.¼W. | | | S.byE.¼E. | | | S byW.¼W | | | | | |
|---|---|---|---|---|---|---|---|---|---|---|---|---|---|---|
| Dist. | Lat. | Dep. | Dist. | Lat. | Dep. | Dist. | Lat. | Dep. | Dist. | Lat. | Dep. | Dist. | Lat. | Dep. |
| 1 | 01.0 | 00.2 | 61 | 59.2 | 14.8 | 121 | 117.4 | 29.4 | 181 | 175.6 | 44.0 | 241 | 233.8 | 58.6 |
| 2 | 01.9 | 00.5 | 62 | 60.1 | 15.1 | 22 | 118.3 | 29.6 | 82 | 176.5 | 44.2 | 42 | 234.7 | 58.8 |
| 3 | 02.9 | 00.7 | 63 | 61.1 | 15.3 | 23 | 119.3 | 29.9 | 83 | 177.5 | 44.5 | 43 | 235.7 | 59.0 |
| 4 | 03.9 | 01.0 | 64 | 62.1 | 15.6 | 24 | 120.3 | 30.1 | 84 | 178.5 | 44.7 | 44 | 236.7 | 59.3 |
| 5 | 04.9 | 01.2 | 65 | 63.1 | 15.8 | 25 | 121.3 | 30.4 | 85 | 179.5 | 45.0 | 45 | 237.7 | 59.5 |
| 6 | 05.8 | 01.5 | 66 | 64.0 | 16.0 | 26 | 122.2 | 30.6 | 86 | 180.4 | 45.2 | 46 | 238.6 | 59.8 |
| 7 | 06.8 | 01.7 | 67 | 65.0 | 16.3 | 27 | 123.2 | 30.9 | 87 | 181.4 | 45.4 | 47 | 239.6 | 60.0 |
| 8 | 07.8 | 01.9 | 68 | 66.0 | 16.5 | 28 | 124.2 | 31.1 | 88 | 182.4 | 45.7 | 48 | 240.6 | 60.3 |
| 9 | 08.7 | 02.2 | 69 | 66.9 | 16.8 | 29 | 125.1 | 31.3 | 89 | 183.3 | 45.9 | 49 | 241.5 | 60.5 |
| 10 | 09.7 | 02.4 | 70 | 67.9 | 17.0 | 30 | 126.1 | 31.6 | 90 | 184.3 | 46.2 | 50 | 242.5 | 60.7 |
| 11 | 10.7 | 02.7 | 71 | 68.9 | 17.3 | 131 | 127.1 | 31.8 | 191 | 185.3 | 46.4 | 251 | 243.5 | 61.0 |
| 12 | 11.6 | 02.9 | 72 | 69.8 | 17.5 | 32 | 128.0 | 32.1 | 92 | 186.2 | 46.7 | 52 | 244.4 | 61.2 |
| 13 | 12.6 | 03.2 | 73 | 70.8 | 17.7 | 33 | 129.0 | 32.3 | 93 | 187.2 | 46.9 | 53 | 245.4 | 61.5 |
| 14 | 13.6 | 03.4 | 74 | 71.8 | 18.0 | 34 | 130.0 | 32.6 | 94 | 188.2 | 47.1 | 54 | 246.4 | 61.7 |
| 15 | 14.6 | 03.6 | 75 | 72.8 | 18.2 | 35 | 131.0 | 32.8 | 95 | 189.2 | 47.4 | 55 | 247.4 | 62.0 |
| 16 | 15.5 | 03.9 | 76 | 73.7 | 18.5 | 36 | 131.9 | 33.0 | 96 | 190.1 | 47.6 | 56 | 248.3 | 62.2 |
| 17 | 16.5 | 04.1 | 77 | 74.7 | 18.7 | 37 | 132.9 | 33.3 | 97 | 191.1 | 47.9 | 57 | 249.3 | 62.4 |
| 18 | 17.5 | 04.4 | 78 | 75.7 | 19.0 | 38 | 133.9 | 33.5 | 98 | 192.1 | 48.1 | 58 | 250.3 | 62.7 |
| 19 | 18.4 | 04.6 | 79 | 76.6 | 19.2 | 39 | 134.8 | 33.8 | 99 | 193.0 | 48.4 | 59 | 251.2 | 62.9 |
| 20 | 19.4 | 04.9 | 80 | 77.6 | 19.4 | 40 | 135.8 | 34.0 | 200 | 194.0 | 48.6 | 60 | 252.2 | 63.2 |
| 21 | 20.4 | 05.1 | 81 | 78.6 | 19.7 | 141 | 136.8 | 34.3 | 201 | 195.0 | 48.8 | 261 | 253.2 | 63.4 |
| 22 | 21.3 | 05.3 | 82 | 79.5 | 19.9 | 42 | 137.7 | 34.5 | 02 | 195.9 | 49.1 | 62 | 254.1 | 63.7 |
| 23 | 22.3 | 05.6 | 83 | 80.5 | 20.2 | 43 | 138.7 | 34.7 | 03 | 196.9 | 49.3 | 63 | 255.1 | 63.9 |
| 24 | 23.3 | 05.8 | 84 | 81.5 | 20.4 | 44 | 139.7 | 35.0 | 04 | 197.9 | 49.6 | 64 | 256.1 | 64.1 |
| 25 | 24.3 | 06.1 | 85 | 82.5 | 20.7 | 45 | 140.7 | 35.2 | 05 | 198.9 | 49.8 | 65 | 257.1 | 64.4 |
| 26 | 25.2 | 06.3 | 86 | 83.4 | 20.9 | 46 | 141.6 | 35.5 | 06 | 199.8 | 50.1 | 66 | 258.0 | 64.6 |
| 27 | 26.2 | 06.6 | 87 | 84.4 | 21.1 | 47 | 142.6 | 35.7 | 07 | 200.8 | 50.3 | 67 | 259.0 | 64.9 |
| 28 | 27.2 | 06.8 | 88 | 85.4 | 21.4 | 48 | 143.6 | 36.0 | 08 | 201.8 | 50.5 | 68 | 260.0 | 65.1 |
| 29 | 28.1 | 07.0 | 89 | 86.3 | 21.6 | 49 | 144.5 | 36.2 | 09 | 202.7 | 50.8 | 69 | 260.9 | 65.4 |
| 30 | 29.1 | 07.3 | 90 | 87.3 | 21.9 | 50 | 145.5 | 36.4 | 10 | 203.7 | 51.0 | 70 | 261.9 | 65.6 |
| 31 | 30.1 | 07.5 | 91 | 88.3 | 22.1 | 151 | 146.5 | 36.7 | 211 | 204.7 | 51.3 | 271 | 262.9 | 65.8 |
| 32 | 31.0 | 07.8 | 92 | 89.2 | 22.4 | 52 | 147.4 | 36.9 | 12 | 205.6 | 51.5 | 72 | 263.8 | 66.1 |
| 33 | 32.0 | 08.0 | 93 | 90.2 | 22.6 | 53 | 148.4 | 37.2 | 13 | 206.6 | 51.8 | 73 | 264.8 | 66.3 |
| 34 | 33.0 | 08.3 | 94 | 91.2 | 22.8 | 54 | 149.4 | 37.4 | 14 | 207.6 | 52.0 | 74 | 265.8 | 66.6 |
| 35 | 34.0 | 08.5 | 95 | 92.2 | 23.1 | 55 | 150.4 | 37.7 | 15 | 208.6 | 52.2 | 75 | 266.8 | 66.8 |
| 36 | 34.9 | 08.7 | 96 | 93.1 | 23.3 | 56 | 151.3 | 37.9 | 16 | 209.5 | 52.5 | 76 | 267.7 | 67.1 |
| 37 | 35.9 | 09.0 | 97 | 94.1 | 23.6 | 57 | 152.3 | 38.1 | 17 | 210.5 | 52.7 | 77 | 268.7 | 67.3 |
| 38 | 36.9 | 09.2 | 98 | 95.1 | 23.8 | 58 | 153.3 | 38.4 | 18 | 211.5 | 53.0 | 78 | 269.7 | 67.5 |
| 39 | 37.8 | 09.5 | 99 | 96.0 | 24.1 | 59 | 154.2 | 38.6 | 19 | 212.4 | 53.2 | 79 | 270.6 | 67.8 |
| 40 | 38.8 | 09.7 | 100 | 97.0 | 24.3 | 60 | 155.2 | 38.9 | 20 | 213.4 | 53.5 | 80 | 271.6 | 68.0 |
| 41 | 39.8 | 10.0 | 101 | 98.0 | 24.5 | 161 | 156.2 | 39.1 | 221 | 214.4 | 53.7 | 281 | 272.6 | 68.3 |
| 42 | 40.7 | 10.2 | 02 | 98.9 | 24.8 | 62 | 157.1 | 39.4 | 22 | 215.3 | 53.9 | 82 | 273.5 | 68.5 |
| 43 | 41.7 | 10.4 | 03 | 99.9 | 25.0 | 63 | 158.1 | 39.6 | 23 | 216.3 | 54.2 | 83 | 274.5 | 68.8 |
| 44 | 42.7 | 10.7 | 04 | 100.9 | 25.3 | 64 | 159.1 | 39.8 | 24 | 217.3 | 54.4 | 84 | 275.5 | 69.0 |
| 45 | 43.7 | 10.9 | 05 | 101.9 | 25.5 | 65 | 160.1 | 40.1 | 25 | 218.3 | 54.7 | 85 | 276.5 | 69.2 |
| 46 | 44.6 | 11.2 | 06 | 102.8 | 25.8 | 66 | 161.0 | 40.3 | 26 | 219.2 | 54.9 | 86 | 277.4 | 69.5 |
| 47 | 45.6 | 11.4 | 07 | 103.8 | 26.0 | 67 | 162.0 | 40.6 | 27 | 220.2 | 55.2 | 87 | 278.4 | 69.7 |
| 48 | 46.6 | 11.7 | 08 | 104.8 | 26.2 | 68 | 163.0 | 40.8 | 28 | 221.2 | 55.4 | 88 | 279.4 | 70.0 |
| 49 | 47.5 | 11.9 | 09 | 105.7 | 26.5 | 69 | 163.9 | 41.1 | 29 | 222.1 | 55.6 | 89 | 280.3 | 70.2 |
| 50 | 48.5 | 12.1 | 10 | 106.7 | 26.7 | 70 | 164.9 | 41.3 | 30 | 223.1 | 55.9 | 90 | 281.3 | 70.5 |
| 51 | 49.5 | 12.4 | 111 | 107.7 | 27.0 | 171 | 165.9 | 41.5 | 231 | 224.1 | 56.1 | 291 | 282.3 | 70.7 |
| 52 | 50.4 | 12.6 | 12 | 108.6 | 27.2 | 72 | 166.8 | 41.8 | 32 | 225.0 | 56.4 | 92 | 283.2 | 71.0 |
| 53 | 51.4 | 12.9 | 13 | 109.6 | 27.5 | 73 | 167.8 | 42.0 | 33 | 226.0 | 56.6 | 93 | 284.2 | 71.2 |
| 54 | 52.4 | 13.1 | 14 | 110.6 | 27.7 | 74 | 168.8 | 42.3 | 34 | 227.0 | 56.9 | 94 | 285.2 | 71.4 |
| 55 | 53.4 | 13.4 | 15 | 111.6 | 27.9 | 75 | 169.8 | 42.5 | 35 | 228.0 | 57.1 | 95 | 286.2 | 71.7 |
| 56 | 54.3 | 13.6 | 16 | 112.5 | 28.2 | 76 | 170.7 | 42.8 | 36 | 228.9 | 57.3 | 96 | 287.1 | 71.9 |
| 57 | 55.3 | 13.8 | 17 | 113.5 | 28.4 | 77 | 171.7 | 43.0 | 37 | 229.9 | 57.6 | 97 | 288.1 | 72.2 |
| 58 | 56.3 | 14.1 | 18 | 114.5 | 28.7 | 78 | 172.7 | 43.3 | 38 | 230.9 | 57.8 | 98 | 289.1 | 72.4 |
| 59 | 57.2 | 14.3 | 19 | 115.4 | 28.9 | 79 | 173.6 | 43.5 | 39 | 231.8 | 58.1 | 99 | 290.0 | 72.7 |
| 60 | 58.2 | 14.6 | 20 | 116.4 | 29.2 | 80 | 174.6 | 43.7 | 40 | 232.8 | 58.3 | 300 | 291.0 | 72.9 |
| Dist. | Dep. | Lat. | Dist. | Dep. | Lat. | Dist. | Dep. | Lat. | Dist. | Dep. | Lat. | Dist. | Dep. | Lat. |
| E.N.E.¾E. | | | E.S.E.¾E. | | | W.N.W.¾W. | | | W.S.W.¾W. | | | [For 6¾ Points. | | |

# TABLE I.

## Difference of Latitude and Departure for 1½ Points.

| N.byE.½E. | | | N.byW.½W. | | | S.byE.½E. | | | S.byW.½W. | | |
|---|---|---|---|---|---|---|---|---|---|---|---|

| Dist. | Lat. | Dep. | Dist. | Lat. | Dep. | Dist. | Lat. | Dep. | Dist. | Lat. | Dep. | Dist. | Lat. | Dep. |
|---|---|---|---|---|---|---|---|---|---|---|---|---|---|---|
| 1 | 01.0 | 00.3 | 61 | 58.4 | 17.7 | 121 | 115.8 | 35.1 | 181 | 173.2 | 52.5 | 241 | 230.6 | 70.0 |
| 2 | 01.9 | 00.6 | 62 | 59.3 | 18.0 | 22 | 116.7 | 35.4 | 82 | 174.2 | 52.8 | 42 | 231.6 | 70.2 |
| 3 | 02.9 | 00.9 | 63 | 60.3 | 18.3 | 23 | 117.7 | 35.7 | 83 | 175.1 | 53.1 | 43 | 232.5 | 70.5 |
| 4 | 03.8 | 01.2 | 64 | 61.2 | 18.6 | 24 | 118.7 | 36.0 | 84 | 176.1 | 53.4 | 44 | 233.5 | 70.8 |
| 5 | 04.8 | 01.5 | 65 | 62.2 | 18.9 | 25 | 119.6 | 36.3 | 85 | 177.0 | 53.7 | 45 | 234.5 | 71.1 |
| 6 | 05.7 | 01.7 | 66 | 63.2 | 19.2 | 26 | 120.6 | 36.6 | 86 | 178.0 | 54.0 | 46 | 235.4 | 71.4 |
| 7 | 06.7 | 02.0 | 67 | 64.1 | 19.4 | 27 | 121.5 | 36.9 | 87 | 178.9 | 54.3 | 47 | 236.4 | 71.7 |
| 8 | 07.7 | 02.3 | 68 | 65.1 | 19.7 | 28 | 122.5 | 37.2 | 88 | 179.9 | 54.6 | 48 | 237.3 | 72.0 |
| 9 | 08.6 | 02.6 | 69 | 66.0 | 20.0 | 29 | 123.4 | 37.4 | 89 | 180.9 | 54.9 | 49 | 238.3 | 72.3 |
| 10 | 09.6 | 02.9 | 70 | 67.0 | 20.3 | 30 | 124.4 | 37.7 | 90 | 181.8 | 55.2 | 50 | 239.2 | 72.6 |
| 11 | 10.5 | 03.2 | 71 | 67.9 | 20.6 | 131 | 125.4 | 38.0 | 191 | 182.8 | 55.4 | 251 | 240.2 | 72.9 |
| 12 | 11.5 | 03.5 | 72 | 68.9 | 20.9 | 32 | 126.3 | 38.3 | 92 | 183.7 | 55.7 | 52 | 241.1 | 73.2 |
| 13 | 12.4 | 03.8 | 73 | 69.9 | 21.2 | 33 | 127.3 | 38.6 | 93 | 184.7 | 56.0 | 53 | 242.1 | 73.4 |
| 14 | 13.4 | 04.1 | 74 | 70.8 | 21.5 | 34 | 128.2 | 38.9 | 94 | 185.6 | 56.3 | 54 | 243.1 | 73.7 |
| 15 | 14.4 | 04.4 | 75 | 71.8 | 21.8 | 35 | 129.2 | 39.2 | 95 | 186.6 | 56.6 | 55 | 244.0 | 74.0 |
| 16 | 15.3 | 04.6 | 76 | 72.7 | 22.1 | 36 | 130.1 | 39.5 | 96 | 187.6 | 56.9 | 56 | 245.0 | 74.3 |
| 17 | 16.3 | 04.9 | 77 | 73.7 | 22.4 | 37 | 131.1 | 39.8 | 97 | 188.5 | 57.2 | 57 | 245.9 | 74.6 |
| 18 | 17.2 | 05.2 | 78 | 74.6 | 22.6 | 38 | 132.1 | 40.1 | 98 | 189.5 | 57.5 | 58 | 246.9 | 74.9 |
| 19 | 18.2 | 05.5 | 79 | 75.6 | 22.9 | 39 | 133.0 | 40.3 | 99 | 190.4 | 57.8 | 59 | 247.8 | 75.2 |
| 20 | 19.1 | 05.8 | 80 | 76.6 | 23.2 | 40 | 134.0 | 40.6 | 200 | 191.4 | 58.1 | 60 | 248.8 | 75.5 |
| 21 | 20.1 | 06.1 | 81 | 77.5 | 23.5 | 141 | 134.9 | 40.9 | 201 | 192.3 | 58.3 | 261 | 249.8 | 75.8 |
| 22 | 21.1 | 06.4 | 82 | 78.5 | 23.8 | 42 | 135.9 | 41.2 | 02 | 193.3 | 58.6 | 62 | 250.7 | 76.1 |
| 23 | 22.0 | 06.7 | 83 | 79.4 | 24.1 | 43 | 136.8 | 41.5 | 03 | 194.3 | 58.9 | 63 | 251.7 | 76.3 |
| 24 | 23.0 | 07.0 | 84 | 80.4 | 24.4 | 44 | 137.8 | 41.8 | 04 | 195.2 | 59.2 | 64 | 252.6 | 76.6 |
| 25 | 23.9 | 07.3 | 85 | 81.3 | 24.7 | 45 | 138.8 | 42.1 | 05 | 196.2 | 59.5 | 65 | 253.6 | 76.9 |
| 26 | 24.9 | 07.5 | 86 | 82.3 | 25.0 | 46 | 139.7 | 42.4 | 06 | 197.1 | 59.8 | 66 | 254.5 | 77.2 |
| 27 | 25.8 | 07.8 | 87 | 83.3 | 25.3 | 47 | 140.7 | 42.7 | 07 | 198.1 | 60.1 | 67 | 255.5 | 77.5 |
| 28 | 26.8 | 08.1 | 88 | 84.2 | 25.5 | 48 | 141.6 | 43.0 | 08 | 199.0 | 60.4 | 68 | 256.5 | 77.8 |
| 29 | 27.8 | 08.4 | 89 | 85.2 | 25.8 | 49 | 142.6 | 43.3 | 09 | 200.0 | 60.7 | 69 | 257.4 | 78.1 |
| 30 | 28.7 | 08.7 | 90 | 86.1 | 26.1 | 50 | 143.5 | 43.5 | 10 | 201.0 | 61.0 | 70 | 258.4 | 78.4 |
| 31 | 29.7 | 09.0 | 91 | 87.1 | 26.4 | 151 | 144.5 | 43.8 | 211 | 201.9 | 61.3 | 271 | 259.3 | 78.7 |
| 32 | 30.6 | 09.3 | 92 | 88.0 | 26.7 | 52 | 145.5 | 44.1 | 12 | 202.9 | 61.5 | 72 | 260.3 | 79.0 |
| 33 | 31.6 | 09.6 | 93 | 89.0 | 27.0 | 53 | 146.4 | 44.4 | 13 | 203.8 | 61.8 | 73 | 261.2 | 79.2 |
| 34 | 32.5 | 09.9 | 94 | 90.0 | 27.3 | 54 | 147.4 | 44.7 | 14 | 204.8 | 62.1 | 74 | 262.2 | 79.5 |
| 35 | 33.5 | 10.2 | 95 | 90.9 | 27.6 | 55 | 148.3 | 45.0 | 15 | 205.7 | 62.4 | 75 | 263.2 | 79.8 |
| 36 | 34.4 | 10.5 | 96 | 91.9 | 27.9 | 56 | 149.3 | 45.3 | 16 | 206.7 | 62.7 | 76 | 264.1 | 80.1 |
| 37 | 35.4 | 10.7 | 97 | 92.8 | 28.2 | 57 | 150.2 | 45.6 | 17 | 207.7 | 63.0 | 77 | 265.1 | 80.4 |
| 38 | 36.4 | 11.0 | 98 | 93.8 | 28.4 | 58 | 151.2 | 45.9 | 18 | 208.6 | 63.3 | 78 | 266.0 | 80.7 |
| 39 | 37.3 | 11.3 | 99 | 94.7 | 28.7 | 59 | 152.2 | 46.2 | 19 | 209.6 | 63.6 | 79 | 267.0 | 81.0 |
| 40 | 38.3 | 11.6 | 100 | 95.7 | 29.0 | 60 | 153.1 | 46.4 | 20 | 210.5 | 63.9 | 80 | 267.9 | 81.3 |
| 41 | 39.2 | 11.9 | 101 | 96.7 | 29.3 | 161 | 154.1 | 46.7 | 221 | 211.5 | 64.2 | 281 | 268.9 | 81.6 |
| 42 | 40.2 | 12.2 | 02 | 97.6 | 29.6 | 62 | 155.0 | 47.0 | 22 | 212.4 | 64.4 | 82 | 269.9 | 81.9 |
| 43 | 41.1 | 12.5 | 03 | 98.6 | 29.9 | 63 | 156.0 | 47.3 | 23 | 213.4 | 64.7 | 83 | 270.8 | 82.2 |
| 44 | 42.1 | 12.8 | 04 | 99.5 | 30.2 | 64 | 156.9 | 47.6 | 24 | 214.4 | 65.0 | 84 | 271.8 | 82.4 |
| 45 | 43.1 | 13.1 | 05 | 100.5 | 30.5 | 65 | 157.9 | 47.9 | 25 | 215.3 | 65.3 | 85 | 272.7 | 82.7 |
| 46 | 44.0 | 13.4 | 06 | 101.4 | 30.8 | 66 | 158.9 | 48.2 | 26 | 216.3 | 65.6 | 86 | 273.7 | 83.0 |
| 47 | 45.0 | 13.6 | 07 | 102.4 | 31.1 | 67 | 159.8 | 48.5 | 27 | 217.2 | 65.9 | 87 | 274.6 | 83.3 |
| 48 | 45.9 | 13.9 | 08 | 103.3 | 31.4 | 68 | 160.8 | 48.8 | 28 | 218.2 | 66.2 | 88 | 275.6 | 83.6 |
| 49 | 46.9 | 14.2 | 09 | 104.3 | 31.6 | 69 | 161.7 | 49.1 | 29 | 219.1 | 66.5 | 89 | 276.6 | 83.9 |
| 50 | 47.8 | 14.5 | 10 | 105.3 | 31.9 | 70 | 162.7 | 49.3 | 30 | 220.1 | 66.8 | 90 | 277.5 | 84.2 |
| 51 | 48.8 | 14.8 | 111 | 106.2 | 32.2 | 171 | 163.6 | 49.6 | 231 | 221.1 | 67.1 | 291 | 278.5 | 84.5 |
| 52 | 49.8 | 15.1 | 12 | 107.2 | 32.5 | 72 | 164.6 | 49.9 | 32 | 222.0 | 67.3 | 92 | 279.4 | 84.8 |
| 53 | 50.7 | 15.4 | 13 | 108.1 | 32.8 | 73 | 165.6 | 50.2 | 33 | 223.0 | 67.6 | 93 | 280.4 | 85.1 |
| 54 | 51.7 | 15.7 | 14 | 109.1 | 33.1 | 74 | 166.5 | 50.5 | 34 | 223.9 | 67.9 | 94 | 281.3 | 85.3 |
| 55 | 52.6 | 16.0 | 15 | 110.0 | 33.4 | 75 | 167.5 | 50.8 | 35 | 224.9 | 68.2 | 95 | 282.3 | 85.6 |
| 56 | 53.6 | 16.3 | 16 | 111.0 | 33.7 | 76 | 168.4 | 51.1 | 36 | 225.8 | 68.5 | 96 | 283.3 | 85.9 |
| 57 | 54.5 | 16.5 | 17 | 112.0 | 34.0 | 77 | 169.4 | 51.4 | 37 | 226.8 | 68.8 | 97 | 284.2 | 86.2 |
| 58 | 55.5 | 16.8 | 18 | 112.9 | 34.3 | 78 | 170.3 | 51.7 | 38 | 227.8 | 69.1 | 98 | 285.2 | 86.5 |
| 59 | 56.5 | 17.1 | 19 | 113.9 | 34.5 | 79 | 171.3 | 52.0 | 39 | 228.7 | 69.4 | 99 | 286.1 | 86.8 |
| 60 | 57.4 | 17.4 | 20 | 114.8 | 34.8 | 80 | 172.2 | 52.3 | 40 | 229.7 | 69.7 | 300 | 287.1 | 87.1 |
| Dis. | Dep. | Lat. | Dist. | Dep. | Lat. | Dist. | Dep. | Lat. | Dist. | Dep. | Lat. | Dist. | Dep. | Lat. |

| E.N.E.½E. | E.S.E.½E. | W.N.W.½W. | W.S.W.½W. | [For 6½ Points. |
|---|---|---|---|---|

# TABLE I.

## Difference of Latitude and Departure for 1¾ Points.

| N.by E.¾E. | | | N.by W.¾W. | | | S.by E.¾E. | | | S.by W.¾W. | | | | | |
|---|---|---|---|---|---|---|---|---|---|---|---|---|---|---|
| Dist. | Lat. | Dep. | Dist. | Lat. | Dep. | Dist. | Lat. | Dep. | Dist. | Lat. | Dep. | Dist. | Lat. | Dep. |
| 1 | 00.9 | 00.3 | 61 | 57.4 | 20.6 | 121 | 113.9 | 40.8 | 181 | 170.4 | 61.0 | 241 | 226.9 | 81.2 |
| 2 | 01.9 | 00.7 | 62 | 58.4 | 20.9 | 22 | 114.9 | 41.1 | 82 | 171.4 | 61.3 | 42 | 227.9 | 81.5 |
| 3 | 02.8 | 01.0 | 63 | 59.3 | 21.2 | 23 | 115.8 | 41.4 | 83 | 172.3 | 61.7 | 43 | 228.8 | 81.9 |
| 4 | 03.8 | 01.3 | 64 | 60.3 | 21.6 | 24 | 116.8 | 41.8 | 84 | 173.2 | 62.0 | 44 | 229.7 | 82.2 |
| 5 | 04.7 | 01.7 | 65 | 61.2 | 21.9 | 25 | 117.7 | 42.1 | 85 | 174.2 | 62.3 | 45 | 230.7 | 82.5 |
| 6 | 05.6 | 02.0 | 66 | 62.1 | 22.2 | 26 | 118.6 | 42.4 | 86 | 175.1 | 62.7 | 46 | 231.6 | 82.9 |
| 7 | 06.6 | 02.4 | 67 | 63.1 | 22.6 | 27 | 119.6 | 42.8 | 87 | 176.1 | 63.0 | 47 | 232.6 | 83.2 |
| 8 | 07.5 | 02.7 | 68 | 64.0 | 22.9 | 28 | 120.5 | 43.1 | 88 | 177.0 | 63.3 | 48 | 233.5 | 83.5 |
| 9 | 08.5 | 03.0 | 69 | 65.0 | 23.2 | 29 | 121.5 | 43.5 | 89 | 178.0 | 63.7 | 49 | 234.4 | 83.9 |
| 10 | 09.4 | 03.4 | 70 | 65.9 | 23.6 | 30 | 122.4 | 43.8 | 90 | 178.9 | 64.0 | 50 | 235.4 | 84.2 |
| 11 | 10.4 | 03.7 | 71 | 66.8 | 23.9 | 131 | 123.3 | 44.1 | 191 | 179.8 | 64.3 | 251 | 236.3 | 84.6 |
| 12 | 11.3 | 04.0 | 72 | 67.8 | 24.3 | 32 | 124.3 | 44.5 | 92 | 180.8 | 64.7 | 52 | 237.3 | 84.9 |
| 13 | 12.2 | 04.4 | 73 | 68.7 | 24.6 | 33 | 125.2 | 44.8 | 93 | 181.7 | 65.0 | 53 | 238.2 | 85.2 |
| 14 | 13.2 | 04.7 | 74 | 69.7 | 24.9 | 34 | 126.2 | 45.1 | 94 | 182.7 | 65.4 | 54 | 239.2 | 85.6 |
| 15 | 14.1 | 05.1 | 75 | 70.6 | 25.3 | 35 | 127.1 | 45.5 | 95 | 183.6 | 65.7 | 55 | 240.1 | 85.9 |
| 16 | 15.1 | 05.4 | 76 | 71.6 | 25.6 | 36 | 128.0 | 45.8 | 96 | 184.5 | 66.0 | 56 | 241.0 | 86.2 |
| 17 | 16.0 | 05.7 | 77 | 72.5 | 25.9 | 37 | 129.0 | 46.2 | 97 | 185.5 | 66.4 | 57 | 242.0 | 86.6 |
| 18 | 16.9 | 06.1 | 78 | 73.4 | 26.3 | 38 | 129.9 | 46.5 | 98 | 186.4 | 66.7 | 58 | 242.9 | 86.9 |
| 19 | 17.9 | 06.4 | 79 | 74.4 | 26.6 | 39 | 130.9 | 46.8 | 99 | 187.4 | 67.0 | 59 | 243.9 | 87.3 |
| 20 | 18.8 | 06.7 | 80 | 75.3 | 27.0 | 40 | 131.8 | 47.2 | 200 | 188.3 | 67.4 | 60 | 244.8 | 87.6 |
| 21 | 19.8 | 07.1 | 81 | 76.3 | 27.3 | 141 | 132.8 | 47.5 | 201 | 189.3 | 67.7 | 261 | 245.7 | 87.9 |
| 22 | 20.7 | 07.4 | 82 | 77.2 | 27.6 | 42 | 133.7 | 47.8 | 02 | 190.2 | 68.1 | 62 | 246.7 | 88.3 |
| 23 | 21.7 | 07.7 | 83 | 78.1 | 28.0 | 43 | 134.6 | 48.2 | 03 | 191.1 | 68.4 | 63 | 247.6 | 88.6 |
| 24 | 22.6 | 08.1 | 84 | 79.1 | 28.3 | 44 | 135.6 | 48.5 | 04 | 192.1 | 68.7 | 64 | 248.6 | 88.9 |
| 25 | 23.5 | 08.4 | 85 | 80.0 | 28.6 | 45 | 136.5 | 48.8 | 05 | 193.0 | 69.1 | 65 | 249.5 | 89.3 |
| 26 | 24.5 | 08.8 | 86 | 81.0 | 29.0 | 46 | 137.5 | 49.2 | 06 | 194.0 | 69.4 | 66 | 250.5 | 89.6 |
| 27 | 25.4 | 09.1 | 87 | 81.9 | 29.3 | 47 | 138.4 | 49.5 | 07 | 194.9 | 69.7 | 67 | 251.4 | 89.9 |
| 28 | 26.4 | 09.4 | 88 | 82.9 | 29.6 | 48 | 139.3 | 49.9 | 08 | 195.8 | 70.1 | 68 | 252.3 | 90.3 |
| 29 | 27.3 | 09.8 | 89 | 83.8 | 30.0 | 49 | 140.3 | 50.2 | 09 | 196.8 | 70.4 | 69 | 253.3 | 90.6 |
| 30 | 28.2 | 10.1 | 90 | 84.7 | 30.3 | 50 | 141.2 | 50.5 | 10 | 197.7 | 70.7 | 70 | 254.2 | 91.0 |
| 31 | 29.2 | 10.4 | 91 | 85.7 | 30.7 | 151 | 142.2 | 50.9 | 211 | 198.7 | 71.1 | 271 | 255.2 | 91.3 |
| 32 | 30.1 | 10.8 | 92 | 86.6 | 31.0 | 52 | 143.1 | 51.2 | 12 | 199.6 | 71.4 | 72 | 256.1 | 91.6 |
| 33 | 31.1 | 11.1 | 93 | 87.6 | 31.3 | 53 | 144.1 | 51.5 | 13 | 200.5 | 71.8 | 73 | 257.0 | 92.0 |
| 34 | 32.0 | 11.5 | 94 | 88.5 | 31.7 | 54 | 145.0 | 51.9 | 14 | 201.5 | 72.1 | 74 | 258.0 | 92.3 |
| 35 | 33.0 | 11.8 | 95 | 89.4 | 32.0 | 55 | 145.9 | 52.2 | 15 | 202.4 | 72.4 | 75 | 258.9 | 92.6 |
| 36 | 33.9 | 12.1 | 96 | 90.4 | 32.3 | 56 | 146.9 | 52.6 | 16 | 203.4 | 72.8 | 76 | 259.9 | 93.0 |
| 37 | 34.8 | 12.5 | 97 | 91.3 | 32.7 | 57 | 147.8 | 52.9 | 17 | 204.3 | 73.1 | 77 | 260.8 | 93.3 |
| 38 | 35.8 | 12.8 | 98 | 92.3 | 33.0 | 58 | 148.8 | 53.2 | 18 | 205.3 | 73.4 | 78 | 261.7 | 93.7 |
| 39 | 36.7 | 13.1 | 99 | 93.2 | 33.4 | 59 | 149.7 | 53.6 | 19 | 206.2 | 73.8 | 79 | 262.7 | 94.0 |
| 40 | 37.7 | 13.5 | 100 | 94.2 | 33.7 | 60 | 150.6 | 53.9 | 20 | 207.1 | 74.1 | 80 | 263.6 | 94.3 |
| 41 | 38.6 | 13.8 | 101 | 95.1 | 34.0 | 161 | 151.6 | 54.2 | 221 | 208.1 | 74.5 | 281 | 264.6 | 94.7 |
| 42 | 39.5 | 14.1 | 02 | 96.0 | 34.4 | 62 | 152.5 | 54.6 | 22 | 209.0 | 74.8 | 82 | 265.5 | 95.0 |
| 43 | 40.5 | 14.5 | 03 | 97.0 | 34.7 | 63 | 153.5 | 54.9 | 23 | 210.0 | 75.1 | 83 | 266.5 | 95.3 |
| 44 | 41.4 | 14.8 | 04 | 97.9 | 35.0 | 64 | 154.4 | 55.2 | 24 | 210.9 | 75.5 | 84 | 267.4 | 95.7 |
| 45 | 42.4 | 15.2 | 05 | 98.9 | 35.4 | 65 | 155.4 | 55.6 | 25 | 211.8 | 75.8 | 85 | 268.3 | 96.0 |
| 46 | 43.3 | 15.5 | 06 | 99.8 | 35.7 | 66 | 156.3 | 55.9 | 26 | 212.8 | 76.1 | 86 | 269.3 | 96.4 |
| 47 | 44.3 | 15.8 | 07 | 100.7 | 36.0 | 67 | 157.2 | 56.3 | 27 | 213.7 | 76.5 | 87 | 270.2 | 96.7 |
| 48 | 45.2 | 16.2 | 08 | 101.7 | 36.4 | 68 | 158.2 | 56.6 | 28 | 214.7 | 76.8 | 88 | 271.2 | 97.0 |
| 49 | 46.1 | 16.5 | 09 | 102.6 | 36.7 | 69 | 159.1 | 56.9 | 29 | 215.6 | 77.1 | 89 | 272.1 | 97.4 |
| 50 | 47.1 | 16.8 | 10 | 103.6 | 37.1 | 70 | 160.1 | 57.3 | 30 | 216.6 | 77.5 | 90 | 273.0 | 97.7 |
| 51 | 48.0 | 17.2 | 111 | 104.5 | 37.4 | 171 | 161.0 | 57.6 | 231 | 217.5 | 77.8 | 291 | 274.0 | 98.0 |
| 52 | 49.0 | 17.5 | 12 | 105.5 | 37.7 | 72 | 161.9 | 57.9 | 32 | 218.4 | 78.2 | 92 | 274.9 | 98.4 |
| 53 | 49.9 | 17.9 | 13 | 106.4 | 38.1 | 73 | 162.9 | 58.3 | 33 | 219.4 | 78.5 | 93 | 275.9 | 98.7 |
| 54 | 50.8 | 18.2 | 14 | 107.3 | 38.4 | 74 | 163.8 | 58.6 | 34 | 220.3 | 78.8 | 94 | 276.8 | 99.0 |
| 55 | 51.8 | 18.5 | 15 | 108.3 | 38.7 | 75 | 164.8 | 59.0 | 35 | 221.3 | 79.2 | 95 | 277.8 | 99.4 |
| 56 | 52.7 | 18.9 | 16 | 109.2 | 39.1 | 76 | 165.7 | 59.3 | 36 | 222.2 | 79.5 | 96 | 278.7 | 99.7 |
| 57 | 53.7 | 19.2 | 17 | 110.2 | 39.4 | 77 | 166.7 | 59.6 | 37 | 223.1 | 79.8 | 97 | 279.6 | 100.1 |
| 58 | 54.6 | 19.5 | 18 | 111.1 | 39.8 | 78 | 167.6 | 60.0 | 38 | 224.1 | 80.2 | 98 | 280.6 | 100.4 |
| 59 | 55.6 | 19.9 | 19 | 112.0 | 40.1 | 79 | 168.5 | 60.3 | 39 | 225.0 | 80.5 | 99 | 281.5 | 100.7 |
| 60 | 56.5 | 20.2 | 20 | 113.0 | 40.4 | 80 | 169.5 | 60.6 | 40 | 226.0 | 80.9 | 300 | 282.5 | 101.1 |
| Dist. | Dep. | Lat. | Dist. | Dep. | Lat. | Dist. | Dep. | Lat. | Dist. | Dep. | Lat. | Dist. | Dep. | Lat. |
| E.N.E.¼E. | | | E.S.E.¼E. | | | W.N.W.¼W. | | | W.S.W.¼W. | | | [For 6¼ Points. | | |

# TABLE I.

## Difference of Latitude and Departure for 2 Points.

N.N.E. N.N.W. S.S.E. S.S.W.

| Dist. | Lat. | Dep. | Dist. | Lat. | Dep. | Dist. | Lat. | Dep. | Dist. | Lat. | Dep. | Dist. | Lat. | Dep. |
|---|---|---|---|---|---|---|---|---|---|---|---|---|---|---|
| 1 | 00.9 | 00.4 | 61 | 56.4 | 23.3 | 121 | 111.8 | 46.3 | 181 | 167.2 | 69.3 | 241 | 222.7 | 92.2 |
| 2 | 01.8 | 00.8 | 62 | 57.3 | 23.7 | 22 | 112.7 | 46.7 | 82 | 168.1 | 69.6 | 42 | 223.6 | 92.6 |
| 3 | 02.8 | 01.1 | 63 | 58.2 | 24.1 | 23 | 113.6 | 47.1 | 83 | 169.1 | 70.0 | 43 | 224.5 | 93.0 |
| 4 | 03.7 | 01.5 | 64 | 59.1 | 24.5 | 24 | 114.6 | 47.5 | 84 | 170.0 | 70.4 | 44 | 225.4 | 93.4 |
| 5 | 04.6 | 01.9 | 65 | 60.1 | 24.9 | 25 | 115.5 | 47.8 | 85 | 170.9 | 70.8 | 45 | 226.4 | 93.8 |
| 6 | 05.5 | 02.3 | 66 | 61.0 | 25.3 | 26 | 116.4 | 48.2 | 86 | 171.8 | 71.2 | 46 | 227.3 | 94.1 |
| 7 | 06.5 | 02.7 | 67 | 61.9 | 25.6 | 27 | 117.3 | 48.6 | 87 | 172.8 | 71.6 | 47 | 228.2 | 94.5 |
| 8 | 07.4 | 03.1 | 68 | 62.8 | 26.0 | 28 | 118.3 | 49.0 | 88 | 173.7 | 71.9 | 48 | 229.1 | 94.9 |
| 9 | 08.3 | 03.4 | 69 | 63.7 | 26.4 | 29 | 119.2 | 49.4 | 89 | 174.6 | 72.3 | 49 | 230.0 | 95.3 |
| 10 | 09.2 | 03.8 | 70 | 64.7 | 26.8 | 30 | 120.1 | 49.7 | 90 | 175.5 | 72.7 | 50 | 231.0 | 95.7 |
| 11 | 10.2 | 04.2 | 71 | 65.6 | 27.2 | 131 | 121.0 | 50.1 | 191 | 176.5 | 73.1 | 251 | 231.9 | 96.1 |
| 12 | 11.1 | 04.6 | 72 | 66.5 | 27.6 | 32 | 122.0 | 50.5 | 92 | 177.4 | 73.5 | 52 | 232.8 | 96.4 |
| 13 | 12.0 | 05.0 | 73 | 67.4 | 27.9 | 33 | 122.9 | 50.9 | 93 | 178.3 | 73.9 | 53 | 233.7 | 96.8 |
| 14 | 12.9 | 05.4 | 74 | 68.4 | 28.3 | 34 | 123.8 | 51.3 | 94 | 179.2 | 74.2 | 54 | 234.7 | 97.2 |
| 15 | 13.9 | 05.7 | 75 | 69.3 | 28.7 | 35 | 124.7 | 51.7 | 95 | 180.2 | 74.6 | 55 | 235.6 | 97.6 |
| 16 | 14.8 | 06.1 | 76 | 70.2 | 29.1 | 36 | 125.6 | 52.0 | 96 | 181.1 | 75.0 | 56 | 236.5 | 98.0 |
| 17 | 15.7 | 06.5 | 77 | 71.1 | 29.5 | 37 | 126.6 | 52.4 | 97 | 182.0 | 75.4 | 57 | 237.4 | 98.3 |
| 18 | 16.6 | 06.9 | 78 | 72.1 | 29.8 | 38 | 127.5 | 52.8 | 98 | 182.9 | 75.8 | 58 | 238.4 | 98.7 |
| 19 | 17.6 | 07.3 | 79 | 73.0 | 30.2 | 39 | 128.4 | 53.2 | 99 | 183.9 | 76.2 | 59 | 239.3 | 99.1 |
| 20 | 18.5 | 07.7 | 80 | 73.9 | 30.6 | 40 | 129.3 | 53.6 | 200 | 184.8 | 76.5 | 60 | 240.2 | 99.5 |
| 21 | 19.4 | 08.0 | 81 | 74.8 | 31.0 | 141 | 130.3 | 54.0 | 201 | 185.7 | 76.9 | 261 | 241.1 | 99.9 |
| 22 | 20.3 | 08.4 | 82 | 75.8 | 31.4 | 42 | 131.2 | 54.3 | 02 | 186.6 | 77.3 | 62 | 242.1 | 100.3 |
| 23 | 21.2 | 08.8 | 83 | 76.7 | 31.8 | 43 | 132.1 | 54.7 | 03 | 187.5 | 77.7 | 63 | 243.0 | 100.6 |
| 24 | 22.2 | 09.2 | 84 | 77.6 | 32.1 | 44 | 133.0 | 55.1 | 04 | 188.5 | 78.1 | 64 | 243.9 | 101.0 |
| 25 | 23.1 | 09.6 | 85 | 78.5 | 32.5 | 45 | 134.0 | 55.5 | 05 | 189.4 | 78.5 | 65 | 244.8 | 101.4 |
| 26 | 24.0 | 09.9 | 86 | 79.5 | 32.9 | 46 | 134.9 | 55.9 | 06 | 190.3 | 78.8 | 66 | 245.8 | 101.8 |
| 27 | 24.9 | 10.3 | 87 | 80.4 | 33.3 | 47 | 135.8 | 56.3 | 07 | 191.2 | 79.2 | 67 | 246.7 | 102.2 |
| 28 | 25.9 | 10.7 | 88 | 81.3 | 33.7 | 48 | 136.7 | 56.6 | 08 | 192.2 | 79.6 | 68 | 247.6 | 102.6 |
| 29 | 26.8 | 11.1 | 89 | 82.2 | 34.1 | 49 | 137.7 | 57.0 | 09 | 193.1 | 80.0 | 69 | 248.5 | 102.9 |
| 30 | 27.7 | 11.5 | 90 | 83.1 | 34.4 | 50 | 138.6 | 57.4 | 10 | 194.0 | 80.4 | 70 | 249.4 | 103.3 |
| 31 | 28.6 | 11.9 | 91 | 84.1 | 34.8 | 151 | 139.5 | 57.8 | 211 | 194.9 | 80.7 | 271 | 250.4 | 103.7 |
| 32 | 29.6 | 12.2 | 92 | 85.0 | 35.2 | 52 | 140.4 | 58.2 | 12 | 195.9 | 81.1 | 72 | 251.3 | 104.1 |
| 33 | 30.5 | 12.6 | 93 | 85.9 | 35.6 | 53 | 141.4 | 58.6 | 13 | 196.8 | 81.5 | 73 | 252.2 | 104.5 |
| 34 | 31.4 | 13.0 | 94 | 86.8 | 36.0 | 54 | 142.3 | 58.9 | 14 | 197.7 | 81.9 | 74 | 253.1 | 104.9 |
| 35 | 32.3 | 13.4 | 95 | 87.8 | 36.4 | 55 | 143.2 | 59.3 | 15 | 198.6 | 82.3 | 75 | 254.1 | 105.2 |
| 36 | 33.3 | 13.8 | 96 | 88.7 | 36.7 | 56 | 144.1 | 59.7 | 16 | 199.6 | 82.7 | 76 | 255.0 | 105.6 |
| 37 | 34.2 | 14.2 | 97 | 89.6 | 37.1 | 57 | 145.0 | 60.1 | 17 | 200.5 | 83.0 | 77 | 255.9 | 106,0 |
| 38 | 35.1 | 14.5 | 98 | 90.5 | 37.5 | 58 | 146.0 | 60.5 | 18 | 201.4 | 83.4 | 78 | 256.8 | 106.4 |
| 39 | 36.0 | 14.9 | 99 | 91.5 | 37.9 | 59 | 146.9 | 60.8 | 19 | 202.3 | 83.8 | 79 | 257.8 | 106.8 |
| 40 | 37.0 | 15.3 | 100 | 92.4 | 38.3 | 60 | 147.8 | 61.2 | 20 | 203.3 | 84.2 | 80 | 258.7 | 107.2 |
| 41 | 37.9 | 15.7 | 101 | 93.3 | 38.7 | 161 | 148.7 | 61.6 | 221 | 204.2 | 84.6 | 281 | 259.6 | 107.5 |
| 42 | 38.8 | 16.1 | 02 | 94.2 | 39.0 | 62 | 149.7 | 62.0 | 22 | 205.1 | 85.0 | 82 | 260.5 | 107.9 |
| 43 | 39.7 | 16.5 | 03 | 95.2 | 39.4 | 63 | 150.6 | 62.4 | 23 | 206.0 | 85.3 | 83 | 261.5 | 108.3 |
| 44 | 40.7 | 16.8 | 04 | 96.1 | 39.8 | 64 | 151.5 | 62.8 | 24 | 206.9 | 85.7 | 84 | 262.4 | 108.7 |
| 45 | 41.6 | 17.2 | 05 | 97.0 | 40.2 | 65 | 152.4 | 63.1 | 25 | 207.9 | 86.1 | 85 | 263.3 | 109.1 |
| 46 | 42.5 | 17.6 | 06 | 97.9 | 40.6 | 66 | 153.4 | 63.5 | 26 | 208.8 | 86.5 | 86 | 264.2 | 109.4 |
| 47 | 43.4 | 18.0 | 07 | 98.9 | 40.9 | 67 | 154.3 | 63.9 | 27 | 209.7 | 86.9 | 87 | 265.2 | 109.8 |
| 48 | 44.3 | 18.4 | 08 | 99.8 | 41.3 | 68 | 155.2 | 64.3 | 28 | 210.6 | 87.3 | 88 | 266.1 | 110.2 |
| 49 | 45.3 | 18.8 | 09 | 100.7 | 41.7 | 69 | 156.1 | 64.7 | 29 | 211.6 | 87.6 | 89 | 267.0 | 110.6 |
| 50 | 46.2 | 19.1 | 10 | 101.6 | 42.1 | 70 | 157.1 | 65.1 | 30 | 212.5 | 88.0 | 90 | 267.9 | 111.0 |
| 51 | 47.1 | 19.5 | 111 | 102.6 | 42.5 | 171 | 158.0 | 65.4 | 231 | 213.4 | 88.4 | 291 | 268.8 | 111.4 |
| 52 | 48.0 | 19.9 | 12 | 103.5 | 42.9 | 72 | 158.9 | 65.8 | 32 | 214.3 | 88.8 | 92 | 269.8 | 111.7 |
| 53 | 49.0 | 20.3 | 13 | 104.4 | 43.2 | 73 | 159.8 | 66.2 | 33 | 215.3 | 89.2 | 93 | 270.7 | 112.1 |
| 54 | 49.9 | 20.7 | 14 | 105.3 | 43.6 | 74 | 160.8 | 66.6 | 34 | 216.2 | 89.5 | 94 | 271.6 | 112.5 |
| 55 | 50.8 | 21.0 | 15 | 106.2 | 44.0 | 75 | 161.7 | 67.0 | 35 | 217.1 | 89.9 | 95 | 272.5 | 112.9 |
| 56 | 51.7 | 21.4 | 16 | 107.2 | 44.4 | 76 | 162.6 | 67.4 | 36 | 218.0 | 90.3 | 96 | 273.5 | 113.3 |
| 57 | 52.7 | 21.8 | 17 | 108.1 | 44.8 | 77 | 163.5 | 67.7 | 37 | 219.0 | 90.7 | 97 | 274.4 | 113.7 |
| 58 | 53.6 | 22.2 | 18 | 109.0 | 45.2 | 78 | 164.5 | 68.1 | 38 | 219.9 | 91.1 | 98 | 275.3 | 114.0 |
| 59 | 54.5 | 22.6 | 19 | 109.9 | 45.5 | 79 | 165.4 | 68.5 | 39 | 220.8 | 91.5 | 99 | 276.2 | 114.4 |
| 60 | 55.4 | 23.0 | 20 | 110.9 | 45.9 | 80 | 166.3 | 68.9 | 40 | 221.7 | 91.8 | 300 | 277.2 | 114.8 |
| Dist. | Dep. | Lat. | Dist. | Dep. | Lat. | Dist. | Dep. | Lat. | Dist. | Dep. | Lat. | Dist. | Dep. | Lat. |

E.N.E. E.S.E. W.N.W. W.S.W.

[For 6 Points.

# TABLE I.

## Difference of Latitude and Departure for 2¼ Points.

| N.N.E.¼E. | | | N.N.W.¼W. | | | S.S.E.¼E. | | | S.S.W.¼W. | | | | | |
|---|---|---|---|---|---|---|---|---|---|---|---|---|---|---|
| Dist. | Lat. | Dep. | Dist. | Lat. | Dep. | Dist. | Lat. | Dep. | Dist. | Lat. | Dep. | Dist. | Lat. | Dep. |
| 1 | 00.9 | 00.4 | 61 | 55.1 | 26.1 | 121 | 109.4 | 51.7 | 181 | 163.6 | 77.4 | 241 | 217.9 | 103.0 |
| 2 | 01.8 | 00.9 | 62 | 56.0 | 26.5 | 22 | 110.3 | 52.2 | 82 | 164.5 | 77.8 | 42 | 218.8 | 103.5 |
| 3 | 02.7 | 01.3 | 63 | 57.0 | 26.9 | 23 | 111.2 | 52.6 | 83 | 165.4 | 78.2 | 43 | 219.7 | 103.9 |
| 4 | 03.6 | 01.7 | 64 | 57.9 | 27.4 | 24 | 112.1 | 53.0 | 84 | 166.3 | 78.7 | 44 | 220.6 | 104.3 |
| 5 | 04.5 | 02.1 | 65 | 58.8 | 27.8 | 25 | 113.0 | 53.4 | 85 | 167.2 | 79.1 | 45 | 221.5 | 104.8 |
| 6 | 05.4 | 02.6 | 66 | 59.7 | 28.2 | 26 | 113.9 | 53.9 | 86 | 168.1 | 79.5 | 46 | 222.4 | 105.2 |
| 7 | 06.3 | 03.0 | 67 | 60.6 | 28.6 | 27 | 114.8 | 54.3 | 87 | 169.0 | 80.0 | 47 | 223.3 | 105.6 |
| 8 | 07.2 | 03.4 | 68 | 61.5 | 29.1 | 28 | 115.7 | 54.7 | 88 | 169.9 | 80.4 | 48 | 224.2 | 106.0 |
| 9 | 08.1 | 03.8 | 69 | 62.4 | 29.5 | 29 | 116.6 | 55.2 | 89 | 170.9 | 80.8 | 49 | 225.1 | 106.5 |
| 10 | 09.0 | 04.3 | 70 | 63.3 | 29.9 | 30 | 117.5 | 55.6 | 90 | 171.8 | 81.2 | 50 | 226.0 | 106.9 |
| 11 | 09.9 | 04.7 | 71 | 64.2 | 30.4 | 131 | 118.4 | 56.0 | 191 | 172.7 | 81.7 | 251 | 226.9 | 107.3 |
| 12 | 10.8 | 05.1 | 72 | 65.1 | 30.8 | 32 | 119.3 | 56.4 | 92 | 173.6 | 82.1 | 52 | 227.8 | 107.7 |
| 13 | 11.8 | 05.6 | 73 | 66.0 | 31.2 | 33 | 120.2 | 56.9 | 93 | 174.5 | 82.5 | 53 | 228.7 | 108.2 |
| 14 | 12.7 | 06.0 | 74 | 66.9 | 31.6 | 34 | 121.1 | 57.3 | 94 | 175.4 | 82.9 | 54 | 229.6 | 108.6 |
| 15 | 13.6 | 06.4 | 75 | 67.8 | 32.1 | 35 | 122.0 | 57.7 | 95 | 176.3 | 83.4 | 55 | 230.5 | 109.0 |
| 16 | 14.5 | 06.8 | 76 | 68.7 | 32.5 | 36 | 122.9 | 58.1 | 96 | 177.2 | 83.8 | 56 | 231.4 | 109.5 |
| 17 | 15.4 | 07.3 | 77 | 69.6 | 32.9 | 37 | 123.8 | 58.6 | 97 | 178.1 | 84.2 | 57 | 232.3 | 109.9 |
| 18 | 16.3 | 07.7 | 78 | 70.5 | 33.3 | 38 | 124.8 | 59.0 | 98 | 179.0 | 84.7 | 58 | 233.2 | 110.3 |
| 19 | 17.2 | 08.1 | 79 | 71.4 | 33.8 | 39 | 125.7 | 59.4 | 99 | 179.9 | 85.1 | 59 | 234.1 | 110.7 |
| 20 | 18.1 | 08.6 | 80 | 72.3 | 34.2 | 40 | 126.6 | 59.9 | 200 | 180.8 | 85.5 | 60 | 235.0 | 111.2 |
| 21 | 19.0 | 09.0 | 81 | 73.2 | 34.6 | 141 | 127.5 | 60.3 | 201 | 181.7 | 85.9 | 261 | 235.9 | 111.6 |
| 22 | 19.9 | 09.4 | 82 | 74.1 | 35.1 | 42 | 128.4 | 60.7 | 02 | 182.6 | 86.4 | 62 | 236.8 | 112.0 |
| 23 | 20.8 | 09.8 | 83 | 75.0 | 35.5 | 43 | 129.3 | 61.1 | 03 | 183.5 | 86.8 | 63 | 237.7 | 112.4 |
| 24 | 21.7 | 10.3 | 84 | 75.9 | 35.9 | 44 | 130.2 | 61.6 | 04 | 184.4 | 87.2 | 64 | 238.7 | 112.9 |
| 25 | 22.6 | 10.7 | 85 | 76.8 | 36.3 | 45 | 131.1 | 62.0 | 05 | 185.3 | 87.6 | 65 | 239.6 | 113.3 |
| 26 | 23.5 | 11.1 | 86 | 77.7 | 36.8 | 46 | 132.0 | 62.4 | 06 | 186.2 | 88.1 | 66 | 240.5 | 113.7 |
| 27 | 24.4 | 11.5 | 87 | 78.6 | 37.2 | 47 | 132.9 | 62.9 | 07 | 187.1 | 88.5 | 67 | 241.4 | 114.2 |
| 28 | 25.3 | 12.0 | 88 | 79.6 | 37.6 | 48 | 133.8 | 63.3 | 08 | 188.0 | 88.9 | 68 | 242.3 | 114.6 |
| 29 | 26.2 | 12.4 | 89 | 80.5 | 38.1 | 49 | 134.7 | 63.7 | 09 | 188.9 | 89.4 | 69 | 243.2 | 115.0 |
| 30 | 27.1 | 12.8 | 90 | 81.4 | 38.5 | 50 | 135.6 | 64.1 | 10 | 189.8 | 89.8 | 70 | 244.1 | 115.4 |
| 31 | 28.0 | 13.3 | 91 | 82.3 | 38.9 | 151 | 136.5 | 64.6 | 211 | 190.7 | 90.2 | 271 | 245.0 | 115.9 |
| 32 | 28.9 | 13.7 | 92 | 83.2 | 39.3 | 52 | 137.4 | 65.0 | 12 | 191.6 | 90.6 | 72 | 245.9 | 116.3 |
| 33 | 29.8 | 14.1 | 93 | 84.1 | 39.8 | 53 | 138.3 | 65.4 | 13 | 192.5 | 91.1 | 73 | 246.8 | 116.7 |
| 34 | 30.7 | 14.5 | 94 | 85.0 | 40.2 | 54 | 139.2 | 65.8 | 14 | 193.5 | 91.5 | 74 | 247.7 | 117.2 |
| 35 | 31.6 | 15.0 | 95 | 85.9 | 40.6 | 55 | 140.1 | 66.3 | 15 | 194.4 | 91.9 | 75 | 248.6 | 117.6 |
| 36 | 32.5 | 15.4 | 96 | 86.8 | 41.0 | 56 | 141.0 | 66.7 | 16 | 195.3 | 92.4 | 76 | 249.5 | 118.0 |
| 37 | 33.4 | 15.8 | 97 | 87.7 | 41.5 | 57 | 141.9 | 67.1 | 17 | 196.2 | 92.8 | 77 | 250.4 | 118.4 |
| 38 | 34.4 | 16.2 | 98 | 88.6 | 41.9 | 58 | 142.8 | 67.6 | 18 | 197.1 | 93.2 | 78 | 251.3 | 118.9 |
| 39 | 35.3 | 16.7 | 99 | 89.5 | 42.3 | 59 | 143.7 | 68.0 | 19 | 198.0 | 93.6 | 79 | 252.2 | 119.3 |
| 40 | 36.2 | 17.1 | 100 | 90.4 | 42.8 | 60 | 144.6 | 68.4 | 20 | 198.9 | 94.1 | 80 | 253.1 | 119.7 |
| 41 | 37.1 | 17.5 | 101 | 91.3 | 43.2 | 161 | 145.5 | 68.8 | 221 | 199.8 | 94.5 | 281 | 254.0 | 120.1 |
| 42 | 38.0 | 18.0 | 02 | 92.2 | 43.6 | 62 | 146.4 | 69.3 | 22 | 200.7 | 94.9 | 82 | 254.9 | 120.6 |
| 43 | 38.9 | 18.4 | 03 | 93.1 | 44.0 | 63 | 147.4 | 69.7 | 23 | 201.6 | 95.3 | 83 | 255.8 | 121.0 |
| 44 | 39.8 | 18.8 | 04 | 94.0 | 44.5 | 64 | 148.3 | 70.1 | 24 | 202.5 | 95.8 | 84 | 256.7 | 121.4 |
| 45 | 40.7 | 19.2 | 05 | 94.9 | 44.9 | 65 | 149.2 | 70.5 | 25 | 203.4 | 96.2 | 85 | 257.6 | 121.9 |
| 46 | 41.6 | 19.7 | 06 | 95.8 | 45.3 | 66 | 150.1 | 71.0 | 26 | 204.3 | 96.6 | 86 | 258.5 | 122.3 |
| 47 | 42.5 | 20.1 | 07 | 96.7 | 45.7 | 67 | 151.0 | 71.4 | 27 | 205.2 | 97.1 | 87 | 259.4 | 122.7 |
| 48 | 43.4 | 20.5 | 08 | 97.6 | 46.2 | 68 | 151.9 | 71.8 | 28 | 206.1 | 97.5 | 88 | 260.3 | 123.1 |
| 49 | 44.3 | 21.0 | 09 | 98.5 | 46.6 | 69 | 152.8 | 72.3 | 29 | 207.0 | 97.9 | 89 | 261.3 | 123.6 |
| 50 | 45.2 | 21.4 | 10 | 99.4 | 47.0 | 70 | 153.7 | 72.7 | 30 | 207.9 | 98.3 | 90 | 262.2 | 124.0 |
| 51 | 46.1 | 21.8 | 111 | 100.3 | 47.5 | 171 | 154.6 | 73.1 | 231 | 208.8 | 98.8 | 291 | 263.1 | 124.4 |
| 52 | 47.0 | 22.2 | 12 | 101.2 | 47.9 | 72 | 155.5 | 73.5 | 32 | 209.7 | 99.2 | 92 | 264.0 | 124.8 |
| 53 | 47.9 | 22.7 | 13 | 102.2 | 48.3 | 73 | 156.4 | 74.0 | 33 | 210.6 | 99.6 | 93 | 264.9 | 125.3 |
| 54 | 48.8 | 23.1 | 14 | 103.1 | 48.7 | 74 | 157.3 | 74.4 | 34 | 211.5 | 100.0 | 94 | 265.8 | 125.7 |
| 55 | 49.7 | 23.5 | 15 | 104.0 | 49.2 | 75 | 158.2 | 74.8 | 35 | 212.4 | 100.5 | 95 | 266.7 | 126.1 |
| 56 | 50.6 | 23.9 | 16 | 104.9 | 49.6 | 76 | 159.1 | 75.2 | 36 | 213.3 | 100.9 | 96 | 267.6 | 126.6 |
| 57 | 51.5 | 24.4 | 17 | 105.8 | 50.0 | 77 | 160.0 | 75.7 | 37 | 214.2 | 101.3 | 97 | 268.5 | 127.0 |
| 58 | 52.4 | 24.8 | 18 | 106.7 | 50.5 | 78 | 160.9 | 76.1 | 38 | 215.1 | 101.8 | 98 | 269.4 | 127.4 |
| 59 | 53 3 | 25.2 | 19 | 107.6 | 50.9 | 79 | 161.8 | 76.5 | 39 | 216.1 | 102.2 | 99 | 270.3 | 127.8 |
| 60 | 54.2 | 25.7 | 20 | 108.5 | 51.3 | 80 | 162.7 | 77.0 | 40 | 217.0 | 102.6 | 300 | 271.2 | 128.3 |
| Dist. | Dep. | Lat. | Dist. | Dep. | Lat. | Dist. | Dep. | Lat. | Dist. | Dep. | Lat. | Dist. | Dep. | Lat. |
| N.E.byE.¾E. | | | S.E.byE.¾E. | | | N.W.byW.¾W. | | | S.W.byW.¾W. | | | [For 5¾ Points. | | |

# TABLE I.

## Difference of Latitude and Departure for 2½ Points.

N.N.E.½E. N.N.W.½W. S.S.E.½E. S.S.W.½W.

| Dist. | Lat. | Dep. | Dist. | Lat. | Dep. | Dist. | Lat. | Dep. | Dist. | Lat. | Dep. | Dist. | Lat. | Dep. |
|---|---|---|---|---|---|---|---|---|---|---|---|---|---|---|
| 1 | 00.9 | 00.5 | 61 | 53.8 | 28.8 | 121 | 106.7 | 57.0 | 181 | 159.6 | 85.3 | 241 | 212.5 | 113.6 |
| 2 | 01.8 | 00.9 | 62 | 54 7 | 29.2 | 22 | 107.6 | 57.5 | 82 | 160.5 | 85.8 | 42 | 213.4 | 114.1 |
| 3 | 02.6 | 01.4 | 63 | 55.6 | 29.7 | 23 | 108.5 | 58.0 | 83 | 161.4 | 86.3 | 43 | 214.3 | 114.5 |
| 4 | 03.5 | 01.9 | 64 | 56.4 | 30.2 | 24 | 109.4 | 58.5 | 84 | 162.3 | 86.7 | 44 | 215.2 | 115.0 |
| 5 | 04.4 | 02.4 | 65 | 57.3 | 30.6 | 25 | 110.2 | 58.9 | 85 | 163.2 | 87.2 | 45 | 216.1 | 115.5 |
| 6 | 05.3 | 02.8 | 66 | 58.2 | 31.1 | 26 | 111.1 | 59.4 | 86 | 164.0 | 87.7 | 46 | 217.0 | 116.0 |
| 7 | 06.2 | 03.3 | 67 | 59.1 | 31.6 | 27 | 112.0 | 59.9 | 87 | 164.9 | 88.2 | 47 | 217.8 | 116.4 |
| 8 | 07.1 | 03.8 | 68 | 60.0 | 32.1 | 28 | 112.9 | 60.3 | 88 | 165.8 | 88.6 | 48 | 218.7 | 116.9 |
| 9 | 07.9 | 04.2 | 69 | 60.9 | 32.5 | 29 | 113.8 | 60.8 | 89 | 166.7 | 89.1 | 49 | 219.6 | 117.4 |
| 10 | 08.8 | 04.7 | 70 | 61.7 | 33.0 | 30 | 114.6 | 61.3 | 90 | 167.6 | 89.6 | 50 | 220.5 | 117.8 |
| 11 | 09.7 | 05.2 | 71 | 62.6 | 33.5 | 131 | 115.5 | 61.8 | 191 | 168.4 | 90.0 | 251 | 221.4 | 118.3 |
| 12 | 10.6 | 05.7 | 72 | 63.5 | 33.9 | 32 | 116.4 | 62.2 | 92 | 169.3 | 90.5 | 52 | 222.2 | 118.8 |
| 13 | 11.5 | 06.1 | 73 | 64.4 | 34.4 | 33 | 117.3 | 62.7 | 93 | 170.2 | 91.0 | 53 | 223.1 | 119.3 |
| 14 | 12.3 | 06.6 | 74 | 65.3 | 34.9 | 34 | 118.2 | 63.2 | 94 | 171.1 | 91.5 | 54 | 224.0 | 119.7 |
| 15 | 13.2 | 07.1 | 75 | 66.1 | 35.4 | 35 | 119.1 | 63.6 | 95 | 172.0 | 91.9 | 55 | 224.9 | 120.2 |
| 16 | 14.1 | 07.5 | 76 | 67.0 | 35.8 | 36 | 119.9 | 64.1 | 96 | 172.9 | 92.4 | 56 | 225.8 | 120.7 |
| 17 | 15.0 | 08.0 | 77 | 67.9 | 36.3 | 37 | 120.8 | 64.6 | 97 | 173.7 | 92.9 | 57 | 226.7 | 121.1 |
| 18 | 15.9 | 08.5 | 78 | 68.8 | 36.8 | 38 | 121.7 | 65.1 | 98 | 174.6 | 93.3 | 58 | 227.5 | 121.6 |
| 19 | 16.8 | 09.0 | 79 | 69.7 | 37.2 | 39 | 122.6 | 65.5 | 99 | 175.5 | 93.8 | 59 | 228.4 | 122.1 |
| 20 | 17.6 | 09.4 | 80 | 70.6 | 37.7 | 40 | 123.5 | 66.0 | 200 | 176.4 | 94.3 | 60 | 229.3 | 122.6 |
| 21 | 18.5 | 09.9 | 81 | 71.4 | 38.2 | 141 | 124.4 | 66.5 | 201 | 177.3 | 94.8 | 261 | 230.2 | 123.0 |
| 22 | 19.4 | 10.4 | 82 | 72.3 | 38.7 | 42 | 125.2 | 66.9 | 02 | 178.1 | 95.2 | 62 | 231.1 | 123.5 |
| 23 | 20.3 | 10.8 | 83 | 73.2 | 39.1 | 43 | 126.1 | 67.4 | 03 | 179.0 | 95.7 | 63 | 231.9 | 124.0 |
| 24 | 21.2 | 11.3 | 84 | 74.1 | 39.6 | 44 | 127.0 | 67.9 | 04 | 179.9 | 96.2 | 64 | 232.8 | 124.4 |
| 25 | 22.0 | 11.8 | 85 | 75.0 | 40.1 | 45 | 127.9 | 68.4 | 05 | 180.8 | 96.6 | 65 | 233.7 | 124.9 |
| 26 | 22.9 | 12.3 | 86 | 75.8 | 40.5 | 46 | 128.8 | 68.8 | 06 | 181.7 | 97.1 | 66 | 234.6 | 125.4 |
| 27 | 23.8 | 12.7 | 87 | 76.7 | 41.0 | 47 | 129.6 | 69.3 | 07 | 182.6 | 97.6 | 67 | 235.5 | 125.9 |
| 28 | 24.7 | 13.2 | 88 | 77.6 | 41.5 | 48 | 130.5 | 69.8 | 08 | 183.4 | 98.1 | 68 | 236.4 | 126.3 |
| 29 | 25.6 | 13.7 | 89 | 78.5 | 42.0 | 49 | 131.4 | 70.2 | 09 | 184.3 | 98.5 | 69 | 237.2 | 126.8 |
| 30 | 26.5 | 14.1 | 90 | 79.4 | 42.4 | 50 | 132.3 | 70.7 | 10 | 185.2 | 99.0 | 70 | 238.1 | 127.3 |
| 31 | 27.3 | 14.6 | 91 | 80.3 | 42.9 | 151 | 133.2 | 71.2 | 211 | 186.1 | 99.5 | 271 | 239.0 | 127.7 |
| 32 | 28.2 | 15.1 | 92 | 81.1 | 43.4 | 52 | 134.1 | 71.7 | 12 | 187.0 | 99.9 | 72 | 239.9 | 128.2 |
| 33 | 29.1 | 15.6 | 93 | 82.0 | 43.8 | 53 | 134.9 | 72.1 | 13 | 187.8 | 100.4 | 73 | 240.8 | 128.7 |
| 34 | 30.0 | 16.0 | 94 | 82.9 | 44.3 | 54 | 135.8 | 72.6 | 14 | 188.7 | 100.9 | 74 | 241.6 | 129.2 |
| 35 | 30.9 | 16.5 | 95 | 83.8 | 44.8 | 55 | 136.7 | 73.1 | 15 | 189.6 | 101.4 | 75 | 242.5 | 129.6 |
| 36 | 31.7 | 17.0 | 96 | 84.7 | 45.3 | 56 | 137.6 | 73.5 | 16 | 190.5 | 101.8 | 76 | 243.4 | 130.1 |
| 37 | 32.6 | 17.4 | 97 | 85.5 | 45.7 | 57 | 138.5 | 74.0 | 17 | 191.4 | 102.3 | 77 | 244.3 | 130.6 |
| 38 | 33.5 | 17.9 | 98 | 86.4 | 46.2 | 58 | 139.3 | 74.5 | 18 | 192.3 | 102.8 | 78 | 245.2 | 131.0 |
| 39 | 34.4 | 18.4 | 99 | 87.3 | 46.7 | 59 | 140.2 | 75.0 | 19 | 193.1 | 103.2 | 79 | 246.1 | 131.5 |
| 40 | 35.3 | 18.9 | 100 | 88.2 | 47.1 | 60 | 141.1 | 75.4 | 20 | 194.0 | 103.7 | 80 | 246.9 | 132.0 |
| 41 | 36.2 | 19.3 | 101 | 89.1 | 47.6 | 161 | 142.0 | 75.9 | 221 | 194.9 | 104.2 | 281 | 247.8 | 132.5 |
| 42 | 37.0 | 19.8 | 02 | 90.0 | 48.1 | 62 | 142.9 | 76.4 | 22 | 195.8 | 104.7 | 82 | 248.7 | 132.9 |
| 43 | 37.9 | 20.3 | 03 | 90.8 | 48.6 | 63 | 143.8 | 76.8 | 23 | 196.7 | 105.1 | 83 | 249.6 | 133.4 |
| 44 | 38.8 | 20.7 | 04 | 91.7 | 49.0 | 64 | 144.6 | 77.3 | 24 | 197.6 | 105.6 | 84 | 250.5 | 133.9 |
| 45 | 39.7 | 21.2 | 05 | 92.6 | 49.5 | 65 | 145.5 | 77.8 | 25 | 198.4 | 106.1 | 85 | 251.3 | 134.3 |
| 46 | 40.6 | 21.7 | 06 | 93.5 | 50.0 | 66 | 146.4 | 78.3 | 26 | 199.3 | 106.5 | 86 | 252.2 | 134.8 |
| 47 | 41.5 | 22.2 | 07 | 94.4 | 50.4 | 67 | 147.3 | 78.7 | 27 | 200.2 | 107.0 | 87 | 253.1 | 135.3 |
| 48 | 42.3 | 22.6 | 08 | 95.2 | 50.9 | 68 | 148.2 | 79.2 | 28 | 201.1 | 107.5 | 88 | 254.0 | 135.8 |
| 49 | 43.2 | 23.1 | 09 | 96.1 | 51.4 | 69 | 149.0 | 79.7 | 29 | 202.0 | 107.9 | 89 | 254.9 | 136.2 |
| 50 | 44.1 | 23.6 | 10 | 97.0 | 51.9 | 70 | 149.9 | 80.1 | 30 | 202.8 | 108.4 | 90 | 255.8 | 136.7 |
| 51 | 45.0 | 24.0 | 111 | 97.9 | 52.3 | 171 | 150.8 | 80.6 | 231 | 203.7 | 108.9 | 291 | 256.6 | 137.2 |
| 52 | 45.9 | 24.5 | 12 | 98.8 | 52.8 | 72 | 151.7 | 81.1 | 32 | 204.6 | 109.4 | 92 | 257.5 | 137.6 |
| 53 | 46.7 | 25.0 | 13 | 99.7 | 53.3 | 73 | 152.6 | 81.6 | 33 | 205.5 | 109.8 | 93 | 258.4 | 138.1 |
| 54 | 47.6 | 25.5 | 14 | 100.5 | 53.7 | 74 | 153.5 | 82.0 | 34 | 206.4 | 110.3 | 94 | 259.3 | 138.6 |
| 55 | 48.5 | 25.9 | 15 | 101.4 | 54.2 | 75 | 154.3 | 82.5 | 35 | 207.3 | 110.8 | 95 | 260.2 | 139.1 |
| 56 | 49.4 | 26.4 | 16 | 102.3 | 54.7 | 76 | 155.2 | 83.0 | 36 | 208.1 | 111.2 | 96 | 261.0 | 139.5 |
| 57 | 50.3 | 26.9 | 17 | 103.2 | 55.2 | 77 | 156.1 | 83.4 | 37 | 209.0 | 111.7 | 97 | 261.9 | 140.0 |
| 58 | 51.2 | 27.3 | 18 | 104.1 | 55.6 | 78 | 157.0 | 83.9 | 38 | 209.9 | 112.2 | 98 | 262.8 | 140 5 |
| 59 | 52.0 | 27.8 | 19 | 104.9 | 56.1 | 79 | 157.9 | 84.4 | 39 | 210.8 | 112.7 | 99 | 263.7 | 140.9 |
| 60 | 52.9 | 28.3 | 20 | 105.8 | 56.6 | 80 | 158.7 | 84.9 | 40 | 211.7 | 113.1 | 300 | 264.6 | 141.4 |
| Dist. | Dep. | Lat. | Dist. | Dep. | Lat. | Dist. | Dep. | Lat. | Dist. | Dep. | Lat. | Dist. | Dep. | Lat. |

N.E.byE.½E. S.E.byE.½E. N.W.byW.½W. S.W.byW.½W. [For 5½ Points.

# TABLE I.

## Difference of Latitude and Departure for 2¾ Points.

| N.N.E.¾E. | | | N.N.W.¾W. | | | S.S.E.¾E. | | | S.S.W.¾W. | | | | | |
|---|---|---|---|---|---|---|---|---|---|---|---|---|---|---|
| Dist. | Lat. | Dep. | Dist. | Lat. | Dep. | Dist. | Lat. | Dep. | Dist. | Lat. | Dep. | Dist. | Lat. | Dep. |
| 1 | 00.9 | 00.5 | 61 | 52.3 | 31.4 | 121 | 103.8 | 62.2 | 181 | 155.2 | 93.1 | 241 | 206.7 | 123.9 |
| 2 | 01.7 | 01.0 | 62 | 53.2 | 31.9 | 22 | 104.6 | 62.7 | 82 | 156.1 | 93.6 | 42 | 207.6 | 124.4 |
| 3 | 02.6 | 01.5 | 63 | 54.0 | 32.4 | 23 | 105.5 | 63.2 | 83 | 157.0 | 94.1 | 43 | 208.4 | 124.9 |
| 4 | 03.4 | 02.1 | 64 | 54.9 | 32.9 | 24 | 106.4 | 63.7 | 84 | 157.8 | 94.6 | 44 | 209.3 | 125.4 |
| 5 | 04.3 | 02.6 | 65 | 55.8 | 33.4 | 25 | 107.2 | 64.3 | 85 | 158.7 | 95.1 | 45 | 210.1 | 126.0 |
| 6 | 05.1 | 03.1 | 66 | 56.6 | 33.9 | 26 | 108.1 | 64.8 | 86 | 159.5 | 95.6 | 46 | 211.0 | 126.5 |
| 7 | 06.0 | 03.6 | 67 | 57.5 | 34.4 | 27 | 108.9 | 65.3 | 87 | 160.4 | 96.1 | 47 | 211.9 | 127.0 |
| 8 | 06.9 | 04.1 | 68 | 58.3 | 35.0 | 28 | 109.8 | 65.8 | 88 | 161.3 | 96.7 | 48 | 212.7 | 127.5 |
| 9 | 07.7 | 04.6 | 69 | 59.2 | 35.5 | 29 | 110.6 | 66.3 | 89 | 162.1 | 97.2 | 49 | 213.6 | 128.0 |
| 10 | 08.6 | 05.1 | 70 | 60.0 | 36.0 | 30 | 111.5 | 66.8 | 90 | 163.0 | 97.7 | 50 | 214.4 | 128.5 |
| 11 | 09.4 | 05.7 | 71 | 60.9 | 36.5 | 131 | 112.4 | 67.3 | 191 | 163.8 | 98.2 | 251 | 215.3 | 129.0 |
| 12 | 10.3 | 06.2 | 72 | 61.8 | 37.0 | 32 | 113.2 | 67.9 | 92 | 164.7 | 98.7 | 52 | 216.1 | 129.6 |
| 13 | 11.2 | 06.7 | 73 | 62.6 | 37.5 | 33 | 114.1 | 68.4 | 93 | 165.5 | 99.2 | 53 | 217.0 | 130.1 |
| 14 | 12.0 | 07.2 | 74 | 63.5 | 38.0 | 34 | 114.9 | 68.9 | 94 | 166.4 | 99.7 | 54 | 217.9 | 130.6 |
| 15 | 12.9 | 07.7 | 75 | 64.3 | 38.6 | 35 | 115.8 | 69.4 | 95 | 167.3 | 100.3 | 55 | 218.7 | 131.1 |
| 16 | 13.7 | 08.2 | 76 | 65.2 | 39.1 | 36 | 116.7 | 69.9 | 96 | 168.1 | 100.8 | 56 | 219.6 | 131.6 |
| 17 | 14.6 | 08.7 | 77 | 66.0 | 39.6 | 37 | 117.5 | 70.4 | 97 | 169.0 | 101.3 | 57 | 220.4 | 132.1 |
| 18 | 15.4 | 09.3 | 78 | 66.9 | 40.1 | 38 | 118.4 | 70.9 | 98 | 169.8 | 101.8 | 58 | 221.3 | 132.6 |
| 19 | 16.3 | 09.8 | 79 | 67.8 | 40.6 | 39 | 119.2 | 71.5 | 99 | 170.7 | 102.3 | 59 | 222.2 | 133.2 |
| 20 | 17.2 | 10.3 | 80 | 68.6 | 41.1 | 40 | 120.1 | 72.0 | 200 | 171.5 | 102.8 | 60 | 223.0 | 133.7 |
| 21 | 18.0 | 10.8 | 81 | 69.5 | 41.6 | 141 | 120.9 | 72.5 | 201 | 172.4 | 103.3 | 261 | 223.9 | 134.2 |
| 22 | 18.9 | 11.3 | 82 | 70.3 | 42.2 | 42 | 121.8 | 73.0 | 02 | 173.3 | 103.8 | 62 | 224.7 | 134.7 |
| 23 | 19.7 | 11.8 | 83 | 71.2 | 42.7 | 43 | 122.7 | 73.5 | 03 | 174.1 | 104.4 | 63 | 225.6 | 135.2 |
| 24 | 20.6 | 12.3 | 84 | 72.0 | 43.2 | 44 | 123.5 | 74.0 | 04 | 175.0 | 104.9 | 64 | 226.4 | 135.7 |
| 25 | 21.4 | 12.9 | 85 | 72.9 | 43.7 | 45 | 124.4 | 74.5 | 05 | 175.8 | 105.4 | 65 | 227.3 | 136.2 |
| 26 | 22.3 | 13.4 | 86 | 73.8 | 44.2 | 46 | 125.2 | 75.1 | 06 | 176.7 | 105.9 | 66 | 228.2 | 136.8 |
| 27 | 23.2 | 13.9 | 87 | 74.6 | 44.7 | 47 | 126.1 | 75.6 | 07 | 177.5 | 106.4 | 67 | 229.0 | 137.3 |
| 28 | 24.0 | 14.4 | 88 | 75.5 | 45.2 | 48 | 126.9 | 76.1 | 08 | 178.4 | 106.9 | 68 | 229.9 | 137.8 |
| 29 | 24.9 | 14.9 | 89 | 76.3 | 45.8 | 49 | 127.8 | 76.6 | 09 | 179.3 | 107.4 | 69 | 230.7 | 138.3 |
| 30 | 25.7 | 15.4 | 90 | 77.2 | 46.3 | 50 | 128.7 | 77.1 | 10 | 180.1 | 108.0 | 70 | 231.6 | 138.8 |
| 31 | 26.6 | 15.9 | 91 | 78.1 | 46.8 | 151 | 129.5 | 77.6 | 211 | 181.0 | 108.5 | 271 | 232.4 | 139.3 |
| 32 | 27.4 | 16.5 | 92 | 78.9 | 47.3 | 52 | 130.4 | 78.1 | 12 | 181.8 | 109.0 | 72 | 233.3 | 139.8 |
| 33 | 28.3 | 17.0 | 93 | 79.8 | 47.8 | 53 | 131.2 | 78.7 | 13 | 182.7 | 109.5 | 73 | 234.2 | 140.4 |
| 34 | 29.2 | 17.5 | 94 | 80.6 | 48.3 | 54 | 132.1 | 79.2 | 14 | 183.6 | 110.0 | 74 | 235.0 | 140.9 |
| 35 | 30.0 | 18.0 | 95 | 81.5 | 48.8 | 55 | 132.9 | 79.7 | 15 | 184.4 | 110.5 | 75 | 235.9 | 141.4 |
| 36 | 30.9 | 18.5 | 96 | 82.3 | 49.4 | 56 | 133.8 | 80.2 | 16 | 185.3 | 111.0 | 76 | 236.7 | 141.9 |
| 37 | 31.7 | 19.0 | 97 | 83.2 | 49.9 | 57 | 134.7 | 80.7 | 17 | 186.1 | 111.6 | 77 | 237.6 | 142.4 |
| 38 | 32.6 | 19.5 | 98 | 84.1 | 50.4 | 58 | 135.5 | 81.2 | 18 | 187.0 | 112.1 | 78 | 238.4 | 142.9 |
| 39 | 33.5 | 20.1 | 99 | 84.9 | 50.9 | 59 | 136.4 | 81.7 | 19 | 187.8 | 112.6 | 79 | 239.3 | 143.4 |
| 40 | 34.3 | 20.6 | 100 | 85.8 | 51.4 | 60 | 137.2 | 82.3 | 20 | 188.7 | 113.1 | 80 | 240.2 | 143.9 |
| 41 | 35.2 | 21.1 | 101 | 86.6 | 51.9 | 161 | 138.1 | 82.8 | 221 | 189.6 | 113.6 | 281 | 241.0 | 144.5 |
| 42 | 36.0 | 21.6 | 02 | 87.5 | 52.4 | 62 | 139.0 | 83.3 | 22 | 190.4 | 114.1 | 82 | 241.9 | 145.0 |
| 43 | 36.9 | 22.1 | 03 | 88.3 | 53.0 | 63 | 139.8 | 83.8 | 23 | 191.3 | 114.6 | 83 | 242.7 | 145.5 |
| 44 | 37.7 | 22.6 | 04 | 89.2 | 53.5 | 64 | 140.7 | 84.3 | 24 | 192.1 | 115.2 | 84 | 243.6 | 146.0 |
| 45 | 38.6 | 23.1 | 05 | 90.1 | 54.0 | 65 | 141.5 | 84.8 | 25 | 193.0 | 115.7 | 85 | 244.5 | 146.5 |
| 46 | 39.5 | 23.6 | 06 | 90.9 | 54.5 | 66 | 142.4 | 85.3 | 26 | 193.8 | 116.2 | 86 | 245.3 | 147.0 |
| 47 | 40.3 | 24.2 | 07 | 91.8 | 55.0 | 67 | 143.2 | 85.9 | 27 | 194.7 | 116.7 | 87 | 246.2 | 147.5 |
| 48 | 41.2 | 24.7 | 08 | 92.6 | 55.5 | 68 | 144.1 | 86.4 | 28 | 195.6 | 117.2 | 88 | 247.0 | 148.1 |
| 49 | 42.0 | 25.2 | 09 | 93.5 | 56.0 | 69 | 145.0 | 86.9 | 29 | 196.4 | 117.7 | 89 | 247.9 | 148.6 |
| 50 | 42.9 | 25.7 | 10 | 94.4 | 56.6 | 70 | 145.8 | 87.4 | 30 | 197.3 | 118.2 | 90 | 248.7 | 149.1 |
| 51 | 43.7 | 26.2 | 111 | 95.2 | 57.1 | 171 | 146.7 | 87.9 | 231 | 198.1 | 118.8 | 291 | 249.6 | 149.6 |
| 52 | 44.6 | 26.7 | 12 | 96.1 | 57.6 | 72 | 147.5 | 88.4 | 32 | 199.0 | 119.3 | 92 | 250.5 | 150.1 |
| 53 | 45.5 | 27.2 | 13 | 96.9 | 58.1 | 73 | 148.4 | 88.9 | 33 | 199.9 | 119.8 | 93 | 251.3 | 150.6 |
| 54 | 46.3 | 27.8 | 14 | 97.8 | 58.6 | 74 | 149.2 | 89.5 | 34 | 200.7 | 120.3 | 94 | 252.2 | 151.1 |
| 55 | 47.2 | 28.3 | 15 | 98.6 | 59.1 | 75 | 150.1 | 90.0 | 35 | 201.6 | 120.8 | 95 | 253.0 | 151.7 |
| 56 | 48.0 | 28.8 | 16 | 99.5 | 59.6 | 76 | 151.0 | 90.5 | 36 | 202.4 | 121.3 | 96 | 253.9 | 152.2 |
| 57 | 48.9 | 29.3 | 17 | 100.4 | 60.2 | 77 | 151.8 | 91.0 | 37 | 203.3 | 121.8 | 97 | 254.7 | 152.7 |
| 58 | 49.7 | 29.8 | 18 | 101.2 | 60.7 | 78 | 152.7 | 91.5 | 38 | 204.1 | 122.4 | 98 | 255.6 | 153.2 |
| 59 | 50.6 | 30.3 | 19 | 102.1 | 61.2 | 79 | 153.5 | 92.0 | 39 | 205.0 | 122.9 | 99 | 256.5 | 153.7 |
| 60 | 51.5 | 30.8 | 20 | 102.9 | 61.7 | 80 | 154.4 | 92.5 | 40 | 205.9 | 123.4 | 300 | 257.3 | 154.2 |
| Dist. | Dep. | Lat. | Dist. | Dep. | Lat. | Dist. | Dep. | Lat. | Dist. | Dep. | Lat. | Dist. | Dep. | Lat. |
| N.E.byE.¼E. | | | S.E.byE.¼E. | | | N.W.byW.¼W. | | | S.W.byW.¼W. | | | [For 5¼ Points. | | |

# TABLE I.

## Difference of Latitude and Departure for 3 Points.

N.E.byN. N.W.byN. S.E.byS. S.W.byS.

| Dist. | Lat. | Dep. | Dist. | Lat. | Dep. | Dist. | Lat. | Dep. | Dist. | Lat. | Dep. | Dist. | Lat. | Dep. |
|---|---|---|---|---|---|---|---|---|---|---|---|---|---|---|
| 1 | 00.8 | 00.6 | 61 | 50.7 | 33.9 | 121 | 100.6 | 67.2 | 181 | 150.5 | 100.6 | 241 | 200.4 | 133.9 |
| 2 | 01.7 | 01.1 | 62 | 51.6 | 34.4 | 22 | 101.4 | 67.8 | 82 | 151.3 | 101.1 | 42 | 201.2 | 134.4 |
| 3 | 02.5 | 01.7 | 63 | 52.4 | 35.0 | 23 | 102.3 | 68.3 | 83 | 152.2 | 101.7 | 43 | 202.0 | 135.0 |
| 4 | 03.3 | 02.2 | 64 | 53.2 | 35.6 | 24 | 103.1 | 68.9 | 84 | 153.0 | 102.2 | 44 | 202.9 | 135 6 |
| 5 | 04.2 | 02.8 | 65 | 54.0 | 36.1 | 25 | 103.9 | 69.4 | 85 | 153.8 | 102.8 | 45 | 203.7 | 136.1 |
| 6 | 05.0 | 03.3 | 66 | 54.9 | 36.7 | 26 | 104.8 | 70.0 | 86 | 154.7 | 103.3 | 46 | 204.5 | 136.7 |
| 7 | 05.8 | 03.9 | 67 | 55.7 | 37.2 | 27 | 105.6 | 70.6 | 87 | 155.5 | 103.9 | 47 | 205.4 | 137.2 |
| 8 | 06.7 | 04.4 | 68 | 56.5 | 37.8 | 28 | 106.4 | 71.1 | 88 | 156.3 | 104.4 | 48 | 206.2 | 137.8 |
| 9 | 07.5 | 05.0 | 69 | 57.4 | 38.3 | 29 | 107.3 | 71.7 | 89 | 157.1 | 105.0 | 49 | 207.0 | 138.3 |
| 10 | 08.3 | 05.6 | 70 | 58.2 | 38.9 | 30 | 108.1 | 72.2 | 90 | 158.0 | 105.6 | 50 | 207.9 | 138.9 |
| 11 | 09.1 | 06.1 | 71 | 59.0 | 39.4 | 131 | 108.9 | 72.8 | 191 | 158.8 | 106.1 | 251 | 208.7 | 139.4 |
| 12 | 10.0 | 06.7 | 72 | 59.9 | 40.0 | 32 | 109.8 | 73.3 | 92 | 159.6 | 106.7 | 52 | 209.5 | 140.0 |
| 13 | 10.8 | 07.2 | 73 | 60.7 | 40.6 | 33 | 110.6 | 73.9 | 93 | 160.5 | 107.2 | 53 | 210.4 | 140.6 |
| 14 | 11.6 | 07.8 | 74 | 61.5 | 41.1 | 34 | 111.4 | 74.4 | 94 | 161.3 | 107.8 | 54 | 211.2 | 141.1 |
| 15 | 12.5 | 08.3 | 75 | 62.4 | 41.7 | 35 | 112.2 | 75.0 | 95 | 162.1 | 108.3 | 55 | 212.0 | 141.7 |
| 16 | 13.3 | 08.9 | 76 | 63.2 | 42.2 | 36 | 113.1 | 75.6 | 96 | 163.0 | 108.9 | 56 | 212.9 | 142.2 |
| 17 | 14.1 | 09.4 | 77 | 64.0 | 42.8 | 37 | 113.9 | 76.1 | 97 | 163.8 | 109.4 | 57 | 213.7 | 142.8 |
| 18 | 15.0 | 10.0 | 78 | 64.9 | 43.3 | 38 | 114.7 | 76.7 | 98 | 164.6 | 110.0 | 58 | 214.5 | 143.3 |
| 19 | 15.8 | 10.6 | 79 | 65.7 | 43.9 | 39 | 115.6 | 77.2 | 99 | 165.5 | 110.6 | 59 | 215.4 | 143.9 |
| 20 | 16.6 | 11.1 | 80 | 66.5 | 44.4 | 40 | 116.4 | 77.8 | 200 | 166.3 | 111.1 | 60 | 216.2 | 144.4 |
| 21 | 17.5 | 11.7 | 81 | 67.3 | 45.0 | 141 | 117.2 | 78.3 | 201 | 167.1 | 111.7 | 261 | 217.0 | 145.0 |
| 22 | 18.3 | 12.2 | 82 | 68.2 | 45.6 | 42 | 118.1 | 78.9 | 02 | 168.0 | 112.2 | 62 | 217.8 | 145.6 |
| 23 | 19.1 | 12.8 | 83 | 69.0 | 46.1 | 43 | 118.9 | 79.4 | 03 | 168.8 | 112.8 | 63 | 218.7 | 146.1 |
| 24 | 20.0 | 13.3 | 84 | 69.8 | 46.7 | 44 | 119.7 | 80.0 | 04 | 169.6 | 113.3 | 64 | 219.5 | 146.7 |
| 25 | 20.8 | 13.9 | 85 | 70.7 | 47.2 | 45 | 120.6 | 80.6 | 05 | 170.5 | 113.9 | 65 | 220.3 | 147.2 |
| 26 | 21.6 | 14.4 | 86 | 71.5 | 47.8 | 46 | 121.4 | 81.1 | 06 | 171.3 | 114.4 | 66 | 221.2 | 147.8 |
| 27 | 22.4 | 15.0 | 87 | 72.3 | 48.3 | 47 | 122.2 | 81.7 | 07 | 172.1 | 115.0 | 67 | 222.0 | 148.3 |
| 28 | 23.3 | 15.6 | 88 | 73.2 | 48.9 | 48 | 123.1 | 82.2 | 08 | 172.9 | 115.6 | 68 | 222.8 | 148.9 |
| 29 | 24.1 | 16.1 | 89 | 74.0 | 49.4 | 49 | 123.9 | 82.8 | 09 | 173.8 | 116.1 | 69 | 223.7 | 149.4 |
| 30 | 24.9 | 16.7 | 90 | 74.8 | 50.0 | 50 | 124.7 | 83.3 | 10 | 174.6 | 116.7 | 70 | 224.5 | 150.0 |
| 31 | 25.8 | 17.2 | 91 | 75.7 | 50.6 | 151 | 125.6 | 83.9 | 211 | 175.4 | 117.2 | 271 | 225.3 | 150.6 |
| 32 | 26.6 | 17.8 | 92 | 76.5 | 51.1 | 52 | 126.4 | 84.4 | 12 | 176.3 | 117.8 | 72 | 226.2 | 151.1 |
| 33 | 27.4 | 18.3 | 93 | 77.3 | 51.7 | 53 | 127.2 | 85.0 | 13 | 177.1 | 118.3 | 73 | 227.0 | 151.7 |
| 34 | 28.3 | 18.9 | 94 | 78.2 | 52.2 | 54 | 128.0 | 85.6 | 14 | 177.9 | 118.9 | 74 | 227.8 | 152.2 |
| 35 | 29.1 | 19.4 | 95 | 79.0 | 52.8 | 55 | 128.9 | 86.1 | 15 | 178.8 | 119.4 | 75 | 228.7 | 152.8 |
| 36 | 29.9 | 20.0 | 96 | 79.8 | 53.3 | 56 | 129.7 | 86.7 | 16 | 179.6 | 120.0 | 76 | 229.5 | 153.3 |
| 37 | 30.8 | 20.6 | 97 | 80.7 | 53.9 | 57 | 130.5 | 87.2 | 17 | 180.4 | 120.6 | 77 | 230.3 | 153.9 |
| 38 | 31.6 | 21.1 | 98 | 81.5 | 54.4 | 58 | 131.4 | 87.8 | 18 | 181.3 | 121.1 | 78 | 231.1 | 154.4 |
| 39 | 32.4 | 21.7 | 99 | 82.3 | 55.0 | 59 | 132.2 | 88.3 | 19 | 182.1 | 121.7 | 79 | 232.0 | 155.0 |
| 40 | 33.3 | 22.2 | 100 | 83.1 | 55.6 | 60 | 133.0 | 88.9 | 20 | 182.9 | 122.2 | 80 | 232.8 | 155.6 |
| 41 | 34.1 | 22.8 | 101 | 84.0 | 56.1 | 161 | 133.9 | 89.4 | 221 | 183.8 | 122.8 | 281 | 233.6 | 156.1 |
| 42 | 34.9 | 23.3 | 02 | 84.8 | 56.7 | 62 | 134.7 | 90.0 | 22 | 184.6 | 123.3 | 82 | 234.5 | 156.7 |
| 43 | 35.8 | 23.9 | 03 | 85.6 | 57.2 | 63 | 135.5 | 90.6 | 23 | 185.4 | 123.9 | 83 | 235.3 | 157.2 |
| 44 | 36.6 | 24.4 | 04 | 86.5 | 57.8 | 64 | 136.4 | 91.1 | 24 | 186.2 | 124.4 | 84 | 236.1 | 157 8 |
| 45 | 37.4 | 25.0 | 05 | 87.3 | 58.3 | 65 | 137.2 | 91.7 | 25 | 187.1 | 125.0 | 85 | 237.0 | 158.3 |
| 46 | 38.2 | 25.6 | 06 | 88.1 | 58.9 | 66 | 138.0 | 92.2 | 26 | 187.9 | 125.6 | 86 | 237.8 | 158.9 |
| 47 | 39.1 | 26.1 | 07 | 89.0 | 59.4 | 67 | 138.9 | 92.8 | 27 | 188.7 | 126.1 | 87 | 238.6 | 159.4 |
| 48 | 39.9 | 26.7 | 08 | 89.8 | 60.0 | 68 | 139.7 | 93.3 | 28 | 189.6 | 126.7 | 88 | 239.5 | 160.0 |
| 49 | 40.7 | 27.2 | 09 | 90.6 | 60.6 | 69 | 140.5 | 93.9 | 29 | 190.4 | 127.2 | 89 | 240.3 | 160.6 |
| 50 | 41.6 | 27.8 | 10 | 91.5 | 61.1 | 70 | 141.3 | 94.4 | 30 | 191.2 | 127.8 | 90 | 241.1 | 161.1 |
| 51 | 42.4 | 28.3 | 111 | 92.3 | 61.7 | 171 | 142.2 | 95.0 | 231 | 192.1 | 128.3 | 291 | 242.0 | 161.7 |
| 52 | 43.2 | 28.9 | 12 | 93.1 | 62.2 | 72 | 143.0 | 95.6 | 32 | 192.9 | 128.9 | 92 | 242.8 | 162.2 |
| 53 | 44.1 | 29.4 | 13 | 94.0 | 62.8 | 73 | 143.8 | 96.1 | 33 | 193.7 | 129.4 | 93 | 243.6 | 162.8 |
| 54 | 44.9 | 30.0 | 14 | 94.8 | 63.3 | 74 | 144.7 | 96.7 | 34 | 194.6 | 130.0 | 94 | 244.5 | 163.3 |
| 55 | 45.7 | 30.6 | 15 | 95.6 | 63.9 | 75 | 145.5 | 97.2 | 35 | 195.4 | 130.6 | 95 | 245.3 | 163.9 |
| 56 | 46.6 | 31.1 | 16 | 96.5 | 64.4 | 76 | 146.3 | 97.8 | 36 | 196.2 | 131.1 | 96 | 246.1 | 164.4 |
| 57 | 47.4 | 31.7 | 17 | 97.3 | 65.0 | 77 | 147.2 | 98.3 | 37 | 197.1 | 131.7 | 97 | 246.9 | 165.0 |
| 58 | 48.2 | 32.2 | 18 | 98.1 | 65.6 | 78 | 148.0 | 98.9 | 38 | 197.9 | 132.2 | 98 | 247.8 | 165.6 |
| 59 | 49.1 | 32.8 | 19 | 98.9 | 66.1 | 79 | 148.8 | 99.4 | 39 | 198.7 | 132.8 | 99 | 248.6 | 166.1 |
| 60 | 49.9 | 33.3 | 20 | 99.8 | 66.7 | 80 | 149.7 | 100.0 | 40 | 199.6 | 133.3 | 300 | 249.4 | 166.7 |
| Dist. | Dep. | Lat. | Dist. | Dep. | Lat. | Dist. | Dep. | Lat. | Dist. | Dep. | Lat. | Dist. | Dep. | Lat. |

N.E.byE. S.E.byE. N.W.byW. S.W.byW. [For 5 Points.

# TABLE I.

## Difference of Latitude and Departure for 3¼ Points.

N.E.¾N. N.W.¾N. S.E.¾S. S.W.¾S.

| Dist. | Lat. | Dep. | Dist. | Lat. | Dep. | Dist. | Lat. | Dep. | Dist. | Lat. | Dep. | Dist. | Lat. | Dep. |
|---|---|---|---|---|---|---|---|---|---|---|---|---|---|---|
| 1 | 00.8 | 00.6 | 61 | 49.0 | 36.3 | 121 | 97.2 | 72.1 | 181 | 145.4 | 107.8 | 241 | 193.6 | 143.6 |
| 2 | 01.6 | 01.2 | 62 | 49.8 | 36.9 | 22 | 98.0 | 72.7 | 82 | 146.2 | 108.4 | 42 | 194.4 | 144.2 |
| 3 | 02.4 | 01.8 | 63 | 50.6 | 37.5 | 23 | 98.8 | 73.3 | 83 | 147.0 | 109.0 | 43 | 195.2 | 144.8 |
| 4 | 03.2 | 02.4 | 64 | 51.4 | 38.1 | 24 | 99.6 | 73.9 | 84 | 147.8 | 109.6 | 44 | 196.0 | 145.4 |
| 5 | 04.0 | 03.0 | 65 | 52.2 | 38.7 | 25 | 100.4 | 74.5 | 85 | 148.6 | 110.2 | 45 | 196.8 | 145.9 |
| 6 | 04.8 | 03.6 | 66 | 53.0 | 39.3 | 26 | 101.2 | 75.1 | 86 | 149.4 | 110.8 | 46 | 197.6 | 146.5 |
| 7 | 05.6 | 04.2 | 67 | 53.8 | 39.9 | 27 | 102.0 | 75.7 | 87 | 150.2 | 111.4 | 47 | 198.4 | 147.1 |
| 8 | 06.4 | 04.8 | 68 | 54.6 | 40.5 | 28 | 102.8 | 76.2 | 88 | 151.0 | 112.0 | 48 | 199.2 | 147.7 |
| 9 | 07.2 | 05.4 | 69 | 55.4 | 41.1 | 29 | 103.6 | 76.8 | 89 | 151.8 | 112.6 | 49 | 200.0 | 148.3 |
| 10 | 08.0 | 06.0 | 70 | 56.2 | 41.7 | 30 | 104.4 | 77.4 | 90 | 152.6 | 113.2 | 50 | 200.8 | 148.9 |
| 11 | 08.8 | 06.6 | 71 | 57.0 | 42.3 | 131 | 105.2 | 78.0 | 191 | 153.4 | 113.8 | 251 | 201.6 | 149.5 |
| 12 | 09.6 | 07.1 | 72 | 57.8 | 42.9 | 32 | 106.0 | 78.6 | 92 | 154.2 | 114.4 | 52 | 202.4 | 150.1 |
| 13 | 10.4 | 07.7 | 73 | 58.6 | 43.5 | 33 | 106.8 | 79.2 | 93 | 155.0 | 115.0 | 53 | 203.2 | 150.7 |
| 14 | 11.2 | 08.3 | 74 | 59.4 | 44.1 | 34 | 107.6 | 79.8 | 94 | 155.8 | 115.6 | 54 | 204.0 | 151.3 |
| 15 | 12.0 | 08.9 | 75 | 60.2 | 44.7 | 35 | 108.4 | 80.4 | 95 | 156.6 | 116.2 | 55 | 204.8 | 151.9 |
| 16 | 12.9 | 09.5 | 76 | 61.0 | 45.3 | 36 | 109.2 | 81.0 | 96 | 157.4 | 116.8 | 56 | 205.6 | 152.5 |
| 17 | 13.7 | 10.1 | 77 | 61.8 | 45.9 | 37 | 110.0 | 81.6 | 97 | 158.2 | 117.4 | 57 | 206.4 | 153.1 |
| 18 | 14.5 | 10.7 | 78 | 62.7 | 46.5 | 38 | 110.8 | 82.2 | 98 | 159.0 | 117.9 | 58 | 207.2 | 153.7 |
| 19 | 15.3 | 11.3 | 79 | 63.5 | 47.1 | 39 | 111.6 | 82.8 | 99 | 159.8 | 118.5 | 59 | 208.0 | 154.3 |
| 20 | 16.1 | 11.9 | 80 | 64.3 | 47.7 | 40 | 112.4 | 83.4 | 200 | 160.6 | 119.1 | 60 | 208.8 | 154.9 |
| 21 | 16.9 | 12.5 | 81 | 65.1 | 48.3 | 141 | 113.3 | 84.0 | 201 | 161.4 | 119.7 | 261 | 209.6 | 155.5 |
| 22 | 17.7 | 13.1 | 82 | 65.9 | 48.8 | 42 | 114.1 | 84.6 | 02 | 162.2 | 120.3 | 62 | 210.4 | 156.1 |
| 23 | 18.5 | 13.7 | 83 | 66.7 | 49.4 | 43 | 114.9 | 85.2 | 03 | 163.1 | 120.9 | 63 | 211.2 | 156.7 |
| 24 | 19.3 | 14.3 | 84 | 67.5 | 50.0 | 44 | 115.7 | 85.8 | 04 | 163.9 | 121.5 | 64 | 212.0 | 157.3 |
| 25 | 20.1 | 14.9 | 85 | 68.3 | 50.6 | 45 | 116.5 | 86.4 | 05 | 164.7 | 122.1 | 65 | 212.8 | 157.9 |
| 26 | 20.9 | 15.5 | 86 | 69.1 | 51.2 | 46 | 117.3 | 87.0 | 06 | 165.5 | 122.7 | 66 | 213.7 | 158.5 |
| 27 | 21.7 | 16.1 | 87 | 69.9 | 51.8 | 47 | 118.1 | 87.6 | 07 | 166.3 | 123.3 | 67 | 214.5 | 159.1 |
| 28 | 22.5 | 16.7 | 88 | 70.7 | 52.4 | 48 | 118.9 | 88.2 | 08 | 167.1 | 123.9 | 68 | 215.3 | 159.6 |
| 29 | 23.3 | 17.3 | 89 | 71.5 | 53.0 | 49 | 119.7 | 88.8 | 09 | 167.9 | 124.5 | 69 | 216.1 | 160.2 |
| 30 | 24.1 | 17.9 | 90 | 72.3 | 53.6 | 50 | 120.5 | 89.4 | 10 | 168.7 | 125.1 | 70 | 216.9 | 160.8 |
| 31 | 24.9 | 18.5 | 91 | 73.1 | 54.2 | 151 | 121.3 | 90.0 | 211 | 169.5 | 125.7 | 271 | 217.7 | 161.4 |
| 32 | 25.7 | 19.1 | 92 | 73.9 | 54.8 | 52 | 122.1 | 90.5 | 12 | 170.3 | 126.3 | 72 | 218.5 | 162.0 |
| 33 | 26.5 | 19.7 | 93 | 74.7 | 55.4 | 53 | 122.9 | 91.1 | 13 | 171.1 | 126.9 | 73 | 219.3 | 162.6 |
| 34 | 27.3 | 20.3 | 94 | 75.5 | 56.0 | 54 | 123.7 | 91.7 | 14 | 171.9 | 127.5 | 74 | 220.1 | 163.2 |
| 35 | 28.1 | 20.8 | 95 | 76.3 | 56.6 | 55 | 124.5 | 92.3 | 15 | 172.7 | 128.1 | 75 | 220.9 | 163.8 |
| 36 | 28.9 | 21.4 | 96 | 77.1 | 57.2 | 56 | 125.3 | 92.9 | 16 | 173.5 | 128.7 | 76 | 221.7 | 164.4 |
| 37 | 29.7 | 22.0 | 97 | 77.9 | 57.8 | 57 | 126.1 | 93.5 | 17 | 174.3 | 129.3 | 77 | 222.5 | 165.0 |
| 38 | 30.5 | 22.6 | 98 | 78.7 | 58.4 | 58 | 126.9 | 94.1 | 18 | 175.1 | 129.9 | 78 | 223.3 | 165.6 |
| 39 | 31.3 | 23.2 | 99 | 79.5 | 59.0 | 59 | 127.7 | 94.7 | 19 | 175.9 | 130.5 | 79 | 224.1 | 166.2 |
| 40 | 32.1 | 23.8 | 100 | 80.3 | 59.6 | 60 | 128.5 | 95.3 | 20 | 176.7 | 131.1 | 80 | 224.9 | 166.8 |
| 41 | 32.9 | 24.4 | 101 | 81.1 | 60.2 | 161 | 129.3 | 95.9 | 221 | 177.5 | 131.6 | 281 | 225.7 | 167.4 |
| 42 | 33.7 | 25.0 | 02 | 81.9 | 60.8 | 62 | 130.1 | 96.5 | 22 | 178.3 | 132.2 | 82 | 226.5 | 168.0 |
| 43 | 34.5 | 25.6 | 03 | 82.7 | 61.4 | 63 | 130.9 | 97.1 | 23 | 179.1 | 132.8 | 83 | 227.3 | 168.6 |
| 44 | 35.3 | 26.2 | 04 | 83.5 | 62.0 | 64 | 131.7 | 97.7 | 24 | 179.9 | 133.4 | 84 | 228.1 | 169.2 |
| 45 | 36.1 | 26.8 | 05 | 84.3 | 62.5 | 65 | 132.5 | 98.3 | 25 | 180.7 | 134.0 | 85 | 228.9 | 169.8 |
| 46 | 36.9 | 27.4 | 06 | 85.1 | 63.1 | 66 | 133.3 | 98.9 | 26 | 181.5 | 134.6 | 86 | 229.7 | 170.4 |
| 47 | 37.8 | 28.0 | 07 | 85.9 | 63.7 | 67 | 134.1 | 99.5 | 27 | 182.3 | 135.2 | 87 | 230.5 | 171.0 |
| 48 | 38.6 | 28.6 | 08 | 86.7 | 64.3 | 68 | 134.9 | 100.1 | 28 | 183.1 | 135.8 | 88 | 231.3 | 171.6 |
| 49 | 39.4 | 29.2 | 09 | 87.5 | 64.9 | 69 | 135.7 | 100.7 | 29 | 183.9 | 136.4 | 89 | 232.1 | 172.2 |
| 50 | 40.2 | 29.8 | 10 | 88.4 | 65.5 | 70 | 136.5 | 101.3 | 30 | 184.7 | 137.0 | 90 | 232.9 | 172.8 |
| 51 | 41.0 | 30.4 | 111 | 89.2 | 66.1 | 171 | 137.3 | 101.9 | 231 | 185.5 | 137.6 | 291 | 233.7 | 173.3 |
| 52 | 41.8 | 31.0 | 12 | 90.0 | 66.7 | 72 | 138.2 | 102.5 | 32 | 186.3 | 138.2 | 92 | 234.5 | 173.9 |
| 53 | 42.6 | 31.6 | 13 | 90.8 | 67.3 | 73 | 139.0 | 103.1 | 33 | 187.1 | 138.8 | 93 | 235.3 | 174.5 |
| 54 | 43.4 | 32.2 | 14 | 91.6 | 67.9 | 74 | 139.8 | 103.7 | 34 | 188.0 | 139.4 | 94 | 236.1 | 175.1 |
| 55 | 44.2 | 32.8 | 15 | 92.4 | 68.5 | 75 | 140.6 | 104.2 | 35 | 188.8 | 140.0 | 95 | 236.9 | 175.7 |
| 56 | 45.0 | 33.4 | 16 | 93.2 | 69.1 | 76 | 141.4 | 104.8 | 36 | 189.6 | 140.6 | 96 | 237.7 | 176.3 |
| 57 | 45.8 | 34.0 | 17 | 94.0 | 69.7 | 77 | 142.2 | 105.4 | 37 | 190.4 | 141.2 | 97 | 238.6 | 176.9 |
| 58 | 46.6 | 34.6 | 18 | 94.8 | 70.3 | 78 | 143.0 | 106.0 | 38 | 191.2 | 141.8 | 98 | 239.4 | 177.5 |
| 59 | 47.4 | 35.1 | 19 | 95.6 | 70.9 | 79 | 143.8 | 106.6 | 39 | 192.0 | 142.4 | 99 | 240.2 | 178.1 |
| 60 | 48.2 | 35.7 | 20 | 96.4 | 71.5 | 80 | 144.6 | 107.2 | 40 | 192.8 | 143.0 | 300 | 241.0 | 178.7 |
| Dist. | Dep. | Lat. | Dist. | Dep. | Lat. | Dist. | Dep. | Lat. | Dist. | Dep. | Lat. | Dist. | Dep. | Lat. |

N.E.¾E. S.E.¾E. N.W.¾W. S.W.¾W.

# TABLE I.

## Difference of Latitude and Departure for 3½ Points.

| N.E.½N. | | | N.W.½N. | | | S.E.½S. | | | S.W.½S. | | | | | |
|---|---|---|---|---|---|---|---|---|---|---|---|---|---|---|
| Dist. | Lat. | Dep. | Dist. | Lat. | Dep. | Dist. | Lat. | Dep. | Dist. | Lat. | Dep. | Dist. | Lat. | Dep. |
| 1 | 00.8 | 00.6 | 61 | 47.2 | 38.7 | 121 | 93.5 | 76.8 | 181 | 139.9 | 114.8 | 241 | 186.3 | 152.9 |
| 2 | 01.5 | 01.3 | 62 | 47.9 | 39.3 | 22 | 94.3 | 77.4 | 82 | 140.7 | 115.5 | 42 | 187.1 | 153.5 |
| 3 | 02.3 | 01.9 | 63 | 48.7 | 40.0 | 23 | 95.1 | 78.0 | 83 | 141.5 | 116.1 | 43 | 187.8 | 154.2 |
| 4 | 03.1 | 02.5 | 64 | 49.5 | 40.6 | 24 | 95.9 | 78.7 | 84 | 142.2 | 116.7 | 44 | 188.6 | 154.8 |
| 5 | 03.9 | 03.2 | 65 | 50.2 | 41.2 | 25 | 96.6 | 79.3 | 85 | 143.0 | 117.4 | 45 | 189.4 | 155.4 |
| 6 | 04.6 | 03.8 | 66 | 51.0 | 41.9 | 26 | 97.4 | 79.9 | 86 | 143.8 | 118.0 | 46 | 190.2 | 156.1 |
| 7 | 05.4 | 04.4 | 67 | 51.8 | 42.5 | 27 | 98.2 | 80.6 | 87 | 144.6 | 118.6 | 47 | 190.9 | 156.7 |
| 8 | 06.2 | 05.1 | 68 | 52.6 | 43.1 | 28 | 98.9 | 81.2 | 88 | 145.3 | 119.3 | 48 | 191.7 | 157.3 |
| 9 | 07.0 | 05.7 | 69 | 53.3 | 43.8 | 29 | 99.7 | 81.8 | 89 | 146.1 | 119.9 | 49 | 192.5 | 158.0 |
| 10 | 07.7 | 06.3 | 70 | 54.1 | 44.4 | 30 | 100.5 | 82.5 | 90 | 146.9 | 120.5 | 50 | 193.3 | 158.6 |
| 11 | 08.5 | 07.0 | 71 | 54.9 | 45.0 | 131 | 101.3 | 83.1 | 191 | 147.6 | 121.2 | 251 | 194.0 | 159.2 |
| 12 | 09.3 | 07.6 | 72 | 55.7 | 45.7 | 32 | 102.0 | 83.7 | 92 | 148.4 | 121.8 | 52 | 194.8 | 159.9 |
| 13 | 10.0 | 08.2 | 73 | 56.4 | 46.3 | 33 | 102.8 | 84.4 | 93 | 149.2 | 122.4 | 53 | 195.6 | 160.5 |
| 14 | 10.8 | 08.9 | 74 | 57.2 | 46.9 | 34 | 103.6 | 85.0 | 94 | 150.0 | 123.1 | 54 | 196.3 | 161.1 |
| 15 | 11.6 | 09.5 | 75 | 58.0 | 47.6 | 35 | 104.4 | 85.6 | 95 | 150.7 | 123.7 | 55 | 197.1 | 161.8 |
| 16 | 12.4 | 10.2 | 76 | 58.7 | 48.2 | 36 | 105.1 | 86.3 | 96 | 151.5 | 124.3 | 56 | 197.9 | 162.4 |
| 17 | 13.1 | 10.8 | 77 | 59.5 | 48.8 | 37 | 105.9 | 86.9 | 97 | 152.3 | 125.0 | 57 | 198.7 | 163.0 |
| 18 | 13.9 | 11.4 | 78 | 60.3 | 49.5 | 38 | 106.7 | 87.5 | 98 | 153.1 | 125.6 | 58 | 199.4 | 163.7 |
| 19 | 14.7 | 12.1 | 79 | 61.1 | 50.1 | 39 | 107.4 | 88.2 | 99 | 153.8 | 126.2 | 59 | 200.2 | 164.3 |
| 20 | 15.5 | 12.7 | 80 | 61.8 | 50.8 | 40 | 108.2 | 88.8 | 200 | 154.6 | 126.9 | 60 | 201.0 | 164.9 |
| 21 | 16.2 | 13.3 | 81 | 62.6 | 51.4 | 141 | 109.0 | 89.4 | 201 | 155.4 | 127.5 | 261 | 201.8 | 165.6 |
| 22 | 17.0 | 14.0 | 82 | 63.4 | 52.0 | 42 | 109.8 | 90.1 | 02 | 156.1 | 128.1 | 62 | 202.5 | 166.2 |
| 23 | 17.8 | 14.6 | 83 | 64.2 | 52.7 | 43 | 110.5 | 90.7 | 03 | 156.9 | 128.8 | 63 | 203.3 | 166.8 |
| 24 | 18.6 | 15.2 | 84 | 64.9 | 53.3 | 44 | 111.3 | 91.4 | 04 | 157.7 | 129.4 | 64 | 204.1 | 167.5 |
| 25 | 19.3 | 15.9 | 85 | 65.7 | 53.9 | 45 | 112.1 | 92.0 | 05 | 158.5 | 130.1 | 65 | 204.8 | 168.1 |
| 26 | 20.1 | 16.5 | 86 | 66.5 | 54.6 | 46 | 112.9 | 92.6 | 06 | 159.2 | 130.7 | 66 | 205.6 | 168.7 |
| 27 | 20.9 | 17.1 | 87 | 67.3 | 55.2 | 47 | 113.6 | 93.3 | 07 | 160.0 | 131.3 | 67 | 206.4 | 169.4 |
| 28 | 21.6 | 17.8 | 88 | 68.0 | 55.8 | 48 | 114.4 | 93.9 | 08 | 160.8 | 132.0 | 68 | 207.2 | 170.0 |
| 29 | 22.4 | 18.4 | 89 | 68.8 | 56.5 | 49 | 115.2 | 94.5 | 09 | 161.6 | 132.6 | 69 | 207.9 | 170.7 |
| 30 | 23.2 | 19.0 | 90 | 69.6 | 57.1 | 50 | 116.0 | 95.2 | 10 | 162.3 | 133.2 | 70 | 208.7 | 171.3 |
| 31 | 24.0 | 19.7 | 91 | 70.3 | 57.7 | 151 | 116.7 | 95.8 | 211 | 163.1 | 133.9 | 271 | 209.5 | 171.9 |
| 32 | 24.7 | 20.3 | 92 | 71.1 | 58.4 | 52 | 117.5 | 96.4 | 12 | 163.9 | 134.5 | 72 | 210.3 | 172.6 |
| 33 | 25.5 | 20.9 | 93 | 71.9 | 59.0 | 53 | 118.3 | 97.1 | 13 | 164.7 | 135.1 | 73 | 211.0 | 173.2 |
| 34 | 26.3 | 21.6 | 94 | 72.7 | 59.6 | 54 | 119.0 | 97.7 | 14 | 165.4 | 135.8 | 74 | 211.8 | 173.8 |
| 35 | 27.1 | 22.2 | 95 | 73.4 | 60.3 | 55 | 119.8 | 98.3 | 15 | 166.2 | 136.4 | 75 | 212.6 | 174.5 |
| 36 | 27.8 | 22.8 | 96 | 74.2 | 60.9 | 56 | 120.6 | 99.0 | 16 | 167.0 | 137.0 | 76 | 213.4 | 175.1 |
| 37 | 28.6 | 23.5 | 97 | 75.0 | 61.5 | 57 | 121.4 | 99.6 | 17 | 167.7 | 137.7 | 77 | 214.1 | 175.7 |
| 38 | 29.4 | 24.1 | 98 | 75.8 | 62.2 | 58 | 122.1 | 100.2 | 18 | 168.5 | 138.3 | 78 | 214.9 | 176.4 |
| 39 | 30.1 | 24.7 | 99 | 76.5 | 62.8 | 59 | 122.9 | 100.9 | 19 | 169.3 | 138.9 | 79 | 215.7 | 177.0 |
| 40 | 30.9 | 25.4 | 100 | 77.3 | 63.4 | 60 | 123.7 | 101.5 | 20 | 170.1 | 139.6 | 80 | 216.4 | 177.6 |
| 41 | 31.7 | 26.0 | 101 | 78.1 | 64.1 | 161 | 124.5 | 102.1 | 221 | 170.8 | 140.2 | 281 | 217.2 | 178.3 |
| 42 | 32.5 | 26.6 | 02 | 78.8 | 64.7 | 62 | 125.2 | 102.8 | 22 | 171.6 | 140.8 | 82 | 218.0 | 178.9 |
| 43 | 33.2 | 27.3 | 03 | 79.6 | 65.3 | 63 | 126.0 | 103.4 | 23 | 172.4 | 141.5 | 83 | 218.8 | 179.5 |
| 44 | 34.0 | 27.9 | 04 | 80.4 | 66.0 | 64 | 126.8 | 104.0 | 24 | 173.2 | 142.1 | 84 | 219.5 | 180.2 |
| 45 | 34.8 | 28.5 | 05 | 81.2 | 66.6 | 65 | 127.5 | 104.7 | 25 | 173.9 | 142.7 | 85 | 220.3 | 180.8 |
| 46 | 35.6 | 29.2 | 06 | 81.9 | 67.2 | 66 | 128.3 | 105.3 | 26 | 174.7 | 143.4 | 86 | 221.1 | 181.4 |
| 47 | 36.3 | 29.8 | 07 | 82.7 | 67.9 | 67 | 129.1 | 105.9 | 27 | 175.5 | 144.0 | 87 | 221.9 | 182.1 |
| 48 | 37.1 | 30.5 | 08 | 83.5 | 68.5 | 68 | 129.9 | 106.6 | 28 | 176.2 | 144.6 | 88 | 222.6 | 182.7 |
| 49 | 37.9 | 31.1 | 09 | 84.3 | 69.1 | 69 | 130.6 | 107.2 | 29 | 177.0 | 145.3 | 89 | 223.4 | 183.3 |
| 50 | 38.7 | 31.7 | 10 | 85.0 | 69.8 | 70 | 131.4 | 107.8 | 30 | 177.8 | 145.9 | 90 | 224.2 | 184.0 |
| 51 | 39.4 | 32.4 | 111 | 85.8 | 70.4 | 171 | 132.2 | 108.5 | 231 | 178.6 | 146.5 | 291 | 224.9 | 184.6 |
| 52 | 40.2 | 33.0 | 12 | 86.6 | 71.1 | 72 | 133.0 | 109.1 | 32 | 179.3 | 147.2 | 92 | 225.7 | 185.2 |
| 53 | 41.0 | 33.6 | 13 | 87.4 | 71.7 | 73 | 133.7 | 109.8 | 33 | 180.1 | 147.8 | 93 | 226.5 | 185.9 |
| 54 | 41.7 | 34.3 | 14 | 88.1 | 72.3 | 74 | 134.5 | 110.4 | 34 | 180.9 | 148.4 | 94 | 227.3 | 186.5 |
| 55 | 42.5 | 34.9 | 15 | 88.9 | 73.0 | 75 | 135.3 | 111.0 | 35 | 181.7 | 149.1 | 95 | 228.0 | 187.1 |
| 56 | 43.3 | 35.5 | 16 | 89.7 | 73.6 | 76 | 136.0 | 111.7 | 36 | 182.4 | 149.7 | 96 | 228.8 | 187.8 |
| 57 | 44.1 | 36.2 | 17 | 90.4 | 74.2 | 77 | 136.8 | 112.3 | 37 | 183.2 | 150.4 | 97 | 229.6 | 188.4 |
| 58 | 44.8 | 36.8 | 18 | 91.2 | 74.9 | 78 | 137.6 | 112.9 | 38 | 184.0 | 151.0 | 98 | 230.4 | 189.0 |
| 59 | 45.6 | 37.4 | 19 | 92.0 | 75.5 | 79 | 138.4 | 113.6 | 39 | 184.7 | 151.6 | 99 | 231.1 | 189.7 |
| 60 | 46.4 | 38.1 | 20 | 92.8 | 76.1 | 80 | 139.1 | 114.2 | 40 | 185.5 | 152.3 | 300 | 231.9 | 190.3 |
| Dist. | Dep. | Lat. | Dist. | Dep. | Lat. | Dist. | Dep. | Lat. | Dist. | Dep. | Lat. | Dist. | Dep. | Lat. |
| N.E.½E. | | | S.E.½E. | | | N.W.½W. | | | S.W.½W. | | | | | |

[For 4½ Points.

# TABLE I.

## Difference of Latitude and Departure for 3¾ Points.

N.E.¼N. N.W.¼N. S.E.¼S. S.W.¼S.

| Dist. | Lat. | Dep. | Dist. | Lat. | Dep. | Dist. | Lat. | Dep. | Dist. | Lat. | Dep. | Dist. | Lat. | Dep. |
|---|---|---|---|---|---|---|---|---|---|---|---|---|---|---|
| 1 | 00.7 | 00.7 | 61 | 45.2 | 41.0 | 121 | 89.7 | 81.3 | 181 | 134.1 | 121.6 | 241 | 178.6 | 161.8 |
| 2 | 01.5 | 01.3 | 62 | 45.9 | 41.6 | 22 | 90.4 | 81.9 | 82 | 134.9 | 122.2 | 42 | 179.3 | 162.5 |
| 3 | 02.2 | 02.0 | 63 | 46.7 | 42.3 | 23 | 91.1 | 82.6 | 83 | 135.6 | 122.9 | 43 | 180.1 | 163.2 |
| 4 | 03.0 | 02.7 | 64 | 47.4 | 43.0 | 24 | 91.9 | 83.3 | 84 | 136.3 | 123.6 | 44 | 180.8 | 163.9 |
| 5 | 03.7 | 03.4 | 65 | 48.2 | 43.7 | 25 | 92.6 | 83.9 | 85 | 137.1 | 124.2 | 45 | 181.5 | 164.5 |
| 6 | 04.4 | 04.0 | 66 | 48.9 | 44.3 | 26 | 93.4 | 84.6 | 86 | 137.8 | 124.9 | 46 | 182.3 | 165.2 |
| 7 | 05.2 | 04.7 | 67 | 49.6 | 45.0 | 27 | 94.1 | 85.3 | 87 | 138.6 | 125.6 | 47 | 183.0 | 165.9 |
| 8 | 05.9 | 05.4 | 68 | 50.4 | 45.7 | 28 | 94.8 | 86.0 | 88 | 139.3 | 126.3 | 48 | 183.8 | 166.5 |
| 9 | 06.7 | 06.0 | 69 | 51.1 | 46.3 | 29 | 95.6 | 86.6 | 89 | 140.0 | 126.9 | 49 | 184.5 | 167.2 |
| 10 | 07.4 | 06.7 | 70 | 51.9 | 47.0 | 30 | 96.3 | 87.3 | 90 | 140.8 | 127.6 | 50 | 185.2 | 167.9 |
| 11 | 08.2 | 07.4 | 71 | 52.6 | 47.7 | 131 | 97.1 | 88.0 | 191 | 141.5 | 128.3 | 251 | 186.0 | 168.6 |
| 12 | 08.9 | 08.1 | 72 | 53.3 | 48.4 | 32 | 97.8 | 88.6 | 92 | 142.3 | 128.9 | 52 | 186.7 | 169.2 |
| 13 | 09.6 | 08.7 | 73 | 54.1 | 49.0 | 33 | 98.5 | 89.3 | 93 | 143.0 | 129.6 | 53 | 187.5 | 169.9 |
| 14 | 10.4 | 09.4 | 74 | 54.8 | 49.7 | 34 | 99.3 | 90.0 | 94 | 143.7 | 130.3 | 54 | 188.2 | 170.6 |
| 15 | 11.1 | 10.1 | 75 | 55.6 | 50.4 | 35 | 100.0 | 90.7 | 95 | 144.5 | 131.0 | 55 | 188.9 | 171.2 |
| 16 | 11.9 | 10.7 | 76 | 56.3 | 51.0 | 36 | 100.8 | 91.3 | 96 | 145.2 | 131.6 | 56 | 189.7 | 171.9 |
| 17 | 12.6 | 11.4 | 77 | 57.1 | 51.7 | 37 | 101.5 | 92.0 | 97 | 146.0 | 132.3 | 57 | 190.4 | 172.6 |
| 18 | 13.3 | 12.1 | 78 | 57.8 | 52.4 | 38 | 102.3 | 92.7 | 98 | 146.7 | 133.0 | 58 | 191.2 | 173.3 |
| 19 | 14.1 | 12.8 | 79 | 58.5 | 53.1 | 39 | 103.0 | 93.3 | 99 | 147.4 | 133.6 | 59 | 191.9 | 173.9 |
| 20 | 14.8 | 13.4 | 80 | 59.3 | 53.7 | 40 | 103.7 | 94.0 | 200 | 148.2 | 134.3 | 60 | 192.6 | 174.6 |
| 21 | 15.6 | 14.1 | 81 | 60.0 | 54.4 | 141 | 104.5 | 94.7 | 201 | 148.9 | 135.0 | 261 | 193.4 | 175.3 |
| 22 | 16.3 | 14.8 | 82 | 60.8 | 55.1 | 42 | 105.2 | 95.4 | 02 | 149.7 | 135.7 | 62 | 194.1 | 175.9 |
| 23 | 17.0 | 15.4 | 83 | 61.5 | 55.7 | 43 | 106.0 | 96.0 | 03 | 150.4 | 136.3 | 63 | 194.9 | 176.6 |
| 24 | 17.8 | 16.1 | 84 | 62.2 | 56.4 | 44 | 106.7 | 96.7 | 04 | 151.2 | 137.0 | 64 | 195.6 | 177.3 |
| 25 | 18.5 | 16.8 | 85 | 63.0 | 57.1 | 45 | 107.4 | 97.4 | 05 | 151.9 | 137.7 | 65 | 196.4 | 178.0 |
| 26 | 19.3 | 17.5 | 86 | 63.7 | 57.8 | 46 | 108.2 | 98.0 | 06 | 152.6 | 138.3 | 66 | 197.1 | 178.6 |
| 27 | 20.0 | 18.1 | 87 | 64.5 | 58.4 | 47 | 108.9 | 98.7 | 07 | 153.4 | 139.0 | 67 | 197.8 | 179.3 |
| 28 | 20.7 | 18.8 | 88 | 65.2 | 59.1 | 48 | 109.7 | 99.4 | 08 | 154.1 | 139.7 | 68 | 198.6 | 180.0 |
| 29 | 21.5 | 19.5 | 89 | 65.9 | 59.8 | 49 | 110.4 | 100.1 | 09 | 154.9 | 140.4 | 69 | 199.3 | 180.6 |
| 30 | 22.2 | 20.1 | 90 | 66.7 | 60.4 | 50 | 111.1 | 100.7 | 10 | 155.6 | 141.0 | 70 | 200.1 | 181.3 |
| 31 | 23.0 | 20.8 | 91 | 67.4 | 61.1 | 151 | 111.9 | 101.4 | 211 | 156.3 | 141.7 | 271 | 200.8 | 182.0 |
| 32 | 23.7 | 21.5 | 92 | 68.2 | 61.8 | 52 | 112.6 | 102.1 | 12 | 157.1 | 142.4 | 72 | 201.5 | 182.7 |
| 33 | 24.5 | 22.2 | 93 | 68.9 | 62.5 | 53 | 113.4 | 102.7 | 13 | 157.8 | 143.0 | 73 | 202.3 | 183.3 |
| 34 | 25.2 | 22.8 | 94 | 69.6 | 63.1 | 54 | 114.1 | 103.4 | 14 | 158.6 | 143.7 | 74 | 203.0 | 184.0 |
| 35 | 25.9 | 23.5 | 95 | 70.4 | 63.8 | 55 | 114.8 | 104.1 | 15 | 159.3 | 144.4 | 75 | 203.8 | 184.7 |
| 36 | 26.7 | 24.2 | 96 | 71.1 | 64.5 | 56 | 115.6 | 104.8 | 16 | 160.0 | 145.1 | 76 | 204.5 | 185.4 |
| 37 | 27.4 | 24.8 | 97 | 71.9 | 65.1 | 57 | 116.3 | 105.4 | 17 | 160.8 | 145.7 | 77 | 205.2 | 186.0 |
| 38 | 28.2 | 25.5 | 98 | 72.6 | 65.8 | 58 | 117.1 | 106.1 | 18 | 161.5 | 146.4 | 78 | 206.0 | 186.7 |
| 39 | 28.9 | 26.2 | 99 | 73.4 | 66.5 | 59 | 117.8 | 106.8 | 19 | 162.3 | 147.1 | 79 | 206.7 | 187.4 |
| 40 | 29.6 | 26.9 | 100 | 74.1 | 67.2 | 60 | 118.6 | 107.4 | 20 | 163.0 | 147.7 | 80 | 207.5 | 188.0 |
| 41 | 30.4 | 27.5 | 101 | 74.8 | 67.8 | 161 | 119.3 | 108.1 | 221 | 163.8 | 148.4 | 281 | 208.2 | 188.7 |
| 42 | 31.1 | 28.2 | 02 | 75.6 | 68.5 | 62 | 120.0 | 108.8 | 22 | 164.5 | 149.1 | 82 | 208.9 | 189.4 |
| 43 | 31.9 | 28.9 | 03 | 76.3 | 69.2 | 63 | 120.8 | 109.5 | 23 | 165.2 | 149.8 | 83 | 209.7 | 190.1 |
| 44 | 32.6 | 29.5 | 04 | 77.1 | 69.8 | 64 | 121.5 | 110.1 | 24 | 166.0 | 150.4 | 84 | 210.4 | 190.7 |
| 45 | 33.3 | 30.2 | 05 | 77.8 | 70.5 | 65 | 122.3 | 110.8 | 25 | 166.7 | 151.1 | 85 | 211.2 | 191.4 |
| 46 | 34.1 | 30.9 | 06 | 78.5 | 71.2 | 66 | 123.0 | 111.5 | 26 | 167.5 | 151.8 | 86 | 211.9 | 192.1 |
| 47 | 34.8 | 31.6 | 07 | 79.3 | 71.9 | 67 | 123.7 | 112.2 | 27 | 168.2 | 152.4 | 87 | 212.7 | 192.7 |
| 48 | 35.6 | 32.2 | 08 | 80.0 | 72.5 | 68 | 124.5 | 112.8 | 28 | 168.9 | 153.1 | 88 | 213.4 | 193.4 |
| 49 | 36.3 | 32.9 | 09 | 80.8 | 73.2 | 69 | 125.2 | 113.5 | 29 | 169.7 | 153.8 | 89 | 214.1 | 194.1 |
| 50 | 37.0 | 33.6 | 10 | 81.5 | 73.9 | 70 | 126.0 | 114.2 | 30 | 170.4 | 154.5 | 90 | 214.9 | 194.8 |
| 51 | 37.8 | 34.2 | 111 | 82.2 | 74.5 | 171 | 126.7 | 114.8 | 231 | 171.2 | 155.1 | 291 | 215.6 | 195.4 |
| 52 | 38.5 | 34.9 | 12 | 83.0 | 75.2 | 72 | 127.4 | 115.5 | 32 | 171.9 | 155.8 | 92 | 216.4 | 196.1 |
| 53 | 39.3 | 35.6 | 13 | 83.7 | 75.9 | 73 | 128.2 | 116.2 | 33 | 172.6 | 156.5 | 93 | 217.1 | 196.8 |
| 54 | 40.0 | 36.3 | 14 | 84.5 | 76.6 | 74 | 128.9 | 116.9 | 34 | 173.4 | 157.1 | 94 | 217.8 | 197.4 |
| 55 | 40.8 | 36.9 | 15 | 85.2 | 77.2 | 75 | 129.7 | 117.5 | 35 | 174.1 | 157.8 | 95 | 218.6 | 198.1 |
| 56 | 41.5 | 37.6 | 16 | 86.0 | 77.9 | 76 | 130.4 | 118.2 | 36 | 174.9 | 158.5 | 96 | 219.3 | 198.8 |
| 57 | 42.2 | 38.3 | 17 | 86.7 | 78.6 | 77 | 131.1 | 118.9 | 37 | 175.6 | 159.2 | 97 | 220.1 | 199.5 |
| 58 | 43.0 | 39.0 | 18 | 87.4 | 79.2 | 78 | 131.9 | 119.5 | 38 | 176.3 | 159.8 | 98 | 220.8 | 200.1 |
| 59 | 43.7 | 39.6 | 19 | 88.2 | 79.9 | 79 | 132.6 | 120.2 | 39 | 177.1 | 160.5 | 99 | 221.5 | 200.8 |
| 60 | 44.5 | 40.3 | 20 | 88.9 | 80.6 | 80 | 133.4 | 120.9 | 40 | 177.8 | 161.2 | 300 | 222.3 | 201.5 |
| Dist. | Dep. | Lat. | Dist. | Dep. | Lat. | Dist. | Dep. | Lat. | Dist. | Dep. | Lat. | Dist. | Dep. | Lat. |

N.E.¼E. S.E.¼E. N.W.¼W. S.W.¼W.

[For 4¼ Points.

# TABLE I.

## Difference of Latitude and Departure for 4 Points.

| | N.E. | | | N.W. | | | S.E. | | | S.W. | | | | |
|---|---|---|---|---|---|---|---|---|---|---|---|---|---|---|
| Dist. | Lat. | Dep. | Dist. | Lat. | Dep. | Dist. | Lat. | Dep. | Dist. | Lat. | Dep. | Dist. | Lat. | Dep. |
| 1 | 00.7 | 00.7 | 61 | 43.1 | 43.1 | 121 | 85.6 | 85.6 | 181 | 128.0 | 128.0 | 241 | 170.4 | 170.4 |
| 2 | 01.4 | 01.4 | 62 | 43.8 | 43.8 | 22 | 86.3 | 86.3 | 82 | 128.7 | 128.7 | 42 | 171.1 | 171.1 |
| 3 | 02.1 | 02.1 | 63 | 44.5 | 44.5 | 23 | 87.0 | 87.0 | 83 | 129.4 | 129.4 | 43 | 171.8 | 171.8 |
| 4 | 02.8 | 02.8 | 64 | 45.3 | 45.3 | 24 | 87.7 | 87.7 | 84 | 130.1 | 130.1 | 44 | 172.5 | 172.5 |
| 5 | 03.5 | 03.5 | 65 | 46.0 | 46.0 | 25 | 88.4 | 88.4 | 85 | 130.8 | 130.8 | 45 | 173.2 | 173.2 |
| 6 | 04.2 | 04.2 | 66 | 46.7 | 46.7 | 26 | 89.1 | 89.1 | 86 | 131.5 | 131.5 | 46 | 173.9 | 173.9 |
| 7 | 04.9 | 04.9 | 67 | 47.4 | 47.4 | 27 | 89.8 | 89.8 | 87 | 132.2 | 132.2 | 47 | 174.7 | 174.7 |
| 8 | 05.7 | 05.7 | 68 | 48.1 | 48.1 | 28 | 90.5 | 90.5 | 88 | 132.9 | 132.9 | 48 | 175.4 | 175.4 |
| 9 | 06.4 | 06.4 | 69 | 48.8 | 48.8 | 29 | 91.2 | 91.2 | 89 | 133.6 | 133.6 | 49 | 176.1 | 176.1 |
| 10 | 07.1 | 07.1 | 70 | 49.5 | 49.5 | 30 | 91.9 | 91.9 | 90 | 134.4 | 134.4 | 50 | 176.8 | 176.8 |
| 11 | 07.8 | 07.8 | 71 | 50.2 | 50.2 | 131 | 92.6 | 92.6 | 191 | 135.1 | 135.1 | 251 | 177.5 | 177.5 |
| 12 | 08.5 | 08.5 | 72 | 50.9 | 50.9 | 32 | 93.3 | 93.3 | 92 | 135.8 | 135.8 | 52 | 178.2 | 178.2 |
| 13 | 09.2 | 09.2 | 73 | 51.6 | 51.6 | 33 | 94.0 | 94.0 | 93 | 136.5 | 136.5 | 53 | 178.9 | 178.9 |
| 14 | 09.9 | 09.9 | 74 | 52.3 | 52.3 | 34 | 94.8 | 94.8 | 94 | 137.2 | 137.2 | 54 | 179.6 | 179.6 |
| 15 | 10.6 | 10.6 | 75 | 53.0 | 53.0 | 35 | 95.5 | 95.5 | 95 | 137.9 | 137.9 | 55 | 180.3 | 180.3 |
| 16 | 11.3 | 11.3 | 76 | 53.7 | 53.7 | 36 | 96.2 | 96.2 | 96 | 138.6 | 138.6 | 56 | 181.0 | 181.0 |
| 17 | 12.0 | 12.0 | 77 | 54.4 | 54.4 | 37 | 96.9 | 96.9 | 97 | 139.3 | 139.3 | 57 | 181.7 | 181.7 |
| 18 | 12.7 | 12.7 | 78 | 55.2 | 55.2 | 38 | 97.6 | 97.6 | 98 | 140.0 | 140.0 | 58 | 182.4 | 182.4 |
| 19 | 13.4 | 13.4 | 79 | 55.9 | 55.9 | 39 | 98.3 | 98.3 | 99 | 140.7 | 140.7 | 59 | 183.1 | 183.1 |
| 20 | 14.1 | 14.1 | 80 | 56.6 | 56.6 | 40 | 99.0 | 99.0 | 200 | 141.4 | 141.4 | 60 | 183.8 | 183.8 |
| 21 | 14.8 | 14.8 | 81 | 57.3 | 57.3 | 141 | 99.7 | 99.7 | 201 | 142.1 | 142.1 | 261 | 184.6 | 184.6 |
| 22 | 15.6 | 15.6 | 82 | 58.0 | 58.0 | 42 | 100.4 | 100.4 | 02 | 142.8 | 142.8 | 62 | 185.3 | 185.3 |
| 23 | 16.3 | 16.3 | 83 | 58.7 | 58.7 | 43 | 101.1 | 101.1 | 03 | 143.5 | 143.5 | 63 | 186.0 | 186.0 |
| 24 | 17.0 | 17.0 | 84 | 59.4 | 59.4 | 44 | 101.8 | 101.8 | 04 | 144.2 | 144.2 | 64 | 186.7 | 186.7 |
| 25 | 17.7 | 17.7 | 85 | 60.1 | 60.1 | 45 | 102.5 | 102.5 | 05 | 145.0 | 145.0 | 65 | 187.4 | 187.4 |
| 26 | 18.4 | 18.4 | 86 | 60.8 | 60.8 | 46 | 103.2 | 103.2 | 06 | 145.7 | 145.7 | 66 | 188.1 | 188.1 |
| 27 | 19.1 | 19.1 | 87 | 61.5 | 61.5 | 47 | 103.9 | 103.9 | 07 | 146.4 | 146.4 | 67 | 188.8 | 188.8 |
| 28 | 19.8 | 19.8 | 88 | 62.2 | 62.2 | 48 | 104.7 | 104.7 | 08 | 147.1 | 147.1 | 68 | 189.5 | 189.5 |
| 29 | 20.5 | 20.5 | 89 | 62.9 | 62.9 | 49 | 105.4 | 105.4 | 09 | 147.8 | 147.8 | 69 | 190.2 | 190.2 |
| 30 | 21.2 | 21.2 | 90 | 63.6 | 63.6 | 50 | 106.1 | 106.1 | 10 | 148.5 | 148.5 | 70 | 190.9 | 190.9 |
| 31 | 21.9 | 21.9 | 91 | 64.3 | 64.3 | 151 | 106.8 | 106.8 | 211 | 149.2 | 149.2 | 271 | 191.6 | 191.6 |
| 32 | 22.6 | 22.6 | 92 | 65.1 | 65.1 | 52 | 107.5 | 107.5 | 12 | 149.9 | 149.9 | 72 | 192.3 | 192.3 |
| 33 | 23.3 | 23.3 | 93 | 65.8 | 65.8 | 53 | 108.2 | 108.2 | 13 | 150.6 | 150.6 | 73 | 193.0 | 193.0 |
| 34 | 24.0 | 24.0 | 94 | 66.5 | 66.5 | 54 | 108.9 | 108.9 | 14 | 151.3 | 151.3 | 74 | 193.7 | 193.7 |
| 35 | 24.7 | 24.7 | 95 | 67.2 | 67.2 | 55 | 109.6 | 109.6 | 15 | 152.0 | 152.0 | 75 | 194.5 | 194.5 |
| 36 | 25.5 | 25.5 | 96 | 67.9 | 67.9 | 56 | 110.3 | 110.3 | 16 | 152.7 | 152.7 | 76 | 195.2 | 195.2 |
| 37 | 26.2 | 26.2 | 97 | 68.6 | 68.6 | 57 | 111.0 | 111.0 | 17 | 153.4 | 153.4 | 77 | 195.9 | 195.9 |
| 38 | 26.9 | 26.9 | 98 | 69.3 | 69.3 | 58 | 111.7 | 111.7 | 18 | 154.1 | 154.1 | 78 | 196.6 | 196.6 |
| 39 | 27.6 | 27.6 | 99 | 70.0 | 70.0 | 59 | 112.4 | 112.4 | 19 | 154.9 | 154.9 | 79 | 197.3 | 197.3 |
| 40 | 28.3 | 28.3 | 100 | 70.7 | 70.7 | 60 | 113.1 | 113.1 | 20 | 155.6 | 155.6 | 80 | 198.0 | 198.0 |
| 41 | 29.0 | 29.0 | 101 | 71.4 | 71.4 | 161 | 113.8 | 113.8 | 221 | 156.3 | 156.3 | 281 | 198.7 | 198.7 |
| 42 | 29.7 | 29.7 | 02 | 72.1 | 72.1 | 62 | 114.6 | 114.6 | 22 | 157.0 | 157.0 | 82 | 199.4 | 199.4 |
| 43 | 30.4 | 30.4 | 03 | 72.8 | 72.8 | 63 | 115.3 | 115.3 | 23 | 157.7 | 157.7 | 83 | 200.1 | 200.1 |
| 44 | 31.1 | 31.1 | 04 | 73.5 | 73.5 | 64 | 116.0 | 116.0 | 24 | 158.4 | 158.4 | 84 | 200.8 | 200.8 |
| 45 | 31.8 | 31.8 | 05 | 74.2 | 74.2 | 65 | 116.7 | 116.7 | 25 | 159.1 | 159.1 | 85 | 201.5 | 201.5 |
| 46 | 32.5 | 32.5 | 06 | 75.0 | 75.0 | 66 | 117.4 | 117.4 | 26 | 159.8 | 159.8 | 86 | 202.2 | 202.2 |
| 47 | 33.2 | 33.2 | 07 | 75.7 | 75.7 | 67 | 118.1 | 118.1 | 27 | 160.5 | 160.5 | 87 | 202.9 | 202.9 |
| 48 | 33.9 | 33.9 | 08 | 76.4 | 76.4 | 68 | 118.8 | 118.8 | 28 | 161.2 | 161.2 | 88 | 203.6 | 203.6 |
| 49 | 34.6 | 34.6 | 09 | 77.1 | 77.1 | 69 | 119.5 | 119.5 | 29 | 161.9 | 161.9 | 89 | 204.4 | 204.4 |
| 50 | 35.4 | 35.4 | 10 | 77.8 | 77.8 | 70 | 120.2 | 120.2 | 30 | 162.6 | 162.6 | 90 | 205.1 | 205.1 |
| 51 | 36.1 | 36.1 | 111 | 78.5 | 78.5 | 171 | 120.9 | 120.9 | 231 | 163.3 | 163.3 | 291 | 205.8 | 205.8 |
| 52 | 36.8 | 36.8 | 12 | 79.2 | 79.2 | 72 | 121.6 | 121.6 | 32 | 164.0 | 164.0 | 92 | 206.5 | 206.5 |
| 53 | 37.5 | 37.5 | 13 | 79.9 | 79.9 | 73 | 122.3 | 122.3 | 33 | 164.8 | 164.8 | 93 | 207.2 | 207.2 |
| 54 | 38.2 | 38.2 | 14 | 80.6 | 80.6 | 74 | 123.0 | 123.0 | 34 | 165.5 | 165.5 | 94 | 207.9 | 207.9 |
| 55 | 38.9 | 38.9 | 15 | 81.3 | 81.3 | 75 | 123.7 | 123.7 | 35 | 166.2 | 166.2 | 95 | 208.6 | 208.6 |
| 56 | 39.6 | 39.6 | 16 | 82.0 | 82.0 | 76 | 124.5 | 124.5 | 36 | 166.9 | 166.9 | 96 | 209.3 | 209.3 |
| 57 | 40.3 | 40.3 | 17 | 82.7 | 82.7 | 77 | 125.2 | 125.2 | 37 | 167.6 | 167.6 | 97 | 210.0 | 210.0 |
| 58 | 41.0 | 41.0 | 18 | 83.4 | 83.4 | 78 | 125.9 | 125.9 | 38 | 168.3 | 168.3 | 98 | 210.7 | 210.7 |
| 59 | 41.7 | 41.7 | 19 | 84.1 | 84.1 | 79 | 126.6 | 126.6 | 39 | 169.0 | 169.0 | 99 | 211.4 | 211.4 |
| 60 | 42.4 | 42.4 | 20 | 84.9 | 84.9 | 80 | 127.3 | 127.3 | 40 | 169.7 | 169.7 | 300 | 212.1 | 212.1 |
| Dist. | Dep. | Lat. | Dist. | Dep. | Lat. | Dist. | Dep. | Lat. | Dist. | Dep. | Lat. | Dist. | Dep. | Lat. |
| | N.E. | | | N.W. | | | S.E. | | | S.W. | | | [For 4 Points. | |

# TABLE II.

## Difference of Latitude and Departure for 1 Degree.

| Dist. | Lat. | Dep. | Dist. | Lat. | Dep. | Dist. | Lat. | Dep. | Dist. | Lat. | Dep. | Dist. | Lat. | Dep. |
|---|---|---|---|---|---|---|---|---|---|---|---|---|---|---|
| 1 | 01.0 | 00.0 | 61 | 61.0 | 01.1 | 121 | 121.0 | 02.1 | 181 | 181.0 | 03.2 | 241 | 241.0 | 04.2 |
| 2 | 02.0 | 00.0 | 62 | 62.0 | 01.1 | 22 | 122.0 | 02.1 | 82 | 182.0 | 03.2 | 42 | 242.0 | 04.2 |
| 3 | 03.0 | 00.1 | 63 | 63.0 | 01.1 | 23 | 123.0 | 02.1 | 83 | 183.0 | 03.2 | 43 | 243.0 | 04.2 |
| 4 | 04.0 | 00 1 | 64 | 64.0 | 01.1 | 24 | 124.0 | 02.2 | 84 | 184.0 | 03.2 | 44 | 244.0 | 04.3 |
| 5 | 05.0 | 00.1 | 65 | 65.0 | 01.1 | 25 | 125.0 | 02.2 | 85 | 185.0 | 03.2 | 45 | 245.0 | 04.3 |
| 6 | 06.0 | 00.1 | 66 | 66.0 | 01.2 | 26 | 126.0 | 02.2 | 86 | 186.0 | 03.2 | 46 | 246.0 | 04.3 |
| 7 | 07.0 | 00.1 | 67 | 67.0 | 01.2 | 27 | 127.0 | 02.2 | 87 | 187.0 | 03.3 | 47 | 247.0 | 04.3 |
| 8 | 08.0 | 00.1 | 68 | 68.0 | 01.2 | 28 | 128.0 | 02.2 | 88 | 188.0 | 03.3 | 48 | 248.0 | 04.3 |
| 9 | 09.0 | 00.2 | 69 | 69.0 | 01.2 | 29 | 129.0 | 02.3 | 89 | 189.0 | 03.3 | 49 | 249.0 | 04.3 |
| 10 | 10.0 | 00.2 | 70 | 70.0 | 01.2 | 30 | 130.0 | 02.3 | 90 | 190.0 | 03.3 | 50 | 250.0 | 04.4 |
| 11 | 11.0 | 00.2 | 71 | 71.0 | 01.2 | 131 | 131.0 | 02.3 | 191 | 191.0 | 03.3 | 251 | 251.0 | 04.4 |
| 12 | 12.0 | 00.2 | 72 | 72.0 | 01 3 | 32 | 132.0 | 02.3 | 92 | 192.0 | 03.4 | 52 | 252.0 | 04.4 |
| 13 | 13.0 | 00.2 | 73 | 73.0 | 01 3 | 33 | 133.0 | 02.3 | 93 | 193.0 | 03.4 | 53 | 253.0 | 04.4 |
| 14 | 14.0 | 00.2 | 74 | 74.0 | 01.3 | 34 | 134.0 | 02.3 | 94 | 194.0 | 03.4 | 54 | 254.0 | 04.4 |
| 15 | 15.0 | 00.3 | 75 | 75.0 | 01.3 | 35 | 135.0 | 02.4 | 95 | 195.0 | 03.4 | 55 | 255.0 | 04.5 |
| 16 | 16.0 | 00.3 | 76 | 76.0 | 01.3 | 36 | 136.0 | 02.4 | 96 | 196.0 | 03.4 | 56 | 256.0 | 04.5 |
| 17 | 17.0 | 00.3 | 77 | 77.0 | 01.3 | 37 | 137.0 | 02.4 | 97 | 197.0 | 03.4 | 57 | 257.0 | 04.5 |
| 18 | 18.0 | 00.3 | 78 | 78.0 | 01.4 | 38 | 138.0 | 02.4 | 98 | 198.0 | 03.5 | 58 | 258.0 | 04.5 |
| 19 | 19.0 | 00.3 | 79 | 79.0 | 01.4 | 39 | 139.0 | 02.4 | 99 | 199.0 | 03.5 | 59 | 259.0 | 04.5 |
| 20 | 20.0 | 00.3 | 80 | 80.0 | 01.4 | 40 | 140.0 | 02.4 | 200 | 200.0 | 03.5 | 60 | 260.0 | 04.5 |
| 21 | 21.0 | 00.4 | 81 | 81.0 | 01.4 | 141 | 141.0 | 02.5 | 201 | 201.0 | 03.5 | 261 | 261.0 | 04.6 |
| 22 | 22.0 | 00.4 | 82 | 82.0 | 01.4 | 42 | 142.0 | 02.5 | 02 | 202.0 | 03.5 | 62 | 262.0 | 04.6 |
| 23 | 23.0 | 00.4 | 83 | 83.0 | 01.4 | 43 | 143.0 | 02.5 | 03 | 203.0 | 03.5 | 63 | 263.0 | 04.6 |
| 24 | 24.0 | 00.4 | 84 | 84.0 | 01.5 | 44 | 144.0 | 02.5 | 04 | 204.0 | 03.6 | 64 | 264.0 | 04.6 |
| 25 | 25.0 | 00.4 | 85 | 85.0 | 01.5 | 45 | 145.0 | 02.5 | 05 | 205.0 | 03.6 | 65 | 265.0 | 04.6 |
| 26 | 26.0 | 00.5 | 86 | 86.0 | 01.5 | 46 | 146.0 | 02.5 | 06 | 206.0 | 03.6 | 66 | 266.0 | 04.6 |
| 27 | 27.0 | 00.5 | 87 | 87.0 | 01.5 | 47 | 147.0 | 02.6 | 07 | 207.0 | 03.6 | 67 | 267.0 | 04.7 |
| 28 | 28.0 | 00.5 | 88 | 88.0 | 01.5 | 48 | 148.0 | 02.6 | 08 | 208.0 | 03.6 | 68 | 268.0 | 04.7 |
| 29 | 29.0 | 00.5 | 89 | 89.0 | 01.6 | 49 | 149.0 | 02.6 | 09 | 209.0 | 03.6 | 69 | 269.0 | 04.7 |
| 30 | 30.0 | 00.5 | 90 | 90.0 | 01.6 | 50 | 150.0 | 02.6 | 10 | 210.0 | 03.7 | 70 | 270.0 | 04.7 |
| 31 | 31.0 | 00.5 | 91 | 91.0 | 01.6 | 151 | 151.0 | 02.6 | 211 | 211.0 | 03.7 | 271 | 271.0 | 04.7 |
| 32 | 32.0 | 00.6 | 92 | 92.0 | 01.6 | 52 | 152.0 | 02.7 | 12 | 212.0 | 03.7 | 72 | 272.0 | 04.7 |
| 33 | 33.0 | 00.6 | 93 | 93.0 | 01.6 | 53 | 153.0 | 02.7 | 13 | 213.0 | 03.7 | 73 | 273.0 | 04.8 |
| 34 | 34.0 | 00.6 | 94 | 94.0 | 01.6 | 54 | 154.0 | 02.7 | 14 | 214.0 | 03.7 | 74 | 274.0 | 04.8 |
| 35 | 35.0 | 00.6 | 95 | 95.0 | 01.7 | 55 | 155.0 | 02.7 | 15 | 215.0 | 03.8 | 75 | 275.0 | 04.8 |
| 36 | 36.0 | 00.6 | 96 | 96.0 | 01.7 | 56 | 156.0 | 02.7 | 16 | 216.0 | 03.8 | 76 | 276.0 | 04.8 |
| 37 | 37.0 | 00.6 | 97 | 97.0 | 01.7 | 57 | 157.0 | 02.7 | 17 | 217.0 | 03.8 | 77 | 277.0 | 04.8 |
| 38 | 38.0 | 00.7 | 98 | 98.0 | 01.7 | 58 | 158.0 | 02.8 | 18 | 218.0 | 03.8 | 78 | 278.0 | 04.9 |
| 39 | 39.0 | 00.7 | 99 | 99.0 | 01.7 | 59 | 159.0 | 02.8 | 19 | 219.0 | 03.8 | 79 | 279.0 | 04.9 |
| 40 | 40.0 | 00.7 | 100 | 100.0 | 01.7 | 60 | 160.0 | 02.8 | 20 | 220.0 | 03.8 | 80 | 280.0 | 04.9 |
| 41 | 41.0 | 00.7 | 101 | 101.0 | 01.8 | 161 | 161.0 | 02.8 | 221 | 221.0 | 03.9 | 281 | 281.0 | 04.9 |
| 42 | 42.0 | 00.7 | 02 | 102.0 | 01.8 | 62 | 162.0 | 02.8 | 22 | 222.0 | 03.9 | 82 | 282.0 | 04.9 |
| 43 | 43.0 | 00.8 | 03 | 103.0 | 01.8 | 63 | 163.0 | 02.8 | 23 | 223.0 | 03.9 | 83 | 283.0 | 04.9 |
| 44 | 44.0 | 00.8 | 04 | 104.0 | 01.8 | 64 | 164.0 | 02.9 | 24 | 224.0 | 03.9 | 84 | 284.0 | 05.0 |
| 45 | 45.0 | 00.8 | 05 | 105.0 | 01.8 | 65 | 165.0 | 02.9 | 25 | 225.0 | 03.9 | 85 | 285.0 | 05.0 |
| 46 | 46.0 | 00.8 | 06 | 106.0 | 01.8 | 66 | 166.0 | 02.9 | 26 | 226.0 | 03.9 | 86 | 286.0 | 05.0 |
| 47 | 47.0 | 00.8 | 07 | 107.0 | 01.9 | 67 | 167.0 | 02.9 | 27 | 227.0 | 04.0 | 87 | 287.0 | 05.0 |
| 48 | 48.0 | 00.8 | 08 | 108.0 | 01.9 | 68 | 168.0 | 02.9 | 28 | 228.0 | 04.0 | 88 | 288.0 | 05.0 |
| 49 | 49.0 | 00.9 | 09 | 109.0 | 01.9 | 69 | 169.0 | 02.9 | 29 | 229.0 | 04.0 | 89 | 289.0 | 05.0 |
| 50 | 50.0 | 00.9 | 10 | 110.0 | 01.9 | 70 | 170.0 | 03.0 | 30 | 230.0 | 04.0 | 90 | 290.0 | 05.1 |
| 51 | 51.0 | 00.9 | 111 | 111.0 | 01.9 | 171 | 171.0 | 03.0 | 231 | 231.0 | 04.0 | 291 | 291.0 | 05.1 |
| 52 | 52.0 | 00.9 | 12 | 112.0 | 02.0 | 72 | 172.0 | 03.0 | 32 | 232.0 | 04.0 | 92 | 292.0 | 05.1 |
| 53 | 53.0 | 00.9 | 13 | 113.0 | 02.0 | 73 | 173.0 | 03.0 | 33 | 233.0 | 04.1 | 93 | 293.0 | 05.1 |
| 54 | 54.0 | 00.9 | 14 | 114.0 | 02.0 | 74 | 174.0 | 03.0 | 34 | 234.0 | 04.1 | 94 | 294.0 | 05.1 |
| 55 | 55.0 | 01.0 | 15 | 115.0 | 02.0 | 75 | 175.0 | 03.1 | 35 | 235.0 | 04.1 | 95 | 295.0 | 05.1 |
| 56 | 56.0 | 01.0 | 16 | 116.0 | 02.0 | 76 | 176.0 | 03.1 | 36 | 236.0 | 04.1 | 96 | 296.0 | 05.2 |
| 57 | 57.0 | 01.0 | 17 | 117.0 | 02.0 | 77 | 177.0 | 03.1 | 37 | 237.0 | 04.1 | 97 | 297.0 | 05.2 |
| 58 | 58.0 | 01.0 | 18 | 118.0 | 02.1 | 78 | 178.0 | 03.1 | 38 | 238.0 | 04.2 | 98 | 298.0 | 05.2 |
| 59 | 59.0 | 01.0 | 19 | 119.0 | 02.1 | 79 | 179.0 | 03.1 | 39 | 239.0 | 04.2 | 99 | 299.0 | 05.2 |
| 60 | 60.0 | 01.0 | 20 | 120.0 | 02.1 | 80 | 180.0 | 03.1 | 40 | 240.0 | 04.2 | 300 | 300.0 | 05.2 |
| Dist. | Dep. | Lat. | Dist. | Dep. | Lat. | Dist. | Dep. | Lat. | Dist. | Dep. | Lat. | Dist. | Dep. | Lat. |

[For 89 Degrees.

# TABLE II.

## Difference of Latitude and Departure for 2 Degrees.

| Dist. | Lat. | Dep. | Dist. | Lat. | Dep. | Dist. | Lat. | Dep. | Dist. | Lat. | Dep. | Dist. | Lat. | Dep. |
|---|---|---|---|---|---|---|---|---|---|---|---|---|---|---|
| 1 | 01.0 | 00.0 | 61 | 61.0 | 02.1 | 121 | 120.9 | 04.2 | 181 | 180.9 | 06.3 | 241 | 240.9 | 08.4 |
| 2 | 02.0 | 00.1 | 62 | 62.0 | 02.2 | 22 | 121.9 | 04.3 | 82 | 181.9 | 06.4 | 42 | 241.9 | 08.4 |
| 3 | 03.0 | 00.1 | 63 | 63.0 | 02.2 | 23 | 122.9 | 04.3 | 83 | 182.9 | 06.4 | 43 | 242.9 | 08.5 |
| 4 | 04.0 | 00.1 | 64 | 64.0 | 02.2 | 24 | 123.9 | 04.3 | 84 | 183.9 | 06.4 | 44 | 243.9 | 08.5 |
| 5 | 05.0 | 00.2 | 65 | 65.0 | 02.3 | 25 | 124.9 | 04.4 | 85 | 184.9 | 06.5 | 45 | 244.9 | 08 6 |
| 6 | 06.0 | 00.2 | 66 | 66.0 | 02.3 | 26 | 125.9 | 04.4 | 86 | 185.9 | 06.5 | 46 | 245.9 | 08.6 |
| 7 | 07.0 | 00.2 | 67 | 67.0 | 02.3 | 27 | 126.9 | 04.4 | 87 | 186.9 | 06.5 | 47 | 246.8 | 08.6 |
| 8 | 08.0 | 00.3 | 68 | 68.0 | 02.4 | 28 | 127.9 | 04.5 | 88 | 187.9 | 06.6 | 48 | 247.8 | 08.7 |
| 9 | 09.0 | 00.3 | 69 | 69.0 | 02.4 | 29 | 128.9 | 04.5 | 89 | 188.9 | 06.6 | 49 | 248.8 | 08.7 |
| 10 | 10.0 | 00.3 | 70 | 70.0 | 02.4 | 30 | 129.9 | 04.5 | 90 | 189.9 | 06.6 | 50 | 249.8 | 08.7 |
| 11 | 11.0 | 00.4 | 71 | 71.0 | 02.5 | 131 | 130.9 | 04.6 | 191 | 190.9 | 06.7 | 251 | 250.8 | 08.8 |
| 12 | 12.0 | 00.4 | 72 | 72.0 | 02.5 | 32 | 131.9 | 04.6 | 92 | 191.9 | 06.7 | 52 | 251.8 | 08.8 |
| 13 | 13.0 | 00.5 | 73 | 73.0 | 02.5 | 33 | 132.9 | 04.6 | 93 | 192.9 | 06.7 | 53 | 252.8 | 08.8 |
| 14 | 14.0 | 00.5 | 74 | 74.0 | 02.6 | 34 | 133.9 | 04.7 | 94 | 193.9 | 06.8 | 54 | 253.8 | 08.9 |
| 15 | 15.0 | 00.5 | 75 | 75.0 | 02.6 | 35 | 134.9 | 04.7 | 95 | 194.9 | 06.8 | 55 | 254.8 | 08.9 |
| 16 | 16.0 | 00.6 | 76 | 76.0 | 02.7 | 36 | 135.9 | 04.7 | 96 | 195.9 | 06.8 | 56 | 255.8 | 08.9 |
| 17 | 17.0 | 00.6 | 77 | 77.0 | 02.7 | 37 | 136.9 | 04.8 | 97 | 196.9 | 06.9 | 57 | 256.8 | 09.0 |
| 18 | 18.0 | 00.6 | 78 | 78.0 | 02.7 | 38 | 137.9 | 04.8 | 98 | 197.9 | 06.9 | 58 | 257.8 | 09.0 |
| 19 | 19.0 | 00.7 | 79 | 79.0 | 02.8 | 39 | 138.9 | 04.9 | 99 | 198.9 | 06.9 | 59 | 258.8 | 09.0 |
| 20 | 20.0 | 00.7 | 80 | 80.0 | 02.8 | 40 | 139.9 | 04.9 | 200 | 199.9 | 07.0 | 60 | 259.8 | 09.1 |
| 21 | 21.0 | 00.7 | 81 | 81.0 | 02.8 | 141 | 140.9 | 04.9 | 201 | 200.9 | 07.0 | 261 | 260.8 | 09.1 |
| 22 | 22.0 | 00.8 | 82 | 82.0 | 02.9 | 42 | 141.9 | 05.0 | 02 | 201.9 | 07.0 | 62 | 261.8 | 09.1 |
| 23 | 23.0 | 00.8 | 83 | 82.9 | 02.9 | 43 | 142.9 | 05.0 | 03 | 202.9 | 07.1 | 63 | 262.8 | 09.2 |
| 24 | 24.0 | 00.8 | 84 | 83.9 | 02.9 | 44 | 143.9 | 05.0 | 04 | 203.9 | 07.1 | 64 | 263.8 | 09.2 |
| 25 | 25.0 | 00.9 | 85 | 84.9 | 03.0 | 45 | 144.9 | 05.1 | 05 | 204.9 | 07.2 | 65 | 264.8 | 09.2 |
| 26 | 26.0 | 00.9 | 86 | 85.9 | 03.0 | 46 | 145.9 | 05.1 | 06 | 205.9 | 07.2 | 66 | 265.8 | 09.3 |
| 27 | 27.0 | 00.9 | 87 | 86.9 | 03.0 | 47 | 146.9 | 05.1 | 07 | 206.9 | 07.2 | 67 | 266.8 | 09.3 |
| 28 | 28.0 | 01.0 | 88 | 87.9 | 03.1 | 48 | 147.9 | 05.2 | 08 | 207.9 | 07.3 | 68 | 267.8 | 09.4 |
| 29 | 29.0 | 01.0 | 89 | 88.9 | 03.1 | 49 | 148.9 | 05.2 | 09 | 208.9 | 07.3 | 69 | 268.8 | 09.4 |
| 30 | 30.0 | 01.0 | 90 | 89.9 | 03.1 | 50 | 149.9 | 05.2 | 10 | 209.9 | 07.3 | 70 | 269.8 | 09.4 |
| 31 | 31.0 | 01.1 | 91 | 90.9 | 03.2 | 151 | 150.9 | 05.3 | 211 | 210.9 | 07.4 | 271 | 270.8 | 09.5 |
| 32 | 32.0 | 01.1 | 92 | 91.9 | 03.2 | 52 | 151.9 | 05.3 | 12 | 211.9 | 07.4 | 72 | 271.8 | 09.5 |
| 33 | 33.0 | 01.2 | 93 | 92.9 | 03.2 | 53 | 152.9 | 05.3 | 13 | 212.9 | 07.4 | 73 | 272.8 | 09.5 |
| 34 | 34.0 | 01.2 | 94 | 93.9 | 03.3 | 54 | 153.9 | 05.4 | 14 | 213.9 | 07.5 | 74 | 273.8 | 09.6 |
| 35 | 35.0 | 01.2 | 95 | 94.9 | 03.3 | 55 | 154.9 | 05.4 | 15 | 214.9 | 07.5 | 75 | 274.8 | 09.6 |
| 36 | 36.0 | 01.3 | 96 | 95.9 | 03.4 | 56 | 155.9 | 05.4 | 16 | 215.9 | 07.5 | 76 | 275.8 | 09.6 |
| 37 | 37.0 | 01.3 | 97 | 96.9 | 03.4 | 57 | 156.9 | 05.5 | 17 | 216.9 | 07.6 | 77 | 276.8 | 09.7 |
| 38 | 38.0 | 01.3 | 98 | 97.9 | 03.4 | 58 | 157.9 | 05.5 | 18 | 217.9 | 07.6 | 78 | 277.8 | 09.7 |
| 39 | 39.0 | 01.4 | 99 | 98.9 | 03.5 | 59 | 158.9 | 05.5 | 19 | 218.9 | 07.6 | 79 | 278.8 | 09.7 |
| 40 | 40.0 | 01.4 | 100 | 99.9 | 03.5 | 60 | 159.9 | 05.6 | 20 | 219.9 | 07.7 | 80 | 279.8 | 09.8 |
| 41 | 41.0 | 01.4 | 101 | 100.9 | 03.5 | 161 | 160.9 | 05.6 | 221 | 220.9 | 07.7 | 281 | 280.8 | 09.8 |
| 42 | 42.0 | 01.5 | 02 | 101.9 | 03.6 | 62 | 161.9 | 05.7 | 22 | 221.9 | 07.7 | 82 | 281.8 | 09.8 |
| 43 | 43.0 | 01.5 | 03 | 102.9 | 03.6 | 63 | 162.9 | 05.7 | 23 | 222.9 | 07.8 | 83 | 282.8 | 09.9 |
| 44 | 44.0 | 01.5 | 04 | 103.9 | 03.6 | 64 | 163.9 | 05.7 | 24 | 223.9 | 07.8 | 84 | 283.8 | 09.9 |
| 45 | 45.0 | 01.6 | 05 | 104.9 | 03.7 | 65 | 164.9 | 05.8 | 25 | 224.9 | 07.9 | 85 | 284.8 | 09.9 |
| 46 | 46.0 | 01.6 | 06 | 105.9 | 03.7 | 66 | 165.9 | 05.8 | 26 | 225.9 | 07.9 | 86 | 285.8 | 10.0 |
| 47 | 47.0 | 01.6 | 07 | 106.9 | 03.7 | 67 | 166.9 | 05.8 | 27 | 226.9 | 07.9 | 87 | 286.8 | 10.0 |
| 48 | 48.0 | 01.7 | 08 | 107.9 | 03.8 | 68 | 167.9 | 05.9 | 28 | 227.9 | 08.0 | 88 | 287.8 | 10.1 |
| 49 | 49.0 | 01.7 | 09 | 108.9 | 03.8 | 69 | 168.9 | 05.9 | 29 | 228.9 | 08.0 | 89 | 288.8 | 10.1 |
| 50 | 50.0 | 01.7 | 10 | 109.9 | 03.8 | 70 | 169.9 | 05.9 | 30 | 229.9 | 08.0 | 90 | 289.8 | 10.1 |
| 51 | 51.0 | 01.8 | 111 | 110.9 | 03.9 | 171 | 170.9 | 06.0 | 231 | 230.9 | 08.1 | 291 | 290.8 | 10.2 |
| 52 | 52.0 | 01.8 | 12 | 111.9 | 03.9 | 72 | 171.9 | 06.0 | 32 | 231.9 | 08.1 | 92 | 291.8 | 10.2 |
| 53 | 53.0 | 01.8 | 13 | 112.9 | 03.9 | 73 | 172.9 | 06.0 | 33 | 232.9 | 08.1 | 93 | 292.8 | 10.2 |
| 54 | 54.0 | 01.9 | 14 | 113.9 | 04.0 | 74 | 173.9 | 06.1 | 34 | 233.9 | 08.2 | 94 | 293.8 | 10.3 |
| 55 | 55.0 | 01.9 | 15 | 114.9 | 04.0 | 75 | 174.9 | 06.1 | 35 | 234.9 | 08.2 | 95 | 294.8 | 10.3 |
| 56 | 56.0 | 02.0 | 16 | 115.9 | 04.0 | 76 | 175.9 | 06.1 | 36 | 235.9 | 08.2 | 96 | 295.8 | 10 3 |
| 57 | 57.0 | 02.0 | 17 | 116.9 | 04.1 | 77 | 176.9 | 06.2 | 37 | 236.9 | 08.3 | 97 | 296.8 | 10.4 |
| 58 | 58.0 | 02.0 | 18 | 117.9 | 04.1 | 78 | 177.9 | 06.2 | 38 | 237.9 | 08.3 | 98 | 297.8 | 10.4 |
| 59 | 59.0 | 02.1 | 19 | 118.9 | 04.2 | 79 | 178.9 | 06.2 | 39 | 238.9 | 08.3 | 99 | 298.8 | 10.4 |
| 60 | 60.0 | 02.1 | 20 | 119.9 | 04.2 | 80 | 179.9 | 06.3 | 40 | 239.9 | 08.4 | 300 | 299.8 | 10.5 |
| Dist. | Dep. | Lat. | Dist. | Dep. | Lat. | Dist. | Dep. | Lat. | Dist. | Dep. | Lat. | Dist. | Dep. | Lat. |

# TABLE II.

## Difference of Latitude and Departure for 3 Degrees.

| Dist. | Lat. | Dep. | Dist. | Lat. | Dep. | Dist. | Lat. | Dep. | Dist. | Lat. | Dep. | Dist. | Lat. | Dep. |
|---|---|---|---|---|---|---|---|---|---|---|---|---|---|---|
| 1 | 01.0 | 00.1 | 61 | 60.9 | 03.2 | 121 | 120.8 | 06.3 | 181 | 180.8 | 09.5 | 241 | 240.7 | 12.6 |
| 2 | 02.0 | 00.1 | 62 | 61.9 | 03.2 | 22 | 121.8 | 06.4 | 82 | 181.8 | 09.5 | 42 | 241.7 | 12.7 |
| 3 | 03.0 | 00.2 | 63 | 62.9 | 03.3 | 23 | 122.8 | 06.4 | 83 | 182.7 | 09.6 | 43 | 242.7 | 12.7 |
| 4 | 04.0 | 00 2 | 64 | 63.9 | 03.3 | 24 | 123.8 | 06.5 | 84 | 183.7 | 09.6 | 44 | 243.7 | 12.8 |
| 5 | 05.0 | 00.3 | 65 | 64.9 | 03.4 | 25 | 124.8 | 06.5 | 85 | 184.7 | 09.7 | 45 | 244.7 | 12.8 |
| 6 | 06.0 | 00.3 | 66 | 65.9 | 03.5 | 26 | 125.8 | 06.6 | 86 | 185.7 | 09.7 | 46 | 245.7 | 12.9 |
| 7 | 07.0 | 00.4 | 67 | 66.9 | 03.5 | 27 | 126.8 | 06.6 | 87 | 186.7 | 09.8 | 47 | 246.7 | 12.9 |
| 8 | 08.0 | 00.4 | 68 | 67.9 | 03.6 | 28 | 127.8 | 06.7 | 88 | 187.7 | 09.8 | 48 | 247.7 | 13.0 |
| 9 | 09.0 | 00.5 | 69 | 68.9 | 03.6 | 29 | 128.8 | 06.8 | 89 | 188.7 | 09.9 | 49 | 248.7 | 13.0 |
| 10 | 10.0 | 00.5 | 70 | 69.9 | 03.7 | 30 | 129.8 | 06.8 | 90 | 189.7 | 09.9 | 50 | 249.7 | 13.1 |
| 11 | 11.0 | 00.6 | 71 | 70.9 | 03.7 | 131 | 130.8 | 06.9 | 191 | 190.7 | 10.0 | 251 | 250.7 | 13.1 |
| 12 | 12.0 | 00.6 | 72 | 71.9 | 03.8 | 32 | 131.8 | 06.9 | 92 | 191.7 | 10.0 | 52 | 251.7 | 13.2 |
| 13 | 13.0 | 00.7 | 73 | 72.9 | 03.8 | 33 | 132.8 | 07.0 | 93 | 192.7 | 10.1 | 53 | 252.7 | 13.2 |
| 14 | 14.0 | 00.7 | 74 | 73.9 | 03.9 | 34 | 133.8 | 07.0 | 94 | 193.7 | 10.2 | 54 | 253.7 | 13.3 |
| 15 | 15.0 | 00.8 | 75 | 74.9 | 03.9 | 35 | 134.8 | 07.1 | 95 | 194.7 | 10.2 | 55 | 254.7 | 13.3 |
| 16 | 16.0 | 00.8 | 76 | 75.9 | 04.0 | 36 | 135.8 | 07.1 | 96 | 195.7 | 10.3 | 56 | 255.6 | 13.4 |
| 17 | 17.0 | 00.9 | 77 | 76.9 | 04.0 | 37 | 136.8 | 07.2 | 97 | 196.7 | 10.3 | 57 | 256.6 | 13.5 |
| 18 | 18.0 | 00.9 | 78 | 77.9 | 04.1 | 38 | 137.8 | 07.2 | 98 | 197.7 | 10.4 | 58 | 257.6 | 13.5 |
| 19 | 19.0 | 01.0 | 79 | 78.9 | 04.1 | 39 | 138.8 | 07.3 | 99 | 198.7 | 10.4 | 59 | 258.6 | 13.6 |
| 20 | 20.0 | 01.0 | 80 | 79.9 | 04.2 | 40 | 139.8 | 07.3 | 200 | 199.7 | 10.5 | 60 | 259.6 | 13.6 |
| 21 | 21.0 | 01.1 | 81 | 80.9 | 04.2 | 141 | 140.8 | 07.4 | 201 | 200.7 | 10.5 | 261 | 260.6 | 13.7 |
| 22 | 22.0 | 01.2 | 82 | 81.9 | 04.3 | 42 | 141.8 | 07.4 | 02 | 201.7 | 10.6 | 62 | 261.6 | 13.7 |
| 23 | 23.0 | 01.2 | 83 | 82.9 | 04.3 | 43 | 142.8 | 07.5 | 03 | 202.7 | 10.6 | 63 | 262.6 | 13.8 |
| 24 | 24.0 | 01.3 | 84 | 83.9 | 04.4 | 44 | 143.8 | 07.5 | 04 | 203.7 | 10.7 | 64 | 263.6 | 13.8 |
| 25 | 25.0 | 01.3 | 85 | 84.9 | 04.4 | 45 | 144.8 | 07.6 | 05 | 204.7 | 10.7 | 65 | 264.6 | 13.9 |
| 26 | 26.0 | 01.4 | 86 | 85.9 | 04.5 | 46 | 145.8 | 07.6 | 06 | 205.7 | 10.8 | 66 | 265.6 | 13.9 |
| 27 | 27.0 | 01.4 | 87 | 86.9 | 04.6 | 47 | 146.8 | 07.7 | 07 | 206.7 | 10.8 | 67 | 266.6 | 14.0 |
| 28 | 28.0 | 01.5 | 88 | 87.9 | 04.6 | 48 | 147.8 | 07.7 | 08 | 207.7 | 10.9 | 68 | 267.6 | 14.0 |
| 29 | 29.0 | 01.5 | 89 | 88.9 | 04.7 | 49 | 148.8 | 07.8 | 09 | 208.7 | 10.9 | 69 | 268.6 | 14.1 |
| 30 | 30.0 | 01.6 | 90 | 89.9 | 04.7 | 50 | 149.8 | 07.9 | 10 | 209.7 | 11.0 | 70 | 269.6 | 14.1 |
| 31 | 31.0 | 01.6 | 91 | 90.9 | 04.8 | 151 | 150.8 | 07.9 | 211 | 210.7 | 11.0 | 271 | 270.6 | 14.2 |
| 32 | 32.0 | 01.7 | 92 | 91.9 | 04.8 | 52 | 151.8 | 08.0 | 12 | 211.7 | 11.1 | 72 | 271.6 | 14.2 |
| 33 | 33.0 | 01.7 | 93 | 92.9 | 04.9 | 53 | 152.8 | 08.0 | 13 | 212.7 | 11.1 | 73 | 272.6 | 14.3 |
| 34 | 34.0 | 01.8 | 94 | 93.9 | 04.9 | 54 | 153.8 | 08.1 | 14 | 213.7 | 11.2 | 74 | 273.6 | 14.3 |
| 35 | 35.0 | 01.8 | 95 | 94.9 | 05.0 | 55 | 154.8 | 08.1 | 15 | 214.7 | 11.3 | 75 | 274.6 | 14.4 |
| 36 | 36.0 | 01.9 | 96 | 95.9 | 05.0 | 56 | 155.8 | 08.2 | 16 | 215.7 | 11.3 | 76 | 275.6 | 14.4 |
| 37 | 36.9 | 01.9 | 97 | 96.9 | 05.1 | 57 | 156.8 | 08.2 | 17 | 216.7 | 11.4 | 77 | 276.6 | 14.5 |
| 38 | 37.9 | 02.0 | 98 | 97.9 | 05.1 | 58 | 157.8 | 08.3 | 18 | 217.7 | 11.4 | 78 | 277.6 | 14.5 |
| 39 | 38.9 | 02.0 | 99 | 98.9 | 05.2 | 59 | 158.8 | 08.3 | 19 | 218.7 | 11.5 | 79 | 278.6 | 14.6 |
| 40 | 39.9 | 02.1 | 100 | 99.9 | 05.2 | 60 | 159.8 | 08.4 | 20 | 219.7 | 11.5 | 80 | 279.6 | 14.7 |
| 41 | 40.9 | 02.1 | 101 | 100.9 | 05.3 | 161 | 160.8 | 08.4 | 221 | 220.7 | 11.6 | 281 | 280.6 | 14.7 |
| 42 | 41.9 | 02.2 | 02 | 101.9 | 05.3 | 62 | 161.8 | 08.5 | 22 | 221.7 | 11.6 | 82 | 281.6 | 14.8 |
| 43 | 42.9 | 02.3 | 03 | 102.9 | 05.4 | 63 | 162.8 | 08.5 | 23 | 222.7 | 11.7 | 83 | 282.6 | 14.8 |
| 44 | 43.9 | 02.3 | 04 | 103.9 | 05.4 | 64 | 163.8 | 08.6 | 24 | 223.7 | 11.7 | 84 | 283.6 | 14.9 |
| 45 | 44.9 | 02.4 | 05 | 104.9 | 05.5 | 65 | 164.8 | 08.6 | 25 | 224.7 | 11.8 | 85 | 284.6 | 14.9 |
| 46 | 45.9 | 02.4 | 06 | 105.9 | 05.5 | 66 | 165.8 | 08.7 | 26 | 225.7 | 11.8 | 86 | 285.6 | 15.0 |
| 47 | 46.9 | 02.5 | 07 | 106.9 | 05.6 | 67 | 166.8 | 08.7 | 27 | 226.7 | 11.9 | 87 | 286.6 | 15.0 |
| 48 | 47.9 | 02.5 | 08 | 107.9 | 05.7 | 68 | 167.8 | 08.8 | 28 | 227.7 | 11.9 | 88 | 287.6 | 15.1 |
| 49 | 48.9 | 02.6 | 09 | 108.9 | 05.7 | 69 | 168.8 | 08.8 | 29 | 228.7 | 12.0 | 89 | 288.6 | 15.1 |
| 50 | 49.9 | 02.6 | 10 | 109.8 | 05.8 | 70 | 169.8 | 08.9 | 30 | 229.7 | 12.0 | 90 | 289.6 | 15.2 |
| 51 | 50.9 | 02.7 | 111 | 110.8 | 05.8 | 171 | 170.8 | 08.9 | 231 | 230.7 | 12.1 | 291 | 290.6 | 15.2 |
| 52 | 51.9 | 02.7 | 12 | 111.8 | 05.9 | 72 | 171.8 | 09.0 | 32 | 231.7 | 12.1 | 92 | 291.6 | 15.3 |
| 53 | 52.9 | 02.8 | 13 | 112.8 | 05.9 | 73 | 172.8 | 09.1 | 33 | 232.7 | 12.2 | 93 | 292.6 | 15.3 |
| 54 | 53.9 | 02.8 | 14 | 113.8 | 06.0 | 74 | 173.8 | 09.1 | 34 | 233.7 | 12.2 | 94 | 293.6 | 15.4 |
| 55 | 54.9 | 02.9 | 15 | 114.8 | 06.0 | 75 | 174.8 | 09.2 | 35 | 234.7 | 12.3 | 95 | 294.6 | 15.4 |
| 56 | 55.9 | 02.9 | 16 | 115.8 | 06.1 | 76 | 175.8 | 09.2 | 36 | 235.7 | 12.4 | 96 | 295.6 | 15.5 |
| 57 | 56.9 | 03.0 | 17 | 116.8 | 06.1 | 77 | 176.8 | 09.3 | 37 | 236.7 | 12.4 | 97 | 296.6 | 15.5 |
| 58 | 57.9 | 03.0 | 18 | 117.8 | 06.2 | 78 | 177.8 | 09.3 | 38 | 237.7 | 12.5 | 98 | 297.6 | 15.6 |
| 59 | 58.9 | 03.1 | 19 | 118.8 | 06.2 | 79 | 178.8 | 09.4 | 39 | 238.7 | 12.5 | 99 | 298.6 | 15.6 |
| 60 | 59.9 | 03.1 | 20 | 119.8 | 06.3 | 80 | 179.8 | 09.4 | 40 | 239.7 | 12.6 | 300 | 299.6 | 15.7 |
| Dist. | Dep. | Lat. | Dist. | Dep. | Lat. | Dist. | Dep. | Lat. | Dist. | Dep. | Lat. | Dist. | Dep. | Lat. |

# TABLE II.

## Difference of Latitude and Departure for 4 Degrees.

| Dist. | Lat. | Dep. | Dist. | Lat. | Dep. | Dist. | Lat. | Dep. | Dist. | Lat. | Dep. | Dist. | Lat. | Dep. |
|---|---|---|---|---|---|---|---|---|---|---|---|---|---|---|
| 1 | 01.0 | 00.1 | 61 | 60.9 | 04.3 | 121 | 120.7 | 08.4 | 181 | 180.6 | 12.6 | 241 | 240.4 | 16.8 |
| 2 | 02.0 | 00.1 | 62 | 61.8 | 04.3 | 22 | 121.7 | 08.5 | 82 | 181.6 | 12.7 | 42 | 241.4 | 16.9 |
| 3 | 03.0 | 00.2 | 63 | 62.8 | 04.4 | 23 | 122.7 | 08.6 | 83 | 182.6 | 12.8 | 43 | 242.4 | 17.0 |
| 4 | 04.0 | 00.3 | 64 | 63.8 | 04.5 | 24 | 123.7 | 08.6 | 84 | 183.6 | 12.8 | 44 | 243.4 | 17.0 |
| 5 | 05.0 | 00.3 | 65 | 64.8 | 04.5 | 25 | 124.7 | 08.7 | 85 | 184.5 | 12.9 | 45 | 244.4 | 17.1 |
| 6 | 06.0 | 00.4 | 66 | 65.8 | 04.6 | 26 | 125.7 | 08.8 | 86 | 185.5 | 13.0 | 46 | 245.4 | 17.2 |
| 7 | 07.0 | 00.5 | 67 | 66.8 | 04.7 | 27 | 126.7 | 08.9 | 87 | 186.5 | 13.0 | 47 | 246.4 | 17.2 |
| 8 | 08.0 | 00.6 | 68 | 67.8 | 04.7 | 28 | 127.7 | 08.9 | 88 | 187.5 | 13.1 | 48 | 247.4 | 17.3 |
| 9 | 09.0 | 00.6 | 69 | 68.8 | 04.8 | 29 | 128.7 | 09.0 | 89 | 188.5 | 13.2 | 49 | 248.4 | 17.4 |
| 10 | 10.0 | 00.7 | 70 | 69.8 | 04.9 | 30 | 129.7 | 09.1 | 90 | 189.5 | 13.3 | 50 | 249.4 | 17.4 |
| 11 | 11.0 | 00.8 | 71 | 70.8 | 05.0 | 131 | 130.7 | 09.1 | 191 | 190.5 | 13.3 | 251 | 250.4 | 17.5 |
| 12 | 12.0 | 00.8 | 72 | 71.8 | 05.0 | 32 | 131.7 | 09.2 | 92 | 191.5 | 13.4 | 52 | 251.4 | 17.6 |
| 13 | 13.0 | 00.9 | 73 | 72.8 | 05.1 | 33 | 132.7 | 09.3 | 93 | 192.5 | 13.5 | 53 | 252.4 | 17.6 |
| 14 | 14.0 | 01.0 | 74 | 73.8 | 05.2 | 34 | 133.7 | 09.3 | 94 | 193.5 | 13.5 | 54 | 253.4 | 17.7 |
| 15 | 15.0 | 01.0 | 75 | 74.8 | 05.2 | 35 | 134.7 | 09.4 | 95 | 194.5 | 13.6 | 55 | 254.4 | 17.8 |
| 16 | 16.0 | 01.1 | 76 | 75.8 | 05.3 | 36 | 135.7 | 09.5 | 96 | 195.5 | 13.7 | 56 | 255.4 | 17.9 |
| 17 | 17.0 | 01.2 | 77 | 76.8 | 05.4 | 37 | 136.7 | 09.6 | 97 | 196.5 | 13.7 | 57 | 256.4 | 17.9 |
| 18 | 18.0 | 01.3 | 78 | 77.8 | 05.4 | 38 | 137.7 | 09.6 | 98 | 197.5 | 13.8 | 58 | 257.4 | 18.0 |
| 19 | 19.0 | 01.3 | 79 | 78.8 | 05.5 | 39 | 138.7 | 09.7 | 99 | 198.5 | 13.9 | 59 | 258.4 | 18.1 |
| 20 | 20.0 | 01.4 | 80 | 79.8 | 05.6 | 40 | 139.7 | 09.8 | 200 | 199.5 | 14.0 | 60 | 259.4 | 18.1 |
| 21 | 20.9 | 01.5 | 81 | 80.8 | 05.7 | 141 | 140.7 | 09.8 | 201 | 200.5 | 14.0 | 261 | 260.4 | 18.2 |
| 22 | 21.9 | 01.5 | 82 | 81.8 | 05.7 | 42 | 141.7 | 09.9 | 02 | 201.5 | 14.1 | 62 | 261.4 | 18.3 |
| 23 | 22.9 | 01.6 | 83 | 82.8 | 05.8 | 43 | 142.7 | 10.0 | 03 | 202.5 | 14.2 | 63 | 262.4 | 18.3 |
| 24 | 23.9 | 01.7 | 84 | 83.8 | 05.9 | 44 | 143.6 | 10.0 | 04 | 203.5 | 14.2 | 64 | 263.4 | 18.4 |
| 25 | 24.9 | 01.7 | 85 | 84.8 | 05.9 | 45 | 144.6 | 10.1 | 05 | 204.5 | 14.3 | 65 | 264.4 | 18.5 |
| 26 | 25.9 | 01.8 | 86 | 85.8 | 06.0 | 46 | 145.6 | 10.2 | 06 | 205.5 | 14.4 | 66 | 265.4 | 18.6 |
| 27 | 26.9 | 01.9 | 87 | 86.8 | 06.1 | 47 | 146.6 | 10.3 | 07 | 206.5 | 14.4 | 67 | 266.3 | 18.6 |
| 28 | 27.9 | 02.0 | 88 | 87.8 | 06.1 | 48 | 147.6 | 10.3 | 08 | 207.5 | 14.5 | 68 | 267.3 | 18.7 |
| 29 | 28.9 | 02.0 | 89 | 88.8 | 06.2 | 49 | 148.6 | 10.4 | 09 | 208.5 | 14.6 | 69 | 268.3 | 18.8 |
| 30 | 29.9 | 02.1 | 90 | 89.8 | 06.3 | 50 | 149.6 | 10.5 | 10 | 209.5 | 14.6 | 70 | 269.3 | 18.8 |
| 31 | 30.9 | 02.2 | 91 | 90.8 | 06.3 | 151 | 150.6 | 10.5 | 211 | 210.5 | 14.7 | 271 | 270.3 | 18.9 |
| 32 | 31.9 | 02.2 | 92 | 91.8 | 06.4 | 52 | 151.6 | 10.6 | 12 | 211.5 | 14.8 | 72 | 271.3 | 19.0 |
| 33 | 32.9 | 02.3 | 93 | 92.8 | 06.5 | 53 | 152.6 | 10.7 | 13 | 212.5 | 14.9 | 73 | 272.3 | 19.0 |
| 34 | 33.9 | 02.4 | 94 | 93.8 | 06.6 | 54 | 153.6 | 10.7 | 14 | 213.5 | 14.9 | 74 | 273.3 | 19.1 |
| 35 | 34.9 | 02.4 | 95 | 94.8 | 06.6 | 55 | 154.6 | 10.8 | 15 | 214.5 | 15.0 | 75 | 274.3 | 19.2 |
| 36 | 35.9 | 02.5 | 96 | 95.8 | 06.7 | 56 | 155.6 | 10.9 | 16 | 215.5 | 15.1 | 76 | 275.3 | 19.3 |
| 37 | 36.9 | 02.6 | 97 | 96.8 | 06.8 | 57 | 156.6 | 11.0 | 17 | 216.5 | 15.1 | 77 | 276.3 | 19.3 |
| 38 | 37.9 | 02.7 | 98 | 97.8 | 06.8 | 58 | 157.6 | 11.0 | 18 | 217.5 | 15.2 | 78 | 277.3 | 19.4 |
| 39 | 38.9 | 02.7 | 99 | 98.8 | 06.9 | 59 | 158.6 | 11.1 | 19 | 218.5 | 15.3 | 79 | 278.3 | 19.5 |
| 40 | 39.9 | 02.8 | 100 | 99.8 | 07.0 | 60 | 159.6 | 11.2 | 20 | 219.5 | 15.3 | 80 | 279.3 | 19.5 |
| 41 | 40.9 | 02.9 | 101 | 100.8 | 07.0 | 161 | 160.6 | 11.2 | 221 | 220.5 | 15.4 | 281 | 280.3 | 19.6 |
| 42 | 41.9 | 02.9 | 02 | 101.8 | 07.1 | 62 | 161.6 | 11.3 | 22 | 221.5 | 15.5 | 82 | 281.3 | 19.7 |
| 43 | 42.9 | 03.0 | 03 | 102.7 | 07.2 | 63 | 162.6 | 11.4 | 23 | 222.5 | 15.6 | 83 | 282.3 | 19.7 |
| 44 | 43.9 | 03.1 | 04 | 103.7 | 07.3 | 64 | 163.6 | 11.4 | 24 | 223.5 | 15.6 | 84 | 283.3 | 19.8 |
| 45 | 44.9 | 03.1 | 05 | 104.7 | 07.3 | 65 | 164.6 | 11.5 | 25 | 224.5 | 15.7 | 85 | 284.3 | 19.9 |
| 46 | 45.9 | 03.2 | 06 | 105.7 | 07.4 | 66 | 165.6 | 11.6 | 26 | 225.4 | 15.8 | 86 | 285.3 | 20.0 |
| 47 | 46.9 | 03.3 | 07 | 106.7 | 07.5 | 67 | 166.6 | 11.6 | 27 | 226.4 | 15.8 | 87 | 286.3 | 20.0 |
| 48 | 47.9 | 03.3 | 08 | 107.7 | 07.5 | 68 | 167.6 | 11.7 | 28 | 227.4 | 15.9 | 88 | 287.3 | 20.1 |
| 49 | 48.9 | 03.4 | 09 | 108.7 | 07.6 | 69 | 168.6 | 11.8 | 29 | 228.4 | 16.0 | 89 | 288.3 | 20.2 |
| 50 | 49.9 | 03.5 | 10 | 109.7 | 07.7 | 70 | 169.6 | 11.9 | 30 | 229.4 | 16.0 | 90 | 289 3 | 20.2 |
| 51 | 50.9 | 03.6 | 111 | 110.7 | 07.7 | 171 | 170.6 | 11.9 | 231 | 230.4 | 16.1 | 291 | 290.3 | 20.3 |
| 52 | 51.9 | 03.6 | 12 | 111.7 | 07.8 | 72 | 171.6 | 12.0 | 32 | 231.4 | 16.2 | 92 | 291.3 | 20.4 |
| 53 | 52.9 | 03.7 | 13 | 112.7 | 07.9 | 73 | 172.6 | 12.1 | 33 | 232.4 | 16.3 | 93 | 292.3 | 20.4 |
| 54 | 53.9 | 03.8 | 14 | 113.7 | 08.0 | 74 | 173.6 | 12.1 | 34 | 233.4 | 16.3 | 94 | 293.3 | 20.5 |
| 55 | 54.9 | 03.8 | 15 | 114.7 | 08.0 | 75 | 174.6 | 12.2 | 35 | 234.4 | 16.4 | 95 | 294.3 | 20.6 |
| 56 | 55.9 | 03.9 | 16 | 115.7 | 08.1 | 76 | 175.6 | 12.3 | 36 | 235.4 | 16.5 | 96 | 295.3 | 20.6 |
| 57 | 56.9 | 04.0 | 17 | 116.7 | 08.2 | 77 | 176.6 | 12.3 | 37 | 236.4 | 16.5 | 97 | 296.3 | 20.7 |
| 58 | 57.9 | 04.0 | 18 | 117.7 | 08.2 | 78 | 177.6 | 12.4 | 38 | 237.4 | 16.6 | 98 | 297.3 | 20.8 |
| 59 | 58.9 | 04.1 | 19 | 118.7 | 08.3 | 79 | 178.6 | 12.5 | 39 | 238.4 | 16.7 | 99 | 298.3 | 20.9 |
| 60 | 59.9 | 04.2 | 20 | 119.7 | 08.4 | 80 | 179.6 | 12.6 | 40 | 239.4 | 16.7 | 300 | 299.3 | 20.9 |
| Dist. | Dep. | Lat. | Dist. | Dep. | Lat. | Dist. | Dep. | Lat. | Dist. | Dep. | Lat. | Dist. | Dep. | Lat. |

# TABLE II.

## Difference of Latitude and Departure for 5 Degrees.

| Dist. | Lat. | Dep. | Dist. | Lat. | Dep. | Dist. | Lat. | Dep. | Dist. | Lat. | Dep. | Dist. | Lat. | Dep. |
|---|---|---|---|---|---|---|---|---|---|---|---|---|---|---|
| 1 | 01.0 | 00.1 | 61 | 60.8 | 05.3 | 121 | 120.5 | 10.5 | 181 | 180.3 | 15.8 | 241 | 240.1 | 21.0 |
| 2 | 02.0 | 00.2 | 62 | 61.8 | 05.4 | 22 | 121.5 | 10.6 | 82 | 181.3 | 15.9 | 42 | 241.1 | 21.1 |
| 3 | 03.0 | 00.3 | 63 | 62.8 | 05.5 | 23 | 122.5 | 10.7 | 83 | 182.3 | 15.9 | 43 | 242.1 | 21.2 |
| 4 | 04.0 | 00.3 | 64 | 63.8 | 05.6 | 24 | 123.5 | 10.8 | 84 | 183.3 | 16.0 | 44 | 243.1 | 21.3 |
| 5 | 05.0 | 00.4 | 65 | 64.8 | 05.7 | 25 | 124.5 | 10.9 | 85 | 184.3 | 16.1 | 45 | 244.1 | 21.4 |
| 6 | 06.0 | 00.5 | 66 | 65.7 | 05.8 | 26 | 125.5 | 11.0 | 86 | 185.3 | 16.2 | 46 | 245.1 | 21.4 |
| 7 | 07.0 | 00.6 | 67 | 66.7 | 05.8 | 27 | 126.5 | 11.1 | 87 | 186.3 | 16.3 | 47 | 246.1 | 21.5 |
| 8 | 08.0 | 00.7 | 68 | 67.7 | 05.9 | 28 | 127.5 | 11.2 | 88 | 187.3 | 16.4 | 48 | 247.1 | 21.6 |
| 9 | 09.0 | 00.8 | 69 | 68.7 | 06.0 | 29 | 128.5 | 11.2 | 89 | 188.3 | 16.5 | 49 | 248.1 | 21.7 |
| 10 | 10.0 | 00.9 | 70 | 69.7 | 06.1 | 30 | 129.5 | 11.3 | 90 | 189.3 | 16.6 | 50 | 249.0 | 21.8 |
| 11 | 11.0 | 01.0 | 71 | 70.7 | 06.2 | 131 | 130.5 | 11.4 | 191 | 190.3 | 16.6 | 251 | 250.0 | 21.9 |
| 12 | 12.0 | 01.0 | 72 | 71.7 | 06.3 | 32 | 131.5 | 11.5 | 92 | 191.3 | 16.7 | 52 | 251.0 | 22.0 |
| 13 | 13.0 | 01.1 | 73 | 72.7 | 06.4 | 33 | 132.5 | 11.6 | 93 | 192.3 | 16.8 | 53 | 252.0 | 22.1 |
| 14 | 13.9 | 01.2 | 74 | 73.7 | 06.4 | 34 | 133.5 | 11.7 | 94 | 193.3 | 16.9 | 54 | 253.0 | 22.1 |
| 15 | 14.9 | 01.3 | 75 | 74.7 | 06.5 | 35 | 134.5 | 11.8 | 95 | 194.3 | 17.0 | 55 | 254.0 | 22.2 |
| 16 | 15.9 | 01.4 | 76 | 75.7 | 06.6 | 36 | 135.5 | 11.9 | 96 | 195.3 | 17.1 | 56 | 255.0 | 22.3 |
| 17 | 16.9 | 01.5 | 77 | 76.7 | 06.7 | 37 | 136.5 | 11.9 | 97 | 196.3 | 17.2 | 57 | 256.0 | 22.4 |
| 18 | 17.9 | 01.6 | 78 | 77.7 | 06.8 | 38 | 137.5 | 12.0 | 98 | 197.2 | 17.3 | 58 | 257.0 | 22.5 |
| 19 | 18.9 | 01.7 | 79 | 78.7 | 06.9 | 39 | 138.5 | 12.1 | 99 | 198.2 | 17.3 | 59 | 258.0 | 22.6 |
| 20 | 19.9 | 01.7 | 80 | 79.7 | 07.0 | 40 | 139.5 | 12.2 | 200 | 199.2 | 17.4 | 60 | 259.0 | 22.7 |
| 21 | 20.9 | 01.8 | 81 | 80.7 | 07.1 | 141 | 140.5 | 12.3 | 201 | 200.2 | 17.5 | 261 | 260.0 | 22.7 |
| 22 | 21.9 | 01.9 | 82 | 81.7 | 07.1 | 42 | 141.5 | 12.4 | 02 | 201.2 | 17.6 | 62 | 261.0 | 22.8 |
| 23 | 22.9 | 02.0 | 83 | 82.7 | 07.2 | 43 | 142.5 | 12.5 | 03 | 202.2 | 17.7 | 63 | 262.0 | 22.9 |
| 24 | 23.9 | 02.1 | 84 | 83.7 | 07.3 | 44 | 143.5 | 12.6 | 04 | 203.2 | 17.8 | 64 | 263.0 | 23.0 |
| 25 | 24.9 | 02.2 | 85 | 84.7 | 07.4 | 45 | 144.4 | 12.6 | 05 | 204.2 | 17.9 | 65 | 264.0 | 23.1 |
| 26 | 25.9 | 02.3 | 86 | 85.7 | 07.5 | 46 | 145.4 | 12.7 | 06 | 205.2 | 18.0 | 66 | 265.0 | 23.2 |
| 27 | 26.9 | 02.4 | 87 | 86.7 | 07.6 | 47 | 146.4 | 12.8 | 07 | 206.2 | 18.0 | 67 | 266.0 | 23.3 |
| 28 | 27.9 | 02.4 | 88 | 87.7 | 07.7 | 48 | 147.4 | 12.9 | 08 | 207.2 | 18.1 | 68 | 267.0 | 23.4 |
| 29 | 28.9 | 02.5 | 89 | 88.7 | 07.8 | 49 | 148.4 | 13.0 | 09 | 208.2 | 18.2 | 69 | 268.0 | 23.4 |
| 30 | 29.9 | 02.6 | 90 | 89.7 | 07.8 | 50 | 149.4 | 13.1 | 10 | 209.2 | 18.3 | 70 | 269.0 | 23.5 |
| 31 | 30.9 | 02.7 | 91 | 90.7 | 07.9 | 151 | 150.4 | 13.2 | 211 | 210.2 | 18.4 | 271 | 270.0 | 23.6 |
| 32 | 31.9 | 02.8 | 92 | 91.6 | 08.0 | 52 | 151.4 | 13.2 | 12 | 211.2 | 18.5 | 72 | 271.0 | 23.7 |
| 33 | 32.9 | 02.9 | 93 | 92.6 | 08.1 | 53 | 152.4 | 13.3 | 13 | 212.2 | 18.6 | 73 | 272.0 | 23.8 |
| 34 | 33.9 | 03.0 | 94 | 93.6 | 08.2 | 54 | 153.4 | 13.4 | 14 | 213.2 | 18.7 | 74 | 273.0 | 23.9 |
| 35 | 34.9 | 03.1 | 95 | 94.6 | 08.3 | 55 | 154.4 | 13.5 | 15 | 214.2 | 18.7 | 75 | 274.0 | 24.0 |
| 36 | 35.9 | 03.1 | 96 | 95.6 | 08.4 | 56 | 155.4 | 13.6 | 16 | 215.2 | 18.8 | 76 | 274.9 | 24.1 |
| 37 | 36.9 | 03.2 | 97 | 96.6 | 08.5 | 57 | 156.4 | 13.7 | 17 | 216.2 | 18.9 | 77 | 275.9 | 24.1 |
| 38 | 37.9 | 03.3 | 98 | 97.6 | 08.5 | 58 | 157.4 | 13.8 | 18 | 217.2 | 19.0 | 78 | 276.9 | 24.2 |
| 39 | 38.9 | 03.4 | 99 | 98.6 | 08.6 | 59 | 158.4 | 13.9 | 19 | 218.2 | 19.1 | 79 | 277.9 | 24.3 |
| 40 | 39.8 | 03.5 | 100 | 99.6 | 08.7 | 60 | 159.4 | 13.9 | 20 | 219.2 | 19.2 | 80 | 278.9 | 24.4 |
| 41 | 40.8 | 03.6 | 101 | 100.6 | 08.8 | 161 | 160.4 | 14.0 | 221 | 220.2 | 19.3 | 281 | 279.9 | 24.5 |
| 42 | 41.8 | 03.7 | 02 | 101.6 | 08.9 | 62 | 161.4 | 14.1 | 22 | 221.2 | 19.3 | 82 | 280.9 | 24.6 |
| 43 | 42.8 | 03.7 | 03 | 102.6 | 09.0 | 63 | 162.4 | 14.2 | 23 | 222.2 | 19.4 | 83 | 281.9 | 24.7 |
| 44 | 43.8 | 03.8 | 04 | 103.6 | 09.1 | 64 | 163.4 | 14.3 | 24 | 223.1 | 19.5 | 84 | 282.9 | 24.8 |
| 45 | 44.8 | 03.9 | 05 | 104.6 | 09.2 | 65 | 164.4 | 14.4 | 25 | 224.1 | 19.6 | 85 | 283.9 | 24.8 |
| 46 | 45.8 | 04.0 | 06 | 105.6 | 09.2 | 66 | 165.4 | 14.5 | 26 | 225.1 | 19.7 | 86 | 284.9 | 24.9 |
| 47 | 46.8 | 04.1 | 07 | 106.6 | 09.3 | 67 | 166.4 | 14.6 | 27 | 226.1 | 19.8 | 87 | 285.9 | 25.0 |
| 48 | 47.8 | 04.2 | 08 | 107.6 | 09.4 | 68 | 167.4 | 14.6 | 28 | 227.1 | 19.9 | 88 | 286.9 | 25.1 |
| 49 | 48.8 | 04.3 | 09 | 108.6 | 09.5 | 69 | 168.4 | 14.7 | 29 | 228.1 | 20.0 | 89 | 287.9 | 25.2 |
| 50 | 49.8 | 04.4 | 10 | 109.6 | 09.6 | 70 | 169.4 | 14.8 | 30 | 229.1 | 20.0 | 90 | 288.9 | 25.3 |
| 51 | 50.8 | 04.4 | 111 | 110.6 | 09.7 | 171 | 170.3 | 14.9 | 231 | 230.1 | 20.1 | 291 | 289.9 | 25.4 |
| 52 | 51.8 | 04.5 | 12 | 111.6 | 09.8 | 72 | 171.3 | 15.0 | 32 | 231.1 | 20.2 | 92 | 290.9 | 25.4 |
| 53 | 52.8 | 04.6 | 13 | 112.6 | 09.8 | 73 | 172.3 | 15.1 | 33 | 232.1 | 20.3 | 93 | 291.9 | 25.5 |
| 54 | 53.8 | 04.7 | 14 | 113.6 | 09.9 | 74 | 173.3 | 15.2 | 34 | 233.1 | 20.4 | 94 | 292.9 | 25.6 |
| 55 | 54.8 | 04.8 | 15 | 114.6 | 10.0 | 75 | 174.3 | 15.3 | 35 | 234.1 | 20.5 | 95 | 293.9 | 25.7 |
| 56 | 55.8 | 04.9 | 16 | 115.6 | 10.1 | 76 | 175.3 | 15.3 | 36 | 235.1 | 20.6 | 96 | 294.9 | 25.8 |
| 57 | 56.8 | 05.0 | 17 | 116.6 | 10.2 | 77 | 176.3 | 15.4 | 37 | 236.1 | 20.7 | 97 | 295.9 | 25.9 |
| 58 | 57.8 | 05.1 | 18 | 117.6 | 10.3 | 78 | 177.3 | 15.5 | 38 | 237.1 | 20.7 | 98 | 296.9 | 26.0 |
| 59 | 58.8 | 05.1 | 19 | 118.5 | 10.4 | 79 | 178.3 | 15.6 | 39 | 238.1 | 20.8 | 99 | 297.9 | 26.1 |
| 60 | 59.8 | 05.2 | 20 | 119.5 | 10.5 | 80 | 179.3 | 15.7 | 40 | 239.1 | 20.9 | 300 | 298.9 | 26.1 |
| Dist. | Dep. | Lat. | Dist. | Dep. | Lat. | Dist. | Dep. | Lat. | Dist. | Dep. | Lat. | Dist. | Dep. | Lat. |

[For 85 Degrees.

# TABLE II.

## Difference of Latitude and Departure for 6 Degrees.

| Dist. | Lat. | Dep. | Dist. | Lat. | Dep. | Dist. | Lat. | Dep. | Dist. | Lat. | Dep. | Dist. | Lat. | Dep. |
|---|---|---|---|---|---|---|---|---|---|---|---|---|---|---|
| 1 | 01.0 | 00.1 | 61 | 60.7 | 06.4 | 121 | 120.3 | 12.6 | 181 | 180.0 | 18.9 | 241 | 239.7 | 25.2 |
| 2 | 02.0 | 00.2 | 62 | 61.7 | 06.5 | 22 | 121.3 | 12.8 | 82 | 181.0 | 19.0 | 42 | 240.7 | 25.3 |
| 3 | 03.0 | 00.3 | 63 | 62.7 | 06.6 | 23 | 122.3 | 12.9 | 83 | 182.0 | 19.1 | 43 | 241.7 | 25.4 |
| 4 | 04.0 | 00.4 | 64 | 63.6 | 06.7 | 24 | 123.3 | 13.0 | 84 | 183.0 | 19.2 | 44 | 242.7 | 25.5 |
| 5 | 05.0 | 00.5 | 65 | 64.6 | 06.8 | 25 | 124.3 | 13.1 | 85 | 184.0 | 19.3 | 45 | 243.7 | 25.6 |
| 6 | 06.0 | 00.6 | 66 | 65.6 | 06.9 | 26 | 125.3 | 13.2 | 86 | 185.0 | 19.4 | 46 | 244.7 | 25.7 |
| 7 | 07.0 | 00.7 | 67 | 66.6 | 07.0 | 27 | 126.3 | 13.3 | 87 | 186.0 | 19.5 | 47 | 245.6 | 25.8 |
| 8 | 08.0 | 00.8 | 68 | 67.6 | 07.1 | 28 | 127.3 | 13.4 | 88 | 187.0 | 19.7 | 48 | 246.6 | 25.9 |
| 9 | 09.0 | 00.9 | 69 | 68.6 | 07.2 | 29 | 128.3 | 13.5 | 89 | 188.0 | 19.8 | 49 | 247.6 | 26.0 |
| 10 | 09.9 | 01.0 | 70 | 69.6 | 07.3 | 30 | 129.3 | 13.6 | 90 | 189.0 | 19.9 | 50 | 248.6 | 26.1 |
| 11 | 10.9 | 01.1 | 71 | 70.6 | 07.4 | 131 | 130.3 | 13.7 | 191 | 190.0 | 20.0 | 251 | 249.6 | 26.2 |
| 12 | 11.9 | 01.3 | 72 | 71.6 | 07.5 | 32 | 131.3 | 13.8 | 92 | 190.9 | 20.1 | 52 | 250.6 | 26.3 |
| 13 | 12.9 | 01.4 | 73 | 72.6 | 07.6 | 33 | 132.3 | 13.9 | 93 | 191.9 | 20.2 | 53 | 251.6 | 26.4 |
| 14 | 13.9 | 01.5 | 74 | 73.6 | 07.7 | 34 | 133.3 | 14.0 | 94 | 192.9 | 20.3 | 54 | 252.6 | 26.6 |
| 15 | 14.9 | 01.6 | 75 | 74.6 | 07.8 | 35 | 134.3 | 14.1 | 95 | 193.9 | 20.4 | 55 | 253.6 | 26.7 |
| 16 | 15.9 | 01.7 | 76 | 75.6 | 07.9 | 36 | 135.3 | 14.2 | 96 | 194.9 | 20.5 | 56 | 254.6 | 26.8 |
| 17 | 16.9 | 01.8 | 77 | 76.6 | 08.0 | 37 | 136.2 | 14.3 | 97 | 195.9 | 20.6 | 57 | 255.6 | 26.9 |
| 18 | 17.9 | 01.9 | 78 | 77.6 | 08.2 | 38 | 137.2 | 14.4 | 98 | 196.9 | 20.7 | 58 | 256.6 | 27.0 |
| 19 | 18.9 | 02.0 | 79 | 78.6 | 08.3 | 39 | 138.2 | 14.5 | 99 | 197.9 | 20.8 | 59 | 257.6 | 27.1 |
| 20 | 19.9 | 02.1 | 80 | 79.6 | 08.4 | 40 | 139.2 | 14.6 | 200 | 198.9 | 20.9 | 60 | 258.6 | 27.2 |
| 21 | 20.9 | 02.2 | 81 | 80.6 | 08.5 | 141 | 140.2 | 14.7 | 201 | 199.9 | 21.0 | 261 | 259.6 | 27.3 |
| 22 | 21.9 | 02.3 | 82 | 81.6 | 08.6 | 42 | 141.2 | 14.8 | 02 | 200.9 | 21.1 | 62 | 260.6 | 27.4 |
| 23 | 22.9 | 02.4 | 83 | 82.5 | 08.7 | 43 | 142.2 | 14.9 | 03 | 201.9 | 21.2 | 63 | 261.6 | 27.5 |
| 24 | 23.9 | 02.5 | 84 | 83.5 | 08.8 | 44 | 143.2 | 15.1 | 04 | 202.9 | 21.3 | 64 | 262.6 | 27.6 |
| 25 | 24.9 | 02.6 | 85 | 84.5 | 08.9 | 45 | 144.2 | 15.2 | 05 | 203.9 | 21.4 | 65 | 263.5 | 27.7 |
| 26 | 25.9 | 02.7 | 86 | 85.5 | 09.0 | 46 | 145.2 | 15.3 | 06 | 204.9 | 21.5 | 66 | 264.5 | 27.8 |
| 27 | 26.9 | 02.8 | 87 | 86.5 | 09.1 | 47 | 146.2 | 15.4 | 07 | 205.9 | 21.6 | 67 | 265.5 | 27.9 |
| 28 | 27.8 | 02.9 | 88 | 87.5 | 09.2 | 48 | 147.2 | 15.5 | 08 | 206.9 | 21.7 | 68 | 266.5 | 28.0 |
| 29 | 28.8 | 03.0 | 89 | 88.5 | 09.3 | 49 | 148.2 | 15.6 | 09 | 207.9 | 21.8 | 69 | 267.5 | 28.1 |
| 30 | 29.8 | 03.1 | 90 | 89.5 | 09.4 | 50 | 149.2 | 15.7 | 10 | 208.8 | 22.0 | 70 | 268.5 | 28.2 |
| 31 | 30.8 | 03.2 | 91 | 90.5 | 09.5 | 151 | 150.2 | 15.8 | 211 | 209.8 | 22.1 | 271 | 269.5 | 28.3 |
| 32 | 31.8 | 03.3 | 92 | 91.5 | 09.6 | 52 | 151.2 | 15.9 | 12 | 210.8 | 22.2 | 72 | 270.5 | 28.4 |
| 33 | 32.8 | 03.4 | 93 | 92.5 | 09.7 | 53 | 152.2 | 16.0 | 13 | 211.8 | 22.3 | 73 | 271.5 | 28.5 |
| 34 | 33.8 | 03.6 | 94 | 93.5 | 09.8 | 54 | 153.2 | 16.1 | 14 | 212.8 | 22.4 | 74 | 272.5 | 28.6 |
| 35 | 34.8 | 03.7 | 95 | 94.5 | 09.9 | 55 | 154.2 | 16.2 | 15 | 213.8 | 22.5 | 75 | 273.5 | 28.7 |
| 36 | 35.8 | 03.8 | 96 | 95.5 | 10.0 | 56 | 155.1 | 16.3 | 16 | 214.8 | 22.6 | 76 | 274.5 | 28.8 |
| 37 | 36.8 | 03.9 | 97 | 96.5 | 10.1 | 57 | 156.1 | 16.4 | 17 | 215.8 | 22.7 | 77 | 275.5 | 29.0 |
| 38 | 37.8 | 04.0 | 98 | 97.5 | 10.2 | 58 | 157.1 | 16.5 | 18 | 216.8 | 22.8 | 78 | 276.5 | 29.1 |
| 39 | 38.8 | 04.1 | 99 | 98.5 | 10.3 | 59 | 158.1 | 16.6 | 19 | 217.8 | 22.9 | 79 | 277.5 | 29.2 |
| 40 | 39.8 | 04.2 | 100 | 99.5 | 10.5 | 60 | 159.1 | 16.7 | 20 | 218.8 | 23.0 | 80 | 278.5 | 29.3 |
| 41 | 40.8 | 04.3 | 101 | 100.4 | 10.6 | 161 | 160.1 | 16.8 | 221 | 219.8 | 23.1 | 281 | 279.5 | 29.4 |
| 42 | 41.8 | 04.4 | 02 | 101.4 | 10.7 | 62 | 161.1 | 16.9 | 22 | 220.8 | 23.2 | 82 | 280.5 | 29.5 |
| 43 | 42.8 | 04.5 | 03 | 102.4 | 10.8 | 63 | 162.1 | 17.0 | 23 | 221.8 | 23.3 | 83 | 281.4 | 29.6 |
| 44 | 43.8 | 04.6 | 04 | 103.4 | 10.9 | 64 | 163.1 | 17.1 | 24 | 222.8 | 23.4 | 84 | 282.4 | 29.7 |
| 45 | 44.8 | 04.7 | 05 | 104.4 | 11.0 | 65 | 164.1 | 17.2 | 25 | 223.8 | 23.5 | 85 | 283.4 | 29.8 |
| 46 | 45.7 | 04.8 | 06 | 105.4 | 11.1 | 66 | 165.1 | 17.4 | 26 | 224.8 | 23.6 | 86 | 284.4 | 29.9 |
| 47 | 46.7 | 04.9 | 07 | 106.4 | 11.2 | 67 | 166.1 | 17.5 | 27 | 225.8 | 23.7 | 87 | 285.4 | 30.0 |
| 48 | 47.7 | 05.0 | 08 | 107.4 | 11.3 | 68 | 167.1 | 17.6 | 28 | 226.8 | 23.8 | 88 | 286.4 | 30.1 |
| 49 | 48.7 | 05.1 | 09 | 108.4 | 11.4 | 69 | 168.1 | 17.7 | 29 | 227.7 | 23.9 | 89 | 287.4 | 30.2 |
| 50 | 49.7 | 05.2 | 10 | 109.4 | 11.5 | 70 | 169.1 | 17.8 | 30 | 228.7 | 24.0 | 90 | 288.4 | 30.3 |
| 51 | 50.7 | 05.3 | 111 | 110.4 | 11.6 | 171 | 170.1 | 17.9 | 231 | 229.7 | 24.1 | 291 | 289.4 | 30.4 |
| 52 | 51.7 | 05.4 | 12 | 111.4 | 11.7 | 72 | 171.1 | 18.0 | 32 | 230.7 | 24.3 | 92 | 290.4 | 30.5 |
| 53 | 52.7 | 05.5 | 13 | 112.4 | 11.8 | 73 | 172.1 | 18.1 | 33 | 231.7 | 24.4 | 93 | 291.4 | 30.6 |
| 54 | 53.7 | 05.6 | 14 | 113.4 | 11.9 | 74 | 173.0 | 18.2 | 34 | 232.7 | 24.5 | 94 | 292.4 | 30.7 |
| 55 | 54.7 | 05.7 | 15 | 114.4 | 12.0 | 75 | 174.0 | 18.3 | 35 | 233.7 | 24.6 | 95 | 293.4 | 30.8 |
| 56 | 55.7 | 05.9 | 16 | 115.4 | 12.1 | 76 | 175.0 | 18.4 | 36 | 234.7 | 24.7 | 96 | 294.4 | 30.9 |
| 57 | 56.7 | 06.0 | 17 | 116.4 | 12.2 | 77 | 176.0 | 18.5 | 37 | 235.7 | 24.8 | 97 | 295.4 | 31.0 |
| 58 | 57.7 | 06.1 | 18 | 117.4 | 12.3 | 78 | 177.0 | 18.6 | 38 | 236.7 | 24.9 | 98 | 296.4 | 31.1 |
| 59 | 58.7 | 06.2 | 19 | 118.3 | 12.4 | 79 | 178.0 | 18.7 | 39 | 237.7 | 25.0 | 99 | 297.4 | 31.3 |
| 60 | 59.7 | 06.3 | 20 | 119.3 | 12.5 | 80 | 179.0 | 18.8 | 40 | 238.7 | 25.1 | 300 | 298.4 | 31.4 |
| Dist. | Dep. | Lat. | Dist. | Dep. | Lat. | Dist. | Dep. | Lat. | Dist. | Dep. | Lat. | Dist. | Dep. | Lat. |

[For 84 Degrees.

# TABLE II.

## Difference of Latitude and Departure for 7 Degrees.

| Dist. | Lat. | Dep. | Dist. | Lat. | Dep. | Dist. | Lat. | Dep. | Dist. | Lat. | Dep. | Dist. | Lat. | Dep. |
|---|---|---|---|---|---|---|---|---|---|---|---|---|---|---|
| 1 | 01.0 | 00.1 | 61 | 60.5 | 07.4 | 121 | 120.1 | 14.7 | 181 | 179.7 | 22.1 | 241 | 239.2 | 29.4 |
| 2 | 02.0 | 00.2 | 62 | 61.5 | 07.6 | 22 | 121.1 | 14.9 | 82 | 180.6 | 22.2 | 42 | 240.2 | 29.5 |
| 3 | 03.0 | 00.4 | 63 | 62.5 | 07.7 | 23 | 122.1 | 15.0 | 83 | 181.6 | 22.3 | 43 | 241.2 | 29.6 |
| 4 | 04.0 | 00.5 | 64 | 63.5 | 07.8 | 24 | 123.1 | 15.1 | 84 | 182.6 | 22.4 | 44 | 242.2 | 29.7 |
| 5 | 05.0 | 00.6 | 65 | 64.5 | 07.9 | 25 | 124.1 | 15.2 | 85 | 183.6 | 22.5 | 45 | 243.2 | 29.9 |
| 6 | 06.0 | 00.7 | 66 | 65.5 | 08.0 | 26 | 125.1 | 15.4 | 86 | 184.6 | 22.7 | 46 | 244.2 | 30.0 |
| 7 | 06.9 | 00.9 | 67 | 66.5 | 08.2 | 27 | 126.1 | 15.5 | 87 | 185.6 | 22.8 | 47 | 245.2 | 30.1 |
| 8 | 07.9 | 01.0 | 68 | 67.5 | 08.3 | 28 | 127.0 | 15.6 | 88 | 186.6 | 22.9 | 48 | 246.2 | 30.2 |
| 9 | 08.9 | 01.1 | 69 | 68.5 | 08.4 | 29 | 128.0 | 15.7 | 89 | 187.6 | 23.0 | 49 | 247.1 | 30.3 |
| 10 | 09.9 | 01.2 | 70 | 69.5 | 08.5 | 30 | 129.0 | 15.8 | 90 | 188.6 | 23.2 | 50 | 248.1 | 30.5 |
| 11 | 10.9 | 01.3 | 71 | 70.5 | 08.7 | 131 | 130.0 | 16.0 | 191 | 189.6 | 23.3 | 251 | 249.1 | 30.6 |
| 12 | 11.9 | 01.5 | 72 | 71.5 | 08.8 | 32 | 131.0 | 16.1 | 92 | 190.6 | 23.4 | 52 | 250.1 | 30.7 |
| 13 | 12.9 | 01.6 | 73 | 72.5 | 08.9 | 33 | 132.0 | 16.2 | 93 | 191.6 | 23.5 | 53 | 251.1 | 30.8 |
| 14 | 13.9 | 01.7 | 74 | 73.4 | 09.0 | 34 | 133.0 | 16.3 | 94 | 192.6 | 23.6 | 54 | 252.1 | 31.0 |
| 15 | 14.9 | 01.8 | 75 | 74.4 | 09.1 | 35 | 134.0 | 16.5 | 95 | 193.5 | 23.8 | 55 | 253.1 | 31.1 |
| 16 | 15.9 | 01.9 | 76 | 75.4 | 09.3 | 36 | 135.0 | 16.6 | 96 | 194.5 | 23.9 | 56 | 254.1 | 31.2 |
| 17 | 16.9 | 02.1 | 77 | 76.4 | 09.4 | 37 | 136.0 | 16.7 | 97 | 195.5 | 24.0 | 57 | 255.1 | 31.3 |
| 18 | 17.9 | 02.2 | 78 | 77.4 | 09.5 | 38 | 137.0 | 16.8 | 98 | 196.5 | 24.1 | 58 | 256.1 | 31.4 |
| 19 | 18.9 | 02.3 | 79 | 78.4 | 09.6 | 39 | 138.0 | 16.9 | 99 | 197.5 | 24.3 | 59 | 257.1 | 31.6 |
| 20 | 19.9 | 02.4 | 80 | 79.4 | 09.7 | 40 | 139.0 | 17.1 | 200 | 198.5 | 24.4 | 60 | 258.1 | 31.7 |
| 21 | 20.8 | 02.6 | 81 | 80.4 | 09.9 | 141 | 139.9 | 17.2 | 201 | 199.5 | 24.5 | 261 | 259.1 | 31.8 |
| 22 | 21.8 | 02.7 | 82 | 81.4 | 10.0 | 42 | 140.9 | 17.3 | 02 | 200.5 | 24.6 | 62 | 260.0 | 31.9 |
| 23 | 22.8 | 02.8 | 83 | 82.4 | 10.1 | 43 | 141.9 | 17.4 | 03 | 201.5 | 24.7 | 63 | 261.0 | 32.1 |
| 24 | 23.8 | 02.9 | 84 | 83.4 | 10.2 | 44 | 142.9 | 17.5 | 04 | 202.5 | 24.9 | 64 | 262.0 | 32.2 |
| 25 | 24.8 | 03.0 | 85 | 84.4 | 10.4 | 45 | 143.9 | 17.7 | 05 | 203.5 | 25.0 | 65 | 263.0 | 32.3 |
| 26 | 25.8 | 03.2 | 86 | 85.4 | 10.5 | 46 | 144.9 | 17.8 | 06 | 204.5 | 25.1 | 66 | 264.0 | 32.4 |
| 27 | 26.8 | 03.3 | 87 | 86.4 | 10.6 | 47 | 145.9 | 17.9 | 07 | 205.5 | 25.2 | 67 | 265.0 | 32.5 |
| 28 | 27.8 | 03.4 | 88 | 87.3 | 10.7 | 48 | 146.9 | 18.0 | 08 | 206.4 | 25.3 | 68 | 266.0 | 32.7 |
| 29 | 28.8 | 03.5 | 89 | 88.3 | 10.8 | 49 | 147.9 | 18.2 | 09 | 207.4 | 25.5 | 69 | 267.0 | 32.8 |
| 30 | 29.8 | 03.7 | 90 | 89.3 | 11.0 | 50 | 148.9 | 18.3 | 10 | 208.4 | 25.6 | 70 | 268.0 | 32.9 |
| 31 | 30.8 | 03.8 | 91 | 90.3 | 11.1 | 151 | 149.9 | 18.4 | 211 | 209.4 | 25.7 | 271 | 269.0 | 33.0 |
| 32 | 31.8 | 03.9 | 92 | 91.3 | 11.2 | 52 | 150.9 | 18.5 | 12 | 210.4 | 25.8 | 72 | 270.0 | 33.1 |
| 33 | 32.8 | 04.0 | 93 | 92.3 | 11.3 | 53 | 151.9 | 18.6 | 13 | 211.4 | 26.0 | 73 | 271.0 | 33.3 |
| 34 | 33.7 | 04.1 | 94 | 93.3 | 11.5 | 54 | 152.9 | 18.8 | 14 | 212.4 | 26.1 | 74 | 272.0 | 33.4 |
| 35 | 34.7 | 04.3 | 95 | 94.3 | 11.6 | 55 | 153.8 | 18.9 | 15 | 213.4 | 26.2 | 75 | 273.0 | 33.5 |
| 36 | 35.7 | 04.4 | 96 | 95.3 | 11.7 | 56 | 154.8 | 19.0 | 16 | 214.4 | 26.3 | 76 | 273.9 | 33.6 |
| 37 | 36.7 | 04.5 | 97 | 96.3 | 11.8 | 57 | 155.8 | 19.1 | 17 | 215.4 | 26.4 | 77 | 274.9 | 33.8 |
| 38 | 37.7 | 04.6 | 98 | 97.3 | 11.9 | 58 | 156.8 | 19.3 | 18 | 216.4 | 26.6 | 78 | 275.9 | 33.9 |
| 39 | 38.7 | 04.8 | 99 | 98.3 | 12.1 | 59 | 157.8 | 19.4 | 19 | 217.4 | 26.7 | 79 | 276.9 | 34.0 |
| 40 | 39.7 | 04.9 | 100 | 99.3 | 12.2 | 60 | 158.8 | 19.5 | 20 | 218.4 | 26.8 | 80 | 277.9 | 34.1 |
| 41 | 40.7 | 05.0 | 101 | 100.2 | 12.3 | 161 | 159.8 | 19.6 | 221 | 219.4 | 26.9 | 281 | 278.9 | 34.2 |
| 42 | 41.7 | 05.1 | 02 | 101.2 | 12.4 | 62 | 160.8 | 19.7 | 22 | 220.3 | 27.1 | 82 | 279.9 | 34.4 |
| 43 | 42.7 | 05.2 | 03 | 102.2 | 12.6 | 63 | 161.8 | 19.9 | 23 | 221.3 | 27.2 | 83 | 280.9 | 34.5 |
| 44 | 43.7 | 05.4 | 04 | 103.2 | 12.7 | 64 | 162.8 | 20.0 | 24 | 222.3 | 27.3 | 84 | 281.9 | 34.6 |
| 45 | 44.7 | 05.5 | 05 | 104.2 | 12.8 | 65 | 163.8 | 20.1 | 25 | 223.3 | 27.4 | 85 | 282.9 | 34.7 |
| 46 | 45.7 | 05.6 | 06 | 105.2 | 12.9 | 66 | 164.8 | 20.2 | 26 | 224.3 | 27.5 | 86 | 283.9 | 34.9 |
| 47 | 46.6 | 05.7 | 07 | 106.2 | 13.0 | 67 | 165.8 | 20.4 | 27 | 225.3 | 27.7 | 87 | 284.9 | 35.0 |
| 48 | 47.6 | 05.8 | 08 | 107.2 | 13.2 | 68 | 166.7 | 20.5 | 28 | 226.3 | 27.8 | 88 | 285.9 | 35.1 |
| 49 | 48.6 | 06.0 | 09 | 108.2 | 13.3 | 69 | 167.7 | 20.6 | 29 | 227.3 | 27.9 | 89 | 286.8 | 35.2 |
| 50 | 49.6 | 06.1 | 10 | 109.2 | 13.4 | 70 | 168.7 | 20.7 | 30 | 228.3 | 28.0 | 90 | 287.8 | 35.3 |
| 51 | 50.6 | 06.2 | 111 | 110.2 | 13.5 | 171 | 169.7 | 20.8 | 231 | 229.3 | 28.2 | 291 | 288.8 | 35.5 |
| 52 | 51.6 | 06.3 | 12 | 111.2 | 13.6 | 72 | 170.7 | 21.0 | 32 | 230.3 | 28.3 | 92 | 289.8 | 35.6 |
| 53 | 52.6 | 06.5 | 13 | 112.2 | 13.8 | 73 | 171.7 | 21.1 | 33 | 231.3 | 28.4 | 93 | 290.8 | 35.7 |
| 54 | 53.6 | 06.6 | 14 | 113.2 | 13.9 | 74 | 172.7 | 21.2 | 34 | 232.3 | 28.5 | 94 | 291.8 | 35.8 |
| 55 | 54.6 | 06.7 | 15 | 114.1 | 14.0 | 75 | 173.7 | 21.3 | 35 | 233.2 | 28.6 | 95 | 292.8 | 36.0 |
| 56 | 55.6 | 06.8 | 16 | 115.1 | 14.1 | 76 | 174.7 | 21.4 | 36 | 234.2 | 28.8 | 96 | 293.8 | 36.1 |
| 57 | 56.6 | 06.9 | 17 | 116.1 | 14.3 | 77 | 175.7 | 21.6 | 37 | 235.2 | 28.9 | 97 | 294.8 | 36.2 |
| 58 | 57.6 | 07.1 | 18 | 117.1 | 14.4 | 78 | 176.7 | 21.7 | 38 | 236.2 | 29.0 | 98 | 295.8 | 36.3 |
| 59 | 58.6 | 07.2 | 19 | 118.1 | 14.5 | 79 | 177.7 | 21.8 | 39 | 237.2 | 29.1 | 99 | 296.8 | 36.4 |
| 60 | 59.6 | 07.3 | 20 | 119.1 | 14.6 | 80 | 178.7 | 21.9 | 40 | 238.2 | 29.2 | 300 | 297.8 | 36.6 |
| Dist. | Dep. | Lat. | Dist. | Dep. | Lat. | Dist. | Dep. | Lat. | Dist. | Dep. | Lat. | Dist. | Dep. | Lat. |

[For 83 Degrees.

# TABLE II.

## Difference of Latitude and Departure for 8 Degrees.

| Dist. | Lat. | Dep. | Dist. | Lat. | Dep. | Dist. | Lat. | Dep. | Dist. | Lat. | Dep. | Dist. | Lat. | Dep. |
|---|---|---|---|---|---|---|---|---|---|---|---|---|---|---|
| 1 | 01.0 | 00.1 | 61 | 60.4 | 08.5 | 121 | 119.8 | 16.8 | 181 | 179.2 | 25.2 | 241 | 238.7 | 33.5 |
| 2 | 02.0 | 00.3 | 62 | 61.4 | 08.6 | 22 | 120.8 | 17.0 | 82 | 180.2 | 25.3 | 42 | 239.6 | 33.7 |
| 3 | 03.0 | 00.4 | 63 | 62.4 | 08.8 | 23 | 121.8 | 17.1 | 83 | 181.2 | 25.5 | 43 | 240.6 | 33.8 |
| 4 | 04.0 | 00.6 | 64 | 63.4 | 08.9 | 24 | 122.8 | 17.3 | 84 | 182.2 | 25.6 | 44 | 241.6 | 34.0 |
| 5 | 05.0 | 00.7 | 65 | 64.4 | 09.0 | 25 | 123.8 | 17.4 | 85 | 183.2 | 25.7 | 45 | 242.6 | 34.1 |
| 6 | 05.9 | 00.8 | 66 | 65.4 | 09.2 | 26 | 124.8 | 17.5 | 86 | 184.2 | 25.9 | 46 | 243.6 | 34.2 |
| 7 | 06.9 | 01.0 | 67 | 66.3 | 09.3 | 27 | 125.8 | 17.7 | 87 | 185.2 | 26.0 | 47 | 244.6 | 34.4 |
| 8 | 07.9 | 01.1 | 68 | 67.3 | 09.5 | 28 | 126.8 | 17.8 | 88 | 186.2 | 26.2 | 48 | 245.6 | 34.5 |
| 9 | 08.9 | 01.3 | 69 | 68.3 | 09.6 | 29 | 127.7 | 18.0 | 89 | 187.2 | 26.3 | 49 | 246.6 | 34.7 |
| 10 | 09.9 | 01.4 | 70 | 69.3 | 09.7 | 30 | 128.7 | 18.1 | 90 | 188.2 | 26.4 | 50 | 247.6 | 34.8 |
| 11 | 10.9 | 01.5 | 71 | 70.3 | 09.9 | 131 | 129.7 | 18.2 | 191 | 189.1 | 26.6 | 251 | 248.6 | 34.9 |
| 12 | 11.9 | 01.7 | 72 | 71.3 | 10.0 | 32 | 130.7 | 18.4 | 92 | 190.1 | 26.7 | 52 | 249.5 | 35.1 |
| 13 | 12.9 | 01.8 | 73 | 72.3 | 10.2 | 33 | 131.7 | 18.5 | 93 | 191.1 | 26.9 | 53 | 250.5 | 35.2 |
| 14 | 13.9 | 01.9 | 74 | 73.3 | 10.3 | 34 | 132.7 | 18.6 | 94 | 192.1 | 27.0 | 54 | 251.5 | 35.3 |
| 15 | 14.9 | 02.1 | 75 | 74.3 | 10.4 | 35 | 133.7 | 18.8 | 95 | 193.1 | 27.1 | 55 | 252.5 | 35.5 |
| 16 | 15.8 | 02.2 | 76 | 75.3 | 10.6 | 36 | 134.7 | 18.9 | 96 | 194.1 | 27.3 | 56 | 253.5 | 35.6 |
| 17 | 16.8 | 02.4 | 77 | 76.3 | 10.7 | 37 | 135.7 | 19.1 | 97 | 195.1 | 27.4 | 57 | 254.5 | 35.8 |
| 18 | 17.8 | 02.5 | 78 | 77.2 | 10.9 | 38 | 136.7 | 19.2 | 98 | 196.1 | 27.6 | 58 | 255.5 | 35.9 |
| 19 | 18.8 | 02.6 | 79 | 78.2 | 11.0 | 39 | 137.7 | 19.3 | 99 | 197.1 | 27.7 | 59 | 256.5 | 36.0 |
| 20 | 19.8 | 02.8 | 80 | 79.2 | 11.1 | 40 | 138.6 | 19.5 | 200 | 198.1 | 27.8 | 60 | 257.5 | 36.2 |
| 21 | 20.8 | 02.9 | 81 | 80.2 | 11.3 | 141 | 139.6 | 19.6 | 201 | 199.0 | 28.0 | 261 | 258.5 | 36.3 |
| 22 | 21.8 | 03.1 | 82 | 81.2 | 11.4 | 42 | 140.6 | 19.8 | 02 | 200.0 | 28 1 | 62 | 259.5 | 36.5 |
| 23 | 22.8 | 03.2 | 83 | 82.2 | 11.6 | 43 | 141.6 | 19.9 | 03 | 201.0 | 28.3 | 63 | 260.4 | 36.6 |
| 24 | 23.8 | 03.3 | 84 | 83.2 | 11.7 | 44 | 142.6 | 20.0 | 04 | 202.0 | 28.4 | 64 | 261.4 | 36.7 |
| 25 | 24.8 | 03.5 | 85 | 84.2 | 11.8 | 45 | 143.6 | 20.2 | 05 | 203.0 | 28.5 | 65 | 262.4 | 36.9 |
| 26 | 25.7 | 03.6 | 86 | 85.2 | 12.0 | 46 | 144.6 | 20.3 | 06 | 204.0 | 28.7 | 66 | 263.4 | 37.0 |
| 27 | 26.7 | 03.8 | 87 | 86.2 | 12.1 | 47 | 145.6 | 20.5 | 07 | 205.0 | 28.8 | 67 | 264.4 | 37.2 |
| 28 | 27.7 | 03.9 | 88 | 87.1 | 12.2 | 48 | 146.6 | 20.6 | 08 | 206.0 | 28.9 | 68 | 265.4 | 37.3 |
| 29 | 28.7 | 04.0 | 89 | 88.1 | 12.4 | 49 | 147.5 | 20.7 | 09 | 207.0 | 29.1 | 69 | 266.4 | 37.4 |
| 30 | 29.7 | 04.2 | 90 | 89.1 | 12.5 | 50 | 148.5 | 20.9 | 10 | 208.0 | 29.2 | 70 | 267.4 | 37.6 |
| 31 | 30.7 | 04.3 | 91 | 90.1 | 12.7 | 151 | 149.5 | 21.0 | 211 | 208.9 | 29.4 | 271 | 268.4 | 37.7 |
| 32 | 31.7 | 04.5 | 92 | 91.1 | 12.8 | 52 | 150.5 | 21.2 | 12 | 209.9 | 29.5 | 72 | 269.4 | 37 9 |
| 33 | 32.7 | 04.6 | 93 | 92.1 | 12.9 | 53 | 151.5 | 21.3 | 13 | 210.9 | 29.6 | 73 | 270.3 | 38.0 |
| 34 | 33.7 | 04.7 | 94 | 93.1 | 13.1 | 54 | 152.5 | 21.4 | 14 | 211.9 | 29.8 | 74 | 271.3 | 38.1 |
| 35 | 34.7 | 04.9 | 95 | 94.1 | 13.2 | 55 | 153.5 | 21.6 | 15 | 212.9 | 29.9 | 75 | 272.3 | 38.3 |
| 36 | 35.6 | 05.0 | 96 | 95.1 | 13.4 | 56 | 154.5 | 21.7 | 16 | 213.9 | 30.1 | 76 | 273.3 | 38.4 |
| 37 | 36.6 | 05.1 | 97 | 96.1 | 13.5 | 57 | 155.5 | 21.9 | 17 | 214.9 | 30.2 | 77 | 274.3 | 38 6 |
| 38 | 37.6 | 05.3 | 98 | 97.0 | 13.6 | 58 | 156.5 | 22.0 | 18 | 215.9 | 30.3 | 78 | 275.3 | 38.7 |
| 39 | 38.6 | 05.4 | 99 | 98.0 | 13.8 | 59 | 157.5 | 22.1 | 19 | 216.9 | 30.5 | 79 | 276.3 | 38.8 |
| 40 | 39.6 | 05.6 | 100 | 99.0 | 13.9 | 60 | 158.4 | 22.3 | 20 | 217.9 | 30.6 | 80 | 277.3 | 39.0 |
| 41 | 40.6 | 05.7 | 101 | 100.0 | 14.1 | 161 | 159.4 | 22.4 | 221 | 218.8 | 30.8 | 281 | 278.3 | 39.1 |
| 42 | 41.6 | 05.8 | 02 | 101.0 | 14.2 | 62 | 160.4 | 22.5 | 22 | 219.8 | 30.9 | 82 | 279.3 | 39.2 |
| 43 | 42.6 | 06.0 | 03 | 102.0 | 14.3 | 63 | 161.4 | 22.7 | 23 | 220.8 | 31.0 | 83 | 280.2 | 39.4 |
| 44 | 43.6 | 06.1 | 04 | 103.0 | 14.5 | 64 | 162.4 | 22.8 | 24 | 221.8 | 31.2 | 84 | 281.2 | 39.5 |
| 45 | 44.6 | 06.3 | 05 | 104.0 | 14.6 | 65 | 163.4 | 23.0 | 25 | 222.8 | 31.3 | 85 | 282.2 | 39.7 |
| 46 | 45.6 | 06.4 | 06 | 105.0 | 14.8 | 66 | 164.4 | 23.1 | 26 | 223.8 | 31.5 | 86 | 283.2 | 39.8 |
| 47 | 46.5 | 06.5 | 07 | 106.0 | 14.9 | 67 | 165.4 | 23.2 | 27 | 224.8 | 31.6 | 87 | 284.2 | 39.9 |
| 48 | 47.5 | 06.7 | 08 | 106.9 | 15.0 | 68 | 166.4 | 23.4 | 28 | 225.8 | 31.7 | 88 | 285.2 | 40.1 |
| 49 | 48.5 | 06.8 | 09 | 107.9 | 15.2 | 69 | 167.4 | 23.5 | 29 | 226.8 | 31.9 | 89 | 286.2 | 40.2 |
| 50 | 49.5 | 07.0 | 10 | 108.9 | 15.3 | 70 | 168.3 | 23.7 | 30 | 227.8 | 32.0 | 90 | 287.2 | 40.4 |
| 51 | 50.5 | 07.1 | 111 | 109.9 | 15.4 | 171 | 169.3 | 23.8 | 231 | 228.8 | 32.1 | 291 | 288.2 | 40.5 |
| 52 | 51.5 | 07.2 | 12 | 110.9 | 15.6 | 72 | 170.3 | 23.9 | 32 | 229.7 | 32.3 | 92 | 289.2 | 40.6 |
| 53 | 52.5 | 07.4 | 13 | 111.9 | 15.7 | 73 | 171.3 | 24.1 | 33 | 230.7 | 32.4 | 93 | 290.1 | 40.8 |
| 54 | 53.5 | 07.5 | 14 | 112.9 | 15.9 | 74 | 172.3 | 24.2 | 34 | 231.7 | 32.6 | 94 | 291.1 | 40.9 |
| 55 | 54.5 | 07.7 | 15 | 113.9 | 16.0 | 75 | 173.3 | 24.4 | 35 | 232.7 | 32.7 | 95 | 292.1 | 41.1 |
| 56 | 55.5 | 07.8 | 16 | 114.9 | 16.1 | 76 | 174.3 | 24.5 | 36 | 233.7 | 32.8 | 96 | 293.1 | 41.2 |
| 57 | 56.4 | 07.9 | 17 | 115.9 | 16.3 | 77 | 175.3 | 24.6 | 37 | 234.7 | 33.0 | 97 | 294.1 | 41.3 |
| 58 | 57.4 | 08.1 | 18 | 116.9 | 16.4 | 78 | 176.3 | 24.8 | 38 | 235.7 | 33.1 | 98 | 295.1 | 41.5 |
| 59 | 58.4 | 08.2 | 19 | 117.8 | 16.6 | 79 | 177.3 | 24.9 | 39 | 236.7 | 33.3 | 99 | 296.1 | 41 6 |
| 60 | 59.4 | 08.4 | 20 | 118.8 | 16.7 | 80 | 178.2 | 25.1 | 40 | 237.7 | 33.4 | 300 | 297.1 | 41.8 |
| Dist. | Dep. | Lat. | Dist. | Dep. | Lat. | Dist. | Dep. | Lat. | Dist. | Dep. | Lat. | Dist. | Dep. | Lat. |

[For 82 Degrees.

# TABLE II



## Difference of Latitude and Departure for 9 Degrees.

| Dist. | Lat. | Dep. | Dist. | Lat. | Dep. | Dist. | Lat. | Dep. | Dist. | Lat. | Dep. | Dist. | Lat. | Dep. |
|---|---|---|---|---|---|---|---|---|---|---|---|---|---|---|
| 1 | 01.0 | 00.2 | 61 | 60.2 | 09.5 | 121 | 119.5 | 18.9 | 181 | 178.8 | 28.3 | 241 | 238.0 | 37.7 |
| 2 | 02.0 | 00.3 | 62 | 61.2 | 09.7 | 22 | 120.5 | 19.1 | 82 | 179.8 | 28.5 | 42 | 239.0 | 37.9 |
| 3 | 03.0 | 00.5 | 63 | 62.2 | 09.9 | 23 | 121.5 | 19.2 | 83 | 180.7 | 28.6 | 43 | 240.0 | 38.0 |
| 4 | 04.0 | 00.6 | 64 | 63.2 | 10.0 | 24 | 122.5 | 19.4 | 84 | 181.7 | 28.8 | 44 | 241.0 | 38.2 |
| 5 | 04.9 | 00.8 | 65 | 64.2 | 10.2 | 25 | 123.5 | 19.6 | 85 | 182.7 | 28.9 | 45 | 242.0 | 38.3 |
| 6 | 05.9 | 00.9 | 66 | 65.2 | 10.3 | 26 | 124.4 | 19.7 | 86 | 183.7 | 29.1 | 46 | 243.0 | 38.5 |
| 7 | 06.9 | 01.1 | 67 | 66.2 | 10.5 | 27 | 125.4 | 19.9 | 87 | 184.7 | 29.3 | 47 | 244.0 | 38.6 |
| 8 | 07.9 | 01.3 | 68 | 67.2 | 10.6 | 28 | 126.4 | 20.0 | 88 | 185.7 | 29.4 | 48 | 244.9 | 38.8 |
| 9 | 08.9 | 01.4 | 69 | 68.2 | 10.8 | 29 | 127.4 | 20.2 | 89 | 186.7 | 29.6 | 49 | 245.9 | 39.0 |
| 10 | 09.9 | 01.6 | 70 | 69.1 | 11.0 | 30 | 128.4 | 20.3 | 90 | 187.7 | 29.7 | 50 | 246.9 | 39.1 |
| 11 | 10.9 | 01.7 | 71 | 70.1 | 11.1 | 131 | 129.4 | 20.5 | 191 | 188.6 | 29.9 | 251 | 247.9 | 39.3 |
| 12 | 11.9 | 01.9 | 72 | 71.1 | 11.3 | 32 | 130.4 | 20.6 | 92 | 189.6 | 30.0 | 52 | 248.9 | 39.4 |
| 13 | 12.8 | 02.0 | 73 | 72.1 | 11.4 | 33 | 131.4 | 20.8 | 93 | 190.6 | 30.2 | 53 | 249.9 | 39.6 |
| 14 | 13.8 | 02.2 | 74 | 73.1 | 11.6 | 34 | 132.4 | 21.0 | 94 | 191.6 | 30.3 | 54 | 250.9 | 39.7 |
| 15 | 14.8 | 02.3 | 75 | 74.1 | 11.7 | 35 | 133.3 | 21.1 | 95 | 192.6 | 30.5 | 55 | 251.9 | 39.9 |
| 16 | 15.8 | 02.5 | 76 | 75.1 | 11.9 | 36 | 134.3 | 21.3 | 96 | 193.6 | 30.7 | 56 | 252.8 | 40.0 |
| 17 | 16.8 | 02.7 | 77 | 76.1 | 12.0 | 37 | 135.3 | 21.4 | 97 | 194.6 | 30.8 | 57 | 253.8 | 40.2 |
| 18 | 17.8 | 02.8 | 78 | 77.0 | 12.2 | 38 | 136.3 | 21.6 | 98 | 195.6 | 31.0 | 58 | 254.8 | 40.4 |
| 19 | 18.8 | 03.0 | 79 | 78.0 | 12.4 | 39 | 137.3 | 21.7 | 99 | 196.5 | 31.1 | 59 | 255.8 | 40.5 |
| 20 | 19.8 | 03.1 | 80 | 79.0 | 12.5 | 40 | 138.3 | 21.9 | 200 | 197.5 | 31.3 | 60 | 256.8 | 40.7 |
| 21 | 20.7 | 03.3 | 81 | 80.0 | 12.7 | 141 | 139.3 | 22.1 | 201 | 198.5 | 31.4 | 261 | 257.8 | 40.8 |
| 22 | 21.7 | 03.4 | 82 | 81.0 | 12.8 | 42 | 140.3 | 22.2 | 02 | 199.5 | 31.6 | 62 | 258.8 | 41.0 |
| 23 | 22.7 | 03.6 | 83 | 82.0 | 13.0 | 43 | 141.2 | 22.4 | 03 | 200.5 | 31.8 | 63 | 259.8 | 41.1 |
| 24 | 23.7 | 03.8 | 84 | 83.0 | 13.1 | 44 | 142.2 | 22.5 | 04 | 201.5 | 31.9 | 64 | 260.7 | 41.3 |
| 25 | 24.7 | 03.9 | 85 | 84.0 | 13.3 | 45 | 143.2 | 22.7 | 05 | 202.5 | 32.1 | 65 | 261.7 | 41.5 |
| 26 | 25.7 | 04.1 | 86 | 84.9 | 13.5 | 46 | 144.2 | 22.8 | 06 | 203.5 | 32.2 | 66 | 262.7 | 41.6 |
| 27 | 26.7 | 04.2 | 87 | 85.9 | 13.6 | 47 | 145.2 | 23.0 | 07 | 204.5 | 32.4 | 67 | 263.7 | 41.8 |
| 28 | 27.7 | 04.4 | 88 | 86.9 | 13.8 | 48 | 146.2 | 23.2 | 08 | 205.4 | 32.5 | 68 | 264.7 | 41.9 |
| 29 | 28.6 | 04.5 | 89 | 87.9 | 13.9 | 49 | 147.2 | 23.3 | 09 | 206.4 | 32.7 | 69 | 265.7 | 42.1 |
| 30 | 29.6 | 04.7 | 90 | 88.9 | 14.1 | 50 | 148.2 | 23.5 | 10 | 207.4 | 32.9 | 70 | 266.7 | 42.2 |
| 31 | 30.6 | 04.8 | 91 | 89.9 | 14.2 | 151 | 149.1 | 23.6 | 211 | 208.4 | 33.0 | 271 | 267.7 | 42.4 |
| 32 | 31.6 | 05.0 | 92 | 90.9 | 14.4 | 52 | 150.1 | 23.8 | 12 | 209.4 | 33.2 | 72 | 268.7 | 42.6 |
| 33 | 32.6 | 05.2 | 93 | 91.9 | 14.5 | 53 | 151.1 | 23.9 | 13 | 210.4 | 33.3 | 73 | 269.6 | 42.7 |
| 34 | 33.6 | 05.3 | 94 | 92.8 | 14.7 | 54 | 152.1 | 24.1 | 14 | 211.4 | 33.5 | 74 | 270.6 | 42.9 |
| 35 | 34.6 | 05.5 | 95 | 93.8 | 14.9 | 55 | 153.1 | 24.2 | 15 | 212.4 | 33.6 | 75 | 271.6 | 43.0 |
| 36 | 35.6 | 05.6 | 96 | 94.8 | 15.0 | 56 | 154.1 | 24.4 | 16 | 213.3 | 33.8 | 76 | 272.6 | 43.2 |
| 37 | 36.5 | 05.8 | 97 | 95.8 | 15.2 | 57 | 155.1 | 24.6 | 17 | 214.3 | 33.9 | 77 | 273.6 | 43.3 |
| 38 | 37.5 | 05.9 | 98 | 96.8 | 15.3 | 58 | 156.1 | 24.7 | 18 | 215.3 | 34.1 | 78 | 274.6 | 43.5 |
| 39 | 38.5 | 06.1 | 99 | 97.8 | 15.5 | 59 | 157.0 | 24.9 | 19 | 216.3 | 34.3 | 79 | 275.6 | 43.6 |
| 40 | 39.5 | 06.3 | 100 | 98.8 | 15.6 | 60 | 158.0 | 25.0 | 20 | 217.3 | 34.4 | 80 | 276.6 | 43.8 |
| 41 | 40.5 | 06.4 | 101 | 99.8 | 15.8 | 161 | 159.0 | 25.2 | 221 | 218.3 | 34.6 | 281 | 277.5 | 44.0 |
| 42 | 41.5 | 06.6 | 02 | 100.7 | 16.0 | 62 | 160.0 | 25.3 | 22 | 219.3 | 34.7 | 82 | 278.5 | 44.1 |
| 43 | 42.5 | 06.7 | 03 | 101.7 | 16.1 | 63 | 161.0 | 25.5 | 23 | 220.3 | 34.9 | 83 | 279.5 | 44.3 |
| 44 | 43.5 | 06.9 | 04 | 102.7 | 16.3 | 64 | 162.0 | 25.7 | 24 | 221.2 | 35.0 | 84 | 280.5 | 44.4 |
| 45 | 44.4 | 07.0 | 05 | 103.7 | 16.4 | 65 | 163.0 | 25.8 | 25 | 222.2 | 35.2 | 85 | 281.5 | 44.6 |
| 46 | 45.4 | 07.2 | 06 | 104.7 | 16.6 | 66 | 164.0 | 26.0 | 26 | 223.2 | 35.4 | 86 | 282.5 | 44.7 |
| 47 | 46.4 | 07.4 | 07 | 105.7 | 16.7 | 67 | 164.9 | 26.1 | 27 | 224.2 | 35.5 | 87 | 283.5 | 44.9 |
| 48 | 47.4 | 07.5 | 08 | 106.7 | 16.9 | 68 | 165.9 | 26.3 | 28 | 225.2 | 35.7 | 88 | 284.5 | 45.1 |
| 49 | 48.4 | 07.7 | 09 | 107.7 | 17.1 | 69 | 166.9 | 26.4 | 29 | 226.2 | 35.8 | 89 | 285.4 | 45.2 |
| 50 | 49.4 | 07.8 | 10 | 108.6 | 17.2 | 70 | 167.9 | 26.6 | 30 | 227.2 | 36.0 | 90 | 286.4 | 45.4 |
| 51 | 50.4 | 08.0 | 111 | 109.6 | 17.4 | 171 | 168.9 | 26.8 | 231 | 228.2 | 36.1 | 291 | 287.4 | 45.5 |
| 52 | 51.4 | 08.1 | 12 | 110.6 | 17.5 | 72 | 169.9 | 26.9 | 32 | 229.1 | 36.3 | 92 | 288.4 | 45.7 |
| 53 | 52.3 | 08.3 | 13 | 111.6 | 17.7 | 73 | 170.9 | 27.1 | 33 | 230.1 | 36.4 | 93 | 289.4 | 45.8 |
| 54 | 53.3 | 08.4 | 14 | 112.6 | 17.8 | 74 | 171.9 | 27.2 | 34 | 231.1 | 36.6 | 94 | 290.4 | 46.0 |
| 55 | 54.3 | 08.6 | 15 | 113.6 | 18.0 | 75 | 172.8 | 27.4 | 35 | 232.1 | 36.8 | 95 | 291.4 | 46.1 |
| 56 | 55.3 | 08.8 | 16 | 114.6 | 18.1 | 76 | 173.8 | 27.5 | 36 | 233.1 | 36.9 | 96 | 292.4 | 46.3 |
| 57 | 56.3 | 08.9 | 17 | 115.6 | 18.3 | 77 | 174.8 | 27.7 | 37 | 234.1 | 37.1 | 97 | 293.3 | 46.5 |
| 58 | 57.3 | 09.1 | 18 | 116.5 | 18.5 | 78 | 175.8 | 27.8 | 38 | 235.1 | 37.2 | 98 | 294.3 | 46.6 |
| 59 | 58.3 | 09.2 | 19 | 117.5 | 18.6 | 79 | 176.8 | 28.0 | 39 | 236.1 | 37.4 | 99 | 295.3 | 46.8 |
| 60 | 59.3 | 09.4 | 20 | 118.5 | 18.8 | 80 | 177.8 | 28.2 | 40 | 237.0 | 37.5 | 300 | 296.3 | 46.9 |
| Dist. | Dep. | Lat. | Dist. | Dep. | Lat. | Dist. | Dep. | Lat. | Dist. | Dep. | Lat. | Dist. | Dep. | Lat. |

[For 81 Degrees.

# TABLE II.

## Difference of Latitude and Departure for 10 Degrees.

| Dist. | Lat. | Dep. | Dist. | Lat. | Dep. | Dist. | Lat. | Dep. | Dist. | Lat. | Dep. | Dist. | Lat. | Dep. |
|---|---|---|---|---|---|---|---|---|---|---|---|---|---|---|
| 1 | 01.0 | 00.2 | 61 | 60.1 | 10.6 | 121 | 119.2 | 21.0 | 181 | 178.3 | 31.4 | 241 | 237.3 | 41.8 |
| 2 | 02.0 | 00.3 | 62 | 61.1 | 10.8 | 22 | 120.1 | 21.2 | 82 | 179.2 | 31.6 | 42 | 238.3 | 42.0 |
| 3 | 03.0 | 00.5 | 63 | 62.0 | 10.9 | 23 | 121.1 | 21.4 | 83 | 180.2 | 31.8 | 43 | 239.3 | 42.2 |
| 4 | 03.9 | 00.7 | 64 | 63.0 | 11.1 | 24 | 122.1 | 21.5 | 84 | 181.2 | 32.0 | 44 | 240.3 | 42.4 |
| 5 | 04.9 | 00.9 | 65 | 64.0 | 11.3 | 25 | 123.1 | 21.7 | 85 | 182.2 | 32.1 | 45 | 241.3 | 42.5 |
| 6 | 05.9 | 01.0 | 66 | 65.0 | 11.5 | 26 | 124.1 | 21.9 | 86 | 183.2 | 32.3 | 46 | 242.3 | 42.7 |
| 7 | 06.9 | 01.2 | 67 | 66.0 | 11.6 | 27 | 125.1 | 22.1 | 87 | 184.2 | 32.5 | 47 | 243.2 | 42.9 |
| 8 | 07.9 | 01.4 | 68 | 67.0 | 11.8 | 28 | 126.1 | 22.2 | 88 | 185.1 | 32.6 | 48 | 244.2 | 43.1 |
| 9 | 08.9 | 01.6 | 69 | 68.0 | 12.0 | 29 | 127.0 | 22.4 | 89 | 186.1 | 32.8 | 49 | 245.2 | 43.2 |
| 10 | 09.8 | 01.7 | 70 | 68.9 | 12.2 | 30 | 128.0 | 22.6 | 90 | 187.1 | 33.0 | 50 | 246.2 | 43.4 |
| 11 | 10.8 | 01.9 | 71 | 69.9 | 12.3 | 131 | 129.0 | 22.7 | 191 | 188.1 | 33.2 | 251 | 247.2 | 43.6 |
| 12 | 11.8 | 02.1 | 72 | 70.9 | 12.5 | 32 | 130.0 | 22.9 | 92 | 189.1 | 33.3 | 52 | 248.2 | 43.8 |
| 13 | 12.8 | 02.3 | 73 | 71.9 | 12.7 | 33 | 131.0 | 23.1 | 93 | 190.1 | 33.5 | 53 | 249.2 | 43.9 |
| 14 | 13.8 | 02.4 | 74 | 72.9 | 12.8 | 34 | 132.0 | 23.3 | 94 | 191.1 | 33.7 | 54 | 250.1 | 44.1 |
| 15 | 14.8 | 02.6 | 75 | 73.9 | 13.0 | 35 | 132.9 | 23.4 | 95 | 192.0 | 33.9 | 55 | 251.1 | 44.3 |
| 16 | 15.8 | 02.8 | 76 | 74.8 | 13.2 | 36 | 133.9 | 23.6 | 96 | 193.0 | 34.0 | 56 | 252.1 | 44.5 |
| 17 | 16.7 | 03.0 | 77 | 75.8 | 13.4 | 37 | 134.9 | 23.8 | 97 | 194.0 | 34.2 | 57 | 253.1 | 44.6 |
| 18 | 17.7 | 03.1 | 78 | 76.8 | 13.5 | 38 | 135.9 | 24.0 | 98 | 195.0 | 34.4 | 58 | 254.1 | 44.8 |
| 19 | 18.7 | 03.3 | 79 | 77.8 | 13.7 | 39 | 136.9 | 24.1 | 99 | 196.0 | 34.6 | 59 | 255.1 | 45.0 |
| 20 | 19.7 | 03.5 | 80 | 78.8 | 13.9 | 40 | 137.9 | 24.3 | 200 | 197.0 | 34.7 | 60 | 256.1 | 45.1 |
| 21 | 20.7 | 03.6 | 81 | 79.8 | 14.1 | 141 | 138.9 | 24.5 | 201 | 197.9 | 34.9 | 261 | 257.0 | 45.3 |
| 22 | 21.7 | 03.8 | 82 | 80.8 | 14.2 | 42 | 139.8 | 24.7 | 02 | 198.9 | 35.1 | 62 | 258.0 | 45.5 |
| 23 | 22.7 | 04.0 | 83 | 81.7 | 14.4 | 43 | 140.8 | 24.8 | 03 | 199.9 | 35.3 | 63 | 259.0 | 45.7 |
| 24 | 23.6 | 04.2 | 84 | 82.7 | 14.6 | 44 | 141.8 | 25.0 | 04 | 200.9 | 35.4 | 64 | 260.0 | 45.8 |
| 25 | 24.6 | 04.3 | 85 | 83.7 | 14.8 | 45 | 142.8 | 25.2 | 05 | 201.9 | 35.6 | 65 | 261.0 | 46.0 |
| 26 | 25.6 | 04.5 | 86 | 84.7 | 14.9 | 46 | 143.8 | 25.4 | 06 | 202.9 | 35.8 | 66 | 262.0 | 46.2 |
| 27 | 26.6 | 04.7 | 87 | 85.7 | 15.1 | 47 | 144.8 | 25.5 | 07 | 203.9 | 35.9 | 67 | 262.9 | 46.4 |
| 28 | 27.6 | 04.9 | 88 | 86.7 | 15.3 | 48 | 145.8 | 25.7 | 08 | 204.8 | 36.1 | 68 | 263.9 | 46.5 |
| 29 | 28.6 | 05.0 | 89 | 87.6 | 15.5 | 49 | 146.7 | 25.9 | 09 | 205.8 | 36.3 | 69 | 264.9 | 46.7 |
| 30 | 29.5 | 05.2 | 90 | 88.6 | 15.6 | 50 | 147.7 | 26.0 | 10 | 206.8 | 36.5 | 70 | 265.9 | 46.9 |
| 31 | 30.5 | 05.4 | 91 | 89.6 | 15.8 | 151 | 148.7 | 26.2 | 211 | 207.8 | 36.6 | 271 | 266.9 | 47.1 |
| 32 | 31.5 | 05.6 | 92 | 90.6 | 16.0 | 52 | 149.7 | 26.4 | 12 | 208.8 | 36.8 | 72 | 267.9 | 47.2 |
| 33 | 32.5 | 05.7 | 93 | 91.6 | 16.1 | 53 | 150.7 | 26.6 | 13 | 209.8 | 37.0 | 73 | 268.9 | 47.4 |
| 34 | 33.5 | 05.9 | 94 | 92.6 | 16.3 | 54 | 151.7 | 26.7 | 14 | 210.7 | 37.2 | 74 | 269.8 | 47.6 |
| 35 | 34.5 | 06.1 | 95 | 93.6 | 16.5 | 55 | 152.6 | 26.9 | 15 | 211.7 | 37.3 | 75 | 270.8 | 47.8 |
| 36 | 35.5 | 06.3 | 96 | 94.5 | 16.7 | 56 | 153.6 | 27.1 | 16 | 212.7 | 37.5 | 76 | 271.8 | 47.9 |
| 37 | 36.4 | 06.4 | 97 | 95.5 | 16.8 | 57 | 154.6 | 27.3 | 17 | 213.7 | 37.7 | 77 | 272.8 | 48.1 |
| 38 | 37.4 | 06.6 | 98 | 96.5 | 17.0 | 58 | 155.6 | 27.4 | 18 | 214.7 | 37.9 | 78 | 273.8 | 48.3 |
| 39 | 38.4 | 06.8 | 99 | 97.5 | 17.2 | 59 | 156.6 | 27.6 | 19 | 215.7 | 38.0 | 79 | 274.8 | 48.4 |
| 40 | 39.4 | 06.9 | 100 | 98.5 | 17.4 | 60 | 157.6 | 27.8 | 20 | 216.7 | 38.2 | 80 | 275.7 | 48.6 |
| 41 | 40.4 | 07.1 | 101 | 99.5 | 17.5 | 161 | 158.6 | 28.0 | 221 | 217.6 | 38.4 | 281 | 276.7 | 48.8 |
| 42 | 41.4 | 07.3 | 02 | 100.5 | 17.7 | 62 | 159.5 | 28.1 | 22 | 218.6 | 38.5 | 82 | 277.7 | 49.0 |
| 43 | 42.3 | 07.5 | 03 | 101.4 | 17.9 | 63 | 160.5 | 28.3 | 23 | 219.6 | 38.7 | 83 | 278.7 | 49.1 |
| 44 | 43.3 | 07.6 | 04 | 102.4 | 18.1 | 64 | 161.5 | 28.5 | 24 | 220.6 | 38.9 | 84 | 279.7 | 49.3 |
| 45 | 44.3 | 07.8 | 05 | 103.4 | 18.2 | 65 | 162.5 | 28.7 | 25 | 221.6 | 39.1 | 85 | 280.7 | 49.5 |
| 46 | 45.3 | 08.0 | 06 | 104.4 | 18.4 | 66 | 163.5 | 28.8 | 26 | 222.6 | 39.2 | 86 | 281.7 | 49.7 |
| 47 | 46.3 | 08.2 | 07 | 105.4 | 18.6 | 67 | 164.5 | 29.0 | 27 | 223.6 | 39.4 | 87 | 282.6 | 49.8 |
| 48 | 47.3 | 08.3 | 08 | 106.4 | 18.8 | 68 | 165.4 | 29.2 | 28 | 224.5 | 39.6 | 88 | 283.6 | 50.0 |
| 49 | 48.3 | 08.5 | 09 | 107.3 | 18.9 | 69 | 166.4 | 29.3 | 29 | 225.5 | 39.8 | 89 | 284.6 | 50.2 |
| 50 | 49.2 | 08.7 | 10 | 108.3 | 19.1 | 70 | 167.4 | 29.5 | 30 | 226.5 | 39.9 | 90 | 285.6 | 50.4 |
| 51 | 50.2 | 08.9 | 111 | 109.3 | 19.3 | 171 | 168.4 | 29.7 | 231 | 227.5 | 40.1 | 291 | 286.6 | 50.5 |
| 52 | 51.2 | 09.0 | 12 | 110.3 | 19.4 | 72 | 169.4 | 29.9 | 32 | 228.5 | 40.3 | 92 | 287.6 | 50.7 |
| 53 | 52.2 | 09.2 | 13 | 111.3 | 19.6 | 73 | 170.4 | 30.0 | 33 | 229.5 | 40.5 | 93 | 288.5 | 50.9 |
| 54 | 53.2 | 09.4 | 14 | 112.3 | 19.8 | 74 | 171.4 | 30.2 | 34 | 230.4 | 40.6 | 94 | 289.5 | 51.1 |
| 55 | 54.2 | 09.6 | 15 | 113.3 | 20.0 | 75 | 172.3 | 30.4 | 35 | 231.4 | 40.8 | 95 | 290.5 | 51.2 |
| 56 | 55.1 | 09.7 | 16 | 114.2 | 20.1 | 76 | 173.3 | 30.6 | 36 | 232.4 | 41.0 | 96 | 291.5 | 51.4 |
| 57 | 56.1 | 09.9 | 17 | 115.2 | 20.3 | 77 | 174.3 | 30.7 | 37 | 233.4 | 41.2 | 97 | 292.5 | 51.6 |
| 58 | 57.1 | 10.1 | 18 | 116.2 | 20.5 | 78 | 175.3 | 30.9 | 38 | 234.4 | 41.3 | 98 | 293.5 | 51.7 |
| 59 | 58.1 | 10.2 | 19 | 117.2 | 20.7 | 79 | 176.3 | 31.1 | 39 | 235.4 | 41.5 | 99 | 294.5 | 51.9 |
| 60 | 59.1 | 10.4 | 20 | 118.2 | 20.8 | 80 | 177.3 | 31.3 | 40 | 236.4 | 41.7 | 300 | 295.4 | 52.1 |
| Dist. | Dep. | Lat. | Dist. | Dep. | Lat. | Dist. | Dep. | Lat. | Dist. | Dep. | Lat. | Dist. | Dep. | Lat. |

[For 80 Degrees.

# TABLE II.

## Difference of Latitude and Departure for 11 Degrees.

| Dist. | Lat. | Dep. | Dist. | Lat. | Dep. | Dist. | Lat. | Dep. | Dist. | Lat. | Dep. | Dist. | Lat | Dep. |
|---|---|---|---|---|---|---|---|---|---|---|---|---|---|---|
| 1 | 01.0 | 00.2 | 61 | 59.9 | 11.6 | 121 | 118.8 | 23.1 | 181 | 177.7 | 34.5 | 241 | 236.6 | 46.0 |
| 2 | 02.0 | 00.4 | 62 | 60.9 | 11.8 | 22 | 119.8 | 23.3 | 82 | 178.7 | 34.7 | 42 | 237.6 | 46.2 |
| 3 | 02.9 | 00.6 | 63 | 61.8 | 12.0 | 23 | 120.7 | 23.5 | 83 | 179.6 | 34.9 | 43 | 238.5 | 46.4 |
| 4 | 03.9 | 00.8 | 64 | 62.8 | 12.2 | 24 | 121.7 | 23.7 | 84 | 180.6 | 35.1 | 44 | 239.5 | 46.6 |
| 5 | 04.9 | 01.0 | 65 | 63.8 | 12.4 | 25 | 122.7 | 23.9 | 85 | 181.6 | 35.3 | 45 | 240.5 | 46.7 |
| 6 | 05.9 | 01.1 | 66 | 64.8 | 12.6 | 26 | 123.7 | 24.0 | 86 | 182.6 | 35.5 | 46 | 241.5 | 46.9 |
| 7 | 06.9 | 01.3 | 67 | 65.8 | 12.8 | 27 | 124.7 | 24.2 | 87 | 183.6 | 35.7 | 47 | 242.5 | 47.1 |
| 8 | 07.9 | 01.5 | 68 | 66.8 | 13.0 | 28 | 125.6 | 24.4 | 88 | 184.5 | 35.9 | 48 | 243.4 | 47.3 |
| 9 | 08.8 | 01.7 | 69 | 67.7 | 13.2 | 29 | 126.6 | 24.6 | 89 | 185.5 | 36.1 | 49 | 244.4 | 47.5 |
| 10 | 09.8 | 01.9 | 70 | 68.7 | 13.4 | 30 | 127.6 | 24.8 | 90 | 186.5 | 36.3 | 50 | 245.4 | 47.7 |
| 11 | 10.8 | 02.1 | 71 | 69.7 | 13.5 | 131 | 128.6 | 25.0 | 191 | 187.5 | 36.4 | 251 | 246.4 | 47.9 |
| 12 | 11.8 | 02.3 | 72 | 70.7 | 13.7 | 32 | 129.6 | 25.2 | 92 | 188.5 | 36.6 | 52 | 247.4 | 48.1 |
| 13 | 12.8 | 02.5 | 73 | 71.7 | 13.9 | 33 | 130.6 | 25.4 | 93 | 189.5 | 36.8 | 53 | 248.4 | 48.3 |
| 14 | 13.7 | 02.7 | 74 | 72.6 | 14.1 | 34 | 131.5 | 25.6 | 94 | 190.4 | 37.0 | 54 | 249.3 | 48.5 |
| 15 | 14.7 | 02.9 | 75 | 73.6 | 14.3 | 35 | 132.5 | 25.8 | 95 | 191.4 | 37.2 | 55 | 250.3 | 48.7 |
| 16 | 15.7 | 03.1 | 76 | 74.6 | 14.5 | 36 | 133.5 | 26.0 | 96 | 192.4 | 37.4 | 56 | 251.3 | 48.8 |
| 17 | 16.7 | 03.2 | 77 | 75.6 | 14.7 | 37 | 134.5 | 26.1 | 97 | 193.4 | 37.6 | 57 | 252.3 | 49.0 |
| 18 | 17.7 | 03.4 | 78 | 76.6 | 14.9 | 38 | 135.5 | 26.3 | 98 | 194.4 | 37.8 | 58 | 253.3 | 49.2 |
| 19 | 18.7 | 03.6 | 79 | 77.5 | 15.1 | 39 | 136.4 | 26.5 | 99 | 195.3 | 38.0 | 59 | 254.2 | 49.4 |
| 20 | 19.6 | 03.8 | 80 | 78.5 | 15.3 | 40 | 137.4 | 26.7 | 200 | 196.3 | 38.2 | 60 | 255.2 | 49.6 |
| 21 | 20.6 | 04.0 | 81 | 79.5 | 15.5 | 141 | 138.4 | 26.9 | 201 | 197.3 | 38.4 | 261 | 256.2 | 49.8 |
| 22 | 21.6 | 04.2 | 82 | 80.5 | 15.6 | 42 | 139.4 | 27.1 | 02 | 198.3 | 38.5 | 62 | 257.2 | 50.0 |
| 23 | 22.6 | 04.4 | 83 | 81.5 | 15.8 | 43 | 140.4 | 27.3 | 03 | 199.3 | 38.7 | 63 | 258.2 | 50.2 |
| 24 | 23.6 | 04.6 | 84 | 82.5 | 16.0 | 44 | 141.4 | 27.5 | 04 | 200.3 | 38.9 | 64 | 259.1 | 50.4 |
| 25 | 24.5 | 04.8 | 85 | 83.4 | 16.2 | 45 | 142.3 | 27.7 | 05 | 201.2 | 39.1 | 65 | 260.1 | 50.6 |
| 26 | 25.5 | 05.0 | 86 | 84.4 | 16.4 | 46 | 143.3 | 27.9 | 06 | 202.2 | 39.3 | 66 | 261.1 | 50.8 |
| 27 | 26.5 | 05.2 | 87 | 85.4 | 16.6 | 47 | 144.3 | 28.0 | 07 | 203.2 | 39.5 | 67 | 262.1 | 50.9 |
| 28 | 27.5 | 05.3 | 88 | 86.4 | 16.8 | 48 | 145.3 | 28.2 | 08 | 204.2 | 39.7 | 68 | 263.1 | 51.1 |
| 29 | 28.5 | 05.5 | 89 | 87.4 | 17.0 | 49 | 146.3 | 28.4 | 09 | 205.2 | 39.9 | 69 | 264.1 | 51.3 |
| 30 | 29.4 | 05.7 | 90 | 88.3 | 17.2 | 50 | 147.2 | 28.6 | 10 | 206.1 | 40.1 | 70 | 265.0 | 51.5 |
| 31 | 30.4 | 05.9 | 91 | 89.3 | 17.4 | 151 | 148.2 | 28.8 | 211 | 207.1 | 40.3 | 271 | 266.0 | 51.7 |
| 32 | 31.4 | 06.1 | 92 | 90.3 | 17.6 | 52 | 149.2 | 29.0 | 12 | 208.1 | 40.5 | 72 | 267.0 | 51.9 |
| 33 | 32.4 | 06.3 | 93 | 91.3 | 17.7 | 53 | 150.2 | 29.2 | 13 | 209.1 | 40.6 | 73 | 268.0 | 52.1 |
| 34 | 33.4 | 06.5 | 94 | 92.3 | 17.9 | 54 | 151.2 | 29.4 | 14 | 210.1 | 40.8 | 74 | 269.0 | 52.3 |
| 35 | 34.4 | 06.7 | 95 | 93.3 | 18.1 | 55 | 152.2 | 29.6 | 15 | 211.0 | 41.0 | 75 | 269.9 | 52.5 |
| 36 | 35.3 | 06.9 | 96 | 94.2 | 18.3 | 56 | 153.1 | 29.8 | 16 | 212.0 | 41.2 | 76 | 270.9 | 52.7 |
| 37 | 36.3 | 07.1 | 97 | 95.2 | 18.5 | 57 | 154.1 | 30.0 | 17 | 213.0 | 41.4 | 77 | 271.9 | 52.9 |
| 38 | 37.3 | 07.3 | 98 | 96.2 | 18.7 | 58 | 155.1 | 30.1 | 18 | 214.0 | 41.6 | 78 | 272.9 | 53.0 |
| 39 | 38.3 | 07.4 | 99 | 97.2 | 18.9 | 59 | 156.1 | 30.3 | 19 | 215.0 | 41.8 | 79 | 273.9 | 53.2 |
| 40 | 39.3 | 07.6 | 100 | 98.2 | 19.1 | 60 | 157.1 | 30.5 | 20 | 216.0 | 42.0 | 80 | 274.9 | 53.4 |
| 41 | 40.2 | 07.8 | 101 | 99.1 | 19.3 | 161 | 158.0 | 30.7 | 221 | 216.9 | 42.2 | 281 | 275.8 | 53.6 |
| 42 | 41.2 | 08.0 | 02 | 100.1 | 19.5 | 62 | 159.0 | 30.9 | 22 | 217.9 | 42.4 | 82 | 276.8 | 53.8 |
| 43 | 42.2 | 08.2 | 03 | 101.1 | 19.7 | 63 | 160.0 | 31.1 | 23 | 218.9 | 42.6 | 83 | 277.8 | 54.0 |
| 44 | 43.2 | 08.4 | 04 | 102.1 | 19.8 | 64 | 161.0 | 31.3 | 24 | 219.9 | 42.7 | 84 | 278.8 | 54.2 |
| 45 | 44.2 | 08.6 | 05 | 103.1 | 20.0 | 65 | 162.0 | 31.5 | 25 | 220.9 | 42.9 | 85 | 279.8 | 54.4 |
| 46 | 45.2 | 08.8 | 06 | 104.1 | 20.2 | 66 | 163.0 | 31.7 | 26 | 221.8 | 43.1 | 86 | 280.7 | 54.6 |
| 47 | 46.1 | 09.0 | 07 | 105.0 | 20.4 | 67 | 163.9 | 31.9 | 27 | 222.8 | 43.3 | 87 | 281.7 | 54.8 |
| 48 | 47.1 | 09.2 | 08 | 106.0 | 20.6 | 68 | 164.9 | 32.1 | 28 | 223.8 | 43.5 | 88 | 282.7 | 55.0 |
| 49 | 48.1 | 09.3 | 09 | 107.0 | 20.8 | 69 | 165.9 | 32.2 | 29 | 224.8 | 43.7 | 89 | 283.7 | 55.1 |
| 50 | 49.1 | 09.5 | 10 | 108.0 | 21.0 | 70 | 166.9 | 32.4 | 30 | 225.8 | 43.9 | 90 | 284.7 | 55.3 |
| 51 | 50.1 | 09.7 | 111 | 109.0 | 21.2 | 171 | 167.9 | 32.6 | 231 | 226.8 | 44.1 | 291 | 285.7 | 55.5 |
| 52 | 51.0 | 09.9 | 12 | 109.9 | 21.4 | 72 | 168.8 | 32.8 | 32 | 227.7 | 44.3 | 92 | 286.6 | 55.7 |
| 53 | 52.0 | 10.1 | 13 | 110.9 | 21.6 | 73 | 169.8 | 33.0 | 33 | 228.7 | 44.5 | 93 | 287.6 | 55.9 |
| 54 | 53.0 | 10.3 | 14 | 111.9 | 21.8 | 74 | 170.8 | 33.2 | 34 | 229.7 | 44.6 | 94 | 288.6 | 56.1 |
| 55 | 54.0 | 10.5 | 15 | 112.9 | 21.9 | 75 | 171.8 | 33.4 | 35 | 230.7 | 44.8 | 95 | 289.6 | 56.3 |
| 56 | 55.0 | 10.7 | 16 | 113.9 | 22.1 | 76 | 172.8 | 33.6 | 36 | 231.7 | 45.0 | 96 | 290.6 | 56.5 |
| 57 | 56.0 | 10.9 | 17 | 114.9 | 22.3 | 77 | 173.7 | 33.8 | 37 | 232.6 | 45.2 | 97 | 291.5 | 56.7 |
| 58 | 56.9 | 11.1 | 18 | 115.8 | 22.5 | 78 | 174.7 | 34.0 | 38 | 233.6 | 45.4 | 98 | 292.5 | 56.9 |
| 59 | 57.9 | 11.3 | 19 | 116.8 | 22.7 | 79 | 175.7 | 34.2 | 39 | 234.6 | 45.6 | 99 | 293.5 | 57.1 |
| 60 | 58.9 | 11.4 | 20 | 117.8 | 22.9 | 80 | 176.7 | 34.3 | 40 | 235.6 | 45.8 | 300 | 294.5 | 57.2 |
| Dist. | Dep. | Lat. | Dist. | Dep. | Lat. | Dist. | Dep. | Lat. | Dist. | Dep. | Lat. | Dist. | Dep. | Lat. |

[For 79 Degrees.

# TABLE II.

## Difference of Latitude and Departure for 12 Degrees.

| Dist. | Lat. | Dep. | Dist. | Lat. | Dep. | Dist. | Lat. | Dep. | Dist. | Lat. | Dep. | Dist. | Lat. | Dep. |
|---|---|---|---|---|---|---|---|---|---|---|---|---|---|---|
| 1 | 01.0 | 00.2 | 61 | 59.7 | 12.7 | 121 | 118.4 | 25.2 | 181 | 177.0 | 37.6 | 241 | 235.7 | 50.1 |
| 2 | 02.0 | 00.4 | 62 | 60.6 | 12.9 | 22 | 119.3 | 25.4 | 82 | 178.0 | 37.8 | 42 | 236.7 | 50.3 |
| 3 | 02.9 | 00.6 | 63 | 61.6 | 13.1 | 23 | 120.3 | 25.6 | 83 | 179.0 | 38.0 | 43 | 237.7 | 50.5 |
| 4 | 03.9 | 00.8 | 64 | 62.6 | 13.3 | 24 | 121.3 | 25.8 | 84 | 180.0 | 38.3 | 44 | 238.7 | 50.7 |
| 5 | 04.9 | 01.0 | 65 | 63.6 | 13.5 | 25 | 122.3 | 26.0 | 85 | 181.0 | 38.5 | 45 | 239.6 | 50.9 |
| 6 | 05.9 | 01.2 | 66 | 64.6 | 13.7 | 26 | 123.2 | 26.2 | 86 | 181.9 | 38.7 | 46 | 240.6 | 51.1 |
| 7 | 06.8 | 01.5 | 67 | 65.5 | 13.9 | 27 | 124.2 | 26.4 | 87 | 182.9 | 38.9 | 47 | 241.6 | 51.4 |
| 8 | 07.8 | 01.7 | 68 | 66.5 | 14.1 | 28 | 125.2 | 26.6 | 88 | 183.9 | 39.1 | 48 | 242.6 | 51.6 |
| 9 | 08.8 | 01.9 | 69 | 67.5 | 14.3 | 29 | 126.2 | 26.8 | 89 | 184.9 | 39.3 | 49 | 243.6 | 51.8 |
| 10 | 09.8 | 02.1 | 70 | 68.5 | 14.6 | 30 | 127.2 | 27.0 | 90 | 185.8 | 39.5 | 50 | 244.5 | 52.0 |
| 11 | 10.8 | 02.3 | 71 | 69.4 | 14.8 | 131 | 128.1 | 27.2 | 191 | 186.8 | 39.7 | 251 | 245.5 | 52.2 |
| 12 | 11.7 | 02.5 | 72 | 70.4 | 15.0 | 32 | 129.1 | 27.4 | 92 | 187.8 | 39.9 | 52 | 246.5 | 52.4 |
| 13 | 12.7 | 02.7 | 73 | 71.4 | 15.2 | 33 | 130.1 | 27.7 | 93 | 188.8 | 40.1 | 53 | 247.5 | 52.6 |
| 14 | 13.7 | 02.9 | 74 | 72.4 | 15.4 | 34 | 131.1 | 27.9 | 94 | 189.8 | 40.3 | 54 | 248.4 | 52.8 |
| 15 | 14.7 | 03.1 | 75 | 73.4 | 15.6 | 35 | 132.0 | 28.1 | 95 | 190.7 | 40.5 | 55 | 249.4 | 53.0 |
| 16 | 15.7 | 03.3 | 76 | 74.3 | 15.8 | 36 | 133.0 | 28.3 | 96 | 191.7 | 40.8 | 56 | 250.4 | 53.2 |
| 17 | 16.6 | 03.5 | 77 | 75.3 | 16.0 | 37 | 134.0 | 28.5 | 97 | 192.7 | 41.0 | 57 | 251.4 | 53.4 |
| 18 | 17.6 | 03.7 | 78 | 76.3 | 16.2 | 38 | 135.0 | 28.7 | 98 | 193.7 | 41.2 | 58 | 252.4 | 53.6 |
| 19 | 18.6 | 04.0 | 79 | 77.3 | 16.4 | 39 | 136.0 | 28.9 | 99 | 194.7 | 41.4 | 59 | 253.3 | 53.8 |
| 20 | 19.6 | 04.2 | 80 | 78.3 | 16.6 | 40 | 136.9 | 29.1 | 200 | 195.6 | 41.6 | 60 | 254.3 | 54.1 |
| 21 | 20.5 | 04.4 | 81 | 79.2 | 16.8 | 141 | 137.9 | 29.3 | 201 | 196.6 | 41.8 | 261 | 255.3 | 54.3 |
| 22 | 21.5 | 04.6 | 82 | 80.2 | 17.0 | 42 | 138.9 | 29.5 | 02 | 197.6 | 42.0 | 62 | 256.3 | 54.5 |
| 23 | 22.5 | 04.8 | 83 | 81.2 | 17.3 | 43 | 139.9 | 29.7 | 03 | 198.6 | 42.2 | 63 | 257.3 | 54.7 |
| 24 | 23.5 | 05.0 | 84 | 82.2 | 17.5 | 44 | 140.9 | 29.9 | 04 | 199.5 | 42.4 | 64 | 258.2 | 54.9 |
| 25 | 24.5 | 05.2 | 85 | 83.1 | 17.7 | 45 | 141.8 | 30.1 | 05 | 200.5 | 42.6 | 65 | 259.2 | 55.1 |
| 26 | 25.4 | 05.4 | 86 | 84.1 | 17.9 | 46 | 142.8 | 30.4 | 06 | 201.5 | 42.8 | 66 | 260.2 | 55.3 |
| 27 | 26.4 | 05.6 | 87 | 85.1 | 18.1 | 47 | 143.8 | 30.6 | 07 | 202.5 | 43.0 | 67 | 261.2 | 55.5 |
| 28 | 27.4 | 05.8 | 88 | 86.1 | 18.3 | 48 | 144.8 | 30.8 | 08 | 203.5 | 43.2 | 68 | 262.1 | 55.7 |
| 29 | 28.4 | 06.0 | 89 | 87.1 | 18.5 | 49 | 145.7 | 31.0 | 09 | 204.4 | 43.5 | 69 | 263.1 | 55.9 |
| 30 | 29.3 | 06.2 | 90 | 88.0 | 18.7 | 50 | 146.7 | 31.2 | 10 | 205.4 | 43.7 | 70 | 264.1 | 56.1 |
| 31 | 30.3 | 06.4 | 91 | 89.0 | 18.9 | 151 | 147.7 | 31.4 | 211 | 206.4 | 43.9 | 271 | 265.1 | 56.3 |
| 32 | 31.3 | 06.7 | 92 | 90.0 | 19.1 | 52 | 148.7 | 31.6 | 12 | 207.4 | 44.1 | 72 | 266.1 | 56.6 |
| 33 | 32.3 | 06.9 | 93 | 91.0 | 19.3 | 53 | 149.7 | 31.8 | 13 | 208.3 | 44.3 | 73 | 267.0 | 56.8 |
| 34 | 33.3 | 07.1 | 94 | 91.9 | 19.5 | 54 | 150.6 | 32.0 | 14 | 209.3 | 44.5 | 74 | 268.0 | 57.0 |
| 35 | 34.2 | 07.3 | 95 | 92.9 | 19.8 | 55 | 151.6 | 32.2 | 15 | 210.3 | 44.7 | 75 | 269.0 | 57.2 |
| 36 | 35.2 | 07.5 | 96 | 93.9 | 20.0 | 56 | 152.6 | 32.4 | 16 | 211.3 | 44.9 | 76 | 270.0 | 57.4 |
| 37 | 36.2 | 07.7 | 97 | 94.9 | 20.2 | 57 | 153.6 | 32.6 | 17 | 212.3 | 45.1 | 77 | 270.9 | 57.6 |
| 38 | 37.2 | 07.9 | 98 | 95.9 | 20.4 | 58 | 154.5 | 32.9 | 18 | 213.2 | 45.3 | 78 | 271.9 | 57.8 |
| 39 | 38.1 | 08.1 | 99 | 96.8 | 20.6 | 59 | 155.5 | 33.1 | 19 | 214.2 | 45.5 | 79 | 272.9 | 58.0 |
| 40 | 39.1 | 08.3 | 100 | 97.8 | 20.8 | 60 | 156.5 | 33.3 | 20 | 215.2 | 45.7 | 80 | 273.9 | 58.2 |
| 41 | 40.1 | 08.5 | 101 | 98.8 | 21.0 | 161 | 157.5 | 33.5 | 221 | 216.2 | 45.9 | 281 | 274.9 | 58.4 |
| 42 | 41.1 | 08.7 | 02 | 99.8 | 21.2 | 62 | 158.5 | 33.7 | 22 | 217.1 | 46.2 | 82 | 275.8 | 58.6 |
| 43 | 42.1 | 08.9 | 03 | 100.7 | 21.4 | 63 | 159.4 | 33.9 | 23 | 218.1 | 46.4 | 83 | 276.8 | 58.8 |
| 44 | 43.0 | 09.1 | 04 | 101.7 | 21.6 | 64 | 160.4 | 34.1 | 24 | 219.1 | 46.6 | 84 | 277.8 | 59.0 |
| 45 | 44.0 | 09.4 | 05 | 102.7 | 21.8 | 65 | 161.4 | 34.3 | 25 | 220.1 | 46.8 | 85 | 278.8 | 59.3 |
| 46 | 45.0 | 09.6 | 06 | 103.7 | 22.0 | 66 | 162.4 | 34.5 | 26 | 221.1 | 47.0 | 86 | 279.8 | 59.5 |
| 47 | 46.0 | 09.8 | 07 | 104.7 | 22.2 | 67 | 163.4 | 34.7 | 27 | 222.0 | 47.2 | 87 | 280.7 | 59.7 |
| 48 | 47.0 | 10.0 | 08 | 105.7 | 22.5 | 68 | 164.3 | 34.9 | 28 | 223.0 | 47.4 | 88 | 281.7 | 59.9 |
| 49 | 47.9 | 10.2 | 09 | 106.6 | 22.7 | 69 | 165.3 | 35.1 | 29 | 224.0 | 47.6 | 89 | 282.7 | 60.1 |
| 50 | 48.9 | 10.4 | 10 | 107.6 | 22.9 | 70 | 166.3 | 35.3 | 30 | 225.0 | 47.8 | 90 | 283.7 | 60.3 |
| 51 | 49.9 | 10.6 | 111 | 108.6 | 23.1 | 171 | 167.3 | 35.6 | 231 | 226.0 | 48.0 | 291 | 284.6 | 60.5 |
| 52 | 50.9 | 10.8 | 12 | 109.6 | 23.3 | 72 | 168.2 | 35.8 | 32 | 226.9 | 48.2 | 92 | 285.6 | 60.7 |
| 53 | 51.8 | 11.0 | 13 | 110.5 | 23.5 | 73 | 169.2 | 36.0 | 33 | 227.9 | 48.4 | 93 | 286.6 | 60.9 |
| 54 | 52.8 | 11.2 | 14 | 111.5 | 23.7 | 74 | 170.2 | 36.2 | 34 | 228.9 | 48.7 | 94 | 287.6 | 61.1 |
| 55 | 53.8 | 11.4 | 15 | 112.5 | 23.9 | 75 | 171.2 | 36.4 | 35 | 229.9 | 48.9 | 95 | 288.6 | 61.3 |
| 56 | 54.8 | 11.6 | 16 | 113.5 | 24.1 | 76 | 172.2 | 36.6 | 36 | 230.8 | 49.1 | 96 | 289.5 | 61.5 |
| 57 | 55.8 | 11.9 | 17 | 114.4 | 24.3 | 77 | 173.1 | 36.8 | 37 | 231.8 | 49.3 | 97 | 290.5 | 61.7 |
| 58 | 56.7 | 12.1 | 18 | 115.4 | 24.5 | 78 | 174.1 | 37.0 | 38 | 232.8 | 49.5 | 98 | 291.5 | 62.0 |
| 59 | 57.7 | 12.3 | 19 | 116.4 | 24.7 | 79 | 175.1 | 37.2 | 39 | 233.8 | 49.7 | 99 | 292.5 | 62.2 |
| 60 | 58.7 | 12.5 | 20 | 117.4 | 24.9 | 80 | 176.1 | 37.4 | 40 | 234.8 | 49.9 | 300 | 293.4 | 62.4 |
| Dist. | Dep. | Lat. | Dist. | Dep. | Lat. | Dist. | Dep. | Lat. | Dist. | Dep. | Lat. | Dist. | Dep. | Lat. |

# TABLE II.

## Difference of Latitude and Departure for 13 Degrees.

| Dist. | Lat. | Dep. | Dist. | Lat. | Dep. | Dist. | Lat. | Dep. | Dist. | Lat. | Dep. | Dist. | Lat. | Dep. |
|---|---|---|---|---|---|---|---|---|---|---|---|---|---|---|
| 1 | 01.0 | 00.2 | 61 | 59.4 | 13.7 | 121 | 117.9 | 27.2 | 181 | 176.4 | 40.7 | 241 | 234.8 | 54.2 |
| 2 | 01.9 | 00.4 | 62 | 60.4 | 13.9 | 22 | 118.9 | 27.4 | 82 | 177.3 | 40.9 | 42 | 235.8 | 54.4 |
| 3 | 02.9 | 00.7 | 63 | 61.4 | 14.2 | 23 | 119.8 | 27.7 | 83 | 178.3 | 41.2 | 43 | 236.8 | 54.7 |
| 4 | 03.9 | 00.9 | 64 | 62.4 | 14.4 | 24 | 120.8 | 27.9 | 84 | 179.3 | 41.4 | 44 | 237.7 | 54.9 |
| 5 | 04.9 | 01.1 | 65 | 63.3 | 14.6 | 25 | 121.8 | 28.1 | 85 | 180.3 | 41.6 | 45 | 238.7 | 55.1 |
| 6 | 05.8 | 01.3 | 66 | 64.3 | 14.8 | 26 | 122.8 | 28.3 | 86 | 181.2 | 41.8 | 46 | 239.7 | 55.3 |
| 7 | 06.8 | 01.6 | 67 | 65.3 | 15.1 | 27 | 123.7 | 28.6 | 87 | 182.2 | 42.1 | 47 | 240.7 | 55.6 |
| 8 | 07.8 | 01.8 | 68 | 66.3 | 15.3 | 28 | 124.7 | 28.8 | 88 | 183.2 | 42.3 | 48 | 241.6 | 55.8 |
| 9 | 08.8 | 02.0 | 69 | 67.2 | 15.5 | 29 | 125.7 | 29.0 | 89 | 184.2 | 42.5 | 49 | 242.6 | 56.0 |
| 10 | 09.7 | 02.2 | 70 | 68.2 | 15.7 | 30 | 126.7 | 29.2 | 90 | 185.1 | 42.7 | 50 | 243.6 | 56.2 |
| 11 | 10.7 | 02.5 | 71 | 69.2 | 16.0 | 131 | 127.6 | 29.5 | 191 | 186.1 | 43.0 | 251 | 244.6 | 56.5 |
| 12 | 11.7 | 02.7 | 72 | 70.2 | 16.2 | 32 | 128.6 | 29.7 | 92 | 187.1 | 43.2 | 52 | 245.5 | 56.7 |
| 13 | 12.7 | 02.9 | 73 | 71.1 | 16.4 | 33 | 129.6 | 29.9 | 93 | 188.1 | 43.4 | 53 | 246.5 | 56.9 |
| 14 | 13.6 | 03.1 | 74 | 72.1 | 16.6 | 34 | 130.6 | 30.1 | 94 | 189.0 | 43.6 | 54 | 247.5 | 57.1 |
| 15 | 14.6 | 03.4 | 75 | 73.1 | 16.9 | 35 | 131.5 | 30.4 | 95 | 190.0 | 43.9 | 55 | 248.5 | 57.4 |
| 16 | 15.6 | 03.6 | 76 | 74.1 | 17.1 | 36 | 132.5 | 30.6 | 96 | 191.0 | 44.1 | 56 | 249.4 | 57.6 |
| 17 | 16.6 | 03.8 | 77 | 75.0 | 17.3 | 37 | 133.5 | 30.8 | 97 | 192.0 | 44.3 | 57 | 250.4 | 57.8 |
| 18 | 17.5 | 04.0 | 78 | 76.0 | 17.5 | 38 | 134.5 | 31.0 | 98 | 192.9 | 44.5 | 58 | 251.4 | 58.0 |
| 19 | 18.5 | 04.3 | 79 | 77.0 | 17.8 | 39 | 135.4 | 31.3 | 99 | 193.9 | 44.8 | 59 | 252.4 | 58.3 |
| 20 | 19.5 | 04.5 | 80 | 77.9 | 18.0 | 40 | 136.4 | 31.5 | 200 | 194.9 | 45.0 | 60 | 253.3 | 58.5 |
| 21 | 20.5 | 04.7 | 81 | 78.9 | 18.2 | 141 | 137.4 | 31.7 | 201 | 195.8 | 45.2 | 261 | 254.3 | 58.7 |
| 22 | 21.4 | 04.9 | 82 | 79.9 | 18.4 | 42 | 138.4 | 31.9 | 02 | 196.8 | 45.4 | 62 | 255.3 | 58.9 |
| 23 | 22.4 | 05.2 | 83 | 80.9 | 18.7 | 43 | 139.3 | 32.2 | 03 | 197.8 | 45.7 | 63 | 256.3 | 59.2 |
| 24 | 23.4 | 05.4 | 84 | 81.8 | 18.9 | 44 | 140.3 | 32.4 | 04 | 198.8 | 45.9 | 64 | 257.2 | 59.4 |
| 25 | 24.4 | 05.6 | 85 | 82.8 | 19.1 | 45 | 141.3 | 32.6 | 05 | 199.7 | 46.1 | 65 | 258.2 | 59.6 |
| 26 | 25.3 | 05.8 | 86 | 83.8 | 19.3 | 46 | 142.3 | 32.8 | 06 | 200.7 | 46.3 | 66 | 259.2 | 59.8 |
| 27 | 26.3 | 06.1 | 87 | 84.8 | 19.6 | 47 | 143.2 | 33.1 | 07 | 201.7 | 46.6 | 67 | 260.2 | 60.1 |
| 28 | 27.3 | 06.3 | 88 | 85.7 | 19.8 | 48 | 144.2 | 33.3 | 08 | 202.7 | 46.8 | 68 | 261.1 | 60.3 |
| 29 | 28.3 | 06.5 | 89 | 86.7 | 20.0 | 49 | 145.2 | 33.5 | 09 | 203.6 | 47.0 | 69 | 262.1 | 60.5 |
| 30 | 29.2 | 06.7 | 90 | 87.7 | 20.2 | 50 | 146.2 | 33.7 | 10 | 204.6 | 47.2 | 70 | 263.1 | 60.7 |
| 31 | 30.2 | 07.0 | 91 | 88.7 | 20.5 | 151 | 147.1 | 34.0 | 211 | 205.6 | 47.5 | 271 | 264.1 | 61.0 |
| 32 | 31.2 | 07.2 | 92 | 89.6 | 20.7 | 52 | 148.1 | 34.2 | 12 | 206.6 | 47.7 | 72 | 265.0 | 61.2 |
| 33 | 32.2 | 07.4 | 93 | 90.6 | 20.9 | 53 | 149.1 | 34.4 | 13 | 207.5 | 47.9 | 73 | 266.0 | 61.4 |
| 34 | 33.1 | 07.6 | 94 | 91.6 | 21.1 | 54 | 150.1 | 34.6 | 14 | 208.5 | 48.1 | 74 | 267.0 | 61.6 |
| 35 | 34.1 | 07.9 | 95 | 92.6 | 21.4 | 55 | 151.0 | 34.9 | 15 | 209.5 | 48.4 | 75 | 268.0 | 61.9 |
| 36 | 35.1 | 08.1 | 96 | 93.5 | 21.6 | 56 | 152.0 | 35.1 | 16 | 210.5 | 48.6 | 76 | 268.9 | 62.1 |
| 37 | 36.1 | 08.3 | 97 | 94.5 | 21.8 | 57 | 153.0 | 35.3 | 17 | 211.4 | 48.8 | 77 | 269.9 | 62.3 |
| 38 | 37.0 | 08.5 | 98 | 95.5 | 22.0 | 58 | 154.0 | 35.5 | 18 | 212.4 | 49.0 | 78 | 270.9 | 62.5 |
| 39 | 38.0 | 08.8 | 99 | 96.5 | 22.3 | 59 | 154.9 | 35.8 | 19 | 213.4 | 49.3 | 79 | 271.8 | 62.8 |
| 40 | 39.0 | 09.0 | 100 | 97.4 | 22.5 | 60 | 155.9 | 36.0 | 20 | 214.4 | 49.5 | 80 | 272.8 | 63.0 |
| 41 | 39.9 | 09.2 | 101 | 98.4 | 22.7 | 161 | 156.9 | 36.2 | 221 | 215.3 | 49.7 | 281 | 273.8 | 63.2 |
| 42 | 40.9 | 09.4 | 02 | 99.4 | 22.9 | 62 | 157.8 | 36.4 | 22 | 216.3 | 49.9 | 82 | 274.8 | 63.4 |
| 43 | 41.9 | 09.7 | 03 | 100.4 | 23.2 | 63 | 158.8 | 36.7 | 23 | 217.3 | 50.2 | 83 | 275.7 | 63.7 |
| 44 | 42.9 | 09.9 | 04 | 101.3 | 23.4 | 64 | 159.8 | 36.9 | 24 | 218.3 | 50.4 | 84 | 276.7 | 63.9 |
| 45 | 43.8 | 10.1 | 05 | 102.3 | 23.6 | 65 | 160.8 | 37.1 | 25 | 219.2 | 50.6 | 85 | 277.7 | 64.1 |
| 46 | 44.8 | 10.3 | 06 | 103.3 | 23.8 | 66 | 161.7 | 37.3 | 26 | 220.2 | 50.8 | 86 | 278.7 | 64.3 |
| 47 | 45.8 | 10.6 | 07 | 104.3 | 24.1 | 67 | 162.7 | 37.6 | 27 | 221.2 | 51.1 | 87 | 279.6 | 64.6 |
| 48 | 46.8 | 10.8 | 08 | 105.2 | 24.3 | 68 | 163.7 | 37.8 | 28 | 222.2 | 51.3 | 88 | 280.6 | 64.8 |
| 49 | 47.7 | 11.0 | 09 | 106.2 | 24.5 | 69 | 164.7 | 38.0 | 29 | 223.1 | 51.5 | 89 | 281.6 | 65.0 |
| 50 | 48.7 | 11.2 | 10 | 107.2 | 24.7 | 70 | 165.6 | 38.2 | 30 | 224.1 | 51.7 | 90 | 282.6 | 65.2 |
| 51 | 49.7 | 11.5 | 111 | 108.2 | 25.0 | 171 | 166.6 | 38.5 | 231 | 225.1 | 52.0 | 291 | 283.5 | 65.5 |
| 52 | 50.7 | 11.7 | 12 | 109.1 | 25.2 | 72 | 167.6 | 38.7 | 32 | 226.1 | 52.2 | 92 | 284.5 | 65.7 |
| 53 | 51.6 | 11.9 | 13 | 110.1 | 25.4 | 73 | 168.6 | 38.9 | 33 | 227.0 | 52.4 | 93 | 285.5 | 65.9 |
| 54 | 52.6 | 12.1 | 14 | 111.1 | 25.6 | 74 | 169.5 | 39.1 | 34 | 228.0 | 52.6 | 94 | 286.5 | 66.1 |
| 55 | 53.6 | 12.4 | 15 | 112.1 | 25.9 | 75 | 170.5 | 39.4 | 35 | 229.0 | 52.9 | 95 | 287.4 | 66.4 |
| 56 | 54.6 | 12.6 | 16 | 113.0 | 26.1 | 76 | 171.5 | 39.6 | 36 | 230.0 | 53.1 | 96 | 288.4 | 66.6 |
| 57 | 55.5 | 12.8 | 17 | 114.0 | 26.3 | 77 | 172.5 | 39.8 | 37 | 230.9 | 53.3 | 97 | 289.4 | 66.8 |
| 58 | 56.5 | 13.0 | 18 | 115.0 | 26.5 | 78 | 173.4 | 40.0 | 38 | 231.9 | 53.5 | 98 | 290.4 | 67.0 |
| 59 | 57.5 | 13.3 | 19 | 116.0 | 26.8 | 79 | 174.4 | 40.3 | 39 | 232.9 | 53.8 | 99 | 291.3 | 67.3 |
| 60 | 58.5 | 13.5 | 20 | 116.9 | 27.0 | 80 | 175.4 | 40.5 | 40 | 233.8 | 54.0 | 300 | 292.3 | 67.5 |
| Dist. | Dep. | Lat. | Dist. | Dep | Lat. | Dist. | Dep. | Lat. | Dist. | Dep. | Lat. | Dist. | Dep. | Lat. |

[For 77 Degrees.

# TABLE II.

## Difference of Latitude and Departure for 14 Degrees.

| Dist. | Lat. | Dep. | Dist. | Lat. | Dep. | Dist. | Lat. | Dep. | Dist. | Lat. | Dep. | Dist. | Lat. | Dep. |
|---|---|---|---|---|---|---|---|---|---|---|---|---|---|---|
| 1 | 01.0 | 00.2 | 61 | 59.2 | 14.8 | 121 | 117.4 | 29.3 | 181 | 175.6 | 43.8 | 241 | 233.8 | 58.3 |
| 2 | 01.9 | 00.5 | 62 | 60.2 | 15.0 | 22 | 118.4 | 29.5 | 82 | 176.6 | 44.0 | 42 | 234.8 | 58.5 |
| 3 | 02.9 | 00.7 | 63 | 61.1 | 15.2 | 23 | 119.3 | 29.8 | 83 | 177.6 | 44.3 | 43 | 235.8 | 58.8 |
| 4 | 03.9 | 01.0 | 64 | 62.1 | 15.5 | 24 | 120.3 | 30.0 | 84 | 178.5 | 44.5 | 44 | 236.8 | 59.0 |
| 5 | 04.9 | 01.2 | 65 | 63.1 | 15.7 | 25 | 121.3 | 30.2 | 85 | 179.5 | 44.8 | 45 | 237.7 | 59.3 |
| 6 | 05.8 | 01.5 | 66 | 64.0 | 16.0 | 26 | 122.3 | 30.5 | 86 | 180.5 | 45.0 | 46 | 238.7 | 59.5 |
| 7 | 06.8 | 01.7 | 67 | 65.0 | 16.2 | 27 | 123.2 | 30.7 | 87 | 181.4 | 45.2 | 47 | 239.7 | 59.8 |
| 8 | 07.8 | 01.9 | 68 | 66.0 | 16.5 | 28 | 124.2 | 31.0 | 88 | 182.4 | 45.5 | 48 | 240.6 | 60.0 |
| 9 | 08.7 | 02.2 | 69 | 67.0 | 16.7 | 29 | 125.2 | 31.2 | 89 | 183.4 | 45.7 | 49 | 241.6 | 60.2 |
| 10 | 09.7 | 02.4 | 70 | 67.9 | 16.9 | 30 | 126.1 | 31.4 | 90 | 184.4 | 46.0 | 50 | 242.6 | 60.5 |
| 11 | 10.7 | 02.7 | 71 | 68.9 | 17.2 | 131 | 127.1 | 31.7 | 191 | 185.3 | 46.2 | 251 | 243.5 | 60.7 |
| 12 | 11.6 | 02.9 | 72 | 69.9 | 17.4 | 32 | 128.1 | 31.9 | 92 | 186.3 | 46.4 | 52 | 244.5 | 61.0 |
| 13 | 12.6 | 03.1 | 73 | 70.8 | 17.7 | 33 | 129.0 | 32.2 | 93 | 187.3 | 46.7 | 53 | 245.5 | 61.2 |
| 14 | 13.6 | 03.4 | 74 | 71.8 | 17.9 | 34 | 130.0 | 32.4 | 94 | 188.2 | 46.9 | 54 | 246.5 | 61.4 |
| 15 | 14.6 | 03.6 | 75 | 72.8 | 18.1 | 35 | 131.0 | 32.7 | 95 | 189.2 | 47.2 | 55 | 247.4 | 61.7 |
| 16 | 15.5 | 03.9 | 76 | 73.7 | 18.4 | 36 | 132.0 | 32.9 | 96 | 190.2 | 47.4 | 56 | 248.4 | 61.9 |
| 17 | 16.5 | 04.1 | 77 | 74.7 | 18.6 | 37 | 132.9 | 33.1 | 97 | 191.1 | 47.7 | 57 | 249.4 | 62.2 |
| 18 | 17.5 | 04.4 | 78 | 75.7 | 18.9 | 38 | 133.9 | 33.4 | 98 | 192.1 | 47.9 | 58 | 250.3 | 62.4 |
| 19 | 18.4 | 04.6 | 79 | 76.7 | 19.1 | 39 | 134.9 | 33.6 | 99 | 193.1 | 48.1 | 59 | 251.3 | 62.7 |
| 20 | 19.4 | 04.8 | 80 | 77.6 | 19.4 | 40 | 135.8 | 33.9 | 200 | 194.1 | 48.4 | 60 | 252.3 | 62.9 |
| 21 | 20.4 | 05.1 | 81 | 78.6 | 19.6 | 141 | 136.8 | 34.1 | 201 | 195.0 | 48.6 | 261 | 253.2 | 63.1 |
| 22 | 21.3 | 05.3 | 82 | 79.6 | 19.8 | 42 | 137.8 | 34.4 | 02 | 196.0 | 48.9 | 62 | 254.2 | 63.4 |
| 23 | 22.3 | 05.6 | 83 | 80.5 | 20.1 | 43 | 138.8 | 34.6 | 03 | 197.0 | 49.1 | 63 | 255.2 | 63.6 |
| 24 | 23.3 | 05.8 | 84 | 81.5 | 20.3 | 44 | 139.7 | 34.8 | 04 | 197.9 | 49.4 | 64 | 256.2 | 63.9 |
| 25 | 24.3 | 06.0 | 85 | 82.5 | 20.6 | 45 | 140.7 | 35.1 | 05 | 198.9 | 49.6 | 65 | 257.1 | 64.1 |
| 26 | 25.2 | 06.3 | 86 | 83.4 | 20.8 | 46 | 141.7 | 35.3 | 06 | 199.9 | 49.8 | 66 | 258.1 | 64.4 |
| 27 | 26.2 | 06.5 | 87 | 84.4 | 21.0 | 47 | 142.6 | 35.6 | 07 | 200.9 | 50.1 | 67 | 259.1 | 64.6 |
| 28 | 27.2 | 06.8 | 88 | 85.4 | 21.3 | 48 | 143.6 | 35.8 | 08 | 201.8 | 50.3 | 68 | 260.0 | 64.8 |
| 29 | 28.1 | 07.0 | 89 | 86.4 | 21.5 | 49 | 144.6 | 36.0 | 09 | 202.8 | 50.6 | 69 | 261.0 | 65.1 |
| 30 | 29.1 | 07.3 | 90 | 87.3 | 21.8 | 50 | 145.5 | 36.3 | 10 | 203.8 | 50.8 | 70 | 262.0 | 65.3 |
| 31 | 30.1 | 07.5 | 91 | 88.3 | 22.0 | 151 | 146.5 | 36.5 | 211 | 204.7 | 51.0 | 271 | 263.0 | 65.6 |
| 32 | 31.0 | 07.7 | 92 | 89.3 | 22.3 | 52 | 147.5 | 36.8 | 12 | 205.7 | 51.3 | 72 | 263.9 | 65.8 |
| 33 | 32.0 | 08.0 | 93 | 90.2 | 22.5 | 53 | 148.5 | 37.0 | 13 | 206.7 | 51.5 | 73 | 264.9 | 66.0 |
| 34 | 33.0 | 08.2 | 94 | 91.2 | 22.7 | 54 | 149.4 | 37.3 | 14 | 207.6 | 51.8 | 74 | 265.9 | 66.3 |
| 35 | 34.0 | 08.5 | 95 | 92.2 | 23.0 | 55 | 150.4 | 37.5 | 15 | 208.6 | 52.0 | 75 | 266.8 | 66.5 |
| 36 | 34.9 | 08.7 | 96 | 93.1 | 23.2 | 56 | 151.4 | 37.7 | 16 | 209.6 | 52.3 | 76 | 267.8 | 66.8 |
| 37 | 35.9 | 09.0 | 97 | 94.1 | 23.5 | 57 | 152.3 | 38.0 | 17 | 210.6 | 52.5 | 77 | 268.8 | 67.0 |
| 38 | 36.9 | 09.2 | 98 | 95.1 | 23.7 | 58 | 153.3 | 38.2 | 18 | 211.5 | 52.7 | 78 | 269.7 | 67.3 |
| 39 | 37.8 | 09.4 | 99 | 96.1 | 24.0 | 59 | 154.3 | 38.5 | 19 | 212.5 | 53.0 | 79 | 270.7 | 67.5 |
| 40 | 38.8 | 09.7 | 100 | 97.0 | 24.2 | 60 | 155.2 | 38.7 | 20 | 213.5 | 53.2 | 80 | 271.7 | 67.7 |
| 41 | 39.8 | 09.9 | 101 | 98.0 | 24.4 | 161 | 156.2 | 38.9 | 221 | 214.4 | 53.5 | 281 | 272.7 | 68.0 |
| 42 | 40.8 | 10.2 | 02 | 99.0 | 24.7 | 62 | 157.2 | 39.2 | 22 | 215.4 | 53.7 | 82 | 273.6 | 68.2 |
| 43 | 41.7 | 10.4 | 03 | 99.9 | 24.9 | 63 | 158.2 | 39.4 | 23 | 216.4 | 53.9 | 83 | 274.6 | 68.5 |
| 44 | 42.7 | 10.6 | 04 | 100.9 | 25.2 | 64 | 159.1 | 39.7 | 24 | 217.3 | 54.2 | 84 | 275.6 | 68.7 |
| 45 | 43.7 | 10.9 | 05 | 101.9 | 25.4 | 65 | 160.1 | 39.9 | 25 | 218.3 | 54.4 | 85 | 276.5 | 68.9 |
| 46 | 44.6 | 11.1 | 06 | 102.9 | 25.6 | 66 | 161.1 | 40.2 | 26 | 219.3 | 54.7 | 86 | 277.5 | 69.2 |
| 47 | 45.6 | 11.4 | 07 | 103.8 | 25.9 | 67 | 162.0 | 40.4 | 27 | 220.3 | 54.9 | 87 | 278.5 | 69.4 |
| 48 | 46.6 | 11.6 | 08 | 104.8 | 26.1 | 68 | 163.0 | 40.6 | 28 | 221.2 | 55.2 | 88 | 279.4 | 69.7 |
| 49 | 47.5 | 11.9 | 09 | 105.8 | 26.4 | 69 | 164.0 | 40.9 | 29 | 222.2 | 55.4 | 89 | 280.4 | 69.9 |
| 50 | 48.5 | 12.1 | 10 | 106.7 | 26.6 | 70 | 165.0 | 41.1 | 30 | 223.2 | 55.6 | 90 | 281.4 | 70.2 |
| 51 | 49.5 | 12.3 | 111 | 107.7 | 26.9 | 171 | 165.9 | 41.4 | 231 | 224.1 | 55.9 | 291 | 282.4 | 70.4 |
| 52 | 50.5 | 12.6 | 12 | 108.7 | 27.1 | 72 | 166.9 | 41.6 | 32 | 225.1 | 56.1 | 92 | 283.3 | 70.6 |
| 53 | 51.4 | 12.8 | 13 | 109.6 | 27.3 | 73 | 167.9 | 41.9 | 33 | 226.1 | 56.4 | 93 | 284.3 | 70.9 |
| 54 | 52.4 | 13.1 | 14 | 110.6 | 27.6 | 74 | 168.8 | 42.1 | 34 | 227.0 | 56.6 | 94 | 285.3 | 71.1 |
| 55 | 53.4 | 13.3 | 15 | 111.6 | 27.8 | 75 | 169.8 | 42.3 | 35 | 228.0 | 56.9 | 95 | 286.2 | 71.4 |
| 56 | 54.3 | 13.5 | 16 | 112.6 | 28.1 | 76 | 170.8 | 42.6 | 36 | 229.0 | 57.1 | 96 | 287.2 | 71.6 |
| 57 | 55.3 | 13.8 | 17 | 113.5 | 28.3 | 77 | 171.7 | 42.8 | 37 | 230.0 | 57.3 | 97 | 288.2 | 71.9 |
| 58 | 56.3 | 14.0 | 18 | 114.5 | 28.5 | 78 | 172.7 | 43.1 | 38 | 230.9 | 57.6 | 98 | 289.1 | 72.1 |
| 59 | 57.2 | 14.3 | 19 | 115.5 | 28.8 | 79 | 173.7 | 43.3 | 39 | 231.9 | 57.8 | 99 | 290.1 | 72.3 |
| 60 | 58.2 | 14.5 | 20 | 116.4 | 29.0 | 80 | 174.7 | 43.5 | 40 | 232.9 | 58.1 | 300 | 291.1 | 72.6 |
| Dist. | Dep. | Lat. | Dist. | Dep. | Lat. | Dist. | Dep. | Lat. | Dist. | Dep. | Lat. | Dist. | Dep. | Lat. |

[For 76 Degrees.

# TABLE II.

## Difference of Latitude and Departure for 15 Degrees.

| Dist. | Lat. | Dep. | Dist. | Lat. | Dep. | Dist. | Lat. | Dep. | Dist. | Lat. | Dep. | Dist. | Lat. | Dep. |
|---|---|---|---|---|---|---|---|---|---|---|---|---|---|---|
| 1 | 01.0 | 00.3 | 61 | 58.9 | 15.8 | 121 | 116.9 | 31.3 | 181 | 174.8 | 46.8 | 241 | 232.8 | 62.4 |
| 2 | 01.9 | 00.5 | 62 | 59.9 | 16.0 | 22 | 117.8 | 31.6 | 82 | 175.8 | 47.1 | 42 | 233.8 | 62.6 |
| 3 | 02.9 | 00.8 | 63 | 60.9 | 16.3 | 23 | 118.8 | 31.8 | 83 | 176.8 | 47.4 | 43 | 234.7 | 62.9 |
| 4 | 03.9 | 01.0 | 64 | 61.8 | 16.6 | 24 | 119.8 | 32.1 | 84 | 177.7 | 47.6 | 44 | 235.7 | 63.2 |
| 5 | 04.8 | 01.3 | 65 | 62.8 | 16.8 | 25 | 120.7 | 32.4 | 85 | 178.7 | 47.9 | 45 | 236.7 | 63.4 |
| 6 | 05.8 | 01.6 | 66 | 63.8 | 17.1 | 26 | 121.7 | 32.6 | 86 | 179.7 | 48.1 | 46 | 237.6 | 63.7 |
| 7 | 06.8 | 01.8 | 67 | 64.7 | 17.3 | 27 | 122.7 | 32.9 | 87 | 180.6 | 48.4 | 47 | 238.6 | 63.9 |
| 8 | 07.7 | 02.1 | 68 | 65.7 | 17.6 | 28 | 123.6 | 33.1 | 88 | 181.6 | 48.7 | 48 | 239.5 | 64.2 |
| 9 | 08.7 | 02.3 | 69 | 66.6 | 17.9 | 29 | 124.6 | 33.4 | 89 | 182.6 | 48.9 | 49 | 240.3 | 64.4 |
| 10 | 09.7 | 02.6 | 70 | 67.6 | 18.1 | 30 | 125.6 | 33.6 | 90 | 183.5 | 49.2 | 50 | 241.5 | 64.7 |
| 11 | 10.6 | 02.8 | 71 | 68.6 | 18.4 | 131 | 126.5 | 33.9 | 191 | 184.5 | 49.4 | 251 | 242.4 | 65.0 |
| 12 | 11.6 | 03.1 | 72 | 69.5 | 18.6 | 32 | 127.5 | 34.2 | 92 | 185.5 | 49.7 | 52 | 243.4 | 65.2 |
| 13 | 12.6 | 03.4 | 73 | 70.5 | 18.9 | 33 | 128.5 | 34.4 | 93 | 186.4 | 50.0 | 53 | 244.4 | 65.5 |
| 14 | 13.5 | 03.6 | 74 | 71.5 | 19.2 | 34 | 129.4 | 34.7 | 94 | 187.4 | 50.2 | 54 | 245.3 | 65.7 |
| 15 | 14.5 | 03.9 | 75 | 72.4 | 19.4 | 35 | 130.4 | 34.9 | 95 | 188.4 | 50.5 | 55 | 246.3 | 66.0 |
| 16 | 15.5 | 04.1 | 76 | 73.4 | 19.7 | 36 | 131.4 | 35.2 | 96 | 189.3 | 50.7 | 56 | 247.3 | 66.3 |
| 17 | 16.4 | 04.4 | 77 | 74.4 | 19.9 | 37 | 132.3 | 35.5 | 97 | 190.3 | 51.0 | 57 | 248.2 | 66.5 |
| 18 | 17.4 | 04.7 | 78 | 75.3 | 20.2 | 38 | 133.3 | 35.7 | 98 | 191.3 | 51.2 | 58 | 249.2 | 66.8 |
| 19 | 18.4 | 04.9 | 79 | 76.3 | 20.4 | 39 | 134.3 | 36.0 | 99 | 192.2 | 51.5 | 59 | 250.2 | 67.0 |
| 20 | 19.3 | 05.2 | 80 | 77.3 | 20.7 | 40 | 135.2 | 36.2 | 200 | 193.2 | 51.8 | 60 | 251.1 | 67.3 |
| 21 | 20.3 | 05.4 | 81 | 78.2 | 21.0 | 141 | 136.2 | 36.5 | 201 | 194.2 | 52.0 | 261 | 252.1 | 67.6 |
| 22 | 21.3 | 05.7 | 82 | 79.2 | 21.2 | 42 | 137.2 | 36.8 | 02 | 195.1 | 52.3 | 62 | 253.1 | 67.8 |
| 23 | 22.2 | 06.0 | 83 | 80.2 | 21.5 | 43 | 138.1 | 37.0 | 03 | 196.1 | 52.5 | 63 | 254.0 | 68.1 |
| 24 | 23.2 | 06.2 | 84 | 81.1 | 21.7 | 44 | 139.1 | 37.3 | 04 | 197.0 | 52.8 | 64 | 255.0 | 68.3 |
| 25 | 24.1 | 06.5 | 85 | 82.1 | 22.0 | 45 | 140.1 | 37.5 | 05 | 198.0 | 53.1 | 65 | 256.0 | 68.6 |
| 26 | 25.1 | 06.7 | 86 | 83.1 | 22.3 | 46 | 141.0 | 37.8 | 06 | 199.0 | 53.3 | 66 | 256.9 | 68.8 |
| 27 | 26.1 | 07.0 | 87 | 84.0 | 22.5 | 47 | 142.0 | 38.0 | 07 | 199.9 | 53.6 | 67 | 257.9 | 69.1 |
| 28 | 27.0 | 07.2 | 88 | 85.0 | 22.8 | 48 | 143.0 | 38.3 | 08 | 200.9 | 53.8 | 68 | 258.9 | 69.4 |
| 29 | 28.0 | 07.5 | 89 | 86.0 | 23.0 | 49 | 143.9 | 38.6 | 09 | 201.9 | 54.1 | 69 | 259.8 | 69.6 |
| 30 | 29.0 | 07.8 | 90 | 86.9 | 23.3 | 50 | 144.9 | 38.8 | 10 | 202.8 | 54.4 | 70 | 260.8 | 69.9 |
| 31 | 29.9 | 08.0 | 91 | 87.9 | 23.6 | 151 | 145.9 | 39.1 | 211 | 203.8 | 54.6 | 271 | 261.8 | 70.1 |
| 32 | 30.9 | 08.3 | 92 | 88.9 | 23.8 | 52 | 146.8 | 39.3 | 12 | 204.8 | 54.9 | 72 | 262.7 | 70.4 |
| 33 | 31.9 | 08.5 | 93 | 89.8 | 24.1 | 53 | 147.8 | 39.6 | 13 | 205.7 | 55.1 | 73 | 263.7 | 70.7 |
| 34 | 32.8 | 08.8 | 94 | 90.8 | 24.3 | 54 | 148.8 | 39.9 | 14 | 206.7 | 55.4 | 74 | 264.7 | 70.9 |
| 35 | 33.8 | 09.1 | 95 | 91.8 | 24.6 | 55 | 149.7 | 40.1 | 15 | 207.7 | 55.6 | 75 | 265.6 | 71.2 |
| 36 | 34.8 | 09.3 | 96 | 92.7 | 24.8 | 56 | 150.7 | 40.4 | 16 | 208.6 | 55.9 | 76 | 266.6 | 71.4 |
| 37 | 35.7 | 09.6 | 97 | 93.7 | 25.1 | 57 | 151.7 | 40.6 | 17 | 209.6 | 56.2 | 77 | 267.6 | 71.7 |
| 38 | 36.7 | 09.8 | 98 | 94.7 | 25.4 | 58 | 152.6 | 40.9 | 18 | 210.6 | 56.4 | 78 | 268.5 | 72.0 |
| 39 | 37.7 | 10.1 | 99 | 95.6 | 25.6 | 59 | 153.6 | 41.2 | 19 | 211.5 | 56.7 | 79 | 269.5 | 72.2 |
| 40 | 38.6 | 10.4 | 100 | 96.6 | 25.9 | 60 | 154.5 | 41.4 | 20 | 212.5 | 56.9 | 80 | 270.5 | 72.5 |
| 41 | 39.6 | 10.6 | 101 | 97.6 | 26.1 | 161 | 155.5 | 41.7 | 221 | 213.5 | 57.2 | 281 | 271.4 | 72.7 |
| 42 | 40.6 | 10.9 | 02 | 98.5 | 26.4 | 62 | 156.5 | 41.9 | 22 | 214.4 | 57.5 | 82 | 272.4 | 73.0 |
| 43 | 41.5 | 11.1 | 03 | 99.5 | 26.7 | 63 | 157.4 | 42.2 | 23 | 215.4 | 57.7 | 83 | 273.4 | 73.2 |
| 44 | 42.5 | 11.4 | 04 | 100.5 | 26.9 | 64 | 158.4 | 42.4 | 24 | 216.4 | 58.0 | 84 | 274.3 | 73.5 |
| 45 | 43.5 | 11.6 | 05 | 101.4 | 27.2 | 65 | 159.4 | 42.7 | 25 | 217.3 | 58.2 | 85 | 275.3 | 73.8 |
| 46 | 44.4 | 11.9 | 06 | 102.4 | 27.4 | 66 | 160.3 | 43.0 | 26 | 218.3 | 58.5 | 86 | 276.3 | 74.0 |
| 47 | 45.4 | 12.2 | 07 | 103.4 | 27.7 | 67 | 161.3 | 43.2 | 27 | 219.3 | 58.8 | 87 | 277.2 | 74.3 |
| 48 | 46.4 | 12.4 | 08 | 104.3 | 28.0 | 68 | 162.3 | 43.5 | 28 | 220.2 | 59.0 | 88 | 278.2 | 74.5 |
| 49 | 47.3 | 12.7 | 09 | 105.3 | 28.2 | 69 | 163.2 | 43.7 | 29 | 221.2 | 59.3 | 89 | 279.2 | 74.8 |
| 50 | 48.3 | 12.9 | 10 | 106.3 | 28.5 | 70 | 164.2 | 44.0 | 30 | 222.2 | 59.5 | 90 | 280.1 | 75.1 |
| 51 | 49.3 | 13.2 | 111 | 107.2 | 28.7 | 171 | 165.2 | 44.3 | 231 | 223.1 | 59.8 | 291 | 281.1 | 75.3 |
| 52 | 50.2 | 13.5 | 12 | 108.2 | 29.0 | 72 | 166.1 | 44.5 | 32 | 224.1 | 60.0 | 92 | 282.1 | 75.6 |
| 53 | 51.2 | 13.7 | 13 | 109.1 | 29.2 | 73 | 167.1 | 44.8 | 33 | 225.1 | 60.3 | 93 | 283.0 | 75.8 |
| 54 | 52.2 | 14.0 | 14 | 110.1 | 29.5 | 74 | 168.1 | 45.0 | 34 | 226.0 | 60.6 | 94 | 284.0 | 76.1 |
| 55 | 53.1 | 14.2 | 15 | 111.1 | 29.8 | 75 | 169.0 | 45.3 | 35 | 227.0 | 60.8 | 95 | 284.9 | 76.4 |
| 56 | 54.1 | 14.5 | 16 | 112.0 | 30.0 | 76 | 170.0 | 45.6 | 36 | 228.0 | 61.1 | 96 | 285.9 | 76.6 |
| 57 | 55.1 | 14.8 | 17 | 113.0 | 30.3 | 77 | 171.0 | 45.8 | 37 | 228.9 | 61.3 | 97 | 286.9 | 76.9 |
| 58 | 56.0 | 15.0 | 18 | 114.0 | 30.5 | 78 | 171.9 | 46.1 | 38 | 229.9 | 61.6 | 98 | 287.8 | 77.1 |
| 59 | 57.0 | 15.3 | 19 | 114.9 | 30.8 | 79 | 172.9 | 46.3 | 39 | 230.9 | 61.9 | 99 | 288.8 | 77.4 |
| 60 | 58.0 | 15.5 | 20 | 115.9 | 31.1 | 80 | 173.9 | 46.6 | 40 | 231.8 | 62.1 | 300 | 289.8 | 77.6 |
| Dist. | Dep. | Lat. | Dist. | Dep. | Lat. | Dist. | Dep. | Lat. | Dist. | Dep. | Lat. | Dist. | Dep. | Lat. |

# TABLE II.

## Difference of Latitude and Departure for 16 Degrees

| Dist. | Lat. | Dep. | Dist. | Lat. | Dep. | Dist. | Lat. | Dep. | Dist. | Lat. | Dep. | Dist. | Lat. | Dep. |
|---|---|---|---|---|---|---|---|---|---|---|---|---|---|---|
| 1 | 01.0 | 00.3 | 61 | 58.6 | 16.8 | 121 | 116.3 | 33.4 | 181 | 174.0 | 49.9 | 241 | 231.7 | 66.4 |
| 2 | 01.9 | 00.6 | 62 | 59.6 | 17.1 | 22 | 117.3 | 33.6 | 82 | 174.9 | 50.2 | 42 | 232.6 | 66.7 |
| 3 | 02.9 | 00.8 | 63 | 60.6 | 17.4 | 23 | 118.2 | 33.9 | 83 | 175.9 | 50.4 | 43 | 233.6 | 67.0 |
| 4 | 03.8 | 01.1 | 64 | 61.5 | 17.6 | 24 | 119.2 | 34.2 | 84 | 176.9 | 50.7 | 44 | 234.5 | 67.3 |
| 5 | 04.8 | 01.4 | 65 | 62.5 | 17.9 | 25 | 120.2 | 34.5 | 85 | 177.8 | 51.0 | 45 | 235.5 | 67.5 |
| 6 | 05.8 | 01.7 | 66 | 63.4 | 18.2 | 26 | 121.1 | 34.7 | 86 | 178.8 | 51.3 | 46 | 236.5 | 67.8 |
| 7 | 06.7 | 01.9 | 67 | 64.4 | 18.5 | 27 | 122.1 | 35.0 | 87 | 179.8 | 51.5 | 47 | 237.4 | 68.1 |
| 8 | 07.7 | 02.2 | 68 | 65.4 | 18.7 | 28 | 123.0 | 35.3 | 88 | 180.7 | 51.8 | 48 | 238.4 | 68.4 |
| 9 | 08.7 | 02.5 | 69 | 66.3 | 19.0 | 29 | 124.0 | 35.6 | 89 | 181.7 | 52.1 | 49 | 239.4 | 68.6 |
| 10 | 09.6 | 02.8 | 70 | 67.3 | 19.3 | 30 | 125.0 | 35.8 | 90 | 182.6 | 52.4 | 50 | 240.3 | 68.9 |
| 11 | 10.6 | 03.0 | 71 | 68.2 | 19.6 | 131 | 125.9 | 36.1 | 191 | 183.6 | 52.6 | 251 | 241.3 | 69.2 |
| 12 | 11.5 | 03.3 | 72 | 69.2 | 19.8 | 32 | 126.9 | 36.4 | 92 | 184.6 | 52.9 | 52 | 242.2 | 69.5 |
| 13 | 12.5 | 03.6 | 73 | 70.2 | 20.1 | 33 | 127.8 | 36.7 | 93 | 185.5 | 53.2 | 53 | 243.2 | 69.7 |
| 14 | 13.5 | 03.9 | 74 | 71.1 | 20.4 | 34 | 128.8 | 36.9 | 94 | 186.5 | 53.5 | 54 | 244.2 | 70.0 |
| 15 | 14.4 | 04.1 | 75 | 72.1 | 20.7 | 35 | 129.8 | 37.2 | 95 | 187.4 | 53.7 | 55 | 245.1 | 70.3 |
| 16 | 15.4 | 04.4 | 76 | 73.1 | 20.9 | 36 | 130.7 | 37.5 | 96 | 188.4 | 54.0 | 56 | 246.1 | 70.6 |
| 17 | 16.3 | 04.7 | 77 | 74.0 | 21.2 | 37 | 131.7 | 37.8 | 97 | 189.4 | 54.3 | 57 | 247.0 | 70.8 |
| 18 | 17.3 | 05.0 | 78 | 75.0 | 21.5 | 38 | 132.7 | 38.0 | 98 | 190.3 | 54.6 | 58 | 248.0 | 71.1 |
| 19 | 18.3 | 05.2 | 79 | 75.9 | 21.8 | 39 | 133.6 | 38.3 | 99 | 191.3 | 54.9 | 59 | 249.0 | 71.4 |
| 20 | 19.2 | 05.5 | 80 | 76.9 | 22.1 | 40 | 134.6 | 38.6 | 200 | 192.3 | 55.1 | 60 | 249.9 | 71.7 |
| 21 | 20.2 | 05.8 | 81 | 77.9 | 22.3 | 141 | 135.5 | 38.9 | 201 | 193.2 | 55.4 | 261 | 250.9 | 71.9 |
| 22 | 21.1 | 06.1 | 82 | 78.8 | 22.6 | 42 | 136.5 | 39.1 | 02 | 194.2 | 55.7 | 62 | 251.9 | 72.2 |
| 23 | 22.1 | 06.3 | 83 | 79.8 | 22.9 | 43 | 137.5 | 39.4 | 03 | 195.1 | 56.0 | 63 | 252.8 | 72.5 |
| 24 | 23.1 | 06.6 | 84 | 80.7 | 23.2 | 44 | 138.4 | 39.7 | 04 | 196.1 | 56.2 | 64 | 253.8 | 72.8 |
| 25 | 24.0 | 06.9 | 85 | 81.7 | 23.4 | 45 | 139.4 | 40.0 | 05 | 197.1 | 56.5 | 65 | 254.7 | 73.0 |
| 26 | 25.0 | 07.2 | 86 | 82.7 | 23.7 | 46 | 140.3 | 40.2 | 06 | 198.0 | 56.8 | 66 | 255.7 | 73.3 |
| 27 | 26.0 | 07.4 | 87 | 83.6 | 24.0 | 47 | 141.3 | 40.5 | 07 | 199.0 | 57.1 | 67 | 256.7 | 73.6 |
| 28 | 26.9 | 07.7 | 88 | 84.6 | 24.3 | 48 | 142.3 | 40.8 | 08 | 199.9 | 57.3 | 68 | 257.6 | 73.9 |
| 29 | 27.9 | 08.0 | 89 | 85.6 | 24.5 | 49 | 143.2 | 41.1 | 09 | 200.9 | 57.6 | 69 | 258.6 | 74.1 |
| 30 | 28.8 | 08.3 | 90 | 86.5 | 24.8 | 50 | 144.2 | 41.3 | 10 | 201.9 | 57.9 | 70 | 259.5 | 74.4 |
| 31 | 29.8 | 08.5 | 91 | 87.5 | 25.1 | 151 | 145.2 | 41.6 | 211 | 202.8 | 58.2 | 271 | 260.5 | 74.7 |
| 32 | 30.8 | 08.8 | 92 | 88.4 | 25.4 | 52 | 146.1 | 41.9 | 12 | 203.8 | 58.4 | 72 | 261.5 | 75.0 |
| 33 | 31.7 | 09.1 | 93 | 89.4 | 25.6 | 53 | 147.1 | 42.2 | 13 | 204.7 | 58.7 | 73 | 262.4 | 75.2 |
| 34 | 32.7 | 09.4 | 94 | 90.4 | 25.9 | 54 | 148.0 | 42.4 | 14 | 205.7 | 59.0 | 74 | 263.4 | 75.5 |
| 35 | 33.6 | 09.6 | 95 | 91.3 | 26.2 | 55 | 149.0 | 42.7 | 15 | 206.7 | 59.3 | 75 | 264.3 | 75.8 |
| 36 | 34.6 | 09.9 | 96 | 92.3 | 26.5 | 56 | 150.0 | 43.0 | 16 | 207.6 | 59.5 | 76 | 265.3 | 76.1 |
| 37 | 35.6 | 10.2 | 97 | 93.2 | 26.7 | 57 | 150.9 | 43.3 | 17 | 208.6 | 59.8 | 77 | 266.3 | 76.4 |
| 38 | 36.5 | 10.5 | 98 | 94.2 | 27.0 | 58 | 151.9 | 43.6 | 18 | 209.6 | 60.1 | 78 | 267.2 | 76.6 |
| 39 | 37.5 | 10.7 | 99 | 95.2 | 27.3 | 59 | 152.8 | 43.8 | 19 | 210.5 | 60.4 | 79 | 268.2 | 76.9 |
| 40 | 38.5 | 11.0 | 100 | 96.1 | 27.6 | 60 | 153.8 | 44.1 | 20 | 211.5 | 60.6 | 80 | 269.2 | 77.2 |
| 41 | 39.4 | 11.3 | 101 | 97.1 | 27.8 | 161 | 154.8 | 44.4 | 221 | 212.4 | 60.9 | 281 | 270.1 | 77.5 |
| 42 | 40.4 | 11.6 | 02 | 98.0 | 28.1 | 62 | 155.7 | 44.7 | 22 | 213.4 | 61.2 | 82 | 271.1 | 77.7 |
| 43 | 41.3 | 11.9 | 03 | 99.0 | 28.4 | 63 | 156.7 | 44.9 | 23 | 214.4 | 61.5 | 83 | 272.0 | 78.0 |
| 44 | 42.3 | 12.1 | 04 | 100.0 | 28.7 | 64 | 157.6 | 45.2 | 24 | 215.3 | 61.7 | 84 | 273.0 | 78.3 |
| 45 | 43.3 | 12.4 | 05 | 100.9 | 28.9 | 65 | 158.6 | 45.5 | 25 | 216.3 | 62.0 | 85 | 274.0 | 78.6 |
| 46 | 44.2 | 12.7 | 06 | 101.9 | 29.2 | 66 | 159.6 | 45.8 | 26 | 217.2 | 62.3 | 86 | 274.9 | 78.8 |
| 47 | 45.2 | 13.0 | 07 | 102.9 | 29.5 | 67 | 160.5 | 46.0 | 27 | 218.2 | 62.6 | 87 | 275.9 | 79.1 |
| 48 | 46.1 | 13.2 | 08 | 103.8 | 29.8 | 68 | 161.5 | 46.3 | 28 | 219.2 | 62.8 | 88 | 276.8 | 79.4 |
| 49 | 47.1 | 13.5 | 09 | 104.8 | 30.0 | 69 | 162.5 | 46.6 | 29 | 220.1 | 63.1 | 89 | 277.8 | 79.7 |
| 50 | 48.1 | 13.8 | 10 | 105.7 | 30.3 | 70 | 163.4 | 46.9 | 30 | 221.1 | 63.4 | 90 | 278.8 | 79.9 |
| 51 | 49.0 | 14.1 | 111 | 106.7 | 30.6 | 171 | 164.4 | 47.1 | 231 | 222.1 | 63.7 | 291 | 279.7 | 80.2 |
| 52 | 50.0 | 14.3 | 12 | 107.7 | 30.9 | 72 | 165.3 | 47.4 | 32 | 223.0 | 63.9 | 92 | 280.7 | 80.5 |
| 53 | 50.9 | 14.6 | 13 | 108.6 | 31.1 | 73 | 166.3 | 47.7 | 33 | 224.0 | 64.2 | 93 | 281.6 | 80.8 |
| 54 | 51.9 | 14.9 | 14 | 109.6 | 31.4 | 74 | 167.3 | 48.0 | 34 | 224.9 | 64.5 | 94 | 282.6 | 81.0 |
| 55 | 52.9 | 15.2 | 15 | 110.5 | 31.7 | 75 | 168.2 | 48.2 | 35 | 225.9 | 64.8 | 95 | 283.6 | 81.3 |
| 56 | 53.8 | 15.4 | 16 | 111.5 | 32.0 | 76 | 169.2 | 48.5 | 36 | 226.9 | 65.1 | 96 | 284.5 | 81.6 |
| 57 | 54.8 | 15.7 | 17 | 112.5 | 32.2 | 77 | 170.1 | 48.8 | 37 | 227.8 | 65.3 | 97 | 285.5 | 81.9 |
| 58 | 55.8 | 16.0 | 18 | 113.4 | 32.5 | 78 | 171.1 | 49.1 | 38 | 228.8 | 65.6 | 98 | 286.5 | 82.1 |
| 59 | 56.7 | 16.3 | 19 | 114.4 | 32.8 | 79 | 172.1 | 49.3 | 39 | 229.7 | 65.9 | 99 | 287.4 | 82.4 |
| 60 | 57.7 | 16.5 | 20 | 115.4 | 33.1 | 80 | 173.0 | 49.6 | 40 | 230.7 | 66.2 | 300 | 288.4 | 82.7 |
| Dist. | Dep. | Lat. | Dist. | Dep. | Lat. | Dist. | Dep. | Lat. | Dist. | Dep. | Lat. | Dist. | Dep. | Lat. |

# TABLE II.

## Difference of Latitude and Departure for 17 Degrees.

| Dist. | Lat. | Dep. | Dist. | Lat. | Dep. | Dist. | Lat. | Dep. | Dist. | Lat. | Dep. | Dist. | Lat. | Dep. |
|---|---|---|---|---|---|---|---|---|---|---|---|---|---|---|
| 1 | 01.0 | 00.3 | 61 | 58.3 | 17.8 | 121 | 115.7 | 35.4 | 181 | 173.1 | 52.9 | 241 | 230.5 | 70.5 |
| 2 | 01.9 | 00.6 | 62 | 59.3 | 18.1 | 22 | 116.7 | 35.7 | 82 | 174.0 | 53.2 | 42 | 231.4 | 70.8 |
| 3 | 02.9 | 00.9 | 63 | 60.2 | 18.4 | 23 | 117.6 | 36.0 | 83 | 175.0 | 53.5 | 43 | 232.4 | 71.0 |
| 4 | 03.8 | 01.2 | 64 | 61.2 | 18.7 | 24 | 118.6 | 36.3 | 84 | 176.0 | 53.8 | 44 | 233.3 | 71.3 |
| 5 | 04.8 | 01.5 | 65 | 62.2 | 19.0 | 25 | 119.5 | 36.5 | 85 | 176.9 | 54.1 | 45 | 234.3 | 71.6 |
| 6 | 05.7 | 01.8 | 66 | 63.1 | 19.3 | 26 | 120.5 | 36.8 | 86 | 177.9 | 54.4 | 46 | 235.3 | 71.9 |
| 7 | 06.7 | 02.0 | 67 | 64.1 | 19.6 | 27 | 121.5 | 37.1 | 87 | 178.8 | 54.7 | 47 | 236.2 | 72.2 |
| 8 | 07.7 | 02.3 | 68 | 65.0 | 19.9 | 28 | 122.4 | 37.4 | 88 | 179.8 | 55.0 | 48 | 237.2 | 72.5 |
| 9 | 08.6 | 02.6 | 69 | 66.0 | 20.2 | 29 | 123.4 | 37.7 | 89 | 180.7 | 55.3 | 49 | 238.1 | 72.8 |
| 10 | 09.6 | 02.9 | 70 | 66.9 | 20.5 | 30 | 124.3 | 38.0 | 90 | 181.7 | 55.6 | 50 | 239.1 | 73.1 |
| 11 | 10.5 | 03.2 | 71 | 67.9 | 20.8 | 131 | 125.3 | 38.3 | 191 | 182.7 | 55.8 | 251 | 240.0 | 73.4 |
| 12 | 11.5 | 03.5 | 72 | 68.9 | 21.1 | 32 | 126.2 | 38.6 | 92 | 183.6 | 56.1 | 52 | 241.0 | 73.7 |
| 13 | 12.4 | 03.8 | 73 | 69.8 | 21.3 | 33 | 127.2 | 38.9 | 93 | 184.6 | 56.4 | 53 | 241.9 | 74.0 |
| 14 | 13.4 | 04.1 | 74 | 70.8 | 21.6 | 34 | 128.1 | 39.2 | 94 | 185.5 | 56.7 | 54 | 242.9 | 74.3 |
| 15 | 14.3 | 04.4 | 75 | 71.7 | 21.9 | 35 | 129.1 | 39.5 | 95 | 186.5 | 57.0 | 55 | 243.9 | 74.6 |
| 16 | 15.3 | 04.7 | 76 | 72.7 | 22.2 | 36 | 130.1 | 39.8 | 96 | 187.4 | 57.3 | 56 | 244.8 | 74.8 |
| 17 | 16.3 | 05.0 | 77 | 73.6 | 22.5 | 37 | 131.0 | 40.1 | 97 | 188.4 | 57.6 | 57 | 245.8 | 75.1 |
| 18 | 17.2 | 05.3 | 78 | 74.6 | 22.8 | 38 | 132.0 | 40.3 | 98 | 189.3 | 57.9 | 58 | 246.7 | 75.4 |
| 19 | 18.2 | 05.6 | 79 | 75.5 | 23.1 | 39 | 132.9 | 40.6 | 99 | 190.3 | 58.2 | 59 | 247.7 | 75.7 |
| 20 | 19.1 | 05.8 | 80 | 76.5 | 23.4 | 40 | 133.9 | 40.9 | 200 | 191.3 | 58.5 | 60 | 248.6 | 76.0 |
| 21 | 20.1 | 06.1 | 81 | 77.5 | 23.7 | 141 | 134.8 | 41.2 | 201 | 192.2 | 58.8 | 261 | 249.6 | 76.3 |
| 22 | 21.0 | 06.4 | 82 | 78.4 | 24.0 | 42 | 135.8 | 41.5 | 02 | 193.2 | 59.1 | 62 | 250.6 | 76.6 |
| 23 | 22.0 | 06.7 | 83 | 79.4 | 24.3 | 43 | 136.8 | 41.8 | 03 | 194.1 | 59.4 | 63 | 251.5 | 76.9 |
| 24 | 23.0 | 07.0 | 84 | 80.3 | 24.6 | 44 | 137.7 | 42.1 | 04 | 195.1 | 59.6 | 64 | 252.5 | 77.2 |
| 25 | 23.9 | 07.3 | 85 | 81.3 | 24.9 | 45 | 138.7 | 42.4 | 05 | 196.0 | 59.9 | 65 | 253.4 | 77.5 |
| 26 | 24.9 | 07.6 | 86 | 82.2 | 25.1 | 46 | 139.6 | 42.7 | 06 | 197.0 | 60.2 | 66 | 254.4 | 77.8 |
| 27 | 25.8 | 07.9 | 87 | 83.2 | 25.4 | 47 | 140.6 | 43.0 | 07 | 198.0 | 60.5 | 67 | 255.3 | 78.1 |
| 28 | 26.8 | 08.2 | 88 | 84.2 | 25.7 | 48 | 141.5 | 43.3 | 08 | 198.9 | 60.8 | 68 | 256.3 | 78.4 |
| 29 | 27.7 | 08.5 | 89 | 85.1 | 26.0 | 49 | 142.5 | 43.6 | 09 | 199.9 | 61.1 | 69 | 257.2 | 78.6 |
| 30 | 28.7 | 08.8 | 90 | 86.1 | 26.3 | 50 | 143.4 | 43.9 | 10 | 200.8 | 61.4 | 70 | 258.2 | 78.9 |
| 31 | 29.6 | 09.1 | 91 | 87.0 | 26.6 | 151 | 144.4 | 44.1 | 211 | 201.8 | 61.7 | 271 | 259.2 | 79.2 |
| 32 | 30.6 | 09.4 | 92 | 88.0 | 26.9 | 52 | 145.4 | 44.4 | 12 | 202.7 | 62.0 | 72 | 260.1 | 79.5 |
| 33 | 31.6 | 09.6 | 93 | 88.9 | 27.2 | 53 | 146.3 | 44.7 | 13 | 203.7 | 62.3 | 73 | 261.1 | 79.8 |
| 34 | 32.5 | 09.9 | 94 | 89.9 | 27.5 | 54 | 147.3 | 45.0 | 14 | 204.6 | 62.6 | 74 | 262.0 | 80.1 |
| 35 | 33.5 | 10.2 | 95 | 90.8 | 27.8 | 55 | 148.2 | 45.3 | 15 | 205.6 | 62.9 | 75 | 263.0 | 80.4 |
| 36 | 34.4 | 10.5 | 96 | 91.8 | 28.1 | 56 | 149.2 | 45.6 | 16 | 206.6 | 63.2 | 76 | 263.9 | 80.7 |
| 37 | 35.4 | 10.8 | 97 | 92.8 | 28.4 | 57 | 150.1 | 45.9 | 17 | 207.5 | 63.4 | 77 | 264.9 | 81.0 |
| 38 | 36.3 | 11.1 | 98 | 93.7 | 28.7 | 58 | 151.1 | 46.2 | 18 | 208.5 | 63.7 | 78 | 265.9 | 81.3 |
| 39 | 37.3 | 11.4 | 99 | 94.7 | 28.9 | 59 | 152.1 | 46.5 | 19 | 209.4 | 64.0 | 79 | 266.8 | 81.6 |
| 40 | 38.3 | 11.7 | 100 | 95.6 | 29.2 | 60 | 153.0 | 46.8 | 20 | 210.4 | 64.3 | 80 | 267.8 | 81.9 |
| 41 | 39.2 | 12.0 | 101 | 96.6 | 29.5 | 161 | 154.0 | 47.1 | 221 | 211.3 | 64.6 | 281 | 268.7 | 82.2 |
| 42 | 40.2 | 12.3 | 02 | 97.5 | 29.8 | 62 | 154.9 | 47.4 | 22 | 212.3 | 64.9 | 82 | 269.7 | 82.4 |
| 43 | 41.1 | 12.6 | 03 | 98.5 | 30.1 | 63 | 155.9 | 47.7 | 23 | 213.3 | 65.2 | 83 | 270.6 | 82.7 |
| 44 | 42.1 | 12.9 | 04 | 99.5 | 30.4 | 64 | 156.8 | 47.9 | 24 | 214.2 | 65.5 | 84 | 271.6 | 83.0 |
| 45 | 43.0 | 13.2 | 05 | 100.4 | 30.7 | 65 | 157.8 | 48.2 | 25 | 215.2 | 65.8 | 85 | 272.5 | 83.3 |
| 46 | 44.0 | 13.4 | 06 | 101.4 | 31.0 | 66 | 158.7 | 48.5 | 26 | 216.1 | 66.1 | 86 | 273.5 | 83.6 |
| 47 | 44.9 | 13.7 | 07 | 102.3 | 31.3 | 67 | 159.7 | 48.8 | 27 | 217.1 | 66.4 | 87 | 274.5 | 83.9 |
| 48 | 45.9 | 14.0 | 08 | 103.3 | 31.6 | 68 | 160.7 | 49.1 | 28 | 218.0 | 66.7 | 88 | 275.4 | 84.2 |
| 49 | 46.9 | 14.3 | 09 | 104.2 | 31.9 | 69 | 161.6 | 49.4 | 29 | 219.0 | 67.0 | 89 | 276.4 | 84.5 |
| 50 | 47.8 | 14.6 | 10 | 105.2 | 32.2 | 70 | 162.6 | 49.7 | 30 | 220.0 | 67.2 | 90 | 277.3 | 84.8 |
| 51 | 48.8 | 14.9 | 111 | 106.1 | 32.5 | 171 | 163.5 | 50.0 | 231 | 220.9 | 67.5 | 291 | 278.3 | 85.1 |
| 52 | 49.7 | 15.2 | 12 | 107.1 | 32.7 | 72 | 164.5 | 50.3 | 32 | 221.9 | 67.8 | 92 | 279.2 | 85.4 |
| 53 | 50.7 | 15.5 | 13 | 108.1 | 33.0 | 73 | 165.4 | 50.6 | 33 | 222.8 | 68.1 | 93 | 280.2 | 85.7 |
| 54 | 51.6 | 15.8 | 14 | 109.0 | 33.3 | 74 | 166.4 | 50.9 | 34 | 223.8 | 68.4 | 94 | 281.2 | 86.0 |
| 55 | 52.6 | 16.1 | 15 | 110.0 | 33.6 | 75 | 167.4 | 51.2 | 35 | 224.7 | 68.7 | 95 | 282.1 | 86.2 |
| 56 | 53.6 | 16.4 | 16 | 110.9 | 33.9 | 76 | 168.3 | 51.5 | 36 | 225.7 | 69.0 | 96 | 283.1 | 86.5 |
| 57 | 54.5 | 16.7 | 17 | 111.9 | 34.2 | 77 | 169.3 | 51.7 | 37 | 226.6 | 69.3 | 97 | 284.0 | 86.8 |
| 58 | 55.5 | 17.0 | 18 | 112.8 | 34.5 | 78 | 170.2 | 52.0 | 38 | 227.6 | 69.6 | 98 | 285.0 | 87.1 |
| 59 | 56.4 | 17.2 | 19 | 113.8 | 34.8 | 79 | 171.2 | 52.3 | 39 | 228.6 | 69.9 | 99 | 285.9 | 87.4 |
| 60 | 57.4 | 17.5 | 20 | 114.8 | 35.1 | 80 | 172.1 | 52.6 | 40 | 229.5 | 70.2 | 300 | 286.9 | 87.7 |
| Dist. | Dep. | Lat. | Dist. | Dep. | Lat. | Dist. | Dep. | Lat. | Dist. | Dep. | Lat. | Dist. | Dep. | Lat. |

[For 73 Degrees.

# TABLE II.

## Difference of Latitude and Departure for 18 Degrees.

| Dist. | Lat. | Dep. | Dist. | Lat. | Dep. | Dist. | Lat. | Dep. | Dist. | Lat. | Dep. | Dist. | Lat. | Dep. |
|---|---|---|---|---|---|---|---|---|---|---|---|---|---|---|
| 1 | 01.0 | 00.3 | 61 | 58.0 | 18.9 | 121 | 115.1 | 37.4 | 181 | 172.1 | 55.9 | 241 | 229.2 | 74.5 |
| 2 | 01.9 | 00.6 | 62 | 59.0 | 19.2 | 22 | 116.0 | 37.7 | 82 | 173.1 | 56.2 | 42 | 230.2 | 74.8 |
| 3 | 02.9 | 00.9 | 63 | 59.9 | 19.5 | 23 | 117.0 | 38.0 | 83 | 174.0 | 56.6 | 43 | 231.1 | 75.1 |
| 4 | 03.8 | 01.2 | 64 | 60.9 | 19.8 | 24 | 117.9 | 38.3 | 84 | 175.0 | 56.9 | 44 | 232.1 | 75.4 |
| 5 | 04.8 | 01.5 | 65 | 61.8 | 20.1 | 25 | 118.9 | 38.6 | 85 | 175.9 | 57.2 | 45 | 233.0 | 75.7 |
| 6 | 05.7 | 01.9 | 66 | 62.8 | 20.4 | 26 | 119.8 | 38.9 | 86 | 176.9 | 57.5 | 46 | 234.0 | 76.0 |
| 7 | 06.7 | 02.2 | 67 | 63.7 | 20.7 | 27 | 120.8 | 39.2 | 87 | 177.8 | 57.8 | 47 | 234.9 | 76.3 |
| 8 | 07.6 | 02.5 | 68 | 64.7 | 21.0 | 28 | 121.7 | 39.6 | 88 | 178.8 | 58.1 | 48 | 235.9 | 76.6 |
| 9 | 08.6 | 02.8 | 69 | 65.6 | 21.3 | 29 | 122.7 | 39.9 | 89 | 179.7 | 58.4 | 49 | 236.8 | 76.9 |
| 10 | 09.5 | 03.1 | 70 | 66.6 | 21.6 | 30 | 123.6 | 40.2 | 90 | 180.7 | 58.7 | 50 | 237.8 | 77.3 |
| 11 | 10.5 | 03.4 | 71 | 67.5 | 21.9 | 131 | 124.6 | 40.5 | 191 | 181.7 | 59.0 | 251 | 238.7 | 77.6 |
| 12 | 11.4 | 03.7 | 72 | 68.5 | 22.2 | 32 | 125.5 | 40.8 | 92 | 182.6 | 59.3 | 52 | 239.7 | 77.9 |
| 13 | 12.4 | 04.0 | 73 | 69.4 | 22.6 | 33 | 126.5 | 41.1 | 93 | 183.6 | 59.6 | 53 | 240.6 | 78.2 |
| 14 | 13.3 | 04.3 | 74 | 70.4 | 22.9 | 34 | 127.4 | 41.4 | 94 | 184.5 | 59.9 | 54 | 241.6 | 78.5 |
| 15 | 14.3 | 04.6 | 75 | 71.3 | 23.2 | 35 | 128.4 | 41.7 | 95 | 185.5 | 60.3 | 55 | 242.5 | 78.8 |
| 16 | 15.2 | 04.9 | 76 | 72.3 | 23.5 | 36 | 129.3 | 42.0 | 96 | 186.4 | 60.6 | 56 | 243.5 | 79.1 |
| 17 | 16.2 | 05.3 | 77 | 73.2 | 23.8 | 37 | 130.3 | 42.3 | 97 | 187.4 | 60.9 | 57 | 244.4 | 79.4 |
| 18 | 17.1 | 05.6 | 78 | 74.2 | 24.1 | 38 | 131.2 | 42.6 | 98 | 188.3 | 61.2 | 58 | 245.4 | 79.7 |
| 19 | 18.1 | 05.9 | 79 | 75.1 | 24.4 | 39 | 132.2 | 43.0 | 99 | 189.3 | 61.5 | 59 | 246.3 | 80.0 |
| 20 | 19.0 | 06.2 | 80 | 76.1 | 24.7 | 40 | 133.1 | 43.3 | 200 | 190.2 | 61.8 | 60 | 247.3 | 80.3 |
| 21 | 20.0 | 06.5 | 81 | 77.0 | 25.0 | 141 | 134.1 | 43.6 | 201 | 191.2 | 62.1 | 261 | 248.2 | 80.7 |
| 22 | 20.9 | 06.8 | 82 | 78.0 | 25.3 | 42 | 135.1 | 43.9 | 02 | 192.1 | 62.4 | 62 | 249.2 | 81.0 |
| 23 | 21.9 | 07.1 | 83 | 78.9 | 25.6 | 43 | 136.0 | 44.2 | 03 | 193.1 | 62.7 | 63 | 250.1 | 81.3 |
| 24 | 22.8 | 07.4 | 84 | 79.9 | 26.0 | 44 | 137.0 | 44.5 | 04 | 194.0 | 63.0 | 64 | 251.1 | 81.6 |
| 25 | 23.8 | 07.7 | 85 | 80.8 | 26.3 | 45 | 137.9 | 44.8 | 05 | 195.0 | 63.3 | 65 | 252.0 | 81.9 |
| 26 | 24.7 | 08.0 | 86 | 81.8 | 26.6 | 46 | 138.9 | 45.1 | 06 | 195.9 | 63.7 | 66 | 253.0 | 82.2 |
| 27 | 25.7 | 08.3 | 87 | 82.7 | 26.9 | 47 | 139.8 | 45.4 | 07 | 196.9 | 64.0 | 67 | 253.9 | 82.5 |
| 28 | 26.6 | 08.7 | 88 | 83.7 | 27.2 | 48 | 140.8 | 45.7 | 08 | 197.8 | 64.3 | 68 | 254.9 | 82.8 |
| 29 | 27.6 | 09.0 | 89 | 84.6 | 27.5 | 49 | 141.7 | 46.0 | 09 | 198.8 | 64.6 | 69 | 255.8 | 83.1 |
| 30 | 28.5 | 09.3 | 90 | 85.6 | 27.8 | 50 | 142.7 | 46.4 | 10 | 199.7 | 64.9 | 70 | 256.8 | 83.4 |
| 31 | 29.5 | 09.6 | 91 | 86.5 | 28.1 | 151 | 143.6 | 46.7 | 211 | 200.7 | 65.2 | 271 | 257.7 | 83.7 |
| 32 | 30.4 | 09.9 | 92 | 87.5 | 28.4 | 52 | 144.6 | 47.0 | 12 | 201.6 | 65.5 | 72 | 258.7 | 84.1 |
| 33 | 31.4 | 10.2 | 93 | 88.4 | 28.7 | 53 | 145.5 | 47.3 | 13 | 202.6 | 65.8 | 73 | 259.6 | 84.4 |
| 34 | 32.3 | 10.5 | 94 | 89.4 | 29.0 | 54 | 146.5 | 47.6 | 14 | 203.5 | 66.1 | 74 | 260.6 | 84.7 |
| 35 | 33.3 | 10.8 | 95 | 90.4 | 29.4 | 55 | 147.4 | 47.9 | 15 | 204.5 | 66.4 | 75 | 261.5 | 85.0 |
| 36 | 34.2 | 11.1 | 96 | 91.3 | 29.7 | 56 | 148.4 | 48.2 | 16 | 205.4 | 66.7 | 76 | 262.5 | 85.3 |
| 37 | 35.2 | 11.4 | 97 | 92.3 | 30.0 | 57 | 149.3 | 48.5 | 17 | 206.4 | 67.1 | 77 | 263.4 | 85.6 |
| 38 | 36.1 | 11.7 | 98 | 93.2 | 30.3 | 58 | 150.3 | 48.8 | 18 | 207.3 | 67.4 | 78 | 264.4 | 85.9 |
| 39 | 37.1 | 12.1 | 99 | 94.2 | 30.6 | 59 | 151.2 | 49.1 | 19 | 208.3 | 67.7 | 79 | 265.3 | 86.2 |
| 40 | 38.0 | 12.4 | 100 | 95.1 | 30.9 | 60 | 152.2 | 49.4 | 20 | 209.2 | 68.0 | 80 | 266.3 | 86.5 |
| 41 | 39.0 | 12.7 | 101 | 96.1 | 31.2 | 161 | 153.1 | 49.8 | 221 | 210.2 | 68.3 | 281 | 267.2 | 86.8 |
| 42 | 39.9 | 13.0 | 02 | 97.0 | 31.5 | 62 | 154.1 | 50.1 | 22 | 211.1 | 68.6 | 82 | 268.2 | 87.1 |
| 43 | 40.9 | 13.3 | 03 | 98.0 | 31.8 | 63 | 155.0 | 50.4 | 23 | 212.1 | 68.9 | 83 | 269.1 | 87.5 |
| 44 | 41.8 | 13.6 | 04 | 98.9 | 32.1 | 64 | 156.0 | 50.7 | 24 | 213.0 | 69.2 | 84 | 270.1 | 87.8 |
| 45 | 42.8 | 13.9 | 05 | 99.9 | 32.4 | 65 | 156.9 | 51.0 | 25 | 214.0 | 69.5 | 85 | 271.1 | 88.1 |
| 46 | 43.7 | 14.2 | 06 | 100.8 | 32.8 | 66 | 157.9 | 51.3 | 26 | 214.9 | 69.8 | 86 | 272.0 | 88.4 |
| 47 | 44.7 | 14.5 | 07 | 101.8 | 33.1 | 67 | 158.8 | 51.6 | 27 | 215.9 | 70.1 | 87 | 273.0 | 88.7 |
| 48 | 45.7 | 14.8 | 08 | 102.7 | 33.4 | 68 | 159.8 | 51.9 | 28 | 216.8 | 70.5 | 88 | 273.9 | 89.0 |
| 49 | 46.6 | 15.1 | 09 | 103.7 | 33.7 | 69 | 160.7 | 52.2 | 29 | 217.8 | 70.8 | 89 | 274.9 | 89.3 |
| 50 | 47.6 | 15.5 | 10 | 104.6 | 34.0 | 70 | 161.7 | 52.5 | 30 | 218.7 | 71.1 | 90 | 275.8 | 89.6 |
| 51 | 48.5 | 15.8 | 111 | 105.6 | 34.3 | 171 | 162.6 | 52.8 | 231 | 219.7 | 71.4 | 291 | 276.8 | 89.9 |
| 52 | 49.5 | 16.1 | 12 | 106.5 | 34.6 | 72 | 163.6 | 53.2 | 32 | 220.6 | 71.7 | 92 | 277.7 | 90.2 |
| 53 | 50.4 | 16.4 | 13 | 107.5 | 34.9 | 73 | 164.5 | 53.5 | 33 | 221.6 | 72.0 | 93 | 278.7 | 90.5 |
| 54 | 51.4 | 16.7 | 14 | 108.4 | 35.2 | 74 | 165.5 | 53.8 | 34 | 222.5 | 72.3 | 94 | 279.6 | 90.9 |
| 55 | 52.3 | 17.0 | 15 | 109.4 | 35.5 | 75 | 166.4 | 54.1 | 35 | 223.5 | 72.6 | 95 | 280.6 | 91.2 |
| 56 | 53.3 | 17.3 | 16 | 110.3 | 35.8 | 76 | 167.4 | 54.4 | 36 | 224.4 | 72.9 | 96 | 281.5 | 91.5 |
| 57 | 54.2 | 17.6 | 17 | 111.3 | 36.2 | 77 | 168.3 | 54.7 | 37 | 225.4 | 73.2 | 97 | 282.5 | 91.8 |
| 58 | 55.2 | 17.9 | 18 | 112.2 | 36.5 | 78 | 169.3 | 55.0 | 38 | 226.4 | 73.5 | 98 | 283.4 | 92.1 |
| 59 | 56.1 | 18.2 | 19 | 113.2 | 36.8 | 79 | 170.2 | 55.3 | 39 | 227.3 | 73.9 | 99 | 284.4 | 92.4 |
| 60 | 57.1 | 18.5 | 20 | 114.1 | 37.1 | 80 | 171.2 | 55.6 | 40 | 228.3 | 74.2 | 300 | 285.3 | 92.7 |
| **Dist.** | Dep. | Lat. | Dist. | Dep. | Lat. | Dist. | Dep. | Lat. | Dist. | Dep. | Lat. | Dist. | Dep. | Lat. |

[For 72 Degrees.

# TABLE II.

## Difference of Latitude and Departure for 19 Degrees.

| Dist. | Lat. | Dep. | Dist. | Lat. | Dep. | Dist. | Lat. | Dep. | Dist. | Lat. | Dep. | Dist. | Lat. | Dep. |
|---|---|---|---|---|---|---|---|---|---|---|---|---|---|---|
| 1 | 00.9 | 00.3 | 61 | 57.7 | 19.9 | 121 | 114.4 | 39.4 | 181 | 171.1 | 58.9 | 241 | 227.9 | 78.5 |
| 2 | 01.9 | 00.7 | 62 | 58.6 | 20.2 | 22 | 115.4 | 39.7 | 82 | 172.1 | 59.3 | 42 | 228.8 | 78.8 |
| 3 | 02.8 | 01.0 | 63 | 59.6 | 20.5 | 23 | 116.3 | 40.0 | 83 | 173.0 | 59.6 | 43 | 229.8 | 79.1 |
| 4 | 03.8 | 01.3 | 64 | 60.5 | 20.8 | 24 | 117.2 | 40.4 | 84 | 174.0 | 59.9 | 44 | 230.7 | 79.4 |
| 5 | 04.7 | 01.6 | 65 | 61.5 | 21.2 | 25 | 118.2 | 40.7 | 85 | 174.9 | 60.2 | 45 | 231.7 | 79.8 |
| 6 | 05.7 | 02.0 | 66 | 62.4 | 21.5 | 26 | 119.1 | 41.0 | 86 | 175.9 | 60.6 | 46 | 232.6 | 80.1 |
| 7 | 06.6 | 02.3 | 67 | 63.3 | 21.8 | 27 | 120.1 | 41.3 | 87 | 176.8 | 60.9 | 47 | 233.5 | 80.4 |
| 8 | 07.6 | 02.6 | 68 | 64.3 | 22.1 | 28 | 121.0 | 41.7 | 88 | 177.8 | 61.2 | 48 | 234.5 | 80.7 |
| 9 | 08.5 | 02.9 | 69 | 65.2 | 22.5 | 29 | 122.0 | 42.0 | 89 | 178.7 | 61.5 | 49 | 235.4 | 81.1 |
| 10 | 09.5 | 03.3 | 70 | 66.2 | 22.8 | 30 | 122.9 | 42.3 | 90 | 179.6 | 61.9 | 50 | 236.4 | 81.4 |
| 11 | 10.4 | 03.6 | 71 | 67.1 | 23.1 | 131 | 123.9 | 42.6 | 191 | 180.6 | 62.2 | 251 | 237.3 | 81.7 |
| 12 | 11.3 | 03.9 | 72 | 68.1 | 23.4 | 32 | 124.8 | 43.0 | 92 | 181.5 | 62.5 | 52 | 238.3 | 82.0 |
| 13 | 12.3 | 04.2 | 73 | 69.0 | 23.8 | 33 | 125.8 | 43.3 | 93 | 182.5 | 62.8 | 53 | 239.2 | 82.4 |
| 14 | 13.2 | 04.6 | 74 | 70.0 | 24.1 | 34 | 126.7 | 43.6 | 94 | 183.4 | 63.2 | 54 | 240.2 | 82.7 |
| 15 | 14.2 | 04.9 | 75 | 70.9 | 24.4 | 35 | 127.6 | 44.0 | 95 | 184.4 | 63.5 | 55 | 241.1 | 83.0 |
| 16 | 15.1 | 05.2 | 76 | 71.9 | 24.7 | 36 | 128.6 | 44.3 | 96 | 185.3 | 63.8 | 56 | 242.1 | 83.3 |
| 17 | 16.1 | 05.5 | 77 | 72.8 | 25.1 | 37 | 129.5 | 44.6 | 97 | 186.3 | 64.1 | 57 | 243.0 | 83.7 |
| 18 | 17.0 | 05.9 | 78 | 73.8 | 25.4 | 38 | 130.5 | 44.9 | 98 | 187.2 | 64.5 | 58 | 243.9 | 84.0 |
| 19 | 18.0 | 06.2 | 79 | 74.7 | 25.7 | 39 | 131.4 | 45.3 | 99 | 188.2 | 64.8 | 59 | 244.9 | 84.3 |
| 20 | 18.9 | 06.5 | 80 | 75.6 | 26.0 | 40 | 132.4 | 45.6 | 200 | 189.1 | 65.1 | 60 | 245.8 | 84.6 |
| 21 | 19.9 | 06.8 | 81 | 76.6 | 26.4 | 141 | 133.3 | 45.9 | 201 | 190.0 | 65.4 | 261 | 246.8 | 85.0 |
| 22 | 20.8 | 07.2 | 82 | 77.5 | 26.7 | 42 | 134.3 | 46.2 | 02 | 191.0 | 65.8 | 62 | 247.7 | 85.3 |
| 23 | 21.7 | 07.5 | 83 | 78.5 | 27.0 | 43 | 135.2 | 46.6 | 03 | 191.9 | 66.1 | 63 | 248.7 | 85.6 |
| 24 | 22.7 | 07.8 | 84 | 79.4 | 27.3 | 44 | 136.2 | 46.9 | 04 | 192.9 | 66.4 | 64 | 249.6 | 86.0 |
| 25 | 23.6 | 08.1 | 85 | 80.4 | 27.7 | 45 | 137.1 | 47.2 | 05 | 193.8 | 66.7 | 65 | 250.6 | 86.3 |
| 26 | 24.6 | 08.5 | 86 | 81.3 | 28.0 | 46 | 138.0 | 47.5 | 06 | 194.8 | 67.1 | 66 | 251.5 | 86.6 |
| 27 | 25.5 | 08.8 | 87 | 82.3 | 28.3 | 47 | 139.0 | 47.9 | 07 | 195.7 | 67.4 | 67 | 252.5 | 86.9 |
| 28 | 26.5 | 09.1 | 88 | 83.2 | 28.7 | 48 | 139.9 | 48.2 | 08 | 196.7 | 67.7 | 68 | 253.4 | 87.3 |
| 29 | 27.4 | 09.4 | 89 | 84.2 | 29.0 | 49 | 140.9 | 48.5 | 09 | 197.6 | 68.0 | 69 | 254.3 | 87.6 |
| 30 | 28.4 | 09.8 | 90 | 85.1 | 29.3 | 50 | 141.8 | 48.8 | 10 | 198.6 | 68.4 | 70 | 255.3 | 87.9 |
| 31 | 29.3 | 10.1 | 91 | 86.0 | 29.6 | 151 | 142.8 | 49.2 | 211 | 199.5 | 68.7 | 271 | 256.2 | 88.2 |
| 32 | 30.3 | 10.4 | 92 | 87.0 | 30.0 | 52 | 143.7 | 49.5 | 12 | 200.4 | 69.0 | 72 | 257.2 | 88.6 |
| 33 | 31.2 | 10.7 | 93 | 87.9 | 30.3 | 53 | 144.7 | 49.8 | 13 | 201.4 | 69.3 | 73 | 258.1 | 88.9 |
| 34 | 32.1 | 11.1 | 94 | 88.9 | 30.6 | 54 | 145.6 | 50.1 | 14 | 202.3 | 69.7 | 74 | 259.1 | 89.2 |
| 35 | 33.1 | 11.4 | 95 | 89.8 | 30.9 | 55 | 146.6 | 50.5 | 15 | 203.3 | 70.0 | 75 | 260.0 | 89.5 |
| 36 | 34.0 | 11.7 | 96 | 90.8 | 31.3 | 56 | 147.5 | 50.8 | 16 | 204.2 | 70.3 | 76 | 261.0 | 89.9 |
| 37 | 35.0 | 12.0 | 97 | 91.7 | 31.6 | 57 | 148.4 | 51.1 | 17 | 205.2 | 70.6 | 77 | 261.9 | 90.2 |
| 38 | 35.9 | 12.4 | 98 | 92.7 | 31.9 | 58 | 149.4 | 51.4 | 18 | 206.1 | 71.0 | 78 | 262.9 | 90.5 |
| 39 | 36.9 | 12.7 | 99 | 93.6 | 32.2 | 59 | 150.3 | 51.8 | 19 | 207.1 | 71.3 | 79 | 263.8 | 90.8 |
| 40 | 37.8 | 13.0 | 100 | 94.6 | 32.6 | 60 | 151.3 | 52.1 | 20 | 208.0 | 71.6 | 80 | 264.7 | 91.2 |
| 41 | 38.8 | 13.3 | 101 | 95.5 | 32.9 | 161 | 152.2 | 52.4 | 221 | 209.0 | 72.0 | 281 | 265.7 | 91.5 |
| 42 | 39.7 | 13.7 | 02 | 96.4 | 33.2 | 62 | 153.2 | 52.7 | 22 | 209.9 | 72.3 | 82 | 266.6 | 91.8 |
| 43 | 40.7 | 14.0 | 03 | 97.4 | 33.5 | 63 | 154.1 | 53.1 | 23 | 210.9 | 72.6 | 83 | 267.6 | 92.1 |
| 44 | 41.6 | 14.3 | 04 | 98.3 | 33.9 | 64 | 155.1 | 53.4 | 24 | 211.8 | 72.9 | 84 | 268.5 | 92.5 |
| 45 | 42.5 | 14.7 | 05 | 99.3 | 34.2 | 65 | 156.0 | 53.7 | 25 | 212.7 | 73.3 | 85 | 269.5 | 92.8 |
| 46 | 43.5 | 15.0 | 06 | 100.2 | 34.5 | 66 | 157.0 | 54.0 | 26 | 213.7 | 73.6 | 86 | 270.4 | 93.1 |
| 47 | 44.4 | 15.3 | 07 | 101.2 | 34.8 | 67 | 157.9 | 54.4 | 27 | 214.6 | 73.9 | 87 | 271.4 | 93.4 |
| 48 | 45.4 | 15.6 | 08 | 102.1 | 35.2 | 68 | 158.8 | 54.7 | 28 | 215.6 | 74.2 | 88 | 272.3 | 93.8 |
| 49 | 46.3 | 16.0 | 09 | 103.1 | 35.5 | 69 | 159.8 | 55.0 | 29 | 216.5 | 74.6 | 89 | 273.3 | 94.1 |
| 50 | 47.3 | 16.3 | 10 | 104.0 | 35.8 | 70 | 160.7 | 55.3 | 30 | 217.5 | 74.9 | 90 | 274.2 | 94.4 |
| 51 | 48.2 | 16.6 | 111 | 105.0 | 36.1 | 171 | 161.7 | 55.7 | 231 | 218.4 | 75.2 | 291 | 275.1 | 94.7 |
| 52 | 49.2 | 16.9 | 12 | 105.9 | 36.5 | 72 | 162.6 | 56.0 | 32 | 219.4 | 75.5 | 92 | 276.1 | 95.1 |
| 53 | 50.1 | 17.3 | 13 | 106.8 | 36.8 | 73 | 163.6 | 56.3 | 33 | 220.3 | 75.9 | 93 | 277.0 | 95.4 |
| 54 | 51.1 | 17.6 | 14 | 107.8 | 37.1 | 74 | 164.5 | 56.6 | 34 | 221.3 | 76.2 | 94 | 278.0 | 95.7 |
| 55 | 52.0 | 17.9 | 15 | 108.7 | 37.4 | 75 | 165.5 | 57.0 | 35 | 222.2 | 76.5 | 95 | 278.9 | 96.0 |
| 56 | 52.9 | 18.2 | 16 | 109.7 | 37.8 | 76 | 166.4 | 57.3 | 36 | 223.1 | 76.8 | 96 | 279.9 | 96.4 |
| 57 | 53.9 | 18.6 | 17 | 110.6 | 38.1 | 77 | 167.4 | 57.6 | 37 | 224.1 | 77.2 | 97 | 280.8 | 96.7 |
| 58 | 54.8 | 18.9 | 18 | 111.6 | 38.4 | 78 | 168.3 | 58.0 | 38 | 225.0 | 77.5 | 98 | 281.8 | 97.0 |
| 59 | 55.8 | 19.2 | 19 | 112.5 | 38.7 | 79 | 169.2 | 58.3 | 39 | 226.0 | 77.8 | 99 | 282.7 | 97.3 |
| 60 | 56.7 | 19.5 | 20 | 113.5 | 39.1 | 80 | 170.2 | 58.6 | 40 | 226.9 | 78.1 | 300 | 283.7 | 97.7 |
| Dist. | Dep. | Lat. | Dist. | Dep. | Lat. | Dist. | Dep. | Lat. | Dist. | Dep. | Lat. | Dist. | Dep. | Lat. |

# TABLE II.

## Difference of Latitude and Departure for 20 Degrees.

| Dist. | Lat. | Dep. | Dist. | Lat. | Dep. | Dist. | Lat. | Dep. | Dist. | Lat. | Dep. | Dist. | Lat. | Dep. |
|---|---|---|---|---|---|---|---|---|---|---|---|---|---|---|
| 1 | 00.9 | 00.3 | 61 | 57.3 | 20.9 | 121 | 113.7 | 41.4 | 181 | 170.1 | 61.9 | 241 | 226.5 | 82.4 |
| 2 | 01.9 | 00.7 | 62 | 58.3 | 21.2 | 22 | 114.6 | 41.7 | 82 | 171.0 | 62.2 | 42 | 227.4 | 82.8 |
| 3 | 02.8 | 01.0 | 63 | 59.2 | 21.5 | 23 | 115.6 | 42.1 | 83 | 172.0 | 62.6 | 43 | 228.3 | 83.1 |
| 4 | 03.8 | 01.4 | 64 | 60.1 | 21.9 | 24 | 116.5 | 42.4 | 84 | 172.9 | 62.9 | 44 | 229.3 | 83.5 |
| 5 | 04.7 | 01.7 | 65 | 61.1 | 22.2 | 25 | 117.5 | 42.8 | 85 | 173.8 | 63.3 | 45 | 230.2 | 83.8 |
| 6 | 05.6 | 02.1 | 66 | 62.0 | 22.6 | 26 | 118.4 | 43.1 | 86 | 174.8 | 63.6 | 46 | 231.2 | 84.1 |
| 7 | 06.6 | 02.4 | 67 | 63.0 | 22.9 | 27 | 119.3 | 43.4 | 87 | 175.7 | 64.0 | 47 | 232.1 | 84.5 |
| 8 | 07.5 | 02.7 | 68 | 63.9 | 23.3 | 28 | 120.3 | 43.8 | 88 | 176.7 | 64.3 | 48 | 233.0 | 84.8 |
| 9 | 08.5 | 03.1 | 69 | 64.8 | 23.6 | 29 | 121.2 | 44.1 | 89 | 177.6 | 64.6 | 49 | 234.0 | 85.2 |
| 10 | 09.4 | 03.4 | 70 | 65.8 | 23.9 | 30 | 122.2 | 44.5 | 90 | 178.5 | 65.0 | 50 | 234.9 | 85.5 |
| 11 | 10.3 | 03.8 | 71 | 66.7 | 24.3 | 131 | 123.1 | 44.8 | 191 | 179.5 | 65.3 | 251 | 235.9 | 85.8 |
| 12 | 11.3 | 04.1 | 72 | 67.7 | 24.6 | 32 | 124.0 | 45.1 | 92 | 180.4 | 65.7 | 52 | 236.8 | 86.2 |
| 13 | 12.2 | 04.4 | 73 | 68.6 | 25.0 | 33 | 125.0 | 45.5 | 93 | 181.4 | 66.0 | 53 | 237.7 | 86.5 |
| 14 | 13.2 | 04.8 | 74 | 69.5 | 25.3 | 34 | 125.9 | 45.8 | 94 | 182.3 | 66.4 | 54 | 238.7 | 86.9 |
| 15 | 14.1 | 05.1 | 75 | 70.5 | 25.7 | 35 | 126.9 | 46.2 | 95 | 183.2 | 66.7 | 55 | 239.6 | 87.2 |
| 16 | 15.0 | 05.5 | 76 | 71.4 | 26.0 | 36 | 127.8 | 46.5 | 96 | 184.2 | 67.0 | 56 | 240.6 | 87.6 |
| 17 | 16.0 | 05.8 | 77 | 72.4 | 26.3 | 37 | 128.7 | 46.9 | 97 | 185.1 | 67.4 | 57 | 241.5 | 87.9 |
| 18 | 16.9 | 06.2 | 78 | 73.3 | 26.7 | 38 | 129.7 | 47.2 | 98 | 186.1 | 67.7 | 58 | 242.4 | 88.2 |
| 19 | 17.9 | 06.5 | 79 | 74.2 | 27.0 | 39 | 130.6 | 47.5 | 99 | 187.0 | 68.1 | 59 | 243.4 | 88.6 |
| 20 | 18.8 | 06.8 | 80 | 75.2 | 27.4 | 40 | 131.6 | 47.9 | 200 | 187.9 | 68.4 | 60 | 244.3 | 88.9 |
| 21 | 19.7 | 07.2 | 81 | 76.1 | 27.7 | 141 | 132.5 | 48.2 | 201 | 188.9 | 68.7 | 261 | 245.3 | 89.3 |
| 22 | 20.7 | 07.5 | 82 | 77.1 | 28.0 | 42 | 133.4 | 48.6 | 02 | 189.8 | 69.1 | 62 | 246.2 | 89.6 |
| 23 | 21.6 | 07.9 | 83 | 78.0 | 28.4 | 43 | 134.4 | 48.9 | 03 | 190.8 | 69.4 | 63 | 247.1 | 90.0 |
| 24 | 22.6 | 08.2 | 84 | 78.9 | 28.7 | 44 | 135.3 | 49.3 | 04 | 191.7 | 69.8 | 64 | 248.1 | 90.3 |
| 25 | 23.5 | 08.6 | 85 | 79.9 | 29.1 | 45 | 136.3 | 49.6 | 05 | 192.6 | 70.1 | 65 | 249.0 | 90.6 |
| 26 | 24.4 | 08.9 | 86 | 80.8 | 29.4 | 46 | 137.2 | 49.9 | 06 | 193.6 | 70.5 | 66 | 250.0 | 91.0 |
| 27 | 25.4 | 09.2 | 87 | 81.8 | 29.8 | 47 | 138.1 | 50.3 | 07 | 194.5 | 70.8 | 67 | 250.9 | 91.3 |
| 28 | 26.3 | 09.6 | 88 | 82.7 | 30.1 | 48 | 139.1 | 50.6 | 08 | 195.5 | 71.1 | 68 | 251.8 | 91.7 |
| 29 | 27.3 | 09.9 | 89 | 83.6 | 30.4 | 49 | 140.0 | 51.0 | 09 | 196.4 | 71.5 | 69 | 252.8 | 92.0 |
| 30 | 28.2 | 10.3 | 90 | 84.6 | 30.8 | 50 | 141.0 | 51.3 | 10 | 197.3 | 71.8 | 70 | 253.7 | 92.3 |
| 31 | 29.1 | 10.6 | 91 | 85.5 | 31.1 | 151 | 141.9 | 51.6 | 211 | 198.3 | 72.2 | 271 | 254.7 | 92.7 |
| 32 | 30.1 | 10.9 | 92 | 86.5 | 31.5 | 52 | 142.8 | 52.0 | 12 | 199.2 | 72.5 | 72 | 255.6 | 93.0 |
| 33 | 31.0 | 11.3 | 93 | 87.4 | 31.8 | 53 | 143.8 | 52.3 | 13 | 200.2 | 72.9 | 73 | 256.5 | 93.4 |
| 34 | 31.9 | 11.6 | 94 | 88.3 | 32.1 | 54 | 144.7 | 52.7 | 14 | 201.1 | 73.2 | 74 | 257.5 | 93.7 |
| 35 | 32.9 | 12.0 | 95 | 89.3 | 32.5 | 55 | 145.7 | 53.0 | 15 | 202.0 | 73.5 | 75 | 258.4 | 94.1 |
| 36 | 33.8 | 12.3 | 96 | 90.2 | 32.8 | 56 | 146.6 | 53.4 | 16 | 203.0 | 73.9 | 76 | 259.4 | 94.4 |
| 37 | 34.8 | 12.7 | 97 | 91.2 | 33.2 | 57 | 147.5 | 53.7 | 17 | 203.9 | 74.2 | 77 | 260.3 | 94.7 |
| 38 | 35.7 | 13.0 | 98 | 92.1 | 33.5 | 58 | 148.5 | 54.0 | 18 | 204.9 | 74.6 | 78 | 261.2 | 95.1 |
| 39 | 36.6 | 13.3 | 99 | 93.0 | 33.9 | 59 | 149.4 | 54.4 | 19 | 205.8 | 74.9 | 79 | 262.2 | 95.4 |
| 40 | 37.6 | 13.7 | 100 | 94.0 | 34.2 | 60 | 150.4 | 54.7 | 20 | 206.7 | 75.2 | 80 | 263.1 | 95.8 |
| 41 | 38.5 | 14.0 | 101 | 94.9 | 34.5 | 161 | 151.3 | 55.1 | 221 | 207.7 | 75.6 | 281 | 264.1 | 96.1 |
| 42 | 39.5 | 14.4 | 02 | 95.8 | 34.9 | 62 | 152.2 | 55.4 | 22 | 208.6 | 75.9 | 82 | 265.0 | 96.4 |
| 43 | 40.4 | 14.7 | 03 | 96.8 | 35.2 | 63 | 153.2 | 55.7 | 23 | 209.6 | 76.3 | 83 | 265.9 | 96.8 |
| 44 | 41.3 | 15.0 | 04 | 97.7 | 35.6 | 64 | 154.1 | 56.1 | 24 | 210.5 | 76.6 | 84 | 266.9 | 97.1 |
| 45 | 42.3 | 15.4 | 05 | 98.7 | 35.9 | 65 | 155.0 | 56.4 | 25 | 211.4 | 77.0 | 85 | 267.8 | 97.5 |
| 46 | 43.2 | 15.7 | 06 | 99.6 | 36.3 | 66 | 156.0 | 56.8 | 26 | 212.4 | 77.3 | 86 | 268.8 | 97.8 |
| 47 | 44.2 | 16.1 | 07 | 100.5 | 36.6 | 67 | 156.9 | 57.1 | 27 | 213.3 | 77.6 | 87 | 269.7 | 98.2 |
| 48 | 45.1 | 16.4 | 08 | 101.5 | 36.9 | 68 | 157.9 | 57.5 | 28 | 214.2 | 78.0 | 88 | 270.6 | 98.5 |
| 49 | 46.0 | 16.8 | 09 | 102.4 | 37.3 | 69 | 158.8 | 57.8 | 29 | 215.2 | 78.3 | 89 | 271.6 | 98.8 |
| 50 | 47.0 | 17.1 | 10 | 103.4 | 37.6 | 70 | 159.7 | 58.1 | 30 | 216.1 | 78.7 | 90 | 272.5 | 99.2 |
| 51 | 47.9 | 17.4 | 111 | 104.3 | 38.0 | 171 | 160.7 | 58.5 | 231 | 217.1 | 79.0 | 291 | 273.5 | 99.5 |
| 52 | 48.9 | 17.8 | 12 | 105.2 | 38.3 | 72 | 161.6 | 58.8 | 32 | 218.0 | 79.3 | 92 | 274.4 | 99.9 |
| 53 | 49.8 | 18.1 | 13 | 106.2 | 38.6 | 73 | 162.6 | 59.2 | 33 | 218.9 | 79.7 | 93 | 275.3 | 100.2 |
| 54 | 50.7 | 18.5 | 14 | 107.1 | 39.0 | 74 | 163.5 | 59.5 | 34 | 219.9 | 80.0 | 94 | 276.3 | 100.6 |
| 55 | 51.7 | 18.8 | 15 | 108.1 | 39.3 | 75 | 164.4 | 59.9 | 35 | 220.8 | 80.4 | 95 | 277.2 | 100.9 |
| 56 | 52.6 | 19.2 | 16 | 109.0 | 39.7 | 76 | 165.4 | 60.2 | 36 | 221.8 | 80.7 | 96 | 278.1 | 101.2 |
| 57 | 53.6 | 19.5 | 17 | 109.9 | 40.0 | 77 | 166.3 | 60.5 | 37 | 222.7 | 81.1 | 97 | 279.1 | 101.6 |
| 58 | 54.5 | 19.8 | 18 | 110.9 | 40.4 | 78 | 167.3 | 60.9 | 38 | 223.6 | 81.4 | 98 | 280.0 | 101.9 |
| 59 | 55.4 | 20.2 | 19 | 111.8 | 40.7 | 79 | 168.2 | 61.2 | 39 | 224.6 | 81.7 | 99 | 281.0 | 102.3 |
| 60 | 56.4 | 20.5 | 20 | 112.8 | 41.0 | 80 | 169.1 | 61.6 | 40 | 225.5 | 82.1 | 300 | 281.9 | 102.6 |
| Dist. | Dep. | Lat. | Dist. | Dep. | Lat. | Dist. | Dep. | Lat. | Dist. | Dep. | Lat. | Dist. | Dep. | Lat. |

# TABLE II.



## Difference of Latitude and Departure for 21 Degrees.

| Dist. | Lat. | Dep. | Dist. | Lat. | Dep. | Dist. | Lat. | Dep. | Dist. | Lat. | Dep. | Dist. | Lat. | Dep. |
|---|---|---|---|---|---|---|---|---|---|---|---|---|---|---|
| 1 | 00.9 | 00.4 | 61 | 56.9 | 21.9 | 121 | 113.0 | 43.4 | 181 | 169.0 | 64.9 | 241 | 225.0 | 86.4 |
| 2 | 01.9 | 00.7 | 62 | 57.9 | 22.2 | 22 | 113.9 | 43.7 | 82 | 169.9 | 65.2 | 42 | 225.9 | 86.7 |
| 3 | 02.8 | 01.1 | 63 | 58.8 | 22.6 | 23 | 114.8 | 44.1 | 83 | 170.8 | 65.6 | 43 | 226.9 | 87.1 |
| 4 | 03.7 | 01.4 | 64 | 59.7 | 22.9 | 24 | 115.8 | 44.4 | 84 | 171.8 | 65.9 | 44 | 227.8 | 87.4 |
| 5 | 04.7 | 01.8 | 65 | 60.7 | 23.3 | 25 | 116.7 | 44.8 | 85 | 172.7 | 66.3 | 45 | 228.7 | 87.8 |
| 6 | 05.6 | 02.2 | 66 | 61.6 | 23.7 | 26 | 117.6 | 45.2 | 86 | 173.6 | 66.7 | 46 | 229.7 | 88.2 |
| 7 | 06.5 | 02.5 | 67 | 62.5 | 24.0 | 27 | 118.6 | 45.5 | 87 | 174.6 | 67.0 | 47 | 230.6 | 88.5 |
| 8 | 07.5 | 02.9 | 68 | 63.5 | 24.4 | 28 | 119.5 | 45.9 | 88 | 175.5 | 67.4 | 48 | 231.5 | 88.9 |
| 9 | 08.4 | 03.2 | 69 | 64.4 | 24.7 | 29 | 120.4 | 46.2 | 89 | 176.4 | 67.7 | 49 | 232.5 | 89.2 |
| 10 | 09.3 | 03.6 | 70 | 65.4 | 25.1 | 30 | 121.4 | 46.6 | 90 | 177.4 | 68.1 | 50 | 233.4 | 89.6 |
| 11 | 10.3 | 03.9 | 71 | 66.3 | 25.4 | 131 | 122.3 | 46.9 | 191 | 178.3 | 68.4 | 251 | 234.3 | 90.0 |
| 12 | 11.2 | 04.3 | 72 | 67.2 | 25.8 | 32 | 123.2 | 47.3 | 92 | 179.2 | 68.8 | 52 | 235.3 | 90.3 |
| 13 | 12.1 | 04.7 | 73 | 68.2 | 26.2 | 33 | 124.2 | 47.7 | 93 | 180.2 | 69.2 | 53 | 236.2 | 90.7 |
| 14 | 13.1 | 05.0 | 74 | 69.1 | 26.5 | 34 | 125.1 | 48.0 | 94 | 181.1 | 69.5 | 54 | 237.1 | 91.0 |
| 15 | 14.0 | 05.4 | 75 | 70.0 | 26.9 | 35 | 126.0 | 48.4 | 95 | 182.0 | 69.9 | 55 | 238.1 | 91.4 |
| 16 | 14.9 | 05.7 | 76 | 71.0 | 27.2 | 36 | 127.0 | 48.7 | 96 | 183.0 | 70.2 | 56 | 239.0 | 91.7 |
| 17 | 15.9 | 06.1 | 77 | 71.9 | 27.6 | 37 | 127.9 | 49.1 | 97 | 183.9 | 70.6 | 57 | 239.9 | 92.1 |
| 18 | 16.8 | 06.5 | 78 | 72.8 | 28.0 | 38 | 128.8 | 49.5 | 98 | 184.8 | 71.0 | 58 | 240.9 | 92.5 |
| 19 | 17.7 | 06.8 | 79 | 73.8 | 28.3 | 39 | 129.8 | 49.8 | 99 | 185.8 | 71.3 | 59 | 241.8 | 92.8 |
| 20 | 18.7 | 07.2 | 80 | 74.7 | 28.7 | 40 | 130.7 | 50.2 | 200 | 186.7 | 71.7 | 60 | 242.7 | 93.2 |
| 21 | 19.6 | 07.5 | 81 | 75.6 | 29.0 | 141 | 131.6 | 50.5 | 201 | 187.6 | 72.0 | 261 | 243.7 | 93.5 |
| 22 | 20.5 | 07.9 | 82 | 76.6 | 29.4 | 42 | 132.6 | 50.9 | 02 | 188.6 | 72.4 | 62 | 244.6 | 93.9 |
| 23 | 21.5 | 08.2 | 83 | 77.5 | 29.7 | 43 | 133.5 | 51.2 | 03 | 189.5 | 72.7 | 63 | 245.5 | 94.3 |
| 24 | 22.4 | 08.6 | 84 | 78.4 | 30.1 | 44 | 134.4 | 51.6 | 04 | 190.5 | 73.1 | 64 | 246.5 | 94.6 |
| 25 | 23.3 | 09.0 | 85 | 79.4 | 30.5 | 45 | 135.4 | 52.0 | 05 | 191.4 | 73.5 | 65 | 247.4 | 95.0 |
| 26 | 24.3 | 09.3 | 86 | 80.3 | 30.8 | 46 | 136.3 | 52.3 | 06 | 192.3 | 73.8 | 66 | 248.3 | 95.3 |
| 27 | 25.2 | 09.7 | 87 | 81.2 | 31.2 | 47 | 137.2 | 52.7 | 07 | 193.3 | 74.2 | 67 | 249.3 | 95.7 |
| 28 | 26.1 | 10.0 | 88 | 82.2 | 31.5 | 48 | 138.2 | 53.0 | 08 | 194.2 | 74.5 | 68 | 250.2 | 96.0 |
| 29 | 27.1 | 10.4 | 89 | 83.1 | 31.9 | 49 | 139.1 | 53.4 | 09 | 195.1 | 74.9 | 69 | 251.1 | 96.4 |
| 30 | 28.0 | 10.8 | 90 | 84.0 | 32.3 | 50 | 140.0 | 53.8 | 10 | 196.1 | 75.3 | 70 | 252.1 | 96.8 |
| 31 | 28.9 | 11.1 | 91 | 85.0 | 32.6 | 151 | 141.0 | 54.1 | 211 | 197.0 | 75.6 | 271 | 253.0 | 97.1 |
| 32 | 29.9 | 11.5 | 92 | 85.9 | 33.0 | 52 | 141.9 | 54.5 | 12 | 197.9 | 76.0 | 72 | 253.9 | 97.5 |
| 33 | 30.8 | 11.8 | 93 | 86.8 | 33.3 | 53 | 142.8 | 54.8 | 13 | 198.9 | 76.3 | 73 | 254.9 | 97.8 |
| 34 | 31.7 | 12.2 | 94 | 87.8 | 33.7 | 54 | 143.8 | 55.2 | 14 | 199.8 | 76.7 | 74 | 255.8 | 98.2 |
| 35 | 32.7 | 12.5 | 95 | 88.7 | 34.0 | 55 | 144.7 | 55.5 | 15 | 200.7 | 77.0 | 75 | 256.7 | 98.6 |
| 36 | 33.6 | 12.9 | 96 | 89.6 | 34.4 | 56 | 145.6 | 55.9 | 16 | 201.7 | 77.4 | 76 | 257.7 | 98.9 |
| 37 | 34.5 | 13.3 | 97 | 90.6 | 34.8 | 57 | 146.6 | 56.3 | 17 | 202.6 | 77.8 | 77 | 258.6 | 99.3 |
| 38 | 35.5 | 13.6 | 98 | 91.5 | 35.1 | 58 | 147.5 | 56.6 | 18 | 203.5 | 78.1 | 78 | 259.5 | 99.6 |
| 39 | 36.4 | 14.0 | 99 | 92.4 | 35.5 | 59 | 148.4 | 57.0 | 19 | 204.5 | 78.5 | 79 | 260.5 | 100.0 |
| 40 | 37.3 | 14.3 | 100 | 93.4 | 35.8 | 60 | 149.4 | 57.3 | 20 | 205.4 | 78.8 | 80 | 261.4 | 100.3 |
| 41 | 38.3 | 14.7 | 101 | 94.3 | 36.2 | 161 | 150.3 | 57.7 | 221 | 206.3 | 79.2 | 281 | 262.3 | 100.7 |
| 42 | 39.2 | 15.1 | 02 | 95.2 | 36.6 | 62 | 151.2 | 58.1 | 22 | 207.3 | 79.6 | 82 | 263.3 | 101.1 |
| 43 | 40.1 | 15.4 | 03 | 96.2 | 36.9 | 63 | 152.2 | 58.4 | 23 | 208.2 | 79.9 | 83 | 264.2 | 101.4 |
| 44 | 41.1 | 15.8 | 04 | 97.1 | 37.3 | 64 | 153.1 | 58.8 | 24 | 209.1 | 80.3 | 84 | 265.1 | 101.8 |
| 45 | 42.0 | 16.1 | 05 | 98.0 | 37.6 | 65 | 154.0 | 59.1 | 25 | 210.1 | 80.6 | 85 | 266.1 | 102.1 |
| 46 | 42.9 | 16.5 | 06 | 99.0 | 38.0 | 66 | 155.0 | 59.5 | 26 | 211.0 | 81.0 | 86 | 267.0 | 102.5 |
| 47 | 43.9 | 16.8 | 07 | 99.9 | 38.3 | 67 | 155.9 | 59.8 | 27 | 211.9 | 81.3 | 87 | 267.9 | 102.9 |
| 48 | 44.8 | 17.2 | 08 | 100.8 | 38.7 | 68 | 156.8 | 60.2 | 28 | 212.9 | 81.7 | 88 | 268.9 | 103.2 |
| 49 | 45.7 | 17.6 | 09 | 101.8 | 39.1 | 69 | 157.8 | 60.6 | 29 | 213.8 | 82.1 | 89 | 269.8 | 103.6 |
| 50 | 46.7 | 17.9 | 10 | 102.7 | 39.4 | 70 | 158.7 | 60.9 | 30 | 214.7 | 82.4 | 90 | 270.7 | 103.9 |
| 51 | 47.6 | 18.3 | 111 | 103.6 | 39.8 | 171 | 159.6 | 61.3 | 231 | 215.7 | 82.8 | 291 | 271.7 | 104.3 |
| 52 | 48.5 | 18.6 | 12 | 104.6 | 40.1 | 72 | 160.6 | 61.6 | 32 | 216.6 | 83.1 | 92 | 272.6 | 104.6 |
| 53 | 49.5 | 19.0 | 13 | 105.5 | 40.5 | 73 | 161.5 | 62.0 | 33 | 217.5 | 83.5 | 93 | 273.5 | 105.0 |
| 54 | 50.4 | 19.4 | 14 | 106.4 | 40.9 | 74 | 162.4 | 62.4 | 34 | 218.5 | 83.9 | 94 | 274.5 | 105.4 |
| 55 | 51.3 | 19.7 | 15 | 107.4 | 41.2 | 75 | 163.4 | 62.7 | 35 | 219.4 | 84.2 | 95 | 275.4 | 105.7 |
| 56 | 52.3 | 20.1 | 16 | 108.3 | 41.6 | 76 | 164.3 | 63.1 | 36 | 220.3 | 84.6 | 96 | 276.3 | 106.1 |
| 57 | 53.2 | 20.4 | 17 | 109.2 | 41.9 | 77 | 165.2 | 63.4 | 37 | 221.3 | 84.9 | 97 | 277.3 | 106.4 |
| 58 | 54.1 | 20.8 | 18 | 110.2 | 42.3 | 78 | 166.2 | 63.8 | 38 | 222.2 | 85.3 | 98 | 278.2 | 106.8 |
| 59 | 55.1 | 21.1 | 19 | 111.1 | 42.6 | 79 | 167.1 | 64.1 | 39 | 223.1 | 85.6 | 99 | 279.1 | 107.2 |
| 60 | 56.0 | 21.5 | 20 | 112.0 | 43.0 | 80 | 168.0 | 64.5 | 40 | 224.1 | 86.0 | 300 | 280.1 | 107.5 |
| Dist. | Dep. | Lat. | Dist. | Dep. | Lat. | Dist. | Dep. | Lat. | Dist. | Dep. | Lat. | Dist. | Dep. | Lat. |

[For 69 Degrees.

# TABLE II.

## Difference of Latitude and Departure for 22 Degrees.

| Dist. | Lat. | Dep. | Dist. | Lat. | Dep. | Dist. | Lat. | Dep. | Dist. | Lat. | Dep. | Dist. | Lat. | Dep. |
|---|---|---|---|---|---|---|---|---|---|---|---|---|---|---|
| 1 | 00.9 | 00.4 | 61 | 56.6 | 22.9 | 121 | 112.2 | 45.3 | 181 | 167.8 | 67.8 | 241 | 223.5 | 90.3 |
| 2 | 01.9 | 00.7 | 62 | 57.5 | 23.2 | 22 | 113.1 | 45.7 | 82 | 168.7 | 68.2 | 42 | 224.4 | 90.7 |
| 3 | 02.8 | 01.1 | 63 | 58.4 | 23.6 | 23 | 114.0 | 46.1 | 83 | 169.7 | 68.6 | 43 | 225.3 | 91.0 |
| 4 | 03.7 | 01.5 | 64 | 59.3 | 24.0 | 24 | 115.0 | 46.5 | 84 | 170.6 | 68.9 | 44 | 226.2 | 91.4 |
| 5 | 04.6 | 01.9 | 65 | 60.3 | 24.3 | 25 | 115.9 | 46.8 | 85 | 171.5 | 69.3 | 45 | 227.2 | 91.8 |
| 6 | 05.6 | 02.2 | 66 | 61.2 | 24.7 | 26 | 116.8 | 47.2 | 86 | 172.5 | 69.7 | 46 | 228.1 | 92.2 |
| 7 | 06.5 | 02.6 | 67 | 62.1 | 25.1 | 27 | 117.8 | 47.6 | 87 | 173.4 | 70.1 | 47 | 229.0 | 92.5 |
| 8 | 07.4 | 03.0 | 68 | 63.0 | 25.5 | 28 | 118.7 | 47.9 | 88 | 174.3 | 70.4 | 48 | 229.9 | 92.9 |
| 9 | 08.3 | 03.4 | 69 | 64.0 | 25.8 | 29 | 119.6 | 48.3 | 89 | 175.2 | 70.8 | 49 | 230.9 | 93.3 |
| 10 | 09.3 | 03.7 | 70 | 64.9 | 26.2 | 30 | 120.5 | 48.7 | 90 | 176.2 | 71.2 | 50 | 231.8 | 93.7 |
| 11 | 10.2 | 04.1 | 71 | 65.8 | 26.6 | 131 | 121.5 | 49.1 | 191 | 177.1 | 71.5 | 251 | 232.7 | 94.0 |
| 12 | 11.1 | 04.5 | 72 | 66.8 | 27.0 | 32 | 122.4 | 49.4 | 92 | 178.0 | 71.9 | 52 | 233.7 | 94.4 |
| 13 | 12.1 | 04.9 | 73 | 67.7 | 27.3 | 33 | 123.3 | 49.8 | 93 | 178.9 | 72.3 | 53 | 234.6 | 94.8 |
| 14 | 13.0 | 05.2 | 74 | 68.6 | 27.7 | 34 | 124.2 | 50.2 | 94 | 179.9 | 72.7 | 54 | 235.5 | 95.2 |
| 15 | 13.9 | 05.6 | 75 | 69.5 | 28.1 | 35 | 125.2 | 50.6 | 95 | 180.8 | 73.0 | 55 | 236.4 | 95.5 |
| 16 | 14.8 | 06.0 | 76 | 70.5 | 28.5 | 36 | 126.1 | 50.9 | 96 | 181.7 | 73.4 | 56 | 237.4 | 95.9 |
| 17 | 15.8 | 06.4 | 77 | 71.4 | 28.8 | 37 | 127.0 | 51.3 | 97 | 182.7 | 73.8 | 57 | 238.3 | 96.3 |
| 18 | 16.7 | 06.7 | 78 | 72.3 | 29.2 | 38 | 128.0 | 51.7 | 98 | 183.6 | 74.2 | 58 | 239.2 | 96.6 |
| 19 | 17.6 | 07.1 | 79 | 73.2 | 29.6 | 39 | 128.9 | 52.1 | 99 | 184.5 | 74.5 | 59 | 240.1 | 97.0 |
| 20 | 18.5 | 07.5 | 80 | 74.2 | 30.0 | 40 | 129.8 | 52.4 | 200 | 185.4 | 74.9 | 60 | 241.1 | 97.4 |
| 21 | 19.5 | 07.9 | 81 | 75.1 | 30.3 | 141 | 130.7 | 52.8 | 201 | 186.4 | 75.3 | 261 | 242.0 | 97.8 |
| 22 | 20.4 | 08.2 | 82 | 76.0 | 30.7 | 42 | 131.7 | 53.2 | 02 | 187.3 | 75.7 | 62 | 242.9 | 98.1 |
| 23 | 21.3 | 08.6 | 83 | 77.0 | 31.1 | 43 | 132.6 | 53.6 | 03 | 188.2 | 76.0 | 63 | 243.8 | 98.5 |
| 24 | 22.3 | 09.0 | 84 | 77.9 | 31.5 | 44 | 133.5 | 53.9 | 04 | 189.1 | 76.4 | 64 | 244.8 | 98.9 |
| 25 | 23.2 | 09.4 | 85 | 78.8 | 31.8 | 45 | 134.4 | 54.3 | 05 | 190.1 | 76.8 | 65 | 245.7 | 99.3 |
| 26 | 24.1 | 09.7 | 86 | 79.7 | 32.2 | 46 | 135.4 | 54.7 | 06 | 191.0 | 77.2 | 66 | 246.6 | 99.6 |
| 27 | 25.0 | 10.1 | 87 | 80.7 | 32.6 | 47 | 136.3 | 55.1 | 07 | 191.9 | 77.5 | 67 | 247.6 | 100.0 |
| 28 | 26.0 | 10.5 | 88 | 81.6 | 33.0 | 48 | 137.2 | 55.4 | 08 | 192.9 | 77.9 | 68 | 248.5 | 100.4 |
| 29 | 26.9 | 10.9 | 89 | 82.5 | 33.3 | 49 | 138.2 | 55.8 | 09 | 193.8 | 78.3 | 69 | 249.4 | 100.8 |
| 30 | 27.8 | 11.2 | 90 | 83.4 | 33.7 | 50 | 139.1 | 56.2 | 10 | 194.7 | 78.7 | 70 | 250.3 | 101.1 |
| 31 | 28.7 | 11.6 | 91 | 84.4 | 34.1 | 151 | 140.0 | 56.6 | 211 | 195.6 | 79.0 | 271 | 251.3 | 101.5 |
| 32 | 29.7 | 12.0 | 92 | 85.3 | 34.5 | 52 | 140.9 | 56.9 | 12 | 196.6 | 79.4 | 72 | 252.2 | 101.9 |
| 33 | 30.6 | 12.4 | 93 | 86.2 | 34.8 | 53 | 141.9 | 57.3 | 13 | 197.5 | 79.8 | 73 | 253.1 | 102.3 |
| 34 | 31.5 | 12.7 | 94 | 87.2 | 35.2 | 54 | 142.8 | 57.7 | 14 | 198.4 | 80.2 | 74 | 254.0 | 102.6 |
| 35 | 32.5 | 13.1 | 95 | 88.1 | 35.6 | 55 | 143.7 | 58.1 | 15 | 199.3 | 80.5 | 75 | 255.0 | 103.0 |
| 36 | 33.4 | 13.5 | 96 | 89.0 | 36.0 | 56 | 144.6 | 58.4 | 16 | 200.3 | 80.9 | 76 | 255.9 | 103.4 |
| 37 | 34.3 | 13.9 | 97 | 89.9 | 36.3 | 57 | 145.6 | 58.8 | 17 | 201.2 | 81.3 | 77 | 256.8 | 103.8 |
| 38 | 35.2 | 14.2 | 98 | 90.9 | 36.7 | 58 | 146.5 | 59.2 | 18 | 202.1 | 81.7 | 78 | 257.8 | 104.1 |
| 39 | 36.2 | 14.6 | 99 | 91.8 | 37.1 | 59 | 147.4 | 59.6 | 19 | 203.1 | 82.0 | 79 | 258.7 | 104.5 |
| 40 | 37.1 | 15.0 | 100 | 92.7 | 37.5 | 60 | 148.3 | 59.9 | 20 | 204.0 | 82.4 | 80 | 259.6 | 104.9 |
| 41 | 38.0 | 15.4 | 101 | 93.6 | 37.8 | 161 | 149.3 | 60.3 | 221 | 204.9 | 82.8 | 281 | 260.5 | 105.3 |
| 42 | 38.9 | 15.7 | 02 | 94.6 | 38.2 | 62 | 150.2 | 60.7 | 22 | 205.8 | 83.2 | 82 | 261.5 | 105.6 |
| 43 | 39.9 | 16.1 | 03 | 95.5 | 38.6 | 63 | 151.1 | 61.1 | 23 | 206.8 | 83.5 | 83 | 262.4 | 106.0 |
| 44 | 40.8 | 16.5 | 04 | 96.4 | 39.0 | 64 | 152.1 | 61.4 | 24 | 207.7 | 83.9 | 84 | 263.3 | 106.4 |
| 45 | 41.7 | 16.9 | 05 | 97.4 | 39.3 | 65 | 153.0 | 61.8 | 25 | 208.6 | 84.3 | 85 | 264.2 | 106.8 |
| 46 | 42.7 | 17.2 | 06 | 98.3 | 39.7 | 66 | 153.9 | 62.2 | 26 | 209.5 | 84.7 | 86 | 265.2 | 107.1 |
| 47 | 43.6 | 17.6 | 07 | 99.2 | 40.1 | 67 | 154.8 | 62.6 | 27 | 210.5 | 85.0 | 87 | 266.1 | 107.5 |
| 48 | 44.5 | 18.0 | 08 | 100.1 | 40.5 | 68 | 155.8 | 62.9 | 28 | 211.4 | 85.4 | 88 | 267.0 | 107.9 |
| 49 | 45.4 | 18.4 | 09 | 101.1 | 40.8 | 69 | 156.7 | 63.3 | 29 | 212.3 | 85.8 | 89 | 268.0 | 108.3 |
| 50 | 46.4 | 18.7 | 10 | 102.0 | 41.2 | 70 | 157.6 | 63.7 | 30 | 213.3 | 86.2 | 90 | 268.9 | 108.6 |
| 51 | 47.3 | 19.1 | 111 | 102.9 | 41.6 | 171 | 158.5 | 64.1 | 231 | 214.2 | 86.5 | 291 | 269.8 | 109.0 |
| 52 | 48.2 | 19.5 | 12 | 103.8 | 42.0 | 72 | 159.5 | 64.4 | 32 | 215.1 | 86.9 | 92 | 270.7 | 109.4 |
| 53 | 49.1 | 19.9 | 13 | 104.8 | 42.3 | 73 | 160.4 | 64.8 | 33 | 216.0 | 87.3 | 93 | 271.7 | 109.8 |
| 54 | 50.1 | 20.2 | 14 | 105.7 | 42.7 | 74 | 161.3 | 65.2 | 34 | 217.0 | 87.7 | 94 | 272.6 | 110.1 |
| 55 | 51.0 | 20.6 | 15 | 106.6 | 43.1 | 75 | 162.3 | 65.6 | 35 | 217.9 | 88.0 | 95 | 273.5 | 110.5 |
| 56 | 51.9 | 21.0 | 16 | 107.6 | 43.5 | 76 | 163.2 | 65.9 | 36 | 218.8 | 88.4 | 96 | 274.4 | 110.9 |
| 57 | 52.8 | 21.4 | 17 | 108.5 | 43.8 | 77 | 164.1 | 66.3 | 37 | 219.7 | 88.8 | 97 | 275.4 | 111.3 |
| 58 | 53.8 | 21.7 | 18 | 109.4 | 44.2 | 78 | 165.0 | 66.7 | 38 | 220.7 | 89.2 | 98 | 276.3 | 111.6 |
| 59 | 54.7 | 22.1 | 19 | 110.3 | 44.6 | 79 | 166.0 | 67.1 | 39 | 221.6 | 89.5 | 99 | 277.2 | 112.0 |
| 60 | 55.6 | 22.5 | 20 | 111.3 | 45.0 | 80 | 166.9 | 67.4 | 40 | 222.5 | 89.9 | 300 | 278.2 | 112.4 |
| Dist. | Dep. | Lat. | Dist. | Dep. | Lat. | Dist. | Dep. | Lat. | Dist. | Dep. | Lat. | Dist. | Dep. | Lat. |

# TABLE II.

## Difference of Latitude and Departure for 23 Degrees.

| Dist. | Lat. | Dep. | Dist. | Lat. | Dep. | Dist. | Lat. | Dep. | Dist. | Lat. | Dep. | Dist. | Lat. | Dep. |
|---|---|---|---|---|---|---|---|---|---|---|---|---|---|---|
| 1 | 00.9 | 00.4 | 61 | 56.2 | 23.8 | 121 | 111.4 | 47.3 | 181 | 166.6 | 70.7 | 241 | 221.8 | 94.2 |
| 2 | 01.8 | 00.8 | 62 | 57.1 | 24.2 | 22 | 112.3 | 47.7 | 82 | 167.5 | 71.1 | 42 | 222.8 | 94.6 |
| 3 | 02.8 | 01.2 | 63 | 58.0 | 24.6 | 23 | 113.2 | 48.1 | 83 | 168.5 | 71.5 | 43 | 223.7 | 94.9 |
| 4 | 03.7 | 01.6 | 64 | 58.9 | 25.0 | 24 | 114.1 | 48.5 | 84 | 169.4 | 71.9 | 44 | 224.6 | 95.3 |
| 5 | 04.6 | 02.0 | 65 | 59.8 | 25.4 | 25 | 115.1 | 48.8 | 85 | 170.3 | 72.3 | 45 | 225.5 | 95.7 |
| 6 | 05.5 | 02.3 | 66 | 60.8 | 25.8 | 26 | 116.0 | 49.2 | 86 | 171.2 | 72.7 | 46 | 226.4 | 96.1 |
| 7 | 06.4 | 02.7 | 67 | 61.7 | 26.2 | 27 | 116.9 | 49.6 | 87 | 172.1 | 73.1 | 47 | 227.4 | 96.5 |
| 8 | 07.4 | 03.1 | 68 | 62.6 | 26.6 | 28 | 117.8 | 50.0 | 88 | 173.1 | 73.5 | 48 | 228.3 | 96.9 |
| 9 | 08.3 | 03.5 | 69 | 63.5 | 27.0 | 29 | 118.7 | 50.4 | 89 | 174.0 | 73.8 | 49 | 229.2 | 97.3 |
| 10 | 09.2 | 03.9 | 70 | 64.4 | 27.4 | 30 | 119.7 | 50.8 | 90 | 174.9 | 74.2 | 50 | 230.1 | 97.7 |
| 11 | 10.1 | 04.3 | 71 | 65.4 | 27.7 | 131 | 120.6 | 51.2 | 191 | 175.8 | 74.6 | 251 | 231.0 | 98.1 |
| 12 | 11.0 | 04.7 | 72 | 66.3 | 28.1 | 32 | 121.5 | 51.6 | 92 | 176.7 | 75.0 | 52 | 232.0 | 98.5 |
| 13 | 12.0 | 05.1 | 73 | 67.2 | 28.5 | 33 | 122.4 | 52.0 | 93 | 177.7 | 75.4 | 53 | 232.9 | 98.9 |
| 14 | 12.9 | 05.5 | 74 | 68.1 | 28.9 | 34 | 123.3 | 52.4 | 94 | 178.6 | 75.8 | 54 | 233.8 | 99.2 |
| 15 | 13.8 | 05.9 | 75 | 69.0 | 29.3 | 35 | 124.3 | 52.7 | 95 | 179.5 | 76.2 | 55 | 234.7 | 99.6 |
| 16 | 14.7 | 06.3 | 76 | 70.0 | 29.7 | 36 | 125.2 | 53.1 | 96 | 180.4 | 76.6 | 56 | 235.6 | 100.0 |
| 17 | 15.6 | 06.6 | 77 | 70.9 | 30.1 | 37 | 126.1 | 53.5 | 97 | 181.3 | 77.0 | 57 | 236.6 | 100.4 |
| 18 | 16.6 | 07.0 | 78 | 71.8 | 30.5 | 38 | 127.0 | 53.9 | 98 | 182.3 | 77.4 | 58 | 237.5 | 100.8 |
| 19 | 17.5 | 07.4 | 79 | 72.7 | 30.9 | 39 | 128.0 | 54.3 | 99 | 183.2 | 77.8 | 59 | 238.4 | 101.2 |
| 20 | 18.4 | 07.8 | 80 | 73.6 | 31.3 | 40 | 128.9 | 54.7 | 200 | 184.1 | 78.1 | 60 | 239.3 | 101.6 |
| 21 | 19.3 | 08.2 | 81 | 74.6 | 31.6 | 141 | 129.8 | 55.1 | 201 | 185.0 | 78.5 | 261 | 240.3 | 102.0 |
| 22 | 20.3 | 08.6 | 82 | 75.5 | 32.0 | 42 | 130.7 | 55.5 | 02 | 185.9 | 78.9 | 62 | 241.2 | 102.4 |
| 23 | 21.2 | 09.0 | 83 | 76.4 | 32.4 | 43 | 131.6 | 55.9 | 03 | 186.9 | 79.3 | 63 | 242.1 | 102.8 |
| 24 | 22.1 | 09.4 | 84 | 77.3 | 32.8 | 44 | 132.6 | 56.3 | 04 | 187.8 | 79.7 | 64 | 243.0 | 103.2 |
| 25 | 23.0 | 09.8 | 85 | 78.2 | 33.2 | 45 | 133.5 | 56.7 | 05 | 188.7 | 80.1 | 65 | 243.9 | 103.5 |
| 26 | 23.9 | 10.2 | 86 | 79.2 | 33.6 | 46 | 134.4 | 57.0 | 06 | 189.6 | 80.5 | 66 | 244.9 | 103.9 |
| 27 | 24.9 | 10.5 | 87 | 80.1 | 34.0 | 47 | 135.3 | 57.4 | 07 | 190.5 | 80.9 | 67 | 245.8 | 104.3 |
| 28 | 25.8 | 10.9 | 88 | 81.0 | 34.4 | 48 | 136.2 | 57.8 | 08 | 191.5 | 81.3 | 68 | 246.7 | 104.7 |
| 29 | 26.7 | 11.3 | 89 | 81.9 | 34.8 | 49 | 137.2 | 58.2 | 09 | 192.4 | 81.7 | 69 | 247.6 | 105.1 |
| 30 | 27.6 | 11.7 | 90 | 82.8 | 35.2 | 50 | 138.1 | 58.6 | 10 | 193.3 | 82.1 | 70 | 248.5 | 105.5 |
| 31 | 28.5 | 12.1 | 91 | 83.8 | 35.6 | 151 | 139.0 | 59.0 | 211 | 194.2 | 82.4 | 271 | 249.5 | 105.9 |
| 32 | 29.5 | 12.5 | 92 | 84.7 | 35.9 | 52 | 139.9 | 59.4 | 12 | 195.1 | 82.8 | 72 | 250.4 | 106.3 |
| 33 | 30.4 | 12.9 | 93 | 85.6 | 36.3 | 53 | 140.8 | 59.8 | 13 | 196.1 | 83.2 | 73 | 251.3 | 106.7 |
| 34 | 31.3 | 13.3 | 94 | 86.5 | 36.7 | 54 | 141.8 | 60.2 | 14 | 197.0 | 83.6 | 74 | 252.2 | 107.1 |
| 35 | 32.2 | 13.7 | 95 | 87.4 | 37.1 | 55 | 142.7 | 60.6 | 15 | 197.9 | 84.0 | 75 | 253.1 | 107.5 |
| 36 | 33.1 | 14.1 | 96 | 88.4 | 37.5 | 56 | 143.6 | 61.0 | 16 | 198.8 | 84.4 | 76 | 254.1 | 107.8 |
| 37 | 34.1 | 14.5 | 97 | 89.3 | 37.9 | 57 | 144.5 | 61.3 | 17 | 199.7 | 84.8 | 77 | 255.0 | 108.2 |
| 38 | 35.0 | 14.8 | 98 | 90.2 | 38.3 | 58 | 145.4 | 61.7 | 18 | 200.7 | 85.2 | 78 | 255.9 | 108.6 |
| 39 | 35.9 | 15.2 | 99 | 91.1 | 38.7 | 59 | 146.4 | 62.1 | 19 | 201.6 | 85.6 | 79 | 256.8 | 109.0 |
| 40 | 36.8 | 15.6 | 100 | 92.1 | 39.1 | 60 | 147.3 | 62.5 | 20 | 202.5 | 86.0 | 80 | 257.7 | 109.4 |
| 41 | 37.7 | 16.0 | 101 | 93.0 | 39.5 | 161 | 148.2 | 62.9 | 221 | 203.4 | 86.4 | 281 | 258.7 | 109.8 |
| 42 | 38.7 | 16.4 | 02 | 93.9 | 39.9 | 62 | 149.1 | 63.3 | 22 | 204.4 | 86.7 | 82 | 259.6 | 110.2 |
| 43 | 39.6 | 16.8 | 03 | 94.8 | 40.2 | 63 | 150.0 | 63.7 | 23 | 205.3 | 87.1 | 83 | 260.5 | 110.6 |
| 44 | 40.5 | 17.2 | 04 | 95.7 | 40.6 | 64 | 151.0 | 64.1 | 24 | 206.2 | 87.5 | 84 | 261.4 | 111.0 |
| 45 | 41.4 | 17.6 | 05 | 96.7 | 41.0 | 65 | 151.9 | 64.5 | 25 | 207.1 | 87.9 | 85 | 262.3 | 111.4 |
| 46 | 42.3 | 18.0 | 06 | 97.6 | 41.4 | 66 | 152.8 | 64.9 | 26 | 208.0 | 88.3 | 86 | 263.3 | 111.7 |
| 47 | 43.3 | 18.4 | 07 | 98.5 | 41.8 | 67 | 153.7 | 65.3 | 27 | 209.0 | 88.7 | 87 | 264.2 | 112.1 |
| 48 | 44.2 | 18.8 | 08 | 99.4 | 42.2 | 68 | 154.6 | 65.6 | 28 | 209.9 | 89.1 | 88 | 265.1 | 112.5 |
| 49 | 45.1 | 19.1 | 09 | 100.3 | 42.6 | 69 | 155.6 | 66.0 | 29 | 210.8 | 89.5 | 89 | 266.0 | 112.9 |
| 50 | 46.0 | 19.5 | 10 | 101.3 | 43.0 | 70 | 156.5 | 66.4 | 30 | 211.7 | 89.9 | 90 | 266.9 | 113.3 |
| 51 | 46.9 | 19.9 | 111 | 102.2 | 43.4 | 171 | 157.4 | 66.8 | 231 | 212.6 | 90.3 | 291 | 267.9 | 113.7 |
| 52 | 47.9 | 20.3 | 12 | 103.1 | 43.8 | 72 | 158.3 | 67.2 | 32 | 213.6 | 90.6 | 92 | 268.8 | 114.1 |
| 53 | 48.8 | 20.7 | 13 | 104.0 | 44.2 | 73 | 159.2 | 67.6 | 33 | 214.5 | 91.0 | 93 | 269.7 | 114.5 |
| 54 | 49.7 | 21.1 | 14 | 104.9 | 44.5 | 74 | 160.2 | 68.0 | 34 | 215.4 | 91.4 | 94 | 270.6 | 114.9 |
| 55 | 50.6 | 21.5 | 15 | 105.9 | 44.9 | 75 | 161.1 | 68.4 | 35 | 216.3 | 91.8 | 95 | 271.5 | 115.3 |
| 56 | 51.5 | 21.9 | 16 | 106.8 | 45.3 | 76 | 162.0 | 68.8 | 36 | 217.2 | 92.2 | 96 | 272.5 | 115.7 |
| 57 | 52.5 | 22.3 | 17 | 107.7 | 45.7 | 77 | 162.9 | 69.2 | 37 | 218.2 | 92.6 | 97 | 273.4 | 116.0 |
| 58 | 53.4 | 22.7 | 18 | 108.6 | 46.1 | 78 | 163.8 | 69.6 | 38 | 219.1 | 93.0 | 98 | 274.3 | 116.4 |
| 59 | 54.3 | 23.1 | 19 | 109.5 | 46.5 | 79 | 164.8 | 69.9 | 39 | 220.0 | 93.4 | 99 | 275.2 | 116.8 |
| 60 | 55.2 | 23.4 | 20 | 110.5 | 46.9 | 80 | 165.7 | 70.3 | 40 | 220.9 | 93.8 | 300 | 276.2 | 117.2 |
| Dist. | Dep. | Lat. | Dist. | Dep. | Lat. | Dist. | Dep. | Lat. | Dist. | Dep. | Lat. | Dist. | Dep. | Lat. |

[For 67 Degrees.

# TABLE II.

## Difference of Latitude and Departure for 24 Degrees.

| Dist. | Lat. | Dep. | Dist. | Lat. | Dep. | Dist. | Lat. | Dep. | Dist. | Lat. | Dep. | Dist. | Lat. | Dep. |
|---|---|---|---|---|---|---|---|---|---|---|---|---|---|---|
| 1 | 00.9 | 00.4 | 61 | 55.7 | 24.8 | 121 | 110.5 | 49.2 | 181 | 165.4 | 73.6 | 241 | 220.2 | 98.0 |
| 2 | 01.8 | 00.8 | 62 | 56.6 | 25.2 | 22 | 111.5 | 49.6 | 82 | 166.3 | 74.0 | 42 | 221.1 | 98.4 |
| 3 | 02.7 | 01.2 | 63 | 57.6 | 25.6 | 23 | 112.4 | 50.0 | 83 | 167.2 | 74.4 | 43 | 222.0 | 98.8 |
| 4 | 03.7 | 01.6 | 64 | 58.5 | 26.0 | 24 | 113.3 | 50.4 | 84 | 168.1 | 74.8 | 44 | 222.9 | 99.2 |
| 5 | 04.6 | 02.0 | 65 | 59.4 | 26.4 | 25 | 114.2 | 50.8 | 85 | 169.0 | 75.2 | 45 | 223.8 | 99.7 |
| 6 | 05.5 | 02.4 | 66 | 60.3 | 26.8 | 26 | 115.1 | 51.2 | 86 | 169.9 | 75.7 | 46 | 224.7 | 100.1 |
| 7 | 06.4 | 02.8 | 67 | 61.2 | 27.3 | 27 | 116.0 | 51.7 | 87 | 170.8 | 76.1 | 47 | 225.6 | 100.5 |
| 8 | 07.3 | 03.3 | 68 | 62.1 | 27.7 | 28 | 116.9 | 52.1 | 88 | 171.7 | 76.5 | 48 | 226.6 | 100.9 |
| 9 | 08.2 | 03.7 | 69 | 63.0 | 28.1 | 29 | 117.8 | 52.5 | 89 | 172.7 | 76.9 | 49 | 227.5 | 101.3 |
| 10 | 09.1 | 04.1 | 70 | 63.9 | 28.5 | 30 | 118.8 | 52.9 | 90 | 173.6 | 77.3 | 50 | 228.4 | 101.7 |
| 11 | 10.0 | 04.5 | 71 | 64.9 | 28.9 | 131 | 119.7 | 53.3 | 191 | 174.5 | 77.7 | 251 | 229.3 | 102.1 |
| 12 | 11.0 | 04.9 | 72 | 65.8 | 29.3 | 32 | 120.6 | 53.7 | 92 | 175.4 | 78.1 | 52 | 230.2 | 102.5 |
| 13 | 11.9 | 05.3 | 73 | 66.7 | 29.7 | 33 | 121.5 | 54.1 | 93 | 176.3 | 78.5 | 53 | 231.1 | 102.9 |
| 14 | 12.8 | 05.7 | 74 | 67.6 | 30.1 | 34 | 122.4 | 54.5 | 94 | 177.2 | 78.9 | 54 | 232.0 | 103.3 |
| 15 | 13.7 | 06.1 | 75 | 68.5 | 30.5 | 35 | 123.3 | 54.9 | 95 | 178.1 | 79.3 | 55 | 233.0 | 103.7 |
| 16 | 14.6 | 06.5 | 76 | 69.4 | 30.9 | 36 | 124.2 | 55.3 | 96 | 179.1 | 79.7 | 56 | 233.9 | 104.1 |
| 17 | 15.5 | 06.9 | 77 | 70.3 | 31.3 | 37 | 125.2 | 55.7 | 97 | 180.0 | 80.1 | 57 | 234.8 | 104.5 |
| 18 | 16.4 | 07.3 | 78 | 71.3 | 31.7 | 38 | 126.1 | 56.1 | 98 | 180.9 | 80.5 | 58 | 235.7 | 104.9 |
| 19 | 17.4 | 07.7 | 79 | 72.2 | 32.1 | 39 | 127.0 | 56.5 | 99 | 181.8 | 80.9 | 59 | 236.6 | 105.3 |
| 20 | 18.3 | 08.1 | 80 | 73.1 | 32.5 | 40 | 127.9 | 56.9 | 200 | 182.7 | 81.3 | 60 | 237.5 | 105.8 |
| 21 | 19.2 | 08.5 | 81 | 74.0 | 32.9 | 141 | 128.8 | 57.3 | 201 | 183.6 | 81.8 | 261 | 238.4 | 106.2 |
| 22 | 20.1 | 08.9 | 82 | 74.9 | 33.4 | 42 | 129.7 | 57.8 | 02 | 184.5 | 82.2 | 62 | 239.3 | 106.6 |
| 23 | 21.0 | 09.4 | 83 | 75.8 | 33.8 | 43 | 130.6 | 58.2 | 03 | 185.4 | 82.6 | 63 | 240.3 | 107.0 |
| 24 | 21.9 | 09.8 | 84 | 76.7 | 34.2 | 44 | 131.6 | 58.6 | 04 | 186.4 | 83.0 | 64 | 241.2 | 107.4 |
| 25 | 22.8 | 10.2 | 85 | 77.7 | 34.6 | 45 | 132.5 | 59.0 | 05 | 187.3 | 83.4 | 65 | 242.1 | 107.8 |
| 26 | 23.8 | 10.6 | 86 | 78.6 | 35.0 | 46 | 133.4 | 59.4 | 06 | 188.2 | 83.8 | 66 | 243.0 | 108.2 |
| 27 | 24.7 | 11.0 | 87 | 79.5 | 35.4 | 47 | 134.3 | 59.8 | 07 | 189.1 | 84.2 | 67 | 243.9 | 108.6 |
| 28 | 25.6 | 11.4 | 88 | 80.4 | 35.8 | 48 | 135.2 | 60.2 | 08 | 190.0 | 84.6 | 68 | 244.8 | 109.0 |
| 29 | 26.5 | 11.8 | 89 | 81.3 | 36.2 | 49 | 136.1 | 60.6 | 09 | 190.9 | 85.0 | 69 | 245.7 | 109.4 |
| 30 | 27.4 | 12.2 | 90 | 82.2 | 36.6 | 50 | 137.0 | 61.0 | 10 | 191.8 | 85.4 | 70 | 246.7 | 109.8 |
| 31 | 28.3 | 12.6 | 91 | 83.1 | 37.0 | 151 | 137.9 | 61.4 | 211 | 192.8 | 85.8 | 271 | 247.6 | 110.2 |
| 32 | 29.2 | 13.0 | 92 | 84.0 | 37.4 | 52 | 138.9 | 61.8 | 12 | 193.7 | 86.2 | 72 | 248.5 | 110.6 |
| 33 | 30.1 | 13.4 | 93 | 85.0 | 37.8 | 53 | 139.8 | 62.2 | 13 | 194.6 | 86.6 | 73 | 249.4 | 111.0 |
| 34 | 31.1 | 13.8 | 94 | 85.9 | 38.2 | 54 | 140.7 | 62.6 | 14 | 195.5 | 87.0 | 74 | 250.3 | 111.4 |
| 35 | 32.0 | 14.2 | 95 | 86.8 | 38.6 | 55 | 141.6 | 63.0 | 15 | 196.4 | 87.4 | 75 | 251.2 | 111.9 |
| 36 | 32.9 | 14.6 | 96 | 87.7 | 39.0 | 56 | 142.5 | 63.5 | 16 | 197.3 | 87.9 | 76 | 252.1 | 112.3 |
| 37 | 33.8 | 15.0 | 97 | 88.6 | 39.5 | 57 | 143.4 | 63.9 | 17 | 198.2 | 88.3 | 77 | 253.1 | 112.7 |
| 38 | 34.7 | 15.5 | 98 | 89.5 | 39.9 | 58 | 144.3 | 64.3 | 18 | 199.2 | 88.7 | 78 | 254.0 | 113.1 |
| 39 | 35.6 | 15.9 | 99 | 90.4 | 40.3 | 59 | 145.3 | 64.7 | 19 | 200.1 | 89.1 | 79 | 254.9 | 113.5 |
| 40 | 36.5 | 16.3 | 100 | 91.4 | 40.7 | 60 | 146.2 | 65.1 | 20 | 201.0 | 89.5 | 80 | 255.8 | 113.9 |
| 41 | 37.5 | 16.7 | 101 | 92.3 | 41.1 | 161 | 147.1 | 65.5 | 221 | 201.9 | 89.9 | 281 | 256.7 | 114.3 |
| 42 | 38.4 | 17.1 | 02 | 93.2 | 41.5 | 62 | 148.0 | 65.9 | 22 | 202.8 | 90.3 | 82 | 257.6 | 114.7 |
| 43 | 39.3 | 17.5 | 03 | 94.1 | 41.9 | 63 | 148.9 | 66.3 | 23 | 203.7 | 90.7 | 83 | 258.5 | 115.1 |
| 44 | 40.2 | 17.9 | 04 | 95.0 | 42.3 | 64 | 149.8 | 66.7 | 24 | 204.6 | 91.1 | 84 | 259.4 | 115.5 |
| 45 | 41.1 | 18.3 | 05 | 95.9 | 42.7 | 65 | 150.7 | 67.1 | 25 | 205.5 | 91.5 | 85 | 260.4 | 115.9 |
| 46 | 42.0 | 18.7 | 06 | 96.8 | 43.1 | 66 | 151.6 | 67.5 | 26 | 206.5 | 91.9 | 86 | 261.3 | 116.3 |
| 47 | 42.9 | 19.1 | 07 | 97.7 | 43.5 | 67 | 152.6 | 67.9 | 27 | 207.4 | 92.3 | 87 | 262.2 | 116.7 |
| 48 | 43.9 | 19.5 | 08 | 98.7 | 43.9 | 68 | 153.5 | 68.3 | 28 | 208.3 | 92.7 | 88 | 263.1 | 117.1 |
| 49 | 44.8 | 19.9 | 09 | 99.6 | 44.3 | 69 | 154.4 | 68.7 | 29 | 209.2 | 93.1 | 89 | 264.0 | 117.5 |
| 50 | 45.7 | 20.3 | 10 | 100.5 | 44.7 | 70 | 155.3 | 69.1 | 30 | 210.1 | 93.5 | 90 | 264.9 | 118.0 |
| 51 | 46.6 | 20.7 | 111 | 101.4 | 45.1 | 171 | 156.2 | 69.6 | 231 | 211.0 | 94.0 | 291 | 265.8 | 118.4 |
| 52 | 47.5 | 21.2 | 12 | 102.3 | 45.6 | 72 | 157.1 | 70.0 | 32 | 211.9 | 94.4 | 92 | 266.8 | 118.8 |
| 53 | 48.4 | 21.6 | 13 | 103.2 | 46.0 | 73 | 158.0 | 70.4 | 33 | 212.9 | 94.8 | 93 | 267.7 | 119.2 |
| 54 | 49.3 | 22.0 | 14 | 104.1 | 46.4 | 74 | 159.0 | 70.8 | 34 | 213.8 | 95.2 | 94 | 268.6 | 119.6 |
| 55 | 50.2 | 22.4 | 15 | 105.1 | 46.8 | 75 | 159.9 | 71.2 | 35 | 214.7 | 95.6 | 95 | 269.5 | 120.0 |
| 56 | 51.2 | 22.8 | 16 | 106.0 | 47.2 | 76 | 160.8 | 71.6 | 36 | 215.6 | 96.0 | 96 | 270.4 | 120.4 |
| 57 | 52.1 | 23.2 | 17 | 106.9 | 47.6 | 77 | 161.7 | 72.0 | 37 | 216.5 | 96.4 | 97 | 271.3 | 120.8 |
| 58 | 53.0 | 23.6 | 18 | 107.8 | 48.0 | 78 | 162.6 | 72.4 | 38 | 217.4 | 96.8 | 98 | 272.2 | 121.2 |
| 59 | 53.9 | 24.0 | 19 | 108.7 | 48.4 | 79 | 163.5 | 72.8 | 39 | 218.3 | 97.2 | 99 | 273.2 | 121.6 |
| 60 | 54.8 | 24.4 | 20 | 109.6 | 48.8 | 80 | 164.4 | 73.2 | 40 | 219.3 | 97.6 | 300 | 274.1 | 122.0 |
| Dist. | Dep. | Lat. | Dist. | Dep. | Lat. | Dist. | Dep. | Lat. | Dist. | Dep. | Lat. | Dist. | Dep. | Lat. |

# TABLE II.

## Difference of Latitude and Departure for 25 Degrees.

| Dist. | Lat. | Dep. | Dist. | Lat. | Dep. | Dist. | Lat. | Dep. | Dist. | Lat. | Dep. | Dist. | Lat. | Dep. |
|---|---|---|---|---|---|---|---|---|---|---|---|---|---|---|
| 1 | 00.9 | 00.4 | 61 | 55.3 | 25.8 | 121 | 109.7 | 51.1 | 181 | 164.0 | 76.5 | 241 | 218.4 | 101.9 |
| 2 | 01.8 | 00.8 | 62 | 56.2 | 26.2 | 22 | 110.6 | 51.6 | 82 | 164.9 | 76.9 | 42 | 219.3 | 102.3 |
| 3 | 02.7 | 01.3 | 63 | 57.1 | 26.6 | 23 | 111.5 | 52.0 | 83 | 165.9 | 77.3 | 43 | 220.2 | 102.7 |
| 4 | 03.6 | 01.7 | 64 | 58.0 | 27.0 | 24 | 112.4 | 52.4 | 84 | 166.8 | 77.8 | 44 | 221.1 | 103.1 |
| 5 | 04.5 | 02.1 | 65 | 58.9 | 27.5 | 25 | 113.3 | 52.8 | 85 | 167.7 | 78.2 | 45 | 222.0 | 103.5 |
| 6 | 05.4 | 02.5 | 66 | 59.8 | 27.9 | 26 | 114.2 | 53.2 | 86 | 168.6 | 78.6 | 46 | 223.0 | 104.0 |
| 7 | 06.3 | 03.0 | 67 | 60.7 | 28.3 | 27 | 115.1 | 53.7 | 87 | 169.5 | 79.0 | 47 | 223.9 | 104.4 |
| 8 | 07.3 | 03.4 | 68 | 61.6 | 28.7 | 28 | 116.0 | 54.1 | 88 | 170.4 | 79.5 | 48 | 224.8 | 104.8 |
| 9 | 08.2 | 03.8 | 69 | 62.5 | 29.2 | 29 | 116.9 | 54.5 | 89 | 171.3 | 79.9 | 49 | 225.7 | 105.2 |
| 10 | 09.1 | 04.2 | 70 | 63.4 | 29.6 | 30 | 117.8 | 54.9 | 90 | 172.2 | 80.3 | 50 | 226.6 | 105.7 |
| 11 | 10.0 | 04.6 | 71 | 64.3 | 30.0 | 131 | 118.7 | 55.4 | 191 | 173.1 | 80.7 | 251 | 227.5 | 106.1 |
| 12 | 10.9 | 05.1 | 72 | 65.3 | 30.4 | 32 | 119.6 | 55.8 | 92 | 174.0 | 81.1 | 52 | 228.4 | 106.5 |
| 13 | 11.8 | 05.5 | 73 | 66.2 | 30.9 | 33 | 120.5 | 56.2 | 93 | 174.9 | 81.6 | 53 | 229.3 | 106.9 |
| 14 | 12.7 | 05.9 | 74 | 67.1 | 31.3 | 34 | 121.4 | 56.6 | 94 | 175.8 | 82.0 | 54 | 230.2 | 107.3 |
| 15 | 13.6 | 06.3 | 75 | 68.0 | 31.7 | 35 | 122.4 | 57.1 | 95 | 176.7 | 82.4 | 55 | 231.1 | 107.8 |
| 16 | 14.5 | 06.8 | 76 | 68.9 | 32.1 | 36 | 123.3 | 57.5 | 96 | 177.6 | 82.8 | 56 | 232.0 | 108.2 |
| 17 | 15.4 | 07.2 | 77 | 69.8 | 32.5 | 37 | 124.2 | 57.9 | 97 | 178.5 | 83.3 | 57 | 232.9 | 108.6 |
| 18 | 16.3 | 07.6 | 78 | 70.7 | 33.0 | 38 | 125.1 | 58.3 | 98 | 179.4 | 83.7 | 58 | 233.8 | 109.0 |
| 19 | 17.2 | 08.0 | 79 | 71.6 | 33.4 | 39 | 126.0 | 58.7 | 99 | 180.4 | 84.1 | 59 | 234.7 | 109.5 |
| 20 | 18.1 | 08.5 | 80 | 72.5 | 33.8 | 40 | 126.9 | 59.2 | 200 | 181.3 | 84.5 | 60 | 235.6 | 109.9 |
| 21 | 19.0 | 08.9 | 81 | 73.4 | 34.2 | 141 | 127.8 | 59.6 | 201 | 182.2 | 84.9 | 261 | 236.5 | 110.3 |
| 22 | 19.9 | 09.3 | 82 | 74.3 | 34.7 | 42 | 128.7 | 60.0 | 02 | 183.1 | 85.4 | 62 | 237.5 | 110.7 |
| 23 | 20.8 | 09.7 | 83 | 75.2 | 35.1 | 43 | 129.6 | 60.4 | 03 | 184.0 | 85.8 | 63 | 238.4 | 111.1 |
| 24 | 21.8 | 10.1 | 84 | 76.1 | 35.5 | 44 | 130.5 | 60.9 | 04 | 184.9 | 86.2 | 64 | 239.3 | 111.6 |
| 25 | 22.7 | 10.6 | 85 | 77.0 | 35.9 | 45 | 131.4 | 61.3 | 05 | 185.8 | 86.6 | 65 | 240.2 | 112.0 |
| 26 | 23.6 | 11.0 | 86 | 77.9 | 36.3 | 46 | 132.3 | 61.7 | 06 | 186.7 | 87.1 | 66 | 241.1 | 112.4 |
| 27 | 24.5 | 11.4 | 87 | 78.8 | 36.8 | 47 | 133.2 | 62.1 | 07 | 187.6 | 87.5 | 67 | 242.0 | 112.8 |
| 28 | 25.4 | 11.8 | 88 | 79.8 | 37.2 | 48 | 134.1 | 62.5 | 08 | 188.5 | 87.9 | 68 | 242.9 | 113.3 |
| 29 | 26.3 | 12.3 | 89 | 80.7 | 37.6 | 49 | 135.0 | 63.0 | 09 | 189.4 | 88.3 | 69 | 243.8 | 113.7 |
| 30 | 27.2 | 12.7 | 90 | 81.6 | 38.0 | 50 | 135.9 | 63.4 | 10 | 190.3 | 88.7 | 70 | 244.7 | 114.1 |
| 31 | 28.1 | 13.1 | 91 | 82.5 | 38.5 | 151 | 136.9 | 63.8 | 211 | 191.2 | 89.2 | 271 | 245.6 | 114.5 |
| 32 | 29.0 | 13.5 | 92 | 83.4 | 38.9 | 52 | 137.8 | 64.2 | 12 | 192.1 | 89.6 | 72 | 246.5 | 115.0 |
| 33 | 29.9 | 13.9 | 93 | 84.3 | 39.3 | 53 | 138.7 | 64.7 | 13 | 193.0 | 90.0 | 73 | 247.4 | 115.4 |
| 34 | 30.8 | 14.4 | 94 | 85.2 | 39.7 | 54 | 139.6 | 65.1 | 14 | 193.9 | 90.4 | 74 | 248.3 | 115.8 |
| 35 | 31.7 | 14.8 | 95 | 86.1 | 40.1 | 55 | 140.5 | 65.5 | 15 | 194.9 | 90.9 | 75 | 249.2 | 116.2 |
| 36 | 32.6 | 15.2 | 96 | 87.0 | 40.6 | 56 | 141.4 | 65.9 | 16 | 195.8 | 91.3 | 76 | 250.1 | 116.6 |
| 37 | 33.5 | 15.6 | 97 | 87.9 | 41.0 | 57 | 142.3 | 66.4 | 17 | 196.7 | 91.7 | 77 | 251.0 | 117.1 |
| 38 | 34.4 | 16.1 | 98 | 88.8 | 41.4 | 58 | 143.2 | 66.8 | 18 | 197.6 | 92.1 | 78 | 252.0 | 117.5 |
| 39 | 35.3 | 16.5 | 99 | 89.7 | 41.8 | 59 | 144.1 | 67.2 | 19 | 198.5 | 92.6 | 79 | 252.9 | 117.9 |
| 40 | 36.3 | 16.9 | 100 | 90.6 | 42.3 | 60 | 145.0 | 67.6 | 20 | 199.4 | 93.0 | 80 | 253.8 | 118.3 |
| 41 | 37.2 | 17.3 | 101 | 91.5 | 42.7 | 161 | 145.9 | 68.0 | 221 | 200.3 | 93.4 | 281 | 254.7 | 118.8 |
| 42 | 38.1 | 17.7 | 02 | 92.4 | 43.1 | 62 | 146.8 | 68.5 | 22 | 201.2 | 93.8 | 82 | 255.6 | 119.2 |
| 43 | 39.0 | 18.2 | 03 | 93.3 | 43.5 | 63 | 147.7 | 68.9 | 23 | 202.1 | 94.2 | 83 | 256.5 | 119.6 |
| 44 | 39.9 | 18.6 | 04 | 94.3 | 44.0 | 64 | 148.6 | 69.3 | 24 | 203.0 | 94.7 | 84 | 257.4 | 120.0 |
| 45 | 40.8 | 19.0 | 05 | 95.2 | 44.4 | 65 | 149.5 | 69.7 | 25 | 203.9 | 95.1 | 85 | 258.3 | 120.4 |
| 46 | 41.7 | 19.4 | 06 | 96.1 | 44.8 | 66 | 150.4 | 70.2 | 26 | 204.8 | 95.5 | 86 | 259.2 | 120.9 |
| 47 | 42.6 | 19.9 | 07 | 97.0 | 45.2 | 67 | 151.4 | 70.6 | 27 | 205.7 | 95.9 | 87 | 260.1 | 121.3 |
| 48 | 43.5 | 20.3 | 08 | 97.9 | 45.6 | 68 | 152.3 | 71.0 | 28 | 206.6 | 96.4 | 88 | 261.0 | 121.7 |
| 49 | 44.4 | 20.7 | 09 | 98.8 | 46.1 | 69 | 153.2 | 71.4 | 29 | 207.5 | 96.8 | 89 | 261.9 | 122.1 |
| 50 | 45.3 | 21.1 | 10 | 99.7 | 46.5 | 70 | 154.1 | 71.8 | 30 | 208.5 | 97.2 | 90 | 262.8 | 122.6 |
| 51 | 46.2 | 21.6 | 111 | 100.6 | 46.9 | 171 | 155.0 | 72.3 | 231 | 209.4 | 97.6 | 291 | 263.7 | 123.0 |
| 52 | 47.1 | 22.0 | 12 | 101.5 | 47.3 | 72 | 155.9 | 72.7 | 32 | 210.3 | 98.0 | 92 | 264.6 | 123.4 |
| 53 | 48.0 | 22.4 | 13 | 102.4 | 47.8 | 73 | 156.8 | 73.1 | 33 | 211.2 | 98.5 | 93 | 265.5 | 123.8 |
| 54 | 48.9 | 22.8 | 14 | 103.3 | 48.2 | 74 | 157.7 | 73.5 | 34 | 212.1 | 98.9 | 94 | 266.5 | 124.2 |
| 55 | 49.8 | 23.2 | 15 | 104.2 | 48.6 | 75 | 158.6 | 74.0 | 35 | 213.0 | 99.3 | 95 | 267.4 | 124.7 |
| 56 | 50.8 | 23.7 | 16 | 105.1 | 49.0 | 76 | 159.5 | 74.4 | 36 | 213.9 | 99.7 | 96 | 268.3 | 125.1 |
| 57 | 51.7 | 24.1 | 17 | 106.0 | 49.4 | 77 | 160.4 | 74.8 | 37 | 214.8 | 100.2 | 97 | 269.2 | 125.5 |
| 58 | 52.6 | 24.5 | 18 | 106.9 | 49.9 | 78 | 161.3 | 75.2 | 38 | 215.7 | 100.6 | 98 | 270.1 | 125.9 |
| 59 | 53.5 | 24.9 | 19 | 107.9 | 50.3 | 79 | 162.2 | 75.6 | 39 | 216.6 | 101.0 | 99 | 271.0 | 126.4 |
| 60 | 54.4 | 25.4 | 20 | 108.8 | 50.7 | 80 | 163.1 | 76.1 | 40 | 217.5 | 101.4 | 300 | 271.9 | 126.8 |
| Dist. | Dep. | Lat. | Dist. | Dep. | Lat. | Dist. | Dep. | Lat. | Dist. | Dep. | Lat. | Dist. | Dep. | Lat. |

[For 65 Degrees.

# TABLE II.

## Difference of Latitude and Departure for 26 Degrees.

| Dist. | Lat. | Dep. | Dist. | Lat. | Dep. | Dist. | Lat. | Dep. | Dist. | Lat. | Dep. | Dist. | Lat. | Dep. |
|---|---|---|---|---|---|---|---|---|---|---|---|---|---|---|
| 1 | 00.9 | 00.4 | 61 | 54.8 | 26.7 | 121 | 108.8 | 53.0 | 181 | 162.7 | 79.3 | 241 | 216.6 | 105.6 |
| 2 | 01.8 | 00.9 | 62 | 55.7 | 27.2 | 22 | 109.7 | 53.5 | 82 | 163.6 | 79.8 | 42 | 217.5 | 106.1 |
| 3 | 02.7 | 01.3 | 63 | 56.6 | 27.6 | 23 | 110.6 | 53.9 | 83 | 164.5 | 80.2 | 43 | 218.4 | 106.5 |
| 4 | 03.6 | 01.8 | 64 | 57.5 | 28.1 | 24 | 111.5 | 54.4 | 84 | 165.4 | 80.7 | 44 | 219.3 | 107.0 |
| 5 | 04.5 | 02.2 | 65 | 58.4 | 28.5 | 25 | 112.3 | 54.8 | 85 | 166.3 | 81.1 | 45 | 220.2 | 107.4 |
| 6 | 05.4 | 02.6 | 66 | 59.3 | 28.9 | 26 | 113.2 | 55.2 | 86 | 167.2 | 81.5 | 46 | 221.1 | 107.8 |
| 7 | 06.3 | 03.1 | 67 | 60.2 | 29.4 | 27 | 114.1 | 55.7 | 87 | 168.1 | 82.0 | 47 | 222.0 | 108.3 |
| 8 | 07.2 | 03.5 | 68 | 61.1 | 29.8 | 28 | 115.0 | 56.1 | 88 | 169.0 | 82.4 | 48 | 222.9 | 108.7 |
| 9 | 08.1 | 03.9 | 69 | 62.0 | 30.2 | 29 | 115.9 | 56.5 | 89 | 169.9 | 82.9 | 49 | 223.8 | 109.2 |
| 10 | 09.0 | 04.4 | 70 | 62.9 | 30.7 | 30 | 116.8 | 57.0 | 90 | 170.8 | 83.3 | 50 | 224.7 | 109.6 |
| 11 | 09.9 | 04.8 | 71 | 63.8 | 31.1 | 131 | 117.7 | 57.4 | 191 | 171.7 | 83.7 | 251 | 225.6 | 110.0 |
| 12 | 10.8 | 05.3 | 72 | 64.7 | 31.6 | 32 | 118.6 | 57.9 | 92 | 172.6 | 84.2 | 52 | 226.5 | 110.5 |
| 13 | 11.7 | 05.7 | 73 | 65.6 | 32.0 | 33 | 119.5 | 58.3 | 93 | 173.5 | 84.6 | 53 | 227.4 | 110.9 |
| 14 | 12.6 | 06.1 | 74 | 66.5 | 32.4 | 34 | 120.4 | 58.7 | 94 | 174.4 | 85.0 | 54 | 228.3 | 111.3 |
| 15 | 13.5 | 06.6 | 75 | 67.4 | 32.9 | 35 | 121.3 | 59.2 | 95 | 175.3 | 85.5 | 55 | 229.2 | 111.8 |
| 16 | 14.4 | 07.0 | 76 | 68.3 | 33.3 | 36 | 122.2 | 59.6 | 96 | 176.2 | 85.9 | 56 | 230.1 | 112.2 |
| 17 | 15.3 | 07.5 | 77 | 69.2 | 33.8 | 37 | 123.1 | 60.1 | 97 | 177.1 | 86.4 | 57 | 231.0 | 112.7 |
| 18 | 16.2 | 07.9 | 78 | 70.1 | 34.2 | 38 | 124.0 | 60.5 | 98 | 178.0 | 86.8 | 58 | 231.9 | 113.1 |
| 19 | 17.1 | 08.3 | 79 | 71.0 | 34.6 | 39 | 124.9 | 60.9 | 99 | 178.9 | 87.2 | 59 | 232.8 | 113.5 |
| 20 | 18.0 | 08.8 | 80 | 71.9 | 35.1 | 40 | 125.8 | 61.4 | 200 | 179.8 | 87.7 | 60 | 233.7 | 114.0 |
| 21 | 18.9 | 09.2 | 81 | 72.8 | 35.5 | 141 | 126.7 | 61.8 | 201 | 180.7 | 88.1 | 261 | 234.6 | 114.4 |
| 22 | 19.8 | 09.6 | 82 | 73.7 | 35.9 | 42 | 127.6 | 62.2 | 02 | 181.6 | 88.6 | 62 | 235.5 | 114.9 |
| 23 | 20.7 | 10.1 | 83 | 74.6 | 36.4 | 43 | 128.5 | 62.7 | 03 | 182.5 | 89.0 | 63 | 236.4 | 115.3 |
| 24 | 21.6 | 10.5 | 84 | 75.5 | 36.8 | 44 | 129.4 | 63.1 | 04 | 183.4 | 89.4 | 64 | 237.3 | 115.7 |
| 25 | 22.5 | 11.0 | 85 | 76.4 | 37.3 | 45 | 130.3 | 63.6 | 05 | 184.3 | 89.9 | 65 | 238.2 | 116.2 |
| 26 | 23.4 | 11.4 | 86 | 77.3 | 37.7 | 46 | 131.2 | 64.0 | 06 | 185.2 | 90.3 | 66 | 239.1 | 116.6 |
| 27 | 24.3 | 11.8 | 87 | 78.2 | 38.1 | 47 | 132.1 | 64.4 | 07 | 186.1 | 90.7 | 67 | 240.0 | 117.0 |
| 28 | 25.2 | 12.3 | 88 | 79.1 | 38.6 | 48 | 133.0 | 64.9 | 08 | 186.9 | 91.2 | 68 | 240.9 | 117.5 |
| 29 | 26.1 | 12.7 | 89 | 80.0 | 39.0 | 49 | 133.9 | 65.3 | 09 | 187.8 | 91.6 | 69 | 241.8 | 117.9 |
| 30 | 27.0 | 13.2 | 90 | 80.9 | 39.5 | 50 | 134.8 | 65.8 | 10 | 188.7 | 92.1 | 70 | 242.7 | 118.4 |
| 31 | 27.9 | 13.6 | 91 | 81.8 | 39.9 | 151 | 135.7 | 66.2 | 211 | 189.6 | 92.5 | 271 | 243.6 | 118.8 |
| 32 | 28.8 | 14.0 | 92 | 82.7 | 40.3 | 52 | 136.6 | 66.6 | 12 | 190.5 | 92.9 | 72 | 244.5 | 119.2 |
| 33 | 29.7 | 14.5 | 93 | 83.6 | 40.8 | 53 | 137.5 | 67.1 | 13 | 191.4 | 93.4 | 73 | 245.4 | 119.7 |
| 34 | 30.6 | 14.9 | 94 | 84.5 | 41.2 | 54 | 138.4 | 67.5 | 14 | 192.3 | 93.8 | 74 | 246.3 | 120.1 |
| 35 | 31.5 | 15.3 | 95 | 85.4 | 41.6 | 55 | 139.3 | 67.9 | 15 | 193.2 | 94.2 | 75 | 247.2 | 120.6 |
| 36 | 32.4 | 15.8 | 96 | 86.3 | 42.1 | 56 | 140.2 | 68.4 | 16 | 194.1 | 94.7 | 76 | 248.1 | 121.0 |
| 37 | 33.3 | 16.2 | 97 | 87.2 | 42.5 | 57 | 141.1 | 68.8 | 17 | 195.0 | 95.1 | 77 | 249.0 | 121.4 |
| 38 | 34.2 | 16.7 | 98 | 88.1 | 43.0 | 58 | 142.0 | 69.3 | 18 | 195.9 | 95.6 | 78 | 249.9 | 121.9 |
| 39 | 35.1 | 17.1 | 99 | 89.0 | 43.4 | 59 | 142.9 | 69.7 | 19 | 196.8 | 96.0 | 79 | 250.8 | 122.3 |
| 40 | 36.0 | 17.5 | 100 | 89.9 | 43.8 | 60 | 143.8 | 70.1 | 20 | 197.7 | 96.4 | 80 | 251.7 | 122.7 |
| 41 | 36.9 | 18.0 | 101 | 90.8 | 44.3 | 161 | 144.7 | 70.6 | 221 | 198.6 | 96.9 | 281 | 252.6 | 123.2 |
| 42 | 37.7 | 18.4 | 02 | 91.7 | 44.7 | 62 | 145.6 | 71.0 | 22 | 199.5 | 97.3 | 82 | 253.5 | 123.6 |
| 43 | 38.6 | 18.8 | 03 | 92.6 | 45.2 | 63 | 146.5 | 71.5 | 23 | 200.4 | 97.8 | 83 | 254.4 | 124.1 |
| 44 | 39.5 | 19.3 | 04 | 93.5 | 45.6 | 64 | 147.4 | 71.9 | 24 | 201.3 | 98.2 | 84 | 255.3 | 124.5 |
| 45 | 40.4 | 19.7 | 05 | 94.4 | 46.0 | 65 | 148.3 | 72.3 | 25 | 202.2 | 98.6 | 85 | 256.2 | 124.9 |
| 46 | 41.3 | 20.2 | 06 | 95.3 | 46.5 | 66 | 149.2 | 72.8 | 26 | 203.1 | 99.1 | 86 | 257.1 | 125.4 |
| 47 | 42.2 | 20.6 | 07 | 96.2 | 46.9 | 67 | 150.1 | 73.2 | 27 | 204.0 | 99.5 | 87 | 258.0 | 125.8 |
| 48 | 43.1 | 21.0 | 08 | 97.1 | 47.3 | 68 | 151.0 | 73.6 | 28 | 204.9 | 99.9 | 88 | 258.9 | 126.3 |
| 49 | 44.0 | 21.5 | 09 | 98.0 | 47.8 | 69 | 151.9 | 74.1 | 29 | 205.8 | 100.4 | 89 | 259.8 | 126.7 |
| 50 | 44.9 | 21.9 | 10 | 98.9 | 48.2 | 70 | 152.8 | 74.5 | 30 | 206.7 | 100.8 | 90 | 260.7 | 127.1 |
| 51 | 45.8 | 22.4 | 111 | 99.8 | 48.7 | 171 | 153.7 | 75.0 | 231 | 207.6 | 101.3 | 291 | 261.5 | 127.6 |
| 52 | 46.7 | 22.8 | 12 | 100.7 | 49.1 | 72 | 154.6 | 75.4 | 32 | 208.5 | 101.7 | 92 | 262.4 | 128.0 |
| 53 | 47.6 | 23.2 | 13 | 101.6 | 49.5 | 73 | 155.5 | 75.8 | 33 | 209.4 | 102.1 | 93 | 263.3 | 128.4 |
| 54 | 48.5 | 23.7 | 14 | 102.5 | 50.0 | 74 | 156.4 | 76.3 | 34 | 210.3 | 102.6 | 94 | 264.2 | 128.9 |
| 55 | 49.4 | 24.1 | 15 | 103.4 | 50.4 | 75 | 157.3 | 76.7 | 35 | 211.2 | 103.0 | 95 | 265.1 | 129.3 |
| 56 | 50.3 | 24.5 | 16 | 104.3 | 50.9 | 76 | 158.2 | 77.2 | 36 | 212.1 | 103.5 | 96 | 266.0 | 129.8 |
| 57 | 51.2 | 25.0 | 17 | 105.2 | 51.3 | 77 | 159.1 | 77.6 | 37 | 213.0 | 103.9 | 97 | 266.9 | 130.2 |
| 58 | 52.1 | 25.4 | 18 | 106.1 | 51.7 | 78 | 160.0 | 78.0 | 38 | 213.9 | 104.3 | 98 | 267.8 | 130.6 |
| 59 | 53.0 | 25.9 | 19 | 107.0 | 52.2 | 79 | 160.9 | 78.5 | 39 | 214.8 | 104.8 | 99 | 268.7 | 131.1 |
| 60 | 53.9 | 26.3 | 20 | 107.9 | 52.6 | 80 | 161.8 | 78.9 | 40 | 215.7 | 105.2 | 300 | 269.6 | 131.5 |
| Dist. | Dep. | Lat. | Dist. | Dep. | Lat. | Dist. | Dep. | Lat. | Dist. | Dep. | Lat. | Dist. | Dep. | Lat. |

# TABLE II.

## Difference of Latitude and Departure for 27 Degrees.

| Dist. | Lat. | Dep. | Dist. | Lat. | Dep. | Dist. | Lat. | Dep. | Dist. | Lat. | Dep. | Dist. | Lat. | Dep. |
|---|---|---|---|---|---|---|---|---|---|---|---|---|---|---|
| 1 | 00.9 | 00.5 | 61 | 54.4 | 27.7 | 121 | 107.8 | 54.9 | 181 | 161.3 | 82.2 | 241 | 214.7 | 109.4 |
| 2 | 01.8 | 00.9 | 62 | 55.2 | 28.1 | 22 | 108.7 | 55.4 | 82 | 162.2 | 82.6 | 42 | 215.6 | 109.9 |
| 3 | 02.7 | 01.4 | 63 | 56.1 | 28.6 | 23 | 109.6 | 55.8 | 83 | 163.1 | 83.1 | 43 | 216.5 | 110.3 |
| 4 | 03.6 | 01.8 | 64 | 57.0 | 29.1 | 24 | 110.5 | 56.3 | 84 | 163.9 | 83.5 | 44 | 217.4 | 110.8 |
| 5 | 04.5 | 02.3 | 65 | 57.9 | 29.5 | 25 | 111.4 | 56.7 | 85 | 164.8 | 84.0 | 45 | 218.3 | 111.2 |
| 6 | 05.3 | 02.7 | 66 | 58.8 | 30.0 | 26 | 112.3 | 57.2 | 86 | 165.7 | 84.4 | 46 | 219.2 | 111.7 |
| 7 | 06.2 | 03.2 | 67 | 59.7 | 30.4 | 27 | 113.2 | 57.7 | 87 | 166.6 | 84.9 | 47 | 220.1 | 112.1 |
| 8 | 07.1 | 03.6 | 68 | 60.6 | 30.9 | 28 | 114.0 | 58.1 | 88 | 167.5 | 85.4 | 48 | 221.0 | 112.6 |
| 9 | 08.0 | 04.1 | 69 | 61.5 | 31.3 | 29 | 114.9 | 58.6 | 89 | 168.4 | 85.8 | 49 | 221.9 | 113.0 |
| 10 | 08.9 | 04.5 | 70 | 62.4 | 31.8 | 30 | 115.8 | 59.0 | 90 | 169.3 | 86.3 | 50 | 222.8 | 113.5 |
| 11 | 09.8 | 05.0 | 71 | 63.3 | 32.2 | 131 | 116.7 | 59.5 | 191 | 170.2 | 86.7 | 251 | 223.6 | 114.0 |
| 12 | 10.7 | 05.4 | 72 | 64.2 | 32.7 | 32 | 117.6 | 59.9 | 92 | 171.1 | 87.2 | 52 | 224.5 | 114.4 |
| 13 | 11.6 | 05.9 | 73 | 65.0 | 33.1 | 33 | 118.5 | 60.4 | 93 | 172.0 | 87.6 | 53 | 225.4 | 114.9 |
| 14 | 12.5 | 06.4 | 74 | 65.9 | 33.6 | 34 | 119.4 | 60.8 | 94 | 172.9 | 88.1 | 54 | 226.3 | 115.3 |
| 15 | 13.4 | 06.8 | 75 | 66.8 | 34.0 | 35 | 120.3 | 61.3 | 95 | 173.7 | 88.5 | 55 | 227.2 | 115.8 |
| 16 | 14.3 | 07.3 | 76 | 67.7 | 34.5 | 36 | 121.2 | 61.7 | 96 | 174.6 | 89.0 | 56 | 228.1 | 116.2 |
| 17 | 15.1 | 07.7 | 77 | 68.6 | 35.0 | 37 | 122.1 | 62.2 | 97 | 175.5 | 89.4 | 57 | 229.0 | 116.7 |
| 18 | 16.0 | 08.2 | 78 | 69.5 | 35.4 | 38 | 123.0 | 62.7 | 98 | 176.4 | 89.9 | 58 | 229.9 | 117.1 |
| 19 | 16.9 | 08.6 | 79 | 70.4 | 35.9 | 39 | 123.8 | 63.1 | 99 | 177.3 | 90.3 | 59 | 230.8 | 117.6 |
| 20 | 17.8 | 09.1 | 80 | 71.3 | 36.3 | 40 | 124.7 | 63.6 | 200 | 178.2 | 90.8 | 60 | 231.7 | 118.0 |
| 21 | 18.7 | 09.5 | 81 | 72.2 | 36.8 | 141 | 125.6 | 64.0 | 201 | 179.1 | 91.3 | 261 | 232.6 | 118.5 |
| 22 | 19.6 | 10.0 | 82 | 73.1 | 37.2 | 42 | 126.5 | 64.5 | 02 | 180.0 | 91.7 | 62 | 233.4 | 118.9 |
| 23 | 20.5 | 10.4 | 83 | 74.0 | 37.7 | 43 | 127.4 | 64.9 | 03 | 180.9 | 92.2 | 63 | 234.3 | 119.4 |
| 24 | 21.4 | 10.9 | 84 | 74.8 | 38.1 | 44 | 128.3 | 65.4 | 04 | 181.8 | 92.6 | 64 | 235.2 | 119.9 |
| 25 | 22.3 | 11.3 | 85 | 75.7 | 38.6 | 45 | 129.2 | 65.8 | 05 | 182.7 | 93.1 | 65 | 236.1 | 120.3 |
| 26 | 23.2 | 11.8 | 86 | 76.6 | 39.0 | 46 | 130.1 | 66.3 | 06 | 183.5 | 93.5 | 66 | 237.0 | 120.8 |
| 27 | 24.1 | 12.3 | 87 | 77.5 | 39.5 | 47 | 131.0 | 66.7 | 07 | 184.4 | 94.0 | 67 | 237.9 | 121.2 |
| 28 | 24.9 | 12.7 | 88 | 78.4 | 40.0 | 48 | 131.9 | 67.2 | 08 | 185.3 | 94.4 | 68 | 238.8 | 121.7 |
| 29 | 25.8 | 13.2 | 89 | 79.3 | 40.4 | 49 | 132.8 | 67.6 | 09 | 186.2 | 94.9 | 69 | 239.7 | 122.1 |
| 30 | 26.7 | 13.6 | 90 | 80.2 | 40.9 | 50 | 133.7 | 68.1 | 10 | 187.1 | 95.3 | 70 | 240.6 | 122.6 |
| 31 | 27.6 | 14.1 | 91 | 81.1 | 41.3 | 151 | 134.5 | 68.6 | 211 | 188.0 | 95.8 | 271 | 241.5 | 123.0 |
| 32 | 28.5 | 14.5 | 92 | 82.0 | 41.8 | 52 | 135.4 | 69.0 | 12 | 188.9 | 96.2 | 72 | 242.4 | 123.5 |
| 33 | 29.4 | 15.0 | 93 | 82.9 | 42.2 | 53 | 136.3 | 69.5 | 13 | 189.8 | 96.7 | 73 | 243.2 | 123.9 |
| 34 | 30.3 | 15.4 | 94 | 83.8 | 42.7 | 54 | 137.2 | 69.9 | 14 | 190.7 | 97.2 | 74 | 244.1 | 124.4 |
| 35 | 31.2 | 15.9 | 95 | 84.6 | 43.1 | 55 | 138.1 | 70.4 | 15 | 191.6 | 97.6 | 75 | 245.0 | 124.8 |
| 36 | 32.1 | 16.3 | 96 | 85.5 | 43.6 | 56 | 139.0 | 70.8 | 16 | 192.5 | 98.1 | 76 | 245.9 | 125.3 |
| 37 | 33.0 | 16.8 | 97 | 86.4 | 44.0 | 57 | 139.9 | 71.3 | 17 | 193.3 | 98.5 | 77 | 246.8 | 125.8 |
| 38 | 33.9 | 17.3 | 98 | 87.3 | 44.5 | 58 | 140.8 | 71.7 | 18 | 194.2 | 99.0 | 78 | 247.7 | 126.2 |
| 39 | 34.7 | 17.7 | 99 | 88.2 | 44.9 | 59 | 141.7 | 72.2 | 19 | 195.1 | 99.4 | 79 | 248.6 | 126.7 |
| 40 | 35.6 | 18.2 | 100 | 89.1 | 45.4 | 60 | 142.6 | 72.6 | 20 | 196.0 | 99.9 | 80 | 249.5 | 127.1 |
| 41 | 36.5 | 18.6 | 101 | 90.0 | 45.9 | 161 | 143.5 | 73.1 | 221 | 196.9 | 100.3 | 281 | 250.4 | 127.6 |
| 42 | 37.4 | 19.1 | 02 | 90.9 | 46.3 | 62 | 144.3 | 73.5 | 22 | 197.8 | 100.8 | 82 | 251.3 | 128.0 |
| 43 | 38.3 | 19.5 | 03 | 91.8 | 46.8 | 63 | 145.2 | 74.0 | 23 | 198.7 | 101.2 | 83 | 252.2 | 128.5 |
| 44 | 39.2 | 20.0 | 04 | 92.7 | 47.2 | 64 | 146.1 | 74.5 | 24 | 199.6 | 101.7 | 84 | 253.0 | 128.9 |
| 45 | 40.1 | 20.4 | 05 | 93.6 | 47.7 | 65 | 147.0 | 74.9 | 25 | 200.5 | 102.1 | 85 | 253.9 | 129.4 |
| 46 | 41.0 | 20.9 | 06 | 94.4 | 48.1 | 66 | 147.9 | 75.4 | 26 | 201.4 | 102.6 | 86 | 254.8 | 129.8 |
| 47 | 41.9 | 21.3 | 07 | 95.3 | 48.6 | 67 | 148.8 | 75.8 | 27 | 202.3 | 103.1 | 87 | 255.7 | 130.3 |
| 48 | 42.8 | 21.8 | 08 | 96.2 | 49.0 | 68 | 149.7 | 76.3 | 28 | 203.1 | 103.5 | 88 | 256.6 | 130.7 |
| 49 | 43.7 | 22.2 | 09 | 97.1 | 49.5 | 69 | 150.6 | 76.7 | 29 | 204.0 | 104.0 | 89 | 257.5 | 131.2 |
| 50 | 44.6 | 22.7 | 10 | 98.0 | 49.9 | 70 | 151.5 | 77.2 | 30 | 204.9 | 104.4 | 90 | 258.4 | 131.7 |
| 51 | 45.4 | 23.2 | 111 | 98.9 | 50.4 | 171 | 152.4 | 77.6 | 231 | 205.8 | 104.9 | 291 | 259.3 | 132.1 |
| 52 | 46.3 | 23.6 | 12 | 99.8 | 50.8 | 72 | 153.3 | 78.1 | 32 | 206.7 | 105.3 | 92 | 260.2 | 132.6 |
| 53 | 47.2 | 24.1 | 13 | 100.7 | 51.3 | 73 | 154.1 | 78.5 | 33 | 207.6 | 105.8 | 93 | 261.1 | 133.0 |
| 54 | 48.1 | 24.5 | 14 | 101.6 | 51.8 | 74 | 155.0 | 79.0 | 34 | 208.5 | 106.2 | 94 | 262.0 | 133.5 |
| 55 | 49.0 | 25.0 | 15 | 102.5 | 52.2 | 75 | 155.9 | 79.4 | 35 | 209.4 | 106.7 | 95 | 262.8 | 133.9 |
| 56 | 49.9 | 25.4 | 16 | 103.4 | 52.7 | 76 | 156.8 | 79.9 | 36 | 210.3 | 107.1 | 96 | 263.7 | 134.4 |
| 57 | 50.8 | 25.9 | 17 | 104.2 | 53.1 | 77 | 157.7 | 80.4 | 37 | 211.2 | 107.6 | 97 | 264.6 | 134.8 |
| 58 | 51.7 | 26.3 | 18 | 105.1 | 53.6 | 78 | 158.6 | 80.8 | 38 | 212.1 | 108.0 | 98 | 265.5 | 135.3 |
| 59 | 52.6 | 26.8 | 19 | 106.0 | 54.0 | 79 | 159.5 | 81.3 | 39 | 213.0 | 108.5 | 99 | 266.4 | 135.7 |
| 60 | 53.5 | 27.2 | 20 | 106.9 | 54.5 | 80 | 160.4 | 81.7 | 40 | 213.8 | 109.0 | 300 | 267.3 | 136.2 |
| Dist. | Dep. | Lat. | Dist. | Dep. | Lat. | Dist. | Dep. | Lat. | Dist. | Dep. | Lat. | Dist. | Dep. | Lat. |

[For 63 Degrees.

# TABLE II.

## Difference of Latitude and Departure for 28 Degrees.

| Dist. | Lat. | Dep. | Dist. | Lat. | Dep. | Dist. | Lat. | Dep. | Dist. | Lat. | Dep. | Dist. | Lat. | Dep. |
|---|---|---|---|---|---|---|---|---|---|---|---|---|---|---|
| 1 | 00.9 | 00.5 | 61 | 53.9 | 28.6 | 121 | 106.8 | 56.8 | 181 | 159.8 | 85.0 | 241 | 212.8 | 113.1 |
| 2 | 01.8 | 00.9 | 62 | 54.7 | 29.1 | 22 | 107.7 | 57.3 | 82 | 160.7 | 85.4 | 42 | 213.7 | 113.6 |
| 3 | 02.6 | 01.4 | 63 | 55.6 | 29.6 | 23 | 108.6 | 57.7 | 83 | 161.6 | 85.9 | 43 | 214.6 | 114.1 |
| 4 | 03.5 | 01.9 | 64 | 56.5 | 30.0 | 24 | 109.5 | 58.2 | 84 | 162.5 | 86.4 | 44 | 215.4 | 114.6 |
| 5 | 04.4 | 02.3 | 65 | 57.4 | 30.5 | 25 | 110.4 | 58.7 | 85 | 163.3 | 86.9 | 45 | 216.3 | 115.0 |
| 6 | 05.3 | 02.8 | 66 | 58.3 | 31.0 | 26 | 111.3 | 59.2 | 86 | 164.2 | 87.3 | 46 | 217.2 | 115.5 |
| 7 | 06.2 | 03.3 | 67 | 59.2 | 31.5 | 27 | 112.1 | 59.6 | 87 | 165.1 | 87.8 | 47 | 218.1 | 116.0 |
| 8 | 07.1 | 03.8 | 68 | 60.0 | 31.9 | 28 | 113.0 | 60.1 | 88 | 166.0 | 88.3 | 48 | 219.0 | 116.4 |
| 9 | 07.9 | 04.2 | 69 | 60.9 | 32.4 | 29 | 113.9 | 60.6 | 89 | 166.9 | 88.7 | 49 | 219.9 | 116.9 |
| 10 | 08.8 | 04.7 | 70 | 61.8 | 32.9 | 30 | 114.8 | 61.0 | 90 | 167.8 | 89.2 | 50 | 220.7 | 117.4 |
| 11 | 09.7 | 05.2 | 71 | 62.7 | 33.3 | 131 | 115.7 | 61.5 | 191 | 168.6 | 89.7 | 251 | 221.6 | 117.8 |
| 12 | 10.6 | 05.6 | 72 | 63.6 | 33.8 | 32 | 116.5 | 62.0 | 92 | 169.5 | 90.1 | 52 | 222.5 | 118.3 |
| 13 | 11.5 | 06.1 | 73 | 64.5 | 34.3 | 33 | 117.4 | 62.4 | 93 | 170.4 | 90.6 | 53 | 223.4 | 118.8 |
| 14 | 12.4 | 06.6 | 74 | 65.3 | 34.7 | 34 | 118.3 | 62.9 | 94 | 171.3 | 91.1 | 54 | 224.3 | 119.2 |
| 15 | 13.2 | 07.0 | 75 | 66.2 | 35.2 | 35 | 119.2 | 63.4 | 95 | 172.2 | 91.5 | 55 | 225.2 | 119.7 |
| 16 | 14.1 | 07.5 | 76 | 67.1 | 35.7 | 36 | 120.1 | 63.8 | 96 | 173.1 | 92.0 | 56 | 226.0 | 120.2 |
| 17 | 15.0 | 08.0 | 77 | 68.0 | 36.1 | 37 | 121.0 | 64.3 | 97 | 173.9 | 92.5 | 57 | 226.9 | 120.7 |
| 18 | 15.9 | 08.5 | 78 | 68.9 | 36.6 | 38 | 121.8 | 64.8 | 98 | 174.8 | 93.0 | 58 | 227.8 | 121.1 |
| 19 | 16.8 | 08.9 | 79 | 69.8 | 37.1 | 39 | 122.7 | 65.3 | 99 | 175.7 | 93.4 | 59 | 228.7 | 121.6 |
| 20 | 17.7 | 09.4 | 80 | 70.6 | 37.6 | 40 | 123.6 | 65.7 | 200 | 176.6 | 93.9 | 60 | 229.6 | 122.1 |
| 21 | 18.5 | 09.9 | 81 | 71.5 | 38.0 | 141 | 124.5 | 66.2 | 201 | 177.5 | 94.4 | 261 | 230.4 | 122.5 |
| 22 | 19.4 | 10.3 | 82 | 72.4 | 38.5 | 42 | 125.4 | 66.7 | 02 | 178.4 | 94.8 | 62 | 231.3 | 123.0 |
| 23 | 20.3 | 10.8 | 83 | 73.3 | 39.0 | 43 | 126.3 | 67.1 | 03 | 179.2 | 95.3 | 63 | 232.2 | 123.5 |
| 24 | 21.2 | 11.3 | 84 | 74.2 | 39.4 | 44 | 127.1 | 67.6 | 04 | 180.1 | 95.8 | 64 | 233.1 | 123.9 |
| 25 | 22.1 | 11.7 | 85 | 75.1 | 39.9 | 45 | 128.0 | 68.1 | 05 | 181.0 | 96.2 | 65 | 234.0 | 124.4 |
| 26 | 23.0 | 12.2 | 86 | 75.9 | 40.4 | 46 | 128.9 | 68.5 | 06 | 181.9 | 96.7 | 66 | 234.9 | 124.9 |
| 27 | 23.8 | 12.7 | 87 | 76.8 | 40.8 | 47 | 129.8 | 69.0 | 07 | 182.8 | 97.2 | 67 | 235.7 | 125.3 |
| 28 | 24.7 | 13.1 | 88 | 77.7 | 41.3 | 48 | 130.7 | 69.5 | 08 | 183.7 | 97.7 | 68 | 236.6 | 125.8 |
| 29 | 25.6 | 13.6 | 89 | 78.6 | 41.8 | 49 | 131.6 | 70.0 | 09 | 184.5 | 98.1 | 69 | 237.5 | 126.3 |
| 30 | 26.5 | 14.1 | 90 | 79.5 | 42.3 | 50 | 132.4 | 70.4 | 10 | 185.4 | 98.6 | 70 | 238.4 | 126.8 |
| 31 | 27.4 | 14.6 | 91 | 80.3 | 42.7 | 151 | 133.3 | 70.9 | 211 | 186.3 | 99.1 | 271 | 239.3 | 127.2 |
| 32 | 28.3 | 15.0 | 92 | 81.2 | 43.2 | 52 | 134.2 | 71.4 | 12 | 187.2 | 99.5 | 72 | 240.2 | 127.7 |
| 33 | 29.1 | 15.5 | 93 | 82.1 | 43.7 | 53 | 135.1 | 71.8 | 13 | 188.1 | 100.0 | 73 | 241.0 | 128.2 |
| 34 | 30.0 | 16.0 | 94 | 83.0 | 44.1 | 54 | 136.0 | 72.3 | 14 | 189.0 | 100.5 | 74 | 241.9 | 128.6 |
| 35 | 30.9 | 16.4 | 95 | 83.9 | 44.6 | 55 | 136.9 | 72.8 | 15 | 189.8 | 100.9 | 75 | 242.8 | 129.1 |
| 36 | 31.8 | 16.9 | 96 | 84.8 | 45.1 | 56 | 137.7 | 73.2 | 16 | 190.7 | 101.4 | 76 | 243.7 | 129.6 |
| 37 | 32.7 | 17.4 | 97 | 85.6 | 45.5 | 57 | 138.6 | 73.7 | 17 | 191.6 | 101.9 | 77 | 244.6 | 130.0 |
| 38 | 33.6 | 17.8 | 98 | 86.5 | 46.0 | 58 | 139.5 | 74.2 | 18 | 192.5 | 102.3 | 78 | 245.5 | 130.5 |
| 39 | 34.4 | 18.3 | 99 | 87.4 | 46.5 | 59 | 140.4 | 74.6 | 19 | 193.4 | 102.8 | 79 | 246.3 | 131.0 |
| 40 | 35.3 | 18.8 | 100 | 88.3 | 46.9 | 60 | 141.3 | 75.1 | 20 | 194.2 | 103.3 | 80 | 247.2 | 131.5 |
| 41 | 36.2 | 19.2 | 101 | 89.2 | 47.4 | 161 | 142.2 | 75.6 | 221 | 195.1 | 103.8 | 281 | 248.1 | 131.9 |
| 42 | 37.1 | 19.7 | 02 | 90.1 | 47.9 | 62 | 143.0 | 76.1 | 22 | 196.0 | 104.2 | 82 | 249.0 | 132.4 |
| 43 | 38.0 | 20.2 | 03 | 90.9 | 48.4 | 63 | 143.9 | 76.5 | 23 | 196.9 | 104.7 | 83 | 249.9 | 132.9 |
| 44 | 38.8 | 20.7 | 04 | 91.8 | 48.8 | 64 | 144.8 | 77.0 | 24 | 197.8 | 105.2 | 84 | 250.8 | 133.3 |
| 45 | 39.7 | 21.1 | 05 | 92.7 | 49.3 | 65 | 145.7 | 77.5 | 25 | 198.7 | 105.6 | 85 | 251.6 | 133.8 |
| 46 | 40.6 | 21.6 | 06 | 93.6 | 49.8 | 66 | 146.6 | 77.9 | 26 | 199.5 | 106.1 | 86 | 252.5 | 134.3 |
| 47 | 41.5 | 22.1 | 07 | 94.5 | 50.2 | 67 | 147.5 | 78.4 | 27 | 200.4 | 106.6 | 87 | 253.4 | 134.7 |
| 48 | 42.4 | 22.5 | 08 | 95.4 | 50.7 | 68 | 148.3 | 78.9 | 28 | 201.3 | 107.0 | 88 | 254.3 | 135.2 |
| 49 | 43.3 | 23.0 | 09 | 96.2 | 51.2 | 69 | 149.2 | 79.3 | 29 | 202.2 | 107.5 | 89 | 255.2 | 135.7 |
| 50 | 44.1 | 23.5 | 10 | 97.1 | 51.6 | 70 | 150.1 | 79.8 | 30 | 203.1 | 108.0 | 90 | 256.1 | 136.1 |
| 51 | 45.0 | 23.9 | 111 | 98.0 | 52.1 | 171 | 151.0 | 80.3 | 231 | 204.0 | 108.4 | 291 | 256.9 | 136.6 |
| 52 | 45.9 | 24.4 | 12 | 98.9 | 52.6 | 72 | 151.9 | 80.7 | 32 | 204.8 | 108.9 | 92 | 257.8 | 137.1 |
| 53 | 46.8 | 24.9 | 13 | 99.8 | 53.1 | 73 | 152.7 | 81.2 | 33 | 205.7 | 109.4 | 93 | 258.7 | 137.6 |
| 54 | 47.7 | 25.4 | 14 | 100.7 | 53.5 | 74 | 153.6 | 81.7 | 34 | 206.6 | 109.9 | 94 | 259.6 | 138.0 |
| 55 | 48.6 | 25.8 | 15 | 101.5 | 54.0 | 75 | 154.5 | 82.2 | 35 | 207.5 | 110.3 | 95 | 260.5 | 138.5 |
| 56 | 49.4 | 26.3 | 16 | 102.4 | 54.5 | 76 | 155.4 | 82.6 | 36 | 208.4 | 110.8 | 96 | 261.4 | 139.0 |
| 57 | 50.3 | 26.8 | 17 | 103.3 | 54.9 | 77 | 156.3 | 83.1 | 37 | 209.3 | 111.3 | 97 | 262.2 | 139.4 |
| 58 | 51.2 | 27.2 | 18 | 104.2 | 55.4 | 78 | 157.2 | 83.6 | 38 | 210.1 | 111.7 | 98 | 263.1 | 139.9 |
| 59 | 52.1 | 27.7 | 19 | 105.1 | 55.9 | 79 | 158.0 | 84.0 | 39 | 211.0 | 112.2 | 99 | 264.0 | 140.4 |
| 60 | 53.0 | 28.2 | 20 | 106.0 | 56.3 | 80 | 158.9 | 84.5 | 40 | 211.9 | 112.7 | 300 | 264.9 | 140.8 |
| Dist. | Dep. | Lat. | Dist. | Dep. | Lat. | Dist. | Dep. | Lat. | Dist. | Dep. | Lat. | Dist. | Dep. | Lat. |

# TABLE II.

## Difference of Latitude and Departure for 29 Degrees.

| Dist. | Lat. | Dep. | Dist. | Lat. | Dep. | Dist. | Lat. | Dep. | Dist. | Lat. | Dep. | Dist. | Lat. | Dep. |
|---|---|---|---|---|---|---|---|---|---|---|---|---|---|---|
| 1 | 00.9 | 00.5 | 61 | 53.4 | 29.6 | 121 | 105.8 | 58.7 | 181 | 158.3 | 87.8 | 241 | 210.8 | 116.8 |
| 2 | 01.7 | 01.0 | 62 | 54.2 | 30.1 | 22 | 106.7 | 59.1 | 82 | 159.2 | 88.2 | 42 | 211.7 | 117.3 |
| 3 | 02.6 | 01.5 | 63 | 55.1 | 30.5 | 23 | 107.6 | 59.6 | 83 | 160.1 | 88.7 | 43 | 212.5 | 117.8 |
| 4 | 03.5 | 01.9 | 64 | 56.0 | 31.0 | 24 | 108.5 | 60.1 | 84 | 160.9 | 89.2 | 44 | 213.4 | 118.3 |
| 5 | 04.4 | 02.4 | 65 | 56.9 | 31.5 | 25 | 109.3 | 60.6 | 85 | 161.8 | 89.7 | 45 | 214.3 | 118.8 |
| 6 | 05.2 | 02.9 | 66 | 57.7 | 32.0 | 26 | 110.2 | 61.1 | 86 | 162.7 | 90.2 | 46 | 215.2 | 119.3 |
| 7 | 06.1 | 03.4 | 67 | 58.6 | 32.5 | 27 | 111.1 | 61.6 | 87 | 163.6 | 90.7 | 47 | 216.0 | 119.7 |
| 8 | 07.0 | 03.9 | 68 | 59.5 | 33.0 | 28 | 112.0 | 62.1 | 88 | 164.4 | 91.1 | 48 | 216.9 | 120.2 |
| 9 | 07.9 | 04.4 | 69 | 60.3 | 33.5 | 29 | 112.8 | 62.5 | 89 | 165.3 | 91.6 | 49 | 217.8 | 120.7 |
| 10 | 08.7 | 04.8 | 70 | 61.2 | 33.9 | 30 | 113.7 | 63.0 | 90 | 166.2 | 92.1 | 50 | 218.7 | 121.2 |
| 11 | 09.6 | 05.3 | 71 | 62.1 | 34.4 | 131 | 114.6 | 63.5 | 191 | 167.1 | 92.6 | 251 | 219.5 | 121.7 |
| 12 | 10.5 | 05.8 | 72 | 63.0 | 34.9 | 32 | 115.4 | 64.0 | 92 | 167.9 | 93.1 | 52 | 220.4 | 122.2 |
| 13 | 11.4 | 06.3 | 73 | 63.8 | 35.4 | 33 | 116.3 | 64.5 | 93 | 168.8 | 93.6 | 53 | 221.3 | 122.7 |
| 14 | 12.2 | 06.8 | 74 | 64.7 | 35.9 | 34 | 117.2 | 65.0 | 94 | 169.7 | 94.1 | 54 | 222.2 | 123.1 |
| 15 | 13.1 | 07.3 | 75 | 65.6 | 36.4 | 35 | 118.1 | 65.4 | 95 | 170.6 | 94.5 | 55 | 223.0 | 123.6 |
| 16 | 14.0 | 07.8 | 76 | 66.5 | 36.8 | 36 | 118.9 | 65.9 | 96 | 171.4 | 95.0 | 56 | 223.9 | 124.1 |
| 17 | 14.9 | 08.2 | 77 | 67.3 | 37.3 | 37 | 119.8 | 66.4 | 97 | 172.3 | 95.5 | 57 | 224.8 | 124.6 |
| 18 | 15.7 | 08.7 | 78 | 68.2 | 37.8 | 38 | 120.7 | 66.9 | 98 | 173.2 | 96.0 | 58 | 225.7 | 125.1 |
| 19 | 16.6 | 09.2 | 79 | 69.1 | 38.3 | 39 | 121.6 | 67.4 | 99 | 174.0 | 96.5 | 59 | 226.5 | 125.6 |
| 20 | 17.5 | 09.7 | 80 | 70.0 | 38.8 | 40 | 122.4 | 67.9 | 200 | 174.9 | 97.0 | 60 | 227.4 | 126.1 |
| 21 | 18.4 | 10.2 | 81 | 70.8 | 39.3 | 141 | 123.3 | 68.4 | 201 | 175.8 | 97.4 | 261 | 228.3 | 126.5 |
| 22 | 19.2 | 10.7 | 82 | 71.7 | 39.8 | 42 | 124.2 | 68.8 | 02 | 176.7 | 97.9 | 62 | 229.2 | 127.0 |
| 23 | 20.1 | 11.2 | 83 | 72.6 | 40.2 | 43 | 125.1 | 69.3 | 03 | 177.5 | 98.4 | 63 | 230.0 | 127.5 |
| 24 | 21.0 | 11.6 | 84 | 73.5 | 40.7 | 44 | 125.9 | 69.8 | 04 | 178.4 | 98.9 | 64 | 230.9 | 128.0 |
| 25 | 21.9 | 12.1 | 85 | 74.3 | 41.2 | 45 | 126.8 | 70.3 | 05 | 179.3 | 99.4 | 65 | 231.8 | 128.5 |
| 26 | 22.7 | 12.6 | 86 | 75.2 | 41.7 | 46 | 127.7 | 70.8 | 06 | 180.2 | 99.9 | 66 | 232.6 | 129.0 |
| 27 | 23.6 | 13.1 | 87 | 76.1 | 42.2 | 47 | 128.6 | 71.3 | 07 | 181.0 | 100.4 | 67 | 233.5 | 129.4 |
| 28 | 24.5 | 13.6 | 88 | 77.0 | 42.7 | 48 | 129.4 | 71.8 | 08 | 181.9 | 100.8 | 68 | 234.4 | 129.9 |
| 29 | 25.4 | 14.1 | 89 | 77.8 | 43.1 | 49 | 130.3 | 72.2 | 09 | 182.8 | 101.3 | 69 | 235.3 | 130.4 |
| 30 | 26.2 | 14.5 | 90 | 78.7 | 43.6 | 50 | 131.2 | 72.7 | 10 | 183.7 | 101.8 | 70 | 236.1 | 130.9 |
| 31 | 27.1 | 15.0 | 91 | 79.6 | 44.1 | 151 | 132.1 | 73.2 | 211 | 184.5 | 102.3 | 271 | 237.0 | 131.4 |
| 32 | 28.0 | 15.5 | 92 | 80.5 | 44.6 | 52 | 132.9 | 73.7 | 12 | 185.4 | 102.8 | 72 | 237.9 | 131.9 |
| 33 | 28.9 | 16.0 | 93 | 81.3 | 45.1 | 53 | 133.8 | 74.2 | 13 | 186.3 | 103.3 | 73 | 238.8 | 132.4 |
| 34 | 29.7 | 16.5 | 94 | 82.2 | 45.6 | 54 | 134.7 | 74.7 | 14 | 187.2 | 103.7 | 74 | 239.6 | 132.8 |
| 35 | 30.6 | 17.0 | 95 | 83.1 | 46.1 | 55 | 135.6 | 75.1 | 15 | 188.0 | 104.2 | 75 | 240.5 | 133.3 |
| 36 | 31.5 | 17.5 | 96 | 84.0 | 46.5 | 56 | 136.4 | 75.6 | 16 | 188.9 | 104.7 | 76 | 241.4 | 133.8 |
| 37 | 32.4 | 17.9 | 97 | 84.8 | 47.0 | 57 | 137.3 | 76.1 | 17 | 189.8 | 105.2 | 77 | 242.3 | 134.3 |
| 38 | 33.2 | 18.4 | 98 | 85.7 | 47.5 | 58 | 138.2 | 76.6 | 18 | 190.7 | 105.7 | 78 | 243.1 | 134.8 |
| 39 | 34.1 | 18.9 | 99 | 86.6 | 48.0 | 59 | 139.1 | 77.1 | 19 | 191.5 | 106.2 | 79 | 244.0 | 135.3 |
| 40 | 35.0 | 19.4 | 100 | 87.5 | 48.5 | 60 | 139.9 | 77.6 | 20 | 192.4 | 106.7 | 80 | 244.9 | 135.7 |
| 41 | 35.9 | 19.9 | 101 | 88.3 | 49.0 | 161 | 140.8 | 78.1 | 221 | 193.3 | 107.1 | 281 | 245.8 | 136.2 |
| 42 | 36.7 | 20.4 | 02 | 89.2 | 49.5 | 62 | 141.7 | 78.5 | 22 | 194.2 | 107.6 | 82 | 246.6 | 136.7 |
| 43 | 37.6 | 20.8 | 03 | 90.1 | 49.9 | 63 | 142.6 | 79.0 | 23 | 195.0 | 108.1 | 83 | 247.5 | 137.2 |
| 44 | 38.5 | 21.3 | 04 | 91.0 | 50.4 | 64 | 143.4 | 79.5 | 24 | 195.9 | 108.6 | 84 | 248.4 | 137.7 |
| 45 | 39.4 | 21.8 | 05 | 91.8 | 50.9 | 65 | 144.3 | 80.0 | 25 | 196.8 | 109.1 | 85 | 249.3 | 138.2 |
| 46 | 40.2 | 22.3 | 06 | 92.7 | 51.4 | 66 | 145.2 | 80.5 | 26 | 197.7 | 109.6 | 86 | 250.1 | 138.7 |
| 47 | 41.1 | 22.8 | 07 | 93.6 | 51.9 | 67 | 146.1 | 81.0 | 27 | 198.5 | 110.1 | 87 | 251.0 | 139.1 |
| 48 | 42.0 | 23.3 | 08 | 94.5 | 52.4 | 68 | 146.9 | 81.4 | 28 | 199.4 | 110.5 | 88 | 251.9 | 139.6 |
| 49 | 42.9 | 23.8 | 09 | 95.3 | 52.8 | 69 | 147.8 | 81.9 | 29 | 200.3 | 111.0 | 89 | 252.8 | 140.1 |
| 50 | 43.7 | 24.2 | 10 | 96.2 | 53.3 | 70 | 148.7 | 82.4 | 30 | 201.2 | 111.5 | 90 | 253.6 | 140.6 |
| 51 | 44.6 | 24.7 | 111 | 97.1 | 53.8 | 171 | 149.6 | 82.9 | 231 | 202.0 | 112.0 | 291 | 254.5 | 141.1 |
| 52 | 45.5 | 25.2 | 12 | 98.0 | 54.3 | 72 | 150.4 | 83.4 | 32 | 202.9 | 112.5 | 92 | 255.4 | 141.6 |
| 53 | 46.4 | 25.7 | 13 | 98.8 | 54.8 | 73 | 151.3 | 83.9 | 33 | 203.8 | 113.0 | 93 | 256.3 | 142.0 |
| 54 | 47.2 | 26.2 | 14 | 99.7 | 55.3 | 74 | 152.2 | 84.4 | 34 | 204.7 | 113.4 | 94 | 257.1 | 142.5 |
| 55 | 48.1 | 26.7 | 15 | 100.6 | 55.8 | 75 | 153.1 | 84.8 | 35 | 205.5 | 113.9 | 95 | 258.0 | 143.0 |
| 56 | 49.0 | 27.1 | 16 | 101.5 | 56.2 | 76 | 153.9 | 85.3 | 36 | 206.4 | 114.4 | 96 | 258.9 | 143.5 |
| 57 | 49.9 | 27.6 | 17 | 102.3 | 56.7 | 77 | 154.8 | 85.8 | 37 | 207.3 | 114.9 | 97 | 259.8 | 144.0 |
| 58 | 50.7 | 28.1 | 18 | 103.2 | 57.2 | 78 | 155.7 | 86.3 | 38 | 208.2 | 115.4 | 98 | 260.6 | 144.5 |
| 59 | 51.6 | 28.6 | 19 | 104.1 | 57.7 | 79 | 156.6 | 86.8 | 39 | 209.0 | 115.9 | 99 | 261.5 | 145.0 |
| 60 | 52.5 | 29.1 | 20 | 105.0 | 58.2 | 80 | 157.4 | 87.3 | 40 | 209.9 | 116.4 | 300 | 262.4 | 145.4 |
| Dist. | Dep. | Lat. | Dist. | Dep. | Lat. | Dist. | Dep. | Lat. | Dist. | Dep. | Lat. | Dist. | Dep. | Lat. |

[For 61 Degrees.

# TABLE II

## Difference of Latitude and Departure for 30 Degrees.

| Dist. | Lat. | Dep. | Dist. | Lat. | Dep. | Dist. | Lat. | Dep. | Dist. | Lat. | Dep. | Dist. | Lat. | Dep. |
|---|---|---|---|---|---|---|---|---|---|---|---|---|---|---|
| 1 | 00.9 | 00.5 | 61 | 52.8 | 30.5 | 121 | 104.8 | 60.5 | 181 | 156.8 | 90.5 | 241 | 208.7 | 120.5 |
| 2 | 01.7 | 01.0 | 62 | 53.7 | 31.0 | 22 | 105.7 | 61.0 | 82 | 157.6 | 91.0 | 42 | 209.6 | 121.0 |
| 3 | 02.6 | 01.5 | 63 | 54.6 | 31.5 | 23 | 106.5 | 61.5 | 83 | 158.5 | 91.5 | 43 | 210.4 | 121.5 |
| 4 | 03.5 | 02.0 | 64 | 55.4 | 32.0 | 24 | 107.4 | 62.0 | 84 | 159.3 | 92.0 | 44 | 211.3 | 122.0 |
| 5 | 04.3 | 02.5 | 65 | 56.3 | 32.5 | 25 | 108.3 | 62.5 | 85 | 160.2 | 92.5 | 45 | 212.2 | 122.5 |
| 6 | 05.2 | 03.0 | 66 | 57.2 | 33.0 | 26 | 109.1 | 63.0 | 86 | 161.1 | 93.0 | 46 | 213.0 | 123.0 |
| 7 | 06.1 | 03.5 | 67 | 58.0 | 33.5 | 27 | 110.0 | 63.5 | 87 | 161.9 | 93.5 | 47 | 213.9 | 123.5 |
| 8 | 06.9 | 04.0 | 68 | 58.9 | 34.0 | 28 | 110.9 | 64.0 | 88 | 162.8 | 94.0 | 48 | 214.8 | 124.0 |
| 9 | 07.8 | 04.5 | 69 | 59.8 | 34.5 | 29 | 111.7 | 64.5 | 89 | 163.7 | 94.5 | 49 | 215.6 | 124.5 |
| 10 | 08.7 | 05.0 | 70 | 60.6 | 35.0 | 30 | 112.6 | 65.0 | 90 | 164.5 | 95.0 | 50 | 216.5 | 125.0 |
| 11 | 09.5 | 05.5 | 71 | 61.5 | 35.5 | 131 | 113.4 | 65.5 | 191 | 165.4 | 95.5 | 251 | 217.4 | 125.5 |
| 12 | 10.4 | 06.0 | 72 | 62.4 | 36.0 | 32 | 114.3 | 66.0 | 92 | 166.3 | 96.0 | 52 | 218.2 | 126.0 |
| 13 | 11.3 | 06.5 | 73 | 63.2 | 36.5 | 33 | 115.2 | 66.5 | 93 | 167.1 | 96.5 | 53 | 219.1 | 126.5 |
| 14 | 12.1 | 07.0 | 74 | 64.1 | 37.0 | 34 | 116.0 | 67.0 | 94 | 168.0 | 97.0 | 54 | 220.0 | 127.0 |
| 15 | 13.0 | 07.5 | 75 | 65.0 | 37.5 | 35 | 116.9 | 67.5 | 95 | 168.9 | 97.5 | 55 | 220.8 | 127.5 |
| 16 | 13.9 | 08.0 | 76 | 65.8 | 38.0 | 36 | 117.8 | 68.0 | 96 | 169.7 | 98.0 | 56 | 221.7 | 128.0 |
| 17 | 14.7 | 08.5 | 77 | 66.7 | 38.5 | 37 | 118.6 | 68.5 | 97 | 170.6 | 98.5 | 57 | 222.6 | 128.5 |
| 18 | 15.6 | 09.0 | 78 | 67.5 | 39.0 | 38 | 119.5 | 69.0 | 98 | 171.5 | 99.0 | 58 | 223.4 | 129.0 |
| 19 | 16.5 | 09.5 | 79 | 68.4 | 39.5 | 39 | 120.4 | 69.5 | 99 | 172.3 | 99.5 | 59 | 224.3 | 129.5 |
| 20 | 17.3 | 10.0 | 80 | 69.3 | 40.0 | 40 | 121.2 | 70.0 | 200 | 173.2 | 100.0 | 60 | 225.2 | 130.0 |
| 21 | 18.2 | 10.5 | 81 | 70.1 | 40.5 | 141 | 122.1 | 70.5 | 201 | 174.1 | 100.5 | 261 | 226.0 | 130.5 |
| 22 | 19.1 | 11.0 | 82 | 71.0 | 41.0 | 42 | 123.0 | 71.0 | 02 | 174.9 | 101.0 | 62 | 226.9 | 131.0 |
| 23 | 19.9 | 11.5 | 83 | 71.9 | 41.5 | 43 | 123.8 | 71.5 | 03 | 175.8 | 101.5 | 63 | 227.8 | 131.5 |
| 24 | 20.8 | 12.0 | 84 | 72.7 | 42.0 | 44 | 124.7 | 72.0 | 04 | 176.7 | 102.0 | 64 | 228.6 | 132.0 |
| 25 | 21.7 | 12.5 | 85 | 73.6 | 42.5 | 45 | 125.6 | 72.5 | 05 | 177.5 | 102.5 | 65 | 229.5 | 132.5 |
| 26 | 22.5 | 13.0 | 86 | 74.5 | 43.0 | 46 | 126.4 | 73.0 | 06 | 178.4 | 103.0 | 66 | 230.4 | 133.0 |
| 27 | 23.4 | 13.5 | 87 | 75.3 | 43.5 | 47 | 127.3 | 73.5 | 07 | 179.3 | 103.5 | 67 | 231.2 | 133.5 |
| 28 | 24.2 | 14.0 | 88 | 76.2 | 44.0 | 48 | 128.2 | 74.0 | 08 | 180.1 | 104.0 | 68 | 232.1 | 134.0 |
| 29 | 25.1 | 14.5 | 89 | 77.1 | 44.5 | 49 | 129.0 | 74.5 | 09 | 181.0 | 104.5 | 69 | 233.0 | 134.5 |
| 30 | 26.0 | 15.0 | 90 | 77.9 | 45.0 | 50 | 129.9 | 75.0 | 10 | 181.9 | 105.0 | 70 | 233.8 | 135.0 |
| 31 | 26.8 | 15.5 | 91 | 78.8 | 45.5 | 151 | 130.8 | 75.5 | 211 | 182.7 | 105.5 | 271 | 234.7 | 135.5 |
| 32 | 27.7 | 16.0 | 92 | 79.7 | 46.0 | 52 | 131.6 | 76.0 | 12 | 183.6 | 106.0 | 72 | 235.6 | 136.0 |
| 33 | 28.6 | 16.5 | 93 | 80.5 | 46.5 | 53 | 132.5 | 76.5 | 13 | 184.5 | 106.5 | 73 | 236.4 | 136.5 |
| 34 | 29.4 | 17.0 | 94 | 81.4 | 47.0 | 54 | 133.4 | 77.0 | 14 | 185.3 | 107.0 | 74 | 237.3 | 137.0 |
| 35 | 30.3 | 17.5 | 95 | 82.3 | 47.5 | 55 | 134.2 | 77.5 | 15 | 186.2 | 107.5 | 75 | 238.2 | 137.5 |
| 36 | 31.2 | 18.0 | 96 | 83.1 | 48.0 | 56 | 135.1 | 78.0 | 16 | 187.1 | 108.0 | 76 | 239.0 | 138.0 |
| 37 | 32.0 | 18.5 | 97 | 84.0 | 48.5 | 57 | 136.0 | 78.5 | 17 | 187.9 | 108.5 | 77 | 239.9 | 138.5 |
| 38 | 32.9 | 19.0 | 98 | 84.9 | 49.0 | 58 | 136.8 | 79.0 | 18 | 188.8 | 109.0 | 78 | 240.8 | 139.0 |
| 39 | 33.8 | 19.5 | 99 | 85.7 | 49.5 | 59 | 137.7 | 79.5 | 19 | 189.7 | 109.5 | 79 | 241.6 | 139.5 |
| 40 | 34.6 | 20.0 | 100 | 86.6 | 50.0 | 60 | 138.6 | 80.0 | 20 | 190.5 | 110.0 | 80 | 242.5 | 140.0 |
| 41 | 35.5 | 20.5 | 101 | 87.5 | 50.5 | 161 | 139.4 | 80.5 | 221 | 191.4 | 110.5 | 281 | 243.4 | 140.5 |
| 42 | 36.4 | 21.0 | 02 | 88.3 | 51.0 | 62 | 140.3 | 81.0 | 22 | 192.3 | 111.0 | 82 | 244.2 | 141.0 |
| 43 | 37.2 | 21.5 | 03 | 89.2 | 51.5 | 63 | 141.2 | 81.5 | 23 | 193.1 | 111.5 | 83 | 245.1 | 141.5 |
| 44 | 38.1 | 22.0 | 04 | 90.1 | 52.0 | 64 | 142.0 | 82.0 | 24 | 194.0 | 112.0 | 84 | 246.0 | 142.0 |
| 45 | 39.0 | 22.5 | 05 | 90.9 | 52.5 | 65 | 142.9 | 82.5 | 25 | 194.9 | 112.5 | 85 | 246.8 | 142.5 |
| 46 | 39.8 | 23.0 | 06 | 91.8 | 53.0 | 66 | 143.8 | 83.0 | 26 | 195.7 | 113.0 | 86 | 247.7 | 143.0 |
| 47 | 40.7 | 23.5 | 07 | 92.7 | 53.5 | 67 | 144.6 | 83.5 | 27 | 196.6 | 113.5 | 87 | 248.5 | 143.5 |
| 48 | 41.6 | 24.0 | 08 | 93.5 | 54.0 | 68 | 145.5 | 84.0 | 28 | 197.5 | 114.0 | 88 | 249.4 | 144.0 |
| 49 | 42.4 | 24.5 | 09 | 94.4 | 54.5 | 69 | 146.4 | 84.5 | 29 | 198.3 | 114.5 | 89 | 250.3 | 144.5 |
| 50 | 43.3 | 25.0 | 10 | 95.3 | 55.0 | 70 | 147.2 | 85.0 | 30 | 199.2 | 115.0 | 90 | 251.1 | 145.0 |
| 51 | 44.2 | 25.5 | 111 | 96.1 | 55.5 | 171 | 148.1 | 85.5 | 231 | 200.1 | 115.5 | 291 | 252.0 | 145.5 |
| 52 | 45.0 | 26.0 | 12 | 97.0 | 56.0 | 72 | 149.0 | 86.0 | 32 | 200.9 | 116.0 | 92 | 252.9 | 146.0 |
| 53 | 45.9 | 26.5 | 13 | 97.9 | 56.5 | 73 | 149.8 | 86.5 | 33 | 201.8 | 116.5 | 93 | 253.7 | 146.5 |
| 54 | 46.8 | 27.0 | 14 | 98.7 | 57.0 | 74 | 150.7 | 87.0 | 34 | 202.6 | 117.0 | 94 | 254.6 | 147.0 |
| 55 | 47.6 | 27.5 | 15 | 99.6 | 57.5 | 75 | 151.6 | 87.5 | 35 | 203.5 | 117.5 | 95 | 255.5 | 147.5 |
| 56 | 48.5 | 28.0 | 16 | 100.5 | 58.0 | 76 | 152.4 | 88.0 | 36 | 204.4 | 118.0 | 96 | 256.3 | 148.0 |
| 57 | 49.4 | 28.5 | 17 | 101.3 | 58.5 | 77 | 153.3 | 88.5 | 37 | 205.2 | 118.5 | 97 | 257.2 | 148.5 |
| 58 | 50.2 | 29.0 | 18 | 102.2 | 59.0 | 78 | 154.2 | 89.0 | 38 | 206.1 | 119.0 | 98 | 258.1 | 149.0 |
| 59 | 51.1 | 29.5 | 19 | 103.1 | 59.5 | 79 | 155.0 | 89.5 | 39 | 207.0 | 119.5 | 99 | 258.9 | 149.5 |
| 60 | 52.0 | 30.0 | 20 | 103.9 | 60.0 | 80 | 155.9 | 90.0 | 40 | 207.8 | 120.0 | 300 | 259.8 | 150.0 |
| Dist. | Dep. | Lat. | Dist. | Dep. | Lat. | Dist. | Dep. | Lat. | Dist. | Dep. | Lat. | Dist. | Dep. | Lat. |

# TABLE II.

## Difference of Latitude and Departure for 31 Degrees.

| Dist. | Lat. | Dep. | Dist. | Lat. | Dep. | Dist. | Lat. | Dep. | Dist. | Lat. | Dep. | Dist. | Lat. | Dep. |
|---|---|---|---|---|---|---|---|---|---|---|---|---|---|---|
| 1 | 00.9 | 00.5 | 61 | 52.3 | 31.4 | 121 | 103.7 | 62.3 | 181 | 155.1 | 93.2 | 241 | 206.6 | 124.1 |
| 2 | 01.7 | 01.0 | 62 | 53.1 | 31.9 | 22 | 104.6 | 62.8 | 82 | 156.0 | 93.7 | 42 | 207.4 | 124.6 |
| 3 | 02.6 | 01.5 | 63 | 54.0 | 32.4 | 23 | 105.4 | 63.3 | 83 | 156.9 | 94.3 | 43 | 208.3 | 125.2 |
| 4 | 03.4 | 02.1 | 64 | 54.9 | 33.0 | 24 | 106.3 | 63.9 | 84 | 157.7 | 94.8 | 44 | 209.1 | 125.7 |
| 5 | 04.3 | 02.6 | 65 | 55.7 | 33.5 | 25 | 107.1 | 64.4 | 85 | 158.6 | 95.3 | 45 | 210.0 | 126.2 |
| 6 | 05.1 | 03.1 | 66 | 56.6 | 34.0 | 26 | 108.0 | 64.9 | 86 | 159.4 | 95.8 | 46 | 210.9 | 126.7 |
| 7 | 06.0 | 03.6 | 67 | 57.4 | 34.5 | 27 | 108.9 | 65.4 | 87 | 160.3 | 96.3 | 47 | 211.7 | 127.2 |
| 8 | 06.9 | 04.1 | 68 | 58.3 | 35.0 | 28 | 109.7 | 65.9 | 88 | 161.1 | 96.8 | 48 | 212.6 | 127.7 |
| 9 | 07.7 | 04.6 | 69 | 59.1 | 35.5 | 29 | 110.6 | 66.4 | 89 | 162.0 | 97.3 | 49 | 213.4 | 128.2 |
| 10 | 08.6 | 05.2 | 70 | 60.0 | 36.1 | 30 | 111.4 | 67.0 | 90 | 162.9 | 97.9 | 50 | 214.3 | 128.8 |
| 11 | 09.4 | 05.7 | 71 | 60.9 | 36.6 | 131 | 112.3 | 67.5 | 191 | 163.7 | 98.4 | 251 | 215.1 | 129.3 |
| 12 | 10.3 | 06.2 | 72 | 61.7 | 37.1 | 32 | 113.1 | 68.0 | 92 | 164.6 | 98.9 | 52 | 216.0 | 129.8 |
| 13 | 11.1 | 06.7 | 73 | 62.6 | 37.6 | 33 | 114.0 | 68.5 | 93 | 165.4 | 99.4 | 53 | 216.9 | 130.3 |
| 14 | 12.0 | 07.2 | 74 | 63.4 | 38.1 | 34 | 114.9 | 69.0 | 94 | 166.3 | 99.9 | 54 | 217.7 | 130.8 |
| 15 | 12.9 | 07.7 | 75 | 64.3 | 38.6 | 35 | 115.7 | 69.5 | 95 | 167.1 | 100.4 | 55 | 218.6 | 131.3 |
| 16 | 13.7 | 08.2 | 76 | 65.1 | 39.1 | 36 | 116.6 | 70.0 | 96 | 168.0 | 100.9 | 56 | 219.4 | 131.8 |
| 17 | 14.6 | 08.8 | 77 | 66.0 | 39.7 | 37 | 117.4 | 70.6 | 97 | 168.9 | 101.5 | 57 | 220.3 | 132.4 |
| 18 | 15.4 | 09.3 | 78 | 66.9 | 40.2 | 38 | 118.3 | 71.1 | 98 | 169.7 | 102.0 | 58 | 221.1 | 132.9 |
| 19 | 16.3 | 09.8 | 79 | 67.7 | 40.7 | 39 | 119.1 | 71.6 | 99 | 170.6 | 102.5 | 59 | 222.0 | 133.4 |
| 20 | 17.1 | 10.3 | 80 | 68.6 | 41.2 | 40 | 120.0 | 72.1 | 200 | 171.4 | 103.0 | 60 | 222.9 | 133.9 |
| 21 | 18.0 | 10.8 | 81 | 69.4 | 41.7 | 141 | 120.9 | 72.6 | 201 | 172.3 | 103.5 | 261 | 223.7 | 134.4 |
| 22 | 18.9 | 11.3 | 82 | 70.3 | 42.2 | 42 | 121.7 | 73.1 | 02 | 173.1 | 104.0 | 62 | 224.6 | 134.9 |
| 23 | 19.7 | 11.8 | 83 | 71.1 | 42.7 | 43 | 122.6 | 73.7 | 03 | 174.0 | 104.6 | 63 | 225.4 | 135.5 |
| 24 | 20.6 | 12.4 | 84 | 72.0 | 43.3 | 44 | 123.4 | 74.2 | 04 | 174.9 | 105.1 | 64 | 226.3 | 136.0 |
| 25 | 21.4 | 12.9 | 85 | 72.9 | 43.8 | 45 | 124.3 | 74.7 | 05 | 175.7 | 105.6 | 65 | 227.1 | 136.5 |
| 26 | 22.3 | 13.4 | 86 | 73.7 | 44.3 | 46 | 125.1 | 75.2 | 06 | 176.6 | 106.1 | 66 | 228.0 | 137.0 |
| 27 | 23.1 | 13.9 | 87 | 74.6 | 44.8 | 47 | 126.0 | 75.7 | 07 | 177.4 | 106.6 | 67 | 228.9 | 137.5 |
| 28 | 24.0 | 14.4 | 88 | 75.4 | 45.3 | 48 | 126.9 | 76.2 | 08 | 178.3 | 107.1 | 68 | 229.7 | 138.0 |
| 29 | 24.9 | 14.9 | 89 | 76.3 | 45.8 | 49 | 127.7 | 76.7 | 09 | 179.1 | 107.6 | 69 | 230.6 | 138.5 |
| 30 | 25.7 | 15.5 | 90 | 77.1 | 46.4 | 50 | 128.6 | 77.3 | 10 | 180.0 | 108.2 | 70 | 231.4 | 139.1 |
| 31 | 26.6 | 16.0 | 91 | 78.0 | 46.9 | 151 | 129.4 | 77.8 | 211 | 180.9 | 108.7 | 271 | 232.3 | 139.6 |
| 32 | 27.4 | 16.5 | 92 | 78.9 | 47.4 | 52 | 130.3 | 78.3 | 12 | 181.7 | 109.2 | 72 | 233.1 | 140.1 |
| 33 | 28.3 | 17.0 | 93 | 79.7 | 47.9 | 53 | 131.1 | 78.8 | 13 | 182.6 | 109.7 | 73 | 234.0 | 140.6 |
| 34 | 29.1 | 17.5 | 94 | 80.6 | 48.4 | 54 | 132.0 | 79.3 | 14 | 183.4 | 110.2 | 74 | 234.9 | 141.1 |
| 35 | 30.0 | 18.0 | 95 | 81.4 | 48.9 | 55 | 132.9 | 79.8 | 15 | 184.3 | 110.7 | 75 | 235.7 | 141.6 |
| 36 | 30.9 | 18.5 | 96 | 82.3 | 49.4 | 56 | 133.7 | 80.3 | 16 | 185.1 | 111.2 | 76 | 236.6 | 142.2 |
| 37 | 31.7 | 19.1 | 97 | 83.1 | 50.0 | 57 | 134.6 | 80.9 | 17 | 186.0 | 111.8 | 77 | 237.4 | 142.7 |
| 38 | 32.6 | 19.6 | 98 | 84.0 | 50.5 | 58 | 135.4 | 81.4 | 18 | 186.9 | 112.3 | 78 | 238.3 | 143.2 |
| 39 | 33.4 | 20.1 | 99 | 84.9 | 51.0 | 59 | 136.3 | 81.9 | 19 | 187.7 | 112.8 | 79 | 239.1 | 143.7 |
| 40 | 34.3 | 20.6 | 100 | 85.7 | 51.5 | 60 | 137.1 | 82.4 | 20 | 188.6 | 113.3 | 80 | 240.0 | 144.2 |
| 41 | 35.1 | 21.1 | 101 | 86.6 | 52.0 | 161 | 138.0 | 82.9 | 221 | 189.4 | 113.8 | 281 | 240.9 | 144.7 |
| 42 | 36.0 | 21.6 | 02 | 87.4 | 52.5 | 62 | 138.9 | 83.4 | 22 | 190.3 | 114.3 | 82 | 241.7 | 145.2 |
| 43 | 36.9 | 22.1 | 03 | 88.3 | 53.0 | 63 | 139.7 | 84.0 | 23 | 191.1 | 114.9 | 83 | 242.6 | 145.8 |
| 44 | 37.7 | 22.7 | 04 | 89.1 | 53.6 | 64 | 140.6 | 84.5 | 24 | 192.0 | 115.4 | 84 | 243.4 | 146.3 |
| 45 | 38.6 | 23.2 | 05 | 90.0 | 54.1 | 65 | 141.4 | 85.0 | 25 | 192.9 | 115.9 | 85 | 244.3 | 146.8 |
| 46 | 39.4 | 23.7 | 06 | 90.9 | 54.6 | 66 | 142.3 | 85.5 | 26 | 193.7 | 116.4 | 86 | 245.1 | 147.3 |
| 47 | 40.3 | 24.2 | 07 | 91.7 | 55.1 | 67 | 143.1 | 86.0 | 27 | 194.6 | 116.9 | 87 | 246.0 | 147.8 |
| 48 | 41.1 | 24.7 | 08 | 92.6 | 55.6 | 68 | 144.0 | 86.5 | 28 | 195.4 | 117.4 | 88 | 246.9 | 148.3 |
| 49 | 42.0 | 25.2 | 09 | 93.4 | 56.1 | 69 | 144.9 | 87.0 | 29 | 196.3 | 117.9 | 89 | 247.7 | 148.8 |
| 50 | 42.9 | 25.8 | 10 | 94.3 | 56.7 | 70 | 145.7 | 87.6 | 30 | 197.1 | 118.5 | 90 | 248.6 | 149.4 |
| 51 | 43.7 | 26.3 | 111 | 95.1 | 57.2 | 171 | 146.6 | 88.1 | 231 | 198.0 | 119.0 | 291 | 249.4 | 149.9 |
| 52 | 44.6 | 26.8 | 12 | 96.0 | 57.7 | 72 | 147.4 | 88.6 | 32 | 198.9 | 119.5 | 92 | 250.3 | 150.4 |
| 53 | 45.4 | 27.3 | 13 | 96.9 | 58.2 | 73 | 148.3 | 89.1 | 33 | 199.7 | 120.0 | 93 | 251.2 | 150.9 |
| 54 | 46.3 | 27.8 | 14 | 97.7 | 58.7 | 74 | 149.1 | 89.6 | 34 | 200.6 | 120.5 | 94 | 252.0 | 151.4 |
| 55 | 47.1 | 28.3 | 15 | 98.6 | 59.2 | 75 | 150.0 | 90.1 | 35 | 201.4 | 121.0 | 95 | 252.9 | 151.9 |
| 56 | 48.0 | 28.8 | 16 | 99.4 | 59.7 | 76 | 150.9 | 90.6 | 36 | 202.3 | 121.5 | 96 | 253.7 | 152.5 |
| 57 | 48.9 | 29.4 | 17 | 100.3 | 60.3 | 77 | 151.7 | 91.2 | 37 | 203.1 | 122.1 | 97 | 254.6 | 153.0 |
| 58 | 49.7 | 29.9 | 18 | 101.1 | 60.8 | 78 | 152.6 | 91.7 | 38 | 204.0 | 122.6 | 98 | 255.4 | 153.5 |
| 59 | 50.6 | 30.4 | 19 | 102.0 | 61.3 | 79 | 153.4 | 92.2 | 39 | 204.9 | 123.1 | 99 | 256.3 | 154.0 |
| 60 | 51.4 | 30.9 | 20 | 102.9 | 61.8 | 80 | 154.3 | 92.7 | 40 | 205.7 | 123.6 | 300 | 257.1 | 154.5 |
| Dist. | Dep. | Lat. | Dist. | Dep. | Lat. | Dist. | Dep. | Lat. | Dist. | Dep. | Lat. | Dist. | Dep. | Lat. |

# TABLE II.

## Difference of Latitude and Departure for 32 Degrees.

| Dist. | Lat. | Dep. | Dist. | Lat. | Dep. | Dist. | Lat. | Dep. | Dist. | Lat. | Dep. | Dist. | Lat. | Dep. |
|---|---|---|---|---|---|---|---|---|---|---|---|---|---|---|
| 1 | 00.8 | 00.5 | 61 | 51.7 | 32.3 | 121 | 102.6 | 64.1 | 181 | 153.5 | 95.9 | 241 | 204.4 | 127.7 |
| 2 | 01.7 | 01.1 | 62 | 52.6 | 32.9 | 22 | 103.5 | 64.7 | 82 | 154.3 | 96.4 | 42 | 205.2 | 128.2 |
| 3 | 02.5 | 01.6 | 63 | 53.4 | 33.4 | 23 | 104.3 | 65.2 | 83 | 155.2 | 97.0 | 43 | 206.1 | 128.8 |
| 4 | 03.4 | 02.1 | 64 | 54.3 | 33.9 | 24 | 105.2 | 65.7 | 84 | 156.0 | 97.5 | 44 | 206.9 | 129.3 |
| 5 | 04.2 | 02.6 | 65 | 55.1 | 34.4 | 25 | 106.0 | 66.2 | 85 | 156.9 | 98.0 | 45 | 207.8 | 129.8 |
| 6 | 05.1 | 03.2 | 66 | 56.0 | 35.0 | 26 | 106.9 | 66.8 | 86 | 157.7 | 98.6 | 46 | 208.6 | 130.4 |
| 7 | 05.9 | 03.7 | 67 | 56.8 | 35.5 | 27 | 107.7 | 67.3 | 87 | 158.6 | 99.1 | 47 | 209.5 | 130.9 |
| 8 | 06.8 | 04.2 | 68 | 57.7 | 36.0 | 28 | 108.6 | 67.8 | 88 | 159.4 | 99.6 | 48 | 210.3 | 131.4 |
| 9 | 07.6 | 04.8 | 69 | 58.5 | 36.6 | 29 | 109.4 | 68.4 | 89 | 160.3 | 100.2 | 49 | 211.2 | 131.9 |
| 10 | 08.5 | 05.3 | 70 | 59.4 | 37.1 | 30 | 110.2 | 68.9 | 90 | 161.1 | 100.7 | 50 | 212.0 | 132.5 |
| 11 | 09.3 | 05.8 | 71 | 60.2 | 37.6 | 131 | 111.1 | 69.4 | 191 | 162.0 | 101.2 | 251 | 212.9 | 133.0 |
| 12 | 10.2 | 06.4 | 72 | 61.1 | 38.2 | 32 | 111.9 | 69.9 | 92 | 162.8 | 101.7 | 52 | 213.7 | 133.5 |
| 13 | 11.0 | 06.9 | 73 | 61.9 | 38.7 | 33 | 112.8 | 70.5 | 93 | 163.7 | 102.3 | 53 | 214.6 | 134.1 |
| 14 | 11.9 | 07.4 | 74 | 62.8 | 39.2 | 34 | 113.6 | 71.0 | 94 | 164.5 | 102.8 | 54 | 215.4 | 134.6 |
| 15 | 12.7 | 07.9 | 75 | 63.6 | 39.7 | 35 | 114.5 | 71.5 | 95 | 165.4 | 103.3 | 55 | 216.3 | 135.1 |
| 16 | 13.6 | 08.5 | 76 | 64.5 | 40.3 | 36 | 115.3 | 72.1 | 96 | 166.2 | 103.9 | 56 | 217.1 | 135.7 |
| 17 | 14.4 | 09.0 | 77 | 65.3 | 40.8 | 37 | 116.2 | 72.6 | 97 | 167.1 | 104.4 | 57 | 217.9 | 136.2 |
| 18 | 15.3 | 09.5 | 78 | 66.1 | 41.3 | 38 | 117.0 | 73.1 | 98 | 167.9 | 104.9 | 58 | 218.8 | 136.7 |
| 19 | 16.1 | 10.1 | 79 | 67.0 | 41.9 | 39 | 117.9 | 73.7 | 99 | 168.8 | 105.5 | 59 | 219.6 | 137.2 |
| 20 | 17.0 | 10.6 | 80 | 67.8 | 42.4 | 40 | 118.7 | 74.2 | 200 | 169.6 | 106.0 | 60 | 220.5 | 137.8 |
| 21 | 17.8 | 11.1 | 81 | 68.7 | 42.9 | 141 | 119.6 | 74.7 | 201 | 170.5 | 106.5 | 261 | 221.3 | 138.3 |
| 22 | 18.7 | 11.7 | 82 | 69.5 | 43.5 | 42 | 120.4 | 75.2 | 02 | 171.3 | 107.0 | 62 | 222.2 | 138.8 |
| 23 | 19.5 | 12.2 | 83 | 70.4 | 44.0 | 43 | 121.3 | 75.8 | 03 | 172.2 | 107.6 | 63 | 223.0 | 139.4 |
| 24 | 20.4 | 12.7 | 84 | 71.2 | 44.5 | 44 | 122.1 | 76.3 | 04 | 173.0 | 108.1 | 64 | 223.9 | 139.9 |
| 25 | 21.2 | 13.2 | 85 | 72.1 | 45.0 | 45 | 123.0 | 76.8 | 05 | 173.8 | 108.6 | 65 | 224.7 | 140.4 |
| 26 | 22.0 | 13.8 | 86 | 72.9 | 45.6 | 46 | 123.8 | 77.4 | 06 | 174.7 | 109.2 | 66 | 225.6 | 141.0 |
| 27 | 22.9 | 14.3 | 87 | 73.8 | 46.1 | 47 | 124.7 | 77.9 | 07 | 175.5 | 109.7 | 67 | 226.4 | 141.5 |
| 28 | 23.7 | 14.8 | 88 | 74.6 | 46.6 | 48 | 125.5 | 78.4 | 08 | 176.4 | 110.2 | 68 | 227.3 | 142.0 |
| 29 | 24.6 | 15.4 | 89 | 75.5 | 47.2 | 49 | 126.4 | 79.0 | 09 | 177.2 | 110.8 | 69 | 228.1 | 142.5 |
| 30 | 25.4 | 15.9 | 90 | 76.3 | 47.7 | 50 | 127.2 | 79.5 | 10 | 178.1 | 111.3 | 70 | 229.0 | 143.1 |
| 31 | 26.3 | 16.4 | 91 | 77.2 | 48.2 | 151 | 128.1 | 80.0 | 211 | 178.9 | 111.8 | 271 | 229.8 | 143.6 |
| 32 | 27.1 | 17.0 | 92 | 78.0 | 48.8 | 52 | 128.9 | 80.5 | 12 | 179.8 | 112.3 | 72 | 230.7 | 144.1 |
| 33 | 28.0 | 17.5 | 93 | 78.9 | 49.3 | 53 | 129.8 | 81.1 | 13 | 180.6 | 112.9 | 73 | 231.5 | 144.7 |
| 34 | 28.8 | 18.0 | 94 | 79.7 | 49.8 | 54 | 130.6 | 81.6 | 14 | 181.5 | 113.4 | 74 | 232.4 | 145.2 |
| 35 | 29.7 | 18.5 | 95 | 80.6 | 50.3 | 55 | 131.4 | 82.1 | 15 | 182.3 | 113.9 | 75 | 233.2 | 145.7 |
| 36 | 30.5 | 19.1 | 96 | 81.4 | 50.9 | 56 | 132.3 | 82.7 | 16 | 183.2 | 114.5 | 76 | 234.1 | 146.3 |
| 37 | 31.4 | 19.6 | 97 | 82.3 | 51.4 | 57 | 133.1 | 83.2 | 17 | 184.0 | 115.0 | 77 | 234.9 | 146.8 |
| 38 | 32.2 | 20.1 | 98 | 83.1 | 51.9 | 58 | 134.0 | 83.7 | 18 | 184.9 | 115.5 | 78 | 235.8 | 147.3 |
| 39 | 33.1 | 20.7 | 99 | 84.0 | 52.5 | 59 | 134.8 | 84.3 | 19 | 185.7 | 116.1 | 79 | 236.6 | 147.8 |
| 40 | 33.9 | 21.2 | 100 | 84.8 | 53.0 | 60 | 135.7 | 84.8 | 20 | 186.6 | 116.6 | 80 | 237.5 | 148.4 |
| 41 | 34.8 | 21.7 | 101 | 85.7 | 53.5 | 161 | 136.5 | 85.3 | 221 | 187.4 | 117.1 | 281 | 238.3 | 148.9 |
| 42 | 35.6 | 22.3 | 02 | 86.5 | 54.1 | 62 | 137.4 | 85.8 | 22 | 188.3 | 117.6 | 82 | 239.1 | 149.4 |
| 43 | 36.5 | 22.8 | 03 | 87.3 | 54.6 | 63 | 138.2 | 86.4 | 23 | 189.1 | 118.2 | 83 | 240.0 | 150.0 |
| 44 | 37.3 | 23.3 | 04 | 88.2 | 55.1 | 64 | 139.1 | 86.9 | 24 | 190.0 | 118.7 | 84 | 240.8 | 150.5 |
| 45 | 38.2 | 23.8 | 05 | 89.0 | 55.6 | 65 | 139.9 | 87.4 | 25 | 190.8 | 119.2 | 85 | 241.7 | 151.0 |
| 46 | 39.0 | 24.4 | 06 | 89.9 | 56.2 | 66 | 140.8 | 88.0 | 26 | 191.7 | 119.8 | 86 | 242.5 | 151.6 |
| 47 | 39.9 | 24.9 | 07 | 90.7 | 56.7 | 67 | 141.6 | 88.5 | 27 | 192.5 | 120.3 | 87 | 243.4 | 152.1 |
| 48 | 40.7 | 25.4 | 08 | 91.6 | 57.2 | 68 | 142.5 | 89.0 | 28 | 193.4 | 120.8 | 88 | 244.2 | 152.6 |
| 49 | 41.6 | 26.0 | 09 | 92.4 | 57.8 | 69 | 143.3 | 89.6 | 29 | 194.2 | 121.4 | 89 | 245.1 | 153.1 |
| 50 | 42.4 | 26.5 | 10 | 93.3 | 58.3 | 70 | 144.2 | 90.1 | 30 | 195.1 | 121.9 | 90 | 245.9 | 153.7 |
| 51 | 43.3 | 27.0 | 111 | 94.1 | 58.8 | 171 | 145.0 | 90.6 | 231 | 195.9 | 122.4 | 291 | 246.8 | 154.2 |
| 52 | 44.1 | 27.6 | 12 | 95.0 | 59.4 | 72 | 145.9 | 91.1 | 32 | 196.7 | 122.9 | 92 | 247.6 | 154.7 |
| 53 | 44.9 | 28.1 | 13 | 95.8 | 59.9 | 73 | 146.7 | 91.7 | 33 | 197.6 | 123.5 | 93 | 248.5 | 155.3 |
| 54 | 45.8 | 28.6 | 14 | 96.7 | 60.4 | 74 | 147.6 | 92.2 | 34 | 198.4 | 124.0 | 94 | 249.3 | 155.8 |
| 55 | 46.6 | 29.1 | 15 | 97.5 | 60.9 | 75 | 148.4 | 92.7 | 35 | 199.3 | 124.5 | 95 | 250.2 | 156.3 |
| 56 | 47.5 | 29.7 | 16 | 98.4 | 61.5 | 76 | 149.3 | 93.3 | 36 | 200.1 | 125.1 | 96 | 251.0 | 156.9 |
| 57 | 48.3 | 30.2 | 17 | 99.2 | 62.0 | 77 | 150.1 | 93.8 | 37 | 201.0 | 125.6 | 97 | 251.9 | 157.4 |
| 58 | 49.2 | 30.7 | 18 | 100.1 | 62.5 | 78 | 151.0 | 94.3 | 38 | 201.8 | 126.1 | 98 | 252.7 | 157.9 |
| 59 | 50.0 | 31.3 | 19 | 100.9 | 63.1 | 79 | 151.8 | 94.9 | 39 | 202.7 | 126.7 | 99 | 253.6 | 158.4 |
| 60 | 50.9 | 31.8 | 20 | 101.8 | 63.6 | 80 | 152.6 | 95.4 | 40 | 203.5 | 127.2 | 300 | 254.4 | 159.0 |
| Dist. | Dep. | Lat. | Dist. | Dep. | Lat. | Dist. | Dep. | Lat. | Dist. | Dep. | Lat. | Dist. | Dep. | Lat. |

# TABLE II.

## Difference of Latitude and Departure for 33 Degrees.

| Dist. | Lat. | Dep. | Dist. | Lat. | Dep. | Dist. | Lat. | Dep. | Dist. | Lat. | Dep. | Dist. | Lat. | Dep. |
|---|---|---|---|---|---|---|---|---|---|---|---|---|---|---|
| 1 | 00.8 | 00.5 | 61 | 51.2 | 33.2 | 121 | 101.5 | 65.9 | 181 | 151.8 | 98.6 | 241 | 202.1 | 131.3 |
| 2 | 01.7 | 01.1 | 62 | 52.0 | 33.8 | 22 | 102.3 | 66.4 | 82 | 152.6 | 99.1 | 42 | 203.0 | 131.8 |
| 3 | 02.5 | 01.6 | 63 | 52.8 | 34.3 | 23 | 103.2 | 67.0 | 83 | 153.5 | 99.7 | 43 | 203.8 | 132.3 |
| 4 | 03.4 | 02.2 | 64 | 53.7 | 34.9 | 24 | 104.0 | 67.5 | 84 | 154.3 | 100.2 | 44 | 204.6 | 132.9 |
| 5 | 04.2 | 02.7 | 65 | 54.5 | 35.4 | 25 | 104.8 | 68.1 | 85 | 155.2 | 100.8 | 45 | 205.5 | 133.4 |
| 6 | 05.0 | 03.3 | 66 | 55.4 | 35.9 | 26 | 105.7 | 68.6 | 86 | 156.0 | 101.3 | 46 | 206.3 | 134.0 |
| 7 | 05.9 | 03.8 | 67 | 56.2 | 36.5 | 27 | 106.5 | 69.2 | 87 | 156.8 | 101.8 | 47 | 207.2 | 134.5 |
| 8 | 06.7 | 04.4 | 68 | 57.0 | 37.0 | 28 | 107.3 | 69.7 | 88 | 157.7 | 102.4 | 48 | 208.0 | 135.1 |
| 9 | 07.5 | 04.9 | 69 | 57.9 | 37.6 | 29 | 108.2 | 70.3 | 89 | 158.5 | 102.9 | 49 | 208.8 | 135.6 |
| 10 | 08.4 | 05.4 | 70 | 58.7 | 38.1 | 30 | 109.0 | 70.8 | 90 | 159.3 | 103.5 | 50 | 209.7 | 136.2 |
| 11 | 09.2 | 06.0 | 71 | 59.5 | 38.7 | 131 | 109.9 | 71.3 | 191 | 160.2 | 104.0 | 251 | 210.5 | 136.7 |
| 12 | 10.1 | 06.5 | 72 | 60.4 | 39.2 | 32 | 110.7 | 71.9 | 92 | 161.0 | 104.6 | 52 | 211.3 | 137.2 |
| 13 | 10.9 | 07.1 | 73 | 61.2 | 39.8 | 33 | 111.5 | 72.4 | 93 | 161.9 | 105.1 | 53 | 212.2 | 137.8 |
| 14 | 11.7 | 07.6 | 74 | 62.1 | 40.3 | 34 | 112.4 | 73.0 | 94 | 162.7 | 105.7 | 54 | 213.0 | 138.3 |
| 15 | 12.6 | 08.2 | 75 | 62.9 | 40.8 | 35 | 113.2 | 73.5 | 95 | 163.5 | 106.2 | 55 | 213.9 | 138.9 |
| 16 | 13.4 | 08.7 | 76 | 63.7 | 41.4 | 36 | 114.1 | 74.1 | 96 | 164.4 | 106.7 | 56 | 214.7 | 139.4 |
| 17 | 14.3 | 09.3 | 77 | 64.6 | 41.9 | 37 | 114.9 | 74.6 | 97 | 165.2 | 107.3 | 57 | 215.5 | 140.0 |
| 18 | 15.1 | 09.8 | 78 | 65.4 | 42.5 | 38 | 115.7 | 75.2 | 98 | 166.1 | 107.8 | 58 | 216.4 | 140.5 |
| 19 | 15.9 | 10.3 | 79 | 66.3 | 43.0 | 39 | 116.6 | 75.7 | 99 | 166.9 | 108.4 | 59 | 217.2 | 141.1 |
| 20 | 16.8 | 10.9 | 80 | 67.1 | 43.6 | 40 | 117.4 | 76.2 | 200 | 167.7 | 108.9 | 60 | 218.1 | 141.6 |
| 21 | 17.6 | 11.4 | 81 | 67.9 | 44.1 | 141 | 118.3 | 76.8 | 201 | 168.6 | 109.5 | 261 | 218.9 | 142.2 |
| 22 | 18.5 | 12.0 | 82 | 68.8 | 44.7 | 42 | 119.1 | 77.3 | 02 | 169.4 | 110.0 | 62 | 219.7 | 142.7 |
| 23 | 19.3 | 12.5 | 83 | 69.6 | 45.2 | 43 | 119.9 | 77.9 | 03 | 170.3 | 110.6 | 63 | 220.6 | 143.2 |
| 24 | 20.1 | 13.1 | 84 | 70.4 | 45.7 | 44 | 120.8 | 78.4 | 04 | 171.1 | 111.1 | 64 | 221.4 | 143.8 |
| 25 | 21.0 | 13.6 | 85 | 71.3 | 46.3 | 45 | 121.6 | 79.0 | 05 | 171.9 | 111.7 | 65 | 222.2 | 144.3 |
| 26 | 21.8 | 14.2 | 86 | 72.1 | 46.8 | 46 | 122.4 | 79.5 | 06 | 172.8 | 112.2 | 66 | 223.1 | 144.9 |
| 27 | 22.6 | 14.7 | 87 | 73.0 | 47.4 | 47 | 123.3 | 80.1 | 07 | 173.6 | 112.7 | 67 | 223.9 | 145.4 |
| 28 | 23.5 | 15.2 | 88 | 73.8 | 47.9 | 48 | 124.1 | 80.6 | 08 | 174.4 | 113.3 | 68 | 224.8 | 146 0 |
| 29 | 24.3 | 15.8 | 89 | 74.6 | 48.5 | 49 | 125.0 | 81.2 | 09 | 175.3 | 113.8 | 69 | 225.6 | 146.5 |
| 30 | 25.2 | 16.3 | 90 | 75.5 | 49.0 | 50 | 125.8 | 81.7 | 10 | 176.1 | 114.4 | 70 | 226.4 | 147.1 |
| 31 | 26.0 | 16.9 | 91 | 76.3 | 49.6 | 151 | 126.6 | 82.2 | 211 | 177.0 | 114.9 | 271 | 227.3 | 147.6 |
| 32 | 26.8 | 17.4 | 92 | 77.2 | 50.1 | 52 | 127.5 | 82.8 | 12 | 177.8 | 115.5 | 72 | 228.1 | 148.1 |
| 33 | 27.7 | 18.0 | 93 | 78.0 | 50.7 | 53 | 128.3 | 83.3 | 13 | 178.6 | 116.0 | 73 | 229.0 | 148.7 |
| 34 | 28.5 | 18.5 | 94 | 78.8 | 51.2 | 54 | 129.2 | 83.9 | 14 | 179.5 | 116.6 | 74 | 229.8 | 149.2 |
| 35 | 29.4 | 19.1 | 95 | 79.7 | 51.7 | 55 | 130.0 | 84.4 | 15 | 180.3 | 117.1 | 75 | 230.6 | 149.8 |
| 36 | 30.2 | 19.6 | 96 | 80.5 | 52.3 | 56 | 130.8 | 85.0 | 16 | 181.2 | 117.6 | 76 | 231.5 | 150.3 |
| 37 | 31.0 | 20.2 | 97 | 81.4 | 52.8 | 57 | 131.7 | 85.5 | 17 | 182.0 | 118.2 | 77 | 232.3 | 150.9 |
| 38 | 31.9 | 20.7 | 98 | 82.2 | 53.4 | 58 | 132.5 | 86.1 | 18 | 182.8 | 118.7 | 78 | 233.2 | 151.4 |
| 39 | 32.7 | 21.2 | 99 | 83.0 | 53.9 | 59 | 133.3 | 86.6 | 19 | 183.7 | 119.3 | 79 | 234.0 | 152.0 |
| 40 | 33.5 | 21.8 | 100 | 83.9 | 54.5 | 60 | 134.2 | 87.1 | 20 | 184.5 | 119.8 | 80 | 234.8 | 152.5 |
| 41 | 34.4 | 22.3 | 101 | 84.7 | 55.0 | 161 | 135.0 | 87.7 | 221 | 185.3 | 120.4 | 281 | 235.7 | 153.0 |
| 42 | 35.2 | 22.9 | 02 | 85.5 | 55.6 | 62 | 135.9 | 88.2 | 22 | 186.2 | 120.9 | 82 | 236.5 | 153.6 |
| 43 | 36.1 | 23.4 | 03 | 86.4 | 56.1 | 63 | 136.7 | 88.8 | 23 | 187.0 | 121.5 | 83 | 237.3 | 154.1 |
| 44 | 36.9 | 24.0 | 04 | 87.2 | 56.6 | 64 | 137.5 | 89.3 | 24 | 187.9 | 122.0 | 84 | 238.2 | 154.7 |
| 45 | 37.7 | 24.5 | 05 | 88.1 | 57.2 | 65 | 138.4 | 89.9 | 25 | 188.7 | 122.5 | 85 | 239.0 | 155.2 |
| 46 | 38.6 | 25.1 | 06 | 88.9 | 57.7 | 66 | 139.2 | 90.4 | 26 | 189.5 | 123.1 | 86 | 239.9 | 155.8 |
| 47 | 39.4 | 25.6 | 07 | 89.7 | 58.3 | 67 | 140.1 | 91.0 | 27 | 190.4 | 123.6 | 87 | 240.7 | 156.3 |
| 48 | 40.3 | 26.1 | 08 | 90.6 | 58.8 | 68 | 140.9 | 91.5 | 28 | 191.2 | 124.2 | 88 | 241.5 | 156.9 |
| 49 | 41.1 | 26.7 | 09 | 91.4 | 59.4 | 69 | 141.7 | 92.0 | 29 | 192.1 | 124.7 | 89 | 242.4 | 157.4 |
| 50 | 41.9 | 27.2 | 10 | 92.3 | 59.9 | 70 | 142.6 | 92.6 | 30 | 192.9 | 125.3 | 90 | 243.2 | 157.9 |
| 51 | 42.8 | 27.8 | 111 | 93.1 | 60.5 | 171 | 143.4 | 93.1 | 231 | 193.7 | 125.8 | 291 | 244.1 | 158.5 |
| 52 | 43.6 | 28.3 | 12 | 93.9 | 61.0 | 72 | 144.3 | 93.7 | 32 | 194.6 | 126.4 | 92 | 244.9 | 159.0 |
| 53 | 44.4 | 28.9 | 13 | 94.8 | 61.5 | 73 | 145.1 | 94.2 | 33 | 195.4 | 126.9 | 93 | 245.7 | 159.6 |
| 54 | 45.3 | 29.4 | 14 | 95.6 | 62.1 | 74 | 145.9 | 94.8 | 34 | 196.2 | 127.4 | 94 | 246.6 | 160.1 |
| 55 | 46.1 | 30.0 | 15 | 96.4 | 62.6 | 75 | 146.8 | 95.3 | 35 | 197.1 | 128.0 | 95 | 247.4 | 160.7 |
| 56 | 47.0 | 30.5 | 16 | 97.3 | 63.2 | 76 | 147.6 | 95.9 | 36 | 197.9 | 128.5 | 96 | 248.2 | 161.2 |
| 57 | 47.8 | 31.0 | 17 | 98.1 | 63.7 | 77 | 148.4 | 96.4 | 37 | 198.8 | 129.1 | 97 | 249.1 | 161.8 |
| 58 | 48.6 | 31.6 | 18 | 99.0 | 64.3 | 78 | 149.3 | 96.9 | 38 | 199.6 | 129.6 | 98 | 249.9 | 162.3 |
| 59 | 49.5 | 32.1 | 19 | 99.8 | 64.8 | 79 | 150.1 | 97.5 | 39 | 200.4 | 130.2 | 99 | 250.8 | 162.8 |
| 60 | 50.3 | 32.7 | 20 | 100.6 | 65.4 | 80 | 151.0 | 98.0 | 40 | 201.3 | 130.7 | 300 | 251.6 | 163.4 |
| Dist. | Dep. | Lat. | Dist. | Dep. | Lat. | Dist. | Dep. | Lat. | Dist. | Dep. | Lat. | Dist. | Dep. | Lat. |

[For 57 Degrees.

# TABLE II.

## Difference of Latitude and Departure for 34 Degrees.

| Dist. | Lat. | Dep. | Dist. | Lat. | Dep. | Dist. | Lat. | Dep. | Dist. | Lat. | Dep. | Dist. | Lat. | Dep. |
|---|---|---|---|---|---|---|---|---|---|---|---|---|---|---|
| 1 | 00.8 | 00.6 | 61 | 50.6 | 34.1 | 121 | 100.3 | 67.7 | 181 | 150.1 | 101.2 | 241 | 199.8 | 134.8 |
| 2 | 01.7 | 01.1 | 62 | 51.4 | 34.7 | 22 | 101.1 | 68.2 | 82 | 150.9 | 101.8 | 42 | 200.6 | 135.3 |
| 3 | 02.5 | 01.7 | 63 | 52.2 | 35.2 | 23 | 102.0 | 68.8 | 83 | 151.7 | 102.3 | 43 | 201.5 | 135.9 |
| 4 | 03.3 | 02.2 | 64 | 53.1 | 35.8 | 24 | 102.8 | 69.3 | 84 | 152.5 | 102.9 | 44 | 202.3 | 136.4 |
| 5 | 04.1 | 02.8 | 65 | 53.9 | 36.3 | 25 | 103.6 | 69.9 | 85 | 153.4 | 103.5 | 45 | 203.1 | 137.0 |
| 6 | 05.0 | 03.4 | 66 | 54.7 | 36.9 | 26 | 104.5 | 70.5 | 86 | 154.2 | 104.0 | 46 | 203.9 | 137.6 |
| 7 | 05.8 | 03.9 | 67 | 55.5 | 37.5 | 27 | 105.3 | 71.0 | 87 | 155.0 | 104.6 | 47 | 204.8 | 138.1 |
| 8 | 06.6 | 04.5 | 68 | 56.4 | 38.0 | 28 | 106.1 | 71.6 | 88 | 155.9 | 105.1 | 48 | 205.6 | 138.7 |
| 9 | 07.5 | 05.0 | 69 | 57.2 | 38.6 | 29 | 106.9 | 72.1 | 89 | 156.7 | 105.7 | 49 | 206.4 | 139.2 |
| 10 | 08.3 | 05.6 | 70 | 58.0 | 39.1 | 30 | 107.8 | 72.7 | 90 | 157.5 | 106.2 | 50 | 207.3 | 139.8 |
| 11 | 09.1 | 06.2 | 71 | 58.9 | 39.7 | 131 | 108.6 | 73.3 | 191 | 158.3 | 106.8 | 251 | 208.1 | 140.4 |
| 12 | 09.9 | 06.7 | 72 | 59.7 | 40.3 | 32 | 109.4 | 73.8 | 92 | 159.2 | 107.4 | 52 | 208.9 | 140.9 |
| 13 | 10.8 | 07.3 | 73 | 60.5 | 40.8 | 33 | 110.3 | 74.4 | 93 | 160.0 | 107.9 | 53 | 209.7 | 141.5 |
| 14 | 11.6 | 07.8 | 74 | 61.3 | 41.4 | 34 | 111.1 | 74.9 | 94 | 160.8 | 108.5 | 54 | 210.6 | 142.0 |
| 15 | 12.4 | 08.4 | 75 | 62.2 | 41.9 | 35 | 111.9 | 75.5 | 95 | 161.7 | 109.0 | 55 | 211.4 | 142.6 |
| 16 | 13.3 | 08.9 | 76 | 63.0 | 42.5 | 36 | 112.7 | 76.1 | 96 | 162.5 | 109.6 | 56 | 212.2 | 143.2 |
| 17 | 14.1 | 09.5 | 77 | 63.8 | 43.1 | 37 | 113.6 | 76.6 | 97 | 163.3 | 110.2 | 57 | 213.1 | 143.7 |
| 18 | 14.9 | 10.1 | 78 | 64.7 | 43.6 | 38 | 114.4 | 77.2 | 98 | 164.1 | 110.7 | 58 | 213.9 | 144.3 |
| 19 | 15.8 | 10.6 | 79 | 65.5 | 44.2 | 39 | 115.2 | 77.7 | 99 | 165.0 | 111.3 | 59 | 214.7 | 144.8 |
| 20 | 16.6 | 11.2 | 80 | 66.3 | 44.7 | 40 | 116.1 | 78.3 | 200 | 165.8 | 111.8 | 60 | 215.5 | 145.4 |
| 21 | 17.4 | 11.7 | 81 | 67.2 | 45.3 | 141 | 116.9 | 78.8 | 201 | 166.6 | 112.4 | 261 | 216.4 | 145.9 |
| 22 | 18.2 | 12.3 | 82 | 68.0 | 45.9 | 42 | 117.7 | 79.4 | 02 | 167.5 | 113.0 | 62 | 217.2 | 146.5 |
| 23 | 19.1 | 12.9 | 83 | 68.8 | 46.4 | 43 | 118.6 | 80.0 | 03 | 168.3 | 113.5 | 63 | 218.0 | 147.1 |
| 24 | 19.9 | 13.4 | 84 | 69.6 | 47.0 | 44 | 119.4 | 80.5 | 04 | 169.1 | 114.1 | 64 | 218.9 | 147.6 |
| 25 | 20.7 | 14.0 | 85 | 70.5 | 47.5 | 45 | 120.2 | 81.1 | 05 | 170.0 | 114.6 | 65 | 219.7 | 148.2 |
| 26 | 21.6 | 14.5 | 86 | 71.3 | 48.1 | 46 | 121.0 | 81.6 | 06 | 170.8 | 115.2 | 66 | 220.5 | 148.7 |
| 27 | 22.4 | 15.1 | 87 | 72.1 | 48.6 | 47 | 121.9 | 82.2 | 07 | 171.6 | 115.8 | 67 | 221.4 | 149.3 |
| 28 | 23.2 | 15.7 | 88 | 73.0 | 49.2 | 48 | 122.7 | 82.8 | 08 | 172.4 | 116.3 | 68 | 222.2 | 149.9 |
| 29 | 24.0 | 16.2 | 89 | 73.8 | 49.8 | 49 | 123.5 | 83.3 | 09 | 173.3 | 116.9 | 69 | 223.0 | 150.4 |
| 30 | 24.9 | 16.8 | 90 | 74.6 | 50.3 | 50 | 124.4 | 83.9 | 10 | 174.1 | 117.4 | 70 | 223.8 | 151.0 |
| 31 | 25.7 | 17.3 | 91 | 75.4 | 50.9 | 151 | 125.2 | 84.4 | 211 | 174.9 | 118.0 | 271 | 224.7 | 151.5 |
| 32 | 26.5 | 17.9 | 92 | 76.3 | 51.4 | 52 | 126.0 | 85.0 | 12 | 175.8 | 118.5 | 72 | 225.5 | 152.1 |
| 33 | 27.4 | 18.5 | 93 | 77.1 | 52.0 | 53 | 126.8 | 85.6 | 13 | 176.6 | 119.1 | 73 | 226.3 | 152.7 |
| 34 | 28.2 | 19.0 | 94 | 77.9 | 52.6 | 54 | 127.7 | 86.1 | 14 | 177.4 | 119.7 | 74 | 227.2 | 153.2 |
| 35 | 29.0 | 19.6 | 95 | 78.8 | 53.1 | 55 | 128.5 | 86.7 | 15 | 178.2 | 120.2 | 75 | 228.0 | 153.8 |
| 36 | 29.8 | 20.1 | 96 | 79.6 | 53.7 | 56 | 129.3 | 87.2 | 16 | 179.1 | 120.8 | 76 | 228.8 | 154.3 |
| 37 | 30.7 | 20.7 | 97 | 80.4 | 54.2 | 57 | 130.2 | 87.8 | 17 | 179.9 | 121.3 | 77 | 229.6 | 154.9 |
| 38 | 31.5 | 21.2 | 98 | 81.2 | 54.8 | 58 | 131.0 | 88.4 | 18 | 180.7 | 121.9 | 78 | 230.5 | 155.5 |
| 39 | 32.3 | 21.8 | 99 | 82.1 | 55.4 | 59 | 131.8 | 88.9 | 19 | 181.6 | 122.5 | 79 | 231.3 | 156.0 |
| 40 | 33.2 | 22.4 | 100 | 82.9 | 55.9 | 60 | 132.6 | 89.5 | 20 | 182.4 | 123.0 | 80 | 232.1 | 156.6 |
| 41 | 34.0 | 22.9 | 101 | 83.7 | 56.5 | 161 | 133.5 | 90.0 | 221 | 183.2 | 123.6 | 281 | 233.0 | 157.1 |
| 42 | 34.8 | 23.5 | 02 | 84.6 | 57.0 | 62 | 134.3 | 90.6 | 22 | 184.0 | 124.1 | 82 | 233.8 | 157.7 |
| 43 | 35.6 | 24.0 | 03 | 85.4 | 57.6 | 63 | 135.1 | 91.1 | 23 | 184.9 | 124.7 | 83 | 234.6 | 158.3 |
| 44 | 36.5 | 24.6 | 04 | 86.2 | 58.2 | 64 | 136.0 | 91.7 | 24 | 185.7 | 125.3 | 84 | 235.4 | 158.8 |
| 45 | 37.3 | 25.2 | 05 | 87.0 | 58.7 | 65 | 136.8 | 92.3 | 25 | 186.5 | 125.8 | 85 | 236.3 | 159.4 |
| 46 | 38.1 | 25.7 | 06 | 87.9 | 59.3 | 66 | 137.6 | 92.8 | 26 | 187.4 | 126.4 | 86 | 237.1 | 159.9 |
| 47 | 39.0 | 26.3 | 07 | 88.7 | 59.8 | 67 | 138.4 | 93.4 | 27 | 188.2 | 126.9 | 87 | 237.9 | 160.5 |
| 48 | 39.8 | 26.8 | 08 | 89.5 | 60.4 | 68 | 139.3 | 93.9 | 28 | 189.0 | 127.5 | 88 | 238.8 | 161.0 |
| 49 | 40.6 | 27.4 | 09 | 90.4 | 61.0 | 69 | 140.1 | 94.5 | 29 | 189.8 | 128.1 | 89 | 239.6 | 161.6 |
| 50 | 41.5 | 28.0 | 10 | 91.2 | 61.5 | 70 | 140.9 | 95.1 | 30 | 190.7 | 128.6 | 90 | 240.4 | 162.2 |
| 51 | 42.3 | 28.5 | 111 | 92.0 | 62.1 | 171 | 141.8 | 95.6 | 231 | 191.5 | 129.2 | 291 | 241.2 | 162.7 |
| 52 | 43.1 | 29.1 | 12 | 92.9 | 62.6 | 72 | 142.6 | 96.2 | 32 | 192.3 | 129.7 | 92 | 242.1 | 163.3 |
| 53 | 43.9 | 29.6 | 13 | 93.7 | 63.2 | 73 | 143.4 | 96.7 | 33 | 193.2 | 130.3 | 93 | 242.9 | 163.8 |
| 54 | 44.8 | 30.2 | 14 | 94.5 | 63.7 | 74 | 144.3 | 97.3 | 34 | 194.0 | 130.9 | 94 | 243.7 | 164.4 |
| 55 | 45.6 | 30.8 | 15 | 95.3 | 64.3 | 75 | 145.1 | 97.9 | 35 | 194.8 | 131.4 | 95 | 244.6 | 165.0 |
| 56 | 46.4 | 31.3 | 16 | 96.2 | 64.9 | 76 | 145.9 | 98.4 | 36 | 195.7 | 132.0 | 96 | 245.4 | 165.5 |
| 57 | 47.3 | 31.9 | 17 | 97.0 | 65.4 | 77 | 146.7 | 99.0 | 37 | 196.5 | 132.5 | 97 | 246.2 | 166.1 |
| 58 | 48.1 | 32.4 | 18 | 97.8 | 66.0 | 78 | 147.6 | 99.5 | 38 | 197.3 | 133.1 | 98 | 247.1 | 166.6 |
| 59 | 48.9 | 33.0 | 19 | 98.7 | 66.5 | 79 | 148.4 | 100.1 | 39 | 198.1 | 133.6 | 99 | 247.9 | 167.2 |
| 60 | 49.7 | 33.6 | 20 | 99.5 | 67.1 | 80 | 149.2 | 100.7 | 40 | 199.0 | 134.2 | 300 | 248.7 | 167.8 |
| Dist. | Dep. | Lat. | Dist. | Dep. | Lat. | Dist. | Dep. | Lat. | Dist. | Dep. | Lat. | Dist. | Dep. | Lat. |

# TABLE II.

## Difference of Latitude and Departure for 35 Degrees.

| Dist. | Lat. | Dep. | Dist. | Lat. | Dep. | Dist. | Lat. | Dep. | Dist. | Lat. | Dep. | Dist. | Lat. | Dep. |
|---|---|---|---|---|---|---|---|---|---|---|---|---|---|---|
| 1 | 00.8 | 00.6 | 61 | 50.0 | 35.0 | 121 | 99.1 | 69.4 | 181 | 148.3 | 103.8 | 241 | 197.4 | 138.2 |
| 2 | 01.6 | 01.1 | 62 | 50.8 | 35.6 | 22 | 99.9 | 70.0 | 82 | 149.1 | 104.4 | 42 | 198.2 | 138.8 |
| 3 | 02.5 | 01.7 | 63 | 51.6 | 36.1 | 23 | 100.8 | 70.5 | 83 | 149.9 | 105.0 | 43 | 199.1 | 139.4 |
| 4 | 03.3 | 02.3 | 64 | 52.4 | 36.7 | 24 | 101.6 | 71.1 | 84 | 150.7 | 105.5 | 44 | 199.9 | 140.0 |
| 5 | 04.1 | 02.9 | 65 | 53.2 | 37.3 | 25 | 102.4 | 71.7 | 85 | 151.5 | 106.1 | 45 | 200.7 | 140.5 |
| 6 | 04.9 | 03.4 | 66 | 54.1 | 37.9 | 26 | 103.2 | 72.3 | 86 | 152.4 | 106.7 | 46 | 201.5 | 141.1 |
| 7 | 05.7 | 04.0 | 67 | 54.9 | 38.4 | 27 | 104.0 | 72.8 | 87 | 153.2 | 107.3 | 47 | 202.3 | 141.7 |
| 8 | 06.6 | 04.6 | 68 | 55.7 | 39.0 | 28 | 104.9 | 73.4 | 88 | 154.0 | 107.8 | 48 | 203.1 | 142.2 |
| 9 | 07.4 | 05.2 | 69 | 56.5 | 39.6 | 29 | 105.7 | 74.0 | 89 | 154.8 | 108.4 | 49 | 204.0 | 142.8 |
| 10 | 08.2 | 05.7 | 70 | 57.3 | 40.2 | 30 | 106.5 | 74.6 | 90 | 155.6 | 109.0 | 50 | 204.8 | 143.4 |
| 11 | 09.0 | 06.3 | 71 | 58.2 | 40.7 | 131 | 107.3 | 75.1 | 191 | 156.5 | 109.6 | 251 | 205.6 | 144.0 |
| 12 | 09.8 | 06.9 | 72 | 59.0 | 41.3 | 32 | 108.1 | 75.7 | 92 | 157.3 | 110.1 | 52 | 206.4 | 144.5 |
| 13 | 10.6 | 07.5 | 73 | 59.8 | 41.9 | 33 | 108.9 | 76.3 | 93 | 158.1 | 110.7 | 53 | 207.2 | 145.1 |
| 14 | 11.5 | 08.0 | 74 | 60.6 | 42.4 | 34 | 109.8 | 76.9 | 94 | 158.9 | 111.3 | 54 | 208.1 | 145.7 |
| 15 | 12.3 | 08.6 | 75 | 61.4 | 43.0 | 35 | 110.6 | 77.4 | 95 | 159.7 | 111.8 | 55 | 208.9 | 146.3 |
| 16 | 13.1 | 09.2 | 76 | 62.3 | 43.6 | 36 | 111.4 | 78.0 | 96 | 160.6 | 112.4 | 56 | 209.7 | 146.8 |
| 17 | 13.9 | 09.8 | 77 | 63.1 | 44.2 | 37 | 112.2 | 78.6 | 97 | 161.4 | 113.0 | 57 | 210.5 | 147.4 |
| 18 | 14.7 | 10.3 | 78 | 63.9 | 44.7 | 38 | 113.0 | 79.2 | 98 | 162.2 | 113.6 | 58 | 211.3 | 148.0 |
| 19 | 15.6 | 10.9 | 79 | 64.7 | 45.3 | 39 | 113.9 | 79.7 | 99 | 163.0 | 114.1 | 59 | 212.2 | 148.6 |
| 20 | 16.4 | 11.5 | 80 | 65.5 | 45.9 | 40 | 114.7 | 80.3 | 200 | 163.8 | 114.7 | 60 | 213.0 | 149.1 |
| 21 | 17.2 | 12.0 | 81 | 66.4 | 46.5 | 141 | 115.5 | 80.9 | 201 | 164.6 | 115.3 | 261 | 213.8 | 149.7 |
| 22 | 18.0 | 12.6 | 82 | 67.2 | 47.0 | 42 | 116.3 | 81.4 | 02 | 165.5 | 115.9 | 62 | 214.6 | 150.3 |
| 23 | 18.8 | 13.2 | 83 | 68.0 | 47.6 | 43 | 117.1 | 82.0 | 03 | 166.3 | 116.4 | 63 | 215.4 | 150.9 |
| 24 | 19.7 | 13.8 | 84 | 68.8 | 48.2 | 44 | 118.0 | 82.6 | 04 | 167.1 | 117.0 | 64 | 216.3 | 151.4 |
| 25 | 20.5 | 14.3 | 85 | 69.6 | 48.8 | 45 | 118.8 | 83.2 | 05 | 167.9 | 117.6 | 65 | 217.1 | 152.0 |
| 26 | 21.3 | 14.9 | 86 | 70.4 | 49.3 | 46 | 119.6 | 83.7 | 06 | 168.7 | 118.2 | 66 | 217.9 | 152.6 |
| 27 | 22.1 | 15.5 | 87 | 71.3 | 49.9 | 47 | 120.4 | 84.3 | 07 | 169.6 | 118.7 | 67 | 218.7 | 153.1 |
| 28 | 22.9 | 16.1 | 88 | 72.1 | 50.5 | 48 | 121.2 | 84.9 | 08 | 170.4 | 119.3 | 68 | 219.5 | 153.7 |
| 29 | 23.8 | 16.6 | 89 | 72.9 | 51.0 | 49 | 122.1 | 85.5 | 09 | 171.2 | 119.9 | 69 | 220.4 | 154.3 |
| 30 | 24.6 | 17.2 | 90 | 73.7 | 51.6 | 50 | 122.9 | 86.0 | 10 | 172.0 | 120.5 | 70 | 221.2 | 154.9 |
| 31 | 25.4 | 17.8 | 91 | 74.5 | 52.2 | 151 | 123.7 | 86.6 | 211 | 172.8 | 121.0 | 271 | 222.0 | 155.4 |
| 32 | 26.2 | 18.4 | 92 | 75.4 | 52.8 | 52 | 124.5 | 87.2 | 12 | 173.7 | 121.6 | 72 | 222.8 | 156.0 |
| 33 | 27.0 | 18.9 | 93 | 76.2 | 53.3 | 53 | 125.3 | 87.8 | 13 | 174.5 | 122.2 | 73 | 223.6 | 156.6 |
| 34 | 27.9 | 19.5 | 94 | 77.0 | 53.9 | 54 | 126.1 | 88.3 | 14 | 175.3 | 122.7 | 74 | 224.4 | 157.2 |
| 35 | 28.7 | 20.1 | 95 | 77.8 | 54.5 | 55 | 127.0 | 88.9 | 15 | 176.1 | 123.3 | 75 | 225.3 | 157.7 |
| 36 | 29.5 | 20.6 | 96 | 78.6 | 55.1 | 56 | 127.8 | 89.5 | 16 | 176.9 | 123.9 | 76 | 226.1 | 158.3 |
| 37 | 30.3 | 21.2 | 97 | 79.5 | 55.6 | 57 | 128.6 | 90.1 | 17 | 177.8 | 124.5 | 77 | 226.9 | 158.9 |
| 38 | 31.1 | 21.8 | 98 | 80.3 | 56.2 | 58 | 129.4 | 90.6 | 18 | 178.6 | 125.0 | 78 | 227.7 | 159.5 |
| 39 | 31.9 | 22.4 | 99 | 81.1 | 56.8 | 59 | 130.2 | 91.2 | 19 | 179.4 | 125.6 | 79 | 228.5 | 160.0 |
| 40 | 32.8 | 22.9 | 100 | 81.9 | 57.4 | 60 | 131.1 | 91.8 | 20 | 180.2 | 126.2 | 80 | 229.4 | 160.6 |
| 41 | 33.6 | 23.5 | 101 | 82.7 | 57.9 | 161 | 131.9 | 92.3 | 221 | 181.0 | 126.8 | 281 | 230.2 | 161.2 |
| 42 | 34.4 | 24.1 | 02 | 83.6 | 58.5 | 62 | 132.7 | 92.9 | 22 | 181.9 | 127.3 | 82 | 231.0 | 161.7 |
| 43 | 35.2 | 24.7 | 03 | 84.4 | 59.1 | 63 | 133.5 | 93.5 | 23 | 182.7 | 127.9 | 83 | 231.8 | 162.3 |
| 44 | 36.0 | 25.2 | 04 | 85.2 | 59.7 | 64 | 134.3 | 94.1 | 24 | 183.5 | 128.5 | 84 | 232.6 | 162.9 |
| 45 | 36.9 | 25.8 | 05 | 86.0 | 60.2 | 65 | 135.2 | 94.6 | 25 | 184.3 | 129.1 | 85 | 233.5 | 163.5 |
| 46 | 37.7 | 26.4 | 06 | 86.8 | 60.8 | 66 | 136.0 | 95.2 | 26 | 185.1 | 129.6 | 86 | 234.3 | 164.0 |
| 47 | 38.5 | 27.0 | 07 | 87.6 | 61.4 | 67 | 136.8 | 95.8 | 27 | 185.9 | 130.2 | 87 | 235.1 | 164.6 |
| 48 | 39.3 | 27.5 | 08 | 88.5 | 61.9 | 68 | 137.6 | 96.4 | 28 | 186.8 | 130.8 | 88 | 235.9 | 165.2 |
| 49 | 40.1 | 28.1 | 09 | 89.3 | 62.5 | 69 | 138.4 | 96.9 | 29 | 187.6 | 131.3 | 89 | 236.7 | 165.8 |
| 50 | 41.0 | 28.7 | 10 | 90.1 | 63.1 | 70 | 139.3 | 97.5 | 30 | 188.4 | 131.9 | 90 | 237.6 | 166.3 |
| 51 | 41.8 | 29.3 | 111 | 90.9 | 63.7 | 171 | 140.1 | 98.1 | 231 | 189.2 | 132.5 | 291 | 238.4 | 166.9 |
| 52 | 42.6 | 29.8 | 12 | 91.7 | 64.2 | 72 | 140.9 | 98.7 | 32 | 190.0 | 133.1 | 92 | 239.2 | 167.5 |
| 53 | 43.4 | 30.4 | 13 | 92.6 | 64.8 | 73 | 141.7 | 99.2 | 33 | 190.9 | 133.6 | 93 | 240.0 | 168.1 |
| 54 | 44.2 | 31.0 | 14 | 93.4 | 65.4 | 74 | 142.5 | 99.8 | 34 | 191.7 | 134.2 | 94 | 240.8 | 168.6 |
| 55 | 45.1 | 31.5 | 15 | 94.2 | 66.0 | 75 | 143.4 | 100.4 | 35 | 192.5 | 134.8 | 95 | 241.6 | 169.2 |
| 56 | 45.9 | 32.1 | 16 | 95.0 | 66.5 | 76 | 144.2 | 100.9 | 36 | 193.3 | 135.4 | 96 | 242.5 | 169.8 |
| 57 | 46.7 | 32.7 | 17 | 95.8 | 67.1 | 77 | 145.0 | 101.5 | 37 | 194.1 | 135.9 | 97 | 243.3 | 170.4 |
| 58 | 47.5 | 33.3 | 18 | 96.7 | 67.7 | 78 | 145.8 | 102.1 | 38 | 195.0 | 136.5 | 98 | 244.1 | 170.9 |
| 59 | 48.3 | 33.8 | 19 | 97.5 | 68.3 | 79 | 146.6 | 102.7 | 39 | 195.8 | 137.1 | 99 | 244.9 | 171.5 |
| 60 | 49.1 | 34.4 | 20 | 98.3 | 68.8 | 80 | 147.4 | 103.2 | 40 | 196.6 | 137.7 | 300 | 245.7 | 172.1 |
| Dist. | Dep. | Lat. | Dist. | Dep. | Lat. | Dist. | Dep. | Lat. | Dist. | Dep. | Lat. | Dist. | Dep. | Lat. |

# TABLE II.

## Difference of Latitude and Departure for 36 Degrees.

| Dist. | Lat. | Dep. | Dist. | Lat. | Dep. | Dist. | Lat. | Dep. | Dist. | Lat. | Dep. | Dist. | Lat. | Dep. |
|---|---|---|---|---|---|---|---|---|---|---|---|---|---|---|
| 1 | 00.8 | 00.6 | 61 | 49.4 | 35.9 | 121 | 97.9 | 71.1 | 181 | 146.4 | 106.4 | 241 | 195.0 | 141.7 |
| 2 | 01.6 | 01.2 | 62 | 50.2 | 36.4 | 22 | 98.7 | 71.7 | 82 | 147.2 | 107.0 | 42 | 195.8 | 142.2 |
| 3 | 02.4 | 01.8 | 63 | 51.0 | 37.0 | 23 | 99.5 | 72.3 | 83 | 148.1 | 107.6 | 43 | 196.6 | 142.8 |
| 4 | 03.2 | 02.4 | 64 | 51.8 | 37.6 | 24 | 100.3 | 72.9 | 84 | 148.9 | 108.2 | 44 | 197.4 | 143.4 |
| 5 | 04.0 | 02.9 | 65 | 52.6 | 38.2 | 25 | 101.1 | 73.5 | 85 | 149.7 | 108.7 | 45 | 198.2 | 144.0 |
| 6 | 04.9 | 03.5 | 66 | 53.4 | 38.8 | 26 | 101.9 | 74.1 | 86 | 150.5 | 109.3 | 46 | 199.0 | 144.6 |
| 7 | 05.7 | 04.1 | 67 | 54.2 | 39.4 | 27 | 102.7 | 74.6 | 87 | 151.3 | 109.9 | 47 | 199.8 | 145.2 |
| 8 | 06.5 | 04.7 | 68 | 55.0 | 40.0 | 28 | 103.6 | 75.2 | 88 | 152.1 | 110.5 | 48 | 200.6 | 145.8 |
| 9 | 07.3 | 05.3 | 69 | 55.8 | 40.6 | 29 | 104.4 | 75.8 | 89 | 152.9 | 111.1 | 49 | 201.4 | 146.4 |
| 10 | 08.1 | 05.9 | 70 | 56.6 | 41.1 | 30 | 105.2 | 76.4 | 90 | 153.7 | 111.7 | 50 | 202.3 | 146.9 |
| 11 | 08.9 | 06.5 | 71 | 57.4 | 41.7 | 131 | 106.0 | 77.0 | 191 | 154.5 | 112.3 | 251 | 203.1 | 147.5 |
| 12 | 09.7 | 07.1 | 72 | 58.2 | 42.3 | 32 | 106.8 | 77.6 | 92 | 155.3 | 112.9 | 52 | 203.9 | 148.1 |
| 13 | 10.5 | 07.6 | 73 | 59.1 | 42.9 | 33 | 107.6 | 78.2 | 93 | 156.1 | 113.4 | 53 | 204.7 | 148.7 |
| 14 | 11.3 | 08.2 | 74 | 59.9 | 43.5 | 34 | 108.4 | 78.8 | 94 | 156.9 | 114.0 | 54 | 205.5 | 149.3 |
| 15 | 12.1 | 08.8 | 75 | 60.7 | 44.1 | 35 | 109.2 | 79.4 | 95 | 157.8 | 114.6 | 55 | 206.3 | 149.9 |
| 16 | 12.9 | 09.4 | 76 | 61.5 | 44.7 | 36 | 110.0 | 79.9 | 96 | 158.6 | 115.2 | 56 | 207.1 | 150.5 |
| 17 | 13.8 | 10.0 | 77 | 62.3 | 45.3 | 37 | 110.8 | 80.5 | 97 | 159.4 | 115.8 | 57 | 207.9 | 151.1 |
| 18 | 14.6 | 10.6 | 78 | 63.1 | 45.8 | 38 | 111.6 | 81.1 | 98 | 160.2 | 116.4 | 58 | 208.7 | 151.6 |
| 19 | 15.4 | 11.2 | 79 | 63.9 | 46.4 | 39 | 112.5 | 81.7 | 99 | 161.0 | 117.0 | 59 | 209.5 | 152.2 |
| 20 | 16.2 | 11.8 | 80 | 64.7 | 47.0 | 40 | 113.3 | 82.3 | 200 | 161.8 | 117.6 | 60 | 210.3 | 152.8 |
| 21 | 17.0 | 12.3 | 81 | 65.5 | 47.6 | 141 | 114.1 | 82.9 | 201 | 162.6 | 118.1 | 261 | 211.2 | 153.4 |
| 22 | 17.8 | 12.9 | 82 | 66.3 | 48.2 | 42 | 114.9 | 83.5 | 02 | 163.4 | 118.7 | 62 | 212.0 | 154.0 |
| 23 | 18.6 | 13.5 | 83 | 67.1 | 48.8 | 43 | 115.7 | 84.1 | 03 | 164.2 | 119.3 | 63 | 212.8 | 154.6 |
| 24 | 19.4 | 14.1 | 84 | 68.0 | 49.4 | 44 | 116.5 | 84.6 | 04 | 165.0 | 119.9 | 64 | 213.6 | 155.2 |
| 25 | 20.2 | 14.7 | 85 | 68.8 | 50.0 | 45 | 117.3 | 85.2 | 05 | 165.8 | 120.5 | 65 | 214.4 | 155.8 |
| 26 | 21.0 | 15.3 | 86 | 69.6 | 50.5 | 46 | 118.1 | 85.8 | 06 | 166.7 | 121.1 | 66 | 215.2 | 156.4 |
| 27 | 21.8 | 15.9 | 87 | 70.4 | 51.1 | 47 | 118.9 | 86.4 | 07 | 167.5 | 121.7 | 67 | 216.0 | 156.9 |
| 28 | 22.7 | 16.5 | 88 | 71.2 | 51.7 | 48 | 119.7 | 87.0 | 08 | 168.3 | 122.3 | 68 | 216.8 | 157.5 |
| 29 | 23.5 | 17.0 | 89 | 72.0 | 52.3 | 49 | 120.5 | 87.6 | 09 | 169.1 | 122.8 | 69 | 217.6 | 158.1 |
| 30 | 24.3 | 17.6 | 90 | 72.8 | 52.9 | 50 | 121.4 | 88.2 | 10 | 169.9 | 123.4 | 70 | 218.4 | 158.7 |
| 31 | 25.1 | 18.2 | 91 | 73.6 | 53.5 | 151 | 122.2 | 88.8 | 211 | 170.7 | 124.0 | 271 | 219.2 | 159.3 |
| 32 | 25.9 | 18.8 | 92 | 74.4 | 54.1 | 52 | 123.0 | 89.3 | 12 | 171.5 | 124.6 | 72 | 220.1 | 159.9 |
| 33 | 26.7 | 19.4 | 93 | 75.2 | 54.7 | 53 | 123.8 | 89.9 | 13 | 172.3 | 125.2 | 73 | 220.9 | 160.5 |
| 34 | 27.5 | 20.0 | 94 | 76.0 | 55.3 | 54 | 124.6 | 90.5 | 14 | 173.1 | 125.8 | 74 | 221.7 | 161.1 |
| 35 | 28.3 | 20.6 | 95 | 76.9 | 55.8 | 55 | 125.4 | 91.1 | 15 | 173.9 | 126.4 | 75 | 222.5 | 161.6 |
| 36 | 29.1 | 21.2 | 96 | 77.7 | 56.4 | 56 | 126.2 | 91.7 | 16 | 174.7 | 127.0 | 76 | 223.3 | 162.2 |
| 37 | 29.9 | 21.7 | 97 | 78.5 | 57.0 | 57 | 127.0 | 92.3 | 17 | 175.6 | 127.5 | 77 | 224.1 | 162.8 |
| 38 | 30.7 | 22.3 | 98 | 79.3 | 57.6 | 58 | 127.8 | 92.9 | 18 | 176.4 | 128.1 | 78 | 224.9 | 163.4 |
| 39 | 31.6 | 22.9 | 99 | 80.1 | 58.2 | 59 | 128.6 | 93.5 | 19 | 177.2 | 128.7 | 79 | 225.7 | 164.0 |
| 40 | 32.4 | 23.5 | 100 | 80.9 | 58.8 | 60 | 129.4 | 94.0 | 20 | 178.0 | 129.3 | 80 | 226.5 | 164.6 |
| 41 | 33.2 | 24.1 | 101 | 81.7 | 59.4 | 161 | 130.3 | 94.6 | 221 | 178.8 | 129.9 | 281 | 227.3 | 165.2 |
| 42 | 34.0 | 24.7 | 02 | 82.5 | 60.0 | 62 | 131.1 | 95.2 | 22 | 179.6 | 130.5 | 82 | 228.1 | 165.8 |
| 43 | 34.8 | 25.3 | 03 | 83.3 | 60.5 | 63 | 131.9 | 95.8 | 23 | 180.4 | 131.1 | 83 | 229.0 | 166.3 |
| 44 | 35.6 | 25.9 | 04 | 84.1 | 61.1 | 64 | 132.7 | 96.4 | 24 | 181.2 | 131.7 | 84 | 229.8 | 166.9 |
| 45 | 36.4 | 26.5 | 05 | 84.9 | 61.7 | 65 | 133.5 | 97.0 | 25 | 182.0 | 132.3 | 85 | 230.6 | 167.5 |
| 46 | 37.2 | 27.0 | 06 | 85.8 | 62.3 | 66 | 134.3 | 97.6 | 26 | 182.8 | 132.8 | 86 | 231.4 | 168.1 |
| 47 | 38.0 | 27.6 | 07 | 86.6 | 62.9 | 67 | 135.1 | 98.2 | 27 | 183.6 | 133.4 | 87 | 232.2 | 168.7 |
| 48 | 38.8 | 28.2 | 08 | 87.4 | 63.5 | 68 | 135.9 | 98.7 | 28 | 184.5 | 134.0 | 88 | 233.0 | 169.3 |
| 49 | 39.6 | 28.8 | 09 | 88.2 | 64.1 | 69 | 136.7 | 99.3 | 29 | 185.3 | 134.6 | 89 | 233.8 | 169.9 |
| 50 | 40.5 | 29.4 | 10 | 89.0 | 64.7 | 70 | 137.5 | 99.9 | 30 | 186.1 | 135.2 | 90 | 234.6 | 170.5 |
| 51 | 41.3 | 30.0 | 111 | 89.8 | 65.2 | 171 | 138.3 | 100.5 | 231 | 186.9 | 135.8 | 291 | 235.4 | 171.0 |
| 52 | 42.1 | 30.6 | 12 | 90.6 | 65.8 | 72 | 139.2 | 101.1 | 32 | 187.7 | 136.4 | 92 | 236.2 | 171.6 |
| 53 | 42.9 | 31.2 | 13 | 91.4 | 66.4 | 73 | 140.0 | 101.7 | 33 | 188.5 | 137.0 | 93 | 237.0 | 172.2 |
| 54 | 43.7 | 31.7 | 14 | 92.2 | 67.0 | 74 | 140.8 | 102.3 | 34 | 189.3 | 137.5 | 94 | 237.9 | 172.8 |
| 55 | 44.5 | 32.3 | 15 | 93.0 | 67.6 | 75 | 141.6 | 102.9 | 35 | 190.1 | 138.1 | 95 | 238.7 | 173.4 |
| 56 | 45.3 | 32.9 | 16 | 93.8 | 68.2 | 76 | 142.4 | 103.5 | 36 | 190.9 | 138.7 | 96 | 239.5 | 174.0 |
| 57 | 46.1 | 33.5 | 17 | 94.7 | 68.8 | 77 | 143.2 | 104.0 | 37 | 191.7 | 139.3 | 97 | 240.3 | 174.6 |
| 58 | 46.9 | 34.1 | 18 | 95.5 | 69.4 | 78 | 144.0 | 104.6 | 38 | 192.5 | 139.9 | 98 | 241.1 | 175.2 |
| 59 | 47.7 | 34.7 | 19 | 96.3 | 69.9 | 79 | 144.8 | 105.2 | 39 | 193.4 | 140.5 | 99 | 241.9 | 175.7 |
| 60 | 48.5 | 35.3 | 20 | 97.1 | 70.5 | 80 | 145.6 | 105.8 | 40 | 194.2 | 141.1 | 300 | 242.7 | 176.3 |
| Dist. | Dep. | Lat. | Dist. | Dep. | Lat. | Dist. | Dep. | Lat. | Dist. | Dep. | Lat. | Dist. | Dep. | Lat. |

[For 54 Degrees.

# TABLE II.

## Difference of Latitude and Departure for 37 Degrees.

| Dist. | Lat. | Dep. | Dist. | Lat. | Dep. | Dist. | Lat. | Dep. | Dist. | Lat. | Dep. | Dist. | Lat. | Dep. |
|---|---|---|---|---|---|---|---|---|---|---|---|---|---|---|
| 1 | 00.8 | 00.6 | 61 | 48.7 | 36.7 | 121 | 96.6 | 72.8 | 181 | 144.6 | 108.9 | 241 | 192.5 | 145.0 |
| 2 | 01.6 | 01.2 | 62 | 49.5 | 37.3 | 22 | 97.4 | 73.4 | 82 | 145.4 | 109.5 | 42 | 193.3 | 145.6 |
| 3 | 02.4 | 01.8 | 63 | 50.3 | 37.9 | 23 | 98.2 | 74.0 | 83 | 146.2 | 110.1 | 43 | 194.1 | 146.2 |
| 4 | 03.2 | 02.4 | 64 | 51.1 | 38.5 | 24 | 99.0 | 74.6 | 84 | 146.9 | 110.7 | 44 | 194.9 | 146.8 |
| 5 | 04.0 | 03.0 | 65 | 51.9 | 39.1 | 25 | 99.8 | 75.2 | 85 | 147.7 | 111.3 | 45 | 195.7 | 147.4 |
| 6 | 04.8 | 03.6 | 66 | 52.7 | 39.7 | 26 | 100.6 | 75.8 | 86 | 148.5 | 111.9 | 46 | 196.5 | 148.0 |
| 7 | 05.6 | 04.2 | 67 | 53.5 | 40.3 | 27 | 101.4 | 76.4 | 87 | 149.3 | 112.5 | 47 | 197.3 | 148.6 |
| 8 | 06.4 | 04.8 | 68 | 54.3 | 40.9 | 28 | 102.2 | 77.0 | 88 | 150.1 | 113.1 | 48 | 198.1 | 149.3 |
| 9 | 07.2 | 05.4 | 69 | 55.1 | 41.5 | 29 | 103.0 | 77.6 | 89 | 150.9 | 113.7 | 49 | 198.9 | 149.9 |
| 10 | 08.0 | 06.0 | 70 | 55.9 | 42.1 | 30 | 103.8 | 78.2 | 90 | 151.7 | 114.3 | 50 | 199.7 | 150.5 |
| 11 | 08.8 | 06.6 | 71 | 56.7 | 42.7 | 131 | 104.6 | 78.8 | 191 | 152.5 | 114.9 | 251 | 200.5 | 151.1 |
| 12 | 09.6 | 07.2 | 72 | 57.5 | 43.3 | 32 | 105.4 | 79.4 | 92 | 153.3 | 115.5 | 52 | 201.3 | 151.7 |
| 13 | 10.4 | 07.8 | 73 | 58.3 | 43.9 | 33 | 106.2 | 80.0 | 93 | 154.1 | 116.2 | 53 | 202.1 | 152.3 |
| 14 | 11.2 | 08.4 | 74 | 59.1 | 44.5 | 34 | 107.0 | 80.6 | 94 | 154.9 | 116.8 | 54 | 202.9 | 152.9 |
| 15 | 12.0 | 09.0 | 75 | 59.9 | 45.1 | 35 | 107.8 | 81.2 | 95 | 155.7 | 117.4 | 55 | 203.7 | 153.5 |
| 16 | 12.8 | 09.6 | 76 | 60.7 | 45.7 | 36 | 108.6 | 81.8 | 96 | 156.5 | 118.0 | 56 | 204.5 | 154.1 |
| 17 | 13.6 | 10.2 | 77 | 61.5 | 46.3 | 37 | 109.4 | 82.4 | 97 | 157.3 | 118.6 | 57 | 205.2 | 154.7 |
| 18 | 14.4 | 10.8 | 78 | 62.3 | 46.9 | 38 | 110.2 | 83.1 | 98 | 158.1 | 119.2 | 58 | 206.0 | 155.3 |
| 19 | 15.2 | 11.4 | 79 | 63.1 | 47.5 | 39 | 111.0 | 83.7 | 99 | 158.9 | 119.8 | 59 | 206.8 | 155.9 |
| 20 | 16.0 | 12.0 | 80 | 63.9 | 48.1 | 40 | 111.8 | 84.3 | 200 | 159.7 | 120.4 | 60 | 207.6 | 156.5 |
| 21 | 16.8 | 12.6 | 81 | 64.7 | 48.7 | 141 | 112.6 | 84.9 | 201 | 160.5 | 121.0 | 261 | 208.4 | 157.1 |
| 22 | 17.6 | 13.2 | 82 | 65.5 | 49.3 | 42 | 113.4 | 85.5 | 02 | 161.3 | 121.6 | 62 | 209.2 | 157.7 |
| 23 | 18.4 | 13.8 | 83 | 66.3 | 50.0 | 43 | 114.2 | 86.1 | 03 | 162.1 | 122.2 | 63 | 210.0 | 158.3 |
| 24 | 19.2 | 14.4 | 84 | 67.1 | 50.6 | 44 | 115.0 | 86.7 | 04 | 162.9 | 122.8 | 64 | 210.8 | 158.9 |
| 25 | 20.0 | 15.0 | 85 | 67.9 | 51.2 | 45 | 115.8 | 87.3 | 05 | 163.7 | 123.4 | 65 | 211.6 | 159.5 |
| 26 | 20.8 | 15.6 | 86 | 68.7 | 51.8 | 46 | 116.6 | 87.9 | 06 | 164.5 | 124.0 | 66 | 212.4 | 160.1 |
| 27 | 21.6 | 16.2 | 87 | 69.5 | 52.4 | 47 | 117.4 | 88.5 | 07 | 165.3 | 124.6 | 67 | 213.2 | 160.7 |
| 28 | 22.4 | 16.9 | 88 | 70.3 | 53.0 | 48 | 118.2 | 89.1 | 08 | 166.1 | 125.2 | 68 | 214.0 | 161.3 |
| 29 | 23.2 | 17.5 | 89 | 71.1 | 53.6 | 49 | 119.0 | 89.7 | 09 | 166.9 | 125.8 | 69 | 214.8 | 161.9 |
| 30 | 24.0 | 18.1 | 90 | 71.9 | 54.2 | 50 | 119.8 | 90.3 | 10 | 167.7 | 126.4 | 70 | 215.6 | 162.5 |
| 31 | 24.8 | 18.7 | 91 | 72.7 | 54.8 | 151 | 120.6 | 90.9 | 211 | 168.5 | 127.0 | 271 | 216.4 | 163.1 |
| 32 | 25.6 | 19.3 | 92 | 73.5 | 55.4 | 52 | 121.4 | 91.5 | 12 | 169.3 | 127.6 | 72 | 217.2 | 163.7 |
| 33 | 26.4 | 19.9 | 93 | 74.3 | 56.0 | 53 | 122.2 | 92.1 | 13 | 170.1 | 128.2 | 73 | 218.0 | 164.3 |
| 34 | 27.2 | 20.5 | 94 | 75.1 | 56.6 | 54 | 123.0 | 92.7 | 14 | 170.9 | 128.8 | 74 | 218.8 | 164.9 |
| 35 | 28.0 | 21.1 | 95 | 75.9 | 57.2 | 55 | 123.8 | 93.3 | 15 | 171.7 | 129.4 | 75 | 219.6 | 165.5 |
| 36 | 28.8 | 21.7 | 96 | 76.7 | 57.8 | 56 | 124.6 | 93.9 | 16 | 172.5 | 130.0 | 76 | 220.4 | 166.1 |
| 37 | 29.5 | 22.3 | 97 | 77.5 | 58.4 | 57 | 125.4 | 94.5 | 17 | 173.3 | 130.6 | 77 | 221.2 | 166.7 |
| 38 | 30.3 | 22.9 | 98 | 78.3 | 59.0 | 58 | 126.2 | 95.1 | 18 | 174.1 | 131.2 | 78 | 222.0 | 167.3 |
| 39 | 31.1 | 23.5 | 99 | 79.1 | 59.6 | 59 | 127.0 | 95.7 | 19 | 174.9 | 131.8 | 79 | 222.8 | 167.9 |
| 40 | 31.9 | 24.1 | 100 | 79.9 | 60.2 | 60 | 127.8 | 96.3 | 20 | 175.7 | 132.4 | 80 | 223.6 | 168.5 |
| 41 | 32.7 | 24.7 | 101 | 80.7 | 60.8 | 161 | 128.6 | 96.9 | 221 | 176.5 | 133.0 | 281 | 224.4 | 169.1 |
| 42 | 33.5 | 25.3 | 02 | 81.5 | 61.4 | 62 | 129.4 | 97.5 | 22 | 177.3 | 133.6 | 82 | 225.2 | 169.7 |
| 43 | 34.3 | 25.9 | 03 | 82.3 | 62.0 | 63 | 130.2 | 98.1 | 23 | 178.1 | 134.2 | 83 | 226.0 | 170.3 |
| 44 | 35.1 | 26.5 | 04 | 83.1 | 62.6 | 64 | 131.0 | 98.7 | 24 | 178.9 | 134.8 | 84 | 226.8 | 170.9 |
| 45 | 35.9 | 27.1 | 05 | 83.9 | 63.2 | 65 | 131.8 | 99.3 | 25 | 179.7 | 135.4 | 85 | 227.6 | 171.5 |
| 46 | 36.7 | 27.7 | 06 | 84.7 | 63.8 | 66 | 132.6 | 99.9 | 26 | 180.5 | 136.0 | 86 | 228.4 | 172.1 |
| 47 | 37.5 | 28.3 | 07 | 85.5 | 64.4 | 67 | 133.4 | 100.5 | 27 | 181.3 | 136.6 | 87 | 229.2 | 172.7 |
| 48 | 38.3 | 28.9 | 08 | 86.3 | 65.0 | 68 | 134.2 | 101.1 | 28 | 182.1 | 137.2 | 88 | 230.0 | 173.3 |
| 49 | 39.1 | 29.5 | 09 | 87.1 | 65.6 | 69 | 135.0 | 101.7 | 29 | 182.9 | 137.8 | 89 | 230.8 | 173.9 |
| 50 | 39.9 | 30.1 | 10 | 87.8 | 66.2 | 70 | 135.8 | 102.3 | 30 | 183.7 | 138.4 | 90 | 231.6 | 174.5 |
| 51 | 40.7 | 30.7 | 111 | 88.6 | 66.8 | 171 | 136.6 | 102.9 | 231 | 184.5 | 139.0 | 291 | 232.4 | 175.1 |
| 52 | 41.5 | 31.3 | 12 | 89.4 | 67.4 | 72 | 137.4 | 103.5 | 32 | 185.3 | 139.6 | 92 | 233.2 | 175.7 |
| 53 | 42.3 | 31.9 | 13 | 90.2 | 68.0 | 73 | 138.2 | 104.1 | 33 | 186.1 | 140.2 | 93 | 234.0 | 176.3 |
| 54 | 43.1 | 32.5 | 14 | 91.0 | 68.6 | 74 | 139.0 | 104.7 | 34 | 186.9 | 140.8 | 94 | 234.8 | 176.9 |
| 55 | 43.9 | 33.1 | 15 | 91.8 | 69.2 | 75 | 139.8 | 105.3 | 35 | 187.7 | 141.4 | 95 | 235.6 | 177.5 |
| 56 | 44.7 | 33.7 | 16 | 92.6 | 69.8 | 76 | 140.6 | 105.9 | 36 | 188.5 | 142.0 | 96 | 236.4 | 178.1 |
| 57 | 45.5 | 34.3 | 17 | 93.4 | 70.4 | 77 | 141.4 | 106.5 | 37 | 189.3 | 142.6 | 97 | 237.2 | 178.7 |
| 58 | 46.3 | 34.9 | 18 | 94.2 | 71.0 | 78 | 142.2 | 107.1 | 38 | 190.1 | 143.2 | 98 | 238.0 | 179.3 |
| 59 | 47.1 | 35.5 | 19 | 95.0 | 71.6 | 79 | 143.0 | 107.7 | 39 | 190.9 | 143.8 | 99 | 238.8 | 179.9 |
| 60 | 47.9 | 36.1 | 20 | 95.8 | 72.2 | 80 | 143.8 | 108.3 | 40 | 191.7 | 144.4 | 300 | 239.6 | 180.5 |
| Dist. | Dep. | Lat. | Dist. | Dep. | Lat. | Dist. | Dep. | Lat. | Dist. | Dep. | Lat. | Dist. | Dep. | Lat. |

[For 53 Degrees.

# TABLE II.

## Difference of Latitude and Departure for 38 Degrees.

| Dist. | Lat. | Dep. | Dist. | Lat. | Dep. | Dist. | Lat. | Dep. | Dist. | Lat. | Dep. | Dist. | Lat. | Dep. |
|---|---|---|---|---|---|---|---|---|---|---|---|---|---|---|
| 1 | 00.8 | 00.6 | 61 | 48.1 | 37.6 | 121 | 95.3 | 74.5 | 181 | 142.6 | 111.4 | 241 | 189.9 | 148.4 |
| 2 | 01.6 | 01.2 | 62 | 48.9 | 38.2 | 22 | 96.1 | 75.1 | 82 | 143.4 | 112.1 | 42 | 190.7 | 149.0 |
| 3 | 02.4 | 01.8 | 63 | 49.6 | 38.8 | 23 | 96.9 | 75.7 | 83 | 144.2 | 112.7 | 43 | 191.5 | 149.6 |
| 4 | 03.2 | 02.5 | 64 | 50.4 | 39.4 | 24 | 97.7 | 76.3 | 84 | 145.0 | 113.3 | 44 | 192.3 | 150.2 |
| 5 | 03.9 | 03.1 | 65 | 51.2 | 40.0 | 25 | 98.5 | 77.0 | 85 | 145.8 | 113.9 | 45 | 193.1 | 150.8 |
| 6 | 04.7 | 03.7 | 66 | 52.0 | 40.6 | 26 | 99.3 | 77.6 | 86 | 146.6 | 114.5 | 46 | 193.9 | 151.5 |
| 7 | 05.5 | 04.3 | 67 | 52.8 | 41.2 | 27 | 100.1 | 78.2 | 87 | 147.4 | 115.1 | 47 | 194.6 | 152.1 |
| 8 | 06.3 | 04.9 | 68 | 53.6 | 41.9 | 28 | 100.9 | 78.8 | 88 | 148.1 | 115.7 | 48 | 195.4 | 152.7 |
| 9 | 07.1 | 05.5 | 69 | 54.4 | 42.5 | 29 | 101.7 | 79.4 | 89 | 148.9 | 116.4 | 49 | 196.2 | 153.3 |
| 10 | 07.9 | 06.2 | 70 | 55.2 | 43.1 | 30 | 102.4 | 80.0 | 90 | 149.7 | 117.0 | 50 | 197.0 | 153.9 |
| 11 | 08.7 | 06.8 | 71 | 55.9 | 43.7 | 131 | 103.2 | 80.7 | 191 | 150.5 | 117.6 | 251 | 197.8 | 154.5 |
| 12 | 09.5 | 07.4 | 72 | 56.7 | 44.3 | 32 | 104.0 | 81.3 | 92 | 151.3 | 118.2 | 52 | 198.6 | 155.1 |
| 13 | 10.2 | 08.0 | 73 | 57.5 | 44.9 | 33 | 104.8 | 81.9 | 93 | 152.1 | 118.8 | 53 | 199.4 | 155.8 |
| 14 | 11.0 | 08.6 | 74 | 58.3 | 45.6 | 34 | 105.6 | 82.5 | 94 | 152.9 | 119.4 | 54 | 200.2 | 156.4 |
| 15 | 11.8 | 09.2 | 75 | 59.1 | 46.2 | 35 | 106.4 | 83.1 | 95 | 153.7 | 120.1 | 55 | 200.9 | 157.0 |
| 16 | 12.6 | 09.9 | 76 | 59.9 | 46.8 | 36 | 107.2 | 83.7 | 96 | 154.5 | 120.7 | 56 | 201.7 | 157.6 |
| 17 | 13.4 | 10.5 | 77 | 60.7 | 47.4 | 37 | 108.0 | 84.3 | 97 | 155.2 | 121.3 | 57 | 202.5 | 158.2 |
| 18 | 14.2 | 11.1 | 78 | 61.5 | 48.0 | 38 | 108.7 | 85.0 | 98 | 156.0 | 121.9 | 58 | 203.3 | 158.8 |
| 19 | 15.0 | 11.7 | 79 | 62.3 | 48.6 | 39 | 109.5 | 85.6 | 99 | 156.8 | 122.5 | 59 | 204.1 | 159.5 |
| 20 | 15.8 | 12.3 | 80 | 63.0 | 49.3 | 40 | 110.3 | 86.2 | 200 | 157.6 | 123.1 | 60 | 204.9 | 160.1 |
| 21 | 16.5 | 12.9 | 81 | 63.8 | 49.9 | 141 | 111.1 | 86.8 | 201 | 158.4 | 123.7 | 261 | 205.7 | 160.7 |
| 22 | 17.3 | 13.5 | 82 | 64.6 | 50.5 | 42 | 111.9 | 87.4 | 02 | 159.2 | 124.4 | 62 | 206.5 | 161.3 |
| 23 | 18.1 | 14.2 | 83 | 65.4 | 51.1 | 43 | 112.7 | 88.0 | 03 | 160.0 | 125.0 | 63 | 207.2 | 161.9 |
| 24 | 18.9 | 14.8 | 84 | 66.2 | 51.7 | 44 | 113.5 | 88.7 | 04 | 160.8 | 125.6 | 64 | 208.0 | 162.5 |
| 25 | 19.7 | 15.4 | 85 | 67.0 | 52.3 | 45 | 114.3 | 89.3 | 05 | 161.5 | 126.2 | 65 | 208.8 | 163.2 |
| 26 | 20.5 | 16.0 | 86 | 67.8 | 52.9 | 46 | 115.0 | 89.9 | 06 | 162.3 | 126.8 | 66 | 209.6 | 163.8 |
| 27 | 21.3 | 16.6 | 87 | 68.6 | 53.6 | 47 | 115.8 | 90.5 | 07 | 163.1 | 127.4 | 67 | 210.4 | 164.4 |
| 28 | 22.1 | 17.2 | 88 | 69.3 | 54.2 | 48 | 116.6 | 91.1 | 08 | 163.9 | 128.1 | 68 | 211.2 | 165.0 |
| 29 | 22.9 | 17.9 | 89 | 70.1 | 54.8 | 49 | 117.4 | 91.7 | 09 | 164.7 | 128.7 | 69 | 212.0 | 165.6 |
| 30 | 23.6 | 18.5 | 90 | 70.9 | 55.4 | 50 | 118.2 | 92.3 | 10 | 165.5 | 129.3 | 70 | 212.8 | 166.2 |
| 31 | 24.4 | 19.1 | 91 | 71.7 | 56.0 | 151 | 119.0 | 93.0 | 211 | 166.3 | 129.9 | 271 | 213.6 | 166.8 |
| 32 | 25.2 | 19.7 | 92 | 72.5 | 56.6 | 52 | 119.8 | 93.6 | 12 | 167.1 | 130.5 | 72 | 214.3 | 167.5 |
| 33 | 26.0 | 20.3 | 93 | 73.3 | 57.3 | 53 | 120.6 | 94.2 | 13 | 167.8 | 131.1 | 73 | 215.1 | 168.1 |
| 34 | 26.8 | 20.9 | 94 | 74.1 | 57.9 | 54 | 121.4 | 94.8 | 14 | 168.6 | 131.8 | 74 | 215.9 | 168.7 |
| 35 | 27.6 | 21.5 | 95 | 74.9 | 58.5 | 55 | 122.1 | 95.4 | 15 | 169.4 | 132.4 | 75 | 216.7 | 169.3 |
| 36 | 28.4 | 22.2 | 96 | 75.6 | 59.1 | 56 | 122.9 | 96.0 | 16 | 170.2 | 133.0 | 76 | 217.5 | 169.9 |
| 37 | 29.2 | 22.8 | 97 | 76.4 | 59.7 | 57 | 123.7 | 96.7 | 17 | 171.0 | 133.6 | 77 | 218.3 | 170.5 |
| 38 | 29.9 | 23.4 | 98 | 77.2 | 60.3 | 58 | 124.5 | 97.3 | 18 | 171.8 | 134.2 | 78 | 219.1 | 171.2 |
| 39 | 30.7 | 24.0 | 99 | 78.0 | 61.0 | 59 | 125.3 | 97.9 | 19 | 172.6 | 134.8 | 79 | 219.9 | 171.8 |
| 40 | 31.5 | 24.6 | 100 | 78.8 | 61.6 | 60 | 126.1 | 98.5 | 20 | 173.4 | 135.4 | 80 | 220.6 | 172.4 |
| 41 | 32.3 | 25.2 | 101 | 79.6 | 62.2 | 161 | 126.9 | 99.1 | 221 | 174.2 | 136.1 | 281 | 221.4 | 173.0 |
| 42 | 33.1 | 25.9 | 02 | 80.4 | 62.8 | 62 | 127.7 | 99.7 | 22 | 174.9 | 136.7 | 82 | 222.2 | 173.6 |
| 43 | 33.9 | 26.5 | 03 | 81.2 | 63.4 | 63 | 128.4 | 100.4 | 23 | 175.7 | 137.3 | 83 | 223.0 | 174.2 |
| 44 | 34.7 | 27.1 | 04 | 82.0 | 64.0 | 64 | 129.2 | 101.0 | 24 | 176.5 | 137.9 | 84 | 223.8 | 174.8 |
| 45 | 35.5 | 27.7 | 05 | 82.7 | 64.6 | 65 | 130.0 | 101.6 | 25 | 177.3 | 138.5 | 85 | 224.6 | 175.5 |
| 46 | 36.2 | 28.3 | 06 | 83.5 | 65.3 | 66 | 130.8 | 102.2 | 26 | 178.1 | 139.1 | 86 | 225.4 | 176.1 |
| 47 | 37.0 | 28.9 | 07 | 84.3 | 65.9 | 67 | 131.6 | 102.8 | 27 | 178.9 | 139.8 | 87 | 226.2 | 176.7 |
| 48 | 37.8 | 29.6 | 08 | 85.1 | 66.5 | 68 | 132.4 | 103.4 | 28 | 179.7 | 140.4 | 88 | 226.9 | 177.3 |
| 49 | 38.6 | 30.2 | 09 | 85.9 | 67.1 | 69 | 133.2 | 104.0 | 29 | 180.5 | 141.0 | 89 | 227.7 | 177.9 |
| 50 | 39.4 | 30.8 | 10 | 86.7 | 67.7 | 70 | 134.0 | 104.7 | 30 | 181.2 | 141.6 | 90 | 228.5 | 178.5 |
| 51 | 40.2 | 31.4 | 111 | 87.5 | 68.3 | 171 | 134.7 | 105.3 | 231 | 182.0 | 142.2 | 291 | 229.3 | 179.2 |
| 52 | 41.0 | 32.0 | 12 | 88.3 | 69.0 | 72 | 135.5 | 105.9 | 32 | 182.8 | 142.8 | 92 | 230.1 | 179.8 |
| 53 | 41.8 | 32.6 | 13 | 89.0 | 69.6 | 73 | 136.3 | 106.5 | 33 | 183.6 | 143.4 | 93 | 230.9 | 180.4 |
| 54 | 42.6 | 33.2 | 14 | 89.8 | 70.2 | 74 | 137.1 | 107.1 | 34 | 184.4 | 144.1 | 94 | 231.7 | 181.0 |
| 55 | 43.3 | 33.9 | 15 | 90.6 | 70.8 | 75 | 137.9 | 107.7 | 35 | 185.2 | 144.7 | 95 | 232.5 | 181.6 |
| 56 | 44.1 | 34.5 | 16 | 91.4 | 71.4 | 76 | 138.7 | 108.4 | 36 | 186.0 | 145.3 | 96 | 233.3 | 182.2 |
| 57 | 44.9 | 35.1 | 17 | 92.2 | 72.0 | 77 | 139.5 | 109.0 | 37 | 186.8 | 145.9 | 97 | 234.0 | 182.9 |
| 58 | 45.7 | 35.7 | 18 | 93.0 | 72.6 | 78 | 140.3 | 109.6 | 38 | 187.5 | 146.5 | 98 | 234.8 | 183.5 |
| 59 | 46.5 | 36.3 | 19 | 93.8 | 73.3 | 79 | 141.1 | 110.2 | 39 | 188.3 | 147.1 | 99 | 235.6 | 184.1 |
| 60 | 47.3 | 36.9 | 20 | 94.6 | 73.9 | 80 | 141.8 | 110.8 | 40 | 189.1 | 147.8 | 300 | 236.4 | 184.7 |
| Dist. | Dep. | Lat. | Dist. | Dep. | Lat. | Dist. | Dep. | Lat. | Dist. | Dep. | Lat. | Dist. | Dep. | Lat. |

# TABLE II.

## Difference of Latitude and Departure for 39 Degrees.

| Dist. | Lat. | Dep. | Dist. | Lat. | Dep. | Dist. | Lat. | Dep. | Dist. | Lat. | Dep. | Dist. | Lat. | Dep. |
|---|---|---|---|---|---|---|---|---|---|---|---|---|---|---|
| 1 | 00.8 | 00.6 | 61 | 47.4 | 38.4 | 121 | 94.0 | 76.1 | 181 | 140.7 | 113.9 | 241 | 187.3 | 151.7 |
| 2 | 01.6 | 01.3 | 62 | 48.2 | 39.0 | 22 | 94.8 | 76.8 | 82 | 141.4 | 114.5 | 42 | 188.1 | 152.3 |
| 3 | 02.3 | 01.9 | 63 | 49.0 | 39.6 | 23 | 95.6 | 77.4 | 83 | 142.2 | 115.2 | 43 | 188.8 | 152.9 |
| 4 | 03.1 | 02.5 | 64 | 49.7 | 40.3 | 24 | 96.4 | 78.0 | 84 | 143.0 | 115.8 | 44 | 189.6 | 153.6 |
| 5 | 03.9 | 03.1 | 65 | 50.5 | 40.9 | 25 | 97.1 | 78.7 | 85 | 143.8 | 116.4 | 45 | 190.4 | 154.2 |
| 6 | 04.7 | 03.8 | 66 | 51.3 | 41.5 | 26 | 97.9 | 79.3 | 86 | 144.5 | 117.1 | 46 | 191.2 | 154.8 |
| 7 | 05.4 | 04.4 | 67 | 52.1 | 42.2 | 27 | 98.7 | 79.9 | 87 | 145.3 | 117.7 | 47 | 192.0 | 155.4 |
| 8 | 06.2 | 05.0 | 68 | 52.8 | 42.8 | 28 | 99.5 | 80.6 | 88 | 146.1 | 118.3 | 48 | 192.7 | 156.1 |
| 9 | 07.0 | 05.7 | 69 | 53.6 | 43.4 | 29 | 100.3 | 81.2 | 89 | 146.9 | 118.9 | 49 | 193.5 | 156.7 |
| 10 | 07.8 | 06.3 | 70 | 54.4 | 44.1 | 30 | 101.0 | 81.8 | 90 | 147.7 | 119.6 | 50 | 194.3 | 157.3 |
| 11 | 08.5 | 06.9 | 71 | 55.2 | 44.7 | 131 | 101.8 | 82.4 | 191 | 148.4 | 120.2 | 251 | 195.1 | 158.0 |
| 12 | 09.3 | 07.6 | 72 | 56.0 | 45.3 | 32 | 102.6 | 83.1 | 92 | 149.2 | 120.8 | 52 | 195.8 | 158.6 |
| 13 | 10.1 | 08.2 | 73 | 56.7 | 45.9 | 33 | 103.4 | 83.7 | 93 | 150.0 | 121.5 | 53 | 196.6 | 159.2 |
| 14 | 10.9 | 08.8 | 74 | 57.5 | 46.6 | 34 | 104.1 | 84.3 | 94 | 150.8 | 122.1 | 54 | 197.4 | 159.8 |
| 15 | 11.7 | 09.4 | 75 | 58.3 | 47.2 | 35 | 104.9 | 85.0 | 95 | 151.5 | 122.7 | 55 | 198.2 | 160.5 |
| 16 | 12.4 | 10.1 | 76 | 59.1 | 47.8 | 36 | 105.7 | 85.6 | 96 | 152.3 | 123.3 | 56 | 198.9 | 161.1 |
| 17 | 13.2 | 10.7 | 77 | 59.8 | 48.5 | 37 | 106.5 | 86.2 | 97 | 153.1 | 124.0 | 57 | 199.7 | 161.7 |
| 18 | 14.0 | 11.3 | 78 | 60.6 | 49.1 | 38 | 107.2 | 86.8 | 98 | 153.9 | 124.6 | 58 | 200.5 | 162.4 |
| 19 | 14.8 | 12.0 | 79 | 61.4 | 49.7 | 39 | 108.0 | 87.5 | 99 | 154.7 | 125.2 | 59 | 201.3 | 163.0 |
| 20 | 15.5 | 12.6 | 80 | 62.2 | 50.3 | 40 | 108.8 | 88.1 | 200 | 155.4 | 125.9 | 60 | 202.1 | 163.6 |
| 21 | 16.3 | 13.2 | 81 | 62.9 | 51.0 | 141 | 109.6 | 88.7 | 201 | 156.2 | 126.5 | 261 | 202.8 | 164.3 |
| 22 | 17.1 | 13.8 | 82 | 63.7 | 51.6 | 42 | 110.4 | 89.4 | 02 | 157.0 | 127.1 | 62 | 203.6 | 164.9 |
| 23 | 17.9 | 14.5 | 83 | 64.5 | 52.2 | 43 | 111.1 | 90.0 | 03 | 157.8 | 127.8 | 63 | 204.4 | 165.5 |
| 24 | 18.7 | 15.1 | 84 | 65.3 | 52.9 | 44 | 111.9 | 90.6 | 04 | 158.5 | 128.4 | 64 | 205.2 | 166.1 |
| 25 | 19.4 | 15.7 | 85 | 66.1 | 53.5 | 45 | 112.7 | 91.3 | 05 | 159.3 | 129.0 | 65 | 205.9 | 166.8 |
| 26 | 20.2 | 16.4 | 86 | 66.8 | 54.1 | 46 | 113.5 | 91.9 | 06 | 160.1 | 129.6 | 66 | 206.7 | 167.4 |
| 27 | 21.0 | 17.0 | 87 | 67.6 | 54.8 | 47 | 114.2 | 92.5 | 07 | 160.9 | 130.3 | 67 | 207.5 | 168.0 |
| 28 | 21.8 | 17.6 | 88 | 68.4 | 55.4 | 48 | 115.0 | 93.1 | 08 | 161.6 | 130.9 | 68 | 208.3 | 168.7 |
| 29 | 22.5 | 18.3 | 89 | 69.2 | 56.0 | 49 | 115.8 | 93.8 | 09 | 162.4 | 131.5 | 69 | 209.1 | 169.3 |
| 30 | 23.3 | 18.9 | 90 | 69.9 | 56.6 | 50 | 116.6 | 94.4 | 10 | 163.2 | 132.2 | 70 | 209.8 | 169.9 |
| 31 | 24.1 | 19.5 | 91 | 70.7 | 57.3 | 151 | 117.3 | 95.0 | 211 | 164.0 | 132.8 | 271 | 210.6 | 170.5 |
| 32 | 24.9 | 20.1 | 92 | 71.5 | 57.9 | 52 | 118.1 | 95.7 | 12 | 164.8 | 133.4 | 72 | 211.4 | 171.2 |
| 33 | 25.6 | 20.8 | 93 | 72.3 | 58.5 | 53 | 118.9 | 96.3 | 13 | 165.5 | 134.0 | 73 | 212.2 | 171.8 |
| 34 | 26.4 | 21.4 | 94 | 73.1 | 59.2 | 54 | 119.7 | 96.9 | 14 | 166.3 | 134.7 | 74 | 212.9 | 172.4 |
| 35 | 27.2 | 22.0 | 95 | 73.8 | 59.8 | 55 | 120.5 | 97.5 | 15 | 167.1 | 135.3 | 75 | 213.7 | 173.1 |
| 36 | 28.0 | 22.7 | 96 | 74.6 | 60.4 | 56 | 121.2 | 98.2 | 16 | 167.9 | 135.9 | 76 | 214.5 | 173.7 |
| 37 | 28.8 | 23.3 | 97 | 75.4 | 61.0 | 57 | 122.0 | 98.8 | 17 | 168.6 | 136.6 | 77 | 215.3 | 174.3 |
| 38 | 29.5 | 23.9 | 98 | 76.2 | 61.7 | 58 | 122.8 | 99.4 | 18 | 169.4 | 137.2 | 78 | 216.0 | 175.0 |
| 39 | 30.3 | 24.5 | 99 | 76.9 | 62.3 | 59 | 123.6 | 100.1 | 19 | 170.2 | 137.8 | 79 | 216.8 | 175.6 |
| 40 | 31.1 | 25.2 | 100 | 77.7 | 62.9 | 60 | 124.3 | 100.7 | 20 | 171.0 | 138.5 | 80 | 217.6 | 176.2 |
| 41 | 31.9 | 25.8 | 101 | 78.5 | 63.6 | 161 | 125.1 | 101.3 | 221 | 171.7 | 139.1 | 281 | 218.4 | 176.8 |
| 42 | 32.6 | 26.4 | 02 | 79.3 | 64.2 | 62 | 125.9 | 101.9 | 22 | 172.5 | 139.7 | 82 | 219.2 | 177.5 |
| 43 | 33.4 | 27.1 | 03 | 80.0 | 64.8 | 63 | 126.7 | 102.6 | 23 | 173.3 | 140.3 | 83 | 219.9 | 178.1 |
| 44 | 34.2 | 27.7 | 04 | 80.8 | 65.4 | 64 | 127.5 | 103.2 | 24 | 174.1 | 141.0 | 84 | 220.7 | 178.7 |
| 45 | 35.0 | 28.3 | 05 | 81.6 | 66.1 | 65 | 128.2 | 103.8 | 25 | 174.9 | 141.6 | 85 | 221.5 | 179.4 |
| 46 | 35.7 | 28.9 | 06 | 82.4 | 66.7 | 66 | 129.0 | 104.5 | 26 | 175.6 | 142.2 | 86 | 222.3 | 180.0 |
| 47 | 36.5 | 29.6 | 07 | 83.2 | 67.3 | 67 | 129.8 | 105.1 | 27 | 176.4 | 142.9 | 87 | 223.0 | 180.6 |
| 48 | 37.3 | 30.2 | 08 | 83.9 | 68.0 | 68 | 130.6 | 105.7 | 28 | 177.2 | 143.5 | 88 | 223.8 | 181.2 |
| 49 | 38.1 | 30.8 | 09 | 84.7 | 68.6 | 69 | 131.3 | 106.4 | 29 | 178.0 | 144.1 | 89 | 224.6 | 181.9 |
| 50 | 38.9 | 31.5 | 10 | 85.5 | 69.2 | 70 | 132.1 | 107.0 | 30 | 178.7 | 144.7 | 90 | 225.4 | 182.5 |
| 51 | 39.6 | 32.1 | 111 | 86.3 | 69.9 | 171 | 132.9 | 107.6 | 231 | 179.5 | 145.4 | 291 | 226.1 | 183.1 |
| 52 | 40.4 | 32.7 | 12 | 87.0 | 70.5 | 72 | 133.7 | 108.2 | 32 | 180.3 | 146.0 | 92 | 226.9 | 183.8 |
| 53 | 41.2 | 33.4 | 13 | 87.8 | 71.1 | 73 | 134.4 | 108.9 | 33 | 181.1 | 146.6 | 93 | 227.7 | 184.4 |
| 54 | 42.0 | 34.0 | 14 | 88.6 | 71.7 | 74 | 135.2 | 109.5 | 34 | 181.9 | 147.3 | 94 | 228.5 | 185.0 |
| 55 | 42.7 | 34.6 | 15 | 89.4 | 72.4 | 75 | 136.0 | 110.1 | 35 | 182.6 | 147.9 | 95 | 229.3 | 185.6 |
| 56 | 43.5 | 35.2 | 16 | 90.1 | 73.0 | 76 | 136.8 | 110.8 | 36 | 183.4 | 148.5 | 96 | 230.0 | 186.3 |
| 57 | 44.3 | 35.9 | 17 | 90.9 | 73.6 | 77 | 137.6 | 111.4 | 37 | 184.2 | 149.1 | 97 | 230.8 | 186.9 |
| 58 | 45.1 | 36.5 | 18 | 91.7 | 74.3 | 78 | 138.3 | 112.0 | 38 | 185.0 | 149.8 | 98 | 231.6 | 187.5 |
| 59 | 45.9 | 37.1 | 19 | 92.5 | 74.9 | 79 | 139.1 | 112.6 | 39 | 185.7 | 150.4 | 99 | 232.4 | 188.2 |
| 60 | 46.6 | 37.8 | 20 | 93.3 | 75.5 | 80 | 139.9 | 113.3 | 40 | 186.5 | 151.0 | 300 | 233.1 | 188.8 |
| Dist. | Dep. | Lat. | Dist. | Dep. | Lat. | Dist. | Dep. | Lat. | Dist. | Dep. | Lat. | Dist. | Dep. | Lat. |

[For 51 Degrees

# TABLE II.

## Difference of Latitude and Departure for 40 Degrees.

| Dist. | Lat. | Dep. | Dist. | Lat. | Dep. | Dist. | Lat. | Dep. | Dist. | Lat. | Dep. | Dist. | Lat. | Dep. |
|---|---|---|---|---|---|---|---|---|---|---|---|---|---|---|
| 1 | 00.8 | 00.6 | 61 | 46.7 | 39.2 | 121 | 92.7 | 77.8 | 181 | 138.7 | 116.3 | 241 | 184.6 | 154.9 |
| 2 | 01.5 | 01.3 | 62 | 47.5 | 39.9 | 22 | 93.5 | 78.4 | 82 | 139.4 | 117.0 | 42 | 185.4 | 155.6 |
| 3 | 02.3 | 01.9 | 63 | 48.3 | 40.5 | 23 | 94.2 | 79.1 | 83 | 140.2 | 117.6 | 43 | 186.1 | 156.2 |
| 4 | 03.1 | 02.6 | 64 | 49.0 | 41.1 | 24 | 95.0 | 79.7 | 84 | 141.0 | 118.3 | 44 | 186.9 | 156.8 |
| 5 | 03.8 | 03.2 | 65 | 49.8 | 41.8 | 25 | 95.8 | 80.3 | 85 | 141.7 | 118.9 | 45 | 187.7 | 157.5 |
| 6 | 04.6 | 03.9 | 66 | 50.6 | 42.4 | 26 | 96.5 | 81.0 | 86 | 142.5 | 119.6 | 46 | 188.4 | 158.1 |
| 7 | 05.4 | 04.5 | 67 | 51.3 | 43.1 | 27 | 97.3 | 81.6 | 87 | 143.3 | 120.2 | 47 | 189.2 | 158.8 |
| 8 | 06.1 | 05.1 | 68 | 52.1 | 43.7 | 28 | 98.1 | 82.3 | 88 | 144.0 | 120.8 | 48 | 190.0 | 159.4 |
| 9 | 06.9 | 05.8 | 69 | 52.9 | 44.4 | 29 | 98.8 | 82.9 | 89 | 144.8 | 121.5 | 49 | 190.7 | 160.1 |
| 10 | 07.7 | 06.4 | 70 | 53.6 | 45.0 | 30 | 99.6 | 83.6 | 90 | 145.5 | 122.1 | 50 | 191.5 | 160.7 |
| 11 | 08.4 | 07.1 | 71 | 54.4 | 45.6 | 131 | 100.4 | 84.2 | 191 | 146.3 | 122.8 | 251 | 192.3 | 161.3 |
| 12 | 09.2 | 07.7 | 72 | 55.2 | 46.3 | 32 | 101.1 | 84.8 | 92 | 147.1 | 123.4 | 52 | 193.0 | 162.0 |
| 13 | 10.0 | 08.4 | 73 | 55.9 | 46.9 | 33 | 101.9 | 85.5 | 93 | 147.8 | 124.1 | 53 | 193.8 | 162.6 |
| 14 | 10.7 | 09.0 | 74 | 56.7 | 47.6 | 34 | 102.6 | 86.1 | 94 | 148.6 | 124.7 | 54 | 194.6 | 163.3 |
| 15 | 11.5 | 09.6 | 75 | 57.5 | 48.2 | 35 | 103.4 | 86.8 | 95 | 149.4 | 125.3 | 55 | 195.3 | 163.9 |
| 16 | 12.3 | 10.3 | 76 | 58.2 | 48.9 | 36 | 104.2 | 87.4 | 96 | 150.1 | 126.0 | 56 | 196.1 | 164.6 |
| 17 | 13.0 | 10.9 | 77 | 59.0 | 49.5 | 37 | 104.9 | 88.1 | 97 | 150.9 | 126.6 | 57 | 196.9 | 165.2 |
| 18 | 13.8 | 11.6 | 78 | 59.8 | 50.1 | 38 | 105.7 | 88.7 | 98 | 151.7 | 127.3 | 58 | 197.6 | 165.8 |
| 19 | 14.6 | 12.2 | 79 | 60.5 | 50.8 | 39 | 106.5 | 89.3 | 99 | 152.4 | 127.9 | 59 | 198.4 | 166.5 |
| 20 | 15.3 | 12.9 | 80 | 61.3 | 51.4 | 40 | 107.2 | 90.0 | 200 | 153.2 | 128.6 | 60 | 199.2 | 167.1 |
| 21 | 16.1 | 13.5 | 81 | 62.0 | 52.1 | 141 | 108.0 | 90.6 | 201 | 154.0 | 129.2 | 261 | 199.9 | 167.8 |
| 22 | 16.9 | 14.1 | 82 | 62.8 | 52.7 | 42 | 108.8 | 91.3 | 02 | 154.7 | 129.8 | 62 | 200.7 | 168.4 |
| 23 | 17.6 | 14.8 | 83 | 63.6 | 53.4 | 43 | 109.5 | 91.9 | 03 | 155.5 | 130.5 | 63 | 201.5 | 169.1 |
| 24 | 18.4 | 15.4 | 84 | 64.3 | 54.0 | 44 | 110.3 | 92.6 | 04 | 156.3 | 131.1 | 64 | 202.2 | 169.7 |
| 25 | 19.2 | 16.1 | 85 | 65.1 | 54.6 | 45 | 111.1 | 93.2 | 05 | 157.0 | 131.8 | 65 | 203.0 | 170.3 |
| 26 | 19.9 | 16.7 | 86 | 65.9 | 55.3 | 46 | 111.8 | 93.8 | 06 | 157.8 | 132.4 | 66 | 203.8 | 171.0 |
| 27 | 20.7 | 17.4 | 87 | 66.6 | 55.9 | 47 | 112.6 | 94.5 | 07 | 158.6 | 133.1 | 67 | 204.5 | 171.6 |
| 28 | 21.4 | 18.0 | 88 | 67.4 | 56.6 | 48 | 113.4 | 95.1 | 08 | 159.3 | 133.7 | 68 | 205.3 | 172.3 |
| 29 | 22.2 | 18.6 | 89 | 68.2 | 57.2 | 49 | 114.1 | 95.8 | 09 | 160.1 | 134.3 | 69 | 206.1 | 172.9 |
| 30 | 23.0 | 19.3 | 90 | 68.9 | 57.9 | 50 | 114.9 | 96.4 | 10 | 160.9 | 135.0 | 70 | 206.8 | 173.6 |
| 31 | 23.7 | 19.9 | 91 | 69.7 | 58.5 | 151 | 115.7 | 97.1 | 211 | 161.6 | 135.6 | 271 | 207.6 | 174.2 |
| 32 | 24.5 | 20.6 | 92 | 70.5 | 59.1 | 52 | 116.4 | 97.7 | 12 | 162.4 | 136.3 | 72 | 208.4 | 174.8 |
| 33 | 25.3 | 21.2 | 93 | 71.2 | 59.8 | 53 | 117.2 | 98.3 | 13 | 163.2 | 136.9 | 73 | 209.1 | 175.5 |
| 34 | 26.0 | 21.9 | 94 | 72.0 | 60.4 | 54 | 118.0 | 99.0 | 14 | 163.9 | 137.6 | 74 | 209.9 | 176.1 |
| 35 | 26.8 | 22.5 | 95 | 72.8 | 61.1 | 55 | 118.7 | 99.6 | 15 | 164.7 | 138.2 | 75 | 210.7 | 176.8 |
| 36 | 27.6 | 23.1 | 96 | 73.5 | 61.7 | 56 | 119.5 | 100.3 | 16 | 165.5 | 138.8 | 76 | 211.4 | 177.4 |
| 37 | 28.3 | 23.8 | 97 | 74.3 | 62.4 | 57 | 120.3 | 100.9 | 17 | 166.2 | 139.5 | 77 | 212.2 | 178.1 |
| 38 | 29.1 | 24.4 | 98 | 75.1 | 63.0 | 58 | 121.0 | 101.6 | 18 | 167.0 | 140.1 | 78 | 213.0 | 178.7 |
| 39 | 29.9 | 25.1 | 99 | 75.8 | 63.6 | 59 | 121.8 | 102.2 | 19 | 167.8 | 140.8 | 79 | 213.7 | 179.3 |
| 40 | 30.6 | 25.7 | 100 | 76.6 | 64.3 | 60 | 122.6 | 102.8 | 20 | 168.5 | 141.4 | 80 | 214.5 | 180.0 |
| 41 | 31.4 | 26.4 | 101 | 77.4 | 64.9 | 161 | 123.3 | 103.5 | 221 | 169.3 | 142.1 | 281 | 215.3 | 180.6 |
| 42 | 32.2 | 27.0 | 02 | 78.1 | 65.6 | 62 | 124.1 | 104.1 | 22 | 170.1 | 142.7 | 82 | 216.0 | 181.3 |
| 43 | 32.9 | 27.6 | 03 | 78.9 | 66.2 | 63 | 124.9 | 104.8 | 23 | 170.8 | 143.3 | 83 | 216.8 | 181.9 |
| 44 | 33.7 | 28.3 | 04 | 79.7 | 66.8 | 64 | 125.6 | 105.4 | 24 | 171.6 | 144.0 | 84 | 217.6 | 182.6 |
| 45 | 34.5 | 28.9 | 05 | 80.4 | 67.5 | 65 | 126.4 | 106.1 | 25 | 172.4 | 144.6 | 85 | 218.3 | 183.2 |
| 46 | 35.2 | 29.6 | 06 | 81.2 | 68.1 | 66 | 127.2 | 106.7 | 26 | 173.1 | 145.3 | 86 | 219.1 | 183.8 |
| 47 | 36.0 | 30.2 | 07 | 82.0 | 68.8 | 67 | 127.9 | 107.3 | 27 | 173.9 | 145.9 | 87 | 219.9 | 184.5 |
| 48 | 36.8 | 30.9 | 08 | 82.7 | 69.4 | 68 | 128.7 | 108.0 | 28 | 174.7 | 146.6 | 88 | 220.6 | 185.1 |
| 49 | 37.5 | 31.5 | 09 | 83.5 | 70.1 | 69 | 129.5 | 108.6 | 29 | 175.4 | 147.2 | 89 | 221.4 | 185.8 |
| 50 | 38.3 | 32.1 | 10 | 84.3 | 70.7 | 70 | 130.2 | 109.3 | 30 | 176.2 | 147.8 | 90 | 222.2 | 186.4 |
| 51 | 39.1 | 32.8 | 111 | 85.0 | 71.3 | 171 | 131.0 | 109.9 | 231 | 177.0 | 148.5 | 291 | 222.9 | 187.1 |
| 52 | 39.8 | 33.4 | 12 | 85.8 | 72.0 | 72 | 131.8 | 110.6 | 32 | 177.7 | 149.1 | 92 | 223.7 | 187.7 |
| 53 | 40.6 | 34.1 | 13 | 86.6 | 72.6 | 73 | 132.5 | 111.2 | 33 | 178.5 | 149.8 | 93 | 224.5 | 188.3 |
| 54 | 41.4 | 34.7 | 14 | 87.3 | 73.3 | 74 | 133.3 | 111.8 | 34 | 179.3 | 150.4 | 94 | 225.2 | 189.0 |
| 55 | 42.1 | 35.4 | 15 | 88.1 | 73.9 | 75 | 134.1 | 112.5 | 35 | 180.0 | 151.1 | 95 | 226.0 | 189.6 |
| 56 | 42.9 | 36.0 | 16 | 88.9 | 74.6 | 76 | 134.8 | 113.1 | 36 | 180.8 | 151.7 | 96 | 226.7 | 190.3 |
| 57 | 43.7 | 36.6 | 17 | 89.6 | 75.2 | 77 | 135.6 | 113.8 | 37 | 181.6 | 152.3 | 97 | 227.5 | 190.9 |
| 58 | 44.4 | 37.3 | 18 | 90.4 | 75.8 | 78 | 136.4 | 114.4 | 38 | 182.3 | 153.0 | 98 | 228.3 | 191.6 |
| 59 | 45.2 | 37.9 | 19 | 91.2 | 76.5 | 79 | 137.1 | 115.1 | 39 | 183.1 | 153.6 | 99 | 229.0 | 192.2 |
| 60 | 46.0 | 38.6 | 20 | 91.9 | 77.1 | 80 | 137.9 | 115.7 | 40 | 183.9 | 154.3 | 300 | 229.8 | 192.8 |
| Dist. | Dep. | Lat. | Dist. | Dep. | Lat. | Dist. | Dep. | Lat. | Dist. | Dep. | Lat. | Dist. | Dep. | Lat. |

# TABLE II.

## Difference of Latitude and Departure for 41 Degrees

| Dist. | Lat. | Dep. | Dist. | Lat. | Dep. | Dist. | Lat. | Dep. | Dist | Lat. | Dep. | Dist. | Lat. | Dep. |
|---|---|---|---|---|---|---|---|---|---|---|---|---|---|---|
| 1 | 00.8 | 00.7 | 61 | 46.0 | 40.0 | 121 | 91.3 | 79.4 | 181 | 136.6 | 118.7 | 241 | 181.9 | 158.1 |
| 2 | 01.5 | 01.3 | 62 | 46.8 | 40.7 | 22 | 92.1 | 80.0 | 82 | 137.4 | 119.4 | 42 | 182.6 | 158.8 |
| 3 | 02.3 | 02.0 | 63 | 47.5 | 41.3 | 23 | 92.8 | 80.7 | 83 | 138.1 | 120.1 | 43 | 183.4 | 159.4 |
| 4 | 03.0 | 02.6 | 64 | 48.3 | 42.0 | 24 | 93.6 | 81.4 | 84 | 138.9 | 120.7 | 44 | 184.1 | 160.1 |
| 5 | 03.8 | 03.3 | 65 | 49.1 | 42.6 | 25 | 94.3 | 82.0 | 85 | 139.6 | 121.4 | 45 | 184.9 | 160.7 |
| 6 | 04.5 | 03.9 | 66 | 49.8 | 43.3 | 26 | 95.1 | 82.7 | 86 | 140.4 | 122.0 | 46 | 185.7 | 161.4 |
| 7 | 05.3 | 04.6 | 67 | 50.6 | 44.0 | 27 | 95.8 | 83.3 | 87 | 141.1 | 122.7 | 47 | 186.4 | 162.0 |
| 8 | 06.0 | 05.2 | 68 | 51.3 | 44.6 | 28 | 96.6 | 84.0 | 88 | 141.9 | 123.3 | 48 | 187.2 | 162.7 |
| 9 | 06.8 | 05.9 | 69 | 52.1 | 45.3 | 29 | 97.4 | 84.6 | 89 | 142.6 | 124.0 | 49 | 187.9 | 163.4 |
| 10 | 07.5 | 06.6 | 70 | 52.8 | 45.9 | 30 | 98.1 | 85.3 | 90 | 143.4 | 124.7 | 50 | 188.7 | 164.0 |
| 11 | 08.3 | 07.2 | 71 | 53.6 | 46.6 | 131 | 98.9 | 85.9 | 191 | 144.1 | 125.3 | 251 | 189.4 | 164.7 |
| 12 | 09.1 | 07.9 | 72 | 54.3 | 47.2 | 32 | 99.6 | 86.6 | 92 | 144.9 | 126.0 | 52 | 190.2 | 165.3 |
| 13 | 09.8 | 08.5 | 73 | 55.1 | 47.9 | 33 | 100.4 | 87.3 | 93 | 145.7 | 126.6 | 53 | 190.9 | 166.0 |
| 14 | 10.6 | 09.2 | 74 | 55.8 | 48.5 | 34 | 101.1 | 87.9 | 94 | 146.4 | 127.3 | 54 | 191.7 | 166.6 |
| 15 | 11.3 | 09.8 | 75 | 56.6 | 49.2 | 35 | 101.9 | 88.6 | 95 | 147.2 | 127.9 | 55 | 192.5 | 167.3 |
| 16 | 12.1 | 10.5 | 76 | 57.4 | 49.9 | 36 | 102.6 | 89.2 | 96 | 147.9 | 128.6 | 56 | 193.2 | 168.0 |
| 17 | 12.8 | 11.2 | 77 | 58.1 | 50.5 | 37 | 103.4 | 89.9 | 97 | 148.7 | 129.2 | 57 | 194.0 | 168.6 |
| 18 | 13.6 | 11.8 | 78 | 58.9 | 51.2 | 38 | 104.1 | 90.5 | 98 | 149.4 | 129.9 | 58 | 194.7 | 169.3 |
| 19 | 14.3 | 12.5 | 79 | 59.6 | 51.8 | 39 | 104.9 | 91.2 | 99 | 150.2 | 130.6 | 59 | 195.5 | 169.9 |
| 20 | 15.1 | 13.1 | 80 | 60.4 | 52.5 | 40 | 105.7 | 91.8 | 200 | 150.9 | 131.2 | 60 | 196.2 | 170.6 |
| 21 | 15.8 | 13.8 | 81 | 61.1 | 53.1 | 141 | 106.4 | 92.5 | 201 | 151.7 | 131.9 | 261 | 197.0 | 171.2 |
| 22 | 16.6 | 14.4 | 82 | 61.9 | 53.8 | 42 | 107.2 | 93.2 | 02 | 152.5 | 132.5 | 62 | 197.7 | 171.9 |
| 23 | 17.4 | 15.1 | 83 | 62.6 | 54.5 | 43 | 107.9 | 93.8 | 03 | 153.2 | 133.2 | 63 | 198.5 | 172.5 |
| 24 | 18.1 | 15.7 | 84 | 63.4 | 55.1 | 44 | 108.7 | 94.5 | 04 | 154.0 | 133.8 | 64 | 199.2 | 173.2 |
| 25 | 18.9 | 16.4 | 85 | 64.2 | 55.8 | 45 | 109.4 | 95.1 | 05 | 154.7 | 134.5 | 65 | 200.0 | 173.9 |
| 26 | 19.6 | 17.1 | 86 | 64.9 | 56.4 | 46 | 110.2 | 95.8 | 06 | 155.5 | 135.1 | 66 | 200.8 | 174.5 |
| 27 | 20.4 | 17.7 | 87 | 65.7 | 57.1 | 47 | 110.9 | 96.4 | 07 | 156.2 | 135.8 | 67 | 201.5 | 175.2 |
| 28 | 21.1 | 18.4 | 88 | 66.4 | 57.7 | 48 | 111.7 | 97.1 | 08 | 157.0 | 136.5 | 68 | 202.3 | 175.8 |
| 29 | 21.9 | 19.0 | 89 | 67.2 | 58.4 | 49 | 112.5 | 97.8 | 09 | 157.7 | 137.1 | 69 | 203.0 | 176.5 |
| 30 | 22.6 | 19.7 | 90 | 67.9 | 59.0 | 50 | 113.2 | 98.4 | 10 | 158.5 | 137.8 | 70 | 203.8 | 177.1 |
| 31 | 23.4 | 20.3 | 91 | 68.7 | 59.7 | 151 | 114.0 | 99.1 | 211 | 159.2 | 138.4 | 271 | 204.5 | 177.8 |
| 32 | 24.2 | 21.0 | 92 | 69.4 | 60.4 | 52 | 114.7 | 99.7 | 12 | 160.0 | 139.1 | 72 | 205.3 | 178.4 |
| 33 | 24.9 | 21.6 | 93 | 70.2 | 61.0 | 53 | 115.5 | 100.4 | 13 | 160.8 | 139.7 | 73 | 206.0 | 179.1 |
| 34 | 25.7 | 22.3 | 94 | 70.9 | 61.7 | 54 | 116.2 | 101.0 | 14 | 161.5 | 140.4 | 74 | 206.8 | 179.8 |
| 35 | 26.4 | 23.0 | 95 | 71.7 | 62.3 | 55 | 117.0 | 101.7 | 15 | 162.3 | 141.1 | 75 | 207.5 | 180.4 |
| 36 | 27.2 | 23.6 | 96 | 72.5 | 63.0 | 56 | 117.7 | 102.3 | 16 | 163.0 | 141.7 | 76 | 208.3 | 181.1 |
| 37 | 27.9 | 24.3 | 97 | 73.2 | 63.6 | 57 | 118.5 | 103.0 | 17 | 163.8 | 142.4 | 77 | 209.1 | 181.7 |
| 38 | 28.7 | 24.9 | 98 | 74.0 | 64.3 | 58 | 119.2 | 103.7 | 18 | 164.5 | 143.0 | 78 | 209.8 | 182.4 |
| 39 | 29.4 | 25.6 | 99 | 74.7 | 64.9 | 59 | 120.0 | 104.3 | 19 | 165.3 | 143.7 | 79 | 210.6 | 183.0 |
| 40 | 30.2 | 26.2 | 100 | 75.5 | 65.6 | 60 | 120.8 | 105.0 | 20 | 166.0 | 144.3 | 80 | 211.3 | 183.7 |
| 41 | 30.9 | 26.9 | 101 | 76.2 | 66.3 | 161 | 121.5 | 105.6 | 221 | 166.8 | 145.0 | 281 | 212.1 | 184.4 |
| 42 | 31.7 | 27.6 | 02 | 77.0 | 66.9 | 62 | 122.3 | 106.3 | 22 | 167.5 | 145.6 | 82 | 212.8 | 185.0 |
| 43 | 32.5 | 28.2 | 03 | 77.7 | 67.6 | 63 | 123.0 | 106.9 | 23 | 168.3 | 146.3 | 83 | 213.6 | 185.7 |
| 44 | 33.2 | 28.9 | 04 | 78.5 | 68.2 | 64 | 123.8 | 107.6 | 24 | 169.1 | 147.0 | 84 | 214.3 | 186.3 |
| 45 | 34.0 | 29.5 | 05 | 79.2 | 68.9 | 65 | 124.5 | 108.2 | 25 | 169.8 | 147.6 | 85 | 215.1 | 187.0 |
| 46 | 34.7 | 30.2 | 06 | 80.0 | 69.5 | 66 | 125.3 | 108.9 | 26 | 170.6 | 148.3 | 86 | 215.8 | 187.6 |
| 47 | 35.5 | 30.8 | 07 | 80.8 | 70.2 | 67 | 126.0 | 109.6 | 27 | 171.3 | 148.9 | 87 | 216.6 | 188.3 |
| 48 | 36.2 | 31.5 | 08 | 81.5 | 70.9 | 68 | 126.8 | 110.2 | 28 | 172.1 | 149.6 | 88 | 217.4 | 188.9 |
| 49 | 37.0 | 32.1 | 09 | 82.3 | 71.5 | 69 | 127.5 | 110.9 | 29 | 172.8 | 150.2 | 89 | 218.1 | 189.6 |
| 50 | 37.7 | 32.8 | 10 | 83.0 | 72.2 | 70 | 128.3 | 111.5 | 30 | 173.6 | 150.9 | 90 | 218.9 | 190.3 |
| 51 | 38.5 | 33.5 | 111 | 83.8 | 72.8 | 171 | 129.1 | 112.2 | 231 | 174.3 | 151.5 | 291 | 219.6 | 190.9 |
| 52 | 39.2 | 34.1 | 12 | 84.5 | 73.5 | 72 | 129.8 | 112.8 | 32 | 175.1 | 152.2 | 92 | 220.4 | 191.6 |
| 53 | 40.0 | 34.8 | 13 | 85.3 | 74.1 | 73 | 130.6 | 113.5 | 33 | 175.8 | 152.9 | 93 | 221.1 | 192.2 |
| 54 | 40.8 | 35.4 | 14 | 86.0 | 74.8 | 74 | 131.3 | 114.2 | 34 | 176.6 | 153.5 | 94 | 221.9 | 192.9 |
| 55 | 41.5 | 36.1 | 15 | 86.8 | 75.4 | 75 | 132.1 | 114.8 | 35 | 177.4 | 154.2 | 95 | 222.6 | 193.5 |
| 56 | 42.3 | 36.7 | 16 | 87.5 | 76.1 | 76 | 132.8 | 115.5 | 36 | 178.1 | 154.8 | 96 | 223.4 | 194.2 |
| 57 | 43.0 | 37.4 | 17 | 88.3 | 76.8 | 77 | 133.6 | 116.1 | 37 | 178.9 | 155.5 | 97 | 224.1 | 194.8 |
| 58 | 43.8 | 38.1 | 18 | 89.1 | 77.4 | 78 | 134.3 | 116.8 | 38 | 179.6 | 156.1 | 98 | 224.9 | 195.5 |
| 59 | 44.5 | 38.7 | 19 | 89.8 | 78.1 | 79 | 135.1 | 117.4 | 39 | 180.4 | 156.8 | 99 | 225.7 | 196.2 |
| 60 | 45.3 | 39.4 | 20 | 90.6 | 78.7 | 80 | 135.8 | 118.1 | 40 | 181.1 | 157.5 | 300 | 226.4 | 196.8 |
| Dist. | Dep. | Lat. | Dist. | Dep. | Lat. | Dist. | Dep. | Lat. | Dist. | Dep. | Lat. | Dist. | Dep. | Lat. |

[For 49 Degrees.

# TABLE II.

## Difference of Latitude and Departure for 42 Degrees.

| Dist. | Lat. | Dep. | Dist. | Lat. | Dep. | Dist. | Lat. | Dep. | Dist. | Lat. | Dep. | Dist. | Lat. | Dep. |
|---|---|---|---|---|---|---|---|---|---|---|---|---|---|---|
| 1 | 00.7 | 00.7 | 61 | 45.3 | 40.8 | 121 | 89.9 | 81.0 | 181 | 134.5 | 121.1 | 241 | 179.1 | 161.3 |
| 2 | 01.5 | 01.3 | 62 | 46.1 | 41.5 | 22 | 90.7 | 81.6 | 82 | 135.3 | 121.8 | 42 | 179.8 | 161.9 |
| 3 | 02.2 | 02.0 | 63 | 46.8 | 42.2 | 23 | 91.4 | 82.3 | 83 | 136.0 | 122.5 | 43 | 180.6 | 162.6 |
| 4 | 03.0 | 02.7 | 64 | 47.6 | 42.8 | 24 | 92.1 | 83.0 | 84 | 136.7 | 123.1 | 44 | 181.3 | 163.3 |
| 5 | 03.7 | 03.3 | 65 | 48.3 | 43.5 | 25 | 92.9 | 83.6 | 85 | 137.5 | 123.8 | 45 | 182.1 | 163.9 |
| 6 | 04.5 | 04.0 | 66 | 49.0 | 44.2 | 26 | 93.6 | 84.3 | 86 | 138.2 | 124.5 | 46 | 182.8 | 164.6 |
| 7 | 05.2 | 04.7 | 67 | 49.8 | 44.8 | 27 | 94.4 | 85.0 | 87 | 139.0 | 125.1 | 47 | 183.6 | 165.3 |
| 8 | 05.9 | 05.4 | 68 | 50.5 | 45.5 | 28 | 95.1 | 85.6 | 88 | 139.7 | 125.8 | 48 | 184.3 | 165.9 |
| 9 | 06.7 | 06.0 | 69 | 51.3 | 46.2 | 29 | 95.9 | 86.3 | 89 | 140.5 | 126.5 | 49 | 185.0 | 166.6 |
| 10 | 07.4 | 06.7 | 70 | 52.0 | 46.8 | 30 | 96.6 | 87.0 | 90 | 141.2 | 127.1 | 50 | 185.8 | 167.3 |
| 11 | 08.2 | 07.4 | 71 | 52.8 | 47.5 | 131 | 97.4 | 87.7 | 191 | 141.9 | 127.8 | 251 | 186.5 | 168.0 |
| 12 | 08.9 | 08.0 | 72 | 53.5 | 48.2 | 32 | 98.1 | 88.3 | 92 | 142.7 | 128.5 | 52 | 187.3 | 168.6 |
| 13 | 09.7 | 08.7 | 73 | 54.2 | 48.8 | 33 | 98.8 | 89.0 | 93 | 143.4 | 129.1 | 53 | 188.0 | 169.3 |
| 14 | 10.4 | 09.4 | 74 | 55.0 | 49.5 | 34 | 99.6 | 89.7 | 94 | 144.2 | 129.8 | 54 | 188.8 | 170.0 |
| 15 | 11.1 | 10.0 | 75 | 55.7 | 50.2 | 35 | 100.3 | 90.3 | 95 | 144.9 | 130.5 | 55 | 189.5 | 170.6 |
| 16 | 11.9 | 10.7 | 76 | 56.5 | 50.9 | 36 | 101.1 | 91.0 | 96 | 145.7 | 131.1 | 56 | 190.2 | 171.3 |
| 17 | 12.6 | 11.4 | 77 | 57.2 | 51.5 | 37 | 101.8 | 91.7 | 97 | 146.4 | 131.8 | 57 | 191.0 | 172.0 |
| 18 | 13.4 | 12.0 | 78 | 58.0 | 52.2 | 38 | 102.6 | 92.3 | 98 | 147.1 | 132.5 | 58 | 191.7 | 172.6 |
| 19 | 14.1 | 12.7 | 79 | 58.7 | 52.9 | 39 | 103.3 | 93.0 | 99 | 147.9 | 133.2 | 59 | 192.5 | 173.3 |
| 20 | 14.9 | 13.4 | 80 | 59.5 | 53.5 | 40 | 104.0 | 93.7 | 200 | 148.6 | 133.8 | 60 | 193.2 | 174.0 |
| 21 | 15.6 | 14.1 | 81 | 60.2 | 54.2 | 141 | 104.8 | 94.3 | 201 | 149.4 | 134.5 | 261 | 194.0 | 174.6 |
| 22 | 16.3 | 14.7 | 82 | 60.9 | 54.9 | 42 | 105.5 | 95.0 | 02 | 150.1 | 135.2 | 62 | 194.7 | 175.3 |
| 23 | 17.1 | 15.4 | 83 | 61.7 | 55.5 | 43 | 106.3 | 95.7 | 03 | 150.9 | 135.8 | 63 | 195.4 | 176.0 |
| 24 | 17.8 | 16.1 | 84 | 62.4 | 56.2 | 44 | 107.0 | 96.4 | 04 | 151.6 | 136.5 | 64 | 196.2 | 176.7 |
| 25 | 18.6 | 16.7 | 85 | 63.2 | 56.9 | 45 | 107.8 | 97.0 | 05 | 152.3 | 137.2 | 65 | 196.9 | 177.3 |
| 26 | 19.3 | 17.4 | 86 | 63.9 | 57.5 | 46 | 108.5 | 97.7 | 06 | 153.1 | 137.8 | 66 | 197.7 | 178.0 |
| 27 | 20.1 | 18.1 | 87 | 64.7 | 58.2 | 47 | 109.2 | 98.4 | 07 | 153.8 | 138.5 | 67 | 198.4 | 178.7 |
| 28 | 20.8 | 18.7 | 88 | 65.4 | 58.9 | 48 | 110.0 | 99.0 | 08 | 154.6 | 139.2 | 68 | 199.2 | 179.3 |
| 29 | 21.6 | 19.4 | 89 | 66.1 | 59.6 | 49 | 110.7 | 99.7 | 09 | 155.3 | 139.8 | 69 | 199.9 | 180.0 |
| 30 | 22.3 | 20.1 | 90 | 66.9 | 60.2 | 50 | 111.5 | 100.4 | 10 | 156.1 | 140.5 | 70 | 200.6 | 180.7 |
| 31 | 23.0 | 20.7 | 91 | 67.6 | 60.9 | 151 | 112.2 | 101.0 | 211 | 156.8 | 141.2 | 271 | 201.4 | 181.3 |
| 32 | 23.8 | 21.4 | 92 | 68.4 | 61.6 | 52 | 113.0 | 101.7 | 12 | 157.5 | 141.9 | 72 | 202.1 | 182.0 |
| 33 | 24.5 | 22.1 | 93 | 69.1 | 62.2 | 53 | 113.7 | 102.4 | 13 | 158.3 | 142.5 | 73 | 202.9 | 182.7 |
| 34 | 25.3 | 22.8 | 94 | 69.9 | 62.9 | 54 | 114.4 | 103.0 | 14 | 159.0 | 143.2 | 74 | 203.6 | 183.3 |
| 35 | 26.0 | 23.4 | 95 | 70.6 | 63.6 | 55 | 115.2 | 103.7 | 15 | 159.8 | 143.9 | 75 | 204.4 | 184.0 |
| 36 | 26.8 | 24.1 | 96 | 71.3 | 64.2 | 56 | 115.9 | 104.4 | 16 | 160.5 | 144.5 | 76 | 205.1 | 184.7 |
| 37 | 27.5 | 24.8 | 97 | 72.1 | 64.9 | 57 | 116.7 | 105.1 | 17 | 161.3 | 145.2 | 77 | 205.9 | 185.3 |
| 38 | 28.2 | 25.4 | 98 | 72.8 | 65.6 | 58 | 117.4 | 105.7 | 18 | 162.0 | 145.9 | 78 | 206.6 | 186.0 |
| 39 | 29.0 | 26.1 | 99 | 73.6 | 66.2 | 59 | 118.2 | 106.4 | 19 | 162.7 | 146.5 | 79 | 207.3 | 186.7 |
| 40 | 29.7 | 26.8 | 100 | 74.3 | 66.9 | 60 | 118.9 | 107.1 | 20 | 163.5 | 147.2 | 80 | 208.1 | 187.4 |
| 41 | 30.5 | 27.4 | 101 | 75.1 | 67.6 | 161 | 119.6 | 107.7 | 221 | 164.2 | 147.9 | 281 | 208.8 | 188.0 |
| 42 | 31.2 | 28.1 | 02 | 75.8 | 68.3 | 62 | 120.4 | 108.4 | 22 | 165.0 | 148.5 | 82 | 209.6 | 188.7 |
| 43 | 32.0 | 28.8 | 03 | 76.5 | 68.9 | 63 | 121.1 | 109.1 | 23 | 165.7 | 149.2 | 83 | 210.3 | 189.4 |
| 44 | 32.7 | 29.4 | 04 | 77.3 | 69.6 | 64 | 121.9 | 109.7 | 24 | 166.5 | 149.9 | 84 | 211.1 | 190.0 |
| 45 | 33.4 | 30.1 | 05 | 78.0 | 70.3 | 65 | 122.6 | 110.4 | 25 | 167.2 | 150.6 | 85 | 211.8 | 190.7 |
| 46 | 34.2 | 30.8 | 06 | 78.8 | 70.9 | 66 | 123.4 | 111.1 | 26 | 168.0 | 151.2 | 86 | 212.5 | 191.4 |
| 47 | 34.9 | 31.4 | 07 | 79.5 | 71.6 | 67 | 124.1 | 111.7 | 27 | 168.7 | 151.9 | 87 | 213.3 | 192.0 |
| 48 | 35.7 | 32.1 | 08 | 80.3 | 72.3 | 68 | 124.8 | 112.4 | 28 | 169.4 | 152.6 | 88 | 214.0 | 192.7 |
| 49 | 36.4 | 32.8 | 09 | 81.0 | 72.9 | 69 | 125.6 | 113.1 | 29 | 170.2 | 153.2 | 89 | 214.8 | 193.4 |
| 50 | 37.2 | 33.5 | 10 | 81.7 | 73.6 | 70 | 126.3 | 113.8 | 30 | 170.9 | 153.9 | 90 | 215.5 | 194.0 |
| 51 | 37.9 | 34.1 | 111 | 82.5 | 74.3 | 171 | 127.1 | 114.4 | 231 | 171.7 | 154.6 | 291 | 216.3 | 194.7 |
| 52 | 38.6 | 34.8 | 12 | 83.2 | 74.9 | 72 | 127.8 | 115.1 | 32 | 172.4 | 155.2 | 92 | 217.0 | 195.4 |
| 53 | 39.4 | 35.5 | 13 | 84.0 | 75.6 | 73 | 128.6 | 115.8 | 33 | 173.2 | 155.9 | 93 | 217.7 | 196.1 |
| 54 | 40.1 | 36.1 | 14 | 84.7 | 76.3 | 74 | 129.3 | 116.4 | 34 | 173.9 | 156.6 | 94 | 218.5 | 196.7 |
| 55 | 40.9 | 36.8 | 15 | 85.5 | 77.0 | 75 | 130.1 | 117.1 | 35 | 174.6 | 157.2 | 95 | 219.2 | 197.4 |
| 56 | 41.6 | 37.5 | 16 | 86.2 | 77.6 | 76 | 130.8 | 117.8 | 36 | 175.4 | 157.9 | 96 | 220.0 | 198.1 |
| 57 | 42.4 | 38.1 | 17 | 86.9 | 78.3 | 77 | 131.5 | 118.4 | 37 | 176.1 | 158.6 | 97 | 220.7 | 198.7 |
| 58 | 43.1 | 38.8 | 18 | 87.7 | 79.0 | 78 | 132.3 | 119.1 | 38 | 176.9 | 159.3 | 98 | 221.5 | 199.4 |
| 59 | 43.8 | 39.5 | 19 | 88.4 | 79.6 | 79 | 133.0 | 119.8 | 39 | 177.6 | 159.9 | 99 | 222.2 | 200.1 |
| 60 | 44.6 | 40.1 | 20 | 89.2 | 80.3 | 80 | 133.8 | 120.4 | 40 | 178.4 | 160.6 | 300 | 222.9 | 200.7 |
| Dist. | Dep. | Lat. | Dist. | Dep. | Lat. | Dist. | Dep. | Lat. | Dist. | Dep. | Lat. | Dist. | Dep. | Lat. |

[For 48 Degrees.

# TABLE II.

## Difference of Latitude and Departure for 43 Degrees.

| Dist. | Lat. | Dep. | Dist. | Lat. | Dep. | Dist. | Lat. | Dep. | Dist. | Lat. | Dep. | Dist. | Lat. | Dep. |
|---|---|---|---|---|---|---|---|---|---|---|---|---|---|---|
| 1 | 00.7 | 00.7 | 61 | 44.6 | 41.6 | 121 | 88.5 | 82.5 | 181 | 132.4 | 123.4 | 241 | 176.3 | 164.4 |
| 2 | 01.5 | 01.4 | 62 | 45.3 | 42.3 | 22 | 89.2 | 83.2 | 82 | 133.1 | 124.1 | 42 | 177.0 | 165.0 |
| 3 | 02.2 | 02.0 | 63 | 46.1 | 43.0 | 23 | 90.0 | 83.9 | 83 | 133.8 | 124.8 | 43 | 177.7 | 165.7 |
| 4 | 02.9 | 02.7 | 64 | 46.8 | 43.6 | 24 | 90.7 | 84.6 | 84 | 134.6 | 125.5 | 44 | 178.5 | 166.4 |
| 5 | 03.7 | 03.4 | 65 | 47.5 | 44.3 | 25 | 91.4 | 85.2 | 85 | 135.3 | 126.2 | 45 | 179.2 | 167.1 |
| 6 | 04.4 | 04.1 | 66 | 48.3 | 45.0 | 26 | 92.2 | 85.9 | 86 | 136.0 | 126.9 | 46 | 179.9 | 167.8 |
| 7 | 05.1 | 04.8 | 67 | 49.0 | 45.7 | 27 | 92.9 | 86.6 | 87 | 136.8 | 127.5 | 47 | 180.6 | 168.5 |
| 8 | 05.9 | 05.5 | 68 | 49.7 | 46.4 | 28 | 93.6 | 87.3 | 88 | 137.5 | 128.2 | 48 | 181.4 | 169.1 |
| 9 | 06.6 | 06.1 | 69 | 50.5 | 47.1 | 29 | 94.3 | 88.0 | 89 | 138.2 | 128.9 | 49 | 182.1 | 169.8 |
| 10 | 07.3 | 06.8 | 70 | 51.2 | 47.7 | 30 | 95.1 | 88.7 | 90 | 139.0 | 129.6 | 50 | 182.8 | 170.5 |
| 11 | 08.0 | 07.5 | 71 | 51.9 | 48.4 | 131 | 95.8 | 89.3 | 191 | 139.7 | 130.3 | 251 | 183.6 | 171.2 |
| 12 | 08.8 | 08.2 | 72 | 52.7 | 49.1 | 32 | 96.5 | 90.0 | 92 | 140.4 | 130.9 | 52 | 184.3 | 171.9 |
| 13 | 09.5 | 08.9 | 73 | 53.4 | 49.8 | 33 | 97.3 | 90.7 | 93 | 141.2 | 131.6 | 53 | 185.0 | 172.5 |
| 14 | 10.2 | 09.5 | 74 | 54.1 | 50.5 | 34 | 98.0 | 91.4 | 94 | 141.9 | 132.3 | 54 | 185.8 | 173.2 |
| 15 | 11.0 | 10.2 | 75 | 54.9 | 51.1 | 35 | 98.7 | 92.1 | 95 | 142.6 | 133.0 | 55 | 186.5 | 173.9 |
| 16 | 11.7 | 10.9 | 76 | 55.6 | 51.8 | 36 | 99.5 | 92.8 | 96 | 143.3 | 133.7 | 56 | 187.2 | 174.6 |
| 17 | 12.4 | 11.6 | 77 | 56.3 | 52.5 | 37 | 100.2 | 93.4 | 97 | 144.1 | 134.4 | 57 | 188.0 | 175.3 |
| 18 | 13.2 | 12.3 | 78 | 57.0 | 53.2 | 38 | 100.9 | 94.1 | 98 | 144.8 | 135.0 | 58 | 188.7 | 176.0 |
| 19 | 13.9 | 13.0 | 79 | 57.8 | 53.9 | 39 | 101.7 | 94.8 | 99 | 145.5 | 135.7 | 59 | 189.4 | 176.6 |
| 20 | 14.6 | 13.6 | 80 | 58.5 | 54.6 | 40 | 102.4 | 95.5 | 200 | 146.3 | 136.4 | 60 | 190.2 | 177.3 |
| 21 | 15.4 | 14.3 | 81 | 59.2 | 55.2 | 141 | 103.1 | 96.2 | 201 | 147.0 | 137.1 | 261 | 190.9 | 178.0 |
| 22 | 16.1 | 15.0 | 82 | 60.0 | 55.9 | 42 | 103.9 | 96.8 | 02 | 147.7 | 137.8 | 62 | 191.6 | 178.7 |
| 23 | 16.8 | 15.7 | 83 | 60.7 | 56.6 | 43 | 104.6 | 97.5 | 03 | 148.5 | 138.4 | 63 | 192.3 | 179.4 |
| 24 | 17.6 | 16.4 | 84 | 61.4 | 57.3 | 44 | 105.3 | 98.2 | 04 | 149.2 | 139.1 | 64 | 193.1 | 180.0 |
| 25 | 18.3 | 17.0 | 85 | 62.2 | 58.0 | 45 | 106.0 | 98.9 | 05 | 149.9 | 139.8 | 65 | 193.8 | 180.7 |
| 26 | 19.0 | 17.7 | 86 | 62.9 | 58.7 | 46 | 106.8 | 99.6 | 06 | 150.7 | 140.5 | 66 | 194.5 | 181.4 |
| 27 | 19.7 | 18.4 | 87 | 63.6 | 59.3 | 47 | 107.5 | 100.3 | 07 | 151.4 | 141.2 | 67 | 195.3 | 182.1 |
| 28 | 20.5 | 19.1 | 88 | 64.4 | 60.0 | 48 | 108.2 | 100.9 | 08 | 152.1 | 141.9 | 68 | 196.0 | 182.8 |
| 29 | 21.2 | 19.8 | 89 | 65.1 | 60.7 | 49 | 109.0 | 101.6 | 09 | 152.9 | 142.5 | 69 | 196.7 | 183.5 |
| 30 | 21.9 | 20.5 | 90 | 65.8 | 61.4 | 50 | 109.7 | 102.3 | 10 | 153.6 | 143.2 | 70 | 197.5 | 184.1 |
| 31 | 22.7 | 21.1 | 91 | 66.6 | 62.1 | 151 | 110.4 | 103.0 | 211 | 154.3 | 143.9 | 271 | 198.2 | 184.8 |
| 32 | 23.4 | 21.8 | 92 | 67.3 | 62.7 | 52 | 111.2 | 103.7 | 12 | 155.0 | 144.6 | 72 | 198.9 | 185.5 |
| 33 | 24.1 | 22.5 | 93 | 68.0 | 63.4 | 53 | 111.9 | 104.3 | 13 | 155.8 | 145.3 | 73 | 199.7 | 186.2 |
| 34 | 24.9 | 23.2 | 94 | 68.7 | 64.1 | 54 | 112.6 | 105.0 | 14 | 156.5 | 145.9 | 74 | 200.4 | 186.9 |
| 35 | 25.6 | 23.9 | 95 | 69.5 | 64.8 | 55 | 113.4 | 105.7 | 15 | 157.2 | 146.6 | 75 | 201.1 | 187.5 |
| 36 | 26.3 | 24.6 | 96 | 70.2 | 65.5 | 56 | 114.1 | 106.4 | 16 | 158.0 | 147.3 | 76 | 201.9 | 188.2 |
| 37 | 27.1 | 25.2 | 97 | 70.9 | 66.2 | 57 | 114.8 | 107.1 | 17 | 158.7 | 148.0 | 77 | 202.6 | 188.9 |
| 38 | 27.8 | 25.9 | 98 | 71.7 | 66.8 | 58 | 115.6 | 107.8 | 18 | 159.4 | 148.7 | 78 | 203.3 | 189.6 |
| 39 | 28.5 | 26.6 | 99 | 72.4 | 67.5 | 59 | 116.3 | 108.4 | 19 | 160.2 | 149.4 | 79 | 204.0 | 190.3 |
| 40 | 29.3 | 27.3 | 100 | 73.1 | 68.2 | 60 | 117.0 | 109.1 | 20 | 160.9 | 150.0 | 80 | 204.8 | 191.0 |
| 41 | 30.0 | 28.0 | 101 | 73.9 | 68.9 | 161 | 117.7 | 109.8 | 221 | 161.6 | 150.7 | 281 | 205.5 | 191.6 |
| 42 | 30.7 | 28.6 | 02 | 74.6 | 69.6 | 62 | 118.5 | 110.5 | 22 | 162.4 | 151.4 | 82 | 206.2 | 192.3 |
| 43 | 31.4 | 29.3 | 03 | 75.3 | 70.2 | 63 | 119.2 | 111.2 | 23 | 163.1 | 152.1 | 83 | 207.0 | 193.0 |
| 44 | 32.2 | 30.0 | 04 | 76.1 | 70.9 | 64 | 119.9 | 111.8 | 24 | 163.8 | 152.8 | 84 | 207.7 | 193.7 |
| 45 | 32.9 | 30.7 | 05 | 76.8 | 71.6 | 65 | 120.7 | 112.5 | 25 | 164.6 | 153.4 | 85 | 208.4 | 194.4 |
| 46 | 33.6 | 31.4 | 06 | 77.5 | 72.3 | 66 | 121.4 | 113.2 | 26 | 165.3 | 154.1 | 86 | 209.2 | 195.1 |
| 47 | 34.4 | 32.1 | 07 | 78.3 | 73.0 | 67 | 122.1 | 113.9 | 27 | 166.0 | 154.8 | 87 | 209.9 | 195.7 |
| 48 | 35.1 | 32.7 | 08 | 79.0 | 73.7 | 68 | 122.9 | 114.6 | 28 | 166.7 | 155.5 | 88 | 210.6 | 196.4 |
| 49 | 35.8 | 33.4 | 09 | 79.7 | 74.3 | 69 | 123.6 | 115.3 | 29 | 167.5 | 156.2 | 89 | 211.4 | 197.1 |
| 50 | 36.6 | 34.1 | 10 | 80.4 | 75.0 | 70 | 124.3 | 115.9 | 30 | 168.2 | 156.9 | 90 | 212.1 | 197.8 |
| 51 | 37.3 | 34.8 | 111 | 81.2 | 75.7 | 171 | 125.1 | 116.6 | 231 | 168.9 | 157.5 | 291 | 212.8 | 198.5 |
| 52 | 38.0 | 35.5 | 12 | 81.9 | 76.4 | 72 | 125.8 | 117.3 | 32 | 169.7 | 158.2 | 92 | 213.6 | 199.1 |
| 53 | 38.8 | 36.1 | 13 | 82.6 | 77.1 | 73 | 126.5 | 118.0 | 33 | 170.4 | 158.9 | 93 | 214.3 | 199.8 |
| 54 | 39.5 | 36.8 | 14 | 83.4 | 77.7 | 74 | 127.3 | 118.7 | 34 | 171.1 | 159.6 | 94 | 215.0 | 200.5 |
| 55 | 40.2 | 37.5 | 15 | 84.1 | 78.4 | 75 | 128.0 | 119.3 | 35 | 171.9 | 160.3 | 95 | 215.7 | 201.2 |
| 56 | 41.0 | 38.2 | 16 | 84.8 | 79.1 | 76 | 128.7 | 120.0 | 36 | 172.6 | 161.0 | 96 | 216.5 | 201.9 |
| 57 | 41.7 | 38.9 | 17 | 85.6 | 79.8 | 77 | 129.4 | 120.7 | 37 | 173.3 | 161.6 | 97 | 217.2 | 202.6 |
| 58 | 42.4 | 39.6 | 18 | 86.3 | 80.5 | 78 | 130.2 | 121.4 | 38 | 174.1 | 162.3 | 98 | 217.9 | 203.2 |
| 59 | 43.1 | 40.2 | 19 | 87.0 | 81.2 | 79 | 130.9 | 122.1 | 39 | 174.8 | 163.0 | 99 | 218.7 | 203.9 |
| 60 | 43.9 | 40.9 | 20 | 87.8 | 81.8 | 80 | 131.6 | 122.8 | 40 | 175.5 | 163.7 | 300 | 219.4 | 204.6 |
| Dist. | Dep. | Lat. | Dist. | Dep. | Lat. | Dist. | Dep. | Lat. | Dist. | Dep. | Lat. | Dist. | Dep. | Lat. |

# TABLE II.

## Difference of Latitude and Departure for 44 Degrees.

| Dist. | Lat. | Dep. | Dist. | Lat. | Dep. | Dist. | Lat. | Dep. | Dist. | Lat. | Dep. | Dist. | Lat. | Dep. |
|---|---|---|---|---|---|---|---|---|---|---|---|---|---|---|
| 1 | 00.7 | 00.7 | 61 | 43.9 | 42.4 | 121 | 87.0 | 84.1 | 181 | 130.2 | 125.7 | 241 | 173.4 | [illegible] |
| 2 | 01.4 | 01.4 | 62 | 44.6 | 43.1 | 22 | 87.8 | 84.7 | 82 | 130.9 | 126.4 | 42 | 174.1 | [illegible] |
| 3 | 02.2 | 02.1 | 63 | 45.3 | 43.8 | 23 | 88.5 | 85.4 | 83 | 131.6 | 127.1 | 43 | 174.8 | 168.8 |
| 4 | 02.9 | 02.8 | 64 | 46.0 | 44.5 | 24 | 89.2 | 86.1 | 84 | 132.4 | 127.8 | 44 | 175.5 | 169.5 |
| 5 | 03.6 | 03.5 | 65 | 46.8 | 45.2 | 25 | 89.9 | 86.8 | 85 | 133.1 | 128.5 | 45 | 176.2 | 170.2 |
| 6 | 04.3 | 04.2 | 66 | 47.5 | 45.8 | 26 | 90.6 | 87.5 | 86 | 133.8 | 129.2 | 46 | 177.0 | 170.9 |
| 7 | 05.0 | 04.9 | 67 | 48.2 | 46.5 | 27 | 91.4 | 88.2 | 87 | 134.5 | 129.9 | 47 | 177.7 | 171.6 |
| 8 | 05.8 | 05.6 | 68 | 48.9 | 47.2 | 28 | 92.1 | 88.9 | 88 | 135.2 | 130.6 | 48 | 178.4 | 172.3 |
| 9 | 06.5 | 06.3 | 69 | 49.6 | 47.9 | 29 | 92.8 | 89.6 | 89 | 136.0 | 131.3 | 49 | 179.1 | 173.0 |
| 10 | 07.2 | 06.9 | 70 | 50.4 | 48.6 | 30 | 93.5 | 90.3 | 90 | 136.7 | 132.0 | 50 | 179.8 | 173.7 |
| 11 | 07.9 | 07.6 | 71 | 51.1 | 49.3 | 131 | 94.2 | 91.0 | 191 | 137.4 | 132.7 | 251 | 180.6 | 174.4 |
| 12 | 08.6 | 08.3 | 72 | 51.8 | 50.0 | 32 | 95.0 | 91.7 | 92 | 138.1 | 133.4 | 52 | 181.3 | 175.1 |
| 13 | 09.4 | 09.0 | 73 | 52.5 | 50.7 | 33 | 95.7 | 92.4 | 93 | 138.8 | 134.1 | 53 | 182.0 | 175.7 |
| 14 | 10.1 | 09.7 | 74 | 53.2 | 51.4 | 34 | 96.4 | 93.1 | 94 | 139.6 | 134.8 | 54 | 182.7 | 176.4 |
| 15 | 10.8 | 10.4 | 75 | 54.0 | 52.1 | 35 | 97.1 | 93.8 | 95 | 140.3 | 135.5 | 55 | 183.4 | 177.1 |
| 16 | 11.5 | 11.1 | 76 | 54.7 | 52.8 | 36 | 97.8 | 94.5 | 96 | 141.0 | 136.2 | 56 | 184.2 | 177.8 |
| 17 | 12.2 | 11.8 | 77 | 55.4 | 53.5 | 37 | 98.5 | 95.2 | 97 | 141.7 | 136.8 | 57 | 184.9 | 178.5 |
| 18 | 12.9 | 12.5 | 78 | 56.1 | 54.2 | 38 | 99.3 | 95.9 | 98 | 142.4 | 137.5 | 58 | 185.6 | 179.2 |
| 19 | 13.7 | 13.2 | 79 | 56.8 | 54.9 | 39 | 100.0 | 96.6 | 99 | 143.1 | 138.2 | 59 | 186.3 | 179.9 |
| 20 | 14.4 | 13.9 | 80 | 57.5 | 55.6 | 40 | 100.7 | 97.3 | 200 | 143.9 | 138.9 | 60 | 187.0 | 180.6 |
| 21 | 15.1 | 14.6 | 81 | 58.3 | 56.3 | 141 | 101.4 | 97.9 | 201 | 144.6 | 139.6 | 261 | 187.7 | 181.3 |
| 22 | 15.8 | 15.3 | 82 | 59.0 | 57.0 | 42 | 102.1 | 98.6 | 02 | 145.3 | 140.3 | 62 | 188.5 | 182.0 |
| 23 | 16.5 | 16.0 | 83 | 59.7 | 57.7 | 43 | 102.9 | 99.3 | 03 | 146.0 | 141.0 | 63 | 189.2 | 182.7 |
| 24 | 17.3 | 16.7 | 84 | 60.4 | 58.4 | 44 | 103.6 | 100.0 | 04 | 146.7 | 141.7 | 64 | 189.9 | 183.4 |
| 25 | 18.0 | 17.4 | 85 | 61.1 | 59.0 | 45 | 104.3 | 100.7 | 05 | 147.5 | 142.4 | 65 | 190.6 | 184.1 |
| 26 | 18.7 | 18.1 | 86 | 61.9 | 59.7 | 46 | 105.0 | 101.4 | 06 | 148.2 | 143.1 | 66 | 191.3 | 184.8 |
| 27 | 19.4 | 18.8 | 87 | 62.6 | 60.4 | 47 | 105.7 | 102.1 | 07 | 148.9 | 143.8 | 67 | 192.1 | 185.5 |
| 28 | 20.1 | 19.5 | 88 | 63.3 | 61.1 | 48 | 106.5 | 102.8 | 08 | 149.6 | 144.5 | 68 | 192.8 | 186.2 |
| 29 | 20.9 | 20.1 | 89 | 64.0 | 61.8 | 49 | 107.2 | 103.5 | 09 | 150.3 | 145.2 | 69 | 193.5 | 186.9 |
| 30 | 21.6 | 20.8 | 90 | 64.7 | 62.5 | 50 | 107.9 | 104.2 | 10 | 151.1 | 145.9 | 70 | 194.2 | 187.6 |
| 31 | 22.3 | 21.5 | 91 | 65.5 | 63.2 | 151 | 108.6 | 104.9 | 211 | 151.8 | 146.6 | 271 | 194.9 | 188.3 |
| 32 | 23.0 | 22.2 | 92 | 66.2 | 63.9 | 52 | 109.3 | 105.6 | 12 | 152.5 | 147.3 | 72 | 195.7 | 188.9 |
| 33 | 23.7 | 22.9 | 93 | 66.9 | 64.6 | 53 | 110.1 | 106.3 | 13 | 153.2 | 148.0 | 73 | 196.4 | 189.6 |
| 34 | 24.5 | 23.6 | 94 | 67.6 | 65.3 | 54 | 110.8 | 107.0 | 14 | 153.9 | 148.7 | 74 | 197.1 | 190.3 |
| 35 | 25.2 | 24.3 | 95 | 68.3 | 66.0 | 55 | 111.5 | 107.7 | 15 | 154.7 | 149.4 | 75 | 197.8 | 191.0 |
| 36 | 25.9 | 25.0 | 96 | 69.1 | 66.7 | 56 | 112.2 | 108.4 | 16 | 155.4 | 150.0 | 76 | 198.5 | 191.7 |
| 37 | 26.6 | 25.7 | 97 | 69.8 | 67.4 | 57 | 112.9 | 109.1 | 17 | 156.1 | 150.7 | 77 | 199.3 | 192.4 |
| 38 | 27.3 | 26.4 | 98 | 70.5 | 68.1 | 58 | 113.7 | 109.8 | 18 | 156.8 | 151.4 | 78 | 200.0 | 193.1 |
| 39 | 28.1 | 27.1 | 99 | 71.2 | 68.8 | 59 | 114.4 | 110.5 | 19 | 157.5 | 152.1 | 79 | 200.7 | 193.8 |
| 40 | 28.8 | 27.8 | 100 | 71.9 | 69.5 | 60 | 115.1 | 111.1 | 20 | 158.3 | 152.8 | 80 | 201.4 | 194.5 |
| 41 | 29.5 | 28.5 | 101 | 72.7 | 70.2 | 161 | 115.8 | 111.8 | 221 | 159.0 | 153.5 | 281 | 202.1 | 195.2 |
| 42 | 30.2 | 29.2 | 02 | 73.4 | 70.9 | 62 | 116.5 | 112.5 | 22 | 159.7 | 154.2 | 82 | 202.9 | 195.9 |
| 43 | 30.9 | 29.9 | 03 | 74.1 | 71.5 | 63 | 117.3 | 113.2 | 23 | 160.4 | 154.9 | 83 | 203.6 | 196.6 |
| 44 | 31.7 | 30.6 | 04 | 74.8 | 72.2 | 64 | 118.0 | 113.9 | 24 | 161.1 | 155.6 | 84 | 204.3 | 197.3 |
| 45 | 32.4 | 31.3 | 05 | 75.5 | 72.9 | 65 | 118.7 | 114.6 | 25 | 161.9 | 156.3 | 85 | 205.0 | 198.0 |
| 46 | 33.1 | 32.0 | 06 | 76.3 | 73.6 | 66 | 119.4 | 115.3 | 26 | 162.6 | 157.0 | 86 | 205.7 | 198.7 |
| 47 | 33.8 | 32.6 | 07 | 77.0 | 74.3 | 67 | 120.1 | 116.0 | 27 | 163.3 | 157.7 | 87 | 206.5 | 199.4 |
| 48 | 34.5 | 33.3 | 08 | 77.7 | 75.0 | 68 | 120.8 | 116.7 | 28 | 164.0 | 158.4 | 88 | 207.2 | 200.1 |
| 49 | 35.2 | 34.0 | 09 | 78.4 | 75.7 | 69 | 121.6 | 117.4 | 29 | 164.7 | 159.1 | 89 | 207.9 | 200.8 |
| 50 | 36.0 | 34.7 | 10 | 79.1 | 76.4 | 70 | 122.3 | 118.1 | 30 | 165.4 | 159.8 | 90 | 208.6 | 201.5 |
| 51 | 36.7 | 35.4 | 111 | 79.8 | 77.1 | 171 | 123.0 | 118.8 | 231 | 166.2 | 160.5 | 291 | 209.3 | 202.1 |
| 52 | 37.4 | 36.1 | 12 | 80.6 | 77.8 | 72 | 123.7 | 119.5 | 32 | 166.9 | 161.2 | 92 | 210.0 | 202.8 |
| 53 | 38.1 | 36.8 | 13 | 81.3 | 78.5 | 73 | 124.4 | 120.2 | 33 | 167.6 | 161.9 | 93 | 210.8 | 203.5 |
| 54 | 38.8 | 37.5 | 14 | 82.0 | 79.2 | 74 | 125.2 | 120.9 | 34 | 168.3 | 162.6 | 94 | 211.5 | 204.2 |
| 55 | 39.6 | 38.2 | 15 | 82.7 | 79.9 | 75 | 125.9 | 121.6 | 35 | 169.0 | 163.2 | 95 | 212.2 | 204.9 |
| 56 | 40.3 | 38.9 | 16 | 83.4 | 80.6 | 76 | 126.6 | 122.3 | 36 | 169.8 | 163.9 | 96 | 212.9 | 205.6 |
| 57 | 41.0 | 39.6 | 17 | 84.2 | 81.3 | 77 | 127.3 | 123.0 | 37 | 170.5 | 164.6 | 97 | 213.6 | 206.3 |
| 58 | 41.7 | 40.3 | 18 | 84.9 | 82.0 | 78 | 128.0 | 123.6 | 38 | 171.2 | 165.3 | 98 | 214.4 | 207.0 |
| 59 | 42.4 | 41.0 | 19 | 85.6 | 82.7 | 79 | 128.8 | 124.3 | 39 | 171.9 | 166.0 | 99 | 215.1 | 207.7 |
| 60 | 43.2 | 41.7 | 20 | 86.3 | 83.4 | 80 | 129.5 | 125.0 | 40 | 172.6 | 166.7 | 300 | 215.8 | 208.4 |
| Dist. | Dep. | Lat. | Dist. | Dep. | Lat. | Dist. | Dep. | Lat. | Dist. | Dep. | Lat. | Dist. | Dep. | Lat. |

# TABLE II.

## Difference of Latitude and Departure for 45 Degrees.

| Dist. | Lat. | Dep. | Dist. | Lat. | Dep. | Dist. | Lat. | Dep. | Dist. | Lat. | Dep. | Dist. | Lat. | Dep. |
|---|---|---|---|---|---|---|---|---|---|---|---|---|---|---|
| 1 | 00.7 | 00.7 | 61 | 43.1 | 43.1 | 121 | 85.6 | 85.6 | 181 | 128.0 | 128.0 | 241 | 170.4 | 170.4 |
| 2 | 01.4 | 01.4 | 62 | 43.8 | 43.8 | 22 | 86.3 | 86.3 | 82 | 128.7 | 128.7 | 42 | 171.1 | 171.1 |
| 3 | 02.1 | 02.1 | 63 | 44.5 | 44.5 | 23 | 87.0 | 87.0 | 83 | 129.4 | 129.4 | 43 | 171.8 | 171.8 |
| 4 | 02.8 | 02.8 | 64 | 45.3 | 45.3 | 24 | 87.7 | 87.7 | 84 | 130.1 | 130.1 | 44 | 172.5 | 172.5 |
| 5 | 03.5 | 03.5 | 65 | 46.0 | 46.0 | 25 | 88.4 | 88.4 | 85 | 130.8 | 130.8 | 45 | 173.2 | 173.2 |
| 6 | 04.2 | 04.2 | 66 | 46.7 | 46.7 | 26 | 89.1 | 89.1 | 86 | 131.5 | 131.5 | 46 | 173.9 | 173.9 |
| 7 | 04.9 | 04.9 | 67 | 47.4 | 47.4 | 27 | 89.8 | 89.8 | 87 | 132.2 | 132.2 | 47 | 174.7 | 174.7 |
| 8 | 05.7 | 05.7 | 68 | 48.1 | 48.1 | 28 | 90.5 | 90.5 | 88 | 132.9 | 132.9 | 48 | 175.4 | 175.4 |
| 9 | 06.4 | 06.4 | 69 | 48.8 | 48.8 | 29 | 91.2 | 91.2 | 89 | 133.6 | 133.6 | 49 | 176.1 | 176.1 |
| 10 | 07.1 | 07.1 | 70 | 49.5 | 49.5 | 30 | 91.9 | 91.9 | 90 | 134.4 | 134.4 | 50 | 176.8 | 176.8 |
| 11 | 07.8 | 07.8 | 71 | 50.2 | 50.2 | 131 | 92.6 | 92.6 | 191 | 135.1 | 135.1 | 251 | 177.5 | 177.5 |
| 12 | 08.5 | 08.5 | 72 | 50.9 | 50.9 | 32 | 93.3 | 93.3 | 92 | 135.8 | 135.8 | 52 | 178.2 | 178.2 |
| 13 | 09.2 | 09.2 | 73 | 51.6 | 51.6 | 33 | 94.0 | 94.0 | 93 | 136.5 | 136.5 | 53 | 178.9 | 178.9 |
| 14 | 09.9 | 09.9 | 74 | 52.3 | 52.3 | 34 | 94.8 | 94.8 | 94 | 137.2 | 137.2 | 54 | 179.6 | 179.6 |
| 15 | 10.6 | 10.6 | 75 | 53.0 | 53.0 | 35 | 95.5 | 95.5 | 95 | 137.9 | 137.9 | 55 | 180.3 | 180.3 |
| 16 | 11.3 | 11.3 | 76 | 53.7 | 53.7 | 36 | 96.2 | 96.2 | 96 | 138.6 | 138.6 | 56 | 181.0 | 181.0 |
| 17 | 12.0 | 12.0 | 77 | 54.4 | 54.4 | 37 | 96.9 | 96.9 | 97 | 139.3 | 139.3 | 57 | 181.7 | 181.7 |
| 18 | 12.7 | 12.7 | 78 | 55.2 | 55.2 | 38 | 97.6 | 97.6 | 98 | 140.0 | 140.0 | 58 | 182.4 | 182.4 |
| 19 | 13.4 | 13.4 | 79 | 55.9 | 55.9 | 39 | 98.3 | 98.3 | 99 | 140.7 | 140.7 | 59 | 183.1 | 183.1 |
| 20 | 14.1 | 14.1 | 80 | 56.6 | 56.6 | 40 | 99.0 | 99.0 | 200 | 141.4 | 141.4 | 60 | 183.8 | 183.8 |
| 21 | 14.8 | 14.8 | 81 | 57.3 | 57.3 | 141 | 99.7 | 99.7 | 201 | 142.1 | 142.1 | 261 | 184.6 | 184.6 |
| 22 | 15.6 | 15.6 | 82 | 58.0 | 58.0 | 42 | 100.4 | 100.4 | 02 | 142.8 | 142.8 | 62 | 185.3 | 185.3 |
| 23 | 16.3 | 16.3 | 83 | 58.7 | 58.7 | 43 | 101.1 | 101.1 | 03 | 143.5 | 143.5 | 63 | 186.0 | 186.0 |
| 24 | 17.0 | 17.0 | 84 | 59.4 | 59.4 | 44 | 101.8 | 101.8 | 04 | 144.2 | 144.2 | 64 | 186.7 | 186.7 |
| 25 | 17.7 | 17.7 | 85 | 60.1 | 60.1 | 45 | 102.5 | 102.5 | 05 | 145.0 | 145.0 | 65 | 187.4 | 187.4 |
| 26 | 18.4 | 18.4 | 86 | 60.8 | 60.8 | 46 | 103.2 | 103.2 | 06 | 145.7 | 145.7 | 66 | 188.1 | 188.1 |
| 27 | 19.1 | 19.1 | 87 | 61.5 | 61.5 | 47 | 103.9 | 103.9 | 07 | 146.4 | 146.4 | 67 | 188.8 | 188.8 |
| 28 | 19.8 | 19.8 | 88 | 62.2 | 62.2 | 48 | 104.7 | 104.7 | 08 | 147.1 | 147.1 | 68 | 189.5 | 189.5 |
| 29 | 20.5 | 20.5 | 89 | 62.9 | 62.9 | 49 | 105.4 | 105.4 | 09 | 147.8 | 147.8 | 69 | 190.2 | 190.2 |
| 30 | 21.2 | 21.2 | 90 | 63.6 | 63.6 | 50 | 106.1 | 106.1 | 10 | 148.5 | 148.5 | 70 | 190.9 | 190.9 |
| 31 | 21.9 | 21.9 | 91 | 64.3 | 64.3 | 151 | 106.8 | 106.8 | 211 | 149.2 | 149.2 | 271 | 191.6 | 191.6 |
| 32 | 22.6 | 22.6 | 92 | 65.1 | 65.1 | 52 | 107.5 | 107.5 | 12 | 149.9 | 149.9 | 72 | 192.3 | 192.3 |
| 33 | 23.3 | 23.3 | 93 | 65.8 | 65.8 | 53 | 108.2 | 108.2 | 13 | 150.6 | 150.6 | 73 | 193.0 | 193.0 |
| 34 | 24.0 | 24.0 | 94 | 66.5 | 66.5 | 54 | 108.9 | 108.9 | 14 | 151.3 | 151.3 | 74 | 193.7 | 193.7 |
| 35 | 24.7 | 24.7 | 95 | 67.2 | 67.2 | 55 | 109.6 | 109.6 | 15 | 152.0 | 152.0 | 75 | 194.5 | 194.5 |
| 36 | 25.5 | 25.5 | 96 | 67.9 | 67.9 | 56 | 110.3 | 110.3 | 16 | 152.7 | 152.7 | 76 | 195.2 | 195.2 |
| 37 | 26.2 | 26.2 | 97 | 68.6 | 68.6 | 57 | 111.0 | 111.0 | 17 | 153.4 | 153.4 | 77 | 195.9 | 195.9 |
| 38 | 26.9 | 26.9 | 98 | 69.3 | 69.3 | 58 | 111.7 | 111.7 | 18 | 154.1 | 154.1 | 78 | 196.6 | 196.6 |
| 39 | 27.6 | 27.6 | 99 | 70.0 | 70.0 | 59 | 112.4 | 112.4 | 19 | 154.9 | 154.9 | 79 | 197.3 | 197.3 |
| 40 | 28.3 | 28.3 | 100 | 70.7 | 70.7 | 60 | 113.1 | 113.1 | 20 | 155.6 | 155.6 | 80 | 198.0 | 198.0 |
| 41 | 29.0 | 29.0 | 101 | 71.4 | 71.4 | 161 | 113.8 | 113.8 | 221 | 156.3 | 156.3 | 281 | 198.7 | 198.7 |
| 42 | 29.7 | 29.7 | 02 | 72.1 | 72.1 | 62 | 114.6 | 114.6 | 22 | 157.0 | 157.0 | 82 | 199.4 | 199.4 |
| 43 | 30.4 | 30.4 | 03 | 72.8 | 72.8 | 63 | 115.3 | 115.3 | 23 | 157.7 | 157.7 | 83 | 200.1 | 200.1 |
| 44 | 31.1 | 31.1 | 04 | 73.5 | 73.5 | 64 | 116.0 | 116.0 | 24 | 158.4 | 158.4 | 84 | 200.8 | 200.8 |
| 45 | 31.8 | 31.8 | 05 | 74.2 | 74.2 | 65 | 116.7 | 116.7 | 25 | 159.1 | 159.1 | 85 | 201.5 | 201.5 |
| 46 | 32.5 | 32.5 | 06 | 75.0 | 75.0 | 66 | 117.4 | 117.4 | 26 | 159.8 | 159.8 | 86 | 202.2 | 202.2 |
| 47 | 33.2 | 33.2 | 07 | 75.7 | 75.7 | 67 | 118.1 | 118.1 | 27 | 160.5 | 160.5 | 87 | 202.9 | 202.9 |
| 48 | 33.9 | 33.9 | 08 | 76.4 | 76.4 | 68 | 118.8 | 118.8 | 28 | 161.2 | 161.2 | 88 | 203.6 | 203.6 |
| 49 | 34.6 | 34.6 | 09 | 77.1 | 77.1 | 69 | 119.5 | 119.5 | 29 | 161.9 | 161.9 | 89 | 204.4 | 204.4 |
| 50 | 35.4 | 35.4 | 10 | 77.8 | 77.8 | 70 | 120.2 | 120.2 | 30 | 162.6 | 162.6 | 90 | 205.1 | 205.1 |
| 51 | 36.1 | 36.1 | 111 | 78.5 | 78.5 | 171 | 120.9 | 120.9 | 231 | 163.3 | 163.3 | 291 | 205.8 | 205.8 |
| 52 | 36.8 | 36.8 | 12 | 79.2 | 79.2 | 72 | 121.6 | 121.6 | 32 | 164.0 | 164.0 | 92 | 206.5 | 206.5 |
| 53 | 37.5 | 37.5 | 13 | 79.9 | 79.9 | 73 | 122.3 | 122.3 | 33 | 164.8 | 164.8 | 93 | 207.2 | 207.2 |
| 54 | 38.2 | 38.2 | 14 | 80.6 | 80.6 | 74 | 123.0 | 123.0 | 34 | 165.5 | 165.5 | 94 | 207.9 | 207.9 |
| 55 | 38.9 | 38.9 | 15 | 81.3 | 81.3 | 75 | 123.7 | 123.7 | 35 | 166.2 | 166.2 | 95 | 208.6 | 208.6 |
| 56 | 39.6 | 39.6 | 16 | 82.0 | 82.0 | 76 | 124.5 | 124.5 | 36 | 166.9 | 166.9 | 96 | 209.3 | 209.3 |
| 57 | 40.3 | 40.3 | 17 | 82.7 | 82.7 | 77 | 125.2 | 125.2 | 37 | 167.6 | 167.6 | 97 | 210.0 | 210.0 |
| 58 | 41.0 | 41.0 | 18 | 83.4 | 83.4 | 78 | 125.9 | 125.9 | 38 | 168.3 | 168.3 | 98 | 210.7 | 210.7 |
| 59 | 41.7 | 41.7 | 19 | 84.1 | 84.1 | 79 | 126.6 | 126.6 | 39 | 169.0 | 169.0 | 99 | 211.4 | 211.4 |
| 60 | 42.4 | 42.4 | 20 | 84.9 | 84.9 | 80 | 127.3 | 127.3 | 40 | 169.7 | 169.7 | 300 | 212.1 | 212.1 |
| Dist. | Dep. | Lat. | Dist. | Dep. | Lat. | Dist. | Dep. | Lat. | Dist. | Dep. | Lat. | Dist. | Dep. | Lat. |

# TABLE III.

## Meridional Parts.

| M. | 0° | 1° | 2° | 3° | 4° | 5° | 6° | 7° | 8° | 9° | 10° | 11° | 12° | 13° | M. |
|---|---|---|---|---|---|---|---|---|---|---|---|---|---|---|---|
| 0 | 0 | 60 | 120 | 180 | 240 | 300 | 361 | 421 | 482 | 542 | 603 | 664 | 725 | 787 | 0 |
| 1 | 1 | 61 | 121 | 181 | 241 | 301 | 362 | 422 | 483 | 543 | 604 | 665 | 726 | 788 | 1 |
| 2 | 2 | 62 | 122 | 182 | 242 | 302 | 363 | 423 | 484 | 544 | 605 | 666 | 727 | 789 | 2 |
| 3 | 3 | 63 | 123 | 183 | 243 | 303 | 364 | 424 | 485 | 545 | 606 | 667 | 728 | 790 | 3 |
| 4 | 4 | 64 | 124 | 184 | 244 | 304 | 365 | 425 | 486 | 546 | 607 | 668 | 729 | 791 | 4 |
| 5 | 5 | 65 | 125 | 185 | 245 | 305 | 366 | 426 | 487 | 547 | 608 | 669 | 730 | 792 | 5 |
| 6 | 6 | 66 | 126 | 186 | 246 | 306 | 367 | 427 | 488 | 548 | 609 | 670 | 731 | 793 | 6 |
| 7 | 7 | 67 | 127 | 187 | 247 | 307 | 368 | 428 | 489 | 549 | 610 | 671 | 732 | 794 | 7 |
| 8 | 8 | 68 | 128 | 188 | 248 | 308 | 369 | 429 | 490 | 550 | 611 | 672 | 734 | 795 | 8 |
| 9 | 9 | 69 | 129 | 189 | 249 | 309 | 370 | 430 | 491 | 551 | 612 | 673 | 735 | 796 | 9 |
| 10 | 10 | 70 | 130 | 190 | 250 | 310 | 371 | 431 | 492 | 552 | 613 | 674 | 736 | 797 | 10 |
| 11 | 11 | 71 | 131 | 191 | 251 | 311 | 372 | 432 | 493 | 553 | 614 | 675 | 737 | 798 | 11 |
| 12 | 12 | 72 | 132 | 192 | 252 | 312 | 373 | 433 | 494 | 554 | 615 | 676 | 738 | 799 | 12 |
| 13 | 13 | 73 | 133 | 193 | 253 | 313 | 374 | 434 | 495 | 555 | 616 | 677 | 739 | 800 | 13 |
| 14 | 14 | 74 | 134 | 194 | 254 | 314 | 375 | 435 | 496 | 556 | 617 | 678 | 740 | 801 | 14 |
| 15 | 15 | 75 | 135 | 195 | 255 | 315 | 376 | 436 | 497 | 557 | 618 | 679 | 741 | 802 | 15 |
| 16 | 16 | 76 | 136 | 196 | 256 | 316 | 377 | 437 | 498 | 558 | 619 | 680 | 742 | 803 | 16 |
| 17 | 17 | 77 | 137 | 197 | 257 | 317 | 378 | 438 | 499 | 559 | 620 | 681 | 743 | 804 | 17 |
| 18 | 18 | 78 | 138 | 198 | 258 | 318 | 379 | 439 | 500 | 560 | 621 | 682 | 744 | 805 | 18 |
| 19 | 19 | 79 | 139 | 199 | 259 | 319 | 380 | 440 | 501 | 561 | 622 | 683 | 745 | 806 | 19 |
| 20 | 20 | 80 | 140 | 200 | 260 | 320 | 381 | 441 | 502 | 562 | 623 | 684 | 746 | 807 | 20 |
| 21 | 21 | 81 | 141 | 201 | 261 | 321 | 382 | 442 | 503 | 564 | 624 | 685 | 747 | 808 | 21 |
| 22 | 22 | 82 | 142 | 202 | 262 | 322 | 383 | 443 | 504 | 565 | 625 | 687 | 748 | 809 | 22 |
| 23 | 23 | 83 | 143 | 203 | 263 | 323 | 384 | 444 | 505 | 566 | 626 | 688 | 749 | 810 | 23 |
| 24 | 24 | 84 | 144 | 204 | 264 | 324 | 385 | 445 | 506 | 567 | 627 | 689 | 750 | 811 | 24 |
| 25 | 25 | 85 | 145 | 205 | 265 | 325 | 386 | 446 | 507 | 568 | 628 | 690 | 751 | 812 | 25 |
| 26 | 26 | 86 | 146 | 206 | 266 | 326 | 387 | 447 | 508 | 569 | 629 | 691 | 752 | 813 | 26 |
| 27 | 27 | 87 | 147 | 207 | 267 | 327 | 388 | 448 | 509 | 570 | 631 | 692 | 753 | 815 | 27 |
| 28 | 28 | 88 | 148 | 208 | 268 | 328 | 389 | 449 | 510 | 571 | 632 | 693 | 754 | 816 | 28 |
| 29 | 29 | 89 | 149 | 209 | 269 | 330 | 390 | 450 | 511 | 572 | 633 | 694 | 755 | 817 | 29 |
| 30 | 30 | 90 | 150 | 210 | 270 | 331 | 391 | 451 | 512 | 573 | 634 | 695 | 756 | 818 | 30 |
| 31 | 31 | 91 | 151 | 211 | 271 | 332 | 392 | 452 | 513 | 574 | 635 | 696 | 757 | 819 | 31 |
| 32 | 32 | 92 | 152 | 212 | 272 | 333 | 393 | 453 | 514 | 575 | 636 | 697 | 758 | 820 | 32 |
| 33 | 33 | 93 | 153 | 213 | 273 | 334 | 394 | 454 | 515 | 576 | 637 | 698 | 759 | 821 | 33 |
| 34 | 34 | 94 | 154 | 214 | 274 | 335 | 395 | 455 | 516 | 577 | 638 | 699 | 760 | 822 | 34 |
| 35 | 35 | 95 | 155 | 215 | 275 | 336 | 396 | 456 | 517 | 578 | 639 | 700 | 761 | 823 | 35 |
| 36 | 36 | 96 | 156 | 216 | 276 | 337 | 397 | 457 | 518 | 579 | 640 | 701 | 762 | 824 | 36 |
| 37 | 37 | 97 | 157 | 217 | 277 | 338 | 398 | 458 | 519 | 580 | 641 | 702 | 763 | 825 | 37 |
| 38 | 38 | 98 | 158 | 218 | 278 | 339 | 399 | 459 | 520 | 581 | 642 | 703 | 764 | 826 | 38 |
| 39 | 39 | 99 | 159 | 219 | 279 | 340 | 400 | 460 | 521 | 582 | 643 | 704 | 765 | 827 | 39 |
| 40 | 40 | 100 | 160 | 220 | 280 | 341 | 401 | 461 | 522 | 583 | 644 | 705 | 766 | 828 | 40 |
| 41 | 41 | 101 | 161 | 221 | 281 | 342 | 402 | 462 | 523 | 584 | 645 | 706 | 767 | 829 | 41 |
| 42 | 42 | 102 | 162 | 222 | 282 | 343 | 403 | 463 | 524 | 585 | 646 | 707 | 768 | 830 | 42 |
| 43 | 43 | 103 | 163 | 223 | 283 | 344 | 404 | 464 | 525 | 586 | 647 | 708 | 769 | 831 | 43 |
| 44 | 44 | 104 | 164 | 224 | 284 | 345 | 405 | 465 | 526 | 587 | 648 | 709 | 770 | 832 | 44 |
| 45 | 45 | 105 | 165 | 225 | 285 | 346 | 406 | 466 | 527 | 588 | 649 | 710 | 771 | 833 | 45 |
| 46 | 46 | 106 | 166 | 226 | 286 | 347 | 407 | 467 | 528 | 589 | 650 | 711 | 772 | 834 | 46 |
| 47 | 47 | 107 | 167 | 227 | 287 | 348 | 408 | 468 | 529 | 590 | 651 | 712 | 773 | 835 | 47 |
| 48 | 48 | 108 | 168 | 228 | 288 | 349 | 409 | 469 | 530 | 591 | 652 | 713 | 774 | 836 | 48 |
| 49 | 49 | 109 | 169 | 229 | 289 | 350 | 410 | 470 | 531 | 592 | 653 | 714 | 775 | 837 | 49 |
| 50 | 50 | 110 | 170 | 230 | 290 | 351 | 411 | 471 | 532 | 593 | 654 | 715 | 777 | 838 | 50 |
| 51 | 51 | 111 | 171 | 231 | 291 | 352 | 412 | 472 | 533 | 594 | 655 | 716 | 778 | 839 | 51 |
| 52 | 52 | 112 | 172 | 232 | 292 | 353 | 413 | 473 | 534 | 595 | 656 | 717 | 779 | 840 | 52 |
| 53 | 53 | 113 | 173 | 233 | 293 | 354 | 414 | 474 | 535 | 596 | 657 | 718 | 780 | 841 | 53 |
| 54 | 54 | 114 | 174 | 234 | 294 | 355 | 415 | 476 | 536 | 597 | 658 | 719 | 781 | 842 | 54 |
| 55 | 55 | 115 | 175 | 235 | 295 | 356 | 416 | 477 | 537 | 598 | 659 | 720 | 782 | 843 | 55 |
| 56 | 56 | 116 | 176 | 236 | 296 | 357 | 417 | 478 | 538 | 599 | 660 | 721 | 783 | 844 | 56 |
| 57 | 57 | 117 | 177 | 237 | 297 | 358 | 418 | 479 | 539 | 600 | 661 | 722 | 784 | 845 | 57 |
| 58 | 58 | 118 | 178 | 238 | 298 | 359 | 419 | 480 | 540 | 601 | 662 | 723 | 785 | 846 | 58 |
| 59 | 59 | 119 | 179 | 239 | 299 | 360 | 420 | 481 | 541 | 602 | 663 | 724 | 786 | 847 | 59 |
| M. | 0° | 1° | 2° | 3° | 4° | 5° | 6° | 7° | 8° | 9° | 10° | 11° | 12° | 13° | M. |

# TABLE III.

## Meridional Parts.

| M. | 14° | 15° | 16° | 17° | 18° | 19° | 20° | 21° | 22° | 23° | 24° | 25° | 26° | 27° | M. |
|---|---|---|---|---|---|---|---|---|---|---|---|---|---|---|---|
| 0 | 848 | 910 | 973 | 1035 | 1098 | 1161 | 1225 | 1289 | 1354 | 1419 | 1484 | 1550 | 1616 | 1684 | 0 |
| 1 | 850 | 911 | 974 | 36 | 99 | 63 | 26 | 90 | 55 | 20 | 85 | 51 | 18 | 85 | 1 |
| 2 | 851 | 913 | 975 | 37 | 1100 | 64 | 27 | 91 | 56 | 21 | 86 | 52 | 19 | 86 | 2 |
| 3 | 852 | 914 | 976 | 38 | 01 | 65 | 28 | 92 | 57 | 22 | 87 | 53 | 20 | 87 | 3 |
| 4 | 853 | 915 | 977 | 39 | 02 | 66 | 29 | 93 | 58 | 23 | 88 | 54 | 21 | 88 | 4 |
| 5 | 854 | 916 | 978 | 1041 | 1103 | 1167 | 1230 | 1295 | 1359 | 1424 | 1490 | 1556 | 1622 | 1689 | 5 |
| 6 | 855 | 917 | 979 | 42 | 05 | 68 | 32 | 96 | 60 | 25 | 91 | 57 | 23 | 90 | 6 |
| 7 | 856 | 918 | 980 | 43 | 06 | 69 | 33 | 97 | 61 | 26 | 92 | 58 | 24 | 91 | 7 |
| 8 | 857 | 919 | 981 | 44 | 07 | 70 | 34 | 98 | 62 | 27 | 93 | 59 | 25 | 93 | 8 |
| 9 | 858 | 920 | 982 | 45 | 08 | 71 | 35 | 99 | 63 | 28 | 94 | 60 | 26 | 94 | 9 |
| 10 | 859 | 921 | 983 | 1046 | 1109 | 1172 | 1236 | 1300 | 1364 | 1430 | 1495 | 1561 | 1628 | 1695 | 10 |
| 11 | 860 | 922 | 984 | 47 | 10 | 73 | 37 | 01 | 66 | 31 | 96 | 62 | 29 | 96 | 11 |
| 12 | 861 | 923 | 985 | 48 | 11 | 74 | 38 | 02 | 67 | 32 | 97 | 63 | 30 | 97 | 12 |
| 13 | 862 | 924 | 986 | 49 | 12 | 75 | 39 | 03 | 68 | 33 | 98 | 64 | 31 | 98 | 13 |
| 14 | 863 | 925 | 987 | 50 | 13 | 76 | 40 | 04 | 69 | 34 | 99 | 65 | 32 | 99 | 14 |
| 15 | 864 | 926 | 988 | 1051 | 1114 | 1177 | 1241 | 1305 | 1370 | 1435 | 1500 | 1567 | 1633 | 1700 | 15 |
| 16 | 865 | 927 | 989 | 52 | 15 | 78 | 42 | 06 | 71 | 36 | 02 | 68 | 34 | 01 | 16 |
| 17 | 866 | 928 | 990 | 53 | 16 | 79 | 43 | 07 | 72 | 37 | 03 | 69 | 35 | 03 | 17 |
| 18 | 867 | 929 | 991 | 54 | 17 | 81 | 44 | 08 | 73 | 38 | 04 | 70 | 37 | 04 | 18 |
| 19 | 868 | 930 | 993 | 55 | 18 | 82 | 45 | 10 | 74 | 39 | 05 | 71 | 38 | 05 | 19 |
| 20 | 869 | 931 | 994 | 1056 | 1119 | 1183 | 1246 | 1311 | 1375 | 1440 | 1506 | 1572 | 1639 | 1706 | 20 |
| 21 | 870 | 932 | 995 | 57 | 20 | 84 | 48 | 12 | 76 | 41 | 07 | 73 | 40 | 07 | 21 |
| 22 | 871 | 933 | 996 | 58 | 21 | 85 | 49 | 13 | 77 | 43 | 08 | 74 | 41 | 08 | 22 |
| 23 | 872 | 934 | 997 | 59 | 22 | 86 | 50 | 14 | 79 | 44 | 09 | 75 | 42 | 09 | 23 |
| 24 | 873 | 935 | 998 | 60 | 23 | 87 | 51 | 15 | 80 | 45 | 10 | 77 | 43 | 11 | 24 |
| 25 | 874 | 936 | 999 | 1061 | 1125 | 1188 | 1252 | 1316 | 1381 | 1446 | 1511 | 1578 | 1644 | 1712 | 25 |
| 26 | 875 | 937 | 1000 | 63 | 26 | 89 | 53 | 17 | 82 | 47 | 13 | 79 | 45 | 13 | 26 |
| 27 | 876 | 938 | 01 | 64 | 27 | 90 | 54 | 18 | 83 | 48 | 14 | 80 | 47 | 14 | 27 |
| 28 | 877 | 939 | 02 | 65 | 28 | 91 | 55 | 19 | 84 | 49 | 15 | 81 | 48 | 15 | 28 |
| 29 | 878 | 941 | 03 | 66 | 29 | 92 | 56 | 20 | 85 | 50 | 16 | 82 | 49 | 16 | 29 |
| 30 | 879 | 942 | 1004 | 1067 | 1130 | 1193 | 1257 | 1321 | 1386 | 1451 | 1517 | 1583 | 1650 | 1717 | 30 |
| 31 | 880 | 943 | 05 | 68 | 31 | 94 | 58 | 22 | 87 | 52 | 18 | 84 | 51 | 18 | 31 |
| 32 | 882 | 944 | 06 | 69 | 32 | 95 | 59 | 24 | 88 | 53 | 19 | 85 | 52 | 20 | 32 |
| 33 | 883 | 945 | 07 | 70 | 33 | 96 | 60 | 25 | 89 | 55 | 20 | 86 | 53 | 21 | 33 |
| 34 | 884 | 946 | 08 | 71 | 34 | 98 | 61 | 26 | 90 | 56 | 21 | 88 | 54 | 22 | 34 |
| 35 | 885 | 947 | 1009 | 1072 | 1135 | 1199 | 1262 | 1327 | 1392 | 1457 | 1522 | 1589 | 1656 | 1723 | 35 |
| 36 | 886 | 948 | 10 | 73 | 36 | 1200 | 64 | 28 | 93 | 58 | 24 | 90 | 57 | 24 | 36 |
| 37 | 887 | 949 | 11 | 74 | 37 | 01 | 65 | 29 | 94 | 59 | 25 | 91 | 58 | 25 | 37 |
| 38 | 888 | 950 | 12 | 75 | 38 | 02 | 66 | 30 | 95 | 60 | 26 | 92 | 59 | 26 | 38 |
| 39 | 889 | 951 | 13 | 76 | 39 | 03 | 67 | 31 | 96 | 61 | 27 | 93 | 60 | 27 | 39 |
| 40 | 890 | 952 | 1014 | 1077 | 1140 | 1204 | 1268 | 1332 | 1397 | 1462 | 1528 | 1594 | 1661 | 1729 | 40 |
| 41 | 891 | 953 | 15 | 78 | 41 | 05 | 69 | 33 | 98 | 63 | 29 | 95 | 62 | 30 | 41 |
| 42 | 892 | 954 | 16 | 79 | 42 | 06 | 70 | 34 | 99 | 64 | 30 | 96 | 63 | 31 | 42 |
| 43 | 893 | 955 | 18 | 80 | 44 | 07 | 71 | 35 | 1400 | 65 | 31 | 98 | 64 | 32 | 43 |
| 44 | 894 | 956 | 19 | 81 | 45 | 08 | 72 | 36 | 01 | 67 | 32 | 99 | 66 | 33 | 44 |
| 45 | 895 | 957 | 1020 | 1082 | 1146 | 1209 | 1273 | 1338 | 1402 | 1468 | 1533 | 1600 | 1667 | 1734 | 45 |
| 46 | 896 | 958 | 21 | 84 | 47 | 10 | 74 | 39 | 03 | 69 | 35 | 01 | 68 | 35 | 46 |
| 47 | 897 | 959 | 22 | 85 | 48 | 11 | 75 | 40 | 05 | 70 | 36 | 02 | 69 | 36 | 47 |
| 48 | 898 | 960 | 23 | 86 | 49 | 12 | 76 | 41 | 06 | 71 | 37 | 03 | 70 | 38 | 48 |
| 49 | 899 | 961 | 24 | 87 | 50 | 13 | 77 | 42 | 07 | 72 | 38 | 04 | 71 | 39 | 49 |
| 50 | 900 | 962 | 1025 | 1088 | 1151 | 1215 | 1278 | 1343 | 1408 | 1473 | 1539 | 1605 | 1672 | 1740 | 50 |
| 51 | 901 | 963 | 26 | 89 | 52 | 16 | 80 | 44 | 09 | 74 | 40 | 06 | 73 | 41 | 51 |
| 52 | 902 | 964 | 27 | 90 | 53 | 17 | 81 | 45 | 10 | 75 | 41 | 08 | 75 | 42 | 52 |
| 53 | 903 | 965 | 28 | 91 | 54 | 18 | 82 | 46 | 11 | 76 | 42 | 09 | 76 | 43 | 53 |
| 54 | 904 | 966 | 29 | 92 | 55 | 19 | 83 | 47 | 12 | 77 | 43 | 10 | 77 | 44 | 54 |
| 55 | 905 | 968 | 1030 | 1093 | 1156 | 1220 | 1284 | 1348 | 1413 | 1479 | 1544 | 1611 | 1678 | 1746 | 55 |
| 56 | 906 | 969 | 31 | 94 | 57 | 21 | 85 | 49 | 14 | 80 | 46 | 12 | 79 | 47 | 56 |
| 57 | 907 | 970 | 32 | 95 | 58 | 22 | 86 | 50 | 15 | 81 | 47 | 13 | 80 | 48 | 57 |
| 58 | 908 | 971 | 33 | 96 | 59 | 23 | 87 | 52 | 16 | 82 | 48 | 14 | 81 | 49 | 58 |
| 59 | 909 | 972 | 34 | 97 | 60 | 24 | 88 | 53 | 18 | 83 | 49 | 15 | 82 | 50 | 59 |
| M. | 14° | 15° | 16° | 17° | 18° | 19° | 20° | 21° | 22° | 23° | 24° | 25° | 26° | 27° | M. |

# TABLE III

## Meridional Parts.

| M. | 28° | 29° | 30° | 31° | 32° | 33° | 34° | 35° | 36° | 37° | 38° | 39° | 40° | 41° | M. |
|---|---|---|---|---|---|---|---|---|---|---|---|---|---|---|---|
| 0 | 1751 | 1819 | 1888 | 1958 | 2028 | 2100 | 2171 | 2244 | 2318 | 2393 | 2468 | 2545 | 2623 | 2702 | 0 |
| 1 | 52 | 21 | 90 | 59 | 30 | 01 | 73 | 46 | 19 | 94 | 70 | 46 | 24 | 03 | 1 |
| 2 | 53 | 22 | 91 | 60 | 31 | 02 | 74 | 47 | 20 | 95 | 71 | 48 | 25 | 04 | 2 |
| 3 | 55 | 23 | 92 | 62 | 32 | 03 | 75 | 48 | 22 | 96 | 72 | 49 | 27 | 06 | 3 |
| 4 | 56 | 24 | 93 | 63 | 33 | 04 | 76 | 49 | 23 | 98 | 73 | 50 | 28 | 07 | 4 |
| 5 | 1757 | 1825 | 1894 | 1964 | 2034 | 2105 | 2178 | 2250 | 2324 | 2399 | 2475 | 2551 | 2629 | 2708 | 5 |
| 6 | 58 | 26 | 95 | 65 | 35 | 07 | 79 | 52 | 25 | 2400 | 76 | 53 | 31 | 10 | 6 |
| 7 | 59 | 27 | 96 | 66 | 37 | 08 | 80 | 53 | 27 | 01 | 77 | 54 | 32 | 11 | 7 |
| 8 | 60 | 29 | 98 | 67 | 38 | 09 | 81 | 54 | 28 | 03 | 78 | 55 | 33 | 12 | 8 |
| 9 | 61 | 30 | 99 | 69 | 39 | 10 | 82 | 55 | 29 | 04 | 80 | 57 | 34 | 14 | 9 |
| 10 | 1762 | 1831 | 1900 | 1970 | 2040 | 2111 | 2184 | 2257 | 2330 | 2405 | 2481 | 2558 | 2636 | 2715 | 10 |
| 11 | 64 | 32 | 01 | 71 | 41 | 13 | 85 | 58 | 32 | 06 | 82 | 59 | 37 | 16 | 11 |
| 12 | 65 | 33 | 02 | 72 | 43 | 14 | 86 | 59 | 33 | 08 | 84 | 60 | 38 | 18 | 12 |
| 13 | 66 | 34 | 03 | 73 | 44 | 15 | 87 | 60 | 34 | 09 | 85 | 62 | 40 | 19 | 13 |
| 14 | 67 | 35 | 05 | 74 | 45 | 16 | 88 | 61 | 35 | 10 | 86 | 63 | 41 | 20 | 14 |
| 15 | 1768 | 1837 | 1906 | 1976 | 2046 | 2117 | 2190 | 2263 | 2337 | 2411 | 2487 | 2564 | 2642 | 2722 | 15 |
| 16 | 69 | 38 | 07 | 77 | 47 | 19 | 91 | 64 | 38 | 13 | 89 | 66 | 44 | 23 | 16 |
| 17 | 70 | 39 | 08 | 78 | 48 | 20 | 92 | 65 | 39 | 14 | 90 | 67 | 45 | 24 | 17 |
| 18 | 72 | 40 | 09 | 79 | 50 | 21 | 93 | 66 | 40 | 15 | 91 | 68 | 46 | 26 | 18 |
| 19 | 73 | 41 | 10 | 80 | 51 | 22 | 94 | 68 | 42 | 16 | 92 | 69 | 48 | 27 | 19 |
| 20 | 1774 | 1842 | 1912 | 1981 | 2052 | 2123 | 2196 | 2269 | 2343 | 2418 | 2494 | 2571 | 2649 | 2728 | 20 |
| 21 | 75 | 43 | 13 | 83 | 53 | 25 | 97 | 70 | 44 | 19 | 95 | 72 | 50 | 29 | 21 |
| 22 | 76 | 45 | 14 | 84 | 54 | 26 | 98 | 71 | 45 | 20 | 96 | 73 | 51 | 31 | 22 |
| 23 | 77 | 46 | 15 | 85 | 56 | 27 | 99 | 72 | 46 | 22 | 98 | 75 | 53 | 32 | 23 |
| 24 | 78 | 47 | 16 | 86 | 57 | 28 | 2200 | 74 | 48 | 23 | 99 | 76 | 54 | 33 | 24 |
| 25 | 1780 | 1848 | 1917 | 1987 | 2058 | 2129 | 2202 | 2275 | 2349 | 2424 | 2500 | 2577 | 2655 | 2735 | 25 |
| 26 | 81 | 49 | 18 | 88 | 59 | 31 | 03 | 76 | 50 | 25 | 01 | 78 | 57 | 36 | 26 |
| 27 | 82 | 50 | 20 | 90 | 60 | 32 | 04 | 77 | 51 | 27 | 03 | 80 | 58 | 37 | 27 |
| 28 | 83 | 52 | 21 | 91 | 61 | 33 | 05 | 79 | 53 | 28 | 04 | 81 | 59 | 39 | 28 |
| 29 | 84 | 53 | 22 | 92 | 63 | 34 | 07 | 80 | 54 | 29 | 05 | 82 | 61 | 40 | 29 |
| 30 | 1785 | 1854 | 1923 | 1993 | 2064 | 2135 | 2208 | 2281 | 2355 | 2430 | 2506 | 2584 | 2662 | 2742 | 30 |
| 31 | 86 | 55 | 24 | 94 | 65 | 37 | 09 | 82 | 56 | 32 | 08 | 85 | 63 | 43 | 31 |
| 32 | 87 | 56 | 25 | 95 | 66 | 38 | 10 | 83 | 58 | 33 | 09 | 86 | 65 | 44 | 32 |
| 33 | 89 | 57 | 27 | 97 | 67 | 39 | 11 | 85 | 59 | 34 | 10 | 88 | 66 | 46 | 33 |
| 34 | 90 | 58 | 28 | 98 | 69 | 40 | 13 | 86 | 60 | 35 | 12 | 89 | 67 | 47 | 34 |
| 35 | 1791 | 1860 | 1929 | 1999 | 2070 | 2141 | 2214 | 2287 | 2361 | 2437 | 2513 | 2590 | 2669 | 2748 | 35 |
| 36 | 92 | 61 | 30 | 2000 | 71 | 43 | 15 | 88 | 63 | 38 | 14 | 91 | 70 | 50 | 36 |
| 37 | 93 | 62 | 31 | 01 | 72 | 44 | 16 | 90 | 64 | 39 | 15 | 93 | 71 | 51 | 37 |
| 38 | 94 | 63 | 32 | 02 | 73 | 45 | 17 | 91 | 65 | 40 | 17 | 94 | 73 | 52 | 38 |
| 39 | 95 | 64 | 34 | 04 | 75 | 46 | 19 | 92 | 66 | 42 | 18 | 95 | 74 | 54 | 39 |
| 40 | 1797 | 1865 | 1935 | 2005 | 2076 | 2147 | 2220 | 2293 | 2368 | 2443 | 2519 | 2597 | 2675 | 2755 | 40 |
| 41 | 98 | 66 | 36 | 06 | 77 | 49 | 21 | 95 | 69 | 44 | 21 | 98 | 76 | 56 | 41 |
| 42 | 99 | 68 | 37 | 07 | 78 | 50 | 22 | 96 | 70 | 45 | 22 | 99 | 78 | 58 | 42 |
| 43 | 1800 | 69 | 38 | 08 | 79 | 51 | 24 | 97 | 71 | 47 | 23 | 2601 | 79 | 59 | 43 |
| 44 | 01 | 70 | 39 | 10 | 80 | 52 | 25 | 98 | 73 | 48 | 24 | 02 | 80 | 60 | 44 |
| 45 | 1802 | 1871 | 1941 | 2011 | 2082 | 2153 | 2226 | 2299 | 2374 | 2449 | 2526 | 2603 | 2682 | 2762 | 45 |
| 46 | 03 | 72 | 42 | 12 | 83 | 55 | 27 | 2301 | 75 | 51 | 27 | 04 | 83 | 63 | 46 |
| 47 | 05 | 73 | 43 | 13 | 84 | 56 | 28 | 02 | 76 | 52 | 28 | 06 | 84 | 64 | 47 |
| 48 | 06 | 75 | 44 | 14 | 85 | 57 | 30 | 03 | 78 | 53 | 30 | 07 | 86 | 66 | 48 |
| 49 | 07 | 76 | 45 | 15 | 86 | 58 | 31 | 04 | 79 | 54 | 31 | 08 | 87 | 67 | 49 |
| 50 | 1808 | 1877 | 1946 | 2017 | 2088 | 2159 | 2232 | 2306 | 2380 | 2456 | 2532 | 2610 | 2688 | 2768 | 50 |
| 51 | 09 | 78 | 48 | 18 | 89 | 61 | 33 | 07 | 81 | 57 | 33 | 11 | 90 | 70 | 51 |
| 52 | 10 | 79 | 49 | 19 | 90 | 62 | 35 | 08 | 83 | 58 | 35 | 12 | 91 | 71 | 52 |
| 53 | 11 | 80 | 50 | 20 | 91 | 63 | 36 | 09 | 84 | 59 | 36 | 14 | 92 | 72 | 53 |
| 54 | 13 | 81 | 51 | 21 | 92 | 64 | 37 | 11 | 85 | 61 | 37 | 15 | 94 | 74 | 54 |
| 55 | 1814 | 1883 | 1952 | 2022 | 2094 | 2165 | 2238 | 2312 | 2386 | 2462 | 2538 | 2616 | 2695 | 2775 | 55 |
| 56 | 15 | 84 | 53 | 24 | 95 | 67 | 39 | 13 | 88 | 63 | 40 | 17 | 96 | 76 | 56 |
| 57 | 16 | 85 | 55 | 25 | 96 | 68 | 41 | 14 | 89 | 64 | 41 | 19 | 98 | 78 | 57 |
| 58 | 17 | 86 | 56 | 26 | 97 | 69 | 42 | 16 | 90 | 66 | 42 | 20 | 99 | 79 | 58 |
| 59 | 18 | 87 | 57 | 27 | 98 | 70 | 43 | 17 | 91 | 67 | 44 | 21 | 2700 | 80 | 59 |
| M. | 28° | 29° | 30° | 31° | 32° | 33° | 34° | 35° | 36° | 37° | 38° | 39° | 40° | 41° | M. |

# TABLE III.

## Meridional Parts.

| M. | 42° | 43° | 44° | 45° | 46° | 47° | 48° | 49° | 50° | 51° | 52° | 53° | 54° | 55° | M. |
|---|---|---|---|---|---|---|---|---|---|---|---|---|---|---|---|
| 0 | 2782 | 2863 | 2946 | 3030 | 3116 | 3203 | 3292 | 3382 | 3474 | 3569 | 3665 | 3764 | 3865 | 3968 | 0 |
| 1 | 83 | 64 | 47 | 31 | 17 | 04 | 93 | 84 | 76 | 70 | 67 | 65 | 66 | 70 | 1 |
| 2 | 84 | 66 | 49 | 33 | 18 | 06 | 95 | 85 | 78 | 72 | 68 | 67 | 68 | 71 | 2 |
| 3 | 86 | 67 | 50 | 34 | 20 | 07 | 96 | 87 | 79 | 74 | 70 | 69 | 70 | 73 | 3 |
| 4 | 87 | 69 | 51 | 36 | 21 | 09 | 98 | 88 | 81 | 75 | 72 | 70 | 71 | 75 | 4 |
| 5 | 2788 | 2870 | 2953 | 3037 | 3123 | 3210 | 3299 | 3390 | 3482 | 3577 | 3673 | 3772 | 3873 | 3977 | 5 |
| 6 | 90 | 71 | 54 | 38 | 24 | 12 | 3301 | 91 | 84 | 78 | 75 | 74 | 75 | 78 | 6 |
| 7 | 91 | 73 | 56 | 40 | 26 | 13 | 02 | 93 | 85 | 80 | 77 | 75 | 77 | 80 | 7 |
| 8 | 92 | 74 | 57 | 41 | 27 | 14 | 03 | 94 | 87 | 82 | 78 | 77 | 78 | 82 | 8 |
| 9 | 94 | 75 | 58 | 43 | 29 | 16 | 05 | 96 | 88 | 83 | 80 | 79 | 80 | 84 | 9 |
| 10 | 2795 | 2877 | 2960 | 3044 | 3130 | 3217 | 3306 | 3397 | 3490 | 3585 | 3681 | 3780 | 3882 | 3985 | 10 |
| 11 | 97 | 78 | 61 | 46 | 31 | 19 | 08 | 99 | 92 | 86 | 83 | 82 | 83 | 87 | 11 |
| 12 | 98 | 80 | 63 | 47 | 33 | 20 | 09 | 3400 | 93 | 88 | 85 | 84 | 85 | 89 | 12 |
| 13 | 99 | 81 | 64 | 48 | 34 | 22 | 11 | 02 | 95 | 90 | 86 | 85 | 87 | 91 | 13 |
| 14 | 2801 | 82 | 65 | 50 | 36 | 23 | 12 | 03 | 96 | 91 | 88 | 87 | 89 | 92 | 14 |
| 15 | 2802 | 2884 | 2967 | 3051 | 3137 | 3225 | 3314 | 3405 | 3498 | 3593 | 3690 | 3789 | 3890 | 3994 | 15 |
| 16 | 03 | 85 | 68 | 53 | 39 | 26 | 16 | 07 | 99 | 94 | 91 | 90 | 92 | 96 | 16 |
| 17 | 05 | 86 | 70 | 54 | 40 | 28 | 17 | 08 | 3501 | 96 | 93 | 92 | 94 | 98 | 17 |
| 18 | 06 | 88 | 71 | 55 | 42 | 29 | 19 | 10 | 03 | 98 | 95 | 94 | 95 | 99 | 18 |
| 19 | 07 | 89 | 72 | 57 | 43 | 31 | 20 | 11 | 04 | 99 | 96 | 95 | 97 | 4001 | 19 |
| 20 | 2809 | 2891 | 2974 | 3058 | 3144 | 3232 | 3322 | 3413 | 3506 | 3601 | 3698 | 3797 | 3899 | 4003 | 20 |
| 21 | 10 | 92 | 75 | 60 | 46 | 34 | 23 | 14 | 07 | 02 | 99 | 99 | 3901 | 05 | 21 |
| 22 | 11 | 93 | 76 | 61 | 47 | 35 | 25 | 16 | 09 | 04 | 3701 | 3800 | 02 | 06 | 22 |
| 23 | 13 | 95 | 78 | 63 | 49 | 37 | 26 | 17 | 10 | 06 | 03 | 02 | 04 | 08 | 23 |
| 24 | 14 | 96 | 79 | 64 | 50 | 38 | 28 | 19 | 12 | 07 | 04 | 04 | 06 | 10 | 24 |
| 25 | 2815 | 2897 | 2981 | 3065 | 3152 | 3240 | 3329 | 3420 | 3514 | 3609 | 3706 | 3806 | 3907 | 4012 | 25 |
| 26 | 17 | 99 | 82 | 67 | 53 | 41 | 31 | 22 | 15 | 10 | 08 | 07 | 09 | 14 | 26 |
| 27 | 18 | 2900 | 83 | 68 | 55 | 42 | 32 | 23 | 17 | 12 | 09 | 09 | 11 | 15 | 27 |
| 28 | 20 | 02 | 85 | 70 | 56 | 44 | 34 | 25 | 18 | 14 | 11 | 11 | 13 | 17 | 28 |
| 29 | 21 | 03 | 86 | 71 | 57 | 45 | 35 | 27 | 20 | 15 | 13 | 12 | 14 | 19 | 29 |
| 30 | 2822 | 2904 | 2988 | 3073 | 3159 | 3247 | 3337 | 3428 | 3521 | 3617 | 3714 | 3814 | 3916 | 4021 | 30 |
| 31 | 24 | 06 | 89 | 74 | 60 | 48 | 38 | 30 | 23 | 18 | 16 | 16 | 18 | 22 | 31 |
| 32 | 25 | 07 | 91 | 75 | 62 | 50 | 40 | 31 | 25 | 20 | 17 | 17 | 19 | 24 | 32 |
| 33 | 26 | 08 | 92 | 77 | 63 | 51 | 41 | 33 | 26 | 22 | 19 | 19 | 21 | 26 | 33 |
| 34 | 28 | 10 | 93 | 78 | 65 | 53 | 43 | 34 | 28 | 23 | 21 | 21 | 23 | 28 | 34 |
| 35 | 2829 | 2911 | 2995 | 3080 | 3166 | 3254 | 3344 | 3436 | 3529 | 3625 | 3722 | 3822 | 3925 | 4029 | 35 |
| 36 | 30 | 13 | 96 | 81 | 68 | 56 | 46 | 37 | 31 | 26 | 24 | 24 | 26 | 31 | 36 |
| 37 | 32 | 14 | 98 | 83 | 69 | 57 | 47 | 39 | 32 | 28 | 26 | 26 | 28 | 33 | 37 |
| 38 | 33 | 15 | 99 | 84 | 71 | 59 | 49 | 40 | 34 | 30 | 27 | 27 | 30 | 35 | 38 |
| 39 | 34 | 17 | 3000 | 85 | 72 | 60 | 50 | 42 | 36 | 31 | 29 | 29 | 32 | 37 | 39 |
| 40 | 2836 | 2918 | 3002 | 3087 | 3173 | 3262 | 3352 | 3443 | 3537 | 3633 | 3731 | 3831 | 3933 | 4038 | 40 |
| 41 | 37 | 19 | 03 | 88 | 75 | 63 | 53 | 45 | 39 | 34 | 32 | 32 | 35 | 40 | 41 |
| 42 | 39 | 21 | 05 | 90 | 76 | 65 | 55 | 47 | 40 | 36 | 34 | 34 | 37 | 42 | 42 |
| 43 | 40 | 22 | 06 | 91 | 78 | 66 | 56 | 48 | 42 | 38 | 36 | 36 | 38 | 44 | 43 |
| 44 | 41 | 24 | 07 | 93 | 79 | 68 | 58 | 50 | 43 | 39 | 37 | 38 | 40 | 45 | 44 |
| 45 | 2843 | 2925 | 3009 | 3094 | 3181 | 3269 | 3359 | 3451 | 3545 | 3641 | 3739 | 3839 | 3942 | 4047 | 45 |
| 46 | 44 | 26 | 10 | 95 | 82 | 71 | 61 | 53 | 47 | 43 | 41 | 41 | 44 | 49 | 46 |
| 47 | 45 | 28 | 12 | 97 | 84 | 72 | 62 | 54 | 48 | 44 | 42 | 43 | 45 | 51 | 47 |
| 48 | 47 | 29 | 13 | 98 | 85 | 74 | 64 | 56 | 50 | 46 | 44 | 44 | 47 | 52 | 48 |
| 49 | 48 | 31 | 14 | 3100 | 87 | 75 | 65 | 57 | 51 | 47 | 46 | 46 | 49 | 54 | 49 |
| 50 | 2849 | 2932 | 3016 | 3101 | 3188 | 3277 | 3367 | 3459 | 3553 | 3649 | 3747 | 3848 | 3951 | 4056 | 50 |
| 51 | 51 | 33 | 17 | 03 | 90 | 78 | 68 | 60 | 55 | 51 | 49 | 49 | 52 | 58 | 51 |
| 52 | 52 | 35 | 19 | 04 | 91 | 80 | 70 | 62 | 56 | 52 | 50 | 51 | 54 | 60 | 52 |
| 53 | 54 | 36 | 20 | 05 | 92 | 81 | 71 | 64 | 58 | 54 | 52 | 53 | 56 | 61 | 53 |
| 54 | 55 | 37 | 21 | 07 | 94 | 83 | 73 | 65 | 59 | 55 | 54 | 54 | 58 | 63 | 54 |
| 55 | 2856 | 2939 | 3023 | 3108 | 3195 | 3284 | 3374 | 3467 | 3561 | 3657 | 3755 | 3856 | 3959 | 4065 | 55 |
| 56 | 58 | 40 | 24 | 10 | 97 | 86 | 76 | 68 | 62 | 59 | 57 | 58 | 61 | 67 | 56 |
| 57 | 59 | 42 | 26 | 11 | 98 | 87 | 78 | 70 | 64 | 60 | 59 | 60 | 63 | 69 | 57 |
| 58 | 60 | 43 | 27 | 13 | 3200 | 89 | 79 | 71 | 66 | 62 | 60 | 61 | 64 | 70 | 58 |
| 59 | 62 | 44 | 29 | 14 | 01 | 90 | 81 | 73 | 67 | 64 | 62 | 63 | 66 | 72 | 59 |
| M. | 42° | 43° | 44° | 45° | 46° | 47° | 48° | 49° | 50° | 51° | 52° | 53° | 54° | 55° | M. |

# TABLE III.

## Meridional Parts.

| M. | 56° | 57° | 58° | 59° | 60° | 61° | 62° | 63° | 64° | 65° | 66° | 67° | 68° | 69° | M. |
|---|---|---|---|---|---|---|---|---|---|---|---|---|---|---|---|
| 0 | 4074 | 4183 | 4294 | 4409 | 4527 | 4649 | 4775 | 4905 | 5039 | 5179 | 5324 | 5474 | 5631 | 5795 | 0 |
| 1 | 76 | 84 | 96 | 11 | 29 | 51 | 77 | 07 | 42 | 81 | 26 | 77 | 33 | 97 | 1 |
| 2 | 77 | 86 | 98 | 13 | 31 | 53 | 79 | 09 | 44 | 84 | 28 | 79 | 36 | 5800 | 2 |
| 3 | 79 | 88 | 4300 | 15 | 33 | 55 | 81 | 12 | 46 | 86 | 31 | 82 | 39 | 03 | 3 |
| 4 | 81 | 90 | 02 | 17 | 35 | 57 | 84 | 14 | 49 | 88 | 33 | 84 | 42 | 06 | 4 |
| 5 | 4083 | 4192 | 4304 | 4419 | 4537 | 4660 | 4786 | 4916 | 5051 | 5191 | 5336 | 5487 | 5644 | 5809 | 5 |
| 6 | 85 | 94 | 06 | 21 | 39 | 62 | 88 | 18 | 53 | 93 | 38 | 89 | 47 | 11 | 6 |
| 7 | 86 | 95 | 08 | 23 | 41 | 64 | 90 | 20 | 55 | 95 | 41 | 92 | 50 | 14 | 7 |
| 8 | 88 | 97 | 09 | 25 | 43 | 66 | 92 | 23 | 58 | 98 | 43 | 95 | 52 | 17 | 8 |
| 9 | 90 | 99 | 11 | 27 | 45 | 68 | 94 | 25 | 60 | 5200 | 46 | 97 | 55 | 20 | 9 |
| 10 | 4092 | 4201 | 4313 | 4429 | 4547 | 4670 | 4796 | 4927 | 5062 | 5203 | 5348 | 5500 | 5658 | 5823 | 10 |
| 11 | 94 | 03 | 15 | 31 | 49 | 72 | 98 | 29 | 65 | 05 | 51 | 02 | 60 | 25 | 11 |
| 12 | 95 | 05 | 17 | 33 | 51 | 74 | 4801 | 31 | 67 | 07 | 53 | 05 | 63 | 28 | 12 |
| 13 | 97 | 07 | 19 | 34 | 53 | 76 | 03 | 34 | 69 | 10 | 56 | 07 | 66 | 31 | 13 |
| 14 | 99 | 08 | 21 | 36 | 55 | 78 | 05 | 36 | 71 | 12 | 58 | 10 | 68 | 34 | 14 |
| 15 | 4101 | 4210 | 4323 | 4438 | 4557 | 4680 | 4807 | 4938 | 5074 | 5214 | 5361 | 5513 | 5671 | 5837 | 15 |
| 16 | 03 | 12 | 25 | 40 | 59 | 82 | 09 | 40 | 76 | 17 | 63 | 15 | 74 | 39 | 16 |
| 17 | 04 | 14 | 27 | 42 | 62 | 84 | 11 | 43 | 78 | 19 | 66 | 18 | 76 | 42 | 17 |
| 18 | 06 | 16 | 28 | 44 | 64 | 87 | 14 | 45 | 81 | 22 | 68 | 20 | 79 | 45 | 18 |
| 19 | 08 | 18 | 30 | 46 | 66 | 89 | 16 | 47 | 83 | 24 | 71 | 23 | 82 | 48 | 19 |
| 20 | 4110 | 4220 | 4332 | 4448 | 4568 | 4691 | 4818 | 4949 | 5085 | 5226 | 5373 | 5526 | 5685 | 5851 | 20 |
| 21 | 12 | 21 | 34 | 50 | 70 | 93 | 20 | 51 | 88 | 29 | 76 | 28 | 87 | 54 | 21 |
| 22 | 13 | 23 | 36 | 52 | 72 | 95 | 22 | 54 | 90 | 31 | 78 | 31 | 90 | 56 | 22 |
| 23 | 15 | 25 | 38 | 54 | 74 | 97 | 24 | 56 | 92 | 34 | 80 | 33 | 93 | 59 | 23 |
| 24 | 17 | 27 | 40 | 56 | 76 | 99 | 26 | 58 | 95 | 36 | 83 | 36 | 95 | 62 | 24 |
| 25 | 4119 | 4229 | 4342 | 4458 | 4578 | 4701 | 4829 | 4960 | 5097 | 5238 | 5385 | 5539 | 5698 | 5865 | 25 |
| 26 | 21 | 31 | 44 | 60 | 80 | 03 | 31 | 63 | 99 | 41 | 88 | 41 | 5701 | 68 | 26 |
| 27 | 22 | 32 | 46 | 62 | 82 | 05 | 33 | 65 | 5102 | 43 | 90 | 44 | 04 | 71 | 27 |
| 28 | 24 | 34 | 47 | 64 | 84 | 07 | 35 | 67 | 04 | 46 | 93 | 46 | 06 | 74 | 28 |
| 29 | 26 | 36 | 49 | 66 | 86 | 10 | 37 | 69 | 06 | 48 | 95 | 49 | 09 | 76 | 29 |
| 30 | 4128 | 4238 | 4351 | 4468 | 4588 | 4712 | 4839 | 4972 | 5108 | 5250 | 5398 | 5552 | 5712 | 5879 | 30 |
| 31 | 30 | 40 | 53 | 70 | 90 | 14 | 42 | 74 | 11 | 53 | 5401 | 54 | 15 | 82 | 31 |
| 32 | 32 | 42 | 55 | 72 | 92 | 16 | 44 | 76 | 13 | 55 | 03 | 57 | 17 | 85 | 32 |
| 33 | 33 | 44 | 57 | 74 | 94 | 18 | 46 | 78 | 15 | 58 | 06 | 59 | 20 | 88 | 33 |
| 34 | 35 | 46 | 59 | 76 | 96 | 20 | 48 | 81 | 18 | 60 | 08 | 62 | 23 | 91 | 34 |
| 35 | 4137 | 4247 | 4361 | 4478 | 4598 | 4722 | 4850 | 4983 | 5120 | 5263 | 5411 | 5565 | 5725 | 5894 | 35 |
| 36 | 39 | 49 | 63 | 80 | 4600 | 24 | 52 | 85 | 22 | 65 | 13 | 67 | 28 | 96 | 36 |
| 37 | 41 | 51 | 65 | 82 | 02 | 26 | 55 | 87 | 25 | 67 | 16 | 70 | 31 | 99 | 37 |
| 38 | 42 | 53 | 67 | 84 | 04 | 28 | 57 | 90 | 27 | 70 | 18 | 73 | 34 | 5902 | 38 |
| 39 | 44 | 55 | 69 | 86 | 06 | 31 | 59 | 92 | 29 | 72 | 21 | 75 | 36 | 05 | 39 |
| 40 | 4146 | 4257 | 4370 | 4488 | 4608 | 4733 | 4861 | 4994 | 5132 | 5275 | 5423 | 5578 | 5739 | 5908 | 40 |
| 41 | 48 | 59 | 72 | 90 | 10 | 35 | 63 | 96 | 34 | 77 | 26 | 80 | 42 | 11 | 41 |
| 42 | 50 | 60 | 74 | 92 | 12 | 37 | 65 | 99 | 36 | 80 | 28 | 83 | 45 | 14 | 42 |
| 43 | 52 | 62 | 76 | 94 | 14 | 39 | 68 | 5001 | 39 | 82 | 31 | 86 | 47 | 17 | 43 |
| 44 | 53 | 64 | 78 | 95 | 16 | 41 | 70 | 03 | 41 | 84 | 33 | 88 | 50 | 19 | 44 |
| 45 | 4155 | 4266 | 4380 | 4497 | 4618 | 4743 | 4872 | 5005 | 5143 | 5287 | 5436 | 5591 | 5753 | 5922 | 45 |
| 46 | 57 | 68 | 82 | 99 | 20 | 45 | 74 | 08 | 46 | 89 | 38 | 94 | 56 | 25 | 46 |
| 47 | 59 | 70 | 84 | 4501 | 23 | 47 | 76 | 10 | 48 | 92 | 41 | 96 | 58 | 28 | 47 |
| 48 | 61 | 72 | 86 | 03 | 25 | 50 | 79 | 12 | 51 | 94 | 43 | 99 | 61 | 31 | 48 |
| 49 | 62 | 74 | 88 | 05 | 27 | 52 | 81 | 14 | 53 | 97 | 46 | 5602 | 64 | 34 | 49 |
| 50 | 4164 | 4275 | 4390 | 4507 | 4629 | 4754 | 4883 | 5017 | 5155 | 5299 | 5448 | 5604 | 5767 | 5937 | 50 |
| 51 | 66 | 77 | 92 | 09 | 31 | 56 | 85 | 19 | 58 | 5301 | 51 | 07 | 70 | 40 | 51 |
| 52 | 68 | 79 | 94 | 11 | 33 | 58 | 87 | 21 | 60 | 04 | 54 | 10 | 72 | 43 | 52 |
| 53 | 70 | 81 | 96 | 13 | 35 | 60 | 90 | 23 | 62 | 06 | 56 | 12 | 75 | 46 | 53 |
| 54 | 72 | 83 | 98 | 15 | 37 | 62 | 92 | 26 | 65 | 09 | 59 | 15 | 78 | 48 | 54 |
| 55 | 4173 | 4285 | 4399 | 4517 | 4639 | 4764 | 4894 | 5028 | 5167 | 5311 | 5461 | 5617 | 5781 | 5951 | 55 |
| 56 | 75 | 87 | 4401 | 19 | 41 | 66 | 96 | 30 | 69 | 14 | 64 | 20 | 83 | 54 | 56 |
| 57 | 77 | 89 | 03 | 21 | 43 | 69 | 98 | 33 | 72 | 16 | 66 | 23 | 86 | 57 | 57 |
| 58 | 79 | 91 | 05 | 23 | 45 | 71 | 4901 | 35 | 74 | 19 | 69 | 25 | 89 | 60 | 58 |
| 59 | 81 | 92 | 07 | 25 | 47 | 73 | 03 | 37 | 76 | 21 | 71 | 28 | 92 | 63 | 59 |
| M. | 56° | 57° | 58° | 59° | 60° | 61° | 62° | 63° | 64° | 65° | 66° | 67° | 68° | 69° | M. |

# TABLE III.

## Meridional Parts.

| M. | 70° | 71° | 72° | 73° | 74° | 75° | 76° | 77° | 78° | 79° | 80° | 81° | 82° | 83° | M. |
|---|---|---|---|---|---|---|---|---|---|---|---|---|---|---|---|
| 0 | 5966 | 6146 | 6335 | 6534 | 6746 | 6970 | 7210 | 7467 | 7745 | 8046 | 8375 | 8739 | 9145 | 9606 | 0 |
| 1 | 69 | 49 | 38 | 38 | 49 | 74 | 14 | 72 | 49 | 51 | 81 | 45 | 53 | 14 | 1 |
| 2 | 72 | 52 | 41 | 41 | 53 | 78 | 18 | 76 | 54 | 56 | 87 | 52 | 60 | 22 | 2 |
| 3 | 75 | 55 | 45 | 45 | 57 | 82 | 22 | 81 | 59 | 61 | 93 | 58 | 67 | 31 | 3 |
| 4 | 78 | 58 | 48 | 48 | 60 | 86 | 27 | 85 | 64 | 67 | 98 | 65 | 74 | 39 | 4 |
| 5 | 5981 | 6161 | 6351 | 6552 | 6764 | 6990 | 7231 | 7490 | 7769 | 8072 | 8404 | 8771 | 9182 | 9647 | 5 |
| 6 | 84 | 64 | 54 | 55 | 68 | 94 | 35 | 94 | 74 | 77 | 10 | 78 | 89 | 55 | 6 |
| 7 | 86 | 67 | 58 | 58 | 71 | 97 | 39 | 98 | 78 | 83 | 16 | 84 | 96 | 64 | 7 |
| 8 | 89 | 70 | 61 | 62 | 75 | 7001 | 43 | 7503 | 83 | 88 | 22 | 91 | 9203 | 72 | 8 |
| 9 | 92 | 73 | 64 | 65 | 79 | 05 | 47 | 07 | 88 | 93 | 27 | 97 | 11 | 80 | 9 |
| 10 | 5995 | 6177 | 6367 | 6569 | 6782 | 7009 | 7252 | 7512 | 7793 | 8099 | 8433 | 8804 | 9218 | 9689 | 10 |
| 11 | 98 | 80 | 71 | 72 | 86 | 13 | 56 | 16 | 98 | 8104 | 39 | 10 | 25 | 97 | 11 |
| 12 | 6001 | 83 | 74 | 76 | 90 | 17 | 60 | 21 | 7803 | 09 | 45 | 17 | 33 | 9706 | 12 |
| 13 | 04 | 86 | 77 | 79 | 93 | 21 | 64 | 25 | 08 | 15 | 51 | 23 | 40 | 14 | 13 |
| 14 | 07 | 89 | 80 | 83 | 97 | 25 | 68 | 30 | 13 | 20 | 57 | 30 | 48 | 23 | 14 |
| 15 | 6010 | 6192 | 6384 | 6586 | 6801 | 7029 | 7273 | 7535 | 7817 | 8125 | 8463 | 8836 | 9255 | 9731 | 15 |
| 16 | 13 | 95 | 87 | 90 | 04 | 33 | 77 | 39 | 22 | 31 | 69 | 43 | 62 | 40 | 16 |
| 17 | 16 | 98 | 90 | 93 | 08 | 37 | 81 | 44 | 27 | 36 | 74 | 49 | 70 | 48 | 17 |
| 18 | 19 | 6201 | 94 | 97 | 12 | 41 | 85 | 48 | 32 | 41 | 80 | 56 | 77 | 57 | 18 |
| 19 | 22 | 05 | 97 | 6600 | 15 | 45 | 89 | 53 | 37 | 47 | 86 | 63 | 85 | 65 | 19 |
| 20 | 6025 | 6208 | 6400 | 6603 | 6819 | 7048 | 7294 | 7557 | 7842 | 8152 | 8492 | 8869 | 9292 | 9774 | 20 |
| 21 | 28 | 11 | 03 | 07 | 23 | 52 | 98 | 62 | 47 | 58 | 98 | 76 | 9300 | 83 | 21 |
| 22 | 31 | 14 | 07 | 10 | 26 | 56 | 7302 | 66 | 52 | 63 | 8504 | 83 | 07 | 91 | 22 |
| 23 | 34 | 17 | 10 | 14 | 30 | 60 | 06 | 71 | 57 | 68 | 10 | 89 | 15 | 9800 | 23 |
| 24 | 37 | 20 | 13 | 17 | 34 | 64 | 11 | 76 | 62 | 74 | 16 | 96 | 22 | 09 | 24 |
| 25 | 6040 | 6223 | 6417 | 6621 | 6838 | 7068 | 7315 | 7580 | 7867 | 8179 | 8522 | 8903 | 9330 | 9817 | 25 |
| 26 | 43 | 26 | 20 | 24 | 41 | 72 | 19 | 85 | 72 | 85 | 28 | 09 | 37 | 26 | 26 |
| 27 | 46 | 30 | 23 | 28 | 45 | 76 | 23 | 89 | 77 | 90 | 34 | 16 | 45 | 35 | 27 |
| 28 | 49 | 33 | 27 | 31 | 49 | 80 | 28 | 94 | 82 | 96 | 40 | 23 | 53 | 44 | 28 |
| 29 | 52 | 36 | 30 | 35 | 53 | 84 | 32 | 99 | 87 | 8201 | 46 | 30 | 60 | 52 | 29 |
| 30 | 6055 | 6239 | 6433 | 6639 | 6856 | 7088 | 7336 | 7603 | 7892 | 8207 | 8552 | 8936 | 9368 | 9861 | 30 |
| 31 | 58 | 42 | 37 | 42 | 60 | 92 | 41 | 08 | 97 | 12 | 58 | 43 | 76 | 70 | 31 |
| 32 | 61 | 45 | 40 | 46 | 64 | 96 | 45 | 12 | 7902 | 18 | 65 | 50 | 83 | 79 | 32 |
| 33 | 64 | 49 | 43 | 49 | 68 | 7100 | 49 | 17 | 07 | 23 | 71 | 57 | 91 | 88 | 33 |
| 34 | 67 | 52 | 47 | 53 | 71 | 04 | 53 | 22 | 12 | 29 | 77 | 63 | 99 | 97 | 34 |
| 35 | 6070 | 6255 | 6450 | 6656 | 6875 | 7108 | 7358 | 7626 | 7917 | 8234 | 8583 | 8970 | 9407 | 9906 | 35 |
| 36 | 73 | 58 | 53 | 60 | 79 | 12 | 62 | 31 | 22 | 40 | 89 | 77 | 14 | 15 | 36 |
| 37 | 76 | 61 | 57 | 63 | 83 | 16 | 66 | 36 | 27 | 45 | 95 | 84 | 22 | 24 | 37 |
| 38 | 79 | 64 | 60 | 67 | 86 | 20 | 71 | 40 | 32 | 51 | 8601 | 91 | 30 | 33 | 38 |
| 39 | 82 | 68 | 63 | 70 | 90 | 24 | 75 | 45 | 37 | 56 | 07 | 98 | 38 | 42 | 39 |
| 40 | 6085 | 6271 | 6467 | 6674 | 6894 | 7128 | 7379 | 7650 | 7942 | 8262 | 8614 | 9005 | 9445 | 9951 | 40 |
| 41 | 88 | 74 | 70 | 77 | 98 | 32 | 84 | 54 | 48 | 67 | 20 | 12 | 53 | 60 | 41 |
| 42 | 91 | 77 | 73 | 81 | 6901 | 36 | 88 | 59 | 53 | 73 | 26 | 18 | 61 | 69 | 42 |
| 43 | 94 | 80 | 77 | 85 | 05 | 40 | 92 | 64 | 58 | 79 | 32 | 25 | 69 | 78 | 43 |
| 44 | 97 | 83 | 80 | 88 | 09 | 45 | 97 | 68 | 63 | 84 | 38 | 32 | 77 | 87 | 44 |
| 45 | 6100 | 6287 | 6483 | 6692 | 6913 | 7149 | 7401 | 7673 | 7968 | 8290 | 8644 | 9039 | 9485 | 9996 | 45 |
| 46 | 03 | 90 | 87 | 95 | 17 | 53 | 06 | 78 | 73 | 95 | 51 | 46 | 93 | 10005 | 46 |
| 47 | 06 | 93 | 90 | 99 | 20 | 57 | 10 | 83 | 78 | 8301 | 57 | 53 | 9501 | 10015 | 47 |
| 48 | 09 | 96 | 94 | 6702 | 24 | 61 | 14 | 87 | 83 | 07 | 63 | 60 | 09 | 10024 | 48 |
| 49 | 12 | 99 | 97 | 06 | 28 | 65 | 19 | 92 | 89 | 12 | 69 | 67 | 17 | 10033 | 49 |
| 50 | 6115 | 6303 | 6500 | 6710 | 6932 | 7169 | 7423 | 7697 | 7994 | 8318 | 8676 | 9074 | 9525 | 10043 | 50 |
| 51 | 18 | 06 | 04 | 13 | 36 | 73 | 27 | 7702 | 99 | 24 | 82 | 81 | 33 | 10052 | 51 |
| 52 | 21 | 09 | 07 | 17 | 40 | 77 | 32 | 06 | 8004 | 29 | 88 | 88 | 41 | 10061 | 52 |
| 53 | 24 | 12 | 11 | 20 | 43 | 81 | 36 | 11 | 09 | 35 | 95 | 96 | 49 | 10071 | 53 |
| 54 | 27 | 15 | 14 | 24 | 47 | 85 | 41 | 16 | 14 | 41 | 8701 | 9103 | 57 | 10080 | 54 |
| 55 | 6130 | 6319 | 6517 | 6728 | 6951 | 7189 | 7445 | 7721 | 8020 | 8347 | 8707 | 9110 | 9565 | 10089 | 55 |
| 56 | 33 | 22 | 21 | 31 | 55 | 94 | 49 | 25 | 25 | 52 | 14 | 17 | 73 | 10099 | 56 |
| 57 | 36 | 25 | 24 | 35 | 59 | 98 | 54 | 30 | 30 | 58 | 20 | 24 | 81 | 10108 | 57 |
| 58 | 40 | 28 | 28 | 38 | 63 | 7202 | 58 | 35 | 35 | 64 | 26 | 31 | 89 | 10118 | 58 |
| 59 | 43 | 32 | 31 | 42 | 66 | 06 | 63 | 40 | 40 | 69 | 33 | 38 | 98 | 10127 | 59 |
| M. | 70° | 71° | 72° | 73° | 74° | 75° | 76° | 77° | 78° | 79° | 80° | 81° | 82° | 83° | M. |

# TABLE X.

## For finding the Distance of Terrestrial Objects at Sea, in Statute Miles.

| Height in feet. | Distance. Mil. Dec. | Height in feet. | Distance. Mil. Dec. | Height in feet. | Distance. Mil. Dec. | Height in feet. | Distance. Mil. Dec. | Height in feet. | Distance. Mil. Dec. | Height in feet. | Distance. Mil. Dec. | Height in feet. | Distance. Mil. Dec. |
|---|---|---|---|---|---|---|---|---|---|---|---|---|---|
| 1 | 1.32 | 26 | 6.75 | 55 | 9.81 | 210 | 19.17 | 460 | 28.37 | 920 | 40.13 | 3100 | 73.7 |
| 2 | 1.87 | 27 | 6.87 | 60 | 10.25 | 220 | 19.62 | 470 | 28.68 | 940 | 40.56 | 3200 | 74.8 |
| 3 | 2.29 | 28 | 7.00 | 65 | 10.67 | 230 | 20.06 | 480 | 28.98 | 960 | 40.99 | 3300 | 76.0 |
| 4 | 2.65 | 29 | 7.12 | 70 | 11.07 | 240 | 20.50 | 490 | 29.29 | 980 | 41.42 | 3400 | 77.1 |
| 5 | 2.96 | 30 | 7.25 | 75 | 11.46 | 250 | 20.92 | 500 | 29.58 | 1000 | 41.80 | 3500 | 78.3 |
| 6 | 3.24 | 31 | 7.37 | 80 | 11.83 | 260 | 21.33 | 520 | 30.17 | 1100 | 43.90 | 3600 | 79.4 |
| 7 | 3.50 | 32 | 7.48 | 85 | 12,20 | 270 | 21.74 | 540 | 30.74 | 1200 | 45.80 | 3700 | 80.5 |
| 8 | 3.74 | 33 | 7.60 | 90 | 12.55 | 280 | 22.14 | 560 | 31.31 | 1300 | 47.70 | 3800 | 81.6 |
| 9 | 3.97 | 34 | 7.71 | 95 | 12.89 | 290 | 22.53 | 580 | 31.86 | 1400 | 49.50 | 3900 | 82.6 |
| 10 | 4.18 | 35 | 7.83 | 100 | 13.23 | 300 | 22.91 | 600 | 32.41 | 1500 | 51.20 | 4000 | 83.7 |
| 11 | 4.39 | 36 | 7.94 | 105 | 13.56 | 310 | 23.29 | 620 | 32.94 | 1600 | 52.90 | 4100 | 84.7 |
| 12 | 4.58 | 37 | 8.05 | 110 | 13.88 | 320 | 23.67 | 640 | 33.47 | 1700 | 54.50 | 4200 | 85.7 |
| 13 | 4.77 | 38 | 8.16 | 115 | 14.19 | 330 | 24.03 | 660 | 33.99 | 1800 | 56.10 | 4300 | 86.8 |
| 14 | 4.95 | 39 | 8.26 | 120 | 14.49 | 340 | 24.39 | 680 | 34.50 | 1900 | 57.70 | 4400 | 87.8 |
| 15 | 5.12 | 40 | 8.37 | 125 | 14.79 | 350 | 24.75 | 700 | 35.00 | 2000 | 59.20 | 4500 | 88.7 |
| 16 | 5.29 | 41 | 8.47 | 130 | 15.08 | 360 | 25.10 | 720 | 35.50 | 2100 | 60.60 | 4600 | 89.7 |
| 17 | 5.45 | 42 | 8.57 | 135 | 15.37 | 370 | 25.45 | 740 | 35.99 | 2200 | 62.10 | 4700 | 90.7 |
| 18 | 5.61 | 43 | 8.68 | 140 | 15.65 | 380 | 25.79 | 760 | 36.47 | 2300 | 63.40 | 4800 | 91.7 |
| 19 | 5.77 | 44 | 8.78 | 145 | 15.93 | 390 | 26.13 | 780 | 36.95 | 2400 | 64.80 | 4900 | 92.6 |
| 20 | 5.92 | 45 | 8.87 | 150 | 16.20 | 400 | 26.46 | 800 | 37.42 | 2500 | 66.10 | 5000 | 93.5 |
| 21 | 6.06 | 46 | 8.97 | 160 | 16.73 | 410 | 26.79 | 820 | 37.88 | 2600 | 67.50 | 1 mile | 96.1 |
| 22 | 6.21 | 47 | 9.07 | 170 | 17.25 | 420 | 27.11 | 840 | 38.34 | 2700 | 68.70 | | |
| 23 | 6.34 | 48 | 9.17 | 180 | 17.75 | 430 | 27.43 | 860 | 38.80 | 2800 | 70.00 | | |
| 24 | 6.48 | 49 | 9.26 | 190 | 18.24 | 440 | 27.75 | 880 | 39.25 | 2900 | 71.20 | | |
| 25 | 6.61 | 50 | 9.35 | 200 | 18.71 | 450 | 28.06 | 900 | 39.69 | 3000 | 72.50 | | |

# TABLE X. A.

## Parallax in Altitude of a Planet.

| | Horizontal Parallax of a Planet. | | | | | | | | | | | | | | | | | | | | | | | | | | | | | | |
|---|---|---|---|---|---|---|---|---|---|---|---|---|---|---|---|---|---|---|---|---|---|---|---|---|---|---|---|---|---|---|---|
| Alt. D. | 1 | ″ 2 | ″ 3 | ″ 4 | ″ 5 | ″ 6 | ″ 7 | ″ 8 | ″ 9 | ″ 10 | ″ 11 | ″ 12 | ″ 13 | ″ 14 | ″ 15 | ″ 16 | ″ 17 | ″ 18 | ″ 19 | ″ 20 | ″ 21 | ″ 22 | ″ 23 | ″ 24 | ″ 25 | ″ 26 | ″ 27 | ″ 28 | ″ 30 | ″ 35 | Alt. D. |
| 0 | 1 | 2 | 3 | 4 | 5 | 6 | 7 | 8 | 9 | 10 | 11 | 12 | 13 | 14 | 15 | 16 | 17 | 18 | 19 | 20 | 21 | 22 | 23 | 24 | 25 | 26 | 27 | 28 | 30 | 35 | 0 |
| 10 | 1 | 2 | 3 | 4 | 5 | 6 | 7 | 8 | 9 | 10 | 11 | 12 | 13 | 14 | 15 | 16 | 17 | 18 | 19 | 20 | 21 | 22 | 23 | 24 | 25 | 26 | 27 | 28 | 30 | 35 | 10 |
| 20 | 1 | 2 | 3 | 4 | 5 | 6 | 7 | 8 | 8 | 9 | 10 | 11 | 12 | 13 | 14 | 15 | 16 | 17 | 18 | 19 | 20 | 21 | 22 | 23 | 23 | 24 | 25 | 26 | 28 | 33 | 20 |
| 30 | 1 | 2 | 3 | 3 | 4 | 5 | 6 | 7 | 8 | 9 | 10 | 10 | 11 | 12 | 13 | 14 | 15 | 16 | 16 | 17 | 18 | 19 | 20 | 21 | 22 | 23 | 23 | 24 | 26 | 30 | 30 |
| 35 | 1 | 2 | 2 | 3 | 4 | 5 | 6 | 7 | 7 | 8 | 9 | 10 | 11 | 11 | 12 | 13 | 14 | 15 | 16 | 16 | 17 | 18 | 19 | 20 | 20 | 21 | 22 | 23 | 25 | 29 | 35 |
| 40 | 1 | 2 | 2 | 3 | 4 | 5 | 5 | 6 | 7 | 8 | 8 | 9 | 10 | 11 | 11 | 12 | 13 | 14 | 15 | 15 | 16 | 17 | 18 | 18 | 19 | 20 | 21 | 21 | 23 | 27 | 40 |
| 43 | 1 | 1 | 2 | 3 | 4 | 4 | 5 | 6 | 7 | 7 | 8 | 9 | 10 | 10 | 11 | 12 | 12 | 13 | 14 | 15 | 15 | 16 | 17 | 18 | 18 | 19 | 20 | 20 | 22 | 26 | 43 |
| 46 | 1 | 1 | 2 | 3 | 3 | 4 | 5 | 6 | 6 | 7 | 8 | 8 | 9 | 10 | 10 | 11 | 12 | 13 | 13 | 14 | 15 | 15 | 16 | 17 | 17 | 18 | 19 | 19 | 21 | 24 | 46 |
| 49 | 1 | 1 | 2 | 3 | 3 | 4 | 5 | 5 | 6 | 7 | 7 | 8 | 9 | 9 | 10 | 10 | 11 | 12 | 12 | 13 | 14 | 14 | 15 | 16 | 16 | 17 | 18 | 18 | 20 | 23 | 49 |
| 52 | 1 | 1 | 2 | 2 | 3 | 4 | 4 | 5 | 6 | 6 | 7 | 7 | 8 | 9 | 9 | 10 | 10 | 11 | 12 | 12 | 13 | 14 | 14 | 15 | 15 | 16 | 17 | 17 | 18 | 22 | 52 |
| 55 | 1 | 1 | 2 | 2 | 3 | 3 | 4 | 5 | 5 | 6 | 6 | 7 | 7 | 8 | 9 | 9 | 10 | 10 | 11 | 11 | 12 | 13 | 13 | 14 | 14 | 15 | 15 | 16 | 17 | 20 | 55 |
| 58 | 1 | 1 | 2 | 2 | 3 | 3 | 4 | 4 | 5 | 5 | 6 | 6 | 7 | 7 | 8 | 8 | 9 | 10 | 10 | 11 | 11 | 12 | 12 | 13 | 13 | 14 | 14 | 15 | 16 | 19 | 58 |
| 61 | 0 | 1 | 1 | 2 | 2 | 3 | 3 | 4 | 4 | 5 | 5 | 6 | 6 | 7 | 7 | 8 | 8 | 9 | 9 | 10 | 10 | 11 | 11 | 12 | 12 | 13 | 13 | 14 | 15 | 17 | 61 |
| 64 | 0 | 1 | 1 | 2 | 2 | 3 | 3 | 4 | 4 | 4 | 5 | 5 | 6 | 6 | 7 | 7 | 7 | 8 | 8 | 9 | 9 | 10 | 10 | 11 | 11 | 11 | 12 | 12 | 13 | 15 | 64 |
| 67 | 0 | 1 | 1 | 2 | 2 | 2 | 3 | 3 | 4 | 4 | 4 | 5 | 5 | 5 | 6 | 6 | 7 | 7 | 7 | 8 | 8 | 9 | 9 | 9 | 10 | 10 | 11 | 11 | 12 | 14 | 67 |
| 70 | 0 | 1 | 1 | 1 | 2 | 2 | 2 | 3 | 3 | 3 | 4 | 4 | 4 | 5 | 5 | 5 | 6 | 6 | 6 | 7 | 7 | 8 | 8 | 8 | 9 | 9 | 9 | 10 | 10 | 12 | 70 |
| 72 | 0 | 1 | 1 | 1 | 2 | 2 | 2 | 2 | 3 | 3 | 3 | 4 | 4 | 4 | 5 | 5 | 5 | 6 | 6 | 6 | 6 | 7 | 7 | 7 | 8 | 8 | 8 | 9 | 9 | 11 | 72 |
| 74 | 0 | 1 | 1 | 1 | 1 | 2 | 2 | 2 | 2 | 3 | 3 | 3 | 4 | 4 | 4 | 4 | 5 | 5 | 5 | 6 | 6 | 6 | 6 | 7 | 7 | 7 | 7 | 8 | 8 | 10 | 74 |
| 76 | 0 | 0 | 1 | 1 | 1 | 1 | 2 | 2 | 2 | 2 | 3 | 3 | 3 | 3 | 4 | 4 | 4 | 4 | 5 | 5 | 5 | 5 | 6 | 6 | 6 | 6 | 7 | 7 | 7 | 8 | 76 |
| 78 | 0 | 0 | 1 | 1 | 1 | 1 | 1 | 2 | 2 | 2 | 2 | 2 | 3 | 3 | 3 | 3 | 4 | 4 | 4 | 4 | 4 | 5 | 5 | 5 | 5 | 5 | 6 | 6 | 6 | 7 | 78 |
| 80 | 0 | 0 | 1 | 1 | 1 | 1 | 1 | 1 | 2 | 2 | 2 | 2 | 2 | 2 | 3 | 3 | 3 | 3 | 3 | 3 | 4 | 4 | 4 | 4 | 4 | 5 | 5 | 5 | 5 | 6 | 80 |
| 82 | 0 | 0 | 0 | 1 | 1 | 1 | 1 | 1 | 1 | 1 | 2 | 2 | 2 | 2 | 2 | 2 | 2 | 3 | 3 | 3 | 3 | 3 | 3 | 3 | 3 | 4 | 4 | 4 | 4 | 5 | 82 |
| 84 | 0 | 0 | 0 | 0 | 1 | 1 | 1 | 1 | 1 | 1 | 1 | 1 | 1 | 1 | 2 | 2 | 2 | 2 | 2 | 2 | 2 | 2 | 2 | 3 | 3 | 3 | 3 | 3 | 3 | 4 | 84 |
| 86 | 0 | 0 | 0 | 0 | 0 | 0 | 0 | 1 | 1 | 1 | 1 | 1 | 1 | 1 | 1 | 1 | 1 | 1 | 1 | 1 | 1 | 2 | 2 | 2 | 2 | 2 | 2 | 2 | 2 | 2 | 86 |
| 88 | 0 | 0 | 0 | 0 | 0 | 0 | 0 | 0 | 0 | 0 | 0 | 0 | 0 | 0 | 1 | 1 | 1 | 1 | 1 | 1 | 1 | 1 | 1 | 1 | 1 | 1 | 1 | 1 | 1 | 1 | 88 |
| 90 | 0 | 0 | 0 | 0 | 0 | 0 | 0 | 0 | 0 | 0 | 0 | 0 | 0 | 0 | 0 | 0 | 0 | 0 | 0 | 0 | 0 | 0 | 0 | 0 | 0 | 0 | 0 | 0 | 0 | 0 | 90 |

# TABLES XII, XIII, XIV, XV, AND XVI.

## TABLE XII.
The Refraction of the Heavenly Bodies in Altitude.

| App. Alt. | Ref. | App. Alt. | Ref. | App. Alt. | Ref. |
|---|---|---|---|---|---|
| D. M. | M. S. | D. M. | M. S. | D. | M. S. |
| 0. 0 | 33. 0 | 6.30 | 7.52 | 30 | 1.38 |
| 0. 5 | 32.11 | 6.40 | 7.41 | 31 | 1.35 |
| 0.10 | 31.22 | 6.50 | 7.31 | 32 | 1.31 |
| 0.15 | 30.36 | 7. 0 | 7.21 | 33 | 1.28 |
| 0.20 | 29.50 | 7.10 | 7.12 | 34 | 1.24 |
| 0.25 | 29. 6 | 7.20 | 7. 3 | 35 | 1.21 |
| 0.30 | 28.23 | 7.30 | 6.54 | 36 | 1.18 |
| 0.35 | 27.41 | 7.40 | 6.46 | 37 | 1.16 |
| 0.40 | 27. 0 | 7.50 | 6.38 | 38 | 1.13 |
| 0.45 | 26.20 | 8. 0 | 6.30 | 39 | 1.10 |
| 0.50 | 25.42 | 8.10 | 6.22 | 40 | 1. 8 |
| 0.55 | 25. 5 | 8.20 | 6.15 | 41 | 1. 5 |
| 1. 0 | 24.29 | 8.30 | 6. 8 | 42 | 1. 3 |
| 1. 5 | 23.54 | 8.40 | 6. 1 | 43 | 1. 1 |
| 1.10 | 23.20 | 8.50 | 5.55 | 44 | 0.59 |
| 1.15 | 22.47 | 9. 0 | 5.49 | 45 | 0.57 |
| 1.20 | 22.15 | 9.10 | 5.43 | 46 | 0.55 |
| 1.25 | 21.44 | 9.20 | 5.37 | 47 | 0.53 |
| 1.30 | 21.15 | 9.30 | 5.31 | 48 | 0.51 |
| 1.35 | 20.46 | 9.40 | 5.26 | 49 | 0.50 |
| 1.40 | 20.18 | 9.50 | 5.20 | 50 | 0.48 |
| 1.45 | 19.51 | 10. 0 | 5.15 | 51 | 0.46 |
| 1.50 | 19.25 | 10.15 | 5. 8 | 52 | 0.45 |
| 1.55 | 18.59 | 10.30 | 5. 0 | 53 | 0.43 |
| 2. 0 | 18.35 | 10.45 | 4.54 | 54 | 0.41 |
| 2. 5 | 18.11 | 11. 0 | 4.47 | 55 | 0.40 |
| 2.10 | 17.48 | 11.15 | 4.41 | 56 | 0.38 |
| 2.15 | 17.26 | 11.30 | 4.35 | 57 | 0.37 |
| 2.20 | 17. 4 | 11.45 | 4.29 | 58 | 0.36 |
| 2.25 | 16.44 | 12. 0 | 4.23 | 59 | 0.34 |
| 2.30 | 16.23 | 12.20 | 4.16 | 60 | 0.33 |
| 2.35 | 16. 4 | 12.40 | 4. 9 | 61 | 0.32 |
| 2.40 | 15.45 | 13. 0 | 4. 3 | 62 | 0.30 |
| 2.45 | 15.27 | 13.20 | 3.57 | 63 | 0.29 |
| 2.50 | 15. 9 | 13.40 | 3.51 | 64 | 0.28 |
| 2.55 | 14.52 | 14. 0 | 3.46 | 65 | 0.27 |
| 3. 0 | 14.35 | 14.20 | 3.40 | 66 | 0.25 |
| 3. 5 | 14.19 | 14.40 | 3.35 | 67 | 0.24 |
| 3.10 | 14. 3 | 15. 0 | 3.30 | 68 | 0.23 |
| 3.15 | 13.48 | 15.30 | 3.23 | 69 | 0.22 |
| 3.20 | 13.33 | 16. 0 | 3.17 | 70 | 0.21 |
| 3.25 | 13.19 | 16.30 | 3.11 | 71 | 0.20 |
| 3.30 | 13. 5 | 17. 0 | 3. 5 | 72 | 0.19 |
| 3.40 | 12.39 | 17.30 | 2.59 | 73 | 0.17 |
| 3.50 | 12.14 | 18. 0 | 2.54 | 74 | 0.16 |
| 4. 0 | 11.50 | 18.30 | 2.49 | 75 | 0.15 |
| 4.10 | 11.28 | 19. 0 | 2.44 | 76 | 0.14 |
| 4.20 | 11. 7 | 19.30 | 2.40 | 77 | 0.13 |
| 4.30 | 10.47 | 20. 0 | 2.36 | 78 | 0.12 |
| 4.40 | 10.28 | 20.30 | 2.32 | 79 | 0.11 |
| 4.50 | 10.10 | 21. 0 | 2.28 | 80 | 0.10 |
| 5. 0 | 9.53 | 21.30 | 2.24 | 81 | 0. 9 |
| 5.10 | 9.37 | 22. 0 | 2.20 | 82 | 0. 8 |
| 5.20 | 9.21 | 23. 0 | 2.14 | 83 | 0. 7 |
| 5.30 | 9. 7 | 24. 0 | 2. 7 | 84 | 0. 6 |
| 5.40 | 8.53 | 25. 0 | 2. 2 | 85 | 0. 5 |
| 5.50 | 8.39 | 26. 0 | 1.56 | 86 | 0. 4 |
| 6. 0 | 8.27 | 27. 0 | 1.51 | 87 | 0. 3 |
| 6.10 | 8.15 | 28. 0 | 1.47 | 88 | 0. 2 |
| 6.20 | 8. 3 | 29. 0 | 1.43 | 89 | 0. 1 |

## TABLE XIII.
Depression or Dip of the Horizon of the Sea.

| Height of the Eye. | Dip of the Horizon. |
|---|---|
| Feet. | M. S. |
| 1 | 0.59 |
| 2 | 1.24 |
| 3 | 1.42 |
| 4 | 1.58 |
| 5 | 2.12 |
| 6 | 2.25 |
| 7 | 2.36 |
| 8 | 2.47 |
| 9 | 2.57 |
| 10 | 3. 7 |
| 11 | 3.16 |
| 12 | 3.25 |
| 13 | 3.33 |
| 14 | 3.41 |
| 15 | 3.49 |
| 16 | 3.56 |
| 17 | 4. 3 |
| 18 | 4.11 |
| 19 | 4.17 |
| 20 | 4.24 |
| 21 | 4.31 |
| 22 | 4.37 |
| 23 | 4.43 |
| 24 | 4.49 |
| 26 | 5. 1 |
| 28 | 5.13 |
| 30 | 5.23 |
| 35 | 5.49 |
| 40 | 6.14 |
| 45 | 6.36 |
| 50 | 6.58 |
| 60 | 7.37 |
| 70 | 8.14 |
| 80 | 8.48 |
| 90 | 9.20 |
| 100 | 9.51 |

## TABLE XIV.
The Sun's Parallax in Altitude.

| Sun's Alt. | Sun's Parallax. |
|---|---|
| D. | S. |
| 0 | 9 |
| 10 | 9 |
| 20 | 8 |
| 30 | 8 |
| 40 | 7 |
| 50 | 6 |
| 55 | 5 |
| 60 | 4 |
| 65 | 4 |
| 70 | 3 |
| 75 | 2 |
| 80 | 2 |
| 85 | 1 |
| 90 | 0 |

## TABLE XV.
Augmentation of the Moon's Semi-diameter.

| Moon's Alt. | Augment. |
|---|---|
| D. | S. |
| 0 | 0 |
| 5 | 1 |
| 10 | 3 |
| 15 | 4 |
| 20 | 5 |
| 25 | 7 |
| 30 | 8 |
| 35 | 9 |
| 40 | 10 |
| 45 | 11 |
| 50 | 12 |
| 55 | 13 |
| 60 | 14 |
| 70 | 15 |
| 80 | 15 |
| 90 | 16 |

## TABLE XVI.
Dip of the Sea at different Distances from the Observer.

| Dist of the Land in Sea Miles. | Height of the Eye above the Sea in Feet. | | | | | | | |
|---|---|---|---|---|---|---|---|---|
| | 5 | 10 | 15 | 20 | 25 | 30 | 35 | 40 |
| | Dip. | Dip. | Dip. | Dip. | Dip. | Dip. | Dip. | Dip. |
| | M. | M. | M. | M. | M. | M. | M. | M. |
| ¼ | 11 | 23 | 34 | 45 | 57 | 68 | 79 | 91 |
| ½ | 6 | 12 | 17 | 23 | 28 | 34 | 40 | 45 |
| ¾ | 4 | 8 | 12 | 15 | 19 | 23 | 27 | 30 |
| 1 | 3 | 6 | 9 | 12 | 15 | 17 | 20 | 23 |
| 1¼ | 3 | 5 | 7 | 10 | 12 | 14 | 16 | 19 |
| 1½ | 3 | 4 | 6 | 8 | 10 | 12 | 14 | 16 |
| 2 | 2 | 4 | 5 | 7 | 8 | 9 | 11 | 12 |
| 2½ | 2 | 3 | 4 | 6 | 7 | 8 | 9 | 10 |
| 3 | 2 | 3 | 4 | 5 | 6 | 7 | 8 | 9 |
| 3½ | 2 | 3 | 4 | 5 | 6 | 6 | 7 | 8 |
| 4 | 2 | 3 | 4 | 5 | 5 | 6 | 7 | 7 |
| 5 | 2 | 3 | 4 | 4 | 5 | 6 | 6 | 7 |
| 6 | 2 | 3 | 4 | 4 | 5 | 5 | 6 | 6 |

NOTE TO TABLE XVI.—The numbers of this Table below the black lines, are the same as are given in Table XIII, the visible horizon, corresponding to those heights, not being so far distant as the land.

# TABLE XXI.

## For turning Degrees and Minutes into Time, and the contrary.

| D. | H. M. | D. | H. M. | D. | H. M. | D. | H. M. | D. | H. M. | D. | H. M. |
|---|---|---|---|---|---|---|---|---|---|---|---|
| M. | M. S. | M. | M. S. | M. | M. S. | M. | M. S. | M. | M. S. | M. | M. S. |
| 1 | 0. 4 | 61 | 4. 4 | 121 | 8. 4 | 181 | 12. 4 | 241 | 16. 4 | 301 | 20. 4 |
| 2 | 0. 8 | 62 | 4. 8 | 122 | 8. 8 | 182 | 12. 8 | 242 | 16. 8 | 302 | 20. 8 |
| 3 | 0.12 | 63 | 4.12 | 123 | 8.12 | 183 | 12.12 | 243 | 16.12 | 303 | 20.12 |
| 4 | 0.16 | 64 | 4.16 | 124 | 8.16 | 184 | 12.16 | 244 | 16.16 | 304 | 20.16 |
| 5 | 0.20 | 65 | 4.20 | 125 | 8.20 | 185 | 12.20 | 245 | 16.20 | 305 | 20.20 |
| 6 | 0.24 | 66 | 4.24 | 126 | 8.24 | 186 | 12.24 | 246 | 16.24 | 306 | 20.24 |
| 7 | 0.28 | 67 | 4.28 | 127 | 8.28 | 187 | 12.28 | 247 | 16.28 | 307 | 20.28 |
| 8 | 0.32 | 68 | 4.32 | 128 | 8.32 | 188 | 12.32 | 248 | 16.32 | 308 | 20.32 |
| 9 | 0.36 | 69 | 4.36 | 129 | 8.36 | 189 | 12.36 | 249 | 16.36 | 309 | 20.36 |
| 10 | 0.40 | 70 | 4.40 | 130 | 8.40 | 190 | 12.40 | 250 | 16.40 | 310 | 20.40 |
| 11 | 0.44 | 71 | 4.44 | 131 | 8.44 | 191 | 12.44 | 251 | 16.44 | 311 | 20.44 |
| 12 | 0.48 | 72 | 4.48 | 132 | 8.48 | 192 | 12.48 | 252 | 16.48 | 312 | 20.48 |
| 13 | 0.52 | 73 | 4.52 | 133 | 8.52 | 193 | 12.52 | 253 | 16.52 | 313 | 20.52 |
| 14 | 0.56 | 74 | 4.56 | 134 | 8.56 | 194 | 12.56 | 254 | 16.56 | 314 | 20.56 |
| 15 | 1. 0 | 75 | 5. 0 | 135 | 9. 0 | 195 | 13. 0 | 255 | 17. 0 | 315 | 21. 0 |
| 16 | 1. 4 | 76 | 5. 4 | 136 | 9. 4 | 196 | 13. 4 | 256 | 17. 4 | 316 | 21. 4 |
| 17 | 1. 8 | 77 | 5. 8 | 137 | 9. 8 | 197 | 13. 8 | 257 | 17. 8 | 317 | 21. 8 |
| 18 | 1.12 | 78 | 5.12 | 138 | 9.12 | 198 | 13.12 | 258 | 17.12 | 318 | 21.12 |
| 19 | 1.16 | 79 | 5.16 | 139 | 9.16 | 199 | 13.16 | 259 | 17.16 | 319 | 21.16 |
| 20 | 1.20 | 80 | 5.20 | 140 | 9.20 | 200 | 13.20 | 260 | 17.20 | 320 | 21.20 |
| 21 | 1.24 | 81 | 5.24 | 141 | 9.24 | 201 | 13.24 | 261 | 17.24 | 321 | 21.24 |
| 22 | 1.28 | 82 | 5.28 | 142 | 9.28 | 202 | 13.28 | 262 | 17.28 | 322 | 21.28 |
| 23 | 1.32 | 83 | 5.32 | 143 | 9.32 | 203 | 13.32 | 263 | 17.32 | 323 | 21.32 |
| 24 | 1.36 | 84 | 5.36 | 144 | 9.36 | 204 | 13.36 | 264 | 17.36 | 324 | 21.36 |
| 25 | 1.40 | 85 | 5.40 | 145 | 9.40 | 205 | 13.40 | 265 | 17.40 | 325 | 21.40 |
| 26 | 1.44 | 86 | 5.44 | 146 | 9.44 | 206 | 13.44 | 266 | 17.44 | 326 | 21.44 |
| 27 | 1.48 | 87 | 5.48 | 147 | 9.48 | 207 | 13.48 | 267 | 17.48 | 327 | 21.48 |
| 28 | 1.52 | 88 | 5.52 | 148 | 9.52 | 208 | 13.52 | 268 | 17.52 | 328 | 21.52 |
| 29 | 1.56 | 89 | 5.56 | 149 | 9.56 | 209 | 13.56 | 269 | 17.56 | 329 | 21.56 |
| 30 | 2. 0 | 90 | 6. 0 | 150 | 10. 0 | 210 | 14. 0 | 270 | 18. 0 | 330 | 22. 0 |
| 31 | 2. 4 | 91 | 6. 4 | 151 | 10. 4 | 211 | 14. 4 | 271 | 18. 4 | 331 | 22. 4 |
| 32 | 2. 8 | 92 | 6. 8 | 152 | 10. 8 | 212 | 14. 8 | 272 | 18. 8 | 332 | 22. 8 |
| 33 | 2.12 | 93 | 6.12 | 153 | 10.12 | 213 | 14.12 | 273 | 18.12 | 333 | 22.12 |
| 34 | 2.16 | 94 | 6.16 | 154 | 10.16 | 214 | 14.16 | 274 | 18.16 | 334 | 22.16 |
| 35 | 2.20 | 95 | 6.20 | 155 | 10.20 | 215 | 14.20 | 275 | 18.20 | 335 | 22.20 |
| 36 | 2.24 | 96 | 6.24 | 156 | 10.24 | 216 | 14.24 | 276 | 18.24 | 336 | 22.24 |
| 37 | 2.28 | 97 | 6.28 | 157 | 10.28 | 217 | 14.28 | 277 | 18.28 | 337 | 22.28 |
| 38 | 2.32 | 98 | 6.32 | 158 | 10.32 | 218 | 14.32 | 278 | 18.32 | 338 | 22.32 |
| 39 | 2.36 | 99 | 6.36 | 159 | 10.36 | 219 | 14.36 | 279 | 18.36 | 339 | 22.36 |
| 40 | 2.40 | 100 | 6.40 | 160 | 10.40 | 220 | 14.40 | 280 | 18.40 | 340 | 22.40 |
| 41 | 2.44 | 101 | 6.44 | 161 | 10.44 | 221 | 14.44 | 281 | 18.44 | 341 | 22.44 |
| 42 | 2.48 | 102 | 6.48 | 162 | 10.48 | 222 | 14.48 | 282 | 18.48 | 342 | 22.48 |
| 43 | 2.52 | 103 | 6.52 | 163 | 10.52 | 223 | 14.52 | 283 | 18.52 | 343 | 22.52 |
| 44 | 2.56 | 104 | 6.56 | 164 | 10.56 | 224 | 14.56 | 284 | 18.56 | 344 | 22.56 |
| 45 | 3. 0 | 105 | 7. 0 | 165 | 11. 0 | 225 | 15. 0 | 285 | 19. 0 | 345 | 23. 0 |
| 46 | 3. 4 | 106 | 7. 4 | 166 | 11. 4 | 226 | 15. 4 | 286 | 19. 4 | 346 | 23. 4 |
| 47 | 3. 8 | 107 | 7. 8 | 167 | 11. 8 | 227 | 15. 8 | 287 | 19. 8 | 347 | 23. 8 |
| 48 | 3.12 | 108 | 7.12 | 168 | 11.12 | 228 | 15.12 | 288 | 19.12 | 348 | 23.12 |
| 49 | 3.16 | 109 | 7.16 | 169 | 11.16 | 229 | 15.16 | 289 | 19.16 | 349 | 23.16 |
| 50 | 3.20 | 110 | 7.20 | 170 | 11.20 | 230 | 15.20 | 290 | 19.20 | 350 | 23.20 |
| 51 | 3.24 | 111 | 7.24 | 171 | 11.24 | 231 | 15.24 | 291 | 19.24 | 351 | 23.24 |
| 52 | 3.28 | 112 | 7.28 | 172 | 11.28 | 232 | 15.28 | 292 | 19.28 | 352 | 23.28 |
| 53 | 3.32 | 113 | 7.32 | 173 | 11.32 | 233 | 15.32 | 293 | 19.32 | 353 | 23.32 |
| 54 | 3.36 | 114 | 7.36 | 174 | 11.36 | 234 | 15.36 | 294 | 19.36 | 354 | 23.36 |
| 55 | 3.40 | 115 | 7.40 | 175 | 11.40 | 235 | 15.40 | 295 | 19.40 | 355 | 23.40 |
| 56 | 3.44 | 116 | 7.44 | 176 | 11.44 | 236 | 15.44 | 296 | 19.44 | 356 | 23.44 |
| 57 | 3.48 | 117 | 7.48 | 177 | 11.48 | 237 | 15.48 | 297 | 19.48 | 357 | 23.48 |
| 58 | 3.52 | 118 | 7.52 | 178 | 11.52 | 238 | 15.52 | 298 | 19.52 | 358 | 23.52 |
| 59 | 3.56 | 119 | 7.56 | 179 | 11.56 | 239 | 15.56 | 299 | 19.56 | 359 | 23.56 |
| 60 | 4. 0 | 120 | 8. 0 | 180 | 12. 0 | 240 | 16. 0 | 300 | 20. 0 | 360 | 24. 0 |

# TABLE XXII.

## Proportional Logarithms.

| S. | *h m* 0° 0′ | *h m* 0° 1′ | *h m* 0° 2′ | *h m* 0° 3′ | *h m* 0° 4′ | *h m* 0° 5′ | *h m* 0° 6′ | *h m* 0° 7′ | *h m* 0° 8′ | S. |
|---|---|---|---|---|---|---|---|---|---|---|
| 0 | | 2.2553 | 1.9542 | 1.7782 | 1.6532 | 1.5563 | 1.4771 | 1.4102 | 1.3522 | 0 |
| 1 | 4.0334 | 2481 | 9506 | 7757 | 6514 | 5549 | 4759 | 4091 | 3513 | 1 |
| 2 | 3.7324 | 2410 | 9471 | 7734 | 6496 | 5534 | 4747 | 4081 | 3504 | 2 |
| 3 | 5563 | 2341 | 9435 | 7710 | 6478 | 5520 | 4735 | 4071 | 3495 | 3 |
| 4 | 4314 | 2272 | 9400 | 7686 | 6460 | 5506 | 4723 | 4061 | 3486 | 4 |
| 5 | 3.3345 | 2.2205 | 1.9365 | 1.7663 | 1.6443 | 1.5491 | 1.4711 | 1.4050 | 1.3477 | 5 |
| 6 | 2553 | 2139 | 9331 | 7639 | 6425 | 5477 | 4699 | 4040 | 3468 | 6 |
| 7 | 1883 | 2073 | 9296 | 7616 | 6407 | 5463 | 4688 | 4030 | 3459 | 7 |
| 8 | 1303 | 2009 | 9262 | 7593 | 6390 | 5449 | 4676 | 4020 | 3450 | 8 |
| 9 | 0792 | 1946 | 9228 | 7570 | 6372 | 5435 | 4664 | 4010 | 3441 | 9 |
| 10 | 3.0334 | 2.1883 | 1.9195 | 1.7547 | 1.6355 | 1.5421 | 1.4652 | 1.4000 | 1.3432 | 10 |
| 11 | 2.9920 | 1822 | 9162 | 7524 | 6338 | 5407 | 4640 | 3989 | 3423 | 11 |
| 12 | 9542 | 1761 | 9128 | 7501 | 6320 | 5393 | 4629 | 3979 | 3415 | 12 |
| 13 | 9195 | 1701 | 9096 | 7479 | 6303 | 5379 | 4617 | 3969 | 3406 | 13 |
| 14 | 8873 | 1642 | 9063 | 7456 | 6286 | 5365 | 4606 | 3959 | 3397 | 14 |
| 15 | 2.8573 | 2.1584 | 1.9031 | 1.7434 | 1.6269 | 1.5351 | 1.4594 | 1.3949 | 1.3388 | 15 |
| 16 | 8293 | 1526 | 8999 | 7412 | 6252 | 5337 | 4582 | 3939 | 3379 | 16 |
| 17 | 8030 | 1469 | 8967 | 7390 | 6235 | 5324 | 4571 | 3929 | 3371 | 17 |
| 18 | 7782 | 1413 | 8935 | 7368 | 6218 | 5310 | 4559 | 3919 | 3362 | 18 |
| 19 | 7547 | 1358 | 8904 | 7346 | 6201 | 5296 | 4548 | 3910 | 3353 | 19 |
| 20 | 2.7324 | 2.1303 | 1.8873 | 1.7324 | 1.6185 | 1.5283 | 1.4536 | 1.3900 | 1.3345 | 20 |
| 21 | 7112 | 1249 | 8842 | 7302 | 6168 | 5269 | 4525 | 3890 | 3336 | 21 |
| 22 | 6910 | 1196 | 8811 | 7281 | 6151 | 5256 | 4514 | 3880 | 3327 | 22 |
| 23 | 6717 | 1143 | 8781 | 7259 | 6135 | 5242 | 4502 | 3870 | 3319 | 23 |
| 24 | 6532 | 1091 | 8751 | 7238 | 6118 | 5229 | 4491 | 3860 | 3310 | 24 |
| 25 | 2.6355 | 2.1040 | 1.8721 | 1.7217 | 1.6102 | 1.5215 | 1.4480 | 1.3851 | 1.3301 | 25 |
| 26 | 6185 | 0989 | 8691 | 7196 | 6085 | 5202 | 4468 | 3841 | 3293 | 26 |
| 27 | 6021 | 0939 | 8661 | 7175 | 6069 | 5189 | 4457 | 3831 | 3284 | 27 |
| 28 | 5863 | 0889 | 8632 | 7154 | 6053 | 5175 | 4446 | 3821 | 3276 | 28 |
| 29 | 5710 | 0840 | 8602 | 7133 | 6037 | 5162 | 4435 | 3812 | 3267 | 29 |
| 30 | 2.5563 | 2.0792 | 1.8573 | 1.7112 | 1.6021 | 1.5149 | 1.4424 | 1.3802 | 1.3259 | 30 |
| 31 | 5421 | 0744 | 8544 | 7091 | 6005 | 5136 | 4412 | 3792 | 3250 | 31 |
| 32 | 5283 | 0696 | 8516 | 7071 | 5989 | 5123 | 4401 | 3783 | 3242 | 32 |
| 33 | 5149 | 0649 | 8487 | 7050 | 5973 | 5110 | 4390 | 3773 | 3233 | 33 |
| 34 | 5019 | 0603 | 8459 | 7030 | 5957 | 5097 | 4379 | 3764 | 3225 | 34 |
| 35 | 2.4894 | 2.0557 | 1.8431 | 1.7010 | 1.5941 | 1.5084 | 1.4368 | 1.3754 | 1.3216 | 35 |
| 36 | 4771 | 0512 | 8403 | 6990 | 5925 | 5071 | 4357 | 3745 | 3208 | 36 |
| 37 | 4652 | 0467 | 8375 | 6970 | 5909 | 5058 | 4346 | 3735 | 3199 | 37 |
| 38 | 4536 | 0422 | 8348 | 6950 | 5894 | 5045 | 4335 | 3726 | 3191 | 38 |
| 39 | 4424 | 0378 | 8320 | 6930 | 5878 | 5032 | 4325 | 3716 | 3183 | 39 |
| 40 | 2.4314 | 2.0334 | 1.8293 | 1.6910 | 1.5863 | 1.5019 | 1.4314 | 1.3707 | 1.3174 | 40 |
| 41 | 4206 | 0291 | 8266 | 6890 | 5847 | 5007 | 4303 | 3697 | 3166 | 41 |
| 42 | 4102 | 0248 | 8239 | 6871 | 5832 | 4994 | 4292 | 3688 | 3158 | 42 |
| 43 | 4000 | 0206 | 8212 | 6851 | 5816 | 4981 | 4281 | 3678 | 3149 | 43 |
| 44 | 3900 | 0164 | 8186 | 6832 | 5801 | 4969 | 4270 | 3669 | 3141 | 44 |
| 45 | 2.3802 | 2.0122 | 1.8159 | 1.6812 | 1.5786 | 1.4956 | 1.4260 | 1.3660 | 1.3133 | 45 |
| 46 | 3707 | 0081 | 8133 | 6793 | 5771 | 4943 | 4249 | 3650 | 3124 | 46 |
| 47 | 3613 | 0040 | 8107 | 6774 | 5755 | 4931 | 4238 | 3641 | 3116 | 47 |
| 48 | 3522 | 0000 | 8081 | 6755 | 5740 | 4918 | 4228 | 3632 | 3108 | 48 |
| 49 | 3432 | 1.9960 | 8055 | 6736 | 5725 | 4906 | 4217 | 3623 | 3100 | 49 |
| 50 | 2.3345 | 1.9920 | 1.8030 | 1.6717 | 1.5710 | 1.4894 | 1.4206 | 1.3613 | 1.3091 | 50 |
| 51 | 3259 | 9881 | 8004 | 6698 | 5695 | 4881 | 4196 | 3604 | 3083 | 51 |
| 52 | 3174 | 9842 | 7979 | 6679 | 5680 | 4869 | 4185 | 3595 | 3075 | 52 |
| 53 | 3091 | 9803 | 7954 | 6661 | 5666 | 4856 | 4175 | 3586 | 3067 | 53 |
| 54 | 3010 | 9765 | 7929 | 6642 | 5651 | 4844 | 4164 | 3576 | 3059 | 54 |
| 55 | 2.2931 | 1.9727 | 1.7904 | 1.6624 | 1.5636 | 1.4832 | 1.4154 | 1.3567 | 1.3051 | 55 |
| 56 | 2852 | 9690 | 7879 | 6605 | 5621 | 4820 | 4143 | 3558 | 3043 | 56 |
| 57 | 2775 | 9652 | 7855 | 6587 | 5607 | 4808 | 4133 | 3549 | 3034 | 57 |
| 58 | 2700 | 9615 | 7830 | 6568 | 5592 | 4795 | 4122 | 3540 | 3026 | 58 |
| 59 | 2626 | 9579 | 7806 | 6550 | 5578 | 4783 | 4112 | 3531 | 3018 | 59 |
| S. | 0° 0′ | 0° 1′ | 0° 2′ | 0° 3′ | 0° 4′ | 0° 5′ | 0° 6′ | 0° 7′ | 0° 8′ | S. |

# TABLE XXII.

## Proportional Logarithms.

| S. | *h m* 0° 9′ | *h m* 0° 10′ | *h m* 0° 11′ | *h m* 0° 12′ | *h m* 0° 13′ | *h m* 0° 14′ | *h m* 0° 15′ | *h m* 0° 16′ | *h m* 0° 17′ | S. |
|---|---|---|---|---|---|---|---|---|---|---|
| 0 | 1.3010 | 1.2553 | 1.2139 | 1.1761 | 1.1413 | 1.1091 | 1.0792 | 1.0512 | 1.0248 | 0 |
| 1 | 3002 | 2545 | 2132 | 1755 | 1408 | 1086 | 0787 | 0507 | 0244 | 1 |
| 2 | 2994 | 2538 | 2126 | 1749 | 1402 | 1081 | 0782 | 0502 | 0240 | 2 |
| 3 | 2986 | 2531 | 2119 | 1743 | 1397 | 1076 | 0777 | 0498 | 0235 | 3 |
| 4 | 2978 | 2524 | 2113 | 1737 | 1391 | 1071 | 0773 | 0493 | 0231 | 4 |
| 5 | 1.2970 | 1.2517 | 1.2106 | 1.1731 | 1.1386 | 1.1066 | 1.0768 | 1.0489 | 1.0227 | 5 |
| 6 | 2962 | 2510 | 2099 | 1725 | 1380 | 1061 | 0763 | 0484 | 0223 | 6 |
| 7 | 2954 | 2502 | 2093 | 1719 | 1374 | 1055 | 0758 | 0480 | 0219 | 7 |
| 8 | 2946 | 2495 | 2086 | 1713 | 1369 | 1050 | 0753 | 0475 | 0214 | 8 |
| 9 | 2939 | 2488 | 2080 | 1707 | 1363 | 1045 | 0749 | 0471 | 0210 | 9 |
| 10 | 1.2931 | 1.2481 | 1.2073 | 1.1701 | 1.1358 | 1.1040 | 1.0744 | 1.0467 | 1.0206 | 10 |
| 11 | 2923 | 2474 | 2067 | 1695 | 1352 | 1035 | 0739 | 0462 | 0202 | 11 |
| 12 | 2915 | 2467 | 2061 | 1689 | 1347 | 1030 | 0734 | 0458 | 0197 | 12 |
| 13 | 2907 | 2460 | 2054 | 1683 | 1342 | 1025 | 0730 | 0453 | 0193 | 13 |
| 14 | 2899 | 2453 | 2048 | 1677 | 1336 | 1020 | 0725 | 0449 | 0189 | 14 |
| 15 | 1.2891 | 1.2445 | 1.2041 | 1.1671 | 1.1331 | 1.1015 | 1.0720 | 1.0444 | 1.0185 | 15 |
| 16 | 2883 | 2438 | 2035 | 1665 | 1325 | 1009 | 0715 | 0440 | 0181 | 16 |
| 17 | 2876 | 2431 | 2028 | 1660 | 1320 | 1004 | 0711 | 0435 | 0176 | 17 |
| 18 | 2868 | 2424 | 2022 | 1654 | 1314 | 0999 | 0706 | 0431 | 0172 | 18 |
| 19 | 2860 | 2417 | 2016 | 1648 | 1309 | 0994 | 0701 | 0426 | 0168 | 19 |
| 20 | 1.2852 | 1.2410 | 1.2009 | 1.1642 | 1.1303 | 1.0989 | 1.0696 | 1.0422 | 1.0164 | 20 |
| 21 | 2845 | 2403 | 2003 | 1636 | 1298 | 0984 | 0692 | 0418 | 0160 | 21 |
| 22 | 2837 | 2396 | 1996 | 1630 | 1292 | 0979 | 0687 | 0413 | 0156 | 22 |
| 23 | 2829 | 2389 | 1990 | 1624 | 1287 | 0974 | 0682 | 0409 | 0151 | 23 |
| 24 | 2821 | 2382 | 1984 | 1619 | 1282 | 0969 | 0678 | 0404 | 0147 | 24 |
| 25 | 1.2814 | 1.2375 | 1.1977 | 1.1613 | 1.1276 | 1.0964 | 1.0673 | 1.0400 | 1.0143 | 25 |
| 26 | 2806 | 2368 | 1971 | 1607 | 1271 | 0959 | 0668 | 0395 | 0139 | 26 |
| 27 | 2798 | 2362 | 1965 | 1601 | 1266 | 0954 | 0663 | 0391 | 0135 | 27 |
| 28 | 2791 | 2355 | 1958 | 1595 | 1260 | 0949 | 0659 | 0387 | 0131 | 28 |
| 29 | 2783 | 2348 | 1952 | 1589 | 1255 | 0944 | 0654 | 0382 | 0126 | 29 |
| 30 | 1.2775 | 1.2341 | 1.1946 | 1.1584 | 1.1249 | 1.0939 | 1.0649 | 1.0378 | 1.0122 | 30 |
| 31 | 2768 | 2334 | 1939 | 1578 | 1244 | 0934 | 0645 | 0374 | 0118 | 31 |
| 32 | 2760 | 2327 | 1933 | 1572 | 1239 | 0929 | 0640 | 0369 | 0114 | 32 |
| 33 | 2753 | 2320 | 1927 | 1566 | 1233 | 0924 | 0635 | 0365 | 0110 | 33 |
| 34 | 2745 | 2313 | 1921 | 1561 | 1228 | 0919 | 0631 | 0360 | 0106 | 34 |
| 35 | 1.2738 | 1.2307 | 1.1914 | 1.1555 | 1.1223 | 1.0914 | 1.0626 | 1.0356 | 1.0102 | 35 |
| 36 | 2730 | 2300 | 1908 | 1549 | 1217 | 0909 | 0621 | 0352 | 0098 | 36 |
| 37 | 2722 | 2293 | 1902 | 1543 | 1212 | 0904 | 0617 | 0347 | 0093 | 37 |
| 38 | 2715 | 2286 | 1896 | 1538 | 1207 | 0899 | 0612 | 0343 | 0089 | 38 |
| 39 | 2707 | 2279 | 1889 | 1532 | 1201 | 0894 | 0608 | 0339 | 0085 | 39 |
| 40 | 1.2700 | 1.2272 | 1.1883 | 1.1526 | 1.1196 | 1.0889 | 1.0603 | 1.0334 | 1.0081 | 40 |
| 41 | 2692 | 2266 | 1877 | 1520 | 1191 | 0884 | 0598 | 0330 | 0077 | 41 |
| 42 | 2685 | 2259 | 1871 | 1515 | 1186 | 0880 | 0594 | 0326 | 0073 | 42 |
| 43 | 2678 | 2252 | 1865 | 1509 | 1180 | 0875 | 0589 | 0321 | 0069 | 43 |
| 44 | 2670 | 2245 | 1859 | 1503 | 1175 | 0870 | 0585 | 0317 | 0065 | 44 |
| 45 | 1.2663 | 1.2239 | 1.1852 | 1.1498 | 1.1170 | 1.0865 | 1.0580 | 1.0313 | 1.0061 | 45 |
| 46 | 2655 | 2232 | 1846 | 1492 | 1164 | 0860 | 0575 | 0308 | 0057 | 46 |
| 47 | 2648 | 2225 | 1840 | 1486 | 1159 | 0855 | 0571 | 0304 | 0053 | 47 |
| 48 | 2640 | 2218 | 1834 | 1481 | 1154 | 0850 | 0566 | 0300 | 0049 | 48 |
| 49 | 2633 | 2212 | 1828 | 1475 | 1149 | 0845 | 0562 | 0295 | 0044 | 49 |
| 50 | 1.2626 | 1.2205 | 1.1822 | 1.1469 | 1.1143 | 1.0840 | 1.0557 | 1.0291 | 1.0040 | 50 |
| 51 | 2618 | 2198 | 1816 | 1464 | 1138 | 0835 | 0552 | 0287 | 0036 | 51 |
| 52 | 2611 | 2192 | 1809 | 1458 | 1133 | 0831 | 0548 | 0282 | 0032 | 52 |
| 53 | 2604 | 2185 | 1803 | 1452 | 1128 | 0826 | 0543 | 0278 | 0028 | 53 |
| 54 | 2596 | 2178 | 1797 | 1447 | 1123 | 0821 | 0539 | 0274 | 0024 | 54 |
| 55 | 1.2589 | 1.2172 | 1.1791 | 1.1441 | 1.1117 | 1.0816 | 1.0534 | 1.0270 | 1.0020 | 55 |
| 56 | 2582 | 2165 | 1785 | 1436 | 1112 | 0811 | 0530 | 0265 | 0016 | 56 |
| 57 | 2574 | 2159 | 1779 | 1430 | 1107 | 0806 | 0525 | 0261 | 0012 | 57 |
| 58 | 2567 | 2152 | 1773 | 1424 | 1102 | 0801 | 0521 | 0257 | 0008 | 58 |
| 59 | 2560 | 2145 | 1767 | 1419 | 1097 | 0797 | 0516 | 0252 | 0004 | 59 |
| S. | 0° 9′ | 0° 10′ | 0° 11′ | 0° 12′ | 0° 13′ | 0° 14′ | 0° 15′ | 0° 16′ | 0° 17′ | S. |

# TABLE XXII.

## Proportional Logarithms.

| S. | h m 0° 18′ | h m 0° 19′ | h m 0° 20′ | h m 0° 21′ | h m 0° 22′ | h m 0° 23′ | h m 0° 24′ | h m 0° 25′ | h m 0° 26′ | h m 0° 27′ | h m 0° 28′ | h m 0° 29′ | S. |
|---|---|---|---|---|---|---|---|---|---|---|---|---|---|
| 0 | 10000 | 9765 | 9542 | 9331 | 9128 | 8935 | 8751 | 8573 | 8403 | 8239 | 8081 | 7929 | 0 |
| 1 | 9996 | 9761 | 9539 | 9327 | 9125 | 8932 | 8748 | 8570 | 8400 | 8236 | 8079 | 7926 | 1 |
| 2 | 9992 | 9758 | 9535 | 9324 | 9122 | 8929 | 8745 | 8568 | 8397 | 8234 | 8076 | 7924 | 2 |
| 3 | 9988 | 9754 | 9532 | 9320 | 9119 | 8926 | 8742 | 8565 | 8395 | 8231 | 8073 | 7921 | 3 |
| 4 | 9984 | 9750 | 9528 | 9317 | 9115 | 8923 | 8739 | 8562 | 8392 | 8228 | 8071 | 7919 | 4 |
| 5 | 9980 | 9746 | 9524 | 9313 | 9112 | 8920 | 8736 | 8559 | 8389 | 8226 | 8068 | 7916 | 5 |
| 6 | 9976 | 9742 | 9521 | 9310 | 9109 | 8917 | 8733 | 8556 | 8386 | 8223 | 8066 | 7914 | 6 |
| 7 | 9972 | 9739 | 9517 | 9306 | 9106 | 8913 | 8730 | 8553 | 8384 | 8220 | 8063 | 7911 | 7 |
| 8 | 9968 | 9735 | 9514 | 9303 | 9102 | 8910 | 8727 | 8550 | 8381 | 8218 | 8061 | 7909 | 8 |
| 9 | 9964 | 9731 | 9510 | 9300 | 9099 | 8907 | 8724 | 8547 | 8378 | 8215 | 8058 | 7906 | 9 |
| 10 | 9960 | 9727 | 9506 | 9296 | 9096 | 8904 | 8721 | 8544 | 8375 | 8212 | 8055 | 7904 | 10 |
| 11 | 9956 | 9723 | 9503 | 9293 | 9092 | 8901 | 8718 | 8542 | 8372 | 8210 | 8053 | 7901 | 11 |
| 12 | 9952 | 9720 | 9499 | 9289 | 9089 | 8898 | 8715 | 8539 | 8370 | 8207 | 8050 | 7899 | 12 |
| 13 | 9948 | 9716 | 9496 | 9286 | 9086 | 8895 | 8712 | 8536 | 8367 | 8204 | 8048 | 7896 | 13 |
| 14 | 9944 | 9712 | 9492 | 9283 | 9083 | 8892 | 8709 | 8533 | 8364 | 8202 | 8045 | 7894 | 14 |
| 15 | 9940 | 9708 | 9488 | 9279 | 9079 | 8888 | 8706 | 8530 | 8361 | 8199 | 8043 | 7891 | 15 |
| 16 | 9936 | 9705 | 9485 | 9276 | 9076 | 8885 | 8703 | 8527 | 8359 | 8196 | 8040 | 7889 | 16 |
| 17 | 9932 | 9701 | 9481 | 9272 | 9073 | 8882 | 8700 | 8524 | 8356 | 8194 | 8037 | 7887 | 17 |
| 18 | 9928 | 9697 | 9478 | 9269 | 9070 | 8879 | 8697 | 8522 | 8353 | 8191 | 8035 | 7884 | 18 |
| 19 | 9924 | 9693 | 9474 | 9266 | 9066 | 8876 | 8694 | 8519 | 8350 | 8188 | 8032 | 7882 | 19 |
| 20 | 9920 | 9690 | 9471 | 9262 | 9063 | 8873 | 8691 | 8516 | 8348 | 8186 | 8030 | 7879 | 20 |
| 21 | 9916 | 9686 | 9467 | 9259 | 9060 | 8870 | 8688 | 8513 | 8345 | 8183 | 8027 | 7877 | 21 |
| 22 | 9912 | 9682 | 9464 | 9255 | 9057 | 8867 | 8685 | 8510 | 8342 | 8181 | 8025 | 7874 | 22 |
| 23 | 9908 | 9678 | 9460 | 9252 | 9053 | 8864 | 8682 | 8507 | 8339 | 8178 | 8022 | 7872 | 23 |
| 24 | 9905 | 9675 | 9456 | 9249 | 9050 | 8861 | 8679 | 8504 | 8337 | 8175 | 8020 | 7869 | 24 |
| 25 | 9901 | 9671 | 9453 | 9245 | 9047 | 8857 | 8676 | 8502 | 8334 | 8173 | 8017 | 7867 | 25 |
| 26 | 9897 | 9667 | 9449 | 9242 | 9044 | 8854 | 8673 | 8499 | 8331 | 8170 | 8014 | 7864 | 26 |
| 27 | 9893 | 9664 | 9446 | 9238 | 9041 | 8851 | 8670 | 8496 | 8328 | 8167 | 8012 | 7862 | 27 |
| 28 | 9889 | 9660 | 9442 | 9235 | 9037 | 8848 | 8667 | 8493 | 8326 | 8165 | 8009 | 7859 | 28 |
| 29 | 9885 | 9656 | 9439 | 9232 | 9034 | 8845 | 8664 | 8490 | 8323 | 8162 | 8007 | 7857 | 29 |
| 30 | 9881 | 9652 | 9435 | 9228 | 9031 | 8842 | 8661 | 8487 | 8320 | 8159 | 8004 | 7855 | 30 |
| 31 | 9877 | 9649 | 9432 | 9225 | 9028 | 8839 | 8658 | 8484 | 8318 | 8157 | 8002 | 7852 | 31 |
| 32 | 9873 | 9645 | 9428 | 9222 | 9024 | 8836 | 8655 | 8482 | 8315 | 8154 | 7999 | 7850 | 32 |
| 33 | 9869 | 9641 | 9425 | 9218 | 9021 | 8833 | 8652 | 8479 | 8312 | 8152 | 7997 | 7847 | 33 |
| 34 | 9865 | 9638 | 9421 | 9215 | 9018 | 8830 | 8649 | 8476 | 8309 | 8149 | 7994 | 7845 | 34 |
| 35 | 9861 | 9634 | 9418 | 9212 | 9015 | 8827 | 8646 | 8473 | 8307 | 8146 | 7992 | 7842 | 35 |
| 36 | 9858 | 9630 | 9414 | 9208 | 9012 | 8824 | 8643 | 8470 | 8304 | 8144 | 7989 | 7840 | 36 |
| 37 | 9854 | 9626 | 9411 | 9205 | 9008 | 8821 | 8640 | 8467 | 8301 | 8141 | 7987 | 7837 | 37 |
| 38 | 9850 | 9623 | 9407 | 9201 | 9005 | 8817 | 8637 | 8465 | 8298 | 8138 | 7984 | 7835 | 38 |
| 39 | 9846 | 9619 | 9404 | 9198 | 9002 | 8814 | 8635 | 8462 | 8296 | 8136 | 7981 | 7832 | 39 |
| 40 | 9842 | 9615 | 9400 | 9195 | 8999 | 8811 | 8632 | 8459 | 8293 | 8133 | 7979 | 7830 | 40 |
| 41 | 9838 | 9612 | 9397 | 9191 | 8996 | 8808 | 8629 | 8456 | 8290 | 8131 | 7976 | 7828 | 41 |
| 42 | 9834 | 9608 | 9393 | 9188 | 8992 | 8805 | 8626 | 8453 | 8288 | 8128 | 7974 | 7825 | 42 |
| 43 | 9830 | 9604 | 9390 | 9185 | 8989 | 8802 | 8623 | 8451 | 8285 | 8125 | 7971 | 7823 | 43 |
| 44 | 9827 | 9601 | 9386 | 9181 | 8986 | 8799 | 8620 | 8448 | 8282 | 8123 | 7969 | 7820 | 44 |
| 45 | 9823 | 9597 | 9383 | 9178 | 8983 | 8796 | 8617 | 8445 | 8279 | 8120 | 7966 | 7818 | 45 |
| 46 | 9819 | 9593 | 9379 | 9175 | 8980 | 8793 | 8614 | 8442 | 8277 | 8117 | 7964 | 7815 | 46 |
| 47 | 9815 | 9590 | 9376 | 9171 | 8977 | 8790 | 8611 | 8439 | 8274 | 8115 | 7961 | 7813 | 47 |
| 48 | 9811 | 9586 | 9372 | 9168 | 8973 | 8787 | 8608 | 8437 | 8271 | 8112 | 7959 | 7811 | 48 |
| 49 | 9807 | 9582 | 9369 | 9165 | 8970 | 8784 | 8605 | 8434 | 8269 | 8110 | 7956 | 7808 | 49 |
| 50 | 9803 | 9579 | 9365 | 9162 | 8967 | 8781 | 8602 | 8431 | 8266 | 8107 | 7954 | 7806 | 50 |
| 51 | 9800 | 9575 | 9362 | 9158 | 8964 | 8778 | 8599 | 8428 | 8263 | 8104 | 7951 | 7803 | 51 |
| 52 | 9796 | 9571 | 9358 | 9155 | 8961 | 8775 | 8597 | 8425 | 8261 | 8102 | 7949 | 7801 | 52 |
| 53 | 9792 | 9568 | 9355 | 9152 | 8958 | 8772 | 8594 | 8423 | 8258 | 8099 | 7946 | 7798 | 53 |
| 54 | 9788 | 9564 | 9351 | 9148 | 8954 | 8769 | 8591 | 8420 | 8255 | 8097 | 7944 | 7796 | 54 |
| 55 | 9784 | 9561 | 9348 | 9145 | 8951 | 8766 | 8588 | 8417 | 8253 | 8094 | 7941 | 7794 | 55 |
| 56 | 9780 | 9557 | 9344 | 9142 | 8948 | 8763 | 8585 | 8414 | 8250 | 8091 | 7939 | 7791 | 56 |
| 57 | 9777 | 9553 | 9341 | 9138 | 8945 | 8760 | 8582 | 8411 | 8247 | 8089 | 7936 | 7789 | 57 |
| 58 | 9773 | 9550 | 9337 | 9135 | 8942 | 8757 | 8579 | 8409 | 8244 | 8086 | 7934 | 7786 | 58 |
| 59 | 9769 | 9546 | 9334 | 9132 | 8939 | 8754 | 8576 | 8406 | 8242 | 8084 | 7931 | 7784 | 59 |
| S. | 0° 18′ | 0° 19′ | 0° 20′ | 0° 21′ | 0° 22′ | 0° 23′ | 0° 24′ | 0° 25′ | 0° 26′ | 0° 27′ | 0° 28′ | 0° 29′ | S. |

# TABLE XXII.

## Proportional Logarithms.

| S. | *h m* 0° 30′ | *h m* 0° 31′ | *h m* 0° 32′ | *h m* 0° 33′ | *h m* 0° 34′ | *h m* 0° 35′ | *h m* 0° 36′ | *h m* 0° 37′ | *h m* 0° 38′ | *h m* 0° 39′ | *h m* 0° 40′ | *h m* 0° 41′ | S. |
|---|---|---|---|---|---|---|---|---|---|---|---|---|---|
| 0 | 7782 | 7639 | 7501 | 7368 | 7238 | 7112 | 6990 | 6871 | 6755 | 6642 | 6532 | 6425 | 0 |
| 1 | 7779 | 7637 | 7499 | 7365 | 7236 | 7110 | 6988 | 6869 | 6753 | 6640 | 6530 | 6423 | 1 |
| 2 | 7777 | 7634 | 7497 | 7363 | 7234 | 7108 | 6986 | 6867 | 6751 | 6638 | 6529 | 6421 | 2 |
| 3 | 7774 | 7632 | 7494 | 7361 | 7232 | 7106 | 6984 | 6865 | 6749 | 6637 | 6527 | 6420 | 3 |
| 4 | 7772 | 7630 | 7492 | 7359 | 7229 | 7104 | 6982 | 6863 | 6747 | 6635 | 6525 | 6418 | 4 |
| 5 | 7769 | 7627 | 7490 | 7357 | 7227 | 7102 | 6980 | 6861 | 6745 | 6633 | 6523 | 6416 | 5 |
| 6 | 7767 | 7625 | 7488 | 7354 | 7225 | 7100 | 6978 | 6859 | 6743 | 6631 | 6521 | 6414 | 6 |
| 7 | 7765 | 7623 | 7485 | 7352 | 7223 | 7098 | 6976 | 6857 | 6742 | 6629 | 6519 | 6413 | 7 |
| 8 | 7762 | 7620 | 7483 | 7350 | 7221 | 7096 | 6974 | 6855 | 6740 | 6627 | 6518 | 6411 | 8 |
| 9 | 7760 | 7618 | 7481 | 7348 | 7219 | 7093 | 6972 | 6853 | 6738 | 6625 | 6516 | 6409 | 9 |
| 10 | 7757 | 7616 | 7479 | 7346 | 7217 | 7091 | 6970 | 6851 | 6736 | 6624 | 6514 | 6407 | 10 |
| 11 | 7755 | 7613 | 7476 | 7344 | 7215 | 7089 | 6968 | 6849 | 6734 | 6622 | 6512 | 6406 | 11 |
| 12 | 7753 | 7611 | 7474 | 7341 | 7212 | 7087 | 6966 | 6847 | 6732 | 6620 | 6510 | 6404 | 12 |
| 13 | 7750 | 7609 | 7472 | 7339 | 7210 | 7085 | 6964 | 6845 | 6730 | 6618 | 6509 | 6402 | 13 |
| 14 | 7748 | 7607 | 7470 | 7337 | 7208 | 7083 | 6962 | 6843 | 6728 | 6616 | 6507 | 6400 | 14 |
| 15 | 7745 | 7604 | 7467 | 7335 | 7206 | 7081 | 6960 | 6841 | 6726 | 6614 | 6505 | 6398 | 15 |
| 16 | 7743 | 7602 | 7465 | 7333 | 7204 | 7079 | 6958 | 6840 | 6725 | 6612 | 6503 | 6397 | 16 |
| 17 | 7741 | 7600 | 7463 | 7330 | 7202 | 7077 | 6956 | 6838 | 6723 | 6611 | 6501 | 6395 | 17 |
| 18 | 7738 | 7597 | 7461 | 7328 | 7200 | 7075 | 6954 | 6836 | 6721 | 6609 | 6500 | 6393 | 18 |
| 19 | 7736 | 7595 | 7458 | 7326 | 7198 | 7073 | 6952 | 6834 | 6719 | 6607 | 6498 | 6391 | 19 |
| 20 | 7734 | 7593 | 7456 | 7324 | 7196 | 7071 | 6950 | 6832 | 6717 | 6605 | 6496 | 6390 | 20 |
| 21 | 7731 | 7590 | 7454 | 7322 | 7193 | 7069 | 6948 | 6830 | 6715 | 6603 | 6494 | 6388 | 21 |
| 22 | 7729 | 7588 | 7452 | 7320 | 7191 | 7067 | 6946 | 6828 | 6713 | 6601 | 6492 | 6386 | 22 |
| 23 | 7726 | 7586 | 7450 | 7317 | 7189 | 7065 | 6944 | 6826 | 6711 | 6600 | 6491 | 6384 | 23 |
| 24 | 7724 | 7583 | 7447 | 7315 | 7187 | 7063 | 6942 | 6824 | 6709 | 6598 | 6489 | 6383 | 24 |
| 25 | 7722 | 7581 | 7445 | 7313 | 7185 | 7061 | 6940 | 6822 | 6708 | 6596 | 6487 | 6381 | 25 |
| 26 | 7719 | 7579 | 7443 | 7311 | 7183 | 7059 | 6938 | 6820 | 6706 | 6594 | 6485 | 6379 | 26 |
| 27 | 7717 | 7577 | 7441 | 7309 | 7181 | 7057 | 6936 | 6818 | 6704 | 6592 | 6484 | 6377 | 27 |
| 28 | 7714 | 7574 | 7438 | 7307 | 7179 | 7055 | 6934 | 6816 | 6702 | 6590 | 6482 | 6376 | 28 |
| 29 | 7712 | 7572 | 7436 | 7304 | 7177 | 7052 | 6932 | 6814 | 6700 | 6589 | 6480 | 6374 | 29 |
| 30 | 7710 | 7570 | 7434 | 7302 | 7175 | 7050 | 6930 | 6812 | 6698 | 6587 | 6478 | 6372 | 30 |
| 31 | 7707 | 7567 | 7432 | 7300 | 7172 | 7048 | 6928 | 6810 | 6696 | 6585 | 6476 | 6371 | 31 |
| 32 | 7705 | 7565 | 7429 | 7298 | 7170 | 7046 | 6926 | 6809 | 6694 | 6583 | 6475 | 6369 | 32 |
| 33 | 7703 | 7563 | 7427 | 7296 | 7168 | 7044 | 6924 | 6807 | 6692 | 6581 | 6473 | 6367 | 33 |
| 34 | 7700 | 7560 | 7425 | 7294 | 7166 | 7042 | 6922 | 6805 | 6691 | 6579 | 6471 | 6365 | 34 |
| 35 | 7698 | 7558 | 7423 | 7291 | 7164 | 7040 | 6920 | 6803 | 6689 | 6578 | 6469 | 6364 | 35 |
| 36 | 7696 | 7556 | 7421 | 7289 | 7162 | 7038 | 6918 | 6801 | 6687 | 6576 | 6467 | 6362 | 36 |
| 37 | 7693 | 7554 | 7418 | 7287 | 7160 | 7036 | 6916 | 6799 | 6685 | 6574 | 6466 | 6360 | 37 |
| 38 | 7691 | 7551 | 7416 | 7285 | 7158 | 7034 | 6914 | 6797 | 6683 | 6572 | 6464 | 6358 | 38 |
| 39 | 7688 | 7549 | 7414 | 7283 | 7156 | 7032 | 6912 | 6795 | 6681 | 6570 | 6462 | 6357 | 39 |
| 40 | 7686 | 7547 | 7412 | 7281 | 7154 | 7030 | 6910 | 6793 | 6679 | 6568 | 6460 | 6355 | 40 |
| 41 | 7684 | 7544 | 7409 | 7279 | 7152 | 7028 | 6908 | 6791 | 6677 | 6567 | 6459 | 6353 | 41 |
| 42 | 7681 | 7542 | 7407 | 7276 | 7149 | 7026 | 6906 | 6789 | 6676 | 6565 | 6457 | 6351 | 42 |
| 43 | 7679 | 7540 | 7405 | 7274 | 7147 | 7024 | 6904 | 6787 | 6674 | 6563 | 6455 | 6350 | 43 |
| 44 | 7677 | 7538 | 7403 | 7272 | 7145 | 7022 | 6902 | 6785 | 6672 | 6561 | 6453 | 6348 | 44 |
| 45 | 7674 | 7535 | 7401 | 7270 | 7143 | 7020 | 6900 | 6784 | 6670 | 6559 | 6451 | 6346 | 45 |
| 46 | 7672 | 7533 | 7398 | 7268 | 7141 | 7018 | 6898 | 6782 | 6668 | 6558 | 6450 | 6344 | 46 |
| 47 | 7670 | 7531 | 7396 | 7266 | 7139 | 7016 | 6896 | 6780 | 6666 | 6556 | 6448 | 6343 | 47 |
| 48 | 7667 | 7528 | 7394 | 7264 | 7137 | 7014 | 6894 | 6778 | 6664 | 6554 | 6446 | 6341 | 48 |
| 49 | 7665 | 7526 | 7392 | 7261 | 7135 | 7012 | 6892 | 6776 | 6663 | 6552 | 6444 | 6339 | 49 |
| 50 | 7663 | 7524 | 7390 | 7259 | 7133 | 7010 | 6890 | 6774 | 6661 | 6550 | 6443 | 6338 | 50 |
| 51 | 7660 | 7522 | 7387 | 7257 | 7131 | 7008 | 6888 | 6772 | 6659 | 6548 | 6441 | 6336 | 51 |
| 52 | 7658 | 7519 | 7385 | 7255 | 7129 | 7006 | 6886 | 6770 | 6657 | 6547 | 6439 | 6334 | 52 |
| 53 | 7655 | 7517 | 7383 | 7253 | 7127 | 7004 | 6884 | 6768 | 6655 | 6545 | 6437 | 6332 | 53 |
| 54 | 7653 | 7515 | 7381 | 7251 | 7124 | 7002 | 6882 | 6766 | 6653 | 6543 | 6435 | 6331 | 54 |
| 55 | 7651 | 7513 | 7379 | 7249 | 7122 | 7000 | 6881 | 6764 | 6651 | 6541 | 6434 | 6329 | 55 |
| 56 | 7648 | 7510 | 7376 | 7246 | 7120 | 6998 | 6879 | 6763 | 6650 | 6539 | 6432 | 6327 | 56 |
| 57 | 7646 | 7508 | 7374 | 7244 | 7118 | 6996 | 6877 | 6761 | 6648 | 6538 | 6430 | 6325 | 57 |
| 58 | 7644 | 7506 | 7372 | 7242 | 7116 | 6994 | 6875 | 6759 | 6646 | 6536 | 6428 | 6324 | 58 |
| 59 | 7641 | 7503 | 7370 | 7240 | 7114 | 6992 | 6873 | 6757 | 6644 | 6534 | 6427 | 6322 | 59 |
| S. | 0° 30′ | 0° 31′ | 0° 32′ | 0° 33′ | 0° 34′ | 0° 35′ | 0° 36′ | 0° 37′ | 0° 38′ | 0° 39′ | 0° 40′ | 0° 41′ | S. |

# TABLE XXII.

## Proportional Logarithms.

| S. | h m 0° 42′ | h m 0° 43′ | h m 0° 44′ | h m 0° 45′ | h m 0° 46′ | h m 0° 47′ | h m 0° 48′ | h m 0° 49′ | h m 0° 50 | h m 0° 51′ | h m 0° 52′ | h m 0° 53′ | S. |
|---|---|---|---|---|---|---|---|---|---|---|---|---|---|
| 0 | 6320 | 6218 | 6118 | 6021 | 5925 | 5832 | 5740 | 5651 | 5563 | 5477 | 5393 | 5310 | 0 |
| 1 | 6319 | 6216 | 6117 | 6019 | 5924 | 5830 | 5739 | 5649 | 5562 | 5476 | 5391 | 5309 | 1 |
| 2 | 6317 | 6215 | 6115 | 6017 | 5922 | 5829 | 5737 | 5648 | 5560 | 5474 | 5390 | 5307 | 2 |
| 3 | 6315 | 6213 | 6113 | 6016 | 5920 | 5827 | 5736 | 5646 | 5559 | 5473 | 5389 | 5306 | 3 |
| 4 | 6313 | 6211 | 6112 | 6014 | 5919 | 5826 | 5734 | 5645 | 5557 | 5471 | 5387 | 5305 | 4 |
| 5 | 6312 | 6210 | 6110 | 6013 | 5917 | 5824 | 5733 | 5643 | 5556 | 5470 | 5386 | 5303 | 5 |
| 6 | 6310 | 6208 | 6108 | 6011 | 5916 | 5823 | 5731 | 5642 | 5554 | 5469 | 5384 | 5302 | 6 |
| 7 | 6308 | 6206 | 6107 | 6009 | 5914 | 5821 | 5730 | 5640 | 5553 | 5467 | 5383 | 5300 | 7 |
| 8 | 6306 | 6205 | 6105 | 6008 | 5913 | 5819 | 5728 | 5639 | 5551 | 5466 | 5382 | 5299 | 8 |
| 9 | 6305 | 6203 | 6103 | 6006 | 5911 | 5818 | 5727 | 5637 | 5550 | 5464 | 5380 | 5298 | 9 |
| 10 | 6303 | 6201 | 6102 | 6005 | 5909 | 5816 | 5725 | 5636 | 5549 | 5463 | 5379 | 5296 | 10 |
| 11 | 6301 | 6200 | 6100 | 6003 | 5908 | 5815 | 5724 | 5635 | 5547 | 5461 | 5377 | 5295 | 11 |
| 12 | 6300 | 6198 | 6099 | 6001 | 5906 | 5813 | 5722 | 5633 | 5546 | 5460 | 5376 | 5294 | 12 |
| 13 | 6298 | 6196 | 6097 | 6000 | 5905 | 5812 | 5721 | 5632 | 5544 | 5459 | 5375 | 5292 | 13 |
| 14 | 6296 | 6195 | 6095 | 5998 | 5903 | 5810 | 5719 | 5630 | 5543 | 5457 | 5373 | 5291 | 14 |
| 15 | 6294 | 6193 | 6094 | 5997 | 5902 | 5809 | 5718 | 5629 | 5541 | 5456 | 5372 | 5290 | 15 |
| 16 | 6293 | 6191 | 6092 | 5995 | 5900 | 5807 | 5716 | 5627 | 5540 | 5454 | 5370 | 5288 | 16 |
| 17 | 6291 | 6190 | 6090 | 5993 | 5898 | 5806 | 5715 | 5626 | 5538 | 5453 | 5369 | 5287 | 17 |
| 18 | 6289 | 6188 | 6089 | 5992 | 5897 | 5804 | 5713 | 5624 | 5537 | 5452 | 5368 | 5285 | 18 |
| 19 | 6288 | 6186 | 6087 | 5990 | 5895 | 5803 | 5712 | 5623 | 5536 | 5450 | 5366 | 5284 | 19 |
| 20 | 6286 | 6185 | 6085 | 5989 | 5894 | 5801 | 5710 | 5621 | 5534 | 5449 | 5365 | 5283 | 20 |
| 21 | 6284 | 6183 | 6084 | 5987 | 5892 | 5800 | 5709 | 5620 | 5533 | 5447 | 5364 | 5281 | 21 |
| 22 | 6282 | 6181 | 6082 | 5985 | 5891 | 5798 | 5707 | 5618 | 5531 | 5446 | 5362 | 5280 | 22 |
| 23 | 6281 | 6179 | 6081 | 5984 | 5889 | 5796 | 5706 | 5617 | 5530 | 5445 | 5361 | 5279 | 23 |
| 24 | 6279 | 6178 | 6079 | 5982 | 5888 | 5795 | 5704 | 5615 | 5528 | 5443 | 5359 | 5277 | 24 |
| 25 | 6277 | 6176 | 6077 | 5981 | 5886 | 5793 | 5703 | 5614 | 5527 | 5442 | 5358 | 5276 | 25 |
| 26 | 6276 | 6174 | 6076 | 5979 | 5884 | 5792 | 5701 | 5613 | 5526 | 5440 | 5357 | 5275 | 26 |
| 27 | 6274 | 6173 | 6074 | 5977 | 5883 | 5790 | 5700 | 5611 | 5524 | 5439 | 5355 | 5273 | 27 |
| 28 | 6272 | 6171 | 6072 | 5976 | 5881 | 5789 | 5698 | 5610 | 5523 | 5437 | 5354 | 5272 | 28 |
| 29 | 6271 | 6169 | 6071 | 5974 | 5880 | 5787 | 5697 | 5608 | 5521 | 5436 | 5353 | 5271 | 29 |
| 30 | 6269 | 6168 | 6069 | 5973 | 5878 | 5786 | 5695 | 5607 | 5520 | 5435 | 5351 | 5269 | 30 |
| 31 | 6267 | 6166 | 6067 | 5971 | 5877 | 5784 | 5694 | 5605 | 5518 | 5433 | 5350 | 5268 | 31 |
| 32 | 6265 | 6165 | 6066 | 5969 | 5875 | 5783 | 5692 | 5604 | 5517 | 5432 | 5348 | 5266 | 32 |
| 33 | 6264 | 6163 | 6064 | 5968 | 5874 | 5781 | 5691 | 5602 | 5516 | 5430 | 5347 | 5265 | 33 |
| 34 | 6262 | 6161 | 6063 | 5966 | 5872 | 5780 | 5689 | 5601 | 5514 | 5429 | 5346 | 5264 | 34 |
| 35 | 6260 | 6160 | 6061 | 5965 | 5870 | 5778 | 5688 | 5599 | 5513 | 5428 | 5344 | 5262 | 35 |
| 36 | 6259 | 6158 | 6059 | 5963 | 5869 | 5777 | 5686 | 5598 | 5511 | 5426 | 5343 | 5261 | 36 |
| 37 | 6257 | 6156 | 6058 | 5961 | 5867 | 5775 | 5685 | 5596 | 5510 | 5425 | 5341 | 5260 | 37 |
| 38 | 6255 | 6155 | 6056 | 5960 | 5866 | 5774 | 5683 | 5595 | 5508 | 5423 | 5340 | 5258 | 38 |
| 39 | 6254 | 6153 | 6055 | 5958 | 5864 | 5772 | 5682 | 5594 | 5507 | 5422 | 5339 | 5257 | 39 |
| 40 | 6252 | 6151 | 6053 | 5957 | 5863 | 5771 | 5680 | 5592 | 5506 | 5421 | 5337 | 5256 | 40 |
| 41 | 6250 | 6150 | 6051 | 5955 | 5861 | 5769 | 5679 | 5591 | 5504 | 5419 | 5336 | 5254 | 41 |
| 42 | 6248 | 6148 | 6050 | 5954 | 5860 | 5768 | 5677 | 5589 | 5503 | 5418 | 5335 | 5253 | 42 |
| 43 | 6247 | 6146 | 6048 | 5952 | 5858 | 5766 | 5676 | 5588 | 5501 | 5416 | 5333 | 5252 | 43 |
| 44 | 6245 | 6145 | 6046 | 5950 | 5856 | 5765 | 5674 | 5586 | 5500 | 5415 | 5332 | 5250 | 44 |
| 45 | 6243 | 6143 | 6045 | 5949 | 5855 | 5763 | 5673 | 5585 | 5498 | 5414 | 5331 | 5249 | 45 |
| 46 | 6242 | 6141 | 6043 | 5947 | 5853 | 5761 | 5671 | 5583 | 5497 | 5412 | 5329 | 5248 | 46 |
| 47 | 6240 | 6140 | 6042 | 5946 | 5852 | 5760 | 5670 | 5582 | 5496 | 5411 | 5328 | 5246 | 47 |
| 48 | 6238 | 6138 | 6040 | 5944 | 5850 | 5758 | 5669 | 5580 | 5494 | 5409 | 5326 | 5245 | 48 |
| 49 | 6237 | 6136 | 6038 | 5942 | 5849 | 5757 | 5667 | 5579 | 5493 | 5408 | 5325 | 5244 | 49 |
| 50 | 6235 | 6135 | 6037 | 5941 | 5847 | 5755 | 5666 | 5578 | 5491 | 5407 | 5324 | 5242 | 50 |
| 51 | 6233 | 6133 | 6035 | 5939 | 5846 | 5754 | 5664 | 5576 | 5490 | 5405 | 5322 | 5241 | 51 |
| 52 | 6232 | 6131 | 6033 | 5938 | 5844 | 5752 | 5663 | 5575 | 5488 | 5404 | 5321 | 5240 | 52 |
| 53 | 6230 | 6130 | 6032 | 5936 | 5843 | 5751 | 5661 | 5573 | 5487 | 5402 | 5320 | 5238 | 53 |
| 54 | 6228 | 6128 | 6030 | 5935 | 5841 | 5749 | 5660 | 5572 | 5486 | 5401 | 5318 | 5237 | 54 |
| 55 | 6226 | 6126 | 6029 | 5933 | 5839 | 5748 | 5658 | 5570 | 5484 | 5400 | 5317 | 5235 | 55 |
| 56 | 6225 | 6125 | 6027 | 5931 | 5838 | 5746 | 5657 | 5569 | 5483 | 5398 | 5315 | 5234 | 56 |
| 57 | 6223 | 6123 | 6025 | 5930 | 5836 | 5745 | 5655 | 5567 | 5481 | 5397 | 5314 | 5233 | 57 |
| 58 | 6221 | 6121 | 6024 | 5928 | 5835 | 5743 | 5654 | 5566 | 5480 | 5395 | 5313 | 5231 | 58 |
| 59 | 6220 | 6120 | 6022 | 5927 | 5833 | 5742 | 5652 | 5564 | 5478 | 5394 | 5311 | 5230 | 59 |
| S. | 0° 42′ | 0° 43′ | 0° 44′ | 0° 45′ | 0° 46′ | 0° 47′ | 0° 48′ | 0° 49′ | 0° 50′ | 0° 51′ | 0° 52′ | 0° 53′ | S. |

# TABLE XXII.

## Proportional Logarithms.

| S. | h m 0° 54′ | h m 0° 55′ | h m 0° 56′ | h m 0° 57′ | h m 0° 58′ | h m 0° 59′ | h m 1° 0′ | h m 1° 1′ | h m 1° 2′ | h m 1° 3′ | h m 1° 4′ | h m 1° 5′ | S. |
|---|---|---|---|---|---|---|---|---|---|---|---|---|---|
| 0 | 5229 | 5149 | 5071 | 4994 | 4918 | 4844 | 4771 | 4699 | 4629 | 4559 | 4491 | 4424 | 0 |
| 1 | 5227 | 5148 | 5070 | 4993 | 4917 | 4843 | 4770 | 4698 | 4628 | 4558 | 4490 | 4422 | 1 |
| 2 | 5226 | 5146 | 5068 | 4991 | 4916 | 4842 | 4769 | 4697 | 4626 | 4557 | 4489 | 4421 | 2 |
| 3 | 5225 | 5145 | 5067 | 4990 | 4915 | 4841 | 4768 | 4696 | 4625 | 4556 | 4488 | 4420 | 3 |
| 4 | 5223 | 5144 | 5066 | 4989 | 4913 | 4839 | 4766 | 4695 | 4624 | 4555 | 4486 | 4419 | 4 |
| 5 | 5222 | 5143 | 5064 | 4988 | 4912 | 4838 | 4765 | 4693 | 4623 | 4554 | 4485 | 4418 | 5 |
| 6 | 5221 | 5141 | 5063 | 4986 | 4911 | 4837 | 4764 | 4692 | 4622 | 4552 | 4484 | 4417 | 6 |
| 7 | 5219 | 5140 | 5062 | 4985 | 4910 | 4836 | 4763 | 4691 | 4621 | 4551 | 4483 | 4416 | 7 |
| 8 | 5218 | 5139 | 5061 | 4984 | 4908 | 4834 | 4762 | 4690 | 4619 | 4550 | 4482 | 4415 | 8 |
| 9 | 5217 | 5137 | 5059 | 4983 | 4907 | 4833 | 4760 | 4689 | 4618 | 4549 | 4481 | 4414 | 9 |
| 10 | 5215 | 5136 | 5058 | 4981 | 4906 | 4832 | 4759 | 4688 | 4617 | 4548 | 4480 | 4412 | 10 |
| 11 | 5214 | 5135 | 5057 | 4980 | 4905 | 4831 | 4758 | 4686 | 4616 | 4547 | 4479 | 4411 | 11 |
| 12 | 5213 | 5133 | 5055 | 4979 | 4903 | 4830 | 4757 | 4685 | 4615 | 4546 | 4477 | 4410 | 12 |
| 13 | 5211 | 5132 | 5054 | 4977 | 4902 | 4828 | 4756 | 4684 | 4614 | 4544 | 4476 | 4409 | 13 |
| 14 | 5210 | 5131 | 5053 | 4976 | 4901 | 4827 | 4754 | 4683 | 4612 | 4543 | 4475 | 4408 | 14 |
| 15 | 5209 | 5129 | 5051 | 4975 | 4900 | 4826 | 4753 | 4682 | 4611 | 4542 | 4474 | 4407 | 15 |
| 16 | 5207 | 5128 | 5050 | 4974 | 4899 | 4825 | 4752 | 4680 | 4610 | 4541 | 4473 | 4406 | 16 |
| 17 | 5206 | 5127 | 5049 | 4972 | 4897 | 4823 | 4751 | 4679 | 4609 | 4540 | 4472 | 4405 | 17 |
| 18 | 5205 | 5125 | 5048 | 4971 | 4896 | 4822 | 4750 | 4678 | 4608 | 4539 | 4471 | 4404 | 18 |
| 19 | 5203 | 5124 | 5046 | 4970 | 4895 | 4821 | 4748 | 4677 | 4607 | 4538 | 4469 | 4402 | 19 |
| 20 | 5202 | 5123 | 5045 | 4969 | 4894 | 4820 | 4747 | 4676 | 4606 | 4536 | 4468 | 4401 | 20 |
| 21 | 5201 | 5122 | 5044 | 4967 | 4892 | 4819 | 4746 | 4675 | 4604 | 4535 | 4467 | 4400 | 21 |
| 22 | 5199 | 5120 | 5043 | 4966 | 4891 | 4817 | 4745 | 4673 | 4603 | 4534 | 4466 | 4399 | 22 |
| 23 | 5198 | 5119 | 5041 | 4965 | 4890 | 4816 | 4744 | 4672 | 4602 | 4533 | 4465 | 4398 | 23 |
| 24 | 5197 | 5118 | 5040 | 4964 | 4889 | 4815 | 4742 | 4671 | 4601 | 4532 | 4464 | 4397 | 24 |
| 25 | 5195 | 5116 | 5039 | 4962 | 4887 | 4814 | 4741 | 4670 | 4600 | 4531 | 4463 | 4396 | 25 |
| 26 | 5194 | 5115 | 5037 | 4961 | 4886 | 4812 | 4740 | 4669 | 4599 | 4530 | 4462 | 4395 | 26 |
| 27 | 5193 | 5114 | 5036 | 4960 | 4885 | 4811 | 4739 | 4668 | 4597 | 4528 | 4460 | 4394 | 27 |
| 28 | 5191 | 5112 | 5035 | 4959 | 4884 | 4810 | 4738 | 4666 | 4596 | 4527 | 4459 | 4393 | 28 |
| 29 | 5190 | 5111 | 5034 | 4957 | 4882 | 4809 | 4736 | 4665 | 4595 | 4526 | 4458 | 4391 | 29 |
| 30 | 5189 | 5110 | 5032 | 4956 | 4881 | 4808 | 4735 | 4664 | 4594 | 4525 | 4457 | 4390 | 30 |
| 31 | 5187 | 5108 | 5031 | 4955 | 4880 | 4806 | 4734 | 4663 | 4593 | 4524 | 4456 | 4389 | 31 |
| 32 | 5186 | 5107 | 5030 | 4954 | 4879 | 4805 | 4733 | 4662 | 4592 | 4523 | 4455 | 4388 | 32 |
| 33 | 5185 | 5106 | 5028 | 4952 | 4877 | 4804 | 4732 | 4660 | 4590 | 4522 | 4454 | 4387 | 33 |
| 34 | 5183 | 5105 | 5027 | 4951 | 4876 | 4803 | 4730 | 4659 | 4589 | 4520 | 4453 | 4386 | 34 |
| 35 | 5182 | 5103 | 5026 | 4950 | 4875 | 4801 | 4729 | 4658 | 4588 | 4519 | 4452 | 4385 | 35 |
| 36 | 5181 | 5102 | 5025 | 4949 | 4874 | 4800 | 4728 | 4657 | 4587 | 4518 | 4450 | 4384 | 36 |
| 37 | 5179 | 5101 | 5023 | 4947 | 4873 | 4799 | 4727 | 4656 | 4586 | 4517 | 4449 | 4383 | 37 |
| 38 | 5178 | 5099 | 5022 | 4946 | 4871 | 4798 | 4726 | 4655 | 4585 | 4516 | 4448 | 4381 | 38 |
| 39 | 5177 | 5098 | 5021 | 4945 | 4870 | 4797 | 4724 | 4653 | 4584 | 4515 | 4447 | 4380 | 39 |
| 40 | 5175 | 5097 | 5019 | 4943 | 4869 | 4795 | 4723 | 4652 | 4582 | 4514 | 4446 | 4379 | 40 |
| 41 | 5174 | 5095 | 5018 | 4942 | 4868 | 4794 | 4722 | 4651 | 4581 | 4512 | 4445 | 4378 | 41 |
| 42 | 5173 | 5094 | 5017 | 4941 | 4866 | 4793 | 4721 | 4650 | 4580 | 4511 | 4444 | 4377 | 42 |
| 43 | 5172 | 5093 | 5016 | 4940 | 4865 | 4792 | 4720 | 4649 | 4579 | 4510 | 4443 | 4376 | 43 |
| 44 | 5170 | 5092 | 5014 | 4938 | 4864 | 4791 | 4718 | 4648 | 4578 | 4509 | 4441 | 4375 | 44 |
| 45 | 5169 | 5090 | 5013 | 4937 | 4863 | 4789 | 4717 | 4646 | 4577 | 4508 | 4440 | 4374 | 45 |
| 46 | 5168 | 5089 | 5012 | 4936 | 4861 | 4788 | 4716 | 4645 | 4575 | 4507 | 4439 | 4373 | 46 |
| 47 | 5166 | 5088 | 5011 | 4935 | 4860 | 4787 | 4715 | 4644 | 4574 | 4506 | 4438 | 4372 | 47 |
| 48 | 5165 | 5086 | 5009 | 4933 | 4859 | 4786 | 4714 | 4643 | 4573 | 4505 | 4437 | 4370 | 48 |
| 49 | 5164 | 5085 | 5008 | 4932 | 4858 | 4785 | 4712 | 4642 | 4572 | 4503 | 4436 | 4369 | 49 |
| 50 | 5162 | 5084 | 5007 | 4931 | 4856 | 4783 | 4711 | 4640 | 4571 | 4502 | 4435 | 4368 | 50 |
| 51 | 5161 | 5082 | 5005 | 4930 | 4855 | 4782 | 4710 | 4639 | 4570 | 4501 | 4434 | 4367 | 51 |
| 52 | 5160 | 5081 | 5004 | 4928 | 4854 | 4781 | 4709 | 4638 | 4569 | 4500 | 4433 | 4366 | 52 |
| 53 | 5158 | 5080 | 5003 | 4927 | 4853 | 4780 | 4708 | 4637 | 4567 | 4499 | 4431 | 4365 | 53 |
| 54 | 5157 | 5079 | 5002 | 4926 | 4852 | 4778 | 4707 | 4636 | 4566 | 4498 | 4430 | 4364 | 54 |
| 55 | 5156 | 5077 | 5000 | 4925 | 4850 | 4777 | 4705 | 4635 | 4565 | 4497 | 4429 | 4363 | 55 |
| 56 | 5154 | 5076 | 4999 | 4923 | 4849 | 4776 | 4704 | 4633 | 4564 | 4495 | 4428 | 4362 | 56 |
| 57 | 5153 | 5075 | 4998 | 4922 | 4848 | 4775 | 4703 | 4632 | 4563 | 4494 | 4427 | 4361 | 57 |
| 58 | 5152 | 5073 | 4997 | 4921 | 4847 | 4774 | 4702 | 4631 | 4562 | 4493 | 4426 | 4359 | 58 |
| 59 | 5150 | 5072 | 4995 | 4920 | 4845 | 4772 | 4701 | 4630 | 4560 | 4492 | 4425 | 4358 | 59 |
| S. | 0° 54′ | 0° 55′ | 0° 56′ | 0° 57′ | 0° 58′ | 0° 59′ | 1° 0′ | 1° 1′ | 1° 2′ | 1° 3′ | 1° 4′ | 1° 5′ | S. |

# TABLE XXII.

## Proportional Logarithms.

| S. | *h m* 1° 6′ | *h m* 1° 7′ | *h m* 1° 8′ | *h m* 1° 9′ | *h m* 1° 10′ | *h m* 1° 11′ | *h m* 1° 12′ | *h m* 1° 13′ | *h m* 1° 14′ | *h m* 1° 15′ | *h m* 1° 16′ | *h m* 1° 17′ | S. |
|---|---|---|---|---|---|---|---|---|---|---|---|---|---|
| 0 | 4357 | 4292 | 4228 | 4164 | 4102 | 4040 | 3979 | 3919 | 3860 | 3802 | 3745 | 3688 | 0 |
| 1 | 4356 | 4291 | 4227 | 4163 | 4101 | 4039 | 3978 | 3919 | 3859 | 3801 | 3744 | 3687 | 1 |
| 2 | 4355 | 4290 | 4226 | 4162 | 4100 | 4038 | 3977 | 3918 | 3858 | 3800 | 3743 | 3686 | 2 |
| 3 | 4354 | 4289 | 4224 | 4161 | 4099 | 4037 | 3976 | 3917 | 3857 | 3799 | 3742 | 3685 | 3 |
| 4 | 4353 | 4288 | 4223 | 4160 | 4098 | 4036 | 3975 | 3916 | 3856 | 3798 | 3741 | 3684 | 4 |
| 5 | 4352 | 4287 | 4222 | 4159 | 4097 | 4035 | 3974 | 3915 | 3856 | 3797 | 3740 | 3683 | 5 |
| 6 | 4351 | 4285 | 4221 | 4158 | 4096 | 4034 | 3973 | 3914 | 3855 | 3796 | 3739 | 3682 | 6 |
| 7 | 4350 | 4284 | 4220 | 4157 | 4095 | 4033 | 3972 | 3913 | 3854 | 3795 | 3738 | 3681 | 7 |
| 8 | 4349 | 4283 | 4219 | 4156 | 4093 | 4032 | 3971 | 3912 | 3853 | 3794 | 3737 | 3680 | 8 |
| 9 | 4347 | 4282 | 4218 | 4155 | 4092 | 4031 | 3970 | 3911 | 3852 | 3793 | 3736 | 3679 | 9 |
| 10 | 4346 | 4281 | 4217 | 4154 | 4091 | 4030 | 3969 | 3910 | 3851 | 3792 | 3735 | 3678 | 10 |
| 11 | 4345 | 4280 | 4216 | 4153 | 4090 | 4029 | 3968 | 3909 | 3850 | 3792 | 3734 | 3677 | 11 |
| 12 | 4344 | 4279 | 4215 | 4152 | 4089 | 4028 | 3967 | 3908 | 3849 | 3791 | 3733 | 3677 | 12 |
| 13 | 4343 | 4278 | 4214 | 4151 | 4088 | 4027 | 3966 | 3907 | 3848 | 3790 | 3732 | 3676 | 13 |
| 14 | 4342 | 4277 | 4213 | 4150 | 4087 | 4026 | 3965 | 3906 | 3847 | 3789 | 3731 | 3675 | 14 |
| 15 | 4341 | 4276 | 4212 | 4149 | 4086 | 4025 | 3964 | 3905 | 3846 | 3788 | 3730 | 3674 | 15 |
| 16 | 4340 | 4275 | 4211 | 4147 | 4085 | 4024 | 3963 | 3904 | 3845 | 3787 | 3729 | 3673 | 16 |
| 17 | 4339 | 4274 | 4210 | 4146 | 4084 | 4023 | 3962 | 3903 | 3844 | 3786 | 3728 | 3672 | 17 |
| 18 | 4338 | 4273 | 4209 | 4145 | 4083 | 4022 | 3961 | 3902 | 3843 | 3785 | 3727 | 3671 | 18 |
| 19 | 4336 | 4271 | 4207 | 4144 | 4082 | 4021 | 3960 | 3901 | 3842 | 3784 | 3727 | 3670 | 19 |
| 20 | 4335 | 4270 | 4206 | 4143 | 4081 | 4020 | 3959 | 3900 | 3841 | 3783 | 3726 | 3669 | 20 |
| 21 | 4334 | 4269 | 4205 | 4142 | 4080 | 4019 | 3958 | 3899 | 3840 | 3782 | 3725 | 3668 | 21 |
| 22 | 4333 | 4268 | 4204 | 4141 | 4079 | 4018 | 3957 | 3898 | 3839 | 3781 | 3724 | 3667 | 22 |
| 23 | 4332 | 4267 | 4203 | 4140 | 4078 | 4017 | 3956 | 3897 | 3838 | 3780 | 3723 | 3666 | 23 |
| 24 | 4331 | 4266 | 4202 | 4139 | 4077 | 4016 | 3955 | 3896 | 3837 | 3779 | 3722 | 3665 | 24 |
| 25 | 4330 | 4265 | 4201 | 4138 | 4076 | 4015 | 3954 | 3895 | 3836 | 3778 | 3721 | 3664 | 25 |
| 26 | 4329 | 4264 | 4200 | 4137 | 4075 | 4014 | 3953 | 3894 | 3835 | 3777 | 3720 | 3663 | 26 |
| 27 | 4328 | 4263 | 4199 | 4136 | 4074 | 4013 | 3952 | 3893 | 3834 | 3776 | 3719 | 3663 | 27 |
| 28 | 4327 | 4262 | 4198 | 4135 | 4073 | 4012 | 3951 | 3892 | 3833 | 3775 | 3718 | 3662 | 28 |
| 29 | 4326 | 4261 | 4197 | 4134 | 4072 | 4011 | 3950 | 3891 | 3832 | 3774 | 3717 | 3661 | 29 |
| 30 | 4325 | 4260 | 4196 | 4133 | 4071 | 4010 | 3949 | 3890 | 3831 | 3773 | 3716 | 3660 | 30 |
| 31 | 4323 | 4259 | 4195 | 4132 | 4070 | 4009 | 3948 | 3889 | 3830 | 3772 | 3715 | 3659 | 31 |
| 32 | 4322 | 4258 | 4194 | 4131 | 4069 | 4008 | 3947 | 3888 | 3829 | 3771 | 3714 | 3658 | 32 |
| 33 | 4321 | 4256 | 4193 | 4130 | 4068 | 4007 | 3946 | 3887 | 3828 | 3770 | 3713 | 3657 | 33 |
| 34 | 4320 | 4255 | 4192 | 4129 | 4067 | 4006 | 3945 | 3886 | 3827 | 3769 | 3712 | 3656 | 34 |
| 35 | 4319 | 4254 | 4191 | 4128 | 4066 | 4005 | 3944 | 3885 | 3826 | 3768 | 3711 | 3655 | 35 |
| 36 | 4318 | 4253 | 4189 | 4127 | 4065 | 4004 | 3943 | 3884 | 3825 | 3768 | 3710 | 3654 | 36 |
| 37 | 4317 | 4252 | 4188 | 4126 | 4064 | 4003 | 3942 | 3883 | 3824 | 3767 | 3709 | 3653 | 37 |
| 38 | 4316 | 4251 | 4187 | 4125 | 4063 | 4002 | 3941 | 3882 | 3823 | 3766 | 3709 | 3652 | 38 |
| 39 | 4315 | 4250 | 4186 | 4124 | 4062 | 4001 | 3940 | 3881 | 3822 | 3765 | 3708 | 3651 | 39 |
| 40 | 4314 | 4249 | 4185 | 4122 | 4061 | 4000 | 3939 | 3880 | 3821 | 3764 | 3707 | 3650 | 40 |
| 41 | 4313 | 4248 | 4184 | 4121 | 4060 | 3999 | 3938 | 3879 | 3820 | 3763 | 3706 | 3649 | 41 |
| 42 | 4311 | 4247 | 4183 | 4120 | 4059 | 3998 | 3937 | 3878 | 3820 | 3762 | 3705 | 3649 | 42 |
| 43 | 4310 | 4246 | 4182 | 4119 | 4058 | 3997 | 3936 | 3877 | 3819 | 3761 | 3704 | 3648 | 43 |
| 44 | 4309 | 4245 | 4181 | 4118 | 4056 | 3996 | 3935 | 3876 | 3818 | 3760 | 3703 | 3647 | 44 |
| 45 | 4308 | 4244 | 4180 | 4117 | 4055 | 3995 | 3934 | 3875 | 3817 | 3759 | 3702 | 3646 | 45 |
| 46 | 4307 | 4243 | 4179 | 4116 | 4054 | 3993 | 3933 | 3874 | 3816 | 3758 | 3701 | 3645 | 46 |
| 47 | 4306 | 4241 | 4178 | 4115 | 4053 | 3992 | 3932 | 3873 | 3815 | 3757 | 3700 | 3644 | 47 |
| 48 | 4305 | 4240 | 4177 | 4114 | 4052 | 3991 | 3931 | 3872 | 3814 | 3756 | 3699 | 3643 | 48 |
| 49 | 4304 | 4239 | 4176 | 4113 | 4051 | 3990 | 3930 | 3871 | 3813 | 3755 | 3698 | 3642 | 49 |
| 50 | 4303 | 4238 | 4175 | 4112 | 4050 | 3989 | 3929 | 3870 | 3812 | 3754 | 3697 | 3641 | 50 |
| 51 | 4302 | 4237 | 4174 | 4111 | 4049 | 3988 | 3928 | 3869 | 3811 | 3753 | 3696 | 3640 | 51 |
| 52 | 4301 | 4236 | 4173 | 4110 | 4048 | 3987 | 3927 | 3868 | 3810 | 3752 | 3695 | 3639 | 52 |
| 53 | 4300 | 4235 | 4172 | 4109 | 4047 | 3986 | 3926 | 3867 | 3809 | 3751 | 3694 | 3638 | 53 |
| 54 | 4298 | 4234 | 4171 | 4108 | 4046 | 3985 | 3925 | 3866 | 3808 | 3750 | 3693 | 3637 | 54 |
| 55 | 4297 | 4233 | 4169 | 4107 | 4045 | 3984 | 3924 | 3865 | 3807 | 3749 | 3693 | 3636 | 55 |
| 56 | 4296 | 4232 | 4168 | 4106 | 4044 | 3983 | 3923 | 3864 | 3806 | 3748 | 3692 | 3635 | 56 |
| 57 | 4295 | 4231 | 4167 | 4105 | 4043 | 3982 | 3922 | 3863 | 3805 | 3747 | 3691 | 3635 | 57 |
| 58 | 4294 | 4230 | 4166 | 4104 | 4042 | 3981 | 3921 | 3862 | 3804 | 3746 | 3690 | 3634 | 58 |
| 59 | 4293 | 4229 | 4165 | 4103 | 4041 | 3980 | 3920 | 3861 | 3803 | 3746 | 3689 | 3633 | 59 |
| S. | 1° 6′ | 1° 7′ | 1° 8′ | 1° 9′ | 1° 10′ | 1° 11′ | 1° 12′ | 1° 13′ | 1° 14′ | 1 15′ | 1° 16′ | 1° 17′ | S. |

# TABLE XXII.

## Proportional Logarithms.

| S. | h m 1° 18′ | h m 1° 19′ | h m 1° 20′ | h m 1° 21′ | h m 1° 22′ | h m 1° 23′ | h m 1° 24′ | h m 1° 25′ | h m 1° 26′ | h m 1° 27′ | h m 1° 28′ | h m 1° 29′ | S. |
|---|---|---|---|---|---|---|---|---|---|---|---|---|---|
| 0 | 3632 | 3576 | 3522 | 3468 | 3415 | 3362 | 3310 | 3259 | 3208 | 3158 | 3108 | 3059 | 0 |
| 1 | 3631 | 3576 | 3521 | 3467 | 3414 | 3361 | 3309 | 3258 | 3207 | 3157 | 3107 | 3058 | 1 |
| 2 | 3630 | 3575 | 3520 | 3466 | 3413 | 3360 | 3308 | 3257 | 3206 | 3156 | 3106 | 3057 | 2 |
| 3 | 3629 | 3574 | 3519 | 3465 | 3412 | 3359 | 3307 | 3256 | 3205 | 3155 | 3105 | 3056 | 3 |
| 4 | 3628 | 3573 | 3518 | 3464 | 3411 | 3358 | 3306 | 3255 | 3204 | 3154 | 3105 | 3056 | 4 |
| 5 | 3627 | 3572 | 3517 | 3463 | 3410 | 3358 | 3306 | 3254 | 3204 | 3153 | 3104 | 3055 | 5 |
| 6 | 3626 | 3571 | 3516 | 3463 | 3409 | 3357 | 3305 | 3253 | 3203 | 3153 | 3103 | 3054 | 6 |
| 7 | 3625 | 3570 | 3515 | 3462 | 3408 | 3356 | 3304 | 3253 | 3202 | 3152 | 3102 | 3053 | 7 |
| 8 | 3624 | 3569 | 3515 | 3461 | 3408 | 3355 | 3303 | 3252 | 3201 | 3151 | 3101 | 3052 | 8 |
| 9 | 3623 | 3568 | 3514 | 3460 | 3407 | 3354 | 3302 | 3251 | 3200 | 3150 | 3101 | 3052 | 9 |
| 10 | 3623 | 3567 | 3513 | 3459 | 3406 | 3353 | 3301 | 3250 | 3199 | 3149 | 3100 | 3051 | 10 |
| 11 | 3622 | 3566 | 3512 | 3458 | 3405 | 3352 | 3300 | 3249 | 3198 | 3148 | 3099 | 3050 | 11 |
| 12 | 3621 | 3565 | 3511 | 3457 | 3404 | 3351 | 3300 | 3248 | 3198 | 3148 | 3098 | 3049 | 12 |
| 13 | 3620 | 3565 | 3510 | 3456 | 3403 | 3351 | 3299 | 3247 | 3197 | 3147 | 3097 | 3048 | 13 |
| 14 | 3619 | 3564 | 3509 | 3455 | 3402 | 3350 | 3298 | 3247 | 3196 | 3146 | 3096 | 3047 | 14 |
| 15 | 3618 | 3563 | 3508 | 3454 | 3401 | 3349 | 3297 | 3246 | 3195 | 3145 | 3096 | 3047 | 15 |
| 16 | 3617 | 3562 | 3507 | 3454 | 3400 | 3348 | 3296 | 3245 | 3194 | 3144 | 3095 | 3046 | 16 |
| 17 | 3616 | 3561 | 3506 | 3453 | 3400 | 3347 | 3295 | 3244 | 3193 | 3143 | 3094 | 3045 | 17 |
| 18 | 3615 | 3560 | 3506 | 3452 | 3399 | 3346 | 3294 | 3243 | 3193 | 3143 | 3093 | 3044 | 18 |
| 19 | 3614 | 3559 | 3505 | 3451 | 3398 | 3345 | 3294 | 3242 | 3192 | 3142 | 3092 | 3043 | 19 |
| 20 | 3613 | 3558 | 3504 | 3450 | 3397 | 3345 | 3293 | 3242 | 3191 | 3141 | 3091 | 3043 | 20 |
| 21 | 3612 | 3557 | 3503 | 3449 | 3396 | 3344 | 3292 | 3241 | 3190 | 3140 | 3091 | 3042 | 21 |
| 22 | 3611 | 3556 | 3502 | 3448 | 3395 | 3343 | 3291 | 3240 | 3189 | 3139 | 3090 | 3041 | 22 |
| 23 | 3610 | 3555 | 3501 | 3447 | 3394 | 3342 | 3290 | 3239 | 3188 | 3138 | 3089 | 3040 | 23 |
| 24 | 3610 | 3555 | 3500 | 3446 | 3393 | 3341 | 3289 | 3238 | 3188 | 3138 | 3088 | 3039 | 24 |
| 25 | 3609 | 3554 | 3499 | 3446 | 3393 | 3340 | 3288 | 3237 | 3187 | 3137 | 3087 | 3039 | 25 |
| 26 | 3608 | 3553 | 3498 | 3445 | 3392 | 3339 | 3288 | 3236 | 3186 | 3136 | 3087 | 3038 | 26 |
| 27 | 3607 | 3552 | 3497 | 3444 | 3391 | 3338 | 3287 | 3236 | 3185 | 3135 | 3086 | 3037 | 27 |
| 28 | 3606 | 3551 | 3497 | 3443 | 3390 | 3338 | 3286 | 3235 | 3184 | 3134 | 3085 | 3036 | 28 |
| 29 | 3605 | 3550 | 3496 | 3442 | 3389 | 3337 | 3285 | 3234 | 3183 | 3133 | 3084 | 3035 | 29 |
| 30 | 3604 | 3549 | 3495 | 3441 | 3388 | 3336 | 3284 | 3233 | 3183 | 3133 | 3083 | 3034 | 30 |
| 31 | 3603 | 3548 | 3494 | 3440 | 3387 | 3335 | 3283 | 3232 | 3182 | 3132 | 3082 | 3034 | 31 |
| 32 | 3602 | 3547 | 3493 | 3439 | 3386 | 3334 | 3282 | 3231 | 3181 | 3131 | 3082 | 3033 | 32 |
| 33 | 3601 | 3546 | 3492 | 3438 | 3386 | 3333 | 3282 | 3231 | 3180 | 3130 | 3081 | 3032 | 33 |
| 34 | 3600 | 3545 | 3491 | 3438 | 3385 | 3332 | 3281 | 3230 | 3179 | 3129 | 3080 | 3031 | 34 |
| 35 | 3599 | 3545 | 3490 | 3437 | 3384 | 3332 | 3280 | 3229 | 3178 | 3129 | 3079 | 3030 | 35 |
| 36 | 3598 | 3544 | 3489 | 3436 | 3383 | 3331 | 3279 | 3228 | 3178 | 3128 | 3078 | 3030 | 36 |
| 37 | 3598 | 3543 | 3488 | 3435 | 3382 | 3330 | 3278 | 3227 | 3177 | 3127 | 3078 | 3029 | 37 |
| 38 | 3597 | 3542 | 3488 | 3434 | 3381 | 3329 | 3277 | 3226 | 3176 | 3126 | 3077 | 3028 | 38 |
| 39 | 3596 | 3541 | 3487 | 3433 | 3380 | 3328 | 3276 | 3225 | 3175 | 3125 | 3076 | 3027 | 39 |
| 40 | 3595 | 3540 | 3486 | 3432 | 3379 | 3327 | 3276 | 3225 | 3174 | 3124 | 3075 | 3026 | 40 |
| 41 | 3594 | 3539 | 3485 | 3431 | 3379 | 3326 | 3275 | 3224 | 3173 | 3124 | 3074 | 3026 | 41 |
| 42 | 3593 | 3538 | 3484 | 3431 | 3378 | 3325 | 3274 | 3223 | 3173 | 3123 | 3073 | 3025 | 42 |
| 43 | 3592 | 3537 | 3483 | 3430 | 3377 | 3325 | 3273 | 3222 | 3172 | 3122 | 3073 | 3024 | 43 |
| 44 | 3591 | 3536 | 3482 | 3429 | 3376 | 3324 | 3272 | 3221 | 3171 | 3121 | 3072 | 3023 | 44 |
| 45 | 3590 | 3535 | 3481 | 3428 | 3375 | 3323 | 3271 | 3220 | 3170 | 3120 | 3071 | 3022 | 45 |
| 46 | 3589 | 3535 | 3480 | 3427 | 3374 | 3322 | 3270 | 3220 | 3169 | 3119 | 3070 | 3022 | 46 |
| 47 | 3588 | 3534 | 3480 | 3426 | 3373 | 3321 | 3270 | 3219 | 3168 | 3119 | 3069 | 3021 | 47 |
| 48 | 3587 | 3533 | 3479 | 3425 | 3372 | 3320 | 3269 | 3218 | 3168 | 3118 | 3069 | 3020 | 48 |
| 49 | 3587 | 3532 | 3478 | 3424 | 3372 | 3319 | 3268 | 3217 | 3167 | 3117 | 3068 | 3019 | 49 |
| 50 | 3586 | 3531 | 3477 | 3423 | 3371 | 3319 | 3267 | 3216 | 3166 | 3116 | 3067 | 3018 | 50 |
| 51 | 3585 | 3530 | 3476 | 3423 | 3370 | 3318 | 3266 | 3215 | 3165 | 3115 | 3066 | 3018 | 51 |
| 52 | 3584 | 3529 | 3475 | 3422 | 3369 | 3317 | 3265 | 3214 | 3164 | 3114 | 3065 | 3017 | 52 |
| 53 | 3583 | 3528 | 3474 | 3421 | 3368 | 3316 | 3265 | 3214 | 3163 | 3114 | 3065 | 3016 | 53 |
| 54 | 3582 | 3527 | 3473 | 3420 | 3367 | 3315 | 3264 | 3213 | 3163 | 3113 | 3064 | 3015 | 54 |
| 55 | 3581 | 3526 | 3472 | 3419 | 3366 | 3314 | 3263 | 3212 | 3162 | 3112 | 3063 | 3014 | 55 |
| 56 | 3580 | 3525 | 3471 | 3418 | 3365 | 3313 | 3262 | 3211 | 3161 | 3111 | 3062 | 3014 | 56 |
| 57 | 3579 | 3525 | 3471 | 3417 | 3365 | 3313 | 3261 | 3210 | 3160 | 3110 | 3061 | 3013 | 57 |
| 58 | 3578 | 3524 | 3470 | 3416 | 3364 | 3312 | 3260 | 3209 | 3159 | 3110 | 3060 | 3012 | 58 |
| 59 | 3577 | 3523 | 3469 | 3415 | 3363 | 3311 | 3259 | 3209 | 3158 | 3109 | 3060 | 3011 | 59 |
| S. | 1° 18′ | 1° 19′ | 1° 20′ | 1° 21′ | 1° 22′ | 1° 23′ | 1° 24′ | 1° 25′ | 1° 26′ | 1° 27′ | 1° 28′ | 1° 29′ | S. |

# TABLE XXII.

## Proportional Logarithms.

| S. | h m 1° 30′ | h m 1° 31′ | h m 1° 32′ | h m 1° 33′ | h m 1° 34′ | h m 1° 35′ | h m 1° 36′ | h m 1° 37′ | h m 1° 38′ | h m 1° 39′ | h m 1° 40′ | h m 1° 41′ | S. |
|---|---|---|---|---|---|---|---|---|---|---|---|---|---|
| 0 | 3010 | 2962 | 2915 | 2868 | 2821 | 2775 | 2730 | 2685 | 2640 | 2596 | 2553 | 2510 | 0 |
| 1 | 3009 | 2962 | 2914 | 2867 | 2821 | 2775 | 2729 | 2684 | 2640 | 2596 | 2552 | 2509 | 1 |
| 2 | 3009 | 2961 | 2913 | 2866 | 2820 | 2774 | 2729 | 2684 | 2639 | 2595 | 2551 | 2508 | 2 |
| 3 | 3008 | 2960 | 2912 | 2866 | 2819 | 2773 | 2728 | 2683 | 2638 | 2594 | 2551 | 2507 | 3 |
| 4 | 3007 | 2959 | 2912 | 2865 | 2818 | 2772 | 2727 | 2682 | 2638 | 2593 | 2550 | 2507 | 4 |
| 5 | 3006 | 2958 | 2911 | 2864 | 2818 | 2772 | 2726 | 2681 | 2637 | 2593 | 2549 | 2506 | 5 |
| 6 | 3005 | 2958 | 2910 | 2863 | 2817 | 2771 | 2725 | 2681 | 2636 | 2592 | 2548 | 2505 | 6 |
| 7 | 3005 | 2957 | 2909 | 2862 | 2816 | 2770 | 2725 | 2680 | 2635 | 2591 | 2548 | 2504 | 7 |
| 8 | 3004 | 2956 | 2909 | 2862 | 2815 | 2769 | 2724 | 2679 | 2635 | 2591 | 2547 | 2504 | 8 |
| 9 | 3003 | 2955 | 2908 | 2861 | 2815 | 2769 | 2723 | 2678 | 2634 | 2590 | 2546 | 2503 | 9 |
| 10 | 3002 | 2954 | 2907 | 2860 | 2814 | 2768 | 2722 | 2678 | 2633 | 2589 | 2545 | 2502 | 10 |
| 11 | 3001 | 2954 | 2906 | 2859 | 2813 | 2767 | 2722 | 2677 | 2632 | 2588 | 2545 | 2502 | 11 |
| 12 | 3001 | 2953 | 2905 | 2859 | 2812 | 2766 | 2721 | 2676 | 2632 | 2588 | 2544 | 2501 | 12 |
| 13 | 3000 | 2952 | 2905 | 2858 | 2811 | 2766 | 2720 | 2675 | 2631 | 2587 | 2543 | 2500 | 13 |
| 14 | 2999 | 2951 | 2904 | 2857 | 2811 | 2765 | 2719 | 2675 | 2630 | 2586 | 2543 | 2499 | 14 |
| 15 | 2998 | 2950 | 2903 | 2856 | 2810 | 2764 | 2719 | 2674 | 2629 | 2585 | 2542 | 2499 | 15 |
| 16 | 2997 | 2950 | 2902 | 2855 | 2809 | 2763 | 2718 | 2673 | 2629 | 2585 | 2541 | 2498 | 16 |
| 17 | 2997 | 2949 | 2901 | 2855 | 2808 | 2763 | 2717 | 2672 | 2628 | 2584 | 2540 | 2497 | 17 |
| 18 | 2996 | 2948 | 2901 | 2854 | 2808 | 2762 | 2716 | 2672 | 2627 | 2583 | 2540 | 2497 | 18 |
| 19 | 2995 | 2947 | 2900 | 2853 | 2807 | 2761 | 2716 | 2671 | 2626 | 2583 | 2539 | 2496 | 19 |
| 20 | 2994 | 2946 | 2899 | 2852 | 2806 | 2760 | 2715 | 2670 | 2626 | 2582 | 2538 | 2495 | 20 |
| 21 | 2993 | 2946 | 2898 | 2852 | 2805 | 2760 | 2714 | 2669 | 2625 | 2581 | 2538 | 2494 | 21 |
| 22 | 2993 | 2945 | 2898 | 2851 | 2805 | 2759 | 2713 | 2669 | 2624 | 2580 | 2537 | 2494 | 22 |
| 23 | 2992 | 2944 | 2897 | 2850 | 2804 | 2758 | 2713 | 2668 | 2624 | 2580 | 2536 | 2493 | 23 |
| 24 | 2991 | 2943 | 2896 | 2849 | 2803 | 2757 | 2712 | 2667 | 2623 | 2579 | 2535 | 2492 | 24 |
| 25 | 2990 | 2942 | 2895 | 2848 | 2802 | 2756 | 2711 | 2666 | 2622 | 2578 | 2535 | 2492 | 25 |
| 26 | 2989 | 2942 | 2894 | 2848 | 2801 | 2756 | 2710 | 2666 | 2621 | 2577 | 2534 | 2491 | 26 |
| 27 | 2989 | 2941 | 2894 | 2847 | 2801 | 2755 | 2710 | 2665 | 2621 | 2577 | 2533 | 2490 | 27 |
| 28 | 2988 | 2940 | 2893 | 2846 | 2800 | 2754 | 2709 | 2664 | 2620 | 2576 | 2533 | 2489 | 28 |
| 29 | 2987 | 2939 | 2892 | 2845 | 2799 | 2753 | 2708 | 2663 | 2619 | 2575 | 2532 | 2489 | 29 |
| 30 | 2986 | 2939 | 2891 | 2845 | 2798 | 2753 | 2707 | 2663 | 2618 | 2574 | 2531 | 2488 | 30 |
| 31 | 2985 | 2938 | 2891 | 2844 | 2798 | 2752 | 2707 | 2662 | 2618 | 2574 | 2530 | 2487 | 31 |
| 32 | 2985 | 2937 | 2890 | 2843 | 2797 | 2751 | 2706 | 2661 | 2617 | 2573 | 2530 | 2487 | 32 |
| 33 | 2984 | 2936 | 2889 | 2842 | 2796 | 2750 | 2705 | 2660 | 2616 | 2572 | 2529 | 2486 | 33 |
| 34 | 2983 | 2935 | 2888 | 2842 | 2795 | 2750 | 2704 | 2660 | 2615 | 2572 | 2528 | 2485 | 34 |
| 35 | 2982 | 2935 | 2887 | 2841 | 2795 | 2749 | 2704 | 2659 | 2615 | 2571 | 2527 | 2485 | 35 |
| 36 | 2981 | 2934 | 2887 | 2840 | 2794 | 2748 | 2703 | 2658 | 2614 | 2570 | 2527 | 2484 | 36 |
| 37 | 2981 | 2933 | 2886 | 2839 | 2793 | 2747 | 2702 | 2657 | 2613 | 2569 | 2526 | 2483 | 37 |
| 38 | 2980 | 2932 | 2885 | 2838 | 2792 | 2747 | 2701 | 2657 | 2612 | 2569 | 2525 | 2482 | 38 |
| 39 | 2979 | 2931 | 2884 | 2838 | 2792 | 2746 | 2701 | 2656 | 2612 | 2568 | 2525 | 2482 | 39 |
| 40 | 2978 | 2931 | 2883 | 2837 | 2791 | 2745 | 2700 | 2655 | 2611 | 2567 | 2524 | 2481 | 40 |
| 41 | 2977 | 2930 | 2883 | 2836 | 2790 | 2744 | 2699 | 2655 | 2610 | 2566 | 2523 | 2480 | 41 |
| 42 | 2977 | 2929 | 2882 | 2835 | 2789 | 2744 | 2698 | 2654 | 2610 | 2566 | 2522 | 2480 | 42 |
| 43 | 2976 | 2928 | 2881 | 2835 | 2788 | 2743 | 2698 | 2653 | 2609 | 2565 | 2522 | 2479 | 43 |
| 44 | 2975 | 2927 | 2880 | 2834 | 2788 | 2742 | 2697 | 2652 | 2608 | 2564 | 2521 | 2478 | 44 |
| 45 | 2974 | 2927 | 2880 | 2833 | 2787 | 2741 | 2696 | 2652 | 2607 | 2564 | 2520 | 2477 | 45 |
| 46 | 2973 | 2926 | 2879 | 2832 | 2786 | 2741 | 2695 | 2651 | 2607 | 2563 | 2520 | 2477 | 46 |
| 47 | 2973 | 2925 | 2878 | 2831 | 2785 | 2740 | 2695 | 2650 | 2606 | 2562 | 2519 | 2476 | 47 |
| 48 | 2972 | 2924 | 2877 | 2831 | 2785 | 2739 | 2694 | 2649 | 2605 | 2561 | 2518 | 2475 | 48 |
| 49 | 2971 | 2924 | 2876 | 2830 | 2784 | 2738 | 2693 | 2649 | 2604 | 2561 | 2517 | 2475 | 49 |
| 50 | 2970 | 2923 | 2876 | 2829 | 2783 | 2738 | 2692 | 2648 | 2604 | 2560 | 2517 | 2474 | 50 |
| 51 | 2969 | 2922 | 2875 | 2828 | 2782 | 2737 | 2692 | 2647 | 2603 | 2559 | 2516 | 2473 | 51 |
| 52 | 2969 | 2921 | 2874 | 2828 | 2782 | 2736 | 2691 | 2646 | 2602 | 2559 | 2515 | 2472 | 52 |
| 53 | 2968 | 2920 | 2873 | 2827 | 2781 | 2735 | 2690 | 2646 | 2601 | 2558 | 2515 | 2472 | 53 |
| 54 | 2967 | 2920 | 2873 | 2826 | 2780 | 2735 | 2689 | 2645 | 2601 | 2557 | 2514 | 2471 | 54 |
| 55 | 2966 | 2919 | 2872 | 2825 | 2779 | 2734 | 2689 | 2644 | 2600 | 2556 | 2513 | 2470 | 55 |
| 56 | 2965 | 2918 | 2871 | 2825 | 2779 | 2733 | 2688 | 2643 | 2599 | 2556 | 2512 | 2470 | 56 |
| 57 | 2965 | 2917 | 2870 | 2824 | 2778 | 2732 | 2687 | 2643 | 2599 | 2555 | 2512 | 2469 | 57 |
| 58 | 2964 | 2916 | 2869 | 2823 | 2777 | 2732 | 2687 | 2642 | 2598 | 2554 | 2511 | 2468 | 58 |
| 59 | 2963 | 2916 | 2869 | 2822 | 2776 | 2731 | 2686 | 2641 | 2597 | 2553 | 2510 | 2467 | 59 |
| S. | 1° 30′ | 1° 31′ | 1° 32′ | 1° 33′ | 1° 34′ | 1° 35′ | 1° 36′ | 1° 37′ | 1° 38′ | 1° 39′ | 1° 40′ | 1° 41′ | S. |

# TABLE XXII.

## Proportional Logarithms.

| S. | h m 1° 42′ | h m 1° 43′ | h m 1° 44′ | h m 1° 45′ | h m 1° 46′ | h m 1° 47′ | h m 1° 48′ | h m 1° 49′ | h m 1° 50′ | h m 1° 51′ | h m 1° 52′ | h m 1° 53′ | S. |
|---|---|---|---|---|---|---|---|---|---|---|---|---|---|
| 0 | 2467 | 2424 | 2382 | 2341 | 2300 | 2259 | 2218 | 2178 | 2139 | 2099 | 2061 | 2022 | 0 |
| 1 | 2466 | 2424 | 2382 | 2340 | 2299 | 2258 | 2218 | 2178 | 2138 | 2099 | 2060 | 2021 | 1 |
| 2 | 2465 | 2423 | 2381 | 2339 | 2298 | 2258 | 2217 | 2177 | 2137 | 2098 | 2059 | 2021 | 2 |
| 3 | 2465 | 2422 | 2380 | 2339 | 2298 | 2257 | 2216 | 2176 | 2137 | 2098 | 2059 | 2020 | 3 |
| 4 | 2464 | 2422 | 2380 | 2338 | 2297 | 2256 | 2216 | 2176 | 2136 | 2097 | 2058 | 2019 | 4 |
| 5 | 2463 | 2421 | 2379 | 2337 | 2296 | 2256 | 2215 | 2175 | 2136 | 2096 | 2057 | 2019 | 5 |
| 6 | 2462 | 2420 | 2378 | 2337 | 2296 | 2255 | 2214 | 2174 | 2135 | 2096 | 2057 | 2018 | 6 |
| 7 | 2462 | 2419 | 2378 | 2336 | 2295 | 2254 | 2214 | 2174 | 2134 | 2095 | 2056 | 2017 | 7 |
| 8 | 2461 | 2419 | 2377 | 2335 | 2294 | 2253 | 2213 | 2173 | 2134 | 2094 | 2055 | 2017 | 8 |
| 9 | 2460 | 2418 | 2376 | 2335 | 2294 | 2253 | 2212 | 2172 | 2133 | 2094 | 2055 | 2016 | 9 |
| 10 | 2460 | 2417 | 2375 | 2334 | 2293 | 2252 | 2212 | 2172 | 2132 | 2093 | 2054 | 2016 | 10 |
| 11 | 2459 | 2417 | 2375 | 2333 | 2292 | 2251 | 2211 | 2171 | 2132 | 2092 | 2053 | 2015 | 11 |
| 12 | 2458 | 2416 | 2374 | 2333 | 2291 | 2251 | 2210 | 2170 | 2131 | 2092 | 2053 | 2014 | 12 |
| 13 | 2458 | 2415 | 2373 | 2332 | 2291 | 2250 | 2210 | 2170 | 2130 | 2091 | 2052 | 2014 | 13 |
| 14 | 2457 | 2415 | 2373 | 2331 | 2290 | 2249 | 2209 | 2169 | 2130 | 2090 | 2052 | 2013 | 14 |
| 15 | 2456 | 2414 | 2372 | 2331 | 2289 | 2249 | 2208 | 2169 | 2129 | 2090 | 2051 | 2012 | 15 |
| 16 | 2455 | 2413 | 2371 | 2330 | 2289 | 2248 | 2208 | 2168 | 2128 | 2089 | 2050 | 2012 | 16 |
| 17 | 2455 | 2412 | 2371 | 2329 | 2288 | 2247 | 2207 | 2167 | 2128 | 2088 | 2050 | 2011 | 17 |
| 18 | 2454 | 2412 | 2370 | 2328 | 2287 | 2247 | 2206 | 2167 | 2127 | 2088 | 2049 | 2010 | 18 |
| 19 | 2453 | 2411 | 2369 | 2328 | 2287 | 2246 | 2206 | 2166 | 2126 | 2087 | 2048 | 2010 | 19 |
| 20 | 2453 | 2410 | 2368 | 2327 | 2286 | 2245 | 2205 | 2165 | 2126 | 2086 | 2048 | 2009 | 20 |
| 21 | 2452 | 2410 | 2368 | 2326 | 2285 | 2245 | 2204 | 2165 | 2125 | 2086 | 2047 | 2009 | 21 |
| 22 | 2451 | 2409 | 2367 | 2326 | 2285 | 2244 | 2204 | 2164 | 2124 | 2085 | 2046 | 2008 | 22 |
| 23 | 2450 | 2408 | 2366 | 2325 | 2284 | 2243 | 2203 | 2163 | 2124 | 2085 | 2046 | 2007 | 23 |
| 24 | 2450 | 2408 | 2366 | 2324 | 2283 | 2243 | 2202 | 2163 | 2123 | 2084 | 2045 | 2007 | 24 |
| 25 | 2449 | 2407 | 2365 | 2324 | 2283 | 2242 | 2202 | 2162 | 2122 | 2083 | 2044 | 2006 | 25 |
| 26 | 2448 | 2406 | 2364 | 2323 | 2282 | 2241 | 2201 | 2161 | 2122 | 2083 | 2044 | 2005 | 26 |
| 27 | 2448 | 2405 | 2364 | 2322 | 2281 | 2241 | 2200 | 2161 | 2121 | 2082 | 2043 | 2005 | 27 |
| 28 | 2447 | 2405 | 2363 | 2322 | 2281 | 2240 | 2200 | 2160 | 2120 | 2081 | 2042 | 2004 | 28 |
| 29 | 2446 | 2404 | 2362 | 2321 | 2280 | 2239 | 2199 | 2159 | 2120 | 2081 | 2042 | 2003 | 29 |
| 30 | 2445 | 2403 | 2362 | 2320 | 2279 | 2239 | 2198 | 2159 | 2119 | 2080 | 2041 | 2003 | 30 |
| 31 | 2445 | 2403 | 2361 | 2320 | 2279 | 2238 | 2198 | 2158 | 2118 | 2079 | 2041 | 2002 | 31 |
| 32 | 2444 | 2402 | 2360 | 2319 | 2278 | 2237 | 2197 | 2157 | 2118 | 2079 | 2040 | 2001 | 32 |
| 33 | 2443 | 2401 | 2359 | 2318 | 2277 | 2237 | 2196 | 2157 | 2117 | 2078 | 2039 | 2001 | 33 |
| 34 | 2443 | 2401 | 2359 | 2317 | 2277 | 2236 | 2196 | 2156 | 2116 | 2077 | 2039 | 2000 | 34 |
| 35 | 2442 | 2400 | 2358 | 2317 | 2276 | 2235 | 2195 | 2155 | 2116 | 2077 | 2038 | 2000 | 35 |
| 36 | 2441 | 2399 | 2357 | 2316 | 2275 | 2235 | 2194 | 2155 | 2115 | 2076 | 2037 | 1999 | 36 |
| 37 | 2441 | 2398 | 2357 | 2315 | 2274 | 2234 | 2194 | 2154 | 2115 | 2075 | 2037 | 1998 | 37 |
| 38 | 2440 | 2398 | 2356 | 2315 | 2274 | 2233 | 2193 | 2153 | 2114 | 2075 | 2036 | 1998 | 38 |
| 39 | 2439 | 2397 | 2355 | 2314 | 2273 | 2233 | 2192 | 2153 | 2113 | 2074 | 2035 | 1997 | 39 |
| 40 | 2438 | 2396 | 2355 | 2313 | 2272 | 2232 | 2192 | 2152 | 2113 | 2073 | 2035 | 1996 | 40 |
| 41 | 2438 | 2396 | 2354 | 2313 | 2272 | 2231 | 2191 | 2151 | 2112 | 2073 | 2034 | 1996 | 41 |
| 42 | 2437 | 2395 | 2353 | 2312 | 2271 | 2231 | 2190 | 2151 | 2111 | 2072 | 2033 | 1995 | 42 |
| 43 | 2436 | 2394 | 2353 | 2311 | 2270 | 2230 | 2190 | 2150 | 2111 | 2072 | 2033 | 1994 | 43 |
| 44 | 2436 | 2394 | 2352 | 2311 | 2270 | 2229 | 2189 | 2149 | 2110 | 2071 | 2032 | 1994 | 44 |
| 45 | 2435 | 2393 | 2351 | 2310 | 2269 | 2229 | 2188 | 2149 | 2109 | 2070 | 2032 | 1993 | 45 |
| 46 | 2434 | 2392 | 2350 | 2309 | 2268 | 2228 | 2188 | 2148 | 2109 | 2070 | 2031 | 1993 | 46 |
| 47 | 2433 | 2391 | 2350 | 2309 | 2268 | 2227 | 2187 | 2147 | 2108 | 2069 | 2030 | 1992 | 47 |
| 48 | 2433 | 2391 | 2349 | 2308 | 2267 | 2227 | 2186 | 2147 | 2107 | 2068 | 2030 | 1991 | 48 |
| 49 | 2432 | 2390 | 2348 | 2307 | 2266 | 2226 | 2186 | 2146 | 2107 | 2068 | 2029 | 1991 | 49 |
| 50 | 2431 | 2389 | 2348 | 2307 | 2266 | 2225 | 2185 | 2145 | 2106 | 2067 | 2028 | 1990 | 50 |
| 51 | 2431 | 2389 | 2347 | 2306 | 2265 | 2225 | 2184 | 2145 | 2105 | 2066 | 2028 | 1989 | 51 |
| 52 | 2430 | 2388 | 2346 | 2305 | 2264 | 2224 | 2184 | 2144 | 2105 | 2066 | 2027 | 1989 | 52 |
| 53 | 2429 | 2387 | 2346 | 2304 | 2264 | 2223 | 2183 | 2143 | 2104 | 2065 | 2026 | 1988 | 53 |
| 54 | 2429 | 2387 | 2345 | 2304 | 2263 | 2223 | 2182 | 2143 | 2103 | 2064 | 2026 | 1987 | 54 |
| 55 | 2428 | 2386 | 2344 | 2303 | 2262 | 2222 | 2182 | 2142 | 2103 | 2064 | 2025 | 1987 | 55 |
| 56 | 2427 | 2385 | 2344 | 2302 | 2262 | 2221 | 2181 | 2141 | 2102 | 2063 | 2025 | 1986 | 56 |
| 57 | 2426 | 2384 | 2343 | 2302 | 2261 | 2220 | 2180 | 2141 | 2101 | 2062 | 2024 | 1986 | 57 |
| 58 | 2426 | 2384 | 2342 | 2301 | 2260 | 2220 | 2180 | 2140 | 2101 | 2062 | 2023 | 1985 | 58 |
| 59 | 2425 | 2383 | 2342 | 2300 | 2260 | 2219 | 2179 | 2139 | 2100 | 2061 | 2023 | 1984 | 59 |
| S. | 1° 42′ | 1° 43′ | 1° 44′ | 1° 45′ | 1° 46′ | 1° 47′ | 1° 48′ | 1° 49′ | 1° 50′ | 1° 51′ | 1° 52′ | 1° 53′ | S. |

# TABLE XXII.

## Proportional Logarithms.

| S. | *h m* 1° 54′ | *h m* 1° 55′ | *h m* 1° 56′ | *h m* 1° 57′ | *h m* 1° 58′ | *h m* 1° 59′ | *h m* 2° 0′ | *h m* 2° 1′ | *h m* 2° 2′ | *h m* 2° 3′ | *h m* 2° 4′ | S. |
|---|---|---|---|---|---|---|---|---|---|---|---|---|
| 0 | 1984 | 1946 | 1908 | 1871 | 1834 | 1797 | 1761 | 1725 | 1689 | 1654 | 1619 | 0 |
| 1 | 1983 | 1945 | 1908 | 1870 | 1833 | 1797 | 1760 | 1724 | 1689 | 1653 | 1618 | 1 |
| 2 | 1982 | 1944 | 1907 | 1870 | 1833 | 1796 | 1760 | 1724 | 1688 | 1652 | 1617 | 2 |
| 3 | 1982 | 1944 | 1906 | 1869 | 1832 | 1795 | 1759 | 1723 | 1687 | 1652 | 1617 | 3 |
| 4 | 1981 | 1943 | 1906 | 1868 | 1831 | 1795 | 1759 | 1722 | 1687 | 1651 | 1616 | 4 |
| 5 | 1981 | 1943 | 1905 | 1868 | 1831 | 1794 | 1758 | 1722 | 1686 | 1651 | 1616 | 5 |
| 6 | 1980 | 1942 | 1904 | 1867 | 1830 | 1794 | 1757 | 1721 | 1686 | 1650 | 1615 | 6 |
| 7 | 1979 | 1941 | 1904 | 1867 | 1830 | 1793 | 1757 | 1721 | 1685 | 1650 | 1614 | 7 |
| 8 | 1979 | 1941 | 1903 | 1866 | 1829 | 1792 | 1756 | 1720 | 1684 | 1649 | 1614 | 8 |
| 9 | 1978 | 1940 | 1903 | 1865 | 1828 | 1792 | 1755 | 1719 | 1684 | 1648 | 1613 | 9 |
| 10 | 1977 | 1939 | 1902 | 1865 | 1828 | 1791 | 1755 | 1719 | 1683 | 1648 | 1613 | 10 |
| 11 | 1977 | 1939 | 1901 | 1864 | 1827 | 1791 | 1754 | 1718 | 1683 | 1647 | 1612 | 11 |
| 12 | 1976 | 1938 | 1901 | 1863 | 1827 | 1790 | 1754 | 1718 | 1682 | 1647 | 1612 | 12 |
| 13 | 1975 | 1938 | 1900 | 1863 | 1826 | 1789 | 1753 | 1717 | 1681 | 1646 | 1611 | 13 |
| 14 | 1975 | 1937 | 1899 | 1862 | 1825 | 1789 | 1752 | 1717 | 1681 | 1645 | 1610 | 14 |
| 15 | 1974 | 1936 | 1899 | 1862 | 1825 | 1788 | 1752 | 1716 | 1680 | 1645 | 1610 | 15 |
| 16 | 1974 | 1936 | 1898 | 1861 | 1824 | 1788 | 1751 | 1715 | 1680 | 1644 | 1609 | 16 |
| 17 | 1973 | 1935 | 1898 | 1860 | 1823 | 1787 | 1751 | 1715 | 1679 | 1644 | 1609 | 17 |
| 18 | 1972 | 1934 | 1897 | 1860 | 1823 | 1786 | 1750 | 1714 | 1678 | 1643 | 1608 | 18 |
| 19 | 1972 | 1934 | 1896 | 1859 | 1822 | 1786 | 1749 | 1714 | 1678 | 1643 | 1607 | 19 |
| 20 | 1971 | 1933 | 1896 | 1859 | 1822 | 1785 | 1749 | 1713 | 1677 | 1642 | 1607 | 20 |
| 21 | 1970 | 1933 | 1895 | 1858 | 1821 | 1785 | 1748 | 1712 | 1677 | 1641 | 1606 | 21 |
| 22 | 1970 | 1932 | 1894 | 1857 | 1820 | 1784 | 1748 | 1712 | 1676 | 1641 | 1606 | 22 |
| 23 | 1969 | 1931 | 1894 | 1857 | 1820 | 1783 | 1747 | 1711 | 1676 | 1640 | 1605 | 23 |
| 24 | 1968 | 1931 | 1893 | 1856 | 1819 | 1783 | 1746 | 1711 | 1675 | 1640 | 1605 | 24 |
| 25 | 1968 | 1930 | 1893 | 1855 | 1819 | 1782 | 1746 | 1710 | 1674 | 1639 | 1604 | 25 |
| 26 | 1967 | 1929 | 1892 | 1855 | 1818 | 1781 | 1745 | 1709 | 1674 | 1638 | 1603 | 26 |
| 27 | 1967 | 1929 | 1891 | 1854 | 1817 | 1781 | 1745 | 1709 | 1673 | 1638 | 1603 | 27 |
| 28 | 1966 | 1928 | 1891 | 1854 | 1817 | 1780 | 1744 | 1708 | 1673 | 1637 | 1602 | 28 |
| 29 | 1965 | 1928 | 1890 | 1853 | 1816 | 1780 | 1743 | 1708 | 1672 | 1637 | 1602 | 29 |
| 30 | 1965 | 1927 | 1889 | 1852 | 1816 | 1779 | 1743 | 1707 | 1671 | 1636 | 1601 | 30 |
| 31 | 1964 | 1926 | 1889 | 1852 | 1815 | 1778 | 1742 | 1706 | 1671 | 1635 | 1600 | 31 |
| 32 | 1963 | 1926 | 1888 | 1851 | 1814 | 1778 | 1742 | 1706 | 1670 | 1635 | 1600 | 32 |
| 33 | 1963 | 1925 | 1888 | 1850 | 1814 | 1777 | 1741 | 1705 | 1670 | 1634 | 1599 | 33 |
| 34 | 1962 | 1924 | 1887 | 1850 | 1813 | 1777 | 1740 | 1705 | 1669 | 1634 | 1599 | 34 |
| 35 | 1962 | 1924 | 1886 | 1849 | 1812 | 1776 | 1740 | 1704 | 1668 | 1633 | 1598 | 35 |
| 36 | 1961 | 1923 | 1886 | 1849 | 1812 | 1775 | 1739 | 1703 | 1668 | 1633 | 1598 | 36 |
| 37 | 1960 | 1923 | 1885 | 1848 | 1811 | 1775 | 1739 | 1703 | 1667 | 1632 | 1597 | 37 |
| 38 | 1960 | 1922 | 1884 | 1847 | 1811 | 1774 | 1738 | 1702 | 1667 | 1631 | 1596 | 38 |
| 39 | 1959 | 1921 | 1884 | 1847 | 1810 | 1774 | 1737 | 1702 | 1666 | 1631 | 1596 | 39 |
| 40 | 1958 | 1921 | 1883 | 1846 | 1809 | 1773 | 1737 | 1701 | 1665 | 1630 | 1595 | 40 |
| 41 | 1958 | 1920 | 1883 | 1845 | 1809 | 1772 | 1736 | 1700 | 1665 | 1630 | 1595 | 41 |
| 42 | 1957 | 1919 | 1882 | 1845 | 1808 | 1772 | 1736 | 1700 | 1664 | 1629 | 1594 | 42 |
| 43 | 1956 | 1919 | 1881 | 1844 | 1808 | 1771 | 1735 | 1699 | 1664 | 1628 | 1593 | 43 |
| 44 | 1956 | 1918 | 1881 | 1844 | 1807 | 1771 | 1734 | 1699 | 1663 | 1628 | 1593 | 44 |
| 45 | 1955 | 1918 | 1880 | 1843 | 1806 | 1770 | 1734 | 1698 | 1663 | 1627 | 1592 | 45 |
| 46 | 1955 | 1917 | 1880 | 1843 | 1806 | 1769 | 1733 | 1697 | 1662 | 1627 | 1592 | 46 |
| 47 | 1954 | 1916 | 1879 | 1842 | 1805 | 1769 | 1733 | 1697 | 1661 | 1626 | 1591 | 47 |
| 48 | 1953 | 1916 | 1878 | 1841 | 1805 | 1768 | 1732 | 1696 | 1661 | 1626 | 1591 | 48 |
| 49 | 1953 | 1915 | 1878 | 1841 | 1804 | 1768 | 1731 | 1696 | 1660 | 1625 | 1590 | 49 |
| 50 | 1952 | 1914 | 1877 | 1840 | 1803 | 1767 | 1731 | 1695 | 1660 | 1624 | 1589 | 50 |
| 51 | 1951 | 1914 | 1876 | 1839 | 1803 | 1766 | 1730 | 1694 | 1659 | 1624 | 1589 | 51 |
| 52 | 1951 | 1913 | 1876 | 1839 | 1802 | 1766 | 1730 | 1694 | 1658 | 1623 | 1588 | 52 |
| 53 | 1950 | 1913 | 1875 | 1838 | 1802 | 1765 | 1729 | 1693 | 1658 | 1623 | 1588 | 53 |
| 54 | 1950 | 1912 | 1875 | 1838 | 1801 | 1765 | 1728 | 1693 | 1657 | 1622 | 1587 | 54 |
| 55 | 1949 | 1911 | 1874 | 1837 | 1800 | 1764 | 1728 | 1692 | 1657 | 1621 | 1587 | 55 |
| 56 | 1948 | 1911 | 1873 | 1836 | 1800 | 1763 | 1727 | 1692 | 1656 | 1621 | 1586 | 56 |
| 57 | 1948 | 1910 | 1873 | 1836 | 1799 | 1763 | 1727 | 1691 | 1655 | 1620 | 1585 | 57 |
| 58 | 1947 | 1909 | 1872 | 1835 | 1798 | 1762 | 1726 | 1690 | 1655 | 1620 | 1585 | 58 |
| 59 | 1946 | 1909 | 1871 | 1835 | 1798 | 1762 | 1725 | 1690 | 1654 | 1619 | 1584 | 59 |
| S. | 1° 54′ | 1° 55′ | 1° 56′ | 1° 57′ | 1° 58′ | 1° 59′ | 2° 0′ | 2° 1′ | 2° 2′ | 2° 3′ | 2° 4′ | S. |

# TABLE XXII.

## Proportional Logarithms.

| S. | h m<br>2° 5′ | h m<br>2° 6′ | h m<br>2° 7′ | h m<br>2° 8′ | h m<br>2° 9′ | h m<br>2° 10′ | h m<br>2° 11′ | h m<br>2° 12′ | h m<br>2° 13′ | h m<br>2° 14′ | h m<br>2° 15′ | S. |
|---|---|---|---|---|---|---|---|---|---|---|---|---|
| 0 | 1584 | 1549 | 1515 | 1481 | 1447 | 1413 | 1380 | 1347 | 1314 | 1282 | 1249 | 0 |
| 1 | 1583 | 1548 | 1514 | 1480 | 1446 | 1413 | 1379 | 1346 | 1314 | 1281 | 1249 | 1 |
| 2 | 1582 | 1548 | 1514 | 1479 | 1446 | 1412 | 1379 | 1346 | 1313 | 1281 | 1248 | 2 |
| 3 | 1582 | 1547 | 1513 | 1479 | 1445 | 1412 | 1378 | 1345 | 1313 | 1280 | 1248 | 3 |
| 4 | 1581 | 1547 | 1512 | 1478 | 1445 | 1411 | 1378 | 1345 | 1312 | 1280 | 1247 | 4 |
| 5 | 1581 | 1546 | 1512 | 1478 | 1444 | 1411 | 1377 | 1344 | 1311 | 1279 | 1247 | 5 |
| 6 | 1580 | 1546 | 1511 | 1477 | 1443 | 1410 | 1377 | 1344 | 1311 | 1278 | 1246 | 6 |
| 7 | 1580 | 1545 | 1511 | 1477 | 1443 | 1409 | 1376 | 1343 | 1310 | 1278 | 1246 | 7 |
| 8 | 1579 | 1544 | 1510 | 1476 | 1442 | 1409 | 1376 | 1343 | 1310 | 1277 | 1245 | 8 |
| 9 | 1578 | 1544 | 1510 | 1476 | 1442 | 1408 | 1375 | 1342 | 1309 | 1277 | 1245 | 9 |
| 10 | 1578 | 1543 | 1509 | 1475 | 1441 | 1408 | 1374 | 1342 | 1309 | 1276 | 1244 | 10 |
| 11 | 1577 | 1543 | 1508 | 1474 | 1441 | 1407 | 1374 | 1341 | 1308 | 1276 | 1243 | 11 |
| 12 | 1577 | 1542 | 1508 | 1474 | 1440 | 1407 | 1373 | 1340 | 1308 | 1275 | 1243 | 12 |
| 13 | 1576 | 1542 | 1507 | 1473 | 1440 | 1406 | 1373 | 1340 | 1307 | 1275 | 1242 | 13 |
| 14 | 1576 | 1541 | 1507 | 1473 | 1439 | 1406 | 1372 | 1339 | 1307 | 1274 | 1242 | 14 |
| 15 | 1575 | 1540 | 1506 | 1472 | 1438 | 1405 | 1372 | 1339 | 1306 | 1274 | 1241 | 15 |
| 16 | 1574 | 1540 | 1506 | 1472 | 1438 | 1404 | 1371 | 1338 | 1306 | 1273 | 1241 | 16 |
| 17 | 1574 | 1539 | 1505 | 1471 | 1437 | 1404 | 1371 | 1338 | 1305 | 1273 | 1240 | 17 |
| 18 | 1573 | 1539 | 1504 | 1470 | 1437 | 1403 | 1370 | 1337 | 1304 | 1272 | 1240 | 18 |
| 19 | 1573 | 1538 | 1504 | 1470 | 1436 | 1403 | 1370 | 1337 | 1304 | 1271 | 1239 | 19 |
| 20 | 1572 | 1538 | 1503 | 1469 | 1436 | 1402 | 1369 | 1336 | 1303 | 1271 | 1239 | 20 |
| 21 | 1571 | 1537 | 1503 | 1469 | 1435 | 1402 | 1368 | 1335 | 1303 | 1270 | 1238 | 21 |
| 22 | 1571 | 1536 | 1502 | 1468 | 1435 | 1401 | 1368 | 1335 | 1302 | 1270 | 1238 | 22 |
| 23 | 1570 | 1536 | 1502 | 1468 | 1434 | 1401 | 1367 | 1334 | 1302 | 1269 | 1237 | 23 |
| 24 | 1570 | 1535 | 1501 | 1467 | 1433 | 1400 | 1367 | 1334 | 1301 | 1269 | 1237 | 24 |
| 25 | 1569 | 1535 | 1500 | 1467 | 1433 | 1399 | 1366 | 1333 | 1301 | 1268 | 1236 | 25 |
| 26 | 1569 | 1534 | 1500 | 1466 | 1432 | 1399 | 1366 | 1333 | 1300 | 1268 | 1235 | 26 |
| 27 | 1568 | 1534 | 1499 | 1465 | 1432 | 1398 | 1365 | 1332 | 1300 | 1267 | 1235 | 27 |
| 28 | 1567 | 1533 | 1499 | 1465 | 1431 | 1398 | 1365 | 1332 | 1299 | 1267 | 1234 | 28 |
| 29 | 1567 | 1532 | 1498 | 1464 | 1431 | 1397 | 1364 | 1331 | 1298 | 1266 | 1234 | 29 |
| 30 | 1566 | 1532 | 1498 | 1464 | 1430 | 1397 | 1363 | 1331 | 1298 | 1266 | 1233 | 30 |
| 31 | 1566 | 1531 | 1497 | 1463 | 1429 | 1396 | 1363 | 1330 | 1297 | 1265 | 1233 | 31 |
| 32 | 1565 | 1531 | 1496 | 1463 | 1429 | 1396 | 1362 | 1329 | 1297 | 1264 | 1232 | 32 |
| 33 | 1565 | 1530 | 1496 | 1462 | 1428 | 1395 | 1362 | 1329 | 1296 | 1264 | 1232 | 33 |
| 34 | 1564 | 1530 | 1495 | 1461 | 1428 | 1394 | 1361 | 1328 | 1296 | 1263 | 1231 | 34 |
| 35 | 1563 | 1529 | 1495 | 1461 | 1427 | 1394 | 1361 | 1328 | 1295 | 1263 | 1231 | 35 |
| 36 | 1563 | 1528 | 1494 | 1460 | 1427 | 1393 | 1360 | 1327 | 1295 | 1262 | 1230 | 36 |
| 37 | 1562 | 1528 | 1494 | 1460 | 1426 | 1393 | 1360 | 1327 | 1294 | 1262 | 1230 | 37 |
| 38 | 1562 | 1527 | 1493 | 1459 | 1426 | 1392 | 1359 | 1326 | 1294 | 1261 | 1229 | 38 |
| 39 | 1561 | 1527 | 1493 | 1459 | 1425 | 1392 | 1359 | 1326 | 1293 | 1261 | 1229 | 39 |
| 40 | 1561 | 1526 | 1492 | 1458 | 1424 | 1391 | 1358 | 1325 | 1292 | 1260 | 1228 | 40 |
| 41 | 1560 | 1526 | 1491 | 1458 | 1424 | 1391 | 1357 | 1325 | 1292 | 1260 | 1227 | 41 |
| 42 | 1559 | 1525 | 1491 | 1457 | 1423 | 1390 | 1357 | 1324 | 1291 | 1259 | 1227 | 42 |
| 43 | 1559 | 1524 | 1490 | 1456 | 1423 | 1389 | 1356 | 1323 | 1291 | 1259 | 1226 | 43 |
| 44 | 1558 | 1524 | 1490 | 1456 | 1422 | 1389 | 1356 | 1323 | 1290 | 1258 | 1226 | 44 |
| 45 | 1558 | 1523 | 1489 | 1455 | 1422 | 1388 | 1355 | 1322 | 1290 | 1257 | 1225 | 45 |
| 46 | 1557 | 1523 | 1489 | 1455 | 1421 | 1388 | 1355 | 1322 | 1289 | 1257 | 1225 | 46 |
| 47 | 1556 | 1522 | 1488 | 1454 | 1421 | 1387 | 1354 | 1321 | 1289 | 1256 | 1224 | 47 |
| 48 | 1556 | 1522 | 1487 | 1454 | 1420 | 1387 | 1354 | 1321 | 1288 | 1256 | 1224 | 48 |
| 49 | 1555 | 1521 | 1487 | 1453 | 1419 | 1386 | 1353 | 1320 | 1288 | 1255 | 1223 | 49 |
| 50 | 1555 | 1520 | 1486 | 1452 | 1419 | 1386 | 1352 | 1320 | 1287 | 1255 | 1223 | 50 |
| 51 | 1554 | 1520 | 1486 | 1452 | 1418 | 1385 | 1352 | 1319 | 1287 | 1254 | 1222 | 51 |
| 52 | 1554 | 1519 | 1485 | 1451 | 1418 | 1384 | 1351 | 1319 | 1286 | 1254 | 1222 | 52 |
| 53 | 1553 | 1519 | 1485 | 1451 | 1417 | 1384 | 1351 | 1318 | 1285 | 1253 | 1221 | 53 |
| 54 | 1552 | 1518 | 1484 | 1450 | 1417 | 1383 | 1350 | 1317 | 1285 | 1253 | 1221 | 54 |
| 55 | 1552 | 1518 | 1483 | 1450 | 1416 | 1383 | 1350 | 1317 | 1284 | 1252 | 1220 | 55 |
| 56 | 1551 | 1517 | 1483 | 1449 | 1416 | 1382 | 1349 | 1316 | 1284 | 1252 | 1219 | 56 |
| 57 | 1551 | 1516 | 1482 | 1449 | 1415 | 1382 | 1349 | 1316 | 1283 | 1251 | 1219 | 57 |
| 58 | 1550 | 1516 | 1482 | 1448 | 1414 | 1381 | 1348 | 1315 | 1283 | 1250 | 1218 | 58 |
| 59 | 1550 | 1515 | 1481 | 1447 | 1414 | 1381 | 1348 | 1315 | 1282 | 1250 | 1218 | 59 |
| S. | 2° 5′ | 2° 6′ | 2° 7′ | 2° 8′ | 2° 9′ | 2° 10′ | 2° 11′ | 2° 12′ | 2° 13′ | 2° 14′ | 2° 15′ | S. |

# TABLE XXII.

## Proportional Logarithms.

| S. | h m 2° 16′ | h m 2° 17′ | h m 2° 18′ | h m 2° 19′ | h m 2° 20′ | h m 2° 21′ | h m 2° 22′ | h m 2° 23′ | h m 2° 24′ | h m 2° 25′ | h m 2° 26′ | S. |
|---|---|---|---|---|---|---|---|---|---|---|---|---|
| 0 | 1217 | 1186 | 1154 | 1123 | 1091 | 1061 | 1030 | 0999 | 0969 | 0939 | 0909 | 0 |
| 1 | 1217 | 1185 | 1153 | 1122 | 1091 | 1060 | 1029 | 0999 | 0969 | 0939 | 0909 | 1 |
| 2 | 1216 | 1184 | 1153 | 1122 | 1090 | 1060 | 1029 | 0998 | 0968 | 0938 | 0908 | 2 |
| 3 | 1216 | 1184 | 1152 | 1121 | 1090 | 1059 | 1028 | 0998 | 0968 | 0938 | 0908 | 3 |
| 4 | 1215 | 1183 | 1152 | 1120 | 1089 | 1058 | 1028 | 0997 | 0967 | 0937 | 0907 | 4 |
| 5 | 1215 | 1183 | 1151 | 1120 | 1089 | 1058 | 1027 | 0997 | 0967 | 0937 | 0907 | 5 |
| 6 | 1214 | 1182 | 1151 | 1119 | 1088 | 1057 | 1027 | 0996 | 0966 | 0936 | 0906 | 6 |
| 7 | 1214 | 1182 | 1150 | 1119 | 1088 | 1057 | 1026 | 0996 | 0966 | 0936 | 0906 | 7 |
| 8 | 1213 | 1181 | 1150 | 1118 | 1087 | 1056 | 1026 | 0995 | 0965 | 0935 | 0905 | 8 |
| 9 | 1213 | 1181 | 1149 | 1118 | 1087 | 1056 | 1025 | 0995 | 0965 | 0935 | 0905 | 9 |
| 10 | 1212 | 1180 | 1149 | 1117 | 1086 | 1055 | 1025 | 0994 | 0964 | 0934 | 0904 | 10 |
| 11 | 1211 | 1180 | 1148 | 1117 | 1086 | 1055 | 1024 | 0994 | 0964 | 0934 | 0904 | 11 |
| 12 | 1211 | 1179 | 1148 | 1116 | 1085 | 1054 | 1024 | 0993 | 0963 | 0933 | 0903 | 12 |
| 13 | 1210 | 1179 | 1147 | 1116 | 1085 | 1054 | 1023 | 0993 | 0963 | 0933 | 0903 | 13 |
| 14 | 1210 | 1178 | 1147 | 1115 | 1084 | 1053 | 1023 | 0992 | 0962 | 0932 | 0902 | 14 |
| 15 | 1209 | 1178 | 1146 | 1115 | 1084 | 1053 | 1022 | 0992 | 0962 | 0932 | 0902 | 15 |
| 16 | 1209 | 1177 | 1146 | 1114 | 1083 | 1052 | 1022 | 0991 | 0961 | 0931 | 0901 | 16 |
| 17 | 1208 | 1177 | 1145 | 1114 | 1083 | 1052 | 1021 | 0991 | 0961 | 0931 | 0901 | 17 |
| 18 | 1208 | 1176 | 1145 | 1113 | 1082 | 1051 | 1021 | 0990 | 0960 | 0930 | 0900 | 18 |
| 19 | 1207 | 1175 | 1144 | 1113 | 1082 | 1051 | 1020 | 0990 | 0960 | 0930 | 0900 | 19 |
| 20 | 1207 | 1175 | 1143 | 1112 | 1081 | 1050 | 1020 | 0989 | 0959 | 0929 | 0899 | 20 |
| 21 | 1206 | 1174 | 1143 | 1112 | 1081 | 1050 | 1019 | 0989 | 0959 | 0929 | 0899 | 21 |
| 22 | 1206 | 1174 | 1142 | 1111 | 1080 | 1049 | 1019 | 0988 | 0958 | 0928 | 0898 | 22 |
| 23 | 1205 | 1173 | 1142 | 1111 | 1080 | 1049 | 1018 | 0988 | 0958 | 0928 | 0898 | 23 |
| 24 | 1205 | 1173 | 1141 | 1110 | 1079 | 1048 | 1018 | 0987 | 0957 | 0927 | 0897 | 24 |
| 25 | 1204 | 1172 | 1141 | 1110 | 1079 | 1048 | 1017 | 0987 | 0957 | 0927 | 0897 | 25 |
| 26 | 1204 | 1172 | 1140 | 1109 | 1078 | 1047 | 1017 | 0986 | 0956 | 0926 | 0896 | 26 |
| 27 | 1203 | 1171 | 1140 | 1109 | 1078 | 1047 | 1016 | 0986 | 0956 | 0926 | 0896 | 27 |
| 28 | 1202 | 1171 | 1139 | 1108 | 1077 | 1046 | 1016 | 0985 | 0955 | 0925 | 0895 | 28 |
| 29 | 1202 | 1170 | 1139 | 1108 | 1076 | 1046 | 1015 | 0985 | 0955 | 0925 | 0895 | 29 |
| 30 | 1201 | 1170 | 1138 | 1107 | 1076 | 1045 | 1015 | 0984 | 0954 | 0924 | 0894 | 30 |
| 31 | 1201 | 1169 | 1138 | 1106 | 1075 | 1045 | 1014 | 0984 | 0954 | 0924 | 0894 | 31 |
| 32 | 1200 | 1169 | 1137 | 1106 | 1075 | 1044 | 1014 | 0983 | 0953 | 0923 | 0893 | 32 |
| 33 | 1200 | 1168 | 1137 | 1105 | 1074 | 1044 | 1013 | 0983 | 0953 | 0923 | 0893 | 33 |
| 34 | 1199 | 1168 | 1136 | 1105 | 1074 | 1043 | 1013 | 0982 | 0952 | 0922 | 0892 | 34 |
| 35 | 1199 | 1167 | 1136 | 1104 | 1073 | 1043 | 1012 | 0982 | 0952 | 0922 | 0892 | 35 |
| 36 | 1198 | 1167 | 1135 | 1104 | 1073 | 1042 | 1012 | 0981 | 0951 | 0921 | 0891 | 36 |
| 37 | 1198 | 1166 | 1135 | 1103 | 1072 | 1042 | 1011 | 0981 | 0951 | 0921 | 0891 | 37 |
| 38 | 1197 | 1165 | 1134 | 1103 | 1072 | 1041 | 1011 | 0980 | 0950 | 0920 | 0890 | 38 |
| 39 | 1197 | 1165 | 1134 | 1102 | 1071 | 1041 | 1010 | 0980 | 0950 | 0920 | 0890 | 39 |
| 40 | 1196 | 1164 | 1133 | 1102 | 1071 | 1040 | 1009 | 0979 | 0949 | 0919 | 0889 | 40 |
| 41 | 1196 | 1164 | 1132 | 1101 | 1070 | 1040 | 1009 | 0979 | 0949 | 0919 | 0889 | 41 |
| 42 | 1195 | 1163 | 1132 | 1101 | 1070 | 1039 | 1008 | 0978 | 0948 | 0918 | 0888 | 42 |
| 43 | 1195 | 1163 | 1131 | 1100 | 1069 | 1039 | 1008 | 0978 | 0948 | 0918 | 0888 | 43 |
| 44 | 1194 | 1162 | 1131 | 1100 | 1069 | 1038 | 1007 | 0977 | 0947 | 0917 | 0887 | 44 |
| 45 | 1193 | 1162 | 1130 | 1099 | 1068 | 1037 | 1007 | 0977 | 0947 | 0917 | 0887 | 45 |
| 46 | 1193 | 1161 | 1130 | 1099 | 1068 | 1037 | 1006 | 0976 | 0946 | 0916 | 0886 | 46 |
| 47 | 1192 | 1161 | 1129 | 1098 | 1067 | 1036 | 1006 | 0976 | 0946 | 0916 | 0886 | 47 |
| 48 | 1192 | 1160 | 1129 | 1098 | 1067 | 1036 | 1005 | 0975 | 0945 | 0915 | 0885 | 48 |
| 49 | 1191 | 1160 | 1128 | 1097 | 1066 | 1035 | 1005 | 0975 | 0945 | 0915 | 0885 | 49 |
| 50 | 1191 | 1159 | 1128 | 1097 | 1066 | 1035 | 1004 | 0974 | 0944 | 0914 | 0884 | 50 |
| 51 | 1190 | 1159 | 1127 | 1096 | 1065 | 1034 | 1004 | 0974 | 0944 | 0914 | 0884 | 51 |
| 52 | 1190 | 1158 | 1127 | 1096 | 1065 | 1034 | 1003 | 0973 | 0943 | 0913 | 0883 | 52 |
| 53 | 1189 | 1158 | 1126 | 1095 | 1064 | 1033 | 1003 | 0973 | 0943 | 0913 | 0883 | 53 |
| 54 | 1189 | 1157 | 1126 | 1095 | 1064 | 1033 | 1002 | 0972 | 0942 | 0912 | 0883 | 54 |
| 55 | 1188 | 1157 | 1125 | 1094 | 1063 | 1032 | 1002 | 0972 | 0942 | 0912 | 0882 | 55 |
| 56 | 1188 | 1156 | 1125 | 1094 | 1063 | 1032 | 1001 | 0971 | 0941 | 0911 | 0882 | 56 |
| 57 | 1187 | 1156 | 1124 | 1093 | 1062 | 1031 | 1001 | 0971 | 0941 | 0911 | 0881 | 57 |
| 58 | 1187 | 1155 | 1124 | 1092 | 1062 | 1031 | 1000 | 0970 | 0940 | 0910 | 0881 | 58 |
| 59 | 1186 | 1154 | 1123 | 1092 | 1061 | 1030 | 1000 | 0970 | 0940 | 0910 | 0880 | 59 |
| S. | 2° 16′ | 2° 17′ | 2° 18′ | 2° 19′ | 2° 20′ | 2° 21′ | 2° 22′ | 2° 23′ | 2° 24′ | 2° 25′ | 2° 26′ | S. |

# TABLE XXII.

## Proportional Logarithms

| S. | h m 2° 27′ | h m 2° 28′ | h m 2° 29′ | h m 2° 30′ | h m 2° 31′ | h m 2° 32′ | h m 2° 33′ | h m 2° 34′ | h m 2° 35′ | h m 2° 36′ | h m 2° 37′ | S. |
|---|---|---|---|---|---|---|---|---|---|---|---|---|
| 0 | 0880 | 0850 | 0821 | 0792 | 0763 | 0734 | 0706 | 0678 | 0649 | 0621 | 0594 | 0 |
| 1 | 0879 | 0850 | 0820 | 0791 | 0762 | 0734 | 0705 | 0677 | 0649 | 0621 | 0593 | 1 |
| 2 | 0879 | 0849 | 0820 | 0791 | 0762 | 0733 | 0705 | 0677 | 0648 | 0621 | 0593 | 2 |
| 3 | 0878 | 0849 | 0819 | 0790 | 0762 | 0733 | 0704 | 0676 | 0648 | 0620 | 0592 | 3 |
| 4 | 0878 | 0848 | 0819 | 0790 | 0761 | 0732 | 0704 | 0676 | 0648 | 0620 | 0592 | 4 |
| 5 | 0877 | 0848 | 0818 | 0789 | 0761 | 0732 | 0703 | 0675 | 0647 | 0619 | 0591 | 5 |
| 6 | 0877 | 0847 | 0818 | 0789 | 0760 | 0731 | 0703 | 0675 | 0647 | 0619 | 0591 | 6 |
| 7 | 0876 | 0847 | 0817 | 0788 | 0760 | 0731 | 0703 | 0674 | 0646 | 0618 | 0591 | 7 |
| 8 | 0876 | 0846 | 0817 | 0788 | 0759 | 0730 | 0702 | 0674 | 0646 | 0618 | 0590 | 8 |
| 9 | 0875 | 0846 | 0816 | 0787 | 0759 | 0730 | 0702 | 0673 | 0645 | 0617 | 0590 | 9 |
| 10 | 0875 | 0845 | 0816 | 0787 | 0758 | 0730 | 0701 | 0673 | 0645 | 0617 | 0589 | 10 |
| 11 | 0874 | 0845 | 0816 | 0787 | 0758 | 0729 | 0701 | 0672 | 0644 | 0616 | 0589 | 11 |
| 12 | 0874 | 0844 | 0815 | 0786 | 0757 | 0729 | 0700 | 0672 | 0644 | 0616 | 0588 | 12 |
| 13 | 0873 | 0844 | 0815 | 0786 | 0757 | 0728 | 0700 | 0671 | 0643 | 0615 | 0588 | 13 |
| 14 | 0873 | 0843 | 0814 | 0785 | 0756 | 0728 | 0699 | 0671 | 0643 | 0615 | 0587 | 14 |
| 15 | 0872 | 0843 | 0814 | 0785 | 0756 | 0727 | 0699 | 0670 | 0642 | 0615 | 0587 | 15 |
| 16 | 0872 | 0842 | 0813 | 0784 | 0755 | 0727 | 0698 | 0670 | 0642 | 0614 | 0586 | 16 |
| 17 | 0871 | 0842 | 0813 | 0784 | 0755 | 0726 | 0698 | 0670 | 0641 | 0614 | 0586 | 17 |
| 18 | 0871 | 0841 | 0812 | 0783 | 0754 | 0726 | 0697 | 0669 | 0641 | 0613 | 0585 | 18 |
| 19 | 0870 | 0841 | 0812 | 0783 | 0754 | 0725 | 0697 | 0669 | 0641 | 0613 | 0585 | 19 |
| 20 | 0870 | 0840 | 0811 | 0782 | 0753 | 0725 | 0696 | 0668 | 0640 | 0612 | 0585 | 20 |
| 21 | 0869 | 0840 | 0811 | 0782 | 0753 | 0724 | 0696 | 0668 | 0640 | 0612 | 0584 | 21 |
| 22 | 0869 | 0839 | 0810 | 0781 | 0752 | 0724 | 0695 | 0667 | 0639 | 0611 | 0584 | 22 |
| 23 | 0868 | 0839 | 0810 | 0781 | 0752 | 0723 | 0695 | 0667 | 0639 | 0611 | 0583 | 23 |
| 24 | 0868 | 0838 | 0809 | 0780 | 0751 | 0723 | 0694 | 0666 | 0638 | 0610 | 0583 | 24 |
| 25 | 0867 | 0838 | 0809 | 0780 | 0751 | 0722 | 0694 | 0666 | 0638 | 0610 | 0582 | 25 |
| 26 | 0867 | 0837 | 0808 | 0779 | 0751 | 0722 | 0694 | 0665 | 0637 | 0609 | 0582 | 26 |
| 27 | 0866 | 0837 | 0808 | 0779 | 0750 | 0721 | 0693 | 0665 | 0637 | 0609 | 0581 | 27 |
| 28 | 0866 | 0836 | 0807 | 0778 | 0750 | 0721 | 0693 | 0664 | 0636 | 0609 | 0581 | 28 |
| 29 | 0865 | 0836 | 0807 | 0778 | 0749 | 0721 | 0692 | 0664 | 0636 | 0608 | 0580 | 29 |
| 30 | 0865 | 0835 | 0806 | 0777 | 0749 | 0720 | 0692 | 0663 | 0635 | 0608 | 0580 | 30 |
| 31 | 0864 | 0835 | 0806 | 0777 | 0748 | 0720 | 0691 | 0663 | 0635 | 0607 | 0579 | 31 |
| 32 | 0864 | 0834 | 0805 | 0776 | 0748 | 0719 | 0691 | 0663 | 0634 | 0607 | 0579 | 32 |
| 33 | 0863 | 0834 | 0805 | 0776 | 0747 | 0719 | 0690 | 0662 | 0634 | 0606 | 0579 | 33 |
| 34 | 0863 | 0834 | 0804 | 0775 | 0747 | 0718 | 0690 | 0662 | 0634 | 0606 | 0578 | 34 |
| 35 | 0862 | 0833 | 0804 | 0775 | 0746 | 0718 | 0689 | 0661 | 0633 | 0605 | 0578 | 35 |
| 36 | 0862 | 0833 | 0803 | 0774 | 0746 | 0717 | 0689 | 0661 | 0633 | 0605 | 0577 | 36 |
| 37 | 0861 | 0832 | 0803 | 0774 | 0745 | 0717 | 0688 | 0660 | 0632 | 0604 | 0577 | 37 |
| 38 | 0861 | 0832 | 0802 | 0774 | 0745 | 0716 | 0688 | 0660 | 0632 | 0604 | 0576 | 38 |
| 39 | 0860 | 0831 | 0802 | 0773 | 0744 | 0716 | 0687 | 0659 | 0631 | 0603 | 0576 | 39 |
| 40 | 0860 | 0831 | 0801 | 0773 | 0744 | 0715 | 0687 | 0659 | 0631 | 0603 | 0575 | 40 |
| 41 | 0859 | 0830 | 0801 | 0772 | 0743 | 0715 | 0686 | 0658 | 0630 | 0602 | 0575 | 41 |
| 42 | 0859 | 0830 | 0801 | 0772 | 0743 | 0714 | 0686 | 0658 | 0630 | 0602 | 0574 | 42 |
| 43 | 0858 | 0829 | 0800 | 0771 | 0742 | 0714 | 0686 | 0657 | 0629 | 0602 | 0574 | 43 |
| 44 | 0858 | 0829 | 0800 | 0771 | 0742 | 0713 | 0685 | 0657 | 0629 | 0601 | 0573 | 44 |
| 45 | 0857 | 0828 | 0799 | 0770 | 0741 | 0713 | 0685 | 0656 | 0628 | 0601 | 0573 | 45 |
| 46 | 0857 | 0828 | 0799 | 0770 | 0741 | 0712 | 0684 | 0656 | 0628 | 0600 | 0573 | 46 |
| 47 | 0856 | 0827 | 0798 | 0769 | 0740 | 0712 | 0684 | 0655 | 0628 | 0600 | 0572 | 47 |
| 48 | 0856 | 0827 | 0798 | 0769 | 0740 | 0711 | 0683 | 0655 | 0627 | 0599 | 0572 | 48 |
| 49 | 0855 | 0826 | 0797 | 0768 | 0740 | 0711 | 0683 | 0655 | 0627 | 0599 | 0571 | 49 |
| 50 | 0855 | 0826 | 0797 | 0768 | 0739 | 0711 | 0682 | 0654 | 0626 | 0598 | 0571 | 50 |
| 51 | 0855 | 0825 | 0796 | 0767 | 0739 | 0710 | 0682 | 0654 | 0626 | 0598 | 0570 | 51 |
| 52 | 0854 | 0825 | 0796 | 0767 | 0738 | 0710 | 0681 | 0653 | 0625 | 0597 | 0570 | 52 |
| 53 | 0854 | 0824 | 0795 | 0766 | 0738 | 0709 | 0681 | 0653 | 0625 | 0597 | 0569 | 53 |
| 54 | 0853 | 0824 | 0795 | 0766 | 0737 | 0709 | 0680 | 0652 | 0624 | 0596 | 0569 | 54 |
| 55 | 0853 | 0823 | 0794 | 0765 | 0737 | 0708 | 0680 | 0652 | 0624 | 0596 | 0568 | 55 |
| 56 | 0852 | 0823 | 0794 | 0765 | 0736 | 0708 | 0679 | 0651 | 0623 | 0596 | 0568 | 56 |
| 57 | 0852 | 0822 | 0793 | 0764 | 0736 | 0707 | 0679 | 0651 | 0623 | 0595 | 0568 | 57 |
| 58 | 0851 | 0822 | 0793 | 0764 | 0735 | 0707 | 0678 | 0650 | 0622 | 0595 | 0567 | 58 |
| 59 | 0851 | 0821 | 0792 | 0763 | 0735 | 0706 | 0678 | 0650 | 0622 | 0594 | 0567 | 59 |
| S. | 2° 27′ | 2° 28′ | 2° 29′ | 2° 30′ | 2° 31′ | 2° 32′ | 2° 33′ | 2° 34′ | 2° 35′ | 2° 36′ | 2° 37′ | S. |

# TABLE XXII.

## Proportional Logarithms.

| S. | h m 2° 38′ | h m 2° 39′ | h m 2° 40′ | h m 2° 41′ | h m 2° 42′ | h m 2° 43′ | h m 2° 44′ | h m 2° 45′ | h m 2° 46′ | h m 2° 47′ | h m 2° 48′ | S. |
|---|---|---|---|---|---|---|---|---|---|---|---|---|
| 0 | 0566 | 0539 | 0512 | 0484 | 0458 | 0431 | 0404 | 0378 | 0352 | 0326 | 0300 | 0 |
| 1 | 0566 | 0538 | 0511 | 0484 | 0457 | 0430 | 0404 | 0377 | 0351 | 0325 | 0299 | 1 |
| 2 | 0565 | 0538 | 0511 | 0484 | 0457 | 0430 | 0403 | 0377 | 0351 | 0325 | 0299 | 2 |
| 3 | 0565 | 0537 | 0510 | 0483 | 0456 | 0430 | 0403 | 0377 | 0350 | 0324 | 0298 | 3 |
| 4 | 0564 | 0537 | 0510 | 0483 | 0456 | 0429 | 0403 | 0376 | 0350 | 0324 | 0298 | 4 |
| 5 | 0564 | 0536 | 0509 | 0482 | 0455 | 0429 | 0402 | 0376 | 0349 | 0323 | 0297 | 5 |
| 6 | 0563 | 0536 | 0509 | 0482 | 0455 | 0428 | 0402 | 0375 | 0349 | 0323 | 0297 | 6 |
| 7 | 0563 | 0536 | 0508 | 0481 | 0454 | 0428 | 0401 | 0375 | 0349 | 0323 | 0297 | 7 |
| 8 | 0562 | 0535 | 0508 | 0481 | 0454 | 0427 | 0401 | 0374 | 0348 | 0322 | 0296 | 8 |
| 9 | 0562 | 0535 | 0507 | 0480 | 0454 | 0427 | 0400 | 0374 | 0348 | 0322 | 0296 | 9 |
| 10 | 0562 | 0534 | 0507 | 0480 | 0453 | 0426 | 0400 | 0374 | 0347 | 0321 | 0295 | 10 |
| 11 | 0561 | 0534 | 0507 | 0480 | 0453 | 0426 | 0399 | 0373 | 0347 | 0321 | 0295 | 11 |
| 12 | 0561 | 0533 | 0506 | 0479 | 0452 | 0426 | 0399 | 0373 | 0346 | 0320 | 0294 | 12 |
| 13 | 0560 | 0533 | 0506 | 0479 | 0452 | 0425 | 0399 | 0372 | 0346 | 0320 | 0294 | 13 |
| 14 | 0560 | 0532 | 0505 | 0478 | 0451 | 0425 | 0398 | 0372 | 0346 | 0319 | 0294 | 14 |
| 15 | 0559 | 0532 | 0505 | 0478 | 0451 | 0424 | 0398 | 0371 | 0345 | 0319 | 0293 | 15 |
| 16 | 0559 | 0531 | 0504 | 0477 | 0450 | 0424 | 0397 | 0371 | 0345 | 0319 | 0293 | 16 |
| 17 | 0558 | 0531 | 0504 | 0477 | 0450 | 0423 | 0397 | 0370 | 0344 | 0318 | 0292 | 17 |
| 18 | 0558 | 0531 | 0503 | 0476 | 0450 | 0423 | 0396 | 0370 | 0344 | 0318 | 0292 | 18 |
| 19 | 0557 | 0530 | 0503 | 0476 | 0449 | 0422 | 0396 | 0370 | 0343 | 0317 | 0291 | 19 |
| 20 | 0557 | 0530 | 0502 | 0475 | 0449 | 0422 | 0395 | 0369 | 0343 | 0317 | 0291 | 20 |
| 21 | 0557 | 0529 | 0502 | 0475 | 0448 | 0422 | 0395 | 0369 | 0342 | 0316 | 0291 | 21 |
| 22 | 0556 | 0529 | 0502 | 0475 | 0448 | 0421 | 0395 | 0368 | 0342 | 0316 | 0290 | 22 |
| 23 | 0556 | 0528 | 0501 | 0474 | 0447 | 0421 | 0394 | 0368 | 0342 | 0316 | 0290 | 23 |
| 24 | 0555 | 0528 | 0501 | 0474 | 0447 | 0420 | 0394 | 0367 | 0341 | 0315 | 0289 | 24 |
| 25 | 0555 | 0527 | 0500 | 0473 | 0446 | 0420 | 0393 | 0367 | 0341 | 0315 | 0289 | 25 |
| 26 | 0554 | 0527 | 0500 | 0473 | 0446 | 0419 | 0393 | 0366 | 0340 | 0314 | 0288 | 26 |
| 27 | 0554 | 0526 | 0499 | 0472 | 0446 | 0419 | 0392 | 0366 | 0340 | 0314 | 0288 | 27 |
| 28 | 0553 | 0526 | 0499 | 0472 | 0445 | 0418 | 0392 | 0366 | 0339 | 0313 | 0288 | 28 |
| 29 | 0553 | 0526 | 0498 | 0471 | 0445 | 0418 | 0392 | 0365 | 0339 | 0313 | 0287 | 29 |
| 30 | 0552 | 0525 | 0498 | 0471 | 0444 | 0418 | 0391 | 0365 | 0339 | 0313 | 0287 | 30 |
| 31 | 0552 | 0525 | 0498 | 0471 | 0444 | 0417 | 0391 | 0364 | 0338 | 0312 | 0286 | 31 |
| 32 | 0552 | 0524 | 0497 | 0470 | 0443 | 0417 | 0390 | 0364 | 0338 | 0312 | 0286 | 32 |
| 33 | 0551 | 0524 | 0497 | 0470 | 0443 | 0416 | 0390 | 0363 | 0337 | 0311 | 0285 | 33 |
| 34 | 0551 | 0523 | 0496 | 0469 | 0442 | 0416 | 0389 | 0363 | 0337 | 0311 | 0285 | 34 |
| 35 | 0550 | 0523 | 0496 | 0469 | 0442 | 0415 | 0389 | 0363 | 0336 | 0310 | 0285 | 35 |
| 36 | 0550 | 0522 | 0495 | 0468 | 0442 | 0415 | 0388 | 0362 | 0336 | 0310 | 0284 | 36 |
| 37 | 0549 | 0522 | 0495 | 0468 | 0441 | 0414 | 0388 | 0362 | 0336 | 0310 | 0284 | 37 |
| 38 | 0549 | 0521 | 0494 | 0467 | 0441 | 0414 | 0388 | 0361 | 0335 | 0309 | 0283 | 38 |
| 39 | 0548 | 0521 | 0494 | 0467 | 0440 | 0414 | 0387 | 0361 | 0335 | 0309 | 0283 | 39 |
| 40 | 0548 | 0521 | 0493 | 0467 | 0440 | 0413 | 0387 | 0360 | 0334 | 0308 | 0282 | 40 |
| 41 | 0547 | 0520 | 0493 | 0466 | 0439 | 0413 | 0386 | 0360 | 0334 | 0308 | 0282 | 41 |
| 42 | 0547 | 0520 | 0493 | 0466 | 0439 | 0412 | 0386 | 0359 | 0333 | 0307 | 0282 | 42 |
| 43 | 0546 | 0519 | 0492 | 0465 | 0438 | 0412 | 0385 | 0359 | 0333 | 0307 | 0281 | 43 |
| 44 | 0546 | 0519 | 0492 | 0465 | 0438 | 0411 | 0385 | 0359 | 0333 | 0307 | 0281 | 44 |
| 45 | 0546 | 0518 | 0491 | 0464 | 0438 | 0411 | 0384 | 0358 | 0332 | 0306 | 0280 | 45 |
| 46 | 0545 | 0518 | 0491 | 0464 | 0437 | 0410 | 0384 | 0358 | 0332 | 0306 | 0280 | 46 |
| 47 | 0545 | 0517 | 0490 | 0463 | 0437 | 0410 | 0384 | 0357 | 0331 | 0305 | 0279 | 47 |
| 48 | 0544 | 0517 | 0490 | 0463 | 0436 | 0410 | 0383 | 0357 | 0331 | 0305 | 0279 | 48 |
| 49 | 0544 | 0517 | 0489 | 0462 | 0436 | 0409 | 0383 | 0356 | 0330 | 0304 | 0279 | 49 |
| 50 | 0543 | 0516 | 0489 | 0462 | 0435 | 0409 | 0382 | 0356 | 0330 | 0304 | 0278 | 50 |
| 51 | 0543 | 0516 | 0489 | 0462 | 0435 | 0408 | 0382 | 0356 | 0329 | 0304 | 0278 | 51 |
| 52 | 0542 | 0515 | 0488 | 0461 | 0434 | 0408 | 0381 | 0355 | 0329 | 0303 | 0277 | 52 |
| 53 | 0542 | 0515 | 0488 | 0461 | 0434 | 0407 | 0381 | 0355 | 0329 | 0303 | 0277 | 53 |
| 54 | 0541 | 0514 | 0487 | 0460 | 0434 | 0407 | 0381 | 0354 | 0328 | 0302 | 0276 | 54 |
| 55 | 0541 | 0514 | 0487 | 0460 | 0433 | 0406 | 0380 | 0354 | 0328 | 0302 | 0276 | 55 |
| 56 | 0541 | 0513 | 0486 | 0459 | 0433 | 0406 | 0380 | 0353 | 0327 | 0301 | 0276 | 56 |
| 57 | 0540 | 0513 | 0486 | 0459 | 0432 | 0406 | 0379 | 0353 | 0327 | 0301 | 0275 | 57 |
| 58 | 0540 | 0512 | 0485 | 0458 | 0432 | 0405 | 0379 | 0353 | 0326 | 0300 | 0275 | 58 |
| 59 | 0539 | 0512 | 0485 | 0458 | 0431 | 0405 | 0378 | 0352 | 0326 | 0300 | 0274 | 59 |
| S. | 2° 38′ | 2° 39′ | 2° 40′ | 2° 41′ | 2° 42′ | 2° 43′ | 2° 44′ | 2° 45′ | 2° 46′ | 2° 47′ | 2° 48′ | S. |

# TABLE XXII.

## Proportional Logarithms.

| S. | h m 2° 49′ | h m 2° 50′ | h m 2° 51′ | h m 2° 52′ | h m 2° 53′ | h m 2° 54′ | h m 2° 55′ | h m 2° 56′ | h m 2° 57′ | h m 2° 58′ | h m 2° 59′ | S. |
|---|---|---|---|---|---|---|---|---|---|---|---|---|
| 0 | 0274 | 0248 | 0223 | 0197 | 0172 | 0147 | 0122 | 0098 | 0073 | 0049 | 0024 | 0 |
| 1 | 0273 | 0248 | 0222 | 0197 | 0172 | 0147 | 0122 | 0097 | 0073 | 0048 | 0024 | 1 |
| 2 | 0273 | 0247 | 0222 | 0197 | 0171 | 0146 | 0122 | 0097 | 0072 | 0048 | 0023 | 2 |
| 3 | 0273 | 0247 | 0221 | 0196 | 0171 | 0146 | 0121 | 0096 | 0072 | 0047 | 0023 | 3 |
| 4 | 0272 | 0247 | 0221 | 0196 | 0171 | 0146 | 0121 | 0096 | 0071 | 0047 | 0023 | 4 |
| 5 | 0272 | 0246 | 0221 | 0195 | 0170 | 0145 | 0120 | 0096 | 0071 | 0046 | 0022 | 5 |
| 6 | 0271 | 0246 | 0220 | 0195 | 0170 | 0145 | 0120 | 0095 | 0071 | 0046 | 0022 | 6 |
| 7 | 0271 | 0245 | 0220 | 0194 | 0169 | 0144 | 0119 | 0095 | 0070 | 0046 | 0021 | 7 |
| 8 | 0270 | 0245 | 0219 | 0194 | 0169 | 0144 | 0119 | 0094 | 0070 | 0045 | 0021 | 8 |
| 9 | 0270 | 0244 | 0219 | 0194 | 0169 | 0143 | 0119 | 0094 | 0069 | 0045 | 0021 | 9 |
| 10 | 0270 | 0244 | 0219 | 0193 | 0168 | 0143 | 0118 | 0093 | 0069 | 0044 | 0020 | 10 |
| 11 | 0269 | 0244 | 0218 | 0193 | 0168 | 0143 | 0118 | 0093 | 0068 | 0044 | 0020 | 11 |
| 12 | 0269 | 0243 | 0218 | 0192 | 0167 | 0142 | 0117 | 0093 | 0068 | 0044 | 0019 | 12 |
| 13 | 0268 | 0243 | 0217 | 0192 | 0167 | 0142 | 0117 | 0092 | 0068 | 0043 | 0019 | 13 |
| 14 | 0268 | 0242 | 0217 | 0192 | 0166 | 0141 | 0117 | 0092 | 0067 | 0043 | 0019 | 14 |
| 15 | 0267 | 0242 | 0216 | 0191 | 0166 | 0141 | 0116 | 0091 | 0067 | 0042 | 0018 | 15 |
| 16 | 0267 | 0241 | 0216 | 0191 | 0166 | 0141 | 0116 | 0091 | 0066 | 0042 | 0018 | 16 |
| 17 | 0267 | 0241 | 0216 | 0190 | 0165 | 0140 | 0115 | 0091 | 0066 | 0042 | 0017 | 17 |
| 18 | 0266 | 0241 | 0215 | 0190 | 0165 | 0140 | 0115 | 0090 | 0066 | 0041 | 0017 | 18 |
| 19 | 0266 | 0240 | 0215 | 0189 | 0164 | 0139 | 0114 | 0090 | 0065 | 0041 | 0017 | 19 |
| 20 | 0265 | 0240 | 0214 | 0189 | 0164 | 0139 | 0114 | 0089 | 0065 | 0040 | 0016 | 20 |
| 21 | 0265 | 0239 | 0214 | 0189 | 0163 | 0139 | 0114 | 0089 | 0064 | 0040 | 0016 | 21 |
| 22 | 0264 | 0239 | 0213 | 0188 | 0163 | 0138 | 0113 | 0089 | 0064 | 0040 | 0015 | 22 |
| 23 | 0264 | 0238 | 0213 | 0188 | 0163 | 0138 | 0113 | 0088 | 0064 | 0039 | 0015 | 23 |
| 24 | 0264 | 0238 | 0213 | 0187 | 0162 | 0137 | 0112 | 0088 | 0063 | 0039 | 0015 | 24 |
| 25 | 0263 | 0238 | 0212 | 0187 | 0162 | 0137 | 0112 | 0087 | 0063 | 0038 | 0014 | 25 |
| 26 | 0263 | 0237 | 0212 | 0187 | 0161 | 0136 | 0112 | 0087 | 0062 | 0038 | 0014 | 26 |
| 27 | 0262 | 0237 | 0211 | 0186 | 0161 | 0136 | 0111 | 0087 | 0062 | 0038 | 0013 | 27 |
| 28 | 0262 | 0236 | 0211 | 0186 | 0161 | 0136 | 0111 | 0086 | 0062 | 0037 | 0013 | 28 |
| 29 | 0261 | 0236 | 0211 | 0185 | 0160 | 0135 | 0110 | 0086 | 0061 | 0037 | 0012 | 29 |
| 30 | 0261 | 0235 | 0210 | 0185 | 0160 | 0135 | 0110 | 0085 | 0061 | 0036 | 0012 | 30 |
| 31 | 0261 | 0235 | 0210 | 0184 | 0159 | 0134 | 0110 | 0085 | 0060 | 0036 | 0012 | 31 |
| 32 | 0260 | 0235 | 0209 | 0184 | 0159 | 0134 | 0109 | 0084 | 0060 | 0036 | 0011 | 32 |
| 33 | 0260 | 0234 | 0209 | 0184 | 0158 | 0134 | 0109 | 0084 | 0060 | 0035 | 0011 | 33 |
| 34 | 0259 | 0234 | 0208 | 0183 | 0158 | 0133 | 0108 | 0084 | 0059 | 0035 | 0010 | 34 |
| 35 | 0259 | 0233 | 0208 | 0183 | 0158 | 0133 | 0108 | 0083 | 0059 | 0034 | 0010 | 35 |
| 36 | 0258 | 0233 | 0208 | 0182 | 0157 | 0132 | 0107 | 0083 | 0058 | 0034 | 0010 | 36 |
| 37 | 0258 | 0233 | 0207 | 0182 | 0157 | 0132 | 0107 | 0082 | 0058 | 0034 | 0009 | 37 |
| 38 | 0258 | 0232 | 0207 | 0181 | 0156 | 0131 | 0107 | 0082 | 0057 | 0033 | 0009 | 38 |
| 39 | 0257 | 0232 | 0206 | 0181 | 0156 | 0131 | 0106 | 0082 | 0057 | 0033 | 0008 | 39 |
| 40 | 0257 | 0231 | 0206 | 0181 | 0156 | 0131 | 0106 | 0081 | 0057 | 0032 | 0008 | 40 |
| 41 | 0256 | 0231 | 0205 | 0180 | 0155 | 0130 | 0105 | 0081 | 0056 | 0032 | 0008 | 41 |
| 42 | 0256 | 0230 | 0205 | 0180 | 0155 | 0130 | 0105 | 0080 | 0056 | 0031 | 0007 | 42 |
| 43 | 0255 | 0230 | 0205 | 0179 | 0154 | 0129 | 0105 | 0080 | 0055 | 0031 | 0007 | 43 |
| 44 | 0255 | 0230 | 0204 | 0179 | 0154 | 0129 | 0104 | 0080 | 0055 | 0031 | 0006 | 44 |
| 45 | 0255 | 0229 | 0204 | 0179 | 0153 | 0129 | 0104 | 0079 | 0055 | 0030 | 0006 | 45 |
| 46 | 0254 | 0229 | 0203 | 0178 | 0153 | 0128 | 0103 | 0079 | 0054 | 0030 | 0006 | 46 |
| 47 | 0254 | 0228 | 0203 | 0178 | 0153 | 0128 | 0103 | 0078 | 0054 | 0029 | 0005 | 47 |
| 48 | 0253 | 0228 | 0202 | 0177 | 0152 | 0127 | 0103 | 0078 | 0053 | 0029 | 0005 | 48 |
| 49 | 0253 | 0227 | 0202 | 0177 | 0152 | 0127 | 0102 | 0077 | 0053 | 0029 | 0004 | 49 |
| 50 | 0252 | 0227 | 0202 | 0176 | 0151 | 0126 | 0102 | 0077 | 0053 | 0028 | 0004 | 50 |
| 51 | 0252 | 0227 | 0201 | 0176 | 0151 | 0126 | 0101 | 0077 | 0052 | 0028 | 0004 | 51 |
| 52 | 0252 | 0226 | 0201 | 0176 | 0151 | 0126 | 0101 | 0076 | 0052 | 0027 | 0003 | 52 |
| 53 | 0251 | 0226 | 0200 | 0175 | 0150 | 0125 | 0100 | 0076 | 0051 | 0027 | 0003 | 53 |
| 54 | 0251 | 0225 | 0200 | 0175 | 0150 | 0125 | 0100 | 0075 | 0051 | 0027 | 0002 | 54 |
| 55 | 0250 | 0225 | 0200 | 0174 | 0149 | 0124 | 0100 | 0075 | 0051 | 0026 | 0002 | 55 |
| 56 | 0250 | 0224 | 0199 | 0174 | 0149 | 0124 | 0099 | 0075 | 0050 | 0026 | 0002 | 56 |
| 57 | 0250 | 0224 | 0199 | 0174 | 0148 | 0124 | 0099 | 0074 | 0050 | 0025 | 0001 | 57 |
| 58 | 0249 | 0224 | 0198 | 0173 | 0148 | 0123 | 0098 | 0074 | 0049 | 0025 | 0001 | 58 |
| 59 | 0249 | 0223 | 0198 | 0173 | 0148 | 0123 | 0098 | 0073 | 0049 | 0025 | 0000 | 59 |
| S. | 2° 49′ | 2° 50′ | 2° 51′ | 2° 52′ | 2° 53′ | 2° 54′ | 2° 55′ | 2° 56′ | 2° 57′ | 2° 58′ | 2° 59′ | S. |

# TABLE XXIV.

## Of Natural Sines.

| Prop. parts 29 | M | 0° N. sine. | 0° N. cos. | 1° N. sine. | 1° N. cos. | 2° N. sine. | 2° N. cos. | 3° N. sine. | 3° N. cos. | 4° N. sine. | 4° N. cos. | | Prop. parts 2 |
|---|---|---|---|---|---|---|---|---|---|---|---|---|---|
| 0 | 0 | 00000 | 100000 | 01745 | 99985 | 03490 | 99939 | 05234 | 99863 | 06976 | 99756 | 60 | 2 |
| 0 | 1 | 00029 | 100000 | 01774 | 99984 | 03519 | 99938 | 05263 | 99861 | 07005 | 99754 | 59 | 2 |
| 1 | 2 | 00058 | 100000 | 01803 | 99984 | 03548 | 99937 | 05292 | 99860 | 07034 | 99752 | 58 | 2 |
| 1 | 3 | 00087 | 100000 | 01832 | 99983 | 03577 | 99936 | 05321 | 99858 | 07063 | 99750 | 57 | 2 |
| 2 | 4 | 00116 | 100000 | 01862 | 99983 | 03606 | 99935 | 05350 | 99857 | 07092 | 99748 | 56 | 2 |
| 2 | 5 | 00145 | 100000 | 01891 | 99982 | 03635 | 99934 | 05379 | 99855 | 07121 | 99746 | 55 | 2 |
| 3 | 6 | 00175 | 100000 | 01920 | 99982 | 03664 | 99933 | 05408 | 99854 | 07150 | 99744 | 54 | 2 |
| 3 | 7 | 00204 | 100000 | 01949 | 99981 | 03693 | 99932 | 05437 | 99852 | 07179 | 99742 | 53 | 2 |
| 4 | 8 | 00233 | 100000 | 01978 | 99980 | 03723 | 99931 | 05466 | 99851 | 07208 | 99740 | 52 | 2 |
| 4 | 9 | 00262 | 100000 | 02007 | 99980 | 03752 | 99930 | 05495 | 99849 | 07237 | 99738 | 51 | 2 |
| 5 | 10 | 00291 | 100000 | 02036 | 99979 | 03781 | 99929 | 05524 | 99847 | 07266 | 99736 | 50 | 2 |
| 5 | 11 | 00320 | 99999 | 02065 | 99979 | 03810 | 99927 | 05553 | 99846 | 07295 | 99734 | 49 | 2 |
| 6 | 12 | 00349 | 99999 | 02094 | 99978 | 03839 | 99926 | 05582 | 99844 | 07324 | 99731 | 48 | 2 |
| 6 | 13 | 00378 | 99999 | 02123 | 99977 | 03868 | 99925 | 05611 | 99842 | 07353 | 99729 | 47 | 2 |
| 7 | 14 | 00407 | 99999 | 02152 | 99977 | 03897 | 99924 | 05640 | 99841 | 07382 | 99727 | 46 | 2 |
| 7 | 15 | 00436 | 99999 | 02181 | 99976 | 03926 | 99923 | 05669 | 99839 | 07411 | 99725 | 45 | 2 |
| 8 | 16 | 00465 | 99999 | 02211 | 99976 | 03955 | 99922 | 05698 | 99838 | 07440 | 99723 | 44 | 1 |
| 8 | 17 | 00495 | 99999 | 02240 | 99975 | 03984 | 99921 | 05727 | 99836 | 07469 | 99721 | 43 | 1 |
| 9 | 18 | 00524 | 99999 | 02269 | 99974 | 04013 | 99919 | 05756 | 99834 | 07498 | 99719 | 42 | 1 |
| 9 | 19 | 00553 | 99998 | 02298 | 99974 | 04042 | 99918 | 05785 | 99833 | 07527 | 99716 | 41 | 1 |
| 10 | 20 | 00582 | 99998 | 02327 | 99973 | 04071 | 99917 | 05814 | 99831 | 07556 | 99714 | 40 | 1 |
| 10 | 21 | 00611 | 99998 | 02356 | 99972 | 04100 | 99916 | 05844 | 99829 | 07585 | 99712 | 39 | 1 |
| 11 | 22 | 00640 | 99998 | 02385 | 99972 | 04129 | 99915 | 05873 | 99827 | 07614 | 99710 | 38 | 1 |
| 11 | 23 | 00669 | 99998 | 02414 | 99971 | 04159 | 99913 | 05902 | 99826 | 07643 | 99708 | 37 | 1 |
| 12 | 24 | 00698 | 99998 | 02443 | 99970 | 04188 | 99912 | 05931 | 99824 | 07672 | 99705 | 36 | 1 |
| 12 | 25 | 00727 | 99997 | 02472 | 99969 | 04217 | 99911 | 05960 | 99822 | 07701 | 99703 | 35 | 1 |
| 13 | 26 | 00756 | 99997 | 02501 | 99969 | 04246 | 99910 | 05989 | 99821 | 07730 | 99701 | 34 | 1 |
| 13 | 27 | 00785 | 99997 | 02530 | 99968 | 04275 | 99909 | 06018 | 99819 | 07759 | 99699 | 33 | 1 |
| 14 | 28 | 00814 | 99997 | 02560 | 99967 | 04304 | 99907 | 06047 | 99817 | 07788 | 99696 | 32 | 1 |
| 14 | 29 | 00844 | 99996 | 02589 | 99966 | 04333 | 99906 | 06076 | 99815 | 07817 | 99694 | 31 | 1 |
| 15 | 30 | 00873 | 99996 | 02618 | 99966 | 04362 | 99905 | 06105 | 99813 | 07846 | 99692 | 30 | 1 |
| 15 | 31 | 00902 | 99996 | 02647 | 99965 | 04391 | 99904 | 06134 | 99812 | 07875 | 99689 | 29 | 1 |
| 15 | 32 | 00931 | 99996 | 02676 | 99964 | 04420 | 99902 | 06163 | 99810 | 07904 | 99687 | 28 | 1 |
| 16 | 33 | 00960 | 99995 | 02705 | 99963 | 04449 | 99901 | 06192 | 99808 | 07933 | 99685 | 27 | 1 |
| 16 | 34 | 00989 | 99995 | 02734 | 99963 | 04478 | 99900 | 06221 | 99806 | 07962 | 99683 | 26 | 1 |
| 17 | 35 | 01018 | 99995 | 02763 | 99962 | 04507 | 99898 | 06250 | 99804 | 07991 | 99680 | 25 | 1 |
| 17 | 36 | 01047 | 99995 | 02792 | 99961 | 04536 | 99897 | 06279 | 99803 | 08020 | 99678 | 24 | 1 |
| 18 | 37 | 01076 | 99994 | 02821 | 99960 | 04565 | 99896 | 06308 | 99801 | 08049 | 99676 | 23 | 1 |
| 18 | 38 | 01105 | 99994 | 02850 | 99959 | 04594 | 99894 | 06337 | 99799 | 08078 | 99673 | 22 | 1 |
| 19 | 39 | 01134 | 99994 | 02879 | 99959 | 04623 | 99893 | 06366 | 99797 | 08107 | 99671 | 21 | 1 |
| 19 | 40 | 01164 | 99993 | 02908 | 99958 | 04653 | 99892 | 06395 | 99795 | 08136 | 99668 | 20 | 1 |
| 20 | 41 | 01193 | 99993 | 02938 | 99957 | 04682 | 99890 | 06424 | 99793 | 08165 | 99666 | 19 | 1 |
| 20 | 42 | 01222 | 99993 | 02967 | 99956 | 04711 | 99889 | 06453 | 99792 | 08194 | 99664 | 18 | 1 |
| 21 | 43 | 01251 | 99992 | 02996 | 99955 | 04740 | 99888 | 06482 | 99790 | 08223 | 99661 | 17 | 1 |
| 21 | 44 | 01280 | 99992 | 03025 | 99954 | 04769 | 99886 | 06511 | 99788 | 08252 | 99659 | 16 | 1 |
| 22 | 45 | 01309 | 99991 | 03054 | 99953 | 04798 | 99885 | 06540 | 99786 | 08281 | 99657 | 15 | 1 |
| 22 | 46 | 01338 | 99991 | 03083 | 99952 | 04827 | 99883 | 06569 | 99784 | 08310 | 99654 | 14 | 0 |
| 23 | 47 | 01367 | 99991 | 03112 | 99952 | 04856 | 99882 | 06598 | 99782 | 08339 | 99652 | 13 | 0 |
| 23 | 48 | 01396 | 99990 | 03141 | 99951 | 04885 | 99881 | 06627 | 99780 | 08368 | 99649 | 12 | 0 |
| 24 | 49 | 01425 | 99990 | 03170 | 99950 | 04914 | 99879 | 06656 | 99778 | 08397 | 99647 | 11 | 0 |
| 24 | 50 | 01454 | 99989 | 03199 | 99949 | 04943 | 99878 | 06685 | 99776 | 08426 | 99644 | 10 | 0 |
| 25 | 51 | 01483 | 99989 | 03228 | 99948 | 04972 | 99876 | 06714 | 99774 | 08455 | 99642 | 9 | 0 |
| 25 | 52 | 01513 | 99989 | 03257 | 99947 | 05001 | 99875 | 06743 | 99772 | 08484 | 99639 | 8 | 0 |
| 26 | 53 | 01542 | 99988 | 03286 | 99946 | 05030 | 99873 | 06773 | 99770 | 08513 | 99637 | 7 | 0 |
| 26 | 54 | 01571 | 99988 | 03316 | 99945 | 05059 | 99872 | 06802 | 99768 | 08542 | 99635 | 6 | 0 |
| 27 | 55 | 01600 | 99987 | 03345 | 99944 | 05088 | 99870 | 06831 | 99766 | 08571 | 99632 | 5 | 0 |
| 27 | 56 | 01629 | 99987 | 03374 | 99943 | 05117 | 99869 | 06860 | 99764 | 08600 | 99630 | 4 | 0 |
| 28 | 57 | 01658 | 99986 | 03403 | 99942 | 05146 | 99867 | 06889 | 99762 | 08629 | 99627 | 3 | 0 |
| 28 | 58 | 01687 | 99986 | 03432 | 99941 | 05175 | 99866 | 06918 | 99760 | 08658 | 99625 | 2 | 0 |
| 29 | 59 | 01716 | 99985 | 03461 | 99940 | 05205 | 99864 | 06947 | 99758 | 08687 | 99622 | 1 | 0 |
| 29 | 60 | 01745 | 99985 | 03490 | 99939 | 05234 | 99863 | 06976 | 99756 | 08716 | 99619 | 0 | 0 |
| | | N. cos. | N. sine. | N. cos. | N. sine. | N. cos. | N. sine. | N. cos. | N. sine. | N. cos. | N. sine. | M | |
| | | 89° | | 88° | | 87° | | 86° | | 85° | | | |

# TABLE XXIV.

## Of Natural Sines.

| Prop. parts 29 | M | 5° N. sine. | 5° N. cos. | 6° N. sine. | 6° N. cos. | 7° N. sine. | 7° N. cos. | 8° N. sine. | 8° N. cos. | 9° N. sine. | 9° N. cos. | | Prop. parts 4 |
|---|---|---|---|---|---|---|---|---|---|---|---|---|---|
| 0 | 0 | 08716 | 99619 | 10453 | 99452 | 12187 | 99255 | 13917 | 99027 | 15643 | 98769 | 60 | 4 |
| 0 | 1 | 08745 | 99617 | 10482 | 99449 | 12216 | 99251 | 13946 | 99023 | 15672 | 98764 | 59 | 4 |
| 1 | 2 | 08774 | 99614 | 10511 | 99446 | 12245 | 99248 | 13975 | 99019 | 15701 | 98760 | 58 | 4 |
| 1 | 3 | 08803 | 99612 | 10540 | 99443 | 12274 | 99244 | 14004 | 99015 | 15730 | 98755 | 57 | 4 |
| 2 | 4 | 08831 | 99609 | 10569 | 99440 | 12302 | 99240 | 14033 | 99011 | 15758 | 98751 | 56 | 4 |
| 2 | 5 | 08860 | 99607 | 10597 | 99437 | 12331 | 99237 | 14061 | 99006 | 15787 | 98746 | 55 | 4 |
| 3 | 6 | 08889 | 99604 | 10626 | 99434 | 12360 | 99233 | 14090 | 99002 | 15816 | 98741 | 54 | 4 |
| 3 | 7 | 08918 | 99602 | 10655 | 99431 | 12389 | 99230 | 14119 | 98998 | 15845 | 98737 | 53 | 4 |
| 4 | 8 | 08947 | 99599 | 10684 | 99428 | 12418 | 99226 | 14148 | 98994 | 15873 | 98732 | 52 | 3 |
| 4 | 9 | 08976 | 99596 | 10713 | 99424 | 12447 | 99222 | 14177 | 98990 | 15902 | 98728 | 51 | 3 |
| 5 | 10 | 09005 | 99594 | 10742 | 99421 | 12476 | 99219 | 14205 | 98986 | 15931 | 98723 | 50 | 3 |
| 5 | 11 | 09034 | 99591 | 10771 | 99418 | 12504 | 99215 | 14234 | 98982 | 15959 | 98718 | 49 | 3 |
| 6 | 12 | 09063 | 99588 | 10800 | 99415 | 12533 | 99211 | 14263 | 98978 | 15988 | 98714 | 48 | 3 |
| 6 | 13 | 09092 | 99586 | 10829 | 99412 | 12562 | 99208 | 14292 | 98973 | 16017 | 98709 | 47 | 3 |
| 7 | 14 | 09121 | 99583 | 10858 | 99409 | 12591 | 99204 | 14320 | 98969 | 16046 | 98704 | 46 | 3 |
| 7 | 15 | 09150 | 99580 | 10887 | 99406 | 12620 | 99200 | 14349 | 98965 | 16074 | 98700 | 45 | 3 |
| 8 | 16 | 09179 | 99578 | 10916 | 99402 | 12649 | 99197 | 14378 | 98961 | 16103 | 98695 | 44 | 3 |
| 8 | 17 | 09208 | 99575 | 10945 | 99399 | 12678 | 99193 | 14407 | 98957 | 16132 | 98690 | 43 | 3 |
| 9 | 18 | 09237 | 99572 | 10973 | 99396 | 12706 | 99189 | 14436 | 98953 | 16160 | 98686 | 42 | 3 |
| 9 | 19 | 09266 | 99570 | 11002 | 99393 | 12735 | 99186 | 14464 | 98948 | 16189 | 98681 | 41 | 3 |
| 10 | 20 | 09295 | 99567 | 11031 | 99390 | 12764 | 99182 | 14493 | 98944 | 16218 | 98676 | 40 | 3 |
| 10 | 21 | 09324 | 99564 | 11060 | 99386 | 12793 | 99178 | 14522 | 98940 | 16246 | 98671 | 39 | 3 |
| 11 | 22 | 09353 | 99562 | 11089 | 99383 | 12822 | 99175 | 14551 | 98936 | 16275 | 98667 | 38 | 3 |
| 11 | 23 | 09382 | 99559 | 11118 | 99380 | 12851 | 99171 | 14580 | 98931 | 16304 | 98662 | 37 | 2 |
| 12 | 24 | 09411 | 99556 | 11147 | 99377 | 12880 | 99167 | 14608 | 98927 | 16333 | 98657 | 36 | 2 |
| 12 | 25 | 09440 | 99553 | 11176 | 99374 | 12908 | 99163 | 14637 | 98923 | 16361 | 98652 | 35 | 2 |
| 13 | 26 | 09469 | 99551 | 11205 | 99370 | 12937 | 99160 | 14666 | 98919 | 16390 | 98648 | 34 | 2 |
| 13 | 27 | 09498 | 99548 | 11234 | 99367 | 12966 | 99156 | 14695 | 98914 | 16419 | 98643 | 33 | 2 |
| 14 | 28 | 09527 | 99545 | 11263 | 99364 | 12995 | 99152 | 14723 | 98910 | 16447 | 98638 | 32 | 2 |
| 14 | 29 | 09556 | 99542 | 11291 | 99360 | 13024 | 99148 | 14752 | 98906 | 16476 | 98633 | 31 | 2 |
| 15 | 30 | 09585 | 99540 | 11320 | 99357 | 13053 | 99144 | 14781 | 98902 | 16505 | 98629 | 30 | 2 |
| 15 | 31 | 09614 | 99537 | 11349 | 99354 | 13081 | 99141 | 14810 | 98897 | 16533 | 98624 | 29 | 2 |
| 15 | 32 | 09642 | 99534 | 11378 | 99351 | 13110 | 99137 | 14838 | 98893 | 16562 | 98619 | 28 | 2 |
| 16 | 33 | 09671 | 99531 | 11407 | 99347 | 13139 | 99133 | 14867 | 98889 | 16591 | 98614 | 27 | 2 |
| 16 | 34 | 09700 | 99528 | 11436 | 99344 | 13168 | 99129 | 14896 | 98884 | 16620 | 98609 | 26 | 2 |
| 17 | 35 | 09729 | 99526 | 11465 | 99341 | 13197 | 99125 | 14925 | 98880 | 16648 | 98604 | 25 | 2 |
| 17 | 36 | 09758 | 99523 | 11494 | 99337 | 13226 | 99122 | 14954 | 98876 | 16677 | 98600 | 24 | 2 |
| 18 | 37 | 09787 | 99520 | 11523 | 99334 | 13254 | 99118 | 14982 | 98871 | 16706 | 98595 | 23 | 2 |
| 18 | 38 | 09816 | 99517 | 11552 | 99331 | 13283 | 99114 | 15011 | 98867 | 16734 | 98590 | 22 | 1 |
| 19 | 39 | 09845 | 99514 | 11580 | 99327 | 13312 | 99110 | 15040 | 98863 | 16763 | 98585 | 21 | 1 |
| 19 | 40 | 09874 | 99511 | 11609 | 99324 | 13341 | 99106 | 15069 | 98858 | 16792 | 98580 | 20 | 1 |
| 20 | 41 | 09903 | 99508 | 11638 | 99320 | 13370 | 99102 | 15097 | 98854 | 16820 | 98575 | 19 | 1 |
| 20 | 42 | 09932 | 99506 | 11667 | 99317 | 13399 | 99098 | 15126 | 98849 | 16849 | 98570 | 18 | 1 |
| 21 | 43 | 09961 | 99503 | 11696 | 99314 | 13427 | 99094 | 15155 | 98845 | 16878 | 98565 | 17 | 1 |
| 21 | 44 | 09990 | 99500 | 11725 | 99310 | 13456 | 99091 | 15184 | 98841 | 16906 | 98561 | 16 | 1 |
| 22 | 45 | 10019 | 99497 | 11754 | 99307 | 13485 | 99087 | 15212 | 98836 | 16935 | 98556 | 15 | 1 |
| 22 | 46 | 10048 | 99494 | 11783 | 99303 | 13514 | 99083 | 15241 | 98832 | 16964 | 98551 | 14 | 1 |
| 23 | 47 | 10077 | 99491 | 11812 | 99300 | 13543 | 99079 | 15270 | 98827 | 16992 | 98546 | 13 | 1 |
| 23 | 48 | 10106 | 99488 | 11840 | 99297 | 13572 | 99075 | 15299 | 98823 | 17021 | 98541 | 12 | 1 |
| 24 | 49 | 10135 | 99485 | 11869 | 99293 | 13600 | 99071 | 15327 | 98818 | 17050 | 98536 | 11 | 1 |
| 24 | 50 | 10164 | 99482 | 11898 | 99290 | 13629 | 99067 | 15356 | 98814 | 17078 | 98531 | 10 | 1 |
| 25 | 51 | 10192 | 99479 | 11927 | 99286 | 13658 | 99063 | 15385 | 98809 | 17107 | 98526 | 9 | 1 |
| 25 | 52 | 10221 | 99476 | 11956 | 99283 | 13687 | 99059 | 15414 | 98805 | 17136 | 98521 | 8 | 1 |
| 26 | 53 | 10250 | 99473 | 11985 | 99279 | 13716 | 99055 | 15442 | 98800 | 17164 | 98516 | 7 | 0 |
| 26 | 54 | 10279 | 99470 | 12014 | 99276 | 13744 | 99051 | 15471 | 98796 | 17193 | 98511 | 6 | 0 |
| 27 | 55 | 10308 | 99467 | 12043 | 99272 | 13773 | 99047 | 15500 | 98791 | 17222 | 98506 | 5 | 0 |
| 27 | 56 | 10337 | 99464 | 12071 | 99269 | 13802 | 99043 | 15529 | 98787 | 17250 | 98501 | 4 | 0 |
| 28 | 57 | 10366 | 99461 | 12100 | 99265 | 13831 | 99039 | 15557 | 98782 | 17279 | 98496 | 3 | 0 |
| 28 | 58 | 10395 | 99458 | 12129 | 99262 | 13860 | 99035 | 15586 | 98778 | 17308 | 98491 | 2 | 0 |
| 29 | 59 | 10424 | 99455 | 12158 | 99258 | 13889 | 99031 | 15615 | 98773 | 17336 | 98486 | 1 | 0 |
| 29 | 60 | 10453 | 99452 | 12187 | 99255 | 13917 | 99027 | 15643 | 98769 | 17365 | 98481 | 0 | 0 |
| | | N. cos. | N. sine. | N. cos. | N. sine. | N. cos. | N. sine. | N. cos. | N. sine. | N. cos. | N. sine. | M | |
| | | 84° | | 83° | | 82° | | 81° | | 80° | | | |

# TABLE XXIV.

## Of Natural Sines.

| Prop. parts 28 | M | 10° N. sine. | 10° N. cos. | 11° N. sine. | 11° N. cos. | 12° N. sine. | 12° N. cos. | 13° N. sine. | 13° N. cos. | 14° N. sine. | 14° N. cos. | | Prop. parts 6 |
|---|---|---|---|---|---|---|---|---|---|---|---|---|---|
| 0 | 0 | 17365 | 98481 | 19081 | 98163 | 20791 | 97815 | 22495 | 97437 | 24192 | 97030 | 60 | 6 |
| 0 | 1 | 17393 | 98476 | 19109 | 98157 | 20820 | 97809 | 22523 | 97430 | 24220 | 97023 | 59 | 6 |
| 1 | 2 | 17422 | 98471 | 19138 | 98152 | 20848 | 97803 | 22552 | 97424 | 24249 | 97015 | 58 | 6 |
| 1 | 3 | 17451 | 98466 | 19167 | 98146 | 20877 | 97797 | 22580 | 97417 | 24277 | 97008 | 57 | 6 |
| 2 | 4 | 17479 | 98461 | 19195 | 98140 | 20905 | 97791 | 22608 | 97411 | 24305 | 97001 | 56 | 6 |
| 2 | 5 | 17508 | 98455 | 19224 | 98135 | 20933 | 97784 | 22637 | 97404 | 24333 | 96994 | 55 | 6 |
| 3 | 6 | 17537 | 98450 | 19252 | 98129 | 20962 | 97778 | 22665 | 97398 | 24362 | 96987 | 54 | 5 |
| 3 | 7 | 17565 | 98445 | 19281 | 98124 | 20990 | 97772 | 22693 | 97391 | 24390 | 96980 | 53 | 5 |
| 4 | 8 | 17594 | 98440 | 19309 | 98118 | 21019 | 97766 | 22722 | 97384 | 24418 | 96973 | 52 | 5 |
| 4 | 9 | 17623 | 98435 | 19338 | 98112 | 21047 | 97760 | 22750 | 97378 | 24446 | 96966 | 51 | 5 |
| 5 | 10 | 17651 | 98430 | 19366 | 98107 | 21076 | 97754 | 22778 | 97371 | 24474 | 96959 | 50 | 5 |
| 5 | 11 | 17680 | 98425 | 19395 | 98101 | 21104 | 97748 | 22807 | 97365 | 24503 | 96952 | 49 | 5 |
| 6 | 12 | 17708 | 98420 | 19423 | 98096 | 21132 | 97742 | 22835 | 97358 | 24531 | 96945 | 48 | 5 |
| 6 | 13 | 17737 | 98414 | 19452 | 98090 | 21161 | 97735 | 22863 | 97351 | 24559 | 96937 | 47 | 5 |
| 7 | 14 | 17766 | 98409 | 19481 | 98084 | 21189 | 97729 | 22892 | 97345 | 24587 | 96930 | 46 | 5 |
| 7 | 15 | 17794 | 98404 | 19509 | 98079 | 21218 | 97723 | 22920 | 97338 | 24615 | 96923 | 45 | 5 |
| 7 | 16 | 17823 | 98399 | 19538 | 98073 | 21246 | 97717 | 22948 | 97331 | 24644 | 96916 | 44 | 4 |
| 8 | 17 | 17852 | 98394 | 19566 | 98067 | 21275 | 97711 | 22977 | 97325 | 24672 | 96909 | 43 | 4 |
| 8 | 18 | 17880 | 98389 | 19595 | 98061 | 21303 | 97705 | 23005 | 97318 | 24700 | 96902 | 42 | 4 |
| 9 | 19 | 17909 | 98383 | 19623 | 98056 | 21331 | 97698 | 23033 | 97311 | 24728 | 96894 | 41 | 4 |
| 9 | 20 | 17937 | 98378 | 19652 | 98050 | 21360 | 97692 | 23062 | 97304 | 24756 | 96887 | 40 | 4 |
| 10 | 21 | 17966 | 98373 | 19680 | 98044 | 21388 | 97686 | 23090 | 97298 | 24784 | 96880 | 39 | 4 |
| 10 | 22 | 17995 | 98368 | 19709 | 98039 | 21417 | 97680 | 23118 | 97291 | 24813 | 96873 | 38 | 4 |
| 11 | 23 | 18023 | 98362 | 19737 | 98033 | 21445 | 97673 | 23146 | 97284 | 24841 | 96866 | 37 | 4 |
| 11 | 24 | 18052 | 98357 | 19766 | 98027 | 21474 | 97667 | 23175 | 97278 | 24869 | 96858 | 36 | 4 |
| 12 | 25 | 18081 | 98352 | 19794 | 98021 | 21502 | 97661 | 23203 | 97271 | 24897 | 96851 | 35 | 4 |
| 12 | 26 | 18109 | 98347 | 19823 | 98016 | 21530 | 97655 | 23231 | 97264 | 24925 | 96844 | 34 | 3 |
| 13 | 27 | 18138 | 98341 | 19851 | 98010 | 21559 | 97648 | 23260 | 97257 | 24954 | 96837 | 33 | 3 |
| 13 | 28 | 18166 | 98336 | 19880 | 98004 | 21587 | 97642 | 23288 | 97251 | 24982 | 96829 | 32 | 3 |
| 14 | 29 | 18195 | 98331 | 19908 | 97998 | 21616 | 97636 | 23316 | 97244 | 25010 | 96822 | 31 | 3 |
| 14 | 30 | 18224 | 98325 | 19937 | 97992 | 21644 | 97630 | 23345 | 97237 | 25038 | 96815 | 30 | 3 |
| 14 | 31 | 18252 | 98320 | 19965 | 97987 | 21672 | 97623 | 23373 | 97230 | 25066 | 96807 | 29 | 3 |
| 15 | 32 | 18281 | 98315 | 19994 | 97981 | 21701 | 97617 | 23401 | 97223 | 25094 | 96800 | 28 | 3 |
| 15 | 33 | 18309 | 98310 | 20022 | 97975 | 21729 | 97611 | 23429 | 97217 | 25122 | 96793 | 27 | 3 |
| 16 | 34 | 18338 | 98304 | 20051 | 97969 | 21758 | 97604 | 23458 | 97210 | 25151 | 96786 | 26 | 3 |
| 16 | 35 | 18367 | 98299 | 20079 | 97963 | 21786 | 97598 | 23486 | 97203 | 25179 | 96778 | 25 | 3 |
| 17 | 36 | 18395 | 98294 | 20108 | 97958 | 21814 | 97592 | 23514 | 97196 | 25207 | 96771 | 24 | 2 |
| 17 | 37 | 18424 | 98288 | 20136 | 97952 | 21843 | 97585 | 23542 | 97189 | 25235 | 96764 | 23 | 2 |
| 18 | 38 | 18452 | 98283 | 20165 | 97946 | 21871 | 97579 | 23571 | 97182 | 25263 | 96756 | 22 | 2 |
| 18 | 39 | 18481 | 98277 | 20193 | 97940 | 21899 | 97573 | 23599 | 97176 | 25291 | 96749 | 21 | 2 |
| 19 | 40 | 18509 | 98272 | 20222 | 97934 | 21928 | 97566 | 23627 | 97169 | 25320 | 96742 | 20 | 2 |
| 19 | 41 | 18538 | 98267 | 20250 | 97928 | 21985 | 97553 | 23684 | 97155 | 25376 | 96727 | 18 | 2 |
| 20 | 42 | 18567 | 98261 | 20279 | 97922 | 21956 | 97560 | 23656 | 97162 | 25348 | 96734 | 19 | 2 |
| 20 | 43 | 18595 | 98256 | 20307 | 97916 | 22013 | 97547 | 23712 | 97148 | 25404 | 96719 | 17 | 2 |
| 21 | 44 | 18624 | 98250 | 20336 | 97910 | 22041 | 97541 | 23740 | 97141 | 25432 | 96712 | 16 | 2 |
| 21 | 45 | 18652 | 98245 | 20364 | 97905 | 22070 | 97534 | 23769 | 97134 | 25460 | 96705 | 15 | 2 |
| 21 | 46 | 18681 | 98240 | 20393 | 97899 | 22098 | 97528 | 23797 | 97127 | 25488 | 96697 | 14 | 1 |
| 22 | 47 | 18710 | 98234 | 20421 | 97893 | 22126 | 97521 | 23825 | 97120 | 25516 | 96690 | 13 | 1 |
| 22 | 48 | 18738 | 98229 | 20450 | 97887 | 22155 | 97515 | 23853 | 97113 | 25545 | 96682 | 12 | 1 |
| 23 | 49 | 18767 | 98223 | 20478 | 97881 | 22183 | 97508 | 23882 | 97106 | 25573 | 96675 | 11 | 1 |
| 23 | 50 | 18795 | 98218 | 20507 | 97875 | 22212 | 97502 | 23910 | 97100 | 25601 | 96667 | 10 | 1 |
| 24 | 51 | 18824 | 98212 | 20535 | 97869 | 22240 | 97496 | 23938 | 97093 | 25629 | 96660 | 9 | 1 |
| 24 | 52 | 18852 | 98207 | 20563 | 97863 | 22268 | 97489 | 23966 | 97086 | 25657 | 96653 | 8 | 1 |
| 25 | 53 | 18881 | 98201 | 20592 | 97857 | 22297 | 97483 | 23995 | 97079 | 25685 | 96645 | 7 | 1 |
| 25 | 54 | 18910 | 98196 | 20620 | 97851 | 22325 | 97476 | 24023 | 97072 | 25713 | 96638 | 6 | 1 |
| 26 | 55 | 18938 | 98190 | 20649 | 97845 | 22353 | 97470 | 24051 | 97065 | 25741 | 96630 | 5 | 1 |
| 26 | 56 | 18967 | 98185 | 20677 | 97839 | 22382 | 97463 | 24079 | 97058 | 25769 | 96623 | 4 | 0 |
| 27 | 57 | 18995 | 98179 | 20706 | 97833 | 22410 | 97457 | 24108 | 97051 | 25798 | 96615 | 3 | 0 |
| 27 | 58 | 19024 | 98174 | 20734 | 97827 | 22438 | 97450 | 24136 | 97044 | 25826 | 96608 | 2 | 0 |
| 28 | 59 | 19052 | 98168 | 20763 | 97821 | 22467 | 97444 | 24164 | 97037 | 25854 | 96600 | 1 | 0 |
| 28 | 60 | 19081 | 98163 | 20791 | 97815 | 22495 | 97437 | 24192 | 97030 | 25882 | 96593 | 0 | 0 |
| | | N. cos. | N. sine. | N. cos. | N. sine. | N. cos. | N. sine. | N. cos. | N. sine. | N. cos. | N. sine. | M | |
| | | 79° | | 78° | | 77° | | 76° | | 75° | | | |

# TABLE XXIV.

## Of Natural Sines.

| Prop. parts | | 15° | | 16° | | 17° | | 18° | | 19° | | | Prop. parts |
|---|---|---|---|---|---|---|---|---|---|---|---|---|---|
| 27 | M | N. sine. | N. cos. | N. sine. | N. cos. | N. sine. | N. cos. | N. sine. | N. cos. | N. sine. | N. cos. | | 9 |
| 0 | 0 | 25882 | 96593 | 27564 | 96126 | 29237 | 95630 | 30902 | 95106 | 32557 | 94552 | 60 | 9 |
| 0 | 1 | 25910 | 96585 | 27592 | 96118 | 29265 | 95622 | 30929 | 95097 | 32584 | 94542 | 59 | 9 |
| 1 | 2 | 25938 | 96578 | 27620 | 96110 | 29293 | 95613 | 30957 | 95088 | 32612 | 94533 | 58 | 9 |
| 1 | 3 | 25966 | 96570 | 27648 | 96102 | 29321 | 95605 | 30985 | 95079 | 32639 | 94523 | 57 | 9 |
| 2 | 4 | 25994 | 96562 | 27676 | 96094 | 29348 | 95596 | 31012 | 95070 | 32667 | 94514 | 56 | 8 |
| 2 | 5 | 26022 | 96555 | 27704 | 96086 | 29376 | 95588 | 31040 | 95061 | 32694 | 94504 | 55 | 8 |
| 3 | 6 | 26050 | 96547 | 27731 | 96078 | 29404 | 95579 | 31068 | 95052 | 32722 | 94495 | 54 | 8 |
| 3 | 7 | 26079 | 96540 | 27759 | 96070 | 29432 | 95571 | 31095 | 95043 | 32749 | 94485 | 53 | 8 |
| 4 | 8 | 26107 | 96532 | 27787 | 96062 | 29460 | 95562 | 31123 | 95033 | 32777 | 94476 | 52 | 8 |
| 4 | 9 | 26135 | 96524 | 27815 | 96054 | 29487 | 95554 | 31151 | 95024 | 32804 | 94466 | 51 | 8 |
| 5 | 10 | 26163 | 96517 | 27843 | 96046 | 29515 | 95545 | 31178 | 95015 | 32832 | 94457 | 50 | 8 |
| 5 | 11 | 26191 | 96509 | 27871 | 96037 | 29543 | 95536 | 31206 | 95006 | 32859 | 94447 | 49 | 7 |
| 5 | 12 | 26219 | 96502 | 27899 | 96029 | 29571 | 95528 | 31233 | 94997 | 32887 | 94438 | 48 | 7 |
| 6 | 13 | 26247 | 96494 | 27927 | 96021 | 29599 | 95519 | 31261 | 94988 | 32914 | 94428 | 47 | 7 |
| 6 | 14 | 26275 | 96486 | 27955 | 96013 | 29626 | 95511 | 31289 | 94979 | 32942 | 94418 | 46 | 7 |
| 7 | 15 | 26303 | 96479 | 27983 | 96005 | 29654 | 95502 | 31316 | 94970 | 32969 | 94409 | 45 | 7 |
| 7 | 16 | 26331 | 96471 | 28011 | 95997 | 29682 | 95493 | 31344 | 94961 | 32997 | 94399 | 44 | 7 |
| 8 | 17 | 26359 | 96463 | 28039 | 95989 | 29710 | 95485 | 31372 | 94952 | 33024 | 94390 | 43 | 6 |
| 8 | 18 | 26387 | 96456 | 28067 | 95981 | 29737 | 95476 | 31399 | 94943 | 33051 | 94380 | 42 | 6 |
| 9 | 19 | 26415 | 96448 | 28095 | 95972 | 29765 | 95467 | 31427 | 94933 | 33079 | 94370 | 41 | 6 |
| 9 | 20 | 26443 | 96440 | 28123 | 95964 | 29793 | 95459 | 31454 | 94924 | 33106 | 94361 | 40 | 6 |
| 9 | 21 | 26471 | 96433 | 28150 | 95956 | 29821 | 95450 | 31482 | 94915 | 33134 | 94351 | 39 | 6 |
| 10 | 22 | 26500 | 96425 | 28178 | 95948 | 29849 | 95441 | 31510 | 94906 | 33161 | 94342 | 38 | 6 |
| 10 | 23 | 26528 | 96417 | 28206 | 95940 | 29876 | 95433 | 31537 | 94897 | 33189 | 94332 | 37 | 6 |
| 11 | 24 | 26556 | 96410 | 28234 | 95931 | 29904 | 95424 | 31565 | 94888 | 33216 | 94322 | 36 | 5 |
| 11 | 25 | 26584 | 96402 | 28262 | 95923 | 29932 | 95415 | 31593 | 94878 | 33244 | 94313 | 35 | 5 |
| 12 | 26 | 26612 | 96394 | 28290 | 95915 | 29960 | 95407 | 31620 | 94869 | 33271 | 94303 | 34 | 5 |
| 12 | 27 | 26640 | 96386 | 28318 | 95907 | 29987 | 95398 | 31648 | 94860 | 33298 | 94293 | 33 | 5 |
| 13 | 28 | 26668 | 96379 | 28346 | 95898 | 30015 | 95389 | 31675 | 94851 | 33326 | 94284 | 32 | 5 |
| 13 | 29 | 26696 | 96371 | 28374 | 95890 | 30043 | 95380 | 31703 | 94842 | 33353 | 94274 | 31 | 5 |
| 14 | 30 | 26724 | 96363 | 28402 | 95882 | 30071 | 95372 | 31730 | 94832 | 33381 | 94264 | 30 | 5 |
| 14 | 31 | 26752 | 96355 | 28429 | 95874 | 30098 | 95363 | 31758 | 94823 | 33408 | 94254 | 29 | 4 |
| 14 | 32 | 26780 | 96347 | 28457 | 95865 | 30126 | 95354 | 31786 | 94814 | 33436 | 94245 | 28 | 4 |
| 15 | 33 | 26808 | 96340 | 28485 | 95857 | 30154 | 95345 | 31813 | 94805 | 33463 | 94235 | 27 | 4 |
| 15 | 34 | 26836 | 96332 | 28513 | 95849 | 30182 | 95337 | 31841 | 94795 | 33490 | 94225 | 26 | 4 |
| 16 | 35 | 26864 | 96324 | 28541 | 95841 | 30209 | 95328 | 31868 | 94786 | 33518 | 94215 | 25 | 4 |
| 16 | 36 | 26892 | 96316 | 28569 | 95832 | 30237 | 95319 | 31896 | 94777 | 33545 | 94206 | 24 | 4 |
| 17 | 37 | 26920 | 96308 | 28597 | 95824 | 30265 | 95310 | 31923 | 94768 | 33573 | 94196 | 23 | 3 |
| 17 | 38 | 26948 | 96301 | 28625 | 95816 | 30292 | 95301 | 31951 | 94758 | 33600 | 94186 | 22 | 3 |
| 18 | 39 | 26976 | 96293 | 28652 | 95807 | 30320 | 95293 | 31979 | 94749 | 33627 | 94176 | 21 | 3 |
| 18 | 40 | 27004 | 96285 | 28680 | 95799 | 30348 | 95284 | 32006 | 94740 | 33655 | 94167 | 20 | 3 |
| 18 | 41 | 27032 | 96277 | 28708 | 95791 | 30376 | 95275 | 32034 | 94730 | 33682 | 94157 | 19 | 3 |
| 19 | 42 | 27060 | 96269 | 28736 | 95782 | 30403 | 95266 | 32061 | 94721 | 33710 | 94147 | 18 | 3 |
| 19 | 43 | 27088 | 96261 | 28764 | 95774 | 30431 | 95257 | 32089 | 94712 | 33737 | 94137 | 17 | 3 |
| 20 | 44 | 27116 | 96253 | 28792 | 95766 | 30459 | 95248 | 32116 | 94702 | 33764 | 94127 | 16 | 2 |
| 20 | 45 | 27144 | 96246 | 28820 | 95757 | 30486 | 95240 | 32144 | 94693 | 33792 | 94118 | 15 | 2 |
| 21 | 46 | 27172 | 96238 | 28847 | 95749 | 30514 | 95231 | 32171 | 94684 | 33819 | 94108 | 14 | 2 |
| 21 | 47 | 27200 | 96230 | 28875 | 95740 | 30542 | 95222 | 32199 | 94674 | 33846 | 94098 | 13 | 2 |
| 22 | 48 | 27228 | 96222 | 28903 | 95732 | 30570 | 95213 | 32227 | 94665 | 33874 | 94088 | 12 | 2 |
| 22 | 49 | 27256 | 96214 | 28931 | 95724 | 30597 | 95204 | 32254 | 94656 | 33901 | 94078 | 11 | 2 |
| 23 | 50 | 27284 | 96206 | 28959 | 95715 | 30625 | 95195 | 32282 | 94646 | 33929 | 94068 | 10 | 2 |
| 23 | 51 | 27312 | 96198 | 28987 | 95707 | 30653 | 95186 | 32309 | 94637 | 33956 | 94058 | 9 | 1 |
| 23 | 52 | 27340 | 96190 | 29015 | 95698 | 30680 | 95177 | 32337 | 94627 | 33983 | 94049 | 8 | 1 |
| 24 | 53 | 27368 | 96182 | 29042 | 95690 | 30708 | 95168 | 32364 | 94618 | 34011 | 94039 | 7 | 1 |
| 24 | 54 | 27396 | 96174 | 29070 | 95681 | 30736 | 95159 | 32392 | 94609 | 34038 | 94029 | 6 | 1 |
| 25 | 55 | 27424 | 96166 | 29098 | 95673 | 30763 | 95150 | 32419 | 94599 | 34065 | 94019 | 5 | 1 |
| 25 | 56 | 27452 | 96158 | 29126 | 95664 | 30791 | 95142 | 32447 | 94590 | 34093 | 94009 | 4 | 1 |
| 26 | 57 | 27480 | 96150 | 29154 | 95656 | 30819 | 95133 | 32474 | 94580 | 34120 | 93999 | 3 | 0 |
| 26 | 58 | 27508 | 96142 | 29182 | 95647 | 30846 | 95124 | 32502 | 94571 | 34147 | 93989 | 2 | 0 |
| 27 | 59 | 27536 | 96134 | 29209 | 95639 | 30874 | 95115 | 32529 | 94561 | 34175 | 93979 | 1 | 0 |
| 27 | 60 | 27564 | 96126 | 29237 | 95630 | 30902 | 95106 | 32557 | 94552 | 34202 | 93969 | 0 | 0 |
| | | N. cos. | N. sine. | N. cos. | N. sine. | N. cos. | N. sine. | N. cos. | N. sine. | N. cos. | N. sine. | M | |
| | | 74° | | 73° | | 72° | | 71° | | 70° | | | |

# TABLE XXIV.

## Of Natural Sines.

| Prop. parts 27 | M | 20° N. sine. | 20° N. cos. | 21° N. sine. | 21° N. cos. | 22° N. sine. | 22° N. cos. | 23° N. sine. | 23° N. cos. | 24° N. sine. | 24° N. cos. | | Prop. parts 11 |
|---|---|---|---|---|---|---|---|---|---|---|---|---|---|
| 0 | 0 | 34202 | 93969 | 35837 | 93358 | 37461 | 92718 | 39073 | 92050 | 40674 | 91355 | 60 | 11 |
| 0 | 1 | 34229 | 93959 | 35864 | 93348 | 37488 | 92707 | 39100 | 92039 | 40700 | 91343 | 59 | 11 |
| 1 | 2 | 34257 | 93949 | 35891 | 93337 | 37515 | 92697 | 39127 | 92028 | 40727 | 91331 | 58 | 11 |
| 1 | 3 | 34284 | 93939 | 35918 | 93327 | 37542 | 92686 | 39153 | 92016 | 40753 | 91319 | 57 | 10 |
| 2 | 4 | 34311 | 93929 | 35945 | 93316 | 37569 | 92675 | 39180 | 92005 | 40780 | 91307 | 56 | 10 |
| 2 | 5 | 34339 | 93919 | 35973 | 93306 | 37595 | 92664 | 39207 | 91994 | 40806 | 91295 | 55 | 10 |
| 3 | 6 | 34366 | 93909 | 36000 | 93295 | 37622 | 92653 | 39234 | 91982 | 40833 | 91283 | 54 | 10 |
| 3 | 7 | 34393 | 93899 | 36027 | 93285 | 37649 | 92642 | 39260 | 91971 | 40860 | 91272 | 53 | 10 |
| 4 | 8 | 34421 | 93889 | 36054 | 93274 | 37676 | 92631 | 39287 | 91959 | 40886 | 91260 | 52 | 10 |
| 4 | 9 | 34448 | 93879 | 36081 | 93264 | 37703 | 92620 | 39314 | 91948 | 40913 | 91248 | 51 | 9 |
| 5 | 10 | 34475 | 93869 | 36108 | 93253 | 37730 | 92609 | 39341 | 91936 | 40939 | 91236 | 50 | 9 |
| 5 | 11 | 34503 | 93859 | 36135 | 93243 | 37757 | 92598 | 39367 | 91925 | 40966 | 91224 | 49 | 9 |
| 5 | 12 | 34530 | 93849 | 36162 | 93232 | 37784 | 92587 | 39394 | 91914 | 40992 | 91212 | 48 | 9 |
| 6 | 13 | 34557 | 93839 | 36190 | 93222 | 37811 | 92576 | 39421 | 91902 | 41019 | 91200 | 47 | 9 |
| 6 | 14 | 34584 | 93829 | 36217 | 93211 | 37838 | 92565 | 39448 | 91891 | 41045 | 91188 | 46 | 8 |
| 7 | 15 | 34612 | 93819 | 36244 | 93201 | 37865 | 92554 | 39474 | 91879 | 41072 | 91176 | 45 | 8 |
| 7 | 16 | 34639 | 93809 | 36271 | 93190 | 37892 | 92543 | 39501 | 91868 | 41098 | 91164 | 44 | 8 |
| 8 | 17 | 34666 | 93799 | 36298 | 93180 | 37919 | 92532 | 39528 | 91856 | 41125 | 91152 | 43 | 8 |
| 8 | 18 | 34694 | 93789 | 36325 | 93169 | 37946 | 92521 | 39555 | 91845 | 41151 | 91140 | 42 | 8 |
| 9 | 19 | 34721 | 93779 | 36352 | 93159 | 37973 | 92510 | 39581 | 91833 | 41178 | 91128 | 41 | 8 |
| 9 | 20 | 34748 | 93769 | 36379 | 93148 | 37999 | 92499 | 39608 | 91822 | 41204 | 91116 | 40 | 7 |
| 9 | 21 | 34775 | 93759 | 36406 | 93137 | 38026 | 92488 | 39635 | 91810 | 41231 | 91104 | 39 | 7 |
| 10 | 22 | 34803 | 93748 | 36434 | 93127 | 38053 | 92477 | 39661 | 91799 | 41257 | 91092 | 38 | 7 |
| 10 | 23 | 34830 | 93738 | 36461 | 93116 | 38080 | 92466 | 39688 | 91787 | 41284 | 91080 | 37 | 7 |
| 11 | 24 | 34857 | 93728 | 36488 | 93106 | 38107 | 92455 | 39715 | 91775 | 41310 | 91068 | 36 | 7 |
| 11 | 25 | 34884 | 93718 | 36515 | 93095 | 38134 | 92444 | 39741 | 91764 | 41337 | 91056 | 35 | 6 |
| 12 | 26 | 34912 | 93708 | 36542 | 93084 | 38161 | 92432 | 39768 | 91752 | 41363 | 91044 | 34 | 6 |
| 12 | 27 | 34939 | 93698 | 36569 | 93074 | 38188 | 92421 | 39795 | 91741 | 41390 | 91032 | 33 | 6 |
| 13 | 28 | 34966 | 93688 | 36596 | 93063 | 38215 | 92410 | 39822 | 91729 | 41416 | 91020 | 32 | 6 |
| 13 | 29 | 34993 | 93677 | 36623 | 93052 | 38241 | 92399 | 39848 | 91718 | 41443 | 91008 | 31 | 6 |
| 14 | 30 | 35021 | 93667 | 36650 | 93042 | 38268 | 92388 | 39875 | 91706 | 41469 | 90996 | 30 | 6 |
| 14 | 31 | 35048 | 93657 | 36677 | 93031 | 38295 | 92377 | 39902 | 91694 | 41496 | 90984 | 29 | 5 |
| 14 | 32 | 35075 | 93647 | 36704 | 93020 | 38322 | 92366 | 39928 | 91683 | 41522 | 90972 | 28 | 5 |
| 15 | 33 | 35102 | 93637 | 36731 | 93010 | 38349 | 92355 | 39955 | 91671 | 41549 | 90960 | 27 | 5 |
| 15 | 34 | 35130 | 93626 | 36758 | 92999 | 38376 | 92343 | 39982 | 91660 | 41575 | 90948 | 26 | 5 |
| 16 | 35 | 35157 | 93616 | 36785 | 92988 | 38403 | 92332 | 40008 | 91648 | 41602 | 90936 | 25 | 5 |
| 16 | 36 | 35184 | 93606 | 36812 | 92978 | 38430 | 92321 | 40035 | 91636 | 41628 | 90924 | 24 | 4 |
| 17 | 37 | 35211 | 93596 | 36839 | 92967 | 38456 | 92310 | 40062 | 91625 | 41655 | 90911 | 23 | 4 |
| 17 | 38 | 35239 | 93585 | 36867 | 92956 | 38483 | 92299 | 40088 | 91613 | 41681 | 90899 | 22 | 4 |
| 18 | 39 | 35266 | 93575 | 36894 | 92945 | 38510 | 92287 | 40115 | 91601 | 41707 | 90887 | 21 | 4 |
| 18 | 40 | 35293 | 93565 | 36921 | 92935 | 38537 | 92276 | 40141 | 91590 | 41734 | 90875 | 20 | 4 |
| 18 | 41 | 35320 | 93555 | 36948 | 92924 | 38564 | 92265 | 40168 | 91578 | 41760 | 90863 | 19 | 3 |
| 19 | 42 | 35347 | 93544 | 36975 | 92913 | 38591 | 92254 | 40195 | 91566 | 41787 | 90851 | 18 | 3 |
| 19 | 43 | 35375 | 93534 | 37002 | 92902 | 38617 | 92243 | 40221 | 91555 | 41813 | 90839 | 17 | 3 |
| 20 | 44 | 35402 | 93524 | 37029 | 92892 | 38644 | 92231 | 40248 | 91543 | 41840 | 90826 | 16 | 3 |
| 20 | 45 | 35429 | 93514 | 37056 | 92881 | 38671 | 92220 | 40275 | 91531 | 41866 | 90814 | 15 | 3 |
| 21 | 46 | 35456 | 93503 | 37083 | 92870 | 38698 | 92209 | 40301 | 91519 | 41892 | 90802 | 14 | 3 |
| 21 | 47 | 35484 | 93493 | 37110 | 92859 | 38725 | 92198 | 40328 | 91508 | 41919 | 90790 | 13 | 2 |
| 22 | 48 | 35511 | 93483 | 37137 | 92849 | 38752 | 92186 | 40355 | 91496 | 41945 | 90778 | 12 | 2 |
| 22 | 49 | 35538 | 93472 | 37164 | 92838 | 38778 | 92175 | 40381 | 91484 | 41972 | 90766 | 11 | 2 |
| 23 | 50 | 35565 | 93462 | 37191 | 92827 | 38805 | 92164 | 40408 | 91472 | 41998 | 90753 | 10 | 2 |
| 23 | 51 | 35592 | 93452 | 37218 | 92816 | 38832 | 92152 | 40434 | 91461 | 42024 | 90741 | 9 | 2 |
| 23 | 52 | 35619 | 93441 | 37245 | 92805 | 38859 | 92141 | 40461 | 91449 | 42051 | 90729 | 8 | 1 |
| 24 | 53 | 35647 | 93431 | 37272 | 92794 | 38886 | 92130 | 40488 | 91437 | 42077 | 90717 | 7 | 1 |
| 24 | 54 | 35674 | 93420 | 37299 | 92784 | 38912 | 92119 | 40514 | 91425 | 42104 | 90704 | 6 | 1 |
| 25 | 55 | 3570[illegible] | 93410 | 37326 | 92773 | 38939 | 92107 | 40541 | 91414 | 42130 | 90692 | 5 | 1 |
| 25 | 56 | 35728 | 93400 | 37353 | 92762 | 38966 | 92096 | 40567 | 91402 | 42156 | 90680 | 4 | 1 |
| 26 | 57 | 35755 | 93389 | 37380 | 92751 | 38993 | 92085 | 40594 | 91390 | 42183 | 90668 | 3 | 1 |
| 26 | 58 | 35782 | 93379 | 37407 | 92740 | 39020 | 92073 | 40621 | 91378 | 42209 | 90655 | 2 | 0 |
| 27 | 59 | 35810 | 93368 | 37434 | 92729 | 39046 | 92062 | 40647 | 91366 | 42235 | 90643 | 1 | 0 |
| 27 | 60 | 35837 | 93358 | 37461 | 92718 | 39073 | 92050 | 40674 | 91355 | 42262 | 90631 | 0 | 0 |
| | | N. cos. | N. sine. | N. cos. | N. sine. | N. cos. | N. sine. | N. cos. | N. sine. | N. cos. | N. sine. | M | |
| | | 69° | | 68° | | 67° | | 66° | | 65° | | | |

# TABLE XXIV.

## Of Natural Sines.

| Prop. parts 26 | M | 25° N. sine. | 25° N. cos. | 26° N. sine. | 26° N. cos. | 27° N. sine. | 27° N. cos. | 28° N. sine. | 28° N. cos. | 29° N. sine. | 29° N. cos. | | Prop. parts 14 |
|---|---|---|---|---|---|---|---|---|---|---|---|---|---|
| 0 | 0 | 42262 | 90631 | 43837 | 89879 | 45399 | 89101 | 46947 | 88295 | 48481 | 87462 | 60 | 14 |
| 0 | 1 | 42288 | 90618 | 43863 | 89867 | 45425 | 89087 | 46973 | 88281 | 48506 | 87448 | 59 | 14 |
| 1 | 2 | 42315 | 90606 | 43889 | 89854 | 45451 | 89074 | 46999 | 88267 | 48532 | 87434 | 58 | 14 |
| 1 | 3 | 42341 | 90594 | 43916 | 89841 | 45477 | 89061 | 47024 | 88254 | 48557 | 87420 | 57 | 13 |
| 2 | 4 | 42367 | 90582 | 43942 | 89828 | 45503 | 89048 | 47050 | 88240 | 48583 | 87406 | 56 | 13 |
| 2 | 5 | 42394 | 90569 | 43968 | 89816 | 45529 | 89035 | 47076 | 88226 | 48608 | 87391 | 55 | 13 |
| 3 | 6 | 42420 | 90557 | 43994 | 89803 | 45554 | 89021 | 47101 | 88213 | 48634 | 87377 | 54 | 13 |
| 3 | 7 | 42446 | 90545 | 44020 | 89790 | 45580 | 89008 | 47127 | 88199 | 48659 | 87363 | 53 | 12 |
| 3 | 8 | 42473 | 90532 | 44046 | 89777 | 45606 | 88995 | 47153 | 88185 | 48684 | 87349 | 52 | 12 |
| 4 | 9 | 42499 | 90520 | 44072 | 89764 | 45632 | 88981 | 47178 | 88172 | 48710 | 87335 | 51 | 12 |
| 4 | 10 | 42525 | 90507 | 44098 | 89752 | 45658 | 88968 | 47204 | 88158 | 48735 | 87321 | 50 | 12 |
| 5 | 11 | 42552 | 90495 | 44124 | 89739 | 45684 | 88955 | 47229 | 88144 | 48761 | 87306 | 49 | 11 |
| 5 | 12 | 42578 | 90483 | 44151 | 89726 | 45710 | 88942 | 47255 | 88130 | 48786 | 87292 | 48 | 11 |
| 6 | 13 | 42604 | 90470 | 44177 | 89713 | 45736 | 88928 | 47281 | 88117 | 48811 | 87278 | 47 | 11 |
| 6 | 14 | 42631 | 90458 | 44203 | 89700 | 45762 | 88915 | 47306 | 88103 | 48837 | 87264 | 46 | 11 |
| 7 | 15 | 42657 | 90446 | 44229 | 89687 | 45787 | 88902 | 47332 | 88089 | 48862 | 87250 | 45 | 11 |
| 7 | 16 | 42683 | 90433 | 44255 | 89674 | 45813 | 88888 | 47358 | 88075 | 48888 | 87235 | 44 | 10 |
| 7 | 17 | 42709 | 90421 | 44281 | 89662 | 45839 | 88875 | 47383 | 88062 | 48913 | 87221 | 43 | 10 |
| 8 | 18 | 42736 | 90408 | 44307 | 89649 | 45865 | 88862 | 47409 | 88048 | 48938 | 87207 | 42 | 10 |
| 8 | 19 | 42762 | 90396 | 44333 | 89636 | 45891 | 88848 | 47434 | 88034 | 48964 | 87193 | 41 | 10 |
| 9 | 20 | 42788 | 90383 | 44359 | 89623 | 45917 | 88835 | 47460 | 88020 | 48989 | 87178 | 40 | 9 |
| 9 | 21 | 42815 | 90371 | 44385 | 89610 | 45942 | 88822 | 47486 | 88006 | 49014 | 87164 | 39 | 9 |
| 10 | 22 | 42841 | 90358 | 44411 | 89597 | 45968 | 88808 | 47511 | 87993 | 49040 | 87150 | 38 | 9 |
| 10 | 23 | 42867 | 90346 | 44437 | 89584 | 45994 | 88795 | 47537 | 87979 | 49065 | 87136 | 37 | 9 |
| 10 | 24 | 42894 | 90334 | 44464 | 89571 | 46020 | 88782 | 47562 | 87965 | 49090 | 87121 | 36 | 8 |
| 11 | 25 | 42920 | 90321 | 44490 | 89558 | 46046 | 88768 | 47588 | 87951 | 49116 | 87107 | 35 | 8 |
| 11 | 26 | 42946 | 90309 | 44516 | 89545 | 46072 | 88755 | 47614 | 87937 | 49141 | 87093 | 34 | 8 |
| 12 | 27 | 42972 | 90296 | 44542 | 89532 | 46097 | 88741 | 47639 | 87923 | 49166 | 87079 | 33 | 8 |
| 12 | 28 | 42999 | 90284 | 44568 | 89519 | 46123 | 88728 | 47665 | 87909 | 49192 | 87064 | 32 | 7 |
| 13 | 29 | 43025 | 90271 | 44594 | 89506 | 46149 | 88715 | 47690 | 87896 | 49217 | 87050 | 31 | 7 |
| 13 | 30 | 43051 | 90259 | 44620 | 89493 | 46175 | 88701 | 47716 | 87882 | 49242 | 87036 | 30 | 7 |
| 13 | 31 | 43077 | 90246 | 44646 | 89480 | 46201 | 88688 | 47741 | 87868 | 49268 | 87021 | 29 | 7 |
| 14 | 32 | 43104 | 90233 | 44672 | 89467 | 46226 | 88674 | 47767 | 87854 | 49293 | 87007 | 28 | 7 |
| 14 | 33 | 43130 | 90221 | 44698 | 89454 | 46252 | 88661 | 47793 | 87840 | 49318 | 86993 | 27 | 6 |
| 15 | 34 | 43156 | 90208 | 44724 | 89441 | 46278 | 88647 | 47818 | 87826 | 49344 | 86978 | 26 | 6 |
| 15 | 35 | 43182 | 90196 | 44750 | 89428 | 46304 | 88634 | 47844 | 87812 | 49369 | 86964 | 25 | 6 |
| 16 | 36 | 43209 | 90183 | 44776 | 89415 | 46330 | 88620 | 47869 | 87798 | 49394 | 86949 | 24 | 6 |
| 16 | 37 | 43235 | 90171 | 44802 | 89402 | 46355 | 88607 | 47895 | 87784 | 49419 | 86935 | 23 | 5 |
| 16 | 38 | 43261 | 90158 | 44828 | 89389 | 46381 | 88593 | 47920 | 87770 | 49445 | 86921 | 22 | 5 |
| 17 | 39 | 43287 | 90146 | 44854 | 89376 | 46407 | 88580 | 47946 | 87756 | 49470 | 86906 | 21 | 5 |
| 17 | 40 | 43313 | 90133 | 44880 | 89363 | 46433 | 88566 | 47971 | 87743 | 49495 | 86892 | 20 | 5 |
| 18 | 41 | 43340 | 90120 | 44906 | 89350 | 46458 | 88553 | 47997 | 87729 | 49521 | 86878 | 19 | 4 |
| 18 | 42 | 43366 | 90108 | 44932 | 89337 | 46484 | 88539 | 48022 | 87715 | 49546 | 86863 | 18 | 4 |
| 19 | 43 | 43392 | 90095 | 44958 | 89324 | 46510 | 88526 | 48048 | 87701 | 49571 | 86849 | 17 | 4 |
| 19 | 44 | 43418 | 90082 | 44984 | 89311 | 46536 | 88512 | 48073 | 87687 | 49596 | 86834 | 16 | 4 |
| 20 | 45 | 43445 | 90070 | 45010 | 89298 | 46561 | 88499 | 48099 | 87673 | 49622 | 86820 | 15 | 4 |
| 20 | 46 | 43471 | 90057 | 45036 | 89285 | 46587 | 88485 | 48124 | 87659 | 49647 | 86805 | 14 | 3 |
| 20 | 47 | 43497 | 90045 | 45062 | 89272 | 46613 | 88472 | 48150 | 87645 | 49672 | 86791 | 13 | 3 |
| 21 | 48 | 43523 | 90032 | 45088 | 89259 | 46639 | 88458 | 48175 | 87631 | 49697 | 86777 | 12 | 3 |
| 21 | 49 | 43549 | 90019 | 45114 | 89245 | 46664 | 88445 | 48201 | 87617 | 49723 | 86762 | 11 | 3 |
| 22 | 50 | 43575 | 90007 | 45140 | 89232 | 46690 | 88431 | 48226 | 87603 | 49748 | 86748 | 10 | 2 |
| 22 | 51 | 43602 | 89994 | 45166 | 89219 | 46716 | 88417 | 48252 | 87589 | 49773 | 86733 | 9 | 2 |
| 23 | 52 | 43628 | 89981 | 45192 | 89206 | 46742 | 88404 | 48277 | 87575 | 49798 | 86719 | 8 | 2 |
| 23 | 53 | 43654 | 89968 | 45218 | 89193 | 46767 | 88390 | 48303 | 87561 | 49824 | 86704 | 7 | 2 |
| 23 | 54 | 43680 | 89956 | 45243 | 89180 | 46793 | 88377 | 48328 | 87546 | 49849 | 86690 | 6 | 1 |
| 24 | 55 | 43706 | 89943 | 45269 | 89167 | 46819 | 88363 | 48354 | 87532 | 49874 | 86675 | 5 | 1 |
| 24 | 56 | 43733 | 89930 | 45295 | 89153 | 46844 | 88349 | 48379 | 87518 | 49899 | 86661 | 4 | 1 |
| 25 | 57 | 43759 | 89918 | 45321 | 89140 | 46870 | 88336 | 48405 | 87504 | 49924 | 86646 | 3 | 1 |
| 25 | 58 | 43785 | 89905 | 45347 | 89127 | 46896 | 88322 | 48430 | 87490 | 49950 | 86632 | 2 | 0 |
| 26 | 59 | 43811 | 89892 | 45373 | 89114 | 46921 | 88308 | 48456 | 87476 | 49975 | 86617 | 1 | 0 |
| 26 | 60 | 43837 | 89879 | 45399 | 89101 | 46947 | 88295 | 48481 | 87462 | 50000 | 86603 | 0 | 0 |
| | | N. cos. | N. sine. | N. cos. | N. sine. | N. cos. | N. sine. | N. cos. | N. sine. | N. cos. | N. sine. | M | |
| | | 64° | | 63° | | 62° | | 61° | | 60° | | | |

# TABLE XXIV.

## Of Natural Sines.

| Prop. parts 25 | M | 30° N. sine. | 30° N. cos. | 31° N. sine. | 31° N. cos. | 32° N. sine. | 32° N. cos. | 33° N. sine. | 33° N. cos. | 34° N. sine. | 34° N. cos. | | Prop. parts 16 |
|---|---|---|---|---|---|---|---|---|---|---|---|---|---|
| 0 | 0 | 50000 | 86603 | 51504 | 85717 | 52992 | 84805 | 54464 | 83867 | 55919 | 82904 | 60 | 16 |
| 0 | 1 | 50025 | 86588 | 51529 | 85702 | 53017 | 84789 | 54488 | 83851 | 55943 | 82887 | 59 | 16 |
| 1 | 2 | 50050 | 86573 | 51554 | 85687 | 53041 | 84774 | 54513 | 83835 | 55968 | 82871 | 58 | 15 |
| 1 | 3 | 50076 | 86559 | 51579 | 85672 | 53066 | 84759 | 54537 | 83819 | 55992 | 82855 | 57 | 15 |
| 2 | 4 | 50101 | 86544 | 51604 | 85657 | 53091 | 84743 | 54561 | 83804 | 56016 | 82839 | 56 | 15 |
| 2 | 5 | 50126 | 86530 | 51628 | 85642 | 53115 | 84728 | 54586 | 83788 | 56040 | 82822 | 55 | 15 |
| 3 | 6 | 50151 | 86515 | 51653 | 85627 | 53140 | 84712 | 54610 | 83772 | 56064 | 82806 | 54 | 14 |
| 3 | 7 | 50176 | 86501 | 51678 | 85612 | 53164 | 84697 | 54635 | 83756 | 56088 | 82790 | 53 | 14 |
| 3 | 8 | 50201 | 86486 | 51703 | 85597 | 53189 | 84681 | 54659 | 83740 | 56112 | 82773 | 52 | 14 |
| 4 | 9 | 50227 | 86471 | 51728 | 85582 | 53214 | 84666 | 54683 | 83724 | 56136 | 82757 | 51 | 14 |
| 4 | 10 | 50252 | 86457 | 51753 | 85567 | 53238 | 84650 | 54708 | 83708 | 56160 | 82741 | 50 | 13 |
| 5 | 11 | 50277 | 86442 | 51778 | 85551 | 53263 | 84635 | 54732 | 83692 | 56184 | 82724 | 49 | 13 |
| 5 | 12 | 50302 | 86427 | 51803 | 85536 | 53288 | 84619 | 54756 | 83676 | 56208 | 82708 | 48 | 13 |
| 5 | 13 | 50327 | 86413 | 51828 | 85521 | 53312 | 84604 | 54781 | 83660 | 56232 | 82692 | 47 | 13 |
| 6 | 14 | 50352 | 86398 | 51852 | 85506 | 53337 | 84588 | 54805 | 83645 | 56256 | 82675 | 46 | 12 |
| 6 | 15 | 50377 | 86384 | 51877 | 85491 | 53361 | 84573 | 54829 | 83629 | 56280 | 82659 | 45 | 12 |
| 7 | 16 | 50403 | 86369 | 51902 | 85476 | 53386 | 84557 | 54854 | 83613 | 56305 | 82643 | 44 | 12 |
| 7 | 17 | 50428 | 86354 | 51927 | 85461 | 53411 | 84542 | 54878 | 83597 | 56329 | 82626 | 43 | 11 |
| 8 | 18 | 50453 | 86340 | 51952 | 85446 | 53435 | 84526 | 54902 | 83581 | 56353 | 82610 | 42 | 11 |
| 8 | 19 | 50478 | 86325 | 51977 | 85431 | 53460 | 84511 | 54927 | 83565 | 56377 | 82593 | 41 | 11 |
| 8 | 20 | 50503 | 86310 | 52002 | 85416 | 53484 | 84495 | 54951 | 83549 | 56401 | 82577 | 40 | 11 |
| 9 | 21 | 50528 | 86295 | 52026 | 85401 | 53509 | 84480 | 54975 | 83533 | 56425 | 82561 | 39 | 10 |
| 9 | 22 | 50553 | 86281 | 52051 | 85385 | 53534 | 84464 | 54999 | 83517 | 56449 | 82544 | 38 | 10 |
| 10 | 23 | 50578 | 86266 | 52076 | 85370 | 53558 | 84448 | 55024 | 83501 | 56473 | 82528 | 37 | 10 |
| 10 | 24 | 50603 | 86251 | 52101 | 85355 | 53583 | 84433 | 55048 | 83485 | 56497 | 82511 | 36 | 10 |
| 10 | 25 | 50628 | 86237 | 52126 | 85340 | 53607 | 84417 | 55072 | 83469 | 56521 | 82495 | 35 | 9 |
| 11 | 26 | 50654 | 86222 | 52151 | 85325 | 53632 | 84402 | 55097 | 83453 | 56545 | 82478 | 34 | 9 |
| 11 | 27 | 50679 | 86207 | 52175 | 85310 | 53656 | 84386 | 55121 | 83437 | 56569 | 82462 | 33 | 9 |
| 12 | 28 | 50704 | 86192 | 52200 | 85294 | 53681 | 84370 | 55145 | 83421 | 56593 | 82446 | 32 | 9 |
| 12 | 29 | 50729 | 86178 | 52225 | 85279 | 53705 | 84355 | 55169 | 83405 | 56617 | 82429 | 31 | 8 |
| 13 | 30 | 50754 | 86163 | 52250 | 85264 | 53730 | 84339 | 55194 | 83389 | 56641 | 82413 | 30 | 8 |
| 13 | 31 | 50779 | 86148 | 52275 | 85249 | 53754 | 84324 | 55218 | 83373 | 56665 | 82396 | 29 | 8 |
| 13 | 32 | 50804 | 86133 | 52299 | 85234 | 53779 | 84308 | 55242 | 83356 | 56689 | 82380 | 28 | 7 |
| 14 | 33 | 50829 | 86119 | 52324 | 85218 | 53804 | 84292 | 55266 | 83340 | 56713 | 82363 | 27 | 7 |
| 14 | 34 | 50854 | 86104 | 52349 | 85203 | 53828 | 84277 | 55291 | 83324 | 56736 | 82347 | 26 | 7 |
| 15 | 35 | 50879 | 86089 | 52374 | 85188 | 53853 | 84261 | 55315 | 83308 | 56760 | 82330 | 25 | 7 |
| 15 | 36 | 50904 | 86074 | 52399 | 85173 | 53877 | 84245 | 55339 | 83292 | 56784 | 82314 | 24 | 6 |
| 15 | 37 | 50929 | 86059 | 52423 | 85157 | 53902 | 84230 | 55363 | 83276 | 56808 | 82297 | 23 | 6 |
| 16 | 38 | 50954 | 86045 | 52448 | 85142 | 53926 | 84214 | 55388 | 83260 | 56832 | 82281 | 22 | 6 |
| 16 | 39 | 50979 | 86030 | 52473 | 85127 | 53951 | 84198 | 55412 | 83244 | 56856 | 82264 | 21 | 6 |
| 17 | 40 | 51004 | 86015 | 52498 | 85112 | 53975 | 84182 | 55436 | 83228 | 56880 | 82248 | 20 | 5 |
| 17 | 41 | 51029 | 86000 | 52522 | 85096 | 54000 | 84167 | 55460 | 83212 | 56904 | 82231 | 19 | 5 |
| 18 | 42 | 51054 | 85985 | 52547 | 85081 | 54024 | 84151 | 55484 | 83195 | 56928 | 82214 | 18 | 5 |
| 18 | 43 | 51079 | 85970 | 52572 | 85066 | 54049 | 84135 | 55509 | 83179 | 56952 | 82198 | 17 | 5 |
| 18 | 44 | 51104 | 85956 | 52597 | 85051 | 54073 | 84120 | 55533 | 83163 | 56976 | 82181 | 16 | 4 |
| 19 | 45 | 51129 | 85941 | 52621 | 85035 | 54097 | 84104 | 55557 | 83147 | 57000 | 82165 | 15 | 4 |
| 19 | 46 | 51154 | 85926 | 52646 | 85020 | 54122 | 84088 | 55581 | 83131 | 57024 | 82148 | 14 | 4 |
| 20 | 47 | 51179 | 85911 | 52671 | 85005 | 54146 | 84072 | 55605 | 83115 | 57047 | 82132 | 13 | 3 |
| 20 | 48 | 51204 | 85896 | 52696 | 84989 | 54171 | 84057 | 55630 | 83098 | 57071 | 82115 | 12 | 3 |
| 20 | 49 | 51229 | 85881 | 52720 | 84974 | 54195 | 84041 | 55654 | 83082 | 57095 | 82098 | 11 | 3 |
| 21 | 50 | 51254 | 85866 | 52745 | 84959 | 54220 | 84025 | 55678 | 83066 | 57119 | 82082 | 10 | 3 |
| 21 | 51 | 51279 | 85851 | 52770 | 84943 | 54244 | 84009 | 55702 | 83050 | 57143 | 82065 | 9 | 2 |
| 22 | 52 | 51304 | 85836 | 52794 | 84928 | 54269 | 83994 | 55726 | 83034 | 57167 | 82048 | 8 | 2 |
| 22 | 53 | 51329 | 85821 | 52819 | 84913 | 54293 | 83978 | 55750 | 83017 | 57191 | 82032 | 7 | 2 |
| 23 | 54 | 51354 | 85806 | 52844 | 84897 | 54317 | 83962 | 55775 | 83001 | 57215 | 82015 | 6 | 2 |
| 23 | 55 | 51379 | 85792 | 52869 | 84882 | 54342 | 83946 | 55799 | 82985 | 57238 | 81999 | 5 | 1 |
| 23 | 56 | 51404 | 85777 | 52893 | 84866 | 54366 | 83930 | 55823 | 82969 | 57262 | 81982 | 4 | 1 |
| 24 | 57 | 51429 | 85762 | 52918 | 84851 | 54391 | 83915 | 55847 | 82953 | 57286 | 81965 | 3 | 1 |
| 24 | 58 | 51454 | 85747 | 52943 | 84836 | 54415 | 83899 | 55871 | 82936 | 57310 | 81949 | 2 | 1 |
| 25 | 59 | 51479 | 85732 | 52967 | 84820 | 54440 | 83883 | 55895 | 82920 | 57334 | 81932 | 1 | 0 |
| 25 | 60 | 51504 | 85717 | 52992 | 84805 | 54464 | 83867 | 55919 | 82904 | 0 | 0 |
| | | N. cos. | N. sine. | N. cos. | N. sine. | N. cos. | N. sine. | N. cos. | N. sine. | N. cos. | N. sine. | M | |
| | | 59° | | 58° | | 57° | | 56° | | 55° | | | |

# TABLE XXIV.

## Of Natural Sines.

| Prop. parts 23 | M | 35° N. sine. | 35° N. cos. | 36° N. sine. | 36° N. cos. | 37° N. sine. | 37° N. cos. | 38° N. sine. | 38° N. cos. | 39° N. sine. | 39° N. cos. | | Prop. parts 18 |
|---|---|---|---|---|---|---|---|---|---|---|---|---|---|
| 0 | 0 | 57358 | 81915 | 58779 | 80902 | 60182 | 79864 | 61566 | 78801 | 62932 | 77715 | 60 | 18 |
| 0 | 1 | 57381 | 81899 | 58802 | 80885 | 60205 | 79846 | 61589 | 78783 | 62955 | 77696 | 59 | 18 |
| 1 | 2 | 57405 | 81882 | 58826 | 80867 | 60228 | 79829 | 61612 | 78765 | 62977 | 77678 | 58 | 17 |
| 1 | 3 | 57429 | 81865 | 58849 | 80850 | 60251 | 79811 | 61635 | 78747 | 63000 | 77660 | 57 | 17 |
| 2 | 4 | 57453 | 81848 | 58873 | 80833 | 60274 | 79793 | 61658 | 78729 | 63022 | 77641 | 56 | 17 |
| 2 | 5 | 57477 | 81832 | 58896 | 80816 | 60298 | 79776 | 61681 | 78711 | 63045 | 77623 | 55 | 17 |
| 2 | 6 | 57501 | 81815 | 58920 | 80799 | 60321 | 79758 | 61704 | 78694 | 63068 | 77605 | 54 | 16 |
| 3 | 7 | 57524 | 81798 | 58943 | 80782 | 60344 | 79741 | 61726 | 78676 | 63090 | 77586 | 53 | 16 |
| 3 | 8 | 57548 | 81782 | 58967 | 80765 | 60367 | 79723 | 61749 | 78658 | 63113 | 77568 | 52 | 16 |
| 3 | 9 | 57572 | 81765 | 58990 | 80748 | 60390 | 79706 | 61772 | 78640 | 63135 | 77550 | 51 | 15 |
| 4 | 10 | 57596 | 81748 | 59014 | 80730 | 60414 | 79688 | 61795 | 78622 | 63158 | 77531 | 50 | 15 |
| 4 | 11 | 57619 | 81731 | 59037 | 80713 | 60437 | 79671 | 61818 | 78604 | 63180 | 77513 | 49 | 15 |
| 5 | 12 | 57643 | 81714 | 59061 | 80696 | 60460 | 79653 | 61841 | 78586 | 63203 | 77494 | 48 | 14 |
| 5 | 13 | 57667 | 81698 | 59084 | 80679 | 60483 | 79635 | 61864 | 78568 | 63225 | 77476 | 47 | 14 |
| 5 | 14 | 57691 | 81681 | 59108 | 80662 | 60506 | 79618 | 61887 | 78550 | 63248 | 77458 | 46 | 14 |
| 6 | 15 | 57715 | 81664 | 59131 | 80644 | 60529 | 79600 | 61909 | 78532 | 63271 | 77439 | 45 | 14 |
| 6 | 16 | 57738 | 81647 | 59154 | 80627 | 60553 | 79583 | 61932 | 78514 | 63293 | 77421 | 44 | 13 |
| 7 | 17 | 57762 | 81631 | 59178 | 80610 | 60576 | 79565 | 61955 | 78496 | 63316 | 77402 | 43 | 13 |
| 7 | 18 | 57786 | 81614 | 59201 | 80593 | 60599 | 79547 | 61978 | 78478 | 63338 | 77384 | 42 | 13 |
| 7 | 19 | 57810 | 81597 | 59225 | 80576 | 60622 | 79530 | 62001 | 78460 | 63361 | 77366 | 41 | 12 |
| 8 | 20 | 57833 | 81580 | 59248 | 80558 | 60645 | 79512 | 62024 | 78442 | 63383 | 77347 | 40 | 12 |
| 8 | 21 | 57857 | 81563 | 59[illegible]72 | 80541 | 60668 | 79494 | 62046 | 78424 | 63406 | 77329 | 39 | 12 |
| 8 | 22 | 57881 | 81546 | 59295 | 80524 | 60691 | 79477 | 62069 | 78405 | 63428 | 77310 | 38 | 11 |
| 9 | 23 | 57904 | 81530 | 59318 | 80507 | 60714 | 79459 | 62092 | 78387 | 63451 | 77292 | 37 | 11 |
| 9 | 24 | 57928 | 81513 | 59342 | 80489 | 60738 | 79441 | 62115 | 78369 | 63473 | 77273 | 36 | 11 |
| 10 | 25 | 57952 | 81496 | 59365 | 80472 | 60761 | 79424 | 62138 | 78351 | 63496 | 77255 | 35 | 11 |
| 10 | 26 | 57976 | 81479 | 59389 | 80455 | 60784 | 79406 | 62160 | 78333 | 63518 | 77236 | 34 | 10 |
| 10 | 27 | 57999 | 81462 | 59412 | 80438 | 60807 | 79388 | 62183 | 78315 | 63540 | 77218 | 33 | 10 |
| 11 | 28 | 58023 | 81445 | 59436 | 80420 | 60830 | 79371 | 62206 | 78297 | 63563 | 77199 | 32 | 10 |
| 11 | 29 | 58047 | 81428 | 59459 | 80403 | 60853 | 79353 | 62229 | 78279 | 63585 | 77181 | 31 | 10 |
| 12 | 30 | 58070 | 81412 | 59482 | 80386 | 60876 | 79335 | 62251 | 78261 | 63608 | 77162 | 30 | 9 |
| 12 | 31 | 58094 | 81395 | 59506 | 80368 | 60899 | 79318 | 62274 | 78243 | 63630 | 77144 | 29 | 9 |
| 12 | 32 | 58118 | 81378 | 59529 | 80351 | 60922 | 79300 | 62297 | 78225 | 63653 | 77125 | 28 | 8 |
| 13 | 33 | 58141 | 81361 | 59552 | 80334 | 60945 | 79282 | 62320 | 78206 | 63675 | 77107 | 27 | 8 |
| 13 | 34 | 58165 | 81344 | 59576 | 80316 | 60968 | 79264 | 62342 | 78188 | 63698 | 77088 | 26 | 8 |
| 13 | 35 | 58189 | 81327 | 59599 | 80299 | 60991 | 79247 | 62365 | 78170 | 63720 | 77070 | 25 | 8 |
| 14 | 36 | 58212 | 81310 | 59622 | 80282 | 61015 | 79229 | 62388 | 78152 | 63742 | 77051 | 24 | 7 |
| 14 | 37 | 58236 | 81293 | 59646 | 80264 | 61038 | 79211 | 62411 | 78134 | 63765 | 77033 | 23 | 7 |
| 15 | 38 | 58260 | 81276 | 59669 | 80247 | 61061 | 79193 | 62433 | 78116 | 63787 | 77014 | 22 | 7 |
| 15 | 39 | 58283 | 81259 | 59693 | 80230 | 61084 | 79176 | 62456 | 78098 | 63810 | 76996 | 21 | 6 |
| 15 | 40 | 58307 | 81242 | 59716 | 80212 | 61107 | 79158 | 62479 | 78079 | 63832 | 76977 | 20 | 6 |
| 16 | 41 | 58330 | 81225 | 59739 | 80195 | 61130 | 79140 | 62502 | 78061 | 63854 | 76959 | 19 | 6 |
| 16 | 42 | 58354 | 81208 | 59763 | 80178 | 61153 | 79122 | 62524 | 78043 | 63877 | 76940 | 18 | 5 |
| 16 | 43 | 58378 | 81191 | 59786 | 80160 | 61176 | 79105 | 62547 | 78025 | 63899 | 76921 | 17 | 5 |
| 17 | 44 | 58401 | 81174 | 59809 | 80143 | 61199 | 79087 | 62570 | 78007 | 63922 | 76903 | 16 | 5 |
| 17 | 45 | 58425 | 81157 | 59832 | 80125 | 61222 | 79069 | 62592 | 77988 | 63944 | 76884 | 15 | 5 |
| 18 | 46 | 58449 | 81140 | 59856 | 80108 | 61245 | 79051 | 62615 | 77970 | 63966 | 76866 | 14 | 4 |
| 18 | 47 | 58472 | 81123 | 59879 | 80091 | 61268 | 79033 | 62638 | 77952 | 63989 | 76847 | 13 | 4 |
| 18 | 48 | 58496 | 81106 | 59902 | 80073 | 61291 | 79016 | 62660 | 77934 | 64011 | 76828 | 12 | 4 |
| 19 | 49 | 58519 | 81089 | 59926 | 80056 | 61314 | 78998 | 62683 | 77916 | 64033 | 76810 | 11 | 3 |
| 19 | 50 | 58543 | 81072 | 59949 | 80038 | 61337 | 78980 | 62706 | 77897 | 64056 | 76791 | 10 | 3 |
| 20 | 51 | 58567 | 81055 | 59972 | 80021 | 61360 | 78962 | 62728 | 77879 | 64078 | 76772 | 9 | 3 |
| 20 | 52 | 58590 | 81038 | 59995 | 80003 | 61383 | 78944 | 62751 | 77861 | 64100 | 76754 | 8 | 2 |
| 20 | 53 | 58614 | 81021 | 60019 | 79986 | 61406 | 78926 | 62774 | 77843 | 64123 | 76735 | 7 | 2 |
| 21 | 54 | 58637 | 81004 | 60042 | 79968 | 61429 | 78908 | 62796 | 77824 | 64145 | 76717 | 6 | 2 |
| 21 | 55 | 58661 | 80987 | 60065 | 79951 | 61451 | 78891 | 62819 | 77806 | 64167 | 76698 | 5 | 2 |
| 21 | 56 | 58684 | 80970 | 60089 | 79934 | 61474 | 78873 | 62842 | 77788 | 64190 | 76679 | 4 | 1 |
| 22 | 57 | 58708 | 80953 | 60112 | 79916 | 61497 | 78855 | 62864 | 77769 | 64212 | 76661 | 3 | 1 |
| 22 | 58 | 58731 | 80936 | 60135 | 79899 | 61520 | 78837 | 62887 | 77751 | 64234 | 76642 | 2 | 1 |
| 23 | 59 | 58755 | 80919 | 60158 | 79881 | 61543 | 78819 | 62909 | 77733 | 64256 | 76623 | 1 | 0 |
| 23 | 60 | 58779 | 80902 | 60182 | 79864 | 61566 | 78801 | 62932 | 77715 | 64279 | 76604 | 0 | 0 |
| | | N. cos. | N. sine. | N. cos. | N. sine. | N. cos. | N. sine. | N. cos. | N. sine. | N. cos. | N. sine. | M | |
| | | 54° | | 53° | | 52° | | 51° | | 50° | | | |

# TABLE XXIV.

## Of Natural Sines.

| Prop. parts 22 | M | 40° N. sine. | 40° N. cos. | 41° N. sine. | 41° N. cos. | 42° N. sine. | 42° N. cos. | 43° N. sine. | 43° N. cos. | 44° N. sine. | 44° N. cos. | | Prop. parts 19 |
|---|---|---|---|---|---|---|---|---|---|---|---|---|---|
| 0 | 0 | 64279 | 76604 | 65606 | 75471 | 66913 | 74314 | 68200 | 73135 | 69466 | 71934 | 60 | 19 |
| 0 | 1 | 64301 | 76586 | 65628 | 75452 | 66935 | 74295 | 68221 | 73116 | 69487 | 71914 | 59 | 19 |
| 1 | 2 | 64323 | 76567 | 65650 | 75433 | 66956 | 74276 | 68242 | 73096 | 69508 | 71894 | 58 | 18 |
| 1 | 3 | 64346 | 76548 | 65672 | 75414 | 66978 | 74256 | 68264 | 73076 | 69529 | 71873 | 57 | 18 |
| 1 | 4 | 64368 | 76530 | 65694 | 75395 | 66999 | 74237 | 68285 | 73056 | 69549 | 71853 | 56 | 18 |
| 2 | 5 | 64390 | 76511 | 65716 | 75375 | 67021 | 74217 | 68306 | 73036 | 69570 | 71833 | 55 | 17 |
| 2 | 6 | 64412 | 76492 | 65738 | 75356 | 67043 | 74198 | 68327 | 73016 | 69591 | 71813 | 54 | 17 |
| 3 | 7 | 64435 | 76473 | 65759 | 75337 | 67064 | 74178 | 68349 | 72996 | 69612 | 71792 | 53 | 17 |
| 3 | 8 | 64457 | 76455 | 65781 | 75318 | 67086 | 74159 | 68370 | 72976 | 69633 | 71772 | 52 | 16 |
| 3 | 9 | 64479 | 76436 | 65803 | 75299 | 67107 | 74139 | 68391 | 72957 | 69654 | 71752 | 51 | 16 |
| 4 | 10 | 64501 | 76417 | 65825 | 75280 | 67129 | 74120 | 68412 | 72937 | 69675 | 71732 | 50 | 16 |
| 4 | 11 | 64524 | 76398 | 65847 | 75261 | 67151 | 74100 | 68434 | 72917 | 69696 | 71711 | 49 | 16 |
| 4 | 12 | 64546 | 76380 | 65869 | 75241 | 67172 | 74080 | 68455 | 72897 | 69717 | 71691 | 48 | 15 |
| 5 | 13 | 64568 | 76361 | 65891 | 75222 | 67194 | 74061 | 68476 | 72877 | 69737 | 71671 | 47 | 15 |
| 5 | 14 | 64590 | 76342 | 65913 | 75203 | 67215 | 74041 | 68497 | 72857 | 69758 | 71650 | 46 | 15 |
| 6 | 15 | 64612 | 76323 | 65935 | 75184 | 67237 | 74022 | 68518 | 72837 | 69779 | 71630 | 45 | 14 |
| 6 | 16 | 64635 | 76304 | 65956 | 75165 | 67258 | 74002 | 68539 | 72817 | 69800 | 71610 | 44 | 14 |
| 6 | 17 | 64657 | 76286 | 65978 | 75146 | 67280 | 73983 | 68561 | 72797 | 69821 | 71590 | 43 | 14 |
| 7 | 18 | 64679 | 76267 | 66000 | 75126 | 67301 | 73963 | 68582 | 72777 | 69842 | 71569 | 42 | 13 |
| 7 | 19 | 64701 | 76248 | 66022 | 75107 | 67323 | 73944 | 68603 | 72757 | 69862 | 71549 | 41 | 13 |
| 7 | 20 | 64723 | 76229 | 66044 | 75088 | 67344 | 73924 | 68624 | 72737 | 69883 | 71529 | 40 | 13 |
| 8 | 21 | 64746 | 76210 | 66066 | 75069 | 67366 | 73904 | 68645 | 72717 | 69904 | 71508 | 39 | 12 |
| 8 | 22 | 64768 | 76192 | 66088 | 75050 | 67387 | 73885 | 68666 | 72697 | 69925 | 71488 | 38 | 12 |
| 8 | 23 | 64790 | 76173 | 66109 | 75030 | 67409 | 73865 | 68688 | 72677 | 69946 | 71468 | 37 | 12 |
| 9 | 24 | 64812 | 76154 | 66131 | 75011 | 67430 | 73846 | 68709 | 72657 | 69966 | 71447 | 36 | 11 |
| 9 | 25 | 64834 | 76135 | 66153 | 74992 | 67452 | 73826 | 68730 | 72637 | 69987 | 71427 | 35 | 11 |
| 10 | 26 | 64856 | 76116 | 66175 | 74973 | 67473 | 73806 | 68751 | 72617 | 70008 | 71407 | 34 | 11 |
| 10 | 27 | 64878 | 76097 | 66197 | 74953 | 67495 | 73787 | 68772 | 72597 | 70029 | 71386 | 33 | 10 |
| 10 | 28 | 64901 | 76078 | 66218 | 74934 | 67516 | 73767 | 68793 | 72577 | 70049 | 71366 | 32 | 10 |
| 11 | 29 | 64923 | 76059 | 66240 | 74915 | 67538 | 73747 | 68814 | 72557 | 70070 | 71345 | 31 | 10 |
| 11 | 30 | 64945 | 76041 | 66262 | 74896 | 67559 | 73728 | 68835 | 72537 | 70091 | 71325 | 30 | 10 |
| 11 | 31 | 64967 | 76022 | 66284 | 74876 | 67580 | 73708 | 68857 | 72517 | 70112 | 71305 | 29 | 9 |
| 12 | 32 | 64989 | 76003 | 66306 | 74857 | 67602 | 73688 | 68878 | 72497 | 70132 | 71284 | 28 | 9 |
| 12 | 33 | 65011 | 75984 | 66327 | 74838 | 67623 | 73669 | 68899 | 72477 | 70153 | 71264 | 27 | 9 |
| 12 | 34 | 65033 | 75965 | 66349 | 74818 | 67645 | 73649 | 68920 | 72457 | 70174 | 71243 | 26 | 8 |
| 13 | 35 | 65055 | 75946 | 66371 | 74799 | 67666 | 73629 | 68941 | 72437 | 70195 | 71223 | 25 | 8 |
| 13 | 36 | 65077 | 75927 | 66393 | 74780 | 67688 | 73610 | 68962 | 72417 | 70215 | 71203 | 24 | 8 |
| 14 | 37 | 65100 | 75908 | 66414 | 74760 | 67709 | 73590 | 68983 | 72397 | 70236 | 71182 | 23 | 7 |
| 14 | 38 | 65122 | 75889 | 66436 | 74741 | 67730 | 73570 | 69004 | 72377 | 70257 | 71162 | 22 | 7 |
| 14 | 39 | 65144 | 75870 | 66458 | 74722 | 67752 | 73551 | 69025 | 72357 | 70277 | 71141 | 21 | 7 |
| 15 | 40 | 65166 | 75851 | 66480 | 74703 | 67773 | 73531 | 69046 | 72337 | 70298 | 71121 | 20 | 6 |
| 15 | 41 | 65188 | 75832 | 66501 | 74683 | 67795 | 73511 | 69067 | 72317 | 70319 | 71100 | 19 | 6 |
| 15 | 42 | 65210 | 75813 | 66523 | 74664 | 67816 | 73491 | 69088 | 72297 | 70339 | 71080 | 18 | 6 |
| 16 | 43 | 65232 | 75794 | 66545 | 74644 | 67837 | 73472 | 69109 | 72277 | 70360 | 71059 | 17 | 5 |
| 16 | 44 | 65254 | 75775 | 66566 | 74625 | 67859 | 73452 | 69130 | 72257 | 70381 | 71039 | 16 | 5 |
| 17 | 45 | 65276 | 75756 | 66588 | 74606 | 67880 | 73432 | 69151 | 72236 | 70401 | 71019 | 15 | 5 |
| 17 | 46 | 65298 | 75738 | 66610 | 74586 | 67901 | 73413 | 69172 | 72216 | 70422 | 70998 | 14 | 4 |
| 17 | 47 | 65320 | 75719 | 66632 | 74567 | 67923 | 73393 | 69193 | 72196 | 70443 | 70978 | 13 | 4 |
| 18 | 48 | 65342 | 75700 | 66653 | 74548 | 67944 | 73373 | 69214 | 72176 | 70463 | 70957 | 12 | 4 |
| 18 | 49 | 65364 | 75680 | 66675 | 74528 | 67965 | 73353 | 69235 | 72156 | 70484 | 70937 | 11 | 3 |
| 18 | 50 | 65386 | 75661 | 66697 | 74509 | 67987 | 73333 | 69256 | 72136 | 70505 | 70916 | 10 | 3 |
| 19 | 51 | 65408 | 75642 | 66718 | 74489 | 68008 | 73314 | 69277 | 72116 | 70525 | 70896 | 9 | 3 |
| 19 | 52 | 65430 | 75623 | 66740 | 74470 | 68029 | 73294 | 69298 | 72095 | 70546 | 70875 | 8 | 3 |
| 19 | 53 | 65452 | 75604 | 66762 | 74451 | 68051 | 73274 | 69319 | 72075 | 70567 | 70855 | 7 | 2 |
| 20 | 54 | 65474 | 75585 | 66783 | 74431 | 68072 | 73254 | 69340 | 72055 | 70587 | 70834 | 6 | 2 |
| 20 | 55 | 65496 | 75566 | 66805 | 74412 | 68093 | 73234 | 69361 | 72035 | 70608 | 70813 | 5 | 2 |
| 21 | 56 | 65518 | 75547 | 66827 | 74392 | 68115 | 73215 | 69382 | 72015 | 70628 | 70793 | 4 | 1 |
| 21 | 57 | 65540 | 75528 | 66848 | 74373 | 68136 | 73195 | 69403 | 71995 | 70649 | 70772 | 3 | 1 |
| 21 | 58 | 65562 | 75509 | 66870 | 74353 | 68157 | 73175 | 69424 | 71974 | 70670 | 70752 | 2 | 1 |
| 22 | 59 | 65584 | 75490 | 66891 | 74334 | 68179 | 73155 | 69445 | 71954 | 70690 | 70731 | 1 | 0 |
| 22 | 60 | 65606 | 75471 | 66913 | 74314 | 68200 | 73135 | 69466 | 71934 | 70711 | 70711 | 0 | 0 |
| | | N. cos. | N. sine. | N. cos. | N. sine. | N. cos. | N. sine. | N. cos. | N. sine. | N. cos. | N. sine. | M | |
| | | 49° | | 48° | | 47° | | 46° | | 45° | | | |

# TABLE XXV.

## Of Logarithmic Sines, Tangents, and Secants to every Point and Quarter Point of the Compass.

| Points. | Sine. | Co-sine. | Tangent. | Co-tang. | Secant. | Co-secant. | |
|---|---|---|---|---|---|---|---|
| 0 | Inf. neg. | 10.00000 | Inf. neg. | Infinite. | 10.00000 | Infinite. | 8 |
| 0 ¼ | 8.69080 | 9.99948 | 8.69132 | 11.30868 | 10.00052 | 11.30920 | 7 ¾ |
| 0 ½ | 8.99130 | 9.99790 | 8.99340 | 11.00660 | 10.00210 | 11.00870 | 7 ½ |
| 0 ¾ | 9.16652 | 9.99527 | 9.17125 | 10.82875 | 10.00473 | 10.83348 | 7 ¼ |
| 1 | 9.29024 | 9.99157 | 9.29866 | 10.70134 | 10.00843 | 10.70976 | 7 |
| 1 ¼ | 9.38557 | 9.98679 | 9.39879 | 10.60121 | 10.01321 | 10.61443 | 6 ¾ |
| 1 ½ | 9.46282 | 9.98088 | 9.48194 | 10.51806 | 10.01912 | 10.53718 | 6 ½ |
| 1 ¾ | 9.52749 | 9.97384 | 9.55365 | 10.44635 | 10.02616 | 10.47251 | 6 ¼ |
| 2 | 9.58284 | 9.96562 | 9.61722 | 10.38278 | 10.03438 | 10.41716 | 6 |
| 2 ¼ | 9.63099 | 9.95616 | 9.67483 | 10.32517 | 10.04384 | 10.36901 | 5 ¾ |
| 2 ½ | 9.67339 | 9.94543 | 9.72796 | 10.27204 | 10.05457 | 10.32661 | 5 ½ |
| 2 ¾ | 9.71105 | 9.93335 | 9.77770 | 10.22230 | 10.06665 | 10.28895 | 5 ¼ |
| 3 | 9.74474 | 9.91985 | 9.82489 | 10.17511 | 10.08015 | 10.25526 | 5 |
| 3 ¼ | 9.77503 | 9.90483 | 9.87020 | 10.12980 | 10.09517 | 10.22497 | 4 ¾ |
| 3 ½ | 9.80236 | 9.88819 | 9.91417 | 10.08583 | 10.11181 | 10.19764 | 4 ½ |
| 3 ¾ | 9.82708 | 9.86979 | 9.95729 | 10.04271 | 10.13021 | 10.17292 | 4 ¼ |
| 4 | 9.84949 | 9.84949 | 10.00000 | 10.00000 | 10.15051 | 10.15051 | 4 |
| | Co-sine. | Sine. | Co-tang. | Tangent. | Co-secant. | Secant. | Points. |

# TABLE XXVI.

## Logarithms of Numbers.

| No. 1——100. | | | | | | | | Log. 0.00000——2.00000. | |
|---|---|---|---|---|---|---|---|---|---|
| No. | Log. | No. | Log. | No. | Log. | No. | Log. | No. | Log. |
| 1 | 0.00000 | 21 | 1.32222 | 41 | 1.61278 | 61 | 1.78533 | 81 | 1.90849 |
| 2 | 0.30103 | 22 | 1.34242 | 42 | 1.62325 | 62 | 1.79239 | 82 | 1.91381 |
| 3 | 0.47712 | 23 | 1.36173 | 43 | 1.63347 | 63 | 1.79934 | 83 | 1.91908 |
| 4 | 0.60206 | 24 | 1.38021 | 44 | 1.64345 | 64 | 1.80618 | 84 | 1.92428 |
| 5 | 0.69897 | 25 | 1.39794 | 45 | 1.65321 | 65 | 1.81291 | 85 | 1.92942 |
| 6 | 0.77815 | 26 | 1.41497 | 46 | 1.66276 | 66 | 1.81954 | 86 | 1.93450 |
| 7 | 0.84510 | 27 | 1.43136 | 47 | 1.67210 | 67 | 1.82607 | 87 | 1.93952 |
| 8 | 0.90309 | 28 | 1.44716 | 48 | 1.68124 | 68 | 1.83251 | 88 | 1.94448 |
| 9 | 0.95424 | 29 | 1.46240 | 49 | 1.69020 | 69 | 1.83885 | 89 | 1.94939 |
| 10 | 1.00000 | 30 | 1.47712 | 50 | 1.69897 | 70 | 1.84510 | 90 | 1.95424 |
| 11 | 1.04139 | 31 | 1.49136 | 51 | 1.70757 | 71 | 1.85126 | 91 | 1.95904 |
| 12 | 1.07918 | 32 | 1.50515 | 52 | 1.71600 | 72 | 1.85733 | 92 | 1.96379 |
| 13 | 1.11394 | 33 | 1.51851 | 53 | 1.72428 | 73 | 1.86332 | 93 | 1.96848 |
| 14 | 1.14613 | 34 | 1.53148 | 54 | 1.73239 | 74 | 1.86923 | 94 | 1.97313 |
| 15 | 1.17609 | 35 | 1.54407 | 55 | 1.74036 | 75 | 1.87506 | 95 | 1.97772 |
| 16 | 1.20412 | 36 | 1.55630 | 56 | 1.74819 | 76 | 1.88081 | 96 | 1.98227 |
| 17 | 1.23045 | 37 | 1.56820 | 57 | 1.75587 | 77 | 1.88649 | 97 | 1.98677 |
| 18 | 1.25527 | 38 | 1.57978 | 58 | 1.76343 | 78 | 1.89209 | 98 | 1.99123 |
| 19 | 1.27875 | 39 | 1.59106 | 59 | 1.77085 | 79 | 1.89763 | 99 | 1.99564 |
| 20 | 1.30103 | 40 | 1.60206 | 60 | 1.77815 | 80 | 1.90309 | 100 | 2.00000 |

# TABLE XXVI.

## Logarithms of Numbers.

No. 100——1600. Log. 00000——20412.

| No. | 0 | 1 | 2 | 3 | 4 | 5 | 6 | 7 | 8 | 9 |
|---|---|---|---|---|---|---|---|---|---|---|
| 100 | 00000 | 00043 | 00087 | 00130 | 00173 | 00217 | 00260 | 00303 | 00346 | 00389 |
| 101 | 00432 | 00475 | 00518 | 00561 | 00604 | 00647 | 00689 | 00732 | 00775 | 00817 |
| 102 | 00860 | 00903 | 00945 | 00988 | 01030 | 01072 | 01115 | 01157 | 01199 | 01242 |
| 103 | 01284 | 01326 | 01368 | 01410 | 01452 | 01494 | 01536 | 01578 | 01620 | 01662 |
| 104 | 01703 | 01745 | 01787 | 01828 | 01870 | 01912 | 01953 | 01995 | 02036 | 02078 |
| 105 | 02119 | 02160 | 02202 | 02243 | 02284 | 02325 | 02366 | 02407 | 02449 | 02490 |
| 106 | 02531 | 02572 | 02612 | 02653 | 02694 | 02735 | 02776 | 02816 | 02857 | 02898 |
| 107 | 02938 | 02979 | 03019 | 03060 | 03100 | 03141 | 03181 | 03222 | 03262 | 03302 |
| 108 | 03342 | 03383 | 03423 | 03463 | 03503 | 03543 | 03583 | 03623 | 03663 | 03703 |
| 109 | 03743 | 03782 | 03822 | 03862 | 03902 | 03941 | 03981 | 04021 | 04060 | 04100 |
| 110 | 04139 | 04179 | 04218 | 04258 | 04297 | 04336 | 04376 | 04415 | 04454 | 04493 |
| 111 | 04532 | 04571 | 04610 | 04650 | 04689 | 04727 | 04766 | 04805 | 04844 | 04883 |
| 112 | 04922 | 04961 | 04999 | 05038 | 05077 | 05115 | 05154 | 05192 | 05231 | 05269 |
| 113 | 05308 | 05346 | 05385 | 05423 | 05461 | 05500 | 05538 | 05576 | 05614 | 05652 |
| 114 | 05690 | 05729 | 05767 | 05805 | 05843 | 05881 | 05918 | 05956 | 05994 | 06032 |
| 115 | 06070 | 06108 | 06145 | 06183 | 06221 | 06258 | 06296 | 06333 | 06371 | 06408 |
| 116 | 06446 | 06483 | 06521 | 06558 | 06595 | 06633 | 06670 | 06707 | 06744 | 06781 |
| 117 | 06819 | 06856 | 06893 | 06930 | 06967 | 07004 | 07041 | 07078 | 07115 | 07151 |
| 118 | 07188 | 07225 | 07262 | 07298 | 07335 | 07372 | 07408 | 07445 | 07482 | 07518 |
| 119 | 07555 | 07591 | 07628 | 07664 | 07700 | 07737 | 07773 | 07809 | 07846 | 07882 |
| 120 | 07918 | 07954 | 07990 | 08027 | 08063 | 08099 | 08135 | 08171 | 08207 | 08243 |
| 121 | 08279 | 08314 | 08350 | 08386 | 08422 | 08458 | 08493 | 08529 | 08565 | 08600 |
| 122 | 08636 | 08672 | 08707 | 08743 | 08778 | 08814 | 08849 | 08884 | 08920 | 08955 |
| 123 | 08991 | 09026 | 09061 | 09096 | 09132 | 09167 | 09202 | 09237 | 09272 | 09307 |
| 124 | 09342 | 09377 | 09412 | 09447 | 09482 | 09517 | 09552 | 09587 | 09621 | 09656 |
| 125 | 09691 | 09726 | 09760 | 09795 | 09830 | 09864 | 09899 | 09934 | 09968 | 10003 |
| 126 | 10037 | 10072 | 10106 | 10140 | 10175 | 10209 | 10243 | 10278 | 10312 | 10346 |
| 127 | 10380 | 10415 | 10449 | 10483 | 10517 | 10551 | 10585 | 10619 | 10653 | 10687 |
| 128 | 10721 | 10755 | 10789 | 10823 | 10857 | 10890 | 10924 | 10958 | 10992 | 11025 |
| 129 | 11059 | 11093 | 11126 | 11160 | 11193 | 11227 | 11261 | 11294 | 11327 | 11361 |
| 130 | 11394 | 11428 | 11461 | 11494 | 11528 | 11561 | 11594 | 11628 | 11661 | 11694 |
| 131 | 11727 | 11760 | 11793 | 11826 | 11860 | 11893 | 11926 | 11959 | 11992 | 12024 |
| 132 | 12057 | 12090 | 12123 | 12156 | 12189 | 12222 | 12254 | 12287 | 12320 | 12352 |
| 133 | 12385 | 12418 | 12450 | 12483 | 12516 | 12548 | 12581 | 12613 | 12646 | 12678 |
| 134 | 12710 | 12743 | 12775 | 12808 | 12840 | 12872 | 12905 | 12937 | 12969 | 13001 |
| 135 | 13033 | 13066 | 13098 | 13130 | 13162 | 13194 | 13226 | 13258 | 13290 | 13322 |
| 136 | 13354 | 13386 | 13418 | 13450 | 13481 | 13513 | 13545 | 13577 | 13609 | 13640 |
| 137 | 13672 | 13704 | 13735 | 13767 | 13799 | 13830 | 13862 | 13893 | 13925 | 13956 |
| 138 | 13988 | 14019 | 14051 | 14082 | 14114 | 14145 | 14176 | 14208 | 14239 | 14270 |
| 139 | 14301 | 14333 | 14364 | 14395 | 14426 | 14457 | 14489 | 14520 | 14551 | 14582 |
| 140 | 14613 | 14644 | 14675 | 14706 | 14737 | 14768 | 14799 | 14829 | 14860 | 14891 |
| 141 | 14922 | 14953 | 14983 | 15014 | 15045 | 15076 | 15106 | 15137 | 15168 | 15198 |
| 142 | 15229 | 15259 | 15290 | 15320 | 15351 | 15381 | 15412 | 15442 | 15473 | 15503 |
| 143 | 15534 | 15564 | 15594 | 15625 | 15655 | 15685 | 15715 | 15746 | 15776 | 15806 |
| 144 | 15836 | 15866 | 15897 | 15927 | 15957 | 15987 | 16017 | 16047 | 16077 | 16107 |
| 145 | 16137 | 16167 | 16197 | 16227 | 16256 | 16286 | 16316 | 16346 | 16376 | 16406 |
| 146 | 16435 | 16465 | 16495 | 16524 | 16554 | 16584 | 16613 | 16643 | 16673 | 16702 |
| 147 | 16732 | 16761 | 16791 | 16820 | 16850 | 16879 | 16909 | 16938 | 16967 | 16997 |
| 148 | 17026 | 17056 | 17085 | 17114 | 17143 | 17173 | 17202 | 17231 | 17260 | 17289 |
| 149 | 17319 | 17348 | 17377 | 17406 | 17435 | 17464 | 17493 | 17522 | 17551 | 17580 |
| 150 | 17609 | 17638 | 17667 | 17696 | 17725 | 17754 | 17782 | 17811 | 17840 | 17869 |
| 151 | 17898 | 17926 | 17955 | 17984 | 18013 | 18041 | 18070 | 18099 | 18127 | 18156 |
| 152 | 18184 | 18213 | 18241 | 18270 | 18298 | 18327 | 18355 | 18384 | 18412 | 18441 |
| 153 | 18469 | 18498 | 18526 | 18554 | 18583 | 18611 | 18639 | 18667 | 18696 | 18724 |
| 154 | 18752 | 18780 | 18808 | 18837 | 18865 | 18893 | 18921 | 18949 | 18977 | 19005 |
| 155 | 19033 | 19061 | 19089 | 19117 | 19145 | 19173 | 19201 | 19229 | 19257 | 19285 |
| 156 | 19312 | 19340 | 19368 | 19396 | 19424 | 19451 | 19479 | 19507 | 19535 | 19562 |
| 157 | 19590 | 19618 | 19645 | 19673 | 19700 | 19728 | 19756 | 19783 | 19811 | 19838 |
| 158 | 19866 | 19893 | 19921 | 19948 | 19976 | 20003 | 20030 | 20058 | 20085 | 20112 |
| 159 | 20140 | 20167 | 20194 | 20222 | 20249 | 20276 | 20303 | 20330 | 20358 | 20385 |
| No. | 0 | 1 | 2 | 3 | 4 | 5 | 6 | 7 | 8 | 9 |

| D | 43 | 42 |
|---|---|---|
| 1 | 4 | 4 |
| 2 | 9 | 8 |
| 3 | 13 | 13 |
| 4 | 17 | 17 |
| 5 | 22 | 21 |
| 6 | 26 | 25 |
| 7 | 30 | 29 |
| 8 | 34 | 34 |
| 9 | 39 | 38 |

| | 41 | 40 |
|---|---|---|
| 1 | 4 | 4 |
| 2 | 8 | 8 |
| 3 | 12 | 12 |
| 4 | 16 | 16 |
| 5 | 21 | 20 |
| 6 | 25 | 24 |
| 7 | 29 | 28 |
| 8 | 33 | 32 |
| 9 | 37 | 36 |

| | 39 | 38 |
|---|---|---|
| 1 | 4 | 4 |
| 2 | 8 | 8 |
| 3 | 12 | 11 |
| 4 | 16 | 15 |
| 5 | 20 | 19 |
| 6 | 23 | 23 |
| 7 | 27 | 27 |
| 8 | 31 | 30 |
| 9 | 35 | 34 |

| | 37 | 36 |
|---|---|---|
| 1 | 4 | 4 |
| 2 | 7 | 7 |
| 3 | 11 | 11 |
| 4 | 15 | 14 |
| 5 | 19 | 18 |
| 6 | 22 | 22 |
| 7 | 26 | 25 |
| 8 | 30 | 29 |
| 9 | 33 | 32 |

| | 35 | 34 |
|---|---|---|
| 1 | 4 | 3 |
| 2 | 7 | 7 |
| 3 | 11 | 10 |
| 4 | 14 | 14 |
| 5 | 18 | 17 |
| 6 | 21 | 20 |
| 7 | 25 | 24 |
| 8 | 28 | 27 |
| 9 | 32 | 31 |

| | 33 | 32 |
|---|---|---|
| 1 | 3 | 3 |
| 2 | 7 | 6 |
| 3 | 10 | 10 |
| 4 | 13 | 13 |
| 5 | 17 | 16 |
| 6 | 20 | 19 |
| 7 | 23 | 22 |
| 8 | 26 | 26 |
| 9 | 30 | 29 |

# TABLE XXVI.



## Logarithms of Numbers.

No. 1600——2200. Log. 20412——34242.

| No. | 0 | 1 | 2 | 3 | 4 | 5 | 6 | 7 | 8 | 9 |
|---|---|---|---|---|---|---|---|---|---|---|
| 160 | 20412 | 20439 | 20466 | 20493 | 20520 | 20548 | 20575 | 20602 | 20629 | 20656 |
| 161 | 20683 | 20710 | 20737 | 20763 | 20790 | 20817 | 20844 | 20871 | 20898 | 20925 |
| 162 | 20952 | 20978 | 21005 | 21032 | 21059 | 21085 | 21112 | 21139 | 21165 | 21192 |
| 163 | 21219 | 21245 | 21272 | 21299 | 21325 | 21352 | 21378 | 21405 | 21431 | 21458 |
| 164 | 21484 | 21511 | 21537 | 21564 | 21590 | 21617 | 21643 | 21669 | 21696 | 21722 |
| 165 | 21748 | 21775 | 21801 | 21827 | 21854 | 21880 | 21906 | 21932 | 21958 | 21985 |
| 166 | 22011 | 22037 | 22063 | 22089 | 22115 | 22141 | 22167 | 22194 | 22220 | 22246 |
| 167 | 22272 | 22298 | 22324 | 22350 | 22376 | 22401 | 22427 | 22453 | 22479 | 22505 |
| 168 | 22531 | 22557 | 22583 | 22608 | 22634 | 22660 | 22686 | 22712 | 22737 | 22763 |
| 169 | 22789 | 22814 | 22840 | 22866 | 22891 | 22917 | 22943 | 22968 | 22994 | 23019 |
| 170 | 23045 | 23070 | 23096 | 23121 | 23147 | 23172 | 23198 | 23223 | 23249 | 23274 |
| 171 | 23300 | 23325 | 23350 | 23376 | 23401 | 23426 | 23452 | 23477 | 23502 | 23528 |
| 172 | 23553 | 23578 | 23603 | 23629 | 23654 | 23679 | 23704 | 23729 | 23754 | 23779 |
| 173 | 23805 | 23830 | 23855 | 23880 | 23905 | 23930 | 23955 | 23980 | 24005 | 24030 |
| 174 | 24055 | 24080 | 24105 | 24130 | 24155 | 24180 | 24204 | 24229 | 24254 | 24279 |
| 175 | 24304 | 24329 | 24353 | 24378 | 24403 | 24428 | 24452 | 24477 | 24502 | 24527 |
| 176 | 24551 | 24576 | 24601 | 24625 | 24650 | 24674 | 24699 | 24724 | 24748 | 24773 |
| 177 | 24797 | 24822 | 24846 | 24871 | 24895 | 24920 | 24944 | 24969 | 24993 | 25018 |
| 178 | 25042 | 25066 | 25091 | 25115 | 25139 | 25164 | 25188 | 25212 | 25237 | 25261 |
| 179 | 25285 | 25310 | 25334 | 25358 | 25382 | 25406 | 25431 | 25455 | 25479 | 25503 |
| 180 | 25527 | 25551 | 25575 | 25600 | 25624 | 25648 | 25672 | 25696 | 25720 | 25744 |
| 181 | 25768 | 25792 | 25816 | 25840 | 25864 | 25888 | 25912 | 25935 | 25959 | 25983 |
| 182 | 26007 | 26031 | 26055 | 26079 | 26102 | 26126 | 26150 | 26174 | 26198 | 26221 |
| 183 | 26245 | 26269 | 26293 | 26316 | 26340 | 26364 | 26387 | 26411 | 26435 | 26458 |
| 184 | 26482 | 26505 | 26529 | 26553 | 26576 | 26600 | 26623 | 26647 | 26670 | 26694 |
| 185 | 26717 | 26741 | 26764 | 26788 | 26811 | 26834 | 26858 | 26881 | 26905 | 26928 |
| 186 | 26951 | 26975 | 26998 | 27021 | 27045 | 27068 | 27091 | 27114 | 27138 | 27161 |
| 187 | 27184 | 27207 | 27231 | 27254 | 27277 | 27300 | 27323 | 27346 | 27370 | 27393 |
| 188 | 27416 | 27439 | 27462 | 27485 | 27508 | 27531 | 27554 | 27577 | 27600 | 27623 |
| 189 | 27646 | 27669 | 27692 | 27715 | 27738 | 27761 | 27784 | 27807 | 27830 | 27852 |
| 190 | 27875 | 27898 | 27921 | 27944 | 27967 | 27989 | 28012 | 28035 | 28058 | 28081 |
| 191 | 28103 | 28126 | 28149 | 28171 | 28194 | 28217 | 28240 | 28262 | 28285 | 28307 |
| 192 | 28330 | 28353 | 28375 | 28398 | 28421 | 28443 | 28466 | 28488 | 28511 | 28533 |
| 193 | 28556 | 28578 | 28601 | 28623 | 28646 | 28668 | 28691 | 28713 | 28735 | 28758 |
| 194 | 28780 | 28803 | 28825 | 28847 | 28870 | 28892 | 28914 | 28937 | 28959 | 28981 |
| 195 | 29003 | 29026 | 29048 | 29070 | 29092 | 29115 | 29137 | 29159 | 29181 | 29203 |
| 196 | 29226 | 29248 | 29270 | 29292 | 29314 | 29336 | 29358 | 29380 | 29403 | 29425 |
| 197 | 29447 | 29469 | 29491 | 29513 | 29535 | 29557 | 29579 | 29601 | 29623 | 29645 |
| 198 | 29667 | 29688 | 29710 | 29732 | 29754 | 29776 | 29798 | 29820 | 29842 | 29863 |
| 199 | 29885 | 29907 | 29929 | 29951 | 29973 | 29994 | 30016 | 30038 | 30060 | 30081 |
| 200 | 30103 | 30125 | 30146 | 30168 | 30190 | 30211 | 30233 | 30255 | 30276 | 30298 |
| 201 | 30320 | 30341 | 30363 | 30384 | 30406 | 30428 | 30449 | 30471 | 30492 | 30514 |
| 202 | 30535 | 30557 | 30578 | 30600 | 30621 | 30643 | 30664 | 30685 | 30707 | 30728 |
| 203 | 30750 | 30771 | 30792 | 30814 | 30835 | 30856 | 30878 | 30899 | 30920 | 30942 |
| 204 | 30963 | 30984 | 31006 | 31027 | 31048 | 31069 | 31091 | 31112 | 31133 | 31154 |
| 205 | 31175 | 31197 | 31218 | 31239 | 31260 | 31281 | 31302 | 31323 | 31345 | 31366 |
| 206 | 31387 | 31408 | 31429 | 31450 | 31471 | 31492 | 31513 | 31534 | 31555 | 31576 |
| 207 | 31597 | 31618 | 31639 | 31660 | 31681 | 31702 | 31723 | 31744 | 31765 | 31785 |
| 208 | 31806 | 31827 | 31848 | 31869 | 31890 | 31911 | 31931 | 31952 | 31973 | 31994 |
| 209 | 32015 | 32035 | 32056 | 32077 | 32098 | 32118 | 32139 | 32160 | 32181 | 32201 |
| 210 | 32222 | 32243 | 32263 | 32284 | 32305 | 32325 | 32346 | 32366 | 32387 | 32408 |
| 211 | 32428 | 32449 | 32469 | 32490 | 32510 | 32531 | 32552 | 32572 | 32593 | 32613 |
| 212 | 32634 | 32654 | 32675 | 32695 | 32715 | 32736 | 32756 | 32777 | 32797 | 32818 |
| 213 | 32838 | 32858 | 32879 | 32899 | 32919 | 32940 | 32960 | 32980 | 33001 | 33021 |
| 214 | 33041 | 33062 | 33082 | 33102 | 33122 | 33143 | 33163 | 33183 | 33203 | 33224 |
| 215 | 33244 | 33264 | 33284 | 33304 | 33325 | 33345 | 33365 | 33385 | 33405 | 33425 |
| 216 | 33445 | 33465 | 33486 | 33506 | 33526 | 33546 | 33566 | 33586 | 33606 | 33626 |
| 217 | 33646 | 33666 | 33686 | 33706 | 33726 | 33746 | 33766 | 33786 | 33806 | 33826 |
| 218 | 33846 | 33866 | 33885 | 33905 | 33925 | 33945 | 33965 | 33985 | 34005 | 34025 |
| 219 | 34044 | 34064 | 34084 | 34104 | 34124 | 34143 | 34163 | 34183 | 34203 | 34223 |
| No. | 0 | 1 | 2 | 3 | 4 | 5 | 6 | 7 | 8 | 9 |

| | 31 | 30 | 29 | 28 | 27 | 26 | 25 | 24 | 23 | 22 | 21 | 20 |
|---|---|---|---|---|---|---|---|---|---|---|---|---|
| 1 | 3 | 3 | 3 | 3 | 3 | 3 | 3 | 2 | 2 | 2 | 2 | 2 |
| 2 | 6 | 6 | 6 | 6 | 5 | 5 | 5 | 5 | 5 | 4 | 4 | 4 |
| 3 | 9 | 9 | 9 | 8 | 8 | 8 | 8 | 7 | 7 | 7 | 6 | 6 |
| 4 | 12 | 12 | 12 | 11 | 11 | 10 | 10 | 10 | 9 | 9 | 8 | 8 |
| 5 | 16 | 15 | 15 | 14 | 14 | 13 | 13 | 12 | 12 | 11 | 11 | 10 |
| 6 | 19 | 18 | 17 | 17 | 16 | 16 | 15 | 14 | 14 | 13 | 13 | 12 |
| 7 | 22 | 21 | 20 | 20 | 19 | 18 | 18 | 17 | 16 | 15 | 15 | 14 |
| 8 | 25 | 24 | 23 | 22 | 22 | 21 | 20 | 19 | 18 | 18 | 17 | 16 |
| 9 | 28 | 27 | 26 | 25 | 24 | 23 | 23 | 22 | 21 | 20 | 19 | 18 |

# TABLE XXVI.

## Logarithms of Numbers.

No. 2200——2800. Log. 34242——44716.

| No. | 0 | 1 | 2 | 3 | 4 | 5 | 6 | 7 | 8 | 9 |
|---|---|---|---|---|---|---|---|---|---|---|
| 220 | 34242 | 34262 | 34282 | 34301 | 34321 | 34341 | 34361 | 34380 | 34400 | 34420 |
| 221 | 34439 | 34459 | 34479 | 34498 | 34518 | 34537 | 34557 | 34577 | 34596 | 34616 |
| 222 | 34635 | 34655 | 34674 | 34694 | 34713 | 34733 | 34753 | 34772 | 34792 | 34811 |
| 223 | 34830 | 34850 | 34869 | 34889 | 34908 | 34928 | 34947 | 34967 | 34986 | 35005 |
| 224 | 35025 | 35044 | 35064 | 35083 | 35102 | 35122 | 35141 | 35160 | 35180 | 35199 |
| 225 | 35218 | 35238 | 35257 | 35276 | 35295 | 35315 | 35334 | 35353 | 35372 | 35392 |
| 226 | 35411 | 35430 | 35449 | 35468 | 35488 | 35507 | 35526 | 35545 | 35564 | 35583 |
| 227 | 35603 | 35622 | 35641 | 35660 | 35679 | 35698 | 35717 | 35736 | 35755 | 35774 |
| 228 | 35793 | 35813 | 35832 | 35851 | 35870 | 35889 | 35908 | 35927 | 35946 | 35965 |
| 229 | 35984 | 36003 | 36021 | 36040 | 36059 | 36078 | 36097 | 36116 | 36135 | 36154 |
| 230 | 36173 | 36192 | 36211 | 36229 | 36248 | 36267 | 36286 | 36305 | 36324 | 36342 |
| 231 | 36361 | 36380 | 36399 | 36418 | 36436 | 36455 | 36474 | 36493 | 36511 | 36530 |
| 232 | 36549 | 36568 | 36586 | 36605 | 36624 | 36642 | 36661 | 36680 | 36698 | 36717 |
| 233 | 36736 | 36754 | 36773 | 36791 | 36810 | 36829 | 36847 | 36866 | 36884 | 36903 |
| 234 | 36922 | 36940 | 36959 | 36977 | 36996 | 37014 | 37033 | 37051 | 37070 | 37088 |
| 235 | 37107 | 37125 | 37144 | 37162 | 37181 | 37199 | 37218 | 37236 | 37254 | 37273 |
| 236 | 37291 | 37310 | 37328 | 37346 | 37365 | 37383 | 37401 | 37420 | 37438 | 37457 |
| 237 | 37475 | 37493 | 37511 | 37530 | 37548 | 37566 | 37585 | 37603 | 37621 | 37639 |
| 238 | 37658 | 37676 | 37694 | 37712 | 37731 | 37749 | 37767 | 37785 | 37803 | 37822 |
| 239 | 37840 | 37858 | 37876 | 37894 | 37912 | 37931 | 37949 | 37967 | 37985 | 38003 |
| 240 | 38021 | 38039 | 38057 | 38075 | 38093 | 38112 | 38130 | 38148 | 38166 | 38184 |
| 241 | 38202 | 38220 | 38238 | 38256 | 38274 | 38292 | 38310 | 38328 | 38346 | 38364 |
| 242 | 38382 | 38399 | 38417 | 38435 | 38453 | 38471 | 38489 | 38507 | 38525 | 38543 |
| 243 | 38561 | 38578 | 38596 | 38614 | 38632 | 38650 | 38668 | 38686 | 38703 | 38721 |
| 244 | 38739 | 38757 | 38775 | 38792 | 38810 | 38828 | 38846 | 38863 | 38881 | 38899 |
| 245 | 38917 | 38934 | 38952 | 38970 | 38987 | 39005 | 39023 | 39041 | 39058 | 39076 |
| 246 | 39094 | 39111 | 39129 | 39146 | 39164 | 39182 | 39199 | 39217 | 39235 | 39252 |
| 247 | 39270 | 39287 | 39305 | 39322 | 39340 | 39358 | 39375 | 39393 | 39410 | 39428 |
| 248 | 39445 | 39463 | 39480 | 39498 | 39515 | 39533 | 39550 | 39568 | 39585 | 39602 |
| 249 | 39620 | 39637 | 39655 | 39672 | 39690 | 39707 | 39724 | 39742 | 39759 | 39777 |
| 250 | 39794 | 39811 | 39829 | 39846 | 39863 | 39881 | 39898 | 39915 | 39933 | 39950 |
| 251 | 39967 | 39985 | 40002 | 40019 | 40037 | 40054 | 40071 | 40088 | 40106 | 40123 |
| 252 | 40140 | 40157 | 40175 | 40192 | 40209 | 40226 | 40243 | 40261 | 40278 | 40295 |
| 253 | 40312 | 40329 | 40346 | 40364 | 40381 | 40398 | 40415 | 40432 | 40449 | 40466 |
| 254 | 40483 | 40500 | 40518 | 40535 | 40552 | 40569 | 40586 | 40603 | 40620 | 40637 |
| 255 | 40654 | 40671 | 40688 | 40705 | 40722 | 40739 | 40756 | 40773 | 40790 | 40807 |
| 256 | 40824 | 40841 | 40858 | 40875 | 40892 | 40909 | 40926 | 40943 | 40960 | 40976 |
| 257 | 40993 | 41010 | 41027 | 41044 | 41061 | 41078 | 41095 | 41111 | 41128 | 41145 |
| 258 | 41162 | 41179 | 41196 | 41212 | 41229 | 41246 | 41263 | 41280 | 41296 | 41313 |
| 259 | 41330 | 41347 | 41363 | 41380 | 41397 | 41414 | 41430 | 41447 | 41464 | 41481 |
| 260 | 41497 | 41514 | 41531 | 41547 | 41564 | 41581 | 41597 | 41614 | 41631 | 41647 |
| 261 | 41664 | 41681 | 41697 | 41714 | 41731 | 41747 | 41764 | 41780 | 41797 | 41814 |
| 262 | 41830 | 41847 | 41863 | 41880 | 41896 | 41913 | 41929 | 41946 | 41963 | 41979 |
| 263 | 41996 | 42012 | 42029 | 42045 | 42062 | 42078 | 42095 | 42111 | 42127 | 42144 |
| 264 | 42160 | 42177 | 42193 | 42210 | 42226 | 42243 | 42259 | 42275 | 42292 | 42308 |
| 265 | 42325 | 42341 | 42357 | 42374 | 42390 | 42406 | 42423 | 42439 | 42455 | 42472 |
| 266 | 42488 | 42504 | 42521 | 42537 | 42553 | 42570 | 42586 | 42602 | 42619 | 42635 |
| 267 | 42651 | 42667 | 42684 | 42700 | 42716 | 42732 | 42749 | 42765 | 42781 | 42797 |
| 268 | 42813 | 42830 | 42846 | 42862 | 42878 | 42894 | 42911 | 42927 | 42943 | 42959 |
| 269 | 42975 | 42991 | 43008 | 43024 | 43040 | 43056 | 43072 | 43088 | 43104 | 43120 |
| 270 | 43136 | 43152 | 43169 | 43185 | 43201 | 43217 | 43233 | 43249 | 43265 | 43281 |
| 271 | 43297 | 43313 | 43329 | 43345 | 43361 | 43377 | 43393 | 43409 | 43425 | 43441 |
| 272 | 43457 | 43473 | 43489 | 43505 | 43521 | 43537 | 43553 | 43569 | 43584 | 43600 |
| 273 | 43616 | 43632 | 43648 | 43664 | 43680 | 43696 | 43712 | 43727 | 43743 | 43759 |
| 274 | 43775 | 43791 | 43807 | 43823 | 43838 | 43854 | 43870 | 43886 | 43902 | 43917 |
| 275 | 43933 | 43949 | 43965 | 43981 | 43996 | 44012 | 44028 | 44044 | 44059 | 44075 |
| 276 | 44091 | 44107 | 44122 | 44138 | 44154 | 44170 | 44185 | 44201 | 44217 | 44232 |
| 277 | 44248 | 44264 | 44279 | 44295 | 44311 | 44326 | 44342 | 44358 | 44373 | 44389 |
| 278 | 44404 | 44420 | 44436 | 44451 | 44467 | 44483 | 44498 | 44514 | 44529 | 44545 |
| 279 | 44560 | 44576 | 44592 | 44607 | 44623 | 44638 | 44654 | 44669 | 44685 | 44700 |
| No. | 0 | 1 | 2 | 3 | 4 | 5 | 6 | 7 | 8 | 9 |

| 20 | |
|---|---|
| 1 | 2 |
| 2 | 4 |
| 3 | 6 |
| 4 | 8 |
| 5 | 10 |
| 6 | 12 |
| 7 | 14 |
| 8 | 16 |
| 9 | 18 |

| 19 | |
|---|---|
| 1 | 2 |
| 2 | 4 |
| 3 | 6 |
| 4 | 8 |
| 5 | 10 |
| 6 | 11 |
| 7 | 13 |
| 8 | 15 |
| 9 | 17 |

| 18 | |
|---|---|
| 1 | 2 |
| 2 | 4 |
| 3 | 5 |
| 4 | 7 |
| 5 | 9 |
| 6 | 11 |
| 7 | 13 |
| 8 | 14 |
| 9 | 16 |

| 17 | |
|---|---|
| 1 | 2 |
| 2 | 3 |
| 3 | 5 |
| 4 | 7 |
| 5 | 9 |
| 6 | 10 |
| 7 | 12 |
| 8 | 14 |
| 9 | 15 |

| 16 | |
|---|---|
| 1 | 2 |
| 2 | 3 |
| 3 | 5 |
| 4 | 6 |
| 5 | 8 |
| 6 | 10 |
| 7 | 11 |
| 8 | 13 |
| 9 | 14 |

| 15 | |
|---|---|
| 1 | 2 |
| 2 | 3 |
| 3 | 5 |
| 4 | 6 |
| 5 | 8 |
| 6 | 9 |
| 7 | 11 |
| 8 | 12 |
| 9 | 14 |

# TABLE XXVI.

## Logarithms of Numbers.

**No. 2800——3400.** **Log. 44716——53148.**

| No. | 0 | 1 | 2 | 3 | 4 | 5 | 6 | 7 | 8 | 9 |
|---|---|---|---|---|---|---|---|---|---|---|
| 280 | 44716 | 44731 | 44747 | 44762 | 44778 | 44793 | 44809 | 44824 | 44840 | 44855 |
| 281 | 44871 | 44886 | 44902 | 44917 | 44932 | 44948 | 44963 | 44979 | 44994 | 45010 |
| 282 | 45025 | 45040 | 45056 | 45071 | 45086 | 45102 | 45117 | 45133 | 45148 | 45163 |
| 283 | 45179 | 45194 | 45209 | 45225 | 45240 | 45255 | 45271 | 45286 | 45301 | 45317 |
| 284 | 45332 | 45347 | 45362 | 45378 | 45393 | 45408 | 45423 | 45439 | 45454 | 45469 |
| 285 | 45484 | 45500 | 45515 | 45530 | 45545 | 45561 | 45576 | 45591 | 45606 | 45621 |
| 286 | 45637 | 45652 | 45667 | 45682 | 45697 | 45712 | 45728 | 45743 | 45758 | 45773 |
| 287 | 45788 | 45803 | 45818 | 45834 | 45849 | 45864 | 45879 | 45894 | 45909 | 45924 |
| 288 | 45939 | 45954 | 45969 | 45984 | 46000 | 46015 | 46030 | 46045 | 46060 | 46075 |
| 289 | 46090 | 46105 | 46120 | 46135 | 46150 | 46165 | 46180 | 46195 | 46210 | 46225 |
| 290 | 46240 | 46255 | 46270 | 46285 | 46300 | 46315 | 46330 | 46345 | 46359 | 46374 |
| 291 | 46389 | 46404 | 46419 | 46434 | 46449 | 46464 | 46479 | 46494 | 46509 | 46523 |
| 292 | 46538 | 46553 | 46568 | 46583 | 46598 | 46613 | 46627 | 46642 | 46657 | 46672 |
| 293 | 46687 | 46702 | 46716 | 46731 | 46746 | 46761 | 46776 | 46790 | 46805 | 46820 |
| 294 | 46835 | 46850 | 46864 | 46879 | 46894 | 46909 | 46923 | 46938 | 46953 | 46967 |
| 295 | 46982 | 46997 | 47012 | 47026 | 47041 | 47056 | 47070 | 47085 | 47100 | 47114 |
| 296 | 47129 | 47144 | 47159 | 47173 | 47188 | 47202 | 47217 | 47232 | 47246 | 47261 |
| 297 | 47276 | 47290 | 47305 | 47319 | 47334 | 47349 | 47363 | 47378 | 47392 | 47407 |
| 298 | 47422 | 47436 | 47451 | 47465 | 47480 | 47494 | 47509 | 47524 | 47538 | 47553 |
| 299 | 47567 | 47582 | 47596 | 47611 | 47625 | 47640 | 47654 | 47669 | 47683 | 47698 |
| 300 | 47712 | 47727 | 47741 | 47756 | 47770 | 47784 | 47799 | 47813 | 47828 | 47842 |
| 301 | 47857 | 47871 | 47885 | 47900 | 47914 | 47929 | 47943 | 47958 | 47972 | 47986 |
| 302 | 48001 | 48015 | 48029 | 48044 | 48058 | 48073 | 48087 | 48101 | 48116 | 48130 |
| 303 | 48144 | 48159 | 48173 | 48187 | 48202 | 48216 | 48230 | 48244 | 48259 | 48273 |
| 304 | 48287 | 48302 | 48316 | 48330 | 48344 | 48359 | 48373 | 48387 | 48401 | 48416 |
| 305 | 48430 | 48444 | 48458 | 48473 | 48487 | 48501 | 48515 | 48530 | 48544 | 48558 |
| 306 | 48572 | 48586 | 48601 | 48615 | 48629 | 48643 | 48657 | 48671 | 48686 | 48700 |
| 307 | 48714 | 48728 | 48742 | 48756 | 48770 | 48785 | 48799 | 48813 | 48827 | 48841 |
| 308 | 48855 | 48869 | 48883 | 48897 | 48911 | 48926 | 48940 | 48954 | 48968 | 48982 |
| 309 | 48996 | 49010 | 49024 | 49038 | 49052 | 49066 | 49080 | 49094 | 49108 | 49122 |
| 310 | 49136 | 49150 | 49164 | 49178 | 49192 | 49206 | 49220 | 49234 | 49248 | 49262 |
| 311 | 49276 | 49290 | 49304 | 49318 | 49332 | 49346 | 49360 | 49374 | 49388 | 49402 |
| 312 | 49415 | 49429 | 49443 | 49457 | 49471 | 49485 | 49499 | 49513 | 49527 | 49541 |
| 313 | 49554 | 49568 | 49582 | 49596 | 49610 | 49624 | 49638 | 49651 | 49665 | 49679 |
| 314 | 49693 | 49707 | 49721 | 49734 | 49748 | 49762 | 49776 | 49790 | 49803 | 49817 |
| 315 | 49831 | 49845 | 49859 | 49872 | 49886 | 49900 | 49914 | 49927 | 49941 | 49955 |
| 316 | 49969 | 49982 | 49996 | 50010 | 50024 | 50037 | 50051 | 50065 | 50079 | 50092 |
| 317 | 50106 | 50120 | 50133 | 50147 | 50161 | 50174 | 50188 | 50202 | 50215 | 50229 |
| 318 | 50243 | 50256 | 50270 | 50284 | 50297 | 50311 | 50325 | 50338 | 50352 | 50365 |
| 319 | 50379 | 50393 | 50406 | 50420 | 50433 | 50447 | 50461 | 50474 | 50488 | 50501 |
| 320 | 50515 | 50529 | 50542 | 50556 | 50569 | 50583 | 50596 | 50610 | 50623 | 50637 |
| 321 | 50651 | 50664 | 50678 | 50691 | 50705 | 50718 | 50732 | 50745 | 50759 | 50772 |
| 322 | 50786 | 50799 | 50813 | 50826 | 50840 | 50853 | 50866 | 50880 | 50893 | 50907 |
| 323 | 50920 | 50934 | 50947 | 50961 | 50974 | 50987 | 51001 | 51014 | 51028 | 51041 |
| 324 | 51055 | 51068 | 51081 | 51095 | 51108 | 51121 | 51135 | 51148 | 51162 | 51175 |
| 325 | 51188 | 51202 | 51215 | 51228 | 51242 | 51255 | 51268 | 51282 | 51295 | 51308 |
| 326 | 51322 | 51335 | 51348 | 51362 | 51375 | 51388 | 51402 | 51415 | 51428 | 51441 |
| 327 | 51455 | 51468 | 51481 | 51495 | 51508 | 51521 | 51534 | 51548 | 51561 | 51574 |
| 328 | 51587 | 51601 | 51614 | 51627 | 51640 | 51654 | 51667 | 51680 | 51693 | 51706 |
| 329 | 51720 | 51733 | 51746 | 51759 | 51772 | 51786 | 51799 | 51812 | 51825 | 51838 |
| 330 | 51851 | 51865 | 51878 | 51891 | 51904 | 51917 | 51930 | 51943 | 51957 | 51970 |
| 331 | 51983 | 51996 | 52009 | 52022 | 52035 | 52048 | 52061 | 52075 | 52088 | 52101 |
| 332 | 52114 | 52127 | 52140 | 52153 | 52166 | 52179 | 52192 | 52205 | 52218 | 52231 |
| 333 | 52244 | 52257 | 52270 | 52284 | 52297 | 52310 | 52323 | 52336 | 52349 | 52362 |
| 334 | 52375 | 52388 | 52401 | 52414 | 52427 | 52440 | 52453 | 52466 | 52479 | 52492 |
| 335 | 52504 | 52517 | 52530 | 52543 | 52556 | 52569 | 52582 | 52595 | 52608 | 52621 |
| 336 | 52634 | 52647 | 52660 | 52673 | 52686 | 52699 | 52711 | 52724 | 52737 | 52750 |
| 337 | 52763 | 52776 | 52789 | 52802 | 52815 | 52827 | 52840 | 52853 | 52866 | 52879 |
| 338 | 52892 | 52905 | 52917 | 52930 | 52943 | 52956 | 52969 | 52982 | 52994 | 53007 |
| 339 | 53020 | 53033 | 53046 | 53058 | 53071 | 53084 | 53097 | 53110 | 53122 | 53135 |
| No. | 0 | 1 | 2 | 3 | 4 | 5 | 6 | 7 | 8 | 9 |

| 16 | |
|---|---|
| 1 | 2 |
| 2 | 3 |
| 3 | 5 |
| 4 | 6 |
| 5 | 8 |
| 6 | 10 |
| 7 | 11 |
| 8 | 13 |
| 9 | 14 |

| 15 | |
|---|---|
| 1 | 2 |
| 2 | 3 |
| 3 | 5 |
| 4 | 6 |
| 5 | 8 |
| 6 | 9 |
| 7 | 11 |
| 8 | 12 |
| 9 | 14 |

| 14 | |
|---|---|
| 1 | 1 |
| 2 | 3 |
| 3 | 4 |
| 4 | 6 |
| 5 | 7 |
| 6 | 8 |
| 7 | 10 |
| 8 | 11 |
| 9 | 13 |

| 13 | |
|---|---|
| 1 | 1 |
| 2 | 3 |
| 3 | 4 |
| 4 | 5 |
| 5 | 7 |
| 6 | 8 |
| 7 | 9 |
| 8 | 10 |
| 9 | 12 |

| 12 | |
|---|---|
| 1 | 1 |
| 2 | 2 |
| 3 | 4 |
| 4 | 5 |
| 5 | 6 |
| 6 | 7 |
| 7 | 8 |
| 8 | 10 |
| 9 | 11 |

# TABLE XXVI.

## Logarithms of Numbers.

No. 3400——4000. Log. 53148——60206.

| No. | 0 | 1 | 2 | 3 | 4 | 5 | 6 | 7 | 8 | 9 |
|---|---|---|---|---|---|---|---|---|---|---|
| 340 | 53148 | 53161 | 53173 | 53186 | 53199 | 53212 | 53224 | 53237 | 53250 | 53263 |
| 341 | 53275 | 53288 | 53301 | 53314 | 53326 | 53339 | 53352 | 53364 | 53377 | 53390 |
| 342 | 53403 | 53415 | 53428 | 53441 | 53453 | 53466 | 53479 | 53491 | 53504 | 53517 |
| 343 | 53529 | 53542 | 53555 | 53567 | 53580 | 53593 | 53605 | 53618 | 53631 | 53643 |
| 344 | 53656 | 53668 | 53681 | 53694 | 53706 | 53719 | 53732 | 53744 | 53757 | 53769 |
| 345 | 53782 | 53794 | 53807 | 53820 | 53832 | 53845 | 53857 | 53870 | 53882 | 53895 |
| 346 | 53908 | 53920 | 53933 | 53945 | 53958 | 53970 | 53983 | 53995 | 54008 | 54020 |
| 347 | 54033 | 54045 | 54058 | 54070 | 54083 | 54095 | 54108 | 54120 | 54133 | 54145 |
| 348 | 54158 | 54170 | 54183 | 54195 | 54208 | 54220 | 54233 | 54245 | 54258 | 54270 |
| 349 | 54283 | 54295 | 54307 | 54320 | 54332 | 54345 | 54357 | 54370 | 54382 | 54394 |
| 350 | 54407 | 54419 | 54432 | 54444 | 54456 | 54469 | 54481 | 54494 | 54506 | 54518 |
| 351 | 54531 | 54543 | 54555 | 54568 | 54580 | 54593 | 54605 | 54617 | 54630 | 54642 |
| 352 | 54654 | 54667 | 54679 | 54691 | 54704 | 54716 | 54728 | 54741 | 54753 | 54765 |
| 353 | 54777 | 54790 | 54802 | 54814 | 54827 | 54839 | 54851 | 54864 | 54876 | 54888 |
| 354 | 54900 | 54913 | 54925 | 54937 | 54949 | 54962 | 54974 | 54986 | 54998 | 55011 |
| 355 | 55023 | 55035 | 55047 | 55060 | 55072 | 55084 | 55096 | 55108 | 55121 | 55133 |
| 356 | 55145 | 55157 | 55169 | 55182 | 55194 | 55206 | 55218 | 55230 | 55242 | 55255 |
| 357 | 55267 | 55279 | 55291 | 55303 | 55315 | 55328 | 55340 | 55352 | 55364 | 55376 |
| 358 | 55388 | 55400 | 55413 | 55425 | 55437 | 55449 | 55461 | 55473 | 55485 | 55497 |
| 359 | 55509 | 55522 | 55534 | 55546 | 55558 | 55570 | 55582 | 55594 | 55606 | 55618 |
| 360 | 55630 | 55642 | 55654 | 55666 | 55678 | 55691 | 55703 | 55715 | 55727 | 55739 |
| 361 | 55751 | 55763 | 55775 | 55787 | 55799 | 55811 | 55823 | 55835 | 55847 | 55859 |
| 362 | 55871 | 55883 | 55895 | 55907 | 55919 | 55931 | 55943 | 55955 | 55967 | 55979 |
| 363 | 55991 | 56003 | 56015 | 56027 | 56038 | 56050 | 56062 | 56074 | 56086 | 56098 |
| 364 | 56110 | 56122 | 56134 | 56146 | 56158 | 56170 | 56182 | 56194 | 56205 | 56217 |
| 365 | 56229 | 56241 | 56253 | 56265 | 56277 | 56289 | 56301 | 56312 | 56324 | 56336 |
| 366 | 56348 | 56360 | 56372 | 56384 | 56396 | 56407 | 56419 | 56431 | 56443 | 56455 |
| 367 | 56467 | 56478 | 56490 | 56502 | 56514 | 56526 | 56538 | 56549 | 56561 | 56573 |
| 368 | 56585 | 56597 | 56608 | 56620 | 56632 | 56644 | 56656 | 56667 | 56679 | 56691 |
| 369 | 56703 | 56714 | 56726 | 56738 | 56750 | 56761 | 56773 | 56785 | 56797 | 56808 |
| 370 | 56820 | 56832 | 56844 | 56855 | 56867 | 56879 | 56891 | 56902 | 56914 | 56926 |
| 371 | 56937 | 56949 | 56961 | 56972 | 56984 | 56996 | 57008 | 57019 | 57031 | 57043 |
| 372 | 57054 | 57066 | 57078 | 57089 | 57101 | 57113 | 57124 | 57136 | 57148 | 57159 |
| 373 | 57171 | 57183 | 57194 | 57206 | 57217 | 57229 | 57241 | 57252 | 57264 | 57276 |
| 374 | 57287 | 57299 | 57310 | 57322 | 57334 | 57345 | 57357 | 57368 | 57380 | 57392 |
| 375 | 57403 | 57415 | 57426 | 57438 | 57449 | 57461 | 57473 | 57484 | 57496 | 57507 |
| 376 | 57519 | 57530 | 57542 | 57553 | 57565 | 57576 | 57588 | 57600 | 57611 | 57623 |
| 377 | 57634 | 57646 | 57657 | 57669 | 57680 | 57692 | 57703 | 57715 | 57726 | 57738 |
| 378 | 57749 | 57761 | 57772 | 57784 | 57795 | 57807 | 57818 | 57830 | 57841 | 57852 |
| 379 | 57864 | 57875 | 57887 | 57898 | 57910 | 57921 | 57933 | 57944 | 57955 | 57967 |
| 380 | 57978 | 57990 | 58001 | 58013 | 58024 | 58035 | 58047 | 58058 | 58070 | 58081 |
| 381 | 58092 | 58104 | 58115 | 58127 | 58138 | 58149 | 58161 | 58172 | 58184 | 58195 |
| 382 | 58206 | 58218 | 58229 | 58240 | 58252 | 58263 | 58274 | 58286 | 58297 | 58309 |
| 383 | 58320 | 58331 | 58343 | 58354 | 58365 | 58377 | 58388 | 58399 | 58410 | 58422 |
| 384 | 58433 | 58444 | 58456 | 58467 | 58478 | 58490 | 58501 | 58512 | 58524 | 58535 |
| 385 | 58546 | 58557 | 58569 | 58580 | 58591 | 58602 | 58614 | 58625 | 58636 | 58647 |
| 386 | 58659 | 58670 | 58681 | 58692 | 58704 | 58715 | 58726 | 58737 | 58749 | 58760 |
| 387 | 58771 | 58782 | 58794 | 58805 | 58816 | 58827 | 58838 | 58850 | 58861 | 58872 |
| 388 | 58883 | 58894 | 58906 | 58917 | 58928 | 58939 | 58950 | 58961 | 58973 | 58984 |
| 389 | 58995 | 59006 | 59017 | 59028 | 59040 | 59051 | 59062 | 59073 | 59084 | 59095 |
| 390 | 59106 | 59118 | 59129 | 59140 | 59151 | 59162 | 59173 | 59184 | 59195 | 59207 |
| 391 | 59218 | 59229 | 59240 | 59251 | 59262 | 59273 | 59284 | 59295 | 59306 | 59318 |
| 392 | 59329 | 59340 | 59351 | 59362 | 59373 | 59384 | 59395 | 59406 | 59417 | 59428 |
| 393 | 59439 | 59450 | 59461 | 59472 | 59483 | 59494 | 59506 | 59517 | 59528 | 59539 |
| 394 | 59550 | 59561 | 59572 | 59583 | 59594 | 59605 | 59616 | 59627 | 59638 | 59649 |
| 395 | 59660 | 59671 | 59682 | 59693 | 59704 | 59715 | 59726 | 59737 | 59748 | 59759 |
| 396 | 59770 | 59780 | 59791 | 59802 | 59813 | 59824 | 59835 | 59846 | 59857 | 59868 |
| 397 | 59879 | 59890 | 59901 | 59912 | 59923 | 59934 | 59945 | 59956 | 59966 | 59977 |
| 398 | 59988 | 59999 | 60010 | 60021 | 60032 | 60043 | 60054 | 60065 | 60076 | 60086 |
| 399 | 60097 | 60108 | 60119 | 60130 | 60141 | 60152 | 60163 | 60173 | 60184 | 60195 |
| No. | 0 | 1 | 2 | 3 | 4 | 5 | 6 | 7 | 8 | 9 |

| 13 | |
|---|---|
| 1 | 1 |
| 2 | 3 |
| 3 | 4 |
| 4 | 5 |
| 5 | 7 |
| 6 | 8 |
| 7 | 9 |
| 8 | 10 |
| 9 | 12 |

| 12 | |
|---|---|
| 1 | 1 |
| 2 | 2 |
| 3 | 4 |
| 4 | 5 |
| 5 | 6 |
| 6 | 7 |
| 7 | 8 |
| 8 | 10 |
| 9 | 11 |

| 11 | |
|---|---|
| 1 | 1 |
| 2 | 2 |
| 3 | 3 |
| 4 | 4 |
| 5 | 6 |
| 6 | 7 |
| 7 | 8 |
| 8 | 9 |
| 9 | 10 |

| 10 | |
|---|---|
| 1 | 1 |
| 2 | 2 |
| 3 | 3 |
| 4 | 4 |
| 5 | 5 |
| 6 | 6 |
| 7 | 7 |
| 8 | 8 |
| 9 | 9 |

# TABLE XXVI.

## Logarithms of Numbers.

No. 4000——4600. Log. 60206——66276.

| No. | 0 | 1 | 2 | 3 | 4 | 5 | 6 | 7 | 8 | 9 |
|---|---|---|---|---|---|---|---|---|---|---|
| 400 | 60206 | 60217 | 60228 | 60239 | 60249 | 60260 | 60271 | 60282 | 60293 | 60304 |
| 401 | 60314 | 60325 | 60336 | 60347 | 60358 | 60369 | 60379 | 60390 | 60401 | 60412 |
| 402 | 60423 | 60433 | 60444 | 60455 | 60466 | 60477 | 60487 | 60498 | 60509 | 60520 |
| 403 | 60531 | 60541 | 60552 | 60563 | 60574 | 60584 | 60595 | 60606 | 60617 | 60627 |
| 404 | 60638 | 60649 | 60660 | 60670 | 60681 | 60692 | 60703 | 60713 | 60724 | 60735 |
| 405 | 60746 | 60756 | 60767 | 60778 | 60788 | 60799 | 60810 | 60821 | 60831 | 60842 |
| 406 | 60853 | 60863 | 60874 | 60885 | 60895 | 60906 | 60917 | 60927 | 60938 | 60949 |
| 407 | 60959 | 60970 | 60981 | 60991 | 61002 | 61013 | 61023 | 61034 | 61045 | 61055 |
| 408 | 61066 | 61077 | 61087 | 61098 | 61109 | 61119 | 61130 | 61140 | 61151 | 61162 |
| 409 | 61172 | 61183 | 61194 | 61204 | 61215 | 61225 | 61236 | 61247 | 61257 | 61268 |
| 410 | 61278 | 61289 | 61300 | 61310 | 61321 | 61331 | 61342 | 61352 | 61363 | 61374 |
| 411 | 61384 | 61395 | 61405 | 61416 | 61426 | 61437 | 61448 | 61458 | 61469 | 61479 |
| 412 | 61490 | 61500 | 61511 | 61521 | 61532 | 61542 | 61553 | 61563 | 61574 | 61584 |
| 413 | 61595 | 61606 | 61616 | 61627 | 61637 | 61648 | 61658 | 61669 | 61679 | 61690 |
| 414 | 61700 | 61711 | 61721 | 61731 | 61742 | 61752 | 61763 | 61773 | 61784 | 61794 |
| 415 | 61805 | 61815 | 61826 | 61836 | 61847 | 61857 | 61868 | 61878 | 61888 | 61899 |
| 416 | 61909 | 61920 | 61930 | 61941 | 61951 | 61962 | 61972 | 61982 | 61993 | 62003 |
| 417 | 62014 | 62024 | 62034 | 62045 | 62055 | 62066 | 62076 | 62086 | 62097 | 62107 |
| 418 | 62118 | 62128 | 62138 | 62149 | 62159 | 62170 | 62180 | 62190 | 62201 | 62211 |
| 419 | 62221 | 62232 | 62242 | 62252 | 62263 | 62273 | 62284 | 62294 | 62304 | 62315 |
| 420 | 62325 | 62335 | 62346 | 62356 | 62366 | 62377 | 62387 | 62397 | 62408 | 62418 |
| 421 | 62428 | 62439 | 62449 | 62459 | 62469 | 62480 | 62490 | 62500 | 62511 | 62521 |
| 422 | 62531 | 62542 | 62552 | 62562 | 62572 | 62583 | 62593 | 62603 | 62613 | 62624 |
| 423 | 62634 | 62644 | 62655 | 62665 | 62675 | 62685 | 62696 | 62706 | 62716 | 62726 |
| 424 | 62737 | 62747 | 62757 | 62767 | 62778 | 62788 | 62798 | 62808 | 62818 | 62829 |
| 425 | 62839 | 62849 | 62859 | 62870 | 62880 | 62890 | 62900 | 62910 | 62921 | 62931 |
| 426 | 62941 | 62951 | 62961 | 62972 | 62982 | 62992 | 63002 | 63012 | 63022 | 63033 |
| 427 | 63043 | 63053 | 63063 | 63073 | 63083 | 63094 | 63104 | 63114 | 63124 | 63134 |
| 428 | 63144 | 63155 | 63165 | 63175 | 63185 | 63195 | 63205 | 63215 | 63225 | 63236 |
| 429 | 63246 | 63256 | 63266 | 63276 | 63286 | 63296 | 63306 | 63317 | 63327 | 63337 |
| 430 | 63347 | 63357 | 63367 | 63377 | 63387 | 63397 | 63407 | 63417 | 63428 | 63438 |
| 431 | 63448 | 63458 | 63468 | 63478 | 63488 | 63498 | 63508 | 63518 | 63528 | 63538 |
| 432 | 63548 | 63558 | 63568 | 63579 | 63589 | 63599 | 63609 | 63619 | 63629 | 63639 |
| 433 | 63649 | 63659 | 63669 | 63679 | 63689 | 63699 | 63709 | 63719 | 63729 | 63739 |
| 434 | 63749 | 63759 | 63769 | 63779 | 63789 | 63799 | 63809 | 63819 | 63829 | 63839 |
| 435 | 63849 | 63859 | 63869 | 63879 | 63889 | 63899 | 63909 | 63919 | 63929 | 63939 |
| 436 | 63949 | 63959 | 63969 | 63979 | 63988 | 63998 | 64008 | 64018 | 64028 | 64038 |
| 437 | 64048 | 64058 | 64068 | 64078 | 64088 | 64098 | 64108 | 64118 | 64128 | 64137 |
| 438 | 64147 | 64157 | 64167 | 64177 | 64187 | 64197 | 64207 | 64217 | 64227 | 64237 |
| 439 | 64246 | 64256 | 64266 | 64276 | 64286 | 64296 | 64306 | 64316 | 64326 | 64335 |
| 440 | 64345 | 64355 | 64365 | 64375 | 64385 | 64395 | 64404 | 64414 | 64424 | 64434 |
| 441 | 64444 | 64454 | 64464 | 64473 | 64483 | 64493 | 64503 | 64513 | 64523 | 64532 |
| 442 | 64542 | 64552 | 64562 | 64572 | 64582 | 64591 | 64601 | 64611 | 64621 | 64631 |
| 443 | 64640 | 64650 | 64660 | 64670 | 64680 | 64689 | 64699 | 64709 | 64719 | 64729 |
| 444 | 64738 | 64748 | 64758 | 64768 | 64777 | 64787 | 64797 | 64807 | 64816 | 64826 |
| 445 | 64836 | 64846 | 64856 | 64865 | 64875 | 64885 | 64895 | 64904 | 64914 | 64924 |
| 446 | 64933 | 64943 | 64953 | 64963 | 64972 | 64982 | 64992 | 65002 | 65011 | 65021 |
| 447 | 65031 | 65040 | 65050 | 65060 | 65070 | 65079 | 65089 | 65099 | 65108 | 65118 |
| 448 | 65128 | 65137 | 65147 | 65157 | 65167 | 65176 | 65186 | 65196 | 65205 | 65215 |
| 449 | 65225 | 65234 | 65244 | 65254 | 65263 | 65273 | 65283 | 65292 | 65302 | 65312 |
| 450 | 65321 | 65331 | 65341 | 65350 | 65360 | 65369 | 65379 | 65389 | 65398 | 65408 |
| 451 | 65418 | 65427 | 65437 | 65447 | 65456 | 65466 | 65475 | 65485 | 65495 | 65504 |
| 452 | 65514 | 65523 | 65533 | 65543 | 65552 | 65562 | 65571 | 65581 | 65591 | 65600 |
| 453 | 65610 | 65619 | 65629 | 65639 | 65648 | 65658 | 65667 | 65677 | 65686 | 65696 |
| 454 | 65706 | 65715 | 65725 | 65734 | 65744 | 65753 | 65763 | 65772 | 65782 | 65792 |
| 455 | 65801 | 65811 | 65820 | 65830 | 65839 | 65849 | 65858 | 65868 | 65877 | 65887 |
| 456 | 65896 | 65906 | 65916 | 65925 | 65935 | 65944 | 65954 | 65963 | 65973 | 65982 |
| 457 | 65992 | 66001 | 66011 | 66020 | 66030 | 66039 | 66049 | 66058 | 66068 | 66077 |
| 458 | 66087 | 66096 | 66106 | 66115 | 66124 | 66134 | 66143 | 66153 | 66162 | 66172 |
| 459 | 66181 | 66191 | 66200 | 66210 | 66219 | 66229 | 66238 | 66247 | 66257 | 66266 |
| No. | 0 | 1 | 2 | 3 | 4 | 5 | 6 | 7 | 8 | 9 |

| 11 | |
|---|---|
| 1 | 1 |
| 2 | 2 |
| 3 | 3 |
| 4 | 4 |
| 5 | 6 |
| 6 | 7 |
| 7 | 8 |
| 8 | 9 |
| 9 | 10 |

| 10 | |
|---|---|
| 1 | 1 |
| 2 | 2 |
| 3 | 3 |
| 4 | 4 |
| 5 | 5 |
| 6 | 6 |
| 7 | 7 |
| 8 | 8 |
| 9 | 9 |

| 9 | |
|---|---|
| 1 | 1 |
| 2 | 2 |
| 3 | 3 |
| 4 | 4 |
| 5 | 5 |
| 6 | 5 |
| 7 | 6 |
| 8 | 7 |
| 9 | 8 |

# TABLE XXVI.

## Logarithms of Numbers.

No. 4600——5200. Log. 66276——71600.

| No. | 0 | 1 | 2 | 3 | 4 | 5 | 6 | 7 | 8 | 9 |
|---|---|---|---|---|---|---|---|---|---|---|
| 460 | 66276 | 66285 | 66295 | 66304 | 66314 | 66323 | 66332 | 66342 | 66351 | 66361 |
| 461 | 66370 | 66380 | 66389 | 66398 | 66408 | 66417 | 66427 | 66436 | 66445 | 66455 |
| 462 | 66464 | 66474 | 66483 | 66492 | 66502 | 66511 | 66521 | 66530 | 66539 | 66549 |
| 463 | 66558 | 66567 | 66577 | 66586 | 66596 | 66605 | 66614 | 66624 | 66633 | 66642 |
| 464 | 66652 | 66661 | 66671 | 66680 | 66689 | 66699 | 66708 | 66717 | 66727 | 66736 |
| 465 | 66745 | 66755 | 66764 | 66773 | 66783 | 66792 | 66801 | 66811 | 66820 | 66829 |
| 466 | 66839 | 66848 | 66857 | 66867 | 66876 | 66885 | 66894 | 66904 | 66913 | 66922 |
| 467 | 66932 | 66941 | 66950 | 66960 | 66969 | 66978 | 66987 | 66997 | 67006 | 67015 |
| 468 | 67025 | 67034 | 67043 | 67052 | 67062 | 67071 | 67080 | 67089 | 67099 | 67108 |
| 469 | 67117 | 67127 | 67136 | 67145 | 67154 | 67164 | 67173 | 67182 | 67191 | 67201 |
| 470 | 67210 | 67219 | 67228 | 67237 | 67247 | 67256 | 67265 | 67274 | 67284 | 67293 |
| 471 | 67302 | 67311 | 67321 | 67330 | 67339 | 67348 | 67357 | 67367 | 67376 | 67385 |
| 472 | 67394 | 67403 | 67413 | 67422 | 67431 | 67440 | 67449 | 67459 | 67468 | 67477 |
| 473 | 67486 | 67495 | 67504 | 67514 | 67523 | 67532 | 67541 | 67550 | 67560 | 67569 |
| 474 | 67578 | 67587 | 67596 | 67605 | 67614 | 67624 | 67633 | 67642 | 67651 | 67660 |
| 475 | 67669 | 67679 | 67688 | 67697 | 67706 | 67715 | 67724 | 67733 | 67742 | 67752 |
| 476 | 67761 | 67770 | 67779 | 67788 | 67797 | 67806 | 67815 | 67825 | 67834 | 67843 |
| 477 | 67852 | 67861 | 67870 | 67879 | 67888 | 67897 | 67906 | 67916 | 67925 | 67934 |
| 478 | 67943 | 67952 | 67961 | 67970 | 67979 | 67988 | 67997 | 68006 | 68015 | 68024 |
| 479 | 68034 | 68043 | 68052 | 68061 | 68070 | 68079 | 68088 | 68097 | 68106 | 68115 |
| 480 | 68124 | 68133 | 68142 | 68151 | 68160 | 68169 | 68178 | 68187 | 68196 | 68205 |
| 481 | 68215 | 68224 | 68233 | 68242 | 68251 | 68260 | 68269 | 68278 | 68287 | 68296 |
| 482 | 68305 | 68314 | 68323 | 68332 | 68341 | 68350 | 68359 | 68368 | 68377 | 68386 |
| 483 | 68395 | 68404 | 68413 | 68422 | 68431 | 68440 | 68449 | 68458 | 68467 | 68476 |
| 484 | 68485 | 68494 | 68502 | 68511 | 68520 | 68529 | 68538 | 68547 | 68556 | 68565 |
| 485 | 68574 | 68583 | 68592 | 68601 | 68610 | 68619 | 68628 | 68637 | 68646 | 68655 |
| 486 | 68664 | 68673 | 68681 | 68690 | 68699 | 68708 | 68717 | 68726 | 68735 | 68744 |
| 487 | 68753 | 68762 | 68771 | 68780 | 68789 | 68797 | 68806 | 68815 | 68824 | 68833 |
| 488 | 68842 | 68851 | 68860 | 68869 | 68878 | 68886 | 68895 | 68904 | 68913 | 68922 |
| 489 | 68931 | 68940 | 68949 | 68958 | 68966 | 68975 | 68984 | 68993 | 69002 | 69011 |
| 490 | 69020 | 69028 | 69037 | 69046 | 69055 | 69064 | 69073 | 69082 | 69090 | 69099 |
| 491 | 69108 | 69117 | 69126 | 69135 | 69144 | 69152 | 69161 | 69170 | 69179 | 69188 |
| 492 | 69197 | 69205 | 69214 | 69223 | 69232 | 69241 | 69249 | 69258 | 69267 | 69276 |
| 493 | 69285 | 69294 | 69302 | 69311 | 69320 | 69329 | 69338 | 69346 | 69355 | 69364 |
| 494 | 69373 | 69381 | 69390 | 69399 | 69408 | 69417 | 69425 | 69434 | 69443 | 69452 |
| 495 | 69461 | 69469 | 69478 | 69487 | 69496 | 69504 | 69513 | 69522 | 69531 | 69539 |
| 496 | 69548 | 69557 | 69566 | 69574 | 69583 | 69592 | 69601 | 69609 | 69618 | 69627 |
| 497 | 69636 | 69644 | 69653 | 69662 | 69671 | 69679 | 69688 | 69697 | 69705 | 69714 |
| 498 | 69723 | 69732 | 69740 | 69749 | 69758 | 69767 | 69775 | 69784 | 69793 | 69801 |
| 499 | 69810 | 69819 | 69827 | 69836 | 69845 | 69854 | 69862 | 69871 | 69880 | 69888 |
| 500 | 69897 | 69906 | 69914 | 69923 | 69932 | 69940 | 69949 | 69958 | 69966 | 69975 |
| 501 | 69984 | 69992 | 70001 | 70010 | 70018 | 70027 | 70036 | 70044 | 70053 | 70062 |
| 502 | 70070 | 70079 | 70088 | 70096 | 70105 | 70114 | 70122 | 70131 | 70140 | 70148 |
| 503 | 70157 | 70165 | 70174 | 70183 | 70191 | 70200 | 70209 | 70217 | 70226 | 70234 |
| 504 | 70243 | 70252 | 70260 | 70269 | 70278 | 70286 | 70295 | 70303 | 70312 | 70321 |
| 505 | 70329 | 70338 | 70346 | 70355 | 70364 | 70372 | 70381 | 70389 | 70398 | 70406 |
| 506 | 70415 | 70424 | 70432 | 70441 | 70449 | 70458 | 70467 | 70475 | 70484 | 70492 |
| 507 | 70501 | 70509 | 70518 | 70526 | 70535 | 70544 | 70552 | 70561 | 70569 | 70578 |
| 508 | 70586 | 70595 | 70603 | 70612 | 70621 | 70629 | 70638 | 70646 | 70655 | 70663 |
| 509 | 70672 | 70680 | 70689 | 70697 | 70706 | 70714 | 70723 | 70731 | 70740 | 70749 |
| 510 | 70757 | 70766 | 70774 | 70783 | 70791 | 70800 | 70808 | 70817 | 70825 | 70834 |
| 511 | 70842 | 70851 | 70859 | 70868 | 70876 | 70885 | 70893 | 70902 | 70910 | 70919 |
| 512 | 70927 | 70935 | 70944 | 70952 | 70961 | 70969 | 70978 | 70986 | 70995 | 71003 |
| 513 | 71012 | 71020 | 71029 | 71037 | 71046 | 71054 | 71063 | 71071 | 71079 | 71088 |
| 514 | 71096 | 71105 | 71113 | 71122 | 71130 | 71139 | 71147 | 71155 | 71164 | 71172 |
| 515 | 71181 | 71189 | 71198 | 71206 | 71214 | 71223 | 71231 | 71240 | 71248 | 71257 |
| 516 | 71265 | 71273 | 71282 | 71290 | 71299 | 71307 | 71315 | 71324 | 71332 | 71341 |
| 517 | 71349 | 71357 | 71366 | 71374 | 71383 | 71391 | 71399 | 71408 | 71416 | 71425 |
| 518 | 71433 | 71441 | 71450 | 71458 | 71466 | 71475 | 71483 | 71492 | 71500 | 71508 |
| 519 | 71517 | 71525 | 71533 | 71542 | 71550 | 71559 | 71567 | 71575 | 71584 | 71592 |
| No. | 0 | 1 | 2 | 3 | 4 | 5 | 6 | 7 | 8 | 9 |

| 10 | |
|---|---|
| 1 | 1 |
| 2 | 2 |
| 3 | 3 |
| 4 | 4 |
| 5 | 5 |
| 6 | 6 |
| 7 | 7 |
| 8 | 8 |
| 9 | 9 |

| 9 | |
|---|---|
| 1 | 1 |
| 2 | 2 |
| 3 | 3 |
| 4 | 4 |
| 5 | 5 |
| 6 | 5 |
| 7 | 6 |
| 8 | 7 |
| 9 | 8 |

| 8 | |
|---|---|
| 1 | 1 |
| 2 | 2 |
| 3 | 2 |
| 4 | 3 |
| 5 | 4 |
| 6 | 5 |
| 7 | 6 |
| 8 | 6 |
| 9 | 7 |

# TABLE XXVI.

## Logarithms of Numbers.

No. 5200——5800. Log. 71600——76343.

| No. | 0 | 1 | 2 | 3 | 4 | 5 | 6 | 7 | 8 | 9 |
|---|---|---|---|---|---|---|---|---|---|---|
| 520 | 71600 | 71609 | 71617 | 71625 | 71634 | 71642 | 71650 | 71659 | 71667 | 71675 |
| 521 | 71684 | 71692 | 71700 | 71709 | 71717 | 71725 | 71734 | 71742 | 71750 | 71759 |
| 522 | 71767 | 71775 | 71784 | 71792 | 71800 | 71809 | 71817 | 71825 | 71834 | 71842 |
| 523 | 71850 | 71858 | 71867 | 71875 | 71883 | 71892 | 71900 | 71908 | 71917 | 71925 |
| 524 | 71933 | 71941 | 71950 | 71958 | 71966 | 71975 | 71983 | 71991 | 71999 | 72008 |
| 525 | 72016 | 72024 | 72032 | 72041 | 72049 | 72057 | 72066 | 72074 | 72082 | 72090 |
| 526 | 72099 | 72107 | 72115 | 72123 | 72132 | 72140 | 72148 | 72156 | 72165 | 72173 |
| 527 | 72181 | 72189 | 72198 | 72206 | 72214 | 72222 | 72230 | 72239 | 72247 | 72255 |
| 528 | 72263 | 72272 | 72280 | 72288 | 72296 | 72304 | 72313 | 72321 | 72329 | 72337 |
| 529 | 72346 | 72354 | 72362 | 72370 | 72378 | 72387 | 72395 | 72403 | 72411 | 72419 |
| 530 | 72428 | 72436 | 72444 | 72452 | 72460 | 72469 | 72477 | 72485 | 72493 | 72501 |
| 531 | 72509 | 72518 | 72526 | 72534 | 72542 | 72550 | 72558 | 72567 | 72575 | 72583 |
| 532 | 72591 | 72599 | 72607 | 72616 | 72624 | 72632 | 72640 | 72648 | 72656 | 72665 |
| 533 | 72673 | 72681 | 72689 | 72697 | 72705 | 72713 | 72722 | 72730 | 72738 | 72746 |
| 534 | 72754 | 72762 | 72770 | 72779 | 72787 | 72795 | 72803 | 72811 | 72819 | 72827 |
| 535 | 72835 | 72843 | 72852 | 72860 | 72868 | 72876 | 72884 | 72892 | 72900 | 72908 |
| 536 | 72916 | 72925 | 72933 | 72941 | 72949 | 72957 | 72965 | 72973 | 72981 | 72989 |
| 537 | 72997 | 73006 | 73014 | 73022 | 73030 | 73038 | 73046 | 73054 | 73062 | 73070 |
| 538 | 73078 | 73086 | 73094 | 73102 | 73111 | 73119 | 73127 | 73135 | 73143 | 73151 |
| 539 | 73159 | 73167 | 73175 | 73183 | 73191 | 73199 | 73207 | 73215 | 73223 | 73231 |
| 540 | 73239 | 73247 | 73255 | 73263 | 73272 | 73280 | 73288 | 73296 | 73304 | 73312 |
| 541 | 73320 | 73328 | 73336 | 73344 | 73352 | 73360 | 73368 | 73376 | 73384 | 73392 |
| 542 | 73400 | 73408 | 73416 | 73424 | 73432 | 73440 | 73448 | 73456 | 73464 | 73472 |
| 543 | 73480 | 73488 | 73496 | 73504 | 73512 | 73520 | 73528 | 73536 | 73544 | 73552 |
| 544 | 73560 | 73568 | 73576 | 73584 | 73592 | 73600 | 73608 | 73616 | 73624 | 73632 |
| 545 | 73640 | 73648 | 73656 | 73664 | 73672 | 73679 | 73687 | 73695 | 73703 | 73711 |
| 546 | 73719 | 73727 | 73735 | 73743 | 73751 | 73759 | 73767 | 73775 | 73783 | 73791 |
| 547 | 73799 | 73807 | 73815 | 73823 | 73830 | 73838 | 73846 | 73854 | 73862 | 73870 |
| 548 | 73878 | 73886 | 73894 | 73902 | 73910 | 73918 | 73926 | 73933 | 73941 | 73949 |
| 549 | 73957 | 73965 | 73973 | 73981 | 73989 | 73997 | 74005 | 74013 | 74020 | 74028 |
| 550 | 74036 | 74044 | 74052 | 74060 | 74068 | 74076 | 74084 | 74092 | 74099 | 74107 |
| 551 | 74115 | 74123 | 74131 | 74139 | 74147 | 74155 | 74162 | 74170 | 74178 | 74186 |
| 552 | 74194 | 74202 | 74210 | 74218 | 74225 | 74233 | 74241 | 74249 | 74257 | 74265 |
| 553 | 74273 | 74280 | 74288 | 74296 | 74304 | 74312 | 74320 | 74327 | 74335 | 74343 |
| 554 | 74351 | 74359 | 74367 | 74374 | 74382 | 74390 | 74398 | 74406 | 74414 | 74421 |
| 555 | 74429 | 74437 | 74445 | 74453 | 74461 | 74468 | 74476 | 74484 | 74492 | 74500 |
| 556 | 74507 | 74515 | 74523 | 74531 | 74539 | 74547 | 74554 | 74562 | 74570 | 74578 |
| 557 | 74586 | 74593 | 74601 | 74609 | 74617 | 74624 | 74632 | 74640 | 74648 | 74656 |
| 558 | 74663 | 74671 | 74679 | 74687 | 74695 | 74702 | 74710 | 74718 | 74726 | 74733 |
| 559 | 74741 | 74749 | 74757 | 74764 | 74772 | 74780 | 74788 | 74796 | 74803 | 74811 |
| 560 | 74819 | 74827 | 74834 | 74842 | 74850 | 74858 | 74865 | 74873 | 74881 | 74889 |
| 561 | 74896 | 74904 | 74912 | 74920 | 74927 | 74935 | 74943 | 74950 | 74958 | 74966 |
| 562 | 74974 | 74981 | 74989 | 74997 | 75005 | 75012 | 75020 | 75028 | 75035 | 75043 |
| 563 | 75051 | 75059 | 75066 | 75074 | 75082 | 75089 | 75097 | 75105 | 75113 | 75120 |
| 564 | 75128 | 75136 | 75143 | 75151 | 75159 | 75166 | 75174 | 75182 | 75189 | 75197 |
| 565 | 75205 | 75213 | 75220 | 75228 | 75236 | 75243 | 75251 | 75259 | 75266 | 75274 |
| 566 | 75282 | 75289 | 75297 | 75305 | 75312 | 75320 | 75328 | 75335 | 75343 | 75351 |
| 567 | 75358 | 75366 | 75374 | 75381 | 75389 | 75397 | 75404 | 75412 | 75420 | 75427 |
| 568 | 75435 | 75442 | 75450 | 75458 | 75465 | 75473 | 75481 | 75488 | 75496 | 75504 |
| 569 | 75511 | 75519 | 75526 | 75534 | 75542 | 75549 | 75557 | 75565 | 75572 | 75580 |
| 570 | 75587 | 75595 | 75603 | 75610 | 75618 | 75626 | 75633 | 75641 | 75648 | 75656 |
| 571 | 75664 | 75671 | 75679 | 75686 | 75694 | 75702 | 75709 | 75717 | 75724 | 75732 |
| 572 | 75740 | 75747 | 75755 | 75762 | 75770 | 75778 | 75785 | 75793 | 75800 | 75808 |
| 573 | 75815 | 75823 | 75831 | 75838 | 75846 | 75853 | 75861 | 75868 | 75876 | 75884 |
| 574 | 75891 | 75899 | 75906 | 75914 | 75921 | 75929 | 75937 | 75944 | 75952 | 75959 |
| 575 | 75967 | 75974 | 75982 | 75989 | 75997 | 76005 | 76012 | 76020 | 76027 | 76035 |
| 576 | 76042 | 76050 | 76057 | 76065 | 76072 | 76080 | 76087 | 76095 | 76103 | 76110 |
| 577 | 76118 | 76125 | 76133 | 76140 | 76148 | 76155 | 76163 | 76170 | 76178 | 76185 |
| 578 | 76193 | 76200 | 76208 | 76215 | 76223 | 76230 | 76238 | 76245 | 76253 | 76260 |
| 579 | 76268 | 76275 | 76283 | 76290 | 76298 | 76305 | 76313 | 76320 | 76328 | 76335 |
| No. | 0 | 1 | 2 | 3 | 4 | 5 | 6 | 7 | 8 | 9 |

| 9 | |
|---|---|
| 1 | 1 |
| 2 | 2 |
| 3 | 3 |
| 4 | 4 |
| 5 | 5 |
| 6 | 5 |
| 7 | 6 |
| 8 | 7 |
| 9 | 8 |

| 8 | |
|---|---|
| 1 | 1 |
| 2 | 2 |
| 3 | 2 |
| 4 | 3 |
| 5 | 4 |
| 6 | 5 |
| 7 | 6 |
| 8 | 6 |
| 9 | 7 |

| 7 | |
|---|---|
| 1 | 1 |
| 2 | 1 |
| 3 | 2 |
| 4 | 3 |
| 5 | 4 |
| 6 | 4 |
| 7 | 5 |
| 8 | 6 |
| 9 | 6 |

# TABLE XXVI.

## Logarithms of Numbers.

No. 5800——6400. Log. 76343——80618.

| No. | 0 | 1 | 2 | 3 | 4 | 5 | 6 | 7 | 8 | 9 |
|---|---|---|---|---|---|---|---|---|---|---|
| 580 | 76343 | 76350 | 76358 | 76365 | 76373 | 76380 | 76388 | 76395 | 76403 | 76410 |
| 581 | 76418 | 76425 | 76433 | 76440 | 76448 | 76455 | 76462 | 76470 | 76477 | 76485 |
| 582 | 76492 | 76500 | 76507 | 76515 | 76522 | 76530 | 76537 | 76545 | 76552 | 76559 |
| 583 | 76567 | 76574 | 76582 | 76589 | 76597 | 76604 | 76612 | 76619 | 76626 | 76634 |
| 584 | 76641 | 76649 | 76656 | 76664 | 76671 | 76678 | 76686 | 76693 | 76701 | 76708 |
| 585 | 76716 | 76723 | 76730 | 76738 | 76745 | 76753 | 76760 | 76768 | 76775 | 76782 |
| 586 | 76790 | 76797 | 76805 | 76812 | 76819 | 76827 | 76834 | 76842 | 76849 | 76856 |
| 587 | 76864 | 76871 | 76879 | 76886 | 76893 | 76901 | 76908 | 76916 | 76923 | 76930 |
| 588 | 76938 | 76945 | 76953 | 76960 | 76967 | 76975 | 76982 | 76989 | 76997 | 77004 |
| 589 | 77012 | 77019 | 77026 | 77034 | 77041 | 77048 | 77056 | 77063 | 77070 | 77078 |
| 590 | 77085 | 77093 | 77100 | 77107 | 77115 | 77122 | 77129 | 77137 | 77144 | 77151 |
| 591 | 77159 | 77166 | 77173 | 77181 | 77188 | 77195 | 77203 | 77210 | 77217 | 77225 |
| 592 | 77232 | 77240 | 77247 | 77254 | 77262 | 77269 | 77276 | 77283 | 77291 | 77298 |
| 593 | 77305 | 77313 | 77320 | 77327 | 77335 | 77342 | 77349 | 77357 | 77364 | 77371 |
| 594 | 77379 | 77386 | 77393 | 77401 | 77408 | 77415 | 77422 | 77430 | 77437 | 77444 |
| 595 | 77452 | 77459 | 77466 | 77474 | 77481 | 77488 | 77495 | 77503 | 77510 | 77517 |
| 596 | 77525 | 77532 | 77539 | 77546 | 77554 | 77561 | 77568 | 77576 | 77583 | 77590 |
| 597 | 77597 | 77605 | 77612 | 77619 | 77627 | 77634 | 77641 | 77648 | 77656 | 77663 |
| 598 | 77670 | 77677 | 77685 | 77692 | 77699 | 77706 | 77714 | 77721 | 77728 | 77735 |
| 599 | 77743 | 77750 | 77757 | 77764 | 77772 | 77779 | 77786 | 77793 | 77801 | 77808 |
| 600 | 77815 | 77822 | 77830 | 77837 | 77844 | 77851 | 77859 | 77866 | 77873 | 77880 |
| 601 | 77887 | 77895 | 77902 | 77909 | 77916 | 77924 | 77931 | 77938 | 77945 | 77952 |
| 602 | 77960 | 77967 | 77974 | 77981 | 77988 | 77996 | 78003 | 78010 | 78017 | 78025 |
| 603 | 78032 | 78039 | 78046 | 78053 | 78061 | 78068 | 78075 | 78082 | 78089 | 78097 |
| 604 | 78104 | 78111 | 78118 | 78125 | 78132 | 78140 | 78147 | 78154 | 78161 | 78168 |
| 605 | 78176 | 78183 | 78190 | 78197 | 78204 | 78211 | 78219 | 78226 | 78233 | 78240 |
| 606 | 78247 | 78254 | 78262 | 78269 | 78276 | 78283 | 78290 | 78297 | 78305 | 78312 |
| 607 | 78319 | 78326 | 78333 | 78340 | 78347 | 78355 | 78362 | 78369 | 78376 | 78383 |
| 608 | 78390 | 78398 | 78405 | 78412 | 78419 | 78426 | 78433 | 78440 | 78447 | 78455 |
| 609 | 78462 | 78469 | 78476 | 78483 | 78490 | 78497 | 78504 | 78512 | 78519 | 78526 |
| 610 | 78533 | 78540 | 78547 | 78554 | 78561 | 78569 | 78576 | 78583 | 78590 | 78597 |
| 611 | 78604 | 78611 | 78618 | 78625 | 78633 | 78640 | 78647 | 78654 | 78661 | 78668 |
| 612 | 78675 | 78682 | 78689 | 78696 | 78704 | 78711 | 78718 | 78725 | 78732 | 78739 |
| 613 | 78746 | 78753 | 78760 | 78767 | 78774 | 78781 | 78789 | 78796 | 78803 | 78810 |
| 614 | 78817 | 78824 | 78831 | 78838 | 78845 | 78852 | 78859 | 78866 | 78873 | 78880 |
| 615 | 78888 | 78895 | 78902 | 78909 | 78916 | 78923 | 78930 | 78937 | 78944 | 78951 |
| 616 | 78958 | 78965 | 78972 | 78979 | 78986 | 78993 | 79000 | 79007 | 79014 | 79021 |
| 617 | 79029 | 79036 | 79043 | 79050 | 79057 | 79064 | 79071 | 79078 | 79085 | 79092 |
| 618 | 79099 | 79106 | 79113 | 79120 | 79127 | 79134 | 79141 | 79148 | 79155 | 79162 |
| 619 | 79169 | 79176 | 79183 | 79190 | 79197 | 79204 | 79211 | 79218 | 79225 | 79232 |
| 620 | 79239 | 79246 | 79253 | 79260 | 79267 | 79274 | 79281 | 79288 | 79295 | 79302 |
| 621 | 79309 | 79316 | 79323 | 79330 | 79337 | 79344 | 79351 | 79358 | 79365 | 79372 |
| 622 | 79379 | 79386 | 79393 | 79400 | 79407 | 79414 | 79421 | 79428 | 79435 | 79442 |
| 623 | 79449 | 79456 | 79463 | 79470 | 79477 | 79484 | 79491 | 79498 | 79505 | 79511 |
| 624 | 79518 | 79525 | 79532 | 79539 | 79546 | 79553 | 79560 | 79567 | 79574 | 79581 |
| 625 | 79588 | 79595 | 79602 | 79609 | 79616 | 79623 | 79630 | 79637 | 79644 | 79650 |
| 626 | 79657 | 79664 | 79671 | 79678 | 79685 | 79692 | 79699 | 79706 | 79713 | 79720 |
| 627 | 79727 | 79734 | 79741 | 79748 | 79754 | 79761 | 79768 | 79775 | 79782 | 79789 |
| 628 | 79796 | 79803 | 79810 | 79817 | 79824 | 79831 | 79837 | 79844 | 79851 | 79858 |
| 629 | 79865 | 79872 | 79879 | 79886 | 79893 | 79900 | 79906 | 79913 | 79920 | 79927 |
| 630 | 79934 | 79941 | 79948 | 79955 | 79962 | 79969 | 79975 | 79982 | 79989 | 79996 |
| 631 | 80003 | 80010 | 80017 | 80024 | 80030 | 80037 | 80044 | 80051 | 80058 | 80065 |
| 632 | 80072 | 80079 | 80085 | 80092 | 80099 | 80106 | 80113 | 80120 | 80127 | 80134 |
| 633 | 80140 | 80147 | 80154 | 80161 | 80168 | 80175 | 80182 | 80188 | 80195 | 80202 |
| 634 | 80209 | 80216 | 80223 | 80229 | 80236 | 80243 | 80250 | 80257 | 80264 | 80271 |
| 635 | 80277 | 80284 | 80291 | 80298 | 80305 | 80312 | 80318 | 80325 | 80332 | 80339 |
| 636 | 80346 | 80353 | 80359 | 80366 | 80373 | 80380 | 80387 | 80393 | 80400 | 80407 |
| 637 | 80414 | 80421 | 80428 | 80434 | 80441 | 80448 | 80455 | 80462 | 80468 | 80475 |
| 638 | 80482 | 80489 | 80496 | 80502 | 80509 | 80516 | 80523 | 80530 | 80536 | 80543 |
| 639 | 80550 | 80557 | 80564 | 80570 | 80577 | 80584 | 80591 | 80598 | 80604 | 80611 |
| No. | 0 | 1 | 2 | 3 | 4 | 5 | 6 | 7 | 8 | 9 |

| | 8 |
|---|---|
| 1 | 1 |
| 2 | 2 |
| 3 | 2 |
| 4 | 3 |
| 5 | 4 |
| 6 | 5 |
| 7 | 6 |
| 8 | 6 |
| 9 | 7 |

| | 7 |
|---|---|
| 1 | 1 |
| 2 | 1 |
| 3 | 2 |
| 4 | 3 |
| 5 | 4 |
| 6 | 4 |
| 7 | 5 |
| 8 | 6 |
| 9 | 6 |

| | 6 |
|---|---|
| 1 | 1 |
| 2 | 1 |
| 3 | 2 |
| 4 | 2 |
| 5 | 3 |
| 6 | 4 |
| 7 | 4 |
| 8 | 5 |
| 9 | 5 |

# TABLE XXVI.

## Logarithms of Numbers.

No. 6400———7000. Log. 80618———84510.

| No. | 0 | 1 | 2 | 3 | 4 | 5 | 6 | 7 | 8 | 9 |
|---|---|---|---|---|---|---|---|---|---|---|
| 640 | 80618 | 80625 | 80632 | 80638 | 80645 | 80652 | 80659 | 80665 | 80672 | 80679 |
| 641 | 80686 | 80693 | 80699 | 80706 | 80713 | 80720 | 80726 | 80733 | 80740 | 80747 |
| 642 | 80754 | 80760 | 80767 | 80774 | 80781 | 80787 | 80794 | 80801 | 80808 | 80814 |
| 643 | 80821 | 80828 | 80835 | 80841 | 80848 | 80855 | 80862 | 80868 | 80875 | 80882 |
| 644 | 80889 | 80895 | 80902 | 80909 | 80916 | 80922 | 80929 | 80936 | 80943 | 80949 |
| 645 | 80956 | 80963 | 80969 | 80976 | 80983 | 80990 | 80996 | 81003 | 81010 | 81017 |
| 646 | 81023 | 81030 | 81037 | 81043 | 81050 | 81057 | 81064 | 81070 | 81077 | 81084 |
| 647 | 81090 | 81097 | 81104 | 81111 | 81117 | 81124 | 81131 | 81137 | 81144 | 81151 |
| 648 | 81158 | 81164 | 81171 | 81178 | 81184 | 81191 | 81198 | 81204 | 81211 | 81218 |
| 649 | 81224 | 81231 | 81238 | 81245 | 81251 | 81258 | 81265 | 81271 | 81278 | 81285 |
| 650 | 81291 | 81298 | 81305 | 81311 | 81318 | 81325 | 81331 | 81338 | 81345 | 81351 |
| 651 | 81358 | 81365 | 81371 | 81378 | 81385 | 81391 | 81398 | 81405 | 81411 | 81418 |
| 652 | 81425 | 81431 | 81438 | 81445 | 81451 | 81458 | 81465 | 81471 | 81478 | 81485 |
| 653 | 81491 | 81498 | 81505 | 81511 | 81518 | 81525 | 81531 | 81538 | 81544 | 81551 |
| 654 | 81558 | 81564 | 81571 | 81578 | 81584 | 81591 | 81598 | 81604 | 81611 | 81617 |
| 655 | 81624 | 81631 | 81637 | 81644 | 81651 | 81657 | 81664 | 81671 | 81677 | 81684 |
| 656 | 81690 | 81697 | 81704 | 81710 | 81717 | 81723 | 81730 | 81737 | 81743 | 81750 |
| 657 | 81757 | 81763 | 81770 | 81776 | 81783 | 81790 | 81796 | 81803 | 81809 | 81816 |
| 658 | 81823 | 81829 | 81836 | 81842 | 81849 | 81856 | 81862 | 81869 | 81875 | 81882 |
| 659 | 81889 | 81895 | 81902 | 81908 | 81915 | 81921 | 81928 | 81935 | 81941 | 81948 |
| 660 | 81954 | 81961 | 81968 | 81974 | 81981 | 81987 | 81994 | 82000 | 82007 | 82014 |
| 661 | 82020 | 82027 | 82033 | 82040 | 82046 | 82053 | 82060 | 82066 | 82073 | 82079 |
| 662 | 82086 | 82092 | 82099 | 82105 | 82112 | 82119 | 82125 | 82132 | 82138 | 82145 |
| 663 | 82151 | 82158 | 82164 | 82171 | 82178 | 82184 | 82191 | 82197 | 82204 | 82210 |
| 664 | 82217 | 82223 | 82230 | 82236 | 82243 | 82249 | 82256 | 82263 | 82269 | 82276 |
| 665 | 82282 | 82289 | 82295 | 82302 | 82308 | 82315 | 82321 | 82328 | 82334 | 82341 |
| 666 | 82347 | 82354 | 82360 | 82367 | 82373 | 82380 | 82387 | 82393 | 82400 | 82406 |
| 667 | 82413 | 82419 | 82426 | 82432 | 82439 | 82445 | 82452 | 82458 | 82465 | 82471 |
| 668 | 82478 | 82484 | 82491 | 82497 | 82504 | 82510 | 82517 | 82523 | 82530 | 82536 |
| 669 | 82543 | 82549 | 82556 | 82562 | 82569 | 82575 | 82582 | 82588 | 82595 | 82601 |
| 670 | 82607 | 82614 | 82620 | 82627 | 82633 | 82640 | 82646 | 82653 | 82659 | 82666 |
| 671 | 82672 | 82679 | 82685 | 82692 | 82698 | 82705 | 82711 | 82718 | 82724 | 82730 |
| 672 | 82737 | 82743 | 82750 | 82756 | 82763 | 82769 | 82776 | 82782 | 82789 | 82795 |
| 673 | 82802 | 82808 | 82814 | 82821 | 82827 | 82834 | 82840 | 82847 | 82853 | 82860 |
| 674 | 82866 | 82872 | 82879 | 82885 | 82892 | 82898 | 82905 | 82911 | 82918 | 82924 |
| 675 | 82930 | 82937 | 82943 | 82950 | 82956 | 82963 | 82969 | 82975 | 82982 | 82988 |
| 676 | 82995 | 83001 | 83008 | 83014 | 83020 | 83027 | 83033 | 83040 | 83046 | 83052 |
| 677 | 83059 | 83065 | 83072 | 83078 | 83085 | 83091 | 83097 | 83104 | 83110 | 83117 |
| 678 | 83123 | 83129 | 83136 | 83142 | 83149 | 83155 | 83161 | 83168 | 83174 | 83181 |
| 679 | 83187 | 83193 | 83200 | 83206 | 83213 | 83219 | 83225 | 83232 | 83238 | 83245 |
| 680 | 83251 | 83257 | 83264 | 83270 | 83276 | 83283 | 83289 | 83296 | 83302 | 83308 |
| 681 | 83315 | 83321 | 83327 | 83334 | 83340 | 83347 | 83353 | 83359 | 83366 | 83372 |
| 682 | 83378 | 83385 | 83391 | 83398 | 83404 | 83410 | 83417 | 83423 | 83429 | 83436 |
| 683 | 83442 | 83448 | 83455 | 83461 | 83467 | 83474 | 83480 | 83487 | 83493 | 83499 |
| 684 | 83506 | 83512 | 83518 | 83525 | 83531 | 83537 | 83544 | 83550 | 83556 | 83563 |
| 685 | 83569 | 83575 | 83582 | 83588 | 83594 | 83601 | 83607 | 83613 | 83620 | 83626 |
| 686 | 83632 | 83639 | 83645 | 83651 | 83658 | 83664 | 83670 | 83677 | 83683 | 83689 |
| 687 | 83696 | 83702 | 83708 | 83715 | 83721 | 83727 | 83734 | 83740 | 83746 | 83753 |
| 688 | 83759 | 83765 | 83771 | 83778 | 83784 | 83790 | 83797 | 83803 | 83809 | 83816 |
| 689 | 83822 | 83828 | 83835 | 83841 | 83847 | 83853 | 83860 | 83866 | 83872 | 83879 |
| 690 | 83885 | 83891 | 83897 | 83904 | 83910 | 83916 | 83923 | 83929 | 83935 | 83942 |
| 691 | 83948 | 83954 | 83960 | 83967 | 83973 | 83979 | 83985 | 83992 | 83998 | 84004 |
| 692 | 84011 | 84017 | 84023 | 84029 | 84036 | 84042 | 84048 | 84055 | 84061 | 84067 |
| 693 | 84073 | 84080 | 84086 | 84092 | 84098 | 84105 | 84111 | 84117 | 84123 | 84130 |
| 694 | 84136 | 84142 | 84148 | 84155 | 84161 | 84167 | 84173 | 84180 | 84186 | 84192 |
| 695 | 84198 | 84205 | 84211 | 84217 | 84223 | 84230 | 84236 | 84242 | 84248 | 84255 |
| 696 | 84261 | 84267 | 84273 | 84280 | 84286 | 84292 | 84298 | 84305 | 84311 | 84317 |
| 697 | 84323 | 84330 | 84336 | 84342 | 84348 | 84354 | 84361 | 84367 | 84373 | 84379 |
| 698 | 84386 | 84392 | 84398 | 84404 | 84410 | 84417 | 84423 | 84429 | 84435 | 84442 |
| 699 | 84448 | 84454 | 84460 | 84466 | 84473 | 84479 | 84485 | 84491 | 84497 | 84504 |
| No. | 0 | 1 | 2 | 3 | 4 | 5 | 6 | 7 | 8 | 9 |

| 7 | |
|---|---|
| 1 | 1 |
| 2 | 1 |
| 3 | 2 |
| 4 | 3 |
| 5 | 4 |
| 6 | 4 |
| 7 | 5 |
| 8 | 6 |
| 9 | 6 |

| 6 | |
|---|---|
| 1 | 1 |
| 2 | 1 |
| 3 | 2 |
| 4 | 2 |
| 5 | 3 |
| 6 | 4 |
| 7 | 4 |
| 8 | 5 |
| 9 | 5 |

# TABLE XXVI.

## Logarithms of Numbers.

No. 7000——7600. Log. 84510——88081.

| No. | 0 | 1 | 2 | 3 | 4 | 5 | 6 | 7 | 8 | 9 |
|---|---|---|---|---|---|---|---|---|---|---|
| 700 | 84510 | 84516 | 84522 | 84528 | 84535 | 84541 | 84547 | 84553 | 84559 | 84566 |
| 701 | 84572 | 84578 | 84584 | 84590 | 84597 | 84603 | 84609 | 84615 | 84621 | 84628 |
| 702 | 84634 | 84640 | 84646 | 84652 | 84658 | 84665 | 84671 | 84677 | 84683 | 84689 |
| 703 | 84696 | 84702 | 84708 | 84714 | 84720 | 84726 | 84733 | 84739 | 84745 | 84751 |
| 704 | 84757 | 84763 | 84770 | 84776 | 84782 | 84788 | 84794 | 84800 | 84807 | 84813 |
| 705 | 84819 | 84825 | 84831 | 84837 | 84844 | 84850 | 84856 | 84862 | 84868 | 84874 |
| 706 | 84880 | 84887 | 84893 | 84899 | 84905 | 84911 | 84917 | 84924 | 84930 | 84936 |
| 707 | 84942 | 84948 | 84954 | 84960 | 84967 | 84973 | 84979 | 84985 | 84991 | 84997 |
| 708 | 85003 | 85009 | 85016 | 85022 | 85028 | 85034 | 85040 | 85046 | 85052 | 85058 |
| 709 | 85065 | 85071 | 85077 | 85083 | 85089 | 85095 | 85101 | 85107 | 85114 | 85120 |
| 710 | 85126 | 85132 | 85138 | 85144 | 85150 | 85156 | 85163 | 85169 | 85175 | 85181 |
| 711 | 85187 | 85193 | 85199 | 85205 | 85211 | 85217 | 85224 | 85230 | 85236 | 85242 |
| 712 | 85248 | 85254 | 85260 | 85266 | 85272 | 85278 | 85285 | 85291 | 85297 | 85303 |
| 713 | 85309 | 85315 | 85321 | 85327 | 85333 | 85339 | 85345 | 85352 | 85358 | 85364 |
| 714 | 85370 | 85376 | 85382 | 85388 | 85394 | 85400 | 85406 | 85412 | 85418 | 85425 |
| 715 | 85431 | 85437 | 85443 | 85449 | 85455 | 85461 | 85467 | 85473 | 85479 | 85485 |
| 716 | 85491 | 85497 | 85503 | 85509 | 85516 | 85522 | 85528 | 85534 | 85540 | 85546 |
| 717 | 85552 | 85558 | 85564 | 85570 | 85576 | 85582 | 85588 | 85594 | 85600 | 85606 |
| 718 | 85612 | 85618 | 85625 | 85631 | 85637 | 85643 | 85649 | 85655 | 85661 | 85667 |
| 719 | 85673 | 85679 | 85685 | 85691 | 85697 | 85703 | 85709 | 85715 | 85721 | 85727 |
| 720 | 85733 | 85739 | 85745 | 85751 | 85757 | 85763 | 85769 | 85775 | 85781 | 85788 |
| 721 | 85794 | 85800 | 85806 | 85812 | 85818 | 85824 | 85830 | 85836 | 85842 | 85848 |
| 722 | 85854 | 85860 | 85866 | 85872 | 85878 | 85884 | 85890 | 85896 | 85902 | 85908 |
| 723 | 85914 | 85920 | 85926 | 85932 | 85938 | 85944 | 85950 | 85956 | 85962 | 85968 |
| 724 | 85974 | 85980 | 85986 | 85992 | 85998 | 86004 | 86010 | 86016 | 86022 | 86028 |
| 725 | 86034 | 86040 | 86046 | 86052 | 86058 | 86064 | 86070 | 86076 | 86082 | 86088 |
| 726 | 86094 | 86100 | 86106 | 86112 | 86118 | 86124 | 86130 | 86136 | 86141 | 86147 |
| 727 | 86153 | 86159 | 86165 | 86171 | 86177 | 86183 | 86189 | 86195 | 86201 | 86207 |
| 728 | 86213 | 86219 | 86225 | 86231 | 86237 | 86243 | 86249 | 86255 | 86261 | 86267 |
| 729 | 86273 | 86279 | 86285 | 86291 | 86297 | 86303 | 86308 | 86314 | 86320 | 86326 |
| 730 | 86332 | 86338 | 86344 | 86350 | 86356 | 86362 | 86368 | 86374 | 86380 | 86386 |
| 731 | 86392 | 86398 | 86404 | 86410 | 86415 | 86421 | 86427 | 86433 | 86439 | 86445 |
| 732 | 86451 | 86457 | 86463 | 86469 | 86475 | 86481 | 86487 | 86493 | 86499 | 86504 |
| 733 | 86510 | 86516 | 86522 | 86528 | 86534 | 86540 | 86546 | 86552 | 86558 | 86564 |
| 734 | 86570 | 86576 | 86581 | 86587 | 86593 | 86599 | 86605 | 86611 | 86617 | 86623 |
| 735 | 86629 | 86635 | 86641 | 86646 | 86652 | 86658 | 86664 | 86670 | 86676 | 86682 |
| 736 | 86688 | 86694 | 86700 | 86705 | 86711 | 86717 | 86723 | 86729 | 86735 | 86741 |
| 737 | 86747 | 86753 | 86759 | 86764 | 86770 | 86776 | 86782 | 86788 | 86794 | 86800 |
| 738 | 86806 | 86812 | 86817 | 86823 | 86829 | 86835 | 86841 | 86847 | 86853 | 86859 |
| 739 | 86864 | 86870 | 86876 | 86882 | 86888 | 86894 | 86900 | 86906 | 86911 | 86917 |
| 740 | 86923 | 86929 | 86935 | 86941 | 86947 | 86953 | 86958 | 86964 | 86970 | 86976 |
| 741 | 86982 | 86988 | 86994 | 86999 | 87005 | 87011 | 87017 | 87023 | 87029 | 87035 |
| 742 | 87040 | 87046 | 87052 | 87058 | 87064 | 87070 | 87075 | 87081 | 87087 | 87093 |
| 743 | 87099 | 87105 | 87111 | 87116 | 87122 | 87128 | 87134 | 87140 | 87146 | 87151 |
| 744 | 87157 | 87163 | 87169 | 87175 | 87181 | 87186 | 87192 | 87198 | 87204 | 87210 |
| 745 | 87216 | 87221 | 87227 | 87233 | 87239 | 87245 | 87251 | 87256 | 87262 | 87268 |
| 746 | 87274 | 87280 | 87286 | 87291 | 87297 | 87303 | 87309 | 87315 | 87320 | 87326 |
| 747 | 87332 | 87338 | 87344 | 87349 | 87355 | 87361 | 87367 | 87373 | 87379 | 87384 |
| 748 | 87390 | 87396 | 87402 | 87408 | 87413 | 87419 | 87425 | 87431 | 87437 | 87442 |
| 749 | 87448 | 87454 | 87460 | 87466 | 87471 | 87477 | 87483 | 87489 | 87495 | 87500 |
| 750 | 87506 | 87512 | 87518 | 87523 | 87529 | 87535 | 87541 | 87547 | 87552 | 87558 |
| 751 | 87564 | 87570 | 87576 | 87581 | 87587 | 87593 | 87599 | 87604 | 87610 | 87616 |
| 752 | 87622 | 87628 | 87633 | 87639 | 87645 | 87651 | 87656 | 87662 | 87668 | 87674 |
| 753 | 87679 | 87685 | 87691 | 87697 | 87703 | 87708 | 87714 | 87720 | 87726 | 87731 |
| 754 | 87737 | 87743 | 87749 | 87754 | 87760 | 87766 | 87772 | 87777 | 87783 | 87789 |
| 755 | 87795 | 87800 | 87806 | 87812 | 87818 | 87823 | 87829 | 87835 | 87841 | 87846 |
| 756 | 87852 | 87858 | 87864 | 87869 | 87875 | 87881 | 87887 | 87892 | 87898 | 87904 |
| 757 | 87910 | 87915 | 87921 | 87927 | 87933 | 87938 | 87944 | 87950 | 87955 | 87961 |
| 758 | 87967 | 87973 | 87978 | 87984 | 87990 | 87996 | 88001 | 88007 | 88013 | 88018 |
| 759 | 88024 | 88030 | 88036 | 88041 | 88047 | 88053 | 88058 | 88064 | 88070 | 88076 |
| No. | 0 | 1 | 2 | 3 | 4 | 5 | 6 | 7 | 8 | 9 |

| 7 | |
|---|---|
| 1 | 1 |
| 2 | 1 |
| 3 | 2 |
| 4 | 3 |
| 5 | 4 |
| 6 | 4 |
| 7 | 5 |
| 8 | 6 |
| 9 | 6 |

| 6 | |
|---|---|
| 1 | 1 |
| 2 | 1 |
| 3 | 2 |
| 4 | 2 |
| 5 | 3 |
| 6 | 4 |
| 7 | 4 |
| 8 | 5 |
| 9 | 5 |

| 5 | |
|---|---|
| 1 | 1 |
| 2 | 1 |
| 3 | 2 |
| 4 | 2 |
| 5 | 3 |
| 6 | 3 |
| 7 | 4 |
| 8 | 4 |
| 9 | 5 |

# TABLE XXVI.

## Logarithms of Numbers.

No. 7600——8200. Log. 88081——91381.

| No. | 0 | 1 | 2 | 3 | 4 | 5 | 6 | 7 | 8 | 9 |
|---|---|---|---|---|---|---|---|---|---|---|
| 760 | 88081 | 88087 | 88093 | 88098 | 88104 | 88110 | 88116 | 88121 | 88127 | 88133 |
| 761 | 88138 | 88144 | 88150 | 88156 | 88161 | 88167 | 88173 | 88178 | 88184 | 88190 |
| 762 | 88195 | 88201 | 88207 | 88213 | 88218 | 88224 | 88230 | 88235 | 88241 | 88247 |
| 763 | 88252 | 88258 | 88264 | 88270 | 88275 | 88281 | 88287 | 88292 | 88298 | 88304 |
| 764 | 88309 | 88315 | 88321 | 88326 | 88332 | 88338 | 88343 | 88349 | 88355 | 88360 |
| 765 | 88366 | 88372 | 88377 | 88383 | 88389 | 88395 | 88400 | 88406 | 88412 | 88417 |
| 766 | 88423 | 88429 | 88434 | 88440 | 88446 | 88451 | 88457 | 88463 | 88468 | 88474 |
| 767 | 88480 | 88485 | 88491 | 88497 | 88502 | 88508 | 88513 | 88519 | 88525 | 88530 |
| 768 | 88536 | 88542 | 88547 | 88553 | 88559 | 88564 | 88570 | 88576 | 88581 | 88587 |
| 769 | 88593 | 88598 | 88604 | 88610 | 88615 | 88621 | 88627 | 88632 | 88638 | 88643 |
| 770 | 88649 | 88655 | 88660 | 88666 | 88672 | 88677 | 88683 | 88689 | 88694 | 88700 |
| 771 | 88705 | 88711 | 88717 | 88722 | 88728 | 88734 | 88739 | 88745 | 88750 | 88756 |
| 772 | 88762 | 88767 | 88773 | 88779 | 88784 | 88790 | 88795 | 88801 | 88807 | 88812 |
| 773 | 88818 | 88824 | 88829 | 88835 | 88840 | 88846 | 88852 | 88857 | 88863 | 88868 |
| 774 | 88874 | 88880 | 88885 | 88891 | 88897 | 88902 | 88908 | 88913 | 88919 | 88925 |
| 775 | 88930 | 88936 | 88941 | 88947 | 88953 | 88958 | 88964 | 88969 | 88975 | 88981 |
| 776 | 88986 | 88992 | 88997 | 89003 | 89009 | 89014 | 89020 | 89025 | 89031 | 89037 |
| 777 | 89042 | 89048 | 89053 | 89059 | 89064 | 89070 | 89076 | 89081 | 89087 | 89092 |
| 778 | 89098 | 89104 | 89109 | 89115 | 89120 | 89126 | 89131 | 89137 | 89143 | 89148 |
| 779 | 89154 | 89159 | 89165 | 89170 | 89176 | 89182 | 89187 | 89193 | 89198 | 89204 |
| 780 | 89209 | 89215 | 89221 | 89226 | 89232 | 89237 | 89243 | 89248 | 89254 | 89260 |
| 781 | 89265 | 89271 | 89276 | 89282 | 89287 | 89293 | 89298 | 89304 | 89310 | 89315 |
| 782 | 89321 | 89326 | 89332 | 89337 | 89343 | 89348 | 89354 | 89360 | 89365 | 89371 |
| 783 | 89376 | 89382 | 89387 | 89393 | 89398 | 89404 | 89409 | 89415 | 89421 | 89426 |
| 784 | 89432 | 89437 | 89443 | 89448 | 89454 | 89459 | 89465 | 89470 | 89476 | 89481 |
| 785 | 89487 | 89492 | 89498 | 89504 | 89509 | 89515 | 89520 | 89526 | 89531 | 89537 |
| 786 | 89542 | 89548 | 89553 | 89559 | 89564 | 89570 | 89575 | 89581 | 89586 | 89592 |
| 787 | 89597 | 89603 | 89609 | 89614 | 89620 | 89625 | 89631 | 89636 | 89642 | 89647 |
| 788 | 89653 | 89658 | 89664 | 89669 | 89675 | 89680 | 89686 | 89691 | 89697 | 89702 |
| 789 | 89708 | 89713 | 89719 | 89724 | 89730 | 89735 | 89741 | 89746 | 89752 | 89757 |
| 790 | 89763 | 89768 | 89774 | 89779 | 89785 | 89790 | 89796 | 89801 | 89807 | 89812 |
| 791 | 89818 | 89823 | 89829 | 89834 | 89840 | 89845 | 89851 | 89856 | 89862 | 89867 |
| 792 | 89873 | 89878 | 89883 | 89889 | 89894 | 89900 | 89905 | 89911 | 89916 | 89922 |
| 793 | 89927 | 89933 | 89938 | 89944 | 89949 | 89955 | 89960 | 89966 | 89971 | 89977 |
| 794 | 89982 | 89988 | 89993 | 89998 | 90004 | 90009 | 90015 | 90020 | 90026 | 90031 |
| 795 | 90037 | 90042 | 90048 | 90053 | 90059 | 90064 | 90069 | 90075 | 90080 | 90086 |
| 796 | 90091 | 90097 | 90102 | 90108 | 90113 | 90119 | 90124 | 90129 | 90135 | 90140 |
| 797 | 90146 | 90151 | 90157 | 90162 | 90168 | 90173 | 90179 | 90184 | 90189 | 90195 |
| 798 | 90200 | 90206 | 90211 | 90217 | 90222 | 90227 | 90233 | 90238 | 90244 | 90249 |
| 799 | 90255 | 90260 | 90266 | 90271 | 90276 | 90282 | 90287 | 90293 | 90298 | 90304 |
| 800 | 90309 | 90314 | 90320 | 90325 | 90331 | 90336 | 90342 | 90347 | 90352 | 90358 |
| 801 | 90363 | 90369 | 90374 | 90380 | 90385 | 90390 | 90396 | 90401 | 90407 | 90412 |
| 802 | 90417 | 90423 | 90428 | 90434 | 90439 | 90445 | 90450 | 90455 | 90461 | 90466 |
| 803 | 90472 | 90477 | 90482 | 90488 | 90493 | 90499 | 90504 | 90509 | 90515 | 90520 |
| 804 | 90526 | 90531 | 90536 | 90542 | 90547 | 90553 | 90558 | 90563 | 90569 | 90574 |
| 805 | 90580 | 90585 | 90590 | 90596 | 90601 | 90607 | 90612 | 90617 | 90623 | 90628 |
| 806 | 90634 | 90639 | 90644 | 90650 | 90655 | 90660 | 90666 | 90671 | 90677 | 90682 |
| 807 | 90687 | 90693 | 90698 | 90703 | 90709 | 90714 | 90720 | 90725 | 90730 | 90736 |
| 808 | 90741 | 90747 | 90752 | 90757 | 90763 | 90768 | 90773 | 90779 | 90784 | 90789 |
| 809 | 90795 | 90800 | 90806 | 90811 | 90816 | 90822 | 90827 | 90832 | 90838 | 90843 |
| 810 | 90849 | 90854 | 90859 | 90865 | 90870 | 90875 | 90881 | 90886 | 90891 | 90897 |
| 811 | 90902 | 90907 | 90913 | 90918 | 90924 | 90929 | 90934 | 90940 | 90945 | 90950 |
| 812 | 90956 | 90961 | 90966 | 90972 | 90977 | 90982 | 90988 | 90993 | 90998 | 91004 |
| 813 | 91009 | 91014 | 91020 | 91025 | 91030 | 91036 | 91041 | 91046 | 91052 | 91057 |
| 814 | 91062 | 91068 | 91073 | 91078 | 91084 | 91089 | 91094 | 91100 | 91105 | 91110 |
| 815 | 91116 | 91121 | 91126 | 91132 | 91137 | 91142 | 91148 | 91153 | 91158 | 91164 |
| 816 | 91169 | 91174 | 91180 | 91185 | 91190 | 91196 | 91201 | 91206 | 91212 | 91217 |
| 817 | 91222 | 91228 | 91233 | 91238 | 91243 | 91249 | 91254 | 91259 | 91265 | 91270 |
| 818 | 91275 | 91281 | 91286 | 91291 | 91297 | 91302 | 91307 | 91312 | 91318 | 91323 |
| 819 | 91328 | 91334 | 91339 | 91344 | 91350 | 91355 | 91360 | 91365 | 91371 | 91376 |
| No. | 0 | 1 | 2 | 3 | 4 | 5 | 6 | 7 | 8 | 9 |

| | 6 |
|---|---|
| 1 | 1 |
| 2 | 1 |
| 3 | 2 |
| 4 | 2 |
| 5 | 3 |
| 6 | 4 |
| 7 | 4 |
| 8 | 5 |
| 9 | 5 |

| | 5 |
|---|---|
| 1 | 1 |
| 2 | 1 |
| 3 | 2 |
| 4 | 2 |
| 5 | 3 |
| 6 | 3 |
| 7 | 4 |
| 8 | 4 |
| 9 | 5 |

# TABLE XXVI.

## Logarithms of Numbers.

No. 8200——8800. Log. 91381——94448.

| No. | 0 | 1 | 2 | 3 | 4 | 5 | 6 | 7 | 8 | 9 |
|---|---|---|---|---|---|---|---|---|---|---|
| 820 | 91381 | 91387 | 91392 | 91397 | 91403 | 91408 | 91413 | 91418 | 91424 | 91429 |
| 821 | 91434 | 91440 | 91445 | 91450 | 91455 | 91461 | 91466 | 91471 | 91477 | 91482 |
| 822 | 91487 | 91492 | 91498 | 91503 | 91508 | 91514 | 91519 | 91524 | 91529 | 91535 |
| 823 | 91540 | 91545 | 91551 | 91556 | 91561 | 91566 | 91572 | 91577 | 91582 | 91587 |
| 824 | 91593 | 91598 | 91603 | 91609 | 91614 | 91619 | 91624 | 91630 | 91635 | 91640 |
| 825 | 91645 | 91651 | 91656 | 91661 | 91666 | 91672 | 91677 | 91682 | 91687 | 91693 |
| 826 | 91698 | 91703 | 91709 | 91714 | 91719 | 91724 | 91730 | 91735 | 91740 | 91745 |
| 827 | 91751 | 91756 | 91761 | 91766 | 91772 | 91777 | 91782 | 91787 | 91793 | 91798 |
| 828 | 91803 | 91808 | 91814 | 91819 | 91824 | 91829 | 91834 | 91840 | 91845 | 91850 |
| 829 | 91855 | 91861 | 91866 | 91871 | 91876 | 91882 | 91887 | 91892 | 91897 | 91903 |
| 830 | 91908 | 91913 | 91918 | 91924 | 91929 | 91934 | 91939 | 91944 | 91950 | 91955 |
| 831 | 91960 | 91965 | 91971 | 91976 | 91981 | 91986 | 91991 | 91997 | 92002 | 92007 |
| 832 | 92012 | 92018 | 92023 | 92028 | 92033 | 92038 | 92044 | 92049 | 92054 | 92059 |
| 833 | 92065 | 92070 | 92075 | 92080 | 92085 | 92091 | 92096 | 92101 | 92106 | 92111 |
| 834 | 92117 | 92122 | 92127 | 92132 | 92137 | 92143 | 92148 | 92153 | 92158 | 92163 |
| 835 | 92169 | 92174 | 92179 | 92184 | 92189 | 92195 | 92200 | 92205 | 92210 | 92215 |
| 836 | 92221 | 92226 | 92231 | 92236 | 92241 | 92247 | 92252 | 92257 | 92262 | 92267 |
| 837 | 92273 | 92278 | 92283 | 92288 | 92293 | 92298 | 92304 | 92309 | 92314 | 92319 |
| 838 | 92324 | 92330 | 92335 | 92340 | 92345 | 92350 | 92355 | 92361 | 92366 | 92371 |
| 839 | 92376 | 92381 | 92387 | 92392 | 92397 | 92402 | 92407 | 92412 | 92418 | 92423 |
| 840 | 92428 | 92433 | 92438 | 92443 | 92449 | 92454 | 92459 | 92464 | 92469 | 92474 |
| 841 | 92480 | 92485 | 92490 | 92495 | 92500 | 92505 | 92511 | 92516 | 92521 | 92526 |
| 842 | 92531 | 92536 | 92542 | 92547 | 92552 | 92557 | 92562 | 92567 | 92572 | 92578 |
| 843 | 92583 | 92588 | 92593 | 92598 | 92603 | 92609 | 92614 | 92619 | 92624 | 92629 |
| 844 | 92634 | 92639 | 92645 | 92650 | 92655 | 92660 | 92665 | 92670 | 92675 | 92681 |
| 845 | 92686 | 92691 | 92696 | 92701 | 92706 | 92711 | 92716 | 92722 | 92727 | 92732 |
| 846 | 92737 | 92742 | 92747 | 92752 | 92758 | 92763 | 92768 | 92773 | 92778 | 92783 |
| 847 | 92788 | 92793 | 92799 | 92804 | 92809 | 92814 | 92819 | 92824 | 92829 | 92834 |
| 848 | 92840 | 92845 | 92850 | 92855 | 92860 | 92865 | 92870 | 92875 | 92881 | 92886 |
| 849 | 92891 | 92896 | 92901 | 92906 | 92911 | 92916 | 92921 | 92927 | 92932 | 92937 |
| 850 | 92942 | 92947 | 92952 | 92957 | 92962 | 92967 | 92973 | 92978 | 92983 | 92988 |
| 851 | 92993 | 92998 | 93003 | 93008 | 93013 | 93018 | 93024 | 93029 | 93034 | 93039 |
| 852 | 93044 | 93049 | 93054 | 93059 | 93064 | 93069 | 93075 | 93080 | 93085 | 93090 |
| 853 | 93095 | 93100 | 93105 | 93110 | 93115 | 93120 | 93125 | 93131 | 93136 | 93141 |
| 854 | 93146 | 93151 | 93156 | 93161 | 93166 | 93171 | 93176 | 93181 | 93186 | 93192 |
| 855 | 93197 | 93202 | 93207 | 93212 | 93217 | 93222 | 93227 | 93232 | 93237 | 93242 |
| 856 | 93247 | 93252 | 93258 | 93263 | 93268 | 93273 | 93278 | 93283 | 93288 | 93293 |
| 857 | 93298 | 93303 | 93308 | 93313 | 93318 | 93323 | 93328 | 93334 | 93339 | 93344 |
| 858 | 93349 | 93354 | 93359 | 93364 | 93369 | 93374 | 93379 | 93384 | 93389 | 93394 |
| 859 | 93399 | 93404 | 93409 | 93414 | 93420 | 93425 | 93430 | 93435 | 93440 | 93445 |
| 860 | 93450 | 93455 | 93460 | 93465 | 93470 | 93475 | 93480 | 93485 | 93490 | 93495 |
| 861 | 93500 | 93505 | 93510 | 93515 | 93520 | 93526 | 93531 | 93536 | 93541 | 93546 |
| 862 | 93551 | 93556 | 93561 | 93566 | 93571 | 93576 | 93581 | 93586 | 93591 | 93596 |
| 863 | 93601 | 93606 | 93611 | 93616 | 93621 | 93626 | 93631 | 93636 | 93641 | 93646 |
| 864 | 93651 | 93656 | 93661 | 93666 | 93671 | 93676 | 93682 | 93687 | 93692 | 93697 |
| 865 | 93702 | 93707 | 93712 | 93717 | 93722 | 93727 | 93732 | 93737 | 93742 | 93747 |
| 866 | 93752 | 93757 | 93762 | 93767 | 93772 | 93777 | 93782 | 93787 | 93792 | 93797 |
| 867 | 93802 | 93807 | 93812 | 93817 | 93822 | 93827 | 93832 | 93837 | 93842 | 93847 |
| 868 | 93852 | 93857 | 93862 | 93867 | 93872 | 93877 | 93882 | 93887 | 93892 | 93897 |
| 869 | 93902 | 93907 | 93912 | 93917 | 93922 | 93927 | 93932 | 93937 | 93942 | 93947 |
| 870 | 93952 | 93957 | 93962 | 93967 | 93972 | 93977 | 93982 | 93987 | 93992 | 93997 |
| 871 | 94002 | 94007 | 94012 | 94017 | 94022 | 94027 | 94032 | 94037 | 94042 | 94047 |
| 872 | 94052 | 94057 | 94062 | 94067 | 94072 | 94077 | 94082 | 94086 | 94091 | 94096 |
| 873 | 94101 | 94106 | 94111 | 94116 | 94121 | 94126 | 94131 | 94136 | 94141 | 94146 |
| 874 | 94151 | 94156 | 94161 | 94166 | 94171 | 94176 | 94181 | 94186 | 94191 | 94196 |
| 875 | 94201 | 94206 | 94211 | 94216 | 94221 | 94226 | 94231 | 94236 | 94240 | 94245 |
| 876 | 94250 | 94255 | 94260 | 94265 | 94270 | 94275 | 94280 | 94285 | 94290 | 94295 |
| 877 | 94300 | 94305 | 94310 | 94315 | 94320 | 94325 | 94330 | 94335 | 94340 | 94345 |
| 878 | 94349 | 94354 | 94359 | 94364 | 94369 | 94374 | 94379 | 94384 | 94389 | 94394 |
| 879 | 94399 | 94404 | 94409 | 94414 | 94419 | 94424 | 94429 | 94433 | 94438 | 94443 |
| No. | 0 | 1 | 2 | 3 | 4 | 5 | 6 | 7 | 8 | 9 |

| 6 | |
|---|---|
| 1 | 1 |
| 2 | 1 |
| 3 | 2 |
| 4 | 2 |
| 5 | 3 |
| 6 | 4 |
| 7 | 4 |
| 8 | 5 |
| 9 | 5 |

| 5 | |
|---|---|
| 1 | 1 |
| 2 | 1 |
| 3 | 2 |
| 4 | 2 |
| 5 | 3 |
| 6 | 3 |
| 7 | 4 |
| 8 | 4 |
| 9 | 5 |

| 4 | |
|---|---|
| 1 | 0 |
| 2 | 1 |
| 3 | 1 |
| 4 | 2 |
| 5 | 2 |
| 6 | 2 |
| 7 | 3 |
| 8 | 3 |
| 9 | 4 |

# TABLE XXVI.

## Logarithms of Numbers.

**No. 8800——9400.** **Log. 94448——97313.**

| No. | 0 | 1 | 2 | 3 | 4 | 5 | 6 | 7 | 8 | 9 |
|---|---|---|---|---|---|---|---|---|---|---|
| 880 | 94448 | 94453 | 94458 | 94463 | 94468 | 94473 | 94478 | 94483 | 94488 | 94493 |
| 881 | 94498 | 94503 | 94507 | 94512 | 94517 | 94522 | 94527 | 94532 | 94537 | 94542 |
| 882 | 94547 | 94552 | 94557 | 94562 | 94567 | 94571 | 94576 | 94581 | 94586 | 94591 |
| 883 | 94596 | 94601 | 94606 | 94611 | 94616 | 94621 | 94626 | 94630 | 94635 | 94640 |
| 884 | 94645 | 94650 | 94655 | 94660 | 94665 | 94670 | 94675 | 94680 | 94685 | 94689 |
| 885 | 94694 | 94699 | 94704 | 94709 | 94714 | 94719 | 94724 | 94729 | 94734 | 94738 |
| 886 | 94743 | 94748 | 94753 | 94758 | 94763 | 94768 | 94773 | 94778 | 94783 | 94787 |
| 887 | 94792 | 94797 | 94802 | 94807 | 94812 | 94817 | 94822 | 94827 | 94832 | 94836 |
| 888 | 94841 | 94846 | 94851 | 94856 | 94861 | 94866 | 94871 | 94876 | 94880 | 94885 |
| 889 | 94890 | 94895 | 94900 | 94905 | 94910 | 94915 | 94919 | 94924 | 94929 | 94934 |
| 890 | 94939 | 94944 | 94949 | 94954 | 94959 | 94963 | 94968 | 94973 | 94978 | 94983 |
| 891 | 94988 | 94993 | 94998 | 95002 | 95007 | 95012 | 95017 | 95022 | 95027 | 95032 |
| 892 | 95036 | 95041 | 95046 | 95051 | 95056 | 95061 | 95066 | 95071 | 95075 | 95080 |
| 893 | 95085 | 95090 | 95095 | 95100 | 95105 | 95109 | 95114 | 95119 | 95124 | 95129 |
| 894 | 95134 | 95139 | 95143 | 95148 | 95153 | 95158 | 95163 | 95168 | 95173 | 95177 |
| 895 | 95182 | 95187 | 95192 | 95197 | 95202 | 95207 | 95211 | 95216 | 95221 | 95226 |
| 896 | 95231 | 95236 | 95240 | 95245 | 95250 | 95255 | 95260 | 95265 | 95270 | 95274 |
| 897 | 95279 | 95284 | 95289 | 95294 | 95299 | 95303 | 95308 | 95313 | 95318 | 95323 |
| 898 | 95328 | 95332 | 95337 | 95342 | 95347 | 95352 | 95357 | 95361 | 95366 | 95371 |
| 899 | 95376 | 95381 | 95386 | 95390 | 95395 | 95400 | 95405 | 95410 | 95415 | 95419 |
| 900 | 95424 | 95429 | 95434 | 95439 | 95444 | 95448 | 95453 | 95458 | 95463 | 95468 |
| 901 | 95472 | 95477 | 95482 | 95487 | 95492 | 95497 | 95501 | 95506 | 95511 | 95516 |
| 902 | 95521 | 95525 | 95530 | 95535 | 95540 | 95545 | 95550 | 95554 | 95559 | 95564 |
| 903 | 95569 | 95574 | 95578 | 95583 | 95588 | 95593 | 95598 | 95602 | 95607 | 95612 |
| 904 | 95617 | 95622 | 95626 | 95631 | 95636 | 95641 | 95646 | 95650 | 95655 | 95660 |
| 905 | 95665 | 95670 | 95674 | 95679 | 95684 | 95689 | 95694 | 95698 | 95703 | 95708 |
| 906 | 95713 | 95718 | 95722 | 95727 | 95732 | 95737 | 95742 | 95746 | 95751 | 95756 |
| 907 | 95761 | 95766 | 95770 | 95775 | 95780 | 95785 | 95789 | 95794 | 95799 | 95804 |
| 908 | 95809 | 95813 | 95818 | 95823 | 95828 | 95832 | 95837 | 95842 | 95847 | 95852 |
| 909 | 95856 | 95861 | 95866 | 95871 | 95875 | 95880 | 95885 | 95890 | 95895 | 95899 |
| 910 | 95904 | 95909 | 95914 | 95918 | 95923 | 95928 | 95933 | 95938 | 95942 | 95947 |
| 911 | 95952 | 95957 | 95961 | 95966 | 95971 | 95976 | 95980 | 95985 | 95990 | 95995 |
| 912 | 95999 | 96004 | 96009 | 96014 | 96019 | 96023 | 96028 | 96033 | 96038 | 96042 |
| 913 | 96047 | 96052 | 96057 | 96061 | 96066 | 96071 | 96076 | 96080 | 96085 | 96090 |
| 914 | 96095 | 96099 | 96104 | 96109 | 96114 | 96118 | 96123 | 96128 | 96133 | 96137 |
| 915 | 96142 | 96147 | 96152 | 96156 | 96161 | 96166 | 96171 | 96175 | 96180 | 96185 |
| 916 | 96190 | 96194 | 96199 | 96204 | 96209 | 96213 | 96218 | 96223 | 96227 | 96232 |
| 917 | 96237 | 96242 | 96246 | 96251 | 96256 | 96261 | 96265 | 96270 | 96275 | 96280 |
| 918 | 96284 | 96289 | 96294 | 96298 | 96303 | 96308 | 96313 | 96317 | 96322 | 96327 |
| 919 | 96332 | 96336 | 96341 | 96346 | 96350 | 96355 | 96360 | 96365 | 96369 | 96374 |
| 920 | 96379 | 96384 | 96388 | 96393 | 96398 | 96402 | 96407 | 96412 | 96417 | 96421 |
| 921 | 96426 | 96431 | 96435 | 96440 | 96445 | 96450 | 96454 | 96459 | 96464 | 96468 |
| 922 | 96473 | 96478 | 96483 | 96487 | 96492 | 96497 | 96501 | 96506 | 96511 | 96515 |
| 923 | 96520 | 96525 | 96530 | 96534 | 96539 | 96544 | 96548 | 96553 | 96558 | 96562 |
| 924 | 96567 | 96572 | 96577 | 96581 | 96586 | 96591 | 96595 | 96600 | 96605 | 96609 |
| 925 | 96614 | 96619 | 96624 | 96628 | 96633 | 96638 | 96642 | 96647 | 96652 | 96656 |
| 926 | 96661 | 96666 | 96670 | 96675 | 96680 | 96685 | 96689 | 96694 | 96699 | 96703 |
| 927 | 96708 | 96713 | 96717 | 96722 | 96727 | 96731 | 96736 | 96741 | 96745 | 96750 |
| 928 | 96755 | 96759 | 96764 | 96769 | 96774 | 96778 | 96783 | 96788 | 96792 | 96797 |
| 929 | 96802 | 96806 | 96811 | 96816 | 96820 | 96825 | 96830 | 96834 | 96839 | 96844 |
| 930 | 96848 | 96853 | 96858 | 96862 | 96867 | 96872 | 96876 | 96881 | 96886 | 96890 |
| 931 | 96895 | 96900 | 96904 | 96909 | 96914 | 96918 | 96923 | 96928 | 96932 | 96937 |
| 932 | 96942 | 96946 | 96951 | 96956 | 96960 | 96965 | 96970 | 96974 | 96979 | 96984 |
| 933 | 96988 | 96993 | 96997 | 97002 | 97007 | 97011 | 97016 | 97021 | 97025 | 97030 |
| 934 | 97035 | 97039 | 97044 | 97049 | 97053 | 97058 | 97063 | 97067 | 97072 | 97077 |
| 935 | 97081 | 97086 | 97090 | 97095 | 97100 | 97104 | 97109 | 97114 | 97118 | 97123 |
| 936 | 97128 | 97132 | 97137 | 97142 | 97146 | 97151 | 97155 | 97160 | 97165 | 97169 |
| 937 | 97174 | 97179 | 97183 | 97188 | 97192 | 97197 | 97202 | 97206 | 97211 | 97216 |
| 938 | 97220 | 97225 | 97230 | 97234 | 97239 | 97243 | 97248 | 97253 | 97257 | 97262 |
| 939 | 97267 | 97271 | 97276 | 97280 | 97285 | 97290 | 97294 | 97299 | 97304 | 97308 |
| No. | 0 | 1 | 2 | 3 | 4 | 5 | 6 | 7 | 8 | 9 |

| 5 | |
|---|---|
| 1 | 1 |
| 2 | 1 |
| 3 | 2 |
| 4 | 2 |
| 5 | 3 |
| 6 | 3 |
| 7 | 4 |
| 8 | 4 |
| 9 | 5 |

| 4 | |
|---|---|
| 1 | 0 |
| 2 | 1 |
| 3 | 1 |
| 4 | 2 |
| 5 | 2 |
| 6 | 2 |
| 7 | 3 |
| 8 | 3 |
| 9 | 4 |

# TABLE XXVI.

## Logarithms of Numbers.

No. 9400———10000. Log. 97313———99996.

| No. | 0 | 1 | 2 | 3 | 4 | 5 | 6 | 7 | 8 | 9 |
|---|---|---|---|---|---|---|---|---|---|---|
| 940 | 97313 | 97317 | 97322 | 97327 | 97331 | 97336 | 97340 | 97345 | 97350 | 97354 |
| 941 | 97359 | 97364 | 97368 | 97373 | 97377 | 97382 | 97387 | 97391 | 97396 | 97400 |
| 942 | 97405 | 97410 | 97414 | 97419 | 97424 | 97428 | 97433 | 97437 | 97442 | 97447 |
| 943 | 97451 | 97456 | 97460 | 97465 | 97470 | 97474 | 97479 | 97483 | 97488 | 97493 |
| 944 | 97497 | 97502 | 97506 | 97511 | 97516 | 975[illegible] | 97525 | 97529 | 97534 | 97539 |
| 945 | 97543 | 97548 | 97552 | 97557 | 97562 | 97566 | 97571 | 97575 | 97580 | 97585 |
| 946 | 97589 | 97594 | 97598 | 97603 | 97607 | 97612 | 97617 | 97621 | 97626 | 97630 |
| 947 | 97635 | 97640 | 97644 | 97649 | 97653 | 97658 | 97663 | 97667 | 97672 | 97676 |
| 948 | 97681 | 97685 | 97690 | 97695 | 97699 | 97704 | 97708 | 97713 | 97717 | 97722 |
| 949 | 97727 | 97731 | 97736 | 97740 | 97745 | 97749 | 97754 | 97759 | 97763 | 97768 |
| 950 | 97772 | 97777 | 97782 | 97786 | 97791 | 97795 | 97800 | 97804 | 97809 | 97813 |
| 951 | 97818 | 97823 | 97827 | 97832 | 97836 | 97841 | 97845 | 97850 | 97855 | 97859 |
| 952 | 97864 | 97868 | 97873 | 97877 | 97882 | 97886 | 97891 | 97896 | 97900 | 97905 |
| 953 | 97909 | 97914 | 97918 | 97923 | 97928 | 97932 | 97937 | 97941 | 97946 | 97950 |
| 954 | 97955 | 97959 | 97964 | 97968 | 97973 | 97978 | 97982 | 97987 | 97991 | 97996 |
| 955 | 98000 | 98005 | 98009 | 98014 | 98019 | 98023 | 98028 | 98032 | 98037 | 98041 |
| 956 | 98046 | 98050 | 98055 | 98059 | 98064 | 98068 | 98073 | 98078 | 98082 | 98087 |
| 957 | 98091 | 98096 | 98100 | 98105 | 98109 | 98114 | 98118 | 98123 | 98127 | 98132 |
| 958 | 98137 | 98141 | 98146 | 98150 | 98155 | 98159 | 98164 | 98168 | 98173 | 98177 |
| 959 | 98182 | 98186 | 98191 | 98195 | 98200 | 98204 | 98209 | 98214 | 98218 | 98223 |
| 960 | 98227 | 98232 | 98236 | 98241 | 98245 | 98250 | 98254 | 98259 | 98263 | 98268 |
| 961 | 98272 | 98277 | 98281 | 98286 | 98290 | 98295 | 98299 | 98304 | 98308 | 98313 |
| 962 | 98318 | 98322 | 98327 | 98331 | 98336 | 98340 | 98345 | 98349 | 98354 | 98358 |
| 963 | 98363 | 98367 | 98372 | 98376 | 98381 | 98385 | 98390 | 98394 | 98399 | 98403 |
| 964 | 98408 | 98412 | 98417 | 98421 | 98426 | 98430 | 98435 | 98439 | 98444 | 98448 |
| 965 | 98453 | 98457 | 98462 | 98466 | 98471 | 98475 | 98480 | 98484 | 98489 | 98493 |
| 966 | 98498 | 98502 | 98507 | 98511 | 98516 | 98520 | 98525 | 98529 | 98534 | 98538 |
| 967 | 98543 | 98547 | 98552 | 98556 | 98561 | 98565 | 98570 | 98574 | 98579 | 98583 |
| 968 | 98588 | 98592 | 98597 | 98601 | 98605 | 98610 | 98614 | 98619 | 98623 | 98628 |
| 969 | 98632 | 98637 | 98641 | 98646 | 98650 | 98655 | 98659 | 98664 | 98668 | 98673 |
| 970 | 98677 | 98682 | 98686 | 98691 | 98695 | 98700 | 98704 | 98709 | 98713 | 98717 |
| 971 | 98722 | 98726 | 98731 | 98735 | 98740 | 98744 | 98749 | 98753 | 98758 | 98762 |
| 972 | 98767 | 98771 | 98776 | 98780 | 98784 | 98789 | 98793 | 98798 | 98802 | 98807 |
| 973 | 98811 | 98816 | 98820 | 98825 | 98829 | 98834 | 98838 | 98843 | 98847 | 98851 |
| 974 | 98856 | 98860 | 98865 | 98869 | 98874 | 98878 | 98883 | 98887 | 98892 | 98896 |
| 975 | 98900 | 98905 | 98909 | 98914 | 98918 | 98923 | 98927 | 98932 | 98936 | 98941 |
| 976 | 98945 | 98949 | 98954 | 98958 | 98963 | 98967 | 98972 | 98976 | 98981 | 98985 |
| 977 | 98989 | 98994 | 98998 | 99003 | 99007 | 99012 | 99016 | 99021 | 99025 | 99029 |
| 978 | 99034 | 99038 | 99043 | 99047 | 99052 | 99056 | 99061 | 99065 | 99069 | 99074 |
| 979 | 99078 | 99083 | 99087 | 99092 | 99096 | 99100 | 99105 | 99109 | 99114 | 99118 |
| 980 | 99123 | 99127 | 99131 | 99136 | 99140 | 99145 | 99149 | 99154 | 99158 | 99162 |
| 981 | 99167 | 99171 | 99176 | 99180 | 99185 | 99189 | 99193 | 99198 | 99202 | 99207 |
| 982 | 99211 | 99216 | 99220 | 99224 | 99229 | 99233 | 99238 | 99242 | 99247 | 99251 |
| 983 | 99255 | 99260 | 99264 | 99269 | 99273 | 99277 | 99282 | 99286 | 99291 | 99295 |
| 984 | 99300 | 99304 | 99308 | 99313 | 99317 | 99322 | 99326 | 99330 | 99335 | 99339 |
| 985 | 99344 | 99348 | 99352 | 99357 | 99361 | 99366 | 99370 | 99374 | 99379 | 99383 |
| 986 | 99388 | 99392 | 99396 | 99401 | 99405 | 99410 | 99414 | 99419 | 99423 | 99427 |
| 987 | 99432 | 99436 | 99441 | 99445 | 99449 | 99454 | 99458 | 99463 | 99467 | 99471 |
| 988 | 99476 | 99480 | 99484 | 99489 | 99493 | 99498 | 99502 | 99506 | 99511 | 99515 |
| 989 | 99520 | 99524 | 99528 | 99533 | 99537 | 99542 | 99546 | 99550 | 99555 | 99559 |
| 990 | 99564 | 99568 | 99572 | 99577 | 99581 | 99585 | 99590 | 99594 | 99599 | 99603 |
| 991 | 99607 | 99612 | 99616 | 99621 | 99625 | 99629 | 99634 | 99638 | 99642 | 99647 |
| 992 | 99651 | 99656 | 99660 | 99664 | 99669 | 99673 | 99677 | 99682 | 99686 | 99691 |
| 993 | 99695 | 99699 | 99704 | 99708 | 99712 | 99717 | 99721 | 99726 | 99730 | 99734 |
| 994 | 99739 | 99743 | 99747 | 99752 | 99756 | 99760 | 99765 | 99769 | 99774 | 99778 |
| 995 | 99782 | 99787 | 99791 | 99795 | 99800 | 99804 | 99808 | 99813 | 99817 | 99822 |
| 996 | 99826 | 99830 | 99835 | 99839 | 99843 | 99848 | 99852 | 99856 | 99861 | 99865 |
| 997 | 99870 | 99874 | 99878 | 99883 | 99887 | 99891 | 99896 | 99900 | 99904 | 99909 |
| 998 | 99913 | 99917 | 99922 | 99926 | 99930 | 99935 | 99939 | 99944 | 99948 | 99952 |
| 999 | 99957 | 99961 | 99965 | 99970 | 99974 | 99978 | 99983 | 99987 | 99991 | 99996 |
| No. | 0 | 1 | 2 | 3 | 4 | 5 | 6 | 7 | 8 | 9 |

| | 5 |
|---|---|
| 1 | 1 |
| 2 | 1 |
| 3 | 2 |
| 4 | 2 |
| 5 | 3 |
| 6 | 3 |
| 7 | 4 |
| 8 | 4 |
| 9 | 5 |

| | 4 |
|---|---|
| 1 | 0 |
| 2 | 1 |
| 3 | 1 |
| 4 | 2 |
| 5 | 2 |
| 6 | 2 |
| 7 | 3 |
| 8 | 3 |
| 9 | 4 |

# TABLE XXVII.

## Log. Sines, Tangents, and Secants.

0° | 179°

| M | Hour A.M. | Hour P.M. | Sine. | Diff. 1′ | Cosecant. | Tangent. | Diff. 1′ | Cotangent | Secant. | Cosine. | M |
|---|---|---|---|---|---|---|---|---|---|---|---|
| 0 | 12 0 0 | 0 0 0 | Inf. Neg. | | Infinite. | Inf. Neg. | | Infinite. | 10.00000 | 10.00000 | 60 |
| 1 | 11 59 52 | 0 8 | 6.46373 | 30103 | 13.53627 | 6.46373 | 30103 | 13.53627 | 00000 | 00000 | 59 |
| 2 | 59 44 | 0 16 | 76476 | 17609 | 23524 | 76476 | 17609 | 23524 | 00000 | 00000 | 58 |
| 3 | 59 36 | 0 24 | 94085 | 12494 | 05915 | 94085 | 12494 | 05915 | 00000 | 00000 | 57 |
| 4 | 59 28 | 0 32 | 7.06579 | 9691 | 12.93421 | 7.06579 | 9691 | 12.93421 | 00000 | 00000 | 56 |
| 5 | 11 59 20 | 0 0 40 | 7.16270 | 7918 | 12.83730 | 7.16270 | 7918 | 12.83730 | 10.00000 | 10.00000 | 55 |
| 6 | 59 12 | 0 48 | 24188 | 6694 | 75812 | 24188 | 6694 | 75812 | 00000 | 00000 | 54 |
| 7 | 59 4 | 0 56 | 30882 | 5800 | 69118 | 30882 | 5800 | 69118 | 00000 | 00000 | 53 |
| 8 | 58 56 | 1 4 | 36682 | 5115 | 63318 | 36682 | 5115 | 63318 | 00000 | 00000 | 52 |
| 9 | 58 48 | 1 12 | 41797 | 4576 | 58203 | 41797 | 4576 | 58203 | 00000 | 00000 | 51 |
| 10 | 11 58 40 | 0 1 20 | 7.46373 | 4139 | 12.53627 | 7.46373 | 4139 | 12.53627 | 10.00000 | 10.00000 | 50 |
| 11 | 58 32 | 1 28 | 50512 | 3779 | 49488 | 50512 | 3779 | 49488 | 00000 | 00000 | 49 |
| 12 | 58 24 | 1 36 | 54291 | 3476 | 45709 | 54291 | 3476 | 45709 | 00000 | 00000 | 48 |
| 13 | 58 16 | 1 44 | 57767 | 3218 | 42233 | 57767 | 3219 | 42233 | 00000 | 00000 | 47 |
| 14 | 58 8 | 1 52 | 60985 | 2997 | 39015 | 60986 | 2996 | 39014 | 00000 | 00000 | 46 |
| 15 | 11 58 0 | 0 2 0 | 7.63982 | 2802 | 12.36018 | 7.63982 | 2803 | 12.36018 | 10.00000 | 10.00000 | 45 |
| 16 | 57 52 | 2 8 | 66784 | 2633 | 33216 | 66785 | 2633 | 33215 | 00000 | 00000 | 44 |
| 17 | 57 44 | 2 16 | 69417 | 2483 | 30583 | 69418 | 2482 | 30582 | 00001 | 9.99999 | 43 |
| 18 | 57 36 | 2 24 | 71900 | 2348 | 28100 | 71900 | 2348 | 28100 | 00001 | 99999 | 42 |
| 19 | 57 28 | 2 32 | 74248 | 2227 | 25752 | 74248 | 2228 | 25752 | 00001 | 99999 | 41 |
| 20 | 11 57 20 | 0 2 40 | 7.76475 | 2119 | 12.23525 | 7.76476 | 2119 | 12.23524 | 10.00001 | 9.99999 | 40 |
| 21 | 57 12 | 2 48 | 78594 | 2021 | 21406 | 78595 | 2020 | 21405 | 00001 | 99999 | 39 |
| 22 | 57 4 | 2 56 | 80615 | 1930 | 19385 | 80615 | 1931 | 19385 | 00001 | 99999 | 38 |
| 23 | 56 56 | 3 4 | 82545 | 1848 | 17455 | 82546 | 1848 | 17454 | 00001 | 99999 | 37 |
| 24 | 56 48 | 3 12 | 84393 | 1773 | 15607 | 84394 | 1773 | 15606 | 00001 | 99999 | 36 |
| 25 | 11 56 40 | 0 3 20 | 7.86166 | 1704 | 12.13834 | 7.86167 | 1704 | 12.13833 | 10.00001 | 9.99999 | 35 |
| 26 | 56 32 | 3 28 | 87870 | 1639 | 12130 | 87871 | 1639 | 12129 | 00001 | 99999 | 34 |
| 27 | 56 24 | 3 36 | 89509 | 1579 | 10491 | 89510 | 1579 | 10490 | 00001 | 99999 | 33 |
| 28 | 56 16 | 3 44 | 91088 | 1524 | 08912 | 91089 | 1524 | 08911 | 00001 | 99999 | 32 |
| 29 | 56 8 | 3 52 | 92612 | 1472 | 07388 | 92613 | 1473 | 07387 | 00002 | 99998 | 31 |
| 30 | 11 56 0 | 0 4 0 | 7.94084 | 1424 | 12.05916 | 7.94086 | 1424 | 12.05914 | 10.00002 | 9.99998 | 30 |
| 31 | 55 52 | 4 8 | 95508 | 1379 | 04492 | 95510 | 1379 | 04490 | 00002 | 99998 | 29 |
| 32 | 55 44 | 4 16 | 96887 | 1336 | 03113 | 96889 | 1336 | 03111 | 00002 | 99998 | 28 |
| 33 | 55 36 | 4 24 | 98223 | 1297 | 01777 | 98225 | 1297 | 01775 | 00002 | 99998 | 27 |
| 34 | 55 28 | 4 32 | 99520 | 1259 | 00480 | 99522 | 1259 | 00478 | 00002 | 99998 | 26 |
| 35 | 11 55 20 | 0 4 40 | 8.00779 | 1223 | 11.99221 | 8.00781 | 1223 | 11.99219 | 10.00002 | 9.99998 | 25 |
| 36 | 55 12 | 4 48 | 02002 | 1190 | 97998 | 02004 | 1190 | 97996 | 00002 | 99998 | 24 |
| 37 | 55 4 | 4 56 | 03192 | 1158 | 96808 | 03194 | 1159 | 96806 | 00003 | 99997 | 23 |
| 38 | 54 56 | 5 4 | 04350 | 1128 | 95650 | 04353 | 1128 | 95647 | 00003 | 99997 | 22 |
| 39 | 54 48 | 5 12 | 05478 | 1100 | 94522 | 05481 | 1100 | 94519 | 00003 | 99997 | 21 |
| 40 | 11 54 40 | 0 5 20 | 8.06578 | 1072 | 11.93422 | 8.06581 | 1072 | 11.93419 | 10.00003 | 9.99997 | 20 |
| 41 | 54 32 | 5 28 | 07650 | 1046 | 92350 | 07653 | 1047 | 92347 | 00003 | 99997 | 19 |
| 42 | 54 24 | 5 36 | 08696 | 1022 | 91304 | 08700 | 1022 | 91300 | 00003 | 99997 | 18 |
| 43 | 54 16 | 5 44 | 09718 | 999 | 90282 | 09722 | 998 | 90278 | 00003 | 99997 | 17 |
| 44 | 54 8 | 5 52 | 10717 | 976 | 89283 | 10720 | 976 | 89280 | 00004 | 99996 | 16 |
| 45 | 11 54 0 | 0 6 0 | 8.11693 | 954 | 11.88307 | 8.11696 | 955 | 11.88304 | 10.00004 | 9.99996 | 15 |
| 46 | 53 52 | 6 8 | 12647 | 934 | 87353 | 12651 | 934 | 87349 | 00004 | 99996 | 14 |
| 47 | 53 44 | 6 16 | 13581 | 914 | 86419 | 13585 | 915 | 86415 | 00004 | 99996 | 13 |
| 48 | 53 36 | 6 24 | 14495 | 896 | 85505 | 14500 | 895 | 85500 | 00004 | 99996 | 12 |
| 49 | 53 28 | 6 32 | 15391 | 877 | 84609 | 15395 | 878 | 84605 | 00004 | 99996 | 11 |
| 50 | 11 53 20 | 0 6 40 | 8.16268 | 860 | 11.83732 | 8.16273 | 860 | 11.83727 | 10.00005 | 9.99995 | 10 |
| 51 | 53 12 | 6 48 | 17128 | 843 | 82872 | 17133 | 843 | 82867 | 00005 | 99995 | 9 |
| 52 | 53 4 | 6 56 | 17971 | 827 | 82029 | 17976 | 828 | 82024 | 00005 | 99995 | 8 |
| 53 | 52 56 | 7 4 | 18798 | 812 | 81202 | 18804 | 812 | 81196 | 00005 | 99995 | 7 |
| 54 | 52 48 | 7 12 | 19610 | 797 | 80390 | 19616 | 797 | 80384 | 00005 | 99995 | 6 |
| 55 | 11 52 40 | 0 7 20 | 8.20407 | 782 | 11.79593 | 8.20413 | 782 | 11.79587 | 10.00006 | 9.99994 | 5 |
| 56 | 52 32 | 7 28 | 21189 | 769 | 78811 | 21195 | 769 | 78805 | 00006 | 99994 | 4 |
| 57 | 52 24 | 7 36 | 21958 | 755 | 78042 | 21964 | 756 | 78036 | 00006 | 99994 | 3 |
| 58 | 52 16 | 7 44 | 22713 | 743 | 77287 | 22720 | 742 | 77280 | 00006 | 99994 | 2 |
| 59 | 52 8 | 7 52 | 23456 | 730 | 76544 | 23462 | 730 | 76538 | 00006 | 99994 | 1 |
| 60 | 52 0 | 8 0 | 24186 | 717 | 75814 | 24192 | 718 | 75808 | 00007 | 99993 | 0 |
| M | Hour P.M. | Hour A.M. | Cosine. | Diff. 1′ | Secant. | Cotangent | Diff. 1′ | Tangent. | Cosecant. | Sine. | M |

90° | 89°

# TABLE XXVII.

## Log. Sines, Tangents, and Secants.

1° 178°

| M | Hour A.M. | Hour P.M. | Sine. | Diff. 1′ | Cosecant. | Tangent. | Diff. 1′ | Cotangent | Secant. | Cosine. | M |
|---|---|---|---|---|---|---|---|---|---|---|---|
| 0 | 11 52 0 | 0 8 0 | 8.24186 | 717 | 11.75814 | 8.24192 | 718 | 11.75808 | 10.00007 | 9.99993 | 60 |
| 1 | 51 52 | 8 8 | 24903 | 706 | 75097 | 24910 | 706 | 75090 | 00007 | 99993 | 59 |
| 2 | 51 44 | 8 16 | 25609 | 695 | 74391 | 25616 | 696 | 74384 | 00007 | 99993 | 58 |
| 3 | 51 36 | 8 24 | 26304 | 684 | 73696 | 26312 | 684 | 73688 | 00007 | 99993 | 57 |
| 4 | 51 28 | 8 32 | 26988 | 673 | 73012 | 26996 | 673 | 73004 | 00008 | 99992 | 56 |
| 5 | 11 51 20 | 0 8 40 | 8.27661 | 663 | 11.72339 | 8.27669 | 663 | 11.72331 | 10.00008 | 9.99992 | 55 |
| 6 | 51 12 | 8 48 | 28324 | 653 | 71676 | 28332 | 654 | 71668 | 00008 | 99992 | 54 |
| 7 | 51 4 | 8 56 | 28977 | 644 | 71023 | 28986 | 643 | 71014 | 00008 | 99992 | 53 |
| 8 | 50 56 | 9 4 | 29621 | 634 | 70379 | 29629 | 634 | 70371 | 00008 | 99992 | 52 |
| 9 | 50 48 | 9 12 | 30255 | 624 | 69745 | 30263 | 625 | 69737 | 00009 | 99991 | 51 |
| 10 | 11 50 40 | 0 9 20 | 8.30879 | 616 | 11.69121 | 8.30888 | 617 | 11.69112 | 10.00009 | 9.99991 | 50 |
| 11 | 50 32 | 9 28 | 31495 | 608 | 68505 | 31505 | 607 | 68495 | 00009 | 99991 | 49 |
| 12 | 50 24 | 9 36 | 32103 | 599 | 67897 | 32112 | 599 | 67888 | 00010 | 99990 | 48 |
| 13 | 50 16 | 9 44 | 32702 | 590 | 67298 | 32711 | 591 | 67289 | 00010 | 99990 | 47 |
| 14 | 50 8 | 9 52 | 33292 | 583 | 66708 | 33302 | 584 | 66698 | 00010 | 99990 | 46 |
| 15 | 11 50 0 | 0 10 0 | 8.33875 | 575 | 11.66125 | 8.33886 | 575 | 11.66114 | 10.00010 | 9.99990 | 45 |
| 16 | 49 52 | 10 8 | 34450 | 568 | 65550 | 34461 | 568 | 65539 | 00011 | 99989 | 44 |
| 17 | 49 44 | 10 16 | 35018 | 560 | 64982 | 35029 | 561 | 64971 | 00011 | 99989 | 43 |
| 18 | 49 36 | 10 24 | 35578 | 553 | 64422 | 35590 | 553 | 64410 | 00011 | 99989 | 42 |
| 19 | 49 28 | 10 32 | 36131 | 547 | 63869 | 36143 | 546 | 63857 | 00011 | 99989 | 41 |
| 20 | 11 49 20 | 0 10 40 | 8.36678 | 539 | 11.63322 | 8.36689 | 540 | 11.63311 | 10.00012 | 9.99988 | 40 |
| 21 | 49 12 | 10 48 | 37217 | 533 | 62783 | 37229 | 533 | 62771 | 00012 | 99988 | 39 |
| 22 | 49 4 | 10 56 | 37750 | 526 | 62250 | 37762 | 527 | 62238 | 00012 | 99988 | 38 |
| 23 | 48 56 | 11 4 | 38276 | 520 | 61724 | 38289 | 520 | 61711 | 00013 | 99987 | 37 |
| 24 | 48 48 | 11 12 | 38796 | 514 | 61204 | 38809 | 514 | 61191 | 00013 | 99987 | 36 |
| 25 | 11 48 40 | 0 11 20 | 8.39310 | 508 | 11.60690 | 8.39323 | 509 | 11.60677 | 10.00013 | 9.99987 | 35 |
| 26 | 48 32 | 11 28 | 39818 | 502 | 60182 | 39832 | 502 | 60168 | 00014 | 99986 | 34 |
| 27 | 48 24 | 11 36 | 40320 | 496 | 59680 | 40334 | 496 | 59666 | 00014 | 99986 | 33 |
| 28 | 48 16 | 11 44 | 40816 | 491 | 59184 | 40830 | 491 | 59170 | 00014 | 99986 | 32 |
| 29 | 48 8 | 11 52 | 41307 | 485 | 58693 | 41321 | 486 | 58679 | 00015 | 99985 | 31 |
| 30 | 11 48 0 | 0 12 0 | 8.41792 | 480 | 11.58208 | 8.41807 | 480 | 11.58193 | 10.00015 | 9.99985 | 30 |
| 31 | 47 52 | 12 8 | 42272 | 474 | 57728 | 42287 | 475 | 57713 | 00015 | 99985 | 29 |
| 32 | 47 44 | 12 16 | 42746 | 470 | 57254 | 42762 | 470 | 57238 | 00016 | 99984 | 28 |
| 33 | 47 36 | 12 24 | 43216 | 464 | 56784 | 43232 | 464 | 56768 | 00016 | 99984 | 27 |
| 34 | 47 28 | 12 32 | 43680 | 459 | 56320 | 43696 | 460 | 56304 | 00016 | 99984 | 26 |
| 35 | 11 47 20 | 0 12 40 | 8.44139 | 455 | 11.55861 | 8.44156 | 455 | 11.55844 | 10.00017 | 9.99983 | 25 |
| 36 | 47 12 | 12 48 | 44594 | 450 | 55406 | 44611 | 450 | 55389 | 00017 | 99983 | 24 |
| 37 | 47 4 | 12 56 | 45044 | 445 | 54956 | 45061 | 446 | 54939 | 00017 | 99983 | 23 |
| 38 | 46 56 | 13 4 | 45489 | 441 | 54511 | 45507 | 441 | 54493 | 00018 | 99982 | 22 |
| 39 | 46 48 | 13 12 | 45930 | 436 | 54070 | 45948 | 437 | 54052 | 00018 | 99982 | 21 |
| 40 | 11 46 40 | 0 13 20 | 8.46366 | 433 | 11.53634 | 8.46385 | 432 | 11.53615 | 10.00018 | 9.99982 | 20 |
| 41 | 46 32 | 13 28 | 46799 | 427 | 53201 | 46817 | 428 | 53183 | 00019 | 99981 | 19 |
| 42 | 46 24 | 13 36 | 47226 | 424 | 52774 | 47245 | 424 | 52755 | 00019 | 99981 | 18 |
| 43 | 46 16 | 13 44 | 47650 | 419 | 52350 | 47669 | 420 | 52331 | 00019 | 99981 | 17 |
| 44 | 46 8 | 13 52 | 48069 | 416 | 51931 | 48089 | 416 | 51911 | 00020 | 99980 | 16 |
| 45 | 11 46 0 | 0 14 0 | 8.48485 | 411 | 11.51515 | 8.48505 | 412 | 11.51495 | 10.00020 | 9.99980 | 15 |
| 46 | 45 52 | 14 8 | 48896 | 408 | 51104 | 48917 | 408 | 51083 | 00021 | 99979 | 14 |
| 47 | 45 44 | 14 16 | 49304 | 404 | 50696 | 49325 | 404 | 50675 | 00021 | 99979 | 13 |
| 48 | 45 36 | 14 24 | 49708 | 400 | 50292 | 49729 | 401 | 50271 | 00021 | 99979 | 12 |
| 49 | 45 28 | 14 32 | 50108 | 396 | 49892 | 50130 | 397 | 49870 | 00022 | 99978 | 11 |
| 50 | 11 45 20 | 0 14 40 | 8.50504 | 393 | 11.49496 | 8.50527 | 393 | 11.49473 | 10.00022 | 9.99978 | 10 |
| 51 | 45 12 | 14 48 | 50897 | 390 | 49103 | 50920 | 390 | 49080 | 00023 | 99977 | 9 |
| 52 | 45 4 | 14 56 | 51287 | 386 | 48713 | 51310 | 386 | 48690 | 00023 | 99977 | 8 |
| 53 | 44 56 | 15 4 | 51673 | 382 | 48327 | 51696 | 383 | 48304 | 00023 | 99977 | 7 |
| 54 | 44 48 | 15 12 | 52055 | 379 | 47945 | 52079 | 380 | 47921 | 00024 | 99976 | 6 |
| 55 | 11 44 40 | 0 15 20 | 8.52434 | 376 | 11.47566 | 8.52459 | 376 | 11.47541 | 10.00024 | 9.99976 | 5 |
| 56 | 44 32 | 15 28 | 52810 | 373 | 47190 | 52835 | 373 | 47165 | 00025 | 99975 | 4 |
| 57 | 44 24 | 15 36 | 53183 | 369 | 46817 | 53208 | 370 | 46792 | 00025 | 99975 | 3 |
| 58 | 44 16 | 15 44 | 53552 | 367 | 46448 | 53578 | 367 | 46422 | 00026 | 99974 | 2 |
| 59 | 44 8 | 15 52 | 53919 | 363 | 46081 | 53945 | 363 | 46055 | 00026 | 99974 | 1 |
| 60 | 44 0 | 16 0 | 54282 | 360 | 45718 | 54308 | 361 | 45692 | 00026 | 99974 | 0 |
| M | Hour P.M. | Hour A.M. | Cosine. | Diff. 1′ | Secant. | Cotangent | Diff. 1′ | Tangent. | Cosecant. | Sine. | M |

91° 88°

# TABLE XXVII.

## Log. Sines, Tangents, and Secants.

2° 177°

| M | Hour A.M. | Hour P.M. | Sine. | Diff. 1′ | Cosecant. | Tangent. | Diff. 1′ | Cotangent | Secant. | Cosine. | M |
|---|---|---|---|---|---|---|---|---|---|---|---|
| 0 | 11 44 0 | 0 16 0 | 8.54282 | 360 | 11.45718 | 8.54308 | 361 | 11.45692 | 10.00026 | 9.99974 | 60 |
| 1 | 43 52 | 16 8 | 54642 | 357 | 45358 | 54669 | 358 | 45331 | 00027 | 99973 | 59 |
| 2 | 43 44 | 16 16 | 54999 | 355 | 45001 | 55027 | 355 | 44973 | 00027 | 99973 | 58 |
| 3 | 43 36 | 16 24 | 55354 | 351 | 44646 | 55382 | 352 | 44618 | 00028 | 99972 | 57 |
| 4 | 43 28 | 16 32 | 55705 | 349 | 44295 | 55734 | 349 | 44266 | 00028 | 99972 | 56 |
| 5 | 11 43 20 | 0 16 40 | 8.56054 | 346 | 11.43946 | 8.56083 | 346 | 11.43917 | 10.00029 | 9.99971 | 55 |
| 6 | 43 12 | 16 48 | 56400 | 343 | 43600 | 56429 | 344 | 43571 | 00029 | 99971 | 54 |
| 7 | 43 4 | 16 56 | 56743 | 341 | 43257 | 56773 | 341 | 43227 | 00030 | 99970 | 53 |
| 8 | 42 56 | 17 4 | 57084 | 337 | 42916 | 57114 | 338 | 42886 | 00030 | 99970 | 52 |
| 9 | 42 48 | 17 12 | 57421 | 336 | 42579 | 57452 | 336 | 42548 | 00031 | 99969 | 51 |
| 10 | 11 42 40 | 0 17 20 | 8.57757 | 332 | 11.42243 | 8.57788 | 333 | 11.42212 | 10.00031 | 9.99969 | 50 |
| 11 | 42 32 | 17 28 | 58089 | 330 | 41911 | 58121 | 330 | 41879 | 00032 | 99968 | 49 |
| 12 | 42 24 | 17 36 | 58419 | 328 | 41581 | 58451 | 328 | 41549 | 00032 | 99968 | 48 |
| 13 | 42 16 | 17 44 | 58747 | 325 | 41253 | 58779 | 326 | 41221 | 00033 | 99967 | 47 |
| 14 | 42 8 | 17 52 | 59072 | 323 | 40928 | 59105 | 323 | 40895 | 00033 | 99967 | 46 |
| 15 | 11 42 0 | 0 18 0 | 8.59395 | 320 | 11.40605 | 8.59428 | 321 | 11.40572 | 10.00033 | 9.99967 | 45 |
| 16 | 41 52 | 18 8 | 59715 | 318 | 40285 | 59749 | 319 | 40251 | 00034 | 99966 | 44 |
| 17 | 41 44 | 18 16 | 60033 | 316 | 39967 | 60068 | 316 | 39932 | 00034 | 99966 | 43 |
| 18 | 41 36 | 18 24 | 60349 | 313 | 39651 | 60384 | 314 | 39616 | 00035 | 99965 | 42 |
| 19 | 41 28 | 18 32 | 60662 | 311 | 39338 | 60698 | 311 | 39302 | 00036 | 99964 | 41 |
| 20 | 11 41 20 | 0 18 40 | 8.60973 | 309 | 11.39027 | 8.61009 | 310 | 11.38991 | 10.00036 | 9.99964 | 40 |
| 21 | 41 12 | 18 48 | 61282 | 307 | 38718 | 61319 | 307 | 38681 | 00037 | 99963 | 39 |
| 22 | 41 4 | 18 56 | 61589 | 305 | 38411 | 61626 | 305 | 38374 | 00037 | 99963 | 38 |
| 23 | 40 56 | 19 4 | 61894 | 302 | 38106 | 61931 | 303 | 38069 | 00038 | 99962 | 37 |
| 24 | 40 48 | 19 12 | 62196 | 301 | 37804 | 62234 | 301 | 37766 | 00038 | 99962 | 36 |
| 25 | 11 40 40 | 0 19 20 | 8.62497 | 298 | 11.37503 | 8.62535 | 299 | 11.37465 | 10.00039 | 9.99961 | 35 |
| 26 | 40 32 | 19 28 | 62795 | 296 | 37205 | 62834 | 297 | 37166 | 00039 | 99961 | 34 |
| 27 | 40 24 | 19 36 | 63091 | 294 | 36909 | 63131 | 295 | 36869 | 00040 | 99960 | 33 |
| 28 | 40 16 | 19 44 | 63385 | 293 | 36615 | 63426 | 292 | 36574 | 00040 | 99960 | 32 |
| 29 | 40 8 | 19 52 | 63678 | 290 | 36322 | 63718 | 291 | 36282 | 00041 | 99959 | 31 |
| 30 | 11 40 0 | 0 20 0 | 8.63968 | 288 | 11.36032 | 8.64009 | 289 | 11.35991 | 10.00041 | 9.99959 | 30 |
| 31 | 39 52 | 20 8 | 64256 | 287 | 35744 | 64298 | 287 | 35702 | 00042 | 99958 | 29 |
| 32 | 39 44 | 20 16 | 64543 | 284 | 35457 | 64585 | 285 | 35415 | 00042 | 99958 | 28 |
| 33 | 39 36 | 20 24 | 64827 | 283 | 35173 | 64870 | 284 | 35130 | 00043 | 99957 | 27 |
| 34 | 39 28 | 20 32 | 65110 | 281 | 34890 | 65154 | 281 | 34846 | 00044 | 99956 | 26 |
| 35 | 11 39 20 | 0 20 40 | 8.65391 | 279 | 11.34609 | 8.65435 | 280 | 11.34565 | 10.00044 | 9.99956 | 25 |
| 36 | 39 12 | 20 48 | 65670 | 277 | 34330 | 65715 | 278 | 34285 | 00045 | 99955 | 24 |
| 37 | 39 4 | 20 56 | 65947 | 276 | 34053 | 65993 | 276 | 34007 | 00045 | 99955 | 23 |
| 38 | 38 56 | 21 4 | 66223 | 274 | 33777 | 66269 | 274 | 33731 | 00046 | 99954 | 22 |
| 39 | 38 48 | 21 12 | 66497 | 272 | 33503 | 66543 | 273 | 33457 | 00046 | 99954 | 21 |
| 40 | 11 38 40 | 0 21 20 | 8.66769 | 270 | 11.33231 | 8.66816 | 271 | 11.33184 | 10.00047 | 9.99953 | 20 |
| 41 | 38 32 | 21 28 | 67039 | 269 | 32961 | 67087 | 269 | 32913 | 00048 | 99952 | 19 |
| 42 | 38 24 | 21 36 | 67308 | 267 | 32692 | 67356 | 268 | 32644 | 00048 | 99952 | 18 |
| 43 | 38 16 | 21 44 | 67575 | 266 | 32425 | 67624 | 266 | 32376 | 00049 | 99951 | 17 |
| 44 | 38 8 | 21 52 | 67841 | 263 | 32159 | 67890 | 264 | 32110 | 00049 | 99951 | 16 |
| 45 | 11 38 0 | 0 22 0 | 8.68104 | 263 | 11.31896 | 8.68154 | 263 | 11.31846 | 10.00050 | 9.99950 | 15 |
| 46 | 37 52 | 22 8 | 68367 | 260 | 31633 | 68417 | 261 | 31583 | 00051 | 99949 | 14 |
| 47 | 37 44 | 22 16 | 68627 | 259 | 31373 | 68678 | 260 | 31322 | 00051 | 99949 | 13 |
| 48 | 37 36 | 22 24 | 68886 | 258 | 31114 | 68938 | 258 | 31062 | 00052 | 99948 | 12 |
| 49 | 37 28 | 22 32 | 69144 | 256 | 30856 | 69196 | 257 | 30804 | 00052 | 99948 | 11 |
| 50 | 11 37 20 | 0 22 40 | 8.69400 | 254 | 11.30600 | 8.69453 | 255 | 11.30547 | 10.00053 | 9.99947 | 10 |
| 51 | 37 12 | 22 48 | 69654 | 253 | 30346 | 69708 | 254 | 30292 | 00054 | 99946 | 9 |
| 52 | 37 4 | 22 56 | 69907 | 252 | 30093 | 69962 | 252 | 30038 | 00054 | 99946 | 8 |
| 53 | 36 56 | 23 4 | 70159 | 250 | 29841 | 70214 | 251 | 29786 | 00055 | 99945 | 7 |
| 54 | 36 48 | 23 12 | 70409 | 249 | 29591 | 70465 | 249 | 29535 | 00056 | 99944 | 6 |
| 55 | 11 36 40 | 0 23 20 | 8.70658 | 247 | 11.29342 | 8.70714 | 248 | 11.29286 | 10.00056 | 9.99944 | 5 |
| 56 | 36 32 | 23 28 | 70905 | 246 | 29095 | 70962 | 246 | 29038 | 00057 | 99943 | 4 |
| 57 | 36 24 | 23 36 | 71151 | 244 | 28849 | 71208 | 245 | 28792 | 00058 | 99942 | 3 |
| 58 | 36 16 | 23 44 | 71395 | 243 | 28605 | 71453 | 244 | 28547 | 00058 | 99942 | 2 |
| 59 | 36 8 | 23 52 | 71638 | 242 | 28362 | 71697 | 243 | 28303 | 00059 | 99941 | 1 |
| 60 | 36 0 | 24 0 | 71880 | 240 | 28120 | 71940 | 241 | 28060 | 00060 | 99940 | 0 |
| M | Hour P.M. | Hour A.M. | Cosine. | Diff. 1′ | Secant. | Cotangent | Diff. 1′ | Tangent. | Cosecant. | Sine. | M |

92° 87°

# TABLE XXVII.

## Log. Sines, Tangents, and Secants.

3° | 176°

| M | Hour A.M. | Hour P.M. | Sine. | Diff. 1′ | Cosecant. | Tangent. | Diff. 1′ | Cotangent | Secant. | Cosine. | M |
|---|---|---|---|---|---|---|---|---|---|---|---|
| 0 | 11 36 0 | 0 24 0 | 8.71880 | 240 | 11.28120 | 8.71940 | 241 | 11.28060 | 10.00060 | 9.99940 | 60 |
| 1 | 35 52 | 24 8 | 72120 | 239 | 27880 | 72181 | 239 | 27819 | 00060 | 99940 | 59 |
| 2 | 35 44 | 24 16 | 72359 | 238 | 27641 | 72420 | 239 | 27580 | 00061 | 99939 | 58 |
| 3 | 35 36 | 24 24 | 72597 | 237 | 27403 | 72659 | 237 | 27341 | 00062 | 99938 | 57 |
| 4 | 35 28 | 24 32 | 72834 | 235 | 27166 | 72896 | 236 | 27104 | 00062 | 99938 | 56 |
| 5 | 11 35 20 | 0 24 40 | 8.73069 | 234 | 11.26931 | 8.73132 | 234 | 11.26868 | 10.00063 | 9.99937 | 55 |
| 6 | 35 12 | 24 48 | 73303 | 232 | 26697 | 73366 | 234 | 26634 | 00064 | 99936 | 54 |
| 7 | 35 4 | 24 56 | 73535 | 232 | 26465 | 73600 | 232 | 26400 | 00064 | 99936 | 53 |
| 8 | 34 56 | 25 4 | 73767 | 230 | 26233 | 73832 | 231 | 26168 | 00065 | 99935 | 52 |
| 9 | 34 48 | 25 12 | 73997 | 229 | 26003 | 74063 | 229 | 25937 | 00066 | 99934 | 51 |
| 10 | 11 34 40 | 0 25 20 | 8.74226 | 228 | 11.25774 | 8.74292 | 229 | 11.25708 | 10.00066 | 9.99934 | 50 |
| 11 | 34 32 | 25 28 | 74454 | 226 | 25546 | 74521 | 227 | 25479 | 00067 | 99933 | 49 |
| 12 | 34 24 | 25 36 | 74680 | 226 | 25320 | 74748 | 226 | 25252 | 00068 | 99932 | 48 |
| 13 | 34 16 | 25 44 | 74906 | 224 | 25094 | 74974 | 225 | 25026 | 00068 | 99932 | 47 |
| 14 | 34 8 | 25 52 | 75130 | 223 | 24870 | 75199 | 224 | 24801 | 00069 | 99931 | 46 |
| 15 | 11 34 0 | 0 26 0 | 8.75353 | 222 | 11.24647 | 8.75423 | 222 | 11.24577 | 10.00070 | 9.99930 | 45 |
| 16 | 33 52 | 26 8 | 75575 | 220 | 24425 | 75645 | 222 | 24355 | 00071 | 99929 | 44 |
| 17 | 33 44 | 26 16 | 75795 | 220 | 24205 | 75867 | 220 | 24133 | 00071 | 99929 | 43 |
| 18 | 33 36 | 26 24 | 76015 | 219 | 23985 | 76087 | 219 | 23913 | 00072 | 99928 | 42 |
| 19 | 33 28 | 26 32 | 76234 | 217 | 23766 | 76306 | 219 | 23694 | 00073 | 99927 | 41 |
| 20 | 11 33 20 | 0 26 40 | 8.76451 | 216 | 11.23549 | 8.76525 | 217 | 11.23475 | 10.00074 | 9.99926 | 40 |
| 21 | 33 12 | 26 48 | 76667 | 216 | 23333 | 76742 | 216 | 23258 | 00074 | 99926 | 39 |
| 22 | 33 4 | 26 56 | 76883 | 214 | 23117 | 76958 | 215 | 23042 | 00075 | 99925 | 38 |
| 23 | 32 56 | 27 4 | 77097 | 213 | 22903 | 77173 | 214 | 22827 | 00076 | 99924 | 37 |
| 24 | 32 48 | 27 12 | 77310 | 212 | 22690 | 77387 | 213 | 22613 | 00077 | 99923 | 36 |
| 25 | 11 32 40 | 0 27 20 | 8.77522 | 211 | 11.22478 | 8.77600 | 211 | 11.22400 | 10.00077 | 9.99923 | 35 |
| 26 | 32 32 | 27 28 | 77733 | 210 | 22267 | 77811 | 211 | 22189 | 00078 | 99922 | 34 |
| 27 | 32 24 | 27 36 | 77943 | 209 | 22057 | 78022 | 210 | 21978 | 00079 | 99921 | 33 |
| 28 | 32 16 | 27 44 | 78152 | 208 | 21848 | 78232 | 209 | 21768 | 00080 | 99920 | 32 |
| 29 | 32 8 | 27 52 | 78360 | 208 | 21640 | 78441 | 208 | 21559 | 00080 | 99920 | 31 |
| 30 | 11 32 0 | 0 28 0 | 8.78568 | 206 | 11.21432 | 8.78649 | 206 | 11.21351 | 10.00081 | 9.99919 | 30 |
| 31 | 31 52 | 28 8 | 78774 | 205 | 21226 | 78855 | 206 | 21145 | 00082 | 99918 | 29 |
| 32 | 31 44 | 28 16 | 78979 | 204 | 21021 | 79061 | 205 | 20939 | 00083 | 99917 | 28 |
| 33 | 31 36 | 28 24 | 79183 | 203 | 20817 | 79266 | 204 | 20734 | 00083 | 99917 | 27 |
| 34 | 31 28 | 28 32 | 79386 | 202 | 20614 | 79470 | 203 | 20530 | 00084 | 99916 | 26 |
| 35 | 11 31 20 | 0 28 40 | 8.79588 | 201 | 11.20412 | 8.79673 | 202 | 11.20327 | 10.00085 | 9.99915 | 25 |
| 36 | 31 12 | 28 48 | 79789 | 201 | 20211 | 79875 | 201 | 20125 | 00086 | 99914 | 24 |
| 37 | 31 4 | 28 56 | 79990 | 199 | 20010 | 80076 | 201 | 19924 | 00087 | 99913 | 23 |
| 38 | 30 56 | 29 4 | 80189 | 199 | 19811 | 80277 | 199 | 19723 | 00087 | 99913 | 22 |
| 39 | 30 48 | 29 12 | 80388 | 197 | 19612 | 80476 | 198 | 19524 | 00088 | 99912 | 21 |
| 40 | 11 30 40 | 0 29 20 | 8.80585 | 197 | 11.19415 | 8.80674 | 198 | 11.19326 | 10.00089 | 9.99911 | 20 |
| 41 | 30 32 | 29 28 | 80782 | 196 | 19218 | 80872 | 196 | 19128 | 00090 | 99910 | 19 |
| 42 | 30 24 | 29 36 | 80978 | 195 | 19022 | 81068 | 196 | 18932 | 00091 | 99909 | 18 |
| 43 | 30 16 | 29 44 | 81173 | 194 | 18827 | 81264 | 195 | 18736 | 00091 | 99909 | 17 |
| 44 | 30 8 | 29 52 | 81367 | 193 | 18633 | 81459 | 194 | 18541 | 00092 | 99908 | 16 |
| 45 | 11 30 0 | 0 30 0 | 8.81560 | 192 | 11.18440 | 8.81653 | 193 | 11.18347 | 10.00093 | 9.99907 | 15 |
| 46 | 29 52 | 30 8 | 81752 | 192 | 18248 | 81846 | 192 | 18154 | 00094 | 99906 | 14 |
| 47 | 29 44 | 30 16 | 81944 | 190 | 18056 | 82038 | 192 | 17962 | 00095 | 99905 | 13 |
| 48 | 29 36 | 30 24 | 82134 | 190 | 17866 | 82230 | 190 | 17770 | 00096 | 99904 | 12 |
| 49 | 29 28 | 30 32 | 82324 | 189 | 17676 | 82420 | 190 | 17580 | 00096 | 99904 | 11 |
| 50 | 11 29 20 | 0 30 40 | 8.82513 | 188 | 11.17487 | 8.82610 | 189 | 11.17390 | 10.00097 | 9.99903 | 10 |
| 51 | 29 12 | 30 48 | 82701 | 187 | 17299 | 82799 | 188 | 17201 | 00098 | 99902 | 9 |
| 52 | 29 4 | 30 56 | 82888 | 187 | 17112 | 82987 | 188 | 17013 | 00099 | 99901 | 8 |
| 53 | 28 56 | 31 4 | 83075 | 186 | 16925 | 83175 | 186 | 16825 | 00100 | 99900 | 7 |
| 54 | 28 48 | 31 12 | 83261 | 185 | 16739 | 83361 | 186 | 16639 | 00101 | 99899 | 6 |
| 55 | 11 28 40 | 0 31 20 | 8.83446 | 184 | 11.16554 | 8.83547 | 185 | 11.16453 | 10.00102 | 9.99898 | 5 |
| 56 | 28 32 | 31 28 | 83630 | 183 | 16370 | 83732 | 184 | 16268 | 00102 | 99898 | 4 |
| 57 | 28 24 | 31 36 | 83813 | 183 | 16187 | 83916 | 184 | 16084 | 00103 | 99897 | 3 |
| 58 | 28 16 | 31 44 | 83996 | 181 | 16004 | 84100 | 182 | 15900 | 00104 | 99896 | 2 |
| 59 | 28 8 | 31 52 | 84177 | 181 | 15823 | 84282 | 182 | 15718 | 00105 | 99895 | 1 |
| 60 | 28 0 | 32 0 | 84358 | 181 | 15642 | 84464 | 182 | 15536 | 00106 | 99894 | 0 |
| M | Hour P.M. | Hour A.M. | Cosine. | Diff. 1′ | Secant. | Cotangent | Diff. 1′ | Tangent. | Cosecant. | Sine. | M |

93° | 86°

# TABLE XXVII.

## Log. Sines, Tangents, and Secants.

4° 175°

| M | Hour A.M. | Hour P.M. | Sine. | Diff. 1' | Cosecant. | Tangent. | Diff. 1' | Cotangent | Secant. | Cosine. | M |
|---|---|---|---|---|---|---|---|---|---|---|---|
| 0 | 11 28 0 | 0 32 0 | 8.84358 | 181 | 11.15642 | 8.84464 | 182 | 11.15536 | 10.00106 | 9.99894 | 60 |
| 1 | 27 52 | 32 8 | 84539 | 179 | 15461 | 84646 | 180 | 15354 | 00107 | 99893 | 59 |
| 2 | 27 44 | 32 16 | 84718 | 179 | 15282 | 84826 | 180 | 15174 | 00108 | 99892 | 58 |
| 3 | 27 36 | 32 24 | 84897 | 178 | 15103 | 85006 | 179 | 14994 | 00109 | 99891 | 57 |
| 4 | 27 28 | 32 32 | 85075 | 177 | 14925 | 85185 | 178 | 14815 | 00109 | 99891 | 56 |
| 5 | 11 27 20 | 0 32 40 | 8.85252 | 177 | 11.14748 | 8.85363 | 177 | 11.14637 | 10.00110 | 9.99890 | 55 |
| 6 | 27 12 | 32 48 | 85429 | 176 | 14571 | 85540 | 177 | 14460 | 00111 | 99889 | 54 |
| 7 | 27 4 | 32 56 | 85605 | 175 | 14395 | 85717 | 176 | 14283 | 00112 | 99888 | 53 |
| 8 | 26 56 | 33 4 | 85780 | 175 | 14220 | 85893 | 176 | 14107 | 00113 | 99887 | 52 |
| 9 | 26 48 | 33 12 | 85955 | 173 | 14045 | 86069 | 174 | 13931 | 00114 | 99886 | 51 |
| 10 | 11 26 40 | 0 33 20 | 8.86128 | 173 | 11.13872 | 8.86243 | 174 | 11.13757 | 10.00115 | 9.99885 | 50 |
| 11 | 26 32 | 33 28 | 86301 | 173 | 13699 | 86417 | 174 | 13583 | 00116 | 99884 | 49 |
| 12 | 26 24 | 33 36 | 86474 | 171 | 13526 | 86591 | 172 | 13409 | 00117 | 99883 | 48 |
| 13 | 26 16 | 33 44 | 86645 | 171 | 13355 | 86763 | 172 | 13237 | 00118 | 99882 | 47 |
| 14 | 26 8 | 33 52 | 86816 | 171 | 13184 | 86935 | 171 | 13065 | 00119 | 99881 | 46 |
| 15 | 11 26 0 | 0 34 0 | 8.86987 | 169 | 11.13013 | 8.87106 | 171 | 11.12894 | 10.00120 | 9.99880 | 45 |
| 16 | 25 52 | 34 8 | 87156 | 169 | 12844 | 87277 | 170 | 12723 | 00121 | 99879 | 44 |
| 17 | 25 44 | 34 16 | 87325 | 169 | 12675 | 87447 | 169 | 12553 | 00121 | 99879 | 43 |
| 18 | 25 36 | 34 24 | 87494 | 167 | 12506 | 87616 | 169 | 12384 | 00122 | 99878 | 42 |
| 19 | 25 28 | 34 32 | 87661 | 168 | 12339 | 87785 | 168 | 12215 | 00123 | 99877 | 41 |
| 20 | 11 25 20 | 0 34 40 | 8.87829 | 166 | 11.12171 | 8.87953 | 167 | 11.12047 | 10.00124 | 9.99876 | 40 |
| 21 | 25 12 | 34 48 | 87995 | 166 | 12005 | 88120 | 167 | 11880 | 00125 | 99875 | 39 |
| 22 | 25 4 | 34 56 | 88161 | 165 | 11839 | 88287 | 166 | 11713 | 00126 | 99874 | 38 |
| 23 | 24 56 | 35 4 | 88326 | 164 | 11674 | 88453 | 165 | 11547 | 00127 | 99873 | 37 |
| 24 | 24 48 | 35 12 | 88490 | 164 | 11510 | 88618 | 165 | 11382 | 00128 | 99872 | 36 |
| 25 | 11 24 40 | 0 35 20 | 8.88654 | 163 | 11.11346 | 8.88783 | 165 | 11.11217 | 10.00129 | 9.99871 | 35 |
| 26 | 24 32 | 35 28 | 88817 | 163 | 11183 | 88948 | 163 | 11052 | 00130 | 99870 | 34 |
| 27 | 24 24 | 35 36 | 88980 | 162 | 11020 | 89111 | 163 | 10889 | 00131 | 99869 | 33 |
| 28 | 24 16 | 35 44 | 89142 | 162 | 10858 | 89274 | 163 | 10726 | 00132 | 99868 | 32 |
| 29 | 24 8 | 35 52 | 89304 | 160 | 10696 | 89437 | 161 | 10563 | 00133 | 99867 | 31 |
| 30 | 11 24 0 | 0 36 0 | 8.89464 | 161 | 11.10536 | 8.89598 | 162 | 11.10402 | 10.00134 | 9.99866 | 30 |
| 31 | 23 52 | 36 8 | 89625 | 159 | 10375 | 89760 | 160 | 10240 | 00135 | 99865 | 29 |
| 32 | 23 44 | 36 16 | 89784 | 159 | 10216 | 89920 | 160 | 10080 | 00136 | 99864 | 28 |
| 33 | 23 36 | 36 24 | 89943 | 159 | 10057 | 90080 | 160 | 09920 | 00137 | 99863 | 27 |
| 34 | 23 28 | 36 32 | 90102 | 158 | 09898 | 90240 | 159 | 09760 | 00138 | 99862 | 26 |
| 35 | 11 23 20 | 0 36 40 | 8.90260 | 157 | 11.09740 | 8.90399 | 158 | 11.09601 | 10.00139 | 9.99861 | 25 |
| 36 | 23 12 | 36 48 | 90417 | 157 | 09583 | 90557 | 158 | 09443 | 00140 | 99860 | 24 |
| 37 | 23 4 | 36 56 | 90574 | 156 | 09426 | 90715 | 157 | 09285 | 00141 | 99859 | 23 |
| 38 | 22 56 | 37 4 | 90730 | 155 | 09270 | 90872 | 157 | 09128 | 00142 | 99858 | 22 |
| 39 | 22 48 | 37 12 | 90885 | 155 | 09115 | 91029 | 156 | 08971 | 00143 | 99857 | 21 |
| 40 | 11 22 40 | 0 37 20 | 8.91040 | 155 | 11.08960 | 8.91185 | 155 | 11.08815 | 10.00144 | 9.99856 | 20 |
| 41 | 22 32 | 37 28 | 91195 | 154 | 08805 | 91340 | 155 | 08660 | 00145 | 99855 | 19 |
| 42 | 22 24 | 37 36 | 91349 | 153 | 08651 | 91495 | 155 | 08505 | 00146 | 99854 | 18 |
| 43 | 22 16 | 37 44 | 91502 | 153 | 08498 | 91650 | 153 | 08350 | 00147 | 99853 | 17 |
| 44 | 22 8 | 37 52 | 91655 | 152 | 08345 | 91803 | 154 | 08197 | 00148 | 99852 | 16 |
| 45 | 11 22 0 | 0 38 0 | 8.91807 | 152 | 11.08193 | 8.91957 | 153 | 11.08043 | 10.00149 | 9.99851 | 15 |
| 46 | 21 52 | 38 8 | 91959 | 151 | 08041 | 92110 | 152 | 07890 | 00150 | 99850 | 14 |
| 47 | 21 44 | 38 16 | 92110 | 151 | 07890 | 92262 | 152 | 07738 | 00152 | 99848 | 13 |
| 48 | 21 36 | 38 24 | 92261 | 150 | 07739 | 92414 | 151 | 07586 | 00153 | 99847 | 12 |
| 49 | 21 28 | 38 32 | 92411 | 150 | 07589 | 92565 | 151 | 07435 | 00154 | 99846 | 11 |
| 50 | 11 21 20 | 0 38 40 | 8.92561 | 149 | 11.07439 | 8.92716 | 150 | 11.07284 | 10.00155 | 9.99845 | 10 |
| 51 | 21 12 | 38 48 | 92710 | 149 | 07290 | 92866 | 150 | 07134 | 00156 | 99844 | 9 |
| 52 | 21 4 | 38 56 | 92859 | 148 | 07141 | 93016 | 149 | 06984 | 00157 | 99843 | 8 |
| 53 | 20 56 | 39 4 | 93007 | 147 | 06993 | 93165 | 148 | 06835 | 00158 | 99842 | 7 |
| 54 | 20 48 | 39 12 | 93154 | 147 | 06846 | 93313 | 149 | 06687 | 00159 | 99841 | 6 |
| 55 | 11 20 40 | 0 39 20 | 8.93301 | 147 | 11.06699 | 8.93462 | 147 | 11.06538 | 10.00160 | 9.99840 | 5 |
| 56 | 20 32 | 39 28 | 93448 | 146 | 06552 | 93609 | 147 | 06391 | 00161 | 99839 | 4 |
| 57 | 20 24 | 39 36 | 93594 | 146 | 06406 | 93756 | 147 | 06244 | 00162 | 99838 | 3 |
| 58 | 20 16 | 39 44 | 93740 | 145 | 06260 | 93903 | 146 | 06097 | 00163 | 99837 | 2 |
| 59 | 20 8 | 39 52 | 93885 | 145 | 06115 | 94049 | 146 | 05951 | 00164 | 99836 | 1 |
| 60 | 20 0 | 40 0 | 94030 | 144 | 05970 | 94195 | 145 | 05805 | 00166 | 99834 | 0 |
| M | Hour P.M. | Hour A.M. | Cosine. | Diff. 1' | Secant. | Cotangent | Diff. 1' | Tangent. | Cosecant. | Sine. | M |

94° 85°

# TABLE XXVII.

## Log. Sines, Tangents, and Secants.

5° | 6h. | 174°

| M | Hour A.M. | Hour P.M. | Sine. (A) | Diff. | Cosecant. (A) | Tangent. (B) | Diff. | Cotangent (B) | Secant. (C) | Diff. | Cosine. (C) | M |
|---|---|---|---|---|---|---|---|---|---|---|---|---|
| 0 | 11 20 00 | 0 40 0 | 8.94030 | 0 | 11.05970 | 8.94195 | 0 | 11.05805 | 10.00166 | 0 | 9.99834 | 60 |
| 1 | 19 52 | 40 8 | 94174 | 2 | 05826 | 94340 | 2 | 05660 | 00167 | 0 | 99833 | 59 |
| 2 | 19 44 | 40 16 | 94317 | 4 | 05683 | 94485 | 4 | 05515 | 00168 | 0 | 99832 | 58 |
| 3 | 19 36 | 40 24 | 94461 | 7 | 05539 | 94630 | 7 | 05370 | 00169 | 0 | 99831 | 57 |
| 4 | 19 28 | 40 32 | 94603 | 9 | 05397 | 94773 | 9 | 05227 | 00170 | 0 | 99830 | 56 |
| 5 | 11 19 20 | 0 40 40 | 8.94746 | 11 | 11.05254 | 8.94917 | 11 | 11.05083 | 10.00171 | 0 | 9.99829 | 55 |
| 6 | 19 12 | 40 48 | 94887 | 13 | 05113 | 95060 | 13 | 04940 | 00172 | 0 | 99828 | 54 |
| 7 | 19 4 | 40 56 | 95029 | 15 | 04971 | 95202 | 15 | 04798 | 00173 | 0 | 99827 | 53 |
| 8 | 18 56 | 41 4 | 95170 | 18 | 04830 | 95344 | 18 | 04656 | 00175 | 0 | 99825 | 52 |
| 9 | 18 48 | 41 12 | 95310 | 20 | 04690 | 95486 | 20 | 04514 | 00176 | 0 | 99824 | 51 |
| 10 | 11 18 40 | 0 41 20 | 8.95450 | 22 | 11.04550 | 8.95627 | 22 | 11.04373 | 10.00177 | 0 | 9.99823 | 50 |
| 11 | 18 32 | 41 28 | 95589 | 24 | 04411 | 95767 | 24 | 04233 | 00178 | 0 | 99822 | 49 |
| 12 | 18 24 | 41 36 | 95728 | 26 | 04272 | 95908 | 27 | 04092 | 00179 | 0 | 99821 | 48 |
| 13 | 18 16 | 41 44 | 95867 | 29 | 04133 | 96047 | 29 | 03953 | 00180 | 0 | 99820 | 47 |
| 14 | 18 8 | 41 52 | 96005 | 31 | 03995 | 96187 | 31 | 03813 | 00181 | 0 | 99819 | 46 |
| 15 | 11 18 0 | 0 42 0 | 8.96143 | 33 | 11.03857 | 8.96325 | 33 | 11.03675 | 10.00183 | 0 | 9.99817 | 45 |
| 16 | 17 52 | 42 8 | 96280 | 35 | 03720 | 96464 | 35 | 03536 | 00184 | 0 | 99816 | 44 |
| 17 | 17 44 | 42 16 | 96417 | 37 | 03583 | 96602 | 38 | 03398 | 00185 | 0 | 99815 | 43 |
| 18 | 17 36 | 42 24 | 96553 | 39 | 03447 | 96739 | 40 | 03261 | 00186 | 0 | 99814 | 42 |
| 19 | 17 28 | 42 32 | 96689 | 42 | 03311 | 96877 | 42 | 03123 | 00187 | 0 | 99813 | 41 |
| 20 | 11 17 20 | 0 42 40 | 8.96825 | 44 | 11.03175 | 8.97013 | 44 | 11.02987 | 10.00188 | 0 | 9.99812 | 40 |
| 21 | 17 12 | 42 48 | 96960 | 46 | 03040 | 97150 | 46 | 02850 | 00190 | 0 | 99810 | 39 |
| 22 | 17 4 | 42 56 | 97095 | 48 | 02905 | 97285 | 49 | 02715 | 00191 | 0 | 99809 | 38 |
| 23 | 16 56 | 43 4 | 97229 | 50 | 02771 | 97421 | 51 | 02579 | 00192 | 0 | 99808 | 37 |
| 24 | 16 48 | 43 12 | 97363 | 53 | 02637 | 97556 | 53 | 02444 | 00193 | 0 | 99807 | 36 |
| 25 | 11 16 40 | 0 43 20 | 8.97496 | 55 | 11.02504 | 8.97691 | 55 | 11.02309 | 10.00194 | 1 | 9.99806 | 35 |
| 26 | 16 32 | 43 28 | 97629 | 57 | 02371 | 97825 | 58 | 02175 | 00196 | 1 | 99804 | 34 |
| 27 | 16 24 | 43 36 | 97762 | 59 | 02238 | 97959 | 60 | 02041 | 00197 | 1 | 99803 | 33 |
| 28 | 16 16 | 43 44 | 97894 | 61 | 02106 | 98092 | 62 | 01908 | 00198 | 1 | 99802 | 32 |
| 29 | 16 8 | 43 52 | 98026 | 64 | 01974 | 98225 | 64 | 01775 | 00199 | 1 | 99801 | 31 |
| 30 | 11 16 0 | 0 44 0 | 8.98157 | 66 | 11.01843 | 8.98358 | 66 | 11.01642 | 10.00200 | 1 | 9.99800 | 30 |
| 31 | 15 52 | 44 8 | 98288 | 68 | 01712 | 98490 | 69 | 01510 | 00202 | 1 | 99798 | 29 |
| 32 | 15 44 | 44 16 | 98419 | 70 | 01581 | 98622 | 71 | 01378 | 00203 | 1 | 99797 | 28 |
| 33 | 15 36 | 44 24 | 98549 | 72 | 01451 | 98753 | 73 | 01247 | 00204 | 1 | 99796 | 27 |
| 34 | 15 28 | 44 32 | 98679 | 75 | 01321 | 98884 | 75 | 01116 | 00205 | 1 | 99795 | 26 |
| 35 | 11 15 20 | 0 44 40 | 8.98808 | 77 | 11.01192 | 8.99015 | 77 | 11.00985 | 10.00207 | 1 | 9.99793 | 25 |
| 36 | 15 12 | 44 48 | 98937 | 79 | 01063 | 99145 | 80 | 00855 | 00208 | 1 | 99792 | 24 |
| 37 | 15 4 | 44 56 | 99066 | 81 | 00934 | 99275 | 82 | 00725 | 00209 | 1 | 99791 | 23 |
| 38 | 14 56 | 45 4 | 99194 | 83 | 00806 | 99405 | 84 | 00595 | 00210 | 1 | 99790 | 22 |
| 39 | 14 48 | 45 12 | 99322 | 86 | 00678 | 99534 | 86 | 00466 | 00212 | 1 | 99788 | 21 |
| 40 | 11 14 40 | 0 45 20 | 8.99450 | 88 | 11.00550 | 8.99662 | 89 | 11.00338 | 10.00213 | 1 | 9.99787 | 20 |
| 41 | 14 32 | 45 28 | 99577 | 90 | 00423 | 99791 | 91 | 00209 | 00214 | 1 | 99786 | 19 |
| 42 | 14 24 | 45 36 | 99704 | 92 | 00296 | 99919 | 93 | 00081 | 00215 | 1 | 99785 | 18 |
| 43 | 14 16 | 45 44 | 99830 | 94 | 00170 | 9.00046 | 95 | 10.99954 | 00217 | 1 | 99783 | 17 |
| 44 | 14 8 | 45 52 | 99956 | 96 | 00044 | 00174 | 97 | 99826 | 00218 | 1 | 99782 | 16 |
| 45 | 11 14 0 | 0 46 0 | 9.00082 | 99 | 10.99918 | 9.00301 | 100 | 10.99699 | 10.00219 | 1 | 9.99781 | 15 |
| 46 | 13 52 | 46 8 | 00207 | 101 | 99793 | 00427 | 102 | 99573 | 00220 | 1 | 99780 | 14 |
| 47 | 13 44 | 46 16 | 00332 | 103 | 99668 | 00553 | 104 | 99447 | 00222 | 1 | 99778 | 13 |
| 48 | 13 36 | 46 24 | 00456 | 105 | 99544 | 00679 | 106 | 99321 | 00223 | 1 | 99777 | 12 |
| 49 | 13 28 | 46 32 | 00581 | 107 | 99419 | 00805 | 108 | 99195 | 00224 | 1 | 99776 | 11 |
| 50 | 11 13 20 | 0 46 40 | 9.00704 | 110 | 10.99296 | 9.00930 | 111 | 10.99070 | 10.00225 | 1 | 9.99775 | 10 |
| 51 | 13 12 | 46 48 | 00828 | 112 | 99172 | 01055 | 113 | 98945 | 00227 | 1 | 99773 | 9 |
| 52 | 13 4 | 46 56 | 00951 | 114 | 99049 | 01179 | 115 | 98821 | 00228 | 1 | 99772 | 8 |
| 53 | 12 56 | 47 4 | 01074 | 116 | 98926 | 01303 | 117 | 98697 | 00229 | 1 | 99771 | 7 |
| 54 | 12 48 | 47 12 | 01196 | 118 | 98804 | 01427 | 120 | 98573 | 00231 | 1 | 99769 | 6 |
| 55 | 11 12 40 | 0 47 20 | 9.01318 | 121 | 10.98682 | 9.01550 | 122 | 10.98450 | 10.00232 | 1 | 9.99768 | 5 |
| 56 | 12 32 | 47 28 | 01440 | 123 | 98560 | 01673 | 124 | 98327 | 00233 | 1 | 99767 | 4 |
| 57 | 12 24 | 47 36 | 01561 | 125 | 98439 | 01796 | 126 | 98204 | 00235 | 1 | 99765 | 3 |
| 58 | 12 16 | 47 44 | 01682 | 127 | 98318 | 01918 | 128 | 98082 | 00236 | 1 | 99764 | 2 |
| 59 | 12 8 | 47 52 | 01803 | 129 | 98197 | 02040 | 131 | 97960 | 00237 | 1 | 99763 | 1 |
| 60 | 12 0 | 48 0 | 01923 | 132 | 98077 | 02162 | 133 | 97838 | 00239 | 1 | 99761 | 0 |
| M | Hour P.M. | Hour A.M. | Cosine. (A) | Diff. | Secant. (A) | Cotangent (B) | Diff. | Tangent. (B) | Cosecant. (C) | Diff. | Sine. (C) | M |

95° | | 84°

| Seconds of time ...... | | 1s | 2s | 3s | 4s | 5s | 6s | 7s |
|---|---|---|---|---|---|---|---|---|
| Prop. parts of cols. | A | 16 | 33 | 49 | 66 | 82 | 99 | 115 |
| | B | 17 | 33 | 50 | 66 | 83 | 100 | 116 |
| | C | 0 | 0 | 0 | 1 | 1 | 1 | 1 |

# TABLE XXVII.

## Log. Sines, Tangents, and Secants.

S'. G'.

6° 173°

| M | Hour A.M. | Hour P.M. | Sine. A | Diff. | Cosecant. A | Tangent. B | Diff. | Cotangent B | Secant. C | Diff. | Cosine. C | M |
|---|---|---|---|---|---|---|---|---|---|---|---|---|
| 0 | 11 12 0 | 0 48 0 | 9.01923 | 0 | 10.98077 | 9.02162 | 0 | 10.97838 | 10.00239 | 0 | 9.99761 | 60 |
| 1 | 11 52 | 48 8 | 02043 | 2 | 97957 | 02283 | 2 | 97717 | 00240 | 0 | 99760 | 59 |
| 2 | 11 44 | 48 16 | 02163 | 4 | 97837 | 02404 | 4 | 97596 | 00241 | 0 | 99759 | 58 |
| 3 | 11 36 | 48 24 | 02283 | 6 | 97717 | 02525 | 6 | 97475 | 00243 | 0 | 99757 | 57 |
| 4 | 11 28 | 48 32 | 02402 | 7 | 97598 | 02645 | 8 | 97355 | 00244 | 0 | 99756 | 56 |
| 5 | 11 11 20 | 0 48 40 | 9.02520 | 9 | 10.97480 | 9.02766 | 9 | 10.97234 | 10.00245 | 0 | 9.99755 | 55 |
| 6 | 11 12 | 48 48 | 02639 | 11 | 97361 | 02885 | 11 | 97115 | 00247 | 0 | 99753 | 54 |
| 7 | 11 4 | 48 56 | 02757 | 13 | 97243 | 03005 | 13 | 96995 | 00248 | 0 | 99752 | 53 |
| 8 | 10 56 | 49 4 | 02874 | 15 | 97126 | 03124 | 15 | 96876 | 00249 | 0 | 99751 | 52 |
| 9 | 10 48 | 49 12 | 02992 | 17 | 97008 | 03242 | 17 | 96758 | 00251 | 0 | 99749 | 51 |
| 10 | 11 10 40 | 0 49 20 | 9.03109 | 19 | 10.96891 | 9.03361 | 19 | 10.96639 | 10.00252 | 0 | 9.99748 | 50 |
| 11 | 10 32 | 49 28 | 03226 | 20 | 96774 | 03479 | 21 | 96521 | 00253 | 0 | 99747 | 49 |
| 12 | 10 24 | 49 36 | 03342 | 22 | 96658 | 03597 | 23 | 96403 | 00255 | 0 | 99745 | 48 |
| 13 | 10 16 | 49 44 | 03458 | 24 | 96542 | 03714 | 24 | 96286 | 00256 | 0 | 99744 | 47 |
| 14 | 10 8 | 49 52 | 03574 | 26 | 96426 | 03832 | 26 | 96168 | 00258 | 0 | 99742 | 46 |
| 15 | 11 10 0 | 0 50 0 | 9.03690 | 28 | 10.96310 | 9.03948 | 28 | 10.96052 | 10.00259 | 0 | 9.99741 | 45 |
| 16 | 9 52 | 50 8 | 03805 | 30 | 96195 | 04065 | 30 | 95935 | 00260 | 0 | 99740 | 44 |
| 17 | 9 44 | 50 16 | 03920 | 31 | 96080 | 04181 | 32 | 95819 | 00262 | 0 | 99738 | 43 |
| 18 | 9 36 | 50 24 | 04034 | 33 | 95966 | 04297 | 34 | 95703 | 00263 | 0 | 99737 | 42 |
| 19 | 9 28 | 50 32 | 04149 | 35 | 95851 | 04413 | 36 | 95587 | 00264 | 0 | 99736 | 41 |
| 20 | 11 9 20 | 0 50 40 | 9.04262 | 37 | 10.95738 | 9.04528 | 38 | 10.95472 | 10.00266 | 0 | 9.99734 | 40 |
| 21 | 9 12 | 50 48 | 04376 | 39 | 95624 | 04643 | 39 | 95357 | 00267 | 1 | 99733 | 39 |
| 22 | 9 4 | 50 56 | 04490 | 41 | 95510 | 04758 | 41 | 95242 | 00269 | 1 | 99731 | 38 |
| 23 | 8 56 | 51 4 | 04603 | 43 | 95397 | 04873 | 43 | 95127 | 00270 | 1 | 99730 | 37 |
| 24 | 8 48 | 51 12 | 04715 | 44 | 95285 | 04987 | 45 | 95013 | 00272 | 1 | 99728 | 36 |
| 25 | 11 8 40 | 0 51 20 | 9.04828 | 46 | 10.95172 | 9.05101 | 47 | 10.94899 | 10.00273 | 1 | 9.99727 | 35 |
| 26 | 8 32 | 51 28 | 04940 | 48 | 95060 | 05214 | 49 | 94786 | 00274 | 1 | 99726 | 34 |
| 27 | 8 24 | 51 36 | 05052 | 50 | 94948 | 05328 | 51 | 94672 | 00276 | 1 | 99724 | 33 |
| 28 | 8 16 | 51 44 | 05164 | 52 | 94836 | 05441 | 53 | 94559 | 00277 | 1 | 99723 | 32 |
| 29 | 8 8 | 51 52 | 05275 | 54 | 94725 | 05553 | 54 | 94447 | 00279 | 1 | 99721 | 31 |
| 30 | 11 8 0 | 0 52 0 | 9.05386 | 56 | 10.94614 | 9.05666 | 56 | 10.94334 | 10.00280 | 1 | 9.99720 | 30 |
| 31 | 7 52 | 52 8 | 05497 | 57 | 94503 | 05778 | 58 | 94222 | 00282 | 1 | 99718 | 29 |
| 32 | 7 44 | 52 16 | 05607 | 59 | 94393 | 05890 | 60 | 94110 | 00283 | 1 | 99717 | 28 |
| 33 | 7 36 | 52 24 | 05717 | 61 | 94283 | 06002 | 62 | 93998 | 00284 | 1 | 99716 | 27 |
| 34 | 7 28 | 52 32 | 05827 | 63 | 94173 | 06113 | 64 | 93887 | 00286 | 1 | 99714 | 26 |
| 35 | 11 7 20 | 0 52 40 | 9.05937 | 65 | 10.94063 | 9.06224 | 66 | 10.93776 | 10.00287 | 1 | 9.99713 | 25 |
| 36 | 7 12 | 52 48 | 06046 | 67 | 93954 | 06335 | 68 | 93665 | 00289 | 1 | 99711 | 24 |
| 37 | 7 4 | 52 56 | 06155 | 69 | 93845 | 06445 | 69 | 93555 | 00290 | 1 | 99710 | 23 |
| 38 | 6 56 | 53 4 | 06264 | 70 | 93736 | 06556 | 71 | 93444 | 00292 | 1 | 99708 | 22 |
| 39 | 6 48 | 53 12 | 06372 | 72 | 93628 | 06666 | 73 | 93334 | 00293 | 1 | 99707 | 21 |
| 40 | 11 6 40 | 0 53 20 | 9.06481 | 74 | 10.93519 | 9.06775 | 75 | 10.93225 | 10.00295 | 1 | 9.99705 | 20 |
| 41 | 6 32 | 53 28 | 06589 | 76 | 93411 | 06885 | 77 | 93115 | 00296 | 1 | 99704 | 19 |
| 42 | 6 24 | 53 36 | 06696 | 78 | 93304 | 06994 | 79 | 93006 | 00298 | 1 | 99702 | 18 |
| 43 | 6 16 | 53 44 | 06804 | 80 | 93196 | 07103 | 81 | 92897 | 00299 | 1 | 99701 | 17 |
| 44 | 6 8 | 53 52 | 06911 | 81 | 93089 | 07211 | 83 | 92789 | 00301 | 1 | 99699 | 16 |
| 45 | 11 6 0 | 0 54 0 | 9.07018 | 83 | 10.92982 | 9.07320 | 84 | 10.92680 | 10.00302 | 1 | 9.99698 | 15 |
| 46 | 5 52 | 54 8 | 07124 | 85 | 92876 | 07428 | 86 | 92572 | 00304 | 1 | 99696 | 14 |
| 47 | 5 44 | 54 16 | 07231 | 87 | 92769 | 07536 | 88 | 92464 | 00305 | 1 | 99695 | 13 |
| 48 | 5 36 | 54 24 | 07337 | 89 | 92663 | 07643 | 90 | 92357 | 00307 | 1 | 99693 | 12 |
| 49 | 5 28 | 54 32 | 07442 | 91 | 92558 | 07751 | 92 | 92249 | 00308 | 1 | 99692 | 11 |
| 50 | 11 5 20 | 0 54 40 | 9.07548 | 93 | 10.92452 | 9.07858 | 94 | 10.92142 | 10.00310 | 1 | 9.99690 | 10 |
| 51 | 5 12 | 54 48 | 07653 | 94 | 92347 | 07964 | 96 | 92036 | 00311 | 1 | 99689 | 9 |
| 52 | 5 4 | 54 56 | 07758 | 96 | 92242 | 08071 | 98 | 91929 | 00313 | 1 | 99687 | 8 |
| 53 | 4 56 | 55 4 | 07863 | 98 | 92137 | 08177 | 99 | 91823 | 00314 | 1 | 99686 | 7 |
| 54 | 4 48 | 55 12 | 07968 | 100 | 92032 | 08283 | 101 | 91717 | 00316 | 1 | 99684 | 6 |
| 55 | 11 4 40 | 0 55 20 | 9.08072 | 102 | 10.91928 | 9.08389 | 103 | 10.91611 | 10.00317 | 1 | 9.99683 | 5 |
| 56 | 4 32 | 55 28 | 08176 | 104 | 91824 | 08495 | 105 | 91505 | 00319 | 1 | 99681 | 4 |
| 57 | 4 24 | 55 36 | 08280 | 106 | 91720 | 08600 | 107 | 91400 | 00320 | 1 | 99680 | 3 |
| 58 | 4 16 | 55 44 | 08383 | 107 | 91617 | 08705 | 109 | 91295 | 00322 | 1 | 99678 | 2 |
| 59 | 4 8 | 55 52 | 08486 | 109 | 91514 | 08810 | 111 | 91190 | 00323 | 1 | 99677 | 1 |
| 60 | 4 0 | 56 0 | 08589 | 111 | 91411 | 08914 | 113 | 91086 | 00325 | 1 | 99675 | 0 |
| M | Hour P.M. | Hour A.M. | Cosine. A | Diff. | Secant. A | Cotangent B | Diff. | Tangent. B | Cosecant. C | Diff. | Sine C | M |

96° 83°

| Seconds of time ...... | | 1s | 2s | 3s | 4s | 5s | 6s | 7s |
|---|---|---|---|---|---|---|---|---|
| Prop. parts of cols. | A | 14 | 28 | 42 | 56 | 69 | 83 | 97 |
| | B | 14 | 28 | 42 | 56 | 70 | 84 | 98 |
| | C | 0 | 0 | 1 | 1 | 1 | 1 | 1 |

# TABLE XXVII.

## Log. Sines, Tangents, and Secants.

S. 7° | G'. 172°

| M | Hour A.M. | Hour P.M. | Sine. (A) | Diff. | Cosecant. (A) | Tangent. (B) | Diff. | Cotangent (B) | Secant. (C) | Diff. | Cosine. (C) | M |
|---|---|---|---|---|---|---|---|---|---|---|---|---|
| 0 | 11 4 0 | 0 56 0 | 9.08589 | 0 | 10.91411 | 9.08914 | 0 | 10.91086 | 10.00325 | 0 | 9.99675 | 60 |
| 1 | 3 52 | 56 8 | 08692 | 2 | 91308 | 09019 | 2 | 90981 | 00326 | 0 | 99674 | 59 |
| 2 | 3 44 | 56 16 | 08795 | 3 | 91205 | 09123 | 3 | 90877 | 00328 | 0 | 99672 | 58 |
| 3 | 3 36 | 56 24 | 08897 | 5 | 91103 | 09227 | 5 | 90773 | 00330 | 0 | 99670 | 57 |
| 4 | 3 28 | 56 32 | 08999 | 6 | 91001 | 09330 | 7 | 90670 | 00331 | 0 | 99669 | 56 |
| 5 | 11 3 20 | 0 56 40 | 9.09101 | 8 | 10.90899 | 9.09434 | 8 | 10.90566 | 10.00333 | 0 | 9.99667 | 55 |
| 6 | 3 12 | 56 48 | 09202 | 10 | 90798 | 09537 | 10 | 90463 | 00334 | 0 | 99666 | 54 |
| 7 | 3 4 | 56 56 | 09304 | 11 | 90696 | 09640 | 11 | 90360 | 00336 | 0 | 99664 | 53 |
| 8 | 2 56 | 57 4 | 09405 | 13 | 90595 | 09742 | 13 | 90258 | 00337 | 0 | 99663 | 52 |
| 9 | 2 48 | 57 12 | 09506 | 14 | 90494 | 09845 | 15 | 90155 | 00339 | 0 | 99661 | 51 |
| 10 | 11 2 40 | 0 57 20 | 9.09606 | 16 | 10.90394 | 9.09947 | 16 | 10.90053 | 10.00341 | 0 | 9.99659 | 50 |
| 11 | 2 32 | 57 28 | 09707 | 18 | 90293 | 10049 | 18 | 89951 | 00342 | 0 | 99658 | 49 |
| 12 | 2 24 | 57 36 | 09807 | 19 | 90193 | 10150 | 20 | 89850 | 00344 | 0 | 99656 | 48 |
| 13 | 2 16 | 57 44 | 09907 | 21 | 90093 | 10252 | 21 | 89748 | 00345 | 0 | 99655 | 47 |
| 14 | 2 8 | 57 52 | 10006 | 22 | 89994 | 10353 | 23 | 89647 | 00347 | 0 | 99653 | 46 |
| 15 | 11 2 0 | 0 58 0 | 9.10106 | 24 | 10.89894 | 9.10454 | 24 | 10.89546 | 10.00349 | 0 | 9.99651 | 45 |
| 16 | 1 52 | 58 8 | 10205 | 26 | 89795 | 10555 | 26 | 89445 | 00350 | 0 | 99650 | 44 |
| 17 | 1 44 | 58 16 | 10304 | 27 | 89696 | 10656 | 28 | 89344 | 00352 | 0 | 99648 | 43 |
| 18 | 1 36 | 58 24 | 10402 | 29 | 89598 | 10756 | 29 | 89244 | 00353 | 1 | 99647 | 42 |
| 19 | 1 28 | 58 32 | 10501 | 30 | 89499 | 10856 | 31 | 89144 | 00355 | 1 | 99645 | 41 |
| 20 | 11 1 20 | 0 58 40 | 9.10599 | 32 | 10.89401 | 9.10956 | 33 | 10.89044 | 10.00357 | 1 | 9.99643 | 40 |
| 21 | 1 12 | 58 48 | 10697 | 34 | 89303 | 11056 | 34 | 88944 | 00358 | 1 | 99642 | 39 |
| 22 | 1 4 | 58 56 | 10795 | 35 | 89205 | 11155 | 36 | 88845 | 00360 | 1 | 99640 | 38 |
| 23 | 0 56 | 59 4 | 10893 | 37 | 89107 | 11254 | 37 | 88746 | 00362 | 1 | 99638 | 37 |
| 24 | 0 48 | 59 12 | 10990 | 38 | 89010 | 11353 | 39 | 88647 | 00363 | 1 | 99637 | 36 |
| 25 | 11 0 40 | 0 59 20 | 9.11087 | 40 | 10.88913 | 9.11452 | 41 | 10.88548 | 10.00365 | 1 | 9.99635 | 35 |
| 26 | 0 32 | 59 28 | 11184 | 42 | 88816 | 11551 | 42 | 88449 | 00367 | 1 | 99633 | 34 |
| 27 | 0 24 | 59 36 | 11281 | 43 | 88719 | 11649 | 44 | 88351 | 00368 | 1 | 99632 | 33 |
| 28 | 0 16 | 59 44 | 11377 | 45 | 88623 | 11747 | 46 | 88253 | 00370 | 1 | 99630 | 32 |
| 29 | 0 8 | 59 52 | 11474 | 46 | 88526 | 11845 | 47 | 88155 | 00371 | 1 | 99629 | 31 |
| 30 | 11 0 0 | 1 0 0 | 9.11570 | 48 | 10.88430 | 9.11943 | 49 | 10.88057 | 10.00373 | 1 | 9.99627 | 30 |
| 31 | 10 59 52 | 0 8 | 11666 | 50 | 88334 | 12040 | 51 | 87960 | 00375 | 1 | 99625 | 29 |
| 32 | 59 44 | 0 16 | 11761 | 51 | 88239 | 12138 | 52 | 87862 | 00376 | 1 | 99624 | 28 |
| 33 | 59 36 | 0 24 | 11857 | 53 | 88143 | 12235 | 54 | 87765 | 00378 | 1 | 99622 | 27 |
| 34 | 59 28 | 0 32 | 11952 | 54 | 88048 | 12332 | 55 | 87668 | 00380 | 1 | 99620 | 26 |
| 35 | 10 59 20 | 1 0 40 | 9.12047 | 56 | 10.87953 | 9.12428 | 57 | 10.87572 | 10.00382 | 1 | 9.99618 | 25 |
| 36 | 59 12 | 0 48 | 12142 | 58 | 87858 | 12525 | 59 | 87475 | 00383 | 1 | 99617 | 24 |
| 37 | 59 4 | 0 56 | 12236 | 59 | 87764 | 12621 | 60 | 87379 | 00385 | 1 | 99615 | 23 |
| 38 | 58 56 | 1 4 | 12331 | 61 | 87669 | 12717 | 62 | 87283 | 00387 | 1 | 99613 | 22 |
| 39 | 58 48 | 1 12 | 12425 | 62 | 87575 | 12813 | 64 | 87187 | 00388 | 1 | 99612 | 21 |
| 40 | 10 58 40 | 1 1 20 | 9.12519 | 64 | 10.87481 | 9.12909 | 65 | 10.87091 | 10.00390 | 1 | 9.99610 | 20 |
| 41 | 58 32 | 1 28 | 12612 | 66 | 87388 | 13004 | 67 | 86996 | 00392 | 1 | 99608 | 19 |
| 42 | 58 24 | 1 36 | 12706 | 67 | 87294 | 13099 | 68 | 86901 | 00393 | 1 | 99607 | 18 |
| 43 | 58 16 | 1 44 | 12799 | 69 | 87201 | 13194 | 70 | 86806 | 00395 | 1 | 99605 | 17 |
| 44 | 58 8 | 1 52 | 12892 | 70 | 87108 | 13289 | 72 | 86711 | 00397 | 1 | 99603 | 16 |
| 45 | 10 58 0 | 1 2 0 | 9.12985 | 72 | 10.87015 | 9.13384 | 73 | 10.86616 | 10.00399 | 1 | 9.99601 | 15 |
| 46 | 57 52 | 2 8 | 13078 | 74 | 86922 | 13478 | 75 | 86522 | 00400 | 1 | 99600 | 14 |
| 47 | 57 44 | 2 16 | 13171 | 75 | 86829 | 13573 | 77 | 86427 | 00402 | 1 | 99598 | 13 |
| 48 | 57 36 | 2 24 | 13263 | 77 | 86737 | 13667 | 78 | 86333 | 00404 | 1 | 99596 | 12 |
| 49 | 57 28 | 2 32 | 13355 | 78 | 86645 | 13761 | 80 | 86239 | 00405 | 1 | 99595 | 11 |
| 50 | 10 57 20 | 1 2 40 | 9.13447 | 80 | 10.86553 | 9.13854 | 81 | 10.86146 | 10.00407 | 1 | 9.99593 | 10 |
| 51 | 57 12 | 2 48 | 13539 | 82 | 86461 | 13948 | 83 | 86052 | 00409 | 1 | 99591 | 9 |
| 52 | 57 4 | 2 56 | 13630 | 83 | 86370 | 14041 | 85 | 85959 | 00411 | 1 | 99589 | 8 |
| 53 | 56 56 | 3 4 | 13722 | 85 | 86278 | 14134 | 86 | 85866 | 00412 | 1 | 99588 | 7 |
| 54 | 56 48 | 3 12 | 13813 | 87 | 86187 | 14227 | 88 | 85773 | 00414 | 2 | 99586 | 6 |
| 55 | 10 56 40 | 1 3 20 | 9.13904 | 88 | 10.86096 | 9.14320 | 90 | 10.85680 | 10.00416 | 2 | 9.99584 | 5 |
| 56 | 56 32 | 3 28 | 13994 | 90 | 86006 | 14412 | 91 | 85588 | 00418 | 2 | 99582 | 4 |
| 57 | 56 24 | 3 36 | 14085 | 91 | 85915 | 14504 | 93 | 85496 | 00419 | 2 | 99581 | 3 |
| 58 | 56 16 | 3 44 | 14175 | 93 | 85825 | 14597 | 95 | 85403 | 00421 | 2 | 99579 | 2 |
| 59 | 56 8 | 3 52 | 14266 | 95 | 85734 | 14688 | 96 | 85312 | 00423 | 2 | 99577 | 1 |
| 60 | 56 0 | 4 0 | 14356 | 96 | 85644 | 14780 | 98 | 85220 | 00425 | 2 | 99575 | 0 |
| M | Hour P.M. | Hour A.M. | Cosine. (A) | Diff. | Secant. (A) | Cotangent (B) | Diff. | Tangent. (B) | Cosecant. (C) | Diff. | Sine. (C) | M |

97° | 82°

| Seconds of time ...... | | 1s | 2s | 3s | 4s | 5s | 6s | 7s |
|---|---|---|---|---|---|---|---|---|
| Prop. parts of cols. | A | 12 | 24 | 36 | 48 | 60 | 72 | 84 |
| | B | 12 | 24 | 37 | 49 | 61 | 73 | 86 |
| | C | 0 | 0 | 1 | 1 | 1 | 1 | 1 |

# TABLE XXVII.

## Log. Sines, Tangents, and Secants.

S — G

8° — 171°

| M | Hour A.M. | Hour P.M. | Sine. (A) | Diff. | Cosecant. (A) | Tangent. (B) | Diff. | Cotangent (B) | Secant. (C) | Diff. | Cosine. (C) | M |
|---|---|---|---|---|---|---|---|---|---|---|---|---|
| 0 | 10 56 0 | 1 4 0 | 9.14356 | 0 | 10.85644 | 9.14780 | 0 | 10.85220 | 10.00425 | 0 | 9.99575 | 60 |
| 1 | 55 52 | 4 8 | 14445 | 1 | 85555 | 14872 | 1 | 85128 | 00426 | 0 | 99574 | 59 |
| 2 | 55 44 | 4 16 | 14535 | 3 | 85465 | 14963 | 3 | 85037 | 00428 | 0 | 99572 | 58 |
| 3 | 55 36 | 4 24 | 14624 | 4 | 85376 | 15054 | 4 | 84946 | 00430 | 0 | 99570 | 57 |
| 4 | 55 28 | 4 32 | 14714 | 6 | 85286 | 15145 | 6 | 84855 | 00432 | 0 | 99568 | 56 |
| 5 | 10 55 20 | 1 4 40 | 9.14803 | 7 | 10.85197 | 9.15236 | 7 | 10.84764 | 10.00434 | 0 | 9.99566 | 55 |
| 6 | 55 12 | 4 48 | 14891 | 8 | 85109 | 15327 | 9 | 84673 | 00435 | 0 | 99565 | 54 |
| 7 | 55 4 | 4 56 | 14980 | 10 | 85020 | 15417 | 10 | 84583 | 00437 | 0 | 99563 | 53 |
| 8 | 54 56 | 5 4 | 15069 | 11 | 84931 | 15508 | 12 | 84492 | 00439 | 0 | 99561 | 52 |
| 9 | 54 48 | 5 12 | 15157 | 13 | 84843 | 15598 | 13 | 84402 | 00441 | 0 | 99559 | 51 |
| 10 | 10 54 40 | 1 5 20 | 9.15245 | 14 | 10.84755 | 9.15688 | 14 | 10.84312 | 10.00443 | 0 | 9.99557 | 50 |
| 11 | 54 32 | 5 28 | 15333 | 16 | 84667 | 15777 | 16 | 84223 | 00444 | 0 | 99556 | 49 |
| 12 | 54 24 | 5 36 | 15421 | 17 | 84579 | 15867 | 17 | 84133 | 00446 | 0 | 99554 | 48 |
| 13 | 54 16 | 5 44 | 15508 | 18 | 84492 | 15956 | 19 | 84044 | 00448 | 0 | 99552 | 47 |
| 14 | 54 8 | 5 52 | 15596 | 20 | 84404 | 16046 | 20 | 83954 | 00450 | 0 | 99550 | 46 |
| 15 | 10 54 0 | 1 6 0 | 9.15683 | 21 | 10.84317 | 9.16135 | 22 | 10.83865 | 10.00452 | 0 | 9.99548 | 45 |
| 16 | 53 52 | 6 8 | 15770 | 23 | 84230 | 16224 | 23 | 83776 | 00454 | 1 | 99546 | 44 |
| 17 | 53 44 | 6 16 | 15857 | 24 | 84143 | 16312 | 25 | 83688 | 00455 | 1 | 99545 | 43 |
| 18 | 53 36 | 6 24 | 15944 | 25 | 84056 | 16401 | 26 | 83599 | 00457 | 1 | 99543 | 42 |
| 19 | 53 28 | 6 32 | 16030 | 27 | 83970 | 16489 | 27 | 83511 | 00459 | 1 | 99541 | 41 |
| 20 | 10 53 20 | 1 6 40 | 9.16116 | 28 | 10.83884 | 9.16577 | 29 | 10.83423 | 10.00461 | 1 | 9.99539 | 40 |
| 21 | 53 12 | 6 48 | 16203 | 30 | 83797 | 16665 | 30 | 83335 | 00463 | 1 | 99537 | 39 |
| 22 | 53 4 | 6 56 | 16289 | 31 | 83711 | 16753 | 32 | 83247 | 00465 | 1 | 99535 | 38 |
| 23 | 52 56 | 7 4 | 16374 | 32 | 83626 | 16841 | 33 | 83159 | 00467 | 1 | 99533 | 37 |
| 24 | 52 48 | 7 12 | 16460 | 34 | 83540 | 16928 | 35 | 83072 | 00468 | 1 | 99532 | 36 |
| 25 | 10 52 40 | 1 7 20 | 9.16545 | 35 | 10.83455 | 9.17016 | 36 | 10.82984 | 10.00470 | 1 | 9.99530 | 35 |
| 26 | 52 32 | 7 28 | 16631 | 37 | 83369 | 17103 | 37 | 82897 | 00472 | 1 | 99528 | 34 |
| 27 | 52 24 | 7 36 | 16716 | 38 | 83284 | 17190 | 39 | 82810 | 00474 | 1 | 99526 | 33 |
| 28 | 52 16 | 7 44 | 16801 | 39 | 83199 | 17277 | 40 | 82723 | 00476 | 1 | 99524 | 32 |
| 29 | 52 8 | 7 52 | 16886 | 41 | 83114 | 17363 | 42 | 82637 | 00478 | 1 | 99522 | 31 |
| 30 | 10 52 0 | 1 8 0 | 9.16970 | 42 | 10.83030 | 9.17450 | 43 | 10.82550 | 10.00480 | 1 | 9.99520 | 30 |
| 31 | 51 52 | 8 8 | 17055 | 44 | 82945 | 17536 | 45 | 82464 | 00482 | 1 | 99518 | 29 |
| 32 | 51 44 | 8 16 | 17139 | 45 | 82861 | 17622 | 46 | 82378 | 00483 | 1 | 99517 | 28 |
| 33 | 51 36 | 8 24 | 17223 | 47 | 82777 | 17708 | 48 | 82292 | 00485 | 1 | 99515 | 27 |
| 34 | 51 28 | 8 32 | 17307 | 48 | 82693 | 17794 | 49 | 82206 | 00487 | 1 | 99513 | 26 |
| 35 | 10 51 20 | 1 8 40 | 9.17391 | 49 | 10.82609 | 9.17880 | 50 | 10.82120 | 10.00489 | 1 | 9.99511 | 25 |
| 36 | 51 12 | 8 48 | 17474 | 51 | 82526 | 17965 | 52 | 82035 | 00491 | 1 | 99509 | 24 |
| 37 | 51 4 | 8 56 | 17558 | 52 | 82442 | 18051 | 53 | 81949 | 00493 | 1 | 99507 | 23 |
| 38 | 50 56 | 9 4 | 17641 | 54 | 82359 | 18136 | 55 | 81864 | 00495 | 1 | 99505 | 22 |
| 39 | 50 48 | 9 12 | 17724 | 55 | 82276 | 18221 | 56 | 81779 | 00497 | 1 | 99503 | 21 |
| 40 | 10 50 40 | 1 9 20 | 9.17807 | 56 | 10.82193 | 9.18306 | 58 | 10.81694 | 10.00499 | 1 | 9.99501 | 20 |
| 41 | 50 32 | 9 28 | 17890 | 58 | 82110 | 18391 | 59 | 81609 | 00501 | 1 | 99499 | 19 |
| 42 | 50 24 | 9 36 | 17973 | 59 | 82027 | 18475 | 61 | 81525 | 00503 | 1 | 99497 | 18 |
| 43 | 50 16 | 9 44 | 18055 | 61 | 81945 | 18560 | 62 | 81440 | 00505 | 1 | 99495 | 17 |
| 44 | 50 8 | 9 52 | 18137 | 62 | 81863 | 18644 | 63 | 81356 | 00506 | 1 | 99494 | 16 |
| 45 | 10 50 0 | 1 10 0 | 9.18220 | 63 | 10.81780 | 9.18728 | 65 | 10.81272 | 10.00508 | 1 | 9.99492 | 15 |
| 46 | 49 52 | 10 8 | 18302 | 65 | 81698 | 18812 | 66 | 81188 | 00510 | 1 | 99490 | 14 |
| 47 | 49 44 | 10 16 | 18383 | 66 | 81617 | 18896 | 68 | 81104 | 00512 | 1 | 99488 | 13 |
| 48 | 49 36 | 10 24 | 18465 | 68 | 81535 | 18979 | 69 | 81021 | 00514 | 2 | 99486 | 12 |
| 49 | 49 28 | 10 32 | 18547 | 69 | 81453 | 19063 | 71 | 80937 | 00516 | 2 | 99484 | 11 |
| 50 | 10 49 20 | 1 10 40 | 9.18628 | 71 | 10.81372 | 9.19146 | 72 | 10.80854 | 10.00518 | 2 | 9.99482 | 10 |
| 51 | 49 12 | 10 48 | 18709 | 72 | 81291 | 19229 | 74 | 80771 | 00520 | 2 | 99480 | 9 |
| 52 | 49 4 | 10 56 | 18790 | 73 | 81210 | 19312 | 75 | 80688 | 00522 | 2 | 99478 | 8 |
| 53 | 48 56 | 11 4 | 18871 | 75 | 81129 | 19395 | 76 | 80605 | 00524 | 2 | 99476 | 7 |
| 54 | 48 48 | 11 12 | 18952 | 76 | 81048 | 19478 | 78 | 80522 | 00526 | 2 | 99474 | 6 |
| 55 | 10 48 40 | 1 11 20 | 9.19033 | 78 | 10.80967 | 9.19561 | 79 | 10.80439 | 10.00528 | 2 | 9.99472 | 5 |
| 56 | 48 32 | 11 28 | 19113 | 79 | 80887 | 19643 | 81 | 80357 | 00530 | 2 | 99470 | 4 |
| 57 | 48 24 | 11 36 | 19193 | 80 | 80807 | 19725 | 82 | 80275 | 00532 | 2 | 99468 | 3 |
| 58 | 48 16 | 11 44 | 19273 | 82 | 80727 | 19807 | 84 | 80193 | 00534 | 2 | 99466 | 2 |
| 59 | 48 8 | 11 52 | 19353 | 83 | 80647 | 19889 | 85 | 80111 | 00536 | 2 | 99464 | 1 |
| 60 | 48 0 | 12 0 | 19433 | 85 | 80567 | 19971 | 87 | 80029 | 00538 | 2 | 99462 | 0 |
| M | Hour P.M. | Hour A.M. | Cosine. (A) | Diff. | Secant. (A) | Cotangent (B) | Diff. | Tangent. (B) | Cosecant. (C) | Diff. | Sine. (C) | M |

98° — 81°

| Seconds of time ...... | | 1ˢ | 2ˢ | 3ˢ | 4ˢ | 5ˢ | 6ˢ | 7ˢ |
|---|---|---|---|---|---|---|---|---|
| Prop parts of cols | A | 11 | 21 | 32 | 42 | 53 | 63 | 74 |
| | B | 11 | 22 | 32 | 43 | 54 | 65 | 76 |
| | C | 0 | 0 | 1 | 1 | 1 | 1 | 2 |

# TABLE XXVII.

S'. Log. Sines, Tangents, and Secants. G'.

9° A A B B C C 170°

| M | Hour A.M. | Hour P.M. | Sine. | Diff. | Cosecant. | Tangent. | Diff. | Cotangent | Secant. | Diff. | Cosine. | M |
|---|---|---|---|---|---|---|---|---|---|---|---|---|
| 0 | 10 48 0 | 1 12 0 | 9.19433 | 0 | 10.80567 | 9.19971 | 0 | 10.80029 | 10.00538 | 0 | 9.99462 | 60 |
| 1 | 47 52 | 12 8 | 19513 | 1 | 80487 | 20053 | 1 | 79947 | 00540 | 0 | 99460 | 59 |
| 2 | 47 44 | 12 16 | 19592 | 3 | 80408 | 20134 | 3 | 79866 | 00542 | 0 | 99458 | 58 |
| 3 | 47 36 | 12 24 | 19672 | 4 | 80328 | 20216 | 4 | 79784 | 00544 | 0 | 99456 | 57 |
| 4 | 47 28 | 12 32 | 19751 | 5 | 80249 | 20297 | 5 | 79703 | 00546 | 0 | 99454 | 56 |
| 5 | 10 47 20 | 1 12 40 | 9.19830 | 6 | 10.80170 | 9.20378 | 6 | 10.79622 | 10.00548 | 0 | 9.99452 | 55 |
| 6 | 47 12 | 12 48 | 19909 | 8 | 80091 | 20459 | 8 | 79541 | 00550 | 0 | 99450 | 54 |
| 7 | 47 4 | 12 56 | 19988 | 9 | 80012 | 20540 | 9 | 79460 | 00552 | 0 | 99448 | 53 |
| 8 | 46 56 | 13 4 | 20067 | 10 | 79933 | 20621 | 10 | 79379 | 00554 | 0 | 99446 | 52 |
| 9 | 46 48 | 13 12 | 20145 | 11 | 79855 | 20701 | 12 | 79299 | 00556 | 0 | 99444 | 51 |
| 10 | 10 46 40 | 1 13 20 | 9.20223 | 13 | 10.79777 | 9.20782 | 13 | 10.79218 | 10.00558 | 0 | 9.99442 | 50 |
| 11 | 46 32 | 13 28 | 20302 | 14 | 79698 | 20862 | 14 | 79138 | 00560 | 0 | 99440 | 49 |
| 12 | 46 24 | 13 36 | 20380 | 15 | 79620 | 20942 | 16 | 79058 | 00562 | 0 | 99438 | 48 |
| 13 | 46 16 | 13 44 | 20458 | 16 | 79542 | 21022 | 17 | 78978 | 00564 | 0 | 99436 | 47 |
| 14 | 46 8 | 13 52 | 20535 | 18 | 79465 | 21102 | 18 | 78898 | 00566 | 0 | 99434 | 46 |
| 15 | 10 46 0 | 1 14 0 | 9.20613 | 19 | 10.79387 | 9.21182 | 19 | 10.78818 | 10.00568 | 1 | 9.99432 | 45 |
| 16 | 45 52 | 14 8 | 20691 | 20 | 79309 | 21261 | 21 | 78739 | 00571 | 1 | 99429 | 44 |
| 17 | 45 44 | 14 16 | 20768 | 21 | 79232 | 21341 | 22 | 78659 | 00573 | 1 | 99427 | 43 |
| 18 | 45 36 | 14 24 | 20845 | 23 | 79155 | 21420 | 23 | 78580 | 00575 | 1 | 99425 | 42 |
| 19 | 45 28 | 14 32 | 20922 | 24 | 79078 | 21499 | 25 | 78501 | 00577 | 1 | 99423 | 41 |
| 20 | 10 45 20 | 1 14 40 | 9.20999 | 25 | 10.79001 | 9.21578 | 26 | 10.78422 | 10.00579 | 1 | 9.99421 | 40 |
| 21 | 45 12 | 14 48 | 21076 | 26 | 78924 | 21657 | 27 | 78343 | 00581 | 1 | 99419 | 39 |
| 22 | 45 4 | 14 56 | 21153 | 28 | 78847 | 21736 | 28 | 78264 | 00583 | 1 | 99417 | 38 |
| 23 | 44 56 | 15 4 | 21229 | 29 | 78771 | 21814 | 30 | 78186 | 00585 | 1 | 99415 | 37 |
| 24 | 44 48 | 15 12 | 21306 | 30 | 78694 | 21893 | 31 | 78107 | 00587 | 1 | 99413 | 36 |
| 25 | 10 44 40 | 1 15 20 | 9.21382 | 31 | 10.78618 | 9.21971 | 32 | 10.78029 | 10.00589 | 1 | 9.99411 | 35 |
| 26 | 44 32 | 15 28 | 21458 | 33 | 78542 | 22049 | 34 | 77951 | 00591 | 1 | 99409 | 34 |
| 27 | 44 24 | 15 36 | 21534 | 34 | 78466 | 22127 | 35 | 77873 | 00593 | 1 | 99407 | 33 |
| 28 | 44 16 | 15 44 | 21610 | 35 | 78390 | 22205 | 36 | 77795 | 00596 | 1 | 99404 | 32 |
| 29 | 44 8 | 15 52 | 21685 | 37 | 78315 | 22283 | 38 | 77717 | 00598 | 1 | 99402 | 31 |
| 30 | 10 44 0 | 1 16 0 | 9.21761 | 38 | 10.78239 | 9.22361 | 39 | 10.77639 | 10.00600 | 1 | 9.99400 | 30 |
| 31 | 43 52 | 16 8 | 21836 | 39 | 78164 | 22438 | 40 | 77562 | 00602 | 1 | 99398 | 29 |
| 32 | 43 44 | 16 16 | 21912 | 40 | 78088 | 22516 | 41 | 77484 | 00604 | 1 | 99396 | 28 |
| 33 | 43 36 | 16 24 | 21987 | 42 | 78013 | 22593 | 43 | 77407 | 00606 | 1 | 99394 | 27 |
| 34 | 43 28 | 16 32 | 22062 | 43 | 77938 | 22670 | 44 | 77330 | 00608 | 1 | 99392 | 26 |
| 35 | 10 43 20 | 1 16 40 | 9.22137 | 44 | 10.77863 | 9.22747 | 45 | 10.77253 | 10.00610 | 1 | 9.99390 | 25 |
| 36 | 43 12 | 16 48 | 22211 | 45 | 77789 | 22824 | 47 | 77176 | 00612 | 1 | 99388 | 24 |
| 37 | 43 4 | 16 56 | 22286 | 47 | 77714 | 22901 | 48 | 77099 | 00615 | 1 | 99385 | 23 |
| 38 | 42 56 | 17 4 | 22361 | 48 | 77639 | 22977 | 49 | 77023 | 00617 | 1 | 99383 | 22 |
| 39 | 42 48 | 17 12 | 22435 | 49 | 77565 | 23054 | 50 | 76946 | 00619 | 1 | 99381 | 21 |
| 40 | 10 42 40 | 1 17 20 | 9.22509 | 50 | 10.77491 | 9.23130 | 52 | 10.76870 | 10.00621 | 1 | 9.99379 | 20 |
| 41 | 42 32 | 17 28 | 22583 | 52 | 77417 | 23206 | 53 | 76794 | 00623 | 1 | 99377 | 19 |
| 42 | 42 24 | 17 36 | 22657 | 53 | 77343 | 23283 | 54 | 76717 | 00625 | 1 | 99375 | 18 |
| 43 | 42 16 | 17 44 | 22731 | 54 | 77269 | 23359 | 56 | 76641 | 00628 | 2 | 99372 | 17 |
| 44 | 42 8 | 17 52 | 22805 | 55 | 77195 | 23435 | 57 | 76565 | 00630 | 2 | 99370 | 16 |
| 45 | 10 42 0 | 1 18 0 | 9.22878 | 57 | 10.77122 | 9.23510 | 58 | 10.76490 | 10.00632 | 2 | 9.99368 | 15 |
| 46 | 41 52 | 18 8 | 22952 | 58 | 77048 | 23586 | 60 | 76414 | 00634 | 2 | 99366 | 14 |
| 47 | 41 44 | 18 16 | 23025 | 59 | 76975 | 23661 | 61 | 76339 | 00636 | 2 | 99364 | 13 |
| 48 | 41 36 | 18 24 | 23098 | 60 | 76902 | 23737 | 62 | 76263 | 00638 | 2 | 99362 | 12 |
| 49 | 41 28 | 18 32 | 23171 | 62 | 76829 | 23812 | 63 | 76188 | 00641 | 2 | 99359 | 11 |
| 50 | 10 41 20 | 1 18 40 | 9.23244 | 63 | 10.76756 | 9.23887 | 65 | 10.76113 | 10.00643 | 2 | 9.99357 | 10 |
| 51 | 41 12 | 18 48 | 23317 | 64 | 76683 | 23962 | 66 | 76038 | 00645 | 2 | 99355 | 9 |
| 52 | 41 4 | 18 56 | 23390 | 65 | 76610 | 24037 | 67 | 75963 | 00647 | 2 | 99353 | 8 |
| 53 | 40 56 | 19 4 | 23462 | 67 | 76538 | 24112 | 69 | 75888 | 00649 | 2 | 99351 | 7 |
| 54 | 40 48 | 19 12 | 23535 | 68 | 76465 | 24186 | 70 | 75814 | 00652 | 2 | 99348 | 6 |
| 55 | 10 40 40 | 1 19 20 | 9.23607 | 69 | 10.76393 | 9.24261 | 71 | 10.75739 | 10.00654 | 2 | 9.99346 | 5 |
| 56 | 40 32 | 19 28 | 23679 | 71 | 76321 | 24335 | 73 | 75665 | 00656 | 2 | 99344 | 4 |
| 57 | 40 24 | 19 36 | 23752 | 72 | 76248 | 24410 | 74 | 75590 | 00658 | 2 | 99342 | 3 |
| 58 | 40 16 | 19 44 | 23823 | 73 | 76177 | 24484 | 75 | 75516 | 00660 | 2 | 99340 | 2 |
| 59 | 40 8 | 19 52 | 23895 | 74 | 76105 | 24558 | 76 | 75442 | 00663 | 2 | 99337 | 1 |
| 60 | 40 0 | 20 0 | 23967 | 76 | 76033 | 24632 | 78 | 75368 | 00665 | 2 | 99335 | 0 |
| M | Hour P.M. | Hour A.M. | Cosine. | Diff. | Secant. | Cotangent | Diff. | Tangent. | Cosecant. | Diff. | Sine. | M |

99° A A B B C C 80°

| Seconds of time ...... | 1s | 2s | 3s | 4s | 5s | 6s | 7s |
|---|---|---|---|---|---|---|---|
| Prop. parts of cols. A | 9 | 19 | 28 | 38 | 47 | 57 | 66 |
| Prop. parts of cols. B | 10 | 19 | 29 | 39 | 49 | 58 | 68 |
| Prop. parts of cols. C | 0 | 1 | 1 | 1 | 1 | 2 | 2 |

# TABLE XXVII.

S'. **Log. Sines, Tangents, and Secants.** G'.

| 10° | | | A | | A | B | | B | C | | C | 169° |
|---|---|---|---|---|---|---|---|---|---|---|---|---|
| M | Hour A.M. | Hour P.M. | Sine. | Diff. | Cosecant. | Tangent. | Diff. | Cotangent | Secant. | Diff. | Cosine. | M |
| 0 | 10 40 0 | 1 20 0 | 9.23967 | 0 | 10.76033 | 9.24632 | 0 | 10.75368 | 10.00665 | 0 | 9.99335 | 60 |
| 1 | 39 52 | 20 8 | 24039 | 1 | 75961 | 24706 | 1 | 75294 | 00667 | 0 | 99333 | 59 |
| 2 | 39 44 | 20 16 | 24110 | 2 | 75890 | 24779 | 2 | 75221 | 00669 | 0 | 99331 | 58 |
| 3 | 39 36 | 20 24 | 24181 | 3 | 75819 | 24853 | 4 | 75147 | 00672 | 0 | 99328 | 57 |
| 4 | 39 28 | 20 32 | 24253 | 5 | 75747 | 24926 | 5 | 75074 | 00674 | 0 | 99326 | 56 |
| 5 | 10 39 20 | 1 20 40 | 9.24324 | 6 | 10.75676 | 9.25000 | 6 | 10.75000 | 10.00676 | 0 | 9.99324 | 55 |
| 6 | 39 12 | 20 48 | 24395 | 7 | 75605 | 25073 | 7 | 74927 | 00678 | 0 | 99322 | 54 |
| 7 | 39 4 | 20 56 | 24466 | 8 | 75534 | 25146 | 8 | 74854 | 00681 | 0 | 99319 | 53 |
| 8 | 38 56 | 21 4 | 24536 | 9 | 75464 | 25219 | 9 | 74781 | 00683 | 0 | 99317 | 52 |
| 9 | 38 48 | 21 12 | 24607 | 10 | 75393 | 25292 | 11 | 74708 | 00685 | 0 | 99315 | 51 |
| 10 | 10 38 40 | 1 21 20 | 9.24677 | 11 | 10 75323 | 9.25365 | 12 | 10.74635 | 10.00687 | 0 | 9.99313 | 50 |
| 11 | 38 32 | 21 28 | 24748 | 13 | 75252 | 25437 | 13 | 74563 | 00690 | 0 | 99310 | 49 |
| 12 | 38 24 | 21 36 | 24818 | 14 | 75182 | 25510 | 14 | 74490 | 00692 | 0 | 99308 | 48 |
| 13 | 38 16 | 21 44 | 24888 | 15 | 75112 | 25582 | 15 | 74418 | 00694 | 1 | 99306 | 47 |
| 14 | 38 8 | 21 52 | 24958 | 16 | 75042 | 25655 | 16 | 74345 | 00696 | 1 | 99304 | 46 |
| 15 | 10 38 0 | 1 22 0 | 9.25028 | 17 | 10.74972 | 9.25727 | 18 | 10.74273 | 10.00699 | 1 | 9.99301 | 45 |
| 16 | 37 52 | 22 8 | 25098 | 18 | 74902 | 25799 | 19 | 74201 | 00701 | 1 | 99299 | 44 |
| 17 | 37 44 | 22 16 | 25168 | 19 | 74832 | 25871 | 20 | 74129 | 00703 | 1 | 99297 | 43 |
| 18 | 37 36 | 22 24 | 25237 | 20 | 74763 | 25943 | 21 | 74057 | 00706 | 1 | 99294 | 42 |
| 19 | 37 28 | 22 32 | 25307 | 22 | 74693 | 26015 | 22 | 73985 | 00708 | 1 | 99292 | 41 |
| 20 | 10 37 20 | 1 22 40 | 9.25376 | 23 | 10.74624 | 9.26086 | 24 | 10.73914 | 10.00710 | 1 | 9.99290 | 40 |
| 21 | 37 12 | 22 48 | 25445 | 24 | 74555 | 26158 | 25 | 73842 | 00712 | 1 | 99288 | 39 |
| 22 | 37 4 | 22 56 | 25514 | 25 | 74486 | 26229 | 26 | 73771 | 00715 | 1 | 99285 | 38 |
| 23 | 36 56 | 23 4 | 25583 | 26 | 74417 | 26301 | 27 | 73699 | 00717 | 1 | 99283 | 37 |
| 24 | 36 48 | 23 12 | 25652 | 27 | 74348 | 26372 | 28 | 73628 | 00719 | 1 | 99281 | 36 |
| 25 | 10 36 40 | 1 23 20 | 9.25721 | 28 | 10.74279 | 9.26443 | 29 | 10.73557 | 10.00722 | 1 | 9.99278 | 35 |
| 26 | 36 32 | 23 28 | 25790 | 30 | 74210 | 26514 | 31 | 73486 | 00724 | 1 | 99276 | 34 |
| 27 | 36 24 | 23 36 | 25858 | 31 | 74142 | 26585 | 32 | 73415 | 00726 | 1 | 99274 | 33 |
| 28 | 36 16 | 23 44 | 25927 | 32 | 74073 | 26655 | 33 | 73345 | 00729 | 1 | 99271 | 32 |
| 29 | 36 8 | 23 52 | 25995 | 33 | 74005 | 26726 | 34 | 73274 | 00731 | 1 | 99269 | 31 |
| 30 | 10 36 0 | 1 24 0 | 9.26063 | 34 | 10.73937 | 9.26797 | 35 | 10.73203 | 10.00733 | 1 | 9.99267 | 30 |
| 31 | 35 52 | 24 8 | 26131 | 35 | 73869 | 26867 | 36 | 73133 | 00736 | 1 | 99264 | 29 |
| 32 | 35 44 | 24 16 | 26199 | 36 | 73801 | 26937 | 38 | 73063 | 00738 | 1 | 99262 | 28 |
| 33 | 35 36 | 24 24 | 26267 | 38 | 73733 | 27008 | 39 | 72992 | 00740 | 1 | 99260 | 27 |
| 34 | 35 28 | 24 32 | 26335 | 39 | 73665 | 27078 | 40 | 72922 | 00743 | 1 | 99257 | 26 |
| 35 | 10 35 20 | 1 24 40 | 9.26403 | 40 | 10.73597 | 9.27148 | 41 | 10.72852 | 10.00745 | 1 | 9.99255 | 25 |
| 36 | 35 12 | 24 48 | 26470 | 41 | 73530 | 27218 | 42 | 72782 | 00748 | 1 | 99252 | 24 |
| 37 | 35 4 | 24 56 | 26538 | 42 | 73462 | 27288 | 44 | 72712 | 00750 | 1 | 99250 | 23 |
| 38 | 34 56 | 25 4 | 26605 | 43 | 73395 | 27357 | 45 | 72643 | 00752 | 1 | 99248 | 22 |
| 39 | 34 48 | 25 12 | 26672 | 44 | 73328 | 27427 | 46 | 72573 | 00755 | 2 | 99245 | 21 |
| 40 | 10 34 40 | 1 25 20 | 9.26739 | 45 | 10.73261 | 9.27496 | 47 | 10.72504 | 10.00757 | 2 | 9.99243 | 20 |
| 41 | 34 32 | 25 28 | 26806 | 47 | 73194 | 27566 | 48 | 72434 | 00759 | 2 | 99241 | 19 |
| 42 | 34 24 | 25 36 | 26873 | 48 | 73127 | 27635 | 49 | 72365 | 00762 | 2 | 99238 | 18 |
| 43 | 34 16 | 25 44 | 26940 | 49 | 73060 | 27704 | 51 | 72296 | 00764 | 2 | 99236 | 17 |
| 44 | 34 8 | 25 52 | 27007 | 50 | 72993 | 27773 | 52 | 72227 | 00767 | 2 | 99233 | 16 |
| 45 | 10 34 0 | 1 26 0 | 9.27073 | 51 | 10.72927 | 9.27842 | 53 | 10.72158 | 10.00769 | 2 | 9.99231 | 15 |
| 46 | 33 52 | 26 8 | 27140 | 52 | 72860 | 27911 | 54 | 72089 | 00771 | 2 | 99229 | 14 |
| 47 | 33 44 | 26 16 | 27206 | 53 | 72794 | 27980 | 55 | 72020 | 00774 | 2 | 99226 | 13 |
| 48 | 33 36 | 26 24 | 27273 | 55 | 72727 | 28049 | 56 | 71951 | 00776 | 2 | 99224 | 12 |
| 49 | 33 28 | 26 32 | 27339 | 56 | 72661 | 28117 | 58 | 71883 | 00779 | 2 | 99221 | 11 |
| 50 | 10 33 20 | 1 26 40 | 9.27405 | 57 | 10.72595 | 9.28186 | 59 | 10.71814 | 10.00781 | 2 | 9.99219 | 10 |
| 51 | 33 12 | 26 48 | 27471 | 58 | 72529 | 28254 | 60 | 71746 | 00783 | 2 | 99217 | 9 |
| 52 | 33 4 | 26 56 | 27537 | 59 | 72463 | 28323 | 61 | 71677 | 00786 | 2 | 99214 | 8 |
| 53 | 32 56 | 27 4 | 27602 | 60 | 72398 | 28391 | 62 | 71609 | 00788 | 2 | 99212 | 7 |
| 54 | 32 48 | 27 12 | 27668 | 61 | 72332 | 28459 | 63 | 71541 | 00791 | 2 | 99209 | 6 |
| 55 | 10 32 40 | 1 27 20 | 9.27734 | 63 | 10.72266 | 9.28527 | 65 | 10.71473 | 10.00793 | 2 | 9.99207 | 5 |
| 56 | 32 32 | 27 28 | 27799 | 64 | 72201 | 28595 | 66 | 71405 | 00796 | 2 | 99204 | 4 |
| 57 | 32 24 | 27 36 | 27864 | 65 | 72136 | 28662 | 67 | 71338 | 00798 | 2 | 99202 | 3 |
| 58 | 32 16 | 27 44 | 27930 | 66 | 72070 | 28730 | 68 | 71270 | 00800 | 2 | 99200 | 2 |
| 59 | 32 8 | 27 52 | 27995 | 67 | 72005 | 28798 | 69 | 71202 | 00803 | 2 | 99197 | 1 |
| 60 | 32 0 | 28 0 | 28060 | 68 | 71940 | 28865 | 71 | 71135 | 00805 | 2 | 99195 | 0 |
| M | Hour P.M. | Hour A.M. | Cosine. | Diff. | Secant. | Cotangent | Diff. | Tangent. | Cosecant. | Diff. | Sine. | M |
| 100° | | | A | | A | B | | B | C | | C | 79° |

| Seconds of time ...... | | 1s | 2s | 3s | 4s | 5s | 6s | 7s |
|---|---|---|---|---|---|---|---|---|
| Prop. parts of cols. | A | 9 | 17 | 26 | 34 | 43 | 51 | 60 |
| | B | 9 | 18 | 26 | 35 | 44 | 53 | 62 |
| | C | 0 | 1 | 1 | 1 | 1 | 2 | 2 |

# TABLE XXVII.

G'.

S'.

## Log. Sines, Tangents, and Secants.

11° A A B B C C 168°

| M | Hour A.M. | Hour P.M. | Sine. | Diff. | Cosecant. | Tangent. | Diff. | Cotangent | Secant. | Diff. | Cosine. | M |
|---|---|---|---|---|---|---|---|---|---|---|---|---|
| 0 | 10 32 0 | 1 28 0 | 9.28060 | 0 | 10.71940 | 9.28865 | 0 | 10.71135 | 10.00805 | 0 | 9.99195 | 60 |
| 1 | 31 52 | 28 8 | 28125 | 1 | 71875 | 28933 | 1 | 71067 | 00808 | 0 | 99192 | 59 |
| 2 | 31 44 | 28 16 | 28190 | 2 | 71810 | 29000 | 2 | 71000 | 00810 | 0 | 99190 | 58 |
| 3 | 31 36 | 28 24 | 28254 | 3 | 71746 | 29067 | 3 | 70933 | 00813 | 0 | 99187 | 57 |
| 4 | 31 28 | 28 32 | 28319 | 4 | 71681 | 29134 | 4 | 70866 | 00815 | 0 | 99185 | 56 |
| 5 | 10 31 20 | 1 28 40 | 9.28384 | 5 | 10.71616 | 9.29201 | 5 | 10.70799 | 10.00818 | 0 | 9.99182 | 55 |
| 6 | 31 12 | 28 48 | 28448 | 6 | 71552 | 29268 | 6 | 70732 | 00820 | 0 | 99180 | 54 |
| 7 | 31 4 | 28 56 | 28512 | 7 | 71488 | 29335 | 8 | 70665 | 00823 | 0 | 99177 | 53 |
| 8 | 30 56 | 29 4 | 28577 | 8 | 71423 | 29402 | 9 | 70598 | 00825 | 0 | 99175 | 52 |
| 9 | 30 48 | 29 12 | 28641 | 9 | 71359 | 29468 | 10 | 70532 | 00828 | 0 | 99172 | 51 |
| 10 | 10 30 40 | 1 29 20 | 9.28705 | 10 | 10.71295 | 9.29535 | 11 | 10.70465 | 10.00830 | 0 | 9.99170 | 50 |
| 11 | 30 32 | 29 28 | 28769 | 11 | 71231 | 29601 | 12 | 70399 | 00833 | 0 | 99167 | 49 |
| 12 | 30 24 | 29 36 | 28833 | 12 | 71167 | 29668 | 13 | 70332 | 00835 | 1 | 99165 | 48 |
| 13 | 30 16 | 29 44 | 28896 | 13 | 71104 | 29734 | 14 | 70266 | 00838 | 1 | 99162 | 47 |
| 14 | 30 8 | 29 52 | 28960 | 14 | 71040 | 29800 | 15 | 70200 | 00840 | 1 | 99160 | 46 |
| 15 | 10 30 0 | 1 30 0 | 9.29024 | 16 | 10.70976 | 9.29866 | 16 | 10.70134 | 10.00843 | 1 | 9.99157 | 45 |
| 16 | 29 52 | 30 8 | 29087 | 17 | 70913 | 29932 | 17 | 70068 | 00845 | 1 | 99155 | 44 |
| 17 | 29 44 | 30 16 | 29150 | 18 | 70850 | 29998 | 18 | 70002 | 00848 | 1 | 99152 | 43 |
| 18 | 29 36 | 30 24 | 29214 | 19 | 70786 | 30064 | 19 | 69936 | 00850 | 1 | 99150 | 42 |
| 19 | 29 28 | 30 32 | 29277 | 20 | 70723 | 30130 | 20 | 69870 | 00853 | 1 | 99147 | 41 |
| 20 | 10 29 20 | 1 30 40 | 9.29340 | 21 | 10.70660 | 9.30195 | 22 | 10.69805 | 10.00855 | 1 | 9.99145 | 40 |
| 21 | 29 12 | 30 48 | 29403 | 22 | 70597 | 30261 | 23 | 69739 | 00858 | 1 | 99142 | 39 |
| 22 | 29 4 | 30 56 | 29466 | 23 | 70534 | 30326 | 24 | 69674 | 00860 | 1 | 99140 | 38 |
| 23 | 28 56 | 31 4 | 29529 | 24 | 70471 | 30391 | 25 | 69609 | 00863 | 1 | 99137 | 37 |
| 24 | 28 48 | 31 12 | 29591 | 25 | 70409 | 30457 | 26 | 69543 | 00865 | 1 | 99135 | 36 |
| 25 | 10 28 40 | 1 31 20 | 9.29654 | 26 | 10.70346 | 9.30522 | 27 | 10.69478 | 10.00868 | 1 | 9.99132 | 35 |
| 26 | 28 32 | 31 28 | 29716 | 27 | 70284 | 30587 | 28 | 69413 | 00870 | 1 | 99130 | 34 |
| 27 | 28 24 | 31 36 | 29779 | 28 | 70221 | 30652 | 29 | 69348 | 00873 | 1 | 99127 | 33 |
| 28 | 28 16 | 31 44 | 29841 | 29 | 70159 | 30717 | 30 | 69283 | 00876 | 1 | 99124 | 32 |
| 29 | 28 8 | 31 52 | 29903 | 30 | 70097 | 30782 | 31 | 69218 | 00878 | 1 | 99122 | 31 |
| 30 | 10 28 0 | 1 32 0 | 9.29966 | 31 | 10.70034 | 9.30846 | 32 | 10.69154 | 10.00881 | 1 | 9.99119 | 30 |
| 31 | 27 52 | 32 8 | 30028 | 32 | 69972 | 30911 | 33 | 69089 | 00883 | 1 | 99117 | 29 |
| 32 | 27 44 | 32 16 | 30090 | 33 | 69910 | 30975 | 35 | 69025 | 00886 | 1 | 99114 | 28 |
| 33 | 27 36 | 32 24 | 30151 | 34 | 69849 | 31040 | 36 | 68960 | 00888 | 1 | 99112 | 27 |
| 34 | 27 28 | 32 32 | 30213 | 35 | 69787 | 31104 | 37 | 68896 | 00891 | 1 | 99109 | 26 |
| 35 | 10 27 20 | 1 32 40 | 9.30275 | 36 | 10.69725 | 9.31168 | 38 | 10.68832 | 10.00894 | 2 | 9.99106 | 25 |
| 36 | 27 12 | 32 48 | 30336 | 37 | 69664 | 31233 | 39 | 68767 | 00896 | 2 | 99104 | 24 |
| 37 | 27 4 | 32 56 | 30398 | 38 | 69602 | 31297 | 40 | 68703 | 00899 | 2 | 99101 | 23 |
| 38 | 26 56 | 33 4 | 30459 | 39 | 69541 | 31361 | 41 | 68639 | 00901 | 2 | 99099 | 22 |
| 39 | 26 48 | 33 12 | 30521 | 40 | 69479 | 31425 | 42 | 68575 | 00904 | 2 | 99096 | 21 |
| 40 | 10 26 40 | 1 33 20 | 9.30582 | 41 | 10.69418 | 9.31489 | 43 | 10.68511 | 10.00907 | 2 | 9.99093 | 20 |
| 41 | 26 32 | 33 28 | 30643 | 42 | 69357 | 31552 | 44 | 68448 | 00909 | 2 | 99091 | 19 |
| 42 | 26 24 | 33 36 | 30704 | 43 | 69296 | 31616 | 45 | 68384 | 00912 | 2 | 99088 | 18 |
| 43 | 26 16 | 33 44 | 30765 | 45 | 69235 | 31679 | 46 | 68321 | 00914 | 2 | 99086 | 17 |
| 44 | 26 8 | 33 52 | 30826 | 46 | 69174 | 31743 | 47 | 68257 | 00917 | 2 | 99083 | 16 |
| 45 | 10 26 0 | 1 34 0 | 9.30887 | 47 | 10.69113 | 9.31806 | 49 | 10.68194 | 10.00920 | 2 | 9.99080 | 15 |
| 46 | 25 52 | 34 8 | 30947 | 48 | 69053 | 31870 | 50 | 68130 | 00922 | 2 | 99078 | 14 |
| 47 | 25 44 | 34 16 | 31008 | 49 | 68992 | 31933 | 51 | 68067 | 00925 | 2 | 99075 | 13 |
| 48 | 25 36 | 34 24 | 31068 | 50 | 68932 | 31996 | 52 | 68004 | 00928 | 2 | 99072 | 12 |
| 49 | 25 28 | 34 32 | 31129 | 51 | 68871 | 32059 | 53 | 67941 | 00930 | 2 | 99070 | 11 |
| 50 | 10 25 20 | 1 34 40 | 9.31189 | 52 | 10.68811 | 9.32122 | 54 | 10.67878 | 10.00933 | 2 | 9.99067 | 10 |
| 51 | 25 12 | 34 48 | 31250 | 53 | 68750 | 32185 | 55 | 67815 | 00936 | 2 | 99064 | 9 |
| 52 | 25 4 | 34 56 | 31310 | 54 | 68690 | 32248 | 56 | 67752 | 00938 | 2 | 99062 | 8 |
| 53 | 24 56 | 35 4 | 31370 | 55 | 68630 | 32311 | 57 | 67689 | 00941 | 2 | 99059 | 7 |
| 54 | 24 48 | 35 12 | 31430 | 56 | 68570 | 32373 | 58 | 67627 | 00944 | 2 | 99056 | 6 |
| 55 | 10 24 40 | 1 35 20 | 9.31490 | 57 | 10.68510 | 9.32436 | 59 | 10.67564 | 10.00946 | 2 | 9.99054 | 5 |
| 56 | 24 32 | 35 28 | 31549 | 58 | 68451 | 32498 | 60 | 67502 | 00949 | 2 | 99051 | 4 |
| 57 | 24 24 | 35 36 | 31609 | 59 | 68391 | 32561 | 61 | 67439 | 00952 | 2 | 99048 | 3 |
| 58 | 24 16 | 35 44 | 31669 | 60 | 68331 | 32623 | 63 | 67377 | 00954 | 2 | 99046 | 2 |
| 59 | 24 8 | 35 52 | 31728 | 61 | 68272 | 32685 | 64 | 67315 | 00957 | 3 | 99043 | 1 |
| 60 | 24 0 | 36 0 | 31788 | 62 | 68212 | 32747 | 65 | 67253 | 00960 | 3 | 99040 | 0 |
| M | Hour P.M. | Hour A.M. | Cosine. | Diff. | Secant. | Cotangent | Diff. | Tangent. | Cosecant. | Diff. | Sine. | M |

101° A A B B C C 78°

| Seconds of time ...... | | 1s | 2s | 3s | 4s | 5s | 6s | 7s |
|---|---|---|---|---|---|---|---|---|
| Prop. parts of cols. | A | 8 | 16 | 23 | 31 | 39 | 47 | 54 |
| | B | 8 | 16 | 24 | 32 | 40 | 49 | 57 |
| | C | 0 | 1 | 1 | 1 | 2 | 2 | 2 |

# TABLE XXVII.

## Log. Sines, Tangents, and Secants.

S'. 12° — G'. 167°

| | | | A | | A | B | | B | C | | C | |
|---|---|---|---|---|---|---|---|---|---|---|---|---|
| M | Hour A.M. | Hour P.M. | Sine. | Diff. | Cosecant. | Tangent. | Diff. | Cotangent | Secant. | Diff. | Cosine. | M |
| 0 | 10 24 0 | 1 36 0 | 9.31788 | 0 | 10.68212 | 9.32747 | 0 | 10.67253 | 10.00960 | 0 | 9.99040 | 60 |
| 1 | 23 52 | 36 8 | 31847 | 1 | 68153 | 32810 | 1 | 67190 | 00962 | 0 | 99038 | 59 |
| 2 | 23 44 | 36 16 | 31907 | 2 | 68093 | 32872 | 2 | 67128 | 00965 | 0 | 99035 | 58 |
| 3 | 23 36 | 36 24 | 31966 | 3 | 68034 | 32933 | 3 | 67067 | 00968 | 0 | 99032 | 57 |
| 4 | 23 28 | 36 32 | 32025 | 4 | 67975 | 32995 | 4 | 67005 | 00970 | 0 | 99030 | 56 |
| 5 | 10 23 20 | 1 36 40 | 9.32084 | 5 | 10.67916 | 9.33057 | 5 | 10.66943 | 10.00973 | 0 | 9.99027 | 55 |
| 6 | 23 12 | 36 48 | 32143 | 6 | 67857 | 33119 | 6 | 66881 | 00976 | 0 | 99024 | 54 |
| 7 | 23 4 | 36 56 | 32202 | 7 | 67798 | 33180 | 7 | 66820 | 00978 | 0 | 99022 | 53 |
| 8 | 22 56 | 37 4 | 32261 | 8 | 67739 | 33242 | 8 | 66758 | 00981 | 0 | 99019 | 52 |
| 9 | 22 48 | 37 12 | 32319 | 9 | 67681 | 33303 | 9 | 66697 | 00984 | 0 | 99016 | 51 |
| 10 | 10 22 40 | 1 37 20 | 9.32378 | 10 | 10.67622 | 9.33365 | 10 | 10.66635 | 10.00987 | 0 | 9.99013 | 50 |
| 11 | 22 32 | 37 28 | 32437 | 10 | 67563 | 33426 | 11 | 66574 | 00989 | 1 | 99011 | 49 |
| 12 | 22 24 | 37 36 | 32495 | 11 | 67505 | 33487 | 12 | 66513 | 00992 | 1 | 99008 | 48 |
| 13 | 22 16 | 37 44 | 32553 | 12 | 67447 | 33548 | 13 | 66452 | 00995 | 1 | 99005 | 47 |
| 14 | 22 8 | 37 52 | 32612 | 13 | 67388 | 33609 | 14 | 66391 | 00998 | 1 | 99002 | 46 |
| 15 | 10 22 0 | 1 38 0 | 9.32670 | 14 | 10.67330 | 9.33670 | 15 | 10.66330 | 10.01000 | 1 | 9.99000 | 45 |
| 16 | 21 52 | 38 8 | 32728 | 15 | 67272 | 33731 | 16 | 66269 | 01003 | 1 | 98997 | 44 |
| 17 | 21 44 | 38 16 | 32786 | 16 | 67214 | 33792 | 17 | 66208 | 01006 | 1 | 98994 | 43 |
| 18 | 21 36 | 38 24 | 32844 | 17 | 67156 | 33853 | 18 | 66147 | 01009 | 1 | 98991 | 42 |
| 19 | 21 28 | 38 32 | 32902 | 18 | 67098 | 33913 | 19 | 66087 | 01011 | 1 | 98989 | 41 |
| 20 | 10 21 20 | 1 38 40 | 9.32960 | 19 | 10.67040 | 9.33974 | 20 | 10.66026 | 10.01014 | 1 | 9.98986 | 40 |
| 21 | 21 12 | 38 48 | 33018 | 20 | 66982 | 34034 | 21 | 65966 | 01017 | 1 | 98983 | 39 |
| 22 | 21 4 | 38 56 | 33075 | 21 | 66925 | 34095 | 22 | 65905 | 01020 | 1 | 98980 | 38 |
| 23 | 20 56 | 39 4 | 33133 | 22 | 66867 | 34155 | 23 | 65845 | 01022 | 1 | 98978 | 37 |
| 24 | 20 48 | 39 12 | 33190 | 23 | 66810 | 34215 | 24 | 65785 | 01025 | 1 | 98975 | 36 |
| 25 | 10 20 40 | 1 39 20 | 9.33248 | 24 | 10.66752 | 9.34276 | 25 | 10.65724 | 10.01028 | 1 | 9.98972 | 35 |
| 26 | 20 32 | 39 28 | 33305 | 25 | 66695 | 34336 | 26 | 65664 | 01031 | 1 | 98969 | 34 |
| 27 | 20 24 | 39 36 | 33362 | 26 | 66638 | 34396 | 27 | 65604 | 01033 | 1 | 98967 | 33 |
| 28 | 20 16 | 39 44 | 33420 | 27 | 66580 | 34456 | 28 | 65544 | 01036 | 1 | 98964 | 32 |
| 29 | 20 8 | 39 52 | 33477 | 28 | 66523 | 34516 | 29 | 65484 | 01039 | 1 | 98961 | 31 |
| 30 | 10 20 0 | 1 40 0 | 9.33534 | 29 | 10.66466 | 9.34576 | 30 | 10.65424 | 10.01042 | 1 | 9.98958 | 30 |
| 31 | 19 52 | 40 8 | 33591 | 29 | 66409 | 34635 | 31 | 65365 | 01045 | 1 | 98955 | 29 |
| 32 | 19 44 | 40 16 | 33647 | 30 | 66353 | 34695 | 32 | 65305 | 01047 | 1 | 98953 | 28 |
| 33 | 19 36 | 40 24 | 33704 | 31 | 66296 | 34755 | 33 | 65245 | 01050 | 2 | 98950 | 27 |
| 34 | 19 28 | 40 32 | 33761 | 32 | 66239 | 34814 | 34 | 65186 | 01053 | 2 | 98947 | 26 |
| 35 | 10 19 20 | 1 40 40 | 9.33818 | 33 | 10.66182 | 9.34874 | 35 | 10.65126 | 10.01056 | 2 | 9.98944 | 25 |
| 36 | 19 12 | 40 48 | 33874 | 34 | 66126 | 34933 | 36 | 65067 | 01059 | 2 | 98941 | 24 |
| 37 | 19 4 | 40 56 | 33931 | 35 | 66069 | 34992 | 37 | 65008 | 01062 | 2 | 98938 | 23 |
| 38 | 18 56 | 41 4 | 33987 | 36 | 66013 | 35051 | 38 | 64949 | 01064 | 2 | 98936 | 22 |
| 39 | 18 48 | 41 12 | 34043 | 37 | 65957 | 35111 | 39 | 64889 | 01067 | 2 | 98933 | 21 |
| 40 | 10 18 40 | 1 41 20 | 9.34100 | 38 | 10.65900 | 9.35170 | 40 | 10.64830 | 10.01070 | 2 | 9.98930 | 20 |
| 41 | 18 32 | 41 28 | 34156 | 39 | 65844 | 35229 | 41 | 64771 | 01073 | 2 | 98927 | 19 |
| 42 | 18 24 | 41 36 | 34212 | 40 | 65788 | 35288 | 42 | 64712 | 01076 | 2 | 98924 | 18 |
| 43 | 18 16 | 41 44 | 34268 | 41 | 65732 | 35347 | 43 | 64653 | 01079 | 2 | 98921 | 17 |
| 44 | 18 8 | 41 52 | 34324 | 42 | 65676 | 35405 | 44 | 64595 | 01081 | 2 | 98919 | 16 |
| 45 | 10 18 0 | 1 42 0 | 9.34380 | 43 | 10.65620 | 9.35464 | 45 | 10.64536 | 10.01084 | 2 | 9.98916 | 15 |
| 46 | 17 52 | 42 8 | 34436 | 44 | 65564 | 35523 | 46 | 64477 | 01087 | 2 | 98913 | 14 |
| 47 | 17 44 | 42 16 | 34491 | 45 | 65509 | 35581 | 47 | 64419 | 01090 | 2 | 98910 | 13 |
| 48 | 17 36 | 42 24 | 34547 | 46 | 65453 | 35640 | 48 | 64360 | 01093 | 2 | 98907 | 12 |
| 49 | 17 28 | 42 32 | 34602 | 47 | 65398 | 35698 | 49 | 64302 | 01096 | 2 | 98904 | 11 |
| 50 | 10 17 20 | 1 42 40 | 9.34658 | 48 | 10.65342 | 9.35757 | 50 | 10.64243 | 10.01099 | 2 | 9.98901 | 10 |
| 51 | 17 12 | 42 48 | 34713 | 48 | 65287 | 35815 | 51 | 64185 | 01102 | 2 | 98898 | 9 |
| 52 | 17 4 | 42 56 | 34769 | 49 | 65231 | 35873 | 52 | 64127 | 01104 | 2 | 98896 | 8 |
| 53 | 16 56 | 43 4 | 34824 | 50 | 65176 | 35931 | 53 | 64069 | 01107 | 2 | 98893 | 7 |
| 54 | 16 48 | 43 12 | 34879 | 51 | 65121 | 35989 | 54 | 64011 | 01110 | 3 | 98890 | 6 |
| 55 | 10 16 40 | 1 43 20 | 9.34934 | 52 | 10.65066 | 9.36047 | 55 | 10.63953 | 10.01113 | 3 | 9.98887 | 5 |
| 56 | 16 32 | 43 28 | 34989 | 53 | 65011 | 36105 | 56 | 63895 | 01116 | 3 | 98884 | 4 |
| 57 | 16 24 | 43 36 | 35044 | 54 | 64956 | 36163 | 57 | 63837 | 01119 | 3 | 98881 | 3 |
| 58 | 16 16 | 43 44 | 35099 | 55 | 64901 | 36221 | 58 | 63779 | 01122 | 3 | 98878 | 2 |
| 59 | 16 8 | 43 52 | 35154 | 56 | 64846 | 36279 | 59 | 63721 | 01125 | 3 | 98875 | 1 |
| 60 | 16 0 | 44 0 | 35209 | 57 | 64791 | 36336 | 60 | 63664 | 01128 | 3 | 98872 | 0 |
| M | Hour P.M. | Hour A.M. | Cosine. | Diff. | Secant. | Cotangent | Diff. | Tangent. | Cosecant. | Diff. | Sine. | M. |
| 102° | | | A | | A | B | | B | C | | C | 77° |

| Seconds of time ...... | | 1s | 2s | 3s | 4s | 5s | 6s | 7s |
|---|---|---|---|---|---|---|---|---|
| Prop. parts of cols. | A | 7 | 14 | 21 | 29 | 36 | 43 | 50 |
| | B | 7 | 15 | 22 | 30 | 37 | 45 | 52 |
| | C | 0 | 1 | 1 | 1 | 2 | 2 | 2 |

# TABLE XXVII.

S'. G

## Log. Sines, Tangents, and Secants.

13° 166°

| M | Hour A.M. | Hour P.M. | Sine. (A) | Diff. | Cosecant. (A) | Tangent. (B) | Diff. | Cotangent. (B) | Secant. (C) | Diff. | Cosine. (C) | M |
|---|---|---|---|---|---|---|---|---|---|---|---|---|
| 0 | 10 16 0 | 1 44 0 | 9.35209 | 0 | 10.64791 | 9.36336 | 0 | 10.63664 | 10.01128 | 0 | 9.98872 | 60 |
| 1 | 15 52 | 44 8 | 35263 | 1 | 64737 | 36394 | 1 | 63606 | 01131 | 0 | 98869 | 59 |
| 2 | 15 44 | 44 16 | 35318 | 2 | 64682 | 36452 | 2 | 63548 | 01133 | 0 | 98867 | 58 |
| 3 | 15 36 | 44 24 | 35373 | 3 | 64627 | 36509 | 3 | 63491 | 01136 | 0 | 98864 | 57 |
| 4 | 15 28 | 44 32 | 35427 | 4 | 64573 | 36566 | 4 | 63434 | 01139 | 0 | 98861 | 56 |
| 5 | 10 15 20 | 1 44 40 | 9.35481 | 4 | 10.64519 | 9.36624 | 5 | 10.63376 | 10.01142 | 0 | 9.98858 | 55 |
| 6 | 15 12 | 44 48 | 35536 | 5 | 64464 | 36681 | 6 | 63319 | 01145 | 0 | 98855 | 54 |
| 7 | 15 4 | 44 56 | 35590 | 6 | 64410 | 36738 | 6 | 63262 | 01148 | 0 | 98852 | 53 |
| 8 | 14 56 | 45 4 | 35644 | 7 | 64356 | 36795 | 7 | 63205 | 01151 | 0 | 98849 | 52 |
| 9 | 14 48 | 45 12 | 35698 | 8 | 64302 | 36852 | 8 | 63148 | 01154 | 0 | 98846 | 51 |
| 10 | 10 14 40 | 1 45 20 | 9.35752 | 9 | 10.64248 | 9.36909 | 9 | 10.63091 | 10.01157 | 1 | 9.98843 | 50 |
| 11 | 14 32 | 45 28 | 35806 | 10 | 64194 | 36966 | 10 | 63034 | 01160 | 1 | 98840 | 49 |
| 12 | 14 24 | 45 36 | 35860 | 11 | 64140 | 37023 | 11 | 62977 | 01163 | 1 | 98837 | 48 |
| 13 | 14 16 | 45 44 | 35914 | 11 | 64086 | 37080 | 12 | 62920 | 01166 | 1 | 98834 | 47 |
| 14 | 14 8 | 45 52 | 35968 | 12 | 64032 | 37137 | 13 | 62863 | 01169 | 1 | 98831 | 46 |
| 15 | 10 14 0 | 1 46 0 | 9.36022 | 13 | 10.63978 | 9.37193 | 14 | 10.62807 | 10.01172 | 1 | 9.98828 | 45 |
| 16 | 13 52 | 46 8 | 36075 | 14 | 63925 | 37250 | 15 | 62750 | 01175 | 1 | 98825 | 44 |
| 17 | 13 44 | 46 16 | 36129 | 15 | 63871 | 37306 | 16 | 62694 | 01178 | 1 | 98822 | 43 |
| 18 | 13 36 | 46 24 | 36182 | 16 | 63818 | 37363 | 17 | 62637 | 01181 | 1 | 98819 | 42 |
| 19 | 13 28 | 46 32 | 36236 | 17 | 63764 | 37419 | 18 | 62581 | 01184 | 1 | 98816 | 41 |
| 20 | 10 13 20 | 1 46 40 | 9.36289 | 18 | 10.63711 | 9.37476 | 19 | 10.62524 | 10.01187 | 1 | 9.98813 | 40 |
| 21 | 13 12 | 46 48 | 36342 | 18 | 63658 | 37532 | 19 | 62468 | 01190 | 1 | 98810 | 39 |
| 22 | 13 4 | 46 56 | 36395 | 19 | 63605 | 37588 | 20 | 62412 | 01193 | 1 | 98807 | 38 |
| 23 | 12 56 | 47 4 | 36449 | 20 | 63551 | 37644 | 21 | 62356 | 01196 | 1 | 98804 | 37 |
| 24 | 12 48 | 47 12 | 36502 | 21 | 63498 | 37700 | 22 | 62300 | 01199 | 1 | 98801 | 36 |
| 25 | 10 12 40 | 1 47 20 | 9.36555 | 22 | 10.63445 | 9.37756 | 23 | 10.62244 | 10.01202 | 1 | 9.98798 | 35 |
| 26 | 12 32 | 47 28 | 36608 | 23 | 63392 | 37812 | 24 | 62188 | 01205 | 1 | 98795 | 34 |
| 27 | 12 24 | 47 36 | 36660 | 24 | 63340 | 37868 | 25 | 62132 | 01208 | 1 | 98792 | 33 |
| 28 | 12 16 | 47 44 | 36713 | 25 | 63287 | 37924 | 26 | 62076 | 01211 | 1 | 98789 | 32 |
| 29 | 12 8 | 47 52 | 36766 | 25 | 63234 | 37980 | 27 | 62020 | 01214 | 1 | 98786 | 31 |
| 30 | 10 12 0 | 1 48 0 | 9.36819 | 26 | 10.63181 | 9.38035 | 28 | 10.61965 | 10.01217 | 2 | 9.98783 | 30 |
| 31 | 11 52 | 48 8 | 36871 | 27 | 63129 | 38091 | 29 | 61909 | 01220 | 2 | 98780 | 29 |
| 32 | 11 44 | 48 16 | 36924 | 28 | 63076 | 38147 | 30 | 61853 | 01223 | 2 | 98777 | 28 |
| 33 | 11 36 | 48 24 | 36976 | 29 | 63024 | 38202 | 31 | 61798 | 01226 | 2 | 98774 | 27 |
| 34 | 11 28 | 48 32 | 37028 | 30 | 62972 | 38257 | 32 | 61743 | 01229 | 2 | 98771 | 26 |
| 35 | 10 11 20 | 1 48 40 | 9.37081 | 31 | 10.62919 | 9.38313 | 32 | 10.61687 | 10.01232 | 2 | 9.98768 | 25 |
| 36 | 11 12 | 48 48 | 37133 | 32 | 62867 | 38368 | 33 | 61632 | 01235 | 2 | 98765 | 24 |
| 37 | 11 4 | 48 56 | 37185 | 32 | 62815 | 38423 | 34 | 61577 | 01238 | 2 | 98762 | 23 |
| 38 | 10 56 | 49 4 | 37237 | 33 | 62763 | 38479 | 35 | 61521 | 01241 | 2 | 98759 | 22 |
| 39 | 10 48 | 49 12 | 37289 | 34 | 62711 | 38534 | 36 | 61466 | 01244 | 2 | 98756 | 21 |
| 40 | 10 10 40 | 1 49 20 | 9.37341 | 35 | 10.62659 | 9.38589 | 37 | 10.61411 | 10.01247 | 2 | 9.98753 | 20 |
| 41 | 10 32 | 49 28 | 37393 | 36 | 62607 | 38644 | 38 | 61356 | 01250 | 2 | 98750 | 19 |
| 42 | 10 24 | 49 36 | 37445 | 37 | 62555 | 38699 | 39 | 61301 | 01254 | 2 | 98746 | 18 |
| 43 | 10 16 | 49 44 | 37497 | 38 | 62503 | 38754 | 40 | 61246 | 01257 | 2 | 98743 | 17 |
| 44 | 10 8 | 49 52 | 37549 | 39 | 62451 | 38808 | 41 | 61192 | 01260 | 2 | 98740 | 16 |
| 45 | 10 10 0 | 1 50 0 | 9.37600 | 39 | 10.62400 | 9.38863 | 42 | 10.61137 | 10.01263 | 2 | 9.98737 | 15 |
| 46 | 9 52 | 50 8 | 37652 | 40 | 62348 | 38918 | 43 | 61082 | 01266 | 2 | 98734 | 14 |
| 47 | 9 44 | 50 16 | 37703 | 41 | 62297 | 38972 | 44 | 61028 | 01269 | 2 | 98731 | 13 |
| 48 | 9 36 | 50 24 | 37755 | 42 | 62245 | 39027 | 45 | 60973 | 01272 | 2 | 98728 | 12 |
| 49 | 9 28 | 50 32 | 37806 | 43 | 62194 | 39082 | 45 | 60918 | 01275 | 2 | 98725 | 11 |
| 50 | 10 9 20 | 1 50 40 | 9.37858 | 44 | 10.62142 | 9.39136 | 46 | 10.60864 | 10.01278 | 3 | 9.98722 | 10 |
| 51 | 9 12 | 50 48 | 37909 | 45 | 62091 | 39190 | 47 | 60810 | 01281 | 3 | 98719 | 9 |
| 52 | 9 4 | 50 56 | 37960 | 46 | 62040 | 39245 | 48 | 60755 | 01285 | 3 | 98715 | 8 |
| 53 | 8 56 | 51 4 | 38011 | 47 | 61989 | 39299 | 49 | 60701 | 01288 | 3 | 98712 | 7 |
| 54 | 8 48 | 51 12 | 38062 | 47 | 61938 | 39353 | 50 | 60647 | 01291 | 3 | 98709 | 6 |
| 55 | 10 8 40 | 1 51 20 | 9.38113 | 48 | 10.61887 | 9.39407 | 51 | 10.60593 | 10.01294 | 3 | 9.98706 | 5 |
| 56 | 8 32 | 51 28 | 38164 | 49 | 61836 | 39461 | 52 | 60539 | 01297 | 3 | 98703 | 4 |
| 57 | 8 24 | 51 36 | 38215 | 50 | 61785 | 39515 | 53 | 60485 | 01300 | 3 | 98700 | 3 |
| 58 | 8 16 | 51 44 | 38266 | 51 | 61734 | 39569 | 54 | 60431 | 01303 | 3 | 98697 | 2 |
| 59 | 8 8 | 51 52 | 38317 | 52 | 61683 | 39623 | 55 | 60377 | 01306 | 3 | 98694 | 1 |
| 60 | 8 0 | 52 0 | 38368 | 53 | 61632 | 39677 | 56 | 60323 | 01310 | 3 | 98690 | 0 |
| M | Hour P.M. | Hour A.M. | Cosine. (A) | Diff. | Secant. (A) | Cotangent (B) | Diff. | Tangent. (B) | Cosecant. (C) | Diff. | Sine. (C) | M |

103° 76°

| Seconds of time ...... | | 1s | 2s | 3s | 4s | 5s | 6s | 7s |
|---|---|---|---|---|---|---|---|---|
| Prop. parts of cols. | A | 7 | 13 | 20 | 26 | 33 | 39 | 46 |
| | B | 7 | 14 | 21 | 28 | 35 | 42 | 49 |
| | C | 0 | 1 | 1 | 2 | 2 | 2 | 3 |

## Log. Sines, Tangents, and Secants.

S.ʹ. 14° | Gʹ. 165°

| M | Hour A.M. | Hour P.M. | Sine. (A) | Diff. | Cosecant. (A) | Tangent. (B) | Diff. | Cotangent (B) | Secant. (C) | Diff. | Cosine. (C) | M |
|---|---|---|---|---|---|---|---|---|---|---|---|---|
| 0 | 10 8 0 | 1 52 0 | 9.38368 | 0 | 10.61632 | 9.39677 | 0 | 10.60323 | 10.01310 | 0 | 9.98690 | 60 |
| 1 | 7 52 | 52 8 | 38418 | 1 | 61582 | 39731 | 1 | 60269 | 01313 | 0 | 98687 | 59 |
| 2 | 7 44 | 52 16 | 38469 | 2 | 61531 | 39785 | 2 | 60215 | 01316 | 0 | 98684 | 58 |
| 3 | 7 36 | 52 24 | 38519 | 2 | 61481 | 39838 | 3 | 60162 | 01319 | 0 | 98681 | 57 |
| 4 | 7 28 | 52 32 | 38570 | 3 | 61430 | 39892 | 3 | 60108 | 01322 | 0 | 98678 | 56 |
| 5 | 10 7 20 | 1 52 40 | 9.38620 | 4 | 10.61380 | 9.39945 | 4 | 10.60055 | 10 01325 | 0 | 9.98675 | 55 |
| 6 | 7 12 | 52 48 | 38670 | 5 | 61330 | 39999 | 5 | 60001 | 01329 | 0 | 98671 | 54 |
| 7 | 7 4 | 52 56 | 38721 | 6 | 61279 | 40052 | 6 | 59948 | 01332 | 0 | 98668 | 53 |
| 8 | 6 56 | 53 4 | 38771 | 7 | 61229 | 40106 | 7 | 59894 | 01335 | 0 | 98665 | 52 |
| 9 | 6 48 | 53 12 | 38821 | 7 | 61179 | 40159 | 8 | 59841 | 01338 | 0 | 98662 | 51 |
| 10 | 10 6 40 | 1 53 20 | 9.38871 | 8 | 10.61129 | 9.40212 | 9 | 10.59788 | 10.01341 | 1 | 9.98659 | 50 |
| 11 | 6 32 | 53 28 | 38921 | 9 | 61079 | 40266 | 10 | 59734 | 01344 | 1 | 98656 | 49 |
| 12 | 6 24 | 53 36 | 38971 | 10 | 61029 | 40319 | 10 | 59681 | 01348 | 1 | 98652 | 48 |
| 13 | 6 16 | 53 44 | 39021 | 11 | 60979 | 40372 | 11 | 59628 | 01351 | 1 | 98649 | 47 |
| 14 | 6 8 | 53 52 | 39071 | 11 | 60929 | 40425 | 12 | 59575 | 01354 | 1 | 98646 | 46 |
| 15 | 10 6 0 | 1 54 0 | 9.39121 | 12 | 10.60879 | 9.40478 | 13 | 10.59522 | 10.01357 | 1 | 9.98643 | 45 |
| 16 | 5 52 | 54 8 | 39170 | 13 | 60830 | 40531 | 14 | 59469 | 01360 | 1 | 98640 | 44 |
| 17 | 5 44 | 54 16 | 39220 | 14 | 60780 | 40584 | 15 | 59416 | 01364 | 1 | 98636 | 43 |
| 18 | 5 36 | 54 24 | 39270 | 15 | 60730 | 40636 | 16 | 59364 | 01367 | 1 | 98633 | 42 |
| 19 | 5 28 | 54 32 | 39319 | 15 | 60681 | 40689 | 17 | 59311 | 01370 | 1 | 98630 | 41 |
| 20 | 10 5 20 | 1 54 40 | 9.39369 | 16 | 10.60631 | 9.40742 | 17 | 10.59258 | 10.01373 | 1 | 9.98627 | 40 |
| 21 | 5 12 | 54 48 | 39418 | 17 | 60582 | 40795 | 18 | 59205 | 01377 | 1 | 98623 | 39 |
| 22 | 5 4 | 54 56 | 39467 | 18 | 60533 | 40847 | 19 | 59153 | 01380 | 1 | 98620 | 38 |
| 23 | 4 56 | 55 4 | 39517 | 19 | 60483 | 40900 | 20 | 59100 | 01383 | 1 | 98617 | 37 |
| 24 | 4 48 | 55 12 | 39566 | 20 | 60434 | 40952 | 21 | 59048 | 01386 | 1 | 98614 | 36 |
| 25 | 10 4 40 | 1 55 20 | 9.39615 | 20 | 10.60385 | 9.41005 | 22 | 10.58995 | 10.01390 | 1 | 9.98610 | 35 |
| 26 | 4 32 | 55 28 | 39664 | 21 | 60336 | 41057 | 23 | 58943 | 01393 | 1 | 98607 | 34 |
| 27 | 4 24 | 55 36 | 39713 | 22 | 60287 | 41109 | 23 | 58891 | 01396 | 1 | 98604 | 33 |
| 28 | 4 16 | 55 44 | 39762 | 23 | 60238 | 41161 | 24 | 58839 | 01399 | 2 | 98601 | 32 |
| 29 | 4 8 | 55 52 | 39811 | 24 | 60189 | 41214 | 25 | 58786 | 01403 | 2 | 98597 | 31 |
| 30 | 10 4 0 | 1 56 0 | 9.39860 | 24 | 10.60140 | 9.41266 | 26 | 10.58734 | 10.01406 | 2 | 9.98594 | 30 |
| 31 | 3 52 | 56 8 | 39909 | 25 | 60091 | 41318 | 27 | 58682 | 01409 | 2 | 98591 | 29 |
| 32 | 3 44 | 56 16 | 39958 | 26 | 60042 | 41370 | 28 | 58630 | 01412 | 2 | 98588 | 28 |
| 33 | 3 36 | 56 24 | 40006 | 27 | 59994 | 41422 | 29 | 58578 | 01416 | 2 | 98584 | 27 |
| 34 | 3 28 | 56 32 | 40055 | 28 | 59945 | 41474 | 30 | 58526 | 01419 | 2 | 98581 | 26 |
| 35 | 10 3 20 | 1 56 40 | 9.40103 | 29 | 10.59897 | 9.41526 | 30 | 10.58474 | 10.01422 | 2 | 9.98578 | 25 |
| 36 | 3 12 | 56 48 | 40152 | 29 | 59848 | 41578 | 31 | 58422 | 01426 | 2 | 98574 | 24 |
| 37 | 3 4 | 56 56 | 40200 | 30 | 59800 | 41629 | 32 | 58371 | 01429 | 2 | 98571 | 23 |
| 38 | 2 56 | 57 4 | 40249 | 31 | 59751 | 41681 | 33 | 58319 | 01432 | 2 | 98568 | 22 |
| 39 | 2 48 | 57 12 | 40297 | 32 | 59703 | 41733 | 34 | 58267 | 01435 | 2 | 98565 | 21 |
| 40 | 10 2 40 | 1 57 20 | 9.40346 | 33 | 10.59654 | 9.41784 | 35 | 10.58216 | 10.01439 | 2 | 9.98561 | 20 |
| 41 | 2 32 | 57 28 | 40394 | 33 | 59606 | 41836 | 36 | 58164 | 01442 | 2 | 98558 | 19 |
| 42 | 2 24 | 57 36 | 40442 | 34 | 59558 | 41887 | 36 | 58113 | 01445 | 2 | 98555 | 18 |
| 43 | 2 16 | 57 44 | 40490 | 35 | 59510 | 41939 | 37 | 58061 | 01449 | 2 | 98551 | 17 |
| 44 | 2 8 | 57 52 | 40538 | 36 | 59462 | 41990 | 38 | 58010 | 01452 | 2 | 98548 | 16 |
| 45 | 10 2 0 | 1 58 0 | 9.40586 | 37 | 10.59414 | 9.42041 | 39 | 10.57959 | 10.01455 | 2 | 9.98545 | 15 |
| 46 | 1 52 | 58 8 | 40634 | 37 | 59366 | 42093 | 40 | 57907 | 01459 | 3 | 98541 | 14 |
| 47 | 1 44 | 58 16 | 40682 | 38 | 59318 | 42144 | 41 | 57856 | 01462 | 3 | 98538 | 13 |
| 48 | 1 36 | 58 24 | 40730 | 39 | 59270 | 42195 | 42 | 57805 | 01465 | 3 | 98535 | 12 |
| 49 | 1 28 | 58 32 | 40778 | 40 | 59222 | 42246 | 43 | 57754 | 01469 | 3 | 98531 | 11 |
| 50 | 10 1 20 | 1 58 40 | 9.40825 | 41 | 10.59175 | 9.42297 | 43 | 10.57703 | 10.01472 | 3 | 9.98528 | 10 |
| 51 | 1 12 | 58 48 | 40873 | 42 | 59127 | 42348 | 44 | 57652 | 01475 | 3 | 98525 | 9 |
| 52 | 1 4 | 58 56 | 40921 | 42 | 59079 | 42399 | 45 | 57601 | 01479 | 3 | 98521 | 8 |
| 53 | 0 56 | 59 4 | 40968 | 43 | 59032 | 42450 | 46 | 57550 | 01482 | 3 | 98518 | 7 |
| 54 | 0 48 | 59 12 | 41016 | 44 | 58984 | 42501 | 47 | 57499 | 01485 | 3 | 98515 | 6 |
| 55 | 10 0 40 | 1 59 20 | 9.41063 | 45 | 10.58937 | 9.42552 | 48 | 10.57448 | 10.01489 | 3 | 9.98511 | 5 |
| 56 | 0 32 | 59 28 | 41111 | 46 | 58889 | 42603 | 49 | 57397 | 01492 | 3 | 98508 | 4 |
| 57 | 0 24 | 59 36 | 41158 | 46 | 58842 | 42653 | 50 | 57347 | 01495 | 3 | 98505 | 3 |
| 58 | 0 16 | 59 44 | 41205 | 47 | 58795 | 42704 | 50 | 57296 | 01499 | 3 | 98501 | 2 |
| 59 | 0 8 | 59 52 | 41252 | 48 | 58748 | 42755 | 51 | 57245 | 01502 | 3 | 98498 | 1 |
| 60 | 0 0 | 2 0 0 | 41300 | 49 | 58700 | 42805 | 52 | 57195 | 01506 | 3 | 98494 | 0 |
| M | Hour P.M. | Hour A.M. | Cosine. (A) | Diff. | Secant. (A) | Cotangent (B) | Diff. | Tangent. (B) | Cosecant. (C) | Diff. | Sine. (C) | M |

104° | 75°

| Seconds of time ...... | | 1s | 2s | 3s | 4s | 5s | 6s | 7s |
|---|---|---|---|---|---|---|---|---|
| Prop. parts of cols. | A | 6 | 12 | 18 | 24 | 31 | 37 | 43 |
| | B | 7 | 13 | 20 | 26 | 33 | 39 | 46 |
| | C | 0 | 1 | 1 | 2 | 2 | 2 | 3 |

# TABLE XXVII.

## Log. Sines, Tangents, and Secants.

S' G.

15° 164°

| M | Hour A.M. | Hour P.M. | A Sine. | Diff. | A Cosecant. | B Tangent. | Diff. | B Cotangent | C Secant. | Diff. | C Cosine. | M |
|---|---|---|---|---|---|---|---|---|---|---|---|---|
| 0 | 10 0 0 | 2 0 0 | 9.41300 | 0 | 10.58700 | 9.42805 | 0 | 10.57195 | 10.01506 | 0 | 9.98494 | 60 |
| 1 | 9 59 52 | 0 8 | 41347 | 1 | 58653 | 42856 | 1 | 57144 | 01509 | 0 | 98491 | 59 |
| 2 | 59 44 | 0 16 | 41394 | 2 | 58606 | 42906 | 2 | 57094 | 01512 | 0 | 98488 | 58 |
| 3 | 59 36 | 0 24 | 41441 | 2 | 58559 | 42957 | 2 | 57043 | 01516 | 0 | 98484 | 57 |
| 4 | 59 28 | 0 32 | 41488 | 3 | 58512 | 43007 | 3 | 56993 | 01519 | 0 | 98481 | 56 |
| 5 | 9 59 20 | 2 0 40 | 9.41535 | 4 | 10.58465 | 9.43057 | 4 | 10.56943 | 10.01523 | 0 | 9.98477 | 55 |
| 6 | 59 12 | 0 48 | 41582 | 5 | 58418 | 43108 | 5 | 56892 | 01526 | 0 | 98474 | 54 |
| 7 | 59 4 | 0 56 | 41628 | 5 | 58372 | 43158 | 6 | 56842 | 01529 | 0 | 98471 | 53 |
| 8 | 58 56 | 1 4 | 41675 | 6 | 58325 | 43208 | 7 | 56792 | 01533 | 0 | 98467 | 52 |
| 9 | 58 48 | 1 12 | 41722 | 7 | 58278 | 43258 | 7 | 56742 | 01536 | 1 | 98464 | 51 |
| 10 | 9 58 40 | 2 1 20 | 9.41768 | 8 | 10.58232 | 9.43308 | 8 | 10.56692 | 10.01540 | 1 | 9.98460 | 50 |
| 11 | 58 32 | 1 28 | 41815 | 8 | 58185 | 43358 | 9 | 56642 | 01543 | 1 | 98457 | 49 |
| 12 | 58 24 | 1 36 | 41861 | 9 | 58139 | 43408 | 10 | 56592 | 01547 | 1 | 98453 | 48 |
| 13 | 58 16 | 1 44 | 41908 | 10 | 58092 | 43458 | 11 | 56542 | 01550 | 1 | 98450 | 47 |
| 14 | 58 8 | 1 52 | 41954 | 11 | 58046 | 43508 | 11 | 56492 | 01553 | 1 | 98447 | 46 |
| 15 | 9 58 0 | 2 2 0 | 9.42001 | 11 | 10.57999 | 9.43558 | 12 | 10.56442 | 10.01557 | 1 | 9.98443 | 45 |
| 16 | 57 52 | 2 8 | 42047 | 12 | 57953 | 43607 | 13 | 56393 | 01560 | 1 | 98440 | 44 |
| 17 | 57 44 | 2 16 | 42093 | 13 | 57907 | 43657 | 14 | 56343 | 01564 | 1 | 98436 | 43 |
| 18 | 57 36 | 2 24 | 42140 | 14 | 57860 | 43707 | 15 | 56293 | 01567 | 1 | 98433 | 42 |
| 19 | 57 28 | 2 32 | 42186 | 14 | 57814 | 43756 | 16 | 56244 | 01571 | 1 | 98429 | 41 |
| 20 | 9 57 20 | 2 2 40 | 9.42232 | 15 | 10.57768 | 9.43806 | 16 | 10.56194 | 10.01574 | 1 | 9.98426 | 40 |
| 21 | 57 12 | 2 48 | 42278 | 16 | 57722 | 43855 | 17 | 56145 | 01578 | 1 | 98422 | 39 |
| 22 | 57 4 | 2 56 | 42324 | 17 | 57676 | 43905 | 18 | 56095 | 01581 | 1 | 98419 | 38 |
| 23 | 56 56 | 3 4 | 42370 | 17 | 57630 | 43954 | 19 | 56046 | 01585 | 1 | 98415 | 37 |
| 24 | 56 48 | 3 12 | 42416 | 18 | 57584 | 44004 | 20 | 55996 | 01588 | 1 | 98412 | 36 |
| 25 | 9 56 40 | 2 3 20 | 9.42461 | 19 | 10.57539 | 9.44053 | 20 | 10.55947 | 10.01591 | 1 | 9.98409 | 35 |
| 26 | 56 32 | 3 28 | 42507 | 20 | 57493 | 44102 | 21 | 55898 | 01595 | 2 | 98405 | 34 |
| 27 | 56 24 | 3 36 | 42553 | 21 | 57447 | 44151 | 22 | 55849 | 01598 | 2 | 98402 | 33 |
| 28 | 56 16 | 3 44 | 42599 | 21 | 57401 | 44201 | 23 | 55799 | 01602 | 2 | 98398 | 32 |
| 29 | 56 8 | 3 52 | 42644 | 22 | 57356 | 44250 | 24 | 55750 | 01605 | 2 | 98395 | 31 |
| 30 | 9 56 0 | 2 4 0 | 9.42690 | 23 | 10.57310 | 9.44299 | 25 | 10.55701 | 10.01609 | 2 | 9.98391 | 30 |
| 31 | 55 52 | 4 8 | 42735 | 24 | 57265 | 44348 | 25 | 55652 | 01612 | 2 | 98388 | 29 |
| 32 | 55 44 | 4 16 | 42781 | 24 | 57219 | 44397 | 26 | 55603 | 01616 | 2 | 98384 | 28 |
| 33 | 55 36 | 4 24 | 42826 | 25 | 57174 | 44446 | 27 | 55554 | 01619 | 2 | 98381 | 27 |
| 34 | 55 28 | 4 32 | 42872 | 26 | 57128 | 44495 | 28 | 55505 | 01623 | 2 | 98377 | 26 |
| 35 | 9 55 20 | 2 4 40 | 9.42917 | 27 | 10.57083 | 9.44544 | 29 | 10.55456 | 10.01627 | 2 | 9.98373 | 25 |
| 36 | 55 12 | 4 48 | 42962 | 27 | 57038 | 44592 | 29 | 55408 | 01630 | 2 | 98370 | 24 |
| 37 | 55 4 | 4 56 | 43008 | 28 | 56992 | 44641 | 30 | 55359 | 01634 | 2 | 98366 | 23 |
| 38 | 54 56 | 5 4 | 43053 | 29 | 56947 | 44690 | 31 | 55310 | 01637 | 2 | 98363 | 22 |
| 39 | 54 48 | 5 12 | 43098 | 30 | 56902 | 44738 | 32 | 55262 | 01641 | 2 | 98359 | 21 |
| 40 | 9 54 40 | 2 5 20 | 9.43143 | 30 | 10.56857 | 9.44787 | 33 | 10.55213 | 10.01644 | 2 | 9.98356 | 20 |
| 41 | 54 32 | 5 28 | 43188 | 31 | 56812 | 44836 | 34 | 55164 | 01648 | 2 | 98352 | 19 |
| 42 | 54 24 | 5 36 | 43233 | 32 | 56767 | 44884 | 34 | 55116 | 01651 | 2 | 98349 | 18 |
| 43 | 54 16 | 5 44 | 43278 | 33 | 56722 | 44933 | 35 | 55067 | 01655 | 3 | 98345 | 17 |
| 44 | 54 8 | 5 52 | 43323 | 33 | 56677 | 44981 | 36 | 55019 | 01658 | 3 | 98342 | 16 |
| 45 | 9 54 0 | 2 6 0 | 9.43367 | 34 | 10.56633 | 9.45029 | 37 | 10.54971 | 10.01662 | 3 | 9.98338 | 15 |
| 46 | 53 52 | 6 8 | 43412 | 35 | 56588 | 45078 | 38 | 54922 | 01666 | 3 | 98334 | 14 |
| 47 | 53 44 | 6 16 | 43457 | 36 | 56543 | 45126 | 38 | 54874 | 01669 | 3 | 98331 | 13 |
| 48 | 53 36 | 6 24 | 43502 | 36 | 56498 | 45174 | 39 | 54826 | 01673 | 3 | 98327 | 12 |
| 49 | 53 28 | 6 32 | 43546 | 37 | 56454 | 45222 | 40 | 54778 | 01676 | 3 | 98324 | 11 |
| 50 | 9 53 20 | 2 6 40 | 9.43591 | 38 | 10.56409 | 9.45271 | 41 | 10.54729 | 10.01680 | 3 | 9.98320 | 10 |
| 51 | 53 12 | 6 48 | 43635 | 39 | 56365 | 45319 | 42 | 54681 | 01683 | 3 | 98317 | 9 |
| 52 | 53 4 | 6 56 | 43680 | 39 | 56320 | 45367 | 43 | 54633 | 01687 | 3 | 98313 | 8 |
| 53 | 52 56 | 7 4 | 43724 | 40 | 56276 | 45415 | 43 | 54585 | 01691 | 3 | 98309 | 7 |
| 54 | 52 48 | 7 12 | 43769 | 41 | 56231 | 45463 | 44 | 54537 | 01694 | 3 | 98306 | 6 |
| 55 | 9 52 40 | 2 7 20 | 9.43813 | 42 | 10.56187 | 9.45511 | 45 | 10.54489 | 10.01698 | 3 | 9.98302 | 5 |
| 56 | 52 32 | 7 28 | 43857 | 43 | 56143 | 45559 | 46 | 54441 | 01701 | 3 | 98299 | 4 |
| 57 | 52 24 | 7 36 | 43901 | 43 | 56099 | 45606 | 47 | 54394 | 01705 | 3 | 98295 | 3 |
| 58 | 52 16 | 7 44 | 43946 | 44 | 56054 | 45654 | 47 | 54346 | 01709 | 3 | 98291 | 2 |
| 59 | 52 8 | 7 52 | 43990 | 45 | 56010 | 45702 | 48 | 54298 | 01712 | 3 | 98288 | 1 |
| 60 | 52 0 | 8 0 | 44034 | 46 | 55966 | 45750 | 49 | 54250 | 01716 | 4 | 98284 | 0 |
| M | Hour P.M. | Hour A.M. | A Cosine. | Diff. | A Secant. | B Cotangent | Diff. | B Tangent. | C Cosecant. | Diff. | C Sine. | M |

105° 74°

| Seconds of time ...... | | 1s | 2s | 3s | 4s | 5s | 6s | 7s |
|---|---|---|---|---|---|---|---|---|
| Prop. parts of cols. | A | 6 | 11 | 17 | 23 | 28 | 34 | 40 |
| | B | 6 | 12 | 18 | 25 | 31 | 37 | 43 |
| | C | 0 | 1 | 1 | 2 | 2 | 3 | 3 |

# TABLE XXVII.

## Log. Sines, Tangents, and Secants.

8h — 16° — Gh. — 163°

| M | Hour A.M. | Hour P.M. | A Sine. | Diff. | A Cosecant. | B Tangent. | Diff. | B Cotangent | C Secant. | Diff. | C Cosine. | M |
|---|---|---|---|---|---|---|---|---|---|---|---|---|
| 0 | 9 52 0 | 2 8 0 | 9.44034 | 0 | 10.55966 | 9.45750 | 0 | 10.54250 | 10.01716 | 0 | 9.98284 | 60 |
| 1 | 51 52 | 8 8 | 44078 | 1 | 55922 | 45797 | 1 | 54203 | 01719 | 0 | 98281 | 59 |
| 2 | 51 44 | 8 16 | 44122 | 1 | 55878 | 45845 | 2 | 54155 | 01723 | 0 | 98277 | 58 |
| 3 | 51 36 | 8 24 | 44166 | 2 | 55834 | 45892 | 2 | 54108 | 01727 | 0 | 98273 | 57 |
| 4 | 51 28 | 8 32 | 44210 | 3 | 55790 | 45940 | 3 | 54060 | 01730 | 0 | 98270 | 56 |
| 5 | 9 51 20 | 2 8 40 | 9.44253 | 4 | 10.55747 | 9.45987 | 4 | 10.54013 | 10.01734 | 0 | 9.98266 | 55 |
| 6 | 51 12 | 8 48 | 44297 | 4 | 55703 | 46035 | 5 | 53965 | 01738 | 0 | 98262 | 54 |
| 7 | 51 4 | 8 56 | 44341 | 5 | 55659 | 46082 | 5 | 53918 | 01741 | 0 | 98259 | 53 |
| 8 | 50 56 | 9 4 | 44385 | 6 | 55615 | 46130 | 6 | 53870 | 01745 | 0 | 98255 | 52 |
| 9 | 50 48 | 9 12 | 44428 | 6 | 55572 | 46177 | 7 | 53823 | 01749 | 1 | 98251 | 51 |
| 10 | 9 50 40 | 2 9 20 | 9.44472 | 7 | 10.55528 | 9.46224 | 8 | 10.53776 | 10.01752 | 1 | 9.98248 | 50 |
| 11 | 50 32 | 9 28 | 44516 | 8 | 55484 | 46271 | 9 | 53729 | 01756 | 1 | 98244 | 49 |
| 12 | 50 24 | 9 36 | 44559 | 9 | 55441 | 46319 | 9 | 53681 | 01760 | 1 | 98240 | 48 |
| 13 | 50 16 | 9 44 | 44602 | 9 | 55398 | 46366 | 10 | 53634 | 01763 | 1 | 98237 | 47 |
| 14 | 50 8 | 9 52 | 44646 | 10 | 55354 | 46413 | 11 | 53587 | 01767 | 1 | 98233 | 46 |
| 15 | 9 50 0 | 2 10 0 | 9.44689 | 11 | 10.55311 | 9.46460 | 12 | 10.53540 | 10.01771 | 1 | 9.98229 | 45 |
| 16 | 49 52 | 10 8 | 44733 | 11 | 55267 | 46507 | 12 | 53493 | 01774 | 1 | 98226 | 44 |
| 17 | 49 44 | 10 16 | 44776 | 12 | 55224 | 46554 | 13 | 53446 | 01778 | 1 | 98222 | 43 |
| 18 | 49 36 | 10 24 | 44819 | 13 | 55181 | 46601 | 14 | 53399 | 01782 | 1 | 98218 | 42 |
| 19 | 49 28 | 10 32 | 44862 | 14 | 55138 | 46648 | 15 | 53352 | 01785 | 1 | 98215 | 41 |
| 20 | 9 49 20 | 2 10 40 | 9.44905 | 14 | 10.55095 | 9.46694 | 15 | 10.53306 | 10.01789 | 1 | 9.98211 | 40 |
| 21 | 49 12 | 10 48 | 44948 | 15 | 55052 | 46741 | 16 | 53259 | 01793 | 1 | 98207 | 39 |
| 22 | 49 4 | 10 56 | 44992 | 16 | 55008 | 46788 | 17 | 53212 | 01796 | 1 | 98204 | 38 |
| 23 | 48 56 | 11 4 | 45035 | 16 | 54965 | 46835 | 18 | 53165 | 01800 | 1 | 98200 | 37 |
| 24 | 48 48 | 11 12 | 45077 | 17 | 54923 | 46881 | 19 | 53119 | 01804 | 1 | 98196 | 36 |
| 25 | 9 48 40 | 2 11 20 | 9.45120 | 18 | 10.54880 | 9.46928 | 19 | 10.53072 | 10.01808 | 2 | 9.98192 | 35 |
| 26 | 48 32 | 11 28 | 45163 | 18 | 54837 | 46975 | 20 | 53025 | 01811 | 2 | 98189 | 34 |
| 27 | 48 24 | 11 36 | 45206 | 19 | 54794 | 47021 | 21 | 52979 | 01815 | 2 | 98185 | 33 |
| 28 | 48 16 | 11 44 | 45249 | 20 | 54751 | 47068 | 22 | 52932 | 01819 | 2 | 98181 | 32 |
| 29 | 48 8 | 11 52 | 45292 | 21 | 54708 | 47114 | 22 | 52886 | 01823 | 2 | 98177 | 31 |
| 30 | 9 48 0 | 2 12 0 | 9.45334 | 21 | 10.54666 | 9.47160 | 23 | 10.52840 | 10.01826 | 2 | 9.98174 | 30 |
| 31 | 47 52 | 12 8 | 45377 | 22 | 54623 | 47207 | 24 | 52793 | 01830 | 2 | 98170 | 29 |
| 32 | 47 44 | 12 16 | 45419 | 23 | 54581 | 47253 | 25 | 52747 | 01834 | 2 | 98166 | 28 |
| 33 | 47 36 | 12 24 | 45462 | 23 | 54538 | 47299 | 26 | 52701 | 01838 | 2 | 98162 | 27 |
| 34 | 47 28 | 12 32 | 45504 | 24 | 54496 | 47346 | 26 | 52654 | 01841 | 2 | 98159 | 26 |
| 35 | 9 47 20 | 2 12 40 | 9.45547 | 25 | 10.54453 | 9.47392 | 27 | 10.52608 | 10.01845 | 2 | 9.98155 | 25 |
| 36 | 47 12 | 12 48 | 45589 | 26 | 54411 | 47438 | 28 | 52562 | 01849 | 2 | 98151 | 24 |
| 37 | 47 4 | 12 56 | 45632 | 26 | 54368 | 47484 | 29 | 52516 | 01853 | 2 | 98147 | 23 |
| 38 | 46 56 | 13 4 | 45674 | 27 | 54326 | 47530 | 29 | 52470 | 01856 | 2 | 98144 | 22 |
| 39 | 46 48 | 13 12 | 45716 | 28 | 54284 | 47576 | 30 | 52424 | 01860 | 2 | 98140 | 21 |
| 40 | 9 46 40 | 2 13 20 | 9.45758 | 28 | 10.54242 | 9.47622 | 31 | 10.52378 | 10.01864 | 2 | 9.98136 | 20 |
| 41 | 46 32 | 13 28 | 45801 | 29 | 54199 | 47668 | 32 | 52332 | 01868 | 3 | 98132 | 19 |
| 42 | 46 24 | 13 36 | 45843 | 30 | 54157 | 47714 | 32 | 52286 | 01871 | 3 | 98129 | 18 |
| 43 | 46 16 | 13 44 | 45885 | 31 | 54115 | 47760 | 33 | 52240 | 01875 | 3 | 98125 | 17 |
| 44 | 46 8 | 13 52 | 45927 | 31 | 54073 | 47806 | 34 | 52194 | 01879 | 3 | 98121 | 16 |
| 45 | 9 46 0 | 2 14 0 | 9.45969 | 32 | 10.54031 | 9.47852 | 35 | 10.52148 | 10.01883 | 3 | 9 98117 | 15 |
| 46 | 45 52 | 14 8 | 46011 | 33 | 53989 | 47897 | 36 | 52103 | 01887 | 3 | 98113 | 14 |
| 47 | 45 44 | 14 16 | 46053 | 33 | 53947 | 47943 | 36 | 52057 | 01890 | 3 | 98110 | 13 |
| 48 | 45 36 | 14 24 | 46095 | 34 | 53905 | 47989 | 37 | 52011 | 01894 | 3 | 98106 | 12 |
| 49 | 45 28 | 14 32 | 46136 | 35 | 53864 | 48035 | 38 | 51965 | 01898 | 3 | 98102 | 11 |
| 50 | 9 45 20 | 2 14 40 | 9.46178 | 36 | 10.53822 | 9.48080 | 39 | 10.51920 | 10.01902 | 3 | 9.98098 | 10 |
| 51 | 45 12 | 14 48 | 46220 | 36 | 53780 | 48126 | 39 | 51874 | 01906 | 3 | 98094 | 9 |
| 52 | 45 4 | 14 56 | 46262 | 37 | 53738 | 48171 | 40 | 51829 | 01910 | 3 | 98090 | 8 |
| 53 | 44 56 | 15 4 | 46303 | 38 | 53697 | 48217 | 41 | 51783 | 01913 | 3 | 98087 | 7 |
| 54 | 44 48 | 15 12 | 46345 | 38 | 53655 | 48262 | 42 | 51738 | 01917 | 3 | 98083 | 6 |
| 55 | 9 44 40 | 2 15 20 | 9.46386 | 39 | 10.53614 | 9.48307 | 43 | 10.51693 | 10.01921 | 3 | 9.98079 | 5 |
| 56 | 44 32 | 15 28 | 46428 | 40 | 53572 | 48353 | 43 | 51647 | 01925 | 3 | 98075 | 4 |
| 57 | 44 24 | 15 36 | 46469 | 41 | 53531 | 48398 | 44 | 51602 | 01929 | 4 | 98071 | 3 |
| 58 | 44 16 | 15 44 | 46511 | 41 | 53489 | 48443 | 45 | 51557 | 01933 | 4 | 98067 | 2 |
| 59 | 44 8 | 15 52 | 46552 | 42 | 53448 | 48489 | 46 | 51511 | 01937 | 4 | 98063 | 1 |
| 60 | 44 0 | 16 0 | 46594 | 43 | 53406 | 48534 | 46 | 51466 | 01940 | 4 | 98060 | 0 |
| M | Hour P.M. | Hour A.M. | A Cosine. | Diff. | A Secant. | B Cotangent | Diff. | B Tangent. | C Cosecant. | Diff. | C Sine. | M |

106° — 73°

| Seconds of time …… | | 1s | 2s | 3s | 4s | 5s | 6s | 7s |
|---|---|---|---|---|---|---|---|---|
| Prop. parts of cols. | A | 5 | 11 | 16 | 21 | 27 | 32 | 37 |
| | B | 6 | 12 | 17 | 23 | 29 | 35 | 41 |
| | C | 0 | | 1 | 2 | 2 | 3 | 3 |

# TABLE XXVII.

## Log. Sines, Tangents, and Secants.

S'. G'.

| 17° | | | A | | A | B | | B | C | | C | 162° |
|---|---|---|---|---|---|---|---|---|---|---|---|---|
| M | Hour A.M. | Hour P.M. | Sine. | Diff. | Cosecant. | Tangent. | Diff. | Cotangent | Secant. | Diff. | Cosine. | M |
| 0 | 9 44 0 | 2 16 0 | 9.46594 | 0 | 10.53406 | 9.48534 | 0 | 10.51466 | 10.01940 | 0 | 9.98060 | 60 |
| 1 | 43 52 | 16 8 | 46635 | 1 | 53365 | 48579 | 1 | 51421 | 01944 | 0 | 98056 | 59 |
| 2 | 43 44 | 16 16 | 46676 | 1 | 53324 | 48624 | 1 | 51376 | 01948 | 0 | 98052 | 58 |
| 3 | 43 36 | 16 24 | 46717 | 2 | 53283 | 48669 | 2 | 51331 | 01952 | 0 | 98048 | 57 |
| 4 | 43 28 | 16 32 | 46758 | 3 | 53242 | 48714 | 3 | 51286 | 01956 | 0 | 98044 | 56 |
| 5 | 9 43 20 | 2 16 40 | 9.46800 | 3 | 10.53200 | 9.48759 | 4 | 10.51241 | 10.01960 | 0 | 9.98040 | 55 |
| 6 | 43 12 | 16 48 | 46841 | 4 | 53159 | 48804 | 4 | 51196 | 01964 | 0 | 98036 | 54 |
| 7 | 43 4 | 16 56 | 46882 | 5 | 53118 | 48849 | 5 | 51151 | 01968 | 0 | 98032 | 53 |
| 8 | 42 56 | 17 4 | 46923 | 5 | 53077 | 48894 | 6 | 51106 | 01971 | 1 | 98029 | 52 |
| 9 | 42 48 | 17 12 | 46964 | 6 | 53036 | 48939 | 7 | 51061 | 01975 | 1 | 98025 | 51 |
| 10 | 9 42 40 | 2 17 20 | 9.47005 | 7 | 10.52995 | 9.48984 | 7 | 10.51016 | 10.01979 | 1 | 9.98021 | 50 |
| 11 | 42 32 | 17 28 | 47045 | 7 | 52955 | 49029 | 8 | 50971 | 01983 | 1 | 98017 | 49 |
| 12 | 42 24 | 17 36 | 47086 | 8 | 52914 | 49073 | 9 | 50927 | 01987 | 1 | 98013 | 48 |
| 13 | 42 16 | 17 44 | 47127 | 9 | 52873 | 49118 | 10 | 50882 | 01991 | 1 | 98009 | 47 |
| 14 | 42 8 | 17 52 | 47168 | 9 | 52832 | 49163 | 10 | 50837 | 01995 | 1 | 98005 | 46 |
| 15 | 9 42 0 | 2 18 0 | 9.47209 | 10 | 10.52791 | 9.49207 | 11 | 10.50793 | 10.01999 | 1 | 9.98001 | 45 |
| 16 | 41 52 | 18 8 | 47249 | 11 | 52751 | 49252 | 12 | 50748 | 02003 | 1 | 97997 | 44 |
| 17 | 41 44 | 18 16 | 47290 | 11 | 52710 | 49296 | 12 | 50704 | 02007 | 1 | 97993 | 43 |
| 18 | 41 36 | 18 24 | 47330 | 12 | 52670 | 49341 | 13 | 50659 | 02011 | 1 | 97989 | 42 |
| 19 | 41 28 | 18 32 | 47371 | 13 | 52629 | 49385 | 14 | 50615 | 02014 | 1 | 97986 | 41 |
| 20 | 9 41 20 | 2 18 40 | 9.47411 | 13 | 10.52589 | 9.49430 | 15 | 10.50570 | 10.02018 | 1 | 9.97982 | 40 |
| 21 | 41 12 | 18 48 | 47452 | 14 | 52548 | 49474 | 15 | 50526 | 02022 | 1 | 97978 | 39 |
| 22 | 41 4 | 18 56 | 47492 | 15 | 52508 | 49519 | 16 | 50481 | 02026 | 1 | 97974 | 38 |
| 23 | 40 56 | 19 4 | 47533 | 15 | 52467 | 49563 | 17 | 50437 | 02030 | 2 | 97970 | 37 |
| 24 | 40 48 | 19 12 | 47573 | 16 | 52427 | 49607 | 18 | 50393 | 02034 | 2 | 97966 | 36 |
| 25 | 9 40 40 | 2 19 20 | 9.47613 | 17 | 10.52387 | 9.49652 | 18 | 10.50348 | 10.02038 | 2 | 9.97962 | 35 |
| 26 | 40 32 | 19 28 | 47654 | 17 | 52346 | 49696 | 19 | 50304 | 02042 | 2 | 97958 | 34 |
| 27 | 40 24 | 19 36 | 47694 | 18 | 52306 | 49740 | 20 | 50260 | 02046 | 2 | 97954 | 33 |
| 28 | 40 16 | 19 44 | 47734 | 19 | 52266 | 49784 | 21 | 50216 | 02050 | 2 | 97950 | 32 |
| 29 | 40 8 | 19 52 | 47774 | 19 | 52226 | 49828 | 21 | 50172 | 02054 | 2 | 97946 | 31 |
| 30 | 9 40 0 | 2 20 0 | 9.47814 | 20 | 10.52186 | 9.49872 | 22 | 10.50128 | 10.02058 | 2 | 9.97942 | 30 |
| 31 | 39 52 | 20 8 | 47854 | 21 | 52146 | 49916 | 23 | 50084 | 02062 | 2 | 97938 | 29 |
| 32 | 39 44 | 20 16 | 47894 | 21 | 52106 | 49960 | 24 | 50040 | 02066 | 2 | 97934 | 28 |
| 33 | 39 36 | 20 24 | 47934 | 22 | 52066 | 50004 | 24 | 49996 | 02070 | 2 | 97930 | 27 |
| 34 | 39 28 | 20 32 | 47974 | 23 | 52026 | 50048 | 25 | 49952 | 02074 | 2 | 97926 | 26 |
| 35 | 9 39 20 | 2 20 40 | 9.48014 | 23 | 10.51986 | 9.50092 | 26 | 10.49908 | 10.02078 | 2 | 9.97922 | 25 |
| 36 | 39 12 | 20 48 | 48054 | 24 | 51946 | 50136 | 26 | 49864 | 02082 | 2 | 97918 | 24 |
| 37 | 39 4 | 20 56 | 48094 | 25 | 51906 | 50180 | 27 | 49820 | 02086 | 2 | 97914 | 23 |
| 38 | 38 56 | 21 4 | 48133 | 25 | 51867 | 50223 | 28 | 49777 | 02090 | 3 | 97910 | 22 |
| 39 | 38 48 | 21 12 | 48173 | 26 | 51827 | 50267 | 29 | 49733 | 02094 | 3 | 97906 | 21 |
| 40 | 9 38 40 | 2 21 20 | 9.48213 | 27 | 10.51787 | 9.50311 | 29 | 10.49689 | 10.02098 | 3 | 9.97902 | 20 |
| 41 | 38 32 | 21 28 | 48252 | 27 | 51748 | 50355 | 30 | 49645 | 02102 | 3 | 97898 | 19 |
| 42 | 38 24 | 21 36 | 48292 | 28 | 51708 | 50398 | 31 | 49602 | 02106 | 3 | 97894 | 18 |
| 43 | 38 16 | 21 44 | 48332 | 29 | 51668 | 50442 | 32 | 49558 | 02110 | 3 | 97890 | 17 |
| 44 | 38 8 | 21 52 | 48371 | 29 | 51629 | 50485 | 32 | 49515 | 02114 | 3 | 97886 | 16 |
| 45 | 9 38 0 | 2 22 0 | 9.48411 | 30 | 10.51589 | 9.50529 | 33 | 10.49471 | 10.02118 | 3 | 9.97882 | 15 |
| 46 | 37 52 | 22 8 | 48450 | 31 | 51550 | 50572 | 34 | 49428 | 02122 | 3 | 97878 | 14 |
| 47 | 37 44 | 22 16 | 48490 | 31 | 51510 | 50616 | 35 | 49384 | 02126 | 3 | 97874 | 13 |
| 48 | 37 36 | 22 24 | 48529 | 32 | 51471 | 50659 | 35 | 49341 | 02130 | 3 | 97870 | 12 |
| 49 | 37 28 | 22 32 | 48568 | 33 | 51432 | 50703 | 36 | 49297 | 02134 | 3 | 97866 | 11 |
| 50 | 9 37 20 | 2 22 40 | 9.48607 | 33 | 10.51393 | 9.50746 | 37 | 10.49254 | 10.02139 | 3 | 9.97861 | 10 |
| 51 | 37 12 | 22 48 | 48647 | 34 | 51353 | 50789 | 37 | 49211 | 02143 | 3 | 97857 | 9 |
| 52 | 37 4 | 22 56 | 48686 | 35 | 51314 | 50833 | 38 | 49167 | 02147 | 3 | 97853 | 8 |
| 53 | 36 56 | 23 4 | 48725 | 35 | 51275 | 50876 | 39 | 49124 | 02151 | 4 | 97849 | 7 |
| 54 | 36 48 | 23 12 | 48764 | 36 | 51236 | 50919 | 40 | 49081 | 02155 | 4 | 97845 | 6 |
| 55 | 9 36 40 | 2 23 20 | 9.48803 | 37 | 10.51197 | 9.50962 | 40 | 10.49038 | 10.02159 | 4 | 9.97841 | 5 |
| 56 | 36 32 | 23 28 | 48842 | 37 | 51158 | 51005 | 41 | 48995 | 02163 | 4 | 97837 | 4 |
| 57 | 36 24 | 23 36 | 48881 | 38 | 51119 | 51048 | 42 | 48952 | 02167 | 4 | 97833 | 3 |
| 58 | 36 16 | 23 44 | 48920 | 39 | 51080 | 51092 | 43 | 48908 | 02171 | 4 | 97829 | 2 |
| 59 | 36 8 | 23 52 | 48959 | 39 | 51041 | 51135 | 43 | 48865 | 02175 | 4 | 97825 | 1 |
| 60 | 36 0 | 24 0 | 48998 | 40 | 51002 | 51178 | 44 | 48822 | 02179 | 4 | 97821 | 0 |
| M | Hour P.M. | Hour A.M. | Cosine. | Diff. | Secant. | Cotangent | Diff. | Tangent. | Cosecant. | Diff. | Sine. | M |
| 107° | | | A | | A | B | | B | C | | C | 72° |

| Seconds of time ...... | | 1s | 2s | 3s | 4s | 5s | 6s | 7s |
|---|---|---|---|---|---|---|---|---|
| Prop. parts of cols. | A | 5 | 10 | 15 | 20 | 25 | 30 | 35 |
| | B | 6 | 11 | 17 | 22 | 28 | 33 | 39 |
| | C | 0 | 1 | 1 | 2 | 2 | 3 | 3 |

# TABLE XXVII.

## Log. Sines, Tangents, and Secants.

S'. 18° G'. 161°

| | | | A | | A | B | | B | C | | C | |
|---|---|---|---|---|---|---|---|---|---|---|---|---|
| M | Hour A.M. | Hour P.M. | Sine. | Diff. | Cosecant. | Tangent. | Diff. | Cotangent | Secant. | Diff. | Cosine. | M |
| 0 | 9 36 0 | 2 24 0 | 9.48998 | 0 | 10.51002 | 9.51178 | 0 | 10.48822 | 10.02179 | 0 | 9.97821 | 60 |
| 1 | 35 52 | 24 8 | 49037 | 1 | 50963 | 51221 | 1 | 48779 | 02183 | 0 | 97817 | 59 |
| 2 | 35 44 | 24 16 | 49076 | 1 | 50924 | 51264 | 1 | 48736 | 02188 | 0 | 97812 | 58 |
| 3 | 35 36 | 24 24 | 49115 | 2 | 50885 | 51306 | 2 | 48694 | 02192 | 0 | 97808 | 57 |
| 4 | 35 28 | 24 32 | 49153 | 3 | 50847 | 51349 | 3 | 48651 | 02196 | 0 | 97804 | 56 |
| 5 | 9 35 20 | 2 24 40 | 9.49192 | 3 | 10.50808 | 9.51392 | 3 | 10.48608 | 10.02200 | 0 | 9.97800 | 55 |
| 6 | 35 12 | 24 48 | 49231 | 4 | 50769 | 51435 | 4 | 48565 | 02204 | 0 | 97796 | 54 |
| 7 | 35 4 | 24 56 | 49269 | 4 | 50731 | 51478 | 5 | 48522 | 02208 | 0 | 97792 | 53 |
| 8 | 34 56 | 25 4 | 49308 | 5 | 50692 | 51520 | 6 | 48480 | 02212 | 1 | 97788 | 52 |
| 9 | 34 48 | 25 12 | 49347 | 6 | 50653 | 51563 | 6 | 48437 | 02216 | 1 | 97784 | 51 |
| 10 | 9 34 40 | 2 25 20 | 9.49385 | 6 | 10.50615 | 9.51606 | 7 | 10.48394 | 10.02221 | 1 | 9.97779 | 50 |
| 11 | 34 32 | 25 28 | 49424 | 7 | 50576 | 51648 | 8 | 48352 | 02225 | 1 | 97775 | 49 |
| 12 | 34 24 | 25 36 | 49462 | 8 | 50538 | 51691 | 8 | 48309 | 02229 | 1 | 97771 | 48 |
| 13 | 34 16 | 25 44 | 49500 | 8 | 50500 | 51734 | 9 | 48266 | 02233 | 1 | 97767 | 47 |
| 14 | 34 8 | 25 52 | 49539 | 9 | 50461 | 51776 | 10 | 48224 | 02237 | 1 | 97763 | 46 |
| 15 | 9 34 0 | 2 26 0 | 9.49577 | 9 | 10.50423 | 9.51819 | 10 | 10.48181 | 10.02241 | 1 | 9.97759 | 45 |
| 16 | 33 52 | 26 8 | 49615 | 10 | 50385 | 51861 | 11 | 48139 | 02246 | 1 | 97754 | 44 |
| 17 | 33 44 | 26 16 | 49654 | 11 | 50346 | 51903 | 12 | 48097 | 02250 | 1 | 97750 | 43 |
| 18 | 33 36 | 26 24 | 49692 | 11 | 50308 | 51946 | 13 | 48054 | 02254 | 1 | 97746 | 42 |
| 19 | 33 28 | 26 32 | 49730 | 12 | 50270 | 51988 | 13 | 48012 | 02258 | 1 | 97742 | 41 |
| 20 | 9 33 20 | 2 26 40 | 9.49768 | 13 | 10.50232 | 9.52031 | 14 | 10.47969 | 10.02262 | 1 | 9.97738 | 40 |
| 21 | 33 12 | 26 48 | 49806 | 13 | 50194 | 52073 | 15 | 47927 | 02266 | 1 | 97734 | 39 |
| 22 | 33 4 | 26 56 | 49844 | 14 | 50156 | 52115 | 15 | 47885 | 02271 | 2 | 97729 | 38 |
| 23 | 32 56 | 27 4 | 49882 | 14 | 50118 | 52157 | 16 | 47843 | 02275 | 2 | 97725 | 37 |
| 24 | 32 48 | 27 12 | 49920 | 15 | 50080 | 52200 | 17 | 47800 | 02279 | 2 | 97721 | 36 |
| 25 | 9 32 40 | 2 27 20 | 9.49958 | 16 | 10.50042 | 9.52242 | 17 | 10.47758 | 10.02283 | 2 | 9.97717 | 35 |
| 26 | 32 32 | 27 28 | 49996 | 16 | 50004 | 52284 | 18 | 47716 | 02287 | 2 | 97713 | 34 |
| 27 | 32 24 | 27 36 | 50034 | 17 | 49966 | 52326 | 19 | 47674 | 02292 | 2 | 97708 | 33 |
| 28 | 32 16 | 27 44 | 50072 | 18 | 49928 | 52368 | 20 | 47632 | 02296 | 2 | 97704 | 32 |
| 29 | 32 8 | 27 52 | 50110 | 18 | 49890 | 52410 | 20 | 47590 | 02300 | 2 | 97700 | 31 |
| 30 | 9 32 0 | 2 28 0 | 9.50148 | 19 | 10.49852 | 9.52452 | 21 | 10.47548 | 10.02304 | 2 | 9.97696 | 30 |
| 31 | 31 52 | 28 8 | 50185 | 20 | 49815 | 52494 | 22 | 47506 | 02309 | 2 | 97691 | 29 |
| 32 | 31 44 | 28 16 | 50223 | 20 | 49777 | 52536 | 22 | 47464 | 02313 | 2 | 97687 | 28 |
| 33 | 31 36 | 28 24 | 50261 | 21 | 49739 | 52578 | 23 | 47422 | 02317 | 2 | 97683 | 27 |
| 34 | 31 28 | 28 32 | 50298 | 21 | 49702 | 52620 | 24 | 47380 | 02321 | 2 | 97679 | 26 |
| 35 | 9 31 20 | 2 28 40 | 9.50336 | 22 | 10.49664 | 9.52661 | 24 | 10.47339 | 10.02326 | 2 | 9.97674 | 25 |
| 36 | 31 12 | 28 48 | 50374 | 23 | 49626 | 52703 | 25 | 47297 | 02330 | 3 | 97670 | 24 |
| 37 | 31 4 | 28 56 | 50411 | 23 | 49589 | 52745 | 26 | 47255 | 02334 | 3 | 97666 | 23 |
| 38 | 30 56 | 29 4 | 50449 | 24 | 49551 | 52787 | 27 | 47213 | 02338 | 3 | 97662 | 22 |
| 39 | 30 48 | 29 12 | 50486 | 25 | 49514 | 52829 | 27 | 47171 | 02343 | 3 | 97657 | 21 |
| 40 | 9 30 40 | 2 29 20 | 9.50523 | 25 | 10.49477 | 9.52870 | 28 | 10.47130 | 10.02347 | 3 | 9.97653 | 20 |
| 41 | 30 32 | 29 28 | 50561 | 26 | 49439 | 52912 | 29 | 47088 | 02351 | 3 | 97649 | 19 |
| 42 | 30 24 | 29 36 | 50598 | 26 | 49402 | 52953 | 29 | 47047 | 02355 | 3 | 97645 | 18 |
| 43 | 30 16 | 29 44 | 50635 | 27 | 49365 | 52995 | 30 | 47005 | 02360 | 3 | 97640 | 17 |
| 44 | 30 8 | 29 52 | 50673 | 28 | 49327 | 53037 | 31 | 46963 | 02364 | 3 | 97636 | 16 |
| 45 | 9 30 0 | 2 30 0 | 9.50710 | 28 | 10.49290 | 9.53078 | 31 | 10.46922 | 10.02368 | 3 | 9.97632 | 15 |
| 46 | 29 52 | 30 8 | 50747 | 29 | 49253 | 53120 | 32 | 46880 | 02372 | 3 | 97628 | 14 |
| 47 | 29 44 | 30 16 | 50784 | 30 | 49216 | 53161 | 33 | 46839 | 02377 | 3 | 97623 | 13 |
| 48 | 29 36 | 30 24 | 50821 | 30 | 49179 | 53202 | 34 | 46798 | 02381 | 3 | 97619 | 12 |
| 49 | 29 28 | 30 32 | 50858 | 31 | 49142 | 53244 | 34 | 46756 | 02385 | 3 | 97615 | 11 |
| 50 | 9 29 20 | 2 30 40 | 9.50896 | 31 | 10.49104 | 9.53285 | 35 | 10.46715 | 10.02390 | 4 | 9.97610 | 10 |
| 51 | 29 12 | 30 48 | 50933 | 32 | 49067 | 53327 | 36 | 46673 | 02394 | 4 | 97606 | 9 |
| 52 | 29 4 | 30 56 | 50970 | 33 | 49030 | 53368 | 36 | 46632 | 02398 | 4 | 97602 | 8 |
| 53 | 28 56 | 31 4 | 51007 | 33 | 48993 | 53409 | 37 | 46591 | 02403 | 4 | 97597 | 7 |
| 54 | 28 48 | 31 12 | 51043 | 34 | 48957 | 53450 | 38 | 46550 | 02407 | 4 | 97593 | 6 |
| 55 | 9 28 40 | 2 31 20 | 9.51080 | 35 | 10.48920 | 9.53492 | 38 | 10.46508 | 10.02411 | 4 | 9.97589 | 5 |
| 56 | 28 32 | 31 28 | 51117 | 35 | 48883 | 53533 | 39 | 46467 | 02416 | 4 | 97584 | 4 |
| 57 | 28 24 | 31 36 | 51154 | 36 | 48846 | 53574 | 40 | 46426 | 02420 | 4 | 97580 | 3 |
| 58 | 28 16 | 31 44 | 51191 | 37 | 48809 | 53615 | 41 | 46385 | 02424 | 4 | 97576 | 2 |
| 59 | 28 8 | 31 52 | 51227 | 37 | 48773 | 53656 | 41 | 46344 | 02429 | 4 | 97571 | 1 |
| 60 | 28 0 | 32 0 | 51264 | 38 | 48736 | 53697 | 42 | 46303 | 02433 | 4 | 97567 | 0 |
| M | Hour P.M. | Hour A.M. | Cosine. | Diff. | Secant. | Cotangent | Diff. | Tangent. | Cosecant. | Diff. | Sine. | M |
| 108° | | | A | | A | B | | B | C | | C | 71° |

| Seconds of time ...... | | 1ˢ | 2ˢ | 3ˢ | 4ˢ | 5ˢ | 6ˢ | 7ˢ |
|---|---|---|---|---|---|---|---|---|
| Prop. parts of cols | A | 5 | 9 | 14 | 19 | 24 | 28 | 33 |
| | B | 5 | 10 | 16 | 21 | 26 | 31 | 37 |
| | C | 1 | 1 | 2 | 2 | 3 | 3 | 4 |

# TABLE XXVII.

S′. Log. Sines, Tangents, and Secants. G′.

19° A A B B C C 160°

| M | Hour A.M. | Hour P.M. | Sine. | Diff. | Cosecant. | Tangent. | Diff. | Cotangent | Secant. | Diff. | Cosine. | M |
|---|---|---|---|---|---|---|---|---|---|---|---|---|
| 0 | 9 28 0 | 2 32 0 | 9.51264 | 0 | 10.48736 | 9.53697 | 0 | 10.46303 | 10.02433 | 0 | 9.97567 | 60 |
| 1 | 27 52 | 32 8 | 51301 | 1 | 48699 | 53738 | 1 | 46262 | 02437 | 0 | 97563 | 59 |
| 2 | 27 44 | 32 61 | 51338 | 1 | 48662 | 53779 | 1 | 46221 | 02442 | 0 | 97558 | 58 |
| 3 | 27 36 | 32 24 | 51374 | 2 | 48626 | 53820 | 2 | 46180 | 02446 | 0 | 97554 | 57 |
| 4 | 27 28 | 32 32 | 51411 | 2 | 48589 | 53861 | 3 | 46139 | 02450 | 0 | 97550 | 56 |
| 5 | 9 27 20 | 2 32 40 | 9.51447 | 3 | 10.48553 | 9.53902 | 3 | 10.46098 | 10.02455 | 0 | 9.97545 | 55 |
| 6 | 27 12 | 32 48 | 51484 | 4 | 48516 | 53943 | 4 | 46057 | 02459 | 0 | 97541 | 54 |
| 7 | 27 4 | 32 56 | 51520 | 4 | 48480 | 53984 | 5 | 46016 | 02464 | 1 | 97536 | 53 |
| 8 | 26 56 | 33 4 | 51557 | 5 | 48443 | 54025 | 5 | 45975 | 02468 | 1 | 97532 | 52 |
| 9 | 26 48 | 33 12 | 51593 | 5 | 48407 | 54065 | 6 | 45935 | 02472 | 1 | 97528 | 51 |
| 10 | 9 26 40 | 2 33 20 | 9.51629 | 6 | 10.48371 | 9.54106 | 7 | 10.45894 | 10.02477 | 1 | 9.97523 | 50 |
| 11 | 26 32 | 33 28 | 51666 | 7 | 48334 | 54147 | 7 | 45853 | 02481 | 1 | 97519 | 49 |
| 12 | 26 24 | 33 36 | 51702 | 7 | 48298 | 54187 | 8 | 45813 | 02485 | 1 | 97515 | 48 |
| 13 | 26 16 | 33 44 | 51738 | 8 | 48262 | 54228 | 9 | 45772 | 02490 | 1 | 97510 | 47 |
| 14 | 26 8 | 33 52 | 51774 | 8 | 48226 | 54269 | 9 | 45731 | 02494 | 1 | 97506 | 46 |
| 15 | 9 26 0 | 2 34 0 | 9.51811 | 9 | 10.48189 | 9.54309 | 10 | 10.45691 | 10.02499 | 1 | 9.97501 | 45 |
| 16 | 25 52 | 34 8 | 51847 | 10 | 48153 | 54350 | 11 | 45650 | 02503 | 1 | 97497 | 44 |
| 17 | 25 44 | 34 16 | 51883 | 10 | 48117 | 54390 | 11 | 45610 | 02508 | 1 | 97492 | 43 |
| 18 | 25 36 | 34 24 | 51919 | 11 | 48081 | 54431 | 12 | 45569 | 02512 | 1 | 97488 | 42 |
| 19 | 25 28 | 34 32 | 51955 | 11 | 48045 | 54471 | 13 | 45529 | 02516 | 1 | 97484 | 41 |
| 20 | 9 25 20 | 2 34 40 | 9.51991 | 12 | 10.48009 | 9.54512 | 13 | 10.45488 | 10.02521 | 1 | 9.97479 | 40 |
| 21 | 25 12 | 34 48 | 52027 | 12 | 47973 | 54552 | 14 | 45448 | 02525 | 2 | 97475 | 39 |
| 22 | 25 4 | 34 56 | 52063 | 13 | 47937 | 54593 | 15 | 45407 | 02530 | 2 | 97470 | 38 |
| 23 | 24 56 | 35 4 | 52099 | 14 | 47901 | 54633 | 15 | 45367 | 02534 | 2 | 97466 | 37 |
| 24 | 24 48 | 35 12 | 52135 | 14 | 47865 | 54673 | 16 | 45327 | 02539 | 2 | 97461 | 36 |
| 25 | 9 24 40 | 2 35 20 | 9.52171 | 15 | 10.47829 | 9.54714 | 17 | 10.45286 | 10.02543 | 2 | 9.97457 | 35 |
| 26 | 24 32 | 35 28 | 52207 | 15 | 47793 | 54754 | 17 | 45246 | 02547 | 2 | 97453 | 34 |
| 27 | 24 24 | 35 36 | 52242 | 16 | 47758 | 54794 | 18 | 45206 | 02552 | 2 | 97448 | 33 |
| 28 | 24 16 | 35 44 | 52278 | 17 | 47722 | 54835 | 19 | 45165 | 02556 | 2 | 97444 | 32 |
| 29 | 24 8 | 35 52 | 52314 | 17 | 47686 | 54875 | 19 | 45125 | 02561 | 2 | 97439 | 31 |
| 30 | 9 24 0 | 2 36 0 | 9.52350 | 18 | 10.47650 | 9.54915 | 20 | 10.45085 | 10.02565 | 2 | 9.97435 | 30 |
| 31 | 23 52 | 36 8 | 52385 | 18 | 47615 | 54955 | 21 | 45045 | 02570 | 2 | 97430 | 29 |
| 32 | 23 44 | 36 16 | 52421 | 19 | 47579 | 54995 | 21 | 45005 | 02574 | 2 | 97426 | 28 |
| 33 | 23 36 | 36 24 | 52456 | 20 | 47544 | 55035 | 22 | 44965 | 02579 | 2 | 97421 | 27 |
| 34 | 23 28 | 36 32 | 52492 | 20 | 47508 | 55075 | 23 | 44925 | 02583 | 3 | 97417 | 26 |
| 35 | 9 23 20 | 2 36 40 | 9.52527 | 21 | 10.47473 | 9.55115 | 23 | 10.44885 | 10.02588 | 3 | 9.97412 | 25 |
| 36 | 23 12 | 36 48 | 52563 | 21 | 47437 | 55155 | 24 | 44845 | 02592 | 3 | 97408 | 24 |
| 37 | 23 4 | 36 56 | 52598 | 22 | 47402 | 55195 | 25 | 44805 | 02597 | 3 | 97403 | 23 |
| 38 | 22 56 | 37 4 | 52634 | 23 | 47366 | 55235 | 25 | 44765 | 02601 | 3 | 97399 | 22 |
| 39 | 22 48 | 37 12 | 52669 | 23 | 47331 | 55275 | 26 | 44725 | 02606 | 3 | 97394 | 21 |
| 40 | 9 22 40 | 2 37 20 | 9.52705 | 24 | 10.47295 | 9.55315 | 27 | 10.44685 | 10.02610 | 3 | 9.97390 | 20 |
| 41 | 22 32 | 37 28 | 52740 | 24 | 47260 | 55355 | 27 | 44645 | 02615 | 3 | 97385 | 19 |
| 42 | 22 24 | 37 36 | 52775 | 25 | 47225 | 55395 | 28 | 44605 | 02619 | 3 | 97381 | 18 |
| 43 | 22 16 | 37 44 | 52811 | 26 | 47189 | 55434 | 29 | 44566 | 02624 | 3 | 97376 | 17 |
| 44 | 22 8 | 37 52 | 52846 | 26 | 47154 | 55474 | 29 | 44526 | 02628 | 3 | 97372 | 16 |
| 45 | 9 22 0 | 2 38 0 | 9.52881 | 27 | 10.47119 | 9.55514 | 30 | 10.44486 | 10.02633 | 3 | 9.97367 | 15 |
| 46 | 21 52 | 38 8 | 52916 | 27 | 47084 | 55554 | 31 | 44446 | 02637 | 3 | 97363 | 14 |
| 47 | 21 44 | 38 16 | 52951 | 28 | 47049 | 55593 | 31 | 44407 | 02642 | 3 | 97358 | 13 |
| 48 | 21 36 | 38 24 | 52986 | 29 | 47014 | 55633 | 32 | 44367 | 02647 | 4 | 97353 | 12 |
| 49 | 21 28 | 38 32 | 53021 | 29 | 46979 | 55673 | 33 | 44327 | 02651 | 4 | 97349 | 11 |
| 50 | 9 21 20 | 2 38 40 | 9.53056 | 30 | 10.46944 | 9.55712 | 33 | 10.44288 | 10.02656 | 4 | 9.97344 | 10 |
| 51 | 21 12 | 38 48 | 53092 | 30 | 46908 | 55752 | 34 | 44248 | 02660 | 4 | 97340 | 9 |
| 52 | 21 4 | 38 56 | 53126 | 31 | 46874 | 55791 | 35 | 44209 | 02665 | 4 | 97335 | 8 |
| 53 | 20 56 | 39 4 | 53161 | 32 | 46839 | 55831 | 35 | 44169 | 02669 | 4 | 97331 | 7 |
| 54 | 20 48 | 39 12 | 53196 | 32 | 46804 | 55870 | 36 | 44130 | 02674 | 4 | 97326 | 6 |
| 55 | 9 20 40 | 2 39 20 | 9.53231 | 33 | 10.46769 | 9.55910 | 37 | 10.44090 | 10.02678 | 4 | 9.97322 | 5 |
| 56 | 20 32 | 39 28 | 53266 | 33 | 46734 | 55949 | 37 | 44051 | 02683 | 4 | 97317 | 4 |
| 57 | 20 24 | 39 36 | 53301 | 34 | 46699 | 55989 | 38 | 44011 | 02688 | 4 | 97312 | 3 |
| 58 | 20 16 | 39 44 | 53336 | 34 | 46664 | 56028 | 39 | 43972 | 02692 | 4 | 97308 | 2 |
| 59 | 20 8 | 39 52 | 53370 | 35 | 46630 | 56067 | 39 | 43933 | 02697 | 4 | 97303 | 1 |
| 60 | 20 0 | 40 0 | 53405 | 36 | 46595 | 56107 | 40 | 43893 | 02701 | 4 | 97299 | 0 |
| M | Hour P.M. | Hour A.M. | Cosine. | Diff. | Secant. | Cotangent | Diff. | Tangent. | Cosecant. | Diff. | Sine. | M |

109° A A B B C C 70°

| Seconds of time ...... | | 1s | 2s | 3s | 4s | 5s | 6s | 7s |
|---|---|---|---|---|---|---|---|---|
| Prop. parts of cols. | A | 4 | 9 | 13 | 18 | 22 | 27 | 31 |
| | B | 5 | 10 | 15 | 20 | 25 | 30 | 35 |
| | C | 1 | 1 | 2 | 2 | 3 | 3 | 4 |

# TABLE XXVII.

## Log. Sines, Tangents, and Secants.

S'. 20° | A | A | B | B | C | C 159° G'.

| M | Hour A.M. | Hour P.M. | Sine. | Diff. | Cosecant. | Tangent. | Diff. | Cotangent | Secant. | Diff. | Cosine. | M |
|---|---|---|---|---|---|---|---|---|---|---|---|---|
| 0 | 9 20 0 | 2 40 0 | 9.53405 | 0 | 10.46595 | 9.56107 | 0 | 10.43893 | 10.02701 | 0 | 9.97299 | 60 |
| 1 | 19 52 | 40 8 | 53440 | 1 | 46560 | 56146 | 1 | 43854 | 02706 | 0 | 97294 | 59 |
| 2 | 19 44 | 40 16 | 53475 | 1 | 46525 | 56185 | 1 | 43815 | 02711 | 0 | 97289 | 58 |
| 3 | 19 36 | 40 24 | 53509 | 2 | 46491 | 56224 | 2 | 43776 | 02715 | 0 | 97285 | 57 |
| 4 | 19 28 | 40 32 | 53544 | 2 | 46456 | 56264 | 3 | 43736 | 02720 | 0 | 97280 | 56 |
| 5 | 9 19 20 | 2 40 40 | 9.53578 | 3 | 10.46422 | 9.56303 | 3 | 10.43697 | 10.02724 | 0 | 9.97276 | 55 |
| 6 | 19 12 | 40 48 | 53613 | 3 | 46387 | 56342 | 4 | 43658 | 02729 | 0 | 97271 | 54 |
| 7 | 19 4 | 40 56 | 53647 | 4 | 46353 | 56381 | 4 | 43619 | 02734 | 1 | 97266 | 53 |
| 8 | 18 56 | 41 4 | 53682 | 5 | 46318 | 56420 | 5 | 43580 | 02738 | 1 | 97262 | 52 |
| 9 | 18 48 | 41 12 | 53716 | 5 | 46284 | 56459 | 6 | 43541 | 02743 | 1 | 97257 | 51 |
| 10 | 9 18 40 | 2 41 20 | 9.53751 | 6 | 10.46249 | 9.56498 | 6 | 10.43502 | 10.02748 | 1 | 9.97252 | 50 |
| 11 | 18 32 | 41 28 | 53785 | 6 | 46215 | 56537 | 7 | 43463 | 02752 | 1 | 97248 | 49 |
| 12 | 18 24 | 41 36 | 53819 | 7 | 46181 | 56576 | 8 | 43424 | 02757 | 1 | 97243 | 48 |
| 13 | 18 16 | 41 44 | 53854 | 7 | 46146 | 56615 | 8 | 43385 | 02762 | 1 | 97238 | 47 |
| 14 | 18 8 | 41 52 | 53888 | 8 | 46112 | 56654 | 9 | 43346 | 02766 | 1 | 97234 | 46 |
| 15 | 9 18 0 | 2 42 0 | 9.53922 | 8 | 10.46078 | 9.56693 | 10 | 10.43307 | 10.02771 | 1 | 9.97229 | 45 |
| 16 | 17 52 | 42 8 | 53957 | 9 | 46043 | 56732 | 10 | 43268 | 02776 | 1 | 97224 | 44 |
| 17 | 17 44 | 42 16 | 53991 | 10 | 46009 | 56771 | 11 | 43229 | 02780 | 1 | 97220 | 43 |
| 18 | 17 36 | 42 24 | 54025 | 10 | 45975 | 56810 | 12 | 43190 | 02785 | 1 | 97215 | 42 |
| 19 | 17 28 | 42 32 | 54059 | 11 | 45941 | 56849 | 12 | 43151 | 02790 | 1 | 97210 | 41 |
| 20 | 9 17 20 | 2 42 40 | 9.54093 | 11 | 10.45907 | 9.56887 | 13 | 10.43113 | 10.02794 | 2 | 9.97206 | 40 |
| 21 | 17 12 | 42 48 | 54127 | 12 | 45873 | 56926 | 13 | 43074 | 02799 | 2 | 97201 | 39 |
| 22 | 17 4 | 42 56 | 54161 | 12 | 45839 | 56965 | 14 | 43035 | 02804 | 2 | 97196 | 38 |
| 23 | 16 56 | 43 4 | 54195 | 13 | 45805 | 57004 | 15 | 42996 | 02808 | 2 | 97192 | 37 |
| 24 | 16 48 | 43 12 | 54229 | 14 | 45771 | 57042 | 15 | 42958 | 02813 | 2 | 97187 | 36 |
| 25 | 9 16 40 | 2 43 20 | 9.54263 | 14 | 10.45737 | 9.57081 | 16 | 10.42919 | 10.02818 | 2 | 9.97182 | 35 |
| 26 | 16 32 | 43 28 | 54297 | 15 | 45703 | 57120 | 17 | 42880 | 02822 | 2 | 97178 | 34 |
| 27 | 16 24 | 43 36 | 54331 | 15 | 45669 | 57158 | 17 | 42842 | 02827 | 2 | 97173 | 33 |
| 28 | 16 16 | 43 44 | 54365 | 16 | 45635 | 57197 | 18 | 42803 | 02832 | 2 | 97168 | 32 |
| 29 | 16 8 | 43 52 | 54399 | 16 | 45601 | 57235 | 19 | 42765 | 02837 | 2 | 97163 | 31 |
| 30 | 9 16 0 | 2 44 0 | 9.54433 | 17 | 10.45567 | 9.57274 | 19 | 10.42726 | 10.02841 | 2 | 9.97159 | 30 |
| 31 | 15 52 | 44 8 | 54466 | 17 | 45534 | 57312 | 20 | 42688 | 02846 | 2 | 97154 | 29 |
| 32 | 15 44 | 44 16 | 54500 | 18 | 45500 | 57351 | 21 | 42649 | 02851 | 3 | 97149 | 28 |
| 33 | 15 36 | 44 24 | 54534 | 19 | 45466 | 57389 | 21 | 42611 | 02855 | 3 | 97145 | 27 |
| 34 | 15 28 | 44 32 | 54567 | 19 | 45433 | 57428 | 22 | 42572 | 02860 | 3 | 97140 | 26 |
| 35 | 9 15 20 | 2 44 40 | 9.54601 | 20 | 10.45399 | 9.57466 | 22 | 10.42534 | 10.02865 | 3 | 9.97135 | 25 |
| 36 | 15 12 | 44 48 | 54635 | 20 | 45365 | 57504 | 23 | 42496 | 02870 | 3 | 97130 | 24 |
| 37 | 15 4 | 44 56 | 54668 | 21 | 45332 | 57543 | 24 | 42457 | 02874 | 3 | 97126 | 23 |
| 38 | 14 56 | 45 4 | 54702 | 21 | 45298 | 57581 | 24 | 42419 | 02879 | 3 | 97121 | 22 |
| 39 | 14 48 | 45 12 | 54735 | 22 | 45265 | 57619 | 25 | 42381 | 02884 | 3 | 97116 | 21 |
| 40 | 9 14 40 | 2 45 20 | 9.54769 | 23 | 10.45231 | 9.57658 | 26 | 10.42342 | 10.02889 | 3 | 9.97111 | 20 |
| 41 | 14 32 | 45 28 | 54802 | 23 | 45198 | 57696 | 26 | 42304 | 02893 | 3 | 97107 | 19 |
| 42 | 14 24 | 45 36 | 54836 | 24 | 45164 | 57734 | 27 | 42266 | 02898 | 3 | 97102 | 18 |
| 43 | 14 16 | 45 44 | 54869 | 24 | 45131 | 57772 | 28 | 42228 | 02903 | 3 | 97097 | 17 |
| 44 | 14 8 | 45 52 | 54903 | 25 | 45097 | 57810 | 28 | 42190 | 02908 | 3 | 97092 | 16 |
| 45 | 9 14 0 | 2 46 0 | 9.54936 | 25 | 10.45064 | 9.57849 | 29 | 10.42151 | 10.02913 | 4 | 9.97087 | 15 |
| 46 | 13 52 | 46 8 | 54969 | 26 | 45031 | 57887 | 30 | 42113 | 02917 | 4 | 97083 | 14 |
| 47 | 13 44 | 46 16 | 55003 | 26 | 44997 | 57925 | 30 | 42075 | 02922 | 4 | 97078 | 13 |
| 48 | 13 36 | 46 24 | 55036 | 27 | 44964 | 57963 | 31 | 42037 | 02927 | 4 | 97073 | 12 |
| 49 | 13 28 | 46 32 | 55069 | 28 | 44931 | 58001 | 31 | 41999 | 02932 | 4 | 97068 | 11 |
| 50 | 9 13 20 | 2 46 40 | 9.55102 | 28 | 10.44898 | 9.58039 | 32 | 10.41961 | 10.02937 | 4 | 9.97063 | 10 |
| 51 | 13 12 | 46 48 | 55136 | 29 | 44864 | 58077 | 33 | 41923 | 02941 | 4 | 97059 | 9 |
| 52 | 13 4 | 46 56 | 55169 | 29 | 44831 | 58115 | 33 | 41885 | 02946 | 4 | 97054 | 8 |
| 53 | 12 56 | 47 4 | 55202 | 30 | 44798 | 58153 | 34 | 41847 | 02951 | 4 | 97049 | 7 |
| 54 | 12 48 | 47 12 | 55235 | 30 | 44765 | 58191 | 35 | 41809 | 02956 | 4 | 97044 | 6 |
| 55 | 9 12 40 | 2 47 20 | 9.55268 | 31 | 10.44732 | 9.58229 | 35 | 10.41771 | 10.02961 | 4 | 9.97039 | 5 |
| 56 | 12 32 | 47 28 | 55301 | 32 | 44699 | 58267 | 36 | 41733 | 02965 | 4 | 97035 | 4 |
| 57 | 12 24 | 47 36 | 55334 | 32 | 44666 | 58304 | 37 | 41696 | 02970 | 4 | 97030 | 3 |
| 58 | 12 16 | 47 44 | 55367 | 33 | 44633 | 58342 | 37 | 41658 | 02975 | 5 | 97025 | 2 |
| 59 | 12 8 | 47 52 | 55400 | 33 | 44600 | 58380 | 38 | 41620 | 02980 | 5 | 97020 | 1 |
| 60 | 12 0 | 48 0 | 55433 | 34 | 44567 | 58418 | 39 | 41582 | 02985 | 5 | 97015 | 0 |
| M | Hour P.M. | Hour A.M. | Cosine. | Diff. | Secant. | Cotangent | Diff. | Tangent. | Cosecant. | Diff. | Sine. | M |

110° | A | A | B | B | C | C 69°

| Seconds of time ...... | | 1s | 2s | 3s | 4s | 5s | 6s | 7s |
|---|---|---|---|---|---|---|---|---|
| Prop. parts of cols. | A | 4 | 8 | 13 | 17 | 21 | 25 | 30 |
| | B | 5 | 10 | 14 | 19 | 24 | 29 | 34 |
| | C | 1 | 1 | 2 | 2 | 3 | 4 | 4 |

# TABLE XXVII.

## Log. Sines, Tangents, and Secants.

S′. 21° — G′. 158°

| M | Hour A.M. | Hour P.M. | Sine. (A) | Diff. | Cosecant. (A) | Tangent. (B) | Diff. | Cotangent (B) | Secant. (C) | Diff. | Cosine. (C) | M |
|---|---|---|---|---|---|---|---|---|---|---|---|---|
| 0 | 9 12 0 | 2 48 0 | 9.55433 | 0 | 10.44567 | 9.58418 | 0 | 10.41582 | 10.02985 | 0 | 9.97015 | 60 |
| 1 | 11 52 | 48 8 | 55466 | 1 | 44534 | 58455 | 1 | 41545 | 02990 | 0 | 97010 | 59 |
| 2 | 11 44 | 48 16 | 55499 | 1 | 44501 | 58493 | 1 | 41507 | 02995 | 0 | 97005 | 58 |
| 3 | 11 36 | 48 24 | 55532 | 2 | 44468 | 58531 | 2 | 41469 | 02999 | 0 | 97001 | 57 |
| 4 | 11 28 | 48 32 | 55564 | 2 | 44436 | 58569 | 2 | 41431 | 03004 | 0 | 96996 | 56 |
| 5 | 9 11 20 | 2 48 40 | 9.55597 | 3 | 10.44403 | 9.58606 | 3 | 10.41394 | 10.03009 | 0 | 9.96991 | 55 |
| 6 | 11 12 | 48 48 | 55630 | 3 | 44370 | 58644 | 4 | 41356 | 03014 | 0 | 96986 | 54 |
| 7 | 11 4 | 48 56 | 55663 | 4 | 44337 | 58681 | 4 | 41319 | 03019 | 1 | 96981 | 53 |
| 8 | 10 56 | 49 4 | 55695 | 4 | 44305 | 58719 | 5 | 41281 | 03024 | 1 | 96976 | 52 |
| 9 | 10 48 | 49 12 | 55728 | 5 | 44272 | 58757 | 6 | 41243 | 03029 | 1 | 96971 | 51 |
| 10 | 9 10 40 | 2 49 20 | 9.55761 | 5 | 10.44239 | 9.58794 | 6 | 10.41206 | 10.03034 | 1 | 9.96966 | 50 |
| 11 | 10 32 | 49 28 | 55793 | 6 | 44207 | 58832 | 7 | 41168 | 03038 | 1 | 96962 | 49 |
| 12 | 10 24 | 49 36 | 55826 | 6 | 44174 | 58869 | 7 | 41131 | 03043 | 1 | 96957 | 48 |
| 13 | 10 16 | 49 44 | 55858 | 7 | 44142 | 58907 | 8 | 41093 | 03048 | 1 | 96952 | 47 |
| 14 | 10 8 | 49 52 | 55891 | 7 | 44109 | 58944 | 9 | 41056 | 03053 | 1 | 96947 | 46 |
| 15 | 9 10 0 | 2 50 0 | 9.55923 | 8 | 10.44077 | 9.58981 | 9 | 10.41019 | 10.03058 | 1 | 9.96942 | 45 |
| 16 | 9 52 | 50 8 | 55956 | 9 | 44044 | 59019 | 10 | 40981 | 03063 | 1 | 96937 | 44 |
| 17 | 9 44 | 50 16 | 55988 | 9 | 44012 | 59056 | 10 | 40944 | 03068 | 1 | 96932 | 43 |
| 18 | 9 36 | 50 24 | 56021 | 10 | 43979 | 59094 | 11 | 40906 | 03073 | 1 | 96927 | 42 |
| 19 | 9 28 | 50 32 | 56053 | 10 | 43947 | 59131 | 12 | 40869 | 03078 | 2 | 96922 | 41 |
| 20 | 9 9 20 | 2 50 40 | 9.56085 | 11 | 10.43915 | 9.59168 | 12 | 10.40832 | 10.03083 | 2 | 9.96917 | 40 |
| 21 | 9 12 | 50 48 | 56118 | 11 | 43882 | 59205 | 13 | 40795 | 03088 | 2 | 96912 | 39 |
| 22 | 9 4 | 50 56 | 56150 | 12 | 43850 | 59243 | 14 | 40757 | 03093 | 2 | 96907 | 38 |
| 23 | 8 56 | 51 4 | 56182 | 12 | 43818 | 59280 | 14 | 40720 | 03097 | 2 | 96903 | 37 |
| 24 | 8 48 | 51 12 | 56215 | 13 | 43785 | 59317 | 15 | 40683 | 03102 | 2 | 96898 | 36 |
| 25 | 9 8 40 | 2 51 20 | 9.56247 | 13 | 10.43753 | 9.59354 | 15 | 10.40646 | 10.03107 | 2 | 9.96893 | 35 |
| 26 | 8 32 | 51 28 | 56279 | 14 | 43721 | 59391 | 16 | 40609 | 03112 | 2 | 96888 | 34 |
| 27 | 8 24 | 51 36 | 56311 | 14 | 43689 | 59429 | 17 | 40571 | 03117 | 2 | 96883 | 33 |
| 28 | 8 16 | 51 44 | 56343 | 15 | 43657 | 59466 | 17 | 40534 | 03122 | 2 | 96878 | 32 |
| 29 | 8 8 | 51 52 | 56375 | 16 | 43625 | 59503 | 18 | 40497 | 03127 | 2 | 96873 | 31 |
| 30 | 9 8 0 | 2 52 0 | 9.56408 | 16 | 10.43592 | 9.59540 | 19 | 10.40460 | 10.03132 | 2 | 9.96868 | 30 |
| 31 | 7 52 | 52 8 | 56440 | 17 | 43560 | 59577 | 19 | 40423 | 03137 | 3 | 96863 | 29 |
| 32 | 7 44 | 52 16 | 56472 | 17 | 43528 | 59614 | 20 | 40386 | 03142 | 3 | 96858 | 28 |
| 33 | 7 36 | 52 24 | 56504 | 18 | 43496 | 59651 | 20 | 40349 | 03147 | 3 | 96853 | 27 |
| 34 | 7 28 | 52 32 | 56536 | 18 | 43464 | 59688 | 21 | 40312 | 03152 | 3 | 96848 | 26 |
| 35 | 9 7 20 | 2 52 40 | 9.56568 | 19 | 10.43432 | 9.59725 | 22 | 10.40275 | 10.03157 | 3 | 9.96843 | 25 |
| 36 | 7 12 | 52 48 | 56599 | 19 | 43401 | 59762 | 22 | 40238 | 03162 | 3 | 96838 | 24 |
| 37 | 7 4 | 52 56 | 56631 | 20 | 43369 | 59799 | 23 | 40201 | 03167 | 3 | 96833 | 23 |
| 38 | 6 56 | 53 4 | 56663 | 20 | 43337 | 59835 | 23 | 40165 | 03172 | 3 | 96828 | 22 |
| 39 | 6 48 | 53 12 | 56695 | 21 | 43305 | 59872 | 24 | 40128 | 03177 | 3 | 96823 | 21 |
| 40 | 9 6 40 | 2 53 20 | 9.56727 | 21 | 10.43273 | 9.59909 | 25 | 10.40091 | 10.03182 | 3 | 9.96818 | 20 |
| 41 | 6 32 | 53 28 | 56759 | 22 | 43241 | 59946 | 25 | 40054 | 03187 | 3 | 96813 | 19 |
| 42 | 6 24 | 53 36 | 56790 | 22 | 43210 | 59983 | 26 | 40017 | 03192 | 3 | 96808 | 18 |
| 43 | 6 16 | 53 44 | 56822 | 23 | 43178 | 60019 | 27 | 39981 | 03197 | 4 | 96803 | 17 |
| 44 | 6 8 | 53 52 | 56854 | 24 | 43146 | 60056 | 27 | 39944 | 03202 | 4 | 96798 | 16 |
| 45 | 9 6 0 | 2 54 0 | 9.56886 | 24 | 10.43114 | 9.60093 | 28 | 10.39907 | 10.03207 | 4 | 9.96793 | 15 |
| 46 | 5 52 | 54 8 | 56917 | 25 | 43083 | 60130 | 28 | 39870 | 03212 | 4 | 96788 | 14 |
| 47 | 5 44 | 54 16 | 56949 | 25 | 43051 | 60166 | 29 | 39834 | 03217 | 4 | 96783 | 13 |
| 48 | 5 36 | 54 24 | 56980 | 26 | 43020 | 60203 | 30 | 39797 | 03222 | 4 | 96778 | 12 |
| 49 | 5 28 | 54 32 | 57012 | 26 | 42988 | 60240 | 30 | 39760 | 03228 | 4 | 96772 | 11 |
| 50 | 9 5 20 | 2 54 40 | 9.57044 | 27 | 10.42956 | 9.60276 | 31 | 10.39724 | 10.03233 | 4 | 9.96767 | 10 |
| 51 | 5 12 | 54 48 | 57075 | 27 | 42925 | 60313 | 31 | 39687 | 03238 | 4 | 96762 | 9 |
| 52 | 5 4 | 54 56 | 57107 | 28 | 42893 | 60349 | 32 | 39651 | 03243 | 4 | 96757 | 8 |
| 53 | 4 56 | 55 4 | 57138 | 28 | 42862 | 60386 | 33 | 39614 | 03248 | 4 | 96752 | 7 |
| 54 | 4 48 | 55 12 | 57169 | 29 | 42831 | 60422 | 33 | 39578 | 03253 | 4 | 96747 | 6 |
| 55 | 9 4 40 | 2 55 20 | 9.57201 | 29 | 10.42799 | 9.60459 | 34 | 10.39541 | 10.03258 | 5 | 9.96742 | 5 |
| 56 | 4 32 | 55 28 | 57232 | 30 | 42768 | 60495 | 35 | 39505 | 03263 | 5 | 96737 | 4 |
| 57 | 4 24 | 55 36 | 57264 | 30 | 42736 | 60532 | 35 | 39468 | 03268 | 5 | 96732 | 3 |
| 58 | 4 16 | 55 44 | 57295 | 31 | 42705 | 60568 | 36 | 39432 | 03273 | 5 | 96727 | 2 |
| 59 | 4 8 | 55 52 | 57326 | 32 | 42674 | 60605 | 36 | 39395 | 03278 | 5 | 96722 | 1 |
| 60 | 4 0 | 56 0 | 57358 | 32 | 42642 | 60641 | 37 | 39359 | 03283 | 5 | 96717 | 0 |
| M | Hour P.M. | Hour A.M. | Cosine. (A) | Diff. | Secant. (A) | Cotangent (B) | Diff. | Tangent. (B) | Cosecant. (C) | Diff. | Sine. (C) | M |

111° — 68°

| Seconds of time ...... | | 1s | 2s | 3s | 4s | 5s | 6s | 7s |
|---|---|---|---|---|---|---|---|---|
| Prop. parts of cols. | A | 4 | 8 | 12 | 16 | 20 | 24 | 28 |
| | B | 5 | 9 | 14 | 19 | 23 | 28 | 32 |
| | C | 1 | 1 | 2 | 2 | 3 | 4 | 4 |

# TABLE XXVII.

S'. Log. Sines, Tangents, and Secants. G'.

| 22° | | | A | | A | B | | B | C | | C | 157° |
|---|---|---|---|---|---|---|---|---|---|---|---|---|
| M | Hour A.M. | Hour P.M. | Sine. | Diff. | Cosecant. | Tangent. | Diff. | Cotangent | Secant. | Diff. | Cosine. | M |
| 0 | 9 4 0 | 2 56 0 | 9.57358 | 0 | 10.42642 | 9.60641 | 0 | 10.39359 | 10.03283 | 0 | 9.96717 | 60 |
| 1 | 3 52 | 56 8 | 57389 | 1 | 42611 | 60677 | 1 | 39323 | 03289 | 0 | 96711 | 59 |
| 2 | 3 44 | 56 16 | 57420 | 1 | 42580 | 60714 | 1 | 39286 | 03294 | 0 | 96706 | 58 |
| 3 | 3 36 | 56 24 | 57451 | 2 | 42549 | 60750 | 2 | 39250 | 03299 | 0 | 96701 | 57 |
| 4 | 3 28 | 56 32 | 57482 | 2 | 42518 | 60786 | 2 | 39214 | 03304 | 0 | 96696 | 56 |
| 5 | 9 3 20 | 2 56 40 | 9.57514 | 3 | 10.42486 | 9.60823 | 3 | 10.39177 | 10.03309 | 0 | 9.96691 | 55 |
| 6 | 3 12 | 56 48 | 57545 | 3 | 42455 | 60859 | 4 | 39141 | 03314 | 1 | 96686 | 54 |
| 7 | 3 4 | 56 56 | 57576 | 4 | 42424 | 60895 | 4 | 39105 | 03319 | 1 | 96681 | 53 |
| 8 | 2 56 | 57 4 | 57607 | 4 | 42393 | 60931 | 5 | 39069 | 03324 | 1 | 96676 | 52 |
| 9 | 2 48 | 57 12 | 57638 | 5 | 42362 | 60967 | 5 | 39033 | 03330 | 1 | 96670 | 51 |
| 10 | 9 2 40 | 2 57 20 | 9.57669 | 5 | 10.42331 | 9.61004 | 6 | 10.38996 | 10.03335 | 1 | 9.96665 | 50 |
| 11 | 2 32 | 57 28 | 57700 | 6 | 42300 | 61040 | 7 | 38960 | 03340 | 1 | 96660 | 49 |
| 12 | 2 24 | 57 36 | 57731 | 6 | 42269 | 61076 | 7 | 38924 | 03345 | 1 | 96655 | 48 |
| 13 | 2 16 | 57 44 | 57762 | 7 | 42238 | 61112 | 8 | 38888 | 03350 | 1 | 96650 | 47 |
| 14 | 2 8 | 57 52 | 57793 | 7 | 42207 | 61148 | 8 | 38852 | 03355 | 1 | 96645 | 46 |
| 15 | 9 2 0 | 2 58 0 | 9.57824 | 8 | 10.42176 | 9.61184 | 9 | 10.38816 | 10.03360 | 1 | 9.96640 | 45 |
| 16 | 1 52 | 58 8 | 57855 | 8 | 42145 | 61220 | 10 | 38780 | 03366 | 1 | 96634 | 44 |
| 17 | 1 44 | 58 16 | 57885 | 9 | 42115 | 61256 | 10 | 38744 | 03371 | 1 | 96629 | 43 |
| 18 | 1 36 | 58 24 | 57916 | 9 | 42084 | 61292 | 11 | 38708 | 03376 | 2 | 96624 | 42 |
| 19 | 1 28 | 58 32 | 57947 | 10 | 42053 | 61328 | 11 | 38672 | 03381 | 2 | 96619 | 41 |
| 20 | 9 1 20 | 2 58 40 | 9.57978 | 10 | 10.42022 | 9.61364 | 12 | 10.38636 | 10.03386 | 2 | 9.96614 | 40 |
| 21 | 1 12 | 58 48 | 58008 | 11 | 41992 | 61400 | 13 | 38600 | 03392 | 2 | 96608 | 39 |
| 22 | 1 4 | 58 56 | 58039 | 11 | 41961 | 61436 | 13 | 38564 | 03397 | 2 | 96603 | 38 |
| 23 | 0 56 | 59 4 | 58070 | 12 | 41930 | 61472 | 14 | 38528 | 03402 | 2 | 96598 | 37 |
| 24 | 0 48 | 59 12 | 58101 | 12 | 41899 | 61508 | 14 | 38492 | 03407 | 2 | 96593 | 36 |
| 25 | 9 0 40 | 2 59 20 | 9.58131 | 13 | 10.41869 | 9.61544 | 15 | 10.38456 | 10.03412 | 2 | 9.96588 | 35 |
| 26 | 0 32 | 59 28 | 58162 | 13 | 41838 | 61579 | 15 | 38421 | 03418 | 2 | 96582 | 34 |
| 27 | 0 24 | 59 36 | 58192 | 14 | 41808 | 61615 | 16 | 38385 | 03423 | 2 | 96577 | 33 |
| 28 | 0 16 | 59 44 | 58223 | 14 | 41777 | 61651 | 17 | 38349 | 03428 | 2 | 96572 | 32 |
| 29 | 0 8 | 59 52 | 58253 | 15 | 41747 | 61687 | 17 | 38313 | 03433 | 3 | 96567 | 31 |
| 30 | 9 0 0 | 3 0 0 | 9.58284 | 15 | 10.41716 | 9.61722 | 18 | 10.38278 | 10.03438 | 3 | 9.96562 | 30 |
| 31 | 8 59 52 | 0 8 | 58314 | 16 | 41686 | 61758 | 18 | 38242 | 03444 | 3 | 96556 | 29 |
| 32 | 59 44 | 0 16 | 58345 | 16 | 41655 | 61794 | 19 | 38206 | 03449 | 3 | 96551 | 28 |
| 33 | 59 36 | 0 24 | 58375 | 17 | 41625 | 61830 | 20 | 38170 | 03454 | 3 | 96546 | 27 |
| 34 | 59 28 | 0 32 | 58406 | 17 | 41594 | 61865 | 20 | 38135 | 03459 | 3 | 96541 | 26 |
| 35 | 8 59 20 | 3 0 40 | 9.58436 | 18 | 10.41564 | 9.61901 | 21 | 10.38099 | 10.03465 | 3 | 9.96535 | 25 |
| 36 | 59 12 | 0 48 | 58467 | 18 | 41533 | 61936 | 21 | 38064 | 03470 | 3 | 96530 | 24 |
| 37 | 59 4 | 0 56 | 58497 | 19 | 41503 | 61972 | 22 | 38028 | 03475 | 3 | 96525 | 23 |
| 38 | 58 56 | 1 4 | 58527 | 19 | 41473 | 62008 | 23 | 37992 | 03480 | 3 | 96520 | 22 |
| 39 | 58 48 | 1 12 | 58557 | 20 | 41443 | 62043 | 23 | 37957 | 03486 | 3 | 96514 | 21 |
| 40 | 8 58 40 | 3 1 20 | 9.58588 | 20 | 10.41412 | 9.62079 | 24 | 10.37921 | 10.03491 | 3 | 9.96509 | 20 |
| 41 | 58 32 | 1 28 | 58618 | 21 | 41382 | 62114 | 24 | 37886 | 03496 | 4 | 96504 | 19 |
| 42 | 58 24 | 1 36 | 58648 | 21 | 41352 | 62150 | 25 | 37850 | 03502 | 4 | 96498 | 18 |
| 43 | 58 16 | 1 44 | 58678 | 22 | 41322 | 62185 | 26 | 37815 | 03507 | 4 | 96493 | 17 |
| 44 | 58 8 | 1 52 | 58709 | 22 | 41291 | 62221 | 26 | 37779 | 03512 | 4 | 96488 | 16 |
| 45 | 8 58 0 | 3 2 0 | 9.58739 | 23 | 10.41261 | 9.62256 | 27 | 10.37744 | 10.03517 | 4 | 9.96483 | 15 |
| 46 | 57 52 | 2 8 | 58769 | 23 | 41231 | 62292 | 27 | 37708 | 03523 | 4 | 96477 | 14 |
| 47 | 57 44 | 2 16 | 58799 | 24 | 41201 | 62327 | 28 | 37673 | 03528 | 4 | 96472 | 13 |
| 48 | 57 36 | 2 24 | 58829 | 24 | 41171 | 62362 | 29 | 37638 | 03533 | 4 | 96467 | 12 |
| 49 | 57 28 | 2 32 | 58859 | 25 | 41141 | 62398 | 29 | 37602 | 03539 | 4 | 96461 | 11 |
| 50 | 8 57 20 | 3 2 40 | 9.58889 | 25 | 10.41111 | 9.62433 | 30 | 10.37567 | 10.03544 | 4 | 9.96456 | 10 |
| 51 | 57 12 | 2 48 | 58919 | 26 | 41081 | 62468 | 30 | 37532 | 03549 | 4 | 96451 | 9 |
| 52 | 57 4 | 2 56 | 58949 | 26 | 41051 | 62504 | 31 | 37496 | 03555 | 5 | 96445 | 8 |
| 53 | 56 56 | 3 4 | 58979 | 27 | 41021 | 62539 | 32 | 37461 | 03560 | 5 | 96440 | 7 |
| 54 | 56 48 | 3 12 | 59009 | 27 | 40991 | 62574 | 32 | 37426 | 03565 | 5 | 96435 | 6 |
| 55 | 8 56 40 | 3 3 20 | 9.59039 | 28 | 10.40961 | 9.62609 | 33 | 10.37391 | 10.03571 | 5 | 9.96429 | 5 |
| 56 | 56 32 | 3 28 | 59069 | 28 | 40931 | 62645 | 33 | 37355 | 03576 | 5 | 96424 | 4 |
| 57 | 56 24 | 3 36 | 59098 | 29 | 40902 | 62680 | 34 | 37320 | 03581 | 5 | 96419 | 3 |
| 58 | 56 16 | 3 44 | 59128 | 29 | 40872 | 62715 | 35 | 37285 | 03587 | 5 | 96413 | 2 |
| 59 | 56 8 | 3 52 | 59158 | 30 | 40842 | 62750 | 35 | 37250 | 03592 | 5 | 96408 | 1 |
| 60 | 56 0 | 4 0 | 59188 | 31 | 40812 | 62785 | 36 | 37215 | 03597 | 5 | 96403 | 0 |
| M | Hour P.M. | Hour A.M. | Cosine. | Diff. | Secant. | Cotangent | Diff. | Tangent. | Cosecant. | Diff. | Sine. | M |
| 112° | | | A | | A | B | | B | C | | C | 67° |

| Seconds of time ...... | | 1ˢ | 2ˢ | 3ˢ | 4ˢ | 5ˢ | 6ˢ | 7ˢ |
|---|---|---|---|---|---|---|---|---|
| Prop. parts of cols. | A | 4 | 8 | 11 | 15 | 19 | 23 | 27 |
| | B | 4 | 9 | 13 | 18 | 22 | 27 | 31 |
| | C | 1 | 1 | 2 | 3 | 3 | 4 | 5 |

# TABLE XXVII.

## Log. Sines, Tangents, and Secants.

S'. G'.

23° 156°

| | | | A | | A | B | | B | C | | C | |
|---|---|---|---|---|---|---|---|---|---|---|---|---|
| M | Hour A.M. | Hour P.M. | Sine. | Diff. | Cosecant. | Tangent. | Diff. | Cotangent | Secant. | Diff. | Cosine. | M |
| 0 | 8 56 0 | 3 4 0 | 9.59188 | 0 | 10.40812 | 9.62785 | 0 | 10.37215 | 10.03597 | 0 | 9.96403 | 60 |
| 1 | 55 52 | 4 8 | 59218 | 0 | 40782 | 62820 | 1 | 37180 | 03603 | 0 | 96397 | 59 |
| 2 | 55 44 | 4 16 | 59247 | 1 | 40753 | 62855 | 1 | 37145 | 03608 | 0 | 96392 | 58 |
| 3 | 55 36 | 4 24 | 59277 | 1 | 40723 | 62890 | 2 | 37110 | 03613 | 0 | 96387 | 57 |
| 4 | 55 28 | 4 32 | 59307 | 2 | 40693 | 62926 | 2 | 37074 | 03619 | 0 | 96381 | 56 |
| 5 | 8 55 20 | 3 4 40 | 9.59336 | 2 | 10.40664 | 9.62961 | 3 | 10.37039 | 10.03624 | 0 | 9.96376 | 55 |
| 6 | 55 12 | 4 48 | 59366 | 3 | 40634 | 62996 | 3 | 37004 | 03630 | 1 | 96370 | 54 |
| 7 | 55 4 | 4 56 | 59396 | 3 | 40604 | 63031 | 4 | 36969 | 03635 | 1 | 96365 | 53 |
| 8 | 54 56 | 5 4 | 59425 | 4 | 40575 | 63066 | 5 | 36934 | 03640 | 1 | 96360 | 52 |
| 9 | 54 48 | 5 12 | 59455 | 4 | 40545 | 63101 | 5 | 36899 | 03646 | 1 | 96354 | 51 |
| 10 | 8 54 40 | 3 5 20 | 9.59484 | 5 | 10.40516 | 9.63135 | 6 | 10.36865 | 10.03651 | 1 | 9.96349 | 50 |
| 11 | 54 32 | 5 28 | 59514 | 5 | 40486 | 63170 | 6 | 36830 | 03657 | 1 | 96343 | 49 |
| 12 | 54 24 | 5 36 | 59543 | 6 | 40457 | 63205 | 7 | 36795 | 03662 | 1 | 96338 | 48 |
| 13 | 54 16 | 5 44 | 59573 | 6 | 40427 | 63240 | 7 | 36760 | 03667 | 1 | 96333 | 47 |
| 14 | 54 8 | 5 52 | 59602 | 7 | 40398 | 63275 | 8 | 36725 | 03673 | 1 | 96327 | 46 |
| 15 | 8 54 0 | 3 6 0 | 9.59632 | 7 | 10.40368 | 9.63310 | 9 | 10.36690 | 10.03678 | 1 | 9.96322 | 45 |
| 16 | 53 52 | 6 8 | 59661 | 8 | 40339 | 63345 | 9 | 36655 | 03684 | 1 | 96316 | 44 |
| 17 | 53 44 | 6 16 | 59690 | 8 | 40310 | 63379 | 10 | 36621 | 03689 | 2 | 96311 | 43 |
| 18 | 53 36 | 6 24 | 59720 | 9 | 40280 | 63414 | 10 | 36586 | 03695 | 2 | 96305 | 42 |
| 19 | 53 28 | 6 32 | 59749 | 9 | 40251 | 63449 | 11 | 36551 | 03700 | 2 | 96300 | 41 |
| 20 | 8 53 20 | 3 6 40 | 9.59778 | 10 | 10.40222 | 9.63484 | 12 | 10.36516 | 10 03706 | 2 | 9.96294 | 40 |
| 21 | 53 12 | 6 48 | 59808 | 10 | 40192 | 63519 | 12 | 36481 | 03711 | 2 | 96289 | 39 |
| 22 | 53 4 | 6 56 | 59837 | 11 | 40163 | 63553 | 13 | 36447 | 03716 | 2 | 96284 | 38 |
| 23 | 52 56 | 7 4 | 59866 | 11 | 40134 | 63588 | 13 | 36412 | 03722 | 2 | 96278 | 37 |
| 24 | 52 48 | 7 12 | 59895 | 12 | 40105 | 63623 | 14 | 36377 | 03727 | 2 | 96273 | 36 |
| 25 | 8 52 40 | 3 7 20 | 9.59924 | 12 | 10.40076 | 9.63657 | 14 | 10.36343 | 10.03733 | 2 | 9.96267 | 35 |
| 26 | 52 32 | 7 28 | 59954 | 13 | 40046 | 63692 | 15 | 36308 | 03738 | 2 | 96262 | 34 |
| 27 | 52 24 | 7 36 | 59983 | 13 | 40017 | 63726 | 16 | 36274 | 03744 | 2 | 96256 | 33 |
| 28 | 52 16 | 7 44 | 60012 | 14 | 39988 | 63761 | 16 | 36239 | 03749 | 3 | 96251 | 32 |
| 29 | 52 8 | 7 52 | [illegible] | [illegible] | [illegible] | 63796 | 17 | 36204 | 03755 | 3 | 96245 | 31 |
| 30 | 8 52 0 | 3 8 0 | 9.60070 | 15 | 10.39930 | 9.63830 | 17 | 10.36170 | 10.03760 | 3 | 9.96240 | 30 |
| 31 | 51 52 | 8 8 | 60099 | 15 | 39901 | 63865 | 18 | 36135 | 03766 | 3 | 96234 | 29 |
| 32 | 51 44 | 8 16 | 60128 | 15 | 39872 | 63899 | 18 | 36101 | 03771 | 3 | 96229 | 28 |
| 33 | 51 36 | 8 24 | 60157 | 16 | 39843 | 63934 | 19 | 36066 | 03777 | 3 | 96223 | 27 |
| 34 | 51 28 | 8 32 | 60186 | 16 | 39814 | 63968 | 20 | 36032 | 03782 | 3 | 96218 | 26 |
| 35 | 8 51 20 | 3 8 40 | 9.60215 | 17 | 10.39785 | 9.64003 | 20 | 10.35997 | 10.03788 | 3 | 9.96212 | 25 |
| 36 | 51 12 | 8 48 | 60244 | 17 | 39756 | 64037 | 21 | 35963 | 03793 | 3 | 96207 | 24 |
| 37 | 51 4 | 8 56 | 60273 | 18 | 39727 | 64072 | 21 | 35928 | 03799 | 3 | 96201 | 23 |
| 38 | 50 56 | 9 4 | 60302 | 18 | 39698 | 64106 | 22 | 35894 | 03804 | 3 | 96196 | 22 |
| 39 | 50 48 | 9 12 | 60331 | 19 | 39669 | 64140 | 22 | 35860 | 03810 | 4 | 96190 | 21 |
| 40 | 8 50 40 | 3 9 20 | 9.60359 | 19 | 10.39641 | 9.64175 | 23 | 10.35825 | 10.03815 | 4 | 9.96185 | 20 |
| 41 | 50 32 | 9 28 | 60388 | 20 | 39612 | 64209 | 24 | 35791 | 03821 | 4 | 96179 | 19 |
| 42 | 50 24 | 9 36 | 60417 | 20 | 39583 | 64243 | 24 | 35757 | 03826 | 4 | 96174 | 18 |
| 43 | 50 16 | 9 44 | 60446 | 21 | 39554 | 64278 | 25 | 35722 | 03832 | 4 | 96168 | 17 |
| 44 | 50 8 | 9 52 | 60474 | 21 | 39526 | 64312 | 25 | 35688 | 03838 | 4 | 96162 | 16 |
| 45 | 8 50 0 | 3 10 0 | 9.60503 | 22 | 10.39497 | 9.64346 | 26 | 10.35654 | 10.03843 | 4 | 9.96157 | 15 |
| 46 | 49 52 | 10 8 | 60532 | 22 | 39468 | 64381 | 26 | 35619 | 03849 | 4 | 96151 | 14 |
| 47 | 49 44 | 10 16 | 60561 | 23 | 39439 | 64415 | 27 | 35585 | 03854 | 4 | 96146 | 13 |
| 48 | 49 36 | 10 24 | 60589 | 23 | 39411 | 64449 | 28 | 35551 | 03860 | 4 | 96140 | 12 |
| 49 | 49 28 | 10 32 | 60618 | 24 | 39382 | 64483 | 28 | 35517 | 03865 | 4 | 96135 | 11 |
| 50 | 8 49 20 | 3 10 40 | 9.60646 | 24 | 10.39354 | 9.64517 | 29 | 10.35483 | 10.03871 | 5 | 9.96129 | 10 |
| 51 | 49 12 | 10 48 | 60675 | 25 | 39325 | 64552 | 29 | 35448 | 03877 | 5 | 96123 | 9 |
| 52 | 49 4 | 10 56 | 60704 | 25 | 39296 | 64586 | 30 | 35414 | 03882 | 5 | 96118 | 8 |
| 53 | 48 56 | 11 4 | 60732 | 26 | 39268 | 64620 | 31 | 35380 | 03888 | 5 | 96112 | 7 |
| 54 | 48 48 | 11 12 | 60761 | 26 | 39239 | 64654 | 31 | 35346 | 03893 | 5 | 96107 | 6 |
| 55 | 8 48 40 | 3 11 20 | 9.60789 | 27 | 10.39211 | 9.64688 | 32 | 10.35312 | 10.03899 | 5 | 9.96101 | 5 |
| 56 | 48 32 | 11 28 | 60818 | 27 | 39182 | 64722 | 32 | 35278 | 03905 | 5 | 96095 | 4 |
| 57 | 48 24 | 11 36 | 60846 | 28 | 39154 | 64756 | 33 | 35244 | 03910 | 5 | 96090 | 3 |
| 58 | 48 16 | 11 44 | 60875 | 28 | 39125 | 64790 | 33 | 35210 | 03916 | 5 | 96084 | 2 |
| 59 | 48 8 | 11 52 | 60903 | 29 | 39097 | 64824 | 34 | 35176 | 03921 | 5 | 96079 | 1 |
| 60 | 48 0 | 12 0 | 60931 | 29 | 39069 | 64858 | 35 | 35142 | 03927 | 6 | 96073 | 0 |
| M | Hour P.M. | Hour A.M. | Cosine. | Diff. | Secant. | Cotangent | Diff. | Tangent. | Cosecant. | Diff. | Sine. | M |
| | | | A | | A | B | | B | C | | C | |

113° 66°

| Seconds of time ...... | | 1s | 2s | 3s | 4s | 5s | 6s | 7s |
|---|---|---|---|---|---|---|---|---|
| Prop. parts of cols. | A | 4 | 7 | 11 | 15 | 18 | 22 | 25 |
| | B | 4 | 9 | 13 | 17 | 22 | 26 | 31 |
| | C | 1 | 1 | 2 | 3 | 3 | 4 | 5 |

# TABLE XXVII.

## Log. Sines, Tangents, and Secants.

S′ 24° — G′. 155°

| M | Hour A.M. | Hour P.M. | A Sine. | Diff. | A Cosecant. | B Tangent. | Diff. | B Cotangent | C Secant. | Diff. | C Cosine. | M |
|---|---|---|---|---|---|---|---|---|---|---|---|---|
| 0 | 8 48 0 | 3 12 0 | 9.60931 | 0 | 10.39069 | 9.64858 | 0 | 10.35142 | 10.03927 | 0 | 9.96073 | 60 |
| 1 | 47 52 | 12 8 | 60960 | 0 | 39040 | 64892 | 1 | 35108 | 03933 | 0 | 96067 | 59 |
| 2 | 47 44 | 12 16 | 60988 | 1 | 39012 | 64926 | 1 | 35074 | 03938 | 0 | 96062 | 58 |
| 3 | 47 36 | 12 24 | 61016 | 1 | 38984 | 64960 | 2 | 35040 | 03944 | 0 | 96056 | 57 |
| 4 | 47 28 | 12 32 | 61045 | 2 | 38955 | 64994 | 2 | 35006 | 03950 | 0 | 96050 | 56 |
| 5 | 8 47 20 | 3 12 40 | 9.61073 | 2 | 10.38927 | 9.65028 | 3 | 10.34972 | 10.03955 | 0 | 9.96045 | 55 |
| 6 | 47 12 | 12 48 | 61101 | 3 | 38899 | 65062 | 3 | 34938 | 03961 | 1 | 96039 | 54 |
| 7 | 47 4 | 12 56 | 61129 | 3 | 38871 | 65096 | 4 | 34904 | 03966 | 1 | 96034 | 53 |
| 8 | 46 56 | 13 4 | 61158 | 4 | 38842 | 65130 | 4 | 34870 | 03972 | 1 | 96028 | 52 |
| 9 | 46 48 | 13 12 | 61186 | 4 | 38814 | 65164 | 5 | 34836 | 03978 | 1 | 96022 | 51 |
| 10 | 8 46 40 | 3 13 20 | 9.61214 | 5 | 10.38786 | 9.65197 | 6 | 10.34803 | 10.03983 | 1 | 9.96017 | 50 |
| 11 | 46 32 | 13 28 | 61242 | 5 | 38758 | 65231 | 6 | 34769 | 03989 | 1 | 96011 | 49 |
| 12 | 46 24 | 13 36 | 61270 | 6 | 38730 | 65265 | 7 | 34735 | 03995 | 1 | 96005 | 48 |
| 13 | 46 16 | 13 44 | 61298 | 6 | 38702 | 65299 | 7 | 34701 | 04000 | 1 | 96000 | 47 |
| 14 | 46 8 | 13 52 | 61326 | 6 | 38674 | 65333 | 8 | 34667 | 04006 | 1 | 95994 | 46 |
| 15 | 8 46 0 | 3 14 0 | 9.61354 | 7 | 10.38646 | 9.65366 | 8 | 10.34634 | 10.04012 | 1 | 9.95988 | 45 |
| 16 | 45 52 | 14 8 | 61382 | 7 | 38618 | 65400 | 9 | 34600 | 04018 | 2 | 95982 | 44 |
| 17 | 45 44 | 14 16 | 61411 | 8 | 38589 | 65434 | 9 | 34566 | 04023 | 2 | 95977 | 43 |
| 18 | 45 36 | 14 24 | 61438 | 8 | 38562 | 65467 | 10 | 34533 | 04029 | 2 | 95971 | 42 |
| 19 | 45 28 | 14 32 | 61466 | 9 | 38534 | 65501 | 11 | 34499 | 04035 | 2 | 95965 | 41 |
| 20 | 8 45 20 | 3 14 40 | 9.61494 | 9 | 10.38506 | 9.65535 | 11 | 10.34465 | 10.04040 | 2 | 9.95960 | 40 |
| 21 | 45 12 | 14 48 | 61522 | 10 | 38478 | 65568 | 12 | 34432 | 04046 | 2 | 95954 | 39 |
| 22 | 45 4 | 14 56 | 61550 | 10 | 38450 | 65602 | 12 | 34398 | 04052 | 2 | 95948 | 38 |
| 23 | 44 56 | 15 4 | 61578 | 11 | 38422 | 65636 | 13 | 34364 | 04058 | 2 | 95942 | 37 |
| 24 | 44 48 | 15 12 | 61606 | 11 | 38394 | 65669 | 13 | 34331 | 04063 | 2 | 95937 | 36 |
| 25 | 8 44 40 | 3 15 20 | 9.61634 | 12 | 10.38366 | 9.65703 | 14 | 10.34297 | 10.04069 | 2 | 9.95931 | 35 |
| 26 | 44 32 | 15 28 | 61662 | 12 | 38338 | 65736 | 15 | 34264 | 04075 | 2 | 95925 | 34 |
| 27 | 44 24 | 15 36 | 61689 | 12 | 38311 | 65770 | 15 | 34230 | 04080 | 3 | 95920 | 33 |
| 28 | 44 16 | 15 44 | 61717 | 13 | 38283 | 65803 | 16 | 34197 | 04086 | 3 | 95914 | 32 |
| 29 | 44 8 | 15 52 | 61745 | 13 | 38255 | 65837 | 16 | 34163 | 04092 | 3 | 95908 | 31 |
| 30 | 8 44 0 | 3 16 0 | 9.61773 | 14 | 10.38227 | 9.65870 | 17 | 10.34130 | 10.04098 | 3 | 9.95902 | 30 |
| 31 | 43 52 | 16 8 | 61800 | 14 | 38200 | 65904 | 17 | 34096 | 04103 | 3 | 95897 | 29 |
| 32 | 43 44 | 16 16 | 61828 | 15 | 38172 | 65937 | 18 | 34063 | 04109 | 3 | 95891 | 28 |
| 33 | 43 36 | 16 24 | 61856 | 15 | 38144 | 65971 | 18 | 34029 | 04115 | 3 | 95885 | 27 |
| 34 | 43 28 | 16 32 | 61883 | 16 | 38117 | 66004 | 19 | 33996 | 04121 | 3 | 95879 | 26 |
| 35 | 8 43 20 | 3 16 40 | 9.61911 | 16 | 10.38089 | 9.66038 | 20 | 10.33962 | 10.04127 | 3 | 9.95873 | 25 |
| 36 | 43 12 | 16 48 | 61939 | 17 | 38061 | 66071 | 20 | 33929 | 04132 | 3 | 95868 | 24 |
| 37 | 43 4 | 16 56 | 61966 | 17 | 38034 | 66104 | 21 | 33896 | 04138 | 4 | 95862 | 23 |
| 38 | 42 56 | 17 4 | 61994 | 18 | 38006 | 66138 | 21 | 33862 | 04144 | 4 | 95856 | 22 |
| 39 | 42 48 | 17 12 | 62021 | 18 | 37979 | 66171 | 22 | 33829 | 04150 | 4 | 95850 | 21 |
| 40 | 8 42 40 | 3 17 20 | 9.62049 | 18 | 10.37951 | 9.66204 | 22 | 10.33796 | 10.04156 | 4 | 9.95844 | 20 |
| 41 | 42 32 | 17 28 | 62076 | 19 | 37924 | 66238 | 23 | 33762 | 04161 | 4 | 95839 | 19 |
| 42 | 42 24 | 17 36 | 62104 | 19 | 37896 | 66271 | 23 | 33729 | 04167 | 4 | 95833 | 18 |
| 43 | 42 16 | 17 44 | 62131 | 20 | 37869 | 66304 | 24 | 33696 | 04173 | 4 | 95827 | 17 |
| 44 | 42 8 | 17 52 | 62159 | 20 | 37841 | 66337 | 25 | 33663 | 04179 | 4 | 95821 | 16 |
| 45 | 8 42 0 | 3 18 0 | 9.62186 | 21 | 10.37814 | 9.66371 | 25 | 10.33629 | 10.04185 | 4 | 9.95815 | 15 |
| 46 | 41 52 | 18 8 | 62214 | 21 | 37786 | 66404 | 26 | 33596 | 04190 | 4 | 95810 | 14 |
| 47 | 41 44 | 18 16 | 62241 | 22 | 37759 | 66437 | 26 | 33563 | 04196 | 5 | 95804 | 13 |
| 48 | 41 36 | 18 24 | 62268 | 22 | 37732 | 66470 | 27 | 33530 | 04202 | 5 | 95798 | 12 |
| 49 | 41 28 | 18 32 | 62296 | 23 | 37704 | 66503 | 27 | 33497 | 04208 | 5 | 95792 | 11 |
| 50 | 8 41 20 | 3 18 40 | 9.62323 | 23 | 10.37677 | 9.66537 | 28 | 10.33463 | 10.04214 | 5 | 9.95786 | 10 |
| 51 | 41 12 | 18 48 | 62350 | 24 | 37650 | 66570 | 28 | 33430 | 04220 | 5 | 95780 | 9 |
| 52 | 41 4 | 18 56 | 62377 | 24 | 37623 | 66603 | 29 | 33397 | 04225 | 5 | 95775 | 8 |
| 53 | 40 56 | 19 4 | 62405 | 24 | 37595 | 66636 | 30 | 33364 | 04231 | 5 | 95769 | 7 |
| 54 | 40 48 | 19 12 | 62432 | 25 | 37568 | 66669 | 30 | 33331 | 04237 | 5 | 95763 | 6 |
| 55 | 8 40 40 | 3 19 20 | 9.62459 | 25 | 10.37541 | 9.66702 | 31 | 10.33298 | 10.04243 | 5 | 9.95757 | 5 |
| 56 | 40 32 | 19 28 | 62486 | 26 | 37514 | 66735 | 31 | 33265 | 04249 | 5 | 95751 | 4 |
| 57 | 40 24 | 19 36 | 62513 | 26 | 37487 | 66768 | 32 | 33232 | 04255 | 5 | 95745 | 3 |
| 58 | 40 16 | 19 44 | 62541 | 27 | 37459 | 66801 | 32 | 33199 | 04261 | 6 | 95739 | 2 |
| 59 | 40 8 | 19 52 | 62568 | 27 | 37432 | 66834 | 33 | 33166 | 04267 | 6 | 95733 | 1 |
| 60 | 40 0 | 20 0 | 62595 | 28 | 37405 | 66867 | 33 | 33133 | 04272 | 6 | 95728 | 0 |
| M | Hour P.M. | Hour A.M. | Cosine. A | Diff. | Secant. A | Cotangent B | Diff. | Tangent. B | Cosecant. C | Diff. | Sine. C | M |

114° — 65°

| Seconds of time ...... | | 1s | 2s | 3s | 4s | 5s | 6s | 7s |
|---|---|---|---|---|---|---|---|---|
| Prop. parts of cols. | A | 3 | 7 | 10 | 14 | 17 | 21 | 24 |
| | B | 4 | 8 | 13 | 17 | 21 | 25 | 29 |
| | C | 1 | 1 | 2 | 3 | 4 | 4 | 5 |

# TABLE XXVII.

## Log. Sines, Tangents, and Secants.

S'. 25° | G'. 154°

| M | Hour A.M. | Hour P.M. | A Sine. | Diff. | A Cosecant. | B Tangent. | Diff. | B Cotangent | C Secant. | Diff. | C Cosine. | M |
|---|---|---|---|---|---|---|---|---|---|---|---|---|
| 0 | 8 40 0 | 3 20 0 | 9.62595 | 0 | 10.37405 | 9.66867 | 0 | 10.33133 | 10.04272 | 0 | 9.95728 | 60 |
| 1 | 39 52 | 20 8 | 62622 | 0 | 37378 | 66900 | 1 | 33100 | 04278 | 0 | 95722 | 59 |
| 2 | 39 44 | 20 16 | 62649 | 1 | 37351 | 66933 | 1 | 33067 | 04284 | 0 | 95716 | 58 |
| 3 | 39 36 | 20 24 | 62676 | 1 | 37324 | 66966 | 2 | 33034 | 04290 | 0 | 95710 | 57 |
| 4 | 39 28 | 20 32 | 62703 | 2 | 37297 | 66999 | 2 | 33001 | 04296 | 0 | 95704 | 56 |
| 5 | 8 39 20 | 3 20 40 | 9.62730 | 2 | 10.37270 | 9.67032 | 3 | 10.32968 | 10.04302 | 1 | 9.95698 | 55 |
| 6 | 39 12 | 20 48 | 62757 | 3 | 37243 | 67065 | 3 | 32935 | 04308 | 1 | 95692 | 54 |
| 7 | 39 4 | 20 56 | 62784 | 3 | 37216 | 67098 | 4 | 32902 | 04314 | 1 | 95686 | 53 |
| 8 | 38 56 | 21 4 | 62811 | 4 | 37189 | 67131 | 4 | 32869 | 04320 | 1 | 95680 | 52 |
| 9 | 38 48 | 21 12 | 62838 | 4 | 37162 | 67163 | 5 | 32837 | 04326 | 1 | 95674 | 51 |
| 10 | 8 38 40 | 3 21 20 | 9.62865 | 4 | 10.37135 | 9.67196 | 5 | 10.32804 | 10.04332 | 1 | 9.95668 | 50 |
| 11 | 38 32 | 21 28 | 62892 | 5 | 37108 | 67229 | 6 | 32771 | 04337 | 1 | 95663 | 49 |
| 12 | 38 24 | 21 36 | 62918 | 5 | 37082 | 67262 | 7 | 32738 | 04343 | 1 | 95657 | 48 |
| 13 | 38 16 | 21 44 | 62945 | 6 | 37055 | 67295 | 7 | 32705 | 04349 | 1 | 95651 | 47 |
| 14 | 38 8 | 21 52 | 62972 | 6 | 37028 | 67327 | 8 | 32673 | 04355 | 1 | 95645 | 46 |
| 15 | 8 38 0 | 3 22 0 | 9.62999 | 7 | 10.37001 | 9.67360 | 8 | 10.32640 | 10.04361 | 2 | 9.95639 | 45 |
| 16 | 37 52 | 22 8 | 63026 | 7 | 36974 | 67393 | 9 | 32607 | 04367 | 2 | 95633 | 44 |
| 17 | 37 44 | 22 16 | 63052 | 8 | 36948 | 67426 | 9 | 32574 | 04373 | 2 | 95627 | 43 |
| 18 | 37 36 | 22 24 | 63079 | 8 | 36921 | 67458 | 10 | 32542 | 04379 | 2 | 95621 | 42 |
| 19 | 37 28 | 22 32 | 63106 | 8 | 36894 | 67491 | 10 | 32509 | 04385 | 2 | 95615 | 41 |
| 20 | 8 37 20 | 3 22 40 | 9.63133 | 9 | 10.36867 | 9.67524 | 11 | 10.32476 | 10.04391 | 2 | 9.95609 | 40 |
| 21 | 37 12 | 22 48 | 63159 | 9 | 36841 | 67556 | 11 | 32444 | 04397 | 2 | 95603 | 39 |
| 22 | 37 4 | 22 56 | 63186 | 10 | 36814 | 67589 | 12 | 32411 | 04403 | 2 | 95597 | 38 |
| 23 | 36 56 | 23 4 | 63213 | 10 | 36787 | 67622 | 12 | 32378 | 04409 | 2 | 95591 | 37 |
| 24 | 36 48 | 23 12 | 63239 | 11 | 36761 | 67654 | 13 | 32346 | 04415 | 2 | 95585 | 36 |
| 25 | 8 36 40 | 3 23 20 | 9.63266 | 11 | 10.36734 | 9.67687 | 14 | 10.32313 | 10.04421 | 3 | 9.95579 | 35 |
| 26 | 36 32 | 23 28 | 63292 | 11 | 36708 | 67719 | 14 | 32281 | 04427 | 3 | 95573 | 34 |
| 27 | 36 24 | 23 36 | 63319 | 12 | 36681 | 67752 | 15 | 32248 | 04433 | 3 | 95567 | 33 |
| 28 | 36 16 | 23 44 | 63345 | 12 | 36655 | 67785 | 15 | 32215 | 04439 | 3 | 95561 | 32 |
| 29 | 36 8 | 23 52 | 63372 | 13 | 36628 | 67817 | 16 | 32183 | 04445 | 3 | 95555 | 31 |
| 30 | 8 36 0 | 3 24 0 | 9.63398 | 13 | 10.36602 | 9.67850 | 16 | 10.32150 | 10.04451 | 3 | 9.95549 | 30 |
| 31 | 35 52 | 24 8 | 63425 | 14 | 36575 | 67882 | 17 | 32118 | 04457 | 3 | 95543 | 29 |
| 32 | 35 44 | 24 16 | 63451 | 14 | 36549 | 67915 | 17 | 32085 | 04463 | 3 | 95537 | 28 |
| 33 | 35 36 | 24 24 | 63478 | 15 | 36522 | 67947 | 18 | 32053 | 04469 | 3 | 95531 | 27 |
| 34 | 35 28 | 24 32 | 63504 | 15 | 36496 | 67980 | 18 | 32020 | 04475 | 3 | 95525 | 26 |
| 35 | 8 35 20 | 3 24 40 | 9.63531 | 15 | 10.36469 | 9.68012 | 19 | 10.31988 | 10.04481 | 4 | 9.95519 | 25 |
| 36 | 35 12 | 24 48 | 63557 | 16 | 36443 | 68044 | 20 | 31956 | 04487 | 4 | 95513 | 24 |
| 37 | 35 4 | 24 56 | 63583 | 16 | 36417 | 68077 | 20 | 31923 | 04493 | 4 | 95507 | 23 |
| 38 | 34 56 | 25 4 | 63610 | 17 | 36390 | 68109 | 21 | 31891 | 04500 | 4 | 95500 | 22 |
| 39 | 34 48 | 25 12 | 63636 | 17 | 36364 | 68142 | 21 | 31858 | 04506 | 4 | 95494 | 21 |
| 40 | 8 34 40 | 3 25 20 | 9.63662 | 18 | 10.36338 | 9.68174 | 22 | 10.31826 | 10.04512 | 4 | 9.95488 | 20 |
| 41 | 34 32 | 25 28 | 63689 | 18 | 36311 | 68206 | 22 | 31794 | 04518 | 4 | 95482 | 19 |
| 42 | 34 24 | 25 36 | 63715 | 19 | 36285 | 68239 | 23 | 31761 | 04524 | 4 | 95476 | 18 |
| 43 | 34 16 | 25 44 | 63741 | 19 | 36259 | 68271 | 23 | 31729 | 04530 | 4 | 95470 | 17 |
| 44 | 34 8 | 25 52 | 63767 | 19 | 36233 | 68303 | 24 | 31697 | 04536 | 4 | 95464 | 16 |
| 45 | 8 34 0 | 3 26 0 | 9.63794 | 20 | 10.36206 | 9.68336 | 24 | 10.31664 | 10.04542 | 5 | 9.95458 | 15 |
| 46 | 33 52 | 26 8 | 63820 | 20 | 36180 | 68368 | 25 | 31632 | 04548 | 5 | 95452 | 14 |
| 47 | 33 44 | 26 16 | 63846 | 21 | 36154 | 68400 | 25 | 31600 | 04554 | 5 | 95446 | 13 |
| 48 | 33 36 | 26 24 | 63872 | 21 | 36128 | 68432 | 26 | 31568 | 04560 | 5 | 95440 | 12 |
| 49 | 33 28 | 26 32 | 63898 | 22 | 36102 | 68465 | 27 | 31535 | 04566 | 5 | 95434 | 11 |
| 50 | 8 33 20 | 3 26 40 | 9.63924 | 22 | 10.36076 | 9.68497 | 27 | 10.31503 | 10.04573 | 5 | 9.95427 | 10 |
| 51 | 33 12 | 26 48 | 63950 | 23 | 36050 | 68529 | 28 | 31471 | 04579 | 5 | 95421 | 9 |
| 52 | 33 4 | 26 56 | 63976 | 23 | 36024 | 68561 | 28 | 31439 | 04585 | 5 | 95415 | 8 |
| 53 | 32 56 | 27 4 | 64002 | 23 | 35998 | 68593 | 29 | 31407 | 04591 | 5 | 95409 | 7 |
| 54 | 32 48 | 27 12 | 64028 | 24 | 35972 | 68626 | 29 | 31374 | 04597 | 5 | 95403 | 6 |
| 55 | 8 32 40 | 3 27 20 | 9.64054 | 24 | 10.35946 | 9.68658 | 30 | 10.31342 | 10.04603 | 6 | 9.95397 | 5 |
| 56 | 32 32 | 27 28 | 64080 | 25 | 35920 | 68690 | 30 | 31310 | 04609 | 6 | 95391 | 4 |
| 57 | 32 24 | 27 36 | 64106 | 25 | 35894 | 68722 | 31 | 31278 | 04616 | 6 | 95384 | 3 |
| 58 | 32 16 | 27 44 | 64132 | 26 | 35868 | 68754 | 31 | 31246 | 04622 | 6 | 95378 | 2 |
| 59 | 32 8 | 27 52 | 64158 | 26 | 35842 | 68786 | 32 | 31214 | 04628 | 6 | 95372 | 1 |
| 60 | 32 0 | 28 0 | 64184 | 26 | 35816 | 68818 | 33 | 31182 | 04634 | 6 | 95366 | 0 |
| M | Hour P.M. | Hour A.M. | Cosine. A | Diff. | Secant. A | Cotangent B | Diff. | Tangent. B | Cosecant. C | Diff. | Sine. C | M |

115° | 64°

| Seconds of time ...... | | 1s | 2s | 3s | 4s | 5s | 6s | 7s |
|---|---|---|---|---|---|---|---|---|
| Prop. parts of cols. | A | 3 | 7 | 10 | 13 | 17 | 20 | 23 |
| | B | 4 | 8 | 12 | 16 | 20 | 24 | 28 |
| | C | 1 | 2 | 2 | 3 | 4 | 5 | 5 |

# TABLE XXVII.

## Log. Sines, Tangents, and Secants.

S'. 26° | G'. 153°

| M | Hour A.M. | Hour P.M. | Sine. (A) | Diff. | Cosecant. (A) | Tangent. (B) | Diff. | Cotangent (B) | Secant. (C) | Diff. | Cosine. (C) | M |
|---|---|---|---|---|---|---|---|---|---|---|---|---|
| 0 | 8 32 0 | 3 28 0 | 9.64184 | 0 | 10.35816 | 9.68818 | 0 | 10.31182 | 10.04634 | 0 | 9.95366 | 60 |
| 1 | 31 52 | 28 8 | 64210 | 0 | 35790 | 68850 | 1 | 31150 | 04640 | 0 | 95360 | 59 |
| 2 | 31 44 | 28 16 | 64236 | 1 | 35764 | 68882 | 1 | 31118 | 04646 | 0 | 95354 | 58 |
| 3 | 31 36 | 28 24 | 64262 | 1 | 35738 | 68914 | 2 | 31086 | 04652 | 0 | 95348 | 57 |
| 4 | 31 28 | 28 32 | 64288 | 2 | 35712 | 68946 | 2 | 31054 | 04659 | 0 | 95341 | 56 |
| 5 | 8 31 20 | 3 28 40 | 9.64313 | 2 | 10.35687 | 9.68978 | 3 | 10.31022 | 10.04665 | 1 | 9.95335 | 55 |
| 6 | 31 12 | 28 48 | 64339 | 3 | 35661 | 69010 | 3 | 30990 | 04671 | 1 | 95329 | 54 |
| 7 | 31 4 | 28 56 | 64365 | 3 | 35635 | 69042 | 4 | 30958 | 04677 | 1 | 95323 | 53 |
| 8 | 30 56 | 29 4 | 64391 | 3 | 35609 | 69074 | 4 | 30926 | 04683 | 1 | 95317 | 52 |
| 9 | 30 48 | 29 12 | 64417 | 4 | 35583 | 69106 | 5 | 30894 | 04690 | 1 | 95310 | 51 |
| 10 | 8 30 40 | 3 29 20 | 9.64442 | 4 | 10.35558 | 9.69138 | 5 | 10.30862 | 10.04696 | 1 | 9.95304 | 50 |
| 11 | 30 32 | 29 28 | 64468 | 5 | 35532 | 69170 | 6 | 30830 | 04702 | 1 | 95298 | 49 |
| 12 | 30 24 | 29 36 | 64494 | 5 | 35506 | 69202 | 6 | 30798 | 04708 | 1 | 95292 | 48 |
| 13 | 30 16 | 29 44 | 64519 | 5 | 35481 | 69234 | 7 | 30766 | 04714 | 1 | 95286 | 47 |
| 14 | 30 8 | 29 52 | 64545 | 6 | 35455 | 69266 | 7 | 30734 | 04721 | 1 | 95279 | 46 |
| 15 | 8 30 0 | 3 30 0 | 9.64571 | 6 | 10.35429 | 9.69298 | 8 | 10.30702 | 10.04727 | 2 | 9.95273 | 45 |
| 16 | 29 52 | 30 8 | 64596 | 7 | 35404 | 69329 | 8 | 30671 | 04733 | 2 | 95267 | 44 |
| 17 | 29 44 | 30 16 | 64622 | 7 | 35378 | 69361 | 9 | 30639 | 04739 | 2 | 95261 | 43 |
| 18 | 29 36 | 30 24 | 64647 | 8 | 35353 | 69393 | 9 | 30607 | 04746 | 2 | 95254 | 42 |
| 19 | 29 28 | 30 32 | 64673 | 8 | 35327 | 69425 | 10 | 30575 | 04752 | 2 | 95248 | 41 |
| 20 | 8 29 20 | 3 30 40 | 9.64698 | 8 | 10.35302 | 9.69457 | 11 | 10.30543 | 10.04758 | 2 | 9.95242 | 40 |
| 21 | 29 12 | 30 48 | 64724 | 9 | 35276 | 69488 | 11 | 30512 | 04764 | 2 | 95236 | 39 |
| 22 | 29 4 | 30 56 | 64749 | 9 | 35251 | 69520 | 12 | 30480 | 04771 | 2 | 95229 | 38 |
| 23 | 28 56 | 31 4 | 64775 | 10 | 35225 | 69552 | 12 | 30448 | 04777 | 2 | 95223 | 37 |
| 24 | 28 48 | 31 12 | 64800 | 10 | 35200 | 69584 | 13 | 30416 | 04783 | 3 | 95217 | 36 |
| 25 | 8 28 40 | 3 31 20 | 9.64826 | 11 | 10.35174 | 9.69615 | 13 | 10.30385 | 10.04789 | 3 | 9.95211 | 35 |
| 26 | 28 32 | 31 28 | 64851 | 11 | 35149 | 69647 | 14 | 30353 | 04796 | 3 | 95204 | 34 |
| 27 | 28 24 | 31 36 | 64877 | 11 | 35123 | 69679 | 14 | 30321 | 04802 | 3 | 95198 | 33 |
| 28 | 28 16 | 31 44 | 64902 | 12 | 35098 | 69710 | 15 | 30290 | 04808 | 3 | 95192 | 32 |
| 29 | 28 8 | 31 52 | 64927 | 12 | 35073 | 69742 | 15 | 30258 | 04815 | 3 | 95185 | 31 |
| 30 | 8 28 0 | 3 32 0 | 9.64953 | 13 | 10.35047 | 9.69774 | 16 | 10.30226 | 10.04821 | 3 | 9.95179 | 30 |
| 31 | 27 52 | 32 8 | 64978 | 13 | 35022 | 69805 | 16 | 30195 | 04827 | 3 | 95173 | 29 |
| 32 | 27 44 | 32 16 | 65003 | 14 | 34997 | 69837 | 17 | 30163 | 04833 | 3 | 95167 | 28 |
| 33 | 27 36 | 32 24 | 65029 | 14 | 34971 | 69868 | 17 | 30132 | 04840 | 3 | 95160 | 27 |
| 34 | 27 28 | 32 32 | 65054 | 14 | 34946 | 69900 | 18 | 30100 | 04846 | 4 | 95154 | 26 |
| 35 | 8 27 20 | 3 32 40 | 9.65079 | 15 | 10.34921 | 9.69932 | 18 | 10.30068 | 10.04852 | 4 | 9.95148 | 25 |
| 36 | 27 12 | 32 48 | 65104 | 15 | 34896 | 69963 | 19 | 30037 | 04859 | 4 | 95141 | 24 |
| 37 | 27 4 | 32 56 | 65130 | 16 | 34870 | 69995 | 20 | 30005 | 04865 | 4 | 95135 | 23 |
| 38 | 26 56 | 33 4 | 65155 | 16 | 34845 | 70026 | 20 | 29974 | 04871 | 4 | 95129 | 22 |
| 39 | 26 48 | 33 12 | 65180 | 16 | 34820 | 70058 | 21 | 29942 | 04878 | 4 | 95122 | 21 |
| 40 | 8 26 40 | 3 33 20 | 9.65205 | 17 | 10.34795 | 9.70089 | 21 | 10.29911 | 10.04884 | 4 | 9.95116 | 20 |
| 41 | 26 32 | 33 28 | 65230 | 17 | 34770 | 70121 | 22 | 29879 | 04890 | 4 | 95110 | 19 |
| 42 | 26 24 | 33 36 | 65255 | 18 | 34745 | 70152 | 22 | 29848 | 04897 | 4 | 95103 | 18 |
| 43 | 26 16 | 33 44 | 65281 | 18 | 34719 | 70184 | 23 | 29816 | 04903 | 5 | 95097 | 17 |
| 44 | 26 8 | 33 52 | 65306 | 19 | 34694 | 70215 | 23 | 29785 | 04910 | 5 | 95090 | 16 |
| 45 | 8 26 0 | 3 34 0 | 9.65331 | 19 | 10.34669 | 9.70247 | 24 | 10.29753 | 10.04916 | 5 | 9.95084 | 15 |
| 46 | 25 52 | 34 8 | 65356 | 19 | 34644 | 70278 | 24 | 29722 | 04922 | 5 | 95078 | 14 |
| 47 | 25 44 | 34 16 | 65381 | 20 | 34619 | 70309 | 25 | 29691 | 04929 | 5 | 95071 | 13 |
| 48 | 25 36 | 34 24 | 65406 | 20 | 34594 | 70341 | 25 | 29659 | 04935 | 5 | 95065 | 12 |
| 49 | 25 28 | 34 32 | 65431 | 21 | 34569 | 70372 | 26 | 29628 | 04941 | 5 | 95059 | 11 |
| 50 | 8 25 20 | 3 34 40 | 9.65456 | 21 | 10.34544 | 9.70404 | 26 | 10.29596 | 10.04948 | 5 | 9.95052 | 10 |
| 51 | 25 12 | 34 48 | 65481 | 22 | 34519 | 70435 | 27 | 29565 | 04954 | 5 | 95046 | 9 |
| 52 | 25 4 | 34 56 | 65506 | 22 | 34494 | 70466 | 27 | 29534 | 04961 | 5 | 95039 | 8 |
| 53 | 24 56 | 35 4 | 65531 | 22 | 34469 | 70498 | 28 | 29502 | 04967 | 6 | 95033 | 7 |
| 54 | 24 48 | 35 12 | 65556 | 23 | 34444 | 70529 | 28 | 29471 | 04973 | 6 | 95027 | 6 |
| 55 | 8 24 40 | 3 35 20 | 9.65580 | 23 | 10.34420 | 9.70560 | 29 | 10.29440 | 10.04980 | 6 | 9.95020 | 5 |
| 56 | 24 32 | 35 28 | 65605 | 24 | 34395 | 70592 | 30 | 29408 | 04986 | 6 | 95014 | 4 |
| 57 | 24 24 | 35 36 | 65630 | 24 | 34370 | 70623 | 30 | 29377 | 04993 | 6 | 95007 | 3 |
| 58 | 24 16 | 35 44 | 65655 | 25 | 34345 | 70654 | 31 | 29346 | 04999 | 6 | 95001 | 2 |
| 59 | 24 8 | 35 52 | 65680 | 25 | 34320 | 70685 | 31 | 29315 | 05005 | 6 | 94995 | 1 |
| 60 | 24 0 | 36 0 | 65705 | 25 | 34295 | 70717 | 32 | 29283 | 05012 | 6 | 94988 | 0 |
| M | Hour P.M. | Hour A.M. | Cosine. (A) | Diff. | Secant. (A) | Cotangent (B) | Diff. | Tangent. (B) | Cosecant. (C) | Diff. | Sine. (C) | M |

116° | 63°

| Seconds of time …… | 1s | 2s | 3s | 4s | 5s | 6s | 7s |
|---|---|---|---|---|---|---|---|
| Prop. parts of cols A | 3 | 6 | 10 | 13 | 16 | 19 | 22 |
| B | 4 | 8 | 12 | 16 | 20 | 24 | 28 |
| C | 1 | 1 | 2 | 3 | 4 | 5 | 6 |

# TABLE XXVII.

5h. | Gh.

## Log. Sines, Tangents, and Secants.

27° | C 152°

| | | | A | | A | B | | B | C | | C | |
|---|---|---|---|---|---|---|---|---|---|---|---|---|
| M | Hour A.M. | Hour P.M. | Sine. | Diff. | Cosecant. | Tangent. | Diff. | Cotangent | Secant. | Diff. | Cosine. | M |
| 0 | 8 24 0 | 3 36 0 | 9.65705 | 0 | 10.34295 | 9.70717 | 0 | 10.29283 | 10.05012 | 0 | 9.94988 | 60 |
| 1 | 23 52 | 36 8 | 65729 | 0 | 34271 | 70748 | 1 | 29252 | 05018 | 0 | 94982 | 59 |
| 2 | 23 44 | 36 16 | 65754 | 1 | 34246 | 70779 | 1 | 29221 | 05025 | 0 | 94975 | 58 |
| 3 | 23 36 | 36 24 | 65779 | 1 | 34221 | 70810 | 2 | 29190 | 05031 | 0 | 94969 | 57 |
| 4 | 23 28 | 36 32 | 65804 | 2 | 34196 | 70841 | 2 | 29159 | 05038 | 0 | 94962 | 56 |
| 5 | 8 23 20 | 3 36 40 | 9.65828 | 2 | 10.34172 | 9.70873 | 3 | 10.29127 | 10.05044 | 1 | 9.94956 | 55 |
| 6 | 23 12 | 36 48 | 65853 | 2 | 34147 | 70904 | 3 | 29096 | 05051 | 1 | 94949 | 54 |
| 7 | 23 4 | 36 56 | 65878 | 3 | 34122 | 70935 | 4 | 29065 | 05057 | 1 | 94943 | 53 |
| 8 | 22 56 | 37 4 | 65902 | 3 | 34098 | 70966 | 4 | 29034 | 05064 | 1 | 94936 | 52 |
| 9 | 22 48 | 37 12 | 65927 | 4 | 34073 | 70997 | 5 | 29003 | 05070 | 1 | 94930 | 51 |
| 10 | 8 22 40 | 3 37 20 | 9.65952 | 4 | 10.34048 | 9.71028 | 5 | 10.28972 | 10.05077 | 1 | 9.94923 | 50 |
| 11 | 22 32 | 37 28 | 65976 | 4 | 34024 | 71059 | 6 | 28941 | 05083 | 1 | 94917 | 49 |
| 12 | 22 24 | 37 36 | 66001 | 5 | 33999 | 71090 | 6 | 28910 | 05089 | 1 | 94911 | 48 |
| 13 | 22 16 | 37 44 | 66025 | 5 | 33975 | 71121 | 7 | 28879 | 05096 | 1 | 94904 | 47 |
| 14 | 22 8 | 37 52 | 66050 | 6 | 33950 | 71153 | 7 | 28847 | 05102 | 2 | 94898 | 46 |
| 15 | 8 22 0 | 3 38 0 | 9.66075 | 6 | 10.33925 | 9.71184 | 8 | 10.28816 | 10.05109 | 2 | 9.94891 | 45 |
| 16 | 21 52 | 38 8 | 66099 | 6 | 33901 | 71215 | 8 | 28785 | 05115 | 2 | 94885 | 44 |
| 17 | 21 44 | 38 16 | 66124 | 7 | 33876 | 71246 | 9 | 28754 | 05122 | 2 | 94878 | 43 |
| 18 | 21 36 | 38 24 | 66148 | 7 | 33852 | 71277 | 9 | 28723 | 05129 | 2 | 94871 | 42 |
| 19 | 21 28 | 38 32 | 66173 | 8 | 33827 | 71308 | 10 | 28692 | 05135 | 2 | 94865 | 41 |
| 20 | 8 21 20 | 3 38 40 | 9.66197 | 8 | 10.33803 | 9.71339 | 10 | 10.28661 | 10.05142 | 2 | 9.94858 | 40 |
| 21 | 21 12 | 38 48 | 66221 | 8 | 33779 | 71370 | 11 | 28630 | 05148 | 2 | 94852 | 39 |
| 22 | 21 4 | 38 56 | 66246 | 9 | 33754 | 71401 | 11 | 28599 | 05155 | 2 | 94845 | 38 |
| 23 | 20 56 | 39 4 | 66270 | 9 | 33730 | 71431 | 12 | 28569 | 05161 | 3 | 94839 | 37 |
| 24 | 20 48 | 39 12 | 66295 | 10 | 33705 | 71462 | 12 | 28538 | 05168 | 3 | 94832 | 36 |
| 25 | 8 20 40 | 3 39 20 | 9.66319 | 10 | 10.33681 | 9.71493 | 13 | 10.28507 | 10.05174 | 3 | 9.94826 | 35 |
| 26 | 20 32 | 39 28 | 66343 | 11 | 33657 | 71524 | 13 | 28476 | 05181 | 3 | 94819 | 34 |
| 27 | 20 24 | 39 36 | 66368 | 11 | 33632 | 71555 | 14 | 28445 | 05187 | 3 | 94813 | 33 |
| 28 | 20 16 | 39 44 | 66392 | 11 | 33608 | 71586 | 14 | 28414 | 05194 | 3 | 94806 | 32 |
| 29 | 20 8 | 39 52 | 66416 | 12 | 33584 | 71617 | 15 | 28383 | 05201 | 3 | 94799 | 31 |
| 30 | 8 20 0 | 3 40 0 | 9.66441 | 12 | 10.33559 | 9.71648 | 15 | 10.28352 | 10.05207 | 3 | 9.94793 | 30 |
| 31 | 19 52 | 40 8 | 66465 | 13 | 33535 | 71679 | 16 | 28321 | 05214 | 3 | 94786 | 29 |
| 32 | 19 44 | 40 16 | 66489 | 13 | 33511 | 71709 | 16 | 28291 | 05220 | 4 | 94780 | 28 |
| 33 | 19 36 | 40 24 | 66513 | 13 | 33487 | 71740 | 17 | 28260 | 05227 | 4 | 94773 | 27 |
| 34 | 19 28 | 40 32 | 66537 | 14 | 33463 | 71771 | 17 | 28229 | 05233 | 4 | 94767 | 26 |
| 35 | 8 19 20 | 3 40 40 | 9.66562 | 14 | 10.33438 | 9.71802 | 18 | 10.28198 | 10.05240 | 4 | 9.94760 | 25 |
| 36 | 19 12 | 40 48 | 66586 | 15 | 33414 | 71833 | 19 | 28167 | 05247 | 4 | 94753 | 24 |
| 37 | 19 4 | 40 56 | 66610 | 15 | 33390 | 71863 | 19 | 28137 | 05253 | 4 | 94747 | 23 |
| 38 | 18 56 | 41 4 | 66634 | 15 | 33366 | 71894 | 20 | 28106 | 05260 | 4 | 94740 | 22 |
| 39 | 18 48 | 41 12 | 66658 | 16 | 33342 | 71925 | 20 | 28075 | 05266 | 4 | 94734 | 21 |
| 40 | 8 18 40 | 3 41 20 | 9.66682 | 16 | 10.33318 | 9.71955 | 21 | 10.28045 | 10.05273 | 4 | 9.94727 | 20 |
| 41 | 18 32 | 41 28 | 66706 | 17 | 33294 | 71986 | 21 | 28014 | 05280 | 4 | 94720 | 19 |
| 42 | 18 24 | 41 36 | 66731 | 17 | 33269 | 72017 | 22 | 27983 | 05286 | 5 | 94714 | 18 |
| 43 | 18 16 | 41 44 | 66755 | 17 | 33245 | 72048 | 22 | 27952 | 05293 | 5 | 94707 | 17 |
| 44 | 18 8 | 41 52 | 66779 | 18 | 33221 | 72078 | 23 | 279[illegible] | 05300 | 5 | 94700 | 16 |
| 45 | 8 18 0 | 3 42 0 | 9.66803 | 18 | 10.33197 | 9.72109 | 23 | 10.27891 | 10.05306 | 5 | 9.94694 | 15 |
| 46 | 17 52 | 42 8 | 66827 | 19 | 33173 | 72140 | 24 | 27860 | 05313 | 5 | 94687 | 14 |
| 47 | 17 44 | 42 16 | 66851 | 19 | 33149 | 72170 | 24 | 27830 | 05320 | 5 | 94680 | 13 |
| 48 | 17 36 | 42 24 | 66875 | 19 | 33125 | 72201 | 25 | 27799 | 05326 | 5 | 94674 | 12 |
| 49 | 17 28 | 42 32 | 66899 | 20 | 33101 | 72231 | 25 | 27769 | 05333 | 5 | 94667 | 11 |
| 50 | 8 17 20 | 3 42 40 | 9.66922 | 20 | 10.33078 | 9.72262 | 26 | 10.27738 | 10.05340 | 5 | 9.94660 | 10 |
| 51 | 17 12 | 42 48 | 66946 | 21 | 33054 | 72293 | 26 | 27707 | 05346 | 6 | 94654 | 9 |
| 52 | 17 4 | 42 56 | 66970 | 21 | 33030 | 72323 | 27 | 27677 | 05353 | 6 | 94647 | 8 |
| 53 | 16 56 | 43 4 | 66994 | 21 | 33006 | 72354 | 27 | 27646 | 05360 | 6 | 94640 | 7 |
| 54 | 16 48 | 43 12 | 67018 | 22 | 32982 | 72384 | 28 | 27616 | 05366 | 6 | 94634 | 6 |
| 55 | 8 16 40 | 3 43 20 | 9.67042 | 22 | 10.32958 | 9.72415 | 28 | 10.27585 | 10.05373 | 6 | 9.94627 | 5 |
| 56 | 16 32 | 43 28 | 67066 | 23 | 32934 | 72445 | 29 | 27555 | 05380 | 6 | 94620 | 4 |
| 57 | 16 24 | 43 36 | 67090 | 23 | 32910 | 72476 | 29 | 27524 | 05386 | 6 | 94614 | 3 |
| 58 | 16 16 | 43 44 | 67113 | 23 | 32887 | 72506 | 30 | 27494 | 05393 | 6 | 94607 | 2 |
| 59 | 16 8 | 43 52 | 67137 | 24 | 32863 | 72537 | 30 | 27463 | 05400 | 6 | 94600 | 1 |
| 60 | 16 0 | 44 0 | 67161 | 24 | 32839 | 72567 | 31 | 27433 | 05407 | 7 | 94593 | 0 |
| M | Hour P.M. | Hour A.M. | Cosine. | Diff. | Secant. | Cotangent | Diff. | Tangent. | Cosecant. | Diff. | Sine. | M |
| | | | A | | A | B | | B | C | | C | |

117° | 62°

| Seconds of time ...... | | 1s | 2s | 3s | 4s | 5s | 6s | 7s |
|---|---|---|---|---|---|---|---|---|
| Prop. parts of cols. | A | 3 | 6 | 9 | 12 | 15 | 18 | 21 |
| | B | 4 | 8 | 12 | 15 | 19 | 23 | 27 |
| | C | 1 | 2 | 2 | 3 | 4 | 5 | 6 |

# TABLE XXVII.

## Log. Sines, Tangents, and Secants.

S′. 28° | G′. 151°

| M | Hour A.M. | Hour P.M. | Sine. A | Diff. | Cosecant. A | Tangent. B | Diff. | Cotangent B | Secant. C | Diff. | Cosine. C | M |
|---|---|---|---|---|---|---|---|---|---|---|---|---|
| 0 | 8 16 0 | 3 44 0 | 9.67161 | 0 | 10.32839 | 9.72567 | 0 | 10.27433 | 10.05407 | 0 | 9.94593 | 60 |
| 1 | 15 52 | 44 8 | 67185 | 0 | 32815 | 72598 | 1 | 27402 | 05413 | 0 | 94587 | 59 |
| 2 | 15 44 | 44 16 | 67208 | 1 | 32792 | 72628 | 1 | 27372 | 05420 | 0 | 94580 | 58 |
| 3 | 15 36 | 44 24 | 67232 | 1 | 32768 | 72659 | 2 | 27341 | 05427 | 0 | 94573 | 57 |
| 4 | 15 28 | 44 32 | 67256 | 2 | 32744 | 72689 | 2 | 27311 | 05433 | 0 | 94567 | 56 |
| 5 | 8 15 20 | 3 44 40 | 9.67280 | 2 | 10.32720 | 9.72720 | 3 | 10.27280 | 10.05440 | 1 | 9.94560 | 55 |
| 6 | 15 12 | 44 48 | 67303 | 2 | 32697 | 72750 | 3 | 27250 | 05447 | 1 | 94553 | 54 |
| 7 | 15 4 | 44 56 | 67327 | 3 | 32673 | 72780 | 4 | 27220 | 05454 | 1 | 94546 | 53 |
| 8 | 14 56 | 45 4 | 67350 | 3 | 32650 | 72811 | 4 | 27189 | 05460 | 1 | 94540 | 52 |
| 9 | 14 48 | 45 12 | 67374 | 3 | 32626 | 72841 | 5 | 27159 | 05467 | 1 | 94533 | 51 |
| 10 | 8 14 40 | 3 45 20 | 9.67398 | 4 | 10.32602 | 9.72872 | 5 | 10.27128 | 10.05474 | 1 | 9.94526 | 50 |
| 11 | 14 32 | 45 28 | 67421 | 4 | 32579 | 72902 | 6 | 27098 | 05481 | 1 | 94519 | 49 |
| 12 | 14 24 | 45 36 | 67445 | 5 | 32555 | 72932 | 6 | 27068 | 05487 | 1 | 94513 | 48 |
| 13 | 14 16 | 45 44 | 67468 | 5 | 32532 | 72963 | 7 | 27037 | 05494 | 1 | 94506 | 47 |
| 14 | 14 8 | 45 52 | 67492 | 5 | 32508 | 72993 | 7 | 27007 | 05501 | 2 | 94499 | 46 |
| 15 | 8 14 0 | 3 46 0 | 9.67515 | 6 | 10.32485 | 9.73023 | 8 | 10.26977 | 10.05508 | 2 | 9.94492 | 45 |
| 16 | 13 52 | 46 8 | 67539 | 6 | 32461 | 73054 | 8 | 26946 | 05515 | 2 | 94485 | 44 |
| 17 | 13 44 | 46 16 | 67562 | 7 | 32438 | 73084 | 9 | 26916 | 05521 | 2 | 94479 | 43 |
| 18 | 13 36 | 46 24 | 67586 | 7 | 32414 | 73114 | 9 | 26886 | 05528 | 2 | 94472 | 42 |
| 19 | 13 28 | 46 32 | 67609 | 7 | 32391 | 73144 | 10 | 26856 | 05535 | 2 | 94465 | 41 |
| 20 | 8 13 20 | 3 46 40 | 9.67633 | 8 | 10.32367 | 9.73175 | 10 | 10.26825 | 10.05542 | 2 | 9.94458 | 40 |
| 21 | 13 12 | 46 48 | 67656 | 8 | 32344 | 73205 | 11 | 26795 | 05549 | 2 | 94451 | 39 |
| 22 | 13 4 | 46 56 | 67680 | 9 | 32320 | 73235 | 11 | 26765 | 05555 | 3 | 94445 | 38 |
| 23 | 12 56 | 47 4 | 67703 | 9 | 32297 | 73265 | 12 | 26735 | 05562 | 3 | 94438 | 37 |
| 24 | 12 48 | 47 12 | 67726 | 9 | 32274 | 73295 | 12 | 26705 | 05569 | 3 | 94431 | 36 |
| 25 | 8 12 40 | 3 47 20 | 9.67750 | 10 | 10.32250 | 9.73326 | 13 | 10.26674 | 10.05576 | 3 | 9.94424 | 35 |
| 26 | 12 32 | 47 28 | 67773 | 10 | 32227 | 73356 | 13 | 26644 | 05583 | 3 | 94417 | 34 |
| 27 | 12 24 | 47 36 | 67796 | 10 | 32204 | 73386 | 14 | 26614 | 05590 | 3 | 94410 | 33 |
| 28 | 12 16 | 47 44 | 67820 | 11 | 32180 | 73416 | 14 | 26584 | 05596 | 3 | 94404 | 32 |
| 29 | 12 8 | 47 52 | 67843 | 11 | 32157 | 73446 | 15 | 26554 | 05603 | 3 | 94397 | 31 |
| 30 | 8 12 0 | 3 48 0 | 9.67866 | 12 | 10.32134 | 9.73476 | 15 | 10.26524 | 10.05610 | 3 | 9.94390 | 30 |
| 31 | 11 52 | 48 8 | 67890 | 12 | 32110 | 73507 | 16 | 26493 | 05617 | 4 | 94383 | 29 |
| 32 | 11 44 | 48 16 | 67913 | 12 | 32087 | 73537 | 16 | 26463 | 05624 | 4 | 94376 | 28 |
| 33 | 11 36 | 48 24 | 67936 | 13 | 32064 | 73567 | 17 | 26433 | 05631 | 4 | 94369 | 27 |
| 34 | 11 28 | 48 32 | 67959 | 13 | 32041 | 73597 | 17 | 26403 | 05638 | 4 | 94362 | 26 |
| 35 | 8 11 20 | 3 48 40 | 9.67982 | 14 | 10.32018 | 9.73627 | 18 | 10.26373 | 10.05645 | 4 | 9.94355 | 25 |
| 36 | 11 12 | 48 48 | 68006 | 14 | 31994 | 73657 | 18 | 26343 | 05651 | 4 | 94349 | 24 |
| 37 | 11 4 | 48 56 | 68029 | 14 | 31971 | 73687 | 19 | 26313 | 05658 | 4 | 94342 | 23 |
| 38 | 10 56 | 49 4 | 68052 | 15 | 31948 | 73717 | 19 | 26283 | 05665 | 4 | 94335 | 22 |
| 39 | 10 48 | 49 12 | 68075 | 15 | 31925 | 73747 | 20 | 26253 | 05672 | 4 | 94328 | 21 |
| 40 | 8 10 40 | 3 49 20 | 9.68098 | 16 | 10.31902 | 9.73777 | 20 | 10.26223 | 10.05679 | 5 | 9.94321 | 20 |
| 41 | 10 32 | 49 28 | 68121 | 16 | 31879 | 73807 | 21 | 26193 | 05686 | 5 | 94314 | 19 |
| 42 | 10 24 | 49 36 | 68144 | 16 | 31856 | 73837 | 21 | 26163 | 05693 | 5 | 94307 | 18 |
| 43 | 10 16 | 49 44 | 68167 | 17 | 31833 | 73867 | 22 | 26133 | 05700 | 5 | 94300 | 17 |
| 44 | 10 8 | 49 52 | 68190 | 17 | 31810 | 73897 | 22 | 26103 | 05707 | 5 | 94293 | 16 |
| 45 | 8 10 0 | 3 50 0 | 9.68213 | 17 | 10.31787 | 9.73927 | 23 | 10.26073 | 10.05714 | 5 | 9.94286 | 15 |
| 46 | 9 52 | 50 8 | 68237 | 18 | 31763 | 73957 | 23 | 26043 | 05721 | 5 | 94279 | 14 |
| 47 | 9 44 | 50 16 | 68260 | 18 | 31740 | 73987 | 24 | 26013 | 05727 | 5 | 94273 | 13 |
| 48 | 9 36 | 50 24 | 68283 | 19 | 31717 | 74017 | 24 | 25983 | 05734 | 5 | 94266 | 12 |
| 49 | 9 28 | 50 32 | 68305 | 19 | 31695 | 74047 | 25 | 25953 | 05741 | 6 | 94259 | 11 |
| 50 | 8 9 20 | 3 50 40 | 9.68328 | 19 | 10.31672 | 9.74077 | 25 | 10.25923 | 10.05748 | 6 | 9.94252 | 10 |
| 51 | 9 12 | 50 48 | 68351 | 20 | 31649 | 74107 | 26 | 25893 | 05755 | 6 | 94245 | 9 |
| 52 | 9 4 | 50 56 | 68374 | 20 | 31626 | 74137 | 26 | 25863 | 05762 | 6 | 94238 | 8 |
| 53 | 8 56 | 51 4 | 68397 | 21 | 31603 | 74166 | 27 | 25834 | 05769 | 6 | 94231 | 7 |
| 54 | 8 48 | 51 12 | 68420 | 21 | 31580 | 74196 | 27 | 25804 | 05776 | 6 | 94224 | 6 |
| 55 | 8 8 40 | 3 51 20 | 9.68443 | 21 | 10.31557 | 9.74226 | 28 | 10.25774 | 10.05783 | 6 | 9.94217 | 5 |
| 56 | 8 32 | 51 28 | 68466 | 22 | 31534 | 74256 | 28 | 25744 | 05790 | 6 | 94210 | 4 |
| 57 | 8 24 | 51 36 | 68489 | 22 | 31511 | 74286 | 29 | 25714 | 05797 | 7 | 94203 | 3 |
| 58 | 8 16 | 51 44 | 68512 | 22 | 31488 | 74316 | 29 | 25684 | 05804 | 7 | 94196 | 2 |
| 59 | 8 8 | 51 52 | 68534 | 23 | 31466 | 74345 | 30 | 25655 | 05811 | 7 | 94189 | 1 |
| 60 | 8 0 | 52 0 | 68557 | 23 | 31443 | 74375 | 30 | 25625 | 05818 | 7 | 94182 | 0 |
| M | Hour P.M. | Hour A.M. | Cosine. A | Diff. | Secant. A | Cotangent B | Diff. | Tangent. B | Cosecant. C | Diff. | Sine. C | M |

118° | 61°

| Seconds of time …… | | 1ˢ | 2ˢ | 3ˢ | 4ˢ | 5ˢ | 6ˢ | 7ˢ |
|---|---|---|---|---|---|---|---|---|
| Prop. parts of cols. | A | 3 | 6 | 9 | 12 | 15 | 17 | 20 |
| | B | 4 | 8 | 11 | 15 | 19 | 23 | 26 |
| | C | 1 | 2 | 3 | 3 | 4 | 5 | 6 |

# TABLE XXVII.

S[t]. Log. Sines, Tangents, and Secants. G[t].

29° | A | A | B | B | C | C | 150°

| M | Hour A.M. | Hour P.M. | Sine. A | Diff. | Cosecant. A | Tangent. B | Diff. | Cotangent B | Secant. C | Diff. | Cosine. C | M |
|---|---|---|---|---|---|---|---|---|---|---|---|---|
| 0 | 8 8 0 | 3 52 0 | 9.68557 | 0 | 10.31443 | 9.74375 | 0 | 10.25625 | 10.05818 | 0 | 9.94182 | 60 |
| 1 | 7 52 | 52 8 | 68580 | 0 | 31420 | 74405 | 0 | 25595 | 05825 | 0 | 94175 | 59 |
| 2 | 7 44 | 52 16 | 68603 | 1 | 31397 | 74435 | 1 | 25565 | 05832 | 0 | 94168 | 58 |
| 3 | 7 36 | 52 24 | 68625 | 1 | 31375 | 74465 | 1 | 25535 | 05839 | 0 | 94161 | 57 |
| 4 | 7 28 | 52 32 | 68648 | 1 | 31352 | 74494 | 2 | 25506 | 05846 | 0 | 94154 | 56 |
| 5 | 8 7 20 | 3 52 40 | 9.68671 | 2 | 10.31329 | 9.74524 | 2 | 10.25476 | 10.05853 | 1 | 9.94147 | 55 |
| 6 | 7 12 | 52 48 | 68694 | 2 | 31306 | 74554 | 3 | 25446 | 05860 | 1 | 94140 | 54 |
| 7 | 7 4 | 52 56 | 68716 | 3 | 31284 | 74583 | 3 | 25417 | 05867 | 1 | 94133 | 53 |
| 8 | 6 56 | 53 4 | 68739 | 3 | 31261 | 74613 | 4 | 25387 | 05874 | 1 | 94126 | 52 |
| 9 | 6 48 | 53 12 | 68762 | 3 | 31238 | 74643 | 4 | 25357 | 05881 | 1 | 94119 | 51 |
| 10 | 8 6 40 | 3 53 20 | 9.68784 | 4 | 10.31216 | 9.74673 | 5 | 10.25327 | 10.05888 | 1 | 9.94112 | 50 |
| 11 | 6 32 | 53 28 | 68807 | 4 | 31193 | 74702 | 5 | 25298 | 05895 | 1 | 94105 | 49 |
| 12 | 6 24 | 53 36 | 68829 | 4 | 31171 | 74732 | 6 | 25268 | 05902 | 1 | 94098 | 48 |
| 13 | 6 16 | 53 44 | 68852 | 5 | 31148 | 74762 | 6 | 25238 | 05910 | 2 | 94090 | 47 |
| 14 | 6 8 | 53 52 | 68875 | 5 | 31125 | 74791 | 7 | 25209 | 05917 | 2 | 94083 | 46 |
| 15 | 8 6 0 | 3 54 0 | 9.68897 | 6 | 10.31103 | 9.74821 | 7 | 10.25179 | 10.05924 | 2 | 9.94076 | 45 |
| 16 | 5 52 | 54 8 | 68920 | 6 | 31080 | 74851 | 8 | 25149 | 05931 | 2 | 94069 | 44 |
| 17 | 5 44 | 54 16 | 68942 | 6 | 31058 | 74880 | 8 | 25120 | 05938 | 2 | 94062 | 43 |
| 18 | 5 36 | 54 24 | 68965 | 7 | 31035 | 74910 | 9 | 25090 | 05945 | 2 | 94055 | 42 |
| 19 | 5 28 | 54 32 | 68987 | 7 | 31013 | 74939 | 9 | 25061 | 05952 | 2 | 94048 | 41 |
| 20 | 8 5 20 | 3 54 40 | 9.69010 | 7 | 10.30990 | 9.74969 | 10 | 10.25031 | 10.05959 | 2 | 9.94041 | 40 |
| 21 | 5 12 | 54 48 | 69032 | 8 | 30968 | 74998 | 10 | 25002 | 05966 | 3 | 94034 | 39 |
| 22 | 5 4 | 54 56 | 69055 | 8 | 30945 | 75028 | 11 | 24972 | 05973 | 3 | 94027 | 38 |
| 23 | 4 56 | 55 4 | 69077 | 9 | 30923 | 75058 | 11 | 24942 | 05980 | 3 | 94020 | 37 |
| 24 | 4 48 | 55 12 | 69100 | 9 | 30900 | 75087 | 12 | 24913 | 05988 | 3 | 94012 | 36 |
| 25 | 8 4 40 | 3 55 20 | 9.69122 | 9 | 10.30878 | 9.75117 | 12 | 10.24883 | 10.05995 | 3 | 9.94005 | 35 |
| 26 | 4 32 | 55 28 | 69144 | 10 | 30856 | 75146 | 13 | 24854 | 06002 | 3 | 93998 | 34 |
| 27 | 4 24 | 55 36 | 69167 | 10 | 30833 | 75176 | 13 | 24824 | 06009 | 3 | 93991 | 33 |
| 28 | 4 16 | 55 44 | 69189 | 10 | 30811 | 75205 | 14 | 24795 | 06016 | 3 | 93984 | 32 |
| 29 | 4 8 | 55 52 | 69212 | 11 | 30788 | 75235 | 14 | 24765 | 06023 | 3 | 93977 | 31 |
| 30 | 8 4 0 | 3 56 0 | 9.69234 | 11 | 10.30766 | 9.75264 | 15 | 10.24736 | 10.06030 | 4 | 9.93970 | 30 |
| 31 | 3 52 | 56 8 | 69256 | 12 | 30744 | 75294 | 15 | 24706 | 06037 | 4 | 93963 | 29 |
| 32 | 3 44 | 56 16 | 69279 | 12 | 30721 | 75323 | 16 | 24677 | 06045 | 4 | 93955 | 28 |
| 33 | 3 36 | 56 24 | 69301 | 12 | 30699 | 75353 | 16 | 24647 | 06052 | 4 | 93948 | 27 |
| 34 | 3 28 | 56 32 | 69323 | 13 | 30677 | 75382 | 17 | 24618 | 06059 | 4 | 93941 | 26 |
| 35 | 8 3 20 | 3 56 40 | 9.69345 | 13 | 10.30655 | 9.75411 | 17 | 10.24589 | 10.06066 | 4 | 9.93934 | 25 |
| 36 | 3 12 | 56 48 | 69368 | 13 | 30632 | 75441 | 18 | 24559 | 06073 | 4 | 93927 | 24 |
| 37 | 3 4 | 56 56 | 69390 | 14 | 30610 | 75470 | 18 | 24530 | 06080 | 4 | 93920 | 23 |
| 38 | 2 56 | 57 4 | 69412 | 14 | 30588 | 75500 | 19 | 24500 | 06088 | 5 | 93912 | 22 |
| 39 | 2 48 | 57 12 | 69434 | 15 | 30566 | 75529 | 19 | 24471 | 06095 | 5 | 93905 | 21 |
| 40 | 8 2 40 | 3 57 20 | 9.69456 | 15 | 10.30544 | 9.75558 | 20 | 10.24442 | 10.06102 | 5 | 9.93898 | 20 |
| 41 | 2 32 | 57 28 | 69479 | 15 | 30521 | 75588 | 20 | 24412 | 06109 | 5 | 93891 | 19 |
| 42 | 2 24 | 57 36 | 69501 | 16 | 30499 | 75617 | 21 | 24383 | 06116 | 5 | 93884 | 18 |
| 43 | 2 16 | 57 44 | 69523 | 16 | 30477 | 75647 | 21 | 24353 | 06124 | 5 | 93876 | 17 |
| 44 | 2 8 | 57 52 | 69545 | 16 | 30455 | 75676 | 22 | 24324 | 06131 | 5 | 93869 | 16 |
| 45 | 8 2 0 | 3 58 0 | 9.69567 | 17 | 10.30433 | 9.75705 | 22 | 10.24295 | 10.06138 | 5 | 9.93862 | 15 |
| 46 | 1 52 | 58 8 | 69589 | 17 | 30411 | 75735 | 23 | 24265 | 06145 | 5 | 93855 | 14 |
| 47 | 1 44 | 58 16 | 69611 | 17 | 30389 | 75764 | 23 | 24236 | 06153 | 6 | 93847 | 13 |
| 48 | 1 36 | 58 24 | 69633 | 18 | 30367 | 75793 | 24 | 24207 | 06160 | 6 | 93840 | 12 |
| 49 | 1 28 | 58 32 | 69655 | 18 | 30345 | 75822 | 24 | 24178 | 06167 | 6 | 93833 | 11 |
| 50 | 8 1 20 | 3 58 40 | 9.69677 | 19 | 10.30323 | 9.75852 | 25 | 10.24148 | 10.06174 | 6 | 9.93826 | 10 |
| 51 | 1 12 | 58 48 | 69699 | 19 | 30301 | 75881 | 25 | 24119 | 06181 | 6 | 93819 | 9 |
| 52 | 1 4 | 58 56 | 69721 | 19 | 30279 | 75910 | 26 | 24090 | 06189 | 6 | 93811 | 8 |
| 53 | 0 56 | 59 4 | 69743 | 20 | 30257 | 75939 | 26 | 24061 | 06196 | 6 | 93804 | 7 |
| 54 | 0 48 | 59 12 | 69765 | 20 | 30235 | 75969 | 27 | 24031 | 06203 | 6 | 93797 | 6 |
| 55 | 8 0 40 | 3 59 20 | 9.69787 | 20 | 10.30213 | 9.75998 | 27 | 10.24002 | 10.06211 | 7 | 9.93789 | 5 |
| 56 | 0 32 | 59 28 | 69809 | 21 | 30191 | 76027 | 28 | 23973 | 06218 | 7 | 93782 | 4 |
| 57 | 0 24 | 59 36 | 69831 | 21 | 30169 | 76056 | 28 | 23944 | 06225 | 7 | 93775 | 3 |
| 58 | 0 16 | 59 44 | 69853 | 22 | 30147 | 76086 | 29 | 23914 | 06232 | 7 | 93768 | 2 |
| 59 | 0 8 | 59 52 | 69875 | 22 | 30125 | 76115 | 29 | 23885 | 06240 | 7 | 93760 | 1 |
| 60 | 0 0 | 4 0 0 | 69897 | 22 | 30103 | 76144 | 29 | 23856 | 06247 | 7 | 93753 | 0 |
| M | Hour P.M. | Hour A.M. | Cosine. A | Diff. | Secant. A | Cotangent B | Diff. | Tangent. B | Cosecant. C | Diff. | Sine. C | M |

119° | A | A | B | B | C | C | 60°

| Seconds of time ...... | | 1[s] | 2[s] | 3[s] | 4[s] | 5[s] | 6[s] | 7[s] |
|---|---|---|---|---|---|---|---|---|
| Prop. parts of cols. | A | 3 | 6 | 8 | 11 | 14 | 17 | 20 |
| | B | 4 | 7 | 11 | 15 | 18 | 22 | 26 |
| | C | 1 | 2 | 3 | 4 | 4 | 5 | 6 |

# TABLE XXVII.

## Log. Sines, Tangents, and Secants.

S′. G′.

| 30° | | | A | | A | B | | B | C | | C 149° | |
|---|---|---|---|---|---|---|---|---|---|---|---|---|
| M | Hour A.M. | Hour P.M. | Sine. | Diff. | Cosecant. | Tangent. | Diff. | Cotangent | Secant. | Diff. | Cosine. | M |
| 0 | 8 0 0 | 4 0 0 | 9.69897 | 0 | 10.30103 | 9.76144 | 0 | 10.23856 | 10.06247 | 0 | 9.93753 | 60 |
| 1 | 7 59 52 | 0 8 | 69919 | 0 | 30081 | 76173 | 0 | 23827 | 06254 | 0 | 93746 | 59 |
| 2 | 59 44 | 0 16 | 69941 | 1 | 30059 | 76202 | 1 | 23798 | 06262 | 0 | 93738 | 58 |
| 3 | 59 36 | 0 24 | 69963 | 1 | 30037 | 76231 | 1 | 23769 | 06269 | 0 | 93731 | 57 |
| 4 | 59 28 | 0 32 | 69984 | 1 | 30016 | 76261 | 2 | 23739 | 06276 | 0 | 93724 | 56 |
| 5 | 7 59 20 | 4 0 40 | 9.70006 | 2 | 10.29994 | 9.76290 | 2 | 10.23710 | 10.06283 | 1 | 9.93717 | 55 |
| 6 | 59 12 | 0 48 | 70028 | 2 | 29972 | 76319 | 3 | 23681 | 06291 | 1 | 93709 | 54 |
| 7 | 59 4 | 0 56 | 70050 | 3 | 29950 | 76348 | 3 | 23652 | 06298 | 1 | 93702 | 53 |
| 8 | 58 56 | 1 4 | 70072 | 3 | 29928 | 76377 | 4 | 23623 | 06305 | 1 | 93695 | 52 |
| 9 | 58 48 | 1 12 | 70093 | 3 | 29907 | 76406 | 4 | 23594 | 06313 | 1 | 93687 | 51 |
| 10 | 7 58 40 | 4 1 20 | 9.70115 | 4 | 10.29885 | 9.76435 | 5 | 10.23565 | 10.06320 | 1 | 9.93680 | 50 |
| 11 | 58 32 | 1 28 | 70137 | 4 | 29863 | 76464 | 5 | 23536 | 06327 | 1 | 93673 | 49 |
| 12 | 58 24 | 1 36 | 70159 | 4 | 29841 | 76493 | 6 | 23507 | 06335 | 1 | 93665 | 48 |
| 13 | 58 16 | 1 44 | 70180 | 5 | 29820 | 76522 | 6 | 23478 | 06342 | 2 | 93658 | 47 |
| 14 | 58 8 | 1 52 | 70202 | 5 | 29798 | 76551 | 7 | 23449 | 06350 | 2 | 93650 | 46 |
| 15 | 7 58 0 | 4 2 0 | 9.70224 | 5 | 10.29776 | 9.76580 | 7 | 10.23420 | 10.06357 | 2 | 9.93643 | 45 |
| 16 | 57 52 | 2 8 | 70245 | 6 | 29755 | 76609 | 8 | 23391 | 06364 | 2 | 93636 | 44 |
| 17 | 57 44 | 2 16 | 70267 | 6 | 29733 | 76639 | 8 | 23361 | 06372 | 2 | 93628 | 43 |
| 18 | 57 36 | 2 24 | 70288 | 6 | 29712 | 76668 | 9 | 23332 | 06379 | 2 | 93621 | 42 |
| 19 | 57 28 | 2 32 | 70310 | 7 | 29690 | 76697 | 9 | 23303 | 06386 | 2 | 93614 | 41 |
| 20 | 7 57 20 | 4 2 40 | 9.70332 | 7 | 10.29668 | 9.76725 | 10 | 10.23275 | 10.06394 | 2 | 9.93606 | 40 |
| 21 | 57 12 | 2 48 | 70353 | 8 | 29647 | 76754 | 10 | 23246 | 06401 | 3 | 93599 | 39 |
| 22 | 57 4 | 2 56 | 70375 | 8 | 29625 | 76783 | 11 | 23217 | 06409 | 3 | 93591 | 38 |
| 23 | 56 56 | 3 4 | 70396 | 8 | 29604 | 76812 | 11 | 23188 | 06416 | 3 | 93584 | 37 |
| 24 | 56 48 | 3 12 | 70418 | 9 | 29582 | 76841 | 12 | 23159 | 06423 | 3 | 93577 | 36 |
| 25 | 7 56 40 | 4 3 20 | 9.70439 | 9 | 10.29561 | 9.76870 | 12 | 10.23130 | 10.06431 | 3 | 9.93569 | 35 |
| 26 | 56 32 | 3 28 | 70461 | 9 | 29539 | 76899 | 13 | 23101 | 06438 | 3 | 93562 | 34 |
| 27 | 56 24 | 3 36 | 70482 | 10 | 29518 | 76928 | 13 | 23072 | 06446 | 3 | 93554 | 33 |
| 28 | 56 16 | 3 44 | 70504 | 10 | 29496 | 76957 | 13 | 23043 | 06453 | 3 | 93547 | 32 |
| 29 | 56 8 | 3 52 | 70525 | 10 | 29475 | 76986 | 14 | 23014 | 06461 | 4 | 93539 | 31 |
| 30 | 7 56 0 | 4 4 0 | 9.70547 | 11 | 10.29453 | 9.77015 | 14 | 10.22985 | 10.06468 | 4 | 9.93532 | 30 |
| 31 | 55 52 | 4 8 | 70568 | 11 | 29432 | 77044 | 15 | 22956 | 06475 | 4 | 93525 | 29 |
| 32 | 55 44 | 4 16 | 70590 | 11 | 29410 | 77073 | 15 | 22927 | 06483 | 4 | 93517 | 28 |
| 33 | 55 36 | 4 24 | 70611 | 12 | 29389 | 77101 | 16 | 22899 | 06490 | 4 | 93510 | 27 |
| 34 | 55 28 | 4 32 | 70633 | 12 | 29367 | 77130 | 16 | 22870 | 06498 | 4 | 93502 | 26 |
| 35 | 7 55 20 | 4 4 40 | 9.70654 | 13 | 10.29346 | 9.77159 | 17 | 10.22841 | 10.06505 | 4 | 9.93495 | 25 |
| 36 | 55 12 | 4 48 | 70675 | 13 | 29325 | 77188 | 17 | 22812 | 06513 | 4 | 93487 | 24 |
| 37 | 55 4 | 4 56 | 70697 | 13 | 29303 | 77217 | 18 | 22783 | 06520 | 5 | 93480 | 23 |
| 38 | 54 56 | 5 4 | 70718 | 14 | 29282 | 77246 | 18 | 22754 | 06528 | 5 | 93472 | 22 |
| 39 | 54 48 | 5 12 | 70739 | 14 | 29261 | 77274 | 19 | 22726 | 06535 | 5 | 93465 | 21 |
| 40 | 7 54 40 | 4 5 20 | 9.70761 | 14 | 10.29239 | 9.77303 | 19 | 10.22697 | 10.06543 | 5 | 9.93457 | 20 |
| 41 | 54 32 | 5 28 | 70782 | 15 | 29218 | 77332 | 20 | 22668 | 06550 | 5 | 93450 | 19 |
| 42 | 54 24 | 5 36 | 70803 | 15 | 29197 | 77361 | 20 | 22639 | 06558 | 5 | 93442 | 18 |
| 43 | 54 16 | 5 44 | 70824 | 15 | 29176 | 77390 | 21 | 22610 | 06565 | 5 | 93435 | 17 |
| 44 | 54 8 | 5 52 | 70846 | 16 | 29154 | 77418 | 21 | 22582 | 06573 | 5 | 93427 | 16 |
| 45 | 7 54 0 | 4 6 0 | 9.70867 | 16 | 10.29133 | 9.77447 | 22 | 10.22553 | 10.06580 | 6 | 9.93420 | 15 |
| 46 | 53 52 | 6 8 | 70888 | 16 | 29112 | 77476 | 22 | 22524 | 06588 | 6 | 93412 | 14 |
| 47 | 53 44 | 6 16 | 70909 | 17 | 29091 | 77505 | 23 | 22495 | 06595 | 6 | 93405 | 13 |
| 48 | 53 36 | 6 24 | 70931 | 17 | 29069 | 77533 | 23 | 22467 | 06603 | 6 | 93397 | 12 |
| 49 | 53 28 | 6 32 | 70952 | 18 | 29048 | 77562 | 24 | 22438 | 06610 | 6 | 93390 | 11 |
| 50 | 7 53 20 | 4 6 40 | 9.70973 | 18 | 10.29027 | 9.77591 | 24 | 10.22409 | 10.06618 | 6 | 9.93382 | 10 |
| 51 | 53 12 | 6 48 | 70994 | 18 | 29006 | 77619 | 25 | 22381 | 06625 | 6 | 93375 | 9 |
| 52 | 53 4 | 6 56 | 71015 | 19 | 28985 | 77648 | 25 | 22352 | 06633 | 6 | 93367 | 8 |
| 53 | 52 56 | 7 4 | 71036 | 19 | 28964 | 77677 | 26 | 22323 | 06640 | 7 | 93360 | 7 |
| 54 | 52 48 | 7 12 | 71058 | 19 | 28942 | 77706 | 26 | 22294 | 06648 | 7 | 93352 | 6 |
| 55 | 7 52 40 | 4 7 20 | 9.71079 | 20 | 10.28921 | 9.77734 | 26 | 10.22266 | 10.06656 | 7 | 9.93344 | 5 |
| 56 | 52 32 | 7 28 | 71100 | 20 | 28900 | 77763 | 27 | 22237 | 06663 | 7 | 93337 | 4 |
| 57 | 52 24 | 7 36 | 71121 | 20 | 28879 | 77791 | 27 | 22209 | 06671 | 7 | 93329 | 3 |
| 58 | 52 16 | 7 44 | 71142 | 21 | 28858 | 77820 | 28 | 22180 | 06678 | 7 | 93322 | 2 |
| 59 | 52 8 | 7 52 | 71163 | 21 | 28837 | 77849 | 28 | 22151 | 06686 | 7 | 93314 | 1 |
| 60 | 52 0 | 8 0 | 71184 | 21 | 28816 | 77877 | 29 | 22123 | 06693 | 7 | 93307 | 0 |
| M | Hour P.M. | Hour A.M. | Cosine. | Diff. | Secant. | Cotangent | Diff. | Tangent. | Cosecant. | Diff. | Sine. | M |
| 120° | | | A | | A | B | | B | C | | C | 59° |

| Seconds of time ...... | | 1 | 2 | 3 | 4 | 5 | 6 | 7 |
|---|---|---|---|---|---|---|---|---|
| Prop. parts of cols. | A | 3 | 5 | 8 | 11 | 13 | 16 | 19 |
| | B | 4 | 7 | 11 | 14 | 18 | 22 | 25 |
| | C | 1 | 2 | 3 | 4 | 5 | 6 | 7 |

# TABLE XXVII.

S′. G′

## Log. Sines, Tangents, and Secants.

31° 148°

| M | Hour A.M. | Hour P.M. | Sine. A | Diff. | Cosecant. A | Tangent. B | Diff. | Cotangent B | Secant. C | Diff. | Cosine. C | M |
|---|---|---|---|---|---|---|---|---|---|---|---|---|
| 0 | 7 52 0 | 4 8 0 | 9.71184 | 0 | 10.28816 | 9.77877 | 0 | 10.22123 | 10.06693 | 0 | 9.93307 | 60 |
| 1 | 51 52 | 8 8 | 71205 | 0 | 28795 | 77906 | 0 | 22094 | 06701 | 0 | 93299 | 59 |
| 2 | 51 44 | 8 16 | 71226 | 1 | 28774 | 77935 | 1 | 22065 | 06709 | 0 | 93291 | 58 |
| 3 | 51 36 | 8 24 | 71247 | 1 | 28753 | 77963 | 1 | 22037 | 06716 | 0 | 93284 | 57 |
| 4 | 51 28 | 8 32 | 71268 | 1 | 28732 | 77992 | 2 | 22008 | 06724 | 1 | 93276 | 56 |
| 5 | 7 51 20 | 4 8 40 | 9.71289 | 2 | 10.28711 | 9.78020 | 2 | 10.21980 | 10.06731 | 1 | 9.93269 | 55 |
| 6 | 51 12 | 8 48 | 71310 | 2 | 28690 | 78049 | 3 | 21951 | 06739 | 1 | 93261 | 54 |
| 7 | 51 4 | 8 56 | 71331 | 2 | 28669 | 78077 | 3 | 21923 | 06747 | 1 | 93253 | 53 |
| 8 | 50 56 | 9 4 | 71352 | 3 | 28648 | 78106 | 4 | 21894 | 06754 | 1 | 93246 | 52 |
| 9 | 50 48 | 9 12 | 71373 | 3 | 28627 | 78135 | 4 | 21865 | 06762 | 1 | 93238 | 51 |
| 10 | 7 50 40 | 4 9 20 | 9.71393 | 3 | 10.28607 | 9.78163 | 5 | 10.21837 | 10.06770 | 1 | 9.93230 | 50 |
| 11 | 50 32 | 9 28 | 71414 | 4 | 28586 | 78192 | 5 | 21808 | 06777 | 1 | 93223 | 49 |
| 12 | 50 24 | 9 36 | 71435 | 4 | 28565 | 78220 | 6 | 21780 | 06785 | 2 | 93215 | 48 |
| 13 | 50 16 | 9 44 | 71456 | 4 | 28544 | 78249 | 6 | 21751 | 06793 | 2 | 93207 | 47 |
| 14 | 50 8 | 9 52 | 71477 | 5 | 28523 | 78277 | 7 | 21723 | 06800 | 2 | 93200 | 46 |
| 15 | 7 50 0 | 4 10 0 | 9.71498 | 5 | 10.28502 | 9.78306 | 7 | 10.21694 | 10.06808 | 2 | 9.93192 | 45 |
| 16 | 49 52 | 10 8 | 71519 | 5 | 28481 | 78334 | 8 | 21666 | 06816 | 2 | 93184 | 44 |
| 17 | 49 44 | 10 16 | 71539 | 6 | 28461 | 78363 | 8 | 21637 | 06823 | 2 | 93177 | 43 |
| 18 | 49 36 | 10 24 | 71560 | 6 | 28440 | 78391 | 9 | 21609 | 06831 | 2 | 93169 | 42 |
| 19 | 49 28 | 10 32 | 71581 | 7 | 28419 | 78419 | 9 | 21581 | 06839 | 2 | 93161 | 41 |
| 20 | 7 49 20 | 4 10 40 | 9.71602 | 7 | 10.28398 | 9.78448 | 9 | 10.21552 | 10.06846 | 3 | 9.93154 | 40 |
| 21 | 49 12 | 10 48 | 71622 | 7 | 28378 | 78476 | 10 | 21524 | 06854 | 3 | 93146 | 39 |
| 22 | 49 4 | 10 56 | 71643 | 8 | 28357 | 78505 | 10 | 21495 | 06862 | 3 | 93138 | 38 |
| 23 | 48 56 | 11 4 | 71664 | 8 | 28336 | 78533 | 11 | 21467 | 06869 | 3 | 93131 | 37 |
| 24 | 48 48 | 11 12 | 71685 | 8 | 28315 | 78562 | 11 | 21438 | 06877 | 3 | 93123 | 36 |
| 25 | 7 48 40 | 4 11 20 | 9.71705 | 9 | 10.28295 | 9.78590 | 12 | 10.21410 | 10.06885 | 3 | 9.93115 | 35 |
| 26 | 48 32 | 11 28 | 71726 | 9 | 28274 | 78618 | 12 | 21382 | 06892 | 3 | 93108 | 34 |
| 27 | 48 24 | 11 36 | 71747 | 9 | 28253 | 78647 | 13 | 21353 | 06900 | 3 | 93100 | 33 |
| 28 | 48 16 | 11 44 | 71767 | 10 | 28233 | 78675 | 13 | 21325 | 06908 | 4 | 93092 | 32 |
| 29 | 48 8 | 11 52 | 71788 | 10 | 28212 | 78704 | 14 | 21296 | 06916 | 4 | 93084 | 31 |
| 30 | 7 48 0 | 4 12 0 | 9.71809 | 10 | 10.28191 | 9.78732 | 14 | 10.21268 | 10.06923 | 4 | 9.93077 | 30 |
| 31 | 47 52 | 12 8 | 71829 | 11 | 28171 | 78760 | 15 | 21240 | 06931 | 4 | 93069 | 29 |
| 32 | 47 44 | 12 16 | 71850 | 11 | 28150 | 78789 | 15 | 21211 | 06939 | 4 | 93061 | 28 |
| 33 | 47 36 | 12 24 | 71870 | 11 | 28130 | 78817 | 16 | 21183 | 06947 | 4 | 93053 | 27 |
| 34 | 47 28 | 12 32 | 71891 | 12 | 28109 | 78845 | 16 | 21155 | 06954 | 4 | 93046 | 26 |
| 35 | 7 47 20 | 4 12 40 | 9.71911 | 12 | 10.28089 | 9.78874 | 17 | 10.21126 | 10.06962 | 5 | 9.93038 | 25 |
| 36 | 47 12 | 12 48 | 71932 | 12 | 28068 | 78902 | 17 | 21098 | 06970 | 5 | 93030 | 24 |
| 37 | 47 4 | 12 56 | 71952 | 13 | 28048 | 78930 | 17 | 21070 | 06978 | 5 | 93022 | 23 |
| 38 | 46 56 | 13 4 | 71973 | 13 | 28027 | 78959 | 18 | 21041 | 06986 | 5 | 93014 | 22 |
| 39 | 46 48 | 13 12 | 71994 | 13 | 28006 | 78987 | 18 | 21013 | 06993 | 5 | 93007 | 21 |
| 40 | 7 46 40 | 4 13 20 | 9.72014 | 14 | 10.27986 | 9.79015 | 19 | 10.20985 | 10.07001 | 5 | 9.92999 | 20 |
| 41 | 46 32 | 13 28 | 72034 | 14 | 27966 | 79043 | 19 | 20957 | 07009 | 5 | 92991 | 19 |
| 42 | 46 24 | 13 36 | 72055 | 14 | 27945 | 79072 | 20 | 20928 | 07017 | 5 | 92983 | 18 |
| 43 | 46 16 | 13 44 | 72075 | 15 | 27925 | 79100 | 20 | 20900 | 07024 | 6 | 92976 | 17 |
| 44 | 46 8 | 13 52 | 72096 | 15 | 27904 | 79128 | 21 | 20872 | 07032 | 6 | 92968 | 16 |
| 45 | 7 46 0 | 4 14 0 | 9.72116 | 15 | 10.27884 | 9.79156 | 21 | 10.20844 | 10.07040 | 6 | 9.92960 | 15 |
| 46 | 45 52 | 14 8 | 72137 | 16 | 27863 | 79185 | 22 | 20815 | 07048 | 6 | 92952 | 14 |
| 47 | 45 44 | 14 16 | 72157 | 16 | 27843 | 79213 | 22 | 20787 | 07056 | 6 | 92944 | 13 |
| 48 | 45 36 | 14 24 | 72177 | 16 | 27823 | 79241 | 23 | 20759 | 07064 | 6 | 92936 | 12 |
| 49 | 45 28 | 14 32 | 72198 | 17 | 27802 | 79269 | 23 | 20731 | 07071 | 6 | 92929 | 11 |
| 50 | 7 45 20 | 4 14 40 | 9.72218 | 17 | 10.27782 | 9.79297 | 24 | 10.20703 | 10.07079 | 6 | 9.92921 | 10 |
| 51 | 45 12 | 14 48 | 72238 | 18 | 27762 | 79326 | 24 | 20674 | 07087 | 7 | 92913 | 9 |
| 52 | 45 4 | 14 56 | 72259 | 18 | 27741 | 79354 | 25 | 20646 | 07095 | 7 | 92905 | 8 |
| 53 | 44 56 | 15 4 | 72279 | 18 | 27721 | 79382 | 25 | 20618 | 07103 | 7 | 92897 | 7 |
| 54 | 44 48 | 15 12 | 72299 | 19 | 27701 | 79410 | 26 | 20590 | 07111 | 7 | 92889 | 6 |
| 55 | 7 44 40 | 4 15 20 | 9.72320 | 19 | 10.27680 | 9.79438 | 26 | 10.20562 | 10.07119 | 7 | 9.92881 | 5 |
| 56 | 44 32 | 15 28 | 72340 | 19 | 27660 | 79466 | 26 | 20534 | 07126 | 7 | 92874 | 4 |
| 57 | 44 24 | 15 36 | 72360 | 20 | 27640 | 79495 | 27 | 20505 | 07134 | 7 | 92866 | 3 |
| 58 | 44 16 | 15 44 | 72381 | 20 | 27619 | 79523 | 27 | 20477 | 07142 | 7 | 92858 | 2 |
| 59 | 44 8 | 15 52 | 72401 | 20 | 27599 | 79551 | 28 | 20449 | 07150 | 8 | 92850 | 1 |
| 60 | 44 0 | 16 0 | 72421 | 21 | 27579 | 79579 | 28 | 20421 | 07158 | 8 | 92842 | 0 |
| M | Hour P.M. | Hour A.M. | Cosine. A | Diff. | Secant. A | Cotangent B | Diff. | Tangent. B | Cosecant. C | Diff. | Sine. C | M |

121° 58°

| Seconds of time ...... | | 1ˢ | 2ˢ | 3ˢ | 4ˢ | 5ˢ | 6ˢ | 7ˢ |
|---|---|---|---|---|---|---|---|---|
| Prop. parts of cols | A | 3 | 5 | 8 | 10 | 13 | 15 | 18 |
| | B | 4 | 7 | 11 | 14 | 18 | 21 | 25 |
| | C | 1 | 2 | 3 | 4 | 5 | 6 | 7 |

# TABLE XXVII.

## Log. Sines, Tangents, and Secants.

S'. 32° | G'. 147°

| M | Hour A.M. | Hour P.M. | A<br>Sine. | Diff. | A<br>Cosecant. | B<br>Tangent. | Diff. | B<br>Cotangent | C<br>Secant. | Diff. | C<br>Cosine. | M |
|---|---|---|---|---|---|---|---|---|---|---|---|---|
| 0 | 7 44 0 | 4 16 0 | 9.72421 | 0 | 10.27579 | 9.79579 | 0 | 10.20421 | 10.07158 | 0 | 9.92842 | 60 |
| 1 | 43 52 | 16 8 | 72441 | 0 | 27559 | 79607 | 0 | 20393 | 07166 | 0 | 92834 | 59 |
| 2 | 43 44 | 16 16 | 72461 | 1 | 27539 | 79635 | 1 | 20365 | 07174 | 0 | 92826 | 58 |
| 3 | 43 36 | 16 24 | 72482 | 1 | 27518 | 79663 | 1 | 20337 | 07182 | 0 | 92818 | 57 |
| 4 | 43 28 | 16 32 | 72502 | 1 | 27498 | 79691 | 2 | 20309 | 07190 | 1 | 92810 | 56 |
| 5 | 7 43 20 | 4 16 40 | 9.72522 | 2 | 10.27478 | 9.79719 | 2 | 10.20281 | 10.07197 | 1 | 9.92803 | 55 |
| 6 | 43 12 | 16 48 | 72542 | 2 | 27458 | 79747 | 3 | 20253 | 07205 | 1 | 92795 | 54 |
| 7 | 43 4 | 16 56 | 72562 | 2 | 27438 | 79776 | 3 | 20224 | 07213 | 1 | 92787 | 53 |
| 8 | 42 56 | 17 4 | 72582 | 3 | 27418 | 79804 | 4 | 20196 | 07221 | 1 | 92779 | 52 |
| 9 | 42 48 | 17 12 | 72602 | 3 | 27398 | 79832 | 4 | 20168 | 07229 | 1 | 92771 | 51 |
| 10 | 7 42 40 | 4 17 20 | 9.72622 | 3 | 10.27378 | 9.79860 | 5 | 10.20140 | 10.07237 | 1 | 9.92763 | 50 |
| 11 | 42 32 | 17 28 | 72643 | 4 | 27357 | 79888 | 5 | 20112 | 07245 | 1 | 92755 | 49 |
| 12 | 42 24 | 17 36 | 72663 | 4 | 27337 | 79916 | 6 | 20084 | 07253 | 2 | 92747 | 48 |
| 13 | 42 16 | 17 44 | 72683 | 4 | 27317 | 79944 | 6 | 20056 | 07261 | 2 | 92739 | 47 |
| 14 | 42 8 | 17 52 | 72703 | 5 | 27297 | 79972 | 7 | 20028 | 07269 | 2 | 92731 | 46 |
| 15 | 7 42 0 | 4 18 0 | 9.72723 | 5 | 10.27277 | 9.80000 | 7 | 10.20000 | 10.07277 | 2 | 9.92723 | 45 |
| 16 | 41 52 | 18 8 | 72743 | 5 | 27257 | 80028 | 7 | 19972 | 07285 | 2 | 92715 | 44 |
| 17 | 41 44 | 18 16 | 72763 | 6 | 27237 | 80056 | 8 | 19944 | 07293 | 2 | 92707 | 43 |
| 18 | 41 36 | 18 24 | 72783 | 6 | 27217 | 80084 | 8 | 19916 | 07301 | 2 | 92699 | 42 |
| 19 | 41 28 | 18 32 | 72803 | 6 | 27197 | 80112 | 9 | 19888 | 07309 | 3 | 92691 | 41 |
| 20 | 7 41 20 | 4 18 40 | 9.72823 | 7 | 10.27177 | 9.80140 | 9 | 10.19860 | 10.07317 | 3 | 9.92683 | 40 |
| 21 | 41 12 | 18 48 | 72843 | 7 | 27157 | 80168 | 10 | 19832 | 07325 | 3 | 92675 | 39 |
| 22 | 41 4 | 18 56 | 72863 | 7 | 27137 | 80195 | 10 | 19805 | 07333 | 3 | 92667 | 38 |
| 23 | 40 56 | 19 4 | 72883 | 8 | 27117 | 80223 | 11 | 19777 | 07341 | 3 | 92659 | 37 |
| 24 | 40 48 | 19 12 | 72902 | 8 | 27098 | 80251 | 11 | 19749 | 07349 | 3 | 92651 | 36 |
| 25 | 7 40 40 | 4 19 20 | 9.72922 | 8 | 10.27078 | 9.80279 | 12 | 10.19721 | 10.07357 | 3 | 9.92643 | 35 |
| 26 | 40 32 | 19 28 | 72942 | 9 | 27058 | 80307 | 12 | 19693 | 07365 | 3 | 92635 | 34 |
| 27 | 40 24 | 19 36 | 72962 | 9 | 27038 | 80335 | 13 | 19665 | 07373 | 4 | 92627 | 33 |
| 28 | 40 16 | 19 44 | 72982 | 9 | 27018 | 80363 | 13 | 19637 | 07381 | 4 | 92619 | 32 |
| 29 | 40 8 | 19 52 | 73002 | 10 | 26998 | 80391 | 13 | 19609 | 07389 | 4 | 92611 | 31 |
| 30 | 7 40 0 | 4 20 0 | 9.73022 | 10 | 10.26978 | 9.80419 | 14 | 10.19581 | 10.07397 | 4 | 9.92603 | 30 |
| 31 | 39 52 | 20 8 | 73041 | 10 | 26959 | 80447 | 14 | 19553 | 07405 | 4 | 92595 | 29 |
| 32 | 39 44 | 20 16 | 73061 | 11 | 26939 | 80474 | 15 | 19526 | 07413 | 4 | 92587 | 28 |
| 33 | 39 36 | 20 24 | 73081 | 11 | 26919 | 80502 | 15 | 19498 | 07421 | 4 | 92579 | 27 |
| 34 | 39 28 | 20 32 | 73101 | 11 | 26899 | 80530 | 16 | 19470 | 07429 | 5 | 92571 | 26 |
| 35 | 7 39 20 | 4 20 40 | 9.73121 | 12 | 10.26879 | 9.80558 | 16 | 10.19442 | 10.07437 | 5 | 9.92563 | 25 |
| 36 | 39 12 | 20 48 | 73140 | 12 | 26860 | 80586 | 17 | 19414 | 07445 | 5 | 92555 | 24 |
| 37 | 39 4 | 20 56 | 73160 | 12 | 26840 | 80614 | 17 | 19386 | 07454 | 5 | 92546 | 23 |
| 38 | 38 56 | 21 4 | 73180 | 13 | 26820 | 80642 | 18 | 19358 | 07462 | 5 | 92538 | 22 |
| 39 | 38 48 | 21 12 | 73200 | 13 | 26800 | 80669 | 18 | 19331 | 07470 | 5 | 92530 | 21 |
| 40 | 7 38 40 | 4 21 20 | 9.73219 | 13 | 10.26781 | 9.80697 | 19 | 10.19303 | 10.07478 | 5 | 9.92522 | 20 |
| 41 | 38 32 | 21 28 | 73239 | 14 | 26761 | 80725 | 19 | 19275 | 07486 | 6 | 92514 | 19 |
| 42 | 38 24 | 21 36 | 73259 | 14 | 26741 | 80753 | 20 | 19247 | 07494 | 6 | 92506 | 18 |
| 43 | 38 16 | 21 44 | 73278 | 14 | 26722 | 80781 | 20 | 19219 | 07502 | 6 | 92498 | 17 |
| 44 | 38 8 | 21 52 | 73298 | 15 | 26702 | 80808 | 20 | 19192 | 07510 | 6 | 92490 | 16 |
| 45 | 7 38 0 | 4 22 0 | 9.73318 | 15 | 10.26682 | 9.80836 | 21 | 10.19164 | 10.07518 | 6 | 9.92482 | 15 |
| 46 | 37 52 | 22 8 | 73337 | 15 | 26663 | 80864 | 21 | 19136 | 07527 | 6 | 92473 | 14 |
| 47 | 37 44 | 22 16 | 73357 | 16 | 26643 | 80892 | 22 | 19108 | 07535 | 6 | 92465 | 13 |
| 48 | 37 36 | 22 24 | 73377 | 16 | 26623 | 80919 | 22 | 19081 | 07543 | 6 | 92457 | 12 |
| 49 | 37 28 | 22 32 | 73396 | 16 | 26604 | 80947 | 23 | 19053 | 07551 | 7 | 92449 | 11 |
| 50 | 7 37 20 | 4 22 40 | 9.73416 | 17 | 10.26584 | 9.80975 | 23 | 10.19025 | 10.07559 | 7 | 9.92441 | 10 |
| 51 | 37 12 | 22 48 | 73435 | 17 | 26565 | 81003 | 24 | 18997 | 07567 | 7 | 92433 | 9 |
| 52 | 37 4 | 22 56 | 73455 | 17 | 26545 | 81030 | 24 | 18970 | 07575 | 7 | 92425 | 8 |
| 53 | 36 56 | 23 4 | 73474 | 18 | 26526 | 81058 | 25 | 18942 | 07584 | 7 | 92416 | 7 |
| 54 | 36 48 | 23 12 | 73494 | 18 | 26506 | 81086 | 25 | 18914 | 07592 | 7 | 92408 | 6 |
| 55 | 7 36 40 | 4 23 20 | 9.73513 | 18 | 10.26487 | 9.81113 | 26 | 10.18887 | 10.07600 | 7 | 9.92400 | 5 |
| 56 | 36 32 | 23 28 | 73533 | 19 | 26467 | 81141 | 26 | 18859 | 07608 | 8 | 92392 | 4 |
| 57 | 36 24 | 23 36 | 73552 | 19 | 26448 | 81169 | 26 | 18831 | 07616 | 8 | 92384 | 3 |
| 58 | 36 16 | 23 44 | 73572 | 19 | 26428 | 81196 | 27 | 18804 | 07624 | 8 | 92376 | 2 |
| 59 | 36 8 | 23 52 | 73591 | 20 | 26409 | 81224 | 27 | 18776 | 07633 | 8 | 92367 | 1 |
| 60 | 36 0 | 24 0 | 73611 | 20 | 26389 | 81252 | 28 | 18748 | 07641 | 8 | 92359 | 0 |
| M | Hour P.M. | Hour A.M. | Cosine.<br>A | Diff. | Secant.<br>A | Cotangent<br>B | Diff. | Tangent.<br>B | Cosecant.<br>C | Diff. | Sine.<br>C | M |

122° | 57°

| Seconds of time ...... | 1s | 2s | 3s | 4s | 5s | 6s | 7s |
|---|---|---|---|---|---|---|---|
| Prop. parts of cols. A | 2 | 5 | 7 | 10 | 12 | 15 | 17 |
| Prop. parts of cols. B | 3 | 7 | 10 | 14 | 17 | 21 | 24 |
| Prop. parts of cols. C | 1 | 2 | 3 | 4 | 5 | 6 | 7 |

# TABLE XXVII.

S. — Log. Sines, Tangents, and Secants. — G.

33° — 146°

| M | Hour A.M. | Hour P.M. | Sine. (A) | Diff. | Cosecant. (A) | Tangent. (B) | Diff. | Cotangent (B) | Secant. (C) | Diff. | Cosine. (C) | M |
|---|---|---|---|---|---|---|---|---|---|---|---|---|
| 0 | 7 36 0 | 4 24 0 | 9.73611 | 0 | 10.26389 | 9.81252 | 0 | 10.18748 | 10.07641 | 0 | 9.92359 | 60 |
| 1 | 35 52 | 24 8 | 73630 | 0 | 26370 | 81279 | 0 | 18721 | 07649 | 0 | 92351 | 59 |
| 2 | 35 44 | 24 16 | 73650 | 1 | 26350 | 81307 | 1 | 18693 | 07657 | 0 | 92343 | 58 |
| 3 | 35 36 | 24 24 | 73669 | 1 | 26331 | 81335 | 1 | 18665 | 07665 | 0 | 92335 | 57 |
| 4 | 35 28 | 24 32 | 73689 | 1 | 26311 | 81362 | 2 | 18638 | 07674 | 1 | 92326 | 56 |
| 5 | 7 35 20 | 4 24 40 | 9.73708 | 2 | 10.26292 | 9.81390 | 2 | 10.18610 | 10.07682 | 1 | 9.92318 | 55 |
| 6 | 35 12 | 24 48 | 73727 | 2 | 26273 | 81418 | 3 | 18582 | 07690 | 1 | 92310 | 54 |
| 7 | 35 4 | 24 56 | 73747 | 2 | 26253 | 81445 | 3 | 18555 | 07698 | 1 | 92302 | 53 |
| 8 | 34 56 | 25 4 | 73766 | 3 | 26234 | 81473 | 4 | 18527 | 07707 | 1 | 92293 | 52 |
| 9 | 34 48 | 25 12 | 73785 | 3 | 26215 | 81500 | 4 | 18500 | 07715 | 1 | 92285 | 51 |
| 10 | 7 34 40 | 4 25 20 | 9.73805 | 3 | 10.26195 | 9.81528 | 5 | 10.18472 | 10.07723 | 1 | 9.92277 | 50 |
| 11 | 34 32 | 25 28 | 73824 | 3 | 26176 | 81556 | 5 | 18444 | 07731 | 2 | 92269 | 49 |
| 12 | 34 24 | 25 36 | 73843 | 4 | 26157 | 81583 | 5 | 18417 | 07740 | 2 | 92260 | 48 |
| 13 | 34 16 | 25 44 | 73863 | 4 | 26137 | 81611 | 6 | 18389 | 07748 | 2 | 92252 | 47 |
| 14 | 34 8 | 25 52 | 73882 | 4 | 26118 | 81638 | 6 | 18362 | 07756 | 2 | 92244 | 46 |
| 15 | 7 34 0 | 4 26 0 | 9.73901 | 5 | 10.26099 | 9.81666 | 7 | 10.18334 | 10.07765 | 2 | 9.92235 | 45 |
| 16 | 33 52 | 26 8 | 73921 | 5 | 26079 | 81693 | 7 | 18307 | 07773 | 2 | 92227 | 44 |
| 17 | 33 44 | 26 16 | 73940 | 5 | 26060 | 81721 | 8 | 18279 | 07781 | 2 | 92219 | 43 |
| 18 | 33 36 | 26 24 | 73959 | 6 | 26041 | 81748 | 8 | 18252 | 07789 | 3 | 92211 | 42 |
| 19 | 33 28 | 26 32 | 73978 | 6 | 26022 | 81776 | 9 | 18224 | 07798 | 3 | 92202 | 41 |
| 20 | 7 33 20 | 4 26 40 | 9.73997 | 6 | 10.26003 | 9.81803 | 9 | 10.18197 | 10.07806 | 3 | 9.92194 | 40 |
| 21 | 33 12 | 26 48 | 74017 | 7 | 25983 | 81831 | 10 | 18169 | 07814 | 3 | 92186 | 39 |
| 22 | 33 4 | 26 56 | 74036 | 7 | 25964 | 81858 | 10 | 18142 | 07823 | 3 | 92177 | 38 |
| 23 | 32 56 | 27 4 | 74055 | 7 | 25945 | 81886 | 11 | 18114 | 07831 | 3 | 92169 | 37 |
| 24 | 32 48 | 27 12 | 74074 | 8 | 25926 | 81913 | 11 | 18087 | 07839 | 3 | 92161 | 36 |
| 25 | 7 32 40 | 4 27 20 | 9.74093 | 8 | 10.25907 | 9.81941 | 11 | 10.18059 | 10.07848 | 3 | 9.92152 | 35 |
| 26 | 32 32 | 27 28 | 74113 | 8 | 25887 | 81968 | 12 | 18032 | 07856 | 4 | 92144 | 34 |
| 27 | 32 24 | 27 36 | 74132 | 9 | 25868 | 81996 | 12 | 18004 | 07864 | 4 | 92136 | 33 |
| 28 | 32 16 | 27 44 | 74151 | 9 | 25849 | 82023 | 13 | 17977 | 07873 | 4 | 92127 | 32 |
| 29 | 32 8 | 27 52 | 74170 | 9 | 25830 | 82051 | 13 | 17949 | 07881 | 4 | 92119 | 31 |
| 30 | 7 32 0 | 4 28 0 | 9.74189 | 10 | 10.25811 | 9.82078 | 14 | 10.17922 | 10.07889 | 4 | 9.92111 | 30 |
| 31 | 31 52 | 28 8 | 74208 | 10 | 25792 | 82106 | 14 | 17894 | 07898 | 4 | 92102 | 29 |
| 32 | 31 44 | 28 16 | 74227 | 10 | 25773 | 82133 | 15 | 17867 | 07906 | 4 | 92094 | 28 |
| 33 | 31 36 | 28 24 | 74246 | 10 | 25754 | 82161 | 15 | 17839 | 07914 | 5 | 92086 | 27 |
| 34 | 31 28 | 28 32 | 74265 | 11 | 25735 | 82188 | 16 | 17812 | 07923 | 5 | 92077 | 26 |
| 35 | 7 31 20 | 4 28 40 | 9.74284 | 11 | 10.25716 | 9.82215 | 16 | 10.17785 | 10.07931 | 5 | 9.92069 | 25 |
| 36 | 31 12 | 28 48 | 74303 | 11 | 25697 | 82243 | 16 | 17757 | 07940 | 5 | 92060 | 24 |
| 37 | 31 4 | 28 56 | 74322 | 12 | 25678 | 82270 | 17 | 17730 | 07948 | 5 | 92052 | 23 |
| 38 | 30 56 | 29 4 | 74341 | 12 | 25659 | 82298 | 17 | 17702 | 07956 | 5 | 92044 | 22 |
| 39 | 30 48 | 29 12 | 74360 | 12 | 25640 | 82325 | 18 | 17675 | 07965 | 5 | 92035 | 21 |
| 40 | 7 30 40 | 4 29 20 | 9.74379 | 13 | 10.25621 | 9.82352 | 18 | 10.17648 | 10.07973 | 6 | 9.92027 | 20 |
| 41 | 30 32 | 29 28 | 74398 | 13 | 25602 | 82380 | 19 | 17620 | 07982 | 6 | 92018 | 19 |
| 42 | 30 24 | 29 36 | 74417 | 13 | 25583 | 82407 | 19 | 17593 | 07990 | 6 | 92010 | 18 |
| 43 | 30 16 | 29 44 | 74436 | 14 | 25564 | 82435 | 20 | 17565 | 07998 | 6 | 92002 | 17 |
| 44 | 30 8 | 29 52 | 74455 | 14 | 25545 | 82462 | 20 | 17538 | 08007 | 6 | 91993 | 16 |
| 45 | 7 30 0 | 4 30 0 | 9.74474 | 14 | 10.25526 | 9.82489 | 21 | 10.17511 | 10.08015 | 6 | 9.91985 | 15 |
| 46 | 29 52 | 30 8 | 74493 | 15 | 25507 | 82517 | 21 | 17483 | 08024 | 6 | 91976 | 14 |
| 47 | 29 44 | 30 16 | 74512 | 15 | 25488 | 82544 | 22 | 17456 | 08032 | 7 | 91968 | 13 |
| 48 | 29 36 | 30 24 | 74531 | 15 | 25469 | 82571 | 22 | 17429 | 08041 | 7 | 91959 | 12 |
| 49 | 29 28 | 30 32 | 74549 | 16 | 25451 | 82599 | 22 | 17401 | 08049 | 7 | 91951 | 11 |
| 50 | 7 29 20 | 4 30 40 | 9.74568 | 16 | 10.25432 | 9.82626 | 23 | 10.17374 | 10.08058 | 7 | 9.91942 | 10 |
| 51 | 29 12 | 30 48 | 74587 | 16 | 25413 | 82653 | 23 | 17347 | 08066 | 7 | 91934 | 9 |
| 52 | 29 4 | 30 56 | 74606 | 17 | 25394 | 82681 | 24 | 17319 | 08075 | 7 | 91925 | 8 |
| 53 | 28 56 | 31 4 | 74625 | 17 | 25375 | 82708 | 24 | 17292 | 08083 | 7 | 91917 | 7 |
| 54 | 28 48 | 31 12 | 74644 | 17 | 25356 | 82735 | 25 | 17265 | 08092 | 8 | 91908 | 6 |
| 55 | 7 28 40 | 4 31 20 | 9.74662 | 17 | 10.25338 | 9.82762 | 25 | 10.17238 | 10.08100 | 8 | 9.91900 | 5 |
| 56 | 28 32 | 31 28 | 74681 | 18 | 25319 | 82790 | 26 | 17210 | 08109 | 8 | 91891 | 4 |
| 57 | 28 24 | 31 36 | 74700 | 18 | 25300 | 82817 | 26 | 17183 | 08117 | 8 | 91883 | 3 |
| 58 | 28 16 | 31 44 | 74719 | 18 | 25281 | 82844 | 27 | 17156 | 08126 | 8 | 91874 | 2 |
| 59 | 28 8 | 31 52 | 74737 | 19 | 25263 | 82871 | 27 | 17129 | 08134 | 8 | 91866 | 1 |
| 60 | 28 0 | 32 0 | 74756 | 19 | 25244 | 82899 | 27 | 17101 | 08143 | 8 | 91857 | 0 |
| M | Hour P.M. | Hour A.M. | Cosine. (A) | Diff. | Secant. (A) | Cotangent (B) | Diff. | Tangent. (B) | Cosecant. (C) | Diff. | Sine. (C) | M |

123° — 56°

| Seconds of time ...... | | 1ˢ | 2ˢ | 3ˢ | 4ˢ | 5ˢ | 6ˢ | 7ˢ |
|---|---|---|---|---|---|---|---|---|
| Prop. parts of cols. | A | 2 | 5 | 7 | 10 | 12 | 14 | 17 |
| | B | 3 | 7 | 10 | 14 | 17 | 21 | 24 |
| | C | 1 | 2 | 3 | 4 | 5 | 6 | 7 |

# TABLE XXVII

## Log. Sines, Tangents, and Secants.

S'. 34° | G'. 145°

| M | Hour A.M. | Hour P.M. | A Sine. | Diff. | A Cosecant. | B Tangent. | Diff. | B Cotangent | C Secant. | Diff. | C Cosine. | M |
|---|---|---|---|---|---|---|---|---|---|---|---|---|
| 0 | 7 28 0 | 4 32 0 | 9.74756 | 0 | 10.25244 | 9.82899 | 0 | 10.17101 | 10.08143 | 0 | 9.91857 | 60 |
| 1 | 27 52 | 32 8 | 74775 | 0 | 25225 | 82926 | 0 | 17074 | 08151 | 0 | 91849 | 59 |
| 2 | 27 44 | 32 16 | 74794 | 1 | 25206 | 82953 | 1 | 17047 | 08160 | 0 | 91840 | 58 |
| 3 | 27 36 | 32 24 | 74812 | 1 | 25188 | 82980 | 1 | 17020 | 08168 | 0 | 91832 | 57 |
| 4 | 27 28 | 32 32 | 74831 | 1 | 25169 | 83008 | 2 | 16992 | 08177 | 1 | 91823 | 56 |
| 5 | 7 27 20 | 4 32 40 | 9.74850 | 2 | 10.25150 | 9.83035 | 2 | 10.16965 | 10.08185 | 1 | 9.91815 | 55 |
| 6 | 27 12 | 32 48 | 74868 | 2 | 25132 | 83062 | 3 | 16938 | 08194 | 1 | 91806 | 54 |
| 7 | 27 4 | 32 56 | 74887 | 2 | 25113 | 83089 | 3 | 16911 | 08202 | 1 | 91798 | 53 |
| 8 | 26 56 | 33 4 | 74906 | 2 | 25094 | 83117 | 4 | 16883 | 08211 | 1 | 91789 | 52 |
| 9 | 26 48 | 33 12 | 74924 | 3 | 25076 | 83144 | 4 | 16856 | 08219 | 1 | 91781 | 51 |
| 10 | 7 26 40 | 4 33 20 | 9.74943 | 3 | 10.25057 | 9.83171 | 5 | 10.16829 | 10.08228 | 1 | 9.91772 | 50 |
| 11 | 26 32 | 33 28 | 74961 | 3 | 25039 | 83198 | 5 | 16802 | 08237 | 2 | 91763 | 49 |
| 12 | 26 24 | 33 36 | 74980 | 4 | 25020 | 83225 | 5 | 16775 | 08245 | 2 | 91755 | 48 |
| 13 | 26 16 | 33 44 | 74999 | 4 | 25001 | 83252 | 6 | 16748 | 08254 | 2 | 91746 | 47 |
| 14 | 26 8 | 33 52 | 75017 | 4 | 24983 | 83280 | 6 | 16720 | 08262 | 2 | 91738 | 46 |
| 15 | 7 26 0 | 4 34 0 | 9.75036 | 5 | 10.24964 | 9.83307 | 7 | 10.16693 | 10.08271 | 2 | 9.91729 | 45 |
| 16 | 25 52 | 34 8 | 75054 | 5 | 24946 | 83334 | 7 | 16666 | 08280 | 2 | 91720 | 44 |
| 17 | 25 44 | 34 16 | 75073 | 5 | 24927 | 83361 | 8 | 16639 | 08288 | 2 | 91712 | 43 |
| 18 | 25 36 | 34 24 | 75091 | 6 | 24909 | 83388 | 8 | 16612 | 08297 | 3 | 91703 | 42 |
| 19 | 25 28 | 34 32 | 75110 | 6 | 24890 | 83415 | 9 | 16585 | 08305 | 3 | 91695 | 41 |
| 20 | 7 25 20 | 4 34 40 | 9.75128 | 6 | 10.24872 | 9.83442 | 9 | 10.16558 | 10.08314 | 3 | 9.91686 | 40 |
| 21 | 25 12 | 34 48 | 75147 | 6 | 24853 | 83470 | 9 | 16530 | 08323 | 3 | 91677 | 39 |
| 22 | 25 4 | 34 56 | 75165 | 7 | 24835 | 83497 | 10 | 16503 | 08331 | 3 | 91669 | 38 |
| 23 | 24 56 | 35 4 | 75184 | 7 | 24816 | 83524 | 10 | 16476 | 08340 | 3 | 91660 | 37 |
| 24 | 24 48 | 35 12 | 75202 | 7 | 24798 | 83551 | 11 | 16449 | 08349 | 3 | 91651 | 36 |
| 25 | 7 24 40 | 4 35 20 | 9.75221 | 8 | 10.24779 | 9.83578 | 11 | 10.16422 | 10.08357 | 4 | 9.91643 | 35 |
| 26 | 24 32 | 35 28 | 75239 | 8 | 24761 | 83605 | 12 | 16395 | 08366 | 4 | 91634 | 34 |
| 27 | 24 24 | 35 36 | 75258 | 8 | 24742 | 83632 | 12 | 16368 | 08375 | 4 | 91625 | 33 |
| 28 | 24 16 | 35 44 | 75276 | 9 | 24724 | 83659 | 13 | 16341 | 08383 | 4 | 91617 | 32 |
| 29 | 24 8 | 35 52 | 75294 | 9 | 24706 | 83686 | 13 | 16314 | 08392 | 4 | 91608 | 31 |
| 30 | 7 24 0 | 4 36 0 | 9.75313 | 9 | 10.24687 | 9.83713 | 14 | 10.16287 | 10.08401 | 4 | 9.91599 | 30 |
| 31 | 23 52 | 36 8 | 75331 | 9 | 24669 | 83740 | 14 | 16260 | 08409 | 4 | 91591 | 29 |
| 32 | 23 44 | 36 16 | 75350 | 10 | 24650 | 83768 | 14 | 16232 | 08418 | 5 | 91582 | 28 |
| 33 | 23 36 | 36 24 | 75368 | 10 | 24632 | 83795 | 15 | 16205 | 08427 | 5 | 91573 | 27 |
| 34 | 23 28 | 36 32 | 75386 | 10 | 24614 | 83822 | 15 | 16178 | 08435 | 5 | 91565 | 26 |
| 35 | 7 23 20 | 4 36 40 | 9.75405 | 11 | 10.24595 | 9.83849 | 16 | 10.16151 | 10.08444 | 5 | 9.91556 | 25 |
| 36 | 23 12 | 36 48 | 75423 | 11 | 24577 | 83876 | 16 | 16124 | 08453 | 5 | 91547 | 24 |
| 37 | 23 4 | 36 56 | 75441 | 11 | 24559 | 83903 | 17 | 16097 | 08462 | 5 | 91538 | 23 |
| 38 | 22 56 | 37 4 | 75459 | 12 | 24541 | 83930 | 17 | 16070 | 08470 | 5 | 91530 | 22 |
| 39 | 22 48 | 37 12 | 75478 | 12 | 24522 | 83957 | 18 | 16043 | 08479 | 6 | 91521 | 21 |
| 40 | 7 22 40 | 4 37 20 | 9.75496 | 12 | 10.24504 | 9.83984 | 18 | 10.16016 | 10.08488 | 6 | 9.91512 | 20 |
| 41 | 22 32 | 37 28 | 75514 | 13 | 24486 | 84011 | 18 | 15989 | 08496 | 6 | 91504 | 19 |
| 42 | 22 24 | 37 36 | 75533 | 13 | 24467 | 84038 | 19 | 15962 | 08505 | 6 | 91495 | 18 |
| 43 | 22 16 | 37 44 | 75551 | 13 | 24449 | 84065 | 19 | 15935 | 08514 | 6 | 91486 | 17 |
| 44 | 22 8 | 37 52 | 75569 | 13 | 24431 | 84092 | 20 | 15908 | 08523 | 6 | 91477 | 16 |
| 45 | 7 22 0 | 4 38 0 | 9.75587 | 14 | 10.24413 | 9.84119 | 20 | 10.15881 | 10.08531 | 7 | 9.91469 | 15 |
| 46 | 21 52 | 38 8 | 75605 | 14 | 24395 | 84146 | 21 | 15854 | 08540 | 7 | 91460 | 14 |
| 47 | 21 44 | 38 16 | 75624 | 14 | 24376 | 84173 | 21 | 15827 | 08549 | 7 | 91451 | 13 |
| 48 | 21 36 | 38 24 | 75642 | 15 | 24358 | 84200 | 22 | 15800 | 08558 | 7 | 91442 | 12 |
| 49 | 21 28 | 38 32 | 75660 | 15 | 24340 | 84227 | 22 | 15773 | 08567 | 7 | 91433 | 11 |
| 50 | 7 21 20 | 4 38 40 | 9.75678 | 15 | 10.24322 | 9.84254 | 23 | 10.15746 | 10.08575 | 7 | 9.91425 | 10 |
| 51 | 21 12 | 38 48 | 75696 | 16 | 24304 | 84280 | 23 | 15720 | 08584 | 7 | 91416 | 9 |
| 52 | 21 4 | 38 56 | 75714 | 16 | 24286 | 84307 | 23 | 15693 | 08593 | 8 | 91407 | 8 |
| 53 | 20 56 | 39 4 | 75733 | 16 | 24267 | 84334 | 24 | 15666 | 08602 | 8 | 91398 | 7 |
| 54 | 20 48 | 39 12 | 75751 | 17 | 24249 | 84361 | 24 | 15639 | 08611 | 8 | 91389 | 6 |
| 55 | 7 20 40 | 4 39 20 | 9.75769 | 17 | 10.24231 | 9.84388 | 25 | 10.15612 | 10.08619 | 8 | 9.91381 | 5 |
| 56 | 20 32 | 39 28 | 75787 | 17 | 24213 | 84415 | 25 | 15585 | 08628 | 8 | 91372 | 4 |
| 57 | 20 24 | 39 36 | 75805 | 17 | 24195 | 84442 | 26 | 15558 | 08637 | 8 | 91363 | 3 |
| 58 | 20 16 | 39 44 | 75823 | 18 | 24177 | 84469 | 26 | 15531 | 08646 | 8 | 91354 | 2 |
| 59 | 20 8 | 39 52 | 75841 | 18 | 24159 | 84496 | 27 | 15504 | 08655 | 9 | 91345 | 1 |
| 60 | 20 0 | 40 0 | 75859 | 18 | 24141 | 84523 | 27 | 15477 | 08664 | 9 | 91336 | 0 |
| M | Hour P.M. | Hour A.M. | Cosine. A | Diff. | Secant. A | Cotangent B | Diff. | Tangent. B | Cosecant. C | Diff. | Sine. C | M |

124° | 55°

| Seconds of time ...... | | 1ˢ | 2ˢ | 3ˢ | 4ˢ | 5ˢ | 6ˢ | 7ˢ |
|---|---|---|---|---|---|---|---|---|
| Prop. parts of cols. | A | 2 | 5 | 7 | 9 | 11 | 14 | 16 |
| | B | 3 | 7 | 10 | 14 | 17 | 20 | 24 |
| | C | 1 | 2 | 3 | 4 | 5 | 7 | 8 |

# TABLE XXVII.

S′. Log. Sines, Tangents, and Secants. G′.

35° 144°

| M | Hour A.M. | Hour P.M. | Sine. (A) | Diff. | Cosecant. (A) | Tangent. (B) | Diff. | Cotangent (B) | Secant. (C) | Diff. | Cosine. (C) | M |
|---|---|---|---|---|---|---|---|---|---|---|---|---|
| 0 | 7 20 0 | 4 40 0 | 9.75859 | 0 | 10.24141 | 9.84523 | 0 | 10.15477 | 10.08664 | 0 | 9.91336 | 60 |
| 1 | 19 52 | 40 8 | 75877 | 0 | 24123 | 84550 | 0 | 15450 | 08672 | 0 | 91328 | 59 |
| 2 | 19 44 | 40 16 | 75895 | 1 | 24105 | 84576 | 1 | 15424 | 08681 | 0 | 91319 | 58 |
| 3 | 19 36 | 40 24 | 75913 | 1 | 24087 | 84603 | 1 | 15397 | 08690 | 0 | 91310 | 57 |
| 4 | 19 28 | 40 32 | 75931 | 1 | 24069 | 84630 | 2 | 15370 | 08699 | 1 | 91301 | 56 |
| 5 | 7 19 20 | 4 40 40 | 9.75949 | 1 | 10.24051 | 9.84657 | 2 | 10.15343 | 10.08708 | 1 | 9.91292 | 55 |
| 6 | 19 12 | 40 48 | 75967 | 2 | 24033 | 84684 | 3 | 15316 | 08717 | 1 | 91283 | 54 |
| 7 | 19 4 | 40 56 | 75985 | 2 | 24015 | 84711 | 3 | 15289 | 08726 | 1 | 91274 | 53 |
| 8 | 18 56 | 41 4 | 76003 | 2 | 23997 | 84738 | 4 | 15262 | 08734 | 1 | 91266 | 52 |
| 9 | 18 48 | 41 12 | 76021 | 3 | 23979 | 84764 | 4 | 15236 | 08743 | 1 | 91257 | 51 |
| 10 | 7 18 40 | 4 41 20 | 9.76039 | 3 | 10.23961 | 9.84791 | 4 | 10.15209 | 10.08752 | 2 | 9.91248 | 50 |
| 11 | 18 32 | 41 28 | 76057 | 3 | 23943 | 84818 | 5 | 15182 | 08761 | 2 | 91239 | 49 |
| 12 | 18 24 | 41 36 | 76075 | 4 | 23925 | 84845 | 5 | 15155 | 08770 | 2 | 91230 | 48 |
| 13 | 18 16 | 41 44 | 76093 | 4 | 23907 | 84872 | 6 | 15128 | 08779 | 2 | 91221 | 47 |
| 14 | 18 8 | 41 52 | 76111 | 4 | 23889 | 84899 | 6 | 15101 | 08788 | 2 | 91212 | 46 |
| 15 | 7 18 0 | 4 42 0 | 9.76129 | 4 | 10.23871 | 9.84925 | 7 | 10.15075 | 10.08797 | 2 | 9.91203 | 45 |
| 16 | 17 52 | 42 8 | 76146 | 5 | 23854 | 84952 | 7 | 15048 | 08806 | 2 | 91194 | 44 |
| 17 | 17 44 | 42 16 | 76164 | 5 | 23836 | 84979 | 8 | 15021 | 08815 | 3 | 91185 | 43 |
| 18 | 17 36 | 42 24 | 76182 | 5 | 23818 | 85006 | 8 | 14994 | 08824 | 3 | 91176 | 42 |
| 19 | 17 28 | 42 32 | 76200 | 6 | 23800 | 85033 | 8 | 14967 | 08833 | 3 | 91167 | 41 |
| 20 | 7 17 20 | 4 42 40 | 9.76218 | 6 | 10.23782 | 9.85059 | 9 | 10.14941 | 10.08842 | 3 | 9.91158 | 40 |
| 21 | 17 12 | 42 48 | 76236 | 6 | 23764 | 85086 | 9 | 14914 | 08851 | 3 | 91149 | 39 |
| 22 | 17 4 | 42 56 | 76253 | 6 | 23747 | 85113 | 10 | 14887 | 08859 | 3 | 91141 | 38 |
| 23 | 16 56 | 43 4 | 76271 | 7 | 23729 | 85140 | 10 | 14860 | 08868 | 3 | 91132 | 37 |
| 24 | 16 48 | 43 12 | 76289 | 7 | 23711 | 85166 | 11 | 14834 | 08877 | 4 | 91123 | 36 |
| 25 | 7 16 40 | 4 43 20 | 9.76307 | 7 | 10.23693 | 9.85193 | 11 | 10.14807 | 10.08886 | 4 | 9.91114 | 35 |
| 26 | 16 32 | 43 28 | 76324 | 8 | 23676 | 85220 | 12 | 14780 | 08895 | 4 | 91105 | 34 |
| 27 | 16 24 | 43 36 | 76342 | 8 | 23658 | 85247 | 12 | 14753 | 08904 | 4 | 91096 | 33 |
| 28 | 16 16 | 43 44 | 76360 | 8 | 23640 | 85273 | 12 | 14727 | 08913 | 4 | 91087 | 32 |
| 29 | 16 8 | 43 52 | 76378 | 9 | 23622 | 85300 | 13 | 14700 | 08922 | 4 | 91078 | 31 |
| 30 | 7 16 0 | 4 44 0 | 9.76395 | 9 | 10.23605 | 9.85327 | 13 | 10.14673 | 10.08931 | 5 | 9.91069 | 30 |
| 31 | 15 52 | 44 8 | 76413 | 9 | 23587 | 85354 | 14 | 14646 | 08940 | 5 | 91060 | 29 |
| 32 | 15 44 | 44 16 | 76431 | 9 | 23569 | 85380 | 14 | 14620 | 08949 | 5 | 91051 | 28 |
| 33 | 15 36 | 44 24 | 76448 | 10 | 23552 | 85407 | 15 | 14593 | 08958 | 5 | 91042 | 27 |
| 34 | 15 28 | 44 32 | 76466 | 10 | 23534 | 85434 | 15 | 14566 | 08967 | 5 | 91033 | 26 |
| 35 | 7 15 20 | 4 44 40 | 9.76484 | 10 | 10.23516 | 9.85460 | 16 | 10.14540 | 10.08977 | 5 | 9.91023 | 25 |
| 36 | 15 12 | 44 48 | 76501 | 11 | 23499 | 85487 | 16 | 14513 | 08986 | 5 | 91014 | 24 |
| 37 | 15 4 | 44 56 | 76519 | 11 | 23481 | 85514 | 16 | 14486 | 08995 | 6 | 91005 | 23 |
| 38 | 14 56 | 45 4 | 76537 | 11 | 23463 | 85540 | 17 | 14460 | 09004 | 6 | 90996 | 22 |
| 39 | 14 48 | 45 12 | 76554 | 12 | 23446 | 85567 | 17 | 14433 | 09013 | 6 | 90987 | 21 |
| 40 | 7 14 40 | 4 45 20 | 9.76572 | 12 | 10.23428 | 9.85594 | 18 | 10.14406 | 10.09022 | 6 | 9.90978 | 20 |
| 41 | 14 32 | 45 28 | 76590 | 12 | 23410 | 85620 | 18 | 14380 | 09031 | 6 | 90969 | 19 |
| 42 | 14 24 | 45 36 | 76607 | 12 | 23393 | 85647 | 19 | 14353 | 09040 | 6 | 90960 | 18 |
| 43 | 14 16 | 45 44 | 76625 | 13 | 23375 | 85674 | 19 | 14326 | 09049 | 6 | 90951 | 17 |
| 44 | 14 8 | 45 52 | 76642 | 13 | 23358 | 85700 | 20 | 14300 | 09058 | 7 | 90942 | 16 |
| 45 | 7 14 0 | 4 46 0 | 9.76660 | 13 | 10.23340 | 9.85727 | 20 | 10.14273 | 10.09067 | 7 | 9.90933 | 15 |
| 46 | 13 52 | 46 8 | 76677 | 14 | 23323 | 85754 | 20 | 14246 | 09076 | 7 | 90924 | 14 |
| 47 | 13 44 | 46 16 | 76695 | 14 | 23305 | 85780 | 21 | 14220 | 09085 | 7 | 90915 | 13 |
| 48 | 13 36 | 46 24 | 76712 | 14 | 23288 | 85807 | 21 | 14193 | 09094 | 7 | 90906 | 12 |
| 49 | 13 28 | 46 32 | 76730 | 14 | 23270 | 85834 | 22 | 14166 | 09104 | 7 | 90896 | 11 |
| 50 | 7 13 20 | 4 46 40 | 9.76747 | 15 | 10.23253 | 9.85860 | 22 | 10.14140 | 10.09113 | 8 | 9.90887 | 10 |
| 51 | 13 12 | 46 48 | 76765 | 15 | 23235 | 85887 | 23 | 14113 | 09122 | 8 | 90878 | 9 |
| 52 | 13 4 | 46 56 | 76782 | 15 | 23218 | 85913 | 23 | 14087 | 09131 | 8 | 90869 | 8 |
| 53 | 12 56 | 47 4 | 76800 | 16 | 23200 | 85940 | 24 | 14060 | 09140 | 8 | 90860 | 7 |
| 54 | 12 48 | 47 12 | 76817 | 16 | 23183 | 85967 | 24 | 14033 | 09149 | 8 | 90851 | 6 |
| 55 | 7 12 40 | 4 47 20 | 9.76835 | 16 | 10.23165 | 9.85993 | 24 | 10.14007 | 10.09158 | 8 | 9.90842 | 5 |
| 56 | 12 32 | 47 28 | 76852 | 17 | 23148 | 86020 | 25 | 13980 | 09168 | 8 | 90832 | 4 |
| 57 | 12 24 | 47 36 | 76870 | 17 | 23130 | 86046 | 25 | 13954 | 09177 | 9 | 90823 | 3 |
| 58 | 12 16 | 47 44 | 76887 | 17 | 23113 | 86073 | 26 | 13927 | 09186 | 9 | 90814 | 2 |
| 59 | 12 8 | 47 52 | 76904 | 17 | 23096 | 86100 | 26 | 13900 | 09195 | 9 | 90805 | 1 |
| 60 | 12 0 | 48 0 | 76922 | 18 | 23078 | 86126 | 27 | 13874 | 09204 | 9 | 90796 | 0 |
| M | Hour P.M. | Hour A.M. | Cosine. (A) | Diff. | Secant. (A) | Cotangent (B) | Diff. | Tangent. (B) | Cosecant. (C) | Diff. | Sine. (C) | M |

125° 54°

| Seconds of time ...... | | 1ˢ | 2ˢ | 3ˢ | 4ˢ | 5ˢ | 6ˢ | 7ˢ |
|---|---|---|---|---|---|---|---|---|
| Prop. parts of cols. | A | 2 | 4 | 7 | 9 | 11 | 13 | 16 |
| | B | 3 | 7 | 10 | 13 | 17 | 20 | 23 |
| | C | 1 | 2 | 3 | 5 | 6 | 7 | 8 |

# TABLE XXVII.

## Log. Sines, Tangents, and Secants.

S'. G'.

| 36° | | | A | | A | B | | B | C | | C | 143° |
|---|---|---|---|---|---|---|---|---|---|---|---|---|
| M | Hour A.M. | Hour P.M. | Sine. | Diff. | Cosecant. | Tangent. | Diff. | Cotangent | Secant. | Diff. | Cosine. | M |
| 0 | 7 12 0 | 4 48 0 | 9.76922 | 0 | 10.23078 | 9.86126 | 0 | 10.13874 | 10.09204 | 0 | 9.90796 | 60 |
| 1 | 11 52 | 48 8 | 76939 | 0 | 23061 | 86153 | 0 | 13847 | 09213 | 0 | 90787 | 59 |
| 2 | 11 44 | 48 16 | 76957 | 1 | 23043 | 86179 | 1 | 13821 | 09223 | 0 | 90777 | 58 |
| 3 | 11 36 | 48 24 | 76974 | 1 | 23026 | 86206 | 1 | 13794 | 09232 | 0 | 90768 | 57 |
| 4 | 11 28 | 48 32 | 76991 | 1 | 23009 | 86232 | 2 | 13768 | 09241 | 1 | 90759 | 56 |
| 5 | 7 11 20 | 4 48 40 | 9.77009 | 1 | 10.22991 | 9.86259 | 2 | 10.13741 | 10.09250 | 1 | 9.90750 | 55 |
| 6 | 11 12 | 48 48 | 77026 | 2 | 22974 | 86285 | 3 | 13715 | 09259 | 1 | 90741 | 54 |
| 7 | 11 4 | 48 56 | 77043 | 2 | 22957 | 86312 | 3 | 13688 | 09269 | 1 | 90731 | 53 |
| 8 | 10 56 | 49 4 | 77061 | 2 | 22939 | 86338 | 4 | 13662 | 09278 | 1 | 90722 | 52 |
| 9 | 10 48 | 49 12 | 77078 | 3 | 22922 | 86365 | 4 | 13635 | 09287 | 1 | 90713 | 51 |
| 10 | 7 10 40 | 4 49 20 | 9.77095 | 3 | 10.22905 | 9.86392 | 4 | 10.13608 | 10.09296 | 2 | 9.90704 | 50 |
| 11 | 10 32 | 49 28 | 77112 | 3 | 22888 | 86418 | 5 | 13582 | 09306 | 2 | 90694 | 49 |
| 12 | 10 24 | 49 36 | 77130 | 3 | 22870 | 86445 | 5 | 13555 | 09315 | 2 | 90685 | 48 |
| 13 | 10 16 | 49 44 | 77147 | 4 | 22853 | 86471 | 6 | 13529 | 09324 | 2 | 90676 | 47 |
| 14 | 10 8 | 49 52 | 77164 | 4 | 22836 | 86498 | 6 | 13502 | 09333 | 2 | 90667 | 46 |
| 15 | 7 10 0 | 4 50 0 | 9.77181 | 4 | 10.22819 | 9.86524 | 7 | 10.13476 | 10.09343 | 2 | 9.90657 | 45 |
| 16 | 9 52 | 50 8 | 77199 | 5 | 22801 | 86551 | 7 | 13449 | 09352 | 2 | 90648 | 44 |
| 17 | 9 44 | 50 16 | 77216 | 5 | 22784 | 86577 | 7 | 13423 | 09361 | 3 | 90639 | 43 |
| 18 | 9 36 | 50 24 | 77233 | 5 | 22767 | 86603 | 8 | 13397 | 09370 | 3 | 90630 | 42 |
| 19 | 9 28 | 50 32 | 77250 | 5 | 22750 | 86630 | 8 | 13370 | 09380 | 3 | 90620 | 41 |
| 20 | 7 9 20 | 4 50 40 | 9.77268 | 6 | 10.22732 | 9.86656 | 9 | 10.13344 | 10.09389 | 3 | 9.90611 | 40 |
| 21 | 9 12 | 50 48 | 77285 | 6 | 22715 | 86683 | 9 | 13317 | 09398 | 3 | 90602 | 39 |
| 22 | 9 4 | 50 56 | 77302 | 6 | 22698 | 86709 | 10 | 13291 | 09408 | 3 | 90592 | 38 |
| 23 | 8 56 | 51 4 | 77319 | 7 | 22681 | 86736 | 10 | 13264 | 09417 | 4 | 90583 | 37 |
| 24 | 8 48 | 51 12 | 77336 | 7 | 22664 | 86762 | 11 | 13238 | 09426 | 4 | 90574 | 36 |
| 25 | 7 8 40 | 4 51 20 | 9.77353 | 7 | 10.22647 | 9.86789 | 11 | 10.13211 | 10.09435 | 4 | 9.90565 | 35 |
| 26 | 8 32 | 51 28 | 77370 | 7 | 22630 | 86815 | 11 | 13185 | 09445 | 4 | 90555 | 34 |
| 27 | 8 24 | 51 36 | 77387 | 8 | 22613 | 86842 | 12 | 13158 | 09454 | 4 | 90546 | 33 |
| 28 | 8 16 | 51 44 | 77405 | 8 | 22595 | 86868 | 12 | 13132 | 09463 | 4 | 90537 | 32 |
| 29 | 8 8 | 51 52 | 77422 | 8 | 22578 | 86894 | 13 | 13106 | 09473 | 5 | 90527 | 31 |
| 30 | 7 8 0 | 4 52 0 | 9.77439 | 9 | 10.22561 | 9.86921 | 13 | 10.13079 | 10.09482 | 5 | 9.90518 | 30 |
| 31 | 7 52 | 52 8 | 77456 | 9 | 22544 | 86947 | 14 | 13053 | 09491 | 5 | 90509 | 29 |
| 32 | 7 44 | 52 16 | 77473 | 9 | 22527 | 86974 | 14 | 13026 | 09501 | 5 | 90499 | 28 |
| 33 | 7 36 | 52 24 | 77490 | 9 | 22510 | 87000 | 15 | 13000 | 09510 | 5 | 90490 | 27 |
| 34 | 7 28 | 52 32 | 77507 | 10 | 22493 | 87027 | 15 | 12973 | 09520 | 5 | 90480 | 26 |
| 35 | 7 7 20 | 4 52 40 | 9.77524 | 10 | 10.22476 | 9.87053 | 15 | 10.12947 | 10.09529 | 5 | 9.90471 | 25 |
| 36 | 7 12 | 52 48 | 77541 | 10 | 22459 | 87079 | 16 | 12921 | 09538 | 6 | 90462 | 24 |
| 37 | 7 4 | 52 56 | 77558 | 11 | 22442 | 87106 | 16 | 12894 | 09548 | 6 | 90452 | 23 |
| 38 | 6 56 | 53 4 | 77575 | 11 | 22425 | 87132 | 17 | 12868 | 09557 | 6 | 90443 | 22 |
| 39 | 6 48 | 53 12 | 77592 | 11 | 22408 | 87158 | 17 | 12842 | 09566 | 6 | 90434 | 21 |
| 40 | 7 6 40 | 4 53 20 | 9.77609 | 11 | 10.22391 | 9.87185 | 18 | 10.12815 | 10.09576 | 6 | 9.90424 | 20 |
| 41 | 6 32 | 53 28 | 77626 | 12 | 22374 | 87211 | 18 | 12789 | 09585 | 6 | 90415 | 19 |
| 42 | 6 24 | 53 36 | 77643 | 12 | 22357 | 87238 | 18 | 12762 | 09595 | 7 | 90405 | 18 |
| 43 | 6 16 | 53 44 | 77660 | 12 | 22340 | 87264 | 19 | 12736 | 09604 | 7 | 90396 | 17 |
| 44 | 6 8 | 53 52 | 77677 | 13 | 22323 | 87290 | 19 | 12710 | 09614 | 7 | 90386 | 16 |
| 45 | 7 6 0 | 4 54 0 | 9.77694 | 13 | 10.22306 | 9.87317 | 20 | 10.12683 | 10.09623 | 7 | 9.90377 | 15 |
| 46 | 5 52 | 54 8 | 77711 | 13 | 22289 | 87343 | 20 | 12657 | 09632 | 7 | 90368 | 14 |
| 47 | 5 44 | 54 16 | 77728 | 13 | 22272 | 87369 | 21 | 12631 | 09642 | 7 | 90358 | 13 |
| 48 | 5 36 | 54 24 | 77744 | 14 | 22256 | 87396 | 21 | 12604 | 09651 | 7 | 90349 | 12 |
| 49 | 5 28 | 54 32 | 77761 | 14 | 22239 | 87422 | 22 | 12578 | 09661 | 8 | 90339 | 11 |
| 50 | 7 5 20 | 4 54 40 | 9.77778 | 14 | 10.22222 | 9.87448 | 22 | 10.12552 | 10.09670 | 8 | 9.90330 | 10 |
| 51 | 5 12 | 54 48 | 77795 | 15 | 22205 | 87475 | 22 | 12525 | 09680 | 8 | 90320 | 9 |
| 52 | 5 4 | 54 56 | 77812 | 15 | 22188 | 87501 | 23 | 12499 | 09689 | 8 | 90311 | 8 |
| 53 | 4 56 | 55 4 | 77829 | 15 | 22171 | 87527 | 23 | 12473 | 09699 | 8 | 90301 | 7 |
| 54 | 4 48 | 55 12 | 77846 | 15 | 22154 | 87554 | 24 | 12446 | 09708 | 8 | 90292 | 6 |
| 55 | 7 4 40 | 4 55 20 | 9.77862 | 16 | 10.22138 | 9.87580 | 24 | 10.12420 | 10.09718 | 9 | 9.90282 | 5 |
| 56 | 4 32 | 55 28 | 77879 | 16 | 22121 | 87606 | 25 | 12394 | 09727 | 9 | 90273 | 4 |
| 57 | 4 24 | 55 36 | 77896 | 16 | 22104 | 87633 | 25 | 12367 | 09737 | 9 | 90263 | 3 |
| 58 | 4 16 | 55 44 | 77913 | 16 | 22087 | 87659 | 26 | 12341 | 09746 | 9 | 90254 | 2 |
| 59 | 4 8 | 55 52 | 77930 | 17 | 22070 | 87685 | 26 | 12315 | 09756 | 9 | 90244 | 1 |
| 60 | 4 0 | 56 0 | 77946 | 17 | 22054 | 87711 | 26 | 12289 | 09765 | 9 | 90235 | 0 |
| M | Hour P.M. | Hour A.M. | Cosine. | Diff. | Secant. | Cotangent | Diff. | Tangent. | Cosecant. | Diff. | Sine. | M |
| 126° | | | A | | A | B | | B | C | | C | 53° |

| Seconds of time ...... | | 1s | 2s | 3s | 4s | 5s | 6s | 7s |
|---|---|---|---|---|---|---|---|---|
| Prop. parts of cols. | A | 2 | 4 | 6 | 9 | 11 | 13 | 15 |
| | B | 3 | 7 | 10 | 13 | 17 | 20 | 23 |
| | C | 1 | 2 | 4 | 5 | 6 | 7 | 8 |

# TABLE XXVII.

S.  G'.

## Log. Sines, Tangents, and Secants.

37° — 142°

| M | Hour A.M. | Hour P.M. | Sine. (A) | Diff. | Cosecant. (A) | Tangent. (B) | Diff. | Cotangent (B) | Secant. (C) | Diff. | Cosine. (C) | M |
|---|---|---|---|---|---|---|---|---|---|---|---|---|
| 0 | 7 4 0 | 4 56 0 | 9.77946 | 0 | 10.22054 | 9.87711 | 0 | 10.12289 | 10.09765 | 0 | 9.90235 | 60 |
| 1 | 3 52 | 56 8 | 77963 | 0 | 22037 | 87738 | 0 | 12262 | 09775 | 0 | 90225 | 59 |
| 2 | 3 44 | 56 16 | 77980 | 1 | 22020 | 87764 | 1 | 12236 | 09784 | 0 | 90216 | 58 |
| 3 | 3 36 | 56 24 | 77997 | 1 | 22003 | 87790 | 1 | 12210 | 09794 | 0 | 90206 | 57 |
| 4 | 3 28 | 56 32 | 78013 | 1 | 21987 | 87817 | 2 | 12183 | 09803 | 1 | 90197 | 56 |
| 5 | 7 3 20 | 4 56 40 | 9.78030 | 1 | 10.21970 | 9.87843 | 2 | 10.12157 | 10.09813 | 1 | 9.90187 | 55 |
| 6 | 3 12 | 56 48 | 78047 | 2 | 21953 | 87869 | 3 | 12131 | 09822 | 1 | 90178 | 54 |
| 7 | 3 4 | 56 56 | 78063 | 2 | 21937 | 87895 | 3 | 12105 | 09832 | 1 | 90168 | 53 |
| 8 | 2 56 | 57 4 | 78080 | 2 | 21920 | 87922 | 3 | 12078 | 09841 | 1 | 90159 | 52 |
| 9 | 2 48 | 57 12 | 78097 | 2 | 21903 | 87948 | 4 | 12052 | 09851 | 1 | 90149 | 51 |
| 10 | 7 2 40 | 4 57 20 | 9.78113 | 3 | 10.21887 | 9.87974 | 4 | 10.12026 | 10.09861 | 2 | 9.90139 | 50 |
| 11 | 2 32 | 57 28 | 78130 | 3 | 21870 | 88000 | 5 | 12000 | 09870 | 2 | 90130 | 49 |
| 12 | 2 24 | 57 36 | 78147 | 3 | 21853 | 88027 | 5 | 11973 | 09880 | 2 | 90120 | 48 |
| 13 | 2 16 | 57 44 | 78163 | 4 | 21837 | 88053 | 6 | 11947 | 09889 | 2 | 90111 | 47 |
| 14 | 2 8 | 57 52 | 78180 | 4 | 21820 | 88079 | 6 | 11921 | 09899 | 2 | 90101 | 46 |
| 15 | 7 2 0 | 4 58 0 | 9.78197 | 4 | 10.21803 | 9.88105 | 7 | 10.11895 | 10.09909 | 2 | 9.90091 | 45 |
| 16 | 1 52 | 58 8 | 78213 | 4 | 21787 | 88131 | 7 | 11869 | 09918 | 3 | 90082 | 44 |
| 17 | 1 44 | 58 16 | 78230 | 5 | 21770 | 88158 | 7 | 11842 | 09928 | 3 | 90072 | 43 |
| 18 | 1 36 | 58 24 | 78246 | 5 | 21754 | 88184 | 8 | 11816 | 09937 | 3 | 90063 | 42 |
| 19 | 1 28 | 58 32 | 78263 | 5 | 21737 | 88210 | 8 | 11790 | 09947 | 3 | 90053 | 41 |
| 20 | 7 1 20 | 4 58 40 | 9.78280 | 5 | 10.21720 | 9.88236 | 9 | 10.11764 | 10.09957 | 3 | 9.90043 | 40 |
| 21 | 1 12 | 58 48 | 78296 | 6 | 21704 | 88262 | 9 | 11738 | 09966 | 3 | 90034 | 39 |
| 22 | 1 4 | 58 56 | 78313 | 6 | 21687 | 88289 | 10 | 11711 | 09976 | 4 | 90024 | 38 |
| 23 | 0 56 | 59 4 | 78329 | 6 | 21671 | 88315 | 10 | 11685 | 09986 | 4 | 90014 | 37 |
| 24 | 0 48 | 59 12 | 78346 | 7 | 21654 | 88341 | 10 | 11659 | 09995 | 4 | 90005 | 36 |
| 25 | 7 0 40 | 4 59 20 | 9.78362 | 7 | 10.21638 | 9.88367 | 11 | 10.11633 | 10.10005 | 4 | 9.89995 | 35 |
| 26 | 0 32 | 59 28 | 78379 | 7 | 21621 | 88393 | 11 | 11607 | 10015 | 4 | 89985 | 34 |
| 27 | 0 24 | 59 36 | 78395 | 7 | 21605 | 88420 | 12 | 11580 | 10024 | 4 | 89976 | 33 |
| 28 | 0 16 | 59 44 | 78412 | 8 | 21588 | 88446 | 12 | 11554 | 10034 | 5 | 89966 | 32 |
| 29 | 0 8 | 59 52 | 78428 | 8 | 21572 | 88472 | 13 | 11528 | 10044 | 5 | 89956 | 31 |
| 30 | 7 0 0 | 5 0 0 | 9.78445 | 8 | 10.21555 | 9.88498 | 13 | 10.11502 | 10.10053 | 5 | 9.89947 | 30 |
| 31 | 6 59 52 | 0 8 | 78461 | 9 | 21539 | 88524 | 14 | 11476 | 10063 | 5 | 89937 | 29 |
| 32 | 59 44 | 0 16 | 78478 | 9 | 21522 | 88550 | 14 | 11450 | 10073 | 5 | 89927 | 28 |
| 33 | 59 36 | 0 24 | 78494 | 9 | 21506 | 88577 | 14 | 11423 | 10082 | 5 | 89918 | 27 |
| 34 | 59 28 | 0 32 | 78510 | 9 | 21490 | 88603 | 15 | 11397 | 10092 | 5 | 89908 | 26 |
| 35 | 6 59 20 | 5 0 40 | 9.78527 | 10 | 10.21473 | 9.88629 | 15 | 10.11371 | 10.10102 | 6 | 9.89898 | 25 |
| 36 | 59 12 | 0 48 | 78543 | 10 | 21457 | 88655 | 16 | 11345 | 10112 | 6 | 89888 | 24 |
| 37 | 59 4 | 0 56 | 78560 | 10 | 21440 | 88681 | 16 | 11319 | 10121 | 6 | 89879 | 23 |
| 38 | 58 56 | 1 4 | 78576 | 10 | 21424 | 88707 | 17 | 11293 | 10131 | 6 | 89869 | 22 |
| 39 | 58 48 | 1 12 | 78592 | 11 | 21408 | 88733 | 17 | 11267 | 10141 | 6 | 89859 | 21 |
| 40 | 6 58 40 | 5 1 20 | 9.78609 | 11 | 10.21391 | 9.88759 | 17 | 10.11241 | 10.10151 | 6 | 9.89849 | 20 |
| 41 | 58 32 | 1 28 | 78625 | 11 | 21375 | 88786 | 18 | 11214 | 10160 | 7 | 89840 | 19 |
| 42 | 58 24 | 1 36 | 78642 | 12 | 21358 | 88812 | 18 | 11188 | 10170 | 7 | 89830 | 18 |
| 43 | 58 16 | 1 44 | 78658 | 12 | 21342 | 88838 | 19 | 11162 | 10180 | 7 | 89820 | 17 |
| 44 | 58 8 | 1 52 | 78674 | 12 | 21326 | 88864 | 19 | 11136 | 10190 | 7 | 89810 | 16 |
| 45 | 6 58 0 | 5 2 0 | 9.78691 | 12 | 10.21309 | 9.88890 | 20 | 10.11110 | 10.10199 | 7 | 9.89801 | 15 |
| 46 | 57 52 | 2 8 | 78707 | 13 | 21293 | 88916 | 20 | 11084 | 10209 | 7 | 89791 | 14 |
| 47 | 57 44 | 2 16 | 78723 | 13 | 21277 | 88942 | 20 | 11058 | 10219 | 8 | 89781 | 13 |
| 48 | 57 36 | 2 24 | 78739 | 13 | 21261 | 88968 | 21 | 11032 | 10229 | 8 | 89771 | 12 |
| 49 | 57 28 | 2 32 | 78756 | 13 | 21244 | 88994 | 21 | 11006 | 10239 | 8 | 89761 | 11 |
| 50 | 6 57 20 | 5 2 40 | 9.78772 | 14 | 10.21228 | 9.89020 | 22 | 10.10980 | 10.10248 | 8 | 9.89752 | 10 |
| 51 | 57 12 | 2 48 | 78788 | 14 | 21212 | 89046 | 22 | 10954 | 10258 | 8 | 89742 | 9 |
| 52 | 57 4 | 2 56 | 78805 | 14 | 21195 | 89073 | 23 | 10927 | 10268 | 8 | 89732 | 8 |
| 53 | 56 56 | 3 4 | 78821 | 15 | 21179 | 89099 | 23 | 10901 | 10278 | 9 | 89722 | 7 |
| 54 | 56 48 | 3 12 | 78837 | 15 | 21163 | 89125 | 24 | 10875 | 10288 | 9 | 89712 | 6 |
| 55 | 6 56 40 | 5 3 20 | 9.78853 | 15 | 10.21147 | 9.89151 | 24 | 10.10849 | 10.10298 | 9 | 9.89702 | 5 |
| 56 | 56 32 | 3 28 | 78869 | 15 | 21131 | 89177 | 24 | 10823 | 10307 | 9 | 89693 | 4 |
| 57 | 56 24 | 3 36 | 78886 | 16 | 21114 | 89203 | 25 | 10797 | 10317 | 9 | 89683 | 3 |
| 58 | 56 16 | 3 44 | 78902 | 16 | 21098 | 89229 | 25 | 10771 | 10327 | 9 | 89673 | 2 |
| 59 | 56 8 | 3 52 | 78918 | 16 | 21082 | 89255 | 26 | 10745 | 10337 | 10 | 89663 | 1 |
| 60 | 56 0 | 4 0 | 78934 | 16 | 21066 | 89281 | 26 | 10719 | 10347 | 10 | 89653 | 0 |
| M | Hour P.M. | Hour A.M. | Cosine. (A) | Diff. | Secant. (A) | Cotangent (B) | Diff. | Tangent. (B) | Cosecant. (C) | Diff. | Sine. (C) | M |

127° — 52°

| Seconds of time ...... | | 1s | 2s | 3s | 4s | 5s | 6s | 7s |
|---|---|---|---|---|---|---|---|---|
| Prop. parts of cols. | A | 2 | 4 | 6 | 8 | 10 | 12 | 14 |
| | B | 3 | 7 | 10 | 13 | 16 | 20 | 23 |
| | C | 1 | 2 | 4 | 5 | 6 | 7 | 8 |

# TABLE XXVII.

## Log. Sines, Tangents, and Secants

| S'. 38° | | | A | | A | B | | B | C | | C | G'. 141° |
|---|---|---|---|---|---|---|---|---|---|---|---|---|
| M | Hour A.M. | Hour P.M. | Sine. | Diff. | Cosecant. | Tangent. | Diff. | Cotangent | Secant. | Diff. | Cosine. | M |
| 0 | 6 56 0 | 5 4 0 | 9.78934 | 0 | 10.21066 | 9.89281 | 0 | 10.10719 | 10.10347 | 0 | 9.89653 | 60 |
| 1 | 55 52 | 4 8 | 78950 | 0 | 21050 | 89307 | 0 | 10693 | 10357 | 0 | 89643 | 59 |
| 2 | 55 44 | 4 16 | 78967 | 1 | 21033 | 89333 | 1 | 10667 | 10367 | 0 | 89633 | 58 |
| 3 | 55 36 | 4 24 | 78983 | 1 | 21017 | 89359 | 1 | 10641 | 10376 | 1 | 89624 | 57 |
| 4 | 55 28 | 4 32 | 78999 | 1 | 21001 | 89385 | 2 | 10615 | 10386 | 1 | 89614 | 56 |
| 5 | 6 55 20 | 5 4 40 | 9.79015 | 1 | 10.20985 | 9.89411 | 2 | 10.10589 | 10.10396 | 1 | 9.89604 | 55 |
| 6 | 55 12 | 4 48 | 79031 | 2 | 20969 | 89437 | 3 | 10563 | 10406 | 1 | 89594 | 54 |
| 7 | 55 4 | 4 56 | 79047 | 2 | 20953 | 89463 | 3 | 10537 | 10416 | 1 | 89584 | 53 |
| 8 | 54 56 | 5 4 | 79063 | 2 | 20937 | 89489 | 3 | 10511 | 10426 | 1 | 89574 | 52 |
| 9 | 54 48 | 5 12 | 79079 | 2 | 20921 | 89515 | 4 | 10485 | 10436 | 2 | 89564 | 51 |
| 10 | 6 54 40 | 5 5 20 | 9.79095 | 3 | 10.20905 | 9.89541 | 4 | 10.10459 | 10.10446 | 2 | 9.89554 | 50 |
| 11 | 54 32 | 5 28 | 79111 | 3 | 20889 | 89567 | 5 | 10433 | 10456 | 2 | 89544 | 49 |
| 12 | 54 24 | 5 36 | 79128 | 3 | 20872 | 89593 | 5 | 10407 | 10466 | 2 | 89534 | 48 |
| 13 | 54 16 | 5 44 | 79144 | 3 | 20856 | 89619 | 6 | 10381 | 10476 | 2 | 89524 | 47 |
| 14 | 54 8 | 5 52 | 79160 | 4 | 20840 | 89645 | 6 | 10355 | 10486 | 2 | 89514 | 46 |
| 15 | 6 54 0 | 5 6 0 | 9.79176 | 4 | 10.20824 | 9.89671 | 6 | 10.10329 | 10.10496 | 3 | 9.89504 | 45 |
| 16 | 53 52 | 6 8 | 79192 | 4 | 20808 | 89697 | 7 | 10303 | 10505 | 3 | 89495 | 44 |
| 17 | 53 44 | 6 16 | 79208 | 5 | 20792 | 89723 | 7 | 10277 | 10515 | 3 | 89485 | 43 |
| 18 | 53 36 | 6 24 | 79224 | 5 | 20776 | 89749 | 8 | 10251 | 10525 | 3 | 89475 | 42 |
| 19 | 53 28 | 6 32 | 79240 | 5 | 20760 | 89775 | 8 | 10225 | 10535 | 3 | 89465 | 41 |
| 20 | 6 53 20 | 5 6 40 | 9.79256 | 5 | 10.20744 | 9.89801 | 9 | 10.10199 | 10.10545 | 3 | 9.89455 | 40 |
| 21 | 53 12 | 6 48 | 79272 | 6 | 20728 | 89827 | 9 | 10173 | 10555 | 4 | 89445 | 39 |
| 22 | 53 4 | 6 56 | 79288 | 6 | 20712 | 89853 | 10 | 10147 | 10565 | 4 | 89435 | 38 |
| 23 | 52 56 | 7 4 | 79304 | 6 | 20696 | 89879 | 10 | 10121 | 10575 | 4 | 89425 | 37 |
| 24 | 52 48 | 7 12 | 79319 | 6 | 20681 | 89905 | 10 | 10095 | 10585 | 4 | 89415 | 36 |
| 25 | 6 52 40 | 5 7 20 | 9.79335 | 7 | 10.20665 | 9.89931 | 11 | 10.10069 | 10.10595 | 4 | 9.89405 | 35 |
| 26 | 52 32 | 7 28 | 79351 | 7 | 20649 | 89957 | 11 | 10043 | 10605 | 4 | 89395 | 34 |
| 27 | 52 24 | 7 36 | 79367 | 7 | 20633 | 89983 | 12 | 10017 | 10615 | 5 | 89385 | 33 |
| 28 | 52 16 | 7 44 | 79383 | 7 | 20617 | 90009 | 12 | 09991 | 10625 | 5 | 89375 | 32 |
| 29 | 52 8 | 7 52 | 79399 | 8 | 20601 | 90035 | 13 | 09965 | 10636 | 5 | 89364 | 31 |
| 30 | 6 52 0 | 5 8 0 | 9.79415 | 8 | 10.20585 | 9.90061 | 13 | 10.09939 | 10.10646 | 5 | 9.89354 | 30 |
| 31 | 51 52 | 8 8 | 79431 | 8 | 20569 | 90086 | 13 | 09914 | 10656 | 5 | 89344 | 29 |
| 32 | 51 44 | 8 16 | 79447 | 8 | 20553 | 90112 | 14 | 09888 | 10666 | 5 | 89334 | 28 |
| 33 | 51 36 | 8 24 | 79463 | 9 | 20537 | 90138 | 14 | 09862 | 10676 | 6 | 89324 | 27 |
| 34 | 51 28 | 8 32 | 79478 | 9 | 20522 | 90164 | 15 | 09836 | 10686 | 6 | 89314 | 26 |
| 35 | 6 51 20 | 5 8 40 | 9.79494 | 9 | 10.20506 | 9.90190 | 15 | 10.09810 | 10.10696 | 6 | 9.89304 | 25 |
| 36 | 51 12 | 8 48 | 79510 | 10 | 20490 | 90216 | 16 | 09784 | 10706 | 6 | 89294 | 24 |
| 37 | 51 4 | 8 56 | 79526 | 10 | 20474 | 90242 | 16 | 09758 | 10716 | 6 | 89284 | 23 |
| 38 | 50 56 | 9 4 | 79542 | 10 | 20458 | 90268 | 16 | 09732 | 10726 | 6 | 89274 | 22 |
| 39 | 50 48 | 9 12 | 79558 | 10 | 20442 | 90294 | 17 | 09706 | 10736 | 7 | 89264 | 21 |
| 40 | 6 50 40 | 5 9 20 | 9.79573 | 11 | 10.20427 | 9.90320 | 17 | 10.09680 | 10.10746 | 7 | 9.89254 | 20 |
| 41 | 50 32 | 9 28 | 79589 | 11 | 20411 | 90346 | 18 | 09654 | 10756 | 7 | 89244 | 19 |
| 42 | 50 24 | 9 36 | 79605 | 11 | 20395 | 90371 | 18 | 09629 | 10767 | 7 | 89233 | 18 |
| 43 | 50 16 | 9 44 | 79621 | 11 | 20379 | 90397 | 19 | 09603 | 10777 | 7 | 89223 | 17 |
| 44 | 50 8 | 9 52 | 79636 | 12 | 20364 | 90423 | 19 | 09577 | 10787 | 7 | 89213 | 16 |
| 45 | 6 50 0 | 5 10 0 | 9.79652 | 12 | 10.20348 | 9.90449 | 19 | 10.09551 | 10.10797 | 8 | 9.89203 | 15 |
| 46 | 49 52 | 10 8 | 79668 | 12 | 20332 | 90475 | 20 | 09525 | 10807 | 8 | 89193 | 14 |
| 47 | 49 44 | 10 16 | 79684 | 12 | 20316 | 90501 | 20 | 09499 | 10817 | 8 | 89183 | 13 |
| 48 | 49 36 | 10 24 | 79699 | 13 | 20301 | 90527 | 21 | 09473 | 10827 | 8 | 89173 | 12 |
| 49 | 49 28 | 10 32 | 79715 | 13 | 20285 | 90553 | 21 | 09447 | 10838 | 8 | 89162 | 11 |
| 50 | 6 49 20 | 5 10 40 | 9.79731 | 13 | 10.20269 | 9.90578 | 22 | 10.09422 | 10.10848 | 8 | 9.89152 | 10 |
| 51 | 49 12 | 10 48 | 79746 | 14 | 20254 | 90604 | 22 | 09396 | 10858 | 9 | 89142 | 9 |
| 52 | 49 4 | 10 56 | 79762 | 14 | 20238 | 90630 | 22 | 09370 | 10868 | 9 | 89132 | 8 |
| 53 | 48 56 | 11 4 | 79778 | 14 | 20222 | 90656 | 23 | 09344 | 10878 | 9 | 89122 | 7 |
| 54 | 48 48 | 11 12 | 79793 | 14 | 20207 | 90682 | 23 | 09318 | 10888 | 9 | 89112 | 6 |
| 55 | 6 48 40 | 5 11 20 | 9.79809 | 15 | 10.20191 | 9.90708 | 24 | 10.09292 | 10.10899 | 9 | 9.89101 | 5 |
| 56 | 48 32 | 11 28 | 79825 | 15 | 20175 | 90734 | 24 | 09266 | 10909 | 9 | 89091 | 4 |
| 57 | 48 24 | 11 36 | 79840 | 15 | 20160 | 90759 | 25 | 09241 | 10919 | 10 | 89081 | 3 |
| 58 | 48 16 | 11 44 | 79856 | 15 | 20144 | 90785 | 25 | 09215 | 10929 | 10 | 89071 | 2 |
| 59 | 48 8 | 11 52 | 79872 | 16 | 20128 | 90811 | 26 | 09189 | 10940 | 10 | 89060 | 1 |
| 60 | 48 0 | 12 0 | 79887 | 16 | 20113 | 90837 | 26 | 09163 | 10950 | 10 | 89050 | 0 |
| M | Hour P.M. | Hour A.M. | Cosine. | Diff. | Secant. | Cotangent | Diff. | Tangent. | Cosecant. | Diff. | Sine. | M |
| 128° | | | A | | A | B | | B | C | | C | 51° |

| Seconds of time ...... | | 1s | 2s | 3s | 4s | 5s | 6s | 7s |
|---|---|---|---|---|---|---|---|---|
| Prop. parts of cols. | A | 2 | 4 | 6 | 8 | 10 | 12 | 14 |
| | B | 3 | 6 | 10 | 13 | 16 | 19 | 23 |
| | C | 1 | 3 | 4 | 5 | 6 | 8 | 9 |

# TABLE XXVII.

## Log. Sines, Tangents, and Secants.

S'. 39° | G'. 140°

| M | Hour A.M. | Hour P.M. | Sine. (A) | Diff. | Cosecant. (A) | Tangent. (B) | Diff. | Cotangent (B) | Secant. (C) | Diff. | Cosine. (C) | M |
|---|---|---|---|---|---|---|---|---|---|---|---|---|
| 0 | 6 48 0 | 5 12 0 | 9.79887 | 0 | 10.20113 | 9.90837 | 0 | 10.09163 | 10.10950 | 0 | 9.89050 | 60 |
| 1 | 47 52 | 12 8 | 79903 | 0 | 20097 | 90863 | 0 | 09137 | 10960 | 0 | 89040 | 59 |
| 2 | 47 44 | 12 16 | 79918 | 1 | 20082 | 90889 | 1 | 09111 | 10970 | 0 | 89030 | 58 |
| 3 | 47 36 | 12 24 | 79934 | 1 | 20066 | 90914 | 1 | 09086 | 10980 | 1 | 89020 | 57 |
| 4 | 47 28 | 12 32 | 79950 | 1 | 20050 | 90940 | 2 | 09060 | 10991 | 1 | 89009 | 56 |
| 5 | 6 47 20 | 5 12 40 | 9.79965 | 1 | 10.20035 | 9.90966 | 2 | 10.09034 | 10.11001 | 1 | 9.88999 | 55 |
| 6 | 47 12 | 12 48 | 79981 | 2 | 20019 | 90992 | 3 | 09008 | 11011 | 1 | 88989 | 54 |
| 7 | 47 4 | 12 56 | 79996 | 2 | 20004 | 91018 | 3 | 08982 | 11022 | 1 | 88978 | 53 |
| 8 | 46 56 | 13 4 | 80012 | 2 | 19988 | 91043 | 3 | 08957 | 11032 | 1 | 88968 | 52 |
| 9 | 46 48 | 13 12 | 80027 | 2 | 19973 | 91069 | 4 | 08931 | 11042 | 2 | 88958 | 51 |
| 10 | 6 46 40 | 5 13 20 | 9.80043 | 3 | 10.19957 | 9.91095 | 4 | 10.08905 | 10.11052 | 2 | 9.88948 | 50 |
| 11 | 46 32 | 13 28 | 80058 | 3 | 19942 | 91121 | 5 | 08879 | 11063 | 2 | 88937 | 49 |
| 12 | 46 24 | 13 36 | 80074 | 3 | 19926 | 91147 | 5 | 08853 | 11073 | 2 | 88927 | 48 |
| 13 | 46 16 | 13 44 | 80089 | 3 | 19911 | 91172 | 6 | 08828 | 11083 | 2 | 88917 | 47 |
| 14 | 46 8 | 13 52 | 80105 | 4 | 19895 | 91198 | 6 | 08802 | 11094 | 2 | 88906 | 46 |
| 15 | 6 46 0 | 5 14 0 | 9.80120 | 4 | 10.19880 | 9.91224 | 6 | 10.08776 | 10.11104 | 3 | 9.88896 | 45 |
| 16 | 45 52 | 14 8 | 80136 | 4 | 19864 | 91250 | 7 | 08750 | 11114 | 3 | 88886 | 44 |
| 17 | 45 44 | 14 16 | 80151 | 4 | 19849 | 91276 | 7 | 08724 | 11125 | 3 | 88875 | 43 |
| 18 | 45 36 | 14 24 | 80166 | 5 | 19834 | 91301 | 8 | 08699 | 11135 | 3 | 88865 | 42 |
| 19 | 45 28 | 14 32 | 80182 | 5 | 19818 | 91327 | 8 | 08673 | 11145 | 3 | 88855 | 41 |
| 20 | 6 45 20 | 5 14 40 | 9.80197 | 5 | 10.19803 | 9.91353 | 9 | 10.08647 | 10.11156 | 3 | 9.88844 | 40 |
| 21 | 45 12 | 14 48 | 80213 | 5 | 19787 | 91379 | 9 | 08621 | 11166 | 4 | 88834 | 39 |
| 22 | 45 4 | 14 56 | 80228 | 6 | 19772 | 91404 | 9 | 08596 | 11176 | 4 | 88824 | 38 |
| 23 | 44 56 | 15 4 | 80244 | 6 | 19756 | 91430 | 10 | 08570 | 11187 | 4 | 88813 | 37 |
| 24 | 44 48 | 15 12 | 80259 | 6 | 19741 | 91456 | 10 | 08544 | 11197 | 4 | 88803 | 36 |
| 25 | 6 44 40 | 5 15 20 | 9.80274 | 6 | 10.19726 | 9.91482 | 11 | 10.08518 | 10.11207 | 4 | 9.88793 | 35 |
| 26 | 44 32 | 15 28 | 80290 | 7 | 19710 | 91507 | 11 | 08493 | 11218 | 5 | 88782 | 34 |
| 27 | 44 24 | 15 36 | 80305 | 7 | 19695 | 91533 | 12 | 08467 | 11228 | 5 | 88772 | 33 |
| 28 | 44 16 | 15 44 | 80320 | 7 | 19680 | 91559 | 12 | 08441 | 11239 | 5 | 88761 | 32 |
| 29 | 44 8 | 15 52 | 80336 | 7 | 19664 | 91585 | 12 | 08415 | 11249 | 5 | 88751 | 31 |
| 30 | 6 44 0 | 5 16 0 | 9.80351 | 8 | 10.19649 | 9.91610 | 13 | 10.08390 | 10,11259 | 5 | 9.88741 | 30 |
| 31 | 43 52 | 16 8 | 80366 | 8 | 19634 | 91636 | 13 | 08364 | 11270 | 5 | 88730 | 29 |
| 32 | 43 44 | 16 16 | 80382 | 8 | 19618 | 91662 | 14 | 08338 | 11280 | 6 | 88720 | 28 |
| 33 | 43 36 | 16 24 | 80397 | 8 | 19603 | 91688 | 14 | 08312 | 11291 | 6 | 88709 | 27 |
| 34 | 43 28 | 16 32 | 80412 | 9 | 19588 | 91713 | 15 | 08287 | 11301 | 6 | 88699 | 26 |
| 35 | 6 43 20 | 5 16 40 | 9.80428 | 9 | 10.19572 | 9.91739 | 15 | 10.08261 | 10.11312 | 6 | 9.88688 | 25 |
| 36 | 43 12 | 16 48 | 80443 | 9 | 19557 | 91765 | 15 | 08235 | 11322 | 6 | 88678 | 24 |
| 37 | 43 4 | 16 56 | 80458 | 9 | 19542 | 91791 | 16 | 08209 | 11332 | 6 | 88668 | 23 |
| 38 | 42 56 | 17 4 | 80473 | 10 | 19527 | 91816 | 16 | 08184 | 11343 | 7 | 88657 | 22 |
| 39 | 42 48 | 17 12 | 80489 | 10 | 19511 | 91842 | 17 | 08158 | 11353 | 7 | 88647 | 21 |
| 40 | 6 42 40 | 5 17 20 | 9.80504 | 10 | 10.19496 | 9.91868 | 17 | 10.08132 | 10.11364 | 7 | 9.88636 | 20 |
| 41 | 42 32 | 17 28 | 80519 | 10 | 19481 | 91893 | 18 | 08107 | 11374 | 7 | 88626 | 19 |
| 42 | 42 24 | 17 36 | 80534 | 11 | 19466 | 91919 | 18 | 08081 | 11385 | 7 | 88615 | 18 |
| 43 | 42 16 | 17 44 | 80550 | 11 | 19450 | 91945 | 18 | 08055 | 11395 | 7 | 88605 | 17 |
| 44 | 42 8 | 17 52 | 80565 | 11 | 19435 | 91971 | 19 | 08029 | 11406 | 8 | 88594 | 16 |
| 45 | 6 42 0 | 5 18 0 | 9.80580 | 12 | 10.19420 | 9.91996 | 19 | 10.08004 | 10.11416 | 8 | 9.88584 | 15 |
| 46 | 41 52 | 18 8 | 80595 | 12 | 19405 | 92022 | 20 | 07978 | 11427 | 8 | 88573 | 14 |
| 47 | 41 44 | 18 16 | 80610 | 12 | 19390 | 92048 | 20 | 07952 | 11437 | 8 | 88563 | 13 |
| 48 | 41 36 | 18 24 | 80625 | 12 | 19375 | 92073 | 21 | 07927 | 11448 | 8 | 88552 | 12 |
| 49 | 41 28 | 18 32 | 80641 | 13 | 19359 | 92099 | 21 | 07901 | 11458 | 9 | 88542 | 11 |
| 50 | 6 41 20 | 5 18 40 | 9.80656 | 13 | 10.19344 | 9.92125 | 21 | 10.07875 | 10.11469 | 9 | 9.88531 | 10 |
| 51 | 41 12 | 18 48 | 80671 | 13 | 19329 | 92150 | 22 | 07850 | 11479 | 9 | 88521 | 9 |
| 52 | 41 4 | 18 56 | 80686 | 13 | 19314 | 92176 | 22 | 07824 | 11490 | 9 | 88510 | 8 |
| 53 | 40 56 | 19 4 | 80701 | 14 | 19299 | 92202 | 23 | 07798 | 11501 | 9 | 88499 | 7 |
| 54 | 40 48 | 19 12 | 80716 | 14 | 19284 | 92227 | 23 | 07773 | 11511 | 9 | 88489 | 6 |
| 55 | 6 40 40 | 5 19 20 | 9.80731 | 14 | 10.19269 | 9 92253 | 24 | 10.07747 | 10.11522 | 10 | 9.88478 | 5 |
| 56 | 40 32 | 19 28 | 80746 | 14 | 19254 | 92279 | 24 | 07721 | 11532 | 10 | 88468 | 4 |
| 57 | 40 24 | 19 36 | 80762 | 15 | 19238 | 92304 | 24 | 07696 | 11543 | 10 | 88457 | 3 |
| 58 | 40 16 | 19 44 | 80777 | 15 | 19223 | 92330 | 25 | 07670 | 11553 | 10 | 88447 | 2 |
| 59 | 40 8 | 19 52 | 80792 | 15 | 19208 | 92356 | 25 | 07644 | 11564 | 10 | 88436 | 1 |
| 60 | 40 0 | 20 0 | 80807 | 15 | 19193 | 92381 | 26 | 07619 | 11575 | 10 | 88425 | 0 |
| M | Hour P.M. | Hour A.M. | Cosine. (A) | Diff. | Secant. (A) | Cotangent (B) | Diff. | Tangent. (B) | Cosecant. (C) | Diff. | Sine. (C) | M |

129° | 50°

| Seconds of time ...... | $1^s$ | $2^s$ | $3^s$ | $4^s$ | $5^s$ | $6^s$ | $7^s$ |
|---|---|---|---|---|---|---|---|
| Prop. parts of cols. A | 2 | 4 | 6 | 8 | 10 | 12 | 13 |
| Prop. parts of cols. B | 3 | 6 | 10 | 13 | 16 | 19 | 23 |
| Prop. parts of cols. C | 1 | 3 | 4 | 5 | 7 | 8 | 9 |

# TABLE XXVII.

## Log. Sines, Tangents, and Secants.

S'. 40° G. 139°

| M | Hour A.M. | Hour P.M. | Sine. (A) | Diff. | Cosecant. (A) | Tangent. (B) | Diff. | Cotangent (B) | Secant. (C) | Diff. | Cosine (C) | M |
|---|---|---|---|---|---|---|---|---|---|---|---|---|
| 0 | 6 40 0 | 5 20 0 | 9.80807 | 0 | 10.19193 | 9.92381 | 0 | 10.07619 | 10.11575 | 0 | 9.88425 | 60 |
| 1 | 39 52 | 20 8 | 80822 | 0 | 19178 | 92407 | 0 | 07593 | 11585 | 0 | 88415 | 59 |
| 2 | 39 44 | 20 16 | 80837 | 0 | 19163 | 92433 | 1 | 07567 | 11596 | 0 | 88404 | 58 |
| 3 | 39 36 | 20 24 | 80852 | 1 | 19148 | 92458 | 1 | 07542 | 11606 | 1 | 88394 | 57 |
| 4 | 39 28 | 20 32 | 80867 | 1 | 19133 | 92484 | 2 | 07516 | 11617 | 1 | 88383 | 56 |
| 5 | 6 39 20 | 5 20 40 | 9.80882 | 1 | 10.19118 | 9.92510 | 2 | 10.07490 | 10.11628 | 1 | 9.88372 | 55 |
| 6 | 39 12 | 20 48 | 80897 | 1 | 19103 | 92535 | 3 | 07465 | 11638 | 1 | 88362 | 54 |
| 7 | 39 4 | 20 56 | 80912 | 2 | 19088 | 92561 | 3 | 07439 | 11649 | 1 | 88351 | 53 |
| 8 | 38 56 | 21 4 | 80927 | 2 | 19073 | 92587 | 3 | 07413 | 11660 | 1 | 88340 | 52 |
| 9 | 38 48 | 21 12 | 80942 | 2 | 19058 | 92612 | 4 | 07388 | 11670 | 2 | 88330 | 51 |
| 10 | 6 38 40 | 5 21 20 | 9.80957 | 2 | 10.19043 | 9.92638 | 4 | 10.07362 | 10.11681 | 2 | 9.88319 | 50 |
| 11 | 38 32 | 21 28 | 80972 | 3 | 19028 | 92663 | 5 | 07337 | 11692 | 2 | 88308 | 49 |
| 12 | 38 24 | 21 36 | 80987 | 3 | 19013 | 92689 | 5 | 07311 | 11702 | 2 | 88298 | 48 |
| 13 | 38 16 | 21 44 | 81002 | 3 | 18998 | 92715 | 6 | 07285 | 11713 | 2 | 88287 | 47 |
| 14 | 38 8 | 21 52 | 81017 | 3 | 18983 | 92740 | 6 | 07260 | 11724 | 3 | 88276 | 46 |
| 15 | 6 38 0 | 5 22 0 | 9.81032 | 4 | 10.18968 | 9.92766 | 6 | 10.07234 | 10.11734 | 3 | 9.88266 | 45 |
| 16 | 37 52 | 22 8 | 81047 | 4 | 18953 | 92792 | 7 | 07208 | 11745 | 3 | 88255 | 44 |
| 17 | 37 44 | 22 16 | 81061 | 4 | 18939 | 92817 | 7 | 07183 | 11756 | 3 | 88244 | 43 |
| 18 | 37 36 | 22 24 | 81076 | 4 | 18924 | 92843 | 8 | 07157 | 11766 | 3 | 88234 | 42 |
| 19 | 37 28 | 22 32 | 81091 | 5 | 18909 | 92868 | 8 | 07132 | 11777 | 3 | 88223 | 41 |
| 20 | 6 37 20 | 5 22 40 | 9.81106 | 5 | 10.18894 | 9.92894 | 9 | 10.07106 | 10.11788 | 4 | 9.88212 | 40 |
| 21 | 37 12 | 22 48 | 81121 | 5 | 18879 | 92920 | 9 | 07080 | 11799 | 4 | 88201 | 39 |
| 22 | 37 4 | 22 56 | 81136 | 5 | 18864 | 92945 | 9 | 07055 | 11809 | 4 | 88191 | 38 |
| 23 | 36 56 | 23 4 | 81151 | 6 | 18849 | 92971 | 10 | 07029 | 11820 | 4 | 88180 | 37 |
| 24 | 36 48 | 23 12 | 81166 | 6 | 18834 | 92996 | 10 | 07004 | 11831 | 4 | 88169 | 36 |
| 25 | 6 36 40 | 5 23 20 | 9.81180 | 6 | 10.18820 | 9.93022 | 11 | 10.06978 | 10.11842 | 4 | 9.88158 | 35 |
| 26 | 36 32 | 23 28 | 81195 | 6 | 18805 | 93048 | 11 | 06952 | 11852 | 5 | 88148 | 34 |
| 27 | 36 24 | 23 36 | 81210 | 7 | 18790 | 93073 | 12 | 06927 | 11863 | 5 | 88137 | 33 |
| 28 | 36 16 | 23 44 | 81225 | 7 | 18775 | 93099 | 12 | 06901 | 11874 | 5 | 88126 | 32 |
| 29 | 36 8 | 23 52 | 81240 | 7 | 18760 | 93124 | 12 | 06876 | 11885 | 5 | 88115 | 31 |
| 30 | 6 36 0 | 5 24 0 | 9.81254 | 7 | 10.18746 | 9.93150 | 13 | 10.06850 | 10.11895 | 5 | 9.88105 | 30 |
| 31 | 35 52 | 24 8 | 81269 | 8 | 18731 | 93175 | 13 | 06825 | 11906 | 6 | 88094 | 29 |
| 32 | 35 44 | 24 16 | 81284 | 8 | 18716 | 93201 | 14 | 06799 | 11917 | 6 | 88083 | 28 |
| 33 | 35 36 | 24 24 | 81299 | 8 | 18701 | 93227 | 14 | 06773 | 11928 | 6 | 88072 | 27 |
| 34 | 35 28 | 24 32 | 81314 | 8 | 18686 | 93252 | 14 | 06748 | 11939 | 6 | 88061 | 26 |
| 35 | 6 35 20 | 5 24 40 | 9.81328 | 9 | 10.18672 | 9.93278 | 15 | 10.06722 | 10.11949 | 6 | 9.88051 | 25 |
| 36 | 35 12 | 24 48 | 81343 | 9 | 18657 | 93303 | 15 | 06697 | 11960 | 6 | 88040 | 24 |
| 37 | 35 4 | 24 56 | 81358 | 9 | 18642 | 93329 | 16 | 06671 | 11971 | 7 | 88029 | 23 |
| 38 | 34 56 | 25 4 | 81372 | 9 | 18628 | 93354 | 16 | 06646 | 11982 | 7 | 88018 | 22 |
| 39 | 34 48 | 25 12 | 81387 | 10 | 18613 | 93380 | 17 | 06620 | 11993 | 7 | 88007 | 21 |
| 40 | 6 34 40 | 5 25 20 | 9.81402 | 10 | 10.18598 | 9.93406 | 17 | 10.06594 | 10.12004 | 7 | 9.87996 | 20 |
| 41 | 34 32 | 25 28 | 81417 | 10 | 18583 | 93431 | 17 | 06569 | 12015 | 7 | 87985 | 19 |
| 42 | 34 24 | 25 36 | 81431 | 10 | 18569 | 93457 | 18 | 06543 | 12025 | 8 | 87975 | 18 |
| 43 | 34 16 | 25 44 | 81446 | 11 | 18554 | 93482 | 18 | 06518 | 12036 | 8 | 87964 | 17 |
| 44 | 34 8 | 25 52 | 81461 | 11 | 18539 | 93508 | 19 | 06492 | 12047 | 8 | 87953 | 16 |
| 45 | 6 34 0 | 5 26 0 | 9.81475 | 11 | 10.18525 | 9.93533 | 19 | 10.06467 | 10.12058 | 8 | 9.87942 | 15 |
| 46 | 33 52 | 26 8 | 81490 | 11 | 18510 | 93559 | 20 | 06441 | 12069 | 8 | 87931 | 14 |
| 47 | 33 44 | 26 16 | 81505 | 12 | 18495 | 93584 | 20 | 06416 | 12080 | 8 | 87920 | 13 |
| 48 | 33 36 | 26 24 | 81519 | 12 | 18481 | 93610 | 20 | 06390 | 12091 | 9 | 87909 | 12 |
| 49 | 33 28 | 26 32 | 81534 | 12 | 18466 | 93636 | 21 | 06364 | 12102 | 9 | 87898 | 11 |
| 50 | 6 33 20 | 5 26 40 | 9.81549 | 12 | 10.18451 | 9.93661 | 21 | 10.06339 | 10.12113 | 9 | 9.87887 | 10 |
| 51 | 33 12 | 26 48 | 81563 | 13 | 18437 | 93687 | 22 | 06313 | 12123 | 9 | 87877 | 9 |
| 52 | 33 4 | 26 56 | 81578 | 13 | 18422 | 93712 | 22 | 06288 | 12134 | 9 | 87866 | 8 |
| 53 | 32 56 | 27 4 | 81592 | 13 | 18408 | 93738 | 23 | 06262 | 12145 | 10 | 87855 | 7 |
| 54 | 32 48 | 27 12 | 81607 | 13 | 18393 | 93763 | 23 | 06237 | 12156 | 10 | 87844 | 6 |
| 55 | 6 32 40 | 5 27 20 | 9.81622 | 14 | 10.18378 | 9.93789 | 23 | 10.06211 | 10.12167 | 10 | 9.87833 | 5 |
| 56 | 32 32 | 27 28 | 81636 | 14 | 18364 | 93814 | 24 | 06186 | 12178 | 10 | 87822 | 4 |
| 57 | 32 24 | 27 36 | 81651 | 14 | 18349 | 93840 | 24 | 06160 | 12189 | 10 | 87811 | 3 |
| 58 | 32 16 | 27 44 | 81665 | 14 | 18335 | 93865 | 25 | 06135 | 12200 | 10 | 87800 | 2 |
| 59 | 32 8 | 27 52 | 81680 | 15 | 18320 | 93891 | 25 | 06109 | 12211 | 11 | 87789 | 1 |
| 60 | 32 0 | 28 0 | 81694 | 15 | 18306 | 93916 | 26 | 06084 | 12222 | 11 | 87778 | 0 |
| M | Hour P.M. | Hour A.M. | Cosine. (A) | Diff. | Secant. (A) | Cotangent (B) | Diff. | Tangent. (B) | Cosecant. (C) | Diff. | Sine. (C) | M |

130° 49°

| Seconds of time ...... | | 1ˢ | 2ˢ | 3ˢ | 4ˢ | 5ˢ | 6ˢ | 7ˢ |
|---|---|---|---|---|---|---|---|---|
| Prop. parts of cols. | A | 2 | 4 | 6 | 7 | 9 | 11 | 13 |
| | B | 3 | 6 | 10 | 13 | 16 | 19 | 22 |
| | C | 1 | 3 | 4 | 5 | 7 | 8 | 9 |

# TABLE XXVII.

S'. G

## Log. Sines, Tangents, and Secants.

41° 138°

| M | Hour A.M. | Hour P.M. | A Sine. | Diff. | A Cosecant. | B Tangent. | Diff. | B Cotangent | C Secant. | Diff. | C Cosine. | M |
|---|---|---|---|---|---|---|---|---|---|---|---|---|
| 0 | 6 32 0 | 5 28 0 | 9.81694 | 0 | 10.18306 | 9.93916 | 0 | 10.06084 | 10.12222 | 0 | 9.87778 | 60 |
| 1 | 31 52 | 28 8 | 81709 | 0 | 18291 | 93942 | 0 | 06058 | 12233 | 0 | 87767 | 59 |
| 2 | 31 44 | 28 16 | 81723 | 0 | 18277 | 93967 | 1 | 06033 | 12244 | 0 | 87756 | 58 |
| 3 | 31 36 | 28 24 | 81738 | 1 | 18262 | 93993 | 1 | 06007 | 12255 | 1 | 87745 | 57 |
| 4 | 31 28 | 28 32 | 81752 | 1 | 18248 | 94018 | 2 | 05982 | 12266 | 1 | 87734 | 56 |
| 5 | 6 31 20 | 5 28 40 | 9.81767 | 1 | 10.18233 | 9.94044 | 2 | 10.05956 | 10.12277 | 1 | 9.87723 | 55 |
| 6 | 31 12 | 28 48 | 81781 | 1 | 18219 | 94069 | 3 | 05931 | 12288 | 1 | 87712 | 54 |
| 7 | 31 4 | 28 56 | 81796 | 2 | 18204 | 94095 | 3 | 05905 | 12299 | 1 | 87701 | 53 |
| 8 | 30 56 | 29 4 | 81810 | 2 | 18190 | 94120 | 3 | 05880 | 12310 | 1 | 87690 | 52 |
| 9 | 30 48 | 29 12 | 81825 | 2 | 18175 | 94146 | 4 | 05854 | 12321 | 2 | 87679 | 51 |
| 10 | 6 30 40 | 5 29 20 | 9.81839 | 2 | 10.18161 | 9.94171 | 4 | 10.05829 | 10.12332 | 2 | 9.87668 | 50 |
| 11 | 30 32 | 29 28 | 81854 | 3 | 18146 | 94197 | 5 | 05803 | 12343 | 2 | 87657 | 49 |
| 12 | 30 24 | 29 36 | 81868 | 3 | 18132 | 94222 | 5 | 05778 | 12354 | 2 | 87646 | 48 |
| 13 | 30 16 | 29 44 | 81882 | 3 | 18118 | 94248 | 6 | 05752 | 12365 | 2 | 87635 | 47 |
| 14 | 30 8 | 29 52 | 81897 | 3 | 18103 | 94273 | 6 | 05727 | 12376 | 3 | 87624 | 46 |
| 15 | 6 30 0 | 5 30 0 | 9.81911 | 4 | 10.18089 | 9.94299 | 6 | 10.05701 | 10.12387 | 3 | 9.87613 | 45 |
| 16 | 29 52 | 30 8 | 81926 | 4 | 18074 | 94324 | 7 | 05676 | 12399 | 3 | 87601 | 44 |
| 17 | 29 44 | 30 16 | 81940 | 4 | 18060 | 94350 | 7 | 05650 | 12410 | 3 | 87590 | 43 |
| 18 | 29 36 | 30 24 | 81955 | 4 | 18045 | 94375 | 8 | 05625 | 12421 | 3 | 87579 | 42 |
| 19 | 29 28 | 30 32 | 81969 | 5 | 18031 | 94401 | 8 | 05599 | 12432 | 4 | 87568 | 41 |
| 20 | 6 29 20 | 5 30 40 | 9.81983 | 5 | 10.18017 | 9.94426 | 8 | 10.05574 | 10.12443 | 4 | 9.87557 | 40 |
| 21 | 29 12 | 30 48 | 81998 | 5 | 18002 | 94452 | 9 | 05548 | 12454 | 4 | 87546 | 39 |
| 22 | 29 4 | 30 56 | 82012 | 5 | 17988 | 94477 | 9 | 05523 | 12465 | 4 | 87535 | 38 |
| 23 | 28 56 | 31 4 | 82026 | 5 | 17974 | 94503 | 10 | 05497 | 12476 | 4 | 87524 | 37 |
| 24 | 28 48 | 31 12 | 82041 | 6 | 17959 | 94528 | 10 | 05472 | 12487 | 4 | 87513 | 36 |
| 25 | 6 28 40 | 5 31 20 | 9.82055 | 6 | 10.17945 | 9.94554 | 11 | 10.05446 | 10.12499 | 5 | 9.87501 | 35 |
| 26 | 28 32 | 31 28 | 82069 | 6 | 17931 | 94579 | 11 | 05421 | 12510 | 5 | 87490 | 34 |
| 27 | 28 24 | 31 36 | 82084 | 6 | 17916 | 94604 | 11 | 05396 | 12521 | 5 | 87479 | 33 |
| 28 | 28 16 | 31 44 | 82098 | 7 | 17902 | 94630 | 12 | 05370 | 12532 | 5 | 87468 | 32 |
| 29 | 28 8 | 31 52 | 82112 | 7 | 17888 | 94655 | 12 | 05345 | 12543 | 5 | 87457 | 31 |
| 30 | 6 28 0 | 5 32 0 | 9.82126 | 7 | 10.17874 | 9.94681 | 13 | 10.05319 | 10.12554 | 6 | 9.87446 | 30 |
| 31 | 27 52 | 32 8 | 82141 | 7 | 17859 | 94706 | 13 | 05294 | 12566 | 6 | 87434 | 29 |
| 32 | 27 44 | 32 16 | 82155 | 8 | 17845 | 94732 | 14 | 05268 | 12577 | 6 | 87423 | 28 |
| 33 | 27 36 | 32 24 | 82169 | 8 | 17831 | 94757 | 14 | 05243 | 12588 | 6 | 87412 | 27 |
| 34 | 27 28 | 32 32 | 82184 | 8 | 17816 | 94783 | 14 | 05217 | 12599 | 6 | 87401 | 26 |
| 35 | 6 27 20 | 5 32 40 | 9.82198 | 8 | 10.17802 | 9.94808 | 15 | 10.05192 | 10.12610 | 7 | 9.87390 | 25 |
| 36 | 27 12 | 32 48 | 82212 | 9 | 17788 | 94834 | 15 | 05166 | 12622 | 7 | 87378 | 24 |
| 37 | 27 4 | 32 56 | 82226 | 9 | 17774 | 94859 | 16 | 05141 | 12633 | 7 | 87367 | 23 |
| 38 | 26 56 | 33 4 | 82240 | 9 | 17760 | 94884 | 16 | 05116 | 12644 | 7 | 87356 | 22 |
| 39 | 26 48 | 33 12 | 82255 | 9 | 17745 | 94910 | 17 | 05090 | 12655 | 7 | 87345 | 21 |
| 40 | 6 26 40 | 5 33 20 | 9.82269 | 10 | 10.17731 | 9.94935 | 17 | 10.05065 | 10.12666 | 7 | 9.87334 | 20 |
| 41 | 26 32 | 33 28 | 82283 | 10 | 17717 | 94961 | 17 | 05039 | 12678 | 8 | 87322 | 19 |
| 42 | 26 24 | 33 36 | 82297 | 10 | 17703 | 94986 | 18 | 05014 | 12689 | 8 | 87311 | 18 |
| 43 | 26 16 | 33 44 | 82311 | 10 | 17689 | 95012 | 18 | 04988 | 12700 | 8 | 87300 | 17 |
| 44 | 26 8 | 33 52 | 82326 | 10 | 17674 | 95037 | 19 | 04963 | 12712 | 8 | 87288 | 16 |
| 45 | 6 26 0 | 5 34 0 | 9.82340 | 11 | 10.17660 | 9.95062 | 19 | 10.04938 | 10.12723 | 8 | 9.87277 | 15 |
| 46 | 25 52 | 34 8 | 82354 | 11 | 17646 | 95088 | 20 | 04912 | 12734 | 9 | 87266 | 14 |
| 47 | 25 44 | 34 16 | 82368 | 11 | 17632 | 95113 | 20 | 04887 | 12745 | 9 | 87255 | 13 |
| 48 | 25 36 | 34 24 | 82382 | 11 | 17618 | 95139 | 20 | 04861 | 12757 | 9 | 87243 | 12 |
| 49 | 25 28 | 34 32 | 82396 | 12 | 17604 | 95164 | 21 | 04836 | 12768 | 9 | 87232 | 11 |
| 50 | 6 25 20 | 5 34 40 | 9.82410 | 12 | 10.17590 | 9.95190 | 21 | 10.04810 | 10.12779 | 9 | 9.87221 | 10 |
| 51 | 25 12 | 34 48 | 82424 | 12 | 17576 | 95215 | 22 | 04785 | 12791 | 10 | 87209 | 9 |
| 52 | 25 4 | 34 56 | 82439 | 12 | 17561 | 95240 | 22 | 04760 | 12802 | 10 | 87198 | 8 |
| 53 | 24 56 | 35 4 | 82453 | 13 | 17547 | 95266 | 22 | 04734 | 12813 | 10 | 87187 | 7 |
| 54 | 24 48 | 35 12 | 82467 | 13 | 17533 | 95291 | 23 | 04709 | 12825 | 10 | 87175 | 6 |
| 55 | 6 24 40 | 5 35 20 | 9.82481 | 13 | 10.17519 | 9.95317 | 23 | 10.04683 | 10.12836 | 10 | 9.87164 | 5 |
| 56 | 24 32 | 35 28 | 82495 | 13 | 17505 | 95342 | 24 | 04658 | 12847 | 10 | 87153 | 4 |
| 57 | 24 24 | 35 36 | 82509 | 14 | 17491 | 95368 | 24 | 04632 | 12859 | 11 | 87141 | 3 |
| 58 | 24 16 | 35 44 | 82523 | 14 | 17477 | 95393 | 25 | 04607 | 12870 | 11 | 87130 | 2 |
| 59 | 24 8 | 35 52 | 82537 | 14 | 17463 | 95418 | 25 | 04582 | 12881 | 11 | 87119 | 1 |
| 60 | 24 0 | 36 0 | 82551 | 14 | 17449 | 95444 | 25 | 04556 | 12893 | 11 | 87107 | 0 |
| M | Hour P.M. | Hour A.M. | Cosine. A | Diff. | Secant. A | Cotangent B | Diff. | Tangent. B | Cosecant. C | Diff. | Sine. C | M |

131° 48°

| Seconds of time ...... | | 1s | 2s | 3s | 4s | 5s | 6s | 7s |
|---|---|---|---|---|---|---|---|---|
| Prop. parts of cols. | A | 2 | 4 | 5 | 7 | 9 | 11 | 12 |
| | B | 3 | 6 | 10 | 13 | 16 | 19 | 22 |
| | C | 1 | 3 | 4 | 6 | 7 | 8 | 10 |

# TABLE XXVII.

## Log. Sines, Tangents, and Secants.

42° | A | A | B | B | C | C 137°

| M | Hour A.M. | Hour P.M. | Sine. | Diff. | Cosecant. | Tangent. | Diff. | Cotangent | Secant. | Diff. | Cosine. | M |
|---|---|---|---|---|---|---|---|---|---|---|---|---|
| 0 | 6 24 0 | 5 36 0 | 9.82551 | 0 | 10.17449 | 9.95444 | 0 | 10.04556 | 10.12893 | 0 | 9.87107 | 60 |
| 1 | 23 52 | 36 8 | 82565 | 0 | 17435 | 95469 | 0 | 04531 | 12904 | 0 | 87096 | 59 |
| 2 | 23 44 | 36 16 | 82579 | 0 | 17421 | 95495 | 1 | 04505 | 12915 | 0 | 87085 | 58 |
| 3 | 23 36 | 36 24 | 82593 | 1 | 17407 | 95520 | 1 | 04480 | 12927 | 1 | 87073 | 57 |
| 4 | 23 28 | 36 32 | 82607 | 1 | 17393 | 95545 | 2 | 04455 | 12938 | 1 | 87062 | 56 |
| 5 | 6 23 20 | 5 36 40 | 9.82621 | 1 | 10.17379 | 9.95571 | 2 | 10.04429 | 10.12950 | 1 | 9.87050 | 55 |
| 6 | 23 12 | 36 48 | 82635 | 1 | 17365 | 95596 | 3 | 04404 | 12961 | 1 | 87039 | 54 |
| 7 | 23 4 | 36 56 | 82649 | 2 | 17351 | 95622 | 3 | 04378 | 12972 | 1 | 87028 | 53 |
| 8 | 22 56 | 37 4 | 82663 | 2 | 17337 | 95647 | 3 | 04353 | 12984 | 2 | 87016 | 52 |
| 9 | 22 48 | 37 12 | 82677 | 2 | 17323 | 95672 | 4 | 04328 | 12995 | 2 | 87005 | 51 |
| 10 | 6 22 40 | 5 37 20 | 9.82691 | 2 | 10.17309 | 9.95698 | 4 | 10.04302 | 10.13007 | 2 | 9.86993 | 50 |
| 11 | 22 32 | 37 28 | 82705 | 3 | 17295 | 95723 | 5 | 04277 | 13018 | 2 | 86982 | 49 |
| 12 | 22 24 | 37 36 | 82719 | 3 | 17281 | 95748 | 5 | 04252 | 13030 | 2 | 86970 | 48 |
| 13 | 22 16 | 37 44 | 82733 | 3 | 17267 | 95774 | 5 | 04226 | 13041 | 3 | 86959 | 47 |
| 14 | 22 8 | 37 52 | 82747 | 3 | 17253 | 95799 | 6 | 04201 | 13053 | 3 | 86947 | 46 |
| 15 | 6 22 0 | 5 38 0 | 9.82761 | 3 | 10.17239 | 9.95825 | 6 | 10.04175 | 10.13064 | 3 | 9.86936 | 45 |
| 16 | 21 52 | 38 8 | 82775 | 4 | 17225 | 95850 | 7 | 04150 | 13076 | 3 | 86924 | 44 |
| 17 | 21 44 | 38 16 | 82788 | 4 | 17212 | 95875 | 7 | 04125 | 13087 | 3 | 86913 | 43 |
| 18 | 21 36 | 38 24 | 82802 | 4 | 17198 | 95901 | 8 | 04099 | 13098 | 3 | 86902 | 42 |
| 19 | 21 28 | 38 32 | 82816 | 4 | 17184 | 95926 | 8 | 04074 | 13110 | 4 | 86890 | 41 |
| 20 | 6 21 20 | 5 38 40 | 9.82830 | 5 | 10.17170 | 9.95952 | 8 | 10.04048 | 10.13121 | 4 | 9.86879 | 40 |
| 21 | 21 12 | 38 48 | 82844 | 5 | 17156 | 95977 | 9 | 04023 | 13133 | 4 | 86867 | 39 |
| 22 | 21 4 | 38 56 | 82858 | 5 | 17142 | 96002 | 9 | 03998 | 13145 | 4 | 86855 | 38 |
| 23 | 20 56 | 39 4 | 82872 | 5 | 17128 | 96028 | 10 | 03972 | 13156 | 4 | 86844 | 37 |
| 24 | 20 48 | 39 12 | 82885 | 6 | 17115 | 96053 | 10 | 03947 | 13168 | 5 | 86832 | 36 |
| 25 | 6 20 40 | 5 39 20 | 9.82899 | 6 | 10.17101 | 9.96078 | 11 | 10.03922 | 10.13179 | 5 | 9.86821 | 35 |
| 26 | 20 32 | 39 28 | 82913 | 6 | 17087 | 96104 | 11 | 03896 | 13191 | 5 | 86809 | 34 |
| 27 | 20 24 | 39 36 | 82927 | 6 | 17073 | 96129 | 11 | 03871 | 13202 | 5 | 86798 | 33 |
| 28 | 20 16 | 39 44 | 82941 | 6 | 17059 | 96155 | 12 | 03845 | 13214 | 5 | 86786 | 32 |
| 29 | 20 8 | 39 52 | 82955 | 7 | 17045 | 96180 | 12 | 03820 | 13225 | 6 | 86775 | 31 |
| 30 | 6 20 0 | 5 40 0 | 9.82968 | 7 | 10.17032 | 9.96205 | 13 | 10.03795 | 10.13237 | 6 | 9.86763 | 30 |
| 31 | 19 52 | 40 8 | 82982 | 7 | 17018 | 96231 | 13 | 03769 | 13248 | 6 | 86752 | 29 |
| 32 | 19 44 | 40 16 | 82996 | 7 | 17004 | 96256 | 14 | 03744 | 13260 | 6 | 86740 | 28 |
| 33 | 19 36 | 40 24 | 83010 | 8 | 16990 | 96281 | 14 | 03719 | 13272 | 6 | 86728 | 27 |
| 34 | 19 28 | 40 32 | 83023 | 8 | 16977 | 96307 | 14 | 03693 | 13283 | 7 | 86717 | 26 |
| 35 | 6 19 20 | 5 40 40 | 9.83037 | 8 | 10.16963 | 9.96332 | 15 | 10.03668 | 10.13295 | 7 | 9.86705 | 25 |
| 36 | 19 12 | 40 48 | 83051 | 8 | 16949 | 96357 | 15 | 03643 | 13306 | 7 | 86694 | 24 |
| 37 | 19 4 | 40 56 | 83065 | 8 | 16935 | 96383 | 16 | 03617 | 13318 | 7 | 86682 | 23 |
| 38 | 18 56 | 41 4 | 83078 | 9 | 16922 | 96408 | 16 | 03592 | 13330 | 7 | 86670 | 22 |
| 39 | 18 48 | 41 12 | 83092 | 9 | 16908 | 96433 | 16 | 03567 | 13341 | 8 | 86659 | 21 |
| 40 | 6 18 40 | 5 41 20 | 9.83106 | 9 | 10.16894 | 9.96459 | 17 | 10.03541 | 10.13353 | 8 | 9.86647 | 20 |
| 41 | 18 32 | 41 28 | 83120 | 9 | 16880 | 96484 | 17 | 03516 | 13365 | 8 | 86635 | 19 |
| 42 | 18 24 | 41 36 | 83133 | 10 | 16867 | 96510 | 18 | 03490 | 13376 | 8 | 86624 | 18 |
| 43 | 18 16 | 41 44 | 83147 | 10 | 16853 | 96535 | 18 | 03465 | 13388 | 8 | 86612 | 17 |
| 44 | 18 8 | 41 52 | 83161 | 10 | 16839 | 96560 | 19 | 03440 | 13400 | 8 | 86600 | 16 |
| 45 | 6 18 0 | 5 42 0 | 9.83174 | 10 | 10.16826 | 9.96586 | 19 | 10.03414 | 10.13411 | 9 | 9.86589 | 15 |
| 46 | 17 52 | 42 8 | 83188 | 11 | 16812 | 96611 | 19 | 03389 | 13423 | 9 | 86577 | 14 |
| 47 | 17 44 | 42 16 | 83202 | 11 | 16798 | 96636 | 20 | 03364 | 13435 | 9 | 86565 | 13 |
| 48 | 17 36 | 42 24 | 83215 | 11 | 16785 | 96662 | 20 | 03338 | 13446 | 9 | 86554 | 12 |
| 49 | 17 28 | 42 32 | 83229 | 11 | 16771 | 96687 | 21 | 03313 | 13458 | 9 | 86542 | 11 |
| 50 | 6 17 20 | 5 42 40 | 9.83242 | 11 | 10.16758 | 9.96712 | 21 | 10.03288 | 10.13470 | 10 | 9.86530 | 10 |
| 51 | 17 12 | 42 48 | 83256 | 12 | 16744 | 96738 | 22 | 03262 | 13482 | 10 | 86518 | 9 |
| 52 | 17 4 | 42 56 | 83270 | 12 | 16730 | 96763 | 22 | 03237 | 13493 | 10 | 86507 | 8 |
| 53 | 16 56 | 43 4 | 83283 | 12 | 16717 | 96788 | 22 | 03212 | 13505 | 10 | 86495 | 7 |
| 54 | 16 48 | 43 12 | 83297 | 12 | 16703 | 96814 | 23 | 03186 | 13517 | 10 | 86483 | 6 |
| 55 | 6 16 40 | 5 43 20 | 9.83310 | 13 | 10.16690 | 9.96839 | 23 | 10.03161 | 10.13528 | 11 | 9.86472 | 5 |
| 56 | 16 32 | 43 28 | 83324 | 13 | 16676 | 96864 | 24 | 03136 | 13540 | 11 | 86460 | 4 |
| 57 | 16 24 | 43 36 | 83338 | 13 | 16662 | 96890 | 24 | 03110 | 13552 | 11 | 86448 | 3 |
| 58 | 16 16 | 43 44 | 83351 | 13 | 16649 | 96915 | 25 | 03085 | 13564 | 11 | 86436 | 2 |
| 59 | 16 8 | 43 52 | 83365 | 14 | 16635 | 96940 | 25 | 03060 | 13575 | 11 | 86425 | 1 |
| 60 | 16 0 | 44 0 | 83378 | 14 | 16622 | 96966 | 25 | 03034 | 13587 | 12 | 86413 | 0 |
| M | Hour P.M. | Hour A.M. | Cosine. | Diff. | Secant. | Cotangent | Diff. | Tangent. | Cosecant. | Diff. | Sine. | M |

132° | A | A | B | B | C | C 47°

| Seconds of time ...... | | 1ˢ | 2ˢ | 3ˢ | 4ˢ | 5ˢ | 6ˢ | 7ˢ |
|---|---|---|---|---|---|---|---|---|
| Prop. parts of cols. | A | 2 | 3 | 5 | 7 | 9 | 10 | 12 |
| | B | 3 | 6 | 10 | 13 | 16 | 19 | 22 |
| | C | 1 | 3 | 4 | 6 | 7 | 9 | 10 |

# TABLE XXVII.

## Log. Sines, Tangents, and Secants.

S'. 43° — G'. 136°

| M | Hour A.M. | Hour P.M. | Sine. (A) | Diff. | Cosecant. (A) | Tangent. (B) | Diff. | Cotangent (B) | Secant (C) | Diff. | Cosine. (C) | M |
|---|---|---|---|---|---|---|---|---|---|---|---|---|
| 0 | 6 16 0 | 5 44 0 | 9.83378 | 0 | 10.16622 | 9.96966 | 0 | 10.03034 | 10.13587 | 0 | 9.86413 | 60 |
| 1 | 15 52 | 44 8 | 83392 | 0 | 16608 | 96991 | 0 | 03009 | 13599 | 0 | 86401 | 59 |
| 2 | 15 44 | 44 16 | 83405 | 0 | 16595 | 97016 | 1 | 02984 | 13611 | 0 | 86389 | 58 |
| 3 | 15 36 | 44 24 | 83419 | 1 | 16581 | 97042 | 1 | 02958 | 13623 | 1 | 86377 | 57 |
| 4 | 15 28 | 44 32 | 83432 | 1 | 16568 | 97067 | 2 | 02933 | 13634 | 1 | 86366 | 56 |
| 5 | 6 15 20 | 5 44 40 | 9.83446 | 1 | 10.16554 | 9.97092 | 2 | 10.02908 | 10.13646 | 1 | 9.86354 | 55 |
| 6 | 15 12 | 44 48 | 83459 | 1 | 16541 | 97118 | 3 | 02882 | 13658 | 1 | 86342 | 54 |
| 7 | 15 4 | 44 56 | 83473 | 2 | 16527 | 97143 | 3 | 02857 | 13670 | 1 | 86330 | 53 |
| 8 | 14 56 | 45 4 | 83486 | 2 | 16514 | 97168 | 3 | 02832 | 13682 | 2 | 86318 | 52 |
| 9 | 14 48 | 45 12 | 83500 | 2 | 16500 | 97193 | 4 | 02807 | 13694 | 2 | 86306 | 51 |
| 10 | 6 14 40 | 5 45 20 | 9.83513 | 2 | 10.16487 | 9.97219 | 4 | 10.02781 | 10.13705 | 2 | 9.86295 | 50 |
| 11 | 14 32 | 45 28 | 83527 | 2 | 16473 | 97244 | 5 | 02756 | 13717 | 2 | 86283 | 49 |
| 12 | 14 24 | 45 36 | 83540 | 3 | 16460 | 97269 | 5 | 02731 | 13729 | 2 | 86271 | 48 |
| 13 | 14 16 | 45 44 | 83554 | 3 | 16446 | 97295 | 5 | 02705 | 13741 | 3 | 86259 | 47 |
| 14 | 14 8 | 45 52 | 83567 | 3 | 16433 | 97320 | 6 | 02680 | 13753 | 3 | 86247 | 46 |
| 15 | 6 14 0 | 5 46 0 | 9.83581 | 3 | 10.16419 | 9.97345 | 6 | 10.02655 | 10.13765 | 3 | 9.86235 | 45 |
| 16 | 13 52 | 46 8 | 83594 | 4 | 16406 | 97371 | 7 | 02629 | 13777 | 3 | 86223 | 44 |
| 17 | 13 44 | 46 16 | 83608 | 4 | 16392 | 97396 | 7 | 02604 | 13789 | 3 | 86211 | 43 |
| 18 | 13 36 | 46 24 | 83621 | 4 | 16379 | 97421 | 8 | 02579 | 13800 | 4 | 86200 | 42 |
| 19 | 13 28 | 46 32 | 83634 | 4 | 16366 | 97447 | 8 | 02553 | 13812 | 4 | 86188 | 41 |
| 20 | 6 13 20 | 5 46 40 | 9.83648 | 4 | 10.16352 | 9.97472 | 8 | 10.02528 | 10.13824 | 4 | 9.86176 | 40 |
| 21 | 13 12 | 46 48 | 83661 | 5 | 16339 | 97497 | 9 | 02503 | 13836 | 4 | 86164 | 39 |
| 22 | 13 4 | 46 56 | 83674 | 5 | 16326 | 97523 | 9 | 02477 | 13848 | 4 | 86152 | 38 |
| 23 | 12 56 | 47 4 | 83688 | 5 | 16312 | 97548 | 10 | 02452 | 13860 | 5 | 86140 | 37 |
| 24 | 12 48 | 47 12 | 83701 | 5 | 16299 | 97573 | 10 | 02427 | 13872 | 5 | 86128 | 36 |
| 25 | 6 12 40 | 5 47 20 | 9.83715 | 6 | 10.16285 | 9.97598 | 11 | 10.02402 | 10.13884 | 5 | 9.86116 | 35 |
| 26 | 12 32 | 47 28 | 83728 | 6 | 16272 | 97624 | 11 | 02376 | 13896 | 5 | 86104 | 34 |
| 27 | 12 24 | 47 36 | 83741 | 6 | 16259 | 97649 | 11 | 02351 | 13908 | 5 | 86092 | 33 |
| 28 | 12 16 | 47 44 | 83755 | 6 | 16245 | 97674 | 12 | 02326 | 13920 | 6 | 86080 | 32 |
| 29 | 12 8 | 47 52 | 83768 | 6 | 16232 | 97700 | 12 | 02300 | 13932 | 6 | 86068 | 31 |
| 30 | 6 12 0 | 5 48 0 | 9.83781 | 7 | 10.16219 | 9.97725 | 13 | 10.02275 | 10.13944 | 6 | 9.86056 | 30 |
| 31 | 11 52 | 48 8 | 83795 | 7 | 16205 | 97750 | 13 | 02250 | 13956 | 6 | 86044 | 29 |
| 32 | 11 44 | 48 16 | 83808 | 7 | 16192 | 97776 | 13 | 02224 | 13968 | 6 | 86032 | 28 |
| 33 | 11 36 | 48 24 | 83821 | 7 | 16179 | 97801 | 14 | 02199 | 13980 | 7 | 86020 | 27 |
| 34 | 11 28 | 48 32 | 83834 | 8 | 16166 | 97826 | 14 | 02174 | 13992 | 7 | 86008 | 26 |
| 35 | 6 11 20 | 5 48 40 | 9.83848 | 8 | 10.16152 | 9.97851 | 15 | 10.02149 | 10.14004 | 7 | 9.85996 | 25 |
| 36 | 11 12 | 48 48 | 83861 | 8 | 16139 | 97877 | 15 | 02123 | 14016 | 7 | 85984 | 24 |
| 37 | 11 4 | 48 56 | 83874 | 8 | 16126 | 97902 | 16 | 02098 | 14028 | 7 | 85972 | 23 |
| 38 | 10 56 | 49 4 | 83887 | 8 | 16113 | 97927 | 16 | 02073 | 14040 | 8 | 85960 | 22 |
| 39 | 10 48 | 49 12 | 83901 | 9 | 16099 | 97953 | 16 | 02047 | 14052 | 8 | 85948 | 21 |
| 40 | 6 10 40 | 5 49 20 | 9.83914 | 9 | 10.16086 | 9.97978 | 17 | 10.02022 | 10.14064 | 8 | 9.85936 | 20 |
| 41 | 10 32 | 49 28 | 83927 | 9 | 16073 | 98003 | 17 | 01997 | 14076 | 8 | 85924 | 19 |
| 42 | 10 24 | 49 36 | 83940 | 9 | 16060 | 98029 | 18 | 01971 | 14088 | 8 | 85912 | 18 |
| 43 | 10 16 | 49 44 | 83954 | 10 | 16046 | 98054 | 18 | 01946 | 14100 | 9 | 85900 | 17 |
| 44 | 10 8 | 49 52 | 83967 | 10 | 16033 | 98079 | 19 | 01921 | 14112 | 9 | 85888 | 16 |
| 45 | 6 10 0 | 5 50 0 | 9.83980 | 10 | 10.16020 | 9.98104 | 19 | 10.01896 | 10.14124 | 9 | 9.85876 | 15 |
| 46 | 9 52 | 50 8 | 83993 | 10 | 16007 | 98130 | 19 | 01870 | 14136 | 9 | 85864 | 14 |
| 47 | 9 44 | 50 16 | 84006 | 10 | 15994 | 98155 | 20 | 01845 | 14149 | 9 | 85851 | 13 |
| 48 | 9 36 | 50 24 | 84020 | 11 | 15980 | 98180 | 20 | 01820 | 14161 | 10 | 85839 | 12 |
| 49 | 9 28 | 50 32 | 84033 | 11 | 15967 | 98206 | 21 | 01794 | 14173 | 10 | 85827 | 11 |
| 50 | 6 9 20 | 5 50 40 | 9.84046 | 11 | 10.15954 | 9.98231 | 21 | 10.01769 | 10.14185 | 10 | 9.85815 | 10 |
| 51 | 9 12 | 50 48 | 84059 | 11 | 15941 | 98256 | 22 | 01744 | 14197 | 10 | 85803 | 9 |
| 52 | 9 4 | 50 56 | 84072 | 12 | 15928 | 98281 | 22 | 01719 | 14209 | 10 | 85791 | 8 |
| 53 | 8 56 | 51 4 | 84085 | 12 | 15915 | 98307 | 22 | 01693 | 14221 | 11 | 85779 | 7 |
| 54 | 8 48 | 51 12 | 84098 | 12 | 15902 | 98332 | 23 | 01668 | 14234 | 11 | 85766 | 6 |
| 55 | 6 8 40 | 5 51 20 | 9.84112 | 12 | 10.15888 | 9.98357 | 23 | 10.01643 | 10.14246 | 11 | 9.85754 | 5 |
| 56 | 8 32 | 51 28 | 84125 | 12 | 15875 | 98383 | 24 | 01617 | 14258 | 11 | 85742 | 4 |
| 57 | 8 24 | 51 36 | 84138 | 13 | 15862 | 98408 | 24 | 01592 | 14270 | 11 | 85730 | 3 |
| 58 | 8 16 | 51 44 | 84151 | 13 | 15849 | 98433 | 24 | 01567 | 14282 | 12 | 85718 | 2 |
| 59 | 8 8 | 51 52 | 84164 | 13 | 15836 | 98458 | 25 | 01542 | 14294 | 12 | 85706 | 1 |
| 60 | 8 0 | 52 0 | 84177 | 13 | 15823 | 98484 | 25 | 01516 | 14307 | 12 | 85693 | 0 |
| M | Hour P.M. | Hour A.M. | Cosine. (A) | Diff. | Secant. (A) | Cotangent (B) | Diff. | Tangent. (B) | Cosecant. (C) | Diff. | Sine. (C) | M |

133° — 46°

| Seconds of time ...... | 1s | 2s | 3s | 4s | 5s | 6s | 7s |
|---|---|---|---|---|---|---|---|
| Prop. parts of cols. A | 2 | 3 | 5 | 7 | 8 | 10 | 12 |
| Prop. parts of cols. B | 3 | 6 | 9 | 13 | 16 | 19 | 22 |
| Prop. parts of cols. C | 2 | 3 | 5 | 6 | 8 | 9 | 11 |

# TABLE XXVII.

## Log. Sines, Tangents, and Secants.

S 44° | A | A | B | B | C | C | G′. 135°

| M | Hour A.M. | Hour P.M. | Sine. | Diff. | Cosecant. | Tangent. | Diff. | Cotangent | Secant. | Diff. | Cosine. | M |
|---|---|---|---|---|---|---|---|---|---|---|---|---|
| 0 | 6 8 0 | 5 52 0 | 9.84177 | 0 | 10.15823 | 9.98484 | 0 | 10.01516 | 10.14307 | 0 | 9.85693 | 60 |
| 1 | 7 52 | 52 8 | 84190 | 0 | 15810 | 98509 | 0 | 01491 | 14319 | 0 | 85681 | 59 |
| 2 | 7 44 | 52 16 | 84203 | 0 | 15797 | 98534 | 1 | 01466 | 14331 | 0 | 85669 | 58 |
| 3 | 7 36 | 52 24 | 84216 | 1 | 15784 | 98560 | 1 | 01440 | 14343 | 1 | 85657 | 57 |
| 4 | 7 28 | 52 32 | 84229 | 1 | 15771 | 98585 | 2 | 01415 | 14355 | 1 | 85645 | 56 |
| 5 | 6 7 20 | 5 52 40 | 9.84242 | 1 | 10.15758 | 9.98610 | 2 | 10.01390 | 10.14368 | 1 | 9.85632 | 55 |
| 6 | 7 12 | 52 48 | 84255 | 1 | 15745 | 98635 | 3 | 01365 | 14380 | 1 | 85620 | 54 |
| 7 | 7 4 | 52 56 | 84269 | 2 | 15731 | 98661 | 3 | 01339 | 14392 | 1 | 85608 | 53 |
| 8 | 6 56 | 53 4 | 84282 | 2 | 15718 | 98686 | 3 | 01314 | 14404 | 2 | 85596 | 52 |
| 9 | 6 48 | 53 12 | 84295 | 2 | 15705 | 98711 | 4 | 01289 | 14417 | 2 | 85583 | 51 |
| 10 | 6 6 40 | 5 53 20 | 9.84308 | 2 | 10.15692 | 9.98737 | 4 | 10.01263 | 10.14429 | 2 | 9.85571 | 50 |
| 11 | 6 32 | 53 28 | 84321 | 2 | 15679 | 98762 | 5 | 01238 | 14441 | 2 | 85559 | 49 |
| 12 | 6 24 | 53 36 | 84334 | 3 | 15666 | 98787 | 5 | 01213 | 14453 | 2 | 85547 | 48 |
| 13 | 6 16 | 53 44 | 84347 | 3 | 15653 | 98812 | 5 | 01188 | 14466 | 3 | 85534 | 47 |
| 14 | 6 8 | 53 52 | 84360 | 3 | 15640 | 98838 | 6 | 01162 | 14478 | 3 | 85522 | 46 |
| 15 | 6 6 0 | 5 54 0 | 9.84373 | 3 | 10.15627 | 9.98863 | 6 | 10.01137 | 10.14490 | 3 | 9.85510 | 45 |
| 16 | 5 52 | 54 8 | 84385 | 3 | 15615 | 98888 | 7 | 01112 | 14503 | 3 | 85497 | 44 |
| 17 | 5 44 | 54 16 | 84398 | 4 | 15602 | 98913 | 7 | 01087 | 14515 | 4 | 85485 | 43 |
| 18 | 5 36 | 54 24 | 84411 | 4 | 15589 | 98939 | 8 | 01061 | 14527 | 4 | 85473 | 42 |
| 19 | 5 28 | 54 32 | 84424 | 4 | 15576 | 98964 | 8 | 01036 | 14540 | 4 | 85460 | 41 |
| 20 | 6 5 20 | 5 54 40 | 9.84437 | 4 | 10.15563 | 9.98989 | 8 | 10.01011 | 10.14552 | 4 | 9.85448 | 40 |
| 21 | 5 12 | 54 48 | 84450 | 5 | 15550 | 99015 | 9 | 00985 | 14564 | 4 | 85436 | 39 |
| 22 | 5 4 | 54 56 | 84463 | 5 | 15537 | 99040 | 9 | 00960 | 14577 | 5 | 85423 | 38 |
| 23 | 4 56 | 55 4 | 84476 | 5 | 15524 | 99065 | 10 | 00935 | 14589 | 5 | 85411 | 37 |
| 24 | 4 48 | 55 12 | 84489 | 5 | 15511 | 99090 | 10 | 00910 | 14601 | 5 | 85399 | 36 |
| 25 | 6 4 40 | 5 55 20 | 9.84502 | 5 | 10.15498 | 9.99116 | 11 | 10.00884 | 10.14614 | 5 | 9.85386 | 35 |
| 26 | 4 32 | 55 28 | 84515 | 6 | 15485 | 99141 | 11 | 00859 | 14626 | 5 | 85374 | 34 |
| 27 | 4 24 | 55 36 | 84528 | 6 | 15472 | 99166 | 11 | 00834 | 14639 | 6 | 85361 | 33 |
| 28 | 4 16 | 55 44 | 84540 | 6 | 15460 | 99191 | 12 | 00809 | 14651 | 6 | 85349 | 32 |
| 29 | 4 8 | 55 52 | 84553 | 6 | 15447 | 99217 | 12 | 00783 | 14663 | 6 | 85337 | 31 |
| 30 | 6 4 0 | 5 56 0 | 9.84566 | 6 | 10.15434 | 9.99242 | 13 | 10.00758 | 10.14676 | 6 | 9.85324 | 30 |
| 31 | 3 52 | 56 8 | 84579 | 7 | 15421 | 99267 | 13 | 00733 | 14688 | 6 | 85312 | 29 |
| 32 | 3 44 | 56 16 | 84592 | 7 | 15408 | 99293 | 13 | 00707 | 14701 | 7 | 85299 | 28 |
| 33 | 3 36 | 56 24 | 84605 | 7 | 15395 | 99318 | 14 | 00682 | 14713 | 7 | 85287 | 27 |
| 34 | 3 28 | 56 32 | 84618 | 7 | 15382 | 99343 | 14 | 00657 | 14726 | 7 | 85274 | 26 |
| 35 | 6 3 20 | 5 56 40 | 9.84630 | 8 | 10.15370 | 9.99368 | 15 | 10.00632 | 10.14738 | 7 | 9.85262 | 25 |
| 36 | 3 12 | 56 48 | 84643 | 8 | 15357 | 99394 | 15 | 00606 | 14750 | 7 | 85250 | 24 |
| 37 | 3 4 | 56 56 | 84656 | 8 | 15344 | 99419 | 16 | 00581 | 14763 | 8 | 85237 | 23 |
| 38 | 2 56 | 57 4 | 84669 | 8 | 15331 | 99444 | 16 | 00556 | 14775 | 8 | 85225 | 22 |
| 39 | 2 48 | 57 12 | 84682 | 8 | 15318 | 99469 | 16 | 00531 | 14788 | 8 | 85212 | 21 |
| 40 | 6 2 40 | 5 57 20 | 9.84694 | 9 | 10.15306 | 9.99495 | 17 | 10.00505 | 10.14800 | 8 | 9.85200 | 20 |
| 41 | 2 32 | 57 28 | 84707 | 9 | 15293 | 99520 | 17 | 00480 | 14813 | 8 | 85187 | 19 |
| 42 | 2 24 | 57 36 | 84720 | 9 | 15280 | 99545 | 18 | 00455 | 14825 | 9 | 85175 | 18 |
| 43 | 2 16 | 57 44 | 84733 | 9 | 15267 | 99570 | 18 | 00430 | 14838 | 9 | 85162 | 17 |
| 44 | 2 8 | 57 52 | 84745 | 9 | 15255 | 99596 | 19 | 00404 | 14850 | 9 | 85150 | 16 |
| 45 | 6 2 0 | 5 58 0 | 9.84758 | 10 | 10.15242 | 9.99621 | 19 | 10.00379 | 10.14863 | 9 | 9.85137 | 15 |
| 46 | 1 52 | 58 8 | 84771 | 10 | 15229 | 99646 | 19 | 00354 | 14875 | 10 | 85125 | 14 |
| 47 | 1 44 | 58 16 | 84784 | 10 | 15216 | 99672 | 20 | 00328 | 14888 | 10 | 85112 | 13 |
| 48 | 1 36 | 58 24 | 84796 | 10 | 15204 | 99697 | 20 | 00303 | 14900 | 10 | 85100 | 12 |
| 49 | 1 28 | 58 32 | 84809 | 11 | 15191 | 99722 | 21 | 00278 | 14913 | 10 | 85087 | 11 |
| 50 | 6 1 20 | 5 58 40 | 9.84822 | 11 | 10.15178 | 9.99747 | 21 | 10.00253 | 10.14926 | 10 | 9.85074 | 10 |
| 51 | 1 12 | 58 48 | 84835 | 11 | 15165 | 99773 | 21 | 00227 | 14938 | 11 | 85062 | 9 |
| 52 | 1 4 | 58 56 | 84847 | 11 | 15153 | 99798 | 22 | 00202 | 14951 | 11 | 85049 | 8 |
| 53 | 0 56 | 59 4 | 84860 | 11 | 15140 | 99823 | 22 | 00177 | 14963 | 11 | 85037 | 7 |
| 54 | 0 48 | 59 12 | 84873 | 12 | 15127 | 99848 | 23 | 00152 | 14976 | 11 | 85024 | 6 |
| 55 | 6 0 40 | 5 59 20 | 9.84885 | 12 | 10.15115 | 9.99874 | 23 | 10.00126 | 10.14988 | 11 | 9.85012 | 5 |
| 56 | 0 32 | 59 28 | 84898 | 12 | 15102 | 99899 | 24 | 00101 | 15001 | 12 | 84999 | 4 |
| 57 | 0 24 | 59 36 | 84911 | 12 | 15089 | 99924 | 24 | 00076 | 15014 | 12 | 84986 | 3 |
| 58 | 0 16 | 59 44 | 84923 | 12 | 15077 | 99949 | 24 | 00051 | 15026 | 12 | 84974 | 2 |
| 59 | 0 8 | 59 52 | 84936 | 13 | 15064 | 99975 | 25 | 00025 | 15039 | 12 | 84961 | 1 |
| 60 | 0 0 | 6 0 0 | 84949 | 13 | 15051 | 10.00000 | 25 | 00000 | 15051 | 12 | 84949 | 0 |
| M | Hour P.M. | Hour A.M. | Cosine. | Diff. | Secant. | Cotangent | Diff. | Tangent. | Cosecant. | Diff. | Sine. | M |

134° | A | A | B | B | C | C | 45°

| Seconds of time ...... | | 1ˢ | 2ˢ | 3ˢ | 4ˢ | 5ˢ | 6ˢ | 7ˢ |
|---|---|---|---|---|---|---|---|---|
| Prop. parts of cols. | A | 2 | 3 | 5 | 6 | 8 | 10 | 11 |
| | B | 3 | 6 | 9 | 13 | 16 | 19 | 22 |
| | C | 2 | 3 | 5 | 6 | 8 | 9 | 11 |

# TABLE LI.

To change mean solar time into sideral time.

| Solar Hours. | Add. | Solar Minutes. | Add. | Solar Seconds. | Add. |
|---|---|---|---|---|---|
| | M. S. | | S. | | S. |
| 1 | 0 9.9 | 1 | 0.2 | 1 | 0.0 |
| 2 | 0 19.7 | 2 | 0.3 | 2 | 0.0 |
| 3 | 0 29.6 | 3 | 0.5 | 3 | 0.0 |
| 4 | 0 39.4 | 4 | 0.7 | 4 | 0.0 |
| 5 | 0 49.3 | 5 | 0.8 | 5 | 0.0 |
| 6 | 0 59.1 | 6 | 1.0 | 6 | 0.0 |
| 7 | 1 9.0 | 7 | 1.2 | 7 | 0.0 |
| 8 | 1 18.9 | 8 | 1.3 | 8 | 0.0 |
| 9 | 1 28.7 | 9 | 1.5 | 9 | 0.0 |
| 10 | 1 38.6 | 10 | 1.6 | 10 | 0.0 |
| 11 | 1 48.4 | 11 | 1.8 | 11 | 0.0 |
| 12 | 1 58.3 | 12 | 2.0 | 12 | 0.0 |
| 13 | 2 8.1 | 13 | 2.1 | 13 | 0.0 |
| 14 | 2 18.0 | 14 | 2.3 | 14 | 0.0 |
| 15 | 2 27.8 | 15 | 2.5 | 15 | 0.0 |
| 16 | 2 37.7 | 16 | 2.6 | 16 | 0.0 |
| 17 | 2 47.6 | 17 | 2.8 | 17 | 0.0 |
| 18 | 2 57.4 | 18 | 3.0 | 18 | 0.0 |
| 19 | 3 7.3 | 19 | 3.1 | 19 | 0.1 |
| 20 | 3 17.1 | 20 | 3.3 | 20 | 0.1 |
| 21 | 3 27.0 | 21 | 3.5 | 21 | 0.1 |
| 22 | 3 36.8 | 22 | 3.6 | 22 | 0.1 |
| 23 | 3 46.7 | 23 | 3.8 | 23 | 0.1 |
| 24 | 3 56.6 | 24 | 3.9 | 24 | 0.1 |
| | | 25 | 4.1 | 25 | 0.1 |
| | | 26 | 4.3 | 26 | 0.1 |
| | | 27 | 4.4 | 27 | 0.1 |
| | | 28 | 4.6 | 28 | 0.1 |
| | | 29 | 4.8 | 29 | 0.1 |
| | | 30 | 4.9 | 30 | 0.1 |
| | | 31 | 5.1 | 31 | 0.1 |
| | | 32 | 5.3 | 32 | 0.1 |
| | | 33 | 5.4 | 33 | 0.1 |
| | | 34 | 5.6 | 34 | 0.1 |
| | | 35 | 5.8 | 35 | 0.1 |
| | | 36 | 5.9 | 36 | 0.1 |
| | | 37 | 6.1 | 37 | 0.1 |
| | | 38 | 6.2 | 38 | 0.1 |
| | | 39 | 6.4 | 39 | 0.1 |
| | | 40 | 6.6 | 40 | 0.1 |
| | | 41 | 6.7 | 41 | 0.1 |
| | | 42 | 6.9 | 42 | 0.1 |
| | | 43 | 7.1 | 43 | 0.1 |
| | | 44 | 7.2 | 44 | 0.1 |
| | | 45 | 7.4 | 45 | 0.1 |
| | | 46 | 7.6 | 46 | 0.1 |
| | | 47 | 7.7 | 47 | 0.1 |
| | | 48 | 7.9 | 48 | 0.1 |
| | | 49 | 8.1 | 49 | 0.1 |
| | | 50 | 8.2 | 50 | 0.1 |
| | | 51 | 8.4 | 51 | 0.1 |
| | | 52 | 8.5 | 52 | 0.1 |
| | | 53 | 8.7 | 53 | 0.1 |
| | | 54 | 8.9 | 54 | 0.1 |
| | | 55 | 9.0 | 55 | 0.2 |
| | | 56 | 9.2 | 56 | 0.2 |
| | | 57 | 9.4 | 57 | 0.2 |
| | | 58 | 9.5 | 58 | 0.2 |
| | | 59 | 9.7 | 59 | 0.2 |
| | | 60 | 9.9 | 60 | 0.2 |

# TABLE LII.

To change sideral time into mean solar time.

| Sideral Hours. | Subtract. | Sideral Minutes. | Subtract | Sideral Seconds. | Subtract |
|---|---|---|---|---|---|
| | M. S. | | S. | | S. |
| 1 | 0 9.8 | 1 | 0.2 | 1 | 0.0 |
| 2 | 0 19.7 | 2 | 0.3 | 2 | 0.0 |
| 3 | 0 29.5 | 3 | 0.5 | 3 | 0.0 |
| 4 | 0 39.3 | 4 | 0.7 | 4 | 0.0 |
| 5 | 0 49.1 | 5 | 0.8 | 5 | 0.0 |
| 6 | 0 59.0 | 6 | 1.0 | 6 | 0.0 |
| 7 | 1 8.8 | 7 | 1.1 | 7 | 0.0 |
| 8 | 1 18.6 | 8 | 1.3 | 8 | 0.0 |
| 9 | 1 28.5 | 9 | 1.5 | 9 | 0.0 |
| 10 | 1 38.3 | 10 | 1.6 | 10 | 0.0 |
| 11 | 1 48.1 | 11 | 1.8 | 11 | 0.0 |
| 12 | 1 58.0 | 12 | 2.0 | 12 | 0.0 |
| 13 | 2 7.8 | 13 | 2.1 | 13 | 0.0 |
| 14 | 2 17.6 | 14 | 2.3 | 14 | 0.0 |
| 15 | 2 27.4 | 15 | 2.5 | 15 | 0.0 |
| 16 | 2 37.3 | 16 | 2.6 | 16 | 0.0 |
| 17 | 2 47.1 | 17 | 2.8 | 17 | 0.0 |
| 18 | 2 56.9 | 18 | 2.9 | 18 | 0.0 |
| 19 | 3 6.8 | 19 | 3.1 | 19 | 0.1 |
| 20 | 3 16.6 | 20 | 3.3 | 20 | 0.1 |
| 21 | 3 26.4 | 21 | 3.4 | 21 | 0.1 |
| 22 | 3 36.2 | 22 | 3.6 | 22 | 0.1 |
| 23 | 3 46.1 | 23 | 3.8 | 23 | 0.1 |
| 24 | 3 55.9 | 24 | 3.9 | 24 | 0.1 |
| | | 25 | 4.1 | 25 | 0.1 |
| | | 26 | 4.3 | 26 | 0.1 |
| | | 27 | 4.4 | 27 | 0.1 |
| | | 28 | 4.6 | 28 | 0.1 |
| | | 29 | 4.8 | 29 | 0.1 |
| | | 30 | 4.9 | 30 | 0.1 |
| | | 31 | 5.1 | 31 | 0.1 |
| | | 32 | 5.2 | 32 | 0.1 |
| | | 33 | 5.4 | 33 | 0.1 |
| | | 34 | 5.6 | 34 | 0.1 |
| | | 35 | 5.7 | 35 | 0.1 |
| | | 36 | 5.9 | 36 | 0.1 |
| | | 37 | 6.1 | 37 | 0.1 |
| | | 38 | 6.2 | 38 | 0.1 |
| | | 39 | 6.4 | 39 | 0.1 |
| | | 40 | 6.6 | 40 | 0.1 |
| | | 41 | 6.7 | 41 | 0.1 |
| | | 42 | 6.9 | 42 | 0.1 |
| | | 43 | 7.0 | 43 | 0.1 |
| | | 44 | 7.2 | 44 | 0.1 |
| | | 45 | 7.4 | 45 | 0.1 |
| | | 46 | 7.5 | 46 | 0.1 |
| | | 47 | 7.7 | 47 | 0.1 |
| | | 48 | 7.9 | 48 | 0.1 |
| | | 49 | 8.0 | 49 | 0.1 |
| | | 50 | 8.2 | 50 | 0.1 |
| | | 51 | 8.4 | 51 | 0.1 |
| | | 52 | 8.5 | 52 | 0.1 |
| | | 53 | 8.7 | 53 | 0.1 |
| | | 54 | 8.8 | 54 | 0.1 |
| | | 55 | 9.0 | 55 | 0.2 |
| | | 56 | 9.2 | 56 | 0.2 |
| | | 57 | 9.3 | 57 | 0.2 |
| | | 58 | 9.5 | 58 | 0.2 |
| | | 59 | 9.7 | 59 | 0 2 |
| | | 60 | 9.8 | 60 | 0.2 |

# LOGARITHMS.

---

In order to abbreviate the tedious operations of multiplication and division with large numbers, a series of numbers, called Logarithms, was invented by Lord Napier, Baron of Marchiston in Scotland, and published in Edinburgh in 1614; by means of which the operation of multiplication may be performed by addition, and division by subtraction; numbers may be involved to any power by simple multiplication, and the root of any power extracted by simple division.

In Table XXVI. are given the logarithms of all numbers from 1 to 9999; to each one must be prefixed an index, with a period or dot to separate it from the other part, as in decimal fractions; the numbers from 1 to 100 are published in that table with their indices; but from 100 to 9999 the index is left out for the sake of brevity; but it may be supplied by this general rule, viz. *The index of the logarithm of any integer or mixed number is always one less than the number of integral places in the natural number.* Thus the index of the logarithm of any number (integral or mixed), between 10 and 100, is 1; from 100 to 1000, it is 2; from 1000 to 10000 is 3, &c.; the method of finding the logarithms from this table will be evident from the following examples.

### *To find the logarithm of any number less than* 100.

Rule. Enter the first page of the table, and opposite the given number will be found the logarithm with its index prefixed.

Thus opposite 71 is 1.85126, which is its logarithm.

### *To find the logarithm of any number between* 100 *and* 1000.

Rule. Find the given number in the left-hand column of the table of logarithms, and immediately under 0 in the next column is a number, to which must be prefixed the number 2 as an index (because the number consists of three places of figures) and you will have the sought logarithm.

Thus, if the logarithm of 149 was required; this number being found in the left-hand column, against it, in the column marked 0 at the top (or bottom), is found 17319, to which prefixing the index 2, we have the logarithm of 149 = 2.17319.

### *To find the logarithm of any number between* 1000 *and* 10000.

Rule. Find the three left-hand figures of the given number, in the left-hand column of the table of logarithms, opposite to which, in the column that is marked at the top (or bottom) with the fourth figure, is to be found the sought logarithm; to which must be prefixed the index 3, because the number contains four places of figures.

Thus, if the logarithm of 1495 was required; opposite to 149, and in the column marked 5 at the top (or bottom), is 17464, to which prefix the index 3, and we have the sought logarithm, 3.17464.

### *To find the logarithm of any number above* 10000.

Rule. Find the three first figures of the given number in the left-hand column of the table, and the fourth figure at the top or bottom, and take out the corresponding number as in the preceding rule; take also the difference between this logarithm and the next greater, and multiply it by the given number exclusive of the four first figures; cross off at the right hand of the product as many figures as you had figures of the given number to multiply by; then add the remaining left-hand figures of this product to the logarithm taken from the table, and to the sum prefix an index equal to one less than the number of integral figures in the given number, and you will have the sought logarithm. To facilitate the calculation of these proportional parts, several small tables are placed in the margin, which give the correction corresponding to the difference D, and to the *fifth* figure of the proposed number. The use of these tables will be seen in the following examples.

Thus, if the logarithm of 14957 was required; opposite to 149, and under 5, is 17464; the difference between this and the next greater number, 17493, is 29, the difference D; this multiplied by 7 (the last figure of the given number) gives 203; crossing off the right-hand figure leaves 20.3 or 20 to be added to 17464, which makes 17484; to this prefixing the index 4, we have the sought logarithm, 4.17484. This correction, 20, may also be found by inspection in the small table in the margin, marked at the top with D = 29, and opposite to the *fifth* figure of the number, namely 7, at the side; the corresponding number is the correction, 20.

Again, if the logarithm of 1495738 was required; the logarithm corresponding to 149 at the left, and 5 at the top, is, as in the last example, 17464; the difference between this and the next greater is 29; multiplying this by 738 (which is equal to the given number, excluding the four first figures) gives 21402; crossing off the three right-hand figures of this product (because the number 738 consists of three figures), we have the correction 21 to be added to 17464; and the index to be prefixed is 6, because the given number consists of 7 places of figures; therefore the sought logarithm is 6.17485. This correction, 21, may be found as above, by means of the marginal table, marked at the top with D = 29, and at the side 7.38 or $7\frac{1}{3}$ nearly, to which corresponds 21, as before.

### *To find the logarithm of any mixed decimal number.*

Rule. Find the logarithm of the number, as if it was an integer, by the last rule, to which prefix the index of the integral part of the given number.

Thus, if the logarithm of the mixed decimal 149.5738 was required; find the logarithm of 1495738, without noticing the decimal point; this, in the last example, was found to be 17485; to this we must prefix the index 2, corresponding to the integral part 149; the logarithm sought will therefore be 2.17485.

### *To find the logarithm of any decimal fraction less than unity.*

The index of the logarithm of any number less than unity is negative; but to avoid the mixture of positive and negative quantities, it is common to borrow 10 or 100 in the index, which must afterwards be neglected in summing them with other indices thus, instead of writing the index —1, it is usually written +9, or +99; but in general it is sufficient to borrow 10 in the index; *and it is what we shall do in the rest of this work.* In this way we may find the logarithm of any decimal fraction by the following rule.

Rule. Find the logarithm of a fraction as if it was a whole number; see how many ciphers precede the first figure of the decimal fraction, subtract that number from 9, and the remainder will be the index of the given fraction.

Thus the logarithm of 0,0391 is 8.59218; the logarithm of 0.25 is 9.39794; the logarithm of 0.0000025 is 4.39794, &c.

### *To find the logarithm of a vulgar fraction.*

Rule. Subtract the logarithm of the denominator from the logarithm of the numerator (borrowing 10 in the index when the denominator is the greatest); the remainder will be the logarithm of the fraction sought.

EXAMPLE I.

Required the logarithm of $\frac{3}{8}$.

| | |
|---|---|
| From log. of 3 ............... | 0.47712 |
| Take log. of 8 ............... | 0.90309 |
| Remainder, log. of $\frac{3}{8}$ or .375.... | 9.57403 |

EXAMPLE II.

Required the logarithm of $3\frac{1}{4}$, or $\frac{13}{4}$.

| | |
|---|---|
| From log. of 13............... | 1.11394 |
| Take log. of 4............... | 0.60206 |
| Remainder, log. of $3\frac{1}{4}$ or 3.25... | 0.51188 |

### *To find the number corresponding to any logarithm.*

Rule. In the column marked 0 at the top (and bottom) of the table, seek for the next less logarithm, neglecting the index; note the number against it, and carry your eye along that line until you find the nearest less logarithm to the given one, and you will have the fourth figure of the given number at the top, which is to be placed to the right of the three other figures; if you wish for greater accuracy, you must take the difference, D, between this tabular logarithm and the next greater, also the difference, *d*, between that least tabular logarithm and the given one; to the latter difference, *d*, annex two or more ciphers at the right hand, and divide it by the former difference, D, and place the quotient* to the right hand of the four figures already found, and you will have the number sought, expressed in a mixed decimal, the integral part of which will consist of a number of figures (at the left hand) equal to the index of the logarithm increased by unity.†

Thus, if the number corresponding to the logarithm 1.52634 was required, we find 52634 in the column marked 0 at the top or bottom, and opposite to it is 336; now, the index being 1, the sought number must consist of two integral places; therefore it is 33.6.

If the given logarithm was 2.32838, we find that 32838 stands in the column marked 0 at the top or bottom, directly opposite to 213, which is the number sought, because, the index being 2, the number must consist of three places of figures.

If the number corresponding to the logarithm 2.57345 was required, we must look in the column 0; and we find in it, against the number 374, the logarithm 57287; and, guiding the eye along that line, we find the given logarithm, 57345, in the column marked 5; therefore the mixed number sought is 3745; and, since the index is 2, the integral part must consist of 3 places; therefore the number sought is 374.5. If the index be 1, the number will be 37.45; and if the index be 0, the number will be 3.745. If the index be 8, corresponding to a number less than unity, the answer will be 0.03745, &c.

Again, if the number corresponding to the logarithm 5.57811 was required, look in the column 0, and find in it, against 378, and under 5, the logarithm 57807, the difference between this and the next greater logarithm, 57818, being 11, and the difference between 57807 and the given number, 57811, being 4; to this 4 affix two ciphers, which make 400, and divide it by 11; the quotient is 36 nearly; this number, being connected with the former four figures, makes 378536, which is the number required, since, the index being 5, the number must consist of six places of figures.

To show, at one view, the indices corresponding to mixed and decimal numbers, we have given the following table.

| *Mixed number.* | *Logarithms.* | *Decimal number.* | *Logarithms.* |
|---|---|---|---|
| 40943.0 | Log. 4.61218 | 0.40943 | Log. 9.61218 |
| 4094.3 | Log. 3.61218 | 0.040943 | Log. 8.61218 |
| 409.43 | Log. 2.61218 | 0.0040943 | Log. 7.61218 |
| 40.943 | Log. 1.61218 | 0.00040943 | Log. 6.61218 |
| 4.0943 | Log. 0.61218 | 0.000040943 | Log. 5.61218 |

## MULTIPLICATION BY LOGARITHMS.

Rule. Add the logarithms of the two numbers to be multiplied, and the sum will be the logarithm of their product.

EXAMPLE I.

Multiply 25 by 35.

| | |
|---|---|
| 25 | Log. 1.39794 |
| 35 | Log. 1.54407 |
| Product, 875 | Log. 2.94201 |

EXAMPLE II.

Multiply 22.4 by 1.8.

| | |
|---|---|
| 22.4 | Log. 1.35025 |
| 1.8 | Log. 0.25527 |
| Product, 40.32 | Log. 1.60552 |

* This quotient must consist of as many places of figures as there were ciphers annexed, conformable to the rules of the division of decimals. Thus, if the divisor was 40, and the number to which two ciphers were annexed was 2, making 2.00, the quotient must not be estimated as 5, but as 05, and then two figures must be placed to the right of the four figures before found.

† If the index corresponds to a fraction less than unity, you must place as many ciphers to the left of that number as are equal to the index subtracted from 9, the decimal point being placed to the left of these ciphers; in this manner you will obtain the sought number.

We may find the fifth figure of the required number by means of the marginal tables, by entering the table corresponding at the top to the proposed value of D, and in the right-hand column with *d*; the corresponding number is the fifth figure of the required natural number.

EXAMPLE III.

Multiply 3.26 by 0.0025.

| | | |
|---|---|---|
| 3.26 | Log. | 0.51322 |
| 0.0025 | Log. | 7.39794 |
| Product, 0.00815 | Log. | 7.91116 |

EXAMPLE IV.

Multiply 0.25 by 0.003.

| | | |
|---|---|---|
| 0.25 | Log. | 9.39794 |
| 0.003 | Log. | 7.47712 |
| Product, 0.00075 | Log. | 6.87506 |

In the last example, the sum of the two indices is 16; but since 10 was borrowed in each number, we have neglected 10 in the sum; and the remainder, 6, being less than the other 10, is evidently the index of the logarithm of a fraction less than unity.

## DIVISION BY LOGARITHMS.

Rule. From the logarithm of the dividend subtract the logarithm of the divisor; the remainder will be the logarithm of the quotient.

EXAMPLE I.

Divide 875 by 25.

| | | |
|---|---|---|
| 875 | Log. | 2.94201 |
| 25 | Log. | 1.39794 |
| Quotient, 35 | Log. | 1.54407 |

EXAMPLE II.

Divide 40.32 by 22.4.

| | | |
|---|---|---|
| 40.32 | Log. | 1.60552 |
| 22.4 | Log. | 1.35025 |
| Quotient, 1.8 | Log. | 0.25527 |

EXAMPLE III.

Divide 0.00815 by 0.0025.

| | | |
|---|---|---|
| 0.00815 | Log. | 7.91116 |
| 0.0025 | Log. | 7.39794 |
| Quotient, 3.26 | Log. | 0.51322 |

EXAMPLE IV.

Divide 0.00075 by 0.025.

| | | |
|---|---|---|
| 0.00075 | Log. | 6.87506 |
| 0.025 | Log. | 8.39794 |
| Quotient, 0.03 | Log. | 8.47712 |

In Example III. both the divisor and dividend are fractions less than unity, and the divisor is the least; consequently the quotient is greater than unity. In Example IV. both fractions are less than unity; and, since the divisor is the greatest, its logarithm is greater than that of the dividend; for this reason it is necessary to borrow 10 in the index before making the subtraction; hence the quotient is less than unity.

## INVOLUTION BY LOGARITHMS.

Rule. Multiply the logarithm of the number given, by the index of the power to which the quantity is to be raised; the product will be the logarithm of the power sought. But in raising the powers of any decimal fraction, it must be observed, that the first significant figure of the power must be put as many places below the place of units as the index of its logarithm wants of 10 multiplied by the index of the power.

EXAMPLE I.

Required the square of 18.

| | | |
|---|---|---|
| 18 | Log. | 1.25527 |
| | | 2 |
| Answer, 324 | Log. | 2.51054 |

EXAMPLE II.

Required the cube of 13.

| | | |
|---|---|---|
| 13 | Log. | 1.11394 |
| | | 3 |
| Answer, 2197 | Log. | 3.34182 |

EXAMPLE III.

Required the square of 6.4.

| | | |
|---|---|---|
| 6.4 | Log. | 0.80618 |
| | | 2 |
| Answer, 40.96 | Log. | 1.61236 |

EXAMPLE IV.

Required the cube of 0.25.

| | | |
|---|---|---|
| 0.25 | Log. | 9.39794 |
| | | 3 |
| Answer, 0.015625 | Log. | 28.19382 |

In the last example, the index 28 wants 2 of 30 (the product of 10 by the power 3); therefore the first significant figure of the answer, viz. 1, is placed two figures distant from the place of units.

## EVOLUTION BY LOGARITHMS.

RULE. Divide the logarithm of the number by the index of the power; the quotient will be the logarithm of the root sought. But if the power whose root is to be extracted is a decimal fraction less than unity, prefix to the index of its logarithm a figure less by one than the index of the power,* and divide the whole by the index of the power; the quotient will be the logarithm of the root sought.

EXAMPLE I.

What is the square root of 324?

324............Log. 2)2.51055

Answer, 18............Log. 1.25527

EXAMPLE II.

Required the cube root of 2197.

2197...........Log. 3)3.34183

Answer, 13...........Log. 1.11394

EXAMPLE III.

Required the square root of 40.96.

40.96 ..........Log. 2)1.61236

Answer, 6.4 ...........Log. 0.80618

EXAMPLE IV.

Required the cube root of 0.015625.

0.015625........Log. 8.19382

Prefix 2 to the index......3)28.19382

Answer, 0.25............Log. 9.39794

## TO WORK THE RULE OF THREE BY LOGARITHMS.

When three numbers are given to find a fourth proportional, in arithmetic, we make a statement, and say, As the first number is to the second, so is the third to the fourth; and by multiplying the second and third together, and dividing the product by the first, we obtain the fourth number sought. To obtain the same result by logarithms, we must *add the logarithms of the second and third numbers together, and from the sum subtract the logarithm of the first number; the remainder will be the logarithm of the sought fourth number.*

EXAMPLE I.

If 6 yards of cloth cost 5 dollars, what will 20 yards cost?

As 6.................. Log. 0.77815

Is to 5.................Log. 0.69897

So is 20 ..............Log. 1.30103

Sum of 2d and 3d........... 2.00000

Subtract the first............ 0.77815

To 16.67...............Log. 1.22185

The answer, therefore, is 16 dollars and $\frac{67}{100}$, or 16 dollars and 67 cents.

EXAMPLE II.

If a ship sails 20 miles in 7 hours, how much will she sail in 21 hours at the same rate?

As 7 ..................Log. 0.84510

Is to 20................Log. 1.30103

So is 21 ...............Log. 1.32222

Sum of 2d and 3d........... 2.62325

Subtract the first............ 0.84510

To 60.................Log. 1.77815

The answer is 60 miles.

## TO CALCULATE COMPOUND INTEREST BY LOGARITHMS.

To 100 dollars add its interest for one year; find the logarithm of this sum, and reject 2 in the index; then multiply it by the number of years and parts of a year for which the interest is to be calculated; to the product add the logarithm of the sum put at interest; the sum of these two logarithms will be the logarithm of the amount of the given sum for the given time.

---

* In this rule it is supposed that 10 is borrowed in finding the index to the decimal according to the rule, page 29.

EXAMPLE.

Required the amount of the principal and interest of 355 dollars, let at 6 per cent. compound interest, for 7 years.

| | | |
|---|---|---|
| Adding 6 to 100 gives 106; whose logarithm, rejecting 2 in the index, is | | 0.02531 |
| Multiplied by | | 7 |
| Product | | 0.17717 |
| Principal, 355 dollars | Log. | 2.55023 |
| Sum gives the logarithm of 533.83 | Log. | 2.72740 |

Therefore the amount of principal and interest is 533 dollars and 83 cents.

---

*To find the logarithm of the sine, tangent, or secant, corresponding to any number of degrees and minutes, by Table* XXVII.

The given number of degrees must be found at the bottom of the page when between 45° and 135°, otherwise at the top; the minutes being found in the column marked M, which stands on the side of the page on which the degrees are marked; thus, *if the degrees are less than* 45, *the minutes are to be found in the left-hand column*, &c.; *and it must be noted that if the degrees are found at the top, the names of* hour, sine, cosine, tangent, &c., *must also be found at the top; and if the degrees are found at the bottom, the names* sine, cosine, &c., *must also be found at the bottom.* Then opposite to the number of the minutes will be found the log. sine, log. secant, &c. in the columns marked *sine*, *secant*, &c. respectively.

EXAMPLE I.

Required the log. sine of 28° 37′.

Find 28° at the top of the page, directly below which, in the left-hand column, find 37′; against which, in the column marked *sine*, is 9.68029, the log. sine of the given number of degrees; and in the same manner the tangents, &c. are found.

EXAMPLE II.

Required the log. secant of 126° 20′.

Find 126° at the bottom of the page, directly above which, in the left-hand column, find 20′; against which, in the column marked *secant*, is 10.22732 required.

*To find the logarithm of the sine, cosine, &c. for degrees, minutes, and seconds, by Table* XXVII.

Find the numbers corresponding to the even minutes next above and below the given degrees and minutes, and take their difference, D; then say, As 60″ is to the number of seconds in the proposed number, so is that difference, D, to a correction, *d*, to be applied to the number corresponding to the least number of degrees and minutes; additive if it is the least of the two numbers taken from the table, otherwise subtractive.

EXAMPLE III.

Required the log. sine of 24° 16′ 38″.

| | | |
|---|---|---|
| Sine of 24° 16′ | Log. | 9.61382 |
| Sine of 24 17 | Log. | 9.61411 |
| Difference | | D = 29 |

Then, as 60″ : 38″ :: 29 : 18, which, being added to the number corresponding to 24° 16′, gives 9.61400, the log. sine of 24° 16′ 38″.

EXAMPLE IV.

Required the log. secant of 105° 20′ 16″.

| | | |
|---|---|---|
| Secant of 105° 20′ | Log. | 10.57768 |
| Secant of 105 21 | Log. | 10.57722 |
| Difference | | D = 46 |

Then, as 60″ : 16″ :: 46 : 12, which, being subtracted from the number corresponding to 105° 20′, gives 10.57756, the log. secant of 105° 20′ 16″.

If the given seconds be $\frac{1}{2}$, $\frac{1}{3}$, $\frac{1}{4}$, $\frac{1}{5}$, or $\frac{1}{6}$, or any other even parts of a minute, the like parts may be taken of the difference of the logarithms, and added or subtracted as above, which may be frequently done by inspection. These proportional parts may also be found very nearly by means of the three columns of differences for seconds, given, for the first time, in the ninth edition of this work. The first column of differences, which is to be used with the two columns marked A, A, is placed between these columns. The second column of differences, which is to be used with the two columns B, B, is placed between these two columns. In like manner, the third column of differences, between the columns C, C, is to be used with them. The correction of the tabular logarithms in any of the columns A, B, C, for any number of seconds, is found by entering the left-hand column of the table, *marked* S′ *at the top*, and finding the number of seconds; opposite to this, in the column of differences, will be found the corresponding correction. Thus, in the table, page 215, which contains the log. sines, tangents, &c., for 30°, the corrections corresponding to 25″, are 9 for the columns A, A, 12 for the columns B, B, 3 for the columns C, C; so that, if it were required to find the sine, tangent, or secant of 30° 12′ 25″, we must add these corrections respectively to the numbers corresponding to 30° 12′; thus,

| | Col. A. | | Col. B. | | Col. C. |
|---|---|---|---|---|---|
| Logs. for 30° 12′....Sine | 9.70159 | Tangent.... | 9.76493 | Secant.... | 10.06335 |
| Corrections for 25″ in S′ | +9 | | +12 | | +3 |
| Logs. for 30° 12′ 25″.... | 9.70168 | | 9.76505 | | 10.06338 |

these corrections being all added, because the logarithms increase in proceeding from 30° 12′ to 30° 13′. Instead of taking out the logarithms for 30° 12′, and adding the correction for 25″, we may take out the logarithms for 30° 13′, and subtract the correction for 60″ — 25″, or 35″, found in the margin S′; thus,

| | | | | | |
|---|---|---|---|---|---|
| Logs. for 30° 13′....Sine | 9.70180 | Tangent.... | 9.76522 | Secant.... | 10.06342 |
| Corr. for 35″ in col. S′, or 25″ in col. G′ .... | —13 | | —17 | | —4 |
| Logs. for 30° 12′ 25″.... | 9.70167 | | 9.76505 | | 10.06338 |

The corrections are in this case subtracted, because the logarithms decrease in proceeding backward 35″ from 30° 13′, to attain 30° 12′ 25″. The tangents and secants, in this example, are the same by both methods; the sines differ by one unit, in the last decimal place, and this will frequently happen, because the difference of the logarithms for 1′, sometimes differ one or two units from the mean values which are used in the three columns of differences. The error arising from this cause is generally diminished by using the *smallest* angle* S′, when the seconds of the proposed angle are *smaller* than 30″; or the *greatest* angle G′, when the number of seconds are *greater* than 30″. Thus, in the above example, where the angle S′ = 30° 12′, and the angle G′ = 30° 13′, it is best to use the angle S′ when the given angle is less than 30° 12′ 30″, but the angle G′ when it exceeds 30° 12′ 30″. Thus, if it be required to find the sine of 30° 12′ 51″, it is best to use the angle G′ = 30° 13′, and find the correction by entering the margin marked S′, with the difference 60″ — 51″ = 9″, opposite to which, in the column of differences, is 3, to be subtracted from log. sine of 30° 13′ = 9.70180, to get the log. sine of 30° 12′ 51″ = 9.70177. To save the trouble of subtracting the seconds from 60″, we may use the right-hand margin, marked G′, and the correction may then be found by the following rules:—

Rule 1. When the *smallest* angle S′ is used, *find the seconds in the column* S′, and take out the corresponding correction, which is to be applied to the logarithm corresponding to S′; by adding, if the log. of G′ be greater than the log. of S′; otherwise, by subtracting.

Rule 2. When the *greater* angle G′ is used, *find the seconds in the column* G′, and take out the corresponding correction, which is to be applied to the logarithm corresponding to G′; by adding, if the log. of S′ be greater than the log. of G′; otherwise, by subtracting; so that, in all cases, the required logarithm may fall between the two logarithms corresponding to the angles S′ and G′.

The correctness of these rules will evidently appear by comparing them with the preceding examples; and by the inverse process we may find the angle corresponding to a given logarithm, as in the next article.

We have given at the bottom of the page, in this table, a small table for finding the proportional parts for the odd seconds of time, corresponding to the column of Hours A. M. or P. M.; to facilitate the process of finding the log. sine, cosine, &c., corresponding to the nearest second of time in the column of hours, or, on the contrary, to find the nearest second of time corresponding to any given log. sine, cosine, &c. Thus, in the preceding examples, where the angle S′ = 30° 12′, and the

* If we neglect the seconds in any proposed angle whose sine, &c. is required, we get the angle denoted above by S′, and this angle increased by 1′, is represented by G′; so that the proposed angle falls between S′ and G′; S′ being a *smaller*, and G′ a *greater* angle than that whose log. sine, &c., is required; the letters S′ and G′, accented for minutes, being used because they are easily remembered as the initials of *smaller* and *greater*

angle G′ = 30° 13′; the times corresponding in the column of Hours P. M., are S′ = 4ʰ 1ᵐ 36ˢ; G′ = 4ʰ 1ᵐ 44ˢ; and if we wish to find the log. sine, cosine, &c., corresponding to any intermediate time, as, for example, 4ʰ 1ᵐ 39ˢ, which differs 3ˢ from the angle S′, we must find the tabular logarithm corresponding to S′, and apply the correction for 3ˢ, given by the table at the bottom of the page, as in the following examples:—

| | A. | B. | C. |
|---|---|---|---|
| Logs. for S′ = 4ʰ 1ᵐ 36ˢ | Sine 9.70159 | Tangent 9.76493 | Secant 10.06335 |
| Correction for +3ˢ | +8 | +11 | +3 |
| Logs. for..... 4ʰ 1ᵐ 39ˢ | Sine 9.70167 | Tangent 9.76504 | Secant 10.06338 |

Nearly the same results are obtained by using the angle G′, in the manner we have before explained:—

| | | | |
|---|---|---|---|
| Logs. for G′ = 4ʰ 1ᵐ 44ˢ | Sine 9.70180 | Tangent 9.76522 | Secant 10.06342 |
| Correction for —5ˢ | —13 | —18 | —5 |
| Logs. for. ... 4ʰ 1ᵐ 39ˢ | Sine 9.70167 | Tangent 9.76504 | Secant 10.06337 |

These corrections must be applied by addition or subtraction, according to the directions given above, so as to make the required logarithm fall between those which correspond to the times S′ and G′.

The inverse process will give the time corresponding to any logarithm. Thus, if the log. sine 9.70167 be given, the difference between this and 9.70159, corresponding to S′ = 4ʰ 1ᵐ 36ˢ, is 8; seeking this in the column A, in the second line of the table at the bottom of the page, it is found to correspond to 3ˢ; adding this to the time S′ = 4ʰ 1ᵐ 36ˢ, we get 4ʰ 1ᵐ 39ˢ for the required time. We may proceed in the same manner with the logarithms in the columns B, C; using the numbers corresponding, marked B, C, respectively, in the table at the bottom of the page.

*To find the degrees, minutes, and seconds, corresponding to any given logarithm sine, cosine, &c. by Table* XXVII.

Find the two nearest numbers to the given log. sine, cosine, &c., in the column marked *sine*, *cosine*, &c., respectively, one being greater, and the other less, and take their difference, D; take also the difference, *d*, between the given logarithm and the logarithm corresponding to the smallest number of degrees and minutes; then say, As the first found difference is to the second found difference, so is 60″ to a number of seconds to be annexed to the smallest number of degrees and minutes before found. The three columns of differences may also be used, by an inverse operation to that which we have explained in the preceding article.

EXAMPLE V.

Find the degrees, minutes, and seconds (less than 90°), corresponding to the log. sine 9.61400.

| | | | |
|---|---|---|---|
| Next less log. S′ = 24° 16′ | 9.61382 | Log. of smallest angle S′ = 24° 16′ is | 9.61382 |
| Greater..... G′ = 24 17 | 9.61411 | Given log....................... | 9.61400 |
| | D = 29 | | *d* = 18 |

Then say, As 29 : 18 : : 60″ : 38″, nearly; which, annexed to 24° 16′, give 24° 16′ 38″, answering to log. sine 9.61400. Subtracting 24° 16′ 38″ from 180°, there remain 155° 43′ 22″, the log. sine of which is also 9.61400. The quantity 38″ may also be found by inspection in the side column S′ of the page opposite *d* = 18, in the column of differences between the two columns, A, A. If we use the angle G′, we shall have *d′* equal to 11, the difference of the logarithms 9.61411 and 9.61400, and the corresponding number of seconds in column G′, is 37″, making 24° 16′ 37″.

*To find the arithmetical complement of any logarithm.*

The arithmetical complement of any logarithm is what it wants of 10.00000, and is used to avoid subtraction. For, when working any proportion by logarithms, you may add the arithmetical complement of the logarithm of the first term, instead of subtracting the logarithm itself, observing to neglect 10 in the index of the sum of the logarithms. The arithmetical complement of any logarithm is thus found:—Begin at the index, and *write down what each figure wants of* 9, *except the last significant figure, which take from* 10.* Thus, the arithmetical complement of 9.62595 is 0.37405; that of 1.86567 is 8.13433; and that of 10.33133 is 89.66867, or 9.66867.

* When the index of the given logarithm is greater than 10, as in some of the numbers of Table XXVII., the left-hand figure of it must be neglected; and when there are any ciphers to the right hand of the last significant figure, you may place the same number of ciphers to the right hand of the other figures of the arithmetical complement

## DIVIDING ENGINE.

They have just completed at their establishment, after a labor of over five years, a Dividing Engine, by which they are enabled to divide Astronomical and Nautical Instruments to a degree of precision which they will *guarantee* to be equal to the best of foreign make. The subscribers, therefore, ask that American ships may be navigated by American made instruments.

## INSTRUMENTS.

Chronometers of the best makers, for sale and to hire.
Sextants, Quadrants, &c., of American manufacture.
Spy Glasses.
Night Glasses, new kind.
Aneroid Barometers.
Compasses, Dent's Improved, and others.
Binnacles.
Globes, Terrestrial and Celestial, 16 inch. The Terrestrial with Isothermal Lines of Temperature, and Deep Sea Soundings.
Massey's Patent Logs.
Ogden's, Ericsson's, and Massey's Patent Sounding Instruments.
Improved Compasses with elastic centres.
ABBOTT'S HOROMETER, a new and simple instrument for working the Longitude either by Lunar Observations or the Chronometer.

E. & G. W. BLUNT, 179 Water-Street.

## All the U. S. Coast Surveys and English Admiralty Surveys

### NOTICE TO SHIPMASTERS.

Just published, Massachusetts Bay.

OFFICE OF THE BOARD OF UNDERWRITERS
*New-York, March 20th*, 1858.

There is reason to believe that disasters to vessels have recently occurred on the Southern Coast of the United States, in consequence of the use of old and incorrect CHARTS. This Board would earnestly impress upon Shipmasters the great importance of being provided with those that are of recent date and from a reliable source. BLUNT'S CHARTS of the Coast of the United States are corrected in conformity with the Government Surveys, and have accurately laid down the position of all the Lights now in use, or in process of construction on our coast, and these Charts should be familiar to every Shipmaster in the trade.

ELLWOOD WALTER, *Secretary Board of Underwriters*

*Extract of a letter from Lieut. John Rodgers, commanding U. S. Ship "Hancock," attached to the Surveying Expedition to the China Seas, North Pacific.*

*New-Bedford, January 4th*, 1852.

I had a long discussion on Charts of the extreme North Pacific, Behring's Straits, Sea of Okotsk, &c. All the Whalers say that you are right.

COMPASSES.—Attention is invited to the new Compasses constructed at the establishment of the subscribers. It is a fact now well understood, that most of the losses charged to Currents are due to the imperfect construction of Compasses, and to their deviation not being ascertained.

Compasses of a superior quality, are manufactured by them, and are constantly on hand. Also, Dent's Patent and other approved Compasses.

E. & G. W. BLUNT.

**Agents for Rogers' Signals.—Office of the Marine Register or American Lloyds.**

*November*, 1860.

www.ingramcontent.com/pod-product-compliance
Lightning Source LLC
LaVergne TN
LVHW011237110826
845150LV00006B/1660

* 9 7 8 1 4 2 5 5 1 4 1 1 2 *